Suzuki SV650 & SV650S
Service and Repair Manual

by Matthew Coombs & Phil Mather

Models covered

(3912 - 2AH3 - 360)

SV650	645cc.	1999 to 2008
SV650S	645cc.	1999 to 2008
SV650A/SA	645cc.	2007 to 2008
SV650 Sport	645cc.	2008

ABCDE
FGHIJ
KLMNO

A book in the **Haynes Service and Repair Manual Series**

ISBN 978 1 84425 767 7

British Library Cataloguing in Publication Data
A catalogue record for this book is available from the British Library

Library of Congress Control Number 2008924281

Printed in the USA

Haynes Publishing
Sparkford, Yeovil, Somerset BA22 7JJ, England

Haynes North America, Inc
861 Lawrence Drive, Newbury Park, California 91320, USA

Haynes Publishing Nordiska AB
Box 1504, 751 45 Uppsala, Sweden

Contents

LIVING WITH YOUR SUZUKI SV650

Contents

Suzuki Every Which Way

by Julian Ryder

From Textile Machinery to Motorcycles

Suzuki were the second of Japan's Big Four motorcycle manufacturers to enter the business, and like Honda they started by bolting small two-stroke motors to bicycles. Unlike Honda, they had manufactured other products before turning to transportation in the aftermath of World War II. In fact Suzuki has been in business since the first decade of the 20th-Century when Michio Suzuki manufactured textile machinery.

The desperate need for transport in post-war Japan saw Suzuki make their first motorised bicycle in 1952, and the fact that by 1954 the company had changed its name to Suzuki Motor Company shows how quickly the sideline took over the whole company's activities. In their first full manufacturing year, Suzuki made nearly 4500 bikes and rapidly expanded into the world markets with a range of two-strokes.

Suzuki didn't make a four-stroke until 1977 when the GS750 double-overhead-cam across-the-frame four arrived. This was several years after Honda and Kawasaki had established the air-cooled four as the industry standard, but no motorcycle epitomises the era of what came to be known as the Universal

The T500 two-stroke twin

One of the later GT750 'kettle' models with front disc brakes

Japanese motorcycle better than the GS. So well engineered were the original fours that you can clearly see their genes in the GS500 twins that are still going strong in the mid-1990s. Suzuki's ability to prolong the life of their products this way means that they are often thought of as a conservative company. This is hardly fair if you look at some of their landmark designs, most of which have been commercial as well as critical successes.

Two-stroke Success

Early racing efforts were bolstered by the arrival of Ernst Degner who defected from the East German MZ team at the Swedish GP of 1961, bringing with him the rotary-valve secrets of design genius Walter Kaaden. The new Suzuki 50 cc racer won its first GP on the Isle of Man the following year and winning the title easily. Only Honda and Ralph Bryans interrupted Suzuki's run of 50 cc titles from 1962 to 1968.

The arrival of the twin-cylinder 125 racer in 1963 enabled Hugh Anderson to win both 50 and 125 world titles. You may not think 50 cc racing would be exciting - until you learn that the final incarnation of the thing had 14 gears and could do well over 100 mph on fast circuits. Before pulling out of GPs in 1967 the 50 cc racer won six of the eight world titles chalked up by Suzuki during the 1960s as well as providing Mitsuo Itoh with the distinction of being the only Japanese rider to win an Isle of Man TT. Mr Itoh still works for Suzuki, he's in charge of their racing program.

Europe got the benefit of Suzuki's two-stroke expertise in a succession of air-cooled twins, the six-speed 250 cc Super Six being the most memorable, but the arrival in 1968 of the first of a series of 500 cc twins which were good looking, robust and versatile marked the start of mainstream success.

So confident were Suzuki of their two-stroke expertise that they even applied it to the burgeoning Superbike sector. The GT750 water-cooled triple arrived in 1972. It was big, fast and comfortable although the handling and stopping power did draw some comment. Whatever the drawbacks of the road bike, the engine was immensely successful in Superbike and Formula 750 racing. The roadster has its devotees, though, and is now a sought-after bike on the classic Japanese scene. Do not refer to it as the Water Buffalo in such company. Joking aside, the later disc-braked versions were quite civilised, but the audacious idea of using a big two-stroke motor in what was essentially a touring bike was a surprising success until the fuel crisis of the mid-'70s effectively killed off big strokers.

The same could be said of Suzuki's only real lemon, the RE5. This is still the only mass-produced bike to use the rotary (or Wankel) engine but never sold well. Fuel consumption in the mid-teens allied to frightening complexity and excess weight meant the RE5 was a non-starter in the sales race.

Suzuki's GT250X7 was an instant hit in the popular 250 cc 'learner' sector

The GS400 was the first in a line of four-stroke twins

Development of the Four-stroke range

When Suzuki got round to building a four-stroke they did a very good job of it. The GS fours were built in 550, 650, 750, 850, 1000 and 1100 cc sizes in sports, custom, roadster and even shaft-driven touring forms over many years. The GS1000 was in on the start of Superbike racing in the early 1970s and the GS850 shaft-driven tourer was around nearly 15 years later. The fours spawned a line of 400, 425, 450 and 500 cc GS twins that were essentially the middle half of the four with all their reliability. If there was ever a criticism of the GS models it was that with the exception of the GS1000S of 1980, colloquially known as the ice-cream van, the range was visually uninspiring.

They nearly made the same mistake when they launched the four-valve-head GSX750 in 1979. Fortunately, the original twin-shock version was soon replaced by the 'E'-model with Full-Floater rear suspension and a full set of all the gadgets the Japanese industry was then keen on and has since forgotten about, like 16-inch front wheels and anti-dive forks. The air-cooled GSX was like the GS built in 550, 750 and 1100 cc versions with a variety of half, full and touring fairings, but the GSX that is best remembered is the Katana that first appeared in 1981. The power was provided by an 1000 or 1100 cc GSX motor, but wrapped around it was the most outrageous styling package to come out of Japan. Designed by Hans Muth of Target Design, the Katana looked like nothing seen before or since. At the time there was as much anti feeling as praise, but now it is rightly regarded as a classic, a true milestone in motorcycle design. The factory have even started making 250 and 400 cc fours for the home market with the same styling as the 1981 bike.

Just to remind us that they'd still been building two-strokes for the likes of Barry Sheene, in 1986 Suzuki marketed a road-going version of their RG500 square-four racer which had put an end to the era of the four-stroke in 500 GPs when it appeared in 1974. In 1976 Suzuki not only won their first 500 title with Sheene, they sold RG500s over the counter and won every GP with them - with the exception of the Isle of Man TT which the works riders boycotted. Ten years on, the RG500 Gamma gave road riders the nearest experience they'd ever get to riding a GP bike. The fearsome beast could top 140 mph and only weighed 340 lb - the other alleged GP replicas were pussy cats compared to the Gamma's man-eating tiger.

The RG only lasted a few years and is already firmly in the category of collector's item; its four-stroke equivalent, the GSX-R, is still with us and looks like being so for many years. You have to look back to 1985 and its launch to realise just what a revolutionary step the GSX-R750 was: quite simply it was the first race replica. Not a bike dressed up to look like a race bike, but a genuine racer with lights on, a bike that could be taken straight to the track and win.

The first GSX-R, the 750, had a completely new motor cooled by oil rather than water and an aluminium cradle frame. It was sparse, a little twitchy and very, very fast. This time Suzuki got the looks right, blue and white bodywork based on the factory's racing colours and endurance-racer lookalike twin headlights. And then came the 1100 - the big GSX-R got progressively more brutal as it chased the Yamaha EXUP for the heavyweight championship.

And alongside all these mould-breaking

The GS750 led the way for a series of four cylinder models

Later four-stroke models, like this GSX1100, were fitted with 16v engines

designs, Suzuki were also making the best looking custom bikes to come out of Japan, the Intruders; the first race replica trail bike, the DR350; the sharpest 250 Supersports, the RGV250; and a bargain-basement 600, the Bandit. The Bandit proved so popular they went on to build 1200 and 750 cc versions of it. I suppose that's predictable, a range of four-stroke fours just like the GS and GSXs. It's just like the company really, sometimes predictable, admittedly - but never boring.

Suzuki SV650 and SV650S

A genuinely all-new design is a rare thing these days, and even more so when it is a budget bike we're talking about. Suzuki re-invented the all-round fun roadster with the Bandit back in the mid-1990s, that was a clever hybrid of current and old designs but a kept down to a price by dipping into many spare-parts bins. The Bandit took the market by storm and the original 600 cc model begat a whole range of Bandits as well as competing models from the opposition. Suzuki's record with V-twins isn't quite so inspiring. The factory-custom Intruders never captured the public imagination and the TL1000 suffered from scare stories and lack of race-track credibility.

So how to explain the SV650? It sprung all-new and fully formed from Japan at a bargain price. A fun 70 bhp V-twin in an aluminium frame with looks derived from the undeniably handsome TL1000. There was of course evidence of penny pinching if you looked hard enough, like non-adjustable suspension and narrow wheels – even the plain paint schemes, but all the road tests agreed – here was the heir to the Bandit.

The SV came in an unfaired version and a half-faired S model. The S model had a shorter wheelbase, plus a sportier riding position thanks to the clip-on handlebars and repositioned footrests. Although the engines are identical, the naked model got an extra tooth on the rear sprocket for buzzier acceleration which of course meant it ran out of steam before the slippier S-model. Those seemingly insignificant differences actually produce two quite different motorcycles. The base model is zippy and easy to flick around in town traffic, the S is slightly happier being given its head on country roads and doesn't feel gutless on motorways. Both models can also carry two people without crippling the pillion. If there is a criticism of the bike it's that the saddle is a tad high for those of us with short legs.

Suzuki definitely achieved their objectives. The SVs have been selling well since they appeared in 1999. British weekly Motorcycle News even called the SV 'the best bike ever for the real world'. They have a point. It's a bike the insurance companies aren't afraid of and when it comes to tyre replacement time those narrow rims mean new rubber is cheap. One constituency Suzuki captured is the riders who want a V-twin but either don't want or can't

The 1999 SV650-X

The 1999 SV650S-X

The 2003 SV650S-K3

The 2008 SV650S-K8

afford a Ducati, or who wanted to stick with the Japanese reliability of their previous steeds.

At first the SVs were seen as ideal bikes for the newly qualified rider, a first 'proper' bike but still a stepping stone to a bigger machine. But it didn't take long for the market to realise that they were more than that. An SV was sensible without being boring and eminently practical. You could afford one as well as the mortgage. Mind you, that hasn't stopped some people boring them out to 750 cc and bolting on GSX-R suspension ...

So how have Suzuki managed to build a brand new machine down to a cost? Surely that is an oxymoron? Maybe, but the evidence shows that the SV is here for the long term, and over time Suzuki will recoup the costs of tooling up for a totally new range. In its first four years, the year-on-year model changes were totally negligible, just an odd washer here or there plus the luxury of front-fork spring preload adjustment from 2002 on. Having spent their money wisely, Suzuki was getting the return on their long-term investment. A major revamp came about in 2003, although at a glance only the smaller fairing on S models gave the game away. The structures of the frame and swingarm were revised and the rear brake caliper was repositioned - and electronic fuel injection replaced the old carburettor system, more in a bid to reduce exhaust emissions than to increase power output which rose by only 2 bhp as a result. Further detail changes included the addition of an oil cooler, slung below the front cylinder, new instruments and an LED tail light.

The SV received its third generation revamp in 2007. Although seemingly unchanged from the outside, it had a host of mechanical changes. Most significant was the dual spark ignition and new throttle bodies and for certain markets ABS. After acknowledging that many owners fit aftermarket fairing side panels and belly pans to the S models, Suzuki relented for the UK market and made a version available with full fairing for 2008, called the Sport.

Acknowledgements

Our thanks are due to V & J Motorcycles of Mudford, Yeovil, who supplied the machines featured in the illustrations throughout this manual. We would also like to thank NGK Spark Plugs (UK) Ltd for supplying the colour spark plug condition photographs, the Avon Rubber Company for supplying information on tyre fitting and Draper Tools Ltd for some of the workshop tools shown.

Thanks are also due to Julian Ryder who wrote the introduction 'Every Which Way' and to Suzuki (GB) Ltd who supplied model photographs.

About this Manual

The aim of this manual is to help you get the best value from your motorcycle. It can do so in several ways. It can help you decide what work must be done, even if you choose to have it done by a dealer; it provides information and procedures for routine maintenance and servicing; and it offers diagnostic and repair procedures to follow when trouble occurs.

We hope you use the manual to tackle the work yourself. For many simpler jobs, doing it yourself may be quicker than arranging an appointment to get the motorcycle into a dealer and making the trips to leave it and pick it up. More importantly, a lot of money can be saved by avoiding the expense the shop must pass on to you to cover its labour and overhead costs. An added benefit is the sense of satisfaction and accomplishment that you feel after doing the job yourself.

References to the left or right side of the motorcycle assume you are sitting on the seat, facing forward.

We take great pride in the accuracy of information given in this manual, but motorcycle manufacturers make alterations and design changes during the production run of a particular motorcycle of which they do not inform us. No liability can be accepted by the authors or publishers for loss, damage or injury caused by any errors in, or omissions from, the information given.

Frame and engine numbers

The frame serial number is stamped into the right-hand side of the steering head. The engine number is stamped into the crankcase on the left-hand side of the engine. Both of these numbers should be recorded and kept in a safe place so they can be furnished to law enforcement officials in the event of a theft. The carburettors also have an ID number stamped into them.

The frame serial number, engine serial number, colour code and carburettor ID should also be kept in a handy place (such as with your driver's licence) so they are always available when purchasing or ordering parts for your machine.

Procedures in this manual identify bikes by model code (e.g. SV650S-X). If not known, the model code can be determined from the initial frame numbers given below on UK and US market machines.

UK models

Model	Year	Initial frame no.
SV650-X	1999	JS1AV133200100001
SV650S-X	1999	JS1AV111200100001
SV650-Y	2000	JS1AV133200100771
SV650S-Y	2000	JS1AV111200101206
SV650-K1	2001	JS1AV133200101261
SV650S-K1	2001	JS1AV111200104066
SV650-K2	2002	JS1AV133200101764
SV650S-K2	2002	JS1AV111200106023
SV650-K3	2003	JS1BY111200100001
SV650S-K3	2003	JS1BY132200100001
SV650-K4	2004	JS1BY111200100630
SV650S-K4	2004	JS1BY132200102282
SV650-K5	2005	JS1BY111200100939
SV650S-K5	2005	JS1BY132200103347
SV650-K6	2006	JS1BY111200101345
SV650S-K6	2006	JS1BY132200104865
SV650-K7	2007	JS1BY1112001
SV650A-K7	2007	JS1BY1132001
SV650S-K7	2007	JS1BY1322001
SV650SA-K7	2007	JS1BY1342001
SV650-K8	2008	JS1BY111200101721
SV650S-K8/Sport	2008	JS1BY132200107232
SV650SA-K8	2008	JS1BY134100101354

US models

Model	Year	Initial frame no.
SV650-X	1999	JS1VP52A X2100001
SV650-Y	2000	JS1VP52A Y2100001
SV650-K1	2001	JS1VP52A 12100001
SV650S-K1	2001	JS1VP52A 12100001
SV650-K2	2002	JS1VP52A 22100001
SV650S-K2	2002	JS1VP52A 22100001
SV650-K3	2003	JS1VP53A 32100001
SV650S-K3	2003	JS1VP53A 32100001
SV650-K4	2004	JS1VP53A 42100001
SV650S-K4	2004	JS1VP53A 42100001
SV650-K5	2005	JS1VP53A 52100001
SV650S-K5	2005	JS1VP53A 52100001
SV650-K6/S-K6	2006	JS1VP53A 62100001
SV650-K7/S-K7	2007	JS1VP53A 72100001
SV650A-K7/SA-K7	2007	JS1VP53B 72100001
SV650-K8/S-K8	2008	JS1VP53A 82100001
SV650A-K8/SA-K8	2008	JS1VP53B 82100001

The engine number is stamped into the crankcase on the left-hand side of the engine

The frame number is stamped into the right-hand side of the steering head

Buying spare parts

Once you have found all the identification numbers, record them for reference when buying parts. Since the manufacturers change specifications, parts and vendors (companies that manufacture various components on the machine), providing the ID numbers is the only way to be reasonably sure that you are buying the correct parts.

Whenever possible, take the worn part to the dealer so direct comparison with the new component can be made. Along the trail from the manufacturer to the parts shelf, there are numerous places that the part can end up with the wrong number or be listed incorrectly.

The two places to purchase new parts for your motorcycle the franchised or main dealer and the parts/accessories store differ in the type of parts they carry. While dealers can obtain every single genuine part for your motorcycle, the accessory store is usually limited to normal high wear items such as chains and sprockets, brake pads, spark plugs and cables, and to tune-up parts and various engine gaskets, etc. Rarely will an accessory outlet have major suspension components, camshafts, transmission gears, or engine cases.

Used parts can be obtained from breakers yards for roughly half the price of new ones, but you can't always be sure of what you're getting. Once again, take your worn part to the breaker for direct comparison, or when ordering by mail order make sure that you can return it if you are not happy.

Whether buying new, used or rebuilt parts, the best course is to deal directly with someone who specialises in your particular make.

SV650-X
(1999 model year)

Introduced in 1999, the standard SV650 is unfaired and has conventional one-piece handlebars and a bracket mounted headlight unit.

It has a liquid-cooled 90° V-twin engine with chain drive to its double overhead camshafts which operate four valves per cylinder. Power is transmitted via a conventional wet multi-plate clutch to the horizontally-stacked 6-speed constant mesh gearbox, and then to the rear wheel by chain and sprockets. The engine is fed by two 39 mm CV carburettors, with ignition by a digital electronic system with separate maps for front and rear cylinders.

The engine is mounted in an oval-section aluminium-alloy truss frame and acts as a stressed member. Suspension is provided by conventional 41 mm oil-damped telescopic forks at the front, and a box-section aluminium swingarm acting on a single shock absorber via a three-way linkage at the rear. The shock absorber is adjustable for spring pre-load. Braking is by twin-piston sliding calipers at the front and by an opposed-piston caliper at the rear.

The SV650 was available in candy jay blue, pearl helios red, pearl canyon yellow and saturn black metallic.

SV650S-X
(1999 model year)

Introduced in 1999, the SV650S is a half-faired 'sports' version of the standard model, and has clip-on handlebars and footrests that are positioned higher and further back to provide a sportier riding position. Other detail differences include a fairing mounted twin headlight unit, fairing mounted front turn signals and mirrors, different instrument cluster, different shape top yoke, and a remote reservoir for the front brake master cylinder.

The engine, frame, suspension and braking systems are essentially the same as used on the standard SV650 model. The S model's reduction in wheelbase was achieved by reducing the swingarm length by 10 mm, and the final drive reduction ratio in the transmission was modified by using a smaller rear sprocket, giving a slightly poorer acceleration but a higher top speed.

The SV650S was available in candy jay blue, pearl helios red, pearl canyon yellow and saturn black metallic.

SV650-Y and SV650S-Y
(2000 model year)

Both models are technically unchanged. Colours were candy grand blue, pearl helios red, pearl canyon yellow and saturn black metallic.

SV650-K1 and SV650S-K1
(2001 model year)

With the exception of minor alterations to the water pump and clutch, both models were unchanged. Colours were candy grand blue, candy antares red, pearl lively yellow and saturn black metallic.

SV650-K2 and SV650S-K2
(2002 model year)

Apart from the front forks being fitted with pre-load adjusters, the model was otherwise unchanged from the previous year. Colours were candy grand blue, sonic silver metallic, pearl lively yellow and saturn black metallic.

SV650-K3 and SV650S-K3
(2003 model year)

Fuel injection replaced the carburettors and most market models were fitted with a pulse secondary air system and catalytic converter. An oil cooler was added and the clutch cover was incorporated in a one-piece right-hand engine cover. An anti-judder assembly was added to the clutch.

The frame and swinging arm were redesigned and a new, single piston sliding rear brake caliper was repositioned above the swingarm. The rider's footrest brackets, the sidestand and the exhaust system mountings were revised; a locknut was added to the steering head bearing adjuster and different front suspension pre-load adjusters were fitted.

On SV650S models, the fairing and bodywork were redesigned with more angular styling. The twin headlights incorporated the side light. The instruments were revised on both models and a new LED tail light was fitted.

The SV650 was available in hydranger blue metallic, sonic silver metallic and pearl novelty black; the SV650S was available in hydranger blue metallic, sonic silver metallic and burning copper metallic.

SV650-K4 and SV650S-K4
(2004 model year)

The rear sub-frame mountings are revised, lowering the frame height 40 mm and a thicker seat is fitted as standard - an optional seat, lowering the seat height 15 mm was available.

Colours were candy grand blue, pearl orpiment yellow and pearl nebular black.

SV650-K5 and SV650S-K5
(2005 model year)

A revised fuel level sender was fitted giving an advanced fuel level warning at approximately 4 litres. The radiator dimensions were altered, decreasing the overall width but increasing coolant capacity by 11%. An oil jet was fitted to the cam chain tensioners and the dimensions of the clutch friction material was altered to reduce clutch drag and improve neutral finding.

The SV650 was fitted with an instrument cowling.

The frame and swinging arm were finished in black. Bodywork colours were red, blue and black.

SV650-K6 and SV650S-K6
(2006 model year)

Both models are technically unchanged. Colours: silver, grey, red, blue.

SV650-K7 and SV650S-K7
(2007 model year)

The 2007 models differ in a number of respects from earlier models, although the changes are not obvious externally. These centre around the engine management system, and include a twin spark ignition system (two plugs per head) and new throttle bodies and a heated oxygen sensor. Models sold in certain markets have ABS. Colours: grey, red, blue, black.

SV650-K8 and SV650S-K8
(2008 model year)

No change from 2007 models. A fully faired Sport model was available in the UK. Colours: black, blue, grey, white.

Dimensions and weights

SV650

Overall length
- X, Y, K1 and K2 models
  - Austria, Switzerland, and Scandinavia models . . . 2120 mm
  - UK and all other Europe models . . . 2070 mm
- K3 models . . . 2125 mm
- K4-on models (non-ABS) . . . 2080 mm
- ABS models . . . 2120 mm

Overall width
- X, Y, K1 and K2 models . . . 750 mm
- K3-on models . . . 745 mm

Overall height
- X, Y, K1 and K2 models . . . 1060 mm
- K3-on models . . . 1085 mm

Wheelbase
- X, Y, K1 and K2 models . . . 1430 mm
- K3-on models (non-ABS) . . . 1440 mm
- ABS models . . . 1470 mm

Seat height
- X, Y, K1 and K2 models . . . 805 mm
- K3-on models . . . 800 mm

Ground clearance
- X, Y, K1 and K2 models . . . 140 mm
- K3-on models . . . 150 mm

Weight (dry)
- X, Y, K1 and K2 models . . . 165 kg
- K3 models . . . 167 kg
- K4 to K6 models . . . 165 kg
- K7-on models . . . 168 kg
- ABS models . . . 171 kg

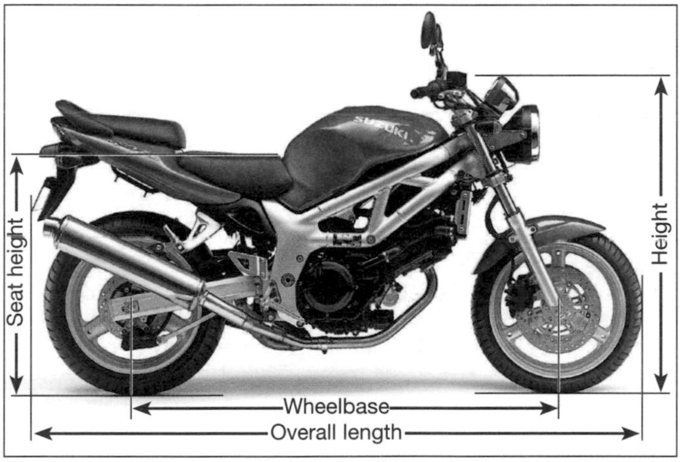

Engine

Type . . . Four stroke 90° V-twin, liquid-cooled, four valves per cylinder
Capacity . . . 645 cc
Bore . . . 81.0 mm
Stroke . . . 62.6 mm
Compression ratio . . . 11.5:1
Camshafts . . . DOHC, chain-driven
Lubrication . . . Wet sump
Fuel system
- X, Y, K1 and K2 models . . . 2 x 39 mm Mikuni CV-type carburettors
- K3-on models . . . Electronic fuel injection

Starter . . . Electric
Ignition system . . . Transistorized with electronic advance
Clutch . . . Wet multi-plate, cable-operated
Gearbox . . . 6-speed constant mesh
Final drive . . . Chain and sprockets

SV650S

Overall length
- X, Y, K1 and K2 models
  - Austria, Switzerland, and Scandinavia models . . . 2120 mm
  - UK and all other Europe models . . . 2045 mm
- K3 models . . . 2130 mm
- K4-on models (non-ABS) . . . 2085 mm
- ABS models . . . 2120 mm

Overall width
- X, Y, K1 and K2 models . . . 740 mm
- K3-on models . . . 730 mm

Overall height
- X, Y, K1 and K2 models . . . 1130 mm
- K3 models . . . 1175 mm
- K4-on models . . . 1170 mm

Wheelbase
- X, Y, K1 and K2 models . . . 1420 mm
- K3 to K6 models . . . 1430 mm
- K7-on models . . . 1425 mm
- ABS models . . . 1470 mm

Seat height
- X, Y, K1 and K2 models . . . 805 mm
- K3-on models . . . 800 mm

Ground clearance
- X, Y, K1 and K2 models . . . 140 mm
- K3-on models . . . 155 mm

Weight (dry)
- X, Y, K1 and K2 models . . . 169 kg
- K3 models . . . 171 kg
- K4 to K6 models . . . 169 kg
- K7-on models . . . 172 kg
- ABS models . . . 175 kg

Chassis

Frame type . . . Aluminium-alloy truss frame, with engine as stressed member
Rake . . . 24.8°
Trail . . . 100 mm
Fuel tank capacity (including reserve)
- X, Y, K1 and K2 models . . . 16 litres
- K3-on Europe models . . . 17 litres
- K3-on US models . . . 16 litres

Front suspension
- Type . . . 41 mm oil-damped telescopic forks
- Travel . . . 130 mm
- Adjustment . . . Spring pre-load from K2 model onwards

Rear suspension
- Type . . . Single shock absorber, rising rate linkage, box section aluminium swingarm
- Travel
  - X, Y, K1 and K2 models . . . 125 mm
  - K3 to K6 models (non-ABS) . . . 137 mm
  - ABS models . . . 147 mm
- Adjustment . . . Spring pre-load

Wheels . . . 17 inch cast aluminium-alloy
Tyres
- Front . . . 120/60ZR17 (55W) tubeless
- Rear . . . 160/60ZR17 (69W) tubeless

Front brake . . . 290 mm discs with Tokico twin piston sliding calipers
Rear brake
- X, Y, K1 and K2 models . . . 240 mm disc with Tokico opposed-piston caliper
- K3-on models . . . 220 mm disc with Nissin single piston sliding caliper

Professional mechanics are trained in safe working procedures. However enthusiastic you may be about getting on with the job at hand, take the time to ensure that your safety is not put at risk. A moment's lack of attention can result in an accident, as can failure to observe simple precautions.

There will always be new ways of having accidents, and the following is not a comprehensive list of all dangers; it is intended rather to make you aware of the risks and to encourage a safe approach to all work you carry out on your bike.

Asbestos

● Certain friction, insulating, sealing and other products - such as brake pads, clutch linings, gaskets, etc. - contain asbestos. Extreme care must be taken to avoid inhalation of dust from such products since it is hazardous to health. If in doubt, assume that they do contain asbestos.

Fire

● Remember at all times that petrol is highly flammable. Never smoke or have any kind of naked flame around, when working on the vehicle. But the risk does not end there - a spark caused by an electrical short-circuit, by two metal surfaces contacting each other, by careless use of tools, or even by static electricity built up in your body under certain conditions, can ignite petrol vapour, which in a confined space is highly explosive. Never use petrol as a cleaning solvent. Use an approved safety solvent.

● Always disconnect the battery earth terminal before working on any part of the fuel or electrical system, and never risk spilling fuel on to a hot engine or exhaust.

● It is recommended that a fire extinguisher of a type suitable for fuel and electrical fires is kept handy in the garage or workplace at all times. Never try to extinguish a fuel or electrical fire with water.

Fumes

● Certain fumes are highly toxic and can quickly cause unconsciousness and even death if inhaled to any extent. Petrol vapour comes into this category, as do the vapours from certain solvents such as trichloro-ethylene. Any draining or pouring of such volatile fluids should be done in a well ventilated area.

● When using cleaning fluids and solvents, read the instructions carefully. Never use materials from unmarked containers - they may give off poisonous vapours.

● Never run the engine of a motor vehicle in an enclosed space such as a garage. Exhaust fumes contain carbon monoxide which is extremely poisonous; if you need to run the engine, always do so in the open air or at least have the rear of the vehicle outside the workplace.

The battery

● Never cause a spark, or allow a naked light near the vehicle's battery. It will normally be giving off a certain amount of hydrogen gas, which is highly explosive.

● Always disconnect the battery ground (earth) terminal before working on the fuel or electrical systems (except where noted).

● If possible, loosen the filler plugs or cover when charging the battery from an external source. Do not charge at an excessive rate or the battery may burst.

● Take care when topping up, cleaning or carrying the battery. The acid electrolyte, evenwhen diluted, is very corrosive and should not be allowed to contact the eyes or skin. Always wear rubber gloves and goggles or a face shield. If you ever need to prepare electrolyte yourself, always add the acid slowly to the water; never add the water to the acid.

Electricity

● When using an electric power tool, inspection light etc., always ensure that the appliance is correctly connected to its plug and that, where necessary, it is properly grounded (earthed). Do not use such appliances in damp conditions and, again, beware of creating a spark or applying excessive heat in the vicinity of fuel or fuel vapour. Also ensure that the appliances meet national safety standards.

● A severe electric shock can result from touching certain parts of the electrical system, such as the spark plug wires (HT leads), when the engine is running or being cranked, particularly if components are damp or the insulation is defective. Where an electronic ignition system is used, the secondary (HT) voltage is much higher and could prove fatal.

Remember...

✗ **Don't** start the engine without first ascertaining that the transmission is in neutral.

✗ **Don't** suddenly remove the pressure cap from a hot cooling system - cover it with a cloth and release the pressure gradually first, or you may get scalded by escaping coolant.

✗ **Don't** attempt to drain oil until you are sure it has cooled sufficiently to avoid scalding you.

✗ **Don't** grasp any part of the engine or exhaust system without first ascertaining that it is cool enough not to burn you.

✗ **Don't** allow brake fluid or antifreeze to contact the machine's paintwork or plastic components.

✗ **Don't** siphon toxic liquids such as fuel, hydraulic fluid or antifreeze by mouth, or allow them to remain on your skin.

✗ **Don't** inhale dust - it may be injurious to health (see Asbestos heading).

✗ **Don't** allow any spilled oil or grease to remain on the floor - wipe it up right away, before someone slips on it.

✗ **Don't** use ill-fitting spanners or other tools which may slip and cause injury.

✗ **Don't** lift a heavy component which may be beyond your capability - get assistance.

✗ **Don't** rush to finish a job or take unverified short cuts.

✗ **Don't** allow children or animals in or around an unattended vehicle.

✗ **Don't** inflate a tyre above the recommended pressure. Apart from overstressing the carcass, in extreme cases the tyre may blow off forcibly.

✔ **Do** ensure that the machine is supported securely at all times. This is especially important when the machine is blocked up to aid wheel or fork removal.

✔ **Do** take care when attempting to loosen a stubborn nut or bolt. It is generally better to pull on a spanner, rather than push, so that if you slip, you fall away from the machine rather than onto it.

✔ **Do** wear eye protection when using power tools such as drill, sander, bench grinder etc.

✔ **Do** use a barrier cream on your hands prior to undertaking dirty jobs - it will protect your skin from infection as well as making the dirt easier to remove afterwards; but make sure your hands aren't left slippery. Note that long-term contact with used engine oil can be a health hazard.

✔ **Do** keep loose clothing (cuffs, ties etc. and long hair) well out of the way of moving mechanical parts.

✔ **Do** remove rings, wristwatch etc., before working on the vehicle - especially the electrical system.

✔ **Do** keep your work area tidy - it is only too easy to fall over articles left lying around.

✔ **Do** exercise caution when compressing springs for removal or installation. Ensure that the tension is applied and released in a controlled manner, using suitable tools which preclude the possibility of the spring escaping violently.

✔ **Do** ensure that any lifting tackle used has a safe working load rating adequate for the job.

✔ **Do** get someone to check periodically that all is well, when working alone on the vehicle.

✔ **Do** carry out work in a logical sequence and check that everything is correctly assembled and tightened afterwards.

✔ **Do** remember that your vehicle's safety affects that of yourself and others. If in doubt on any point, get professional advice.

● If in spite of following these precautions, you are unfortunate enough to injure yourself, seek medical attention as soon as possible.

Note: *The daily (pre-ride) checks outlined in the owner's manual covers those items which should be inspected on a daily basis.*

Engine oil level

Before you start:

✔ Take the motorcycle on a short run to allow it to reach normal operating temperature.

Caution: Do not run the engine in an enclosed space such as a garage or workshop.

✔ Stop the engine and support the motorcycle upright using an auxiliary stand. Allow it to stand undisturbed for a few minutes to allow the oil level to stabilise. Make sure the motorcycle is on level ground.

Bike care:

● If you have to add oil frequently, check whether you have any oil leaks from the engine joints, seals and gaskets. If not, the engine could be burning oil, in which case there will be white smoke coming out of the exhaust (see *Fault Finding* in the Reference section).

The correct oil

● Modern, high-revving engines place great demands on their oil. It is very important that the correct oil for your bike is used.

● Always top up with a good quality oil of the specified type and viscosity and do not overfill the engine.

Oil type	API grade SF or SG or SH/SJ with JASO MA
Oil viscosity	SAE 10W40

1 Wipe the oil level inspection window so that it is clean. it is located on the right-hand side of the engine.

2 With the motorcycle vertical, the oil level should lie between the F (full) and L (low) level lines on the window.

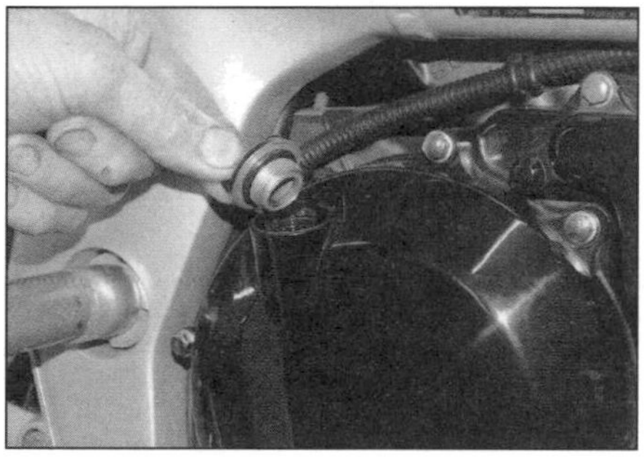

3 If the level is below the L line, unscrew the oil filler cap from the top of the clutch cover.

4 Top up with the recommended grade and type of oil to bring the level up to the F line on the inspection window. Do not overfill. On completion, make sure the filler cap is secure in the cover

Coolant level

> ***Warning: DO NOT remove the radiator pressure cap to add coolant. Topping up is done via the coolant reservoir tank filler. DO NOT leave open containers of coolant about, as it is poisonous.***

Before you start:

✔ The coolant reservoir is located behind the frame on the right-hand side below the fuel tank.

✔ Use a coolant mixture of 50% distilled water and 50% corrosion inhibited ethylene glycol anti-freeze. If the motorcycle is ever exposed to temperatures below minus 31°C, the percentage of anti-freeze can be increased to a maximum of 60% this will prevent freezing up to minus 55°C.

✔ Check the coolant level when the engine is cold and with motorcycle on level ground and supported upright.

Bike care:

● Use anti-freeze in the system all year round, not just in the winter. Do not top up using only water, as the system will become too diluted.

● Do not fill the reservoir tank above the F (full) level line.

● If the coolant level falls steadily, check the system for leaks (see Chapter 1). If no leaks are found and the level continues to fall, take the machine to a Suzuki dealer for a pressure test.

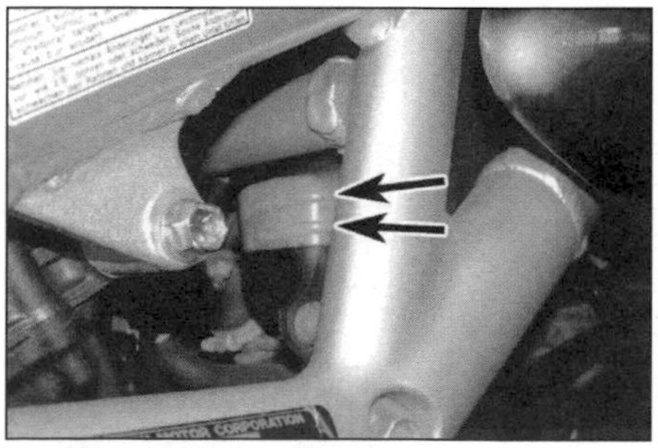

1 With the motorcycle upright, the coolant level should lie between the F (full) and L (low) level lines (arrowed) marked on the reservoir.

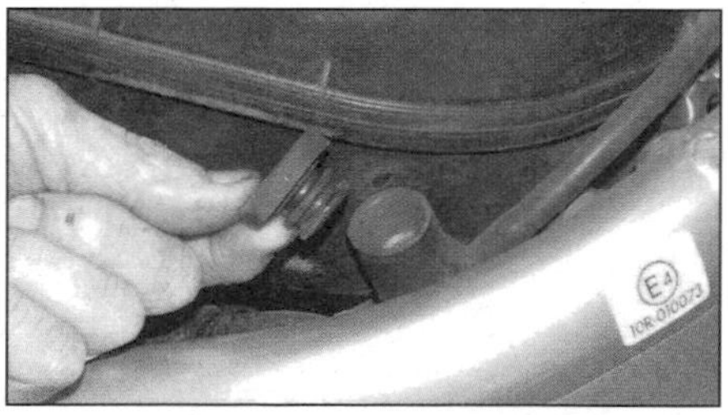

2 If the coolant level is low, raise the fuel tank (see Chapter 4) and support it on the prop, then remove the reservoir filler cap. Note that on X, Y, K1 and K2 models, the filler cap is on the right-hand side of the bike, and on K3-on models it is on the left-hand side.

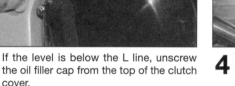

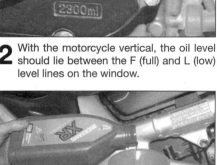

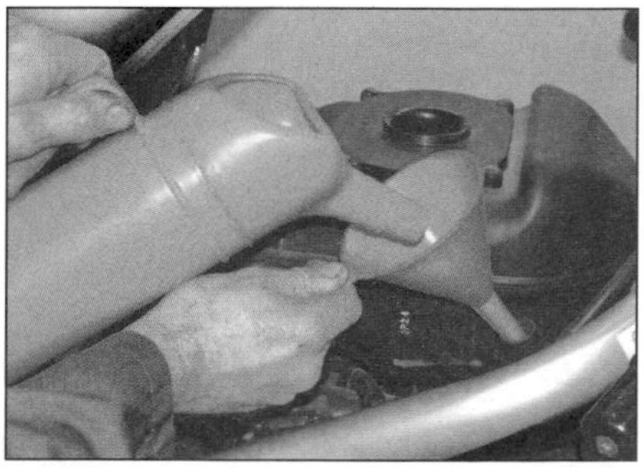

3 Top the coolant level up with the recommended coolant mixture, then fit the cap. Lower the fuel tank.

Suspension, steering and drive chain

- Check that the front and rear suspension operates smoothly without binding (see Chapter 1).
- Check that the steering moves smoothly from lock-to-lock, and that there is no freeplay.
- Check that the chain isn't too loose or too tight, and adjust it if necessary (see Chapter 1). If the chain looks dry, lubricate it (see Chapter 1).

Legal and safety checks

- Check that the headlight, tail light, brake light, licence plate light (where fitted), instrument lights, turn signals and horn work correctly. A working speedometer, graduated in mph, is a statutory requirement in the UK.
- Check that the throttle grip rotates smoothly and snaps shut when released, in all steering positions. Also check for the correct amount of freeplay in the cable (see Chapter 1).
- Check that the clutch operates smoothly in all steering positions. Also check for the correct amount of freeplay in the cable (see Chapter 1).
- Check that sidestand return springs hold the stand up securely when retracted.
- Check the operation of the starter interlock system. It should only be possible to start the engine if the transmission is in neutral and the clutch lever is pulled in, or if the transmission is in gear with the clutch lever pulled in and the sidestand up. Check that the engine shuts off when the kill switch is operated.
- Check that you have enough fuel to complete your journey. If you notice signs of fuel leakage, rectify the cause immediately.

Brakes

> ***Warning: Brake hydraulic fluid can harm your eyes and damage painted surfaces, so use extreme caution when handling and pouring it and cover surrounding surfaces with rag. Do not use fluid that has been standing open for some time, as it is hygroscopic (absorbs moisture from the air) which can cause a dangerous loss of braking effectiveness.***

Before you start:

✔ The front master cylinder reservoir is on the right-hand handlebar. The rear master cylinder reservoir is located under the passenger seat on the right-hand side.

✔ Make sure you have a supply of new DOT 4 hydraulic fluid and support the motorcycle upright so that the reservoirs are level you may have to turn the handlebars when checking the front reservoir.

Bike care:

- The fluid in the front and rear brake master cylinder reservoirs will drop slightly as the brake pads wear down (see Chapter 1 to check pad wear). If either reservoir requires repeated topping-up there could be a leak in the hydraulic system, which must be rectified immediately.
- Check that there is no sign of fluid leakage from the hoses and brake components and check the operation of both brakes before taking the machine on the road; if there is evidence of air in the system (a spongy feel to lever or pedal), the system must be bled (see Chapter 7).

FRONT - SV650

1 The front brake fluid level, visible through the window in the reservoir body, must be above the LOWER level line (arrowed).

2 If the level is below the LOWER line, undo the two reservoir cover screws and remove the cover, diaphragm plate and diaphragm.

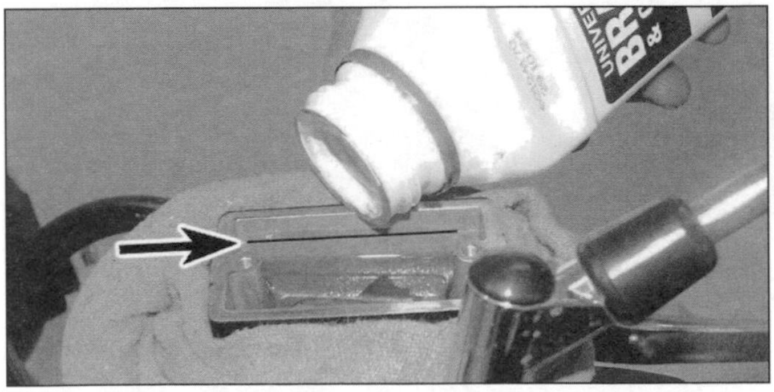

3 Top up with new DOT 4 fluid until the level is up to the ridge along the inside of the front wall of the reservoir (arrowed). Do not overfill.

4 Ensure that the diaphragm is correctly seated before installing the plate and cover. Secure the cover with the two screws.

FRONT - SV650S

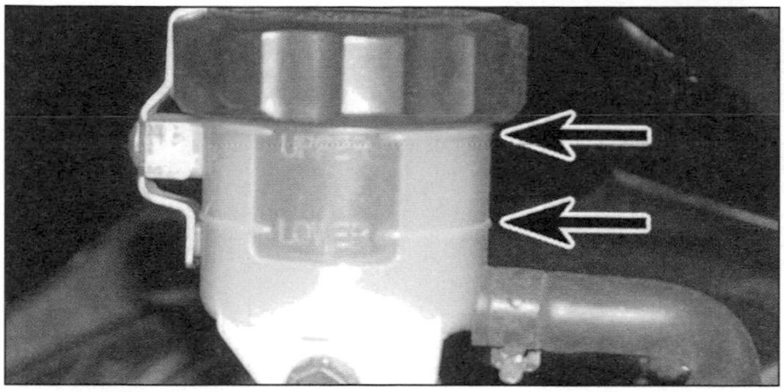

5 The front brake fluid level, visible through the reservoir body, must lie between the UPPER and LOWER level lines (arrowed).

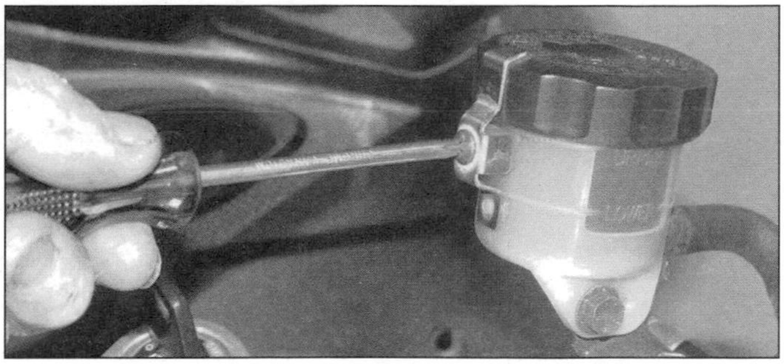

6 If the level is below the LOWER line, undo the reservoir cap clamp screw and remove the clamp, then unscrew the cap and remove the diaphragm plate and diaphragm.

7 Top up with new DOT 4 fluid until the level is up to the UPPER level line on the reservoir. Do not overfill.

8 Ensure that the diaphragm is correctly seated before installing the plate and cap. Secure the cap with the clamp.

REAR - all X, Y, K1 and K2 models

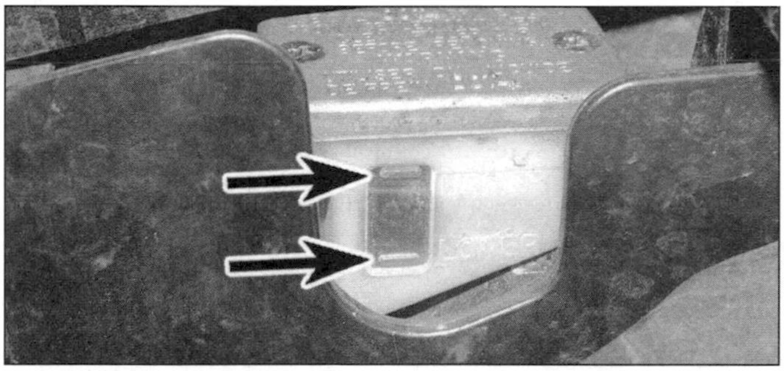

9 Remove the pillion seat (see Chapter 8). The rear brake fluid level, visible through the reservoir body, must lie between the UPPER and LOWER level lines.

10 If the level is below the LOWER level line, angle the reservoir so that a screwdriver can be applied, then undo the two cover screws and remove the cover and diaphragm.

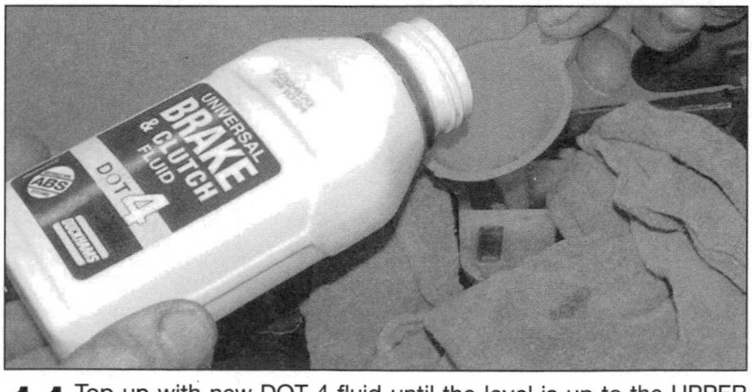

11 Top up with new DOT 4 fluid until the level is up to the UPPER level line. Do not overfill.

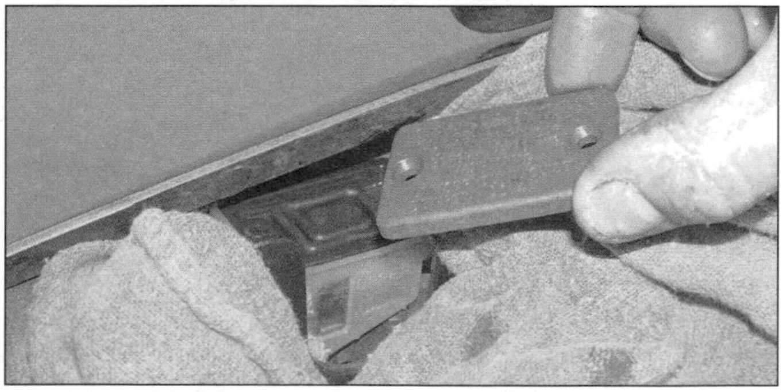

12 Ensure that the diaphragm is correctly seated before installing the cover. Secure the cover with the two screws.

REAR - all K3-on models

13 The rear brake fluid level, visible through the reservoir body, must lie between the UPPER and LOWER level lines.

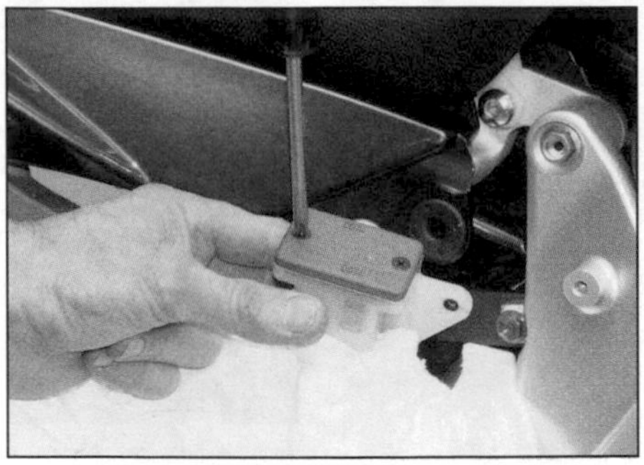

14 If the level is below the LOWER level line, remove the right-hand side panel (see Chapter 8). Undo the mounting bolt and displace the reservoir so that a screwdriver can be applied, then undo the two cover screws.

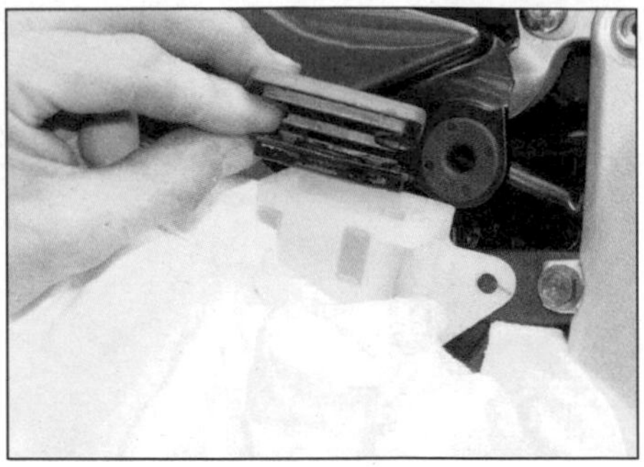

15 Remove the cover and diaphragm, then top up with new DOT 4 fluid until the level is up to the UPPER level line. Do not overfill. Ensure that the diaphragm is correctly seated before installing the cover. Secure the cover with the two screws.

Tyres

The correct pressures:

- The tyres must be checked when cold, not immediately after riding. Note that low tyre pressures may cause the tyre to slip on the rim or come off. High tyre pressures will cause abnormal tread wear and unsafe handling.
- Use an accurate pressure gauge. Many forecourt gauges are wildly inaccurate. If you buy your own, spend as much as you can justify on a quality gauge.
- Proper air pressure will increase tyre life and provide maximum stability and ride comfort.

Front	Rear
33 psi (2.25 Bar)	36 psi (2.50 Bar)

Tyre care:

- Check the tyres carefully for cuts, tears, embedded nails or other sharp objects and excessive wear. Operation of the motorcycle with excessively worn tyres is extremely hazardous, as traction and handling are directly affected.
- Check the condition of the tyre valve and ensure the dust cap is in place.
- Pick out any stones or nails which may have become embedded in the tyre tread. If left, they will eventually penetrate through the casing and cause a puncture.
- If tyre damage is apparent, or unexplained loss of pressure is experienced, seek the advice of a tyre fitting specialist without delay.

Tyre tread depth:

- At the time of writing UK law requires that tread depth must be at least 1 mm over 3/4 of the tread breadth all the way around the tyre, with no bald patches. Many riders, however, consider 2 mm tread depth minimum to be a safer limit. Suzuki recommend a minimum of 1.6 mm on the front and 2 mm on the rear.

- Many tyres now incorporate wear indicators in the tread. Identify the location marking on the tyre sidewall to locate the indicator bar and renew the tyre if the tread has worn down to the bar some tyres have wear bars near the edge as well as in the centre.

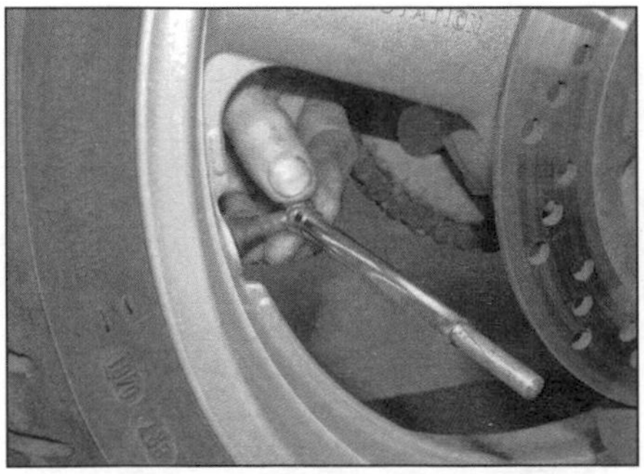

1 Check the tyre pressures when cold. Do not forget to fit the cap after checking the pressure.

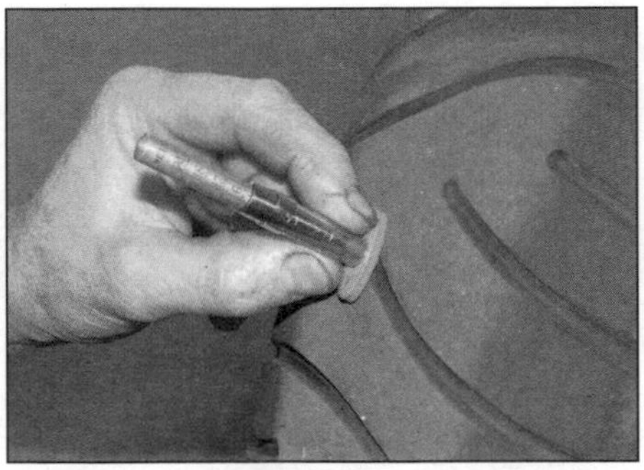

2 Measure tread depth at the centre of the tyre using a depth gauge.

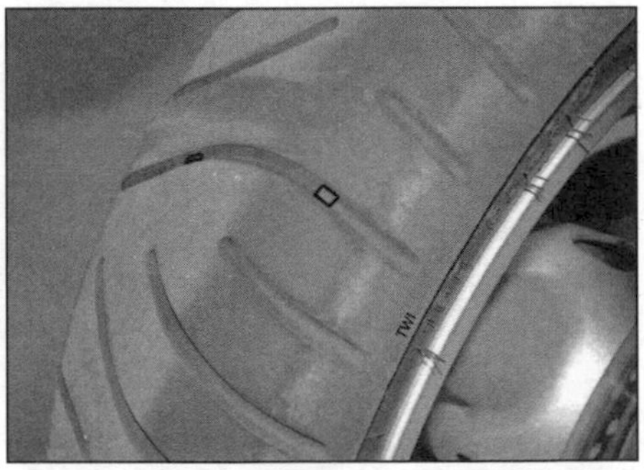

3 Tyre tread wear indicator bars and their location marking (usually either an arrow, a triangle or the letters TWI) on the sidewall.

Chapter 1
Routine maintenance and servicing

Contents

Degrees of difficulty

Easy, suitable for novice with little experience	**Fairly easy,** suitable for beginner with some experience	**Fairly difficult,** suitable for competent DIY mechanic	**Difficult,** suitable for experienced DIY mechanic	**Very difficult,** suitable for expert DIY or professional

Servicing specifications

Engine

Engine idle speed	1300 ± 100 rpm	
Spark plugs	**Type**	**Electrode gap**
Standard	NGK CR8E or Denso U24ESR-N	0.7 to 0.8 mm
For extended high speed riding	NGK CR9E or Denso U27ESR-N	0.7 to 0.8 mm
Valve clearances (COLD engine)		
Intake valves	0.1 to 0.2 mm	
Exhaust valves	0.2 to 0.3 mm	
Carburettor/throttle body synchronisation	20 mm Hg max. difference between readings	
Cylinder compression		
Standard	213 psi (15.0 Bar)	
Service limit	156 psi (11.0 Bar)	
Max. difference between cylinders	28 psi (2.0 Bar)	
Cylinder identification	Front cyl no. 1, rear cyl no. 2	
Oil pressure (at main oil gallery plug, with engine warm)	28 to 85 psi (2.0 to 6.0 Bar) @ 3000 rpm, oil @ 60°C	

Miscellaneous

Drive chain	
Slack	20 to 30 mm with motorcycle on sidestand
Stretch limit (21 pin length – see text)	319.4 mm
Throttle twistgrip freeplay	
Opening (front) cable	2.0 to 4.0 mm
Closing (rear) cable	zero (no freeplay)
Clutch lever freeplay	10 to 15 mm
Clutch release mechanism screw	¼ turn out
Tyre pressures (cold)	see *Daily (pre-ride) checks* on page 0•16
Rear brake pedal height	SV650 – 50 to 60 mm, SV650S – 60 to 70 mm
Gearchange lever height	
SV650	55 to 60 mm
SV650S	60 to 70 mm

Recommended lubricants and fluids

Fuel grade	unleaded, minimum 91 RON (Research Octane Number)
Engine/transmission oil type	API grade SF/ SG or SH/SJ with JASO MA motorcycle oil
Engine/transmission oil viscosity	SAE 10W40
Engine/transmission oil capacity - X to K2 models	
Oil change	2.3 litres
Oil and filter change	2.4 litres
Following engine overhaul – dry engine, new filter	2.7 litres
Engine/transmission oil capacity – K3-on models	
Oil change	2.3 litres
Oil and filter change	2.7 litres
Following engine overhaul – dry engine, new filter	3.1 litres
Coolant type	50% distilled water, 50% corrosion inhibited ethylene glycol anti-freeze
Coolant capacity (inc. reservoir)	Approx. 1.6 litres
Brake fluid	DOT 4
Drive chain	Aerosol chain lube suitable for O-ring and X-ring chains
Steering head bearings	Multi-purpose grease
Swingarm pivot bearings and suspension linkage bearings	Multi-purpose grease
Bearing seal lips	Multi-purpose grease
Gearchange lever/rear brake pedal/footrest pivots	Multi-purpose grease
Brake and clutch lever pivots	Multi-purpose grease or engine oil
Sidestand pivot	Multi-purpose grease
Throttle grip	Multi-purpose grease or dry film lubricant
Front brake lever piston tip	Silicone grease
Cables	Aerosol cable lubricant

Torque settings

Coolant drain plug	13 Nm
Crankshaft end cap	11 Nm
Engine/transmission oil drain plug	21 Nm
Fork bottom yoke clamp bolts	23 Nm
Fork top yoke clamp bolts	23 Nm
Handlebar clamp bolts	23 Nm
Handlebar holder nuts	45 Nm
Main oil gallery plug	18 Nm
Rear axle nut	65 Nm
Rear brake torque arm nut	35 Nm
Spark plugs	11 Nm
Steering stem adjuster locknut (K3, K4 and K5 models)	80 Nm
Steering stem adjuster nut preload	45 Nm
Steering stem nut	
X, Y, K1 and K2 models	65 Nm
K3-on models	90 Nm
Timing mark inspection cap	23 Nm

Note: *The daily (pre-ride) checks outlined in the owner's manual covers those items which should be inspected on a daily basis. Always perform the pre-ride inspection at every maintenance interval (in addition to the procedures listed). The intervals listed below are the intervals recommended by the manufacturer for each particular operation during the model years covered in this manual. Your owner's manual may have different intervals for your model.*

Daily (pre-ride)

- ☐ See 'Daily (pre-ride) checks' at the beginning of this manual.

After the initial 600 miles (1000 km)

Note: *This check is usually performed by a Suzuki dealer after the first 600 miles (1000 km) from new. Thereafter, maintenance is carried out according to the following intervals of the schedule.*

Every 600 miles (1000 km)

- ☐ Check, adjust, clean and lubricate the drive chain (Section 1)

Every 4000 miles (6000 km)

Carry out all the items under the Daily (pre-ride) checks and the 600 mile (1000 km) check, plus the following:

- ☐ Check and clean the air filter element (Section 2)
- ☐ Check the spark plugs (Section 3)
- ☐ Check the fuel hoses, PAIR and EVAP system hoses, and fuel system components (Section 4)
- ☐ Change the engine/transmission oil (Section 5)
- ☐ Check and adjust the engine idle speed – X to K6 models (Section 6)
- ☐ Check throttle/choke cable operation and freeplay (Section 7)
- ☐ Check the operation of the clutch (Section 8)
- ☐ Check the cooling system (Section 9)
- ☐ Check for drive chain wear and stretch (Section 10)
- ☐ Check the brake pads for wear (Section 11)
- ☐ Check the operation of the braking system (Section 12)
- ☐ Check the tyre and wheel condition, and the tyre tread depth (Daily (pre-ride) checks and Section 13)
- ☐ Check the tightness of all nuts and bolts (Section 14)
- ☐ Check and lubricate the sidestand, lever pivots and cables (Section 15)

Every 7500 miles (12,000 km)

Carry out all the items under the 4000 mile (6000 km) check, plus the following:

- ☐ Renew the spark plugs (Section 16)
- ☐ Check carburettor synchronisation – X,Y, K1 and K2 models (Section 17)
- ☐ Check throttle body synchronisation – K3-on models (Section 18)
- ☐ Check the steering head bearing freeplay (Section 19)
- ☐ Check the front and rear suspension (Section 20)

Every 11,000 miles (18,000 km)

Carry out all the items under the 4000 mile (6000 km) check, plus the following:

- ☐ Renew the air filter element (Section 21)
- ☐ Change the engine/transmission oil and renew the oil filter (Section 22)

Every 15,000 miles (24,000 km)

Carry out all the items under the 7500 mile (12,000 km) check, plus the following:

- ☐ Check the valve clearances (Section 23)

Every two years

- ☐ Change the brake fluid (Section 24)
- ☐ Change the coolant (Section 25)

Every four years

- ☐ Renew the brake hoses (Section 26)
- ☐ Renew the fuel hoses, PAIR and EVAP system hoses (Section 27)

Non-scheduled maintenance

- ☐ Check the cylinder compression (Section 28)
- ☐ Check the engine oil pressure (Section 29)
- ☐ Check the wheel bearings (Section 30)
- ☐ Re-grease the steering head bearings (Section 31)
- ☐ Re-grease the swingarm and suspension linkage bearings (Section 32)
- ☐ Renew the brake master cylinder and caliper seals (Section 33)
- ☐ Change the front fork oil (Section 34)
- ☐ Check the battery (Section 35)
- ☐ Check the sidestand and sidestand switch operation (Section 36)
- ☐ Check and adjust the headlight aim (Section 37)

Component locations on the right side – (X, Y, K1 and K2 models)

1 Rear brake fluid reservoir
2 Rear brake light switch
3 Coolant level marks
4 Coolant filler cap
5 Front brake fluid reservoir
6 Radiator pressure cap
7 Coolant drain plug
8 Engine oil level inspection window
9 Engine oil filler cap
10 Rear brake pedal height adjuster
11 Drive chain adjuster

Component locations on the left side – (X, Y, K1 and K2 models)

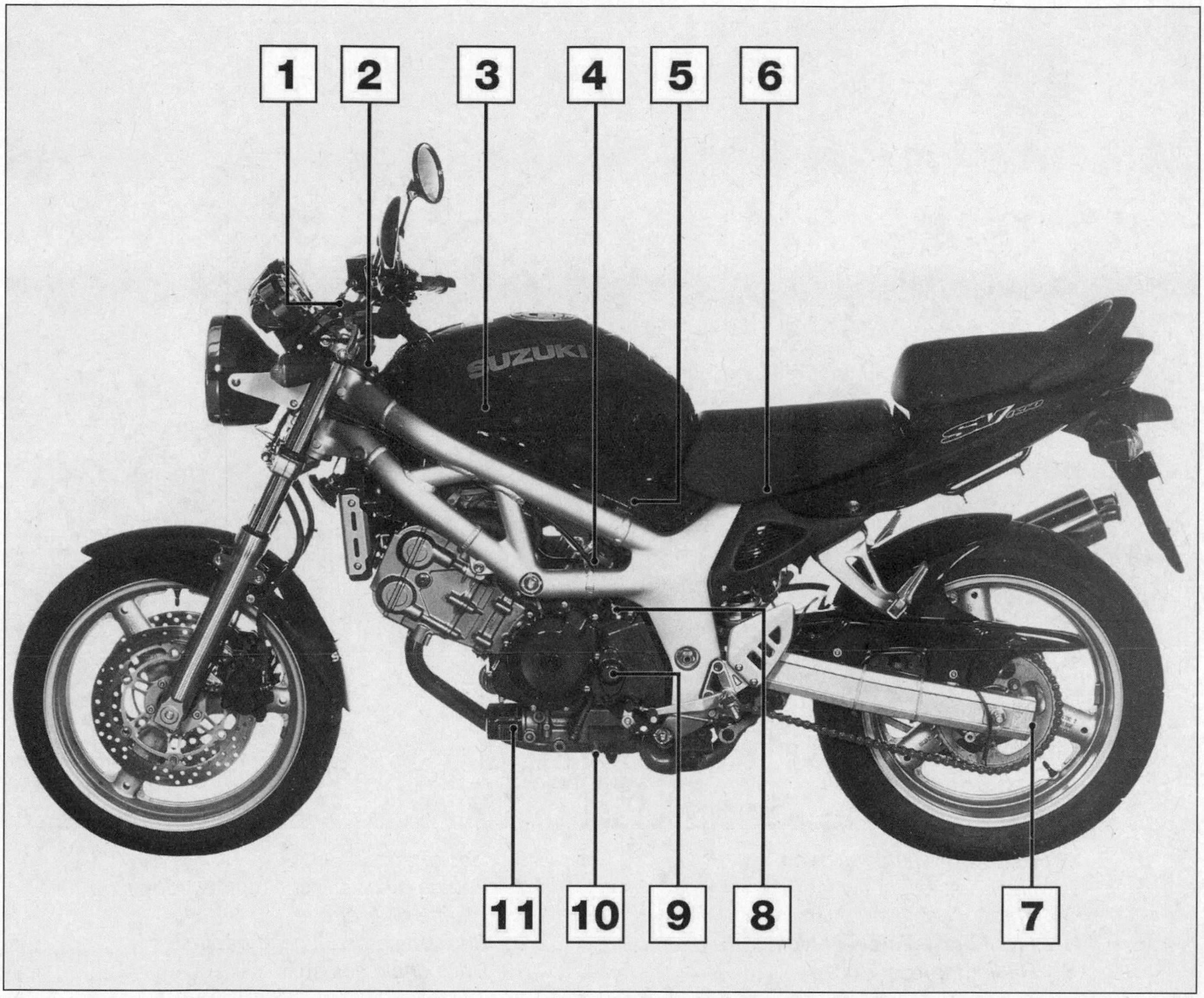

1 *Clutch cable upper adjuster*
2 *Steering head bearing adjuster*
3 *Air filter*
4 *Idle speed adjuster*
5 *Fuel tap filter*
6 *Battery*
7 *Drive chain adjuster*
8 *Clutch cable lower adjuster*
9 *Clutch release mechanism adjuster*
10 *Oil drain plug*
11 *Oil filter*

Component locations on the right side – (K3-on models)

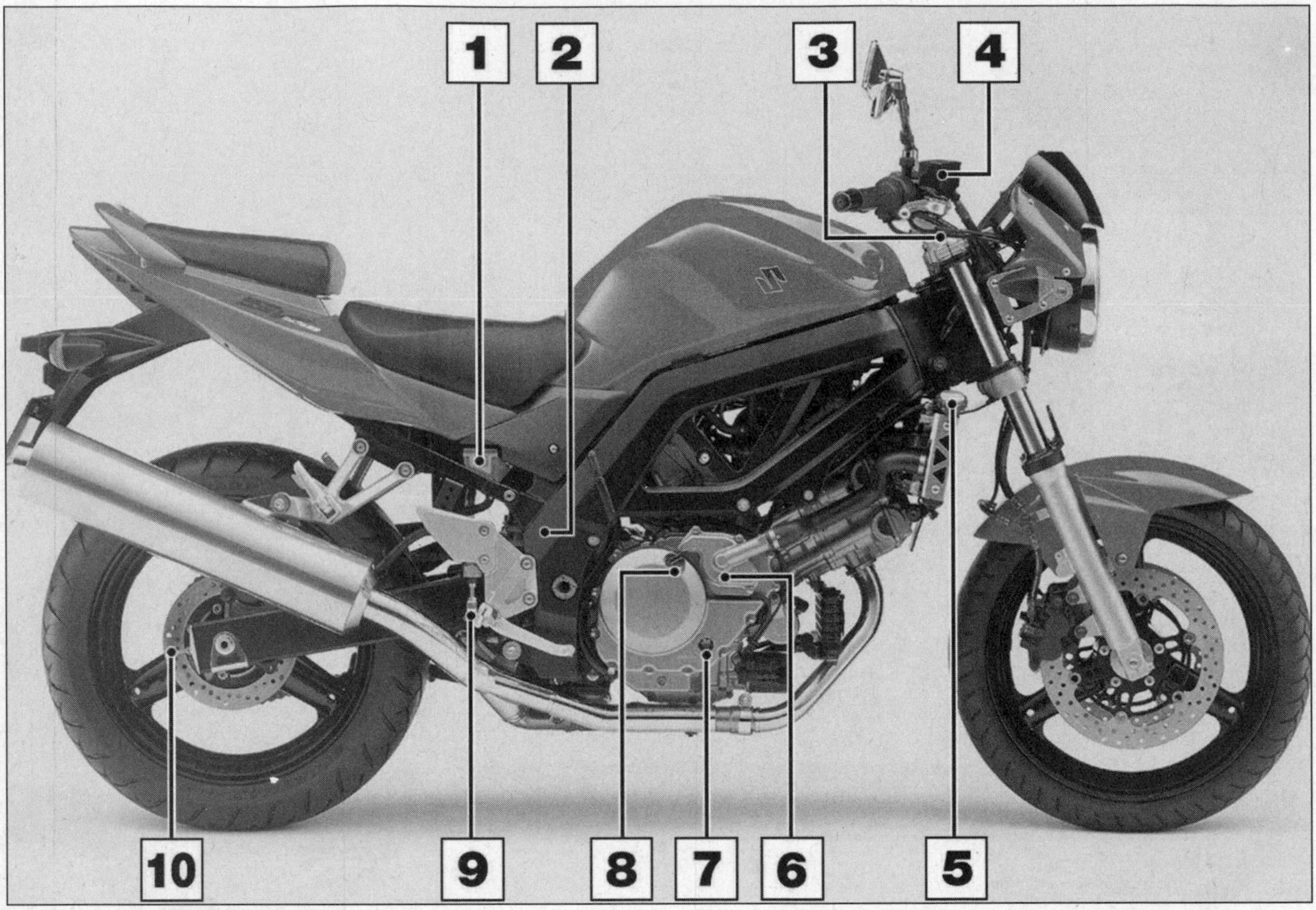

1 *Rear brake fluid reservoir*
2 *Rear brake light switch*
3 *Throttle cable adjusters*
4 *Front brake fluid reservoir*
5 *Radiator pressure cap*
6 *Coolant drain plug*
7 *Engine oil level inspection window*
8 *Engine oil filler cap*
9 *Rear brake pedal height adjuster*
10 *Drive chain adjuster*

Component locations on the left side – (K3-on models)

1 *Clutch cable upper adjuster*
2 *Steering head bearing adjuster*
3 *Air filter*
4 *Idle speed adjuster*
5 *Coolant level marks*
6 *Coolant filler cap*
7 *Drive chain adjuster*
8 *Battery*
9 *Clutch cable lower adjuster*
10 *Clutch release mechanism adjuster*
11 *Oil drain plug*
12 *Oil filter*

Introduction

1 This Chapter is designed to help the home mechanic maintain his/her motorcycle for safety, economy, long life and peak performance.

2 Deciding where to start or plug into the routine maintenance schedule depends on several factors. If your motorcycle has been maintained according to the warranty standards and has just come out of warranty, start routine maintenance as it coincides with the next mileage or calendar interval. If you have owned the machine for some time but have never performed any maintenance on it, start at the nearest interval and include some additional procedures to ensure that nothing important is overlooked. If you have just had a major engine overhaul, then start the maintenance routine from the beginning. If you have a used machine and have no knowledge of its history or maintenance record, combine all the checks into one large service initially and then settle into the specified maintenance schedule.

3 Before beginning any maintenance or repair, the machine should be cleaned thoroughly, especially around the oil filter, spark plugs, valve covers, body panels, carburettors/throttle bodies, etc. Cleaning will help ensure that dirt does not contaminate the engine and will allow you to detect wear and damage that could otherwise easily go unnoticed.

4 Certain maintenance information is sometimes printed on labels attached to the motorcycle. If the information on the labels differs from that included here, use the information on the label.

Every 600 miles (1000 km)

1 Drive chain and sprockets – check, adjustment, cleaning and lubrication

Check

1 A neglected drive chain won't last long and will quickly damage the sprockets. Routine chain adjustment and lubrication isn't difficult and will ensure maximum chain and sprocket life.

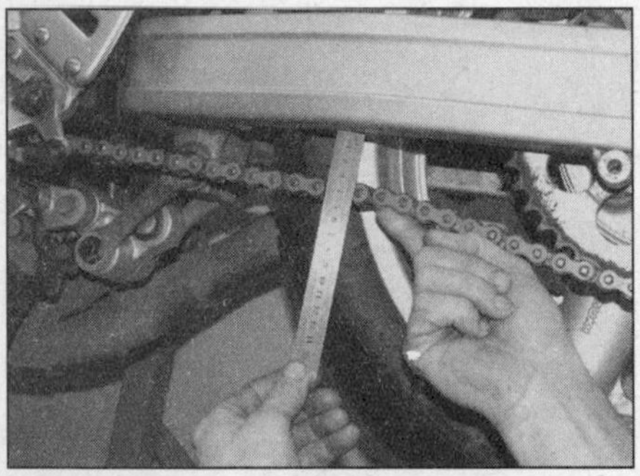

1.3 Push up on the chain and measure the slack

2 To check the chain, place the bike on its sidestand and shift the transmission into neutral. Make sure the ignition switch is OFF.

3 Push up on the bottom run of the chain midway between the two sprockets and measure the amount of slack, then compare your measurement to that listed in this Chapter's Specifications **(see illustration)**. As the chain stretches with wear, adjustment will periodically be necessary (see below). Since the chain will rarely wear evenly, roll the bike forward so that another section of chain can be checked (having an assistant to do this makes the task a lot easier); do this several times to check the entire length of chain, and mark the tightest spot.

4 In some cases where lubrication has been neglected, corrosion and galling may cause the links to bind and kink, which effectively shortens the chain's length. Such links should be thoroughly cleaned and worked free. If the chain is tight between the sprockets, rusty or kinked, it's time to renew it. If you find a tight area, mark it with felt pen or paint, and repeat the measurement after the bike has been ridden. If the chain is still tight in the same area, it may be damaged or worn. Because a tight or kinked chain can damage the transmission bearings, it's a good idea to renew it.

5 Check the entire length of the chain for damaged rollers, loose links and pins, and missing O-rings, and renew it if damage is found. **Note:** *Never install a new chain on old sprockets, and never use the old chain if you install new sprockets – renew the chain and sprockets as a set.*

6 Unscrew the three front sprocket cover bolts and remove the cover **(see illustration)**. Check the teeth on the front sprocket and the rear sprocket for wear **(see illustration)**.

7 Inspect the drive chain slider on the front of the swingarm for excessive wear and damage and renew it if necessary.

Adjustment

8 Move the bike so that the chain is positioned with the tightest point at the centre of its bottom run, then put it on the sidestand.

9 On US models, remove the split pin from the rear axle nut. Discard it as a new one must be used.

10 Slacken the rear axle nut **(see illustration)**. On X, Y, K1 and K2 models, also slacken the nut on the bolt securing the torque arm to the rear brake caliper **(see illustration)**.

11 Turn the adjuster on each side evenly

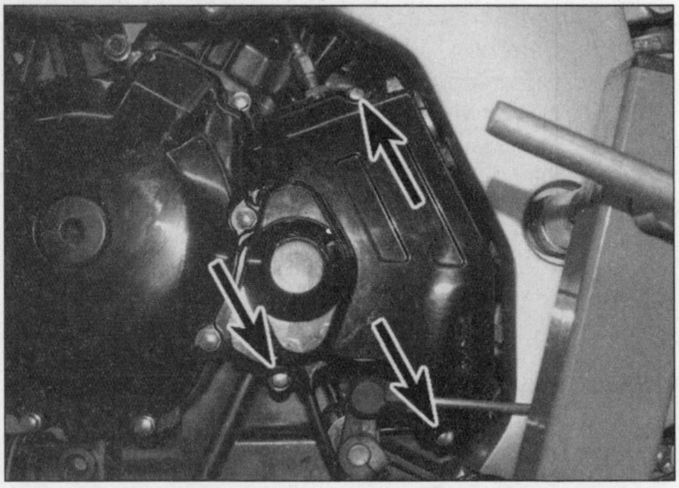

1.6a Unscrew the bolts (arrowed) and remove the cover

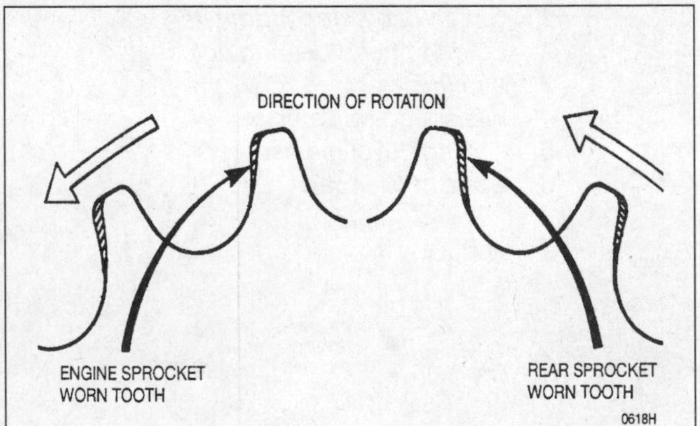

1.6b Check the sprockets in the areas indicated to see if they are worn excessively

1.10a Slacken the axle nut (arrowed)

1.10b On X, Y, K1 and K2 models, slacken the torque arm nut/bolt (arrowed)

1.11a Adjusting the chain on X, Y, K1 and K2 models

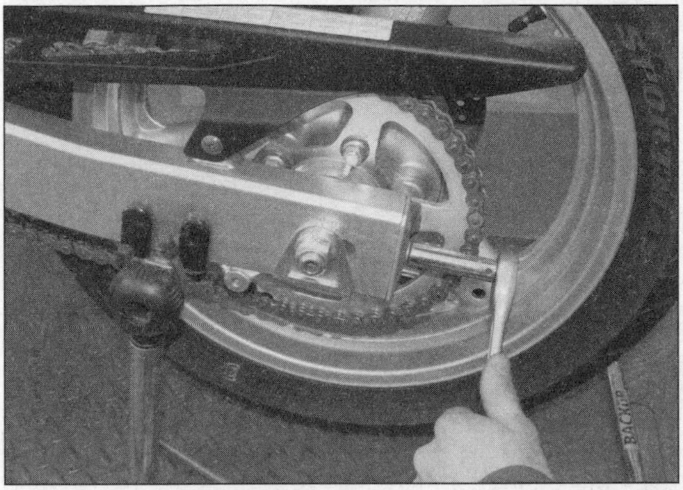

1.11b Adjusting the chain on K3-on models

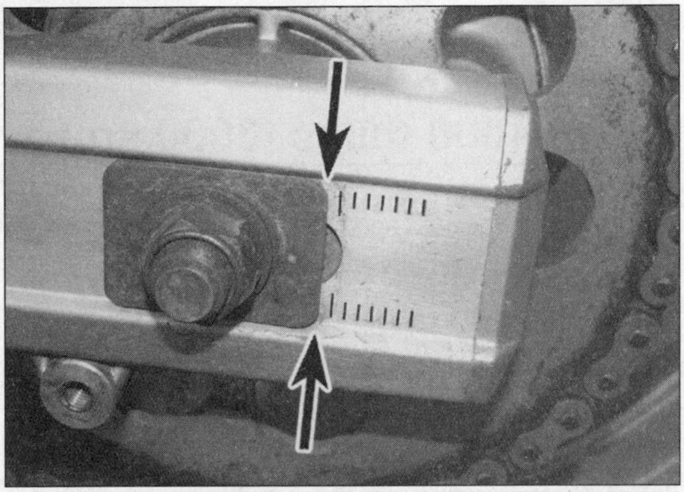

1.11c Align the rear edge of each marker (arrowed) with the same notch on the swingarm – X, Y, K1 and K2 models

until the amount of freeplay specified at the beginning of the Chapter is obtained at the centre of the bottom run of the chain **(see illustrations)**. Following adjustment, check that both chain adjustment markers are in the same position in relation to the index lines on the swingarm **(see illustrations)**. It is important the same index line on each side aligns with the marker; if not, the rear wheel will be out of alignment with the front. If there is a discrepancy in the marker positions, adjust one of them so that its position is exactly the same as the other. Check the chain freeplay as described above and readjust if necessary.

12 Counter-hold the axle head and tighten the axle nut to the torque setting specified at the beginning of the Chapter **(see illustration)**. Recheck the adjustment as above, then check that the wheel runs freely. On X, Y, K1 and K2 models, tighten the brake torque arm nut to the specified torque setting.

13 On US models, fit a new split pin.

Cleaning and lubrication

14 If required, wash the chain in paraffin (kerosene), scrubbing it vigorously with a stiff-bristled brush to work any dirt out if

1.11d Align the central notch on each marker (arrowed) with the same line on the swingarm – K3-on models

1.12 Tighten the axle nut to the specified torque

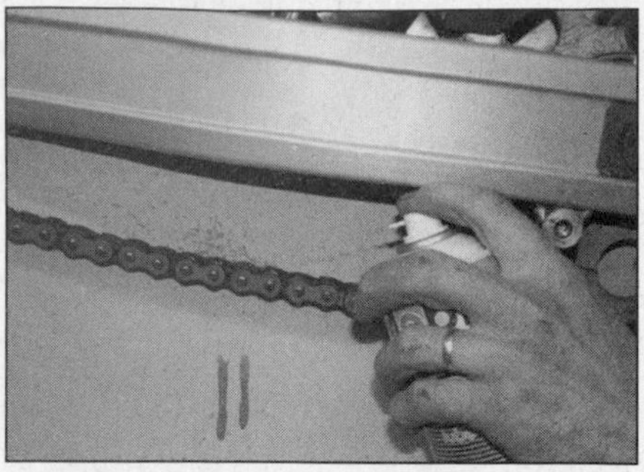
1.15 Use only the correct lubricant and apply it as described

necessary. Cover the rear tyre to prevent it being contaminated. Dry the chain with compressed air or clean rag immediately. If the chain is excessively dirty it should be removed from the machine and soaked in the paraffin for approximately five or six minutes (see Chapter 6).

Caution: Don't use petrol (gasoline), solvent or other cleaning fluids which might damage the chains internal O-ring seals. Don't use high-pressure water. The entire process shouldn't take longer than ten minutes – if it does, the O-ring seals could be damaged.

15 For routine lubrication, the best time to lubricate the chain is after the motorcycle has been ridden. When the chain is warm, the lubricant will penetrate the joints between the sideplates better than when cold. **Note:** *Suzuki specifies a heavy motor oil (such as gear oil) or an aerosol chain lube that it is suitable for O-ring and X-ring (sealed) chains; do not use any other chain lubricants – the solvents could damage the chain's sealing rings.* Apply the oil to the area where the sideplates overlap – not the middle of the rollers **(see illustration)**.

HAYNES HiNT ***Apply the lubricant to the top of the lower chain run, so centrifugal force will work the oil into the chain when the bike is moving. After applying the lubricant, let it soak in a few minutes before wiping off any excess.***

Warning: Take care not to get any lubricant on the tyres or brake system components. If any of the lubricant inadvertently contacts them, clean it off thoroughly using a suitable solvent or dedicated brake cleaner before riding the machine.

Every 4000 miles (6000 km)

2 Air filter – check and clean

Caution: If the machine is constantly used in dirty or dusty conditions the filter should be cleaned and renewed at more frequent intervals than specified.

X, Y, K1 and K2 models

1 Raise the fuel tank (see Chapter 4A) and support it on its prop.

2 Undo the screws securing the air filter and withdraw it from the housing, noting how it fits **(see illustrations)**.

3 To clean the filter, tap it on a hard surface to dislodge any dirt and use compressed air to clear the element, directing the air in the opposite way to normal flow, i.e. from the outside in **(see illustration)**. Do not use any solvents or cleaning agents on the element. Check the element for tears and excessive oil contamination and renew it if necessary.

4 Install the filter in the housing, making sure it is correctly seated, and secure it with its screws.

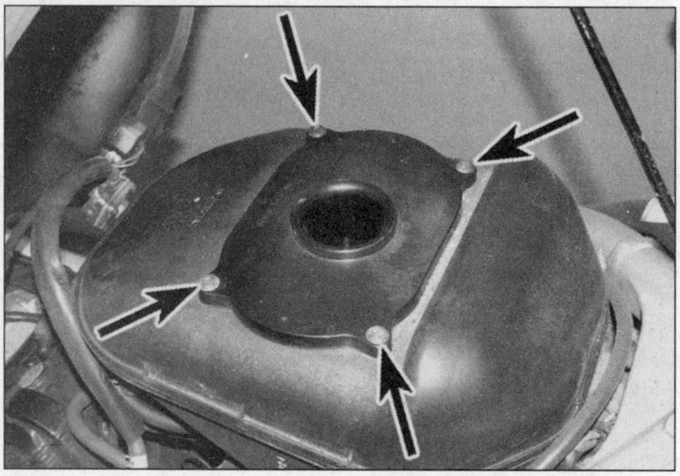
2.2a Undo the screws (arrowed) . . .

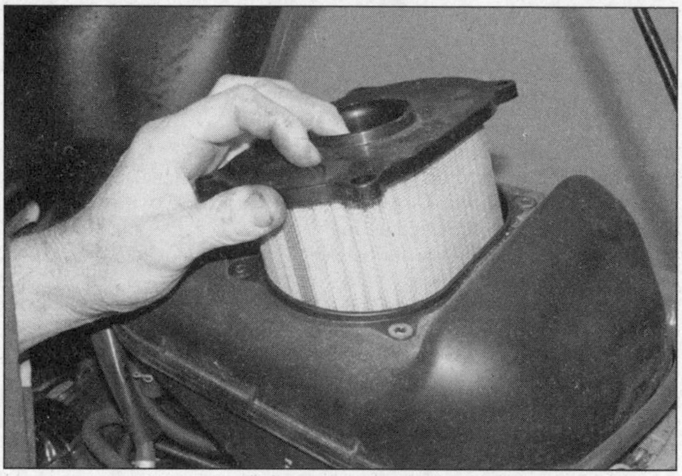
2.2b . . . and withdraw the filter from the housing – X, Y, K1 and K2 models

2.3 Direct the air in the opposite direction of normal flow

2.5a Remove the cap (arrowed) . . .

2.5b . . . and the plug from the drains

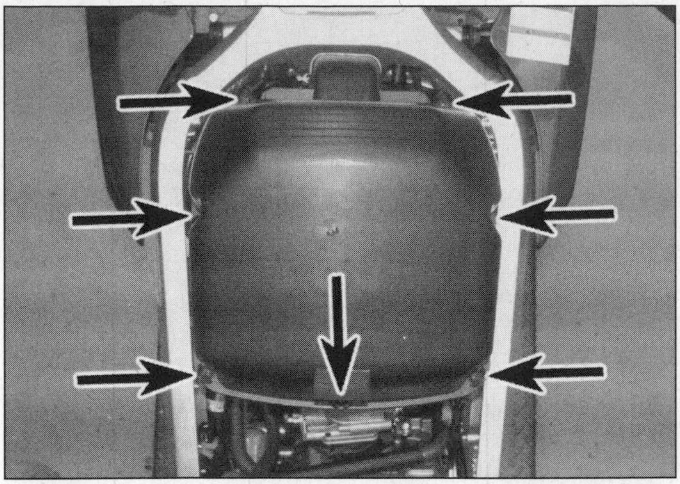

2.8a Undo the screws (arrowed) . . .

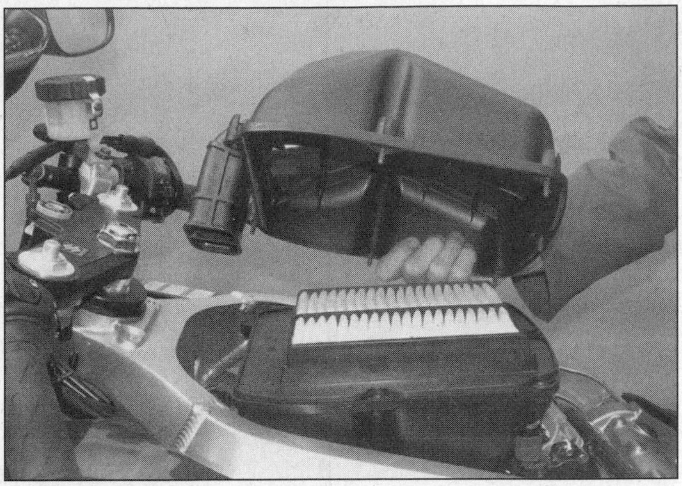

2.8b . . . and remove the cover

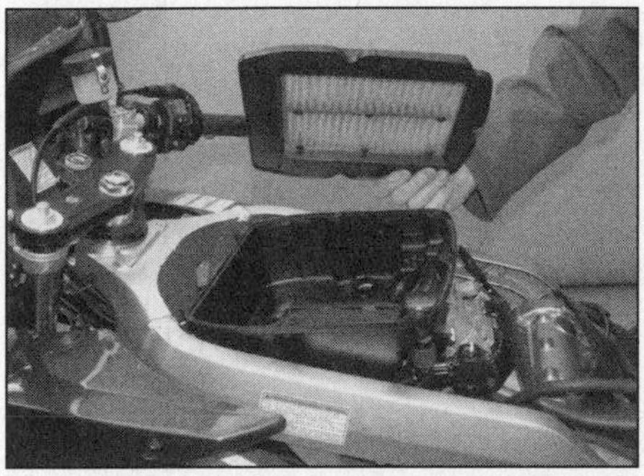

2.8c Lift out the filter element

2.10 Lift out the crankcase breather filter

2.12 Location of the filter housing drain (arrowed)

5 Release the clamps and remove the cap from the drain on the rear right-hand side of the air filter housing and the plug from the drain hose running from the middle of the housing on the right-hand side, and allow any residue to drain from the housing and hose **(see illustrations)**. Refit the plug and cap and secure them in position with the clamps.

6 Lower the fuel tank (see Chapter 4A).

K3-on models

7 Raise the fuel tank (see Chapter 4B) and support it on its prop.

8 Undo the screws securing the air filter cover and remove it **(see illustration)**. Remove the filter from the housing, noting how it fits **(see illustration)**.

9 Use compressed air to clear the element, directing the air in the opposite way to normal flow, i.e. from the throttle body side. Do not use any solvents or cleaning agents on the element. If the element is damaged or cannot be cleaned, or is obviously beyond further use, replace it with a new one.

10 Lift the crankcase breather filter out of the housing **(see illustration)**.

11 Install the filter in the housing, making sure it is correctly seated, then fit the cover and secure it with its screws.

12 Release the clamps and remove the caps from the filter housing drain hose and allow any residue to drain from the housing and hose **(see illustration)**. Refit the caps and secure them in position with the clamps.

13 Lower the fuel tank (see Chapter 4B).

3 Spark plugs – gap check and adjustment

1 Make sure your spark plug socket is the correct size before attempting to remove the plugs – a suitable one is supplied in the motorcycle's tool kit which is stored under the seat.

2 It is advisable to remove the fairing side panels on X, Y, K1 and K2 SV650S models to provide full access to the front cylinder spark plug (see Chapter 8). If care is taken, it is possible to remove the three screws on each side of the fairing and carefully pull the sides away from the radiator to release the pegs from their grommets.

3 On X, Y, K1 and K2 models, remove the horn and its mounting bracket (see Chapter 9). On K3-on SV650 models, remove the radiator guard **(see illustration)**. Unscrew the radiator lower mounting bolt and pivot the bottom of the radiator forward **(see illustrations)**. On X, Y, K1 and K2 SV650S models take care not to damage the fairing if it wasn't removed. Place a block of wood between the radiator and cylinder to keep it

3.3a Undo the bolt (arrowed) and remove the guard – K3-on models

3.3b Unscrew the bolt (arrowed) . . .

3.3c ... and pivot the radiator forward

3.5a Pull the cap (arrowed) off the front plug

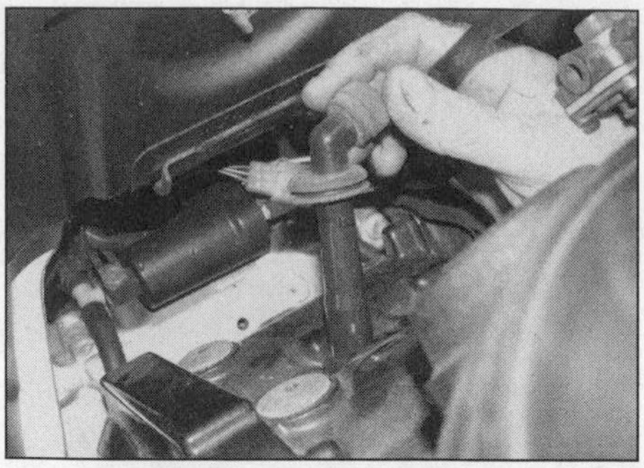

3.5b Pull the cap off the rear plug

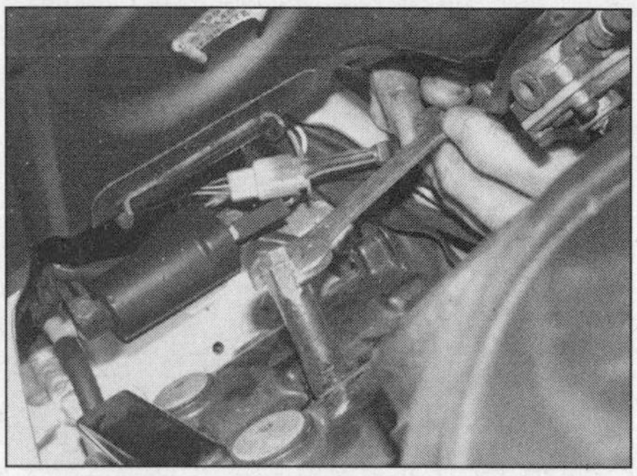

3.5c Unscrew the plug as described ...

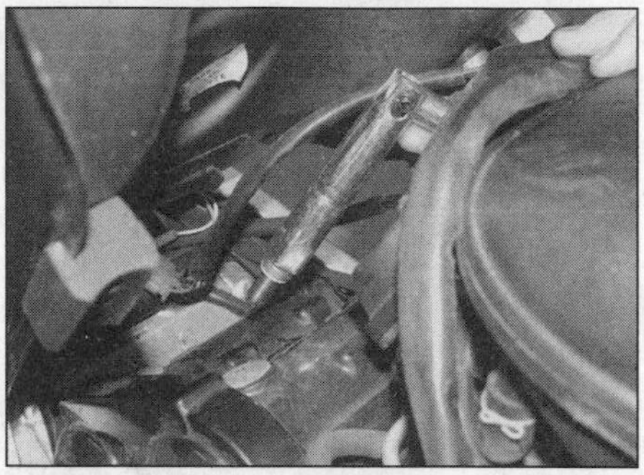

3.5d ... and withdraw it from the head

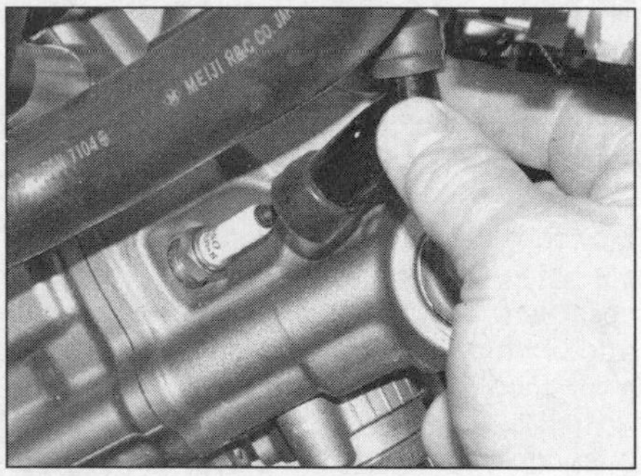

3.5e K7 models onward have a second plug fitted to the right side of the front head ...

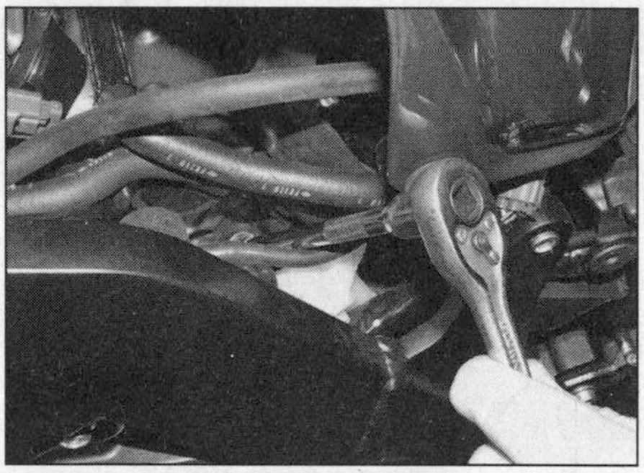

3.5f ... and to the left side of the rear head – use a deep socket and extension to reach it

clear, making sure the block locates so as not to damage the cooling fins, or alternatively hold the radiator back using a cable tie or bungee cord.

4 To access the rear cylinder plug, raise the fuel tank (see Chapter 4B).

5 Pull the cap off the spark plug **(see illustration)**. Using either the plug removal tool from the bike's toolkit or a deep 16 mm plug socket, remove the plug(s) from each cylinder. On X to K6 models there is one plug per cylinder, located in the centre of the head **(see illustrations)**. K7 models onwards have dual spark ignition, which features two plugs per cylinder, the second being located in the side of the head **(see illustrations)**.

6 Inspect the electrodes for wear. Both the centre and side electrodes should have square edges and the side electrode should be of uniform thickness – if not, they are worn. Look for excessive deposits and evidence of a cracked or chipped insulator around the centre electrode. Compare your spark plugs to the colour spark plug reading chart at the end of this manual. Check the threads, the washer and the ceramic insulator body for cracks and other damage.

7 If the electrodes are not excessively worn, if no cracks or chips are visible in the insulator, and if the deposits can be easily removed with a wire brush, the plugs can be re-gapped and re-used. If in doubt concerning the condition of the plugs, renew them.

8 Cleaning spark plugs by sandblasting is permitted, provided you blow out the plugs with compressed air and clean them with a high flash-point solvent afterwards.

9 Before installing the plugs, make sure they are the correct type and heat range and check the gap between the electrodes **(see illustrations)**. Compare the gap to that specified and adjust as necessary. If the gap must be adjusted, bend the side electrodes only and be very careful not to chip or crack the insulator nose **(see illustration)**. Make sure the washer is in place before installing each plug.

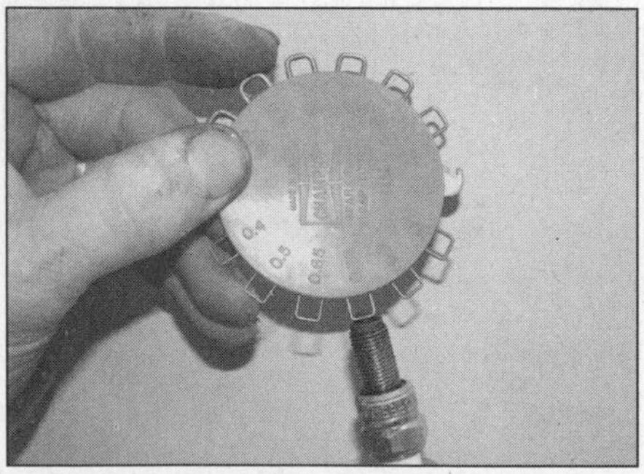

3.9a Using a wire type gauge to measure the spark plug electrode gap

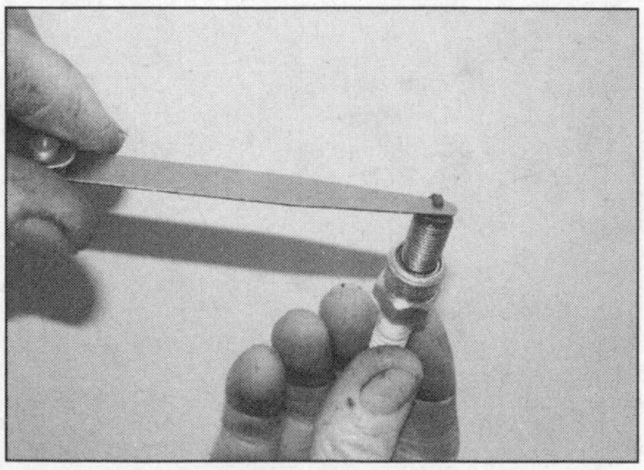

3.9b Using a feeler gauge to measure the spark plug electrode gap

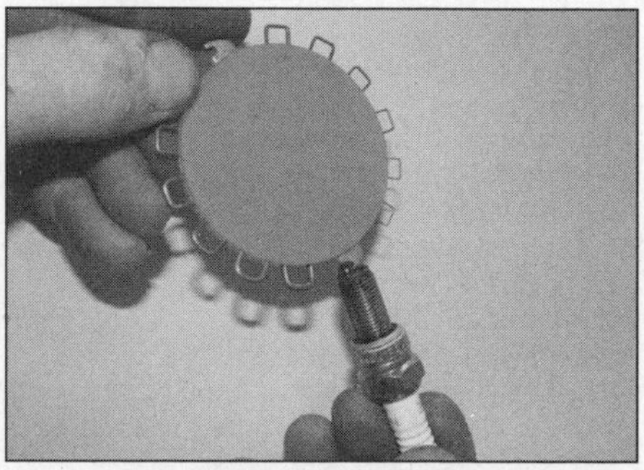

3.9c Adjust the electrode gap by bending the side electrode only

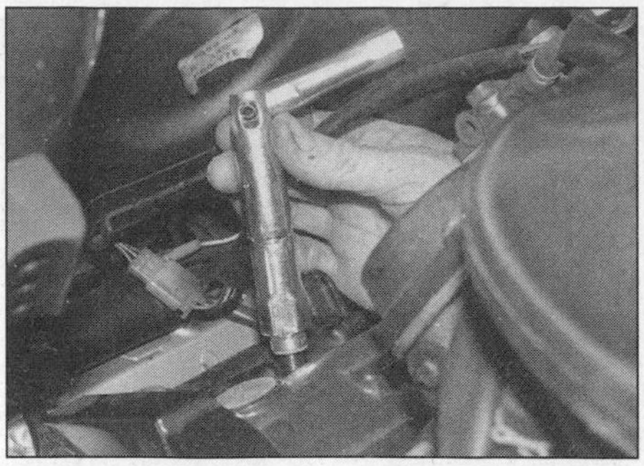

3.10a Fit the plug into the tool – the rubber insert should grip around the plug top . . .

10 Fit the plug into the end of the tool, then use the tool to insert the plug **(see illustration)**. Since the cylinder head is made of aluminium, which is soft and easily damaged, thread the plug as far as possible into the head turning the tool by hand **(see illustration)**. Once the plug is finger-tight, the job can be finished with a spanner on the tool supplied or a socket drive **(see illustration 3.5c)**. If a torque wrench can be applied, tighten the spark plugs to the torque setting specified at the beginning of the Chapter. Otherwise, tighten them according the instructions on the box – generally if new plugs are being used, tighten them by 1/2 a turn after the washer has seated, and if the old plugs are being reused, tighten them by 1/8 to 1/4 turn after they have seated. Do not over-tighten them.

> **HAYNES HiNT** ***You can slip a short length of hose over the end of the plug to use as a tool to thread it into place. The hose will grip the plug well enough to turn it, but will start to slip if the plug begins to cross-thread in the hole – this will prevent damaged threads.***

11 Fit the spark plug cap **(see illustration 3.5a)**, making sure it locates correctly onto the plug and that the triangular mark on the seal is facing the exhaust side of the valve cover **(see illustration)**. Install all other components previously removed.

3.10b . . . and thread it in by hand

> **HAYNES HiNT** ***Stripped plug threads in the cylinder head can be repaired with a Heli-Coil insert – see 'Tools and Workshop Tips' in the Reference section.***

4 Fuel system – check

Warning: Petrol (gasoline) is extremely flammable, so take extra precautions when you work on any part of the fuel system. Don't smoke or allow open flames or bare light bulbs near the work area, and don't work in a garage where a natural gas-type appliance is present. If you spill any fuel on your skin, rinse it off immediately with soap and water. When you perform any kind of work on the fuel system, wear safety glasses and have a fire extinguisher suitable for a Class B type fire (flammable liquids) on hand.

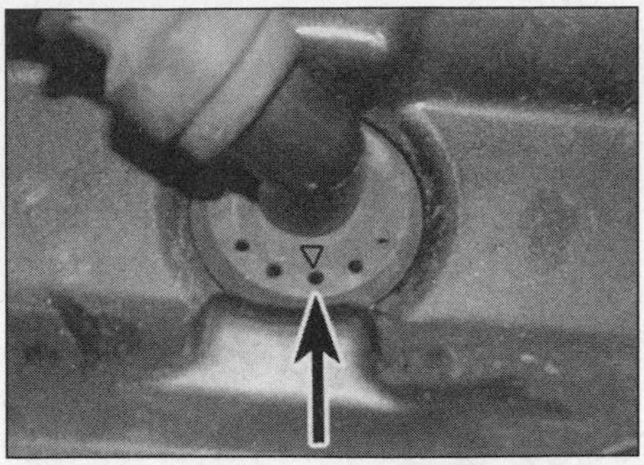

3.11 Make sure the triangular mark (arrowed) points to the exhaust side

X, Y, K1 and K2 models

Check

1 Check the tank, the fuel tap, the fuel pump and the fuel hoses for signs of leakage, deterioration or damage; in particular check that there is no leakage from the fuel hoses **(see illustration)**. Renew any hoses that are cracked or deteriorated. Similarly check the vacuum hoses to the fuel tap and fuel pump **(see illustration)**. On California models also check the EVAP and PAIR emissions control systems hoses (refer to Chapter 4A for details of these systems).

2 If the fuel tap or pump is leaking, tighten the assembly screws **(see illustrations)**. Slacken all the screws a little first, then tighten them evenly and a little at a time to ensure the cover seats properly on the body. If leakage persists remove and disassemble the tap or pump, noting how the components fit (see Chapter 4A). Inspect and clean all components and rebuild the tap or pump. If leakage persists, renew the whole tap or pump – individual components are not available. If the carburettor gaskets are leaking, disassemble the carburettors and rebuild them using new gaskets and seals (see Chapter 4A). Refer to Chapter 4A for checks on the condition and operation of the vacuum diaphragms in the fuel tap and pump.

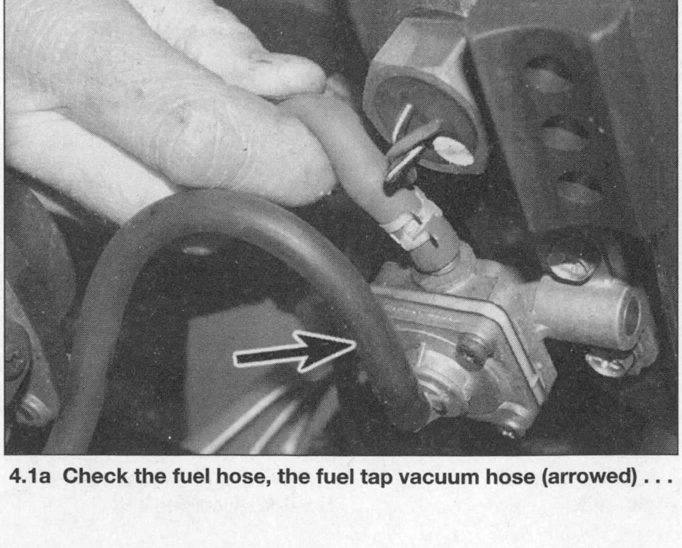

4.1a Check the fuel hose, the fuel tap vacuum hose (arrowed) . . .

4.1b . . . and the fuel pump vacuum hose

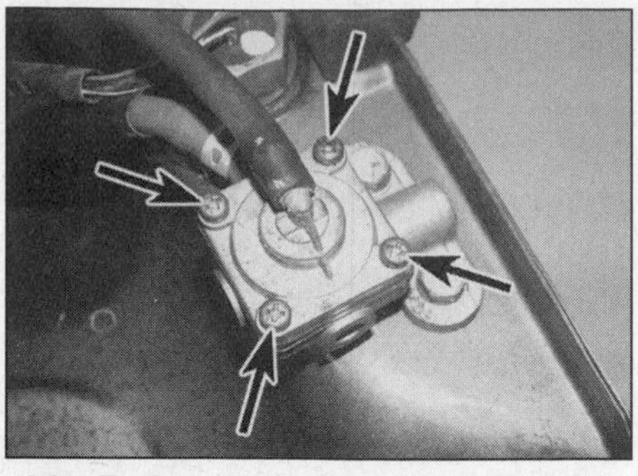

4.2a Fuel tap assembly screws (arrowed)

Filter cleaning

3 A fuel strainer gauze is incorporated in the fuel tap. Cleaning or renewal of the strainer is advised after a particularly high mileage has been covered. It is also necessary if fuel starvation is suspected, or if it looks clogged or dirty. Check the condition of the inside of the tank – if it is old and there is evidence of rust, remove, drain and clean the tank (see Chapter 4A).

4 Remove the fuel tap (see Chapter 4A). Clean all traces of dirt and fuel sediment off the gauze strainer **(see illustration)**. Check the gauze for holes. If any are found, a new tap must be fitted. Install the tap (see Chap-ter 4A).

K3-on models

Check

5 Check the tank, the fuel pump base and

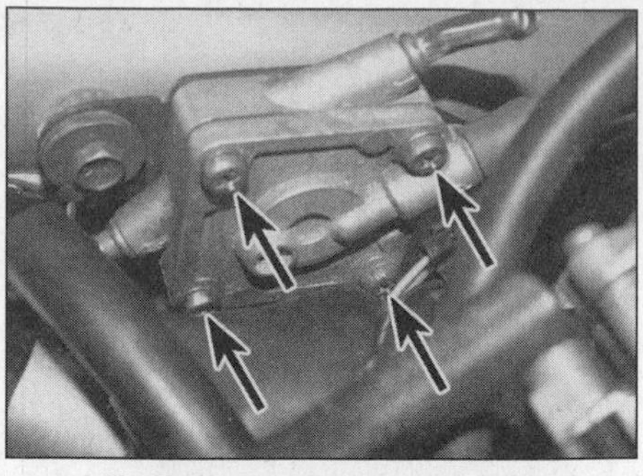

4.2b Fuel pump assembly screws (arrowed)

gasket, the fuel hose and the tank vent and drain hoses for signs of leakage, deterioration or damage; in particular check that there is no leakage from the fuel hose. Renew any hoses that are cracked or deteriorated. Check the PAIR system hoses and on California models also check the EVAP emissions control systems hoses (refer to Chapter 4B for details of these systems).

6 If there is leakage from the fuel pump base, remove the pump and replace the gasket with a new one (see Chapter 4B).

7 Check for signs of fuel leakage between the injectors, the fuel rail and the throttle bodies. If leakage is evident, remove the injectors and install new O-rings and seals (see Chapter 4B).

Filter cleaning

8 A fuel filter is located in the base of the fuel pump – it is advisable to clean the filter after a particularly high mileage has been covered or if fuel starvation is suspected (see Chapter 4B).

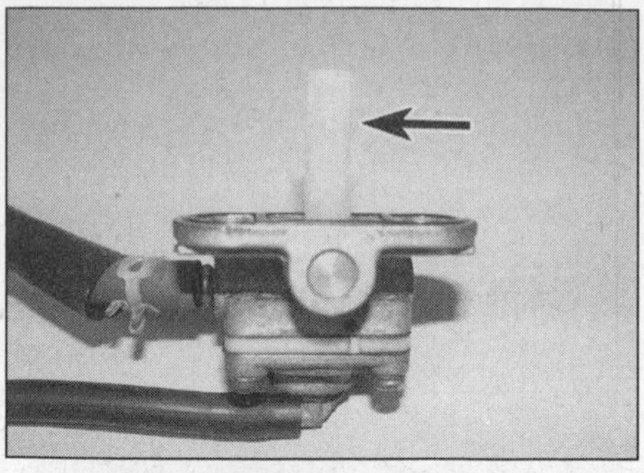

4.4 Check the strainer (arrowed) as described

5 Engine/transmission – oil change

Warning: Be careful when draining the oil, as the exhaust pipes, the engine, and the oil itself can cause severe burns.

1 Regular oil and filter changes are the single most important maintenance procedure you can perform on a motorcycle. The oil not only lubricates the internal parts of the engine, transmission and clutch, but it also acts as a coolant, a cleaner, a sealant, and a protector. Because of these demands, the oil takes a terrific amount of abuse and should be changed often with new oil of the recommended grade and type. Saving a little money on the difference in cost between good oil and cheap oil won't pay off if the engine is damaged. The oil filter should be changed with every third oil change (see Section 22).

2 Before changing the oil, warm up the engine so the oil will drain easily. Make sure the bike is on level ground.

3 Position a clean drain tray below the engine. Unscrew the oil filler cap from the clutch cover to vent the crankcase and to act as a reminder that there is no oil in the engine **(see illustration)**.

4 Unscrew the oil drain plug from the bottom of the engine and allow the oil to flow into the drain tray **(see illustrations)**. Check the condition of the sealing washer on the drain plug and renew it if it is damaged or worn – it is advisable to use a new one whatever the condition of the old one.

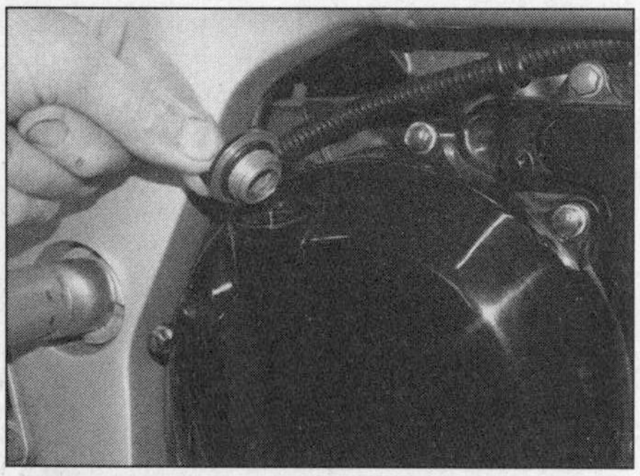

5.3 Unscrew the oil filler cap to act as a vent . . .

5.4a . . . then unscrew the oil drain plug (arrowed) . . .

5.4b . . . and allow the oil to completely drain

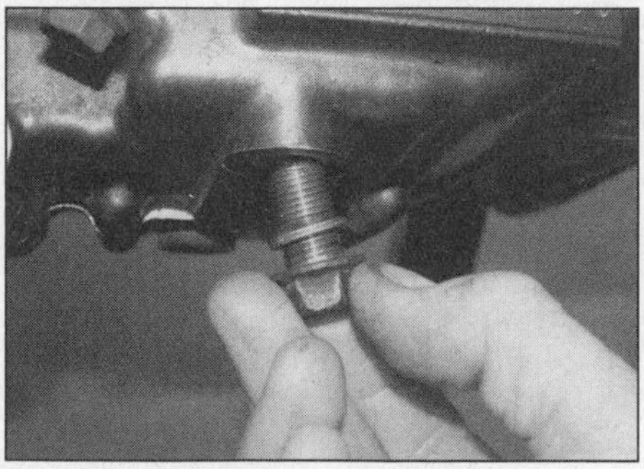

5.5a Install the drain plug, using a new sealing washer if necessary . . .

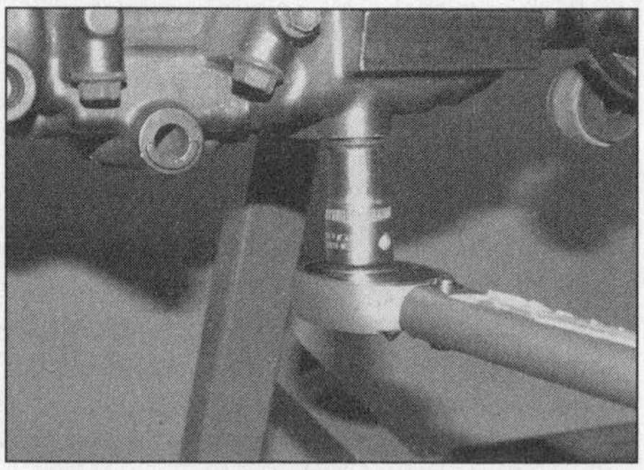

5.5b . . . and tighten it to the specified torque setting

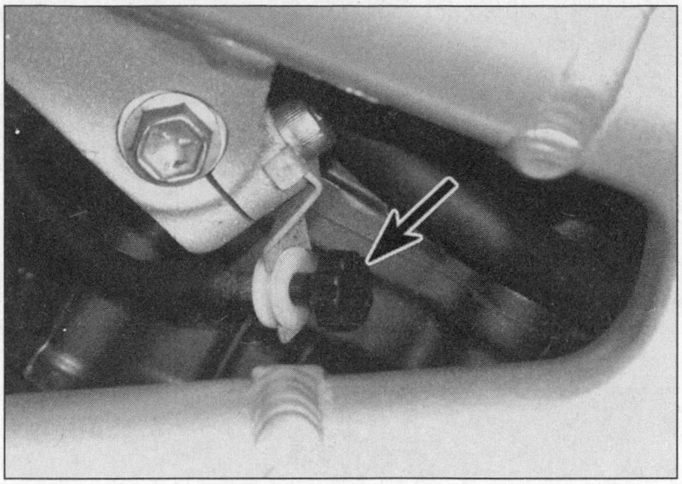

6.3a Idle speed adjuster (arrowed) – X, Y, K1 and K2 models

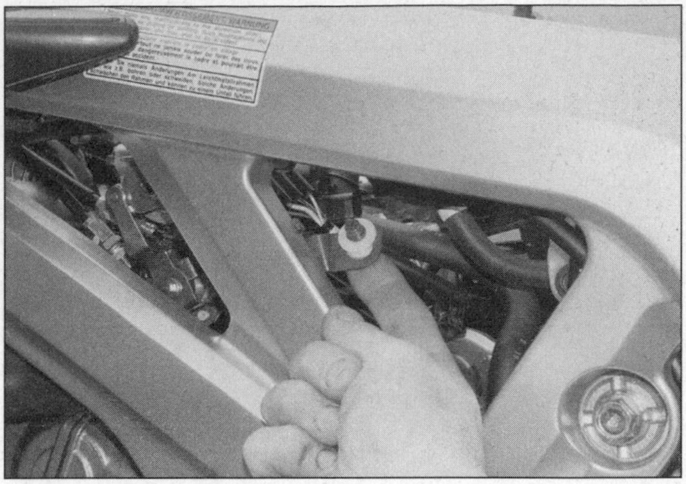

6.3b Idle speed adjuster – K3 to K6 models

5 When the oil has completely drained, fit the plug to the sump, using a new sealing washer if necessary, and tighten it to the torque setting specified at the beginning of the Chapter **(see illustrations)**. Avoid overtightening, as it is quite easy to damage the threads in the sump.

6 Refill the engine to the proper level using the recommended type and amount of oil (see the Specifications at the beginning of this chapter). Install the filler cap **(see illustration 5.3)**. Start the engine and let it run for two or three minutes (make sure that the oil pressure light extinguishes after a few seconds). Shut it off, wait a few minutes, then check the oil level (see *Daily (pre-ride) checks*). If necessary, add more oil to bring the level to the F line on the inspection window. Check that there are no leaks from around the drain plug and the oil filter. A leak around the drain plug probably means a new washer is needed. A leak around the filter probably means it is not tight enough.

7 The old oil drained from the engine cannot be re-used and should be disposed of properly. Check with your local refuse disposal company, disposal facility or environmental agency to see whether they will accept the used oil for recycling. Don't pour used oil into drains or onto the ground.

HAYNES HiNT ***Check the old oil carefully – if it is very metallic coloured, then the engine is experiencing wear from break-in (new engine) or from insufficient lubrication. If there are flakes or chips of metal in the oil, then something is drastically wrong internally and the engine will have to be disassembled for inspection and repair. If there are pieces of fibre-like material in the oil, the clutch is experiencing excessive wear and should be checked.***

OIL CARE – FOLLOW THE CODE

OIL BANK LINE
0800 66 33 66
www.oilbankline.org.uk

Note: It is antisocial and illegal to dump oil down the drain. In the UK, call this number free to find the location of your local recycling bank. in the USA, note that any oil supplier must accept used oil for recycling.

6 Idle speed – check and adjustment

Note: *There is no provision for idle speed adjustment on K7 models onward. Incorrect idle speed will be indicated by the appropriate fault code – see Chapter 4B for more information.*

1 The idle speed should be checked and adjusted before and after the carburettors or throttle bodies are synchronised (balanced), after checking the valve clearances, and when it is obviously too high or too low. Before adjusting the idle speed, turn the handlebars from side-to-side and check the idle speed does not change as you do. If it does, the throttle cables may not be adjusted or routed correctly, or may be worn out. This is a dangerous condition that can cause loss of control of the bike. Be sure to correct this problem before proceeding.

2 The engine should be at normal operating temperature, which is usually reached after 10 to 15 minutes of stop-and-go riding. Place the motorcycle on its sidestand, and make sure the transmission is in neutral.

3 On X, Y, K1 and K2 models, the idle speed adjuster is a knurled knob located on the left-hand side of the engine **(see illustration)**. On K3 to K6 models, the idle speed adjuster is a cross-head screw located on the left-hand side of the engine **(see illustration)**. With the engine idling, turn the adjuster until the idle speed listed in this Chapter's Specifications is obtained. Turn the adjuster clockwise to increase idle speed, and anti-clockwise to decrease it.

4 Snap the throttle open and shut a few times, then recheck the idle speed. If necessary, repeat the adjustment procedure.

5 If a smooth, steady idle can't be achieved, the fuel/air mixture may be incorrect (see Chapter 4A) or the carburettors or throttle bodies may need synchronising (see Section 17 or 18). Also check the intake manifold rubbers for cracks or a loose clamp that will cause an air leak, resulting in a weak mixture.

7 Throttle and choke cables – check and adjustment

Throttle cables

1 Make sure the throttle grip rotates smoothly and freely from fully closed to fully open with the front wheel turned at various angles. The grip should return automatically from fully open to fully closed when released.

2 If the throttle sticks, this is probably due to a cable fault. Remove the cables (see Chap-ter 4A or 4B as applicable) and lubricate them (see Section 15). Check that the inner cables slide freely and easily in the outer cables. If not, renew the cables. With the cables removed, make sure the throttle twistgrip rotates freely on the handlebar. Install the cables, making sure they are correctly routed. If this fails to improve the operation of the throttle, the cables must be renewed. Note that in very rare cases the fault could lie in the carburettors or throttle bodies rather than the cables, necessitating their removal and inspection (see Chapter 4A or 4B as applicable).

3 With the throttle operating smoothly, check for a small amount of freeplay in the cables, measured in terms of the amount of twistgrip rotation before the throttle opens, and compare the amount to that listed in this Chapter's Specifications **(see illustration)**. If it's incorrect, adjust the cables to correct it as follows.

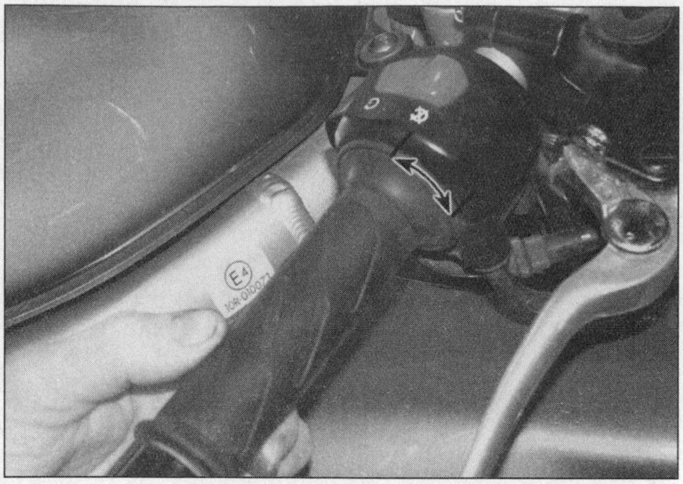

7.3 Throttle cable freeplay is measured in terms of twistgrip rotation

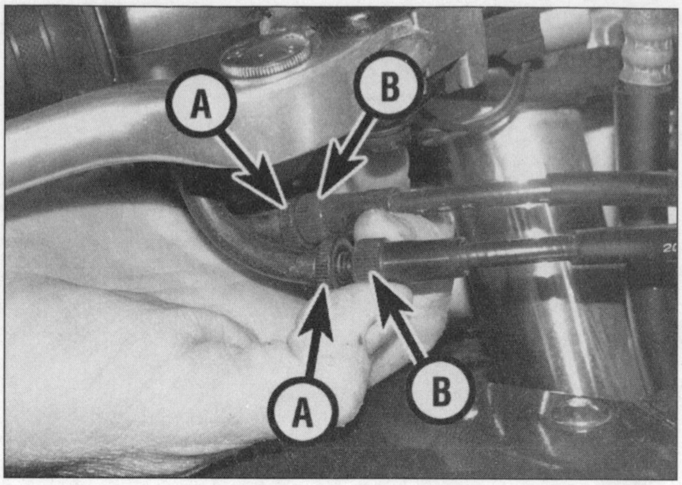

7.5a Slacken the lockrings (A), then turn the adjusters (B) as described

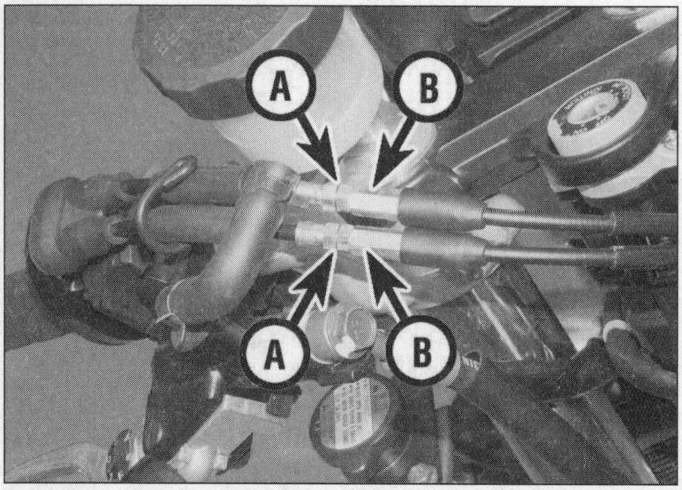

7.5b Slacken the locknuts (A), then turn the adjusters (B) as described – K3-on SV650S models

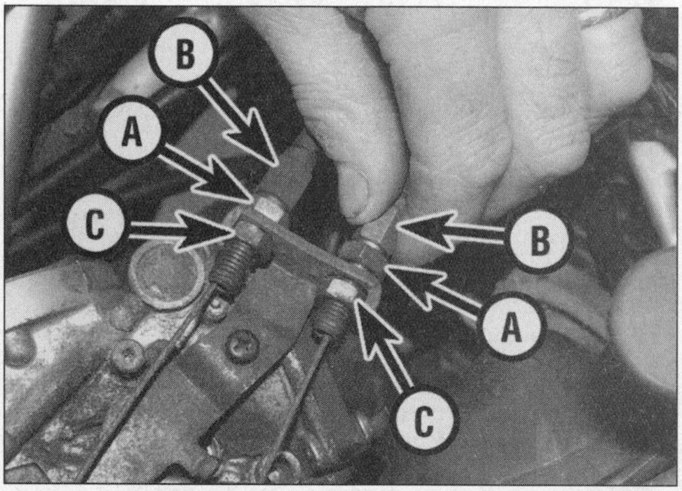

7.6a Slacken the locknuts (A), then turn the adjusters (B), keeping the captive nuts (C) locked – X, Y, K1 and K2 models

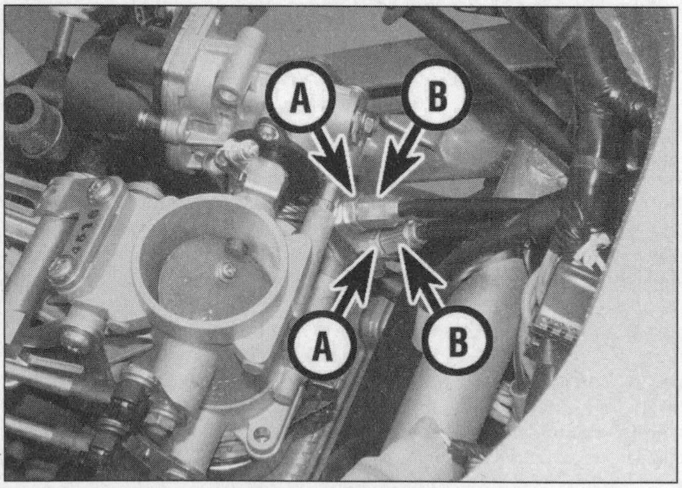

7.6b Slacken the locknuts (A), then turn the adjusters (B) – K3-on models

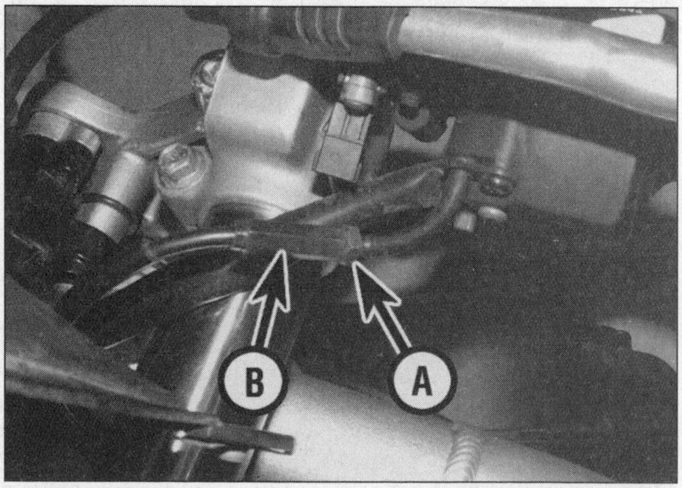

7.9 Slacken the locknut (A), then turn the adjuster (B) as required

4 Freeplay adjustments can be made using the adjusters in the top end of the cables where they leave the throttle/switch housing on the handlebar. Note that on K3 SV650S models onward, the adjusters are in the cables below the fork top yoke inside rubber covers, and employ a locknut rather than a lockring.
5 On all X, Y, K1 and K2 models and K3 SV650 models onward, the front cable in the housing is the opening cable, and the rear is the closing cable. On K3-on SV650S models, the rear cable in the housing is the opening cable, and the front is the closing cable. Loosen the lockring on the closing cable adjuster and turn the adjuster fully in **(see illustrations)**. Now loosen the lockring on the opening cable adjuster and turn the adjuster until the specified amount of freeplay is obtained (see this Chapter's Specifications), then retighten the lockring. Now turn the closing cable adjuster out until a resistance can just be felt – at this point all the freeplay has been taken up. Do not turn the adjuster out any further than the point at which the resistance is felt. Tighten the lockring.
6 If the top end cable adjusters have reached their limit, or if major adjustment is required, adjust the cables at the lower carburettor or throttle body end as follows. Raise the fuel tank and remove the air filter housing (see Chapter 4A or 4B as applicable). First reset the top end adjusters so that the freeplay is at a maximum (i.e. the adjusters are fully turned in), then slacken the lower end adjuster locknuts **(see illustrations)**. Turn the closing cable adjuster out until a resistance can just be felt – at this point all the freeplay has been taken up. Tighten the locknut. Now turn the opening cable adjuster out until the specified amount of freeplay is obtained (see Step 3), and tighten the locknut. Further adjustments can now be made at the throttle end. If the cables cannot be adjusted as specified, install new ones (see Chapter 4A or 4B). Ensure that all the locknuts have been securely tightened before installing the air filter housing.

Warning: Turn the handlebars all the way through their travel with the engine idling. The idle speed should not change. If it does, the cables may be routed incorrectly. Correct this condition before riding the bike.

7 Check that the throttle twistgrip operates smoothly and snaps shut quickly when released.

Choke cable

Note: *No choke cable is fitted to K3-on models – the fuel injection system employs an electronic fast idle mechanism (see Chapter 4B for details).*
8 If the choke does not operate smoothly this is probably due to a cable fault. Remove the cable (see Chapter 4A) and lubricate it (see Section 15). Check that the inner cable slides freely and easily in the outer cable. If not, renew the cable. With the cable removed, make sure the choke lever is able to move freely. Install the cable, making sure it is correctly routed.
9 Check for a small amount of freeplay in the cable before the choke opens and adjust it if necessary using the adjuster at the lever end of the cable. Slacken the locknut, then turn the adjuster as required until a small amount of freeplay is evident, then retighten the locknut **(see illustration)**. If this fails to improve the operation of the choke, the cable must be renewed.
10 If this fails to improve the operation of the choke, the fault could lie in the choke plungers and their bores in the carburettors rather than the cable (see Chapter 4A).

8 Clutch – check and adjustment

Check

1 Check that the clutch lever operates smoothly and easily.
2 If the lever operation is heavy or stiff, remove the cable (see Chapter 2) and lubricate it (see Section 15). Check that the inner cable slides smoothly and freely in the outer cable. If the cable is still stiff, renew it. Install the lubricated or new cable (see Chapter 2). If the cable is good, remove the lever (see Chapter 6) and check the lever, bracket and pivot for wear and damage, and clean and grease all components before reassembling them. If this fails to cure the problem, disassemble the release mechanism on the engine and check it for dirt, wear and damage (see Chapter 2).

Adjustment

3 With the cable operating smoothly, check that it is correctly adjusted. Periodic adjustment is necessary to compensate for wear in the clutch plates and stretch of the cable. Check that the amount of freeplay in the cable, measured in terms of the amount of free movement at the clutch lever end, is within the specifications listed at the beginning of the Chapter **(see illustration)**. If adjustment is required, it can be made both at the lever end of the cable and at the clutch end, but start the procedure at the lever end.
4 To adjust the freeplay at the lever, pull back the rubber boot covering the adjuster, then loosen the adjuster lockring and turn the adjuster in or out until the required amount of freeplay is obtained **(see illustration)**. To increase freeplay, thread the adjuster into the lever bracket. To reduce freeplay, thread the adjuster out of the bracket. Tighten the lockring securely. When adjusting the cable make sure that the slots in the adjuster and lockring are not aligned with each other and the slot in the lever bracket – these slots are to allow removal of the cable. Fit the rubber boot over the adjuster.
5 If all the adjustment has been taken up at the lever, reset the adjuster to give the maximum amount of freeplay (i.e. thread it all the way into the bracket), then set the correct amount of freeplay using the adjusters on the clutch end of cable.

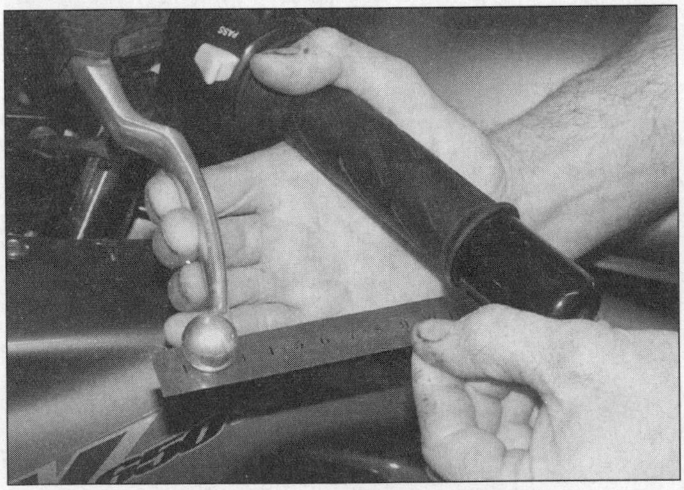

8.3 Measuring clutch lever freeplay

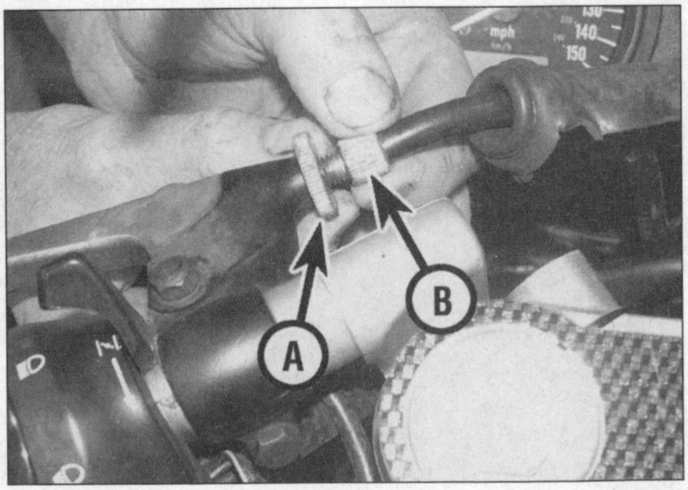

8.4 Slacken the lockring (A) and turn the adjuster (B) in or out as required

8.7 Slacken the locknut and turn the adjuster screw as described

6 Unscrew the three front sprocket cover bolts and remove the cover **(see illustration 1.6a)**.
7 Slacken the locknut on the release mechanism adjuster screw, then undo the adjuster screw a few turns **(see illustration)**.
8 Check the angle of the release mechanism arm in relation to the cable – it should be as shown in the diagram **(see illustration)**. If not, slacken the locknuts on the arm adjuster on the crankcase and position the adjuster so that the angle is correct, then tighten the locknuts. Now turn the release mechanism adjuster screw in until resistance is felt, then back it off 1/4 turn. When doing this, counter-hold the locknut as shown to prevent it from tightening and locking the adjuster **(see illustration 8.7)**. Now counter-hold the adjuster screw to prevent it turning and tighten the locknut.
9 Now check and set the freeplay adjustment at the lever as described in Step 4.
10 On completion, install the sprocket cover.

9 Cooling system – check

Warning: The engine must be cool before beginning this procedure.

1 Check the coolant level (see *Daily (pre-ride) checks*).
2 On X, Y, K1 and K2 SV650S models, remove the fairing side panels (see Chapter 8).
3 Check the entire cooling system for evidence of leakage. Examine each rubber coolant hose along its entire length. Look for

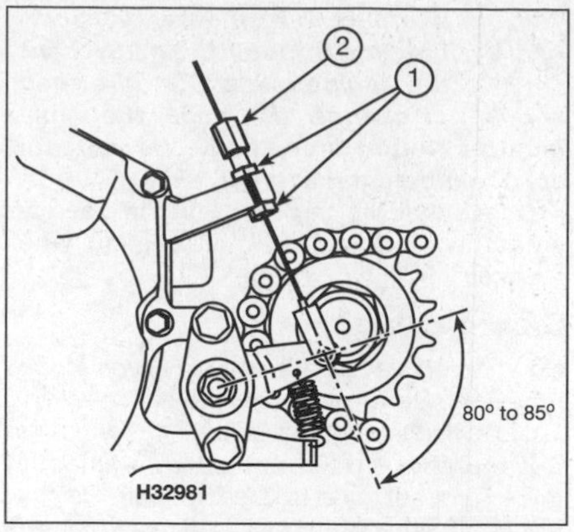

8.8 To alter the arm position, slacken the locknuts (1) and turn the adjuster (2)

cracks, abrasions and other damage. Squeeze each hose at various points to see whether they are dried out or hard **(see illustration)**. They should feel firm, yet pliable, and return to their original shape when released. If necessary, renew them (see Chapter 3).
4 Check for evidence of leaks at each cooling system joint and around the pump on the right-hand side of the engine. Tighten the hose clips carefully to prevent future leaks. If the pump cover is leaking, check that the cover bolts are tight. If they are, renew the O-ring in the cover (see Chapter 3).
5 To prevent leakage of coolant from the cooling system to the lubrication system and vice versa, two seals are fitted on the pump shaft. On the bottom of the pump housing there is a drain hole. If either seal fails, the drain allows the coolant or oil to escape and prevents them mixing. If both seals fail the oil and coolant mix to form a white emulsion. The seal on the water pump side is of the mechanical type which bears on the rear face of the impeller. The second seal, which is mounted behind the mechanical seal is of the normal feathered lip type. Both seals are available separately. If on inspection there is evidence of leakage between the pump housing and the crankcase cover, remove the pump and renew the seal(s) as required (see Chapter 3). If the drain shows signs of coolant leakage, renew the mechanical seal. If there is oil leakage, first check that the pump body O-ring is in good condition, and if that is not the cause of the leak renew the oil seal. If there is a coolant/oil mixture in the form of a white emulsion, renew both seals. Refer to Chapter 3 for details.
6 Check the radiator for leaks and other damage. Leaks in the radiator leave tell-tale scale deposits or coolant stains on the outside of the core below the leak. If leaks are noted, remove the radiator (see Chapter 3) and have it repaired or renew it.

Caution: Do not use a liquid leak stopping compound to try to repair leaks.

7 Check the radiator fins for mud, dirt and insects, which may impede the flow of air through the radiator. If the fins are dirty, remove the radiator (see Chapter 3) and clean it using water or low pressure compressed air directed through the fins from the inner side. If the fins are bent or distorted, straighten them carefully with a screwdriver. If the air flow is restricted by bent or damaged fins over more than 20% of the surface area, renew the radiator.

Warning: Do not remove the pressure cap when the engine is hot. It is good practice to cover the cap with a heavy cloth and turn the cap slowly anti-clockwise. If you hear a hissing sound (indicating that there is still pressure in the system), wait until it stops, then continue turning the cap until it can be removed.

8 On SV650 models unscrew the radiator cap security screw. On all models remove the pressure cap from the radiator filler neck by turning it anti-clockwise until it reaches a stop **(see illustration)**. Now press down on the cap and continue turning it until it can be removed. Check the condition of the coolant in the system. If it is rust-coloured or if accumulations of scale are visible, drain and flush the system and refill it with new coolant (see Section 24). Check the cap seal for cracks and other damage. If in doubt about the pressure cap's condition, have it tested by a Suzuki dealer or renew it.
9 Check the antifreeze content of the coolant with an antifreeze hydrometer. Sometimes coolant looks like it's in good condition, but might be too weak to offer adequate protection. If the hydrometer indicates a weak mixture, drain, flush and refill the system (see Section 24).
10 Install the cap by turning it clockwise until it reaches the first stop then push down on it and continue turning until it can turn no further. On SV650 models tighten the radiator cap security screw. Start the engine and let it reach normal operating temperature, then check for leaks again. As the coolant temperature increases, the electric fan (mounted on the back of the radiator) should come on automatically and the temperature should begin to drop. If it does not, refer to Chapter 3 and check the fan and fan circuit carefully.
11 If the coolant level is consistently low, and no evidence of leaks can be found, have the entire system pressure checked by a Suzuki dealer.

9.3 Check the hoses for evidence of cracks and deterioration

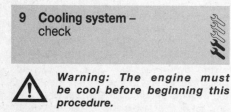

9.8 Remove the pressure cap as described

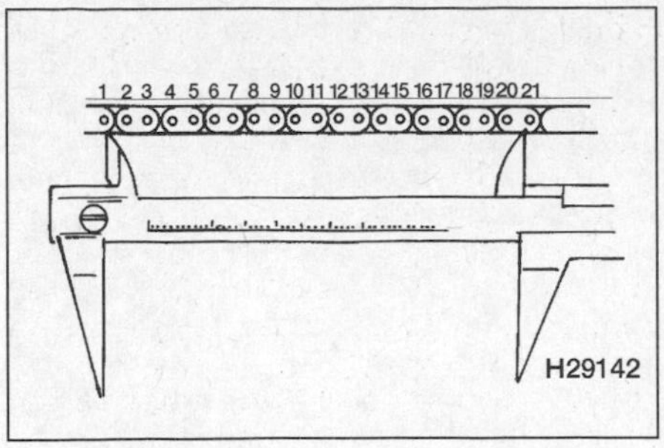

10.3 Measure the distance between the 1st and the 21st pins to determine chain stretch

10 Drive chain – wear and stretch check

1 Check the entire length of the chain for damaged rollers, loose links and pins, and missing O-rings. Fit a new chain if damage is found. **Note:** *Never install a new chain on old sprockets, and never use the old chain if you install new sprockets – renew the chain and sprockets as a set.*

2 Chain stretch is assessed by measuring several sections of the chain with the chain held taut. On US models, remove the split pin from the rear axle nut, then on all models slacken the axle nut **(see illustration 1.10a)**. On X, Y, K1 and K2 models, also slacken the nut on the bolt securing the torque arm to the rear brake caliper. Turn the adjusters evenly until the chain is tight **(see illustration 1.11 a and 11b)**.

3 Measure along the bottom run the length of 21 pins (from the centre of the 1st pin to the centre of the 21st pin) and compare the result with the service limit specified at the beginning of the Chapter **(see illustration)**. Rotate the rear wheel so that several sections of the chain are measured, then calculate the average. If the chain stretch measurement exceeds the service limit it must be renewed (see Chapter 6).

4 If the chain is good, reset the adjusters to the correct amount of freeplay, then tighten the axle nut, and the brake torque arm nut if applicable, to the specified torque settings (see Section 1).

11 Brake pads – wear check

1 Each brake pad has wear indicators in the friction material that should be plainly visible, but note that an accumulation of road dirt and brake dust could make them difficult to see. The wear indicators will be in the form of a cutout or groove in the friction material **(see illustrations)**. **Note:** *Some after-market pads may use different indicators to those on the original equipment*. If the friction material is worn to or beyond the wear indicator, the pads must be renewed. Always renew brake pads as a set (see Chapter 7).

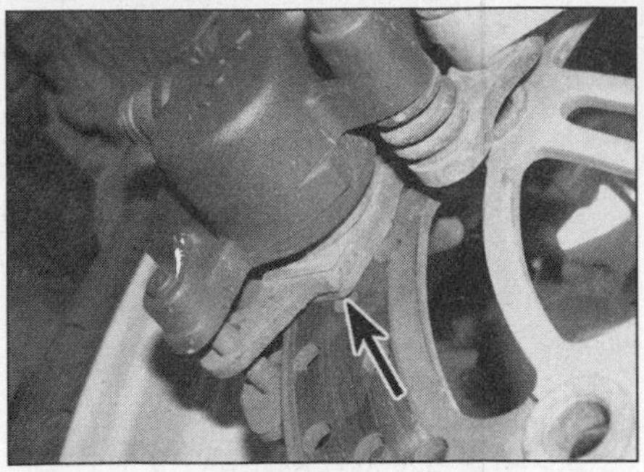

11.1a Brake pad wear indicator (arrowed) – X, Y, K1 and K2 models

11.1b Brake pad wear indicator (arrowed) – K3-on models

2 If the indicators aren't visible because the pads are dirty, or if you are in any doubt as to the amount of friction material remaining, remove the pads for inspection and measure the thickness of the material (see Chapter 7). Suzuki do not specify a minimum thickness, but anything less than 1 mm should be renewed.

3 If the pads are excessively worn, check the brake discs (see Chapter 7).

4 If the pads are damaged or contaminated with oil or grease, they must be renewed.

5 If the pads are worn unevenly, it is likely the caliper is sticking or, due either to dry or corroded slider pins (sliding type caliper) or to corrosion of the caliper pistons – refer to Chapter 7 for overhaul details.

12 Brake system – check

1 A routine general check of the brake system will ensure that any problems are discovered and remedied before the rider's safety is jeopardised.

2 Check the brake lever and pedal for loose mountings, improper or rough action, excessive play, bends, and other damage. Renew any damaged parts (see Chapter 7).

3 Make sure all brake component fasteners are tight. Check the brake pads for wear (see Section 11) and make sure the fluid level in the reservoirs is correct (see *Daily (pre-ride) checks*). Look for leaks at the hose and pipe connections and check for cracks in the hoses and pipes **(see illustration)**. If the lever or pedal is spongy, bleed the brakes (see Chapter 7).

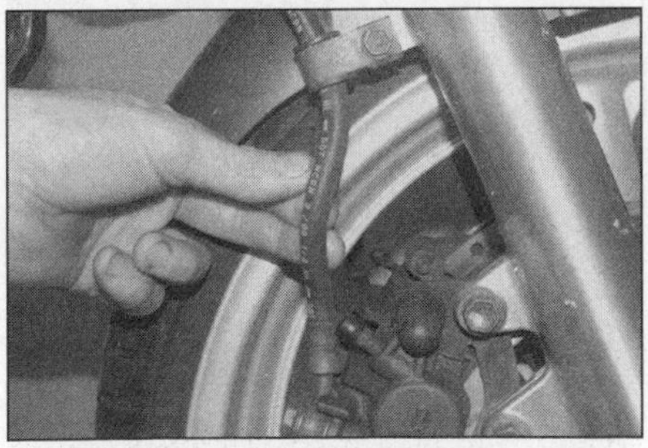

12.3 Flex the hoses and check for cracks, bulges and leaking fluid. Also check the pipes and all connections for leaks

4 Make sure the brake light operates when the front brake lever is pulled in. The front brake light switch, mounted on the underside of the master cylinder, is not adjustable. If it fails to operate properly, check it (see Chapter 9).

5 Make sure the brake light is activated just before the rear brake takes effect. If adjustment is necessary, hold the switch body and turn the adjuster nut until the brake light is activated when required **(see illustration)**. The switch is mounted on the inside of the frame, above the brake pedal and just ahead of the master cylinder. If the brake light comes on too late, turn the nut clockwise. If the brake light comes on too soon or is permanently on, turn the nut anti-clockwise. If the switch doesn't operate the brake light, check it (see Chapter 9).

6 The front brake lever has a span adjuster that alters the distance of the lever from the handlebar **(see illustration)**. Each setting is identified by a number on the adjuster. Pull the lever away from the handlebar and turn the adjuster ring until the setting that best suits the rider is obtained.

7 Measure the height of the rear brake pedal in relation to the top of the rider's footrest and compare it to the range specified at the beginning of the Chapter **(see illustration)**.

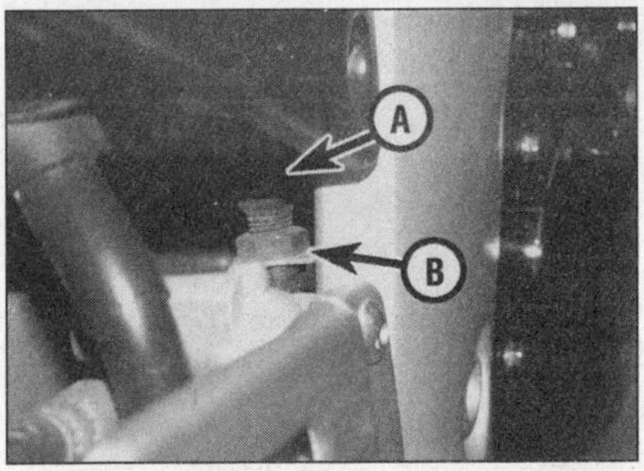

12.5 Hold the rear brake light switch body (A) and turn the adjuster nut (B) as required

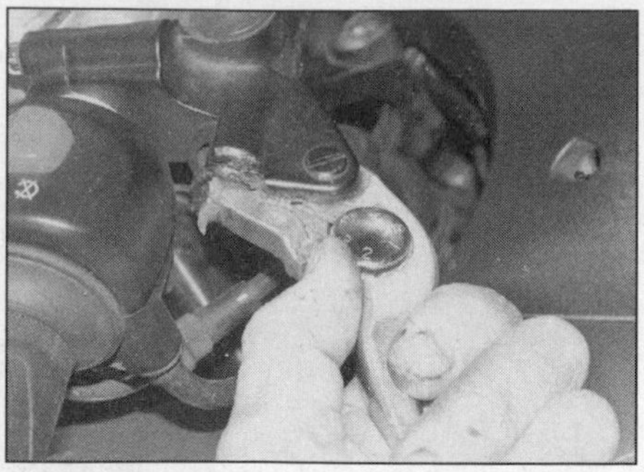

12.6 Adjusting the front brake lever span

12.7a Measure the rear brake pedal height and adjust if required

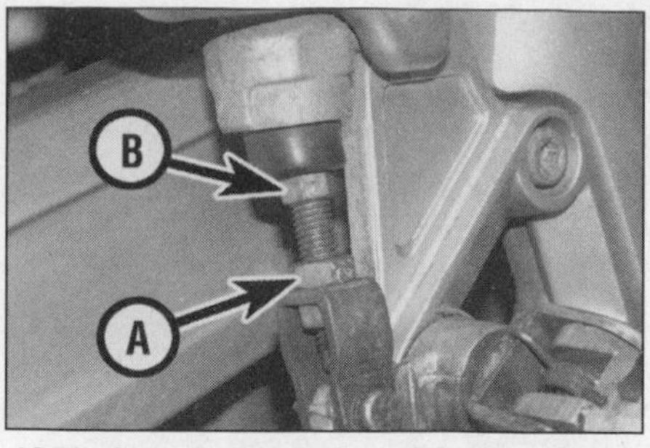

12.7b Slacken the locknut (A) and turn the pushrod using the hex (B) to adjust pedal height

The height can be adjusted to bring it within the range. Slacken the clevis locknut, then turn the pushrod using a spanner on the hex at the top of the rod until the pedal is at the correct or desired height **(see illustration)**. On completion tighten the locknut securely. On all models adjust the rear brake light switch after adjusting the pedal height (see Step 5).

13 Tyres and wheels – general check

Tyres

1 Check the tyre condition and tread depth thoroughly – see *Daily (pre-ride) checks*.

Wheels

2 Cast wheels are virtually maintenance free, but they should be kept clean and checked periodically for cracks and other damage. Also check the wheel runout and alignment (see Chapter 7). Never attempt to repair damaged cast wheels; they must be renewed. Check the valve rubber for signs of damage or deterioration and have it renewed if necessary. Also, make sure the valve stem cap is in place and tight.

14 Nuts and bolts – tightness check

1 Since vibration of the machine tends to loosen fasteners, all nuts, bolts, screws, etc. should be periodically checked for proper tightness.

2 Pay particular attention to the following:

Spark plugs
Engine oil drain plug and coolant drain plug
Lever and pedal bolts
Footrest and sidestand bolts
Engine mounting bolts, adjuster bolts and locknuts (refer to Chapter 2)
Shock absorber and suspension linkage bolts; swingarm pivot bolt, adjuster bolt and locknut (refer to Chapter 6)
Handlebar clamp bolts (all models), holder bolts (SV650) and positioning bolts (SV650S)
Front fork clamp bolts (top and bottom yoke) and fork top bolts
Steering stem nut
Front axle and axle clamp bolts
Rear axle nut
Brake caliper and master cylinder mounting bolts, brake caliper body bolts (rear calliper)
Brake hose banjo bolts and caliper bleed valves
Rear brake torque arm nuts
Brake disc bolts
Exhaust system bolts/nuts

3 If a torque wrench is available, use it along with the torque specifications at the beginning of this and other Chapters.

15 Sidestand, lever pivots and cables – lubrication

1 Since the controls, cables and various other components of a motorcycle are exposed to the elements, they should be checked and lubricated periodically to ensure safe and trouble-free operation.

2 The footrests, clutch and brake levers, brake pedal, gearchange lever and linkage, and sidestand pivot should be lubricated frequently. In order for the lubricant to be applied where it will do the most good, the component should be disassembled. The lubricant recommended by Suzuki for each application is listed at the beginning of the Chapter. If chain or cable lubricant is being used, it can be applied to the pivot joint gaps and will usually work its way into the areas where friction occurs, so less disassembly of the component is needed (however it is always better to do so and clean off all corrosion, dirt and old lubricant first). If motor oil or light grease is being used, apply it sparingly as it may attract dirt (which could cause the controls to bind or wear at an accelerated rate). **Note:** *One of the best lubricants for the control lever pivots is a dry-film lubricant (available from many sources by different names).*

15.3a Lubricating a cable with a pressure lubricator. Make sure the tool seals around the outer cable

3 To lubricate the cables, disconnect the relevant cable at its upper end, then lubricate it with a pressure adapter and aerosol lubricant, or if one is not available, using the set-up shown **(see illustrations)**. See Chapter 4A for choke cable removal on X, Y, K1 and K2 models; Chapter 4A or 4B as applicable for throttle cable removal. See Chapter 2 for clutch cable removal and details of the external clutch release mechanism.

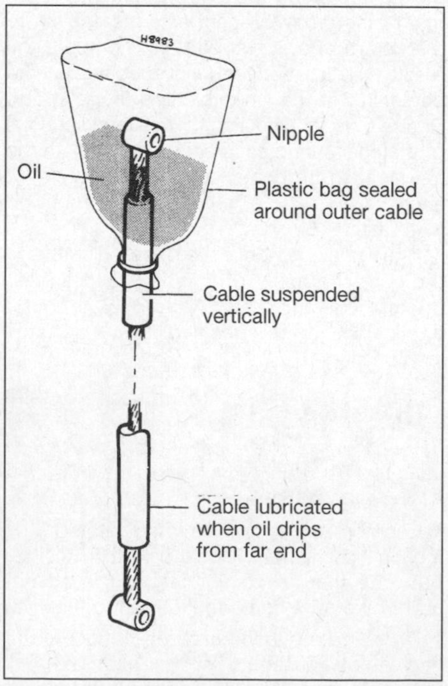

15.3b Lubricating a cable with a makeshift funnel and motor oil

17.5a Detach the vacuum hose from the rear carburettor union . . .

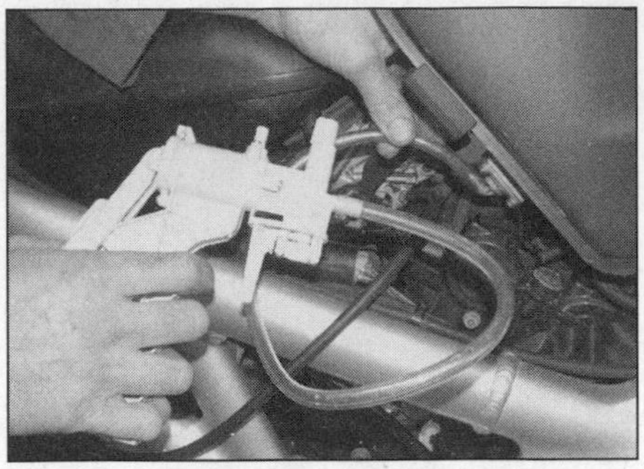

17.5b . . . and apply a vacuum to it to open the fuel tap

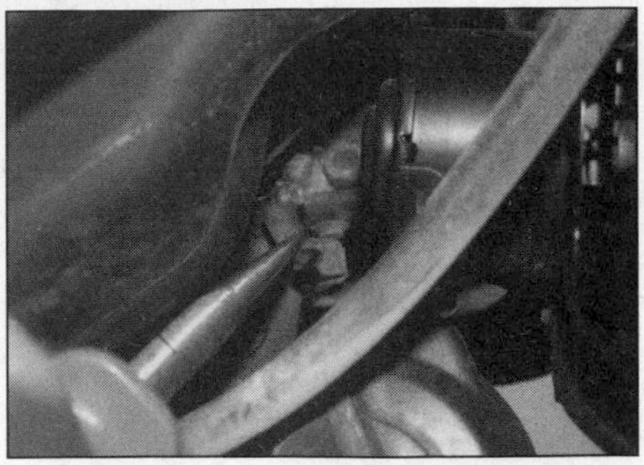

17.7 Remove the blanking cap from the front cylinder take-off point

Every 7500 miles (12,000 km)

Carry out all the items under the 4000 mile (6000 km) check, plus the following:

16 Spark plugs - renewal

1 Remove the old spark plugs as described in Section 3 and install new ones.

17 Carburettors (X, Y, K1 and K2 models) - synchronisation

Warning: Petrol (gasoline) is extremely flammable, so take extra precautions when you work on any part of the fuel system. Don't smoke or allow open flames or bare light bulbs near the work area, and don't work in a garage where a natural gas-type appliance is present. If you spill any fuel on your skin, rinse it off immediately with soap and water. When you perform any kind of work on the fuel system, wear safety glasses and have a fire extinguisher suitable for a Class B type fire (flammable liquids) on hand.

Warning: Take great care not to burn your hand on the hot engine unit when accessing the gauge take-off points on the intake ducts. Do not allow exhaust gases to build up in the work area; either perform the check outside or use an exhaust gas extraction system.

Note: *Suzuki specify that the carburettors should be synchronised with the air filter housing removed. As there is obviously a danger of dirt being drawn into the carburettors it is advisable to obtain an old pair of tights or similar and cut them so a disc of the material can be placed over the intake (and secured with an elastic band) to form a barrier without obstructing airflow.*

1 Carburettor synchronisation is simply the process of adjusting the carburettors so they pass the same amount of fuel/air mixture to each cylinder. This is achieved by measuring the vacuum produced in each intake duct. Carburettors that are out of synchronisation will result in increased fuel consumption, increased engine temperature, less than ideal throttle response and higher vibration levels.

2 To properly synchronise the carburettors, you will need a set of vacuum gauges or calibrated tubes to indicate engine vacuum. The equipment used should be suitable for a twin cylinder engine and come complete with the necessary hoses to fit the take-off points on the front and rear intake ducts. **Note:** *Because of the nature of the synchronisation procedure and the need for special instruments, most owners leave the task to a Suzuki dealer.*

3 Start the engine and let it run until it reaches normal operating temperature, then check that the idle speed is correctly set (1300 rpm), and adjust it if necessary (see Section 6).

4 Raise the fuel tank and remove the air filter housing (see Chapter 4A).

5 Release the fuel tap vacuum hose clamp and detach the hose from the take-off point on the rear cylinder intake duct **(see illustration)**. Using a calibrated vacuum pump if available, apply a vacuum of 1 to 2 psi to the end of the house then clamp it so that the vacuum within is maintained, thereby keeping the diaphragm in the fuel tap open **(see illustration)**. Note that on California models the vacuum hose routing is different and combined with the hose for the PAIR emissions system control valve – refer to the hose routing sticker located on the motorcycle for exact information, or make a careful note of it before disconnection if the sticker is missing.

6 Access the take-off point on the front cylinder intake duct is extremely restricted. On SV650S models, to provide best access and minimise the risk of doing any damage, remove the fairing side panels (see Chapter 8); the alternative is to remove the three screws on each side of it and carefully pull the sides away from the radiator to release the pegs from the grommets (see Chapter 8). On all models, remove the horn along with its mounting bracket (see Chapter 9). Unscrew the radiator lower mounting bolt and pivot the bottom of the radiator forward **(see illustrations 3.3a and b)**. On S models take care not to damage the fairing if it wasn't removed. Place a block of wood between the radiator and cylinder to keep it clear, making sure the block locates so as not to damage the cooling fins, or alternatively hold the radiator back using a cable tie or bungee cord.

7 Remove the blanking cap from the take-off point on the front cylinder intake duct – a pair of long thin-nosed pliers is the best way to access it **(see illustration)**.

8 Connect the gauge hoses to the vacuum take-off points **(see illustrations)**. Make sure they are a good fit because any air leaks will result in false readings.

9 Start the engine. If using vacuum gauges fitted with damping adjustment, set this so that the needle flutter is just eliminated but so that they can still respond to small changes in pressure.

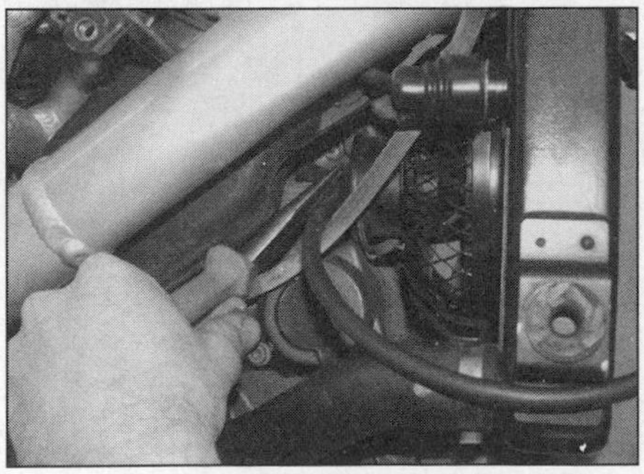

17.8a Connect the gauge hoses to the front union . . .

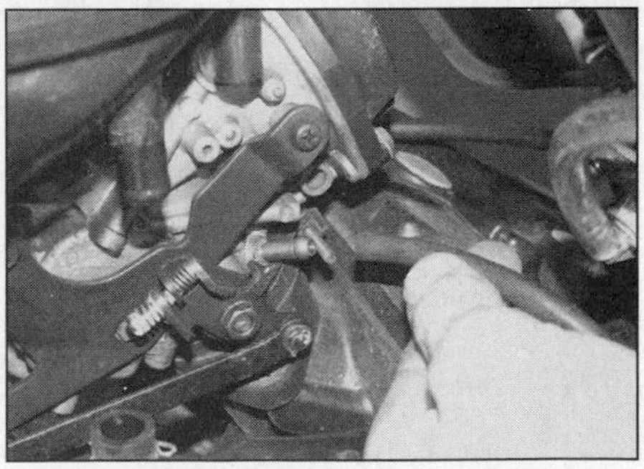

17.8b . . . and the rear union

10 The vacuum readings for both cylinders should be the same, or at least within the maximum difference specified at the beginning of the Chapter **(see illustration)**. If the vacuum readings vary, adjust the carburettors by turning the synchronising screw situated on the left-hand side of the rear carburettor until the readings are the same **(see illustration)**. **Note:** *Do not press hard on the screw whilst adjusting it, otherwise a false reading will be obtained.*

11 When the carburettors are synchronised, open and close the throttle quickly to settle the linkage, and recheck the gauge readings, readjusting if necessary.

12 When the adjustment is complete, adjust the idle speed if necessary by turning the throttle stop screw (see Section 6) until the idle speed listed in this Chapter's Specifications is obtained. Stop the engine.

13 Remove the vacuum gauges. Refit the blanking cap on the front cylinder take-off point **(see illustration 17.7)**. Release the clamp on the fuel tap vacuum hose and attach the hose to the rear cylinder take-off point **(see illustration 17.5a)**. Install the air filter housing, and lower the fuel tank (see Chapter 4A).

14 Fit the radiator back on its lower mounting (see Chapter 3), then install the horn (see Chapter 9) and on S models install or remount the fairing side panels (see Chapter 8).

18 Throttle bodies (K3-on models) – synchronisation

Note: *Synchronisation of the throttle bodies on K3 to K6 models can be carried out using vacuum gauges or calibrated tubes as described below. The procedure for K7 models onward also requires the use of the Suzuki SDS tester to set the ISC (idle speed control) value between the two cylinders – it is thus advised that this maintenance operation be carried out by a Suzuki dealer.*

Warning: Petrol (gasoline) is extremely flammable, so take extra precautions when you work on any part of the fuel system. Don't smoke or allow open flames or bare light bulbs near the work area, and don't work in a garage where a natural gas-type appliance is present. If you spill any fuel on your skin, rinse it off immediately with soap and water. When you perform any kind of work on the fuel system, wear safety glasses and have a fire extinguisher suitable for a Class B type fire (flammable liquids) on hand.

17.10a Check carburettor synchronisation . . .

Warning: Take great care not to burn your hand on the hot engine unit when accessing the gauge take-off points on the throttle bodies. Do not allow exhaust gases to build up in the work area; either perform the check outside or use an exhaust gas extraction system.

Note: *Suzuki specify that the throttle bodies should be synchronised with the air filter housing removed. As there is obviously a danger of dirt being drawn into the throttle bodies it is advisable to obtain an old pair of tights or similar and secure a section of the material over the intake with an elastic band to form a barrier without obstructing airflow.*

1 Throttle body synchronisation is simply the process of adjusting the butterfly valve linkage so they pass the same amount of fuel/air mixture to each cylinder. This is achieved by measuring the vacuum produced in each intake duct. Throttle bodies that are out of synchronisation will result in increased fuel consumption, increased engine temperature, less than ideal throttle response and higher vibration levels.

2 To synchronise the throttle bodies, you will need a set of vacuum gauges or calibrated tubes to indicate engine vacuum. The equipment used should be suitable for a twin cylinder engine and come complete with the necessary hoses to fit the take-off points. **Note:** *Because of the nature of the synchronisation procedure and the need for special instruments, most owners leave the task to a Suzuki dealer.*

3 Start the engine and let it run until it reaches normal operating temperature, then check that the idle speed is correctly set (1300 rpm), and adjust it if necessary (see Section 6).

4 Raise the fuel tank and remove the air filter housing (see Chapter 4B).

5 Remove the intake air temperature and intake air pressure sensors from the air filter housing and reconnect them to the wiring loom (see Chapter 4B). Remove the PAIR control valve from the air filter housing and reconnect the wiring connector and vacuum hose.

6 Check that with the throttle fully closed there is a gap of 0.17 mm between the throttle linkage arm and the stopper screw **(see illustration)**. If necessary, slacken the locknut on the stopper screw and turn the screw to set the gap, then tighten the locknut.

7 Remove the blanking caps from the front and rear cylinder throttle body vacuum take-off points **(see illustration 18.6)**.

8 Connect the gauge hoses to the take-off points. Make sure they are a good fit because any air leaks will result in false readings.

9 Start the engine. If using vacuum gauges fitted with damping adjustment, set this so that the needle flutter is just eliminated but so that they can still respond to small changes in pressure.

10 The vacuum readings for both cylinders should be the same, or at least within the maximum difference specified at the beginning of the Chapter. If the vacuum readings vary, adjust the butterfly valve linkage by turning the synchronising screw situated on the right-hand side of the rear throttle body until the readings are the same **(see illustration)**.

17.10b . . . and adjust if necessary using the synchronisation screw (arrowed)

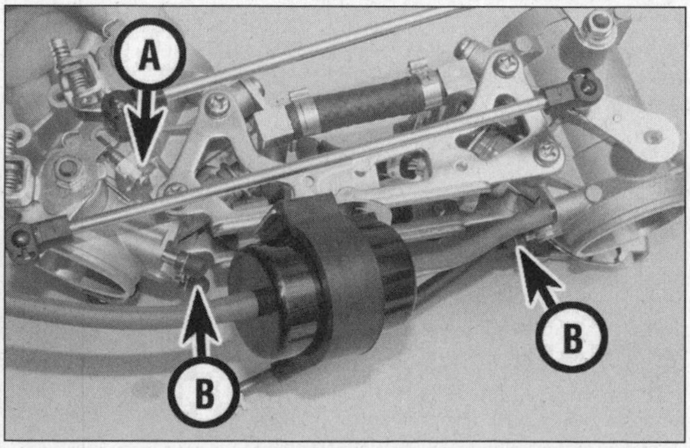

18.6 Location of the throttle stopper screw (A) and blanking caps (B)

Note: *Do not press hard on the screw whilst adjusting it, otherwise a false reading will be obtained.*

11 When the throttle bodies are synchronised, open and close the throttle quickly to settle the linkage, and recheck the gauge readings, readjusting if necessary.

12 When the adjustment is complete, adjust the idle speed if necessary by turning the throttle stop screw (see Section 6) until the idle speed listed in this Chapter's Specifications is obtained. Stop the engine.

13 Refer to Step 6 and recheck the gap between the throttle linkage arm and the stopper screw.

14 Remove the vacuum gauges. Refit the blanking caps on the front and rear cylinder throttle bodies **(see illustration 18.6)**.

15 Install the PAIR control valve, the intake air temperature and intake air pressure sensors in the air filter housing, then install the housing and lower the fuel tank (see Chapter 4B).

19 Steering head bearings – freeplay check and adjustment

1 Steering head bearings can become dented, rough or loose during normal use of the machine. In extreme cases, worn or loose steering head bearings can cause steering wobble – a condition that is potentially dangerous.

Check

2 Support the motorcycle on an auxiliary stand and raise the front wheel off the ground using a jack and block of wood under the engine.

3 Point the front wheel straight-ahead and slowly move the handlebars from side-to-side. Any dents or roughness in the bearing races will be felt and the bars will not move smoothly and freely. Again point the wheel straight-ahead, and tap the front of the wheel to one side. The wheel should 'fall' under its own weight to the limit of its lock, indicating that the bearings are not too tight. Check for similar movement to the other side. If available, attach one end of a spring balance (graduated 100 to 600 grams) to the outer end of the rubber grip on the handlebars. With the steering straight-ahead, pull on the balance and check the reading at which the handlebars start to turn. If the reading is below 200 grams, the steering head is too loose, if the reading is above 500 grams the steering head is too tight. If the steering doesn't perform as described, and it's not due to the resistance of cables or hoses, then the bearings should be adjusted as described below.

4 Next, grasp the bottom of the forks and gently pull and push them forward and backward **(see illustration)**. Any looseness or freeplay in the steering head bearings will be felt as front-to-rear movement of the forks. If play is felt, adjust the bearings as described below.

HAYNES HiNT ***Make sure you are not mistaking any movement between the bike and stand, or between the stand and the ground, for freeplay in the bearings. Do not pull and push the forks too hard – a gentle movement is all that is needed. Freeplay in the forks themselves due to worn bushes can also be misinterpreted as steering head bearing play – do not confuse the two.***

Adjustment

5 As a precaution, remove the fuel tank (see Chapter 4A or 4B). Though not actually necessary, this will prevent the possibility of damage should a tool slip.

6 If required, on SV650 models, displace the handlebars from the top yoke (see Chapter 6). Support them so the brake master cylinder is upright to prevent the possibility of fluid leakage. There is no need to remove assemblies from the handlebars, or to disconnect any cables, hoses or wiring. Note that if you do not have a socket or torque wrench, and are using a spanner to slacken and tighten the steering stem nut, the handlebars can remain in place.

18.10 Location of the synchronising screw

X, Y, K1 and K2 models

7 Slacken the steering stem nut and the fork clamp bolts in the bottom yoke **(see illustrations)**.

8 Using a suitable C-spanner (or a drift) located in one of the notches of the adjuster nut, slacken the nut slightly until pressure is just released, then tighten it until all freeplay is removed, yet the steering is able to move freely as described in Steps 3 and 4 **(see illustrations)**. The object is to set the adjuster nut so that the bearings are under a very light loading, just enough to remove any freeplay, but not so much that the steering does not move freely from side to side as

19.4 Checking for play in the steering head bearings

19.7a Slacken the steering stem nut (arrowed) . . .

19.7b . . . and the bottom yoke fork clamp bolts (arrowed) on each side

19.8a Adjust the bearings as described using a C-spanner . . .

19.8b . . . or a drift

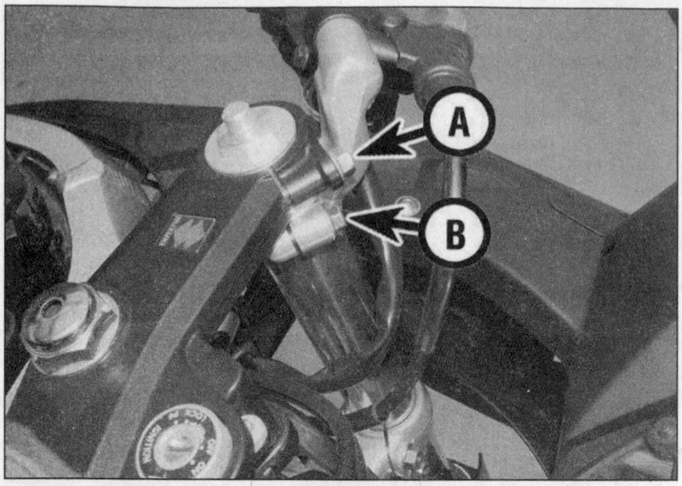

19.13 Slacken the fork clamp bolts (A) and handlebar clamp bolts (B) on each side

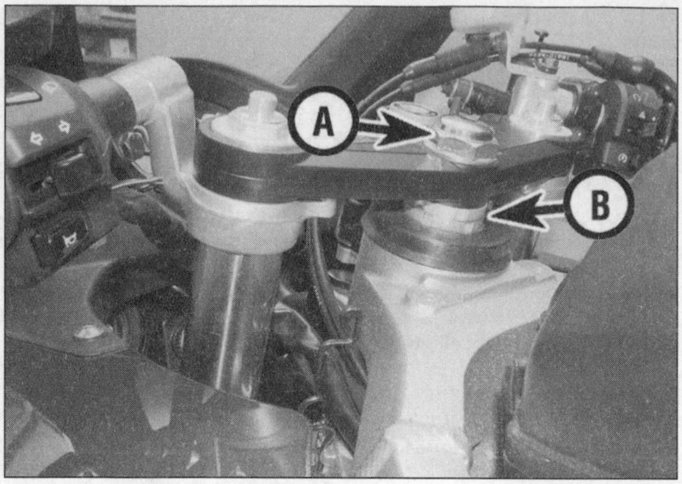

19.14 Slacken the steering stem nut (A) and the bearing adjuster locknut (B)

19.15 Adjusting the bearings using a C-spanner

described in the check procedure above. If you have the spring balance, set the adjuster nut so that the steering starts to move at a load of around 350 grams.

9 If the bearings cannot be correctly adjusted, disassemble the steering head and check the bearings and races (see Chapter 6).

Caution: Take great care not to apply excessive pressure because this will cause premature failure of the bearings.

10 Tighten the steering stem nut to the torque setting specified at the beginning of the Chapter **(see illustration 19.7a)**. Now tighten the fork clamp bolts to the specified torque **(see illustration 19.7b)**.

11 Check the bearing adjustment as described above and re-adjust if necessary.

12 Install the handlebars if displaced (see Chapter 6), and install the fuel tank (see Chapter 4A).

K3-on models

13 Slacken the fork clamp bolts in the top yoke and, on SV650S models, the handlebar clamp bolts **(see illustrations)**. Note that on SV650S models, it may be necessary to loosen the front brake and clutch lever assembly clamps and displace the levers in order to access the fork clamp bolts.

14 Slacken the steering stem nut, then slacken the bearing adjuster locknut using a suitable C-spanner (or a drift) located in one of the notches of the nut **(see illustration)**.

15 Using the C-spanner or drift, slacken the adjuster nut slightly until pressure is just released, then tighten it until all freeplay is removed as described in Step 8 **(see illustration)**.

Caution: Take great care not to apply excessive pressure because this will cause premature failure of the bearings.

16 If the bearings cannot be correctly adjusted, disassemble the steering head and check the bearings and races (see Chapter 6).

17 Tighten the adjuster locknut and the steering stem nut to the torque setting specified at the beginning of the Chapter **(see illustration 19.14)**. Now tighten the fork clamp bolts and, on SV650S models, the handlebar clamp bolts, to the specified torque.

18 Check the bearing adjustment as described above and re-adjust if necessary.

19 Install the handlebars if displaced (see Chapter 6), and install the fuel tank (see Chapter 4B).

20 Suspension – check

1 The suspension components must be maintained in top operating condition to ensure rider safety. Loose, worn or damaged suspension parts decrease the motorcycle's stability and control.

Front suspension

2 While standing alongside the motorcycle, apply the front brake and push on the handlebars to compress the forks several times **(see illustration)**. See if they move up-and-down smoothly without binding. If binding is felt, the forks should be disassembled and inspected (see Chapter 6).

3 Inspect the area around the dust seal for signs of oil leakage, then carefully lever up the seal using a flat-bladed screwdriver and inspect the area around the fork seal **(see illustration)**. If leakage is evident, the seals must be renewed (see Chapter 6).

4 Check the tightness of all suspension nuts and bolts to be sure none have worked loose, applying the torque settings at the beginning of Chapter 6.

Rear suspension

5 Inspect the rear shock absorber for fluid leakage and tightness of its mountings. If leakage is found, the shock must be renewed (see Chapter 6).

6 With the aid of an assistant to support the bike, compress the rear suspension several

20.2 Checking the front suspension

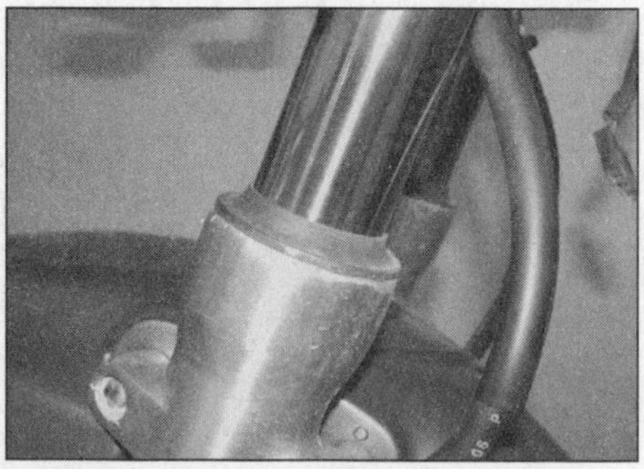

20.3 Check above and below the dust seal for signs of oil leakage

times. It should move up and down freely without binding. If any binding is felt, the worn or faulty component must be identified and checked (see Chapter 6). The problem could be due to either the shock absorber, the suspension linkage components or the swingarm components.

7 Support the motorcycle on an auxiliary stand so that the rear wheel is off the ground. Grab the swingarm and rock it from side to side – there should be no discernible movement at the rear **(see illustration)**. If there's a little movement or a slight clicking can be heard, inspect the tightness of all the swingarm and rear suspension mounting bolts and nuts, referring to the torque settings specified at the beginning of Chapter 6, and re-check for movement.

8 Next, grasp the top of the rear wheel and pull it upwards – there should be no discernible freeplay before the shock absorber begins to compress **(see illustration)**. Any freeplay felt in either check indicates worn bearings or bushes (according to model) in the suspension linkage or swingarm, or worn shock absorber mountings. The worn components must be

20.7 Checking for play in the swingarm bearings

identified and renewed (see Chapter 6).

9 To make an accurate assessment of the swingarm bearings, remove the rear wheel (see Chapter 7) and the bolt securing the suspension linkage assembly to the swingarm (see Chapter 6). Grasp the rear of the swingarm with one hand and place your other hand at the junction of the swingarm and the frame. Try to move the rear of the swingarm from side-to-side. Any wear (play) in the

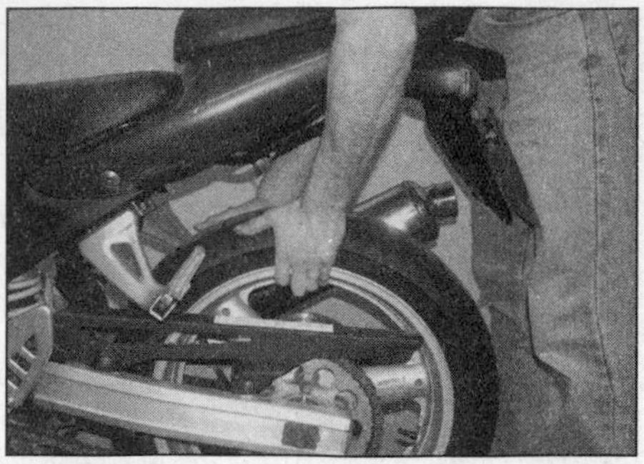

20.8 Checking for play in the rear shock mountings and suspension linkage bearings

bearings should be felt as movement between the swingarm and the frame at the front. If there is any play the swingarm will be felt to move forward and backward at the front (not from side-to-side). Next, move the swingarm up and down through its full travel. It should move freely, without any binding or rough spots. If there is any play in the swingarm or if it does not move freely, remove the bearings for inspection (see Chapter 6).

Every 11,000 miles (18,000 km)

Carry out all the items under the 4000 mile (6000 km) check, plus the following:

21 Air filter – renewal

Caution: If the machine is continually ridden in wet or dusty conditions, the filter should be renewed more frequently.

1 Refer to the procedure in Section 2 and renew the air filter.

22 Engine/transmission – oil and filter change

Warning: Be careful when draining the oil, as the exhaust pipes, the engine, and the oil itself can cause severe burns.

1 Refer to Section 5, Steps 1 to 5 and drain the engine oil.

2 Now place the drain tray below the oil filter, located on the front of the engine. Unscrew the filter using a filter socket such as the Suzuki special tool (Pt. No. 09915-40610) or a commercially available equivalent, a filter removing strap or a chain-wrench, and tip any residual oil into the drain tray **(see illustrations)**. Discard the filter, noting that it should be taken to the disposal site along with the used oil.

3 Smear clean engine oil onto the rubber seal on the new filter and thread it onto the engine until the rubber seal just contacts its mating surface **(see illustrations)**. Now tighten the filter by two full turns (or by the number of turns

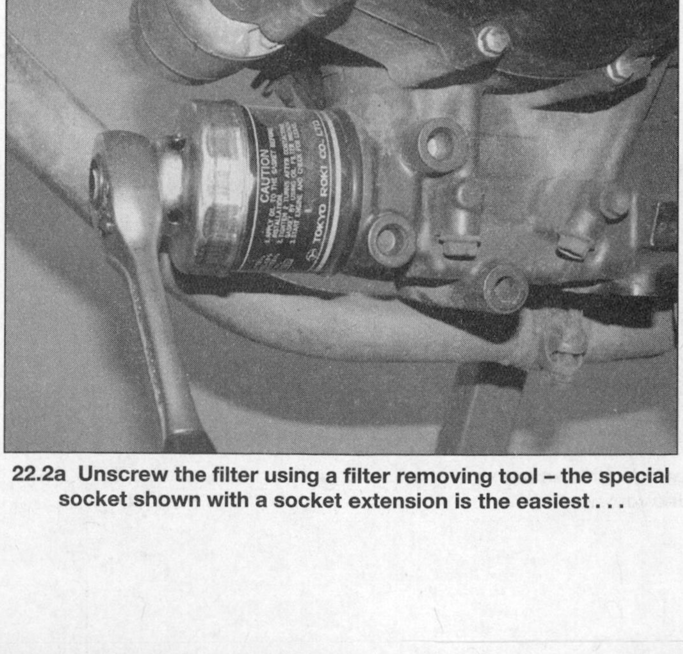

22.2a Unscrew the filter using a filter removing tool – the special socket shown with a socket extension is the easiest . . .

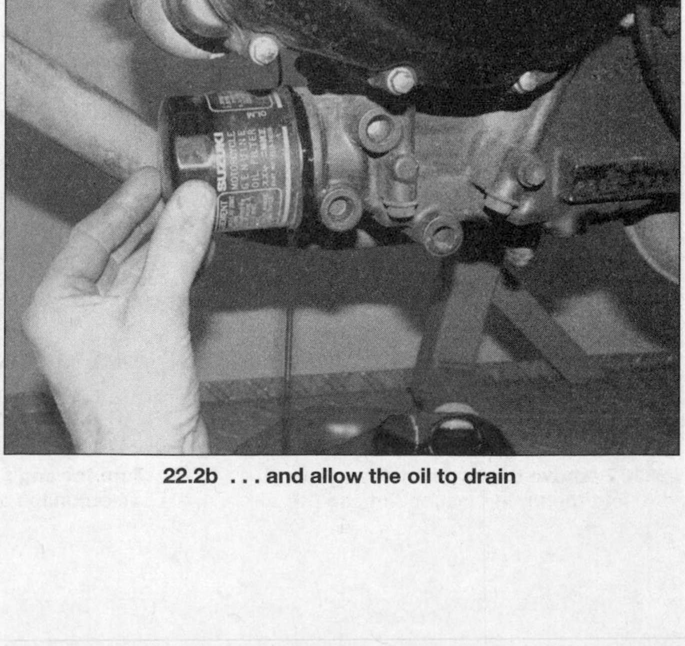

22.2b . . . and allow the oil to drain

22.3a Smear clean oil onto the seal . . .

22.3b . . . then install the filter . . .

22.3c . . . and tighten it using a socket . . .

22.3d . . . or your hands

specified on the filter itself or its packaging) **(see illustrations)**. **Note:** *Do not use a strap or chain filter removing tool to tighten the filter as you will damage it. If you do not have a filter socket you can tighten the filter by hand, but make sure it is tightened by the number of turns specified or it will probably leak.*

4 Refer to Section 5, Steps 6 and 7 and refill the engine to the proper level using the recommended type and amount of oil.

Every 15,000 miles (24,000 km)

Carry out all the items under the 7500 mile (12,000 km) check, plus the following:

23 Valve clearances – check and adjustment

1 The engine must be completely cool for this maintenance procedure, so let the machine sit overnight before beginning.

2 Remove the radiator (see Chapter 3).

3 Remove the spark plugs to allow the engine to be turned over easier (see Section 3).

4 Unscrew the crankshaft end cap and the timing mark inspection cap from the alternator cover **(see illustration)**. Check the condition of the cap O-ring and sealing washer and renew them if they are damaged, deformed or deteriorated.

5 Remove the valve covers (see Chapter 2).

6 Make a chart or sketch of all valve positions so that a note of each clearance can be made against the relevant valve.

7 Start with the front cylinder. Rotate the engine using a 17 mm socket on the alternator rotor bolt, turning it in an anti-clockwise direction only until the line next to the 'F' mark on the flywheel aligns with the notch in the timing mark inspection hole **(see illustrations)**. At this point make sure that the cylinder is at TDC (top dead centre) on the compression stroke (and not the exhaust stroke) by checking the positions of the camshaft lobes – they should be pointing away from each other. If not, turn the engine anti-clockwise through one full turn (360°) until the 'F' mark again aligns with the notch. The camshaft lobes will now be correctly positioned.

8 With the engine in this position all valves will be closed. Check the clearances on both the inlet and exhaust valves. Insert a feeler gauge of the same thickness as the correct valve clearance (see Specifications, noting that there is a difference between inlet and

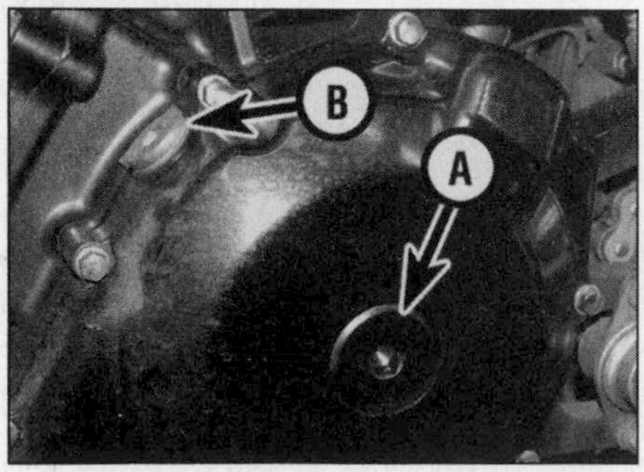

23.4 Remove the crankshaft end cap (A) and the timing inspection cap (B)

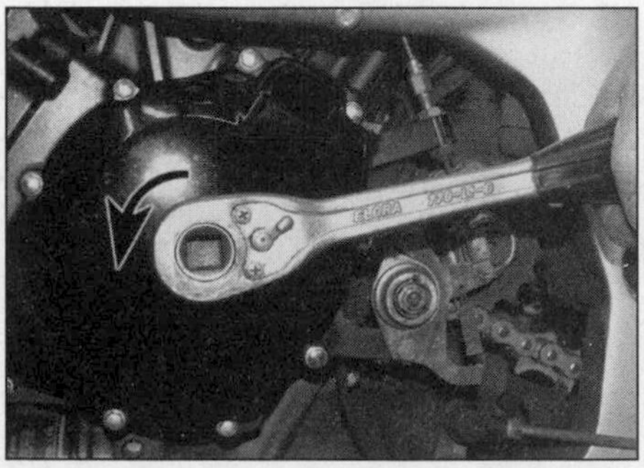

23.7a Turn the engine anti-clockwise using a socket on the timing rotor bolt . . .

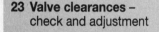

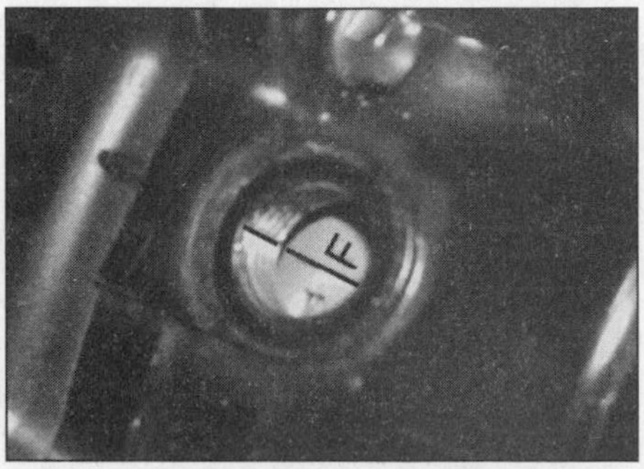

23.7b . . . until the line next to the F mark aligns with the notch

23.8 Insert the feeler gauge between the base of the lobe and the top of the follower as shown

23.9 Turn the engine anti-clockwise until the line next to the R mark aligns with the notch

exhaust) between the base of each camshaft lobe and the top of the cam follower on each valve and check that it is a firm sliding fit – you should feel a slight drag when the you pull the gauge out **(see illustration)**. If not, use the feeler gauges to obtain the exact clearance. Record the measured clearance on the chart.

9 The rear cylinder valve clearances can now be checked. Rotate the engine 270° (3/4 turn) anti-clockwise using the 17 mm socket on the alternator rotor bolt **(see illustration 23.7a)** until the line next to the 'R' mark on the flywheel aligns with the notch in the timing mark inspection hole **(see illustration)**. At this point make sure that the cylinder is at TDC (top dead centre) on the compression stroke (and not the exhaust stroke) by checking the positions of the camshaft lobes – they should be pointing away from each other. If not, turn the engine anti-clockwise through one full turn (360°) until the line next to the 'R' mark again aligns with the notch. The camshaft lobes will now be correctly positioned. Check and adjust the valve clearance as described in Step 8.

10 When all clearances have been measured and charted, identify whether the clearance on any valve falls outside the specified range. If any do, the shim must be changed for one of a thickness that will restore the correct clearance.

11 Shim changing requires removal of the camshaft(s) (see Chapter 2). There is no need to remove both camshafts if shims from only one side of the cylinder need changing. Place rags over the spark plug holes and the cam chain tunnel to prevent a shim from dropping into the engine on removal. Work on one valve at a time to prevent the possibility of mixing up the followers, which must be returned to their original location. If you want to remove more than one shim and follower at a time, store them in a marked container or bag, denoting which cylinder and which valve the follower and shim are from, so that they do not get mixed up.

12 With the camshaft removed, remove the cam follower of the valve in question, then retrieve the shim from the inside of the follower **(see illustrations)**. The follower is best removed with a magnet or using the suction created by a valve lapping tool, but long nosed pliers can be used with care. If the shim is not in the follower, pick it out of the top of the valve spring retainer using either a magnet, a screwdriver with a dab of grease on it (the shim will stick to the grease), or a very small screwdriver and a pair of pliers **(see illustrations)**. Do not allow the shim to fall into the engine.

13 A size mark should be stamped on one face of the shim – a shim marked 175 is 1.75 mm thick. If the mark is not visible measure the shim thickness using a micrometer **(see illustration)**. It is recommended that the shim be measured

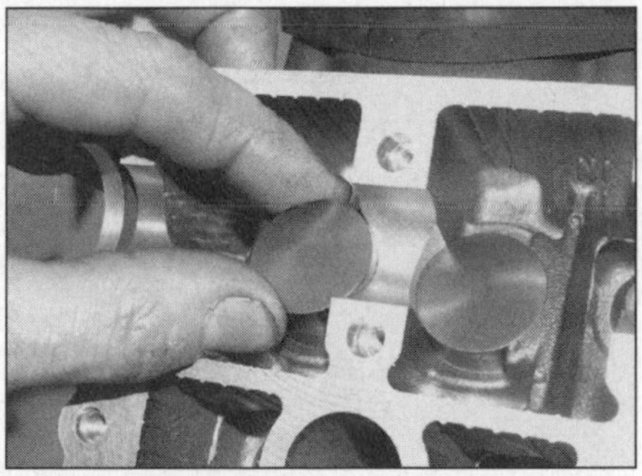

23.12a Carefully lift out the follower . . .

23.12b . . . and retrieve the shim from inside it . . .

23.12c . . . or from the top of the valve using a magnet . . .

23.12d . . . or a screwdriver dabbed with grease

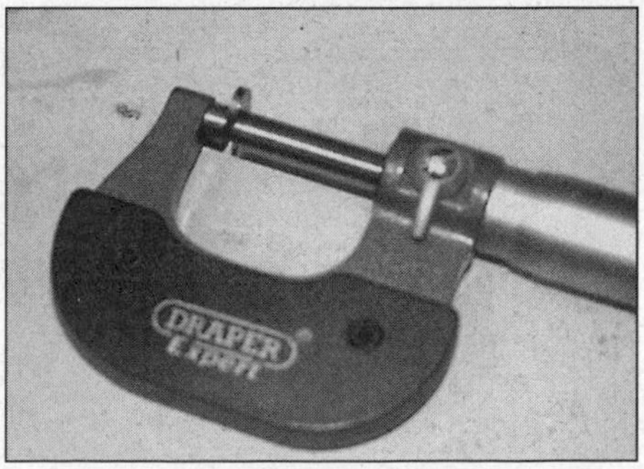

23.13 Check the thickness of the shim using a micrometer

	PRESENT SHIM SIZE (mm)																				
MEASURED TAPPET CLEARANCE (mm)	1.20	1.25	1.30	1.35	1.40	1.45	1.50	1.55	1.60	1.65	1.70	1.75	1.80	1.85	1.90	1.95	2.00	2.05	2.10	2.15	2.20
0.00-0.04			1.20	1.25	1.30	1.35	1.40	1.45	1.50	1.55	1.60	1.65	1.70	1.75	1.80	1.85	1.90	1.95	2.00	2.05	2.10
0.05-0.09		1.20	1.25	1.30	1.35	1.40	1.45	1.50	1.55	1.60	1.65	1.70	1.75	1.80	1.85	1.90	1.95	2.00	2.05	2.10	2.15
0.10-0.20	SPECIFIED CLEARANCE/NO ADJUSTMENT REQUIRED																				
0.21-0.25	1.30	1.35	1.40	1.45	1.50	1.55	1.60	1.65	1.70	1.75	1.80	1.85	1.90	1.95	2.00	2.05	2.10	2.15	2.20	2.20	
0.26-0.30	1.35	1.40	1.45	1.50	1.55	1.60	1.65	1.70	1.75	1.80	1.85	1.90	1.95	2.00	2.05	2.10	2.15	2.20			
0.31-0.35	1.40	1.45	1.50	1.55	1.60	1.65	1.70	1.75	1.80	1.85	1.90	1.95	2.00	2.05	2.10	2.15	2.20				
0.36-0.40	1.45	1.50	1.55	1.60	1.65	1.70	1.75	1.80	1.85	1.90	1.95	2.00	2.05	2.10	2.15	2.20					
0.41-0.45	1.50	1.55	1.60	1.65	1.70	1.75	1.80	1.85	1.90	1.95	2.00	2.05	2.10	2.15	2.20						
0.46-0.50	1.55	1.60	1.65	1.70	1.75	1.80	1.85	1.90	1.95	2.00	2.05	2.10	2.15	2.20							
0.51-0.55	1.60	1.65	1.70	1.75	1.80	1.85	1.90	1.95	2.00	2.05	2.10	2.15	2.20								
0.56-0.60	1.65	1.70	1.75	1.80	1.85	1.90	1.95	2.00	2.05	2.10	2.15	2.20									
0.61-0.65	1.70	1.75	1.80	1.85	1.90	1.95	2.00	2.05	2.10	2.15	2.20										
0.66-0.70	1.75	1.80	1.85	1.90	1.95	2.00	2.05	2.10	2.15	2.20											
0.71-0.75	1.80	1.85	1.90	1.95	2.00	2.05	2.10	2.15	2.20												
0.76-0.80	1.85	1.90	1.95	2.00	2.05	2.10	2.15	2.20													
0.81-0.85	1.90	1.95	2.00	2.05	2.10	2.15	2.20														
0.86-0.90	1.95	2.00	2.05	2.10	2.15	2.20															
0.91-0.95	2.00	2.05	2.10	2.15	2.20																
0.96-1.00	2.05	2.10	2.15	2.20																	
1.01-1.05	2.10	2.15	2.20																		
1.06-1.10	2.15	2.20																			
1.11-1.15	2.20																				

H31236

23.14a Shim selection chart – intake valves

	PRESENT SHIM SIZE (mm)																				
MEASURED TAPPET CLEARANCE (mm)	1.20	1.25	1.30	1.35	1.40	1.45	1.50	1.55	1.60	1.65	1.70	1.75	1.80	1.85	1.90	1.95	2.00	2.05	2.10	2.15	2.20
0.05-0.09				1.20	1.25	1.30	1.35	1.40	1.45	1.50	1.55	1.60	1.65	1.70	1.75	1.80	1.85	1.90	1.95	2.00	2.05
0.10-0.14			1.20	1.25	1.30	1.35	1.40	1.45	1.50	1.55	1.60	1.65	1.70	1.75	1.80	1.85	1.90	1.95	2.00	2.05	2.10
0.15-0.19		1.20	1.25	1.30	1.35	1.40	1.45	1.50	1.55	1.60	1.65	1.70	1.75	1.80	1.85	1.90	1.95	2.00	2.05	2.10	2.15
0.20-0.30	SPECIFIED CLEARANCE/NO ADJUSTMENT REQUIRED																				
0.31-0.35	1.30	1.35	1.40	1.45	1.50	1.55	1.60	1.65	1.70	1.75	1.80	1.85	1.90	1.95	2.00	2.05	2.10	2.15	2.20	2.20	
0.36-0.40	1.35	1.40	1.45	1.50	1.55	1.60	1.65	1.70	1.75	1.80	1.85	1.90	1.95	2.00	2.05	2.10	2.15	2.20			
0.41-0.45	1.40	1.45	1.50	1.55	1.60	1.65	1.70	1.75	1.80	1.85	1.90	1.95	2.00	2.05	2.10	2.15	2.20				
0.46-0.50	1.45	1.50	1.55	1.60	1.65	1.70	1.75	1.80	1.85	1.90	1.95	2.00	2.05	2.10	2.15	2.20					
0.51-0.55	1.50	1.55	1.60	1.65	1.70	1.75	1.80	1.85	1.90	1.95	2.00	2.05	2.10	2.15	2.20						
0.56-0.60	1.55	1.60	1.65	1.70	1.75	1.80	1.85	1.90	1.95	2.00	2.05	2.10	2.15	2.20							
0.61-0.65	1.60	1.65	1.70	1.75	1.80	1.85	1.90	1.95	2.00	2.05	2.10	2.15	2.20								
0.66-0.70	1.65	1.70	1.75	1.80	1.85	1.90	1.95	2.00	2.05	2.10	2.15	2.20									
0.71-0.75	1.70	1.75	1.80	1.85	1.90	1.95	2.00	2.05	2.10	2.15	2.20										
0.76-0.80	1.75	1.80	1.85	1.90	1.95	2.00	2.05	2.10	2.15	2.20											
0.81-0.85	1.80	1.85	1.90	1.95	2.00	2.05	2.10	2.15	2.20												
0.86-0.90	1.85	1.90	1.95	2.00	2.05	2.10	2.15	2.20													
0.91-0.95	1.90	1.95	2.00	2.05	2.10	2.15	2.20														
0.96-1.00	1.95	2.00	2.05	2.10	2.15	2.20															
1.01-1.05	2.00	2.05	2.10	2.15	2.20																
1.06-1.10	2.05	2.10	2.15	2.20																	
1.11-1.15	2.10	2.15	2.20																		
1.16-1.20	2.15	2.20																			
1.21-1.25	2.20																				

H31237

23.14b Shim selection chart – exhaust valves

anyway to check whether it has worn. Shims are available in 0.05 mm increments from 1.200 to 2.200 mm. If the shim thickness is less than its denomination, this must be taken into account when selecting a new shim.

14 Using the appropriate shim selection chart, find where the measured valve clearance and existing shim thickness values intersect and read off the shim size required **(see illustrations)**. **Note:** *If the existing shim is marked with a number not ending in 0 or 5, round it up or down as appropriate to the nearest number ending in 0 or 5 so that the chart can be used.* **Note:** *If the required replacement shim is greater than 2.20 mm (the largest available), the valve is probably not seating correctly due to a build-up of carbon deposits and should be checked and cleaned or resurfaced as required (see Chapter 2).*

15 Obtain the replacement shim, then lubricate it with molybdenum disulphide oil (a 50/50 mixture of molybdenum disulphide grease and engine oil) and fit it into the recess in the top of the valve spring retainer with the size mark facing up **(see illustration 23.12c or d)**.

23.16 Fit the shim into the top of the valve then install the follower

16 Check that the shim is correctly seated, then lubricate the follower with molybdenum disulphide oil and install it onto the valve, making sure it fits squarely in its bore **(see illustration)**. Repeat the process for any other valves until the clearances are correct, then install the camshafts (see Chapter 2).

17 Rotate the crankshaft several turns to seat the new shim(s) **(see illustration 23.7a)**, then check the clearances again.

18 Install all disturbed components in a reverse of the removal sequence, referring to the relevant Chapters. Install the timing inspection cap using a new sealing washer if required, and the crankshaft end cap using a new O-ring if required – smear the O-ring and the cap threads with grease **(see illustration)**. Tighten the caps to the torque settings specified at the beginning of the Chapter.

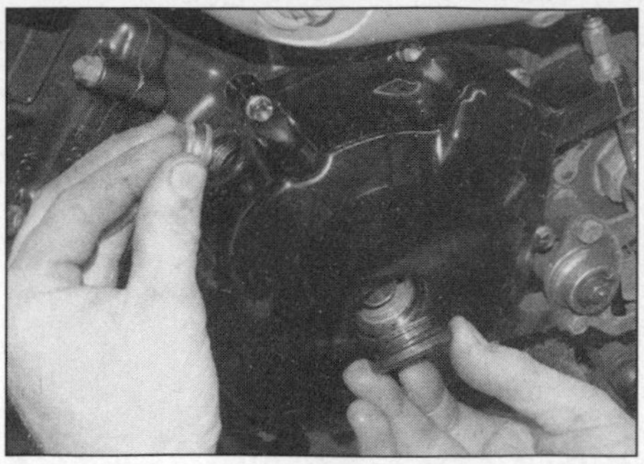

23.18 Fit the caps using a new washer and O-ring

19 Check and adjust the idle speed and carburettor/throttle body balance (synchronisation) (see Sections 6 and 17/18).

Every two years

24 Brake fluid – change

1 The brake fluid should be changed at the prescribed interval or whenever a master cylinder or caliper overhaul is carried out. Refer to the brake bleeding section in Chap-ter 7, noting that all old fluid must be pumped from the fluid reservoir and hydraulic hoses before filling with new fluid.

HAYNES HiNT ***Old brake fluid is invariably much darker in colour than new fluid, making it easy to see when all old fluid has been expelled from the system.***

25 Cooling system – draining, flushing and refilling

Warning: Allow the engine to cool completely before performing this maintenance operation. Also, don't allow antifreeze to come into contact with your skin or the painted surfaces of the motorcycle. Rinse off spills immediately with plenty of water. Antifreeze is highly toxic if ingested. Never leave antifreeze lying around in an open container or in puddles on the floor; children and pets are attracted by its sweet smell and may drink it. Check with local authorities (councils) about disposing of antifreeze. Many communities have collection centres which will see that antifreeze is disposed of safely. Antifreeze is also combustible, so don't store it near open flames.

Warning: Do not remove the pressure cap when the engine is hot. It is good practice to cover the cap with a heavy cloth and turn the cap slowly anti-clockwise. If you hear a hissing sound (indicating that there is still pressure in the system), wait until it stops, then continue turning the cap until it can be removed.

Draining

1 On X, Y, K1 and K2 SV650S models, remove the right-hand fairing side panel (see Chapter 8). On all models raise the fuel tank (see Chapter 4A or 4B as applicable).

2 On SV650 models unscrew the radiator cap security screw. On all models remove the pressure cap from the top of the radiator by turning it anti-clockwise until it reaches a stop **(see illustration 9.8)**. If you hear a hissing sound (indicating there is still pressure in the system), wait until it stops. Now press down on the cap and continue turning the cap until it can be removed. Also remove the coolant reservoir cap.

3 Position a suitable container beneath the water pump on the right-hand side of the engine. Unscrew the drain plug and allow the coolant to completely drain from the system **(see illustrations)**. Retain the old sealing washer for use during flushing.

4 Remove the coolant reservoir cap **(see illustration)**. Disconnect the overflow hose from the radiator filler neck and draw it out of its guide. Drop the end of the hose lower than

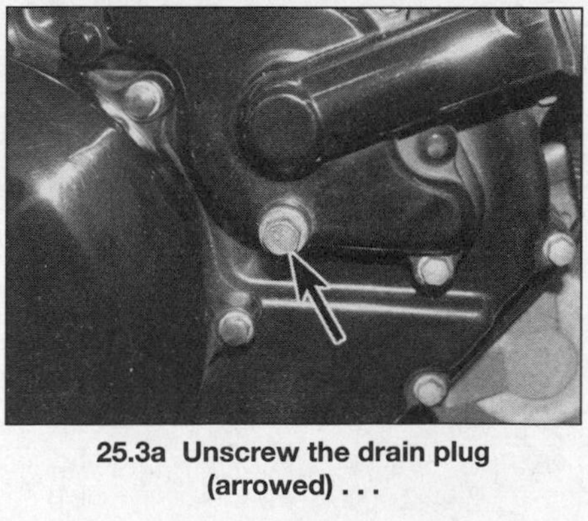

25.3a Unscrew the drain plug (arrowed) . . .

25.3b . . . and allow the coolant to drain

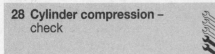

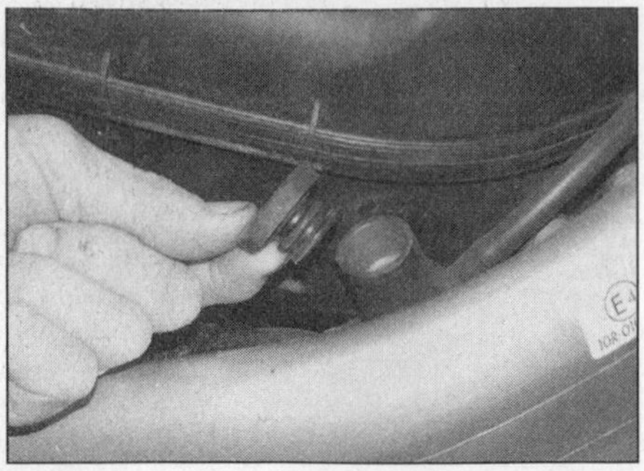

25.4 Remove the reservoir cap to create a vent

the level of the reservoir and allow the coolant to drain into the container. When the reservoir is empty, flush it out with clean water, then reconnect the hose.

Flushing

5 Flush the system with clean tap water by inserting a garden hose in the radiator filler neck. Allow the water to run through the system until it is clear and flows out cleanly. If the radiator is extremely corroded, remove it (see Chapter 3) and have it cleaned by a specialist.

6 Clean the drain hole in the water pump then install the drain plug using the old sealing washer.

7 Fill the cooling system with clean water mixed with a flushing compound. Make sure the flushing compound is compatible with aluminium components, and follow the manufacturer's instructions carefully. Fit the radiator pressure cap and the reservoir cap.

8 Start the engine and allow it to reach normal operating temperature. Let it run for about ten minutes.

9 Stop the engine. Let it cool for a while, then cover the pressure cap with a heavy rag and turn it anti-clockwise to the first stop, releasing any pressure that may be present in the system. Once the hissing stops, push down on the cap and remove it completely.

10 Drain the system once again.

11 Fill the system with clean water and repeat the procedure in Steps 5 to 10.

Refilling

12 Fit a new sealing washer onto the drain plug and tighten it to the torque setting specified at the beginning of the Chapter **(see illustration 25.3a)**.

13 Fill the system with the proper coolant mixture (see this Chapter's Specifications). **Note:** *Pour the coolant in slowly to minimise the amount of air entering the system.*

14 When the system is full (all the way up to the base of the radiator filler neck), start the engine and allow it to idle for 2 to 3 minutes. Flick the throttle twistgrip part open 3 or 4 times, so that the engine speed rises to approximately 4000 – 5000 rpm, then stop the engine. This process will bleed any trapped air bubbles from the system. Lift the bike off its stand and wiggle it about to free any trapped bubbles.

15 If necessary, top up the coolant level to the base of the upper radiator filler neck and install the pressure cap. Also top up the coolant reservoir to the FULL level mark (see *Daily (pre-ride) checks)*.

16 Start the engine and allow it to reach normal operating temperature, then shut it off. Let the engine cool then remove the pressure cap as described in Step 2. Check that the coolant level is still up to the base of the upper radiator filler neck. If it's low, add the specified mixture until it reaches the base of the filler neck. Refit the cap. On SV650 models tighten the radiator cap security screw.

17 Check the coolant level in the reservoir and top up if necessary.

18 Check that there are no leaks from the cooling system. Lower the fuel tank (see Chapter 4A or 4B) and on SV650S models install the fairing side panel (see Chapter 8).

19 Do not dispose of the old coolant by pouring it down the drain. Instead pour it into a heavy plastic container, cap it tightly and take it into an authorised disposal site or service station – see ***Warning*** at the beginning of this Section.

Every four years

26 Brake hoses – renewal

1 The hoses deteriorate with age and should be renewed regardless of their apparent condition. Refer to Chapter 7 and disconnect the brake hoses from the master cylinders and calipers. Always renew the banjo union sealing washers.

27 Fuel hoses – renewal

Warning: Petrol (gasoline) is extremely flammable, so take extra precautions when you work on any part of the fuel system. Don't smoke or allow open flames or bare light bulbs near the work area, and don't work in a garage where a natural gas-type appliance is present. If you spill any fuel on your skin, rinse it off immediately with soap and water. When you perform any kind of work on the fuel system, wear safety glasses and have a fire extinguisher suitable for a Class B type fire (flammable liquids) on hand.

1 The fuel system hoses should be renewed at the first signs of cracking or hardening, or at the specified interval regardless of their apparent condition. This includes all the vent and drain hoses, and the vacuum and PAIR system hoses. On California models you should also renew the EVAP emission control systems hoses.

2 Remove the fuel tank and the air filter housing (see Chapter 4A or 4B as applicable). Disconnect the hoses between the fuel system components and engine unit, noting the routing of each hose and where it connects (see Chapter 4A or 4B as required). It is advisable to make a sketch of the various hoses before removing them to ensure they are correctly installed.

3 Secure each new hose to its unions using new clamps where fitted. Run the engine and check that there are no leaks before taking the machine out on the road.

Non-scheduled maintenance

28 Cylinder compression – check

1 Poor engine performance can be caused by many things, including leaking valves, incorrect valve clearances, a leaking head gasket, loose cylinder head bolts or worn pistons, rings and/or cylinder walls. A cylinder compression check will help pinpoint these conditions and can also indicate the presence of excessive carbon deposits in the cylinder heads.

2 The only tools required are a compression gauge and a spark plug wrench. A compression gauge with a threaded end for the spark plug hole is required. Depending on the outcome of the initial test, a squirt-type oil can may also be needed.

3 Make sure the valve clearances are correctly set (see Section 23).

4 Refer to *Fault Finding Equipment* in the Reference section for details of the compression test. Refer to the specifications at the beginning of the Chapter for compression figures.

29 Engine oil pressure – check

1 The oil pressure warning light should come on when the ignition (main) switch is turned ON and extinguish a few seconds after the engine is started – this serves as a check that the warning light circuit is sound. If the oil pressure light comes on whilst the engine is running, low oil pressure is indicated – stop the engine immediately and check the oil level (see *Daily (pre-ride) checks*).

2 An oil pressure check must be carried out if the warning light comes on when the engine is running yet the oil level is good (Step 1). It can also provide useful information about the condition of the engine's lubrication system.

3 To check the oil pressure, a suitable gauge and adapter (which screws into the crankcase) will be needed. Suzuki provide the components for this purpose – X, Y, K1 and K2 models Pt. Nos. 09915-74520 (hose), 09915-74532 (adapter) and 09915-77330 (gauge); K3-on models Pt. Nos. 09915-74521 (hose), 09915-74532 (adapter) and 09915-77331 (gauge). Alternatively, suitable equipment can be obtained commercially. You will also need a container and some rags to catch and mop up any residual oil that gets lost in between removing the main oil gallery plug and installing the gauge. Check the engine oil level after installing the gauge and replenish if necessary (see *Daily (pre-ride) checks*).

4 Unscrew the main oil gallery plug, located on the left-hand side of the engine just behind the oil filter, and swiftly screw the gauge assembly in its place **(see illustrations)**.

5 Warm the engine up to normal operating temperature – Suzuki specify 10 mins at 2000 rpm in the summer, and 20 mins at 2000 rpm in the winter.

6 Increase the engine speed to 3000 rpm whilst watching the gauge reading. The oil pressure should be similar to that given in the Specifications at the start of this Chapter. Stop the engine.

7 If the pressure is significantly lower than the standard, either the pressure relief valve is stuck open, the oil pump or its drive mechanism is faulty, the oil strainer or filter is blocked, or there is other engine damage. Also make sure the correct grade oil is being used. Begin diagnosis by checking the oil filter, strainer and relief valve, then the oil pump (see Chapter 2). If those items check out okay, chances are the bearing oil clearances are excessive and the engine needs to be overhauled.

8 If the pressure is too high, either an oil passage is clogged, the relief valve is stuck closed or the wrong grade of oil is being used.

9 Unscrew the gauge assembly and immediately install the oil gallery plug, tightening it to the torque setting specified at the beginning of the Chapter.

10 Check the oil level (see *Daily (pre-ride) checks*).

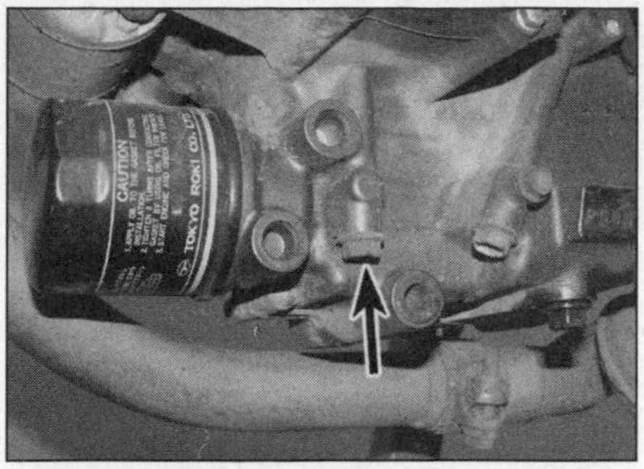

29.4a Main oil gallery plug (arrowed)) – X, Y, K1 and K2 models

29.4b Main oil gallery plug (arrowed)) – K3-on models

30 Wheel bearings – check

1 Wheel bearings will wear over a period of time and result in handling problems.

2 Support the motorcycle upright using an auxiliary stand, and support it so that the wheel being checked is off the ground. Check for any play in the bearings by pushing and pulling the wheel against the axle – turn the steering to full lock to keep it steady when checking the front wheel **(see illustration)**. Also spin the wheel and check that it rotates smoothly.

3 If any play is detected in the hub, or if the wheel does not rotate smoothly (and this is not due to brake or transmission drag), remove the wheel and check the bearings for wear or damage (see Chapter 7). If in doubt renew the bearings.

31 Steering head bearings – re-greasing

1 Over a period of time the grease will harden or may be washed out of the bearings by incorrect use of jet washes.

2 Disassemble the steering head for re-greasing of the bearings. Refer to Chapter 6 for details.

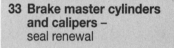

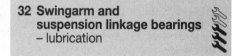

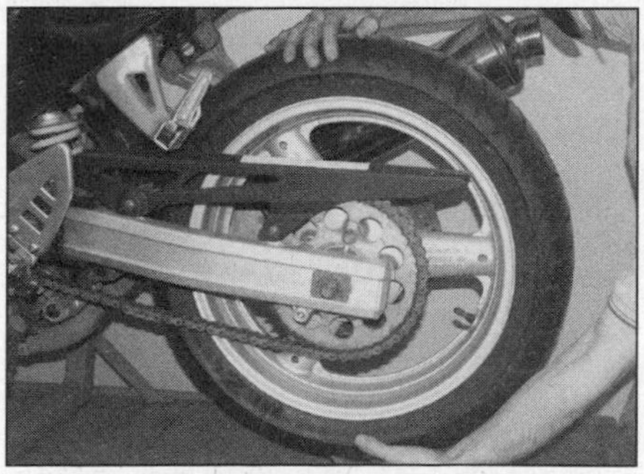

30.2 Checking for play in the wheel bearings

32 Swingarm and suspension linkage bearings – lubrication

1 Over a period of time the grease will harden or dirt will penetrate the bearings due to failed seals.

2 The suspension is not equipped with grease nipples. Remove the swingarm and suspension linkage as described in Chapter 6 for greasing of the bearings.

33 Brake master cylinders and calipers – seal renewal

1 Brake seals will deteriorate over a period of time and lose their effectiveness, leading to sticking operation or fluid loss, or allowing the ingress of air and dirt. Refer to Chapter 7 and dismantle the components for seal renewal.

34 Front forks – oil change

1 Fork oil degrades over a period of time and loses its damping qualities. Refer to the fork oil change procedure in Chapter 6. The forks do not need to be completely disassembled.

35 Battery – check

1 All models are fitted with a sealed MF (maintenance free) battery. **Note:** *Do not attempt to remove the battery caps to check the electrolyte level or battery specific gravity. Removal will damage the caps, resulting in electrolyte leakage and battery damage.* All that should be done is to check that the terminals are clean and tight and that the casing is not damaged or leaking. See Chapter 9 for further details.

2 If the machine is not in regular use, remove the battery and give it a refresher charge every month to six weeks (see Chapter 9).

37.2a Headlight vertical adjustment screw (arrowed) – SV650

37.2b Headlight horizontal adjustment screw (arrowed) – SV650

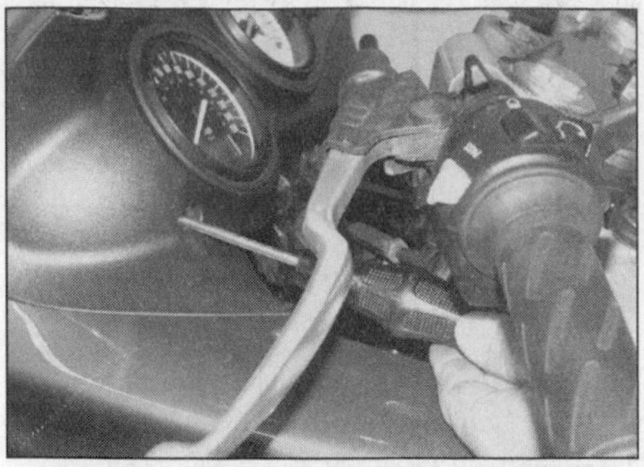

37.3a Access the headlight vertical adjustment screw via the hole in the trim panel – X, Y, K1 and K2 SV650S

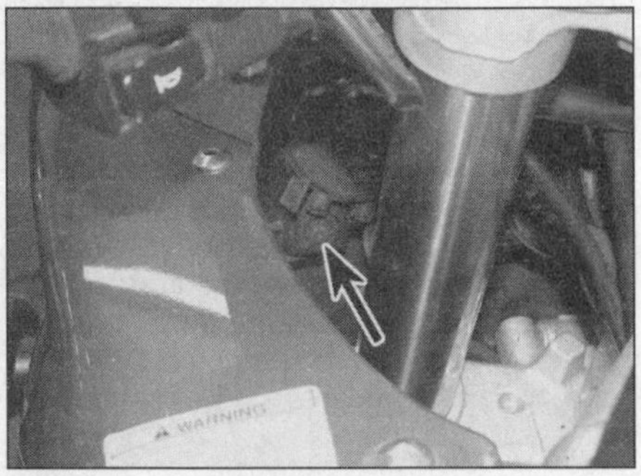

37.3b Headlight horizontal adjustment screw (arrowed) – X, Y, K1 and K2 SV650S

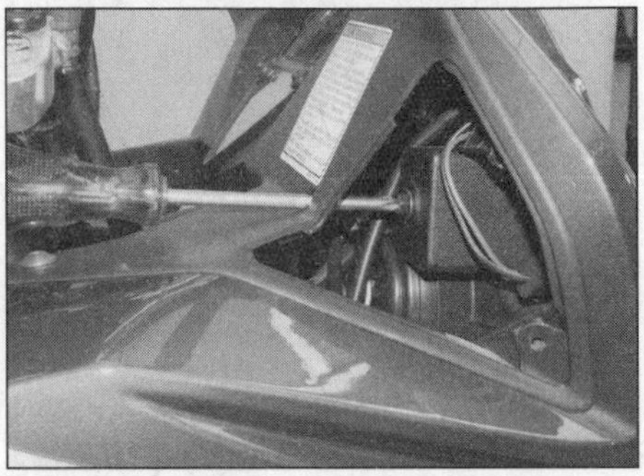

37.3c Headlight vertical adjustment – K3-on SV650S

37.3d Headlight horizontal adjustment (arrowed) – K3-on SV650S

36 Sidestand and sidestand switch – check

1 Check the stand springs for damage and distortion. The springs must be capable of retracting the stand fully and holding it retracted when the motorcycle is in use. If a spring is sagged or broken it must be renewed.

2 Lubricate the stand pivots regularly (see Section 15).

3 Check the stand and its mounting bracket for bends and cracks, and that the bolts and nut are tightened securely.

4 Check the operation of the sidestand switch by shifting the transmission into neutral, retracting the stand, pulling in the clutch lever and starting the engine. With the clutch lever still held in, select a gear. Extend the sidestand. The engine should stop as the sidestand is extended. If the sidestand switch does not operate as described, check its circuit (see Chapter 9).

37 Headlight aim – check and adjustment

Note: *An improperly adjusted headlight may cause problems for oncoming traffic or provide poor, unsafe illumination of the road ahead. Before adjusting the headlight aim, be sure to consult with local traffic laws and regulations – for UK models refer to MOT Test Checks in the Reference section.*

1 The headlight beam(s) can adjusted both horizontally and vertically. Before making any adjustment, check that the tyre pressures are correct and the suspension is adjusted as required. Make any adjustments to the headlight aim with the machine on level ground, with the fuel tank half full and with an assistant sitting on the normal solo riding position. If the bike is usually ridden with a passenger on the back, have a second assistant to do this.

2 On SV650 models, vertical adjustment is made by turning the adjuster screw below the headlight unit using a screwdriver **(see illustration)**. Horizontal adjustment is made by turning the adjuster screw on the left-hand side of the headlight **(see illustration)**.

3 On SV650S models, each headlight can be adjusted individually. On X, Y, K1 and K2 models, vertical adjustment is made by turning the upper adjuster screw using a screwdriver inserted through the access hole in the cockpit trim panel **(see illustration)**. Horizontal adjustment is made by turning the lower adjuster screw **(see illustration)**. On K3-on models, to adjust the headlights vertically, first remove the left or right-hand inspection panel in the cockpit trim panel (see Chapter 8), then turn the adjuster as required **(see illustration)**. To adjust the headlights horizontally, first remove the lower fairing trim panel (see Chapter 8), then turn the adjuster as required using a large cross-head screwdriver **(see illustration)**. Follow the procedure in Chapter 8 to ensure the panels are installed securely.

Chapter 2
Engine, clutch and transmission

Contents

Degrees of difficulty

Easy, suitable for novice with little experience	**Fairly easy,** suitable for beginner with some experience	**Fairly difficult,** suitable for competent DIY mechanic	**Difficult,** suitable for experienced DIY mechanic	**Very difficult,** suitable for expert DIY or professional

Specifications

General

Capacity	645 cc
Bore	81.0 mm
Stroke	62.6 mm
Compression ratio	11.5 to 1
Cylinder identification	Front cyl no. 1, rear cyl no. 2
Cooling system	Liquid cooled
Clutch	Wet multi-plate
Transmission	Six-speed constant mesh
Final drive	Chain and sprockets

Camshafts

	Standard	Service limit
Intake camshaft lobe height		
X, Y, K1 and K2 models	35.480 to 35.530 mm	35.18 mm
K3-on models	36.060 to 36.105 mm	35.76 mm
Exhaust camshaft lobe height		
X, Y, K1 and K2 models	33.480 to 33.530 mm	33.18 mm
K3-on models	34.680 to 34.725 mm	34.38 mm
Camshaft bearing oil clearance	0.032 to 0.066 mm	0.150 mm
Camshaft runout (max)	0.10 mm	
Journal diameter	21.959 to 21.980 mm	
Journal holder internal diameter	22.012 to 22.025 mm	

Cylinder head

Warpage (max)	0.05 mm

Valves, guides and springs

Intake valve	
Stem diameter	4.465 to 4.480 mm
Guide bore diameter	4.500 to 4.512 mm
Stem-to-guide clearance	0.020 to 0.047 mm
Stem deflection (max – see text)	0.35 mm
Seat width	0.9 to 1.1 mm
Head thickness (min)	0.5 mm
Radial runout at head (max)	0.03 mm
Stem runout (max)	0.05 mm
Spring free lengths (min)	
Outer spring	39.8 mm
Inner spring	36.8 mm
Exhaust valve	
Stem diameter	4.455 to 4.470 mm
Guide bore diameter	4.500 to 4.512 mm
Stem-to-guide clearance	0.030 to 0.057 mm
Stem deflection (max – see text)	0.35 mm
Seat width	0.9 to 1.1 mm
Head thickness (min)	0.5 mm
Radial runout at head (max)	0.03 mm
Stem runout (max)	0.05 mm
Spring free lengths (min)	
Outer spring	39.8 mm
Inner spring	36.8 mm
Valve clearances	see Chapter 1

Cylinders

Bore diameter	
Standard	81.000 to 81.015 mm
Wear limit	81.075 mm
Taper (max)	0.05 mm
Ovality (max)	0.05 mm
Warpage (max)	0.05 mm
Cylinder compression	
Standard	213 psi (15.0 Bar)
Service limit	156 psi (11.0 Bar)
Max. difference between cylinders	28 psi (2.0 Bar)

Pistons

Piston diameter (measured 20 mm up from skirt, at 90° to piston pin axis)		
Standard	80.940 to 80.955 mm	
Service limit	80.88 mm	
1st oversize (all models)	+0.50 mm	
2nd oversize (X, Y, K1 and K2 models only)	+1.00 mm	
	Standard	**Service limit**
Piston-to-bore clearance	0.055 to 0.065 mm	0.120 mm
Piston pin diameter	19.992 to 20.000 mm	19.980 mm
Piston pin bore diameter	20.002 to 20.008 mm	20.030 mm
Piston pin-to-bore clearance	0.002 to 0.016 mm	0.05 mm
Connecting rod small-end internal diameter	20.010 to 20.018 mm	20.040 mm
Piston pin-to-connecting rod small-end clearance	0.010 to 0.026 mm	0.06 mm

Piston rings

Ring thickness	
Top ring – K1 to K6 models	1.17 to 1.19 mm
Top ring – K7-on models	0.76 to 0.81 mm and 1.08 to 1.10 mm
2nd ring	0.97 to 0.99 mm
Groove thickness	
Top ring – K1 to K6 models	1.21 to 1.23 mm
Top ring – K7-on models	0.83 to 0.85 mm and 1.30 to 1.32 mm
2nd ring	1.01 to 1.03 mm
Oil ring	2.01 to 2.03 mm

Piston rings (continued)

Ring-to-groove clearance (max)	
Top ring	0.180 mm
2nd ring	0.150 mm
End gap (free)	
X, Y, K1 and K2 models	
Top ring	
Standard	9.9 mm (approx)
Service limit	7.9 mm
2nd ring	
Standard	10.5 mm (approx)
Service limit	8.4 mm
K3-on models	
Top ring – K3 to K6 models	
Standard	9.5 mm (approx)
Service limit	7.6 mm
Top ring – K7-on models	
Standard	7.0 mm
Service limit	5.6 mm
2nd ring	
Standard	11.0 mm (approx)
Service limit	8.8 mm
End gap (installed) – top and second rings	
X to K6 models	
Standard	0.20 to 0.35 mm
Service limit	0.70 mm
K7-on model	
Standard – top ring	0.20 to 0.30 mm
Standard – second ring	0.30 to 0.45 mm
Service limit (both rings)	0.70 mm

Clutch

Friction plate (X, Y, K1 and K2 models)	
Type A (see Section 18 for identification)	
Quantity	6
Thickness	
Standard	2.92 to 3.08 mm
Service limit	2.62 mm
Tab width	
Standard	15.9 to 16.0 mm
Service limit	15.1 mm
Type B (see Section 18 for identification)	
Quantity	1
Thickness	
Standard	3.42 to 3.58 mm
Service limit	3.12 mm
Tab width	
Standard	15.9 to 16.0 mm
Service limit	15.1 mm
Friction plate (K3-on models)	
Quantity	7
Thickness	
Standard	2.92 to 3.08 mm
Service limit	2.62 mm
Tab width	
Standard	13.7 to 13.8 mm
Service limit	12.9 mm
Plain plate (all models)	
Quantity	6
Warpage (max)	0.10 mm
Springs (X, Y, K1 and K2 models)	
Free length	58.9 mm
Service limit	56.0 mm
Springs (K3-on models)	
Free length	53.1 mm
Service limit	50.5 mm

Crankshaft and main bearings

Main bearing oil clearance	
X, Y, K1 and K2 models	
Standard	0.008 to 0.035 mm
Service limit	0.08 mm
K3 models	
Standard	0.005 to 0.015 mm
Service limit	0.08 mm
K4-on models	
Standard	0.002 to 0.029 mm
Service limit	0.08 mm
Main journal diameter	41.985 to 42.000 mm
End-float	0.050 to 0.110 mm
Replacement thrust bearing thickness range	1.925 to 2.175 mm
Runout (max)	0.05 mm

Connecting rods and big-end bearings

Big-end side clearance	
Standard	0.170 to 0.320 mm
Service limit	0.50 mm
Big-end width	20.95 to 21.00 mm
Crankpin width	42.17 to 42.22 mm
Big-end bearing oil clearance	
Standard	0.032 to 0.056 mm
Service limit	0.08 mm
Crankpin diameter	37.976 to 38.000 mm

For connecting rod small-end specifications see under 'Pistons'.

Lubrication system

Oil type, viscosity and capacity	see Chapter 1
Oil pressure (at main oil gallery plug, with engine warm)	see Chapter 1

Selector drum and forks

Selector fork end thickness	5.3 to 5.4 mm
Selector drum groove width	5.5 to 5.6 mm
Fork-to-groove clearance	0.1 to 0.3 mm

Transmission

Primary reduction	2.088 to 1 (71/34T)
Final reduction	
SV650	3.000 to 1 (45/15T)
SV650SX to SK6 models	2.933 to 1 (44/15T)
SV650SK7-on models	3.000 to 1 (45/15T)
1st gear	2.461 to 1 (32/13T)
2nd gear	1.777 to 1 (32/18T)
3rd gear	1.380 to 1 (29/21T)
4th gear	1.125 to 1 (27/24T)
5th gear	0.961 to 1 (25/26T)
6th gear	0.851 to 1 (23/27T)

Torque settings

Cam chain stopper bolt	14 Nm
Cam chain tensioner blade pivot bolt	10 Nm
Cam chain tensioner cap bolt	8 Nm
Cam chain tensioner mounting bolts	10 Nm
Camshaft holder bolts	10 Nm
Clutch cover bolts	10 Nm
Clutch nut	50 Nm
Clutch pressure plate bolts	5.5 Nm
Connecting rod bolts	
Initial setting	35 Nm
Final setting	67 Nm
Crankcase bolts	
8 mm bolts	26 Nm
6 mm bolts	11 Nm
Crankshaft end cap	11 Nm
Cylinder block nuts	10 Nm

Torque settings (continued)

Cylinder head bolts	
10 mm bolts	
Initial setting	25 Nm
Final setting	42 Nm
6 mm bolts	10 Nm
Engine mounting bolts	
Adjuster bolts	10 Nm
Adjuster bolt locknuts	45 Nm
Lower middle mounting bolt nut	93 Nm
Lower rear mounting bolt nut	55 Nm
Front mounting bolts	55 Nm
Upper middle mounting bolts	55 Nm
Upper rear mounting bolt	55 Nm
Spacer pinch bolts	23 Nm
Gearchange mechanism centralising spring locating pin	23 Nm
Gearchange selector drum cam plate bolt	10 Nm
Gearchange stopper arm bolt	10 Nm
Inner crankcase cover bolts	10 Nm
Main bearing retainer plate screws	8 Nm
Oil cooler hose banjo union bolts	23 Nm
Oil cooler mounting bolts	10 Nm
Oil gallery jet bolt	18 Nm
Oil pressure relief valve	27 Nm
Oil pump screws	8 Nm
Oil spray pipe screw	8 Nm
Oil strainer plate bolts	10 Nm
Piston oil jet retainer bolts	10 Nm
Primary drive gear bolt	70 Nm
Timing mark inspection cap	23 Nm
Top cam chain guide bolts	10 Nm
Selector drum bearing retainer screws	8 Nm
Starter clutch bolts	25 Nm
Valve cover bolts	14 Nm

1 General information

The engine/transmission unit is a liquid-cooled 90° V-twin, fitted parallel with the frame. The engine has four valves per cylinder, operated by double overhead camshafts. The camshafts are chain driven off the crankshaft.

The engine/transmission unit is constructed in aluminium alloy and the crankcase is divided vertically. The crankcase incorporates a wet sump, pressure fed lubrication system, and houses an oil pump gear driven off the clutch housing. The water pump is gear driven off the crankshaft. The one-piece forged crankshaft runs in two main bearings. The left-hand end of the crankshaft carries the alternator rotor. The ignition timing triggers are incorporated in the alternator rotor.

The clutch is of the wet multi-plate type and is gear driven off the crankshaft. The transmission is of the six-speed constant mesh type. Final drive to the rear wheel is via a chain and sprockets.

2 Operations possible with the engine in the frame

The components and assemblies listed below can be removed without having to remove the engine/transmission assembly from the frame. If however, a number of areas require attention at the same time, removal of the engine is recommended.

Valve covers
Cam chain tensioners
Camshafts
Cam chains
Cylinder heads
Cylinders
Pistons
Water pump
Pulse generator coil
Clutch
Primary drive gear
Gearchange mechanism
Oil pump
Water pump
Starter motor
Alternator
Starter clutch and idle gear
Oil pressure switch
Neutral switch

3 Operations requiring engine removal

It is necessary to remove the engine/transmission assembly from the frame and separate the crankcase halves to gain access to the following components:

Connecting rod big-ends and bearings
Crankshaft and bearings
Transmission shafts
Selector drum and forks

4 Major engine repair – general note

1 It is not always easy to determine when or if an engine should be completely overhauled, as a number of factors must be considered.

2 High mileage is not necessarily an indication that an overhaul is needed, while low mileage, on the other hand, does not preclude the need for an overhaul. Frequency of servicing is probably the single most important consideration. An engine that has regular and frequent oil and filter changes, as well as other required maintenance, will most likely give many miles of reliable service. Conversely, a neglected engine, or one which has not been run in properly, may require an overhaul very early in its life.

3 Exhaust smoke and excessive oil consumption are both indications that piston rings and/or valve guides are in need of attention, although make sure that the fault is not due to oil leakage.

5.3 Unscrew the bolt (arrowed) and detach the earth lead

5.11 Unscrew the bolt (arrowed) and slide the gearchange arm off the shaft, noting how the punch mark aligns with the slit in the clamp

4 If the engine is making obvious knocking or rumbling noises, the connecting rods and/or main bearings are probably at fault.

5 Loss of power, rough running, excessive valve train noise and high fuel consumption may also point to the need for an overhaul, especially if they are all present at the same time. If a complete tune-up does not remedy the situation, major mechanical work is the only solution.

6 An engine overhaul generally involves restoring the internal parts to the specifications of a new engine. The piston rings and main and connecting rod bearings are usually renewed and the cylinder walls honed or, if necessary, re-bored (oversize pistons are available), during a major overhaul. Generally the valve seats are re-ground, since they are usually in less than perfect condition at this point. The end result should be a like new engine that will give as many trouble-free miles as the original.

7 Before beginning the engine overhaul, read through the related procedures to familiarise yourself with the scope and requirements of the job. Overhauling an engine is not all that difficult, but it is time consuming. Plan on the motorcycle being tied up for a minimum of two weeks. Check on the availability of parts and make sure that any necessary special tools, equipment and supplies are obtained in advance.

8 Most work can be done with typical workshop hand tools, although a number of precision measuring tools are required for inspecting parts to determine if they must be renewed. Often a dealer will handle the inspection of parts and offer advice concerning reconditioning and renewal. As a general rule, time is the primary cost of an overhaul so it does not pay to install worn or substandard parts.

9 As a final note, to ensure maximum life and minimum trouble from a rebuilt engine, everything must be assembled with care in a spotlessly clean environment.

5 Engine – removal and installation

Caution: The engine is very heavy. Engine removal and installation should be carried out with the aid of at least one assistant; personal injury or damage could occur if the engine falls or is dropped. An hydraulic or mechanical floor jack should be used to support and lower or raise the engine if available.

TOOL TIP ***Peg spanners are required to slacken and tighten the adjuster bolts and their locknuts on two of the engine mounting bolts. If the Suzuki service tool (Pt. No. 09940-14990) is not available, suitable ones will have to be fabricated either from a piece of steel tubing, or better still by cutting old sockets. The advantage in using sockets is that a torque wrench can be applied when tightening, which in the case of the adjuster bolts is important. Note that as there are four different sizes required which means cutting up four different sockets (27 mm and 16 mm for the lower middle bolt and 22 mm and 14 mm for the lower rear bolt), and as the Suzuki tool combines all sizes in one tool, it probably worth buying it.***

Removal

1 Support the bike securely in an upright position using an auxiliary stand. Work can be made easier by raising the machine to a suitable working height on an hydraulic ramp or a suitable platform. Make sure the motorcycle is secure and will not topple over (also see *Tools and Workshop Tips* in the Reference section).

2 If the engine is dirty, particularly around its mountings, wash it thoroughly before starting any major dismantling work. This makes working on the engine much easier and rules out the possibility of caked on lumps of dirt falling into some vital component.

3 Remove the seats and the seat cowling (see Chapter 8). Disconnect the negative (-ve) lead from the battery (see Chapter 9). Also unscrew the crankcase bolt that secures the lead to the engine **(see illustration)**.

4 On SV650S models remove the fairing side panels (see Chapter 8).

5 Drain the engine oil and remove the oil filter (see Chapter 1). On K3-on models, remove the oil cooler (see Section 22).

6 Drain the coolant (see Chapter 1).

7 Remove the fuel tank and the air filter housing (see Chapter 4A or 4B). On K3-on models, disconnect the PAIR system hoses from the cylinder heads.

8 On X, Y, K1 and K2 models, remove the carburettors and detach the fuel pump vacuum hose either from the pump or from its union on the cylinder head intake duct (see Chapter 4A). On K3-on models, remove the throttle bodies (see Chapter 4B). Plug the engine intake manifolds with clean rag. On California X, Y, K1 and K2 models, remove the PAIR system control valve, detaching its hoses from the engine rather than the valve itself (see Chapter 4A).

9 Remove the horn (see Chapter 9).

10 Remove the radiator along with its hoses (i.e. detach the hoses from the reservoir, thermostat housing and water pump instead of from the radiator) (see Chapter 3).

11 Unscrew the gearchange linkage arm pinch bolt and slide the arm off the shaft, noting its alignment **(see illustration)**.

12 Remove the front sprocket (see Chapter 6). Tie the clutch release mechanism to the frame so that it is clear of the engine.

13 Remove the exhaust system (see Chapter 4A or 4B).

14 Pull back the rubber boot covering the oil pressure switch terminal, then undo the screw and detach the lead **(see illustration)**.

15 Pull back the rubber boot covering the starter motor terminal, then unscrew the nut and detach the lead **(see illustration)**. Secure the wiring clear of the engine so that it does not impede engine removal. Remove the starter motor now if required (see Chapter 9), or do so after the engine has been removed.

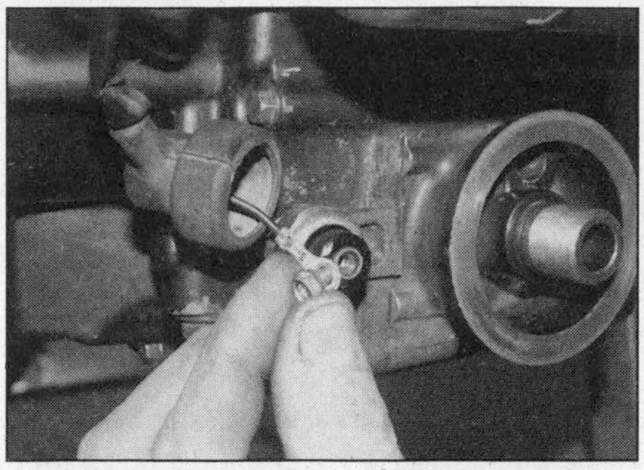

5.14 Detach the oil pressure switch lead . . .

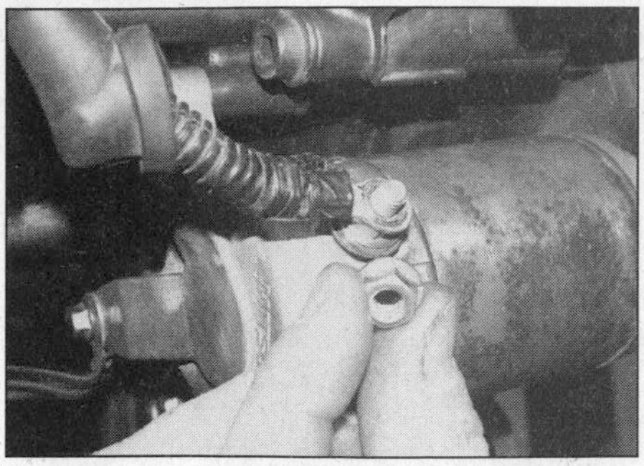

5.15 . . . and the starter motor lead

16 Pull the spark plug caps off the plugs and secure them clear of the engine.

17 Disconnect the coolant temperature sensor wiring connector from the sensor in the thermostat housing **(see illustration)**. Also disconnect the earth wire connector from the housing **(see illustration)**. Remove the housing along with its hoses if required (see Chapter 3), but it is easier after the engine has been removed.

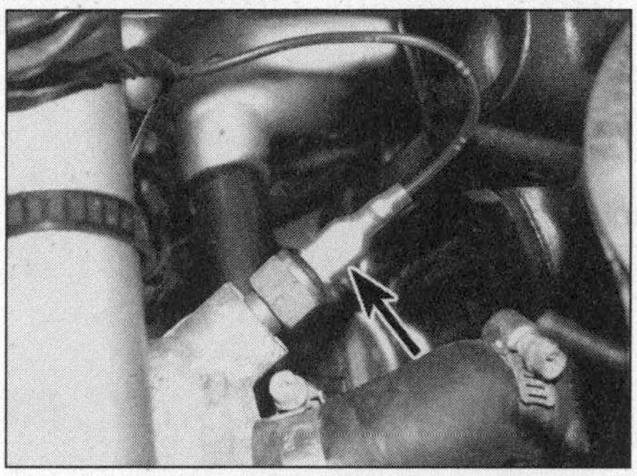

5.17a Detach the coolant temperature sensor wiring connector (arrowed) . . .

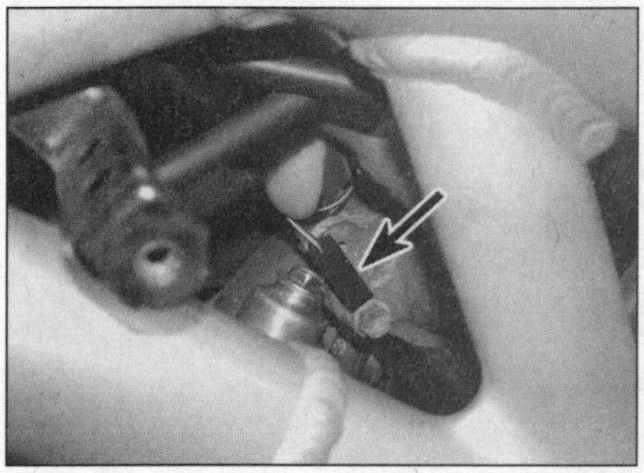

5.17b . . . and the earth wiring connector (arrowed)

18 Trace the alternator and ignition pulse generator/crankshaft position sensor wiring from the cover on the left-hand side of the engine and disconnect it at the connectors near the battery, then feed the wiring through to the engine, noting its routing and releasing it from any ties, and coil it in between the cylinders so that it does not impede engine removal **(see illustration)**.

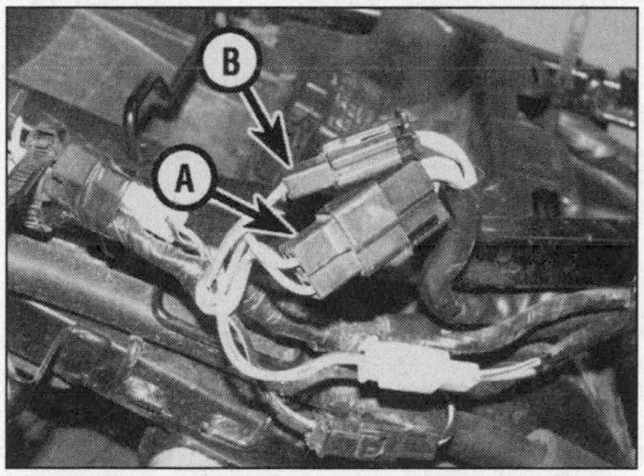

5.18 Disconnect the alternator wiring connector (A) and the pulse generator coil wiring connector (B)

19 Trace the wiring from the neutral switch, noting its routing, and disconnect it at the connector located inside the rubber boot on the left-hand frame tube. Free the wiring from any ties and either tape it to the engine or coil it between the cylinders so that it does not get in the way.

20 At this point, position an hydraulic or mechanical jack under the engine with a block of wood between the jack head and engine. Make sure the jack is centrally positioned so the engine will not topple in any direction when the last mounting bolt is removed. Raise the jack to take the weight of the engine, but make sure it is not lifting the bike and taking the weight of that as well. The idea is to support the engine so that there is no pressure on any of the mounting bolts once they have been slackened, so they can be easily withdrawn. Note that it may be necessary to adjust the jack as some of the bolts are removed to relieve the stress transferred to the other bolts.

> **HAYNES HiNT** ***After removing each engine mounting bolt, fit any adjuster, locknut, washer or spacer that goes with the bolt back onto it, in the correct order and way round, then thread the nut onto the end of the bolt – this ensures that everything can be reassembled with ease later on, and that no washers or spacers can be fitted in the wrong place or the wrong way round. In the case of through-bolts, also make a note of which side of the bike the bolt goes in from.***

X, Y, K1 and K2 models

21 Unscrew the nuts on the left-hand ends of the lower middle and lower rear mounting bolts, noting the washer fitted with the lower rear nut on Y, K1 and K2 models **(see illustrations)**.

22 Slacken the adjuster bolt locknuts on the lower middle and lower rear mounting bolts using a suitable peg spanner (see ***Tool Tip*** above) **(see illustrations)**. The locknuts can remain loose on the adjuster bolts, or they can be removed if required. Now unscrew the

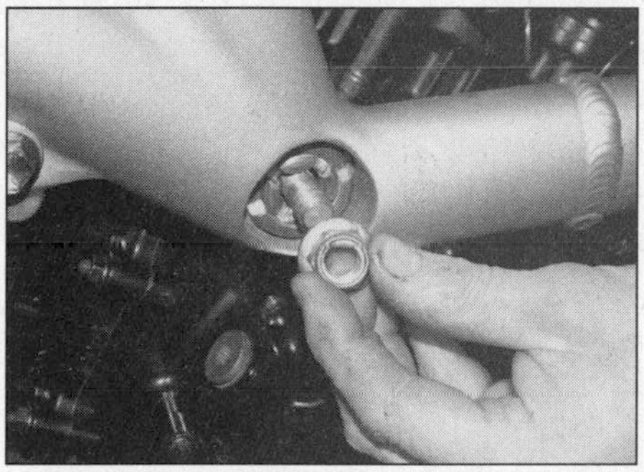

5.21a Unscrew the lower middle mounting bolt nut . . .

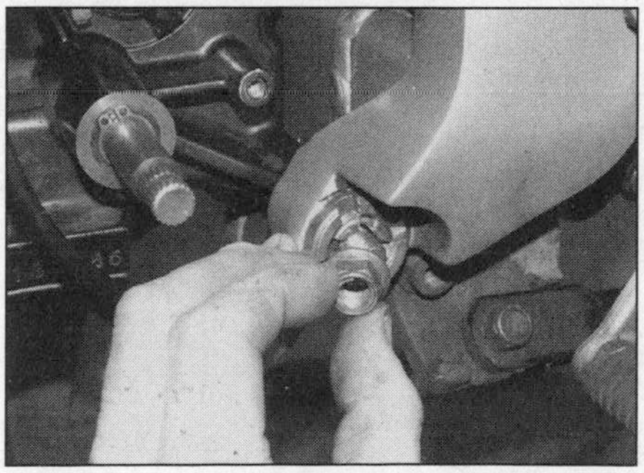

5.21b . . . and the lower rear mounting bolt nut

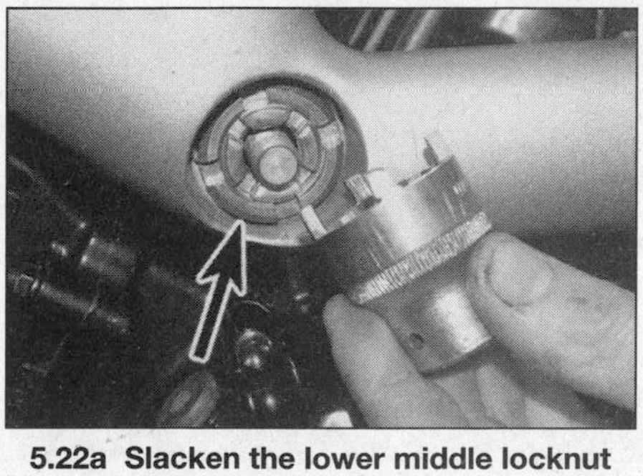

5.22a Slacken the lower middle locknut (arrowed) using a peg spanner or cut-up socket (as shown) . . .

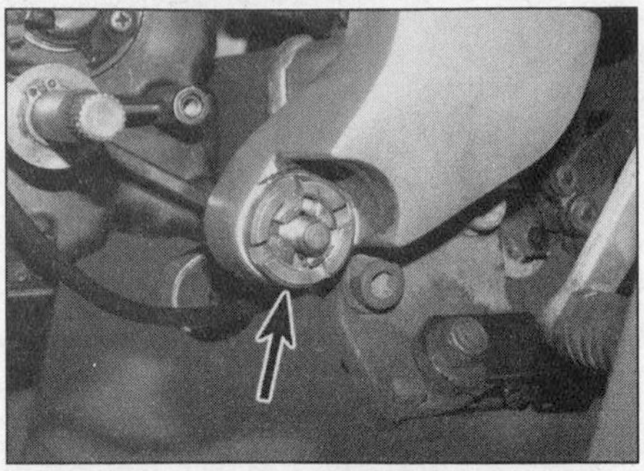

5.22b . . . then slacken the lower rear locknut (arrowed)

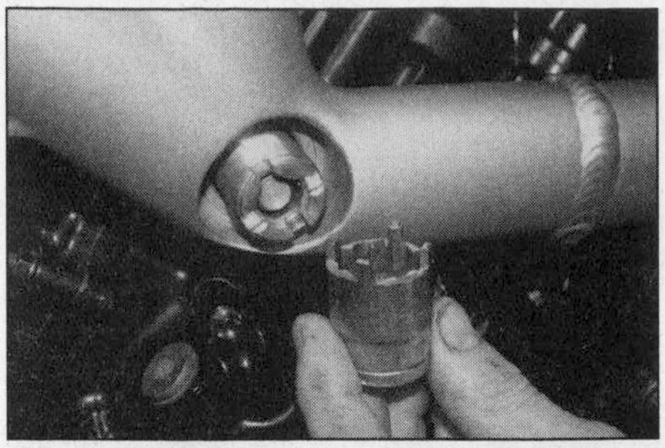

5.22c Unscrew the lower middle and lower rear adjuster bolts using the second peg spanner or cut-up socket

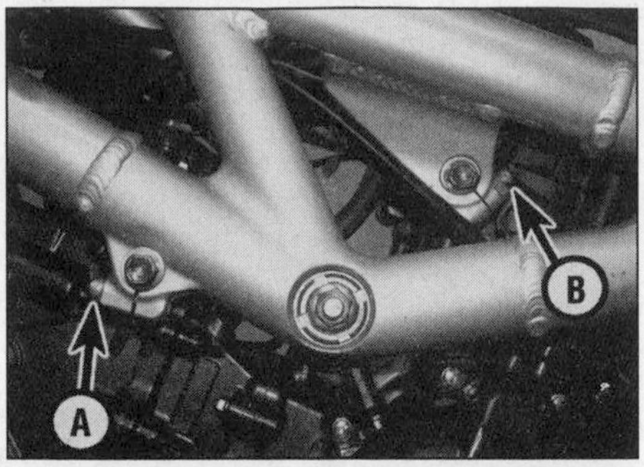

5.23a Slacken the front pinch bolt (A) and the upper middle pinch bolt (B) . . .

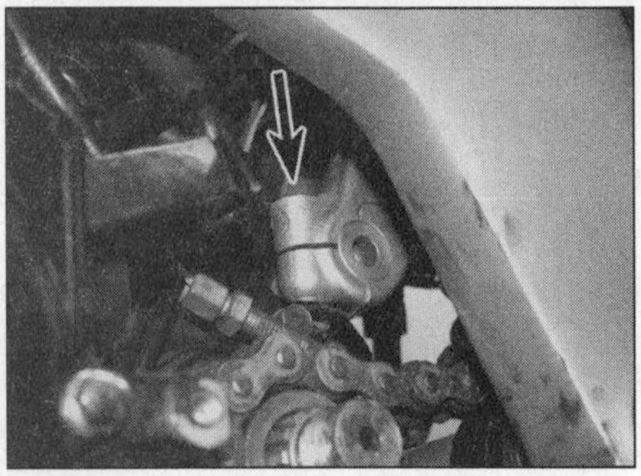

5.23b . . . and the upper rear pinch bolt (arrowed)

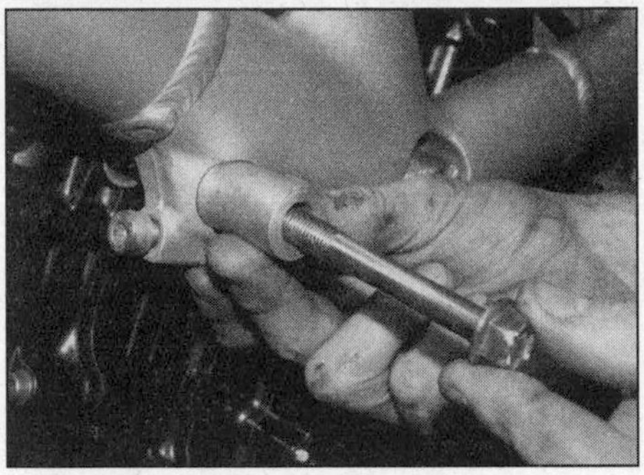

5.23c Unscrew the front left bolt and remove the spacer . . .

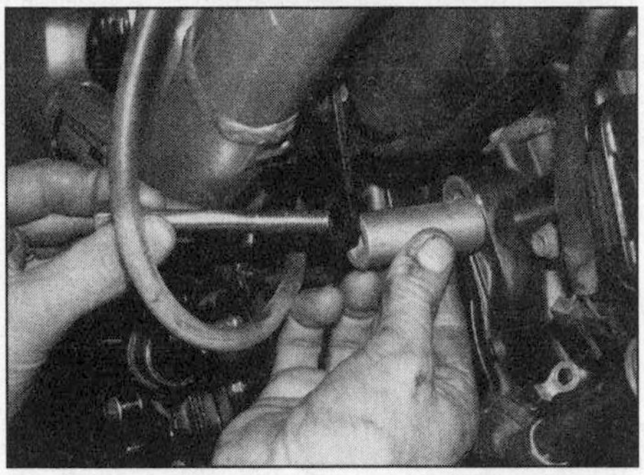

5.23d . . . then unscrew the front right bolt and remove the spacer

adjuster bolts so they are flush with the inside of the frame, but do not remove them **(see illustration)**.

23 Slacken the pinch bolts on the front, upper middle and upper rear mounting bolt spacers on the left-hand side of the frame **(see illustrations)**. Unscrew the front bolt on the left-hand side and remove the spacer **(see illustration)**. Now unscrew the front bolt on the right-hand side and remove the spacer **(see illustration)**.

24 Unscrew the upper middle bolt on the left-hand side and remove the spacer **(see illustration)**. Now unscrew the upper middle bolt on the right-hand side **(see illustration)**.

25 Check that the engine is properly supported by the jack. Unscrew and remove the upper rear mounting bolt on the right-hand side, then slide the spacer on the left-hand side away from the engine and into its lug, noting how it locates **(see illustrations)**. Withdraw the lower middle mounting bolt **(see illustration)**. Check that all wiring, cables and hoses are well clear, then carefully lower the jack allowing the engine to pivot down on the lower rear mounting bolt until the drive chain can be slipped off the end of the output shaft **(see illustration)**. Withdraw the lower rear mounting bolt, then lower the jack more, making sure the rear cylinder exhaust downpipe clears the frame, and that the engine clears all the mounting lugs **(see illustrations)**. Fully lower the jack, then lift the

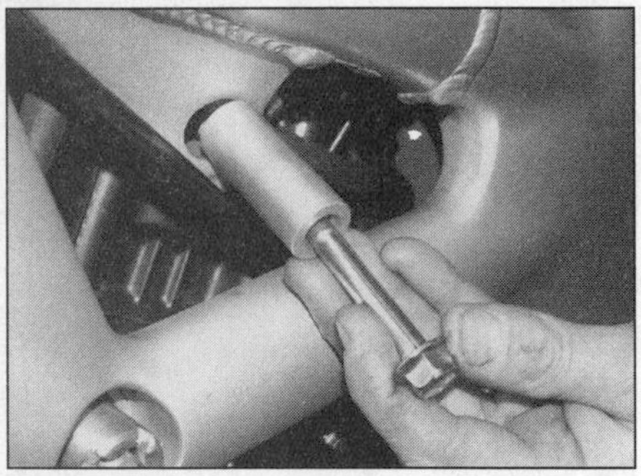

5.24a Unscrew the upper middle bolt on the left and remove the spacer . . .

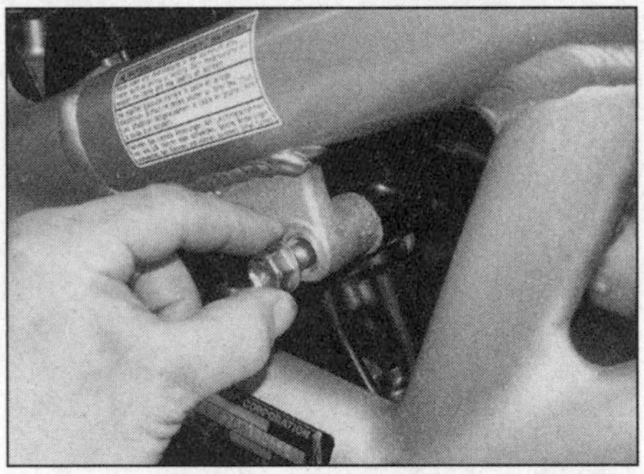

5.24b . . . then unscrew the upper middle bolt on the right

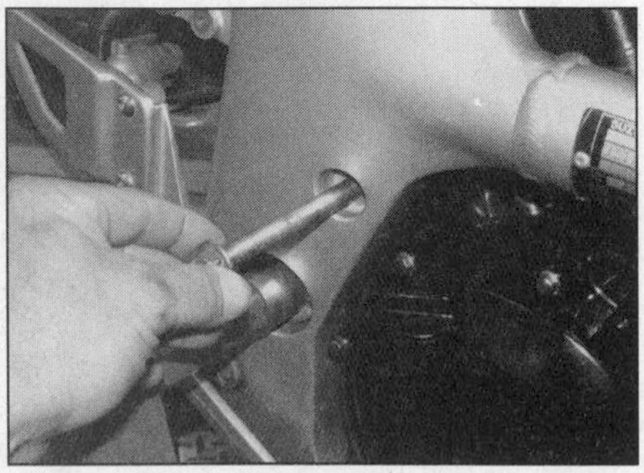

5.25a Unscrew the upper rear mounting bolt . . .

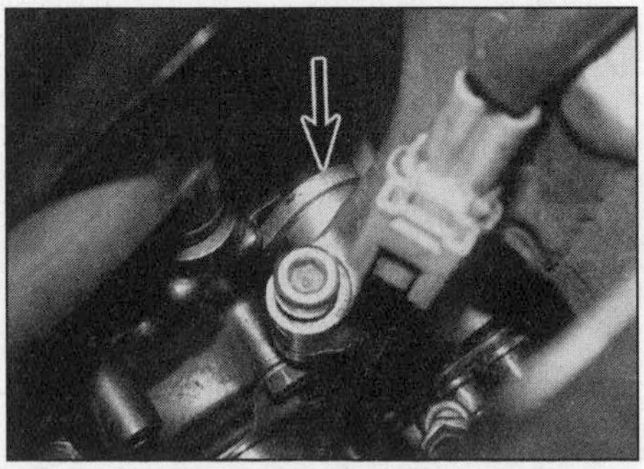

5.25b . . . then slide the spacer (arrowed) across, noting how it locates

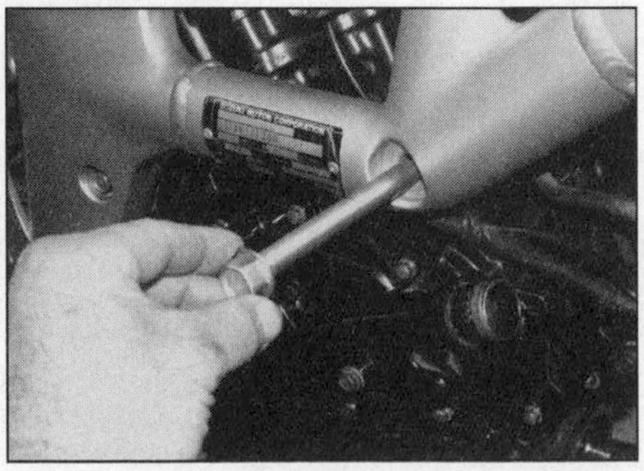

5.25c Withdraw the lower middle mounting bolt

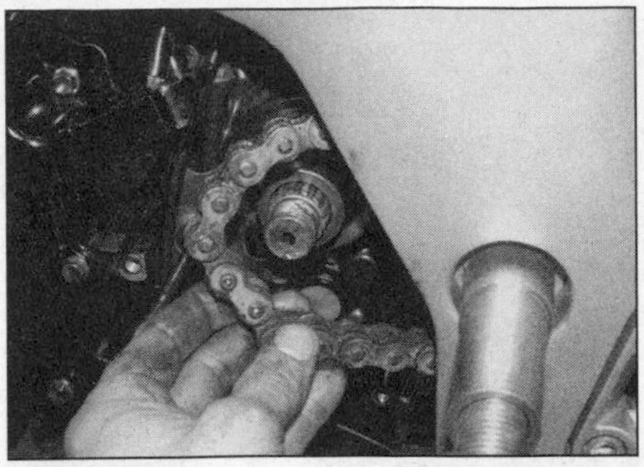

5.25d Draw the chain off the output shaft . . .

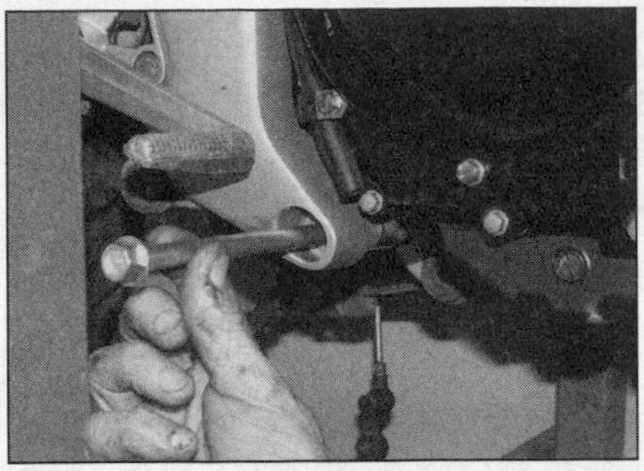

5.25e . . . then withdraw the lower rear mounting bolt . . .

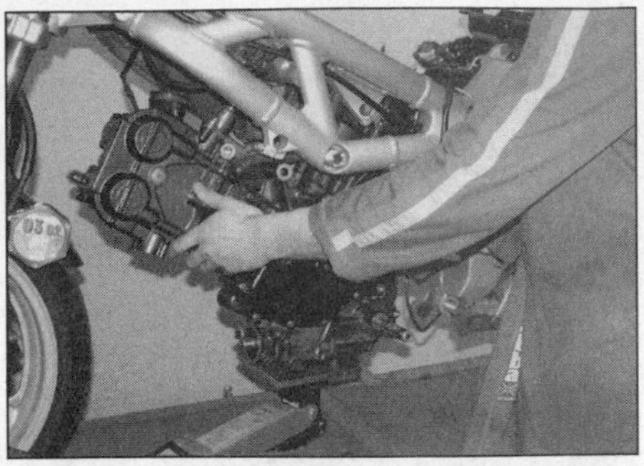

5.25f . . . and manoeuvre the engine out of the frame

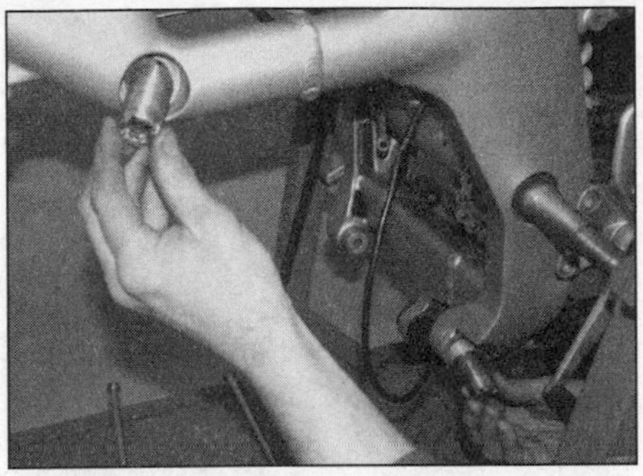

5.25g Remove the two adjuster bolts if required

5.26a Counterhold the lower middle . . .

5.26b . . . and lower rear mounting bolts . . .

engine, remove the jack, and manoeuvre the engine out of the frame. Remove the spacer from the upper rear mounting lug on the left-hand side, noting how it fits. If required, remove the adjuster bolts from the frame **(see illustration)**.

K3-on models

26 Counterhold the lower middle and lower rear mounting bolts, then unscrew the nuts on the right-hand ends of the bolts **(see illustrations)**.

27 Unscrew and remove the left-hand upper middle bolt **(see illustration)**.

28 Slacken the locknuts on the left-hand upper middle and lower middle adjuster bolts using a suitable peg spanner (see ***Tool Tip*** above) **(see illustrations)**. Slacken the locknut on the lower rear and adjuster bolt **(see illustration)**. The locknuts can remain loose on the adjuster bolts, or they can be removed if required. Now unscrew the adjuster bolts so they are flush with the inside of the frame, but do not remove them.

29 Slacken the pinch bolts on the front and upper rear mounting bolt spacers on the left-hand side of the frame **(see illustrations)**. Unscrew the front bolt on the left-hand side and remove the spacer. Now unscrew the front bolt on the right-hand side and remove the spacer **(see illustration)**.

30 Unscrew and remove the right-hand upper middle bolt **(see illustration)**.

31 Check that the engine is properly

5.26c . . . and unscrew the nuts

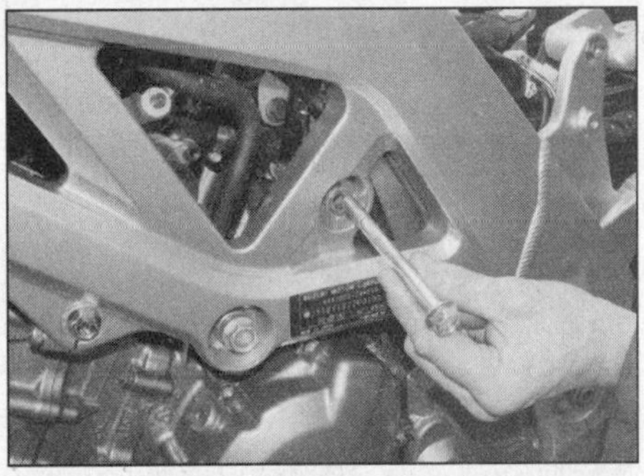

5.27 Unscrew the upper middle bolt on the left

5.28a Slacken the locknuts on the left-hand upper middle (A) and lower middle (B) adjuster bolts . . .

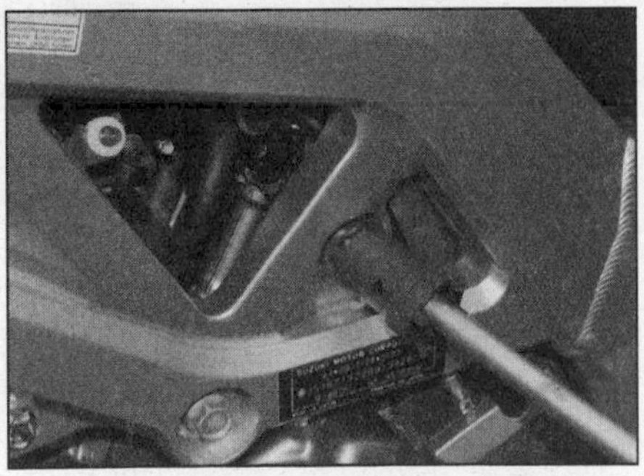

5.28b . . . using a peg spanner as described

5.28c Slacken the locknut on the lower rear adjuster bolt

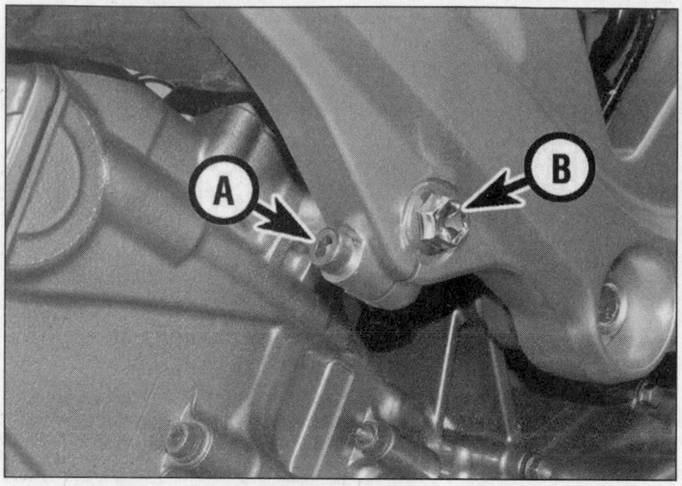

5.29a Pinch bolt (A) and front mounting bolt (B) on the left

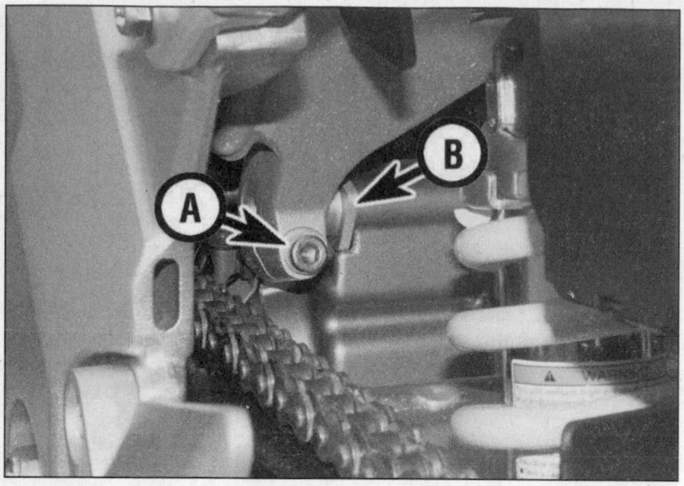

5.29b Upper rear pinch bolt (A); note the location of the spacer (B)

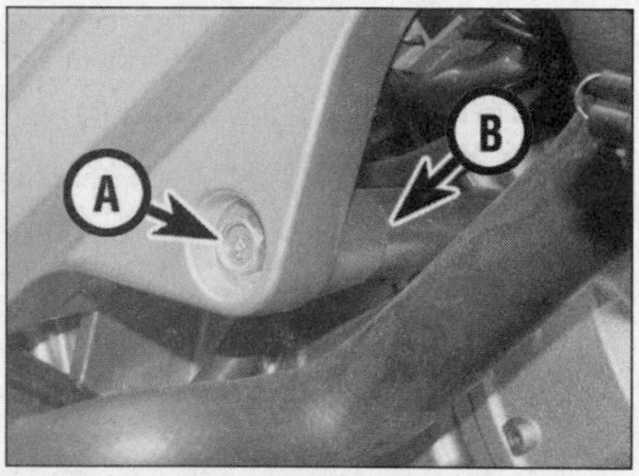

5.29c Front bolt (A) and spacer (B) on the right

5.30 Unscrew the upper middle bolt on the right

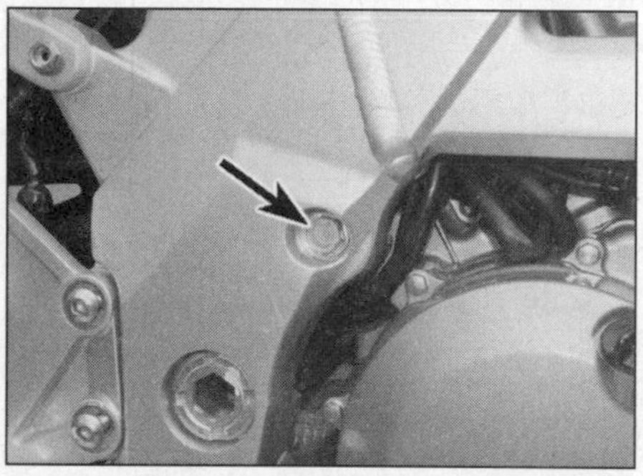
5.31 Unscrew the upper rear bolt on the right

supported by the jack. Unscrew and remove the upper rear mounting bolt on the right-hand side **(see illustration)**. Slide the bolt spacer located in the frame on the left-hand side away from the engine, noting how it locates against the crankcase **(see illustration 5.29b)**.

32 Withdraw the lower middle mounting bolt **(see illustration)**. Check that all wiring, cables and hoses are well clear, then carefully lower the jack allowing the engine to pivot down on the lower rear mounting bolt until the drive chain can be slipped off the end of the output shaft.

33 Withdraw the lower rear mounting bolt **(see illustration)**. Lower the jack carefully, making sure the rear cylinder exhaust downpipe clears the frame, and that the engine clears all the mounting lugs. Manoeuvre the engine out of the frame. Remove the spacer from the upper rear mounting lug on the left-hand side, noting how it fits. If required, remove the adjuster bolts from the frame.

Installation

X, Y, K1 and K2 models

34 If removed, fit the adjuster bolts into the frame, threading them in from the outside until they are flush with the inside **(see illustration 5.25g)**. Also fit the spacer for the upper rear mounting bolt into the lug on the left-hand side of the frame, pointing the triangular section of the flange to the front so that it will align with its locating face on the crankcase **(see illustration 5.25b)**.

35 Manoeuvre the engine into position under the frame and lift it onto the jack **(see illustration 5.25f)**. Raise the engine, taking care not to catch the rear cylinder exhaust downpipe or any part of the engine on the frame, and loop the drive chain around the output shaft as early as possible **(see illustration 5.25d)**. Raise and move the engine as required to align all the mounting bolt holes. Note that it may be necessary to adjust the jack as the bolts are installed.

36 Slide the lower middle and lower rear bolts through from the right-hand side and into the adjuster bolts **(see illustrations 5.25c and e)**.

37 Draw the spacer for the upper rear mounting bolt out of its lug and locate the point of the triangular section into the triangular cutout in the crankcase **(see illustration 5.25b)**. Slide the upper rear bolt through from the right-hand side and thread it finger-tight into the spacer, making sure it stays correctly located against the crankcase **(see illustration 5.25a)**.

38 Install the upper middle bolt into the right-hand side and tighten it finger-tight **(see illustration 5.24b)**. Install the front mounting bolts and the upper middle bolt on the left-hand side with their spacers and tighten them

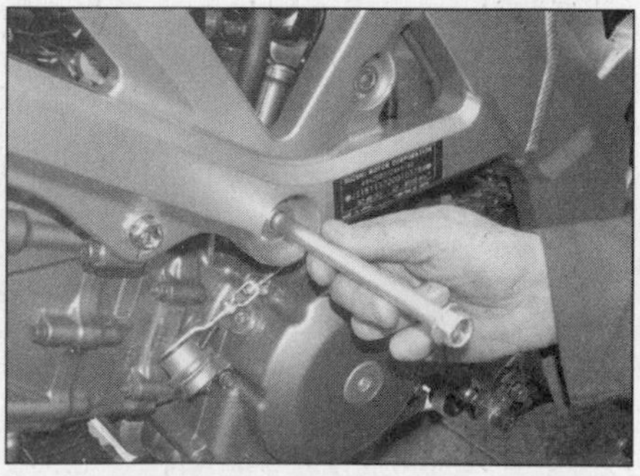
5.32 Withdraw the lower middle mounting bolt

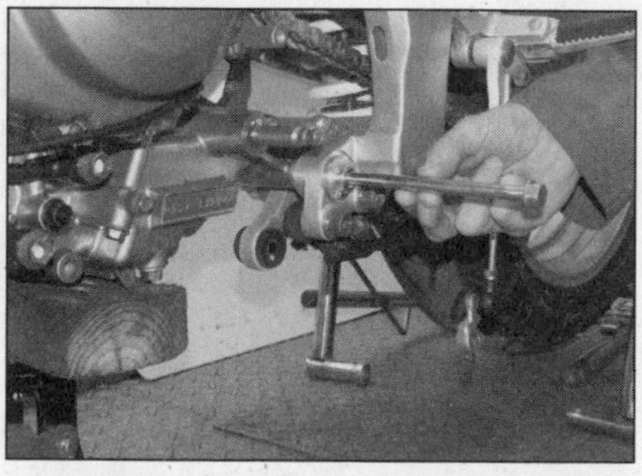
5.33 Withdraw the lower rear mounting bolt

5.39 Tighten the adjuster bolt to the specified torque

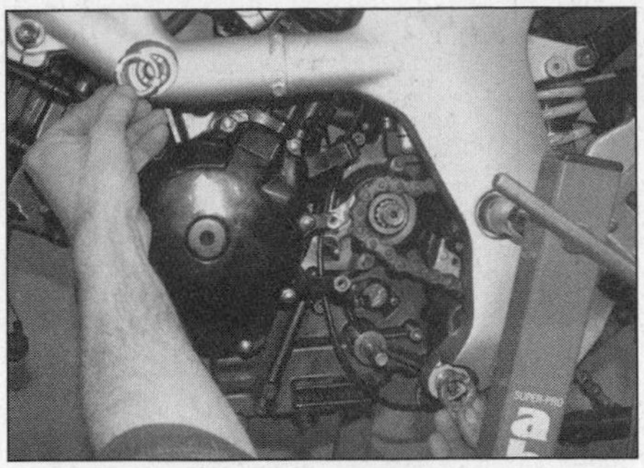

5.40 Thread the locknuts onto the adjuster bolts and tighten them to the specified torque

5.44 Make sure the triangular mark points to the exhaust side

finger-tight **(see illustrations 5.23c and d and 5.24a)**.

39 Tighten the adjuster bolts on the lower middle and lower rear engine mounts to the specified torque using a suitable peg spanner as on removal (see ***Tool Tip*** above) **(see illustration and 5.22c)**.

40 If removed, thread the locknuts onto the adjuster bolts **(see illustration)**. Tighten the locknuts to the specified torque setting using a suitable peg spanner as on removal (see ***Tool Tip*** above) **(see illustrations 5.22a and b)**. It is advisable to make a reference mark between the adjuster bolts and the frame to make sure they do not turn as the locknut is being tightened.

41 Fit the nuts on to the left-hand ends of the lower middle and lower rear mounting bolts, not forgetting the washer where fitted, and tighten them to the specified torque settings **(see illustrations 5.21a and b)**.

42 Tighten the front and upper middle mounting bolts on each side to the torque setting specified at the beginning of the Chapter **(see illustrations 5.24b and a)**. Tighten the upper rear mounting bolt to the specified torque setting.

43 Tighten the pinch bolts for the front, upper middle and upper rear mounting bolt spacers on the left-hand side to the specified torque settings **(see illustrations 5.23a and b)**.

44 The remainder of the installation procedure is the reverse of removal, noting the following points:

- Use new gaskets on the exhaust pipe connections.
- When fitting the gearchange linkage arm onto the gearchange shaft, align the slit in the arm with punch mark on the shaft, and tighten the pinch bolt securely **(see illustration 5.11)**.
- Make sure all wires, cables and hoses are correctly routed and connected, and secured by any clips or ties. When fitting the spark plug caps, make sure the triangular mark on the seal faces the exhaust side of the valve cover **(see illustration)**.
- Refill the engine with oil and coolant (see Chapter 1).
- Adjust the throttle and clutch cable freeplay.
- Adjust the drive chain (see Chapter 1).
- Start the engine and check that there are no oil or coolant leaks. Adjust the idle speed (see Chapter 1).

K3-on models

45 If removed, fit the adjuster bolts into the frame, threading them in from the outside until they are flush with the inside. Also fit the spacer for the upper rear mounting bolt into the lug on the left-hand side of the frame **(see illustration 5.29b)**.

46 Manoeuvre the engine into position under the frame and lift it onto the jack. Raise the engine, taking care not to catch the rear cylinder exhaust downpipe or any part of the engine on the frame, and loop the drive chain around the output shaft as early as possible. Raise and move the engine as required to align all the mounting bolt holes. Note that it may be necessary to adjust the jack as the bolts are installed.

47 Slide the lower middle and lower rear bolts into position from the left-hand side **(see illustrations 5.33 and 5.32)**.

48 Draw the spacer for the upper rear mounting bolt out of its lug and locate the squared section into the cutout in the crankcase **(see illustration 5.29b)**. Slide the upper rear bolt through from the right-hand side and thread it finger-tight into the spacer, making sure it stays correctly located against the crankcase **(see illustration 5.31)**.

49 Install the left and right-hand upper middle bolts and tighten them finger-tight **(see illustrations 5.30 and 5.27)**. Install the front mounting bolts and spacers and tighten them finger-tight **(see illustrations 5.29a and c)**.

50 Tighten the left-hand upper middle, lower middle and lower rear adjuster bolts to the specified torque using a suitable peg spanner as on removal (see ***Tool Tip*** above) **(see illustrations 5.28a, b and c)**.

51 If removed, thread the locknuts onto the adjuster bolts, then tighten the locknuts to the specified torque setting using a suitable peg spanner as on removal (see ***Tool Tip*** above). It is advisable to make a reference mark between the adjuster bolts and the frame to make sure they do not turn as the locknut is being tightened.

52 Fit new nuts on to the right-hand ends of the lower middle and lower rear mounting bolts and tighten them to the specified torque settings **(see illustrations 5.26c, b and a)**.

53 Tighten the front and upper middle mounting bolts on each side to the torque setting specified at the beginning of the Chapter. Tighten the upper rear mounting bolt to the specified torque setting.

54 Tighten the pinch bolts for the front and upper rear mounting bolt spacers on the left-hand side to the specified torque setting.

55 The remainder of the installation procedure is the reverse of removal, noting the points in Step 44.

6 Engine disassembly and reassembly – general information

Disassembly

1 Before disassembling the engine, thoroughly clean and degrease its external surfaces. This will prevent contamination of the engine internals, and will also make working a lot easier and cleaner. A high flash-point solvent, such as paraffin (kerosene) can be used, or better still, a proprietary engine degreaser such as Gunk. Use old paintbrushes and toothbrushes to work the solvent into the various recesses of the casings. Take care to exclude solvent or water from the electrical components and intake and exhaust ports.

⚠ ***Warning: The use of petrol (gasoline) as a cleaning agent should be avoided because of the risk of fire.***

2 When clean and dry, position the engine on the workbench, leaving suitable clear area for working. Gather a selection of small containers, plastic bags and some labels so that parts can be grouped together in an easily identifiable manner. Also get some paper and a pen so that notes can be taken. You will also need a supply of clean rag, which should be as absorbent as possible.

3 Before commencing work, read through the appropriate section so that some idea of the necessary procedure can be gained. When removing components note that great force is seldom required, unless specified (checking the specified torque setting of the particular bolt being removed will indicate how tight it is, and therefore how much force should be needed). In many cases, a component's reluctance to be removed is indicative of an incorrect approach or removal method – if in any doubt, re-check with the text.

4 An engine support stand made from short lengths of 2 x 4 inch wood bolted together into a rectangle will help support the engine **(see illustration)**. The perimeter of the mount should be just big enough to accommodate the lower part of the crankcase. Alternatively place individual blocks under the crankcase as required to ensure the engine is stable.

5 When disassembling the engine, keep 'mated' parts together (including gears, cylinder bores, pistons, connecting rods, valves, etc. that have been in contact with each other during engine operation). These 'mated' parts must be reused or renewed as an assembly.

6 A complete engine/transmission disassembly should be done in the following general order with reference to the appropriate Sections.

Remove the thermostat housing and hoses (if not already done) (see Chapter 3)
Remove the valve covers
Remove the camshafts and cam chain tensioners
Remove the cam chain blades and cam chains
Remove the cylinder heads
Remove the cylinder blocks
Remove the pistons
Remove the water pump (see Chapter 3)
Remove the clutch
Remove the gearchange mechanism
Remove the primary drive gear
Remove the oil pump

6.4 A typical engine support made from pieces of 2 x 4 inch wood – adjust the dimensions as required to suit the engine

Remove the starter motor (see Chapter 9)
Remove the alternator rotor (see Chapter 9)
Remove the starter clutch and idle gear
Separate the crankcase halves
Remove the crankshaft and the connecting rods
Remove the selector drum and forks
Remove the transmission shafts/gears

Reassembly

7 Reassembly is accomplished by reversing the general disassembly sequence.

7 Valve covers

Note: *The valve covers can be removed with the engine in the frame. If the engine has been removed, ignore the steps which do not apply.*

Removal

1 To access the front cylinder valve cover, remove the radiator (see Chapter 3).

2 To access the rear cylinder valve cover, remove the fuel tank (see Chapter 4A or 4B).

3 Disconnect the spark plug lead from the plug and secure it clear of the cover **(see illustration)**. On K3-on models, disconnect the PAIR valve hoses from the unions on the front and rear cylinder heads **(see illustration)**.

4 Unscrew the valve cover bolts, noting the difference in the bolts and their washers **(see illustration)**. Remove the washers with the bolts if they are loose in the cover. Check their condition and renew them if required.

5 Lift the valve cover off the cylinder head **(see illustration)** If it is stuck, do not try to lever it off with a screwdriver. Tap it gently around the sides with a rubber hammer or block of wood to dislodge it. The rubber gasket is normally glued into the groove in the cover, and is best left there if it is reusable (but note that it is always best to use a new gasket). If the gasket is in any way damaged, deformed or deteriorated, renew it.

Installation

6 Clean the mating surface of the cylinder head with solvent, removing all traces of old sealant. On K3-on models, if required, inspect the PAIR valve reeds (see Chapter 4B).

7 Examine the valve cover gasket for any signs of damage or deterioration and replace it with new a one if necessary. If a new one is used, clean all traces of the old sealant from the groove in the cover and clean it with solvent. Apply a smear of a suitable sealant (such as Suzuki Bond no. 1207B) into the groove, then fit the new gasket making sure it locates correctly **(see illustration)**. If the old gasket is being reused, clean off all of the old sealant.

8 Apply the sealant to the cut-outs in the cylinder head where the gasket half-circles fit **(see illustration)**. Position the valve cover on the cylinder head, making sure the gasket stays in place, and that the correct cover is fitted on each head – the front cylinder cover has a threaded bore for the radiator mount in its right-hand end **(see illustration 7.5)**. Smear the washers with clean engine oil. If

7.3a Pull the cap off the spark plug

7.3b Disconnect the PAIR valve hose where fitted

7.4 Unscrew the bolts (arrowed) . . .

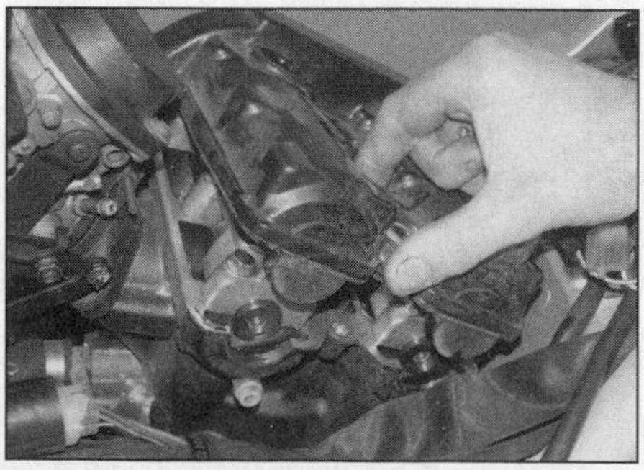

7.5 . . . and remove the cover

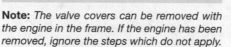

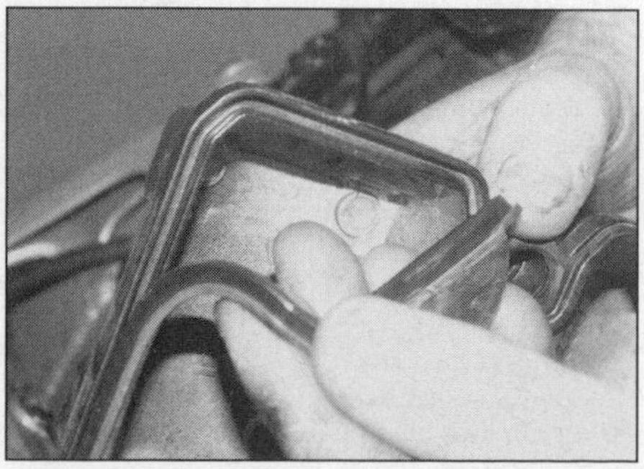

7.7 Make sure the gasket locates in the groove

removed, fit them into the cover, making sure the metallic side of the thicker one faces out and is fitted with the long-shouldered bolt. Install the cover bolts and tighten them to the specified torque setting **(see illustration)**.

9 Fit the spark plug cap, making sure it locates correctly onto the plug and that the triangular mark on the seal is facing the exhaust side of the valve cover **(see illustration 5.36)**. Install all other components previously removed.

7.8a Apply sealant to the cutouts

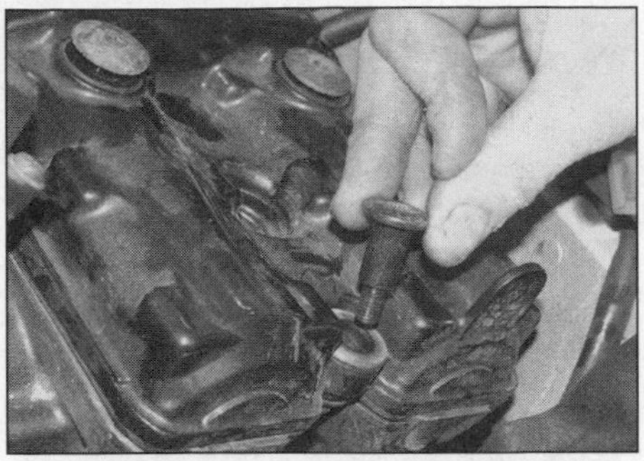

7.8b Install the bolts and tighten them to the specified torque

8 Camshafts and followers

Note: *The camshafts and followers can be removed with the engine in the frame. The camshaft holder bolts are strengthened and must not be replaced by a weaker bolt. The bolts are identified by a 9 on the head. If new bolts are required, make sure you obtain the correct ones from a Suzuki dealer.*

Removal

1 Remove the spark plugs to allow the engine to be turned over easier (see Chapter 1).

2 Remove the valve covers (see Section 7).

3 Unscrew the crankshaft end cap and the timing mark inspection cap from the alternator cover **(see illustration)**. Check the condition of the cap O-ring and sealing washer and discard them if they are damaged, deformed or deteriorated.

4 Start with the front cylinder. Turn the engine using a 17 mm socket on the alternator rotor bolt and turning it in an anti-clockwise direction only until the line next to the 'F' mark on the flywheel aligns with the notch in the timing mark inspection hole **(see illustrations)**. At this point make sure that the cylinder is at TDC (top dead centre) on the compression stroke (and not the exhaust stroke) by checking the camshaft and sprocket markings – the scribe lines on the end of each camshaft should be parallel with the cylinder head and the letter (A for the intake camshaft and B for the exhaust) should be the correct way up **(see illustration)**. Also the arrow between the 1 and the F (1 F mark) on the exhaust camshaft sprocket should be parallel to the head and pointing away from the intake sprocket. As a further check make sure the 2 mark on the exhaust sprocket and the 3 mark on the intake are pointing up. If the marks do not align as described, turn the engine anti-clockwise through one full turn (360°) until the 'F' mark again aligns with the notch – the marks should now all align as described indicating the front cylinder is at TDC on compression.

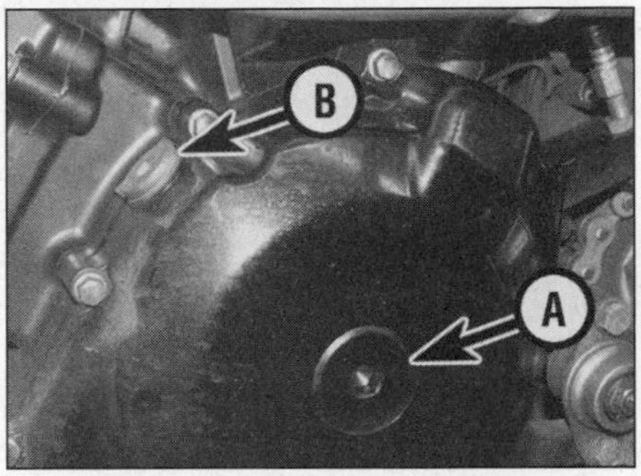

8.3 Remove the crankshaft end cap (A) and the timing inspection cap (B)

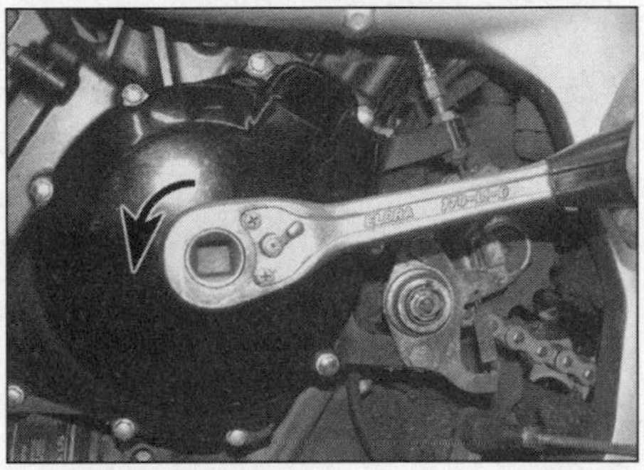

8.4a Turn the engine anti-clockwise using a socket on the timing rotor bolt . . .

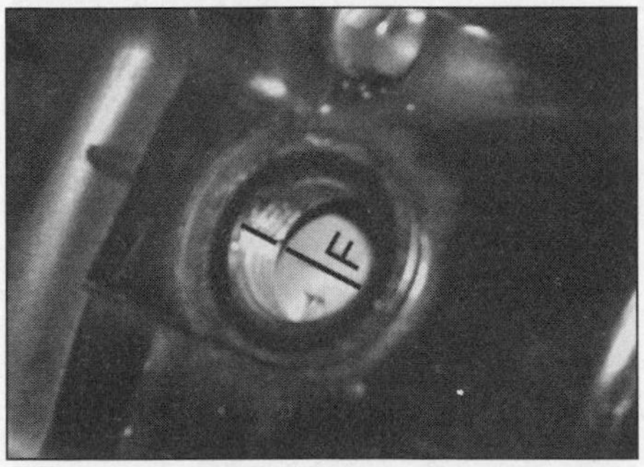

8.4b . . . until the line next to the F mark aligns with the notch

5 Remove the cam chain top guide (see Section 10) and the cam chain tensioner (see Section 9).

6 Mark each camshaft holder according to its cylinder (i.e. front or rear), and its location (i.e. intake or exhaust) – there should already be IN and EX marks, but as the camshaft holders are interchangeable between the cylinders they must be marked F or R as well so they cannot be inadvertently interchanged. Working on one camshaft at a time, unscrew the bolts securing the holder, slackening them evenly and a little at a time in a criss-cross pattern, starting at the ends and working to the middle, then remove the holder **(see illustration)**. Retrieve the two dowels if they are loose.

Caution: Make sure the holder lifts up squarely and is not sticking on a dowel or being distorted by some of the bolts being slackened more than the others as it could easily break.

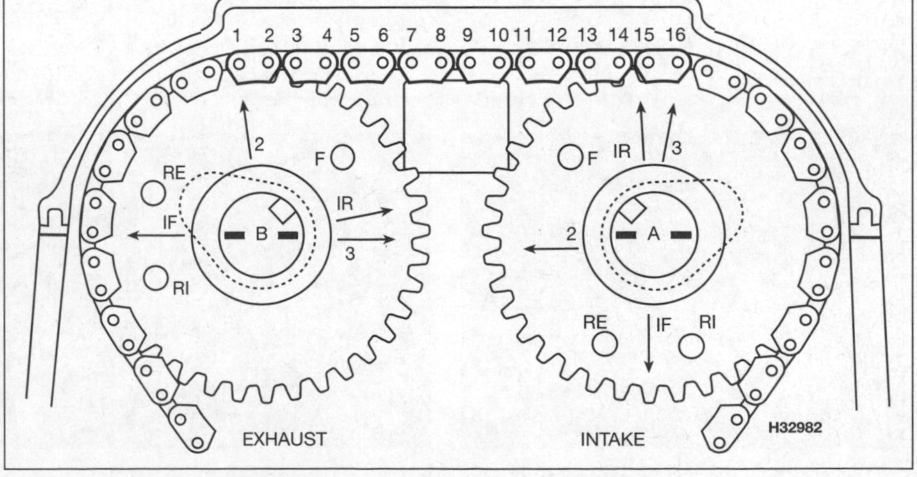

8.4c Front cylinder valve timing marks

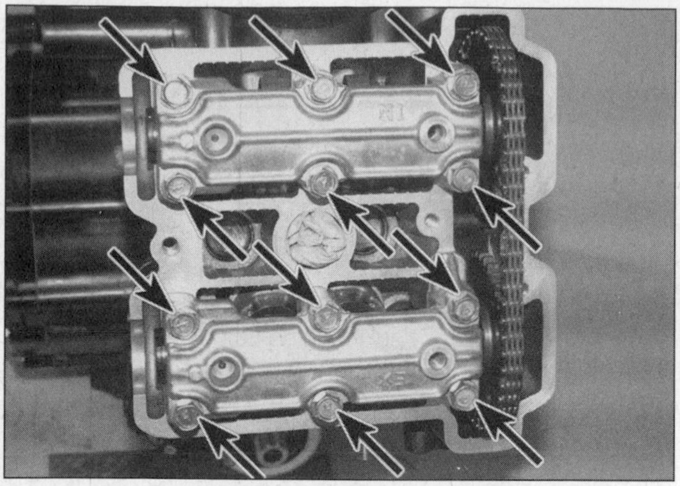

8.6 Camshaft holder bolts (arrowed)

8.7 Lift the camshaft and disengage the chain

7 Remove the intake camshaft, disengaging the cam chain from the sprocket as you do **(see illustration)**. Allow the cam chain to rest on the stopper bolt in the tunnel. The camshafts should be marked for identification – INF (intake camshaft, front cylinder), and EXF (exhaust camshaft, front cylinder) but if these marks are unclear make your own.

8 Repeat Steps 6 and 7 for the exhaust camshaft. On completion cover the top of the cylinder head with a rag to prevent anything falling into the engine.

9 Now do the rear cylinder. Draw the front cylinder cam chain out of the tunnel and hold it tight to prevent it getting trapped between the drive sprocket and the crankcase when turning the engine. Turn the engine anti-clockwise through one full turn (360°) from the TDC position for the front cylinder, until the 'F' mark again aligns with the notch **(see illustrations 8.4a and b)**. At this point the rear cylinder is at 90° ATDC (after top dead centre) on the ignition stroke, and the camshaft and sprocket markings should be as follows – the scribe lines on the end of each camshaft should be parallel with the cylinder head and the letter (C for the intake camshaft and D for the exhaust) should be the correct way up **(see illustration)**. Also the arrow after the 1 and the R (1R↑ mark) on the intake camshaft sprocket should be parallel to the head and pointing away from the exhaust sprocket. As a further check make sure the 2↑ mark on the intake sprocket and the 3↑ mark on the exhaust are pointing up.

10 Repeat Steps 5 to 8 for the rear cylinder, removing the exhaust camshaft before the intake, noting the difference in markings (INR – intake camshaft, rear cylinder, and EXR – exhaust camshaft, rear cylinder) or making your own as required for the rear cylinder identity **(see illustration)**.

11 If you are removing the followers and shims, obtain a container which is divided into eight compartments, and label each compartment with the identity of a valve location in the cylinder head, for example the front cylinder, intake camshaft, left-hand valve could be marked F-I-L. If a container is not available, use labelled plastic bags. Lift

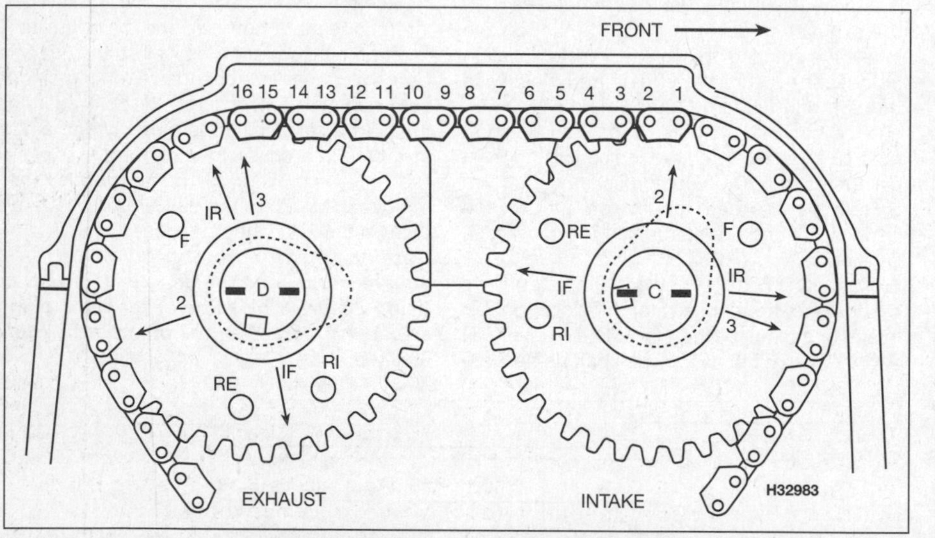

8.9 Rear cylinder valve timing marks

8.10 Lift the camshaft and disengage the chain

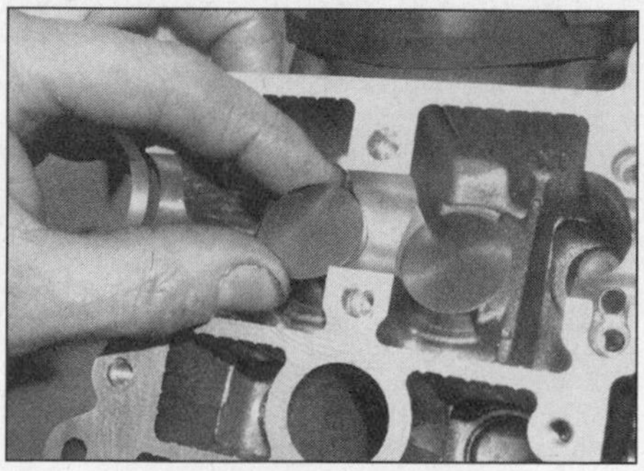

8.11a Lift out the follower . . .

8.11b . . . and remove the shim from inside it . . .

each cam follower out of the cylinder head using either a magnet or a pair of pliers and store it in its corresponding compartment in the container **(see illustration)**. Retrieve the shim from either the inside of the follower **(see illustration)** or pick it out of the top of the valve, using either a magnet, a small screwdriver with a dab of grease on it (the shim will stick to the grease), or a screwdriver and a pair of pliers **(see illustrations)**. Do not allow the shim to fall into the engine.

Inspection

Note: *Before renewing the camshafts or the cylinder head and camshaft holders because of damage, check with local machine shops specialising in motorcycle engineering work. In the case of the camshafts, it may be possible for cam lobes to be welded, reground and hardened, at a cost far lower than that of a new camshaft. If the bearing surfaces in the cylinder head are damaged, it may be possible for them to be bored out to accept bearing inserts. Due to the cost of a new cylinder head, it is recommended that all options be explored.*

12 Inspect the bearing surfaces of the camshaft holders and cylinder head and the corresponding journals on the camshafts. Look for score marks, deep scratches and evidence of spalling (a pitted appearance). Check the oil passages for clogging.

13 Check the camshaft lobes for heat discoloration (blue appearance), score marks, chipped areas, flat spots and spalling. Also check the lobe contact surfaces on the cam followers. Measure the height of each lobe with a micrometer and compare the results to the minimum height listed in this Chapter's Specifications **(see illustration)**. If damage is noted or wear is excessive, the camshaft must be renewed.

14 Check the amount of camshaft runout by supporting each end on V-blocks, and measuring any runout using a dial gauge. If the runout exceeds the specified limit the camshaft must be renewed.

> **HAYNES HiNT** ***Refer to Tools and Workshop Tips in the Reference section for details of how to read a micrometer and dial gauge.***

15 Next, check each camshaft journal oil clearance. Work on one camshaft at a time when doing this. Clean the camshaft and the bearing surfaces in the cylinder head and camshaft holder with a clean lint-free cloth, then lay the camshaft in its correct location in the head (see Step 7), positioning it correctly to prevent the valves contacting the piston (see illustration 8.4c for the front cylinder and 8.9 for the rear cylinder).

16 Cut strips of Plastigauge and lay one piece on each bearing journal parallel with the camshaft centreline. Make sure the camshaft holder dowels are installed then fit the holder,

8.11c . . . or from the top of the valve, using a magnet . . .

making sure it is in its correct location (see Step 6), the flange on the camshaft locates in the groove in the holder, and that the camshaft does not rotate at all **(see illustration 8.29b)**. Install the holder bolts and tighten them evenly and a little at a time in a criss-cross sequence, starting in the middle and working to the ends, to the torque setting specified at the beginning of the Chapter.

17 Now unscrew the bolts, slackening them evenly and a little at a time in a criss-cross pattern starting at the ends and working to the middle, then remove the holder, again making sure the camshaft does not turn.

18 To determine the oil clearance, compare the crushed Plastigauge (at its widest point) on each journal to the scale printed on the Plastigauge container. Compare the results to this Chapter's Specifications.

19 If the oil clearance is greater than specified, measure the diameter of each camshaft bearing journal with a micrometer and renew the camshaft if any journal is worn beyond the service limit specified at the beginning of the Chapter **(see illustration)**. If the camshaft journals are not worn, check the head and holder (see Step 20). If a new camshaft is fitted, check the clearance again with the new one in place. If the clearance is still too great, check the head and holder (see Step 20).

20 Measure the journal bore formed by the cylinder head and the camshaft holder as follows: make sure the camshaft holder dowels are installed then fit the holder, making

8.11d . . . or a screwdriver with a dab of grease

sure it is in its correct location (see Step 6). Tighten the holder bolts evenly and a little at a time in a criss-cross sequence, starting from the middle and working to the ends, to the torque setting specified at the beginning of the Chapter. Using telescoping gauges and a micrometer (see *Tools and Workshop Tips*), measure each journal bore diameter. If it is greater than specified, the cylinder head and holder must be renewed.

21 Except in cases of oil starvation, a cam chain wears very little. If a chain has stretched excessively, which makes it difficult to maintain proper tension, it must be renewed (see Section 11).

22 Check each sprocket for cracks and other damage, renewing the camshaft if necessary – the sprockets are not available separately. If the sprocket teeth are worn, the cam chain is also worn, as will be the drive sprocket on the crankshaft. If wear this severe is apparent, the entire engine should be disassembled for inspection.

Installation

23 Lubricate each shim with molybdenum disulphide oil (a 50/50 mixture of molybdenum disulphide grease and engine oil) and fit it into its recess in the top of the valve spring retainer with the size mark facing up **(see illustration 8.11c and d)**.

24 Check that the shim is correctly seated, then lubricate the follower with molybdenum disulphide oil and install it onto the valve, making sure it fits squarely in its bore **(see**

8.13 Measure the height of each camshaft lobe with a micrometer

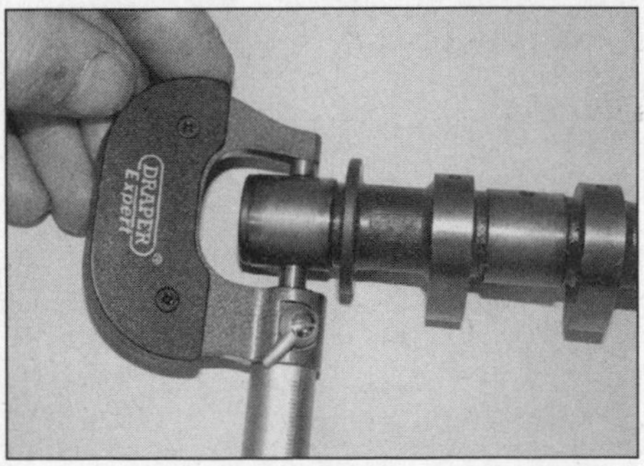

8.19 Measure the diameter of the journal with a micrometer

8.24 Fit the follower onto the valve

8.26a Check the identification letters to make sure you have the correct camshaft

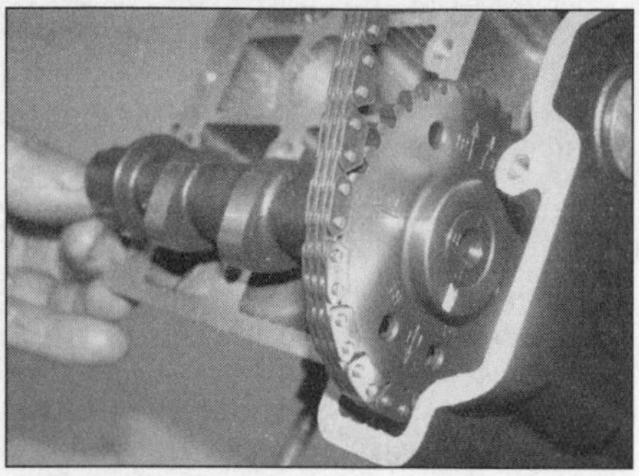

8.26b Lay the exhaust camshaft onto the head and engage the chain

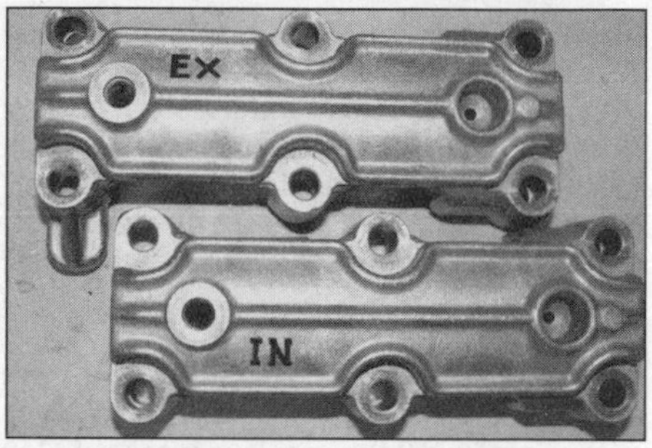

8.29a Check the identification letters to make sure you have the correct camshaft holder

illustration). Repeat the process for all other valves.

25 If only one cylinder has been worked on, the engine should be correctly positioned for installation unless it has been turned for some other reason. If the engine has been turned, align the engine so that the cylinder that has its camshafts installed is positioned with its timing marks correctly aligned as described in Step 4 (front cylinder) or Step 9 (rear cylinder), then turn the engine anti-clockwise one full turn (360°) until the 'F' mark again aligns with the notch, all the time holding the loose cam chain taut so it does not bind around its drive sprocket on the crankshaft. The engine will now be correctly positioned for installation. If both cylinder camshafts have been removed, install the camshafts on the front cylinder first.

26 To install the front cylinder camshafts, check that the cam chain is engaged around the lower sprocket teeth on the crankshaft and that the crankshaft is positioned as described in Step 4. Apply a smear of molybdenum disulphide oil (a mixture of 50% molybdenum disulphide grease and 50% engine oil) to the camshaft journals. Keeping the front run of the cam chain taut, lay the exhaust camshaft (identified by EXF) **(see illustrations)** onto the cylinder head, positioning it so that the scribe lines on the end of the shaft are parallel with the cylinder head and the letter B faces up, the arrow between the 1 and the F (1↑F mark) on the sprocket points forwards and is flush with the top of the cylinder head mating surface, and the ↑2 mark points directly away from the head **(see illustration 8.4c)**. Check that the chain is tight at the front so that there is no slack between the crankshaft sprocket and the exhaust camshaft sprocket – move the chain around the sprocket so that the slack is taken up if required, then check that all marks are still correctly aligned.

27 Starting with and including the cam chain pin that is directly above the ↑2 mark on the exhaust camshaft sprocket, count 16 pins along the chain towards the intake side and mark the pin. Lay the intake camshaft (identified by INF) **(see illustration 8.26a)** onto the cylinder head, positioning it so that the scribe lines on the end of the shaft are parallel with the cylinder head and the letter A faces up, then engage the chain with the sprocket so that the ↑3 mark on the sprocket aligns with the marked 16th pin **(see illustrations 8.7 and 8.4c)**. Again check that the chain is tight at the front and between the sprockets – any slack in the chain must lie in the portion of the chain in the back of the cylinder so that it can be taken up by the tensioner.

28 Before proceeding further, check that every-thing aligns as described in Steps 4, 26 and 27. If it doesn't, the valve timing will be inaccurate and the valves could contact the pistons when the engine is turned over. DO NOT turn the engine until the camshaft holders are installed as the camshafts could jump out of position.

29 If removed, fit the exhaust camshaft holder dowels into the cylinder head or holder (see Step 6 for holder identification), then install the holder, making sure it is the right way round and seats correctly, with the flange on the camshaft locating in the groove in the holder **(see illustrations)**. Install the holder bolts and tighten them evenly and

8.29b Make sure the dowels (arrowed) are fitted in either the head . . .

8.29c . . . or the holder, then fit the holders

a little at a time in a criss-cross pattern, starting in the middle and working to the ends, making sure the holder is drawn down evenly and does not bind on anything, to the torque setting specified at the beginning of the Chapter. Repeat for the intake camshaft holder **(see illustration)**.

Caution: Whilst tightening the bolts, make sure the holder is being pulled squarely down and is not binding on the dowels or tilting to one side – if it does, adjust the relevant bolts until the holder is again square to the head. The holder is likely to break if it's not tightened down evenly and squarely.

30 Install the front cylinder cam chain tensioner (see Section 9).

31 Before installing the rear cylinder camshafts, hold the cam chain to prevent it bunching around the crankshaft sprocket and rotate the crankshaft 360° to realign the F mark with the notch. Check that the cam chain is engaged around the lower sprocket teeth on the crankshaft. Apply a smear of molybdenum disulphide oil (a mixture of 50% molybdenum disulphide grease and 50% engine oil) to the camshaft journals. Keeping the front run of the cam chain taut, lay the intake camshaft (identified by INR) **(see illustrations)** onto the cylinder head, positioning it so that the scribe lines on the end of the shaft are parallel with the cylinder head and the letter C faces up, the arrow after the 1 and the R (1R↑ mark) on the sprocket points forwards and is flush with the top of the cylinder head mating surface, and the ↑2 mark points directly away from the head **(see illustration 8.9)**. Check that the chain is tight at the front so that there is no slack between the crankshaft sprocket and the intake camshaft sprocket, and that all marks are still correctly aligned (see Step 9). If any slack is evident, move the chain around the sprocket so that the slack is taken up.

32 Starting with and including the cam chain pin that is directly above the ↑2 mark on the intake camshaft sprocket, count 16 pins along the chain towards the exhaust side and mark the pin. Lay the exhaust camshaft (identified by EXR) **(see illustration 8.31a)** onto the cylinder head, positioning it so that the scribe lines on the end of the shaft are parallel with the cylinder head and the letter D faces up, then engage the chain with the sprocket so that the ↑3 mark on the sprocket aligns with the marked 16th pin **(see illustrations 8.10 and 8.9)**. Again check that the chain is tight at the front and between the sprockets – any slack in the chain must lie in the portion of the chain in the back of the cylinder so that it can be taken up by the tensioner.

33 Before proceeding further, check that everything aligns as described in Steps 9, 31 and 32. If it doesn't, the valve timing will be inaccurate and the valves could contact the pistons when the engine is turned over. DO NOT turn the engine until the camshaft holders are installed as the camshafts could jump out of position.

8.31a Check the identification letters to make sure you have the correct camshaft

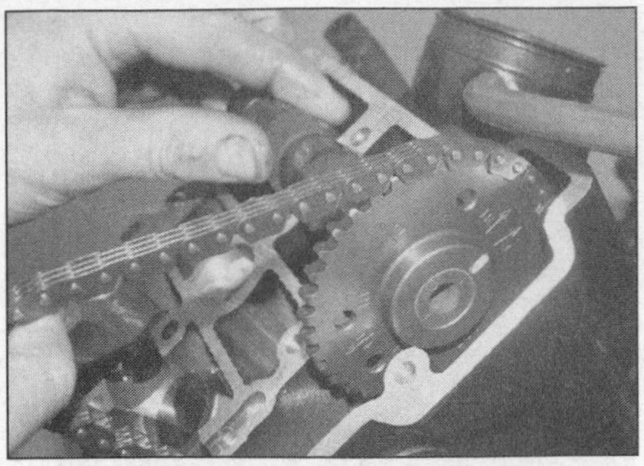
8.31b Lay the intake camshaft onto the head and engage the chain

8.34a Fit the intake camshaft holder . . .

8.34b . . . then the exhaust camshaft holder

34 If removed, fit the intake camshaft holder dowels into the cylinder head or holder (see Step 6 for holder identification) **(see illustration 8.29a)**, then install the holder, making sure it is the right way round and seats correctly, with the flange on the camshaft locating in the groove in the holder **(see illustration)**. Install the holder bolts and tighten them evenly and a little at a time in a criss-cross pattern, starting in the middle and working to the ends, making sure the holder is drawn down evenly and does not bind on anything, to the torque setting specified at the beginning of the Chapter. Repeat for the exhaust camshaft holder **(see illustration)**.

Caution: Whilst tightening the bolts, make sure the holder is being pulled squarely down and is not binding on the dowels or tilting to one side – if it does, adjust the relevant bolts until the holder is again square to the head. The holder is likely to break if it's not tightened down evenly and squarely.

35 Install the rear cylinder cam chain tensioner (see Section 9).

36 Before proceeding further, again check that everything aligns as described in Step 4 for the front cylinder and Step 9 for the rear cylinder. If it doesn't, the valve timing will be inaccurate and the valves will contact the piston when the engine is turned over **(see illustrations 8.4c and 8.9)**.

37 Rotate the engine anti-clockwise through two full turns (720°) and re-check that the valve timing for both cylinders is correct (see Steps 4 and 9). Also recheck the cam chain pin count between the sprockets (see Step 27 for the front cylinder and 32 for the rear cylinder) in case the chain jumped when the engine was being turned. If the chain has jumped, check that the tensioner for that chain has released correctly (see Section 9).

38 Check the valve clearances (Chapter 1) and adjust if necessary.

39 Install the cam chain top guides (see Section 10).

40 Install the timing mark inspection cap using a new sealing washer if required, and the crankshaft end cap using a new O-ring if required – smear the O-ring and the cap threads with grease **(see illustration)**. Tighten the caps to the torque settings specified at the beginning of the Chapter.

41 Install the valve covers (see Section 7).

42 Install the spark plugs (see Chapter 1).

43 Check the engine oil level and top up if necessary (see *Daily (pre-ride) checks*).

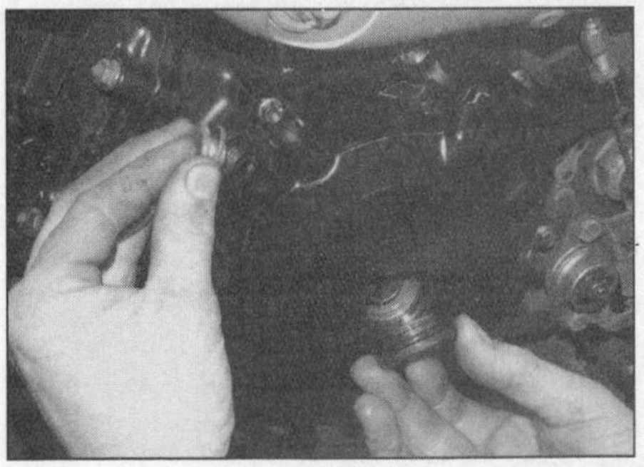
8.40 Fit the caps using a new washer and O-ring if required

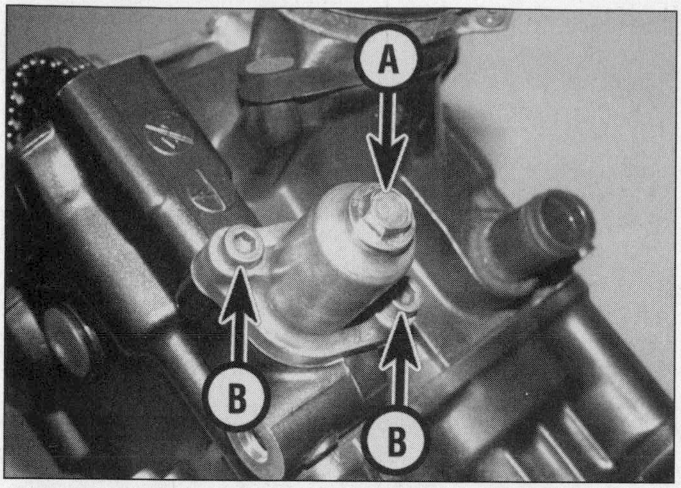

9.4a Cam chain tensioner cap bolt (A) and mounting bolts (B) – front cylinder, engine removed

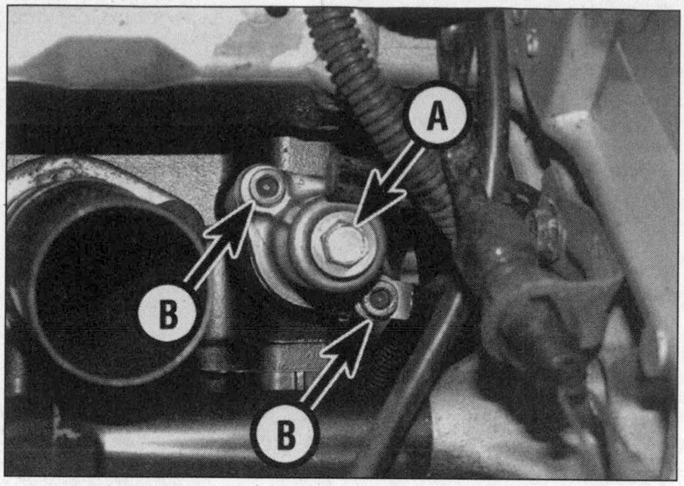

9.4b Cam chain tensioner cap bolt (A) and mounting bolts (B) – rear cylinder, engine installed

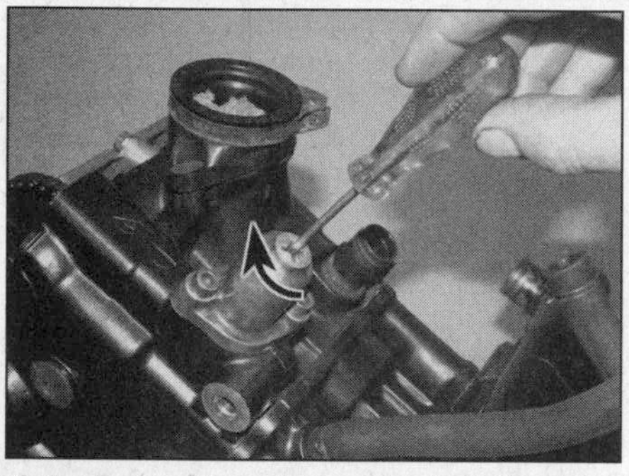

9.4c Retract the plunger as described . . .

9.4d . . . and hold it while removing the mounting bolts . . .

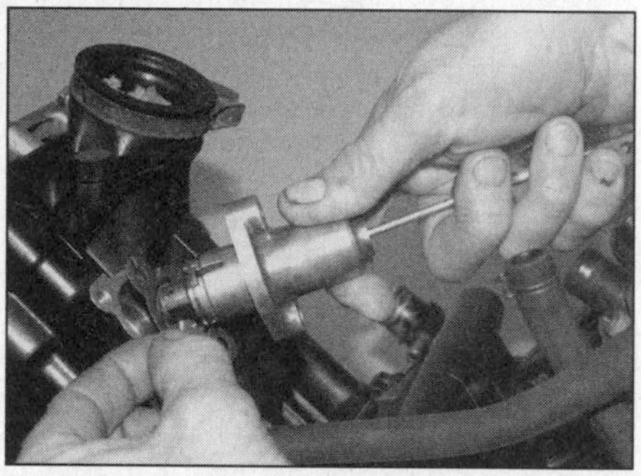

9.4e . . . and lifting off the tensioner assembly

9 Cam chain tensioners

Note: *The cam chain tensioners can be removed with the engine in the frame. If the engine has been removed, ignore the steps that do not apply. On X, Y, K1 and K2 models, a locking tool (Suzuki Pt. No. 09917-62430) that keeps the tensioner retracted can be used when installing the tensioner. While it makes the job slightly easier, it is not essential.*

Caution: Once you start to remove the tensioner bolts, you must remove the tensioner all the way and reset it before tightening the bolts. The tensioner extends itself and locks in place, so if you loosen the bolts partway and then retighten them, the tensioner or cam chain will be damaged.

Removal

1 To access the front cylinder tensioner remove the carburettors or throttle bodies as applicable (see Chapter 4A or 4B).

2 To access the rear cylinder tensioner remove the rear wheel (see Chapter 7). Unscrew the single bolt securing the mud deflector to the swingarm and remove it, noting how it fits.

3 It is advisable to align the valve timing marks before removing the tensioner. Remove the valve cover(s) and the crankshaft end cap and timing mark inspection cap from the alternator cover **(see illustration 8.3)**. Turn the engine in an anti-clockwise direction using a 17 mm socket on the alternator bolt to align the line next to the F mark with the notch in the inspection hole, and check that the marks on the camshafts align (see Section 8, step 4 for the front cylinder marks, and step 9 for the rear cylinder marks).

4 On X, Y, K1 and K2 models, unscrew the tensioner cap bolt and remove the sealing washer **(see illustrations)**. Slacken the tensioner mounting bolts slightly, then insert a small flat-bladed screwdriver in the end of the tensioner so that it engages the slotted plunger. Turn the screwdriver clockwise until the plunger is fully retracted and hold it in this position while unscrewing the mounting bolts and withdrawing the tensioner from the engine **(see illustrations)**. Release the screwdriver – the plunger will spring back out once the screwdriver is removed, but can be easily reset on installation. Do not rotate the engine with the tensioner removed. Remove the tensioner gasket.

5 On K3-on models, unscrew the tensioner cap bolt carefully, then remove the bolt and sealing washer and withdraw the spring from the tensioner body **(see illustrations)**. Remove the

9.5a Remove the cap bolt and washer . . .

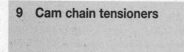

9.5b . . . then withdraw the spring

tensioner mounting bolts and lift the tensioner off. Remove the tensioner gasket.
6 Discard the gasket and sealing washer as new ones must be used on installation. On X, Y, K1 and K2 models, check that the plunger moves smoothly when wound into the tensioner and springs back out freely when released. Do not dismantle the tensioner. On K3-on models, release the tensioner ratchet and check that the plunger moves smoothly in and out of the tensioner body **(see illustration)**. On K5-on models, if the plunger is damaged or seized, the oil jet located in the cylinder block may be blocked. Remove the cylinder (see Section 15) and blow through the oil passage with compressed air.

Installation

7 Ensure the tensioner and cylinder block surfaces are clean and dry.
8 On X, Y, K1 and K2 models, insert a small flat-bladed screwdriver in the end of the tensioner so that it engages the slotted plunger **(see illustration)**. Turn the screwdriver clockwise until the plunger is fully retracted and hold it in this position whilst the tensioner is installed **(see illustration 9.4e)**. If the Suzuki tensioner locking key is available, hold the end of the plunger in the body, then remove the screwdriver and insert the tool in the end of the tensioner so that it engages the slotted plunger and one of the slots in the body and so locks the plunger winder and prevents the plunger springing out.
9 On K3-on models, release the tensioner ratchet and push the plunger all the way into the body **(see illustration 9.6)**.
10 Fit a new gasket onto the tensioner body, then install the tensioner with its mounting bolts and tighten the bolts to the torque setting specified at the beginning of the Chapter. Note that on K3-on models, the UP mark on the tensioner body should face the cylinder head **(see illustration)**.
11 On X, Y, K1 and K2 models, release and remove the screwdriver or the locking tool, making sure the plunger springs out as you do – you should be able to hear as the retractor mechanism unwinds and the plunger contacts the tensioner blade. If you suspect that it hasn't, remove the tensioner again and check (if the valve cover has been removed it is easy to check whether the chain tension has been taken up). Install the tensioner cap bolt with a new sealing washer and tighten it to the specified torque setting **(see illustration)**.
12 On K3-on models, install the tensioner spring, then install the cap bolt with a new sealing washer and tighten it to the specified torque setting. If the valve cover has been removed, check that the cam chain tension has been taken up.
13 Recheck the valve timing marks (see Step 3) and install the valve cover(s). Install the timing mark inspection cap using a new sealing washer if required, and the crank-shaft end cap using a new O-ring if required – smear the O-ring and the cap threads with grease

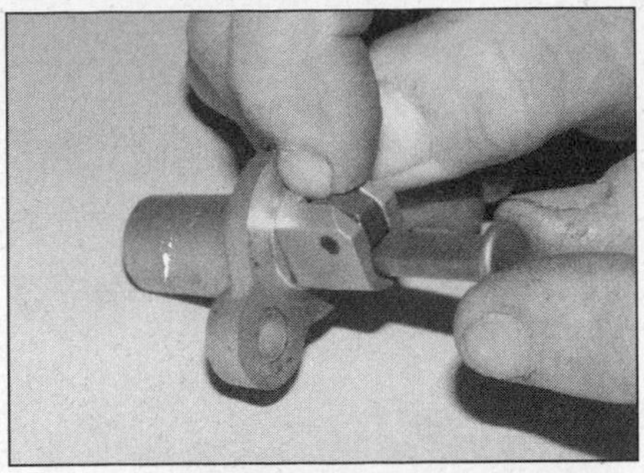

9.6 Check the plunger operation as described

9.8 Insert the screwdriver and turn it clockwise to retract the plunger

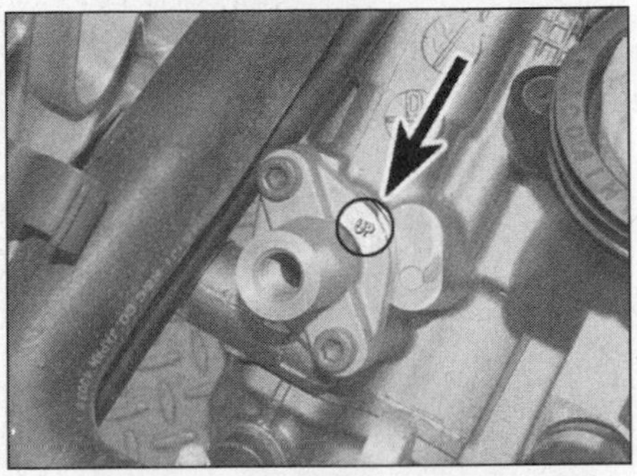

9.10 Note the UP mark – K3, K4 and K5 models

9.11 Install the cap bolt using a new sealing washer

(see illustration 8.40). Tighten the caps to the torque settings specified at the beginning of the Chapter.
14 Install the carburettors or throttle bodies, and/or mudflap and rear wheel as required (see Chapter 4A, 4B or 7). Make sure the peg on the mudflap locates in the hole in the swingarm.

10 Cam chain guides and tensioner blades

Note: *The cam chains, guides and tensioner blades can be removed with the engine in the frame.*

Top guide

1 Remove the valve cover (see Section 7).
2 Unscrew the bolts securing the cam chain top guide and remove it **(see illustration)**. Check the sliding surface and edges of the guide for excessive wear, deep grooves, cracking and other obvious damage, and renew it if necessary.
3 When installing the guide, tighten its bolts to the torque setting specified at the beginning of the Chapter.

Front guide blade

4 Remove the cylinder head (see Section 12).
5 Draw the blade out of the engine, noting how it locates **(see illustration)**. Check the sliding surface and edges of the guide blade for excessive wear, deep grooves, cracking and other obvious damage, and renew it if necessary.
6 When installing the front guide blade, make sure the lugs on the blade locate in the cutouts

10.2 Unscrew the three bolts and remove the top guide

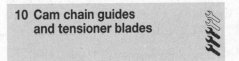

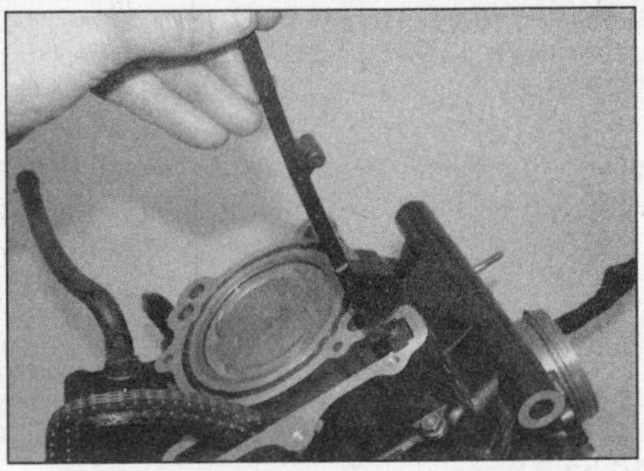

10.5 Removing the front guide blade

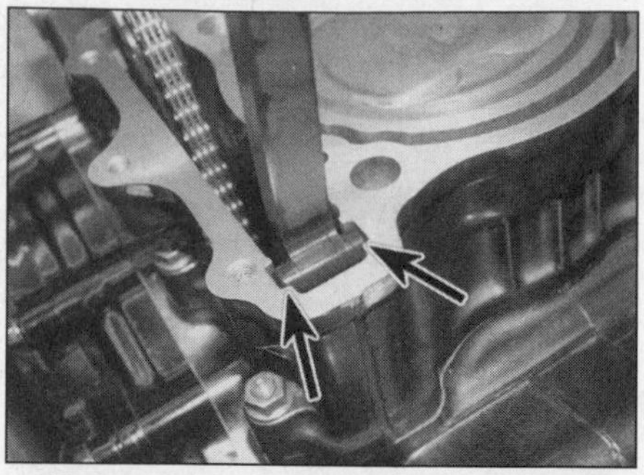

10.6 Make sure the lugs locate correctly in the cutouts

10.11a Installing the front cylinder tensioner blade

in the cylinder block **(see illustration)**. Install the cylinder head as described in Section 12.

Tensioner blade

7 For the front cylinder remove the intake camshaft (see Section 8) and the starter clutch (see Section 22). If the cylinder head is being removed as well, proceed with that now and continue this procedure afterwards, as it makes removing the blade easier.

8 For the rear cylinder remove the exhaust camshaft (see Section 8) and the clutch (see Section 18). If the cylinder head is being removed as well, proceed with that now and continue this procedure afterwards, as it makes removing the blade easier.

9 Unscrew the pivot bolt and draw the blade out of the engine, noting the washer that fits between the blade and the crankcase **(see illustrations)**.

10 Check the sliding surface and edges of the blade for excessive wear, deep grooves, cracking and other obvious damage, and renew it if necessary.

11 When installing the tensioner blade, do not omit the washer that fits between the tensioner blade pivot and the crankcase **(see illustrations)**. Apply a suitable non-permanent thread locking compound to the pivot bolt threads and tighten it to the torque setting specified at the beginning of the Chapter. Install the remaining components in a reverse of the removal procedure.

11.3 Removing the front cylinder cam chain

10.9a Front cylinder tensioner blade pivot bolt (arrowed)

10.11b Installing the rear cylinder tensioner blade

11 Cam chains

Note: *The cam chains can be removed with the engine in the frame.*

Front cylinder cam chain

Removal

1 Drain the engine oil (see Chapter 1).

2 Remove the cylinder head (see Section 12), and the cam chain guide blade and tensioner blade (see Section 10).

3 Drop the cam chain down its tunnel and remove it from the end of the crankshaft **(see illustration)**.

Inspection

4 Check the chain for binding, kinks and any obvious damage and renew it if necessary.

5 Check the sprocket teeth on the crankshaft for wear and damage. The teeth are integral with the crankshaft, so if any significant wear or damage is found, the crankshaft must be renewed. Also check the camshaft sprocket teeth for wear. If the sprockets are worn and new camshafts and/or crankshaft are being fitted, fit a new chain as a matter of course.

10.9b Rear cylinder tensioner blade pivot bolt (arrowed)

Installation

6 Hook the new cam chain onto a piece of wire and draw the chain up through its tunnel, making sure its bottom end engages around the sprocket on the crankshaft **(see illustration 11.3)**. Secure the chain at the top to prevent it falling back down the tunnel.

7 Install the cam chain tensioner blade and guide blade (see Section 10). Install the cylinder head (see Section 12).

8 Replenish the engine oil (see Chapter 1).

Rear cylinder cam chain

Removal

9 Drain the engine oil (see Chapter 1).

10 Remove the cylinder head (see Section 12).

11 Remove the clutch (see Section 18), the primary drive gear (see Section 21), and the cam chain guide blade and tensioner blade (see Section 10).

12 Drop the cam chain down its tunnel and remove it from the end of the crankshaft **(see illustration)**. Slide the cam chain sprocket off the end of the crankshaft **(see illustration)**.

Inspection

13 Check the chain for binding, kinks and any obvious damage and renew it if necessary.

14 Check the cam chain sprocket for wear or damage to both the outer teeth and the inner splines. Also check the camshaft sprocket teeth

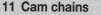

11.12a Removing the rear cylinder cam chain

for wear. If the sprockets are worn and new camshafts and crankshaft sprocket are being fitted, fit a new chain as a matter of course.

Installation

15 Slide the sprocket onto the crankshaft with the flanged end innermost **(see illustration 11.12b)**. Hook the new cam chain onto a piece of wire and draw the chain up through its tunnel, making sure its bottom end engages around the sprocket **(see illustration 11.12a)**. Secure the chain at the top to prevent it falling back down the tunnel.

16 Install the cam chain tensioner blade and guide blade (see Section 10), then the primary drive gear (see Section 21), then the clutch (see Section 18).

17 Install the cylinder head (see Section 12).

18 Replenish the engine oil (see Chapter 1).

12 Cylinder heads – removal and installation

***Caution:** The engine must be completely cool before beginning this procedure or the cylinder head may become warped.*

Note: *The heads can be removed with the engine in the frame. If the engine has been removed, ignore the steps that don't apply.*

11.12b Slide the sprocket off the shaft

Removal

1 Remove the carburettors or throttle bodies as applicable, and the exhaust system (see Chapter 4A or 4B). On X, Y, K1 and K2 models, when removing the rear head, detach the fuel pump vacuum hose from its union on the intake duct.

2 Remove the valve cover (see Section 7).

3 Remove the spark plug (see Chapter 1).

4 Remove the camshafts (see Section 8). If you are planned to overhaul the head, also remove the followers and shims.

5 Slacken the clamp securing the coolant hose to its union on the cylinder head and detach the hose **(see illustration)**.

6 Hook the cam chain off the stopper bolt and let it dangle over the top of head. If removing the front head, unscrew the stopper bolt and remove the washer, noting which way round it fits **(see illustration)**. If removing the rear head, the stopper bolt is obscured by the frame, so this will have to be undone after the head had been raised off the cylinder.

7 First slacken the two nuts securing the cylinder block to the crankcase **(see illustration)**. Tighten the nuts finger-tight only to prevent the block lifting when the cylinder head is removed.

8 The cylinder head is secured by three 6 mm bolts and four 10 mm bolts **(see illustration)**. First unscrew and remove the three 6 mm bolts. Now unscrew the four 10 mm bolts, slackening them evenly and a little at a time in a criss-cross pattern until they are all loose. Remove the bolts and their washers. Take care not to drop any of the washers down the cam chain tunnel.

9 Hold the cam chain up and pull the cylinder head up off the block, then pass the cam chain down through the tunnel **(see illustration)**. If removing the rear head, support it and now unscrew the cam chain stopper bolt. Do not let the chain fall into the crankcase – secure it with a piece of wire or metal bar to prevent it from doing so. If the

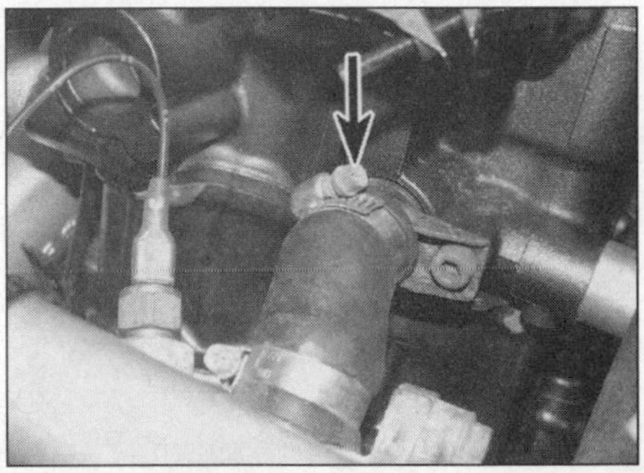

12.5 Slacken the clamp (arrowed) and detach the hose – front cylinder shown

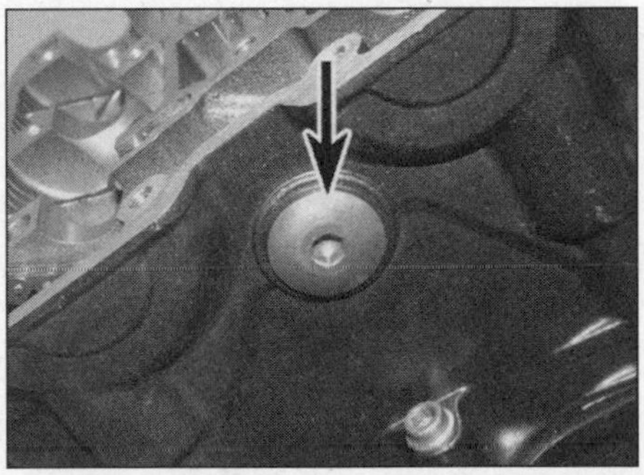

12.6 Unscrew the stopper bolt (arrowed) and remove the washer

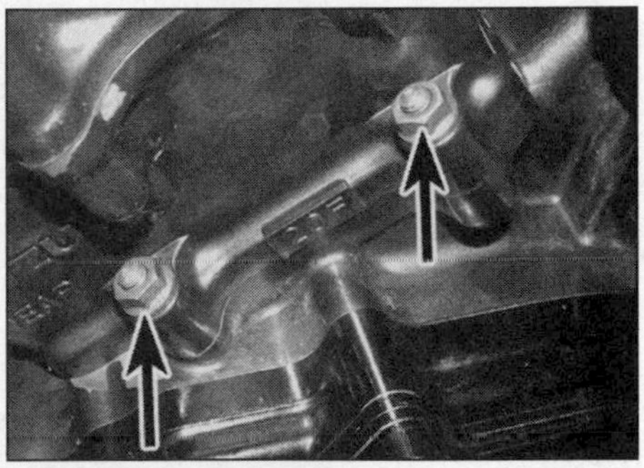

12.7 Slacken the two cylinder block nuts (arrowed)

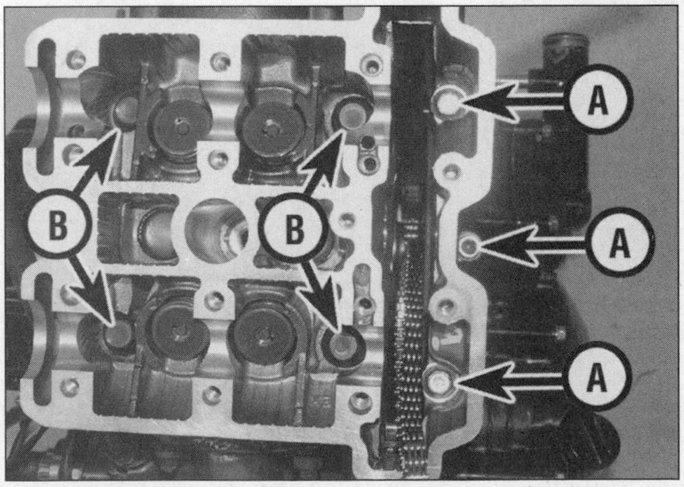

12.8 Cylinder head 6mm bolts (A) and 10mm bolts (B)

12.9 Lift the head up off the block

12.16 Lay the gasket onto the head, locating it over the dowels (arrowed)

12.17 Each cylinder head is marked – make sure you have the correct one

12.18 Install the 10 mm bolts with their washers . . .

12.19 . . . and tighten them as described to the specified torque setting

12.20 Install and tighten the 6 mm bolts

12.22 Fit the chain stopper bolt with its washer

head is stuck, tap around the base of it with a soft-faced mallet. Do not try to free it by inserting a screwdriver between the head and cylinder block – you'll damage the sealing surfaces. Note that each head is marked 'F' or 'R' according to whether it is for the front or rear cylinder **(see illustration 12.17)**.

10 Remove the old gasket **(see illustration 12.16)**.

11 If they are loose, remove the two dowels from the cylinder block **(see illustration 12.16)**. If either appears to be missing it is probably stuck in the underside of the cylinder head. If required, remove the cam chain guide blade from the front of the cam chain tunnel (see Section 10).

12 Check the cylinder head gasket and the mating surfaces on the cylinder head and block for signs of leakage, which could indicate warpage. Refer to Section 14 and check the cylinder head.

13 Clean all traces of old gasket material from the cylinder head and block. If a scraper is used, take care not to scratch or gouge the soft aluminium. Be careful not to let any of the gasket material drop into the crankcase, the cylinder bore or the oil and coolant passages. Unless you are removing the cylinder block, cover it with a clean rag to prevent any debris falling in.

Installation

14 If removed, fit the cam chain guide blade into the front of the cam chain tunnel (see Section 10).

15 If removed, fit the two dowels into the cylinder block **(see illustration 12.16)**. Lubricate the cylinder bores with new engine oil.

16 Ensure both cylinder head and block mating surfaces are clean, then lay the new head gasket in place on the cylinder block, making sure it locates over the dowels **(see illustration)**. The gasket can only fit one way, so if the holes do not line up properly the gasket is upside down. Never re-use the old gasket.

17 Make sure you have the correct head for the cylinder being worked on – the front head is marked 'F' and the rear 'R' **(see illustration)**. Carefully lower the cylinder head onto the block, feeding the cam chain up the tunnel as you do **(see illustration 12.9)**. It is helpful to have an assistant to pass the chain up and slip a piece of wire through it to prevent it falling back into the engine. Keep the chain taut to prevent it becoming disengaged from the crankshaft sprocket.

18 Lubricate the threads of the 10 mm bolts and the washers with clean oil. Install the bolts and washers, with the chamfered side of the washers facing up, and tighten the bolts finger-tight **(see illustration)**.

19 Now tighten the 10 mm bolts evenly and a little at a time in a criss-cross pattern first to the initial torque setting specified at the beginning of the Chapter, and then to the final setting **(see illustration)**.

20 Install the 6 mm bolts and tighten them to the specified torque setting **(see illustration)**.

21 Tighten the cylinder block nuts securely, to the specified torque setting if your torque wrench fits **(see illustration 12.7)**.

22 Fit the cam chain stopper bolt with its washer, making sure the metallic side of the washer faces away from the engine and the chain is around the bolt, and tighten the bolt to the specified torque setting **(see illustration)**.

23 Install all other components that have been removed in a reverse of the removal procedure, referring to the relevant sections and Chapters where necessary.

13 Valves, valve seats and valve guides – servicing

1 Because of the complex nature of this job and the special tools and equipment required, most owners leave servicing of the valves, valve seats and valve guides to a professional. However, once the cylinder head has been removed, you can make an initial assessment of whether the valves are seating correctly, and therefore sealing, by pouring a small amount of solvent into each of the valve ports. If the solvent leaks past any valve into the combustion chamber area the valve is not seating correctly and sealing.

2 You can also remove the valves from the cylinder head, clean the components, check them for wear to assess the extent of the work needed, and, unless a valve service is required, grind in the valves (see Section 14). The head can then be reassembled.

3 A dealer service department will dismantle the valve assemblies, inspect and measure each component for wear, recut the valve seats if necessary, clean and reassemble the valve components using new components where necessary.

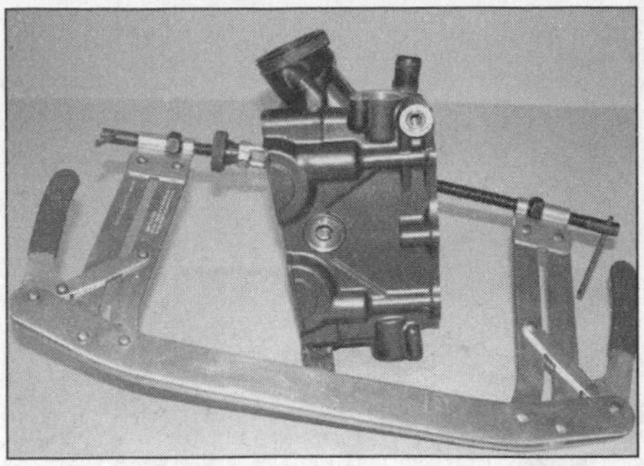

14.5a Fit the valve spring compressor . . .

14.5b . . . making sure it locates correctly on the spring retainer . . .

14.5c . . . and on the valve

4 After the valve service has been performed, the head will be in like-new condition. When the head is returned, be sure to clean it again very thoroughly before installation on the engine to remove any metal particles or abrasive grit that may still be present from the valve service operations. Use compressed air, if available, to blow out all the holes and passages.

14 Cylinder head and valves – disassembly, inspection and reassembly

1 As mentioned in the previous section, valve overhaul should be left to a Suzuki dealer or cylinder head specialist. However, disassembly, cleaning and inspection of the valves and related components can be done (if the necessary special tools are available) by the home mechanic. This way no expense is incurred if the inspection reveals that overhaul is not required at this time.

2 To disassemble the valve components without the risk of damaging them, a valve spring compressor is absolutely essential. Make sure it is suitable for motorcycle work and comes with the correct adapters for your valve size.

Disassembly

3 Before proceeding, arrange to label and store the valves along with their related components in such a way that they can be returned to their original locations without getting mixed up. A good way to do this is to obtain a container which is divided into eight compartments, and label each compartment with the location of a valve, for example the front cylinder, intake camshaft, left-hand valve could be marked F-I-L. If a container is not available, use labelled plastic bags (an egg carton also does very well!).

4 Clean all traces of old gasket material from the cylinder head. If a scraper is used, take care not to scratch or gouge the soft aluminium.

HAYNES HiNT *Refer to Tools and Workshop Tips for details of gasket removal methods.*

5 First locate the valve spring compressor on each end of the valve assembly, making sure it is the correct size **(see illustration)**. On the top of the valve the adaptor needs to be about the same size as the spring retainer – if it is too big it will contact the follower bore and mark it, and if it is too small it will be difficult to remove and install the collets **(see illustration)**. On the underside of the head make sure the plate on the compressor only contacts the valve and not the soft aluminium of the head – if the plate is too big for the valve, use a spacer between them **(see illustration)**.

6 Compress the valve springs on the first valve – do not compress the springs any more than is absolutely necessary. Remove the collets, using either needle-nose pliers, tweezers, a magnet or a screwdriver with a dab of grease on it **(see illustration)**. Carefully release the valve spring compressor and remove it. Remove the spring retainer, noting which way up it fits **(see illustration 14.31c)**. Remove the springs, noting that the closer wound coils are at the bottom **(see illustration 14.31a)**. Press down on the top of the valve stem and draw the valve out from the underside of the head **(see illustration 14.24b)**. If the valve binds in the guide (won't pull through), push it back into the head and deburr the area around the collet groove with a very fine file or whetstone **(see illustration)**.

7 Once the valve has been removed and labelled, pull the valve stem oil seal off the top of the valve guide and discard it (the old seals should never be reused) **(see illustration)**. Now remove the spring seat **(see illustration)**. The seat is difficult to grasp, so either use a small magnet or turn the head upside down and tip it out, taking care not to lose it.

8 Repeat the procedure for the remaining valves. Remember to keep the parts for each valve together and in order so they can be reinstalled in the same location.

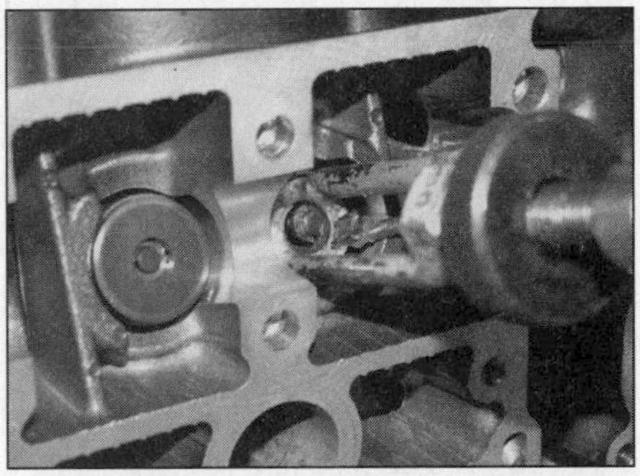

14.6a Remove the collets as described

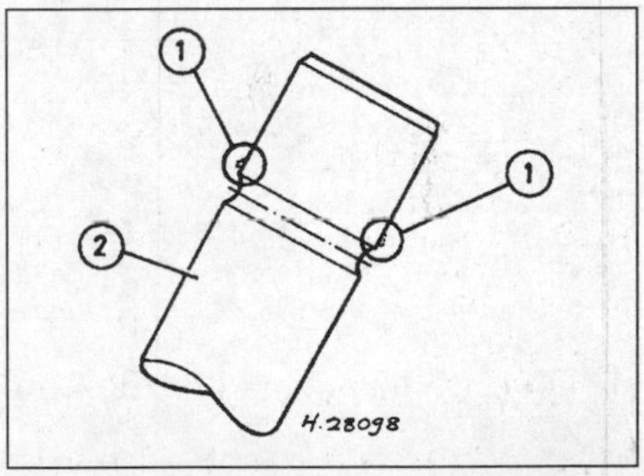

14.6b Remove any burrs (1) if the valve stem (2) won't pull through the guide

14.7a Pull the oil seal off the top of the guide . . .

14.7b . . . then remove the spring seat

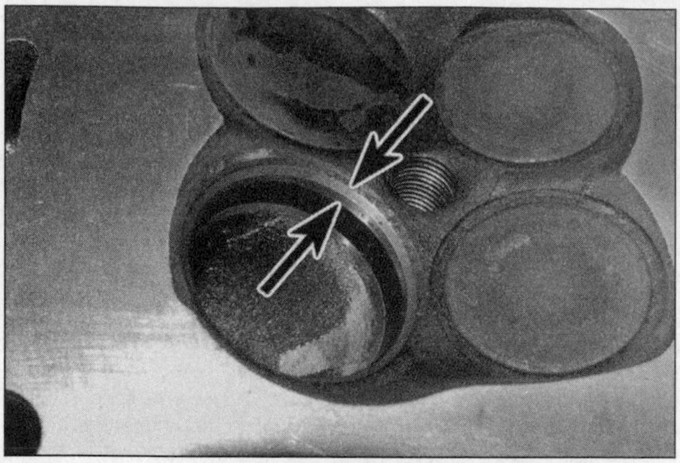

14.15 Measure the valve seat width with a ruler (or for greater precision use a Vernier caliper)

14.16a Measure the amount of stem deflection as shown, relocating the gauge to measure in both directions

9 Next, clean the cylinder head with solvent and dry it thoroughly. Compressed air will speed the drying process and ensure that all holes and recessed areas are reached.

10 Clean all of the valve springs, collets, retainers and spring seats with solvent and dry them thoroughly. Do the parts from one valve at a time so they don't get mixed up.

11 Scrape off any deposits that may have formed on the valve, then use a motorised wire brush to remove deposits from the valve heads and stems. Again, make sure the valves do not get mixed up.

Inspection

12 Inspect the head very carefully for cracks and other damage. If cracks are found, a new head will be required. Check the camshaft bearing surfaces for wear and evidence of seizure. Check the camshafts and holders for wear as well (see Section 8).

13 Inspect the outer surfaces of the cam followers for evidence of scoring or other damage. If a follower is in poor condition, it is probable that the bore in which it works is also damaged. Check for clearance between the followers and their bores. Whilst no specifications are given, if slack is excessive, renew the followers. If the bores are seriously out-of-round or tapered, the cylinder head and the followers must be renewed.

14 Using a precision straight-edge and a feeler gauge set to the warpage limit listed in the specifications at the beginning of the Chapter, check the head gasket mating surface for warpage. Refer to *Tools and Workshop Tips* in the Reference section for details of how to use the straight-edge.

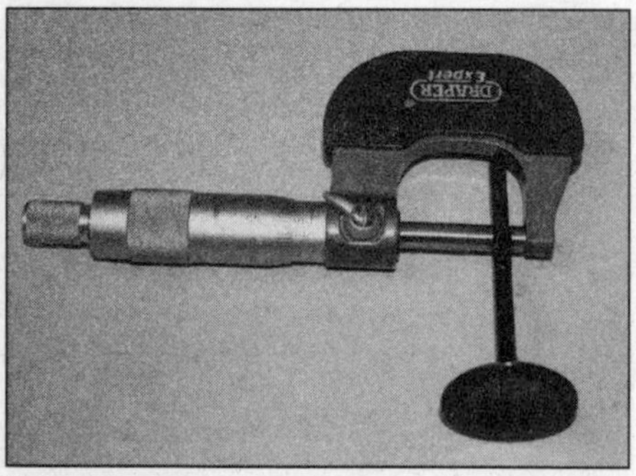

14.16b Measure the valve stem diameter with a micrometer . . .

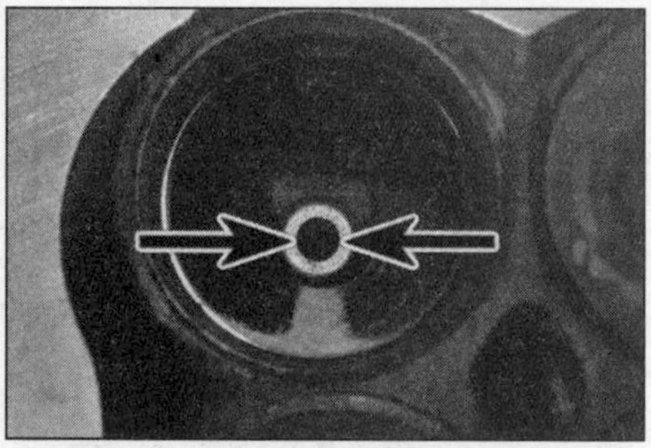

14.16c . . . then measure the guide bore using a small hole gauge, and measure the small hole gauge with a micrometer

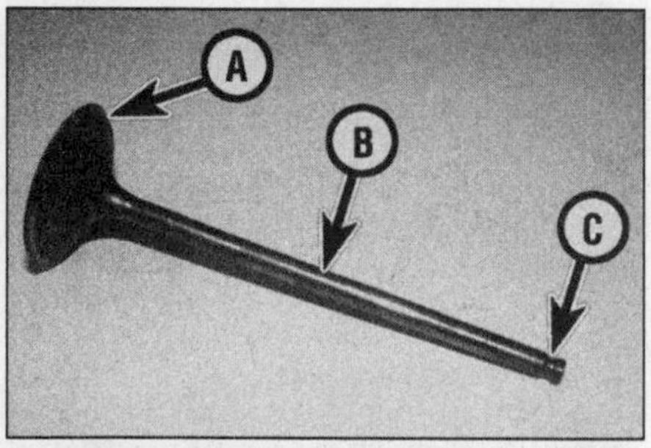

14.17a Check the valve face (A), stem (B) and collet groove (C) for signs of wear and damage

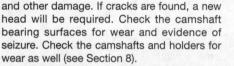

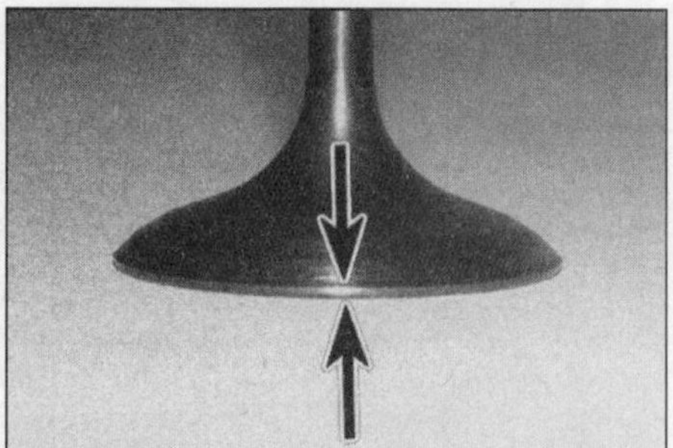

14.17b Measure the thickness of the valve head

15 Examine the valve seats in the combustion chamber. If they are pitted, cracked or burned, the head will require work beyond the scope of the home mechanic. Measure the valve seat width and compare it to this Chapter's Specifications **(see illustration)**. If it exceeds the service limit, or if it varies around its circumference, overhaul is required.

16 Clean the valve guides to remove any carbon build-up, then install each valve in its guide in turn so that its face is 10 mm above the seat. Mount a dial gauge against the side of the valve face and measure the amount of stem deflection (wobble) between the valve stem and its guide – you need to measure in two perpendicular directions, so take the first measurement, then relocate the dial gauge and take a second measurement **(see illustration)**. If the deflection exceeds the limit specified, remove the valve and measure the valve stem diameter **(see illustration)**. Also measure the inside diameter of the guide with a small hole gauge and micrometer **(see illustration)**. Measure the guide at the ends and at the centre to determine if they are worn in a bell-mouth pattern (more wear at the ends). Subtract the stem diameter from the valve guide diameter to obtain the valve stem-to-guide clearance. If the stem-to-guide clearance is greater than listed in this Chapter's Specifications, renew whichever component is worn beyond its specifications. If the valve guide is within specifications, but is worn unevenly, it should be renewed.

17 Carefully inspect each valve face, stem and collet groove area for cracks, pits and burned spots **(see illustration)**. Measure the thickness of the valve head and compare it to the specifications **(see illustration)**. If it is worn below the service limit renew the valve.

18 Rotate the valve and check for any

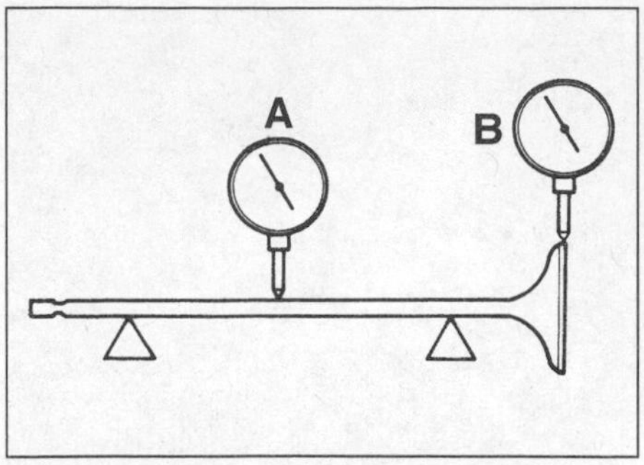

14.18 Measure the valve stem runout (A) and the valve head runout (B)

obvious indication that it is bent, in which case it must be renewed. Using V-blocks and a dial gauge, measure the valve stem runout and the valve head runout and compare the results to the specifications **(see illustration)**. If either measurement exceeds the service limit specified, the valve must be renewed.

19 Check the end of the stem for pitting and excessive wear. The stem end can be ground down, provided that the amount of stem above the collet groove after grinding is sufficient.

20 Check the end of each valve spring for wear and pitting. Measure the spring free lengths and compare them to the specifications **(see illustration)**. If any spring is shorter than specified it has sagged and must be renewed. Also place the spring upright on a flat surface and check it for bend by placing a ruler against it, or alternatively lay it against a set square **(see illustration)**. If the bend in any spring is excessive, it must be renewed. Always new the inner and outer springs as a set, never singly.

21 Check the spring seats, retainers and collets for obvious wear and cracks. Any questionable parts should not be reused, as extensive damage will occur in the event of failure during engine operation.

22 If the inspection indicates that no overhaul work is required, the valve components can be reinstalled in the head.

Reassembly

23 Unless a valve service has been performed, before installing the valves in the head they should be ground in (lapped) to ensure a positive seal between the valves and seats. This procedure requires coarse and fine valve grinding compound and a valve grinding tool (either hand-held or drill driven). If a grinding tool is not available, a piece of rubber or plastic hose can be slipped over the valve stem (after the valve has been installed in the guide) and used to turn the valve.

24 Apply a small amount of coarse grinding compound to the valve face, and some molybdenum disulphide oil (a 50/50 mixture of molybdenum disulphide grease and engine oil) to the valve stem, then slip the valve into the guide **(see illustrations)**. **Note:** *Make sure each valve is installed in its correct guide and be careful not to get any grinding compound on the valve stem.*

14.20a Measure the free length of the valve springs . . .

25 Attach the grinding tool (or hose) to the valve and rotate the tool between the palms of your hands. Use a back-and-forth motion (as though rubbing your hands together) rather than a circular motion (i.e. so that the valve rotates alternately clockwise and anti-clockwise rather than in one direction only) **(see illustration)**. If a motorised tool is being used, take note of the correct drive speed for it – if your drill runs too fast and is not variable, use a hand tool instead. Lift the valve off the seat and turn it at regular intervals to distribute the grinding compound properly. Continue the grinding procedure until the valve face and seat contact area is of uniform and correct width, and unbroken around the entire circumference **(see illustration 14.15)**.

26 Carefully remove the valve from the guide and wipe off all traces of grinding compound, making sure none gets in the guide. Use

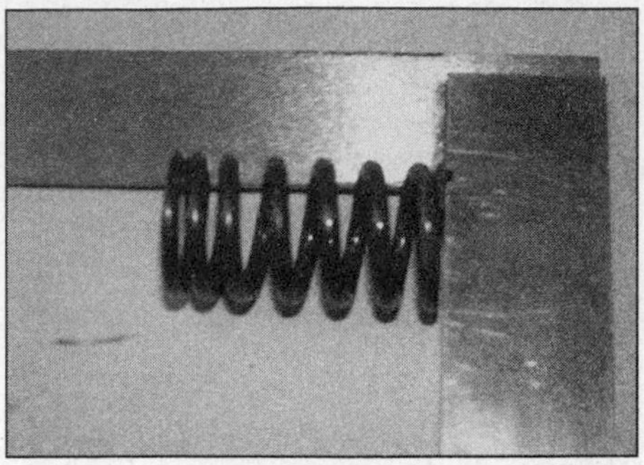

14.20b . . . and check them for squareness

solvent to clean the valve and wipe the seat area thoroughly with a solvent soaked cloth.

27 Repeat the procedure with fine valve grinding compound, then repeat the entire procedure for the remaining valves.

28 Working on one valve at a time, lay the spring seat in place in the cylinder head, making sure the shouldered side faces up – sliding the seat down a rod or screwdriver shaft helps to locate it around the top of the guide and prevents it getting skewed **(see illustration)**.

29 Fit a new valve stem seal onto the guide. Usually finger pressure is sufficient to get it to clip into place, otherwise use a stem seal fitting tool or an appropriate size deep socket to push the seal over the end of the valve guide until it is felt to clip into place **(see illustrations)**. Don't twist or cock the seal, or it will not seal properly against the valve stem. Also, don't remove it again or it will be damaged.

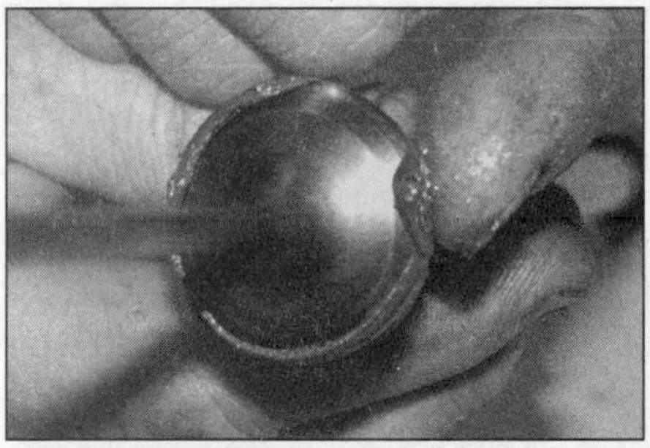

14.24a Apply the lapping compound very sparingly, in small dabs, to the valve face only

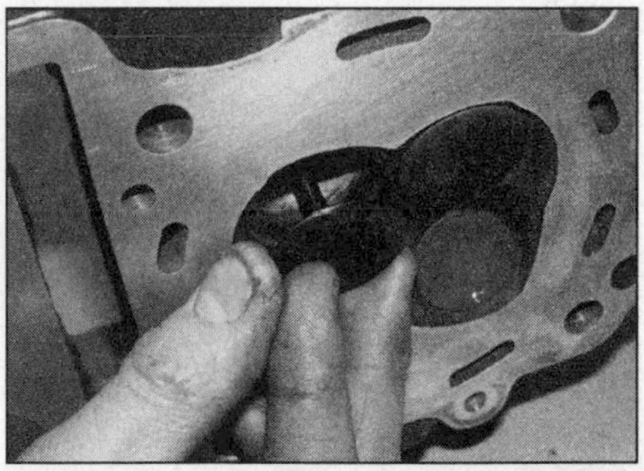

14.24b Lubricate the stem and insert the valve in the guide

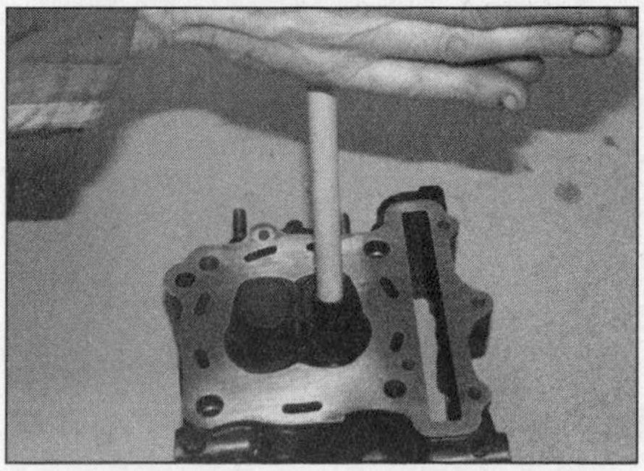

14.25 Rotate the valve grinding tool back and forth between the palms of your hands

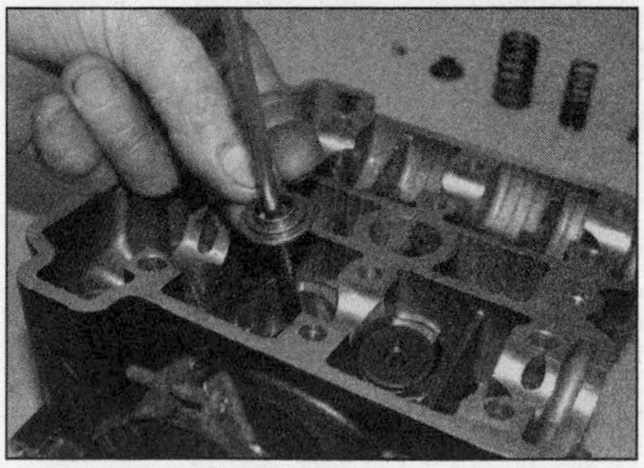

14.28 Fit the spring seat, making sure it is the correct way up

14.29a Fit a new valve stem seal . . .

14.29b . . . using either your finger, . . .

14.29c . . . a deep socket, or seal installation tool to press it squarely into place

14.31a Fit the valve springs . . .

14.31b . . . with their closely spaced coils facing downwards . . .

14.31c . . . then fit the spring retainer

30 Coat the valve stem with molybdenum disulphide oil (a 50/50 mixture of molybdenum disulphide grease and engine oil), then install it into its guide, rotating it slowly to avoid damaging the seal **(see illustration 14.24b)**. Check that the valve moves up and down freely in the guide.

31 Next, install the inner and outer springs, with the closer-wound coils facing down into the cylinder head **(see illustrations)**. Fit the spring retainer, with its shouldered side facing down so that it fits into the top of the springs **(see illustration)**.

32 Compress the valve spring with a spring compressor, making sure it is correctly located onto each end of the valve assembly (see Step 5) **(see illustrations 14.5a, b and c)**. Do not compress the springs any more than is necessary to slip the collets into place. Apply a small amount of grease to the collets to help hold them in place. Locate each collet in turn into the groove in the valve stem, then carefully release the compressor, making sure the collets seat and lock as you do **(see illustration 14.6a)**. Check that the collets are securely locked in the retaining groove.

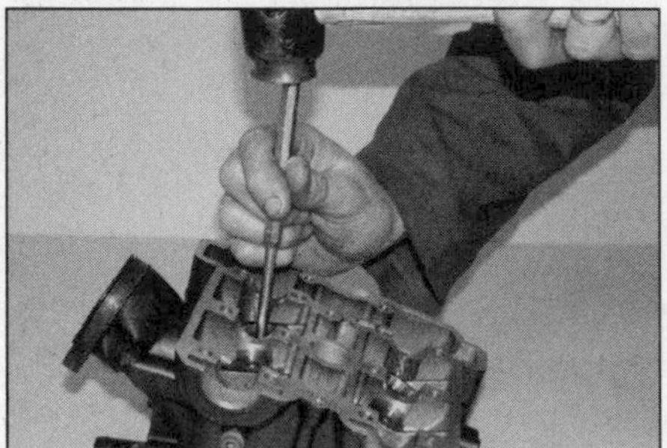

14.33 Tap the end of the valve stem to seat the collets

33 Support the cylinder head on blocks so the valves can't contact the workbench top, then very gently tap the top of the valve stem with a brass drift **(see illustration)**. This will help seat the collets in the groove. If you don't have a brass drift, fit the shim into its recess in the top of the valve spring retainer and use a soft-faced hammer and a piece of wood as an interface.

HAYNES HiNT ***Check for proper sealing of the valves by pouring a small amount of solvent into each of the valve ports. If the solvent leaks past any valve into the combustion chamber area the valve grinding operation on that valve should be repeated.***

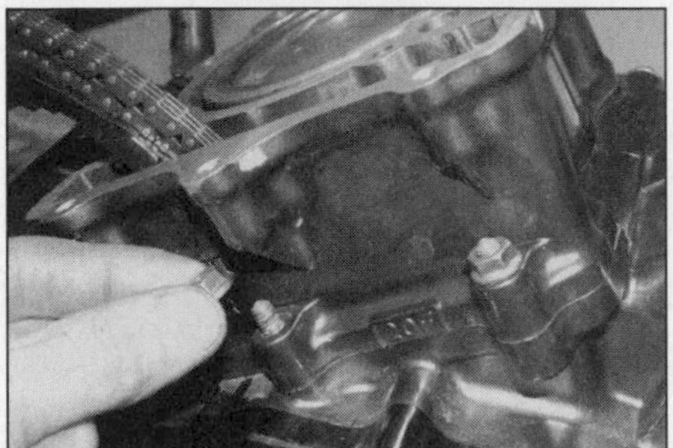

15.3 Unscrew and remove the two nuts

34 Repeat the procedure for the remaining valves. Remember to keep the parts for each valve together, and separate from the other valves, so they can be reinstalled in the same location. After the cylinder head and camshafts have been installed, check the valve clearances and adjust as required (see Chapter 1).

15 Cylinder blocks

Note: *The blocks can be removed with the engine in the frame. If the engine has been removed, ignore the steps that don't apply.*

Removal

1 Remove the cylinder head (see Section 12) and the cam chain guide blade (see Section 10).

2 On California, Austria and Switzerland X, Y, K1 and K2 models, detach the PAIR system hose from the pipe on the block. If required, unscrew the nuts securing the pipe to the block and remove it. Discard the gasket as a new one must be used.

3 Unscrew the two cylinder block nuts **(see illustration)**.

4 Hold the cam chain up and pull the cylinder block up off the crankcase, taking care not to allow the connecting rod to knock against the side of the crankcase once the piston is free, then pass the cam chain down through the tunnel and drape it over the tensioner blade **(see illustration)**. Do not let the chain fall into the crankcase – secure it with a piece of wire or metal bar to prevent it from doing so. If the block is stuck, tap around its base with a soft-faced mallet. Do not try to free it by inserting a screwdriver between the block and crankcase – you'll damage the surfaces. Note that each block is marked 'FRONT' or 'REAR' according to its location. After the block has been removed, stuff clean rags around the piston to prevent anything falling into the crankcase.

5 Remove the old gasket **(see illustration 15.21)**. Pull the oil jet out of the crankcase using a small screwdriver, taking great care not to drop it into the crankcase – make sure the rag covers the hole completely **(see illustration)**. Remove the O-ring and discard it **(see illustration 15.19)**.

6 If they are loose, remove the two dowels from the cylinder block or crankcase **(see illustration 15.21)**.

7 Check the base gasket and the mating surfaces on the cylinder head and block for signs of leakage, which could indicate warpage. Refer below and check the block.

8 Clean all traces of old gasket material from the cylinder block and crankcase. If a scraper is used, take care not to scratch or gouge the soft aluminium. Be careful not to let any of the gasket material drop into the crankcase or the oil passages.

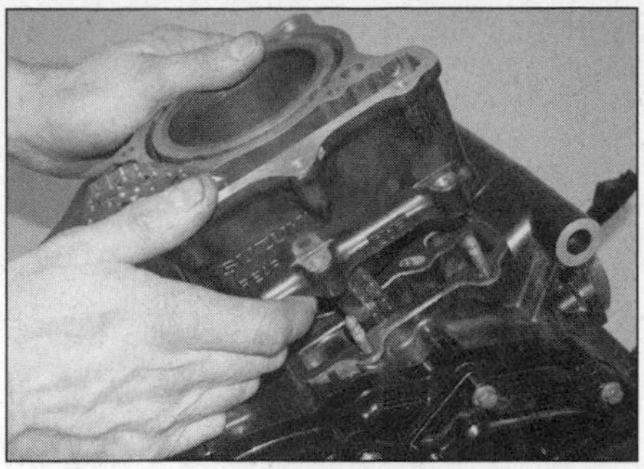

15.4 Lift the block up off the crankcase and remove it

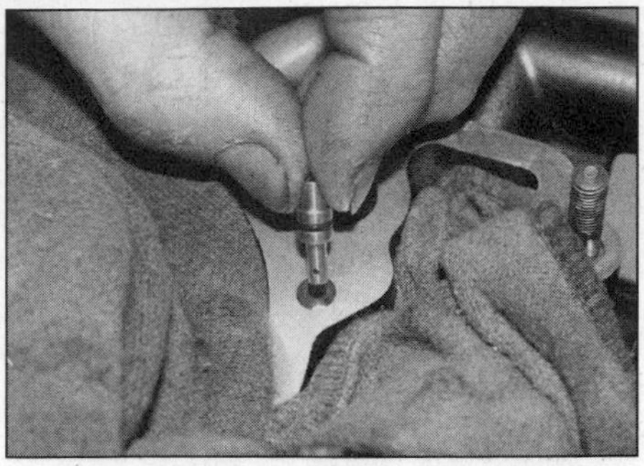

15.5 Pull the oil jet out of its orifice

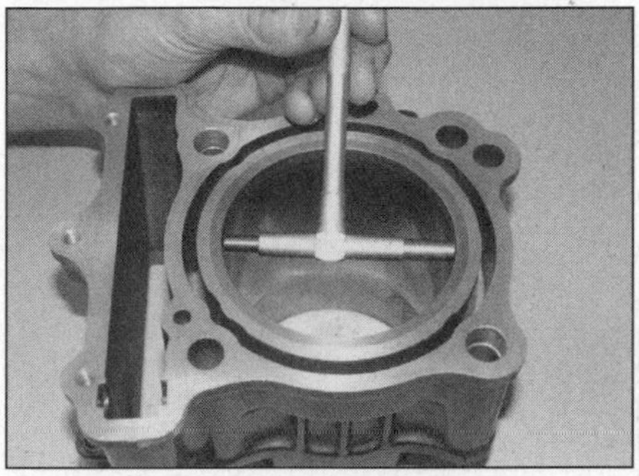

15.12a Use a bore gauge . . .

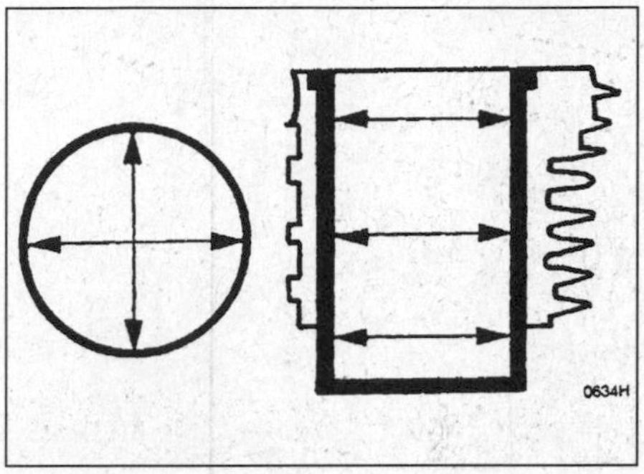

15.12b . . . and measure at the points shown

Inspection

9 Do not attempt to separate the liner from the cylinder block.

10 Check the bore walls carefully for scratches and score marks.

11 Using a precision straight-edge and a feeler gauge set to the warpage limit listed in the specifications at the beginning of the Chapter, check the top mating surface of the cylinder for warpage. Refer to *Tools and Workshop Tips* in the Reference section for details of how to use the straight-edge. If warpage is excessive the cylinder must be renewed.

12 Using a telescoping bore gauge and a micrometer (see *Tools and Workshop Tips*), check the dimensions of each bore to assess the amount of wear, taper and ovality. Measure near the top (but below the level of the top piston ring at TDC), centre and bottom (but above the level of the oil ring at BDC) of the bore, both parallel to and across the crankshaft axis **(see illustrations)**. Compare the results to the specifications at the beginning of the Chapter. If the bores are worn, oval or tapered beyond the service limit they can be rebored, and an oversize (see Specifications) set of pistons and rings are available from Suzuki. Note that the person carrying out the rebore must be aware of the piston-to-bore clearance for the oversize piston (see Specifications).

13 If the precision measuring tools are not available, take the cylinders to a Suzuki dealer or specialist motorcycle repair shop for assessment and advice.

14 If the cylinder bores are in good condition and the piston-to-bore clearance is within specifications (see Section 16), the bores should be honed (de-glazed). To perform this operation you will need the proper size flexible hone with fine stones, or a bottle-brush type hone, plenty of light oil or honing oil, some clean rags and an electric drill motor.

15 Hold the cylinder sideways (so that the bore is horizontal rather than vertical) in a vice with soft jaws or cushioned with wooden blocks. Mount the hone in the drill motor, compress the stones and insert the hone into the bore. Thoroughly lubricate the cylinder walls, then turn on the drill and move the hone up and down in the bore at a pace which produces a fine cross-hatch pattern on the cylinder wall with the lines intersecting at an angle of approximately 60°. Be sure to use plenty of lubricant and do not take off any more material than is necessary to produce the desired effect. Do not withdraw the hone from the cylinder while it is still turning. Switch off the drill and continue to move it up and down in the cylinder until it has stopped turning, then compress the stones and withdraw the hone. Wipe the oil from the cylinder and repeat the procedure on the other one. Remember, do not take too much material from the cylinder wall.

16 Wash the bores thoroughly with warm soapy water to remove all traces of the abrasive grit produced during the honing operation. Be sure to run a brush through the stud holes and flush them with running water. After rinsing, dry the cylinders thoroughly and apply a thin coat of light, rust-preventative oil to all machined surfaces.

17 If you do not have the equipment or desire to perform the honing operation, take the cylinders to a Suzuki dealer or specialist motorcycle repair shop.

Installation

18 Check that the mating surfaces of the cylinder and crankcase are free from oil or pieces of old gasket.

19 Clean the oil jet with solvent and blow it through with compressed air if available. Fit a new O-ring onto the jet, then press it into the passage in the crankcase, making sure the slotted end is at the top **(see illustration and 15.5)**. **Note:** *On K5-on models, an oil jet is fitted behind the cam chain tensioner location – use the same procedure to ensure this jet is clear.*

20 If removed, fit the dowels into the crankcase or into the block, and push them firmly home **(see illustration 15.21)**.

21 Remove the rags from around the piston, taking care not to let the connecting rod fall against the rim of the crankcase, and lay the new base gasket in place, locating it over the dowels

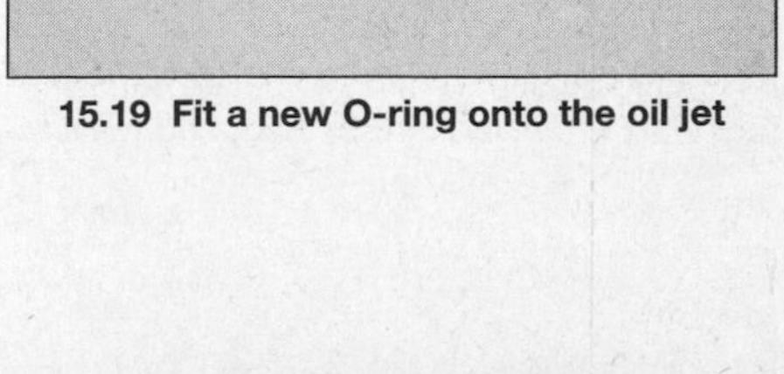

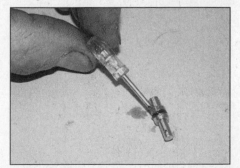

15.19 Fit a new O-ring onto the oil jet

15.21 Fit the two dowels (arrowed) and locate the new gasket over them

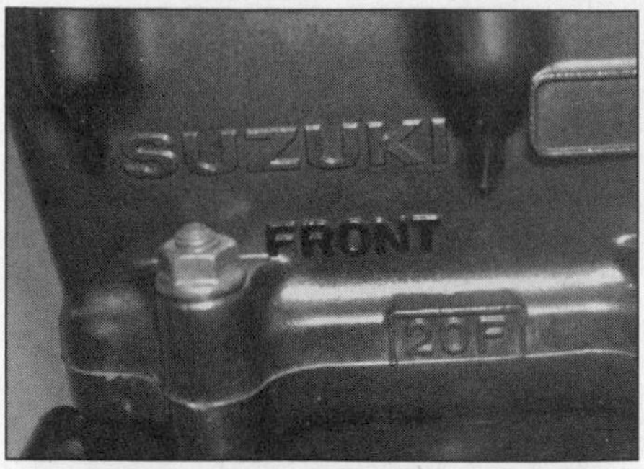

15.23a Make sure you have the correct cylinder

15.23b Lubricate the pistons, rings and bore with new oil

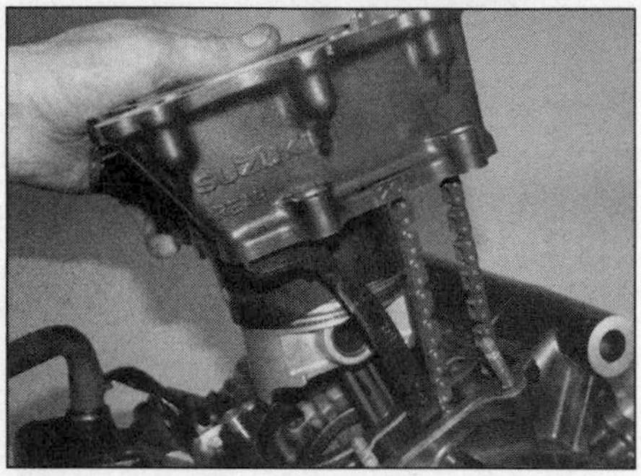

15.24 Carefully lower the block onto the piston . . .

15.25 . . . feeding the piston rings into the bore

(if they are in the crankcase) **(see illustration)**. The gasket can only fit one way, so if all the holes do not line up properly it is either the wrong way round or is not the correct gasket for that cylinder (the front and rear cylinder gaskets are different). Never re-use the old gasket.

22 Ensure the piston ring end gaps are positioned correctly before fitting the cylinder block. If required, fit a piston ring compressor onto the piston to ease its entry into the bore as the cylinder is lowered. This is not essential as there is a good lead-in, enabling the piston rings to be hand-fed into the bore. If possible, have an assistant support the cylinder while this is done.

23 Rotate the crankshaft so that the piston is at its highest point (top dead centre). It is useful to place a support under the piston so that it remains at TDC while the block is fitted, otherwise the downward pressure will turn the crankshaft and the piston will drop. Make sure you have the correct block for the cylinder being worked on – they are marked 'FRONT' and 'REAR' **(see illustration)**. Lubricate the cylinder bore, piston and piston rings with clean engine oil **(see illustration)**.

24 Carefully lower the block onto the piston until the crown fits into the bore, feeding the cam chain up the tunnel as you do so **(see illustration)**. It is helpful to have an assistant to pass the chain up and slip a piece of wire through it to prevent it falling back into the engine. Keep the chain taut to prevent it becoming disengaged from the crankshaft sprocket.

25 Gently push the cylinder down, holding the underside of the piston if you are not using a support to prevent it dropping, and making sure it enters the bore squarely and does not get cocked sideways. If you are doing this without a piston ring compressor, carefully compress and feed each ring into the bore as the cylinder is lowered **(see illustration)**. Do not use force if it appears to be stuck as the piston and/or rings will be damaged. If a compressor was used, remove it once the rings are in the bore.

26 When the piston crown and rings are correctly installed in the bore, remove the support if used then press the cylinder down onto the base gasket, making sure the dowels locate.

27 Fit the two cylinder block nuts and tighten them finger-tight only at this stage **(see illustration 15.3)**.

28 When both blocks are installed, turn the crankshaft (keeping the cam chain taut) and check that everything moves as it should.

29 On California, Austria and Switzerland models, if removed, install the PAIR system pipe using a new gasket and tighten the nuts securely. Connect the hose to the pipe and secure it with its clamp.

30 Install the cam chain guide blade (see Section 10) and the cylinder head (see Section 12).

16 Pistons

Note: *The pistons can be removed with the engine in the frame.*

Removal

1 Remove the cylinder block(s) (see Section 15).

2 Before removing the piston(s) from the connecting rod(s), use a sharp scriber or felt marker pen to write the cylinder identity on the crown of each piston (or on the inside of the skirt if the piston is dirty and going to be cleaned). Each piston crown should already have a circular indent on the crown that faces the exhaust side of the cylinder, though the mark may not be visible until the piston is cleaned **(see illustration)**. Stuff clean rag around the connecting rod to prevent a dropped circlip falling into the crankcase.

3 Carefully prise out the circlip on one side of the piston using needle-nose pliers or a small flat-bladed screwdriver inserted into the notch **(see illustration)**. Push the piston pin out from the other side to free the piston from the connecting rod **(see illustration)**. Remove the other circlip and discard them both as new

16.2 Note the mark on the piston which faces the exhaust side

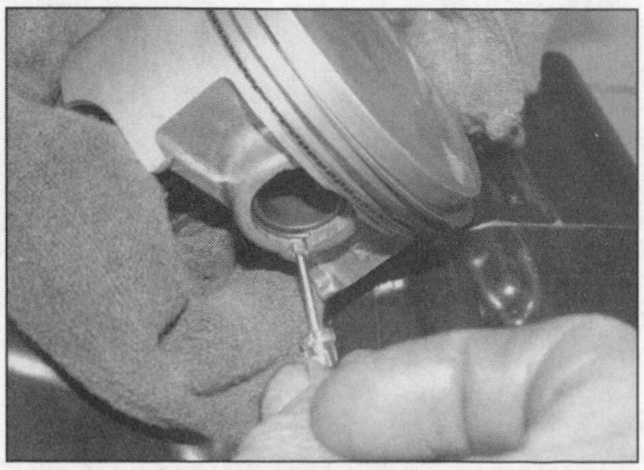

16.3a Prise the circlip out from one side of the piston

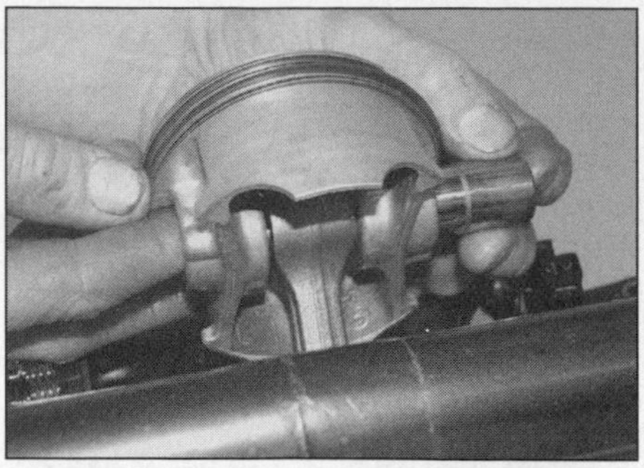

16.3b Push the piston pin out from the other side then withdraw it and remove the piston

HAYNES HiNT

If a piston pin is a tight fit in the piston bosses, soak a rag in boiling water then wring it out and wrap it around the piston – this will expand the alloy piston sufficiently to release its grip on the pin. If the piston pin is particularly stubborn, extract it using a drawbolt tool, but be careful to protect the piston's working surfaces.

ones must be used. When the piston has been removed, slide its pin back into its bore so that related parts do not get mixed up.

Inspection

4 Using your thumbs or a piston ring removal and installation tool, carefully remove the rings from the pistons **(see illustrations 17.12, 11b, and 9c, b and a)**. Do not nick or gouge the pistons in the process. Carefully note which way up each ring fits and in which groove as they must be installed in their original positions if being re-used. The upper surface of the top ring should be marked with the letter R at one end, and the second (middle) ring marked RN. The top and middle rings can also be identified by their different profiles and thickness **(see illustration 17.11a)**.

5 Scrape all traces of carbon from the tops of the pistons. A hand-held wire brush or a piece of fine emery cloth can be used once most of the deposits have been scraped away. Do not, under any circumstances, use a wire brush mounted in a drill motor to remove deposits from the pistons; the piston material is soft and will be eroded away by the wire brush.

6 Use a piston ring groove cleaning tool to remove any carbon deposits from the ring grooves. If a tool is not available, a piece broken off an old ring will do the job. Be very careful to remove only the carbon deposits. Do not remove any metal and do not nick or gouge the sides of the ring grooves.

7 Once the deposits have been removed, clean the pistons with solvent and dry them thoroughly. If the identification previously marked on the piston is cleaned off, be sure to re-mark it with the correct identity. Make sure the oil return holes below the oil ring groove are clear.

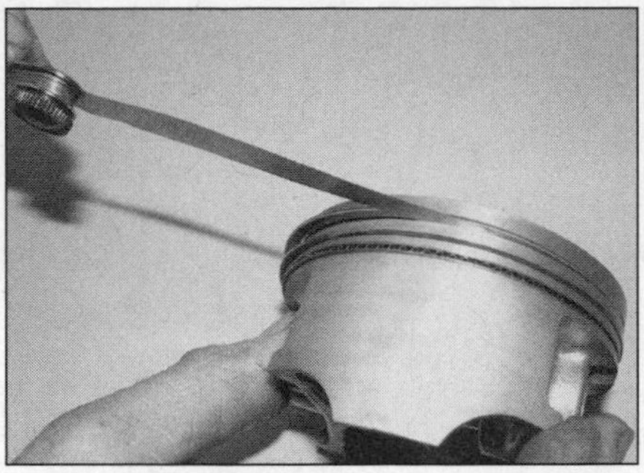

16.10a Either fit the ring into the groove and measure clearance with a feeler gauge . . .

8 Carefully inspect each piston for cracks around the skirt, at the pin bosses and at the ring lands. Normal piston wear appears as even, vertical wear on the thrust surfaces of the piston and slight looseness of the top ring in its groove. If the skirt is scored or scuffed, the engine may have been suffering from overheating and/or abnormal combustion, which caused excessively high operating temperatures. The oil pump should be checked thoroughly. Also check that the circlip grooves are not damaged.

9 A hole in the piston crown, an extreme to be sure, is an indication that abnormal combustion (pre-ignition) was occurring. Burned areas at the edge of the piston crown are usually evidence of spark knock (detonation). If any of the above problems exist, the causes must be corrected or the damage will occur again.

10 Measure the piston ring-to-groove clearance, either by laying each piston ring in its groove and slipping a feeler gauge in beside it, or by measuring the thickness of the ring and the width of the groove and subtracting one from the other **(see illustrations)**. Make sure you have the correct ring for the groove (see Step 4). Check the clearance at three or four locations around the groove. If the clearance is greater than specified, renew both the piston and rings as a set. If new rings are being used anyway, measure the clearance using the new rings. If the clearance is greater than that specified, the piston is worn and must be renewed. Models from the K7 onwards use a stepped top ring, for which two dimensions are given in the Specifications for ring thickness and ring groove width **(see illustration)**.

11 Check the piston-to-bore clearance by measuring the bore (see Section 15) and the piston diameter. Make sure each piston is matched to its correct cylinder. Measure the piston 20 mm up from the bottom of the skirt and at 90° to the piston pin axis **(see illustration)**. Subtract the piston diameter from the bore diameter to obtain the clearance. If it is greater than the specified figure, and if not already done, check the cylinder for wear (see Section 15). If the cylinder is good but the piston is worn, renew the piston. If the cylinder is worn it can be rebored, and then oversize pistons and rings, available from Suzuki, can be fitted.

12 Apply clean engine oil to the piston pin, insert it into the piston and check for any freeplay between the two **(see illustration)**. Measure the pin external diameter and the

16.10b . . . or by measuring the ring width and the groove width and calculating the difference

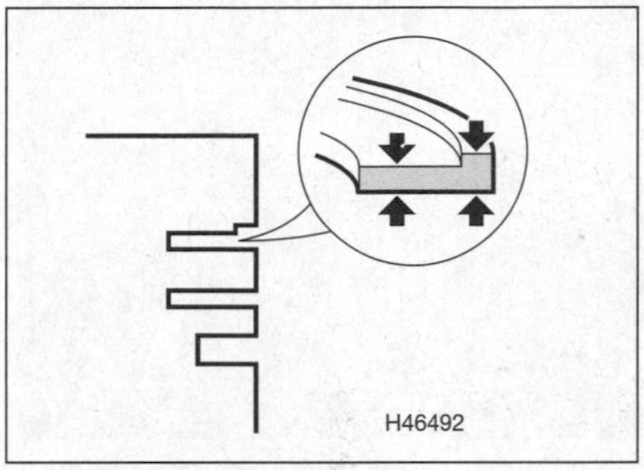

16.10c Note the stepped ring and ring groove profile on K7-on models

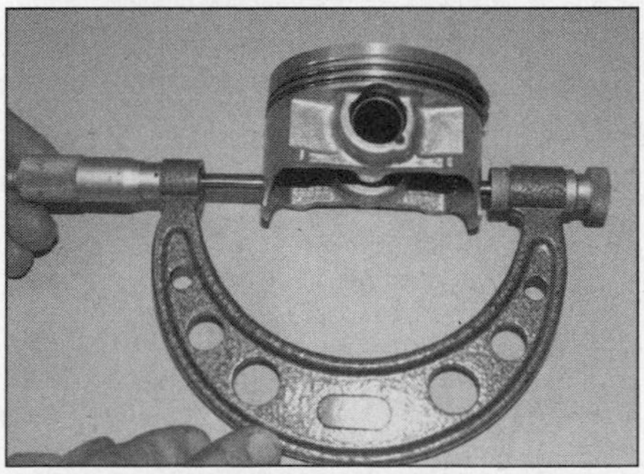

16.11 Measure the piston diameter with a micrometer

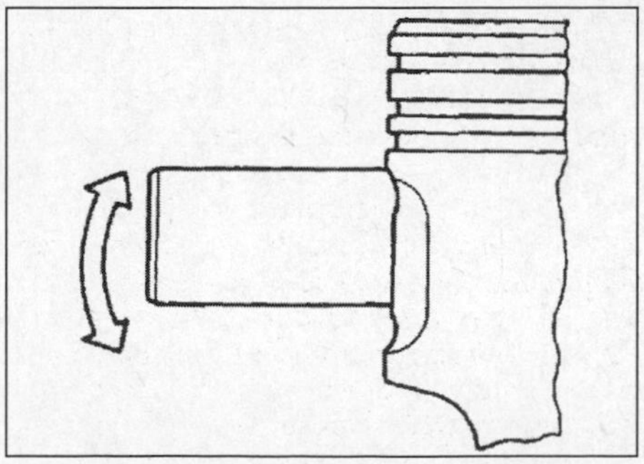

16.12a Slip the pin into the piston and check for freeplay between them

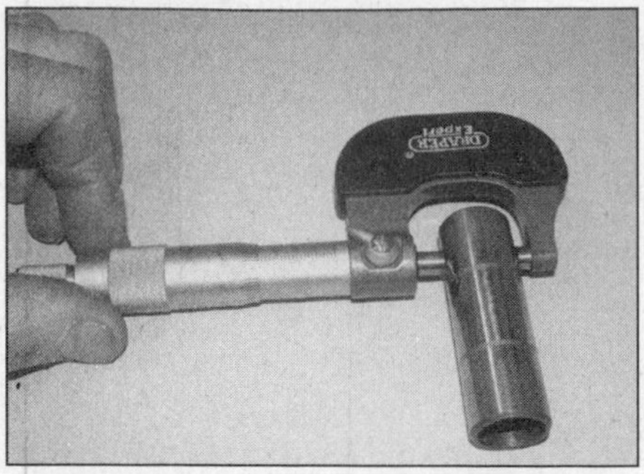

16.12b Measure the external diameter of the pin . . .

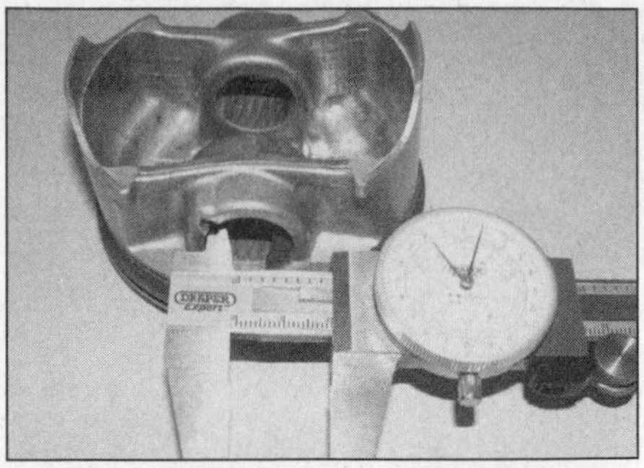

16.12c . . . and the internal diameter of the bore in the piston

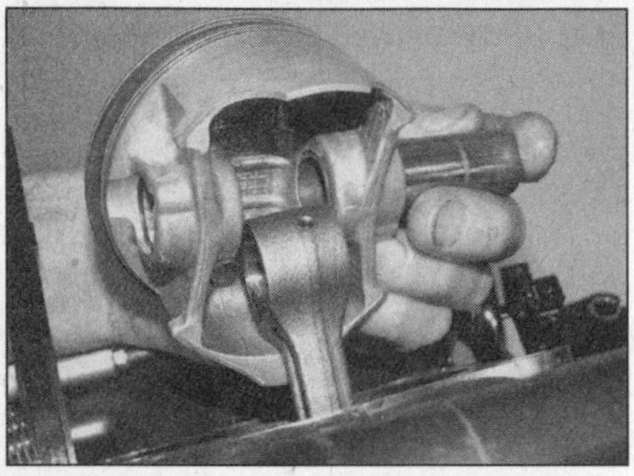

16.16a Slide the pin through the piston and connecting rod . . .

16.16b . . . and secure it with the circlip, locating the open end away from the notch in the piston

pin bore in the piston **(see illustrations)**. Calculate the difference to obtain the piston pin-to-piston pin bore clearance. Compare the result to the specifications at the beginning of the Chapter. If the clearance is greater than specified, renew the components that are worn beyond their specified limits. If not already done, repeat the measurements between the pin and the connecting rod small-end (see Section 28) **(see illustration 28.7)**.

Installation

13 Inspect and install the piston rings (see Section 17).

14 Lubricate the piston pin, the piston pin bore and the connecting rod small-end bore with molybdenum disulphide oil (a 50/50 mixture of molybdenum disulphide grease and clean engine oil).

15 When installing the pistons onto the connecting rods, make sure you have the correct piston for the cylinder being worked on. Note that the small circular indent on the piston crown faces the exhaust side of the cylinder **(see illustration 16.2)**.

16 Stuff clean rag around the connecting rod to prevent a dropped circlip falling into the crankcase. Install a ***new*** circlip in one side of the piston (do not re-use old circlips). Line up the piston on its correct connecting rod, and insert the piston pin from the other side **(see illustration)**. Secure the pin with the other ***new*** circlip **(see illustration)**. When installing the circlips, compress them only just enough to fit them in the piston, and make sure they are properly seated in their grooves with the open end away from the removal notch. Remove the rag the crankcase.

17 Install the cylinder block(s) (see Section 15).

17 Piston rings

1 It is good practice to renew the piston rings when an engine is being overhauled. Before installing the rings (new or old), check the free and installed end gaps of the top and second (middle) rings as follows.

2 If new rings are being used, lay out each piston with a new ring set and keep them together so the rings will be matched with the same piston and bore during the end gap measurement procedure and engine assembly. If the old rings are being reused, make sure they are matched with their correct piston and cylinder.

3 With the ring flat on the work surface, measure its end gap using a Vernier caliper **(see illustration)**. To measure the installed ring end gap, insert the ring into the top of the bore and square it up with the bore walls by pushing it in with the top of the piston **(see illustration)**. The ring should be about 20 mm below the top edge of the bore. Slip a feeler gauge between the ends of the ring and measure the gap. Compare the measurements to the specifications at the beginning of the Chapter **(see illustration)**.

4 If the gap is larger or smaller than specified, double check to make sure that you have the correct rings before proceeding.

5 If the gap is too small, the ring ends may come in contact with each other during engine operation, which can cause serious damage.

6 Excess end gap is not critical unless it exceeds the service limit. Again, double-check to make sure you have the correct rings for your engine and check that the bore is not worn (see Section 15).

7 Repeat the procedure for the other ring. Remember to keep the rings, pistons and bores matched up.

8 Once the ring end gaps have been checked, the rings can be installed on the pistons.

9 Install the oil control ring (lowest on the piston) first. It is composed of three separate components, namely the expander and the upper and lower side rails. Slip the expander into the groove, making sure the ends don't overlap, then install the lower side rail

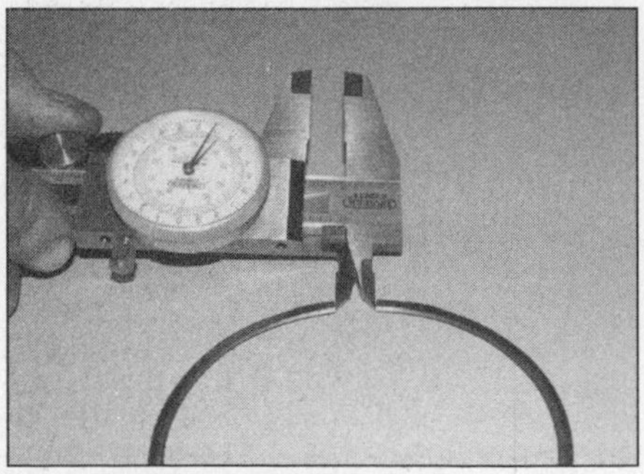

17.3a Measure the free end gap of the piston ring . . .

17.3b . . . then fit the ring into the bore and square it up with the piston . . .

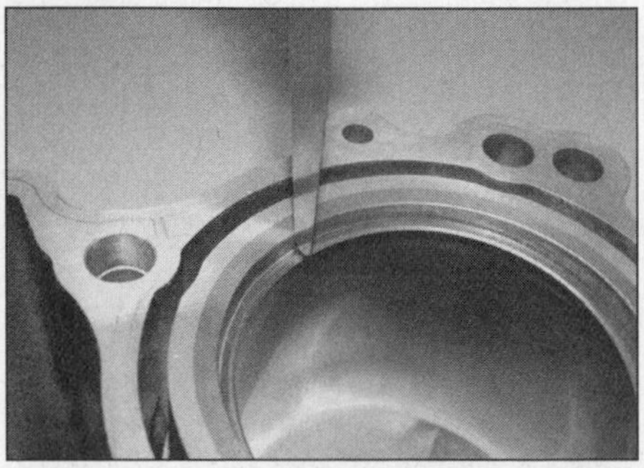

17.3c . . . and measure the installed end gap

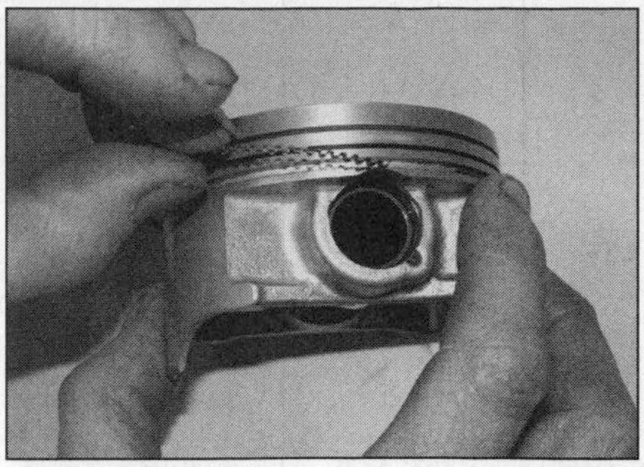

17.9a Install the oil ring expander in its groove . . .

(see illustrations). Do not use a piston ring installation tool on the side rails as they may be damaged. Instead, place one end of the side rail into the groove between the expander and the ring land. Hold it firmly in place and slide a finger around the piston while pushing the rail into the groove. Next, install the upper side rail in the same manner **(see illustration)**. Check that the ends of the expander have not overlapped.

10 After the three oil ring components have been installed, check to make sure that both the upper and lower side rails can be turned smoothly in the ring groove.

11 The upper surface of the top ring is marked with the letter R at one end, and the second (middle) ring is marked RN **(see illustration)**. The top and middle rings can also be identified by their different profiles and thicknesses. Install the second (middle) ring next. Make sure that the identification letter near the end gap is facing up, and the wider edge is at the bottom, as shown in the illustration of the profile. Fit the 2nd ring into the middle groove in the piston **(see illustration)**. Do not expand the ring any more than is necessary to slide it into place. To avoid breaking the ring, use a piston ring installation tool, or alternatively a feeler gauge blade can be used as shown.

12 Finally, install the top ring in the same manner into the top groove in the piston **(see illustration)**. Make sure the identification letter near the end gap is facing up.

13 Once the rings are correctly installed, check they move freely without snagging and stagger their end gaps as shown **(see illustration)**.

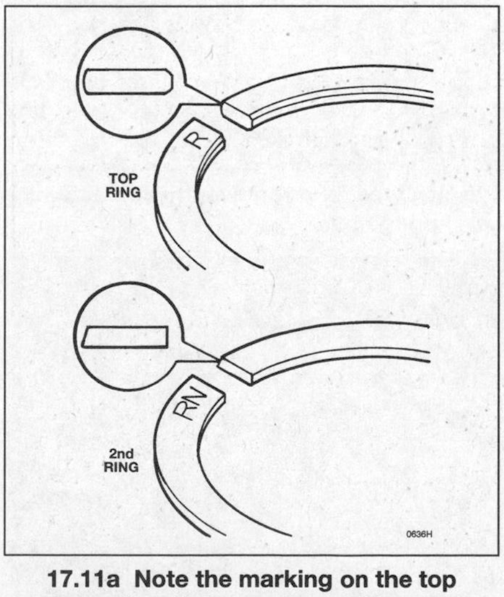

17.11a Note the marking on the top surface of each ring and the different ring profiles

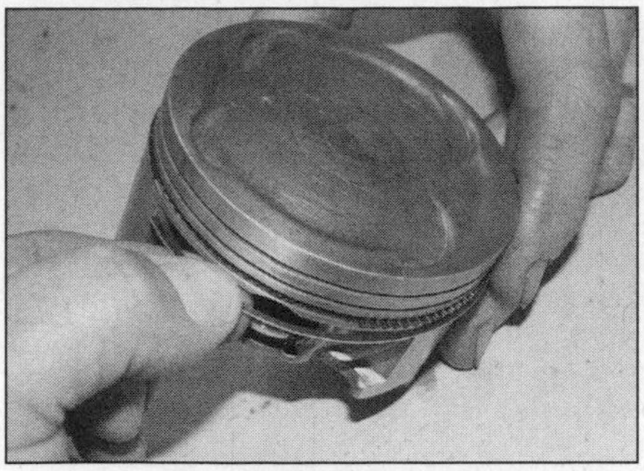

17.9b . . . then fit the lower side rail . . .

17.11b Fit the middle ring into its groove . . .

18 Clutch

Note: *The clutch can be removed with the engine in the frame. If the engine has already been removed, ignore the preliminary steps which don't apply.*

Removal

1 Drain the engine oil (see Chapter 1). On K3-on models, drain the cooling system (see Chapter 3)

2 On X, Y, K1 and K2 models, a separate clutch cover and crankcase cover are fitted. Working in a criss-cross pattern, unscrew the clutch cover bolts, noting the position of the wiring clamp, and lift the cover away from the engine, being prepared to catch any residual oil **(see illustration).** If required, the crankcase cover can be removed instead of the clutch cover to give better access to the clutch, but this means draining the cooling system as the water pump is integral with the cover. If the engine is being fully stripped, or if you need more access, or if you are removing the clutch to access the gearchange mechanism, oil pump or primary drive gear, refer to Chapter 3 and remove the crankcase cover and water pump, leaving the clutch cover attached to it. There is no need to separate the water pump from the cover after removal.

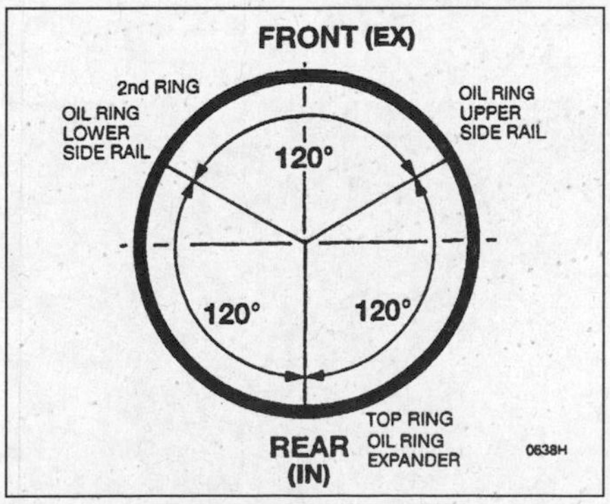

17.13 Arrange the ring end gaps as shown

17.9c . . . and the upper side rail

17.12 . . . then fit the top ring

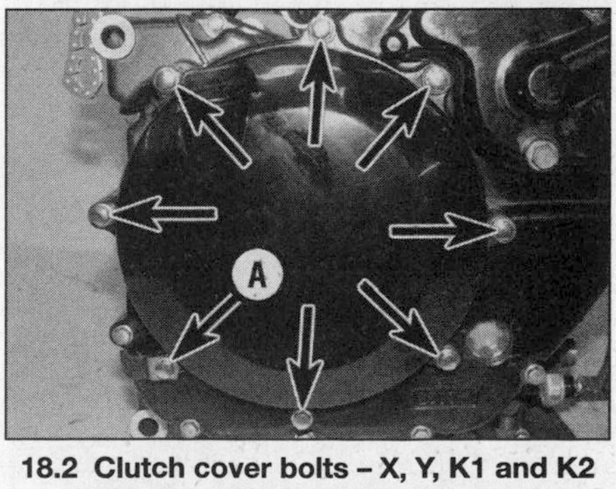

18.2 Clutch cover bolts – X, Y, K1 and K2 models. Note the location of the wiring clamp (A)

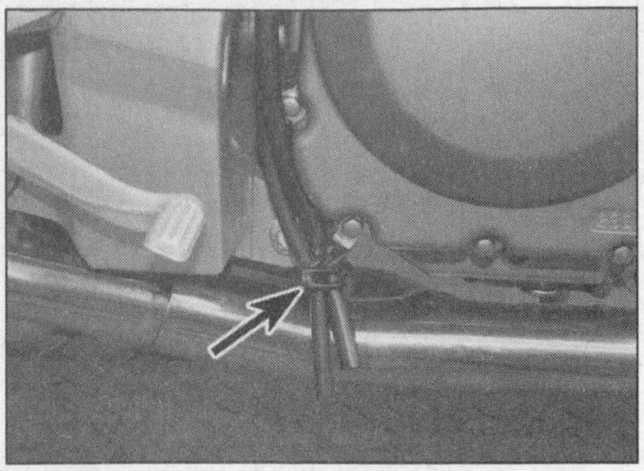

18.3a Release the drain hoses (arrowed) at the back . . .

18.3b . . . and front of the engine

3 On K3-on models, a one-piece crankcase cover is fitted with the water pump bolted to it. Slacken the clamps securing the coolant hoses to the water pump and detach the hoses (see Chapter 3). Release the drain hoses from the clips **(see illustrations)**. Working in a criss-cross pattern, unscrew the cover bolts, noting the position of the hose clip, and lift the cover away from the engine together with the water pump, being prepared to catch any residual oil **(see illustration)**. Note the location of the two dowels and remove them for safekeeping if they are loose.

4 Working in a criss-cross pattern, gradually slacken the clutch pressure plate bolts until spring pressure is released, then remove the bolts, collars, springs and the pressure plate **(see illustrations)**. Withdraw the pressure plate lifter, noting the thrust washer and bearing **(see illustration)**. If the clutch release mechanism has been displaced from the left-hand side of the engine, push the pushrod into the input shaft and withdraw it from the right-hand end **(see illustration)**. Do not withdraw it from the left-hand side as it has a larger diameter knurled section on the right-hand end which could easily damage the oil seal. If the release mechanism is in place, pull the clutch lever in to push the rod as far into the shaft as possible and remove it from the right-hand end of the shaft, using a magnet or hooked piece of wire to draw it out.

5 Grasp the complete set of clutch plates and remove them as a pack **(see illustration)**. Alternatively, remove the plates one by one, keeping them in order, using a bent piece of wire to hook them out where necessary. Unless the plates are being renewed, keep them assembled in their original order. Note that on X, Y, K1 and K2 models, there are two types of friction plate, identified as A and B – the innermost (type B) plate has rubber bands fitted round four of the tabs and is slightly thicker than the type A plates. **Do not** remove the bands from the tabs. On K3-on models, the innermost friction plate is not as wide as the others so that it will fit over the anti-judder spring assembly; remove the anti-judder spring, noting which way round it fits, and the spring seat.

6 Bend down the clutch nut lock washer tab away from the nut **(see illustration)**. To remove the clutch nut the transmission input shaft must be locked. This can be done in several ways. If the engine is in the frame, engage 5th gear and have an assistant hold the rear brake on hard with the rear tyre in firm contact with the ground. Alternatively, the Suzuki service tool (Pt. No. 09920-53740) or a commercially available or home-made equivalent (see ***Tool tip***) can be used to stop the clutch centre from turning whilst the nut is slackened **(see illustration)**. With the shaft locked, unscrew the clutch nut and remove the lockwasher. Discard the washer as a new one must be used.

7 Slide the clutch centre off the shaft **(see illustration 18.25)**.

8 Slide the thrust washer off the shaft **(see illustration 18.24)**.

9 Slide the clutch housing off the shaft, noting

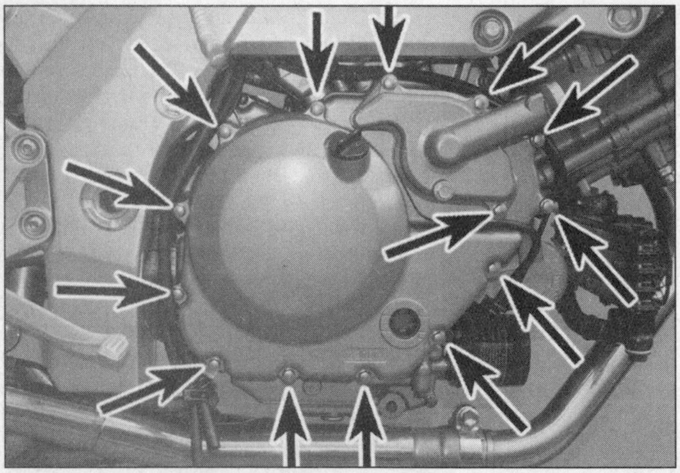

18.3c Clutch cover bolts – K3-on models

18.4a Unscrew the bolts (arrowed) and remove the collars and springs . . .

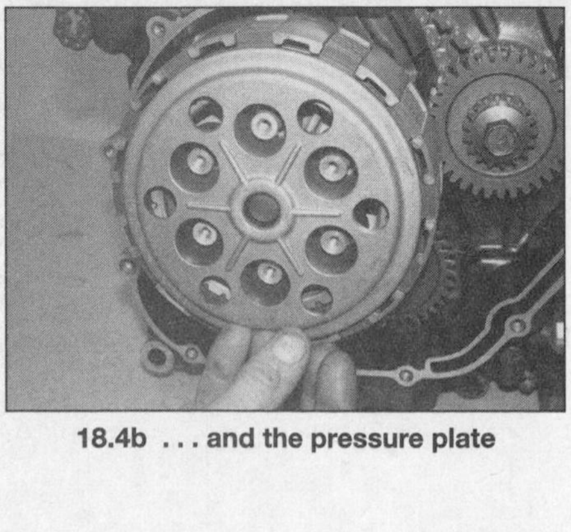

18.4b . . . and the pressure plate

18.4c Withdraw the pressure plate lifter . . .

18.4d . . . and the pushrod

18.5 Remove the clutch plates as a pack

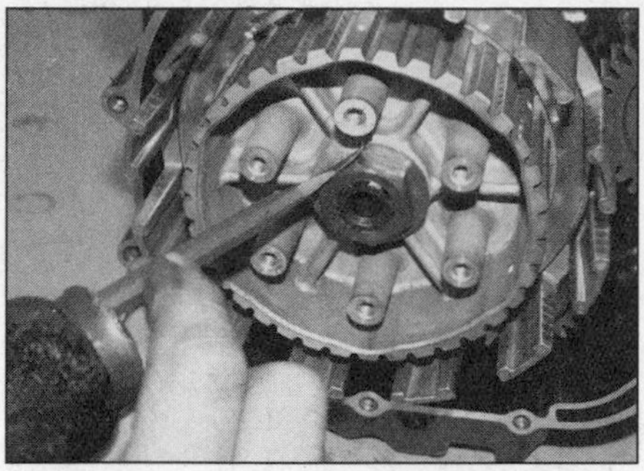
18.6a Release the lockwasher tab from the clutch nut . . .

18.6b . . . then unscrew it as described – here a commercially available holding tool is being used

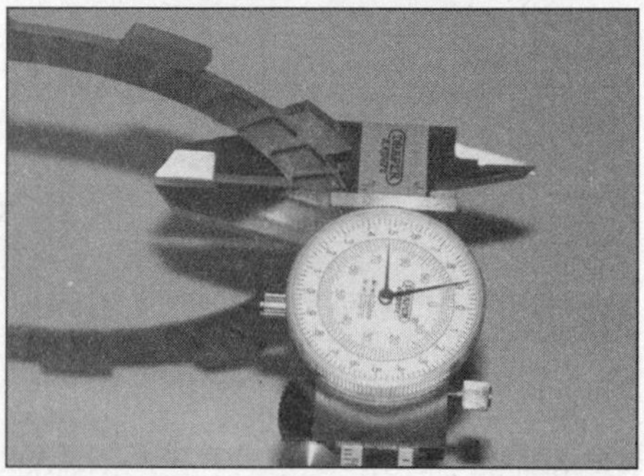
18.11 Measure the thickness of the friction plates . . .

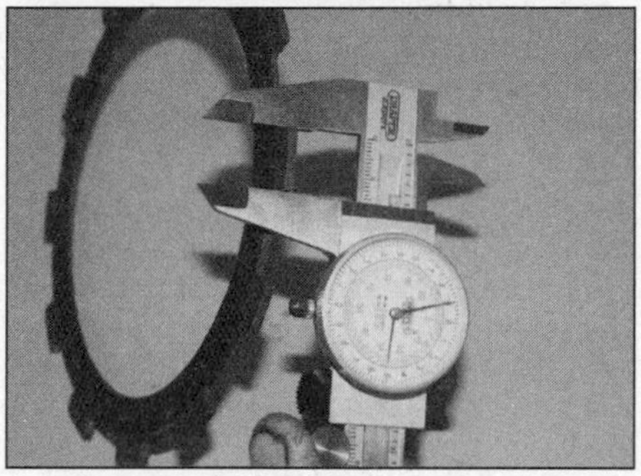
18.12 . . . and the width of the tabs

18.13 Check the plain plates for warpage

that you may have to prevent the spacer in the centre of the housing from sliding with it by pressing on its rim using a very small screwdriver **(see illustration 18.23a)**.

10 On X and Y models, slide the spacer off the shaft, followed by the thrust washer **(see illustrations 18.22b and a)**. On K1 models onwards, slide the shouldered spacer off the shaft.

Inspection

11 After an extended period of service the clutch friction plates will wear and promote clutch slip. Measure the thickness of each friction plate using a Vernier caliper **(see illustration)**. If any plate has worn to or beyond the service limit given in the Specifications at the beginning of the Chapter, the friction plates must be renewed as a set. Also, if any of the plates smell burnt or are glazed, they must be renewed as a set. Note that on X, Y, K1 and K2 models, the type B friction plate (the innermost plate) is thicker than the other six friction plates – ensure the correct dimensions are referred to in the Specifications.

12 Also measure the width of the friction plate tabs **(see illustration)** and renew any plates that are worn beyond the service limit specified.

13 The plain plates should not show any signs of excess heating (bluing). Check for warpage using a flat surface and feeler gauges **(see illustration)**. If any plate exceeds the maximum amount of warpage, or shows signs of bluing, all plain plates must be renewed as a set.

14 Measure the free length of each clutch spring using a Vernier caliper **(see illustration)**. If any spring is below the service limit specified, renew all the springs as a set. Also place the spring upright on a flat surface and check it for bend by placing a ruler against it, or alternatively lay it against a set square **(see illustration)**. If the bend in any spring is excessive, all six springs must be renewed.

15 On K3-on models, inspect the anti-judder spring and the spring seat for signs of wear or distortion and renew if necessary.

16 Inspect the clutch assembly for burrs and indentations on the edges of the protruding tabs of the friction plates and/or slots in the edge of the housing with which they engage. Similarly check for wear between the inner tongues of the plain plates and the slots in the clutch centre. Wear of this nature will cause clutch drag and slow disengagement during gear changes as the plates will snag when the pressure plate is lifted. With care a small amount of wear can be corrected by dressing with a fine file, but if this is excessive the worn components should be renewed.

17 Check the bush in the clutch housing and the spacer it runs on for signs of damage or scoring, and renew them if necessary **(see illustration)**.

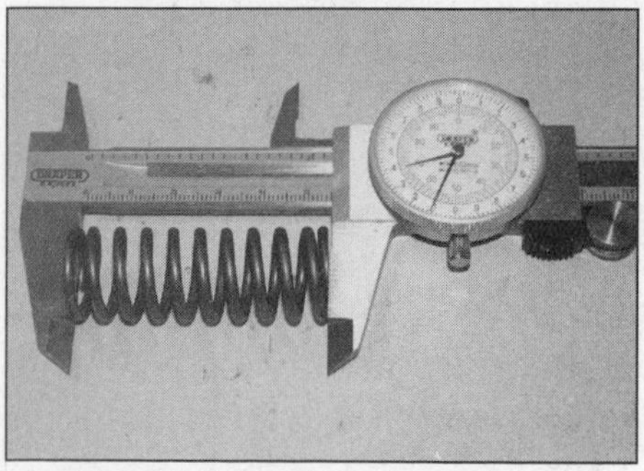
18.14a Measure the free length of the springs . . .

18.14b . . . and check them for squareness

18.17 Check the bush (arrowed) for wear

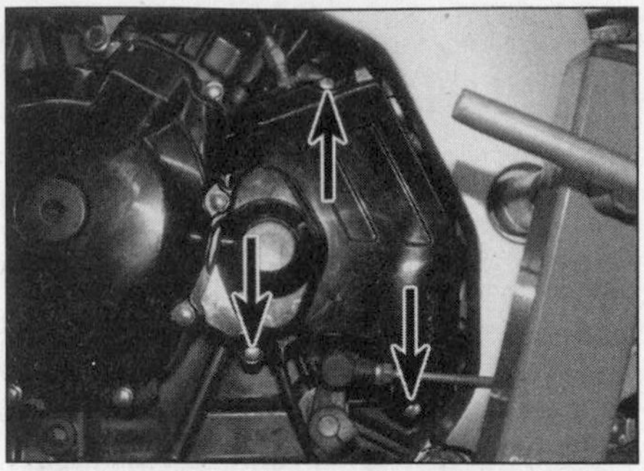

18.18a Unscrew the bolts (arrowed) and remove the cover

18.18b Remove the retainer plate . . .

18.18c . . . to access the oil seal (arrowed)

18 Check the clutch pressure plate, the lifter, the bearing and the thrust washer for signs of roughness, wear or damage, and renew any parts necessary. If not already done, withdraw the clutch pushrod from input shaft (see Step 4) **(see illustration 18.4b)**. Check that the pushrod is straight by rolling it on a flat surface. To access the pushrod oil seal, unscrew the bolts securing the front sprocket cover and remove it **(see illustration)**. Check the pushrod oil seal for signs of leakage and renew it if necessary. First remove the front sprocket (see Chapter 6). Unscrew the bolts securing the oil seal retainer plate and remove the plate **(see illustration)**. Lever out the old seal using a screwdriver, then drive a new seal squarely into place **(see illustration)**. Install the retainer plate, making sure the neutral switch wiring is correctly routed behind it, and tighten its bolts securely. Install the front sprocket (see Chapter 6).

19 Inspect the clutch release mechanism whilst the engine sprocket cover is removed. Check the mechanism for smooth operation and any signs of wear or damage. Detach the clutch cable (see Section 19), then unscrew the two bolts securing the mechanism to the engine and remove it for cleaning and re-greasing if required **(see illustrations)**. Reassemble the mechanism and fit it back onto the crankcase, then attach the clutch cable (see Section 19).

20 Check the teeth of the primary driven gear on the back of the clutch housing and the corresponding teeth of the primary drive gear on the crankshaft. Renew the clutch housing and/or primary drive gear if worn or chipped teeth are discovered (refer to Section 21 for the primary drive gear). To remove the oil pump drive gear refer to Section 22.

Installation

Note: *If the primary drive gear has been removed and not yet installed, do so before installing the clutch (see Section 21).*

21 Remove all traces of old gasket from the crankcase and clutch cover surfaces.

22 Smear the outside of the clutch housing spacer with molybdenum disulphide oil (50% molybdenum grease and 50% engine oil). On X and Y models, slide the thrust washer onto the shaft, followed by the spacer **(see illustrations)**. On K1 models onward slide the shouldered spacer onto the shaft with the shouldered end innermost.

23 Slide the clutch housing onto the spacer on the input shaft, making sure the teeth on the oil pump drive gear engage with those on the driven gear, and the teeth on the primary driven gear engage with those on the primary drive gear **(see illustrations)**.

18.19a Unscrew the bolts and remove the release mechanism . . .

18.19b . . . then disassemble it, clean it and re-grease it

18.22a Slide the thrust washer onto the shaft . . .

18.22b . . . followed by the spacer . . .

18.23a . . . then fit the clutch housing . . .

18.23b . . . making sure related gear teeth engage correctly

18.24 Slide the thrust washer onto the shaft . . .

18.25 . . . followed by the clutch centre

18.26a Fit a new lock washer . . .

18.26b . . . then fit the clutch nut . . .

18.26c . . . and tighten it to the specified torque

18.26d Bend up the lock washer tab to secure the clutch nut

24 Slide the thrust washer onto the shaft **(see illustration)**.

25 Slide the clutch centre onto the shaft **(see illustration)**.

26 Slide a ***new*** clutch nut lock washer onto the shaft then fit the clutch nut, with its chamfered side facing out **(see illustrations)**. Using the method employed on removal to lock the input shaft (see Step 6), tighten the nut to the torque setting specified at the beginning of the Chapter **(see illustration)**. **Note:** *Check that the clutch centre rotates freely after tightening the clutch nut.* Bend up one side of the lock washer against one of the flats on the clutch nut **(see illustration)**.

27 On K3-on models, fit the spring seat and anti-judder spring **(see illustration)**. **Note:** *The anti-judder spring must be fitted the correct way round, with its outer edge raised off the spring seat.*

28 Coat each clutch plate with engine oil, then build up the plates in the housing. On X, Y, K1 and K2 models, start with the type B friction plate with the rubber bands around some of the tabs. On K3-on models, start with the narrow friction plate that fits over the anti-judder spring assembly. Next install a plain plate, then alternating friction plates and plain plates until all are installed **(see illustrations)**.

29 If removed, smear molybdenum grease onto each end of the pushrod and slide it

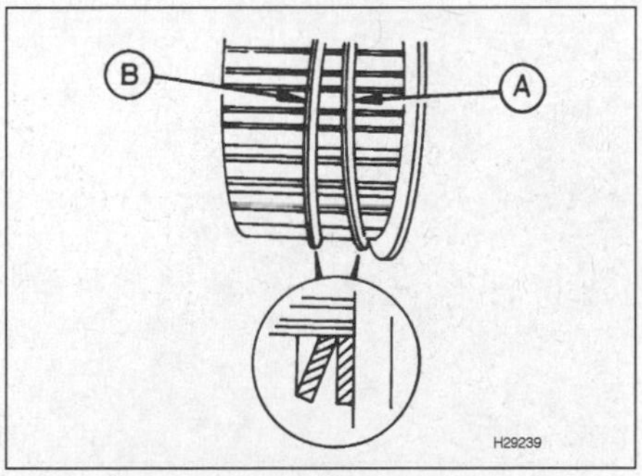

18.27 Correct fitting of spring seat (A) and anti-judder spring (B)

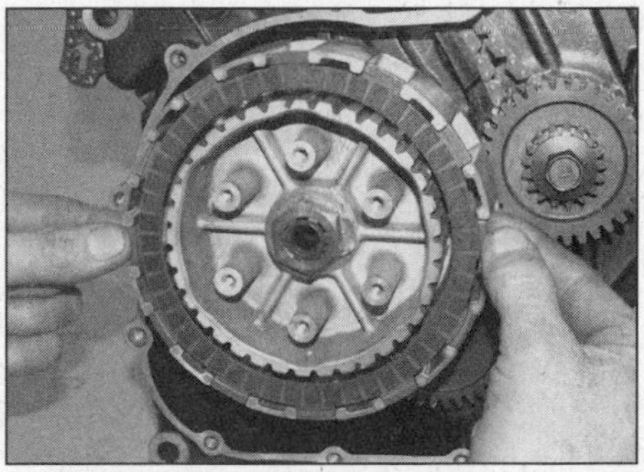

18.28a Fit the friction plate with the rubber bands first . . .

18.28b . . . then alternate plain plates . . .

18.28c . . . and friction plates

18.29a Fit the bearing and washer onto the lifter . . .

18.29b . . . then fit the assembly into the shaft

18.30a Fit the pressure plate, making sure it locates as described . . .

18.30b . . . then fit the springs, collars and bolts

18.31a Fit a new greased O-ring into the groove . . .

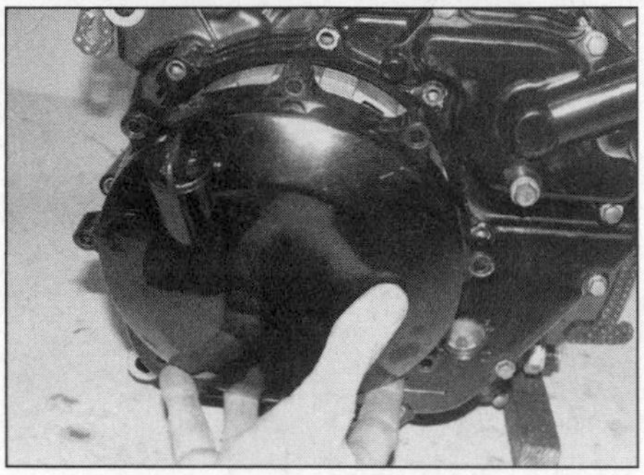
18.31b . . . then install the cover

into the input shaft **(see illustration 18.4b)**. Lubricate the pressure plate lifter, the bearing and thrust washer with clean oil, then fit the bearing and washer onto the lifter **(see illustration)**. Slide the lifter into the input shaft **(see illustration)**.

30 Fit the pressure plate into the clutch centre, making sure it seats correctly with its inner rim castellations locating in the slots in the centre – if there is any clearance between the clutch plates as you push on the pressure plate then it has not located properly **(see illustration)**. Fit the clutch springs, collars and bolts and tighten the bolts evenly in a criss-cross sequence to the specified torque setting **(see illustration)**.

31 On X, Y, K1 and K2 models, if the crankcase cover was removed, refer to Chapter 3 and install the cover and water pump. If just the clutch cover was removed, fit a new O-ring smeared with grease into the groove **(see illustration)**. Apply a suitable non-permanent thread locking compound to the bolts and tighten them evenly in a criss-cross sequence to the specified torque setting **(see illustration)**. Note that if both covers were removed separately, do not tighten the crankcase cover bolts before the clutch cover is fitted – tighten them all finger-tight only until all bolts are in place, then tighten them all to the specified torque. Do not forget the wiring guide with one of the clutch cover bolts **(see illustration 18.2)**.

32 On K3-on models, ensure the dowels are in place in the crankcase, then fit a new cover gasket over the dowels. Follow the procedure in Chapter 3 to install the crankcase cover and water pump, then tighten the cover bolts evenly in a criss-cross sequence to the specified torque setting.

33 Refill the engine with oil (see Chapter 1).

34 Check the clutch lever freeplay and adjust if necessary (see Chapter 1).

19 Clutch cable

Removal

1 Unscrew the bolts securing the sprocket cover and remove it **(see illustration 18.18a)**.

2 Fully slacken the adjuster top locknut **(see illustration)**. Using a small flat-bladed screwdriver, bend back the tab securing the inner cable end in the release arm and slip the cable out of the arm **(see illustrations)**. Thread the bottom locknut off the adjuster and draw the cable out of its bracket **(see illustrations)**.

3 Pull back the rubber cover from the clutch adjuster at the handlebar end of the cable **(see illustration)**. Fully slacken the lockring,

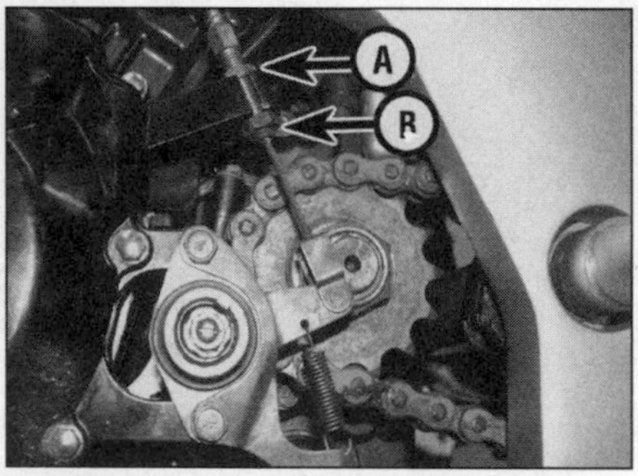

19.2a Top locknut (A), bottom locknut (B)

19.2b Bend down the tab (arrowed) . . .

19.2c . . . and slip the cable end out of the arm

19.2d Remove the bottom locknut . . .

19.2e . . . and withdraw the cable

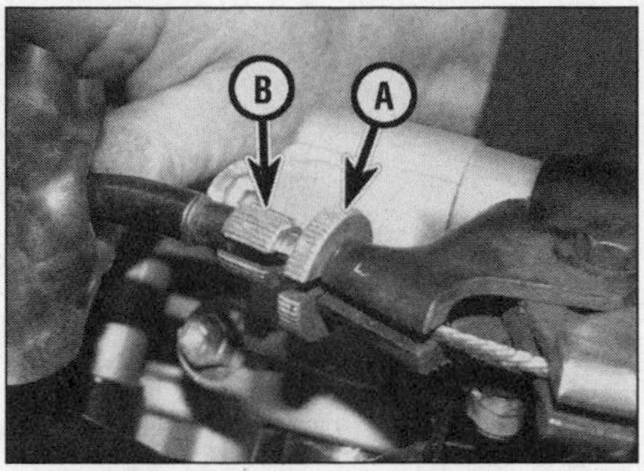

19.3 Pull back the cover, then slacken the lockring (A) and turn the adjuster (B) in

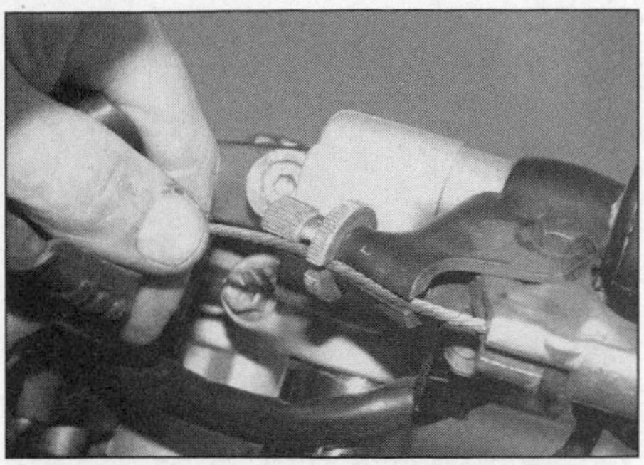
19.4a Align the slots and slip the cable out of the bracket . . .

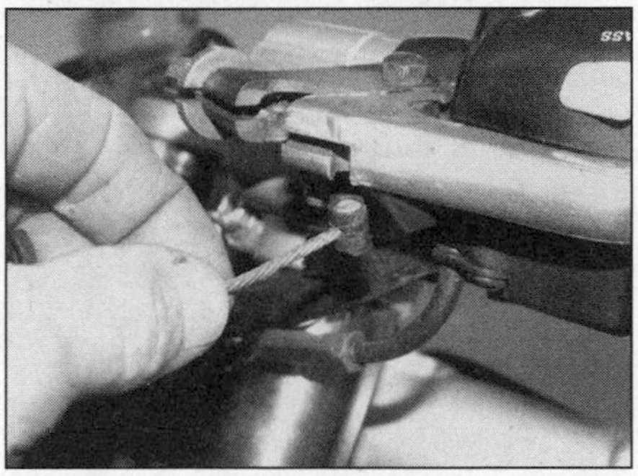
19.4b . . . and detach it from the lever

19.6 Bend up the tab to secure the cable

then screw the adjuster fully in. This resets it to the beginning of its adjustment range.

4 Align the slots in the adjuster and lockring with that in the lever bracket, then pull the outer cable end from the socket in the adjuster and release the inner cable end from the lever **(see illustrations)**.

5 Take note of the exact routing of the cable and any guides that hold it – incorrect installation could result in poor steering movement and affect clutch action. Carefully withdraw the cable – if it gets stuck do not be tempted to pull it out using force as you will only damage something.

> **HAYNES HiNT** ***Before removing the cable from the bike, tape the lower end of the new cable to the upper end of the old cable. Slowly pull the lower end of the old cable out, guiding the new cable down into position. Using this method will ensure the cable is routed correctly.***

Installation

6 Installation is the reverse of removal. Apply grease to the cable ends. Make sure the cable is correctly routed. Do not forget to bend up the tab in the release arm to secure the cable end **(see illustration)**. Adjust the amount of clutch lever freeplay (see Chapter 1).

20 Gearchange mechanism

Note: *The gearchange mechanism can be removed with the engine in the frame. If the engine has already been removed, ignore the preliminary steps.*

Removal

1 Drain the engine oil (see Chapter 1).

2 Unscrew the gearchange linkage arm pinch bolt and slide the arm off the shaft, noting its alignment **(see illustration 5.11)**.

3 Remove the circlip securing the left-hand end of the shaft and slide off the washer **(see illustrations)**.

4 Remove the clutch (see Section 18).

5 Note how the gearchange selector arm locates onto the pins in the selector drum cam plate, and how the gearchange shaft centralising spring ends locate. Withdraw the gearchange shaft from the engine **(see illustration)**.

6 Note how the stopper arm spring ends locate and how the roller on the arm locates in the neutral detent on the selector drum cam, then unscrew the stopper arm bolt and remove the arm, the washer, and the spring, noting how they fit **(see illustration)**.

20.3a Remove the circlip . . .

20.3b . . . and slide the washer off

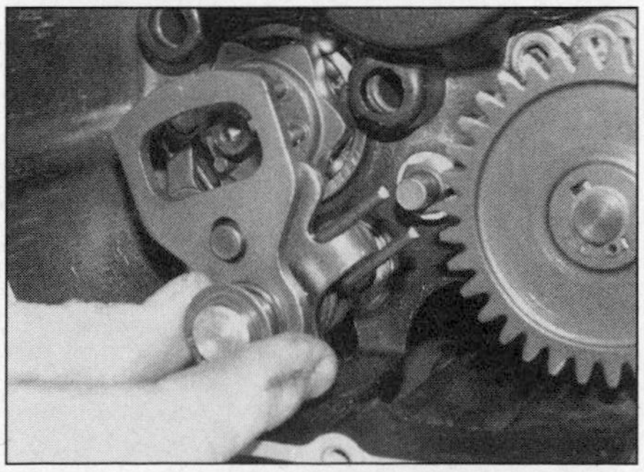
20.5 Note how the spring ends locate then withdraw the shaft

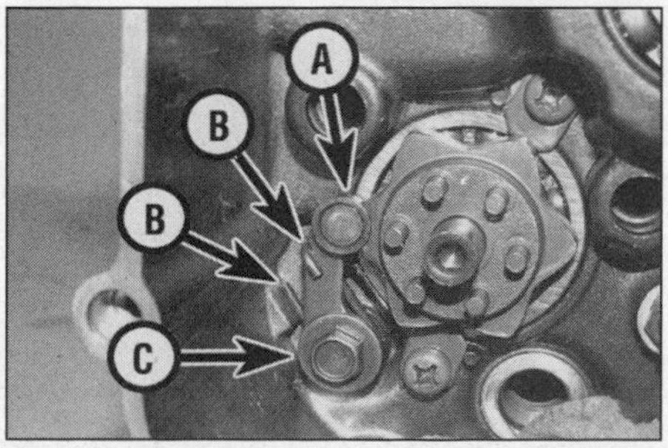

20.6 Note how the roller (A) and the spring ends (B) locate, then unscrew the bolt (C) and remove the arm

20.7a Use a screwdriver located as shown to prevent the drum turning while unscrewing the bolt

20.7b Note the locating pins (arrowed) that fit in the holes in the back of the plate and remove them for safekeeping

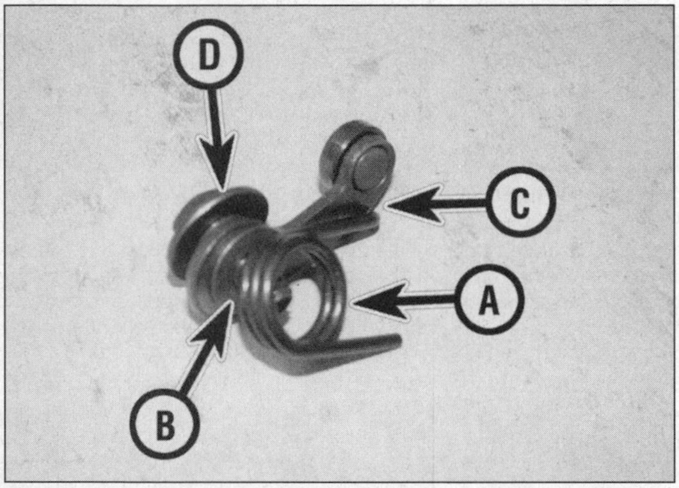

20.8a Stopper arm assembly – return spring (A), washer (B), stopper arm (C), bolt (D)

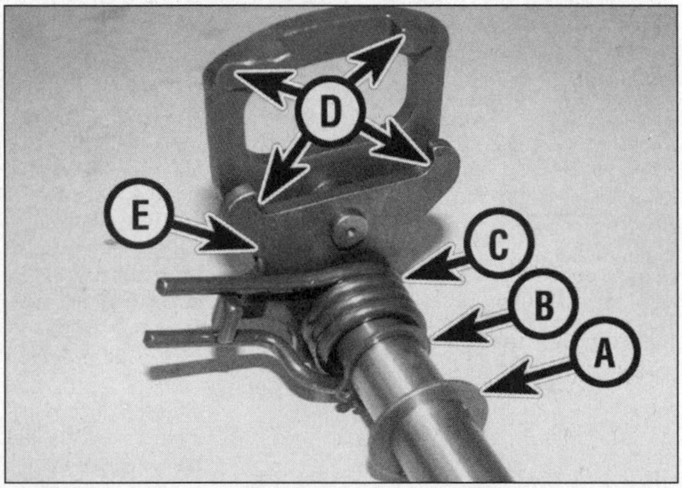

20.8b Selector arm assembly – washer (A), circlip (B), centralising spring (C), pawls (D), lower pawl plate (E) . . .

7 If necessary, unscrew the bolt securing the cam plate to the selector drum and remove the plate – use a screwdriver located between a cam and the bearing retainer plate as shown to prevent the drum turning **(see illustration)**. Note that there are two locating pins that fit between the cam plate and the drum – it is advisable to place some rag in the bottom of the crankcase to catch the pins should they drop out. Otherwise remove the pins for safekeeping **(see illustration)**.

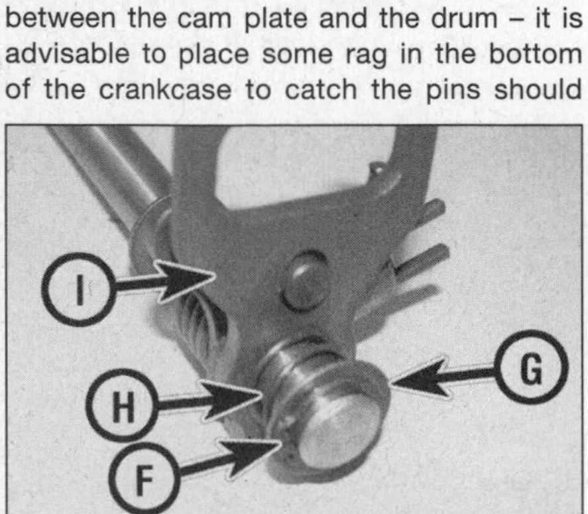

20.8c . . . circlip (F), washer (G), thrust spring (H), upper pawl plate (I)

Inspection

8 Inspect the stopper arm return spring and the shaft centralising spring and thrust spring **(see illustrations)**. If they are fatigued, worn or damaged they must be renewed – each is retained by a circlip. Also check that the centralising spring locating pin in the crankcase is securely tightened. If it is loose, remove it and apply a non-permanent thread locking compound to its threads, then tighten it to the torque setting specified at the beginning of the Chapter.

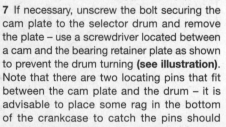

20.9a Lever out the old seal . . .

9 Check the gearchange shaft for straightness and damage to the splines. If the shaft is bent you can attempt to straighten it, but if the splines are damaged the shaft must be renewed. Also check the condition of the shaft oil seal in the left-hand side of the crankcase. If it is damaged, deteriorated or shows signs of leakage it must be renewed. Lever out the old seal with a screwdriver **(see illustration)**. Press or drive the new seal squarely into place, with its lip facing inward, using a seal driver or 16 mm socket – the seal sits below the rim of its bore so make sure it is fully in place **(see illustrations)**.

10 Inspect the selector arm pawls and the pins on the cam plate for wear and renew them if necessary **(see illustrations 20.8b and c)**. The selector arm upper pawl plate can be separated from the lower (which is integral

20.9b . . . then fit the new one with the marked side facing out . . .

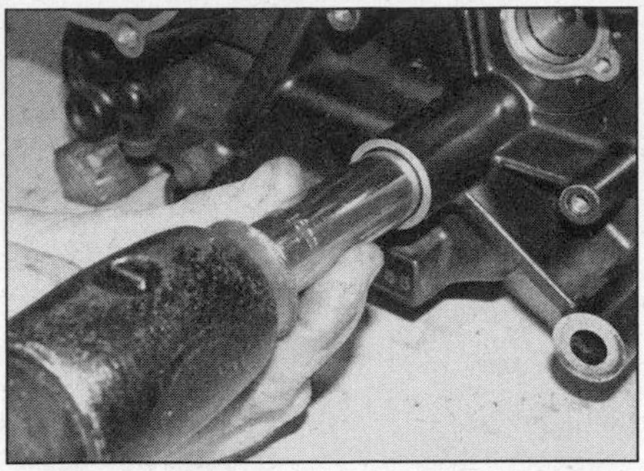

20.9c . . . and press or drive it into place

20.12a Install the threadlocked bolt . . .

20.12b . . . and tighten it to the specified torque, locking the plate as before

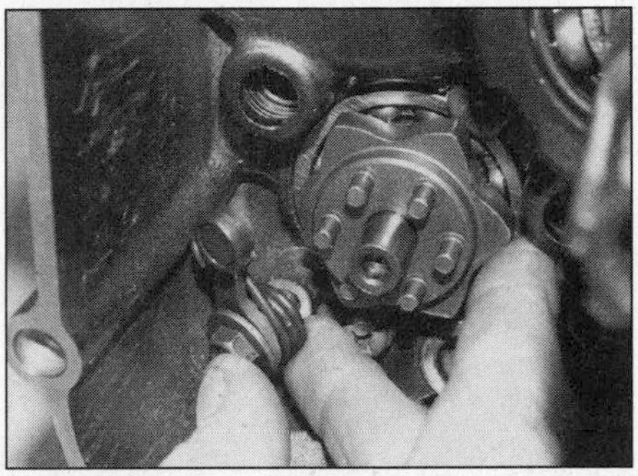

20.13 Install the stopper arm assembly as described

20.14a Slide the shaft into the crankcase . . .

with the shaft) after removing the washer, circlip and thrust spring – note how the hole in the upper plate locates over the pin on the lower one.

11 Check the stopper arm roller and the cam plate detents **(see illustration 20.8a)**. If they are worn or damaged they must be renewed. Check that the roller spins freely.

Installation

12 If removed, fit the locating pins into the end of the selector drum **(see illustration 20.7b)**. Install the cam plate, making sure the holes in the back locate correctly on the pins – they are offset slightly so the cam can only fit one way. Apply a suitable thread locking compound to the threads of the cam bolt and tighten it to the torque setting specified at the beginning of the Chapter, locking the plate to prevent it turning as on removal **(see illustrations)**.

20.14b . . . and locate the spring ends around the pin (arrowed)

13 Fit the stopper arm bolt through the stopper arm, then fit the washer and return spring **(see illustration 20.8a)**. Apply a threadlock to the threads of the bolt. Install the assembly onto the crankcase, making sure the spring ends locate correctly over the stopper arm and against the crankcase, and partially tighten the bolt **(see illustration)**. Lift the stopper arm using a screwdriver as a lever or a pair of pliers, then fully tighten the bolt, locating the roller onto the neutral detent in the cam as they become aligned **(see illustration 20.6)**. Tighten the bolt to the specified torque setting. Afterwards make sure the arm is free to move and is returned by the pressure of the spring.

14 Make sure the inner washer is on the gearchange shaft and the centralising spring ends are correctly located on each side of the tab on the lower pawl plate **(see illustration 20.8b)**. Slide the shaft into its hole in the engine, making sure the centralising spring ends locate correctly each side of the locating pin in the crankcase **(see illustrations)**.

15 Slide the washer onto the left-hand end of the shaft and fit the circlip, making sure it locates in its groove **(see illustrations 20.3b and a)**.

16 Slide the gearchange lever onto the shaft, aligning the punch mark on the shaft end with the slit in the clamp **(see illustration 5.11)**. Tighten the pinch bolt securely and check that the gearchange mechanism works correctly.

17 Install the clutch (see Section 18).

18 Replenish the engine with oil (see Chapter 1).

21 Primary drive gear

Note: *The primary drive gear can be removed with the engine in the frame.*

Caution: The primary drive gear bolt has left-hand threads, meaning that it must be undone in a clockwise direction and tightened in an anti-clockwise direction.

Removal

1 Remove the clutch (see Section 18). Unscrew the crankshaft end cap from the alternator cover **(see illustration)**.

2 To unscrew the primary drive gear bolt the crankshaft must be prevented from turning. To do this, counter-hold the crankshaft using a 17 mm socket on the alternator rotor bolt. Due to the left-hand threads of the primary drive

21.1 Unscrew the end cap (arrowed)

21.3a Unscrew the bolt (arrowed) . . .

21.3b . . . turning it clockwise as it has left-hand threads

21.4a Slide the pump drive gear off the shaft . . .

21.4b . . . followed by the primary drive gear

21.7a Install the bolt . . .

21.7b . . . and tighten it in an anti-clockwise direction to the specified torque

gear bolt the alternator rotor bolt is effectively being tightened by this action, but as it is set to a higher torque setting there is no danger of it tightening more and stripping out.

3 With the crankshaft locked, unscrew the primary drive gear bolt, remembering that it has left-hand threads and so must be slackened by turning it clockwise instead of anti-clockwise **(see illustrations)**.

4 Mark the outer face of the primary drive so that it can be installed the correct way round on refitting. Slide the water pump drive gear and the primary drive gear off the end of the crankshaft **(see illustrations)**.

Inspection

5 Check the teeth of the primary drive gear and the corresponding teeth of the primary driven gear on the back of the clutch housing. Renew the clutch housing and/or primary drive gear if worn or chipped teeth are discovered.

Installation

6 Slide the primary drive gear onto the crankshaft, with the marking made previously facing outwards **(see illustration 21.4b)**. Slide the water pump drive gear onto the shaft, making sure its chamfered side faces out **(see illustration 21.4a)**.

7 Install the bolt and tighten it finger-tight, remembering that it has left-hand threads and so must be tightened in an anti-clockwise direction **(see illustration)**. Lock the crankshaft by counter-holding the alternator bolt as on removal – there is no danger of the bolt coming undone as it is set to a higher torque setting than the primary drive gear bolt is being tightened to. With the crankshaft locked, tighten the primary drive gear bolt to the torque setting specified at the beginning of the Chapter **(see illustration)**, but first check that your torque wrench can be set to tighten left-hand threaded bolts – some of them can't, which means you will keep on tightening, expecting the wrench to click at the correct setting, whereas you will actually be tightening the bolt to a higher setting than the alternator rotor bolt, which will therefore begin to unscrew!

8 Install the crankshaft end cap using a new O-ring if required – smear the O-ring and the cap threads with grease. Tighten the cap to the torque setting specified at the beginning of the Chapter.

9 Install the clutch (see Section 18).

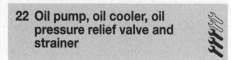

22.3a Remove the circlip . . .

22 Oil pump, oil cooler, oil pressure relief valve and strainer

Note 1: *The oil pump can be removed with the engine in the frame.*

Note 2: *The oil cooler is fitted to K3-on models.*

Note 3: *To access the pressure relief valve and oil strainer the engine must be removed from the frame and the crankcases separated.*

Oil pump

Pressure check

1 Perform an oil pressure check (see Chapter 1). If the pressure is as specified at the beginning of the Chapter then the pump is good. If the pressure is lower than it should be, and all other possible causes (as listed in Chapter 1) have been eliminated, then the pump is worn or faulty and must be renewed. No individual components are available.

Removal

2 Remove the clutch (see Section 18).

3 Remove the circlip securing the driven gear and slide the gear off the shaft, noting how it locates onto the drive pin **(see illustrations)**. Withdraw the pin from the shaft and slide off the washer – it is advisable to place some rag in the bottom of the crankcase to catch the pins should they drop out **(see illustrations)**.

4 Undo the three screws securing the pump to the crankcase and remove the pump **(see illustrations)**.

22.3b . . . and slide the gear off

22.3c Withdraw the drive pin . . .

22.3d . . . and remove the washer

22.4a Undo the screws (arrowed) . . .

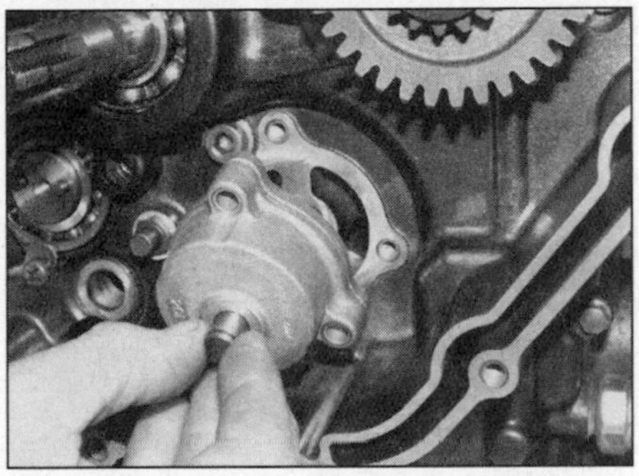
22.4b . . . and remove the pump

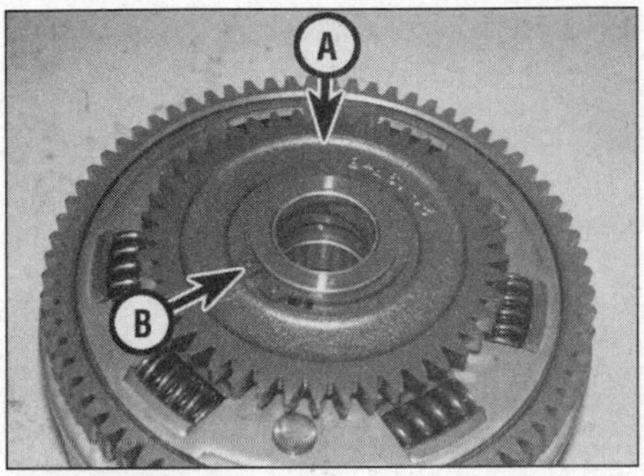

22.6 The drive gear (A) is secured on the back of the clutch housing by a circlip (B)

Inspection

5 Check the pump body for cracks and other damage.

6 Check the driven gear teeth for wear and damage and renew it if necessary. Similarly check the drive gear on the back of the clutch housing **(see illustration)**. The drive gear is secured by a circlip – remove this and lift off the gear, noting the pin that locates between the cutouts in the gear and clutch housing hub to lock them together. Fit the gear back on, making sure the pin locates correctly, and use a new circlip if the old one deforms on removal.

Installation

7 Before installing the pump, prime it by pouring oil into the outlet and turning the shaft by hand **(see illustration)**. This ensures that oil is being pumped as soon as the engine is turned over.

8 Install the pump, making sure it locates correctly into the crankcase **(see illustration)**. Apply a suitable non-permanent thread locking compound to the pump screws and tighten them to the torque setting specified at the beginning of the Chapter **(see illustration)**.

9 Slide the washer onto the shaft end, then fit the drive pin through the hole **(see illustrations 22.3d and c)**. Locate the cutouts in the driven gear over the drive pin ends and secure the gear with the circlip, making sure it locates in its groove **(see illustrations 22.3b and a)**.

10 Install the clutch (see Section 18).

Oil cooler

Removal

11 The oil cooler is located on the front of the engine **(see illustration)**. Drain the engine oil (see Chapter 1).

12 To remove the cooler with its feed and return hoses, first note the alignment of

22.7 Prime the pump with new oil

22.8a Locate the pump on the crankcase . . .

22.8b . . . then threadlock the screws and tighten them to the specified torque

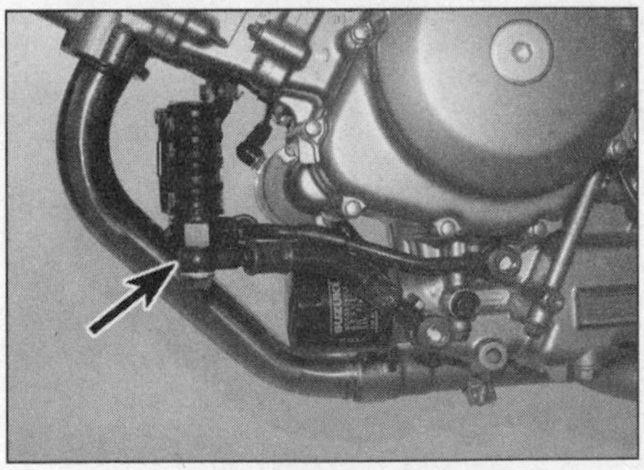
22.11 Location of the oil cooler – K3-on models

22.12 Note the alignment of the hose unions with the crankcase

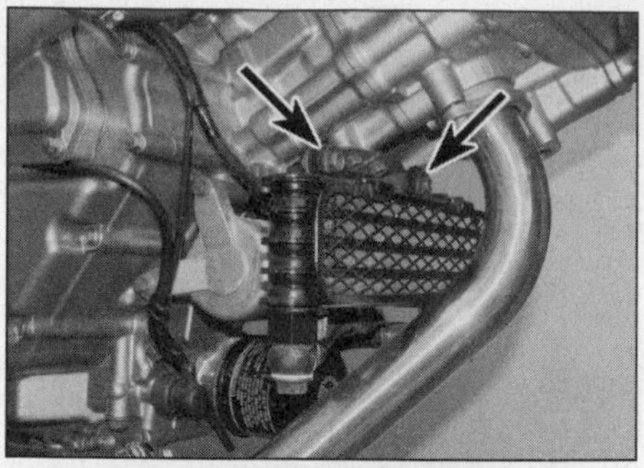

22.14 Note the spacers and grommets on each mounting bolt

22.19 Unscrew the relief valve (arrowed) . . .

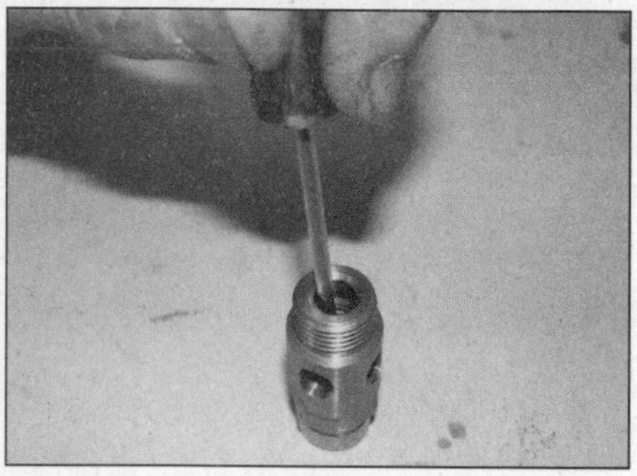

22.30 . . . and check it as described

22.21 Install the valve and tighten it to the specified torque

the banjo unions with the crankcase **(see illustration)**. Position a drain tray below the cooler, then unscrew the banjo bolt securing each hose to the engine and detach the hoses. Discard the banjo union sealing washers as new ones must be used.

13 To remove the cooler without its feed and return hoses, position a drain tray below the cooler. Note the alignment of the banjo unions with the cooler, then unscrew the banjo bolt securing each hose to the cooler and detach the hoses. Discard the banjo union sealing washers as new ones must be used.

14 Unscrew the cooler mounting bolts and remove the cooler, noting the spacers in the mounting grommets **(see illustration)**.

Inspection

15 Undo the screw securing the mesh guard and remove it, noting how it locates at the top.

16 Inspect the cooler fins for mud, dirt and insects which may impede the flow of air. If the fins are dirty, clean them using water or low pressure compressed air directed from the inner side. If the fins are bent or distorted, straighten them carefully with a screwdriver. If the air flow is restricted more then 20% of the surface area, replace the cooler with a new one.

Installation

17 Installation is the reverse of removal, noting the following:

- Check the condition of the cooler mounting grommets and renew them if they are damaged or deteriorated. Ensure the spacers are in the mounting grommets.
- Don't forget to fit the mesh guard before installing the cooler on the bike.
- Always use new sealing washers on each side of the banjo unions.
- Ensure the unions are correctly aligned with the cooler and/or the crankcase.
- Tighten the banjo bolts and the mounting bolts to the torque settings specified at the beginning of this Chapter.
- Replenish the engine oil (see Chapter 1).

Pressure relief valve

Removal

18 Remove the engine from the frame (see Section 5) and separate the crankcase halves (see Section 24).

19 Unscrew the relief valve from the crankcase **(see illustration)**.

Inspection

20 Press down on the plunger and check that it moves freely in the body and returns under spring pressure **(see illustration)**. If it doesn't, renew the valve – it cannot be disassembled and no individual components are available.

Installation

21 Fit the valve into the crankcase and tighten it to the torque setting specified at the beginning of the Chapter **(see illustration)**.

22 Reassemble the crankcase halves (see Section 24).

Oil strainer

Removal

23 Remove the engine from the frame (see Section 5) and separate the crankcase halves (see Section 24).

24 Unscrew the two bolts securing the strainer plate and remove the plate **(see illustration)**.

25 Withdraw the strainer from its housing, noting which way round it fits and how it locates in the slots **(see illustration)**.

Inspection

26 Clean the strainer in solvent and blow it through with compressed air **(see illustration)**. Check the mesh for holes or splits at the edges and renew it if necessary.

Installation

27 Fit the strainer back into its housing, locating the edges in the slots and making sure the protrusion faces down and out **(see illustration)**.

28 Fit the strainer plate, then apply a suitable

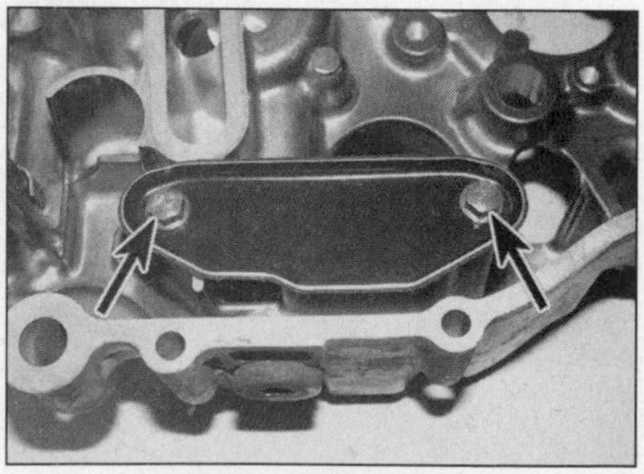

22.24 Unscrew the bolts (arrowed), then remove the plate . . .

22.25 . . . and withdraw the strainer

22.26 Clean the strainer as described

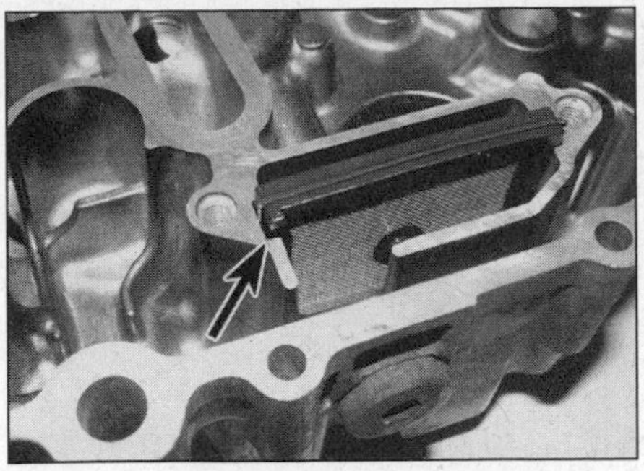

22.27 Install the strainer, making sure the protrusion (arrowed) is as shown . . .

22.28 . . . then fit the plate

non-permanent thread locking compound to its bolts and tighten them to the specified torque setting **(see illustration)**.

29 Reassemble the crankcase halves (see Section 24).

23 Starter clutch

Note: *The starter clutch can be removed with the engine in the frame. If the engine has been removed, ignore the steps which do not apply.*

Check

1 The operation of the starter clutch can be checked while it is in situ. Remove the starter motor (see Chapter 9). Check that the starter drive gear is able to rotate freely clockwise as you look at it via the starter motor aperture, but locks when rotated anti-clockwise. If not, the starter clutch is faulty and should be removed for inspection.

Removal

2 Remove the alternator rotor (see Chapter 9).

3 Remove the Woodruff key from its slot in the end of the crankshaft **(see illustration)**.

4 Slide the starter driven gear off the crankshaft **(see illustration)**.

5 If required, withdraw the idle/reduction gear shaft and remove the gear **(see illustration)**.

Inspection

6 Fit the starter driven gear into the back of the alternator rotor, turning the gear anti-clockwise as you do to spread the clutch sprags and allow it to enter. With the alternator rotor face down on a workbench, check that the starter driven gear rotates freely in an anti-clockwise direction and locks against the rotor in a clockwise direction **(see illustration)**. If it doesn't, the starter clutch should be dismantled for further investigation.

7 Withdraw the starter driven gear from the starter clutch. If the gear appears stuck, rotate it anti-clockwise as you withdraw it to free it from the sprags.

8 Check the condition of the sprags inside the clutch body and the corresponding surface on the driven gear hub **(see illustration)**. If they are damaged, marked or flattened at any point, they should be renewed. To remove the sprag assembly, hold the rotor using a holding strap and unscrew the bolts inside the rotor **(see illustration)**. Remove the sprag housing from the rotor and the sprag assembly from the housing, noting which way round it fits and how it locates. Install the new assembly in a reverse sequence, making sure the sprag assembly flange locates in the rim in the housing. Apply clean engine oil to the sprags. Apply a suitable non-permanent thread locking

23.3 Remove the Woodruff key . . .

23.4 . . . and slide the driven gear off the shaft

23.5 Withdraw the shaft and remove the idle/reduction gear

23.6 Make sure the driven gear turns freely in an anticlockwise direction as shown

23.8a Check the sprags (A) and the surface of the hub (B)

23.8b Unscrew the bolts (arrowed) and separate the sprag assembly from the rotor

23.13 Fit the key into its slot, tapping it into place if necessary

compound to the bolts and tighten them to the torque setting specified at the beginning of the Chapter.

9 Check the bush in the starter driven gear hub and its corresponding surface on the crankshaft. If the bush surfaces show signs of excessive wear replace the gear with a new one.

10 Check the teeth of the starter motor drive shaft, idle/reduction gear and starter driven gear. Renew the gears and/or starter motor if worn or chipped teeth are discovered on related gears. Also check the idle/reduction gear shaft for damage, and check that the gear is not a loose fit on the shaft. Renew the shaft if necessary.

Installation

11 Lubricate the idle/reduction gear shaft with clean engine oil. Locate the gear against the crankcase with the smaller pinion facing out and slide the shaft through and into the crankcase **(see illustration 23.5)**.

12 Slide the starter driven gear onto the end of the crankshaft with the raised section of the hub facing out **(see illustration 23.4)**.

13 Fit the Woodruff key into its slot **(see illustration)**.

14 Install the alternator rotor (see Chapter 9).

24 Crankcase – separation and reassembly

Separation

Note: *All models are fitted with an oil baffle plate that locates inside the crankcase, however the type of plate varies between models. On some models, it is mounted on the outside of the left crankcase half and is secured by the two lower 8 mm crankcase bolts, and has two prongs which locate on each side of one of the crankcase ribs on the inside of the right crankcase half. On other models it has no external mounting and locates between some of the internal crankcase ribs.*

1 To access the crankshaft and connecting rods, bearings and transmission components, the crankcase must be split into two parts. Before doing this, refer to Section 27 and check the crankshaft end-float.

2 To enable the crankcases to be separated, the engine must be removed from the frame (see Section 5). Before the crankcases can be separated, the camshafts, cylinder heads, cylinder blocks, pistons, water pump, starter motor, clutch, gearchange mechanism (including the cam plate), oil pump, primary drive gear, alternator, starter clutch and cam chains must be removed. See the relevant Sections of this and the other Chapters for details.

3 Undo the screw securing the oil spray pipe retainer plate to the right-hand side of the crankcase and remove the plate, noting how it locates against the end of the pipe **(see illustration)**. Withdraw the pipe from the crankcase **(see illustration)**.

4 If the transmission shafts are being removed, unscrew the bolts securing the oil seal retainer plate to the left-hand side of the crankcase and remove the plate, noting how it fits **(see illustration 18.18b)**. Also remove the spacer from the end of the output shaft **(see illustration)**. Discard the O-ring that fits inside the spacer **(see illustration)**.

5 If the selector drum is being removed, remove the neutral switch (see Chapter 9).

6 Lay the engine on its right-hand side. Unscrew the four 8 mm bolts in the left-hand side of the crankcase, slackening them evenly and a little at a time in a criss-cross pattern until they are all loose, then remove the bolts **(see illustration)**. On those models with the externally mounted oil baffle plate remove it from the engine, noting how it fits. **Note:** *As each bolt is removed, store it in its relative position in a cardboard template of the crankcase halves. This will ensure all bolts are installed in the correct location on reassembly. Note the wiring clamp fitted with the top rear bolt and store this in the template with the bolt.*

7 Carefully turn the engine over onto its left-hand side and support it on wooden blocks so the end of the transmission output shaft is off the work surface. Unscrew the nine 6 mm bolts followed by the three 8 mm bolts in the right-hand side of the crankcase, slackening them evenly and a little at a time in a criss-cross pattern until they are all loose, then remove the bolts **(see illustration)**. **Note:** *As each bolt is removed, store it in its relative position in a cardboard template of the crankcase halves. This will ensure all bolts are installed in the correct location on reassembly. Note the sealing washer fitted with the front 6 mm bolt.*

8 Carefully lift the right-hand crankcase half off the left-hand half, if necessary using a soft hammer to tap around the joint and gently on the shaft ends to separate the halves **(see illustration)**. **Note:** *If the halves do not separate easily, make sure all fasteners have been removed. Do not try and separate the halves by levering between the crankcase mating surfaces as they are easily scored and will leak oil afterwards. If the transmission input shaft sticks in its bearing and is lifting with the crankcase, tap the end of it with a soft hammer. If necessary, obtain an expanding clamp (brake piston expanders work very well) and some wood to protect the crankcase, then place the clamp in the cylinder opening and carefully expand the clamp to force the*

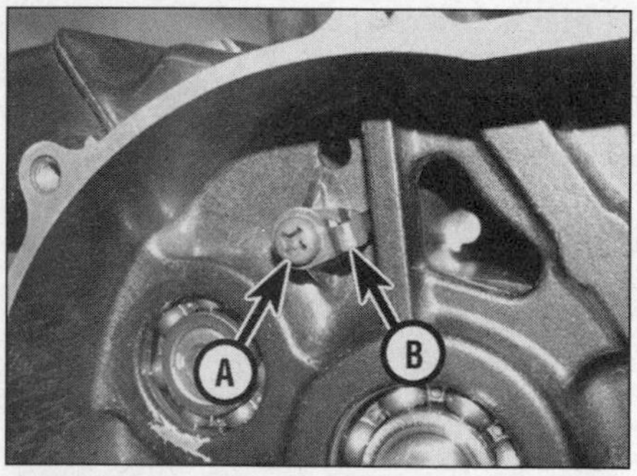

24.3a Undo the screw (A) and remove the retainer plate (B)

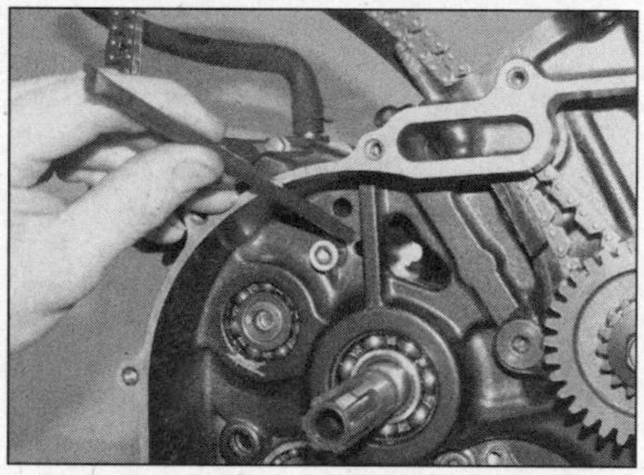

24.3b Withdraw the oil pipe from the crankcase

24.4a Slide the spacer out of the seal and off the shaft . . .

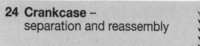

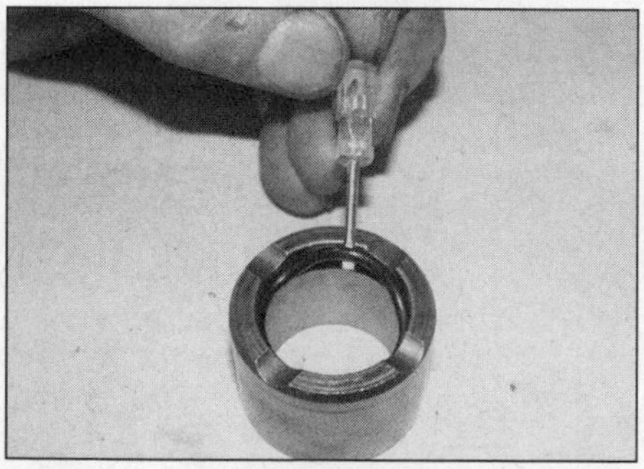

24.4b . . . and remove the O-ring from its inside groove

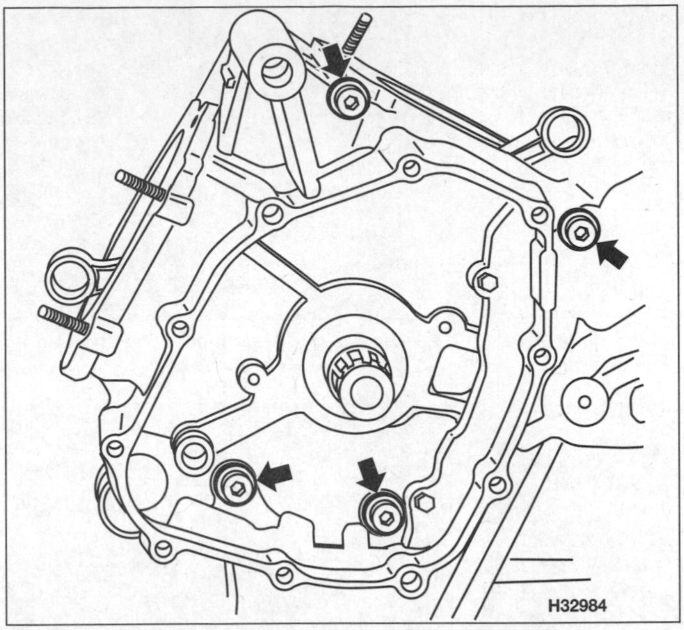

24.6 Left-hand crankcase 8 mm bolts (arrowed)

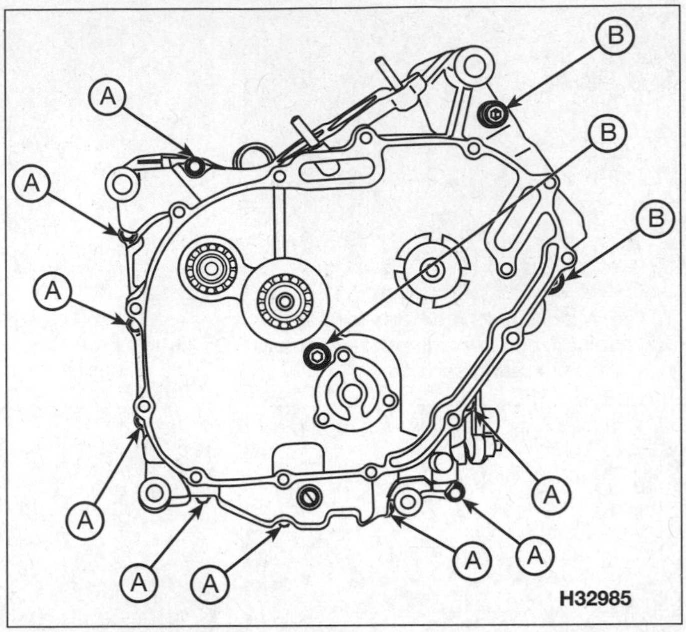

24.7 Right-hand crankcase 6 mm bolts (A) and 8 mm bolts (B)

halves apart **(see illustration)**. The right-hand side crankcase half will come away by itself, leaving the crankshaft, transmission shafts, and selector drum and forks in the left-hand half.

9 Remove the two locating dowels from the crankcase if they are loose (they could be in either crankcase half), noting their locations **(see illustration 24.15)**. Remove the oil passage O-rings – note that on X, Y, K1 and K2 models, one circular and one oval O-ring are fitted, on K3-on models both O-rings are circular **(see illustration 24.11)**. Check that the thrust washer is on the right-hand end of the transmission output shaft and, on X, Y, K1 and K2 models, that the end-float shim is on the right-hand end of the crankshaft; if not, they are probably stuck to the bearings in the right-hand crankcase half.

Reassembly

10 Remove all traces of sealant from the crankcase mating surfaces. If not already done, clean the oil strainer before the cases are assembled (see Section 22).

11 Support the left-hand half on wooden blocks so the end of the transmission output shaft is off the work surface. Ensure that all components and their bearings are in place in the right and left-hand crankcase halves. Fit new O-rings smeared with clean oil into the grooves around the oil passages **(see illustration)**. Check that the transmission output shaft thrust washer is in place on the right-hand end of the shaft. On X, Y, K1 and K2 models, check that the crankshaft end-float shim is on the right-hand end of the crankshaft and make sure the grooves in the shim face the crankshaft web.

12 Generously lubricate the transmission shafts, selector drum and forks, and the crankshaft, particularly around the bearings, with molybdenum disulphide oil (a mixture of 50% molybdenum disulphide grease and 50% engine oil), then use a rag soaked in high flash-point solvent to wipe over the gasket surfaces of both halves to remove all traces of oil.

13 Install the two locating dowels in the left-hand crankcase half **(see illustration 24.15)**.

14 Make sure that each connecting rod is positioned correctly for its cylinder **(see illustration)**.

15 Apply a small amount of suitable sealant (such as Suzuki Bond 1207B or equivalent) to the mating surface of the right-hand crankcase half **(see illustration)**.

Caution: Do not apply an excessive amount of sealant, as it will ooze out when the case

24.8a Carefully separate the crankcase halves

24.8b An expanding clamp can be used as shown if required

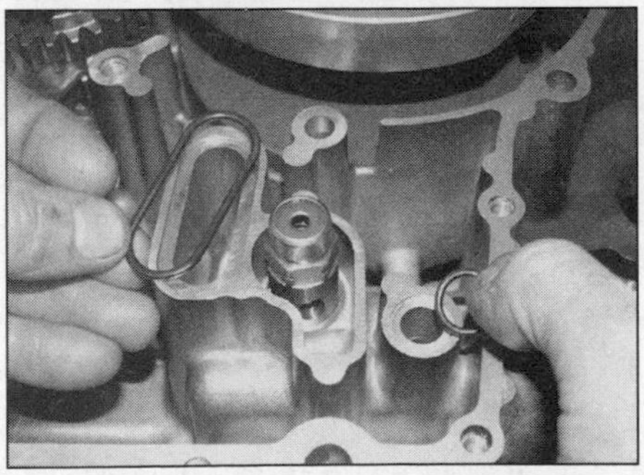

24.11 Fit a new O-ring onto each passage rim – X, Y, K1 and K2 models shown

24.14 Make sure the lower rod is positioned for the front cylinder, and the higher one for the rear

24.15 Make sure the dowels (arrowed) are installed, and apply the sealant to the mating surface

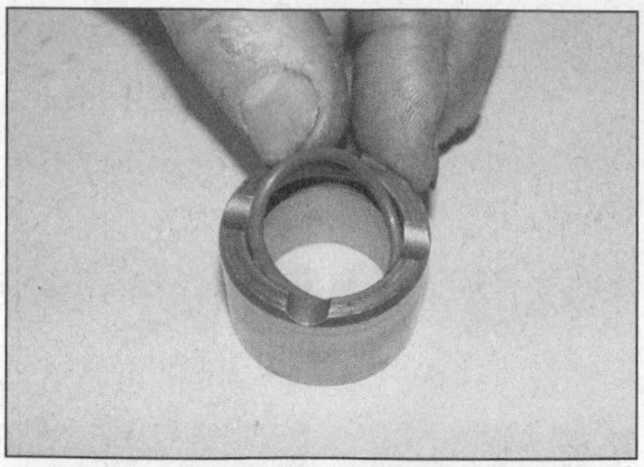

24.23a Fit a new O-ring into the groove, then grease the spacer . . .

24.23b . . . and slide it onto the shaft and into the seal

24.24a Slide the pipe into the crankcase . . .

24.24b . . . then locate the retainer plate . . .

24.24c . . . and secure them with the threadlocked screw

halves are assembled and may obstruct oil passages.

16 Check again that all components are in position, then carefully fit the right-hand crankcase half onto the left-hand half **(see illustration 24.8a)**. Make sure the dowels and shaft ends all locate correctly into the right-hand crankcase half.

17 Check that the right-hand crankcase half is correctly seated. **Note:** *The crankcase halves should fit together without being forced. If the casings are not correctly seated, remove the right-hand half and investigate the problem. Do not attempt to pull them together using the bolts as the casing could crack and be ruined.*

18 Clean the threads of the right-hand crankcase bolts and insert them in their original locations **(see illustration 24.7)**. Secure all bolts finger-tight at first, then tighten the 8 mm bolts followed by the 6 mm bolts evenly and a little at a time in a criss-cross pattern to the torque settings specified at the beginning of the Chapter. When torquing the bolts, be sure to distinguish correctly between the 8 mm bolts and the 6 mm bolts – their settings differ.

19 Turn the engine over. Where fitted, install the externally mounted oil baffle plate, making sure the split prongs locate over the rib in the right-hand crankcase half. Clean the threads of the left-hand crankcase bolts and install them in their original locations, not forgetting the wiring clamp with the top rear bolt **(see illustration 24.6)**. Secure all bolts finger-tight at first, then tighten them evenly and a little at a time in a criss-cross pattern to the torque setting specified at the beginning of the Chapter. All four bolts in the left-hand crankcase half are 8 mm diameter.

20 Stand the engine upright and go round all the 8 mm bolts on each side again and check that they are all at the correct torque setting. Now do the 6 mm bolts.

21 With all crankcase bolts tightened, check that the crankshaft and transmission shafts rotate smoothly and easily. Select each gear in turn (you will have to fit the cam plate onto the selector drum and turn it by hand to do this) and check the operation of the transmission in each gear, then select neutral and check that the shafts can turn freely and independently of each other. If there are any signs of undue stiffness, tight or rough spots, or of any other problem, the fault must be rectified before proceeding further.

22 If removed, install the neutral switch (see Chapter 9).

23 If removed, fit a new O-ring inside the transmission output shaft spacer **(see illustration)**. Smear the inside and outside of the spacer with grease. Slide the spacer onto the shaft and into the seal, making sure the grooved end fits innermost **(see illustration)**. Install the retainer plate, making sure the neutral switch wiring is correctly routed behind it, and tighten its bolts securely **(see illustration 18.18b)**.

24 Slide the oil spray pipe into the crankcase, making sure the protruding section of the end is at the top **(see illustration)**. Fit the retainer plate, making sure it locates correctly, then apply a suitable non-permanent thread locking compound to its screw and tighten it to the specified torque setting **(see illustrations)**.

25 Install all other removed assemblies in the reverse of the sequence given in Step 2.

25 Crankcase – inspection and servicing

1 After the crankcases have been separated, remove the oil strainer (see Section 22), neutral switch (if not already done) and oil pressure switch, the crankshaft and connecting rods, transmission shafts, and selector drum and forks, referring to the relevant Sections of this Chapter, and to Chapter 9 for the neutral and oil pressure switches. Refer to Sections 29 and 30 and to *Tools and Workshop Tips* in the Reference Section for checks and information on the selector drum and transmission shaft bearings. Refer to Sections 26 and 27 and to *Tools and Workshop Tips* in the Reference Section for checks and information on the crankshaft main bearings.

2 Undo the piston oil jet retainer bolts, then pull the oil jets out of the crankcases **(see illustration)**. Remove the O-rings and discard them. Also remove the bolt from the bottom of the angled oil gallery on the outside of the left-hand crankcase half and withdraw the oil jet. Discard its O-ring. Clean the jets with solvent and blow them through with compressed air if available.

3 On models with the internal oil baffle-plate, remove it if required, noting how it fits **(see illustration)**. On all models, if required, remove the baffle-plate from the outside of the left-hand crankcase half **(see illustration)**.

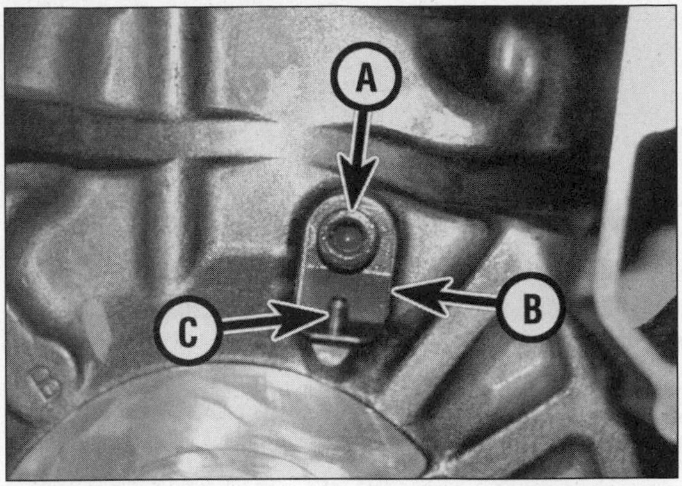

25.2 Unscrew the bolt (A), remove the retainer (B) and withdraw the oil jet (C) – there is one in each crankcase half

25.3a Remove the oil baffle where fitted and if required

4 If not already done, remove the oil seal retainer plate (see Section 24, Step 4). Lever out the transmission output shaft oil seal, clutch pushrod oil seal, and gearchange shaft oil seal with a flat-bladed screwdriver **(see illustrations)**.

5 Remove all traces of old gasket sealant from the mating surfaces. Clean up minor damage to the surfaces with a fine sharpening stone or grindstone.

6 Clean the crankcases thoroughly with new solvent and dry them with compressed air. Blow out all oil passages with compressed air. ***Caution: Be very careful not to nick or gouge the crankcase mating surfaces or oil leaks will result. Check both crankcase halves very carefully for cracks and other damage.***

7 Check that the cylinder block nut studs are tight in each crankcase half. If any are loose, remove them, then clean their threads and apply a suitable non-permanent thread locking compound and tighten them securely. Refer to Section 2 'Fasteners' of *Tools and Workshop Tips* in the Reference section at the end of this manual for details of how to slacken and tighten studs using two nuts locked together.

8 Small cracks or holes in aluminium castings can be repaired with an epoxy resin adhesive as a temporary measure. Permanent repairs can only be done by argon-arc welding, and only a specialist in this process is in a position to advise on the economy or practical aspect of such a repair. If any damage is found that can't be repaired, renew the crankcase halves as a set.

9 Damaged threads can be economically reclaimed using a diamond section wire insert, for example of the Heli-Coil type (though there are other makes), which is easily fitted after drilling and re-tapping the affected thread.

10 Sheared studs or screws can usually be removed with extractors, which consist of a tapered, left-hand thread screw of very hard steel. These are inserted into a pre-drilled hole in the stud, and usually succeed in dislodging the most stubborn stud or screw. If a stud has sheared above its bore line, it can be removed using a conventional stud extractor which avoids the need for drilling.

HAYNES HiNT ***Refer to Tools and Workshop Tips for details of installing a thread insert and using screw extractors.***

11 Fit new transmission output shaft, clutch pushrod and gearchange shaft oil seals **(see illustration 25.4a)**, lubricating their lips with grease and using a suitable socket to drive them into place if required **(see illustrations)**.

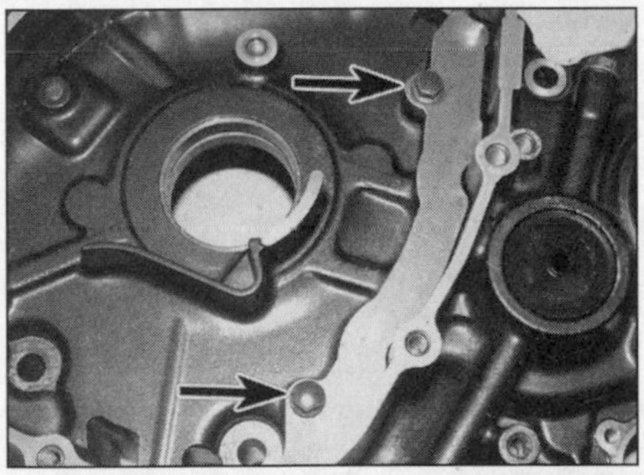
25.3b The external baffle is secured by two bolts (arrowed)

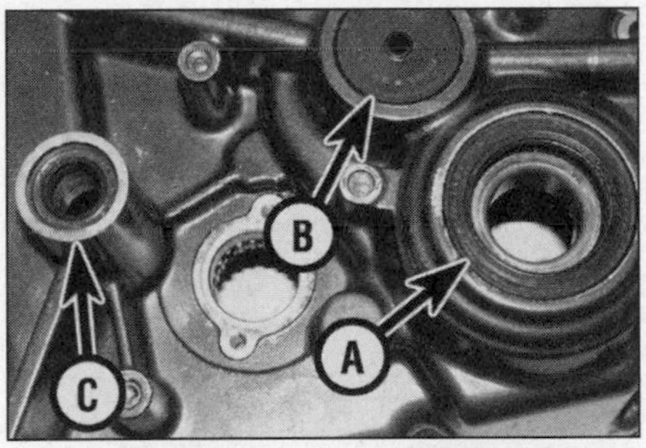

25.4a Lever out the transmission shaft seal (A), the pushrod seal (B) and the gearchange shaft seal (C) . . .

25.4b . . . using a screwdriver

25.11a Lubricate the seal lips with grease . . .

25.11b . . . and drive them in if necessary using a suitable socket

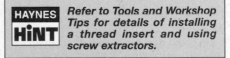

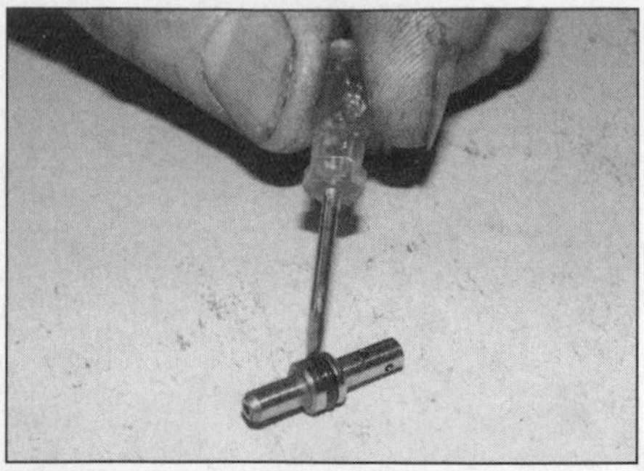
25.12a Fit a new O-ring onto the jet . . .

25.12b . . . then fit it into its passage . . .

25.12c . . . and secure it with the retainer and the threadlocked bolt

Do not fit the seal retainer plate until the neutral switch is installed.

12 Fit new O-rings smeared with oil onto the piston oil jets and fit them into their passages with the tapered ends pointing out **(see illustrations)**. Apply a suitable non-permanent thread locking compound the retainer bolts, then fit the retainers and tighten the bolts to the specified torque setting **(see illustration)**. Fit a new O-ring smeared with oil onto the oil gallery jet and fit it into the gallery, making sure the slotted end goes in first. Fit a new sealing washer onto the gallery bolt and tighten it to the specified torque setting.

13 Install all other components and assemblies, referring to the Steps above and the relevant Sections of this and the other Chapters, before reassembling the crankcase halves. Where fitted, make sure the internal oil baffle-plate locates correctly and is secure **(see illustration 25.3a)**. On all models apply thread-lock to the external baffle-plate bolts **(see illustration 25.3b)**.

26 Main and connecting rod bearings – general information

1 Even though main and connecting rod bearings are generally replaced with new ones during the engine overhaul, the old bearings should be retained for close examination as they may reveal valuable information about the condition of the engine.

2 Bearing failure occurs mainly because of lack of lubrication, the presence of dirt or other foreign particles, overloading the engine and/or corrosion. Regardless of the cause of bearing failure, it must be corrected before the engine is reassembled to prevent it from happening again.

3 When examining the connecting rod bearings, remove them from the connecting rods and caps and lay them out on a clean surface in the same general position as their location on the crankshaft journals. This will enable you to match any noted bearing problems with the corresponding crankshaft journal.

4 Dirt and other foreign particles get into the engine in a variety of ways. It may be left in the engine during assembly or it may pass through filters or breathers. It may get into the oil and from there into the bearings. Metal chips from machining operations and normal engine wear are often present. Abrasives are sometimes left in engine components after reconditioning operations, especially when parts are not thoroughly cleaned using the proper cleaning methods. Whatever the source, these foreign objects often end up imbedded in the soft bearing material and are easily recognised. Large particles will not imbed in the bearing and will score or gouge the bearing and journal. The best prevention for this cause of bearing failure is to clean all parts thoroughly and keep everything spotlessly clean during engine reassembly. Frequent and regular oil and filter changes are also recommended.

5 Lack of lubrication or lubrication breakdown has a number of interrelated causes. Excessive heat (which thins the oil), overloading (which squeezes the oil from the bearing face) and oil leakage or throw off (from excessive bearing clearances, worn oil pump or high engine speeds) all contribute to lubrication breakdown. Blocked oil passages will also starve a bearing and destroy it. When lack of lubrication is the cause of bearing failure, the bearing material is wiped or extruded from the steel backing of the bearing. Temperatures may increase to the point where the steel backing and the journal turn blue from overheating.

HAYNES HiNT *Refer to Tools and Workshop Tips for bearing fault finding.*

27.1 Check crankshaft end-float using a feeler gauge

6 Riding habits can have a definite effect on bearing life. Full throttle low speed operation, or labouring the engine, puts very high loads on bearings, which tend to squeeze out the oil film. These loads cause the bearings to flex, which produces fine cracks in the bearing face (fatigue failure). Eventually the bearing material will loosen in pieces and tear away from the steel backing. Short trip riding leads to corrosion of bearings, as insufficient engine heat is produced to drive off the condensed water and corrosive gases produced. These products collect in the engine oil, forming acid and sludge. As the oil is carried to the engine bearings, the acid attacks and corrodes the bearing material.

7 Incorrect bearing installation during engine assembly will lead to bearing failure as well. Tight fitting bearings that leave insufficient bearing oil clearances result in oil starvation. Dirt or foreign particles trapped behind a bearing insert result in high spots on the bearing that lead to failure.

8 To avoid bearing problems, clean all parts thoroughly before reassembly, double check all bearing clearance measurements and lubricate the new bearings with clean engine oil during installation.

27 Crankshaft and main bearings

Removal

1 Before separating the crankcase halves, check the amount of end-float to determine whether the internal shim is worn or incorrect. To do this refer to Chapter 3 and remove the water pump to give access to the right-hand end of the crankshaft. Grasp the primary drive gear and pull it away from the crankcase. Use a feeler gauge located between the collared end of the cam chain sprocket and the crankcase to determine the amount of end-float **(see illustration)**. If it is not within the range specified at the beginning of the Chapter, refer to the procedure below to select a replacement end-float shim – this is fitted before the crankcase halves are reassembled.

2 Separate the crankcase halves (refer to Section 24). Remove the crankshaft end-float shim from the right-hand end of the crankshaft **(see illustration)**.

3 Lift the crankshaft out of the left-hand crankcase half **(see illustration)**. If it appears stuck, tap it gently using a soft-faced mallet.

4 If required, remove the connecting rods from the crankshaft (see Section 28).

Inspection

5 Clean the crankshaft with solvent, using a rifle-cleaning brush to scrub out the oil passages. If available, blow the crank dry with compressed air, and also blow through the oil passages. Check the cam chain sprockets for wear or damage. If any of the sprocket teeth on the left-hand end are excessively worn, chipped or broken, the crankshaft must be renewed.

6 Refer to Section 26 and examine the main bearings **(see illustration 27.10b)**. If they are scored, badly scuffed or appear to have been seized, new bearing shells must be installed (see below). Always renew the shells as a set. If they are badly damaged, check the corresponding crankshaft journal. Evidence of extreme heat, such as discoloration, indicates that lubrication failure has occurred. Be sure to thoroughly check the oil pump and pressure relief valve as well as all oil holes and passages before reassembling the engine.

7 Inspect the crankshaft journals, paying particular attention where damaged bearings have been discovered. If the journals are scored or pitted in any way a new crankshaft will be required. Note that undersizes are not available, precluding the option of re-grinding the crankshaft.

8 Place the crankshaft on V-blocks and check the runout at the main bearing journals using a dial gauge. Compare the reading to the maximum specified at the beginning of the Chapter. If the runout exceeds the limit, the crankshaft must be renewed.

Oil clearance check

9 Whether new bearing shells are being fitted or the original ones are being re-used, the main bearing oil clearance should be checked prior to reassembly.

10 Using a Vernier caliper, measure the diameter of the crankshaft main bearing journals **(see illustration)**. Using a bore gauge and micrometer, measure the internal diameter of the bore with the main bearings in place **(see illustration)**. Calculate the difference between the two to determine the main bearing oil clearance and compare the results to the specifications at the beginning of the Chapter. If the oil clearance exceeds the service limit, new main bearings must be selected and installed. Note that if the diameter of the crankshaft journal is below the range specified, it is worn and the crankshaft must be renewed. Always fit new main bearings if a new crankshaft is fitted.

Main bearing selection

11 New main bearings are supplied on a selected fit basis according to the code letter

27.2 Remove the end-float shim . . .

stamped into each crankcase half adjacent to the bearing housing **(see illustration)**. If the crankcase code letter is A, the bearing shell colour-code is GREEN; if the letter is B, the colour-code is BLACK; if the letter is C, the colour-code is BROWN. The colour code is marked on the side of each bearing shell. The dimensions relating to the particular codes are given in the table below.

Main bearing selection table

Crankcase code (bearing housing internal diameter)	Bearing colour (thickness)
A (46.000 – 46.006 mm)	Green (1.993 – 1.996 mm)
B (46.0061 – 46.012 mm)	Black (1.996 – 1.999 mm)
C (46.0121 – 46.018 mm)	Brown (1.999 – 2.002 mm)

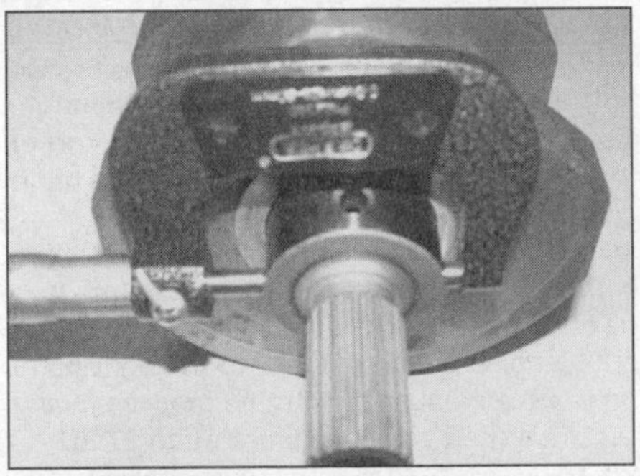

27.10a Measure the journal diameter . . .

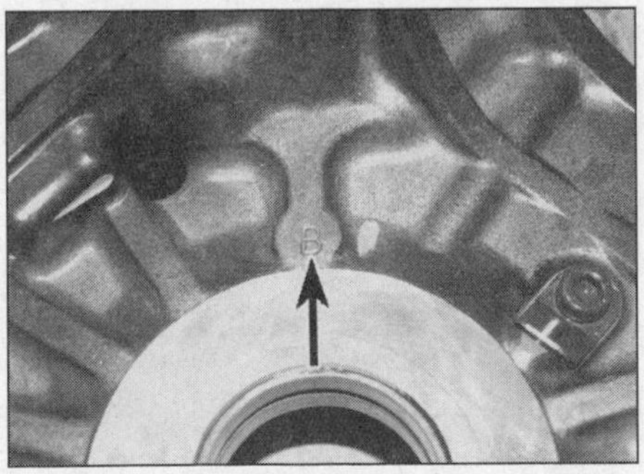

27.11 Main bearing code letter (arrowed)

27.3 . . . then lift the crankshaft out

Main bearing renewal

12 Renewal of the main bearings requires the use of a press and a two-piece Suzuki special tool (Pt. No. 09913-60220 for X, Y, K1 and K2 models and Pt. No. 09913-60221 for K3-on models) in order to avoid damaging either the crankcase or the new bearings, though it is possible to use a drawbolt arrangement in conjunction with the special tool if a press is not available. It is therefore advised that renewal is undertaken by a Suzuki dealer or a suitably equipped specialist.

13 On X, Y, K1 and K2 models, before removing the bearing shells from the left-hand crankcase half, undo the bearing retainer plate screws and remove the plate **(see illustration)**. On installation apply a suitable non-permanent thread locking compound to the screw threads and tighten them to the specified torque setting.

27.10b . . . and the internal diameter of the main bearing

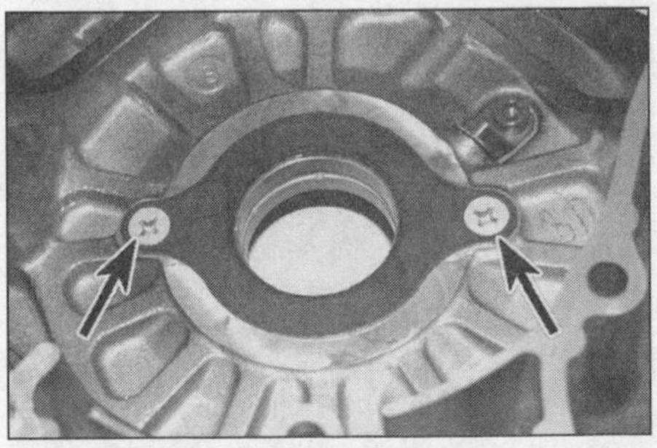

27.13 Undo the screws (arrowed) and remove the retainer plate from the left half – X, Y, K1 and K2 models

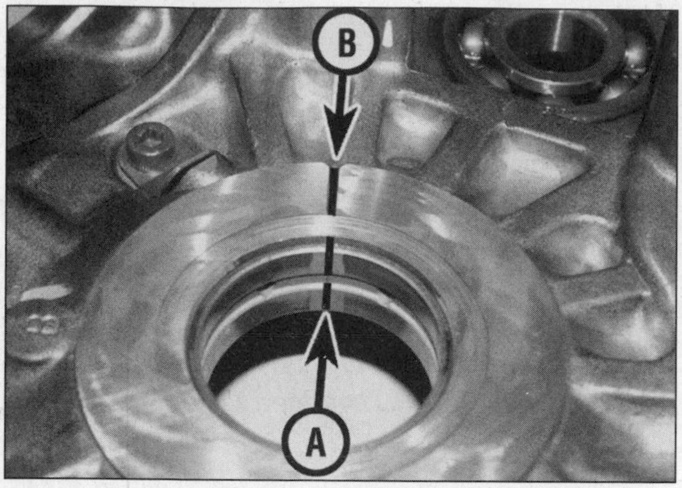

27.14 Align the mating edges (A) with the index line (B)

27.15 Measure the thickness of the shim using a micrometer

14 Remove the old bearings by pressing them out from the inside of the crankcase. Do not reuse the bearings after removal even if they appear to be in good condition. Before installing the new bearings, assemble the bearing shells in the special tool holder and tighten the holder bolts to 23 Nm. Install the new bearings by pressing them in from the inside. Align the mating edges of each shell with the index lines on the inside of the crankcase **(see illustration)**. Apply molybdenum disulphide oil (a mixture of 50% molybdenum disulphide grease and 50% engine oil) to the outside of the bearing to ease its entry into the housing. The special tool will ensure that the new bearings are installed to the correct depth in the bearing housing.

End-float shim selection

15 If the amount of end-float recorded earlier is greater or less than the specified amount, a new shim of the correct thickness to bring the end-float back into range must be selected and fitted. First determine the amount by which the end-float is incorrect by calculating the difference between that recorded (see Step 1) and that specified. Now measure the thickness of the existing shim **(see illustration)**.

16 New shims are available from 1.925 to 2.150 mm, in increments of 0.025 mm. If the current end-float is too great, the existing shim is too thin, and so the amount of excess end-float must be added to the current shim thickness to determine the required thickness of the new shim. In the unlikely event that the current end-float is too small, the existing shim is too thick, and so the amount by which the end-float is too little must be subtracted from the current shim thickness to determine the required thickness of the new shim.

Installation

17 If removed, fit the connecting rods onto the crankshaft (see Section 28).

18 Apply molybdenum disulphide oil (a mixture of 50% molybdenum disulphide grease and 50% engine oil) to the main bearings. Carefully lower the tapered (alternator) end of the crankshaft into position in the left-hand crankcase **(see illustration 27.3)**.

19 Lubricate the crankshaft end-float shim with molybdenum disulphide oil (a mixture of 50% molybdenum disulphide grease and 50% engine oil) and fit it onto the right-hand end of the crankshaft with the grooves facing the crankshaft web **(see illustration 27.2)**.

20 Reassemble the crankcase halves (see Section 24), then recheck the endfloat as described in Step 1.

28.2 Measure the connecting rod side clearance

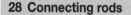

28.3 Note the rod size code numbers

28 Connecting rods

Removal

1 Remove the crankshaft (see Section 27).

2 Before removing the rods from the crankshaft, measure the side clearance between the rods and the crank web with a feeler gauge **(see illustration)**. If the clearance is greater than the service limit listed in this Chapter's Specifications, refer to Step 6.

3 Using paint or a felt marker pen, mark the relevant cylinder identity on each connecting rod (i.e. FRONT or REAR). The left-hand side (alternator end) of the crankpin holds the front cylinder rod, and the right-hand side (primary drive gear end) of the crankpin holds the rear cylinder rod. Mark across the cap-to-connecting rod join to ensure that the cap is fitted the correct way around on reassembly. Do not obscure the existing marking on the intake side of each connecting rod (mark the cylinder ID on the other side – in this way the FRONT marking for the front cylinder rod will in fact be facing the front of the engine, and the REAR marking will be facing the rear). The number already marked is the connecting rod big-end size code **(see illustration)**.

4 Unscrew the big-end cap bolts and separate the connecting rod, cap and both bearing shells from the crankpin **(see illustrations)**. Tap the bolts with a soft hammer to separate them if required. Keep the rod, cap, bolts and (if they are to be re-used) the bearing shells together in their correct positions to ensure correct installation.

Inspection

5 Check the connecting rods for cracks and other obvious damage.

6 If the side clearance measured in Step 1 exceeds the service limit, measure the width of each rod's big-end and the width of the

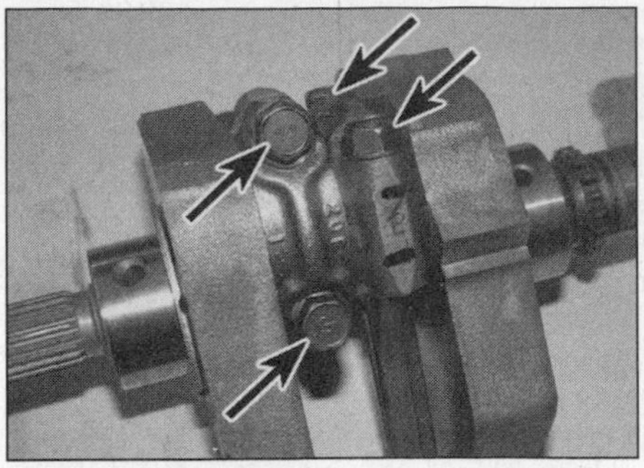

28.4a Unscrew the connecting rod big end cap bolts (arrowed) . . .

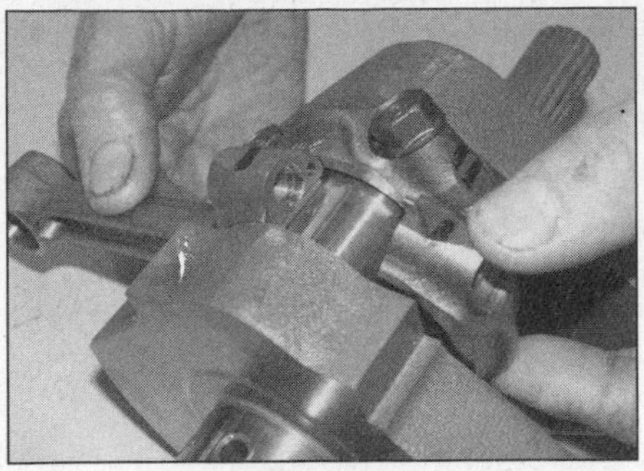

28.4b . . . and separate the rods from the crankpin

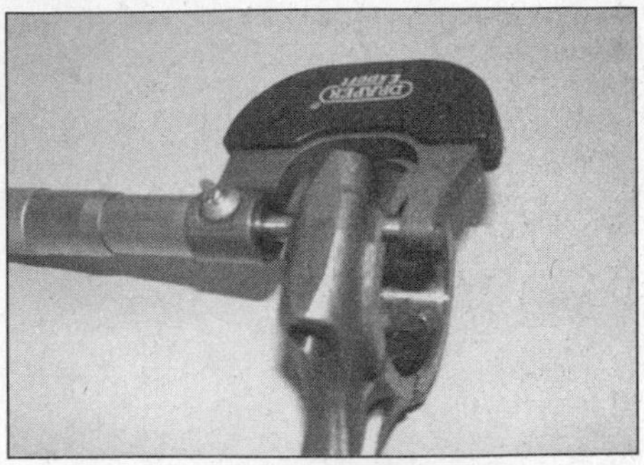

28.6a Measure the width of each rod's big-end . . .

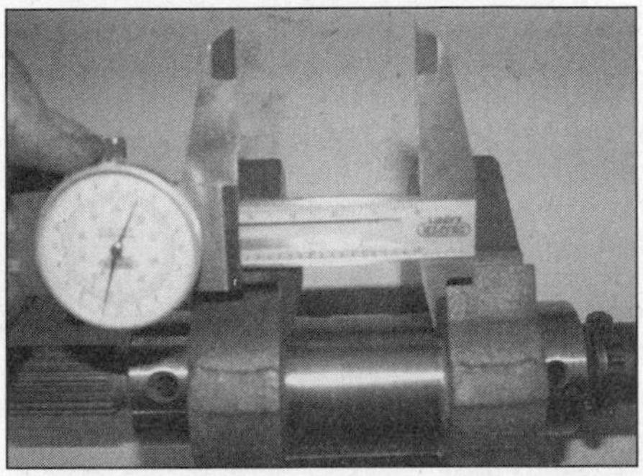

28.6b . . . and the width of the crankpin

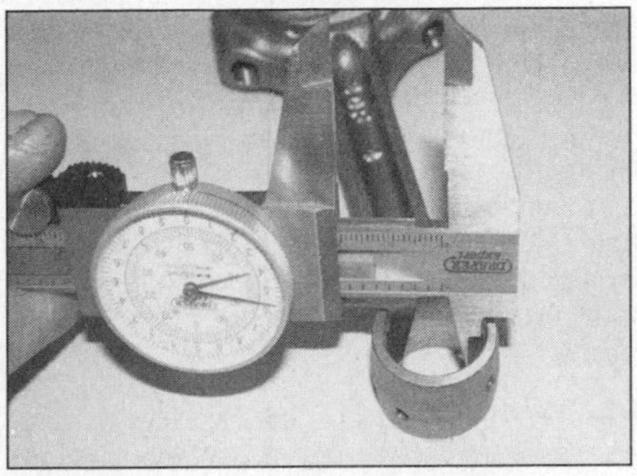

28.7 Measure the connecting rod small end internal diameter

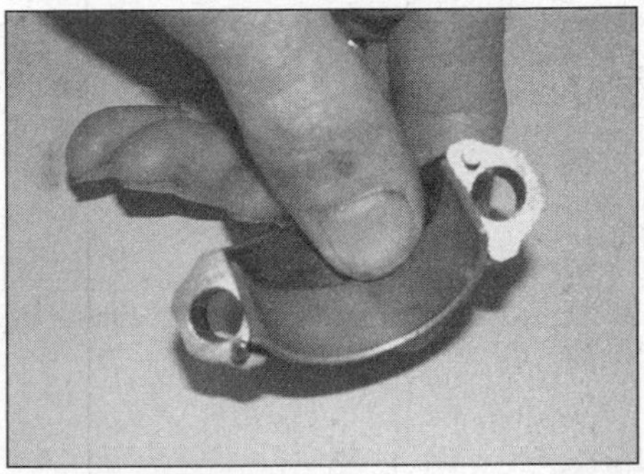

28.11 Remove the shells from the rod and cap

crankpin **(see illustrations)**. If either big-end is narrower than specified renew the rod. If the width of the crankpin is greater than specified renew the crankshaft.

7 If not already done (see Section 16), apply clean engine oil to the piston pin, insert it into the connecting rod small-end and check for any freeplay between the two. Measure the pin OD **(see illustration 16.12b)** and the small-end bore ID **(see illustration)** and compare the measurements to the specifications at the beginning of the Chapter. Calculate the difference between the measurements taken to obtain the piston pin-to-small end clearance and compare the result to the specifications. Replace components that are worn beyond the specified limits.

8 Refer to Section 26 and examine the connecting rod bearing shells. If they are scored, badly scuffed or appear to have seized, new shells must be installed. Always renew the shells in the connecting rods as a set. If they are badly damaged, check the corresponding crankpin. Evidence of extreme heat, such as discoloration, indicates that lubrication failure has occurred. Be sure to thoroughly check the oil pump and pressure relief valve as well as all oil holes and passages before reassembling the engine.

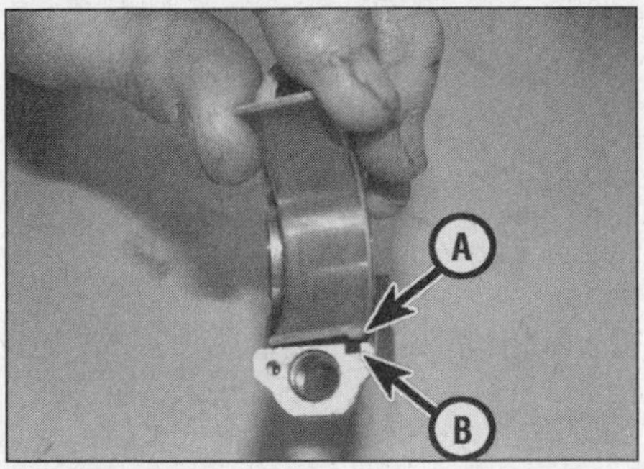

28.12 Fit the shell into its housing making sure the tab (A) locates in the notch (B)

9 Have the rods checked for twist and bend by a Suzuki dealer if you are in doubt about their straightness.

Oil clearance check

10 Whether new bearing shells are being fitted or the original ones are being re-used, the connecting rod bearing oil clearance should be checked prior to reassembly.

11 Remove the bearing shells from the connecting rod and cap **(see illustration)**. Clean the backs of the shells and the bearing locations in both the rod and cap.

12 Press the bearing shells into their locations, ensuring that the tab on each shell engages the notch in the connecting rod/cap **(see illustration)**. Make sure the bearings are fitted in the correct locations and take care not to touch any shell's bearing surface with your fingers.

13 Cut a length of the Plastigauge (it should be slightly shorter than the width of the crankpin) and place it on the (cleaned) crankpin journal. Lubricate the connecting rod bolts with clean engine oil. Fit the (clean) connecting rod assemblies, shells and caps **(see illustration 28.4b)**. Make sure the rods and caps are fitted the correct way around so the previously made markings align (see Step 3), and tighten the bearing cap bolts in two stages, first to the initial torque setting specified at the beginning of the Chapter and then to the final torque setting, whilst ensuring that the connecting rod does not rotate **(see illustration 28.21a and b)**. Now slacken the cap bolts and remove the connecting rod assemblies, again taking great care not to rotate the connecting rod.

14 Compare the width of the crushed Plastigauge at its widest point to the scale printed on the Plastigauge envelope to obtain the connecting rod bearing oil clearance.

15 If the clearance is not within the specified limits, the bearing shells may be the wrong grade (or excessively worn if the original shells are being re-used). Before deciding that different grade shells are needed, make sure that no dirt or oil was trapped between the bearing shells and the connecting rod or cap when the clearance was measured, and be

28.15 Measure the diameter of the crankpin to see if it is worn

28.17 Crankpin journal size numbers

28.21a Lubricate and install the bolts . . .

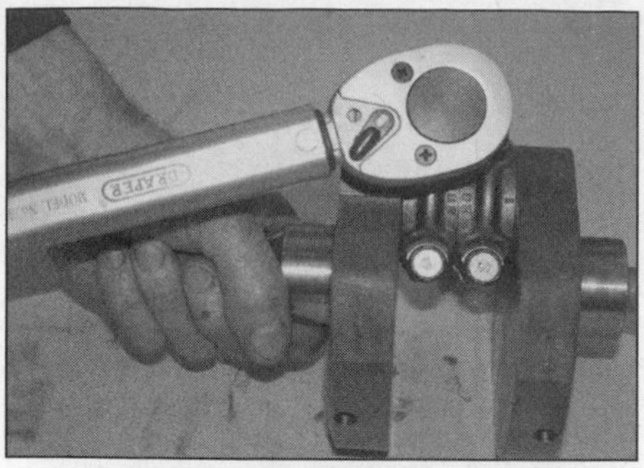
28.21b . . . and tighten them to the specified torque setting as described

certain the neither rod turned in the crankpin and distorted the strand of Plastigauge. If the clearance is excessive, even with new shells (of the correct size), measure the diameter of the crankpin and compare it to the specifications **(see illustration)**. If it is worn beyond the specified range, the crankshaft should be renewed.

16 On completion carefully scrape away all traces of the Plastigauge material from the crankpin and bearing shells using a fingernail or other object which is unlikely to score the shells.

Bearing shell selection

17 New bearing shells for the big-end bearings are supplied on a selected fit basis. Codes stamped on the crankshaft and rods are used to identify the correct replacement bearings. The crankpin journal size number is stamped on one crankshaft web and will be either 1, 2 or 3 – the left-hand number with the L before it corresponds to the left-hand side (alternator end) of the crankpin which holds the front cylinder rod, and the right-hand number with the R after it corresponds to the right-hand side (primary drive gear end) of the crankpin which holds the rear cylinder rod **(see illustration)**. The connecting rod size code is marked on the flat face of the connecting rod and cap and will be either 1 or a 2 **(see illustration 28.3)**.

18 A range of bearing shells is available. Select the correct bearing shells for each connecting rod in accordance with the table below. The bearings themselves are identified by colour (see table). The dimensions relating to the particular codes are given in the table below.

Installation

19 Work on one rod at a time, and make sure it is installed on the correct side of the crank-pin, and the correct way round (see Step 3). Clean the backs of the bearing shells and the bearing housings in both cap and rod. If new shells are being fitted, ensure that all traces of the protective grease are cleaned off using paraffin (kerosene). Wipe the shells, cap and rod dry with a clean lint free cloth. Fit the bearing shells in the connecting rod and cap, making sure the tab on each shell engages the notch in the rod/cap **(see illustrations 28.11 and 12)**.

20 Lubricate each shell's bearing surface with molybdenum disulphide oil (a 50/50 mixture of molybdenum disulphide grease and clean engine oil). Fit the connecting rod onto the crankpin and fit the cap onto the rod **(see illustration 28.4b)**. Make sure the cap is fitted the correct way around so the previously made markings align (see Step 3). Check to make sure that all components have been returned to their original locations using the marks made on disassembly.

21 Apply molybdenum disulphide oil to the threads and under the heads of the connecting rod bolts. Fit the bolts and tighten them in two stages, first to the initial torque setting specified at the beginning of the Chapter and then to the final torque setting **(see illustrations)**.

22 Check that the rod rotates smoothly and freely on the crankpin. If there are any signs of roughness or tightness, remove the rod and re-check the bearing clearance.

23 Install the crankshaft (see Section 27).

Bearing shell selection	Connecting rod code	
Crankpin journal code	1 (41.000 – 41.008 mm)	2 (41.008 – 41.016 mm)
1 (37.992 – 38.000 mm)	Green (1.480 – 1.484 mm)	Black (1.484 – 1.488 mm)
2 (37.984 – 37.992 mm)	Black (1.484 – 1.488 mm)	Brown (1.488 – 1.492 mm)
3 (37.976 – 37.984 mm)	Brown (1.488 – 1.492 mm)	Yellow (1.492 – 1.496 mm)

29.3a Withdraw the shafts (arrowed) . . .

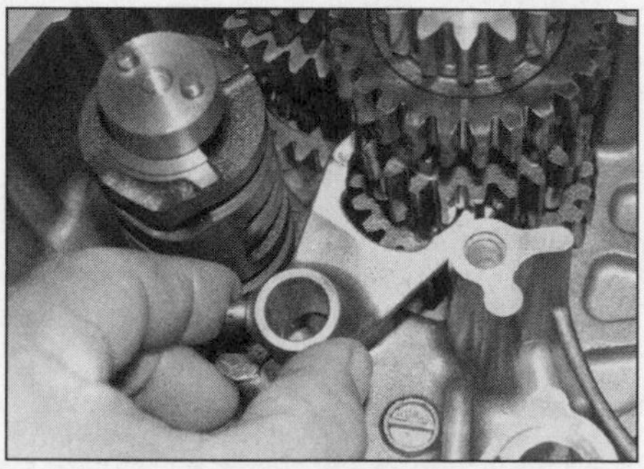
29.3b . . . then remove the forks . . .

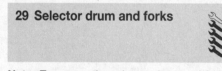

29 Selector drum and forks

Note: *To access the selector drum and forks the engine must be removed from the frame and the crankcases separated.*

Removal

1 Separate the crankcase halves (Section 24). Remove the crankshaft (see Section 27) – though not essential, working with it in place restricts access and makes the procedure fiddly.

2 The selector forks are not marked for identification, so it is best to mark them yourself using a felt pen according to where they fit.

3 Withdraw the selector fork shafts from the crankcase **(see illustration)**. Pivot each fork out of its track in the selector drum and remove it noting how it locates in the groove in its pinion **(see illustration)**. Withdraw the selector drum from the crankcase **(see illustration)**. Once removed, slide the forks back onto the shafts in their correct order and way round **(see illustration)**.

Inspection

4 Inspect the selector forks for any signs of wear or damage, especially around the fork ends where they engage with the groove in the

29.3c . . . and the drum

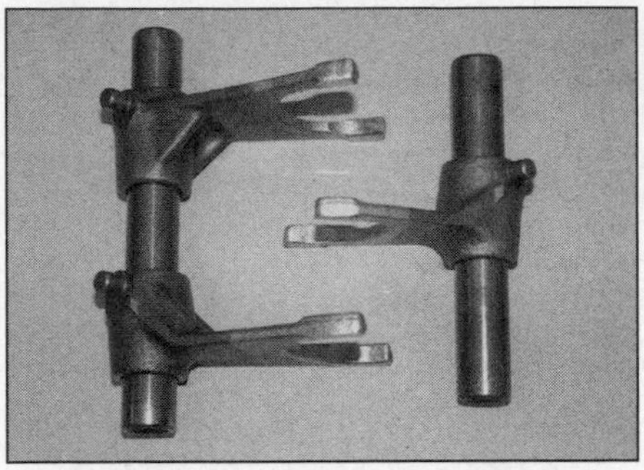
29.3d Slide the forks back on their shafts

29.5a Measure the fork-to-groove side clearance using a feeler gauge

29.5b Measure the thickness of the fork end . . .

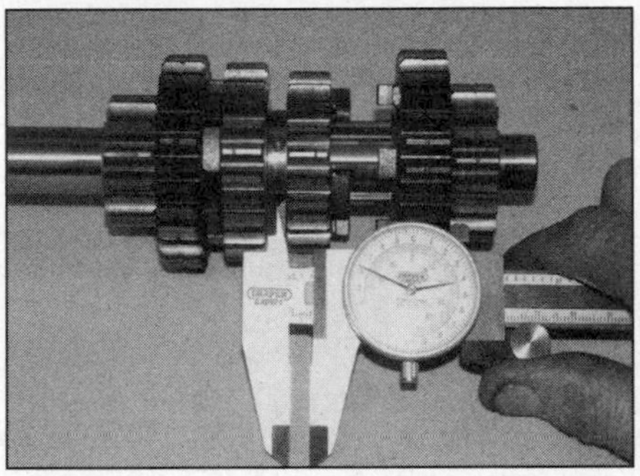
29.5c . . . and the width of the groove

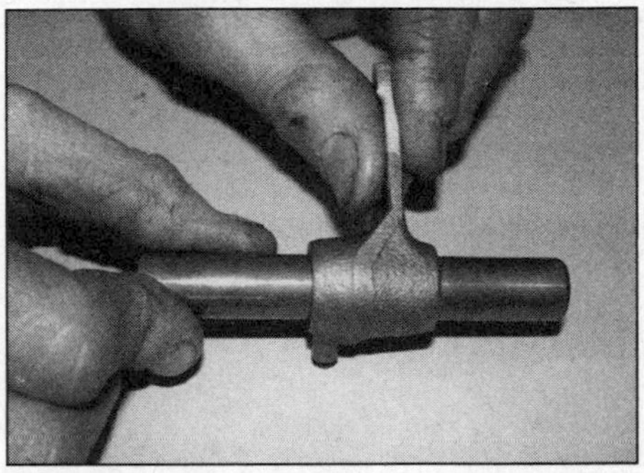
29.6 Check the fit of the fork on the shaft as described

gear pinion. Check that each fork fits correctly in its pinion groove. Check closely to see if the forks are bent. If the forks are in any way damaged they must be renewed.

5 Slip each fork in turn into the groove in its gear pinion on the transmission shaft and measure the fork-to-groove clearance using a feeler gauge **(see illustration)**. Compare the results to the specifications at the beginning of the Chapter. If the clearance exceeds the service limit specified, measure the thickness of the fork ends and the width of the groove and compare the readings to the specifications **(see illustrations)**. Renew whichever components are worn beyond their specifications.

6 Check that the forks fit correctly on their shaft **(see illustration)**. They should move freely with a light fit but no appreciable freeplay. Renew the forks and/or shafts if they are worn. Check that the fork shaft holes in the casing are neither worn nor damaged.

7 Check the selector fork shafts for trueness by rolling them along a flat surface. A bent shaft will cause difficulty in selecting gears and make the gearchange action heavy. Renew the shafts if they are bent.

8 Inspect the selector drum grooves and selector fork guide pins for signs of wear or damage **(see illustration)**. If either component shows signs of wear or damage the fork(s) and drum must be renewed.

9 Check that the selector drum bearings in each crankcase half rotate freely and smoothly and are tight in the casing **(see illustrations)**. Remove the old bearings and fit new ones if necessary (see *Tools and Workshop Tips* in the Reference Section). The bearing in the right crankcase half is held by two retainers, secured by screws **(see illustration 29.9b)**. On installation apply a suitable non-permanent thread locking compound to the screws and tighten them to the specified torque setting.

Installation

10 Apply clean oil to the journal on the left-hand end of the selector drum. Slide the drum into position in the crankcase **(see illustration 29.3c)**, aligning it so that the lowest point in the bottom groove is above the protrusion on the crankcase – this locates it in the neutral position **(see illustration)**.

11 Apply molybdenum disulphide oil (a 50/50 mixture of molybdenum disulphide grease and clean engine oil) to the selector fork ends. Slide each fork into the groove of its gear pinion on the correct transmission shaft and locate the guide pin on the end of each fork into its groove in the selector drum – you may

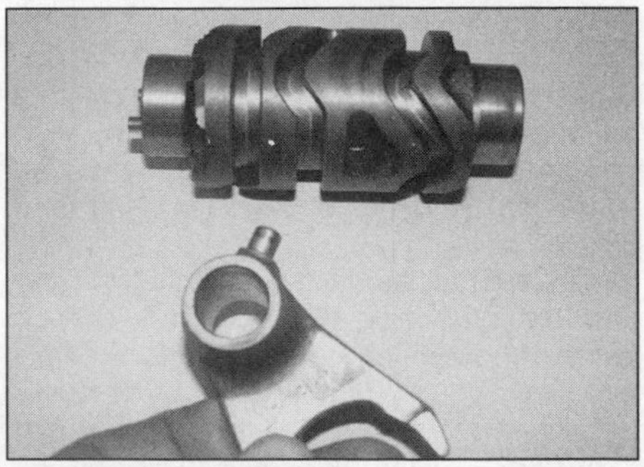
29.8 Check the drum grooves and fork guide pins

29.9a Check the needle bearing (arrowed) in the left half . . .

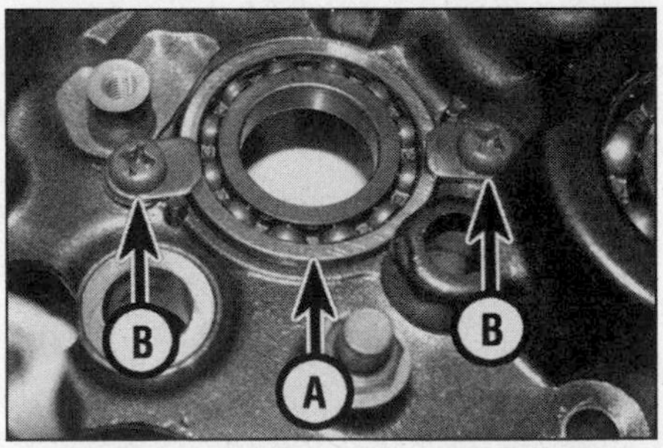

29.9b . . . and the ball bearing (A) in the right half, which is secured by two retainers (B)

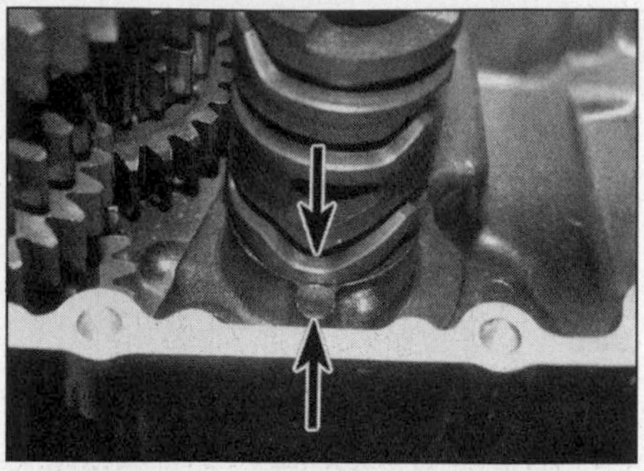

29.10 Align the lowest point of the bottom groove with the protrusion

29.11a Locate the input shaft fork in its pinion and then in the drum

29.11b Locate the lower output shaft fork in its pinion groove . . .

29.11c . . . then locate the guide pin in the selector drum

29.11d Locate the upper output shaft fork in its pinion groove . . .

29.11e . . . then locate the guide pin in the selector drum

29.12a Lubricate each shaft . . .

29.12b . . . then fit them through the fork(s) and into the crankcase

have to move the forks and their pinions up to achieve this **(see illustrations)**.

12 Lubricate the selector fork shafts with molybdenum disulphide oil (a 50/50 mixture of molybdenum disulphide grease and clean engine oil) and slide each through its fork(s) and into its bore in the crankcase **(see illustrations)**.

13 Reassemble the crankcase halves (see Section 24).

30 Transmission shafts – removal and installation

Removal

1 Separate the crankcase halves (Section 24). Remove the crankshaft (see Section 27) – though not essential, working with it in place restricts access and makes the procedure more fiddly.

2 Remove the selector drum and forks (see Section 29).

3 Grasp the input shaft and output shaft and withdraw them from the crankcase as an assembly, noting their relative positions and how they fit together **(see illustration)**. If the output shaft is tight in the crankcase, gently tap the bottom of the shaft using a soft-faced hammer or drift. Separate the shafts. Note the thrust washer on the right-hand end of the output shaft. On K4-on models, note the O-ring and wave washer on the left-hand end of the input shaft.

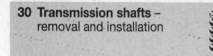

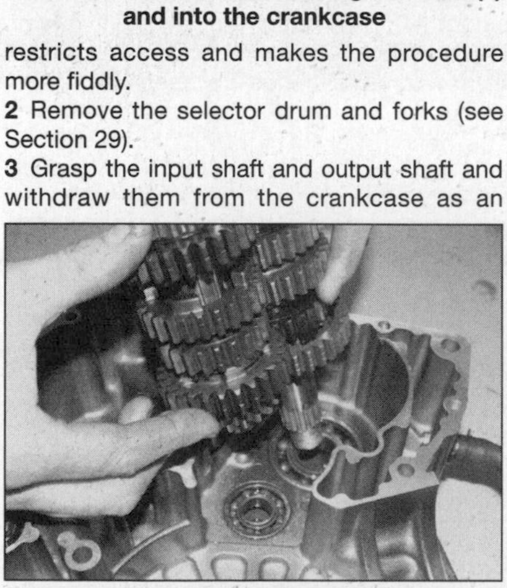

30.3 Grasp the shafts and lift them out of the crankcase

4 Lever the output shaft oil seal out of the crankcase and discard it as a new one must be used **(see illustration 25.4b)**. If necessary, the transmission shafts can be disassembled and inspected for wear or damage (see Section 31).

Installation

5 Smear the lips of a new output shaft oil seal with grease and fit it into the crankcase, using a suitable socket to drive it into place if necessary **(see illustrations 25.11a and b)**.

6 Support the left-hand half of the crankcase on wooden blocks so the end of the transmission output shaft does not contact the work surface as it is installed. Make sure that the wave washer and O-ring are installed on the left-hand end of the input shaft **(see illustration 31.35c)**.

7 Lay the input shaft and output shaft side by side on the bench so that the pinions for each gear mesh together **(see illustration)**. Make sure that the shafts are the correct way round, in which case the smallest pinion on the input shaft meshes with the largest pinion on the output shaft. Lubricate the left-hand end of each shaft with clean engine oil.

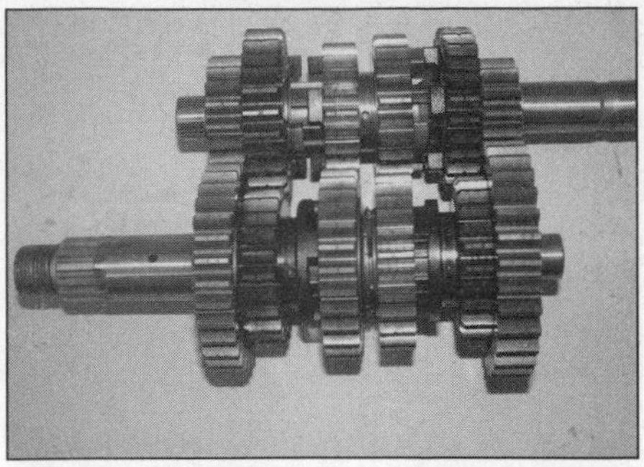
30.7 Position the shafts side by side so the relative pinions mesh

30.8a Make sure the shaft ends locate in their bearings

30.8b Tap the end of the output shaft if it is tight

8 Grasp the input shaft and output shaft and install them into the left-hand crankcase **(see illustration 30.3)**, making sure that both ends engage in their bearings **(see illustration)**. If the output shaft is tight in the bearing, gently tap on the end of the shaft to ease it in **(see illustration)**. Make sure that the thrust washer is installed on the right-hand end of the output shaft **(see illustration 31.35c)**.

9 Install the selector drum and forks (see Section 29).

10 Install the crankshaft if removed (see Section 27). Join the crankcase halves (Section 24).

31 Transmission shafts – disassembly, inspection and reassembly

Note: *References to the right- and left-hand ends of the transmission shafts are made as though they are installed in the engine and the engine is the correct way up.*

HAYNES HiNT ***When disassembling the transmission shafts, place the parts on a long rod or thread a wire through them to keep them in order and facing the proper direction.***

1 Remove the transmission shafts from the crankcase (see Section 30). Always disassemble the transmission shafts separately to avoid mixing up the components.

Input shaft disassembly

2 On K4-on models, first remove the O-ring and wave washer on the left-hand end of the shaft. On all models, reach behind the 6th gear pinion with circlip pliers, spread the circlip and slide it toward the 3rd/4th gear pinion **(see illustration)**. Slide the 6th and 2nd gear pinions back to expose the snap-ring on the end of the shaft, then remove it **(see illustration)**. Slide the 2nd gear pinion off the shaft having marked its outer face as a guide to refitting, then slide the 6th gear pinion off the shaft, followed by the bush and the thrust washer off the shaft **(see illustrations 31.18a and 31.17c, b and a)**.

3 Remove the circlip, then slide the combined 3rd/4th gear pinion off the shaft **(see illustrations 31.16b and a)**.

4 Remove the circlip securing the 5th gear pinion, then slide the thrust washer, the 5th gear pinion and its bush off the shaft **(see illustrations 31.15d, c, b and a)**.

5 The 1st gear pinion is integral with the shaft **(see illustration)**.

Input shaft inspection

6 Wash all of the components in clean solvent and dry them off.

7 Check the gear teeth for cracking chipping, pitting and other obvious wear or damage. Any pinion that is damaged as such must be renewed.

8 Inspect the dogs and the dog holes in the gears for cracks, chips, and excessive wear especially in the form of rounded edges. Make sure mating gears engage properly. Renew the paired gears as a set if necessary.

9 Check for signs of scoring or bluing on the pinions, bushes and shaft. This could be caused by overheating due to inadequate lubrication. Check that all the oil holes and passages are clear. Renew any damaged pinions or bushes.

10 Check that each pinion moves freely on the shaft or bush but without undue freeplay. Check that each bush moves freely on the shaft but without undue freeplay.

11 The shaft is unlikely to sustain damage unless the engine has seized, placing an unusually high loading on the transmission, or the machine has covered a very high mileage. Check the surface of the shaft, especially where a pinion turns on it, and renew the shaft if it has scored or picked up, or if there are any cracks. Damage of any kind can only be cured by renewal.

12 Check that the transmission shaft bearings in each crankcase half rotate freely

31.2a Release the circlip from its groove and slide it along the shaft . . .

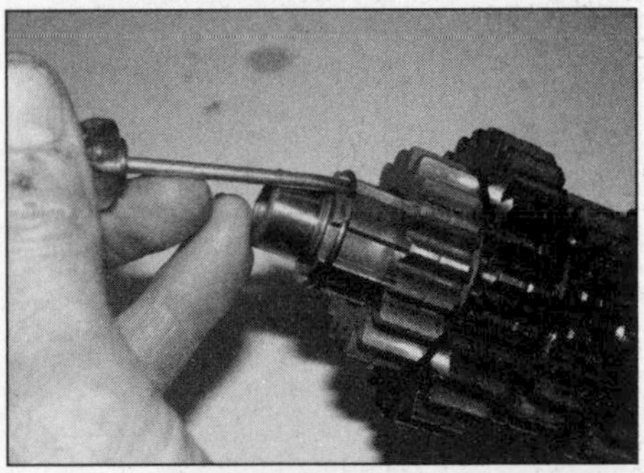
31.2b . . . then slide the pinions along and remove the snap-ring

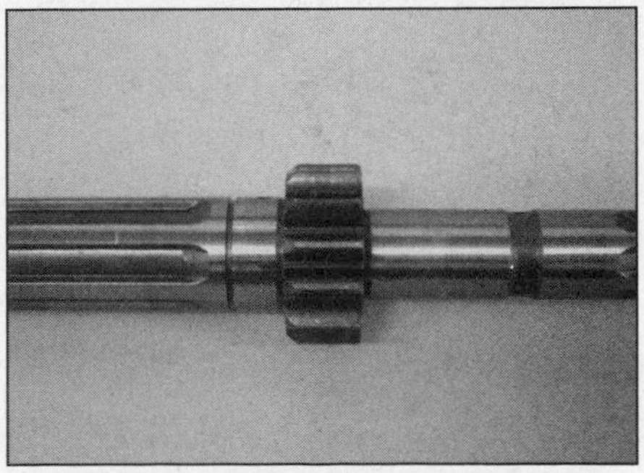
31.5 The 1st gear pinion is integral with the shaft

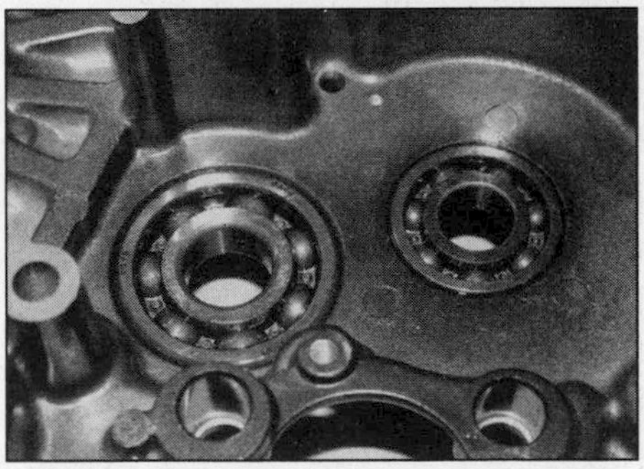
31.12 Check the transmission shaft bearings in each half

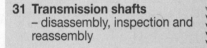

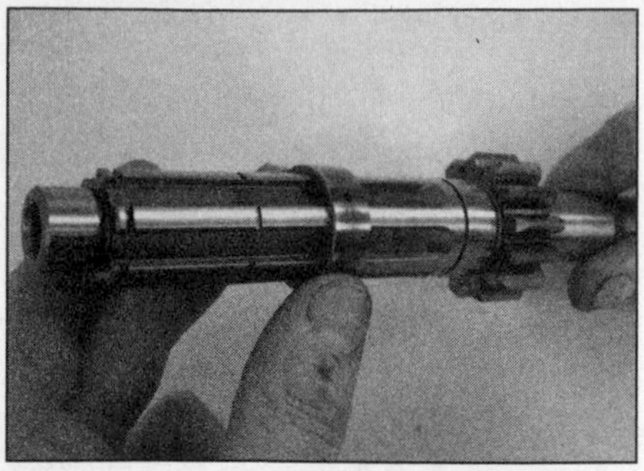

31.15a Slide the 5th gear pinion bush . . .

31.15b . . . the 5th gear pinion . . .

31.15c . . . and the thrust washer onto the shaft . . .

31.15d . . . then fit the circlip . . .

31.15e . . . making sure it locates correctly

31.16a Slide the 3rd/4th gear pinion onto the shaft . . .

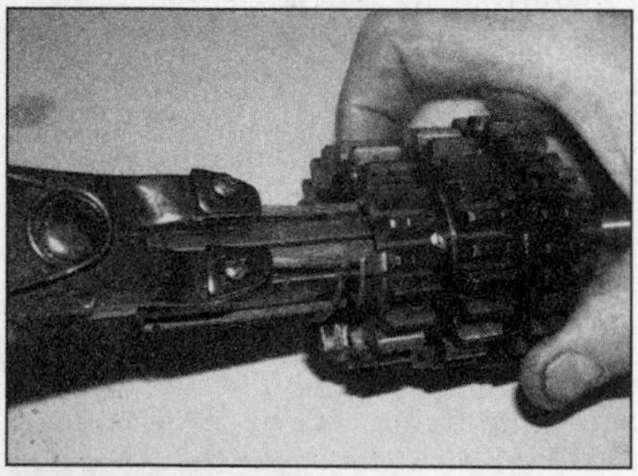

31.16b . . . then fit the circlip, positioning it as described

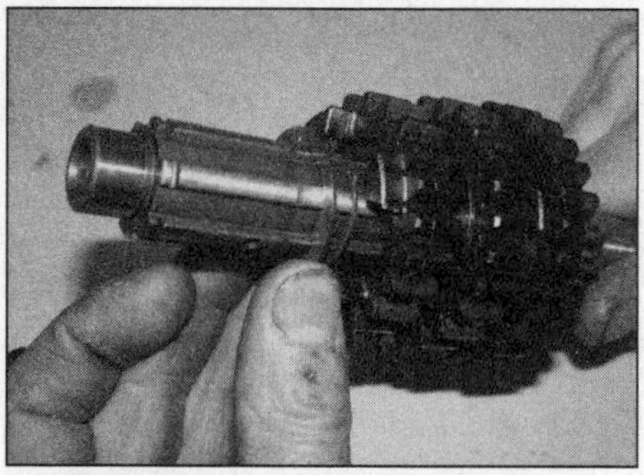

31.17a Slide the splined thrust washer . . .

31.17b . . . the 6th gear pinion splined bush . . .

31.17c . . . and the 6th gear pinion onto the shaft

31.18a Slide the 2nd gear pinion onto the shaft . . .

31.18b . . . then fit the snap-ring . . .

31.18c . . . making sure it locates correctly

31.18d Slide the pinions towards the end of the shaft and fit the circlip into its groove . . .

31.18e . . . making sure it locates correctly

and smoothly and are tight in the casing **(see illustration)**. Remove the old bearings and fit new ones if necessary (see *Tools and Workshop Tips* in the Reference Section).

13 Discard all the circlips and the snap-ring as new ones must be used.

Input shaft reassembly

14 During reassembly, apply molybdenum disulphide oil (a 50/50 mixture of molybdenum disulphide paste or grease and clean engine oil) to the mating surfaces of the shaft, pinions and bushes. When installing the circlips, do not expand the ends any further than is necessary. Install the stamped circlips so that their chamfered side faces the pinion it secures, i.e. so that its sharp edge faces the direction of thrust load (see *correct fitting of a stamped circlip* illustration in Tools and Workshop Tips of the Reference section).

15 Slide the 5th gear pinion bush onto the left-hand end of the shaft, followed by the 5th gear pinion with its dogs facing away from the integral 1st gear **(see illustrations)**. Slide the thrust washer onto the shaft **(see illustration)**. Install the circlip, making sure that it locates correctly in the groove in the shaft **(see illustrations)**.

16 Slide the combined 3rd/4th gear pinion onto the shaft, so that the larger (4th gear) pinion faces the 5th gear pinion dogs **(see illustration)**. Fit the circlip onto the shaft but do not locate it in its groove – slide it past the groove and as far towards the 3rd/4th gear pinion as possible **(see illustration)**.

17 Slide the splined thrust washer onto the shaft, followed by the 6th gear pinion splined bush, aligning the oil hole in the bush with that in the shaft **(see illustration)**. Slide the 6th gear pinion onto the bush, with its dog holes facing the dogs on the 3rd gear pinion **(see illustration)**.

18 Slide the 2nd gear pinion onto the shaft (using the mark made on removal to identify its outer face) and secure it with the snap-ring, making sure it is properly seated in its groove **(see illustrations)**; note that the pinion should have a recess in its outer face to accommodate the snap-ring and the gear teeth on the inner face should have a slight chamfer. Now slide the 6th and 2nd gear pinions along to expose the groove for the 3rd/4th gear pinion circlip, then move the circlip along the shaft and fit it into the groove **(see illustrations)**. On K4-on models, install the wave washer and O-ring on the left-hand end of the input shaft.

19 Check that all components have been correctly installed **(see illustration)**.

Output shaft disassembly

20 Remove the thrust washer from the right-hand end of the shaft **(see illustration 31.35c)**.

21 Slide the 1st gear pinion and its bush off the shaft, followed by the thrust washer and the 5th gear pinion **(see illustrations 31.35b and a and 34b and a)**.

22 Remove the circlip securing the 4th gear pinion, then slide the thrust washer, the pinion and its splined bush off the shaft **(see illustration 31.33d, c, b and a)**.

23 Slide the tabbed lockwasher off the shaft, then turn the slotted splined washer to offset the splines and slide it off the shaft, noting how they fit together **(see illustrations 31.32c and a)**.

24 Slide the 3rd gear pinion, its bush and the thrust washer off the shaft **(see illustrations 31.31c, b and a)**.

25 Remove the circlip securing the 6th gear pinion, then slide the pinion off the shaft **(see illustrations 31.30b and a)**.

26 Remove the circlip securing the 2nd gear pinion, then draw the collared bush out of the pinion and slide it off the shaft, followed by the pinion **(see illustrations 31.29c, b and a)**.

Output shaft inspection

27 Refer to Steps 6 to 13 above.

Output shaft reassembly

28 During reassembly, apply molybdenum disulphide oil (a 50/50 mixture of molybdenum disulphide paste or grease and clean engine oil) to the mating surfaces of the shaft, pinions and bushes. When installing the circlips, do not expand the ends any further than is necessary. Install the stamped circlips so that their chamfered side faces the pinion it secures, i.e. so that its sharp edge faces the direction of thrust load (see *correct fitting of a stamped circlip* illustration in Tools and Workshop Tips of the Reference section).

29 Slide the 2nd gear pinion onto the shaft with its dog holes facing away from the shaft shoulder, then slide its bush into the centre of it **(see illustrations)**. Secure them in place

31.19 The assembled input shaft should look like this

31.29a Slide the 2nd gear pinion onto the shaft . . .

31.29b . . . and fit the bush into its centre

31.29c Fit the circlip . . .

31.29d . . . making sure it locates correctly

31.30a Slide the 6th gear pinion onto the shaft . . .

31.30b . . . then fit the circlip . . .

31.30c . . . making sure it locates correctly

31.31a Slide the splined thrust washer . . .

31.31b . . . the 3rd gear pinion splined bush . . .

31.31c . . . and the 3rd gear pinion onto the shaft

31.32a Slide the slotted splined washer onto the shaft . . .

31.32b . . . and turn it so that it is positioned as shown

31.32c Slide the lock washer onto the shaft with its tabs facing in . . .

31.32d . . . and locate the tabs in the slots

31.33a Slide the 4th gear pinion splined bush . . .

31.33b . . . the 4th gear pinion . . .

31.33c . . . and the splined thrust washer onto the shaft . . .

31.33d . . . then fit the circlip . . .

31.33e . . . making sure it locates correctly

31.34a Slide the 5th gear pinion . . .

with the circlip, making sure it is properly seated in its groove **(see illustrations)**.

30 Slide the 6th gear pinion onto the shaft with its selector fork groove facing away from the 2nd gear pinion, and secure it in place with the circlip, making sure it is properly seated in its groove **(see illustration)**.

31 Slide the splined thrust washer onto the shaft, followed by the 3rd gear pinion splined bush, aligning the oil hole in the bush with that in the shaft **(see illustrations)**. Slide the 3rd gear pinion onto the bush with its dog holes facing the 2nd gear pinion **(see illustration)**.

32 Slide the slotted splined washer onto the shaft and locate it in its groove, then turn it in the groove so that the splines on the washer align with the splines on the shaft and secure the washer in the groove **(see illustrations)**. Slide the lockwasher onto the shaft, so that the tabs on the lockwasher locate into the slots in the outer rim of the splined washer **(see illustrations)**.

33 Slide the 4th gear pinion bush onto the shaft, aligning the oil hole in the bush with that in the shaft, then slide the 4th gear pinion onto the bush with the dog holes facing away from the 3rd gear pinion **(see illustrations)**. Slide the splined washer onto the shaft, then secure them in place with the circlip, making sure it is properly seated in its groove **(see illustrations)**.

34 Slide the 5th gear pinion onto the shaft with its selector fork groove facing the 4th gear pinion, followed by the thrust washer **(see illustrations)**.

35 Slide the 1st gear pinion bush and pinion onto the shaft with the dog holes facing the 5th gear pinion, followed by the thrust washer **(see illustrations)**.

31.34b . . . and the thrust washer onto the shaft

31.35a Slide the 1st gear pinion bush . . .

31.35b . . . and the 1st gear pinion onto the shaft . . .

31.35c . . . then fit the thrust washer

36 Check that all components have been correctly installed **(see illustration)**.

32 Initial start-up after overhaul

1 Make sure the engine oil and coolant levels are correct (see *Daily (pre-ride) checks*). Make sure there is fuel in the tank.

2 Turn the engine kill switch to the ON position and place the transmission in neutral. Turn the ignition ON. Set the choke enough to encourage the bike to start, but not so much as to allow it to race.

3 Pull in the clutch lever and turn the engine over a couple of times on the starter motor to allow the oil to circulate. Now operate the choke and start the engine in the normal way, allowing it to run at a moderately fast idle until it reaches operating temperature.

Warning: If the oil pressure warning light doesn't go off, or it comes on while the engine is running, stop the engine immediately.

4 Check carefully that there are no oil or coolant leaks and make sure the transmission and controls, especially the brakes, function properly before road testing the machine. Refer to Section 33 for the recommended running-in procedure.

5 Upon completion of the road test, and after the engine has cooled down completely, recheck the valve clearances (see Chapter 1) and check the engine oil and coolant levels (see *Daily (pre-ride) checks*).

33 Recommended running-in procedure

1 Treat the machine gently for the first few miles to make sure oil has circulated throughout the engine and any new parts installed have started to seat.

2 Even greater care is necessary if the cylinders have been rebored or a new crankshaft has been fitted. In the case of a rebore, the engine will have to be run in as when new. This means greater use of the transmission and a restraining hand on the throttle until at least 500 miles (800 km) have been covered. There's no point in keeping to any set speed limit – the main idea is to keep from labouring the engine and to gradually increase performance up to the 500 mile (800 km) mark. These recommendations can be lessened to an extent when only a new crankshaft is installed. Experience is the best guide, since it's easy to tell when an engine is running freely. The table below shows the maximum engine speed limitations, which Suzuki provide for new motorcycles, and can be used as a guide.

3 If a lubrication failure is suspected, stop the engine immediately and try to find the cause. If an engine is run without oil, even for a short period of time, severe damage will occur.

31.36 The assembled output shaft should look like this

Maximum engine speed

Up to 500 miles (800 km)	5000 rpm max	Vary throttle position/speed
500 to 1000 miles (800 to 1600 km)	8000 rpm max	Vary throttle position/speed. Use full throttle for short bursts
Over 1000 miles (1600 km)	10,500 rpm max	Do not exceed tachometer red line

Chapter 3
Cooling system

Contents

Degrees of difficulty

Easy, suitable for novice with little experience	**Fairly easy,** suitable for beginner with some experience	**Fairly difficult,** suitable for competent DIY mechanic	**Difficult,** suitable for experienced DIY mechanic	**Very difficult,** suitable for expert DIY or professional

Specifications

Coolant

Mixture type and capacity	see Chapter 1

Cooling fan switch

Switch closes (fan ON)	approx. 96°C
Switch opens (fan OFF)	approx. 91°C

Coolant temperature sensor

X, Y, K1 and K2 models	
Switch closes (warning light ON)	approx. 115°C
Switch opens (warning light OFF)	approx. 108°C
K3, K4 and K5 models	
Resistance at 20°C	approx. 2.450 K-ohms
Resistance at 40°C	approx. 1.148 K-ohms
Resistance at 60°C	approx. 0.587 K-ohms
Resistance at 80°C	approx. 0.322 K-ohms

Thermostat

Opening temperature	
X, Y, K1 and K2 models	80 to 84°C
K3 to K6 models	approx. 88°C
K7-on models	approx. 76.5°C
Fully open	
X, Y, K1 and K2 models	95°C
K3-on models	approx. 100°C
Valve lift	
X to K6 models	8 mm (min) @ 100°C
K7-on models	8 mm (min) @ 90°C

Radiator

Cap valve opening pressure	13.5 to 17.8 psi (0.95 to 1.25 Bar)

Torque settings

Coolant temperature sensor	10 Nm
Crankcase cover bolts (right-hand side)	10 Nm
Fan switch	13 Nm
Water pump cover screws	4.5 Nm
Water pump impeller bolt (X and Y models)	13 Nm

1 General information

The cooling system uses a water/antifreeze coolant to carry away excess heat from the engine and maintain as constant a temperature as possible. Each cylinder is surrounded by a water jacket from which the heated coolant is circulated by thermo-syphonic action in conjunction with a water pump, which is gear driven off the crankshaft. The hot coolant passes upwards to the thermostat and through to the radiator. The coolant then flows down across the core of the radiator, then to the water pump and back to the engine where the cycle is repeated.

A thermostat is fitted in the system to prevent the coolant flowing through the radiator when the engine is cold, therefore accelerating the speed at which the engine reaches normal operating temperature. A coolant temperature sensor mounted in the thermostat housing transmits information to the temperature warning light on the instrument panel. A cooling fan is fitted to the back of the radiator to aid cooling in extreme conditions by drawing extra air through; a thermostatically-controlled switch fitted to the radiator triggers the operation of the fan motor.

The complete cooling system is partially sealed and pressurised, the pressure being controlled by a valve contained in the spring-loaded radiator cap. By pressurising the coolant the boiling point is raised, preventing premature boiling in adverse conditions. The overflow pipe from the system is connected to a reservoir into which excess coolant is expelled under pressure. The discharged coolant automatically returns to the radiator by the vacuum created when the engine cools.

Warning: Do not remove the pressure cap from the radiator when the engine is hot. Scalding hot coolant and steam may be blown out under pressure, which could cause serious injury. When the engine has cooled, place a thick rag, like a towel, over the pressure cap; slowly rotate the cap anti-clockwise to the first stop. This procedure allows any residual pressure to escape. When the steam has stopped escaping, press down on the cap while turning it anti-clockwise and remove it.

Warning: Do not allow antifreeze to come in contact with your skin or painted surfaces of the motorcycle. Rinse off any spills immediately with plenty of water. Antifreeze is highly toxic if ingested. Never leave antifreeze lying around in an open container or in puddles on the floor; children and pets are attracted by its sweet smell and may drink it. Check with the local authorities about disposing of used antifreeze. Many communities will have collection centres which will ensure that antifreeze is disposed of safely.

Caution: At all times use the specified type of antifreeze, and always mix it with distilled water in the correct proportion. The antifreeze contains corrosion inhibitors which are essential to avoid damage to the cooling system. A lack of these inhibitors could lead to a build-up of corrosion which would block the coolant passages, resulting in overheating and severe engine damage. Distilled water must be used as opposed to tap water to avoid a build-up of scale which would also block the passages.

3.5 Unscrew the bolts (arrowed) and remove the fan assembly

2 Radiator pressure cap

1 If problems such as overheating or loss of coolant occur, check the entire system as described in Chapter 1. The radiator cap opening pressure should be checked by a Suzuki dealer with the special tester required to do the job. If the cap is defective, renew it.

3 Cooling fan and fan switch

Cooling fan

Check

1 If the engine is overheating and the cooling fan isn't coming on, first check the fan switch as described below.

2 If the fan does not come on (and the fan switch is good), the fault lies in either the cooling fan motor or the relevant wiring. Test all the wiring and connections as described in Chapter 9, following the relevant Wiring Diagram. Remove the fuel tank and air filter housing for access to the wiring and connectors (see Chapter 4A or 4B as applicable). Trace the wiring from the fan and disconnect it at the connector. Check that there is battery voltage at the orange/yellow wire terminal on the loom side of the connector with the ignition ON. If there is no voltage, check the wiring.

3 To test the cooling fan motor, set up a 12 volt battery and two jumper wires with suitable connectors, and connect the battery positive (+ve) lead to the blue wire terminal on the fan side of the wiring connector, and the battery negative (–ve) lead to the black wire terminal on the wiring. Once connected the fan should operate. If it does not, and the wiring is all good, then the fan motor is faulty.

Renewal

Warning: The engine must be completely cool before carrying out this procedure.

4 Remove the radiator (see Section 6).

5 Undo the bolts securing the fan assembly to the radiator and separate them **(see illustration)**.

6 If required unscrew the fan blade nut and remove the blade, noting how it locates.

7 Installation is the reverse of removal. Apply a suitable non-permanent thread locking compound to the fan blade nut.

8 Install the radiator (see Section 6).

Cooling fan switch

Check

9 On X, Y, K1 and K2 SV650S models, remove the fairing right-hand side panel (see Chapter 8).

10 If the engine is overheating and the cooling fan isn't coming on, either disconnect the wiring connector from the fan switch on the right-hand side of the radiator, or trace the wiring from the fan switch and disconnect it at the connector, according to your model and the switch fitted **(see illustration 3.17)**. Using a jumper wire, connect between the terminals of the wiring connector on the loom side. Turn the ignition switch ON. The fan should come on. If it does, the fan switch is defective and must be renewed. If it does not come on, check for battery voltage at the black/red wire terminal on the switch wiring connector with the ignition ON. If no voltage is present, test the fan motor itself (see above). If there is voltage, check the black/white wire from the loom side of the connector for continuity to earth, and check all wiring and connectors for a fault or break.

11 If the fan is on the whole time, disconnect the switch wiring connector. The fan should stop. If it does, the switch is defective and must be renewed. If it doesn't, check the wiring between the fan and the switch for a short to earth, and the fan itself.

12 If the fan works but is suspected of cutting in at the wrong temperature, a more comprehensive test of the switch can be made as follows.

13 Remove the switch (see Steps 16 and 17). Fill a small heatproof container with oil and place it on a stove. Connect the positive (+ve) probe of an ohmmeter to one terminal of the switch and the negative (–ve) probe to the other terminal, and using some wire or other support suspend the switch in the oil so that just the sensing portion and the threads are

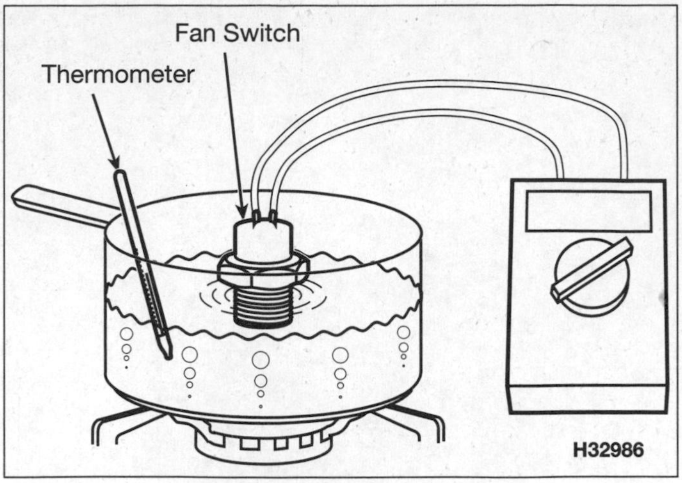

3.13 Cooling fan switch test set-up

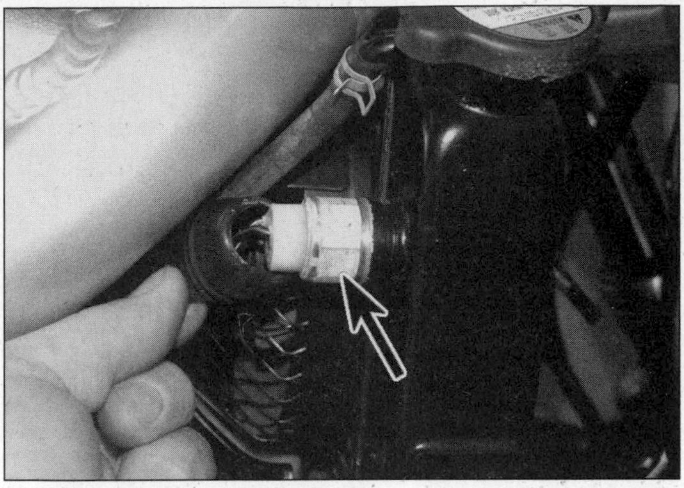

3.17 Fan switch (arrowed) – SV650SY shown

submerged **(see illustration)**. Also place a thermometer capable of reading temperatures up to 110°C in the oil so that its bulb is close to the switch. **Note:** *None of the components should be allowed to directly touch the container or be too close to it.*

14 Initially the ohmmeter reading should be very high indicating that the switch is open (OFF). Heat the oil, stirring it gently.

⚠ ***Warning: This must be done very carefully to avoid the risk of personal injury.***

When the temperature reaches around 96°C the meter reading should drop to around zero ohms, indicating that the switch has closed (ON). Now turn the heat off. As the temperature falls below 91°C the meter reading should show infinite (very high) resistance, indicating that the switch has opened (OFF). If the meter readings obtained are different, or they are obtained at different temperatures, then the switch is faulty and must be renewed.

Renewal

⚠ ***Warning: The engine must be completely cool before carrying out this procedure.***

15 On X, Y, K1 and K2 SV650S models, remove the fairing right-hand side panel (see Chapter 8).

16 Drain the cooling system (see Chapter 1).

17 Either disconnect the wiring connector from the fan switch on the right-hand side of the radiator, or trace the wiring from the fan switch and disconnect it at the connector, according to your model and the switch fitted **(see illustration)**. Unscrew the switch and withdraw it from the radiator. Discard the O-ring as a new one must be used.

18 Install the switch using a new O-ring and tighten it to the torque setting specified at the beginning of the Chapter. Take care not to overtighten the switch as the radiator could be damaged.

19 Reconnect the switch wiring and refill the cooling system (see Chapter 1).

4 Engine coolant temperature sensor and warning LED

Coolant temperature warning LED – X, Y, K1 and K2 models

Check

1 The circuit consists of the sensor mounted in the thermostat housing and the warning light mounted in the instrument cluster. If the system malfunctions first check the signal fuse in the fusebox.

2 If the warning light is not working, raise the fuel tank (see Chapter 4A). Disconnect the wiring connector from the sensor, accessing it from the right-hand side of the bike **(see illustration)**. Turn the ignition switch ON. The warning light should be out. Using a jumper wire attached to the wiring connector terminal, earth the sensor wire on the engine – the light should come on. If the light works as described above, it is proven good, and the sensor could be faulty – check it as described below (Steps 9 to 14).

3 If the light is still faulty, or if it does not come on at all, the fault lies in the wiring or the light itself, which is a light emitting diode (LED) that is integral with the instrument.

4 On SV650 models, remove the headlight beam unit from the shell (see Chapter 9), then disconnect the instrument cluster wiring connectors **(see illustration)**. On SV650S models remove the fairing and the cockpit trim panel (see Chapter 8), then disconnect the wiring connector from the instrument cluster **(see illustration)**.

5 Using an ohmmeter or continuity tester, check for continuity through the LED by connecting the positive (+ve) probe to the orange/green (no. 2) wire terminal and the negative (-ve) probe to the black/green (no. 15) wire terminal on the cluster side of the connectors (SV650) or the cluster socket

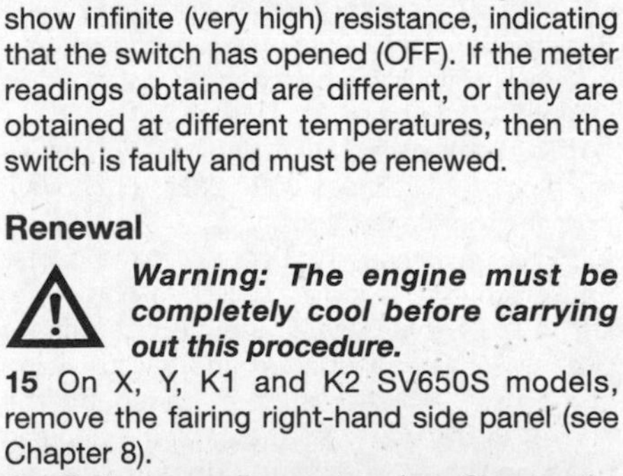

4.2 Coolant temperature sensor wiring connector (arrowed)

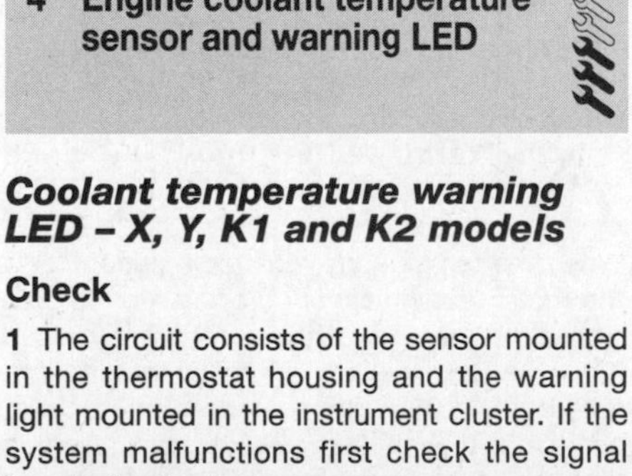

4.4a On SV650 models, disconnect the instrument wiring connectors

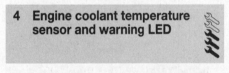

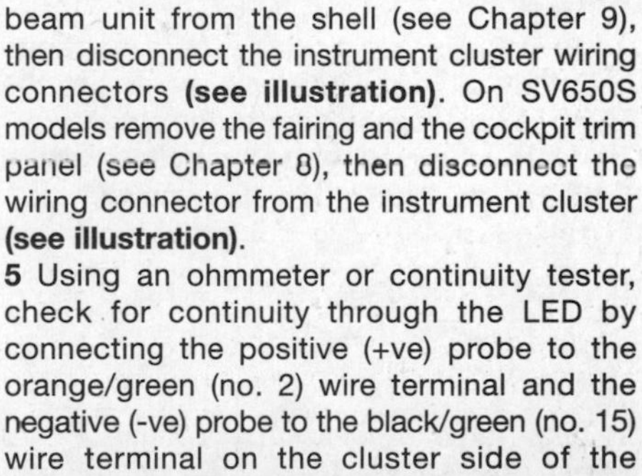

4.4b On SV650S models, disconnect the wiring connector from the instruments

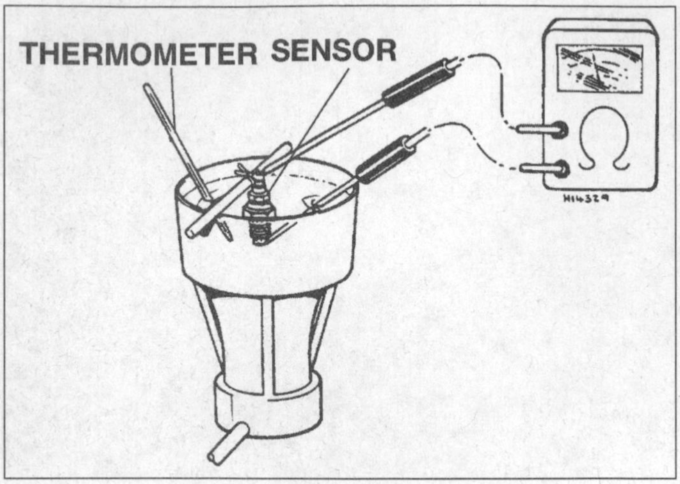

4.13 Coolant temperature sensor test set-up

4.27 Disconnect the ECT wiring connector

(SV650S) **(see illustration 16.3 in Chapter 9)**. If there is no continuity, the LED is faulty.

6 If there is continuity, check for continuity in the black/green wire between the instrument wiring connector (loom side) and the temperature sensor. If there is no continuity, locate the break in the wire and repair it. If there is continuity, check for continuity to earth in the black/white wire from the thermostat housing.

7 Check for battery voltage at the orange/green wire in the instrument wiring connector (loom side) with the ignition ON. If no voltage is present, check the orange/green wire between the instrument cluster wiring connector and the signal fuse in the fusebox.

Renewal

8 The LED is not available as a separate component. In the unlikely event that the LED has failed, either the tachometer (SV650 standard model) or instrument circuit board (SV650S models) must be renewed (see Chapter 9).

Coolant temperature sensor – X, Y, K1 and K2 models

Check

9 If the warning light is not working in normal use but the above checks have proven it to be good, raise the fuel tank (see Chapter 4A). Disconnect the wiring connector from the sensor, accessing it from the right-hand side of the bike **(see illustration 4.2)**.

10 As the warning light/sensor circuit earths itself through the sensor body and thermostat housing, using a continuity tester or multimeter, check for continuity between the sensor terminal and the thermostat housing – if the sensor is cold there will be some resistance, but there should be a complete circuit. If not, the sensor is faulty. If there is a reading, check for continuity between the thermostat housing and the engine or frame. If there is none, check the thermostat cover bolt that secures the black/white (earth) wiring connector for tightness. If the tests prove inconclusive, proceed as follows.

11 Drain the cooling system (see Chapter 1).

12 Remove the sensor (see Steps 15 and 16 below).

13 Fill a small heatproof container with oil and place it on a stove. Using an ohmmeter, connect the positive (+ve) probe of the meter to the terminal on the sensor, and the negative (–ve) probe to the body of the sensor. Using some wire or other support suspend the sensor in the oil so that just the sensing head and the threads are submerged. Also place a thermometer capable of reading temperatures up to 130°C in the water so that its bulb is close to the sensor **(see illustration)**. **Note:** *None of the components should be allowed to directly touch the container or be too close to it.*

14 Initially the ohmmeter reading should be very high indicating that the switch is open (OFF). Heat the oil, stirring it gently.

Warning: This must be done very carefully to avoid the risk of personal injury.

When the temperature reaches around 115°C the meter reading should drop to around zero ohms, indicating that the switch has closed (ON). Now turn the heat off. As the temperature falls below 108°C the meter reading should show infinite (very high) resistance, indicating that the switch has opened (OFF). If the meter readings obtained are different, or they are obtained at different temperatures, then the sensor is faulty and must be renewed.

Renewal

Warning: The engine must be completely cool before carrying out this procedure.

15 The sensor is mounted in the thermostat housing. Drain the cooling system (see Chapter 1). Raise the fuel tank (see Chapter 4A). Disconnect the wiring connector from the sensor, accessing it from the right-hand side of the bike **(see illustration 4.2)**.

16 Unscrew the sensor and remove it from the thermostat housing.

17 Apply a smear of suitable sealant (Suzuki Bond 1207B or equivalent) to the threads of the new sensor, making sure none gets on the sensor head. Install the sensor and tighten it to the torque setting specified at the beginning of the Chapter. Connect the sensor wiring.

18 Lower the fuel tank (see Chapter 4A). Refill the cooling system (see Chapter 1). Check that there are no leaks.

Engine coolant temperature (ECT) sensor – K3-on models

Check

19 The ECT sensor is mounted in the thermostat housing between the engine cylinders. If a sensor fault is indicated by the fuel injection system diagnostic process, carry out the preliminary checks as described in Chapter 4B, Section 11.

20 To check the sensor resistance, first follow the procedure in Steps 25 to 28 and remove it from the thermostat housing.

21 Fill a small heatproof container with water and place it on a stove. Using an ohmmeter set to the K-ohms scale, connect the meter probes to the sensor terminals, and using some wire or other support, suspend the sensor in the water so that just the sensing head and the threads are submerged. Also place a thermometer capable of reading temperatures up to 100°C in the water so that its bulb is close to the sensor **(see illustration 4.13)**. **Note:** *None of the components should be allowed to directly touch the container or be too close to it.*

22 Check the meter reading and compare it with the Specifications at the beginning of this Chapter, then heat the water slowly, stirring it gently.

Warning: This must be done very carefully to avoid the risk of personal injury.

23 As the temperature of the water rises, the sensor resistance should fall. Check that the specified resistance is obtained at the correct temperature (see Specifications). If the readings obtained are different, or are obtained at different temperatures, the sensor is faulty and must be replaced with a new one. If the readings are as specified, the fault could lie in the coolant temperature display circuit in the instrument cluster (see Chapter 9).

Renewal

> ⚠ ***Warning: The engine must be completely cool before carrying out this procedure.***

24 The ECT sensor is mounted in the thermostat housing between the engine cylinders.

25 Drain the cooling system (see Chapter 1).

26 Raise the fuel tank and displace the throttle bodies to gain access to the sensor (see Chapter 4B).

27 Disconnect the ECT sensor wiring connector **(see illustration)**.

28 Place a rag underneath the sensor and unscrew it. Discard the sealing washer as a new one must be used.

29 Installation is the reverse of removal, noting the following:

- Fit a new sealing washer to the sensor.
- Tighten the sensor to the torque setting specified at the beginning of the Chapter.
- Reconnect the wiring connector.
- Refill the cooling system (see Chapter 1).

5 Thermostat and housing

5.4a Detach the hose from the cover

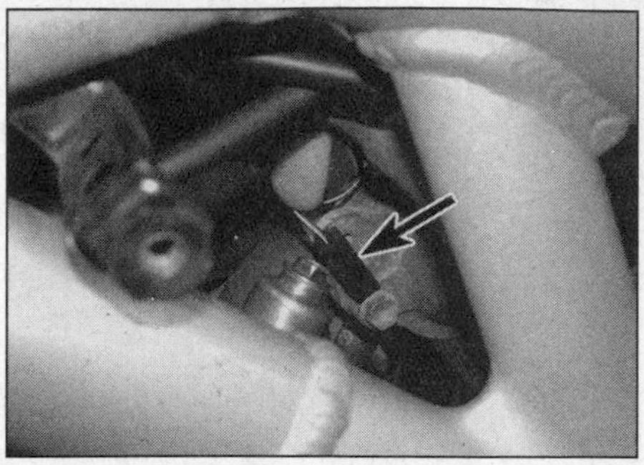

5.4b Disconnect the earth wiring connector (arrowed)

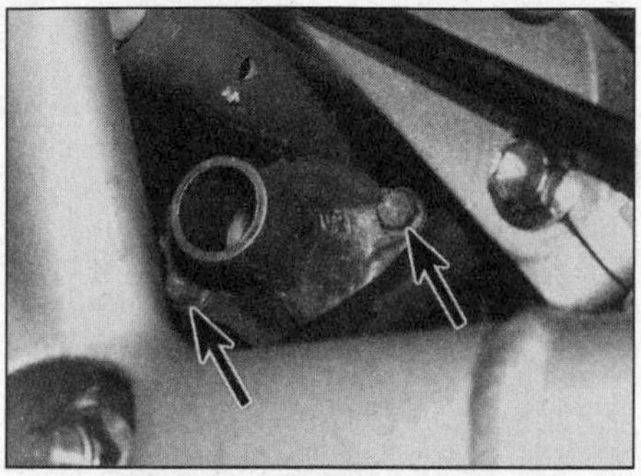

5.4c Unscrew the two bolts (arrowed) and detach the cover . . .

5.4d . . . and remove the thermostat

Removal

Note: *The complete thermostat housing can be removed without removing the thermostat itself.*

> ⚠ ***Warning: The engine must be completely cool before carrying out this procedure.***

1 The thermostat is automatic in operation and should give many years service without requiring attention. In the event of a failure, the valve will probably jam open, in which case the engine will take much longer than normal to warm up. Conversely, if the valve jams shut, the coolant will be unable to circulate and the engine will overheat. Neither condition is acceptable, and the fault must be investigated promptly.

2 On X, Y, K1 and K2 SV650S models, remove the fairing side panels (see Chapter 8).

3 Drain the cooling system (see Chapter 1). Remove the air filter housing and, on K3-on models, remove the throttle body assembly (see Chapter 4A or 4B as applicable).

4 To remove the thermostat, slacken the clamp securing the coolant hose to the thermostat cover and detach the hose **(see illustration)**. On X, Y, K1 and K2 models, disconnect the earth wiring connector **(see illustration)**. Unscrew the two bolts securing the cover to the housing and separate it from the housing **(see illustration)**. Withdraw the thermostat, noting the orientation of the bleed hole and how it fits **(see illustration)**.

5 To remove the thermostat housing, disconnect the coolant temperature sensor and earth wiring connectors as applicable **(see illustration 4.2. 4.27 and 5.4b)**. Slacken the clamp securing the coolant hose to the cover and detach the hose **(see illustration 5.4a)**. Slacken the clamp securing the bypass hose to the inside of the water pump inlet hose union and detach the hose **(see illustration 7.5)**. Slacken the clamp securing the coolant hose to the union on each cylinder head **(see illustrations)**. Detach the hose from the rear cylinder union first, then from the front, and remove the housing with all but the cover hose still attached **(see illustration)**.

Check

6 Examine the thermostat visually before carrying out the test. If it remains in the open position at room temperature, it should be renewed.

7 Suspend the thermostat by a piece of wire in a container of cold water. Place a thermometer capable of reading temperatures

5.5a Slacken the clamps (arrowed) and detach the hose from the rear cylinder . . .

5.5b . . . then the front cylinder . . .

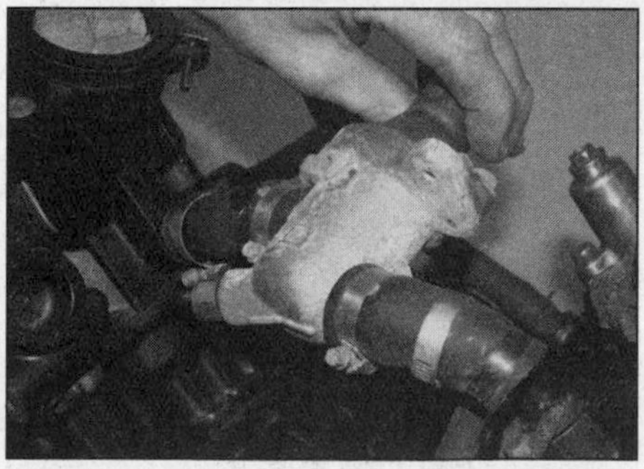

5.5c . . . and remove the housing with the hoses

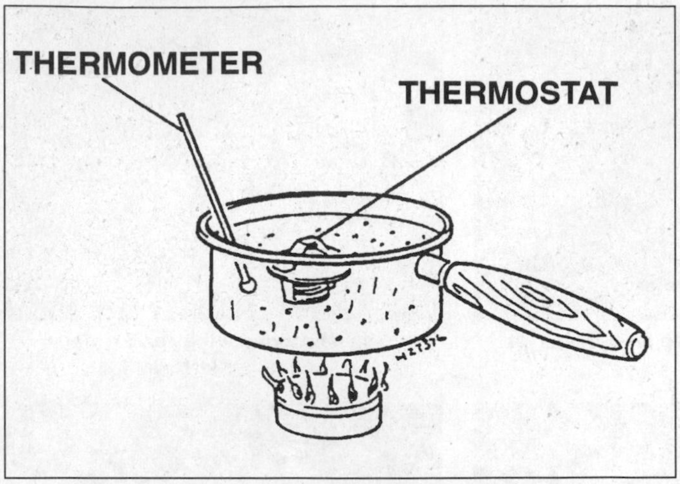

5.7 Thermostat testing set-up

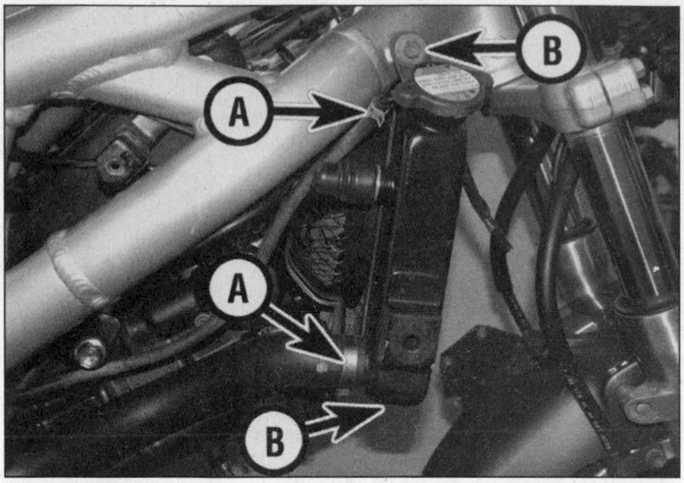

6.5a Radiator hoses (A) and mounting bolts (B) – right-hand side

up to 110°C in the water so that the bulb is close to the thermostat **(see illustration)**. Heat the water, noting the temperature when the thermostat opens, and compare the result with the specifications given at the beginning of the Chapter. Also check the amount the valve opens after it has been heated for a few minutes and compare the measurement to the specifications. **Note:** *None of the components should be allowed to directly touch the container or be too close to it.* If the readings obtained differ from those given, the thermostat is faulty and must be renewed.

8 In the event of thermostat failure, as an emergency measure only, it can be removed and the machine used without it (this is better than leaving a permanently closed thermostat in, but if it is permanently open, you might as well leave it in). **Note:** *Take care when starting the engine from cold as it will take much longer than usual to warm up.* Ensure that a new unit is installed as soon as possible.

Installation

9 Installation is the reverse of removal. Fit the thermostat with the bleed hole at the top, and make sure it locates correctly in the groove in the housing **(see illustration 5.4d)**. Tighten the cover and mounting bolts securely **(see illustration 5.4c)**. Make sure all hoses are pushed fully onto their unions and secured by the clamps **(see illustrations 5.5c, b, a and 5.4a)**. Do not forget to connect the temperature sensor and earth wiring connectors as applicable **(see illustrations 4.2, 4.27 and 5.4b)**. Refill the cooling system (see Chapter 1).

6 Radiator

Removal

Warning: The engine must be completely cool before carrying out this procedure.

Note: *If the radiator is being removed as part of the engine removal procedure, detach the hoses from their unions on the engine rather than on the radiator and remove the radiator with the hoses attached to it. Note the routing of the hoses.*

1 On X, Y, K1 and K2 SV650S models, remove the fairing side panels (see Chapter 8).

2 Drain the cooling system (see Chapter 1).

3 On X, Y, K1 and K2 models, remove the fuel tank and air filter housing (see Chapter 4A), then remove the horn along with its mounting bracket (see Chapter 9). On K3-on models, disconnect the horn wiring connectors.

4 Either disconnect the wiring connector from the fan switch on the right-hand side of the radiator, or trace the wiring from the fan switch and disconnect it at the connector, according to your model and the switch fitted **(see illustration 3.17)**.

5 Slacken the clamps securing all the hoses to the radiator and detach them, noting which fits where **(see illustrations)**.

6 Support the radiator and unscrew its mounting bolts **(see illustrations 6.5a and b)**.

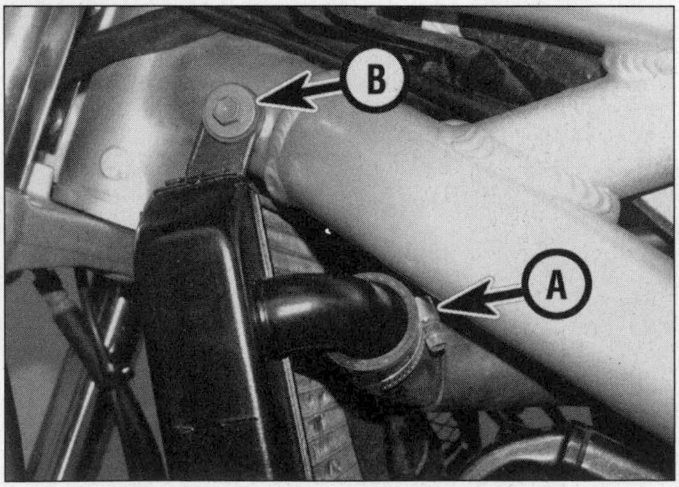

6.5b Radiator hose (A) and mounting bolt (B) – left-hand side

6.6 Carefully remove the radiator

Note that on K3-on models there are only two bolts on the right-hand side. Remove the radiator, noting how it fits **(see illustration)**. Note the arrangement of the collars and rubber grommets in the radiator mounts. If necessary, remove the cooling fan and its switch from the radiator (see Section 3). On K3-on models, remove the horn from the back of the radiator (see Chapter 9).

7 Check the radiator for signs of damage and clear any dirt or debris that might obstruct air flow and inhibit cooling. If the radiator fins are badly damaged or broken the radiator must be renewed. Also check the rubber mounting grommets, and renew them if necessary.

Installation

8 Installation is the reverse of removal, noting the following.

- On K3-on models, ensure the horn is installed before fitting the radiator.
- Make sure the collars are correctly installed in the mounting grommets.
- Make sure that the fan and fan switch wiring is correctly routed and connected.
- Ensure the coolant hoses are in good condition (see Chapter 1), and are securely retained by their clamps, using new ones if necessary.
- On completion refill the cooling system as described in Chapter 1.

7 Water pump

Check

1 The water pump is located on the upper right-hand side of the crankcase. Visually check the area around the pump for signs of leakage.

2 To prevent leakage of coolant from the cooling system to the lubrication system and vice versa, two seals are fitted on the pump shaft. On the bottom of the pump housing there is a drain hole **(see illustration)**. If either seal fails, the drain allows the coolant or oil to escape and prevents them mixing. If both seals fail the oil and coolant mix to form a white emulsion. The seal on the water pump side is of the mechanical type which bears on the rear face of the impeller. The second seal, which is mounted behind the mechanical seal is of the normal feathered lip type. Both seals are available separately.

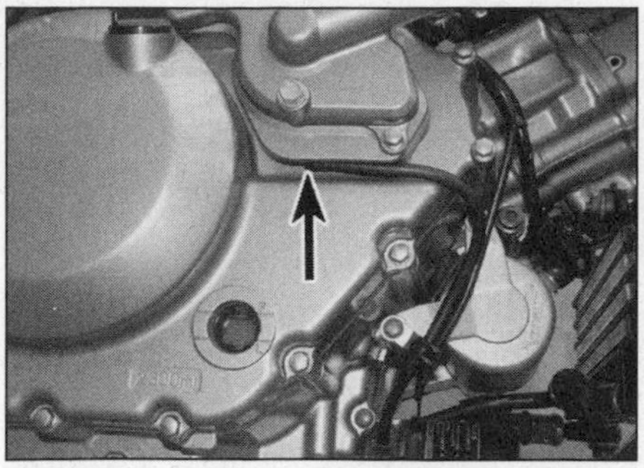

7.2 Check the drain hole (arrowed) for signs of leakage

3 If there is evidence of leakage between the pump housing and the crankcase cover the pump must be overhauled. If the drain shows signs of coolant leakage, renew the mechanical seal. If there is oil leakage, first check that the pump body O-ring is in good condition, and if that is not the cause of the leak renew the oil seal. If there is a coolant/oil mixture in the form of a white emulsion, renew both seals. If you are not sure about their condition, remove the pump and check them visually, looking for signs of damage and leakage.

4 First remove the crankcase cover, then follow the procedure below and remove the pump. Wiggle the water pump impeller back-and-forth and in-and-out, and spin it by hand. If there is excessive movement, or the pump is noisy or rough when turned, the drive shaft bearing(s) must be renewed. Also check for corrosion or a build-up of scale in the pump body and clean or renew the pump as necessary.

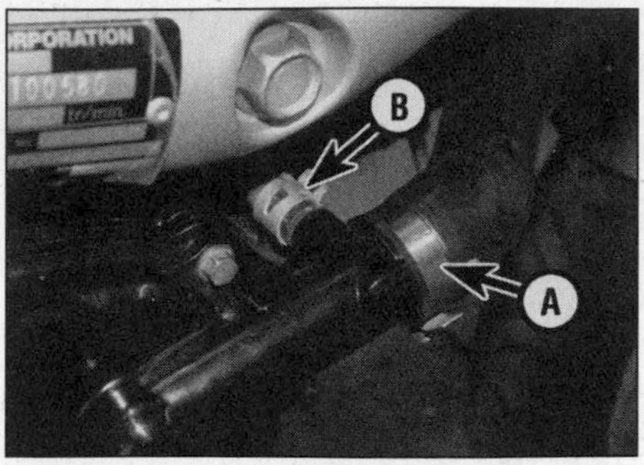

7.5 Slacken the clamps and detach the inlet hose (A) and the bypass hose (B)

Removal

5 Drain the coolant and the engine oil (see Chapter 1). Slacken the clamp securing the inlet hose to the water pump and detach the hose **(see illustration)**. Slacken the clamp securing the bypass hose to the inside of the inlet hose union and detach the hose.

6 Unscrew the bolts securing the crankcase cover remove it **(see illustration)**. Discard the gasket as a new one must be used. Remove the two dowels from the cover or crankcase if they are loose.

Overhaul

7 Remove the circlip securing the pump driven gear and draw the gear off the shaft **(see illustrations)**. Withdraw the drive pin from the shaft and remove the washer **(see illustrations)**.

8 Separate the pump assembly from the crankcase cover **(see illustration)**. Discard the pump body and coolant passage O-rings as new ones must be used **(see illustrations 7.21a and 21b)**.

9 Undo the two screws on the back of the assembly and separate the pump body from the cover **(see illustrations)**. Discard the cover O-ring as a new one must be used.

7.6 Unscrew the bolts (arrowed) and remove the crankcase cover – X, Y, K1 and K2 models shown

7.7a Release the circlip . . .

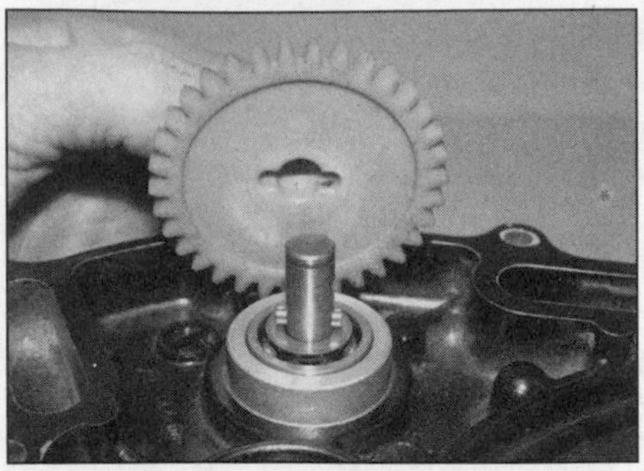

7.7b . . . and remove the gear, noting how it locates on the drive pin

7.7c Withdraw the drive pin . . .

7.7d . . . and remove the washer

7.8 Separate the pump from the cover

7.9a Undo the screws . . .

7.9b . . . and separate the cover from the pump

10 On X and Y models, hold the impeller, then unscrew the bolt securing it to the driveshaft, noting the washers **(see illustration)**. Remove the impeller, noting how it locates on the driveshaft. Remove the seal ring from the back of the impeller, noting how it fits. Withdraw the driveshaft from the back of the pump. Check the condition of the seal ring and the sealing washer and renew them if they are in any way damaged, deformed or deteriorated – it is wise to renew them as a matter of course.

11 On K1 models onward, remove the E-clip from the end of the driveshaft, then grasp the impeller and draw it and the shaft out of the pump body.

12 To renew the bearing(s), use a bearing puller (see *Tools and Workshop Tips* in the reference Section), and draw it/them (X and Y models have one bearing, K1 models onward have two bearings) out from the rear of the body. Note that once the bearings have been removed, they cannot be reused – new ones must be fitted.

13 To remove the mechanical seal, carefully lever it out using a screwdriver or similar. Discard it as a new one must be fitted.

14 To remove the oil seal, first remove the mechanical seal (see above), then carefully lever the oil seal out using a screwdriver or similar. Discard it as a new one must be fitted.

15 Apply a smear of grease to the lips of the new oil seal. Press or carefully drive the new oil seal into the front of the pump body – use a suitable sized socket or seal driver and make sure the seal markings face out.

16 Press or carefully drive the new mechanical seal into the front of the pump body using a suitable sized socket or seal driver that bears only on the rim of the seal and not the sprung centre.

17 Press or drive the new bearing(s) into the rear of the pump body, using a suitable sized socket or bearing driver. Drive the bearing(s) in until properly seated.

18 On X and Y models, wrap a single layer of insulating tape around the impeller end of the driveshaft to protect the seal lips. Slide the driveshaft into the rear of the pump body and push it through until the E-clip seats against the bearing. Fit the seal ring into the back of the impeller, making sure the marked side of the ring faces the impeller, then fit the impeller onto the shaft. Fit the two washers onto the impeller bolt so that the sealing washer will be against the impeller, then apply a suitable non-permanent threadlock to the bolt threads. Counter-hold the impeller as before and tighten the bolt to the torque setting specified at the beginning of the Chapter **(see illustration 7.10)**.

19 On K1 models onward, wrap a single layer of insulating tape around the inner end of the driveshaft to protect the seal lips. Slide the driveshaft into the pump body and through until the clip groove is visible. Fit the E-clip, making sure it locates correctly in the groove.

20 On all models, smear the new cover O-ring with coolant and fit it into its groove **(see illustration)**. Fit the cover onto the pump, then install the two screws and tighten them to the torque setting specified at the beginning of the Chapter **(see illustrations 7.9b and 9a)**.

21 Smear the new coolant passage O-rings with a suitable sealant (such as Suzuki Bond 1207B or equivalent) and fit them into the grooves in the back of the pump **(see illustration)**. Smear the new pump body O-ring with grease and fit it into its groove in the body **(see illustration)**.

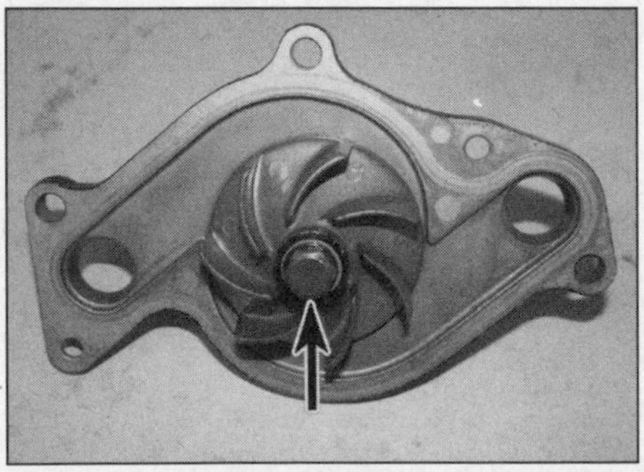

7.10 Unscrew the bolt (arrowed) and draw the impeller off the shaft – X and Y models

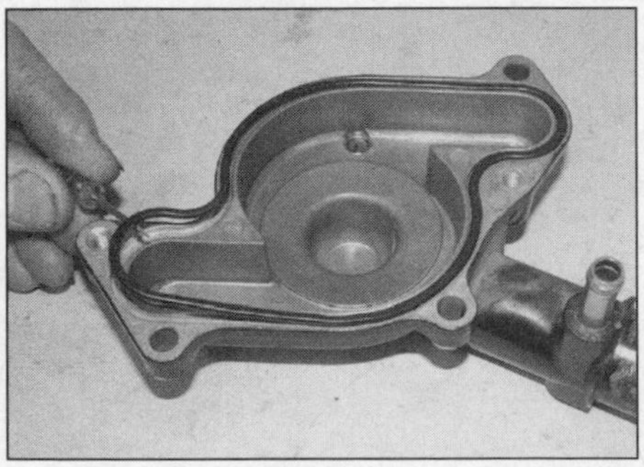

7.20 Fit a new O-ring into the groove in the cover

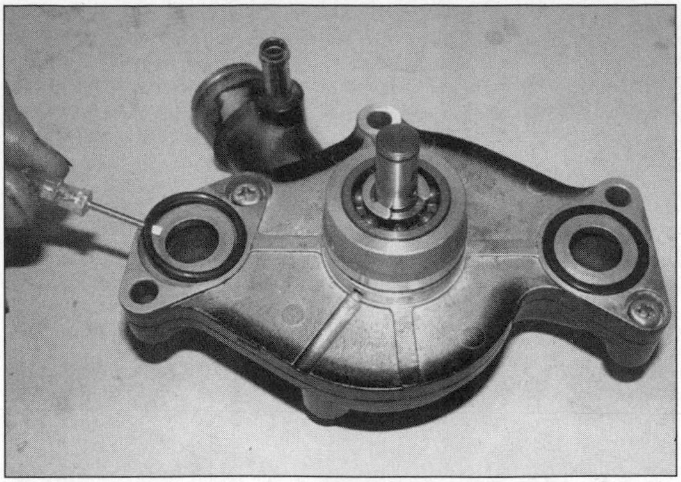

7.21a Use new O-rings for the coolant passages and smear them with sealant

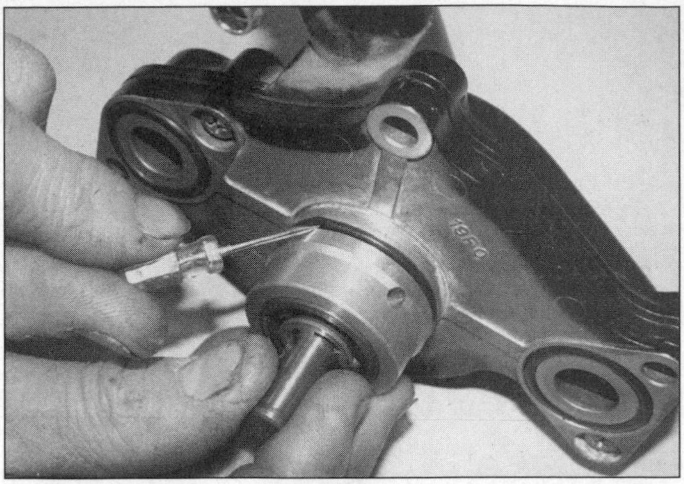

7.21b Use a new O-ring for the pump body and smear it with grease

7.24a Locate the gasket onto the dowels (arrowed) . . .

7.24b . . . then install the cover . . .

7.24c . . . making sure it locates correctly

22 Push the pump into the crankcase cover, aligning the bolt holes **(see illustration 7.8)**.

23 Fit the washer onto the shaft, then slide the drive pin into its hole **(see illustrations 7.7d and 7c)**. Fit the driven gear onto the shaft, locating the cutouts over the drive pin ends, and secure it with the circlip, making sure it locates correctly in its groove **(see illustrations 7.7b and 7a)**.

Installation

24 If removed, fit the dowels into the crankcase. Fit a new gasket, locating it over the dowels **(see illustration)**. Install the crankcase cover, making sure the water pump driven gear engages correctly with its drive gear, and the dowels locate correctly **(see illustrations)**. On X, Y, K1 and K2 models, apply a suitable non-permanent thread locking compound to the cover bolts. On all models, tighten the cover bolts evenly in a criss-cross sequence to the specified torque setting **(see illustration 7.6)**.

25 Fit the coolant bypass hose onto the small union on the inside of the inlet hose union and secure it with its clamp **(see illustration 7.5)**. Fit the inlet hose onto its union and secure it with its clamp.

26 Refill the cooling system and the engine oil (see Chapter 1). Check that there are no leaks.

8 Coolant hoses and unions

Removal

1 Before removing a hose, drain the coolant (see Chapter 1).

2 Use a screwdriver to slacken the larger-bore hose clamps, then slide them back along the hose and clear of the union spigot. The smaller-bore hoses are secured by spring clamps which can be expanded by squeezing their ears together with pliers.

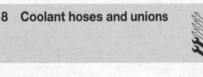

8.4 Each union is secured by a single bolt (arrowed) – X, Y, K1 and K2 models

Caution: The radiator unions are fragile. Do not use excessive force when attempting to remove the hoses.

3 If a hose proves stubborn, release it by rotating it on its union before working it off. If all else fails, cut the hose with a sharp knife. Whilst this means renewing the hose, it is preferable to buying a new radiator.

4 On X, Y, K1 and K2 models, the outlet unions from the cylinder heads can be removed by unscrewing their bolt **(see illustration)**. If a union is removed, its O-ring must be renewed on installation.

Installation

5 Slide the clamps onto the hose and then work the hose on to its union.

> **HAYNES HiNT** ***If the hose is difficult to push on its union, soften it by soaking it in very hot water, or alternatively a little soapy water on the union can be used as a lubricant.***

6 Rotate the hose on its unions to settle it in position before sliding the clamps into place and tightening them securely.

7 If an outlet union from the engine has been removed, install it using a new O-ring smeared with coolant. Install the union and tighten the bolt securely.

Chapter 4 Part A
Fuel and exhaust systems – X, Y, K1 and K2 models

Contents

Degrees of difficulty

Easy, suitable for novice with little experience	**Fairly easy,** suitable for beginner with some experience	**Fairly difficult,** suitable for competent DIY mechanic	**Difficult,** suitable for experienced DIY mechanic	**Very difficult,** suitable for expert DIY or professional

Specifications

Fuel

Grade	Unleaded, minimum 91 RON (Research Octane Number)
Fuel tank capacity	16 litres

Carburettors

Type	2 x Mikuni BDSR39
Heater system resistance (UK models)	12 to 18 ohms
Pilot jet	
Austria and Switzerland models	15
All other European models	17.5
US and Canada models	15
Jet needle	
European models	6E38-54-2
US 49-state and Canada models	6E42-52
California models	6E43-54
Needle jet	
Austria and Switzerland models	P-2
All other European models	P-0
US and Canada models	P-0M
Main jet	137.5
Pilot screw setting (turns out)	
Austria and Switzerland models	2 3/4
Germany restricted models	3 1/2
All other European models	2 1/2
US 49-state and Canada models	3
California models	pre-set and non-adjustable
Float height	7.0 ± 0.5 mm
Fuel level	16.9 ± 0.5 mm
Idle speed	see Chapter 1
Synchronisation vacuum range	see Chapter 1

Torque settings

Carburettor heaters (UK models)	3 Nm
Exhaust system nuts and bolts	23 Nm
Fuel pump bolts	10 Nm

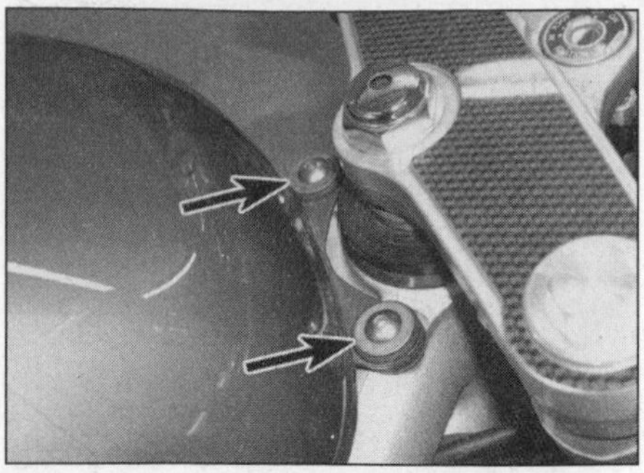

2.3 Unscrew the two bolts (arrowed)

1 General information and precautions

General information

The fuel system consists of the fuel tank, the fuel tap and strainer, the fuel pump, the carburettors, fuel hoses and control cables.

The fuel tap has an automatic vacuum operated valve with an integral strainer inside the fuel tank. The valve opens when a vacuum taken off the rear cylinder inlet duct acts on a diaphragm. The vacuum is created as soon as the engine is turned over by the starter motor. There is no manual facility on the tap. There is also no reserve facility, but a level sensor inside the tank transmits a signal to a low fuel warning light in the instrument cluster.

The fuel pump is automatic, and works using the alternate vacuum and pressure pulses created by the engine as it turns. These pulses act on a diaphragm, which sucks fuel into a chamber via a one-way valve and them pumps it out via another one-way valve. A pressure relief valve allows fuel to flow from the outlet side of the pump to the inlet when necessary. The pump is necessary because the lower section of the fuel tank is below the level of the carburettor float chambers.

The carburettors (one for each cylinder) on all models are 39 mm Mikuni CV. For cold starting, a choke lever mounted on the left-hand handlebar and connected by a cable controls an enrichment circuit in each carburettor.

Air is drawn into the carburettors via an air filter housed under the fuel tank.

The exhaust system is a two-into-one design.

Many of the fuel system service procedures are considered routine maintenance items and for that reason are included in Chapter 1.

Precautions

Warning: Petrol (gasoline) is extremely flammable, so take extra precautions when you work on any part of the fuel system. Don't smoke or allow open flames or bare light bulbs near the work area, and don't work in a garage where a natural gas-type appliance is present. If you spill any fuel on your skin, rinse it off immediately with soap and water. When you perform any kind of work on the fuel system, wear safety glasses and have a fire extinguisher suitable for a class B type fire (flammable liquids) on hand.

Always perform service procedures in a well-ventilated area to prevent a build-up of fumes.

Never work in a building containing a gas appliance with a pilot light, or any other form of naked flame. Ensure that there are no naked light bulbs or any sources of flame or sparks nearby.

Do not smoke (or allow anyone else to smoke) while in the vicinity of petrol or of components containing it. Remember the possible presence of vapour from these sources and move well clear before smoking.

Check all electrical equipment belonging to the house, garage or workshop where work is being undertaken (see the Safety First! section of this manual). Remember that certain electrical appliances such as drills, cutters etc create sparks in the normal course of operation and must not be used near petrol or any component containing it. Again, remember the possible presence of fumes before using electrical equipment.

Always mop up any spilt fuel and safely dispose of the rag used.

Any stored fuel that is drained off during servicing work must be kept in sealed containers that are suitable for holding petrol, and clearly marked as such; the containers themselves should be kept in a safe place. Note that this last point applies equally to the fuel tank if it is removed from the machine; also remember to keep its cap closed at all times.

Note that the fuel system consists of the fuel tank and tap, with its cap and related hoses.

Read the Safety first! section of this manual carefully before starting work.

2 Fuel tank

Warning: Refer to the precautions given in Section 1 before starting work.

Caution: If the fuel tank is full it will be heavy. It is advisable therefore to only remove the tank when it is at least half empty. If the tank is full it is best to drain it before removal. The best way to do this is to obtain a commercially available siphoning tool and a jerry can. Alternatively attach a suitable hose to the tap and feed its open end into a jerry can. Now apply a vacuum to the tap via the vacuum hose – the fuel will now flow out.

Raising

1 Make sure the fuel cap is secure.
2 Remove the seats (see Chapter 8).
3 Unscrew and remove the fuel tank front mounting bolts **(see illustration)**.
4 Remove the tank prop from under the passenger seat, then raise the tank at the front and insert the prop between one of the bolt holes in the tank and the hole in the centre of the steering stem nut **(see illustrations)**.

Removal

5 Make sure the fuel cap is secure.
6 Raise the tank (see above).
7 Release the fuel hose clamp and detach the hose from the either the tap or the pump **(see illustration)**. Detach the vacuum hose from either the tap or the take-off union on the carburettor **(see illustration)**.
8 Disconnect the fuel level sensor wiring connector **(see illustration)**. Also disconnect the breather hose from its union on the tank **(see illustration)**.

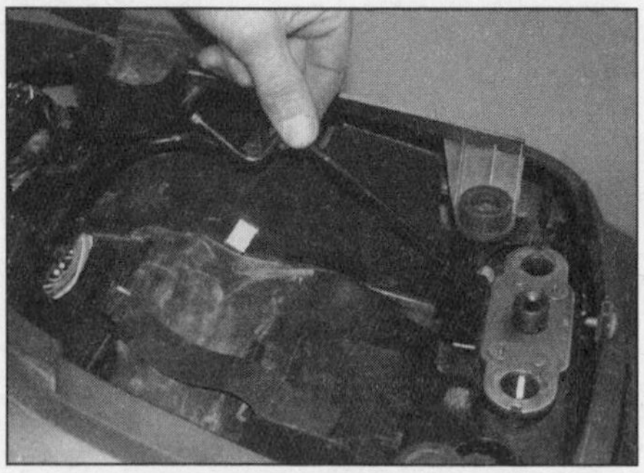

2.4a Remove the prop . . .

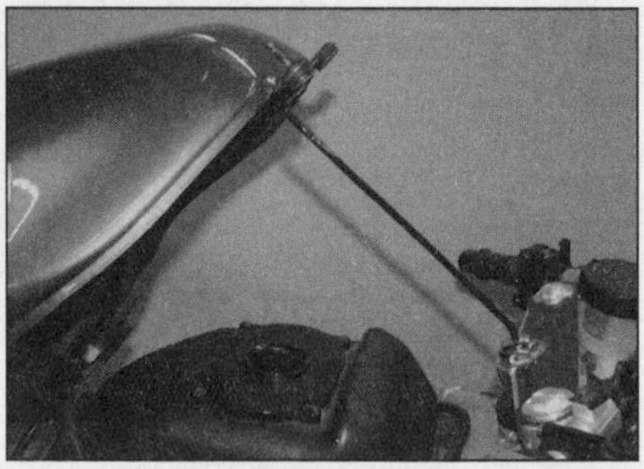

2.4b . . . then raise the front of the tank and support it by locating the prop as described

2.7a Release the clamp . . .

2.7b . . . and detach the fuel hose

2.7c Also detach the vacuum hose from its union

2.8a Disconnect the sensor wiring connector

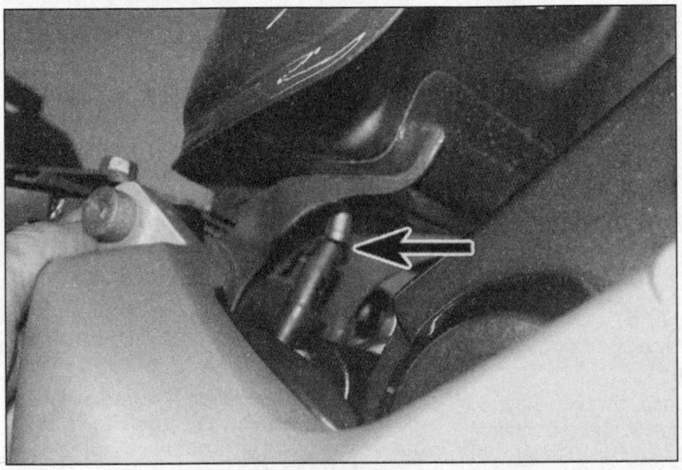

2.8b Detach the breather hose from its union

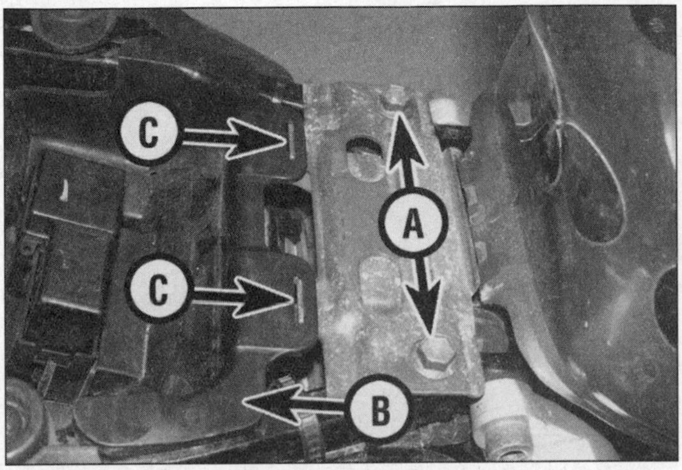

2.9 Unscrew the rear mounting bolts (A), then lift the tray off the bracket (B), noting how its slots locate (C)

9 Remove the tank prop and lower the tank. Unscrew and remove the fuel tank rear mounting bolts **(see illustration)**. Lift the fusebox tray off the tank bracket, noting how its slots locate over the tabs.

10 Carefully remove the tank **(see illustration)**. Note the collars fitted in the front mounting bolt grommets and take care not to lose them.

11 Check the tank mounting grommets and rubbers for damage or deterioration and renew them if necessary.

Installation

12 Installation is the reverse of removal, noting the following:

2.10 Carefully lift the tank off the bike and remove it

- If removed, fit the tank mounting grommets and rubbers. Make sure the rubbers remain in place when installing the tank. Do not omit the collars in the front grommets
- Check that the tank is properly seated and is not pinching any control cables or wires.
- Make sure the fuel hose is fully pushed onto its union and secure it with its clamp.
- Start the engine and check again that there is no sign of fuel leakage, then shut if off.

Repair

13 All repairs to the fuel tank should be carried out by a professional who has experience in this critical and potentially dangerous work. Even after cleaning and flushing of the fuel system, explosive fumes can remain and ignite during repair of the tank.

14 If the fuel tank is removed from the bike, it should not be placed in an area where sparks or open flames could ignite the fumes coming out of the tank. Be especially careful inside garages where a natural gas-type appliance is located, because the pilot light could cause an explosion.

3 Fuel tap

Check

1 If the tap is thought to be faulty, it can be disassembled and inspected. The most likely problem is a hole or split in the diaphragm. Before removing and dismantling the tap, check that there are no splits or cracks in the vacuum hose. If in doubt, raise the fuel tank (see Section 2), then release the clamp securing the fuel hose to the fuel pump and detach the hose **(see illustrations 2.7a and b)**.

2 Place the end in a container suitable for holding fuel. Detach the vacuum hose from the tap. Attach a good spare hose to the vacuum union and apply a vacuum to the hose **(see illustration)**. If fuel does not flow through the tap (and there is definitely fuel in the tank), or

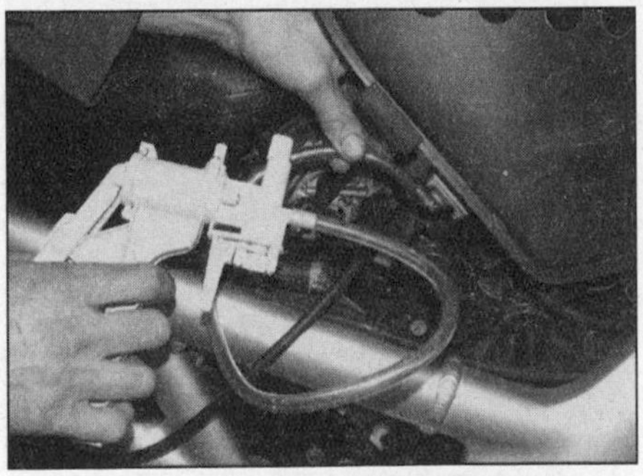

3.2 A commercially available tool is the best way to apply a vacuum

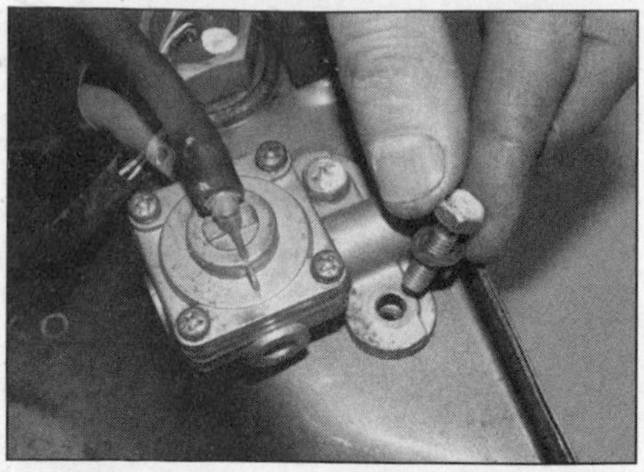

3.4a Unscrew the bolts . . .

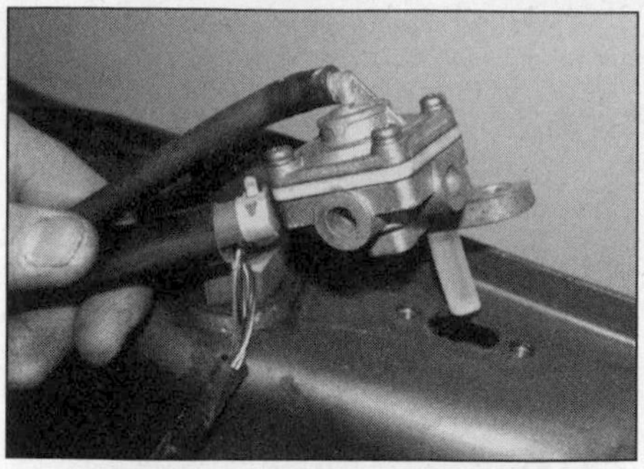

3.4b . . . and remove the tap

3.5 Fuel tap cover screws (arrowed)

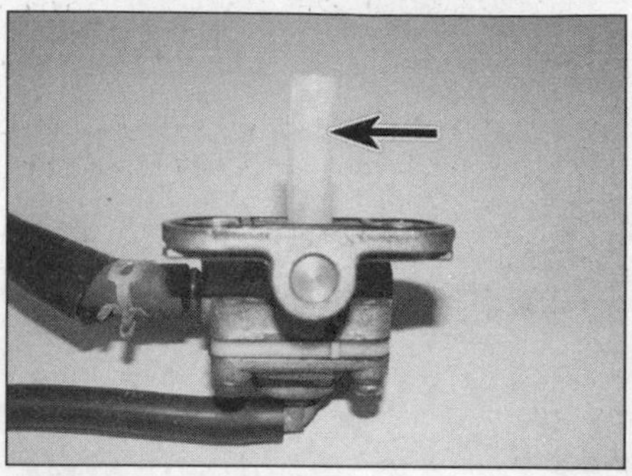

3.6 Check the strainer (arrowed) for damage

3.7 Discard the old O-ring and fit a new one

if fuel flows when there is no vacuum applied, remove and inspect the tap as described below.

Removal

3 Remove the fuel tank as described above.

4 Unscrew the bolts securing the tap to the tank and withdraw the tap assembly, noting its orientation **(see illustrations)**. Discard the O-ring.

Inspection

5 Undo the cover screws and remove the spring and diaphragm, noting how they fit **(see illustration)**. Hold the diaphragm up to a light to check for splits or holes. If any are found a new tap must be fitted – individual components are not available. If the diaphragm is good, reassemble the tap and tighten the cover screws evenly and a little at a time in a criss-cross sequence.

6 Clean the strainer to remove all traces of dirt and fuel sediment **(see illustration)**. Check the gauze for holes. If any are found, a new tap should be fitted – the strainer is not available separately.

Installation

7 Installation is the reverse of removal. Use a new O-ring on the tap and new sealing washers with the mounting bolts **(see illustration)**. Make sure the tap is pointing the correct way **(see illustration 3.4a)**. Tighten the bolts securely.

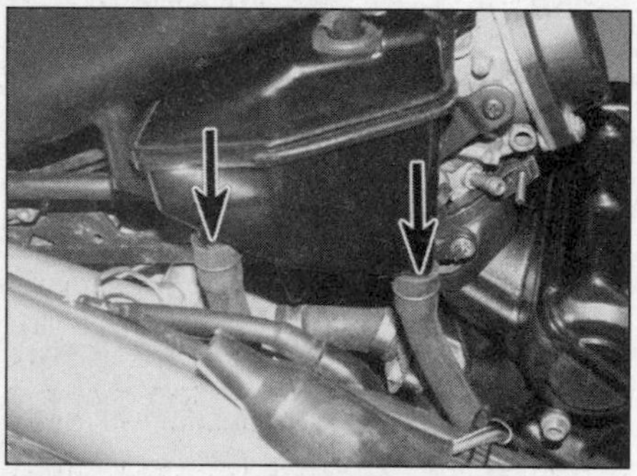

4.2 Detach the breather hoses (arrowed) from their unions

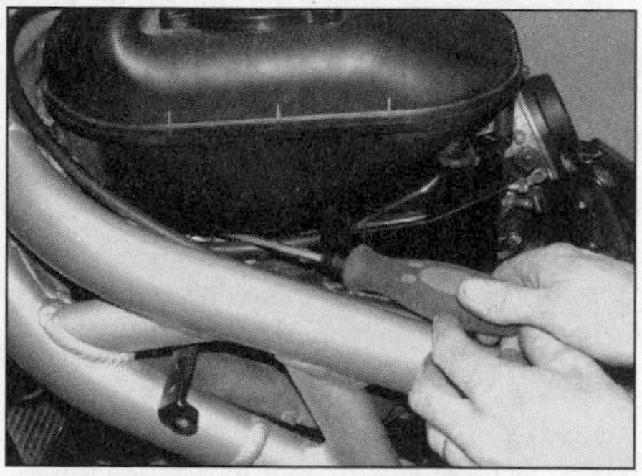

4.3a Slacken the front clamp . . .

4.3b . . . and the rear clamp (arrowed) . . .

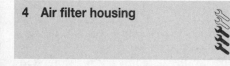

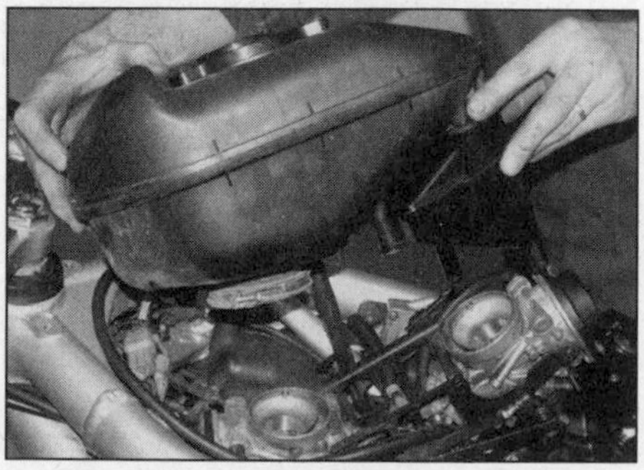

4.3c . . . and lift the housing off the carburettors

4 Air filter housing

Removal

1 Raise or remove the fuel tank (see Section 2).

2 Release the clamps securing the cylinder and crankcase breather hoses to the oil catch tank on the left-hand side of the housing and detach them from their unions **(see illustration)**. On California, Austria and Switzerland models detach the PAIR system hose from the rear of the housing on the right-hand side.

3 Slacken the clamp screws securing the air filter housing to the carburettor intakes **(see illustrations)**. Note the routing of the drain hose attached to the middle of the housing on the right-hand side. Carefully lift the housing up off the carburettors, noting how it fits, bringing the drain hose with it **(see illustration)**.

4 If required, undo the screws securing the catch tank and separate it from the housing **(see illustration)**. Drain and clean the tank.

Installation

5 Installation is the reverse of removal. Make

4.4 Undo the screws (arrowed) and detach the catch tank if required

sure all the hoses are correctly installed and routed and secured by their clamps.

5 Air/fuel mixture adjustment

1 If the engine runs extremely rough at idle or continually stalls, and if a carburettor overhaul does not cure the problem (and it definitely is a carburetion problem – see Section 6), the pilot screws may require adjustment. It is worth noting at this point that unless you have the experience to carry this out it is best to entrust the task to a motorcycle dealer, tuner or fuel systems specialist. The pilot screws are located underneath the carburettors, between the float bowl and the intake duct on the cylinder head **(see illustration 8.11)**, and are best accessed using a purpose-made angled screwdriver, available from any good accessory dealer. Make sure the valve clearances are correct and the carburettors are synchronised before adjusting the pilot screws (see Chapter 1).

2 Before adjusting the pilot screws, warm the engine up to normal working temperature, then stop it. Screw in the pilot screw on both carburettors until they seat lightly, then back them out to the number of turns specified (see this Chapter's Specifications). This is the base position for adjustment.

3 Start the engine and reset the idle speed to the correct level (see Chapter 1). Working on one carburettor at a time, turn the pilot screw by a small amount either side of this position to find the point at which the highest consistent idle speed is obtained. When you've reached this position, reset the idle speed to the specified amount (see Chapter 1). Repeat on the other carburettor.

4 Due to the increased emphasis on controlling exhaust emissions in certain world markets, regulations have been formulated which prevent adjustment of the air/fuel mixture. On such models the pilot screw positions are pre-set at the factory and in some cases have a limiter cap fitted to prevent tampering. Where adjustment is possible, it can only be made in conjunction with an exhaust gas analyser to ensure that the machine does not exceed emissions regulations.

6 Carburettor overhaul – general information

1 Poor engine performance, hesitation, hard starting, stalling, flooding and backfiring are all signs that major carburettor maintenance may be required.

2 Keep in mind that many so-called carburettor problems are really not carburettor problems at all, but mechanical problems within the engine or ignition system or other electrical malfunctions. Try to establish for certain that the carburettors are in need of maintenance before beginning a major overhaul.

3 Check the fuel tap and strainer, the fuel and vacuum hoses, the intake duct joint clamps, the air filter, the ignition system, the spark plugs and carburettor synchronisation before assuming that a carburettor overhaul is required.

4 Most carburettor problems are caused by dirt particles, varnish and other deposits which build up in and block the fuel and air passages. Also, in time, gaskets and O-rings shrink or deteriorate and cause fuel and air leaks which lead to poor performance.

5 When overhauling the carburettors, disassemble them completely and clean the parts thoroughly with a carburettor cleaning solvent and dry them with filtered, unlubricated compressed air. Blow through the fuel and air passages with compressed air to force out any dirt that may have been loosened but not removed by the solvent. Once the cleaning process is complete, reassemble the carburettor using new gaskets and O-rings.

6 Before disassembling the carburettors, make sure you have all necessary O-rings and other parts, some carburettor cleaner, a supply of clean rags, some means of blowing out the carburettor passages and a clean place to work. It is recommended that only one carburettor be overhauled at a time to avoid mixing up parts.

7 Carburettors – removal and installation

Warning: Refer to the precautions given in Section 1 before starting work.

Removal

1 Raise or remove the fuel tank (see Section 2).

2 Remove the air filter housing (see Section 4).

3 Detach the throttle cables from the carburettors (see Section 12). If access is too restricted to detach the cable ends from the throttle cam with the carburettors in situ, just slacken the cable adjuster locknuts at this stage and free the ends after the carburettors have been displaced.

4 Release the tie securing the rear carburettor choke cable to the carburettor joining bracket. Undo the screw securing the choke plunger retainer to the rear carburettor and draw the plunger out **(see illustrations 7.9c and d)**. Discard its O-ring as a new one must be used.

5 If the fuel tank has not been removed, detach the fuel tap vacuum hose from the take-off union on the rear carburettor **(see illustration 2.7c)**.

6 Disconnect the throttle position sensor wiring connector **(see illustration)**. On UK models, disconnect the carburettor heater wiring connector **(see illustration)**.

7 Release the idle speed adjuster from its holder **(see illustration)**.

8 Release the clamp securing the fuel supply

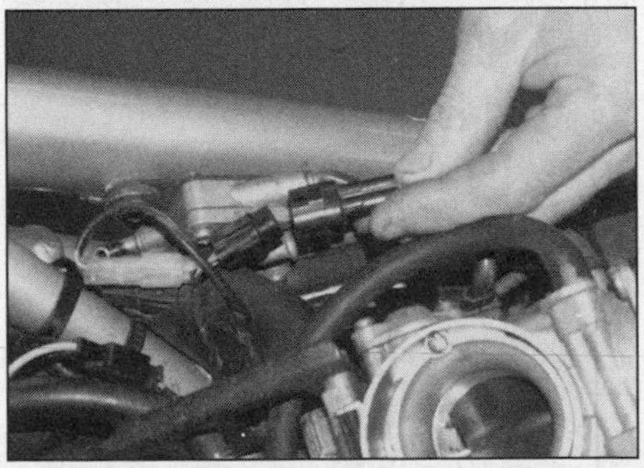

7.6a Disconnect the throttle position sensor wiring connector . . .

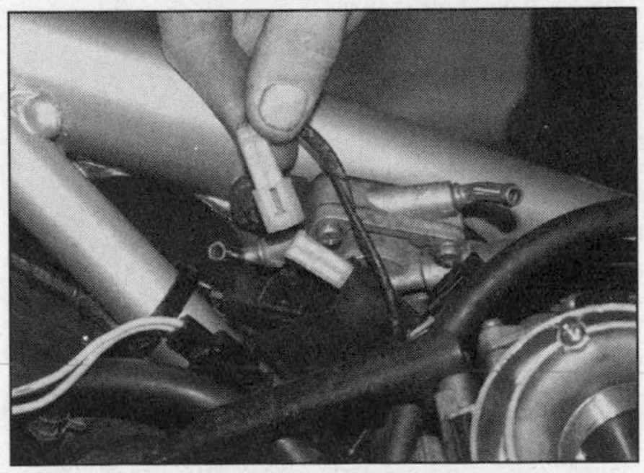

7.6b . . . and on UK models the carburettor heater wiring connector

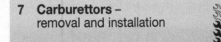

7.7 Release the idle speed adjuster from its holder

7.8 Release the clamp (arrowed) and detach the hose

7.9a Slacken each intake duct clamp screw (rear shown) . . .

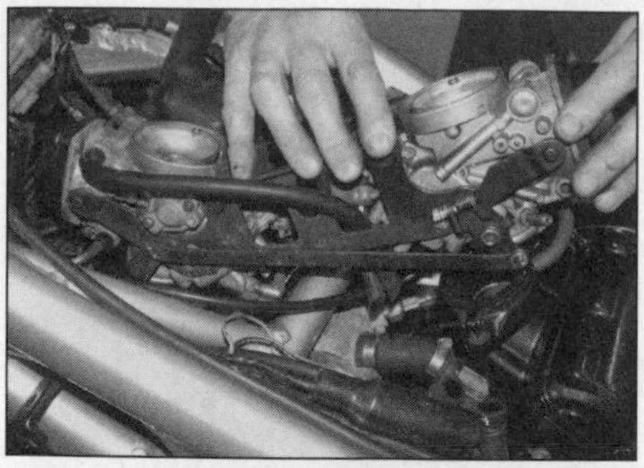

7.9b . . . and ease the carburettors up and out of the ducts

7.9c Undo the choke plunger screw . . .

7.9d . . . and draw the plunger assembly out of the carburettor

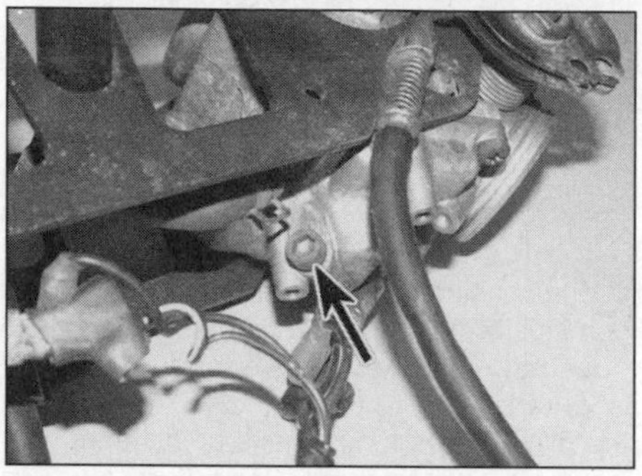

7.11 Slacken each screw in turn and drain the carburettors

hose to its union on the fuel pump and detach it **(see illustration)**.

9 Slacken the clamps securing the carburettors to the cylinder head intake ducts, then ease the carburettors up **(see illustrations)**. When it is accessible, undo the screw securing the choke plunger retainer to the front carburettor and draw the plunger out **(see illustrations)**. Discard its O-ring as a new one must be used. If not already done, detach the throttle cable ends from the cam.

10 Remove the carburettors, on UK models bringing the thermo sensor for the carburettor heaters with them. **Note:** *Keep the carburettors as upright as possible to prevent fuel spillage from the float chambers and the possibility of the piston diaphragms being damaged.*

11 Place a suitable container below the float chambers, then slacken the drain screws and drain all the fuel from the carburettors **(see illustration)**. Once all the fuel has been drained, tighten the drain screws securely.

12 If necessary, undo the screws securing the intake ducts to the cylinder heads and remove them, noting how they fit **(see illustration)**. Discard the O-rings as new ones must be used.

Installation

13 Installation is the reverse of removal, noting the following.

- Check for cracks or splits in the cylinder head intake ducts. If they have been removed from the cylinder head, fit them using a new O-ring smeared with grease. Make sure the one marked UP↑F is installed on the front cylinder, and UP↑R on the rear, with the UP↑ mark at the top **(see illustration 7.12)**. Apply a suitable non-permanent thread locking compound to the screws and tighten them securely.
- Install the front carburettor choke plunger, using a new O-ring smeared lightly with grease, before fitting the carburettors onto the intake ducts **(see illustration and 7.9d and c)**. Make sure the rear carburettor plunger cable is correctly routed under the carburettors, and again fit it using a new O-ring smeared with grease.
- Connect the throttle cables before fitting the carburettors onto the intake ducts.
- Make sure the carburettors are fully engaged with the cylinder head intake ducts and the clamps are securely tightened.
- Do not forget to connect the throttle position sensor wiring connector **(see illustration 7.6a)**. On UK models do not forget to connect the carburettor heater wiring connector **(see illustration 7.6b)**.
- Make sure all hoses are correctly routed and connected and secured, and are not trapped or kinked.
- Check the operation of the choke and throttle cables and adjust them as necessary (see Chapter 1).
- Check idle speed (see Chapter 1).
- If the carburettor bodies have been separated, synchronise the carburettors (see Chapter 1).
- If the pilot screws have been disturbed, or new pilot screws fitted, adjust them as described in Section 5.

7.12 If required, undo the screws (arrowed) and remove the duct

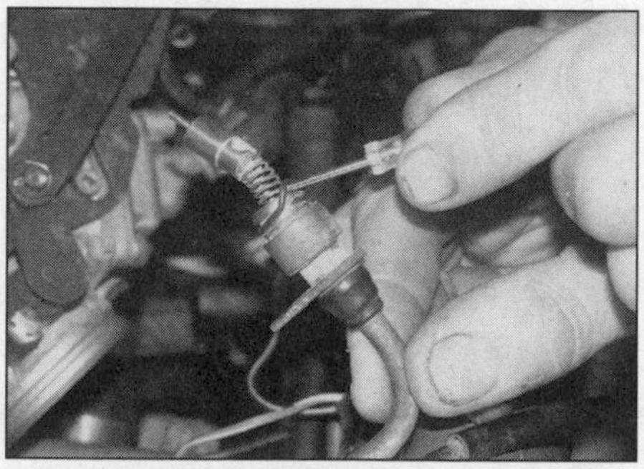

7.13 Fit a new O-ring onto each choke plunger

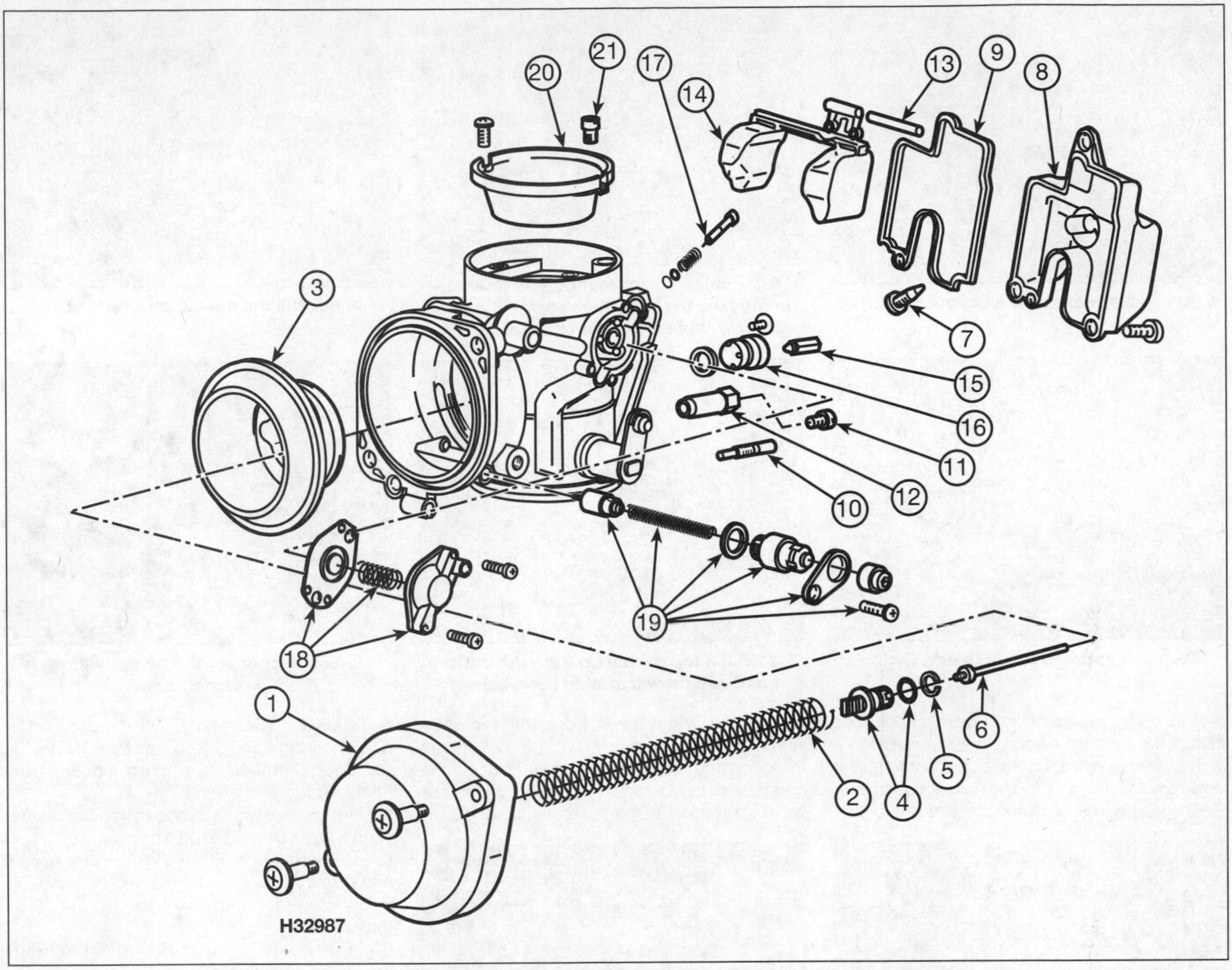

8.1 Carburettor components

1 Top cover
2 Spring
3 Diaphragm/piston assembly
4 Needle retainer, spring and O-ring
5 E-clip
6 Jet needle
7 Drain screw
8 Float chamber
9 Sealing ring
10 Pilot jet
11 Main jet
12 Needle jet
13 Float pin
14 Float
15 Needle valve
16 Needle valve seat and O-ring
17 Pilot screw, spring, washer and O-ring
18 Air cut-off valve cover, spring and diaphragm
19 Choke plunger assembly
20 Funnel
21 Air jet

8 Carburettors – disassembly, cleaning and inspection

***Warning:** Refer to the precautions given in Section 1 before starting work.*

Disassembly

1 Remove the carburettors (see Section 7). **Note:** *Do not separate the carburettors unless absolutely necessary; each carburettor can be dismantled sufficiently for all normal cleaning and adjustments while in place on the mounting brackets. Dismantle the carburettors separately to avoid interchanging parts* **(see illustration).**

2 Unscrew and remove the top cover retaining screws, then remove the cover and withdraw the spring from inside the piston **(see illustrations)**.

3 Carefully peel the diaphragm away from its sealing groove in the carburettor and withdraw the diaphragm and piston assembly **(see illustration).** *Do not use a sharp instrument to displace the diaphragm as it is easily damaged*. Note how the tab on the diaphragm fits in the recess in the carburettor body.

4 Carefully pull the jet needle retainer out of the

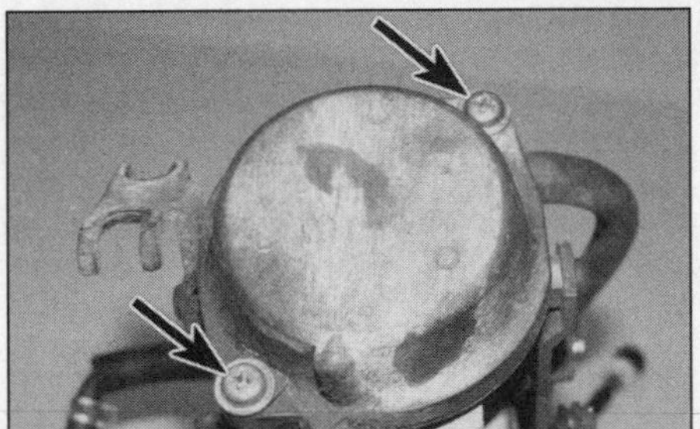

8.2a Undo the screws (arrowed) . . .

8.2b . . . and remove the cover and spring

8.3 Peel the diaphragm off its groove, noting how the tab (arrowed) locates, and withdraw the piston from the carburettor

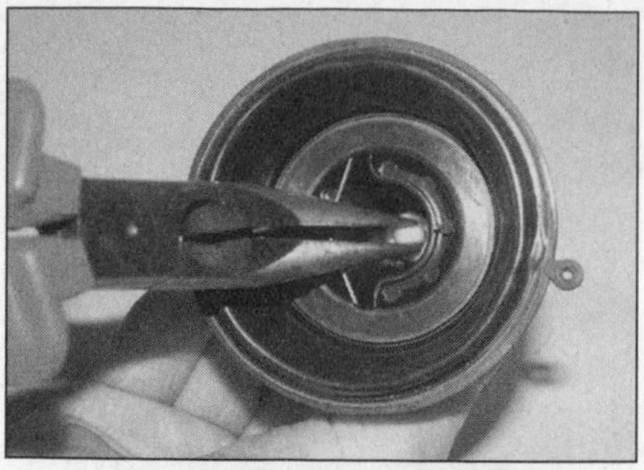
8.4a Pull the needle retainer out . . .

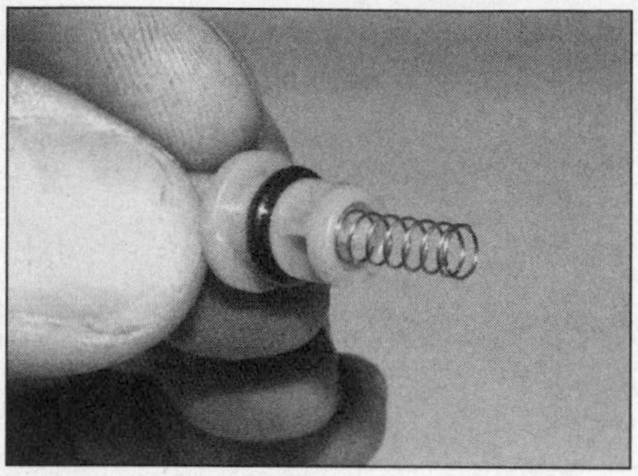
8.4b . . . noting the spring and O-ring

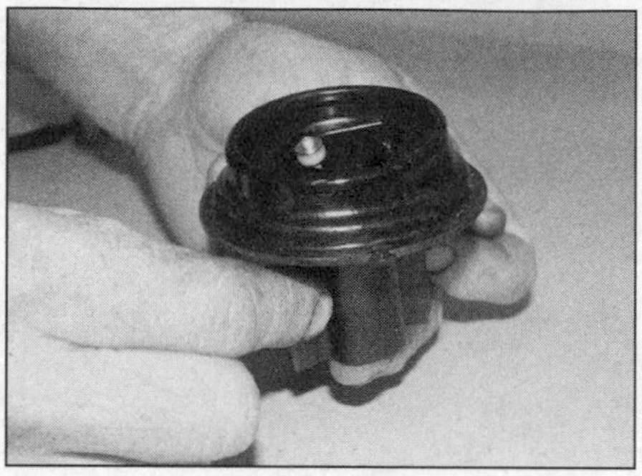
8.4c Push the needle up from the bottom and withdraw it, noting the washer

8.5 Disconnect the heater wiring connectors

piston using a pair of long-nose pliers **(see illustration)**. Note the spring on its underside – it should stay in place, but take care not to lose it and remove it if it is loose **(see illustration)**. Push the needle up from the bottom of the piston and withdraw it from the top **(see illustration)**. Note the washer, E-clip and spacer fitted on the top of the needle. Check the condition of the O-ring on the holder and renew it if it is damaged, deformed or deteriorated.

8.6 Undo the screws (arrowed) and lift off the chamber

8.7 Remove the pilot jet (arrowed) . . .

5 On UK models, disconnect the carburettor heater wiring connectors from the heater on the float chamber. If required, unscrew the heater from the chamber.

6 Undo the screws securing the float chamber to the base of the carburettor and remove it **(see illustration)**. Remove the rubber seal and discard it as a new one must be fitted.

7 Unscrew and remove the pilot jet **(see illustration)**.

8 Unscrew and remove the main jet from the needle jet **(see illustration)**.

9 Unscrew and remove the needle jet **(see illustration)**.

10 Using a pointed instrument, carefully displace the float pin and either push it through the access hole in the carburettor joining bracket, or draw it through using thin-nosed pliers **(see illustrations)**. Remove the float and unhook the float needle valve, noting how it fits onto the tab on the float

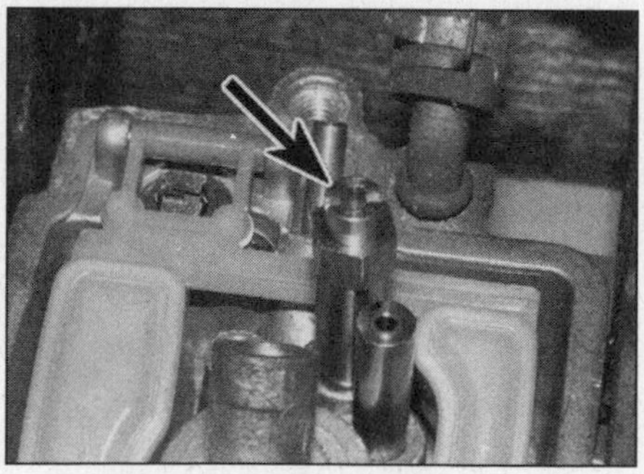
8.8 . . . the main jet (arrowed) . . .

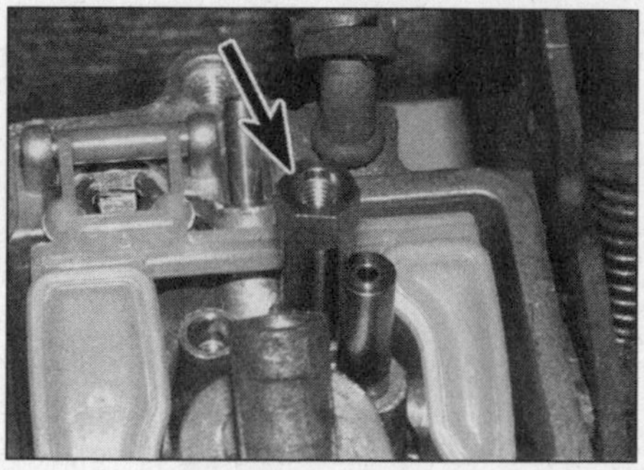
8.9 . . . and the needle jet (arrowed)

8.10a Displace the float pin . . .

8.10b . . . and draw it out the side . . .

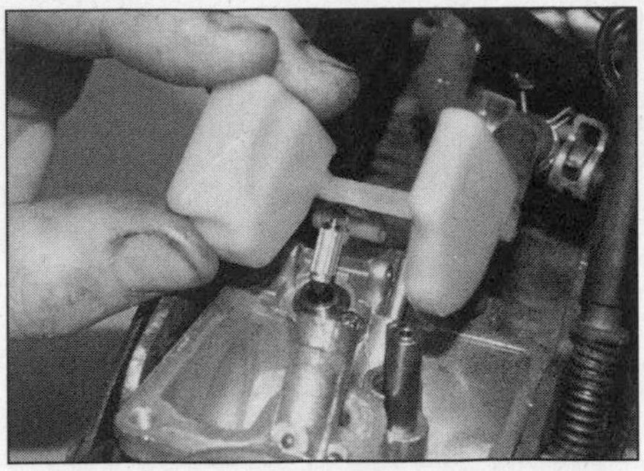

8.10c . . . then remove the float assembly

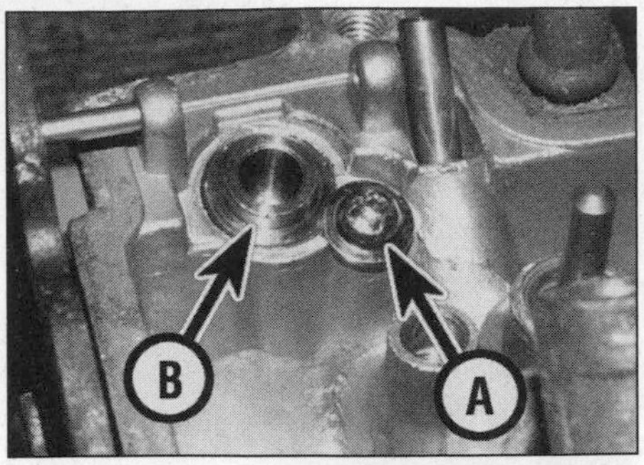

8.10d Undo the screw (A) and pull the float needle valve seat (B) out

(see illustration). Undo the screw securing the float needle valve seat, then carefully pull the seat out, taking care not to damage its gauze filter **(see illustration)**. Check the condition of the O-ring and renew it if it is damaged, deformed or deteriorated.

11 The pilot screw can be removed from the carburettor, but note that its setting will be disturbed (see ***Haynes Hint***). If required, unscrew and remove the pilot screw along with its spring, washer and O-ring **(see illustration)**. Note that models sold in certain markets have a tamperproof cap fitted over the head of the pilot screw, precluding adjustment and access to the screw.

12 Undo the two screws securing the air cut-off valve cover, noting that it is under spring pressure **(see illustration)**. Carefully release the cover and remove the spring and cut-off valve diaphragm, noting how they fit.

13 Do not remove the throttle position sensor unnecessarily. If you do need to remove it, refer to Chapter 5.

14 Undo the screws securing the air intake funnel and remove it, noting how it fits **(see illustration)**. If required, unscrew the pilot air jet.

Cleaning

Caution: Use only a petroleum based solvent for carburettor cleaning. Don't use caustic cleaners.

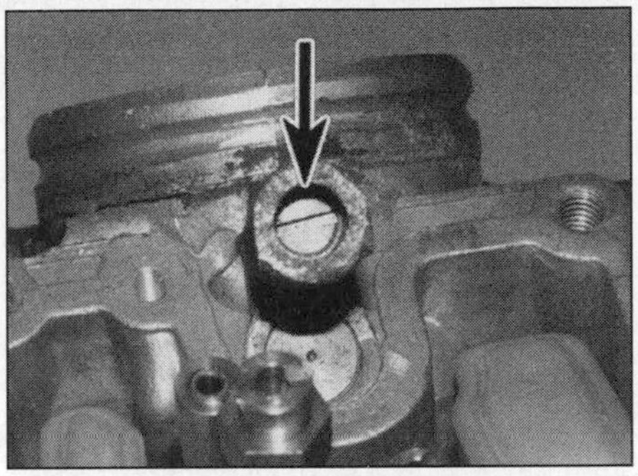

8.11 Pilot screw (arrowed)

15 Submerge the metal components in the solvent for approximately thirty minutes (or longer, if the directions recommend it).

16 After the carburettor has soaked long enough for the cleaner to loosen and dissolve most of the varnish and other deposits, use a nylon-bristled brush to remove the stubborn deposits. Rinse it again, then dry it with compressed air.

17 Use a jet of compressed air to blow out all of the fuel and air passages in the main and upper body, not forgetting the air passages in the carburettor intake.

8.12 Undo the screws (arrowed) then release the cover and remove the spring and diaphragm

Caution: Never clean the jets or passages with a piece of wire or a drill bit, as they will be enlarged, causing the fuel and air metering rates to be upset.

Inspection

18 Inspect the choke plunger assembly for wear and damage **(see illustration)**. If the plunger needle or seat is worn or damaged, renew it. To remove it, draw the spring off the plunger and free the cable end from it. Also renew the spring if it has deformed or sagged.

19 If removed from the carburettor, check the tapered portion of the pilot screw and the

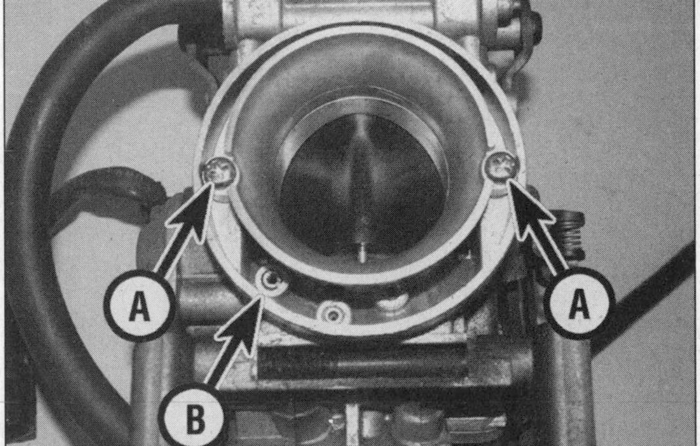

8.14 Undo the screws (A) and remove the funnel to access the pilot air jet (B)

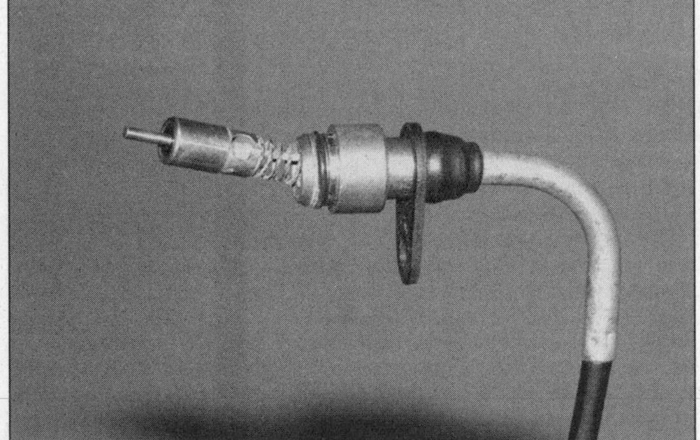

8.18 Check the choke plunger assembly as described

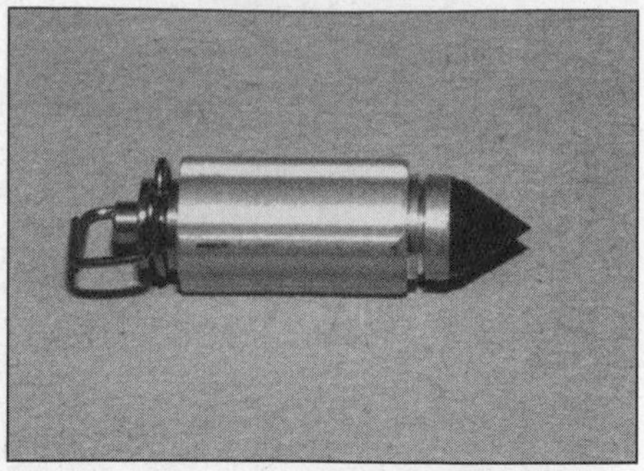

8.24a Check the float needle valve . . .

8.24b . . . and its seat as described

spring and O-ring for wear or damage. Renew them if necessary.

20 Check the carburettor body, float chamber and top cover for cracks, distorted sealing surfaces and other damage. If any defects are found, renew the faulty component, although renewal of the entire carburettor will probably be necessary (check with a Suzuki dealer on the availability of separate components).

21 Check the piston diaphragm for splits, holes and general deterioration. Holding it up to a light will help to reveal problems of this nature.

22 Insert the piston in the carburettor body and check that it moves up-and-down smoothly. Check the surface of the piston for wear. If it's worn excessively or doesn't move smoothly in the guide, renew it.

23 Check the jet needle for straightness by rolling it on a flat surface such as a piece of glass. Renew it if it's bent or if the tip is worn.

24 Check the tip of the float needle valve and the valve seat **(see illustrations)**. If either has grooves or scratches in it, or is in any way worn, they should be renewed as a set. Gently push down on the rod on the top of the needle valve then release it – if it doesn't spring back, renew the valve. Check the gauze strainer on the valve seat for holes or splits and renew it if necessary.

25 Operate the throttle shaft to make sure the throttle butterfly valve opens and closes smoothly. If it doesn't, cleaning the throttle linkage may help. Otherwise, renew the carburettor – spare parts are not available for the throttle linkage.

26 Check the float for damage. This will usually be apparent by the presence of fuel inside the float. If the float is damaged, it must be renewed.

27 Check the air cut-off valve diaphragm for splits and holes – holding it up to a light will help to reveal them. Also check the spring for deformation and weakness and renew it if necessary.

28 On UK models, to check the carburettor heaters and circuit, refer to Section 11.

9 Carburettors – separation and joining

Warning: *Refer to the precautions given in Section 1 before proceeding*

Separation

1 The carburettors do not need to be separated for normal overhaul. You should only need to separate them to renew a carburettor body.

2 Remove the carburettors from the machine (see Section 7). Mark the body of each carburettor with its cylinder location to ensure that it is positioned correctly on reassembly. Make a note of the arrangement of the various hoses and their unions.

3 Remove the throttle position sensor (see Chapter 5).

4 Make a note or mark of the amount that the idle speed adjuster protrudes from its bracket on the front carburettor, then unthread it.

5 Remove the split pin and washer from each end of the throttle linkage arm and remove the arm, noting how and which way round it fits **(see illustration)**. Discard the split pins as new ones should be used.

6 Release the carburettor breather hoses from their holder and draw them out of the joining brackets, noting their routing **(see illustration)**. Release the clamp securing each fuel supply hose to its union and detach each hose. Remove the three-way hose assembly, noting its routing.

9.5 Remove the split pin and washer (arrowed) from each end of the arm and remove the arm

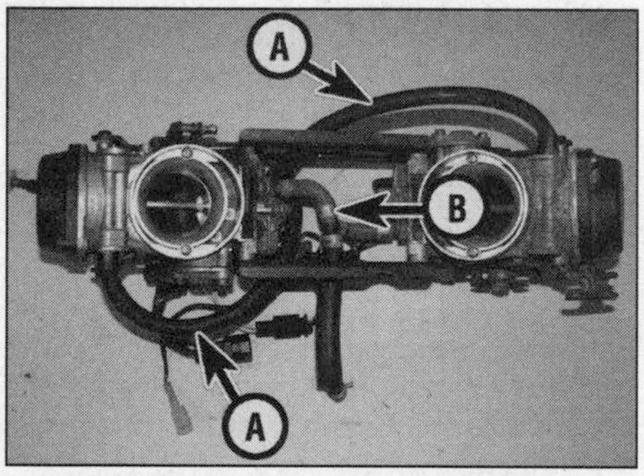

9.6 Release the breather hoses (A) and detach the fuel hose assembly (B)

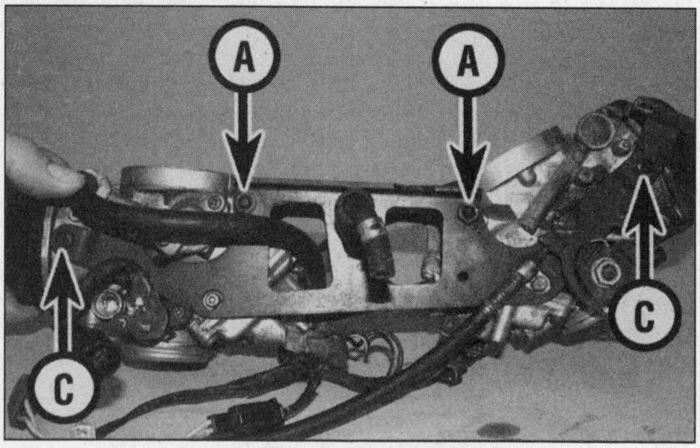

9.7a Unscrew the nuts (A) . . .

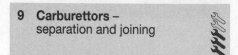

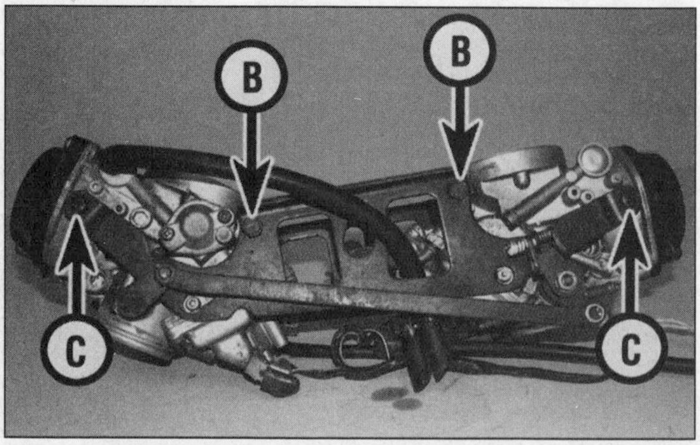

9.7b . . . and withdraw the bolts (B), then undo the screws (C) and remove the brackets

10.2a Fit the diaphragm, locating the point in the passage . . .

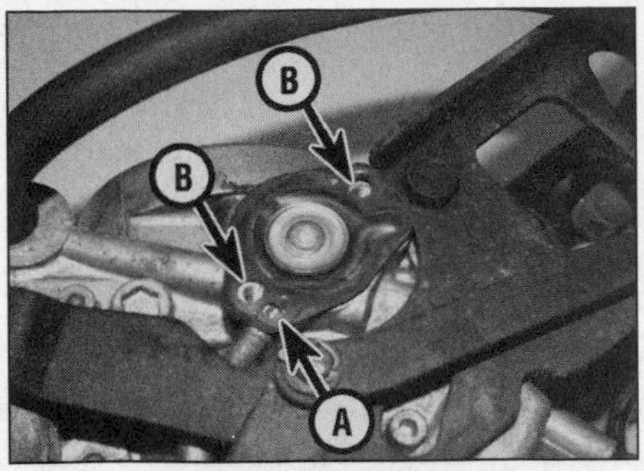

10.2b . . . and making sure the air hole (A) aligns, and the locating pins (B) locate

10.2c Fit the spring then install the cover

7 Unscrew the nuts and withdraw the bolts from the carburettor joining plates **(see illustrations)**. Undo the two screws on the right-hand plate and remove it, noting how it fits. Undo the two screws on the left-hand plate and remove it, noting how it fits.

8 Do not disturb the throttle shafts or butterflies, including the return and synchronisation springs, unless absolutely necessary. If you do, make a careful note of how it all fits and works.

Joining

9 Assembly is the reverse of the disassembly procedure, noting the following.

- Make sure the fuel and breather hoses and elbows are correctly routed and securely connected **(see illustration 9.6)**.
- Check the operation of the throttle linkage ensuring that it operates smoothly and returns quickly under spring pressure.
- Install the carburettors (see Section 7). Check carburettor synchronisation and idle speed (see Chapter 1).

10 Carburettors – reassembly and float height check

Warning: Refer to the precautions given in Section 1 before proceeding.

Note: *When reassembling the carburettors, be sure to use the new O-rings and seals. Do not overtighten the carburettor jets and screws as they are easily damaged.*

1 If removed, screw the pilot air jet into the air intake **(see illustration 8.14)**. Apply a suitable non-permanent thread locking compound to the intake funnel screws, then fit the funnel and tighten the screws securely.

2 Fit the air cut-off valve diaphragm, making sure the pointed centre fits into the passage and is properly seated, the air hole in the diaphragm aligns with the passage in the carburettor, and the two locating pins fit into the holes in the diaphragm **(see illustrations)**. Fit the spring into the cover, then locate the cover, making sure it locates onto the pins, and tighten its screws securely **(see illustration)**.

3 Install the pilot screw (if removed) along with its spring, washer and O-ring, turning it in until it seats lightly **(see illustration 8.11)**. Now turn the screw out the number of turns previously recorded, or as specified at the beginning of the Chapter. Note that where a tamperproof plug was previously fitted (and required by law in that market), the pilot screw must be set to the specified number of turns out and a new plug secured over the screw head – refer to Section 5.

10.4a Fit the needle valve seat . . .

10.4b . . . and secure it with the screw

4 If removed, fit the O-ring onto the float needle valve seat, using a new one if necessary **(see illustration 8.24b)**. Make sure the filter is attached, then press the seat into the carburettor and secure it with the screw **(see illustrations)**.

5 Hook the float needle valve onto the float tab **(see illustration)**. Position the float assembly in the carburettor and slide the pin across, making sure it is secure **(see illustrations 8.10c, b and a)**.

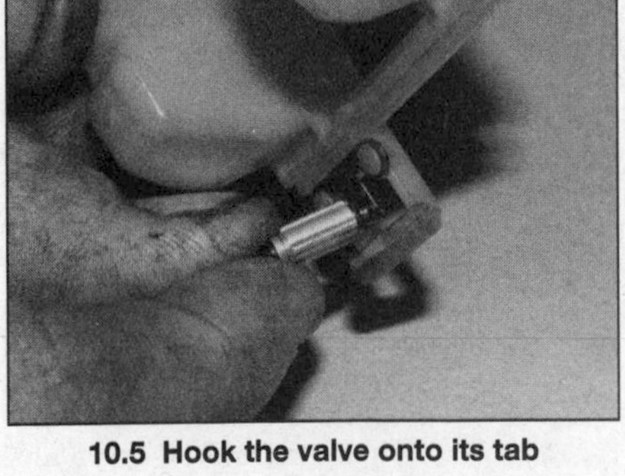

10.5 Hook the valve onto its tab

6 To check the float height, hold the carburettor so the float hangs down, then tilt it back until the needle valve is just seated, but not so far that the needle's spring-loaded tip is compressed. Measure the distance between the base of the carburettor body and the bottom of the float with an accurate ruler **(see illustration)**. The correct setting should be as given in the Specifications at the beginning of the Chapter. If it is incorrect, adjust the float height by carefully bending the float tab a little at a time until the correct height is obtained **(see illustration 10.5)**.

7 Screw the needle jet into the body of the

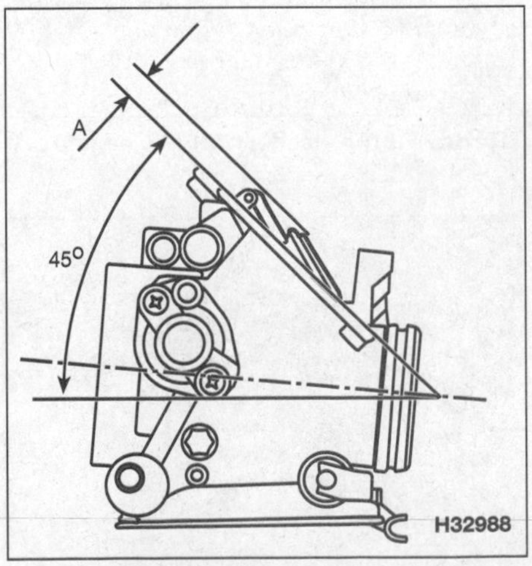

10.6 With the carburettor angled at approximately 45°, measure the float height (A)

10.7a Install the needle jet. . .

10.7b . . . the main jet . . .

10.8 . . . and the pilot jet

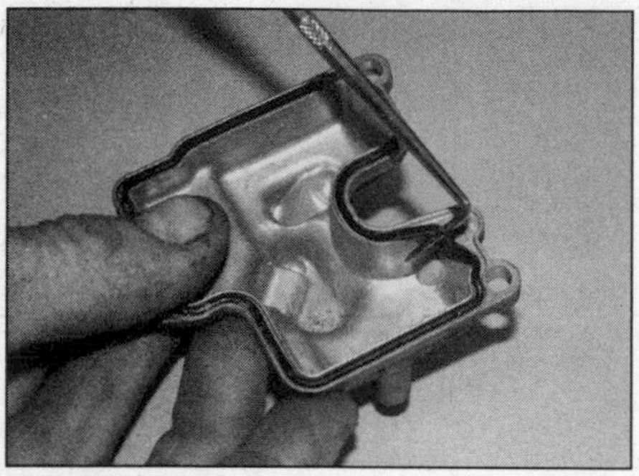
10.9a Fit a new sealing ring into the groove . . .

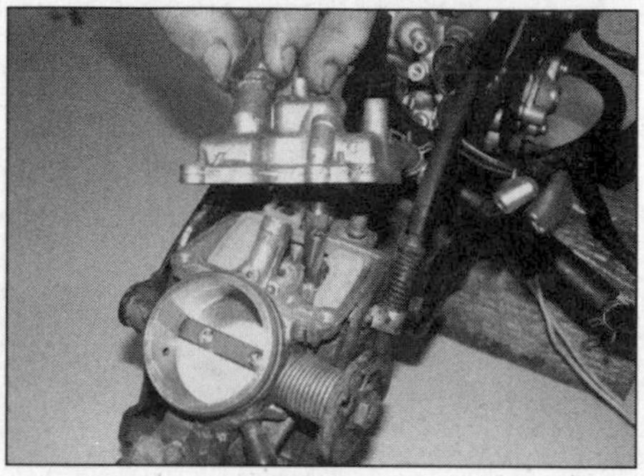
10.9b . . . and install the float chamber

carburettor **(see illustration)**. Screw the main jet into the end of the needle jet **(see illustration)**.

8 Screw the pilot jet into the body of the carburettor **(see illustration)**.

9 Fit a new seal into the groove in the float chamber, then fit the chamber onto the carburettor and secure it with the screws **(see illustrations)**. On UK models, if removed, apply a smear of thermo-grease (Suzuki pt. no. 99000-59029) to the carburettor heater tip, then thread it into the float chamber and tighten it to the torque setting specified at the beginning of the Chapter. Connect the heater wiring connectors **(see illustration 8.5)**.

10 Check that the spacer and E-clip are fitted on the jet needle, then fit the washer onto the top **(see illustration)**. Carefully fit the needle into the piston **(see illustration)**. If removed, fit the O-ring onto the needle retainer, using a new one if necessary **(see illustration 8.4b)**. Check that the spring is fitted to the retainer and is secure. Insert the retainer and carefully press it down until the O-ring is felt to locate **(see illustration)**.

11 Turn the diaphragm inside out so that its rim faces down **(see illustration)**. Insert the piston/diaphragm assembly into the carburettor, ensuring the needle is correctly aligned with the needle jet **(see illustration)**.

10.10a Fit the washer onto the needle . . .

10.10b . . . then insert the needle assembly in the piston

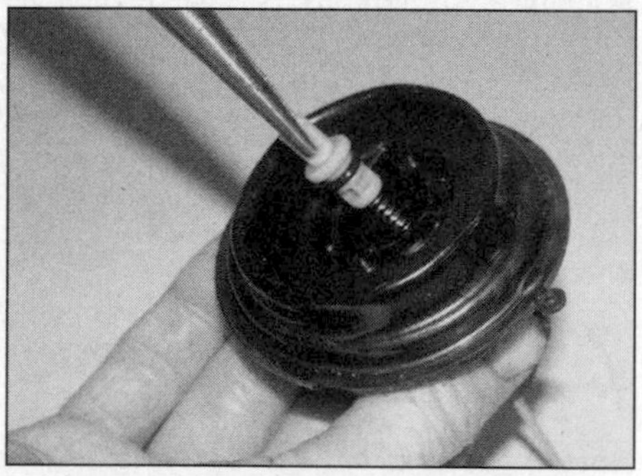
10.10c Fit the retainer onto the needle head

10.11a Turn the diaphragm inside out . . .

10.11b . . . then fit the piston/diaphragm assembly into the carburettor

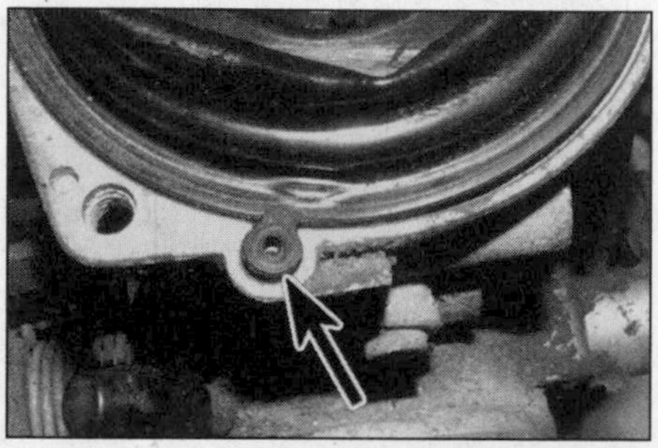
10.11c Fit the rim of the diaphragm into the groove and the tab (arrowed) around the air passage

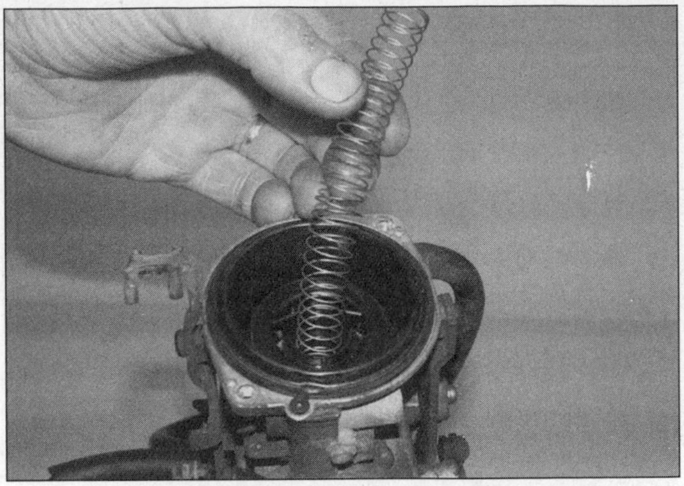

10.12a Fit the spring into the piston . . .

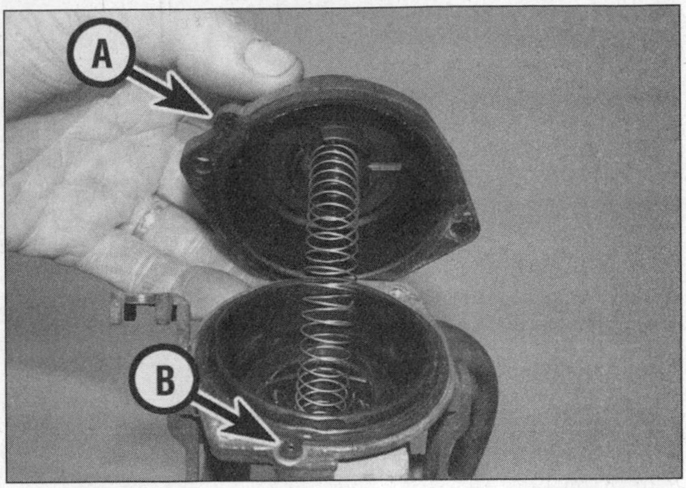

10.12b . . . then fit the cover, aligning the protrusion (A) with the loop (B)

Keep a finger on the bottom of the piston to keep it raised (inserting your finger via the air intake) so the diaphragm stays inside out – this will prevent the rim popping out of the groove. Align the loop on the diaphragm rim with its groove in the carburettor body, then press the diaphragm outer edge into its groove, making sure it is correctly seated **(see illustration)**.

12 Fit the spring, locating it over the needle retainer in the piston **(see illustration)**. Fit the top cover onto the carburettor, locating the top of the spring over the post in the cover and aligning the protrusion on the cover with the loop on the diaphragm **(see illustration)**. Make sure the diaphragm rim stays seated in its groove and does not get pinched by the cover, then install the cover screws and tighten them securely. Check that the piston moves up and down smoothly.

13 If removed, install the throttle position sensor (See Chapter 5).

14 Install the carburettors (see Section 7).

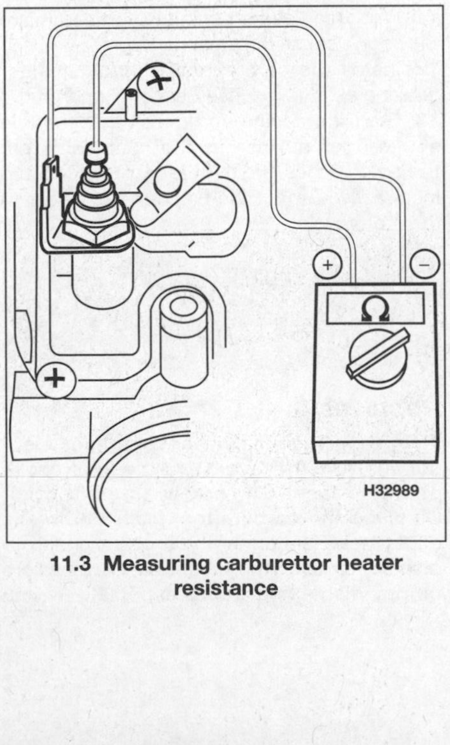

11.3 Measuring carburettor heater resistance

11 Carburettor heater system (UK models)

Warning: Refer to the precautions given in Section 1 before starting work.

1 On UK models, each carburettor has a heater unit threaded into its float chamber. The heaters are controlled by a thermo-switch.

2 To access the heater units, remove the carburettors (see Section 7). To access the thermo switch for the heaters, raise the fuel tank (see Section 2).

3 To check a heater unit, disconnect the wiring connectors from the heater **(see illustration 8.5)**. Using an ohmmeter or multimeter set to the ohms x 1 scale, connect the positive (+ve) probe to the tip of the heater and the negative (-ve) probe to the spade terminal **(see illustration)**. The resistance of each heater should be as specified at the beginning of the Chapter.

4 If a meter is not available, connect a fully charged 12 volt battery to each heater in turn, using the terminals as described above. After about five minutes, the float chamber should be felt to be warm.

5 If any heater does not perform as described, unscrew it from the carburettor. Apply a smear of thermo-grease to a new heater, then thread it into the carburettor and tighten it to the torque setting specified at the beginning of the Chapter.

6 To check the thermo switch, unplug it from the wiring loom **(see illustration)**. Using a continuity tester or multimeter, insert the probes into the switch wiring connector and check for continuity. In normal or warm conditions, there should be no continuity. Now immerse the switch into a bowl of ice. After a few minutes the switch should close and continuity should be shown. If not, the switch is faulty.

7 If the heaters and the switch are all good, turn the ignition switch ON and check for battery voltage at each heater wiring connector, and at the switch wiring connector in the loom. If there is none, refer to the wiring diagrams at the end of Chapter 9 and check the circuits for damaged or broken wiring.

12 Throttle cables

Warning: Refer to the precautions given in Section 1 before proceeding.

Removal

1 Remove the air filter housing (see Section 4). Mark each cable according to its position at each end. Note that access to the throttle cam is restricted and detaching the cable ends is fiddly with the carburettors in situ. If required, displace the carburettors from the intake ducts (see Section 7) – you do not need to disconnect everything from the carburettors before displacing them, especially if you only lift the front carburettor and leave the rear resting on the intake duct, but if any hose, cable or wiring becomes tight while detaching the throttle cables, disconnect the relevant item.

11.6 Carburettor heater system thermo switch and its wiring connector (arrowed) – UK models only

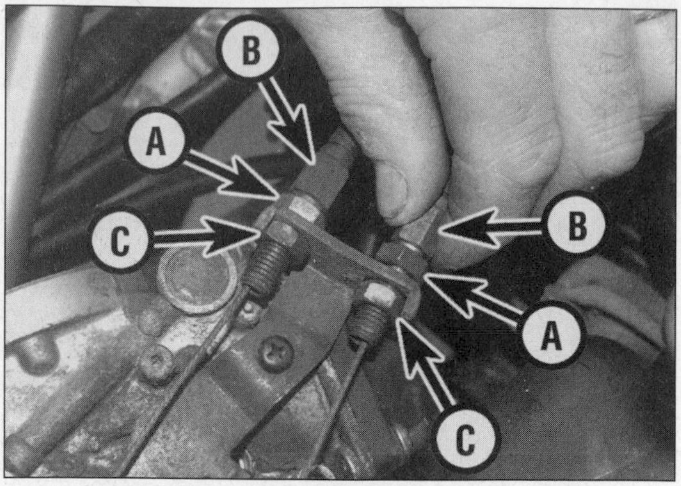

12.2a Adjusters (B), locknuts (A) captive nuts (C)

12.2b Slip the cable out of the bracket . . .

2 Slacken the cable adjuster locknuts and thread them up against the adjusters **(see illustration)**. Move the adjusters down in the bracket until the captive nuts clear the small lugs on the bracket and slip them out of the bracket **(see illustration)**.

3 Detach the inner cable ends from the throttle cam on the carburettor **(see illustration)**.

4 Remove the screw securing the front (opening) cable retaining plate to the handlebar switch/throttle pulley housing, and unscrew the rear (closing) cable retaining ring **(see illustration)**. Remove the handlebar switch/throttle pulley housing screws and separate the halves. Hook the cable ends out of the pulley and remove the cable elbows from the housing **(see illustration)**. Mark each cable to ensure it is connected correctly on installation.

5 Remove the cables from the machine noting their correct routing.

Installation

6 Install the cables making sure they are correctly routed. The cables must not interfere with any other component and should not be kinked or bent sharply.

7 Install the cables into the throttle pulley housing, making sure the opening cable is at the front and the closing cable is at the back. Secure the opening cable elbow with the retainer plate, and thread the closing cable retaining ring into the housing **(see illustration 12.4a)**. Lubricate the end of each inner cable with multi-purpose grease, then locate the lower half of the housing and attach them to the pulley **(see illustration 12.4b)**.

8 Assemble the housing, aligning its locating pin with the hole in the top of the handlebar **(see illustration)**. Install the retaining screws, and tighten them securely.

9 Lubricate the cable lower ends with multi-purpose grease and attach them to the throttle cam on the carburettor **(see illustration 12.3)**. Fit each cable into the mounting bracket and draw it up so the captive nut locates against the lug on the bracket **(see illustration 12.2b)**. Tighten the locknut against the bracket **(see illustration 12.2a)**.

10 Operate the throttle to check that it opens and closes freely.

11 Check the amount of freeplay in the throttle and adjust if necessary (Chapter 1). Turn the handlebars back and forth to make they don't cause the steering to bind.

12 Install the carburettors and/or air filter housing as required (see Section 7 and/or 4).

13 Start the engine and check that the idle speed does not rise as the handlebars are turned. If it does, the throttle cables are routed incorrectly. Correct the problem before riding the motorcycle.

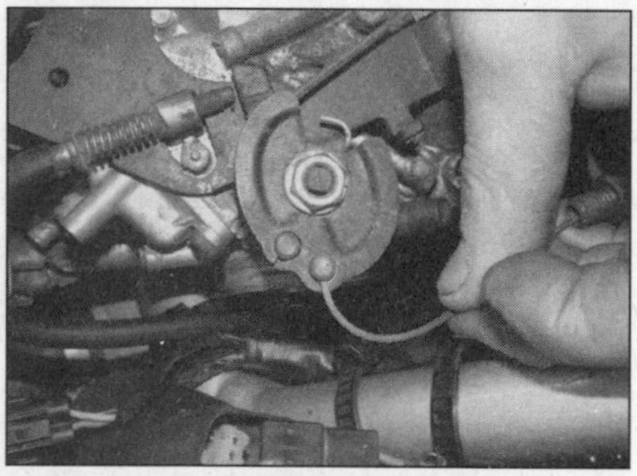

12.3 . . . and detach the cable end from the throttle cam

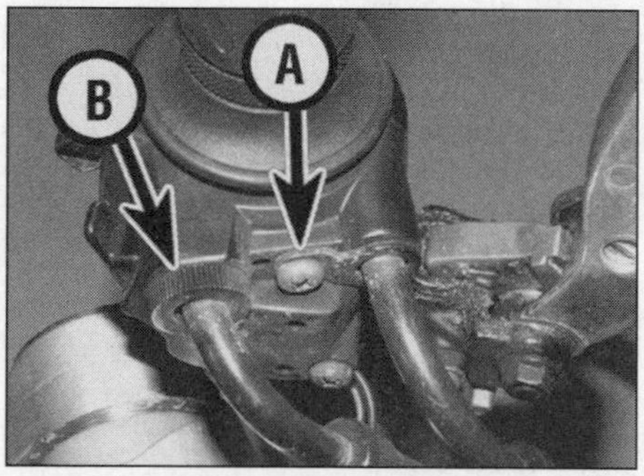

12.4a Undo the retaining plate screw (A) and the ring (B)

12.4b Detach the cable ends from the pulley

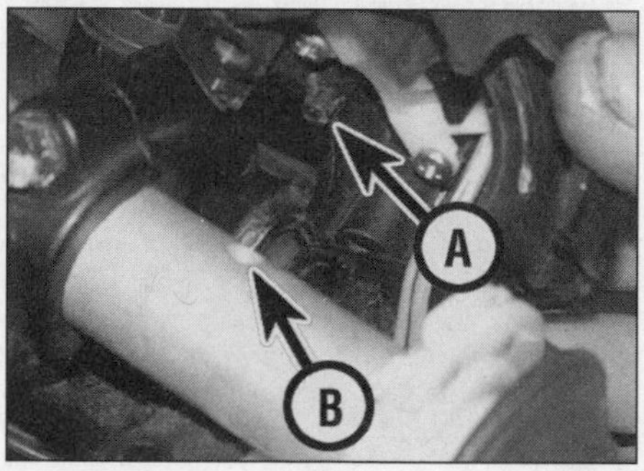

12.8 Locate the pin (A) in the hole (B)

13 Choke cable

Removal

1 Remove the air filter housing (see Section 4). Note that access to the front choke plunger assembly screw is restricted. Displace the carburettors from the intake ducts (see Section 7) – you do not need to disconnect everything from the carburettors before displacing them, especially if you

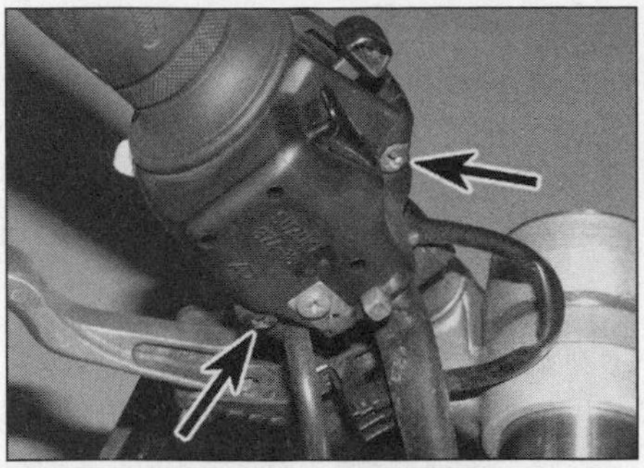

13.4a Undo the screws (arrowed) and separate the switch . . .

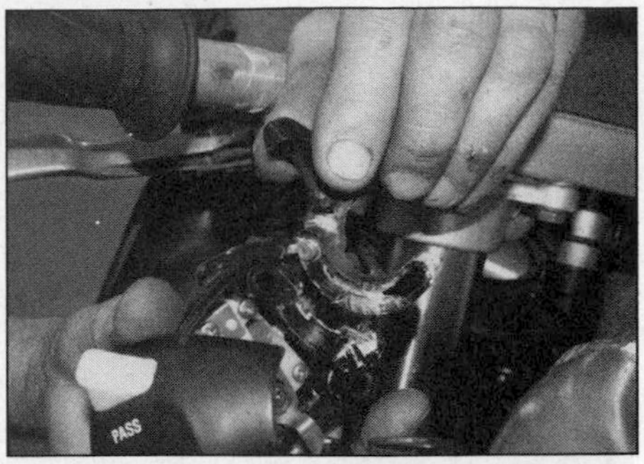

13.4b . . . then detach the lever from the housing and the cable from the lever . . .

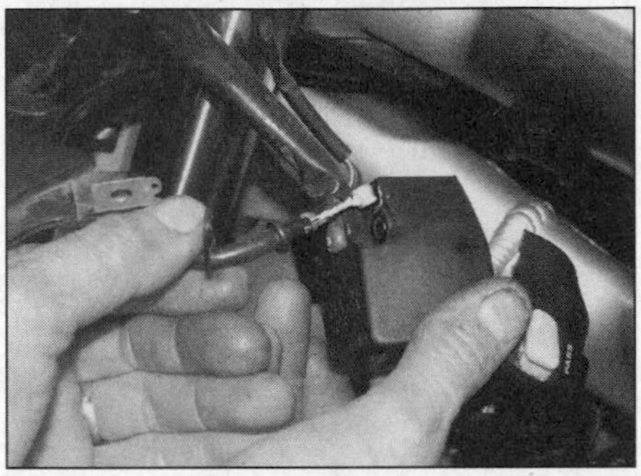

13.4c . . . and draw the cable out of the housing

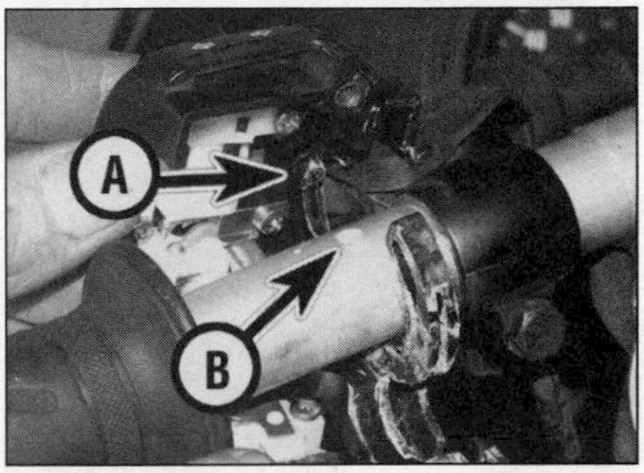

13.7 Assemble the switch on the handlebar, locating the pin (A) in the hole (B)

only lift the front carburettor and leave the rear resting on the intake duct, but if any hose, cable or wiring becomes tight while detaching the throttle cables, disconnect the relevant item.

2 Release the tie securing the rear carburettor choke cable to the carburettor joining bracket. Undo the screws securing the choke plunger retainers to the carburettors and draw the plungers out **(see illustrations 7.9c and d)**. Discard the O-rings as new ones must be used.

3 Compress the spring and detach the cable end from each plunger, noting how it fits **(see illustration 8.18)**. Withdraw the cable from the assembly. If the carburettor is not being disassembled for cleaning, it is advisable to reinstall the choke plunger assembly into the carburettor to avoid losing any of the components.

4 Unscrew the two handlebar switch/choke lever housing screws, one of which secures the choke cable elbow via a retainer plate, and separate the two halves **(see illustration)**. Detach the choke lever from the housing, noting how it fits **(see illustration)**. Detach the choke lever from the cable nipple, then withdraw the cable and elbow from the housing **(see illustration)**.

5 Remove the cable from the machine noting its correct routing.

Installation

6 Install the cable making sure it is correctly routed. The cable must not interfere with any other component and should not be kinked or bent sharply.

7 Lubricate the upper cable nipple with multi-purpose grease. Install the cable in the switch/choke lever housing and attach the nipple to the choke lever **(see illustrations 13.4c and b)**. Locate the lever in the lower half of the housing, then fit the two halves of the housing onto the handlebar, locating the pin in the upper half in the hole in the top of the handlebar **(see illustration)**. Install the screws, making sure the elbow retainer is correctly positioned, and tighten them securely **(see illustration 13.4a)**.

8 Pass the lower end of each inner cable through the rubber boot, cable holder and spring, then attach the nipple to the plunger, making sure it is secure and the spring end locates correctly on the plunger.

9 Fit the choke plungers into the carburettors using new O-rings smeared lightly with grease, then fit the retainer plates and secure them with the screws. Install the carburettors (see Section 7). Check the operation of the choke cable as described in Chapter 1.

14 Exhaust system

Warning: If the engine has been running the exhaust system will be very hot. Allow the system to cool before carrying out any work.

Removal

1 Unscrew the front downpipe flange retaining nuts from the cylinder head studs, then draw the flange off the studs **(see illustration)**. Note that these nuts are very exposed to adverse conditions and are likely to be heavily corroded if the bike is ridden in all weather. It is advisable to apply some penetrating fluid before trying to undo them, and to allow some time for it to work its way in.

2 Slacken the clamp bolt securing the rear cylinder downpipe around the header pipe. Unscrew the rear cylinder downpipe mounting bolt **(see illustration)**.

3 Unscrew the nut on the centre mounting bolt and withdraw the bolt **(see illustration)**. Unscrew the nut on the rear mounting bolt, but leave the bolt in place **(see illustration)**.

4 Support the system, then withdraw the rear mounting bolt and manoeuvre the complete system down to release the rear cylinder downpipe from the header pipe, and the front cylinder downpipe from the port in the cylinder head **(see illustration)**.

14.1 Unscrew the flange nuts and draw the flange off the studs

14.2 Unscrew the rear downpipe bolt (arrowed)

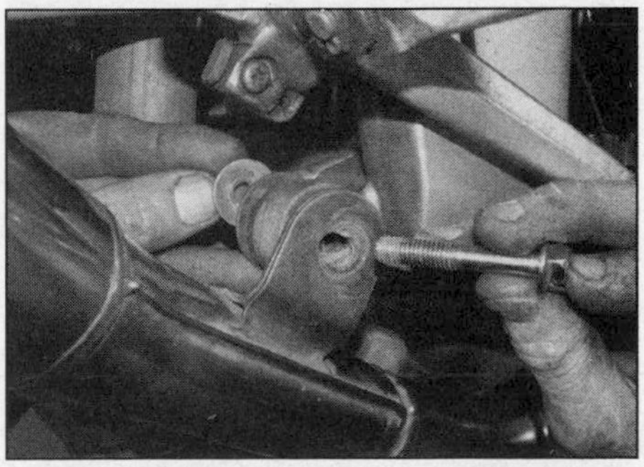

14.3a Unscrew the nut and withdraw the bolt

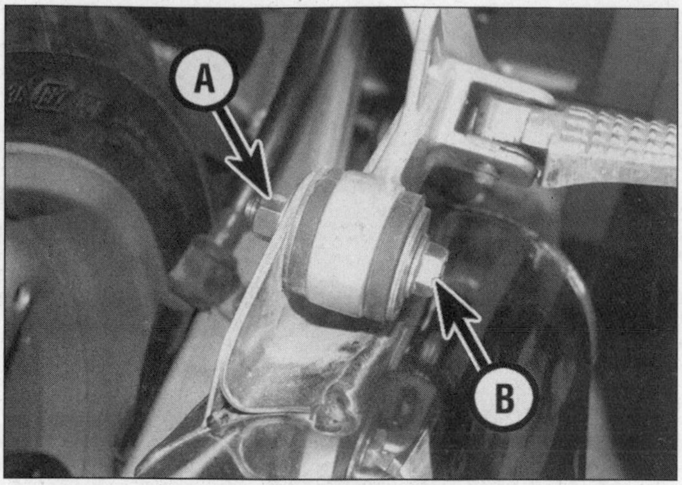

14.3b Unscrew the nut (A) but leave the bolt (B) in place

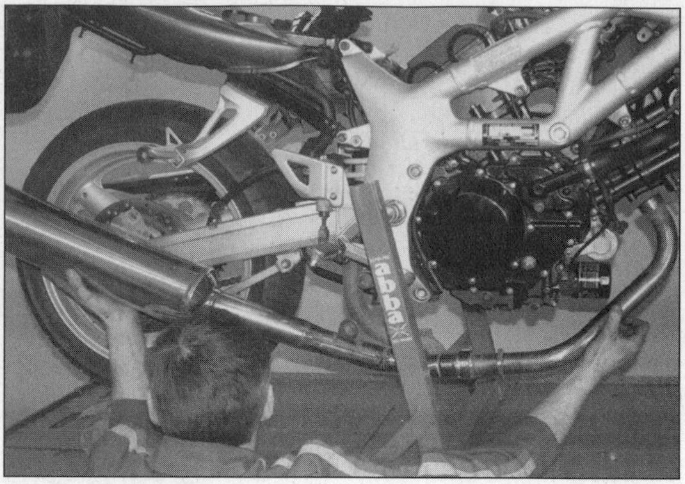

14.4 Manoeuvre the complete system away from the bike

14.5 Remove the gasket from the front cylinder

5 Remove the gasket from the front cylinder head and discard it as a new one must be fitted **(see illustration)**.

6 To access the rear cylinder header pipe bolts, remove the rear wheel (see Chapter 7). Unscrew the single bolt securing the mud deflector to the swingarm and remove it, noting how it fits. To improve access further, remove the rear shock absorber (see Chapter 6). Unscrew the rear downpipe flange retaining bolts from the cylinder head and remove the pipe **(see illustration)**. Remove the gasket from the cylinder head and discard it as a new one must be fitted.

Installation

7 Installation is the reverse of removal, noting the following:

- Use a new gasket in each cylinder head port **(see illustration 14.5)**. Renew any damaged, deformed or deteriorated mounting rubbers with new ones.
- Clean all corrosion off the nuts and bolts using a wire brush. Apply a smear of copper grease to all threads to prevent them from seizing in the future.
- Leave all fasteners loose until the entire system has been installed, making alignment of the various sections easier. Tighten the silencer mounting last.

14.6 Rear cylinder downpipe bolts (arrowed)

- Tighten all nuts and bolts to the torque setting specified at the beginning of the Chapter.
- Run the engine and check that there are no exhaust gas leaks from the exhaust system joints.

15 Fuel pump

Warning: Refer to the precautions given in Section 1 before starting work.

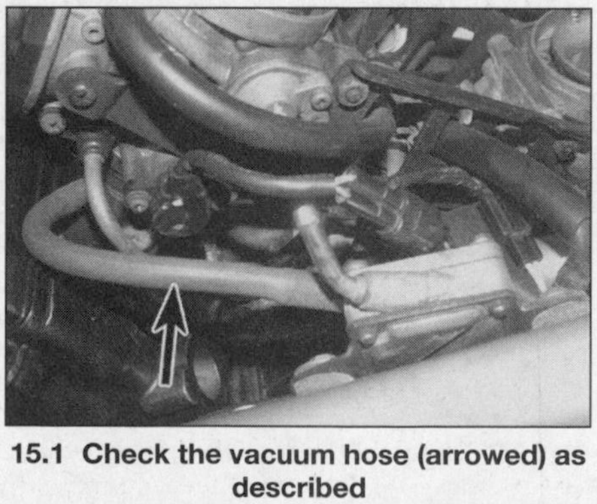

15.1 Check the vacuum hose (arrowed) as described

Check

1 Raise the fuel tank (see Section 2). Before checking the pump, make sure that there are no splits or cracks in the vacuum hose, and that it is securely attached at each end **(see illustration)**.

2 Release the clamp securing the fuel outlet hose on the pump and detach the hose **(see illustration 7.8)**. Connect an auxiliary hose to the union and place the end in a container suitable for holding fuel. Turn the ignition ON and turn the engine on the starter motor. Fuel should flow into the container.

3 If fuel does not flow from the pump (and there is definitely fuel in the tank), first check the fuel tap (see Section 3). If the tap is good, remove and inspect the pump as described below. The most likely problem is a hole or split in the diaphragm.

4 If the pump operates but is thought to be delivering an insufficient amount of fuel, first check that all fuel hoses are in good condition and not pinched or trapped. Check that the strainer on the fuel tap (inside the tank) is not blocked and that fuel delivery hoses are not blocked or pinched at any point.

Renewal

5 Raise the fuel tank (see Section 2).

6 Release the clamps securing the fuel inlet and outlet hoses on the pump and detach the hoses **(see illustration)**. Pull the vacuum hose off its union.

7 Unscrew the bolts securing the pump to the frame and remove the pump **(see illustration 15.6)**. Note the spacers in the rubber grommets.

8 Individual spare parts are not available for the fuel pump – renewal of the pump is the only option if it has failed.

9 Installation is the reverse of removal. Check the condition of the rubber grommets and renew them if they are damaged, deformed or deteriorated. Make sure the tap is fitted the correct way – arrows on the fuel inlet and

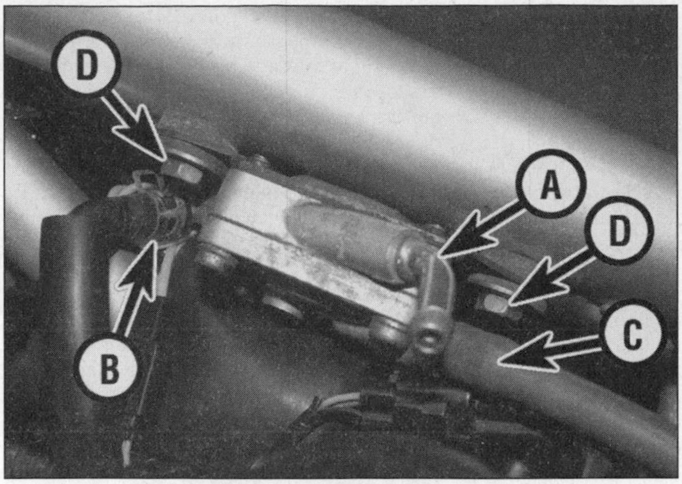

15.6 Inlet hose union (A – hose shown detached), outlet hose (B), vacuum hose (C), mounting bolts (D)

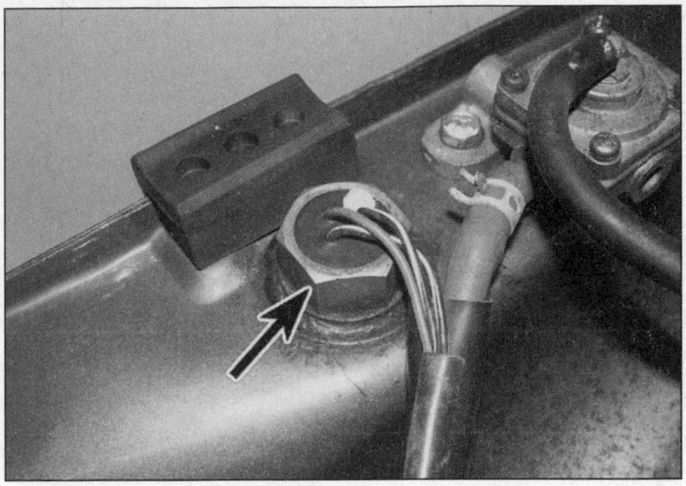

16.5 Fuel level sensor (arrowed)

outlet unions show the direction of fuel flow through the pump **(see illustration 15.6)**. Tighten the bolts to the specified torque setting.

16 Fuel level sensor

Check

1 In normal operation, the fuel level warning light will come on when the ignition is first turned on and extinguish after a few seconds – this serves as a check of the warning light system. The light will start to flicker when the volume of fuel remaining in the tank reaches approximately 3.5 litres, and then stay illuminated when the volume falls to approximately 1.5 litres.

2 If the warning light doesn't come on when the ignition is first turned on, check the electrical circuit to the fuel level warning light in the instrument cluster, and the warning light bulb (see Chapter 9). Raise the fuel tank as described in Section 2 to access the fuel level sensor in the base of the fuel tank. Check the wiring from the sensor wire connector to the instrument cluster (see the wiring diagrams at the end of this manual).

3 If the warning light and wiring are proved good, the sensor is likely to be faulty.

Removal and installation

4 Make sure the ignition is switched OFF. Remove the fuel tank and drain it (see Section 2). Turn the tank upside down and rest it on some clean rag.

5 Unscrew the sensor and withdraw it **(see illustration)**.

6 On installation, apply a smear of suitable sealant to the upper portion of the sensor threads, then screw it into the tank and tighten it securely.

7 Install the tank (see Section 2), and check carefully that there are no leaks before using the bike.

17 PAIR system (Austria, Switzerland and California models)

General information

1 When the engine is running under normal conditions, the control valve is open so whenever there is a negative pulse in the exhaust system filtered fresh air is drawn from the PAIR system air cleaner, through the control valve and reed valves and into the exhaust port of each cylinder head via a flexible hose and metal pipe. This fresh air promotes the burning of any excess fuel present in the exhaust gases, so reducing the amount of harmful hydrocarbons emitted into the atmosphere via the exhaust gases. Exhaust gases are prevented from passing back into the PAIR system by the reed valves.

2 When the throttle is closed the vacuum present in the intake ducts acts on the diaphragm in the PAIR control valve, closing the valve and so cutting off the flow of air, thereby negating the tendency to backfire on overrun **(see illustration)**.

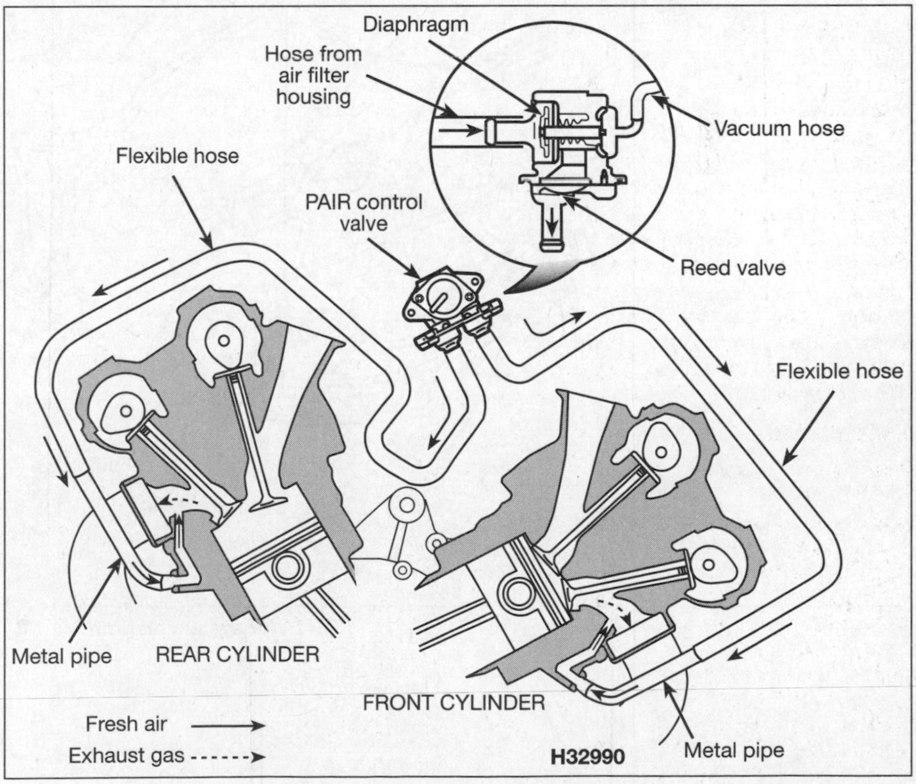

17.2 PAIR system diagram

3 Refer to Chapter 1 for routine checks of the system. The system is not adjustable and requires no maintenance, except to ensure that the hoses are in good condition and are securely connected at each end, and that there is no build-up of carbon fouling the reed valves. Renew any hoses that are cracked, split or generally deteriorated. The reed valves can be checked for a build-up of carbon by unscrewing the control valve cover screws – if any is found, clean up the valves as much as possible, though it is best to install a new control valve (no individual components are available).

4 The control valve should allow air to pass through it when no vacuum is applied to the vacuum union, and should not allow air to pass through it when a vacuum is applied.

5 To test the valve, blow into the air inlet hose union – air should flow out of the four outlet unions. Now apply the correct vacuum via the vacuum hose union, then blow into the air inlet hose union – air should not flow out of the four outlet unions. Release the vacuum and again blow through the inlet union – air should flow from the outlets. As a specific vacuum range is required (270 to 450 mmHg), it is best to have the valve tested by a Suzuki dealer. However If you have a pump and gauge, it is easy to test.

Removal and installation

6 Remove the fuel tank for access to the PAIR control valve, located above the valve cover.

7 Before disconnecting any of the components from their mountings, label the hoses to ensure correct reconnection. If the metal pipes on the cylinder head are removed, use new gaskets on installation.

18 EVAP system (California models)

General information

1 This system prevents the escape of fuel vapour into the atmosphere by storing it in a charcoal-filled canister located on the frame left-hand side at the rear **(see illustration)**.

2 When the engine is stopped, fuel vapour from the tank is directed into the canister where it is absorbed and stored whilst the motorcycle is standing. When the engine is started, vapours that are stored in the canister are drawn into the carburettors to be burned during the normal combustion process.

3 The vent pipe from the fuel tank to the canister incorporates a shut-off valve and a pressure control valve. The tank filler cap has a one way valve which allows air into the tank as the volume of fuel decreases, but prevents any fuel vapour from escaping.

4 The system is not adjustable and should be tested only by a Suzuki dealer. However the owner can check that all the hoses are in good condition and are securely connected at each end. Renew any hoses that are cracked, split or generally deteriorated.

Removal and installation

5 To access the canister remove the seat cowling (see Chapter 8). Prior to their removal, label and disconnect the hoses, then remove the clamp screw and take the canister out. Make sure the hoses are correctly reconnected on installation.

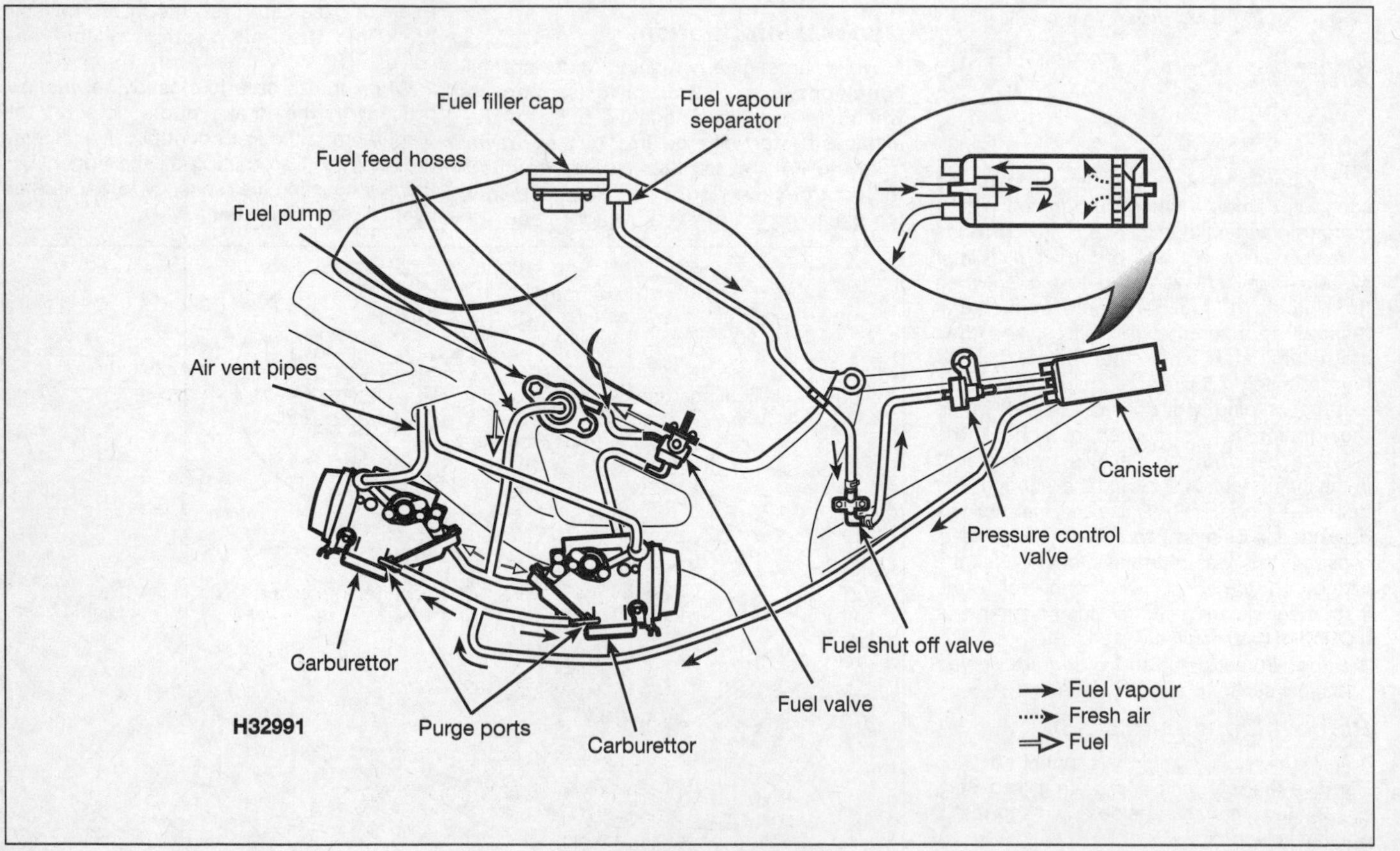

18.1 EVAP system diagram

Chapter 4 Part B
Fuel, engine management and exhaust systems – K3 models onwards

Contents

Degrees of difficulty

Easy, suitable for novice with little experience	**Fairly easy,** suitable for beginner with some experience	**Fairly difficult,** suitable for competent DIY mechanic	**Difficult,** suitable for experienced DIY mechanic	**Very difficult,** suitable for expert DIY or professional

Specifications

Fuel

Grade	
European models	Unleaded, minimum 91 RON (Research Octane Number)
US models and Canada	Unleaded, minimum 87 (R/2+M/2 method)
Fuel tank capacity (including reserve)	
European models	17 litres
US models and Canada	16 litres

Fuel supply system

Operating pressure	43 psi (3.0 Bar)
Pump flow rate	168 ml per 10 seconds at operating pressure

Component test data

Crankshaft position (CKP) sensor	
Resistance	130 to 240 ohms
Peak voltage	above 3.7 V
Engine coolant temperature (ECT) sensor	
Input voltage	4.5 to 5.5 V
Resistance	2.45 K-ohms @ 20°C approx
Gear position (GP) sensor voltage	above 1.0 V
Injector resistance	11 to 13 ohms
Injector voltage	Battery voltage (12 V approx)
Intake air pressure (IAP) sensor	
Input voltage	4.5 to 5.5 V
Output voltage – K3 to K6 models	2.7 V approx at idle speed
Output voltage – K7-on models	2.5 V approx at idle speed
Intake air temperature (IAT) sensor	
Input voltage	4.5 to 5.5 V
Resistance	2.45 K-ohms @ 20°C approx

Component test data (continued)

PAIR solenoid valve	
Resistance – K3 to K6 models	20 to 24 ohms @ 20°C
Resistance – K7-on models	18 to 22 K-ohms @ 25°C
Input voltage	Battery voltage (12 V approx)
Secondary throttle position (STP) sensor – K3 to K6 models	
Input voltage	4.5 to 5.5 V
Output voltage	
Valves closed	0.58 V approx
Valves open	4.38 V approx
Resistance	
Valves closed	0.58 K-ohms approx
Valves open	4.38 K-ohms approx
Secondary throttle position (STP) sensor – K7-on models	
Input voltage	4.5 to 5.5 V
Output voltage	
Valves closed	0.6 V approx
Valves open	4.5 V approx
Secondary throttle valve (STV) sensor	
K3 to K6 models	7.0 to 14.0 ohms approx
K7-on models	7.0 ohms approx
Throttle position (TP) sensor	
Input voltage	4.5 to 5.5 V
Output voltage	
Closed	1.12 V approx
Open	4.26 V approx
Resistance	
Closed	1.12 K-ohms approx
Open	4.26 K-ohms approx
Tip-over (TO) sensor	
Resistance	19.1 to 19.7 K-ohms
Voltage	
Sensor horizontal	0.4 to 1.4 V approx
Sensor tilted (see text)	3.7 to 4.4 V approx

Throttle body

Idle speed	see Chapter 1
Fast idle speed @ 25°C	
K3 to K6 models	1800 to 2400 rpm
K7-on models	1800 to 2200 rpm

Torque settings

Exhaust system (all nuts/bolts)	23 Nm
Fuel pump mounting bolts	10 Nm
Fuel rail screws	5 Nm
Intake air temperature (IAT) sensor – K3 to K6 models	18 Nm
Secondary throttle position (STP) sensor screw	2.0 Nm
Throttle position (TP) sensor screws	3.5 Nm

1 General information and precautions

General information

The fuel system consists of the fuel tank, incorporating the fuel pump, pressure regulator and filter, the fuel hose to the fuel rail on the throttle bodies, and the injectors that are located in each throttle body. The entire fuel injection system is controlled by the engine control module (ECM).

The fuel pump is activated initially by the ignition switch and continues to deliver fuel whilst the engine is running. Fuel pressure is controlled within the pump by the pressure regulator which circulates relieved fuel back into the tank – there is no fuel return hose. In the event of the machine falling over, a tip-over sensor signals the ECM which cuts power to the fuel pump, injectors and ignition coils.

The ECM monitors data sent from the various system sensors and adjusts fuel delivery via the injectors to the engine accordingly. If a fault develops in the injection system, the FI symbol and panel warning LED illuminate on the instrument cluster and an LCD code is displayed. In the case of a minor fault the engine will continue to run enabling the machine to be ridden, although performance will be significantly reduced. For comprehensive fault diagnosis and certain service procedures, a Suzuki mode select switch (Pt. No. 09930-82720) is useful, though not essential, as its function can be copied using a simple jumper wire (see Section 10).

All models have dual valve throttle bodies. The main valve on the front cylinder throttle body is actuated by the throttle cables from the handlebar twistgrip, the secondary valve is actuated by the secondary throttle vale (STV) servo controlled by the ECM. The corresponding valves on the rear cylinder throttle body are actuated by link rods from the front cylinder throttle body. The secondary valves smooth air flow into the throttle body. Throttle position sensors for both valves are located on the rear cylinder throttle body.

For running the engine from cold, a fast idle cam and lever system is actuated by the STV servo. The fast idle is cancelled automatically by the ECM dependant on ambient temperature and engine coolant temperature.

A pulse secondary air (PAIR) system introduces filtered air into the exhaust ports in the cylinder heads to promote the burning of excess fuel in the exhaust gases. The PAIR solenoid valve, located on the underside of the air filter housing, is controlled by the ECM. California models feature an EVAP emission control system that prevents fuel vapour escaping into the atmosphere from the fuel tank.

Precautions

Warning: Petrol (gasoline) is extremely flammable, so take extra precautions when you work on any part of the fuel system. Don't smoke or allow open flames or bare light bulbs near the work area, and don't work in a garage where a natural gas-type appliance is present. If you spill any fuel on your skin, rinse it off immediately with soap and water. When you perform any kind of work on the fuel system, wear safety glasses and have a fire extinguisher suitable for a class B type fire (flammable liquids) on hand.

Always perform service procedures in a well-ventilated area to prevent a build-up of fumes.

Never work in a building containing a gas appliance with a pilot light, or any other form of naked flame. Ensure that there are no naked light bulbs or any sources of flame or sparks nearby.

Do not smoke (or allow anyone else to smoke) while in the vicinity of petrol (gasoline) or of components containing it. Remember the possible presence of vapour from these sources and move well clear before smoking.

Check all electrical equipment belonging to the house, garage or workshop where work is being undertaken (see the Safety first! section of this manual). Remember that certain electrical appliances such as drills, cutters etc. create sparks in the normal course of operation and must not be used near petrol (gasoline) or any component containing it. Again, remember the possible presence of fumes before using electrical equipment.

Always mop up any spilt fuel and safely dispose of the rag used.

Any stored fuel that is drained off during servicing work must be kept in sealed containers that are suitable for holding petrol

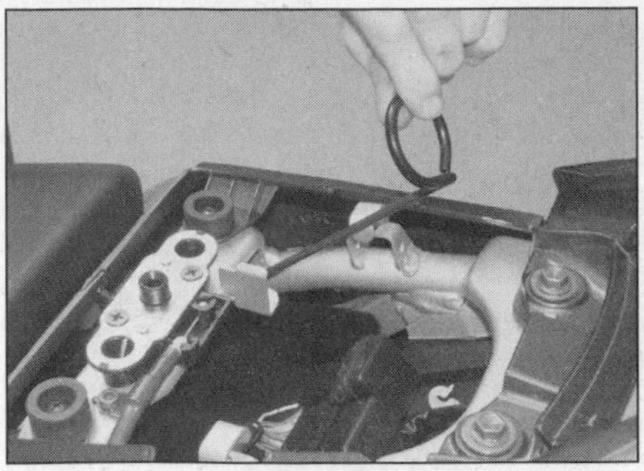

2.2 Remove the prop from under the passenger seat

(gasoline), and clearly marked as such; the containers themselves should be kept in a safe place. Note that this last point applies equally to the fuel tank if it is removed from the machine; also remember to keep its filler cap closed at all times.

Read the Safety first! section of this manual carefully before starting work.

Owners of machines used in the US, particularly California, should note that their machines must comply at all times with Federal or State legislation governing the permissible levels of noise and of pollutants such as unburnt hydrocarbons, carbon monoxide etc. that can be emitted by those machines. All vehicles offered for sale must comply with legislation in force at the date of manufacture and must not subsequently be altered in any way which will affect their emission of noise or of pollutants.

In practice, this means that adjustments may not be made to any part of the fuel, ignition or exhaust systems by anyone who is not authorised or mechanically qualified to do so, or who does not have the tools, equipment and data necessary to properly carry out the task. Also if any part of these systems is to be renewed it must be renewed with only genuine Suzuki components or by components which are approved under the relevant legislation. The machine must never be used with any part of these systems removed, modified or damaged.

2 Fuel tank

Warning: Refer to the precautions given in Section 1 before starting work.

Raise

1 Make sure the fuel cap is secure, then remove the seats (see Chapter 8).

2 Remove the fuel tank prop from the storage space underneath the passenger seat **(see illustration)**.

3 Unscrew the bolts securing the front of the fuel tank to the frame and remove them **(see illustration)**.

4 Raise the front of the tank and support it

2.3 Unscrew the two bolts (arrowed)

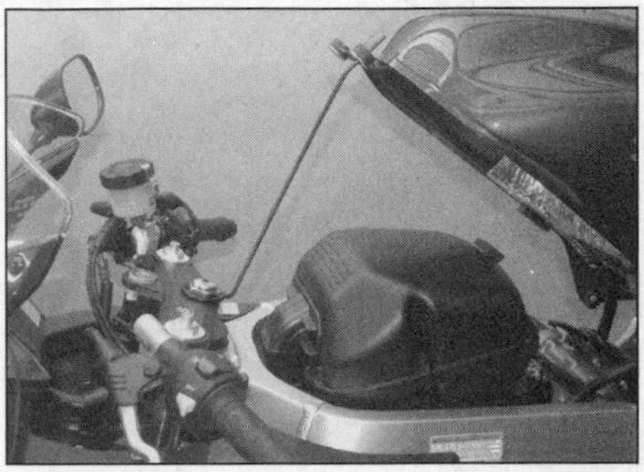

2.4a Support the tank by locating the prop as described

with the prop, locating it between the steering stem nut and one of the fuel tank mounting bolt holes **(see illustration)**. Note the grommet and spacer arrangement for each mounting and take care not lose the spacers **(see illustration)**.

Removal

5 Make sure the ignition is OFF. Raise and support the tank (see above).

6 Disconnect the fuel pump wiring connector **(see illustration)**.

7 Place a rag underneath the fuel supply hose to catch any residual fuel, then release the clip on the hose connector and disconnect it from its union on the bottom of the tank **(see illustration)**. Pull the breather and drain hoses off the unions on the underside of the tank **(see illustration)**.

8 Unscrew the nut and withdraw the pivot bolt securing the rear of the tank to the bracket on

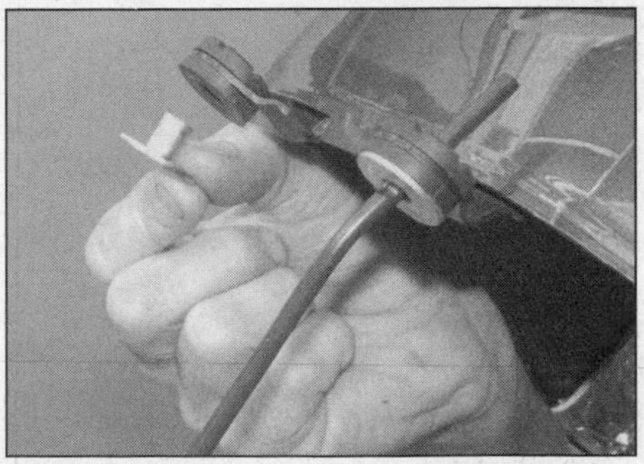

2.4b Note the location of the spacers in the mounting grommets

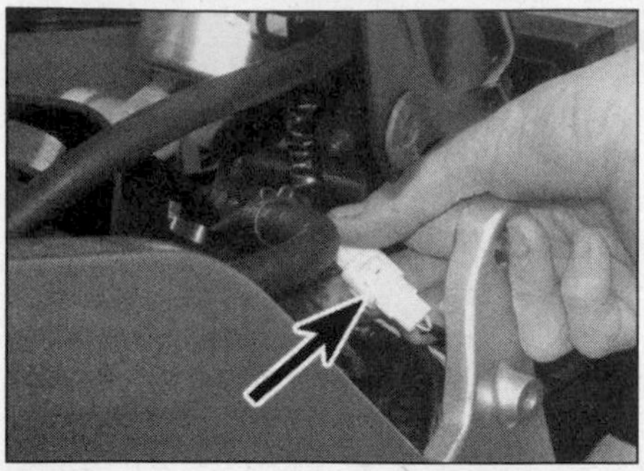

2.6 Fuel pump wiring connector (arrowed)

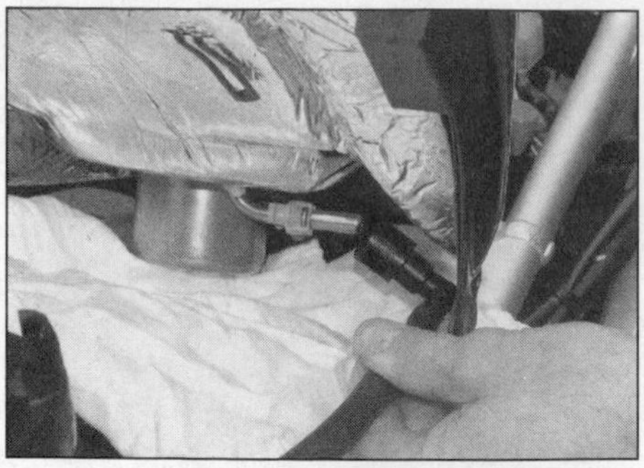

2.7a Disconnect the fuel supply hose

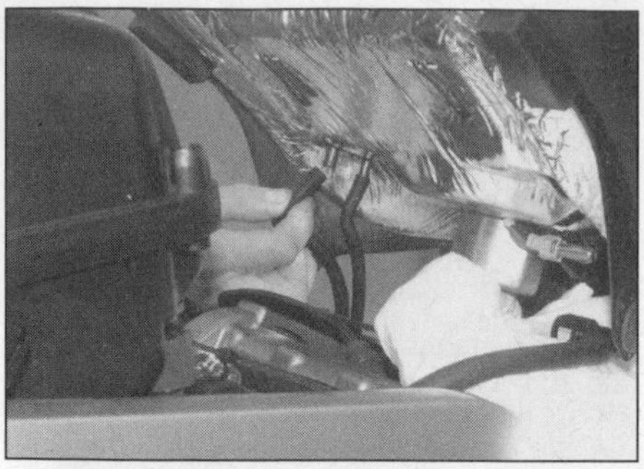

2.7b Pull off the breather and drain hoses

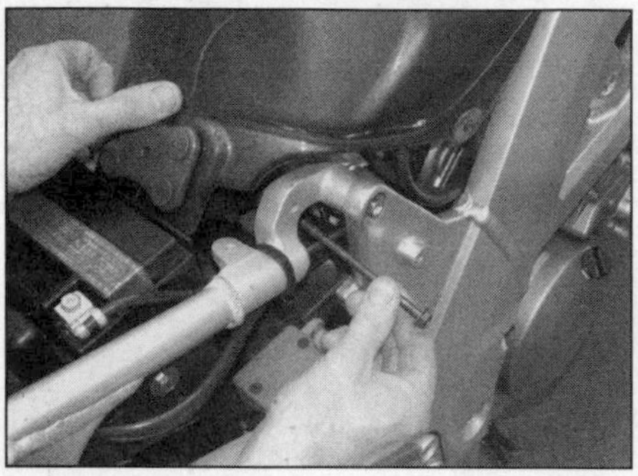

2.8a Remove the pivot bolt . . .

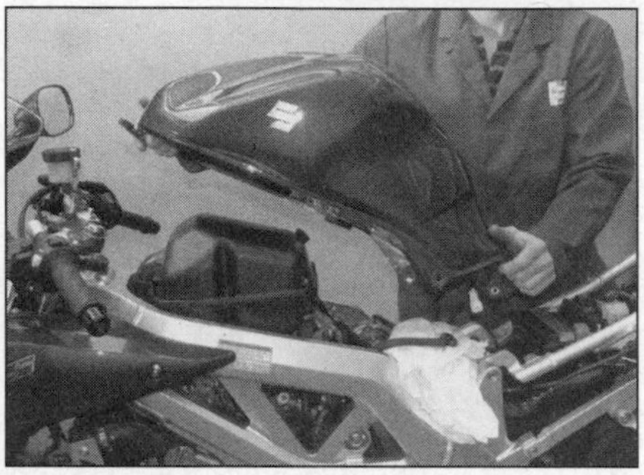

2.8b . . . and lift off the tank

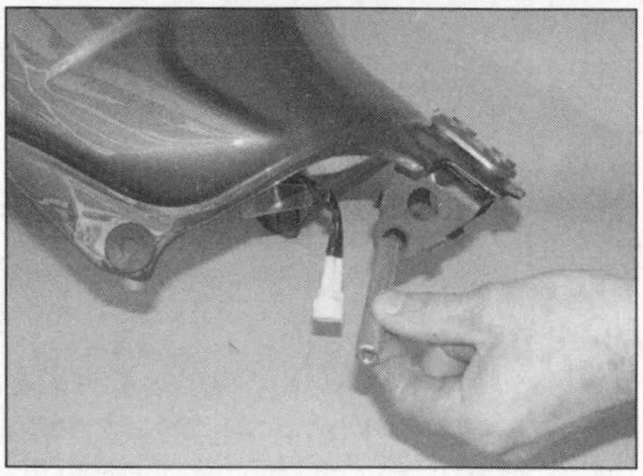

2.8c Note the location of the spacer in the bracket

the frame, then remove the prop and lift the tank away **(see illustrations)**. Note the spacer for the bolt in the bracket **(see illustration)**.

9 Inspect the tank mounting rubbers and the heat shield on the underside of the tank for signs of damage or deterioration and replace them with new ones if necessary.

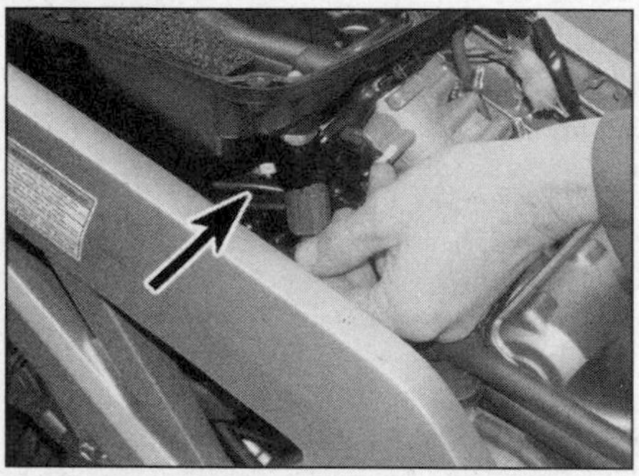

3.2 Disconnect the IAT sensor wiring connector

Installation

10 Installation is the reverse of removal, noting the following.

- Check that the tank mounting rubbers are fitted.
- Ensure that the heat shield is securely clipped in place.
- Refer to Chapter 1 and check the condition of the fuel system hoses before installing the tank.
- Align the fuel supply hose connector with its union on the tank and push it on fully so that the clip engages. Make sure the breather and drain hoses are pushed fully onto their unions.
- Start the engine and check that there is no sign of fuel leakage.

Cleaning and repair

11 All repairs to the fuel tank should be carried out by a professional who has experience in this critical and potentially dangerous work. Even after cleaning and flushing the fuel system, explosive fumes can remain and ignite during repair of the tank.

12 If the fuel tank is removed from the bike, it should not be placed in an area where sparks or open flames could ignite the fumes coming out of the tank. Be especially careful inside garages where a natural gas-type appliance is located, because the pilot light could cause an explosion.

3 Air filter housing

K3 to K6 models

Removal

1 Make sure the ignition is OFF, then raise or remove the fuel tank as required (see Section 2).

2 Disconnect the wiring connector from the intake air temperature (IAT) sensor on the left-hand side of the housing **(see illustration)**.

3 Disconnect the wiring connector and the vacuum hose from the intake air pressure (IAP) sensor on the right-hand side of the housing **(see illustration)**.

4 Disconnect the PAIR solenoid valve wiring connector **(see illustration)**.

5 Loosen the clamp screws securing the housing to the throttle bodies **(see illustrations)**.

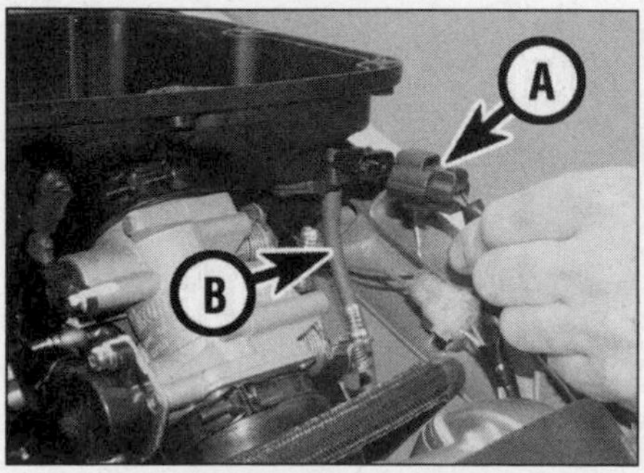

3.3 Disconnect the IAP sensor wiring connector (A) and hose (B)

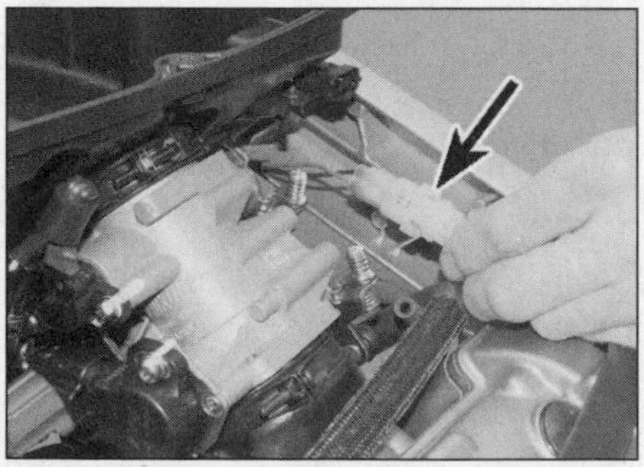

3.4 Disconnect the PAIR solenoid wiring connector

6 Displace the housing, then release the clips and disconnect the crankcase breather hoses from the housing **(see illustration)**.

7 Release the clip and disconnect the PAIR system hose from the solenoid valve on the underside of the housing, then lift off the housing **(see illustration)**.

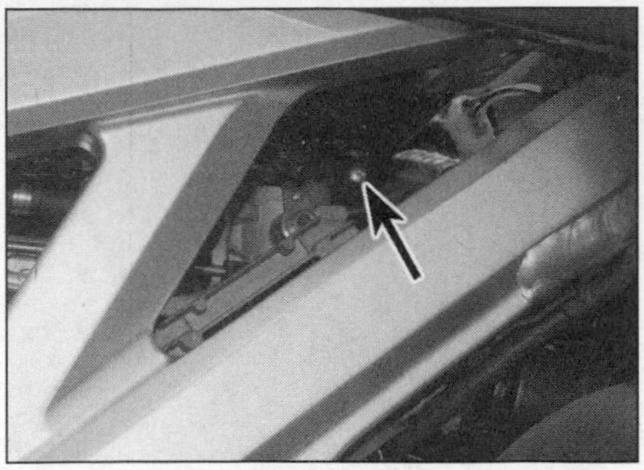

3.5a Loosen the front . . .

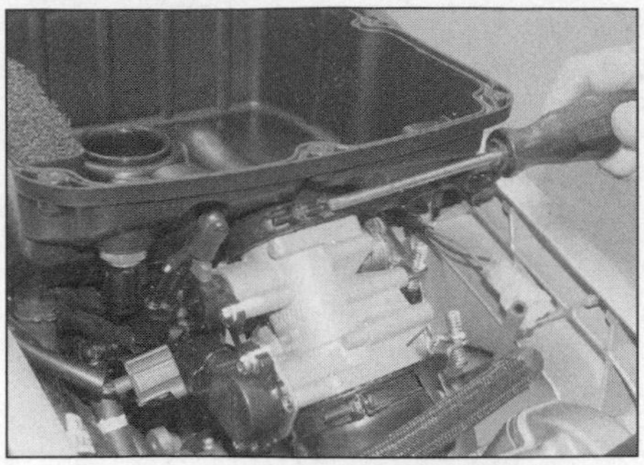

3.5b . . . and rear clamp screws

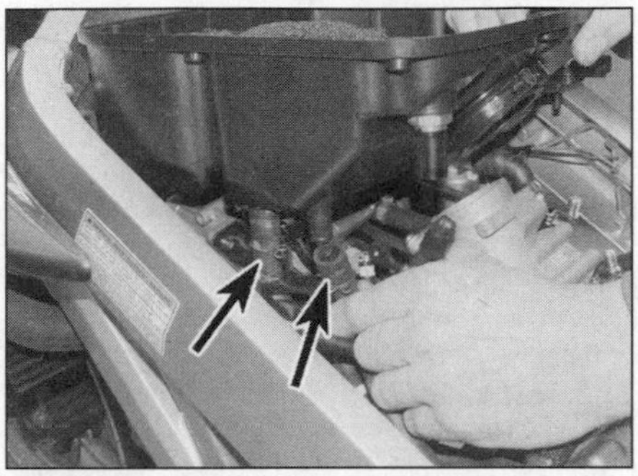

3.6 Disconnect the breather hoses . . .

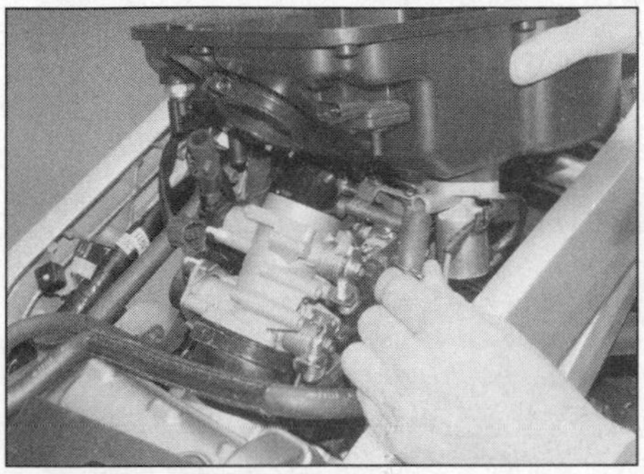

3.7 . . . and the PAIR system hose

Installation

8 Installation is the reverse of removal, noting the following.

- Don't forger to connect the PAIR system hose and the breather hoses before fitting the housing onto the throttle bodies.
- Make sure all hoses are secured with their clips.
- Make sure the housing locates correctly on the throttle bodies and tighten the clamp screws securely.
- Make sure all wiring connectors are securely connected.

K7 models onward

Removal

9 Make sure the ignition is OFF then raise or remove the fuel tank (see Section 2).

10 From the rear of the air filter housing, disconnect the vacuum hoses and wire connectors from both intake air pressure (IAP) sensors or gently ease the sensor mounting rubbers off the air filter housing tabs **(see illustrations)**. Disconnect the wire connector from the intake air temperature (IAT) sensor **(see illustration)**.

11 Loosen the clamp screws which secure the housing to each throttle body. The rear hose clamp is easy to access, but you'll need to pass a long screwdriver through the left side frame aperture to reach the front clamp **(see illustrations)**. The housing can now be lifted up sufficiently to access the hoses and wire connectors on the underside.

12 From the left-hand side of the housing, disconnect the two crankcase breather hoses **(see illustration)**.

13 From the right-hand side of the housing, disconnect the idle speed control (ISC) hose from its stub on the base of the housing

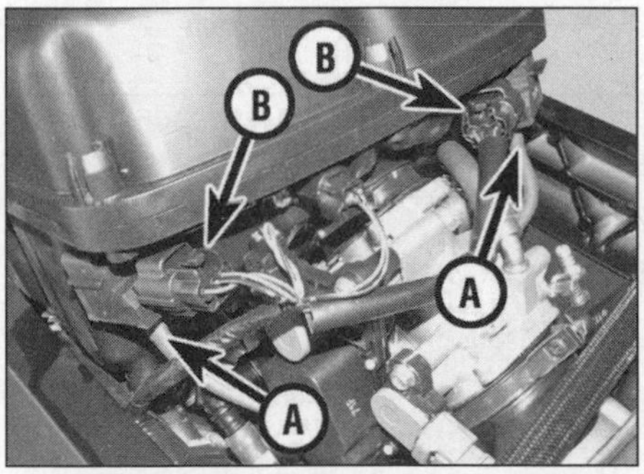

3.10a Disconnect the IAP sensor vacuum hoses (A) and wire connectors (B) . . .

3.10b . . . or pull each sensor mounting rubber off its tab

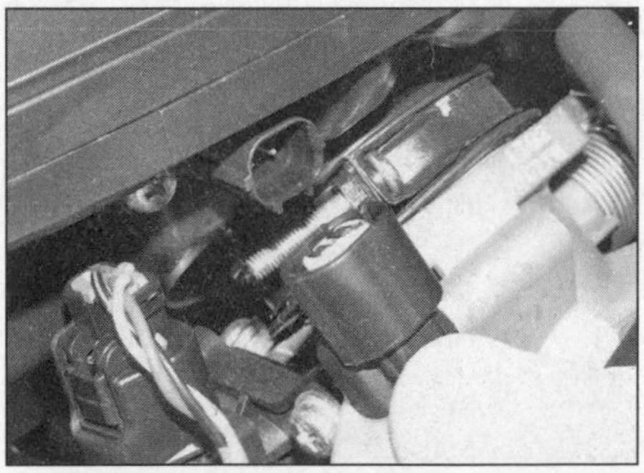

3.10c Disconnect the IAT wire connector

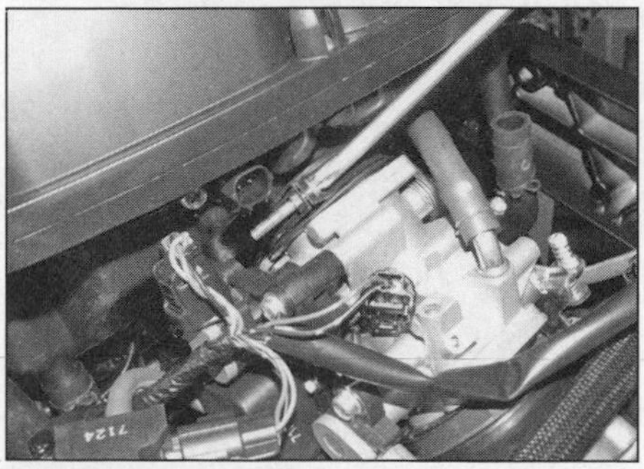

3.11a Slacken off the clamp on the rear . . .

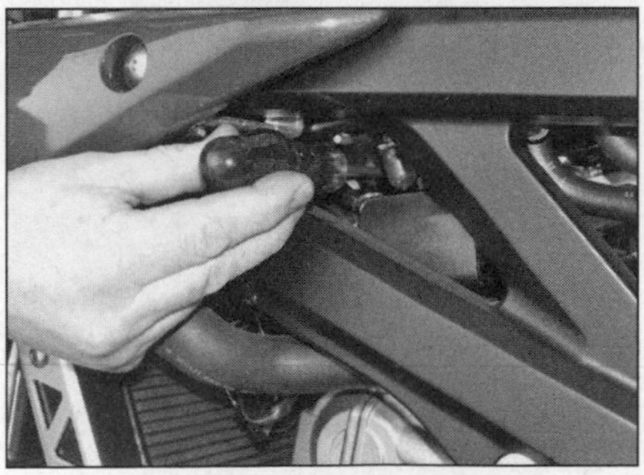

3.11b . . . and front throttle body

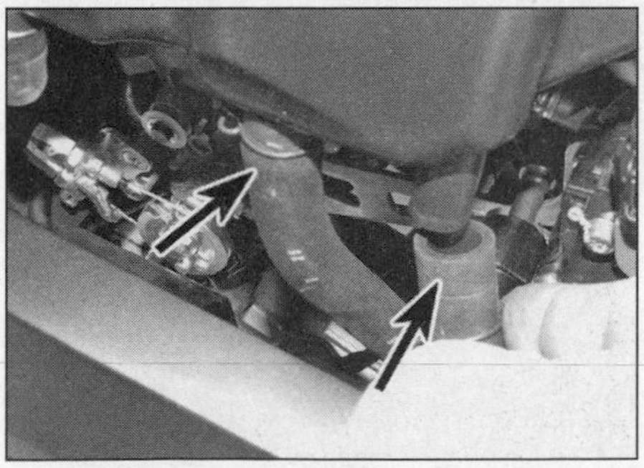

3.12 The crankcase breather hoses (arrowed)

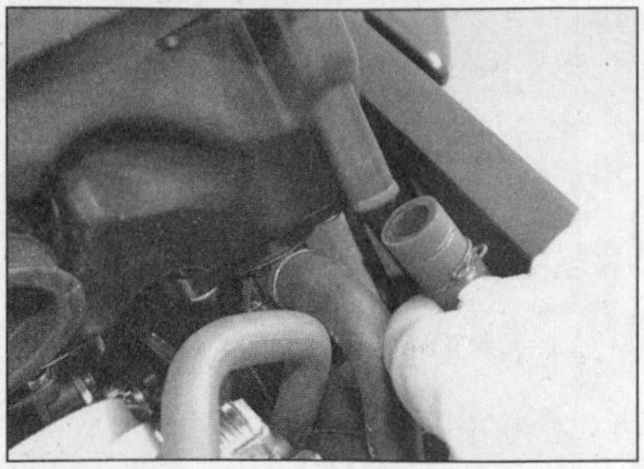

3.13a Release its wire clip and pull the ISC hose off its stub

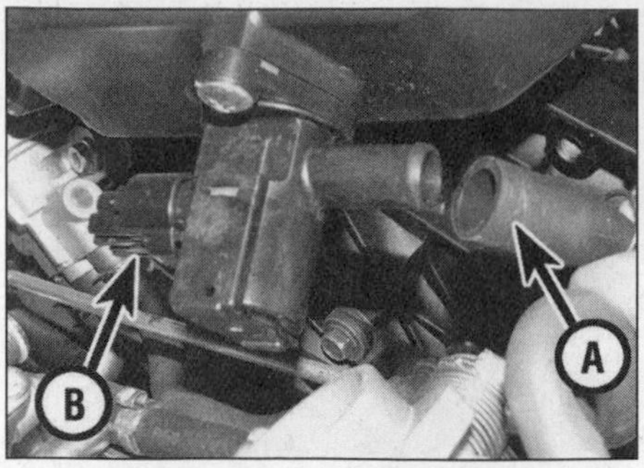

3.13b Disconnect the PAIR valve hose (A) and the wire connector (B)

3.14a If the rubbers have becoming detached, insert them so that the groove (arrowed) locates in the lip of the aperture

(see illustration). Tip the housing back and disconnect the wire connector and vacuum hose from the PAIR solenoid valve **(see illustration)**.

Installation

14 Installation is the reverse of removal, noting the following:

- Check that the rubber stubs are fully engaged in the base of the housing **(see illustration)**. Note that the clamp for the front cylinder has an abutment lug on the housing to locate it correctly **(see illustration)**.
- The housing must fit securely over the throttle bodies so that there are no air leaks. If it tends to spring back rather than seat fully, remove the air filter element (see Chapter 1) and press down on the base of the housing as the clamps are tightened (see illustration).
- Connect all hoses and wiring securely and secure the hoses with their clips, where fitted.

4 Fuel pressure and delivery check

Warning: Refer to the precautions given in Section 1 before starting work.

1 The fuel pump is located inside the fuel tank. When the ignition is switched ON, it should be possible to hear the pump run for a few seconds until the system is up to pressure. If you can't hear anything, first check the fuse (see Chapter 9), then check the relay (see Section 5). If they are good, check the wiring and terminals for physical damage or loose or corroded connections and rectify as necessary (see the *Wiring diagrams* at the end of Chapter 9). If the pump still will not run, fit a new pump assembly (see Section 6). **Note:** *The tip-over sensor switches off the fuel pump if the machine falls over – a sensor fault should be indicated by the fuel injection system diagnostic process (see Section 10).*

Pressure check

2 To check the fuel pressure, a suitable gauge, gauge hose and adapters are needed. Suzuki provides service tools, Pt. Nos. 09915-77331 (gauge), 09915-74521 (gauge hose), 09940-40211 (gauge adapter) and 09940-40220 (gauge hose attachment) for this purpose.

3 Raise the fuel tank and support it with the prop (see Section 2).

4 Place a rag underneath the fuel supply hose to catch any residual fuel, then release the clip on the hose connector and disconnect it from its union on the bottom of the tank **(see illustration 2.7a)**.

5 Connect the gauge hose attachment to the bottom of the tank, then connect hose attachment, the gauge hose and the fuel supply hose via the adapter **(see illustration)**.

6 Turn the ignition switch ON and check the pressure reading on the gauge. The pressure should be as specified at the beginning of this Chapter.

7 Turn the ignition OFF and disconnect the gauge and adapters. Use a rag to catch any residual fuel as before. Align the fuel supply hose connector with its union on the tank and push it on fully so that the clip engages.

8 If the pressure is too low, check for a leak in the fuel supply system, a blocked fuel filter (see Section 7), a faulty pressure regulator (see Section 7) or a faulty fuel pump.

9 If the pressure is too high, either the pressure regulator or the fuel pump check valve is faulty. **Note:** *Suzuki provides no test procedure for the pressure regulator. Disassemble the pump to inspect the regulator (see Section 7). A new regulator is only available as an integral part of the pump filter cartridge. The fuel check valve is an integral part of the regulator and is not available separately.*

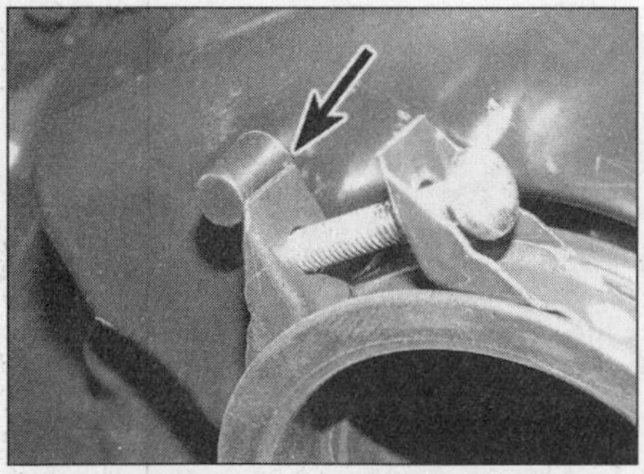

3.14b Locate the ear of the clamp against the lug on the housing (arrowed)

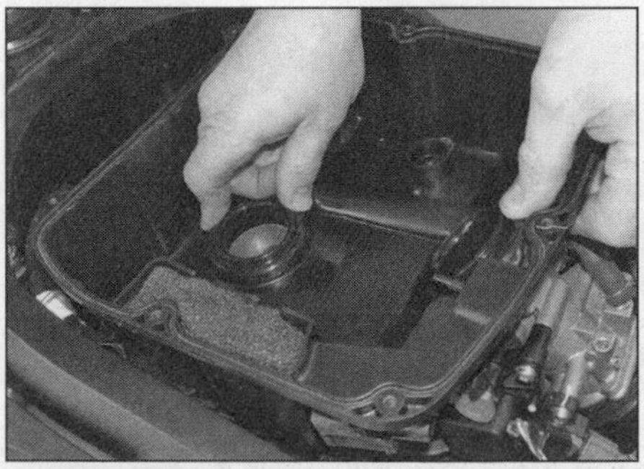

3.14c Remove the element and press down on the housing base to locate the rubbers fully on the throttle bodies

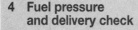

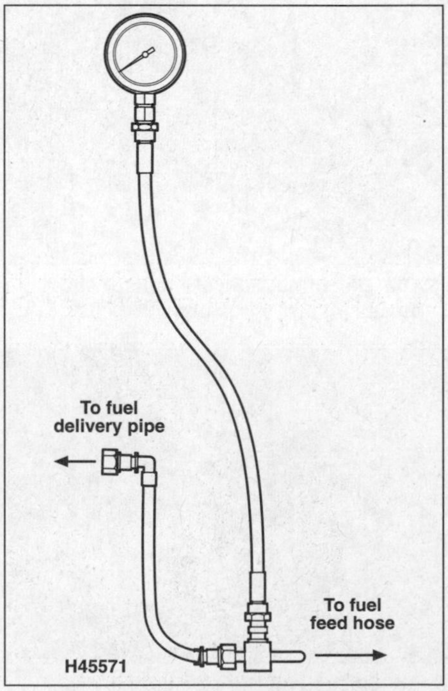

4.5 Set-up for checking fuel pressure

10 On completion run the engine and check for leaks in the fuel hose.

Fuel delivery check

11 Raise the fuel tank, then disconnect the fuel supply hose **(see illustration 2.7a)**.

12 Connect a length of suitable hose to the union on the bottom of the tank and place the open end of the hose in a calibrated container capable for holding approximately 2 litres of fuel.

13 Ensure the ignition is OFF, then disconnect the fuel pump wiring connector **(see illustration 2.6)**. Using a fully charged 12 volt battery and two insulated jumper wires, connect the battery positive (+ve) terminal to the pump's yellow/red wire terminal, and the battery negative (-ve) terminal to the pump's black/white wire terminal. Let fuel flow from the pump into the container for 10 seconds, then disconnect the battery.

14 Measure the amount of fuel that has flowed into the container and compare it to the amount specified at the beginning of this Chapter. If the flow rate recorded is below the minimum required, either the fuel filter is blocked or the pump is defective and must be replaced with a new one (see Section 7).

5 Fuel pump relay

1 The relay is mounted on the right-hand side behind the ECM **(see illustration)** – remove the seat to access it (see Chapter 8).

2 Pull the relay off its mounting and disconnect the wiring connector. Using a multimeter or

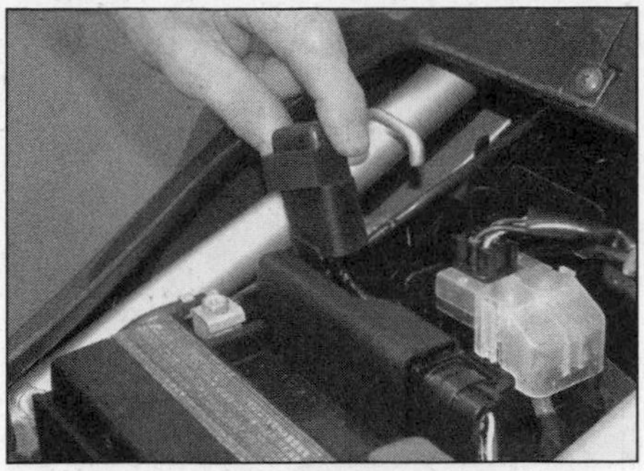

5.1 Location of the fuel pump relay

test light, check for continuity between terminals 1 and 2 on the relay **(see illustration)**. There should be no continuity. Now use jumper wires to connect the positive (+ve) terminal of a fully charged 12 volt battery to terminal 3 on the relay and the negative (-ve) battery terminal to relay terminal 4. There should be continuity shown across terminals 1 and 2. If the relay fails either of the checks, replace it with a new one.

6 Fuel pump – removal and installation

Warning: Refer to the precautions given in Section 1 before starting work.

Removal

1 The fuel pump is located inside the fuel tank. Remove the tank and drain it (see Section 2).

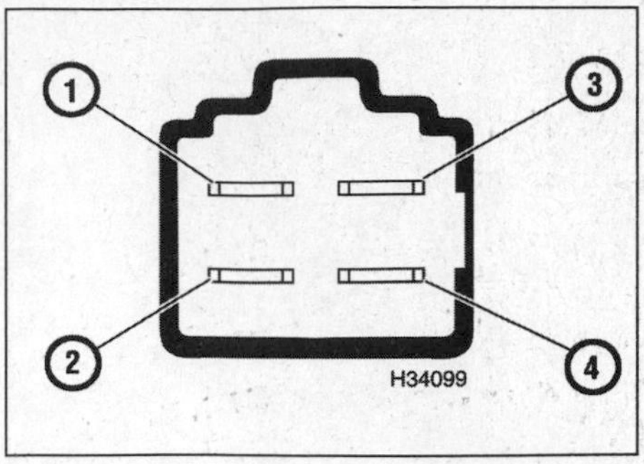

5.2 Fuel pump relay terminal identification

2 Turn the tank upside down and rest it on some clean rag to protect the paintwork. Release the clips securing the heat shield and lift it off **(see illustration)**.

3 Remove the fuel supply hose clip **(see illustration)**.

4 Undo the bolts securing the pump base to the underside of the tank evenly, in a criss-cross pattern, and lift out the pump **(see illustrations)**. Discard the O-ring as a new one must be fitted on reassembly **(see illustration)**.

5 If required, clean the strainer and check the operation of the pressure regulator and level sensor (see Section 7).

6 Check that the wiring terminals for the fuel pump and the level sensor(s) are tight **(see illustration)**.

Installation

7 Fit a new O-ring into the recess around the aperture on the underside of the fuel tank and smear the O-ring lightly with grease. Install the pump and align the holes in the pump

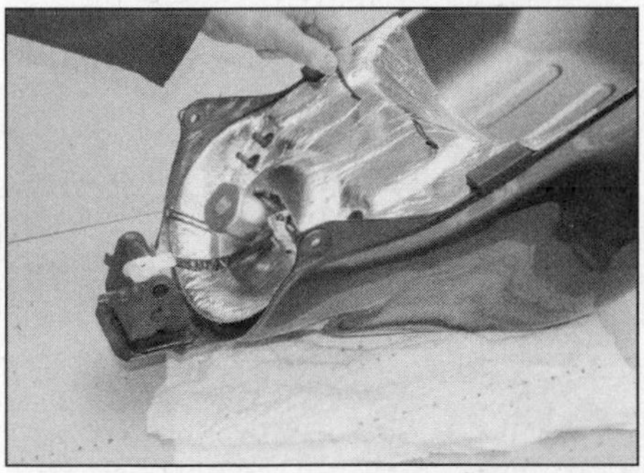

6.2 Lift the clips to release the heat shield

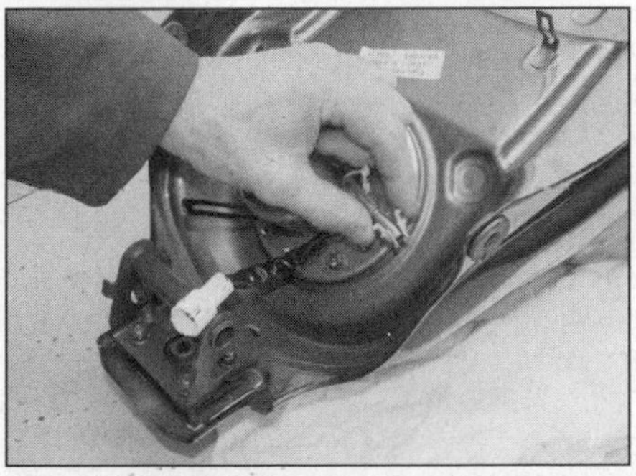

6.3 Remove the fuel supply hose clip

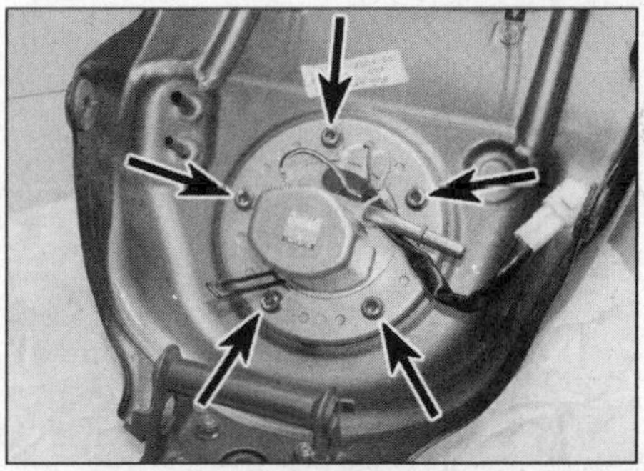

6.4a Undo the bolts (arrowed) . . .

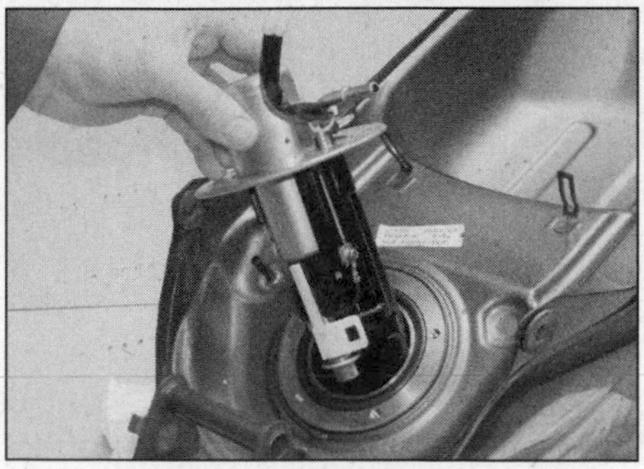

6.4b . . . and lift out the pump

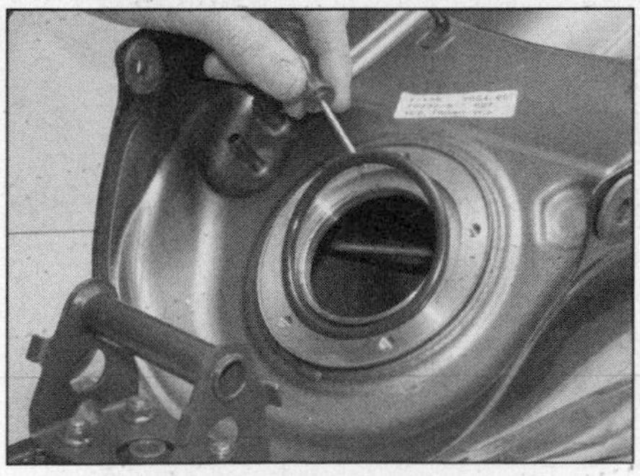

6.4c Discard the pump O-ring

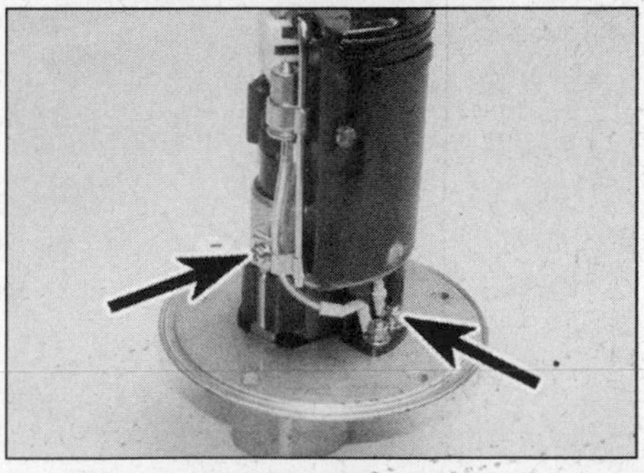

6.6 Ensure the wiring terminals (arrowed) are tight

7.2a Undo the nuts, noting the order of the washers

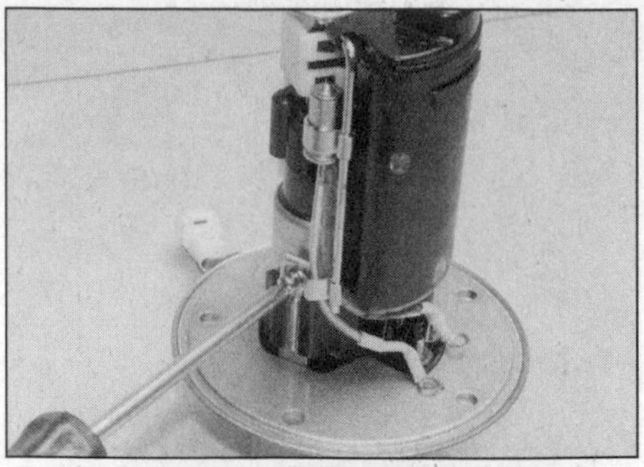

7.2b Undo the pump assembly screws . . .

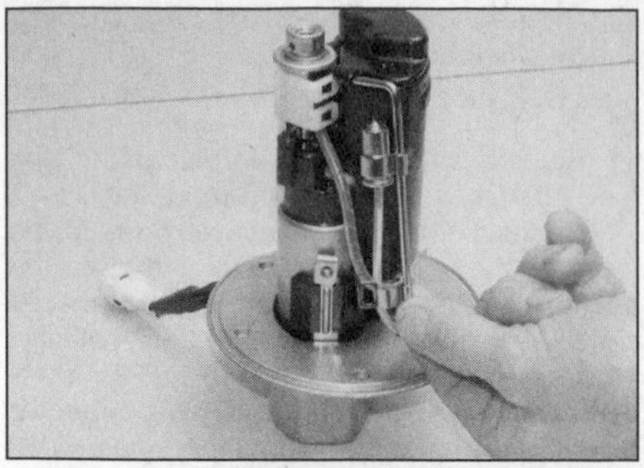

7.2c . . . and lift off the fuel level sensor

base with the threaded holes in the tank. Clean the threads of the bolts, then apply a suitable thread locking compound and install them finger-tight. Now tighten them gradually in a criss-cross pattern to the torque setting specified at the beginning of the Chapter.

8 Install the heat shield and secure it with the clips, then install the fuel supply hose clip **(see illustrations 6.2 and 6.3)**.

9 Install the fuel tank (see Section 2). Fill the tank and ensure there are no signs of fuel leakage around the pump base.

7 Fuel filter and strainer, pressure regulator and level sensor

Warning: Refer to the precautions given in Section 1 before starting work.

Fuel filter and strainer

1 Remove the fuel pump (see Section 6).

2 Undo the nuts securing the pump and level sensor terminals and detach the wires, making a note of which fits where **(see illustration)**. Undo the screws securing the pump assembly to the pump base and lift off the fuel level sensor **(see illustrations)**. Note the wire terminal(s) and clips secured by the assembly screws **(see illustration)**.

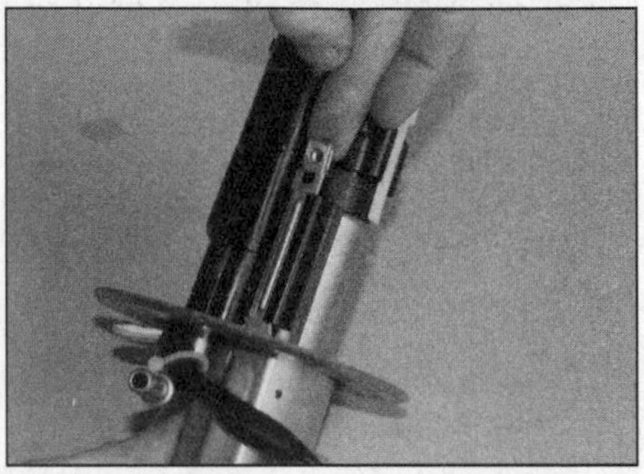

7.2d Note the location of the clips

3 Pull the pump assembly out of the base and discard the O-ring on the base fuel union as a new one must be fitted on reassembly **(see illustrations)**.

4 Clean any sediment out of the pump base. Clean any sediment from the outside of the strainer with a soft brush or low pressure compressed air. If the strainer is damaged, or if there is sediment inside it, remove the clip and the rubber cap, then pull off the strainer and fit a new one **(see illustration)**.

5 If there is sediment inside the strainer, a new filter cartridge should also be fitted. Detach the fuel pressure regulator (see Step 9) then pull the pump and filter cartridge apart. Note the location of the seal between the pump and the filter cartridge and fit a new one on reassembly. **Note:** *The filter cartridge and pressure regulator are supplied as an assembly.*

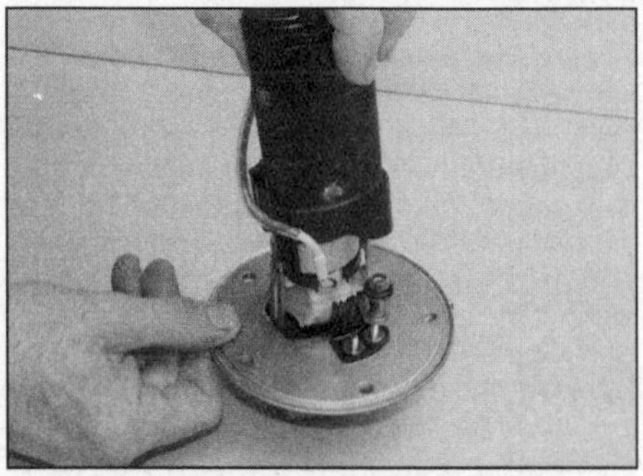

7.3a Pull the pump assembly out of the base

6 Install the components in the reverse order of disassembly, noting the following.

- Fit a new pump seal and smear it with engine oil.
- Fit a new O-ring to the pump base fuel union and smear it with engine oil **(see illustration 7.3b)**.
- Ensure the clips are in place on both the brackets for the pump retaining screws **(see illustration 7.2d)**.

Pressure regulator

7 Suzuki provides no test procedure for the

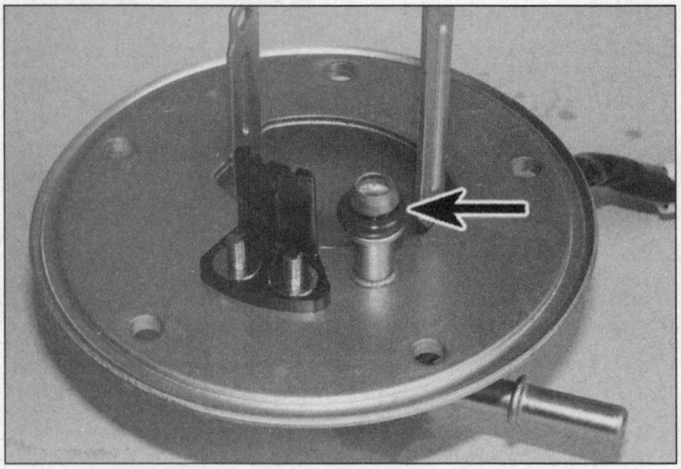

7.3b Note the O-ring (arrowed) on the fuel union

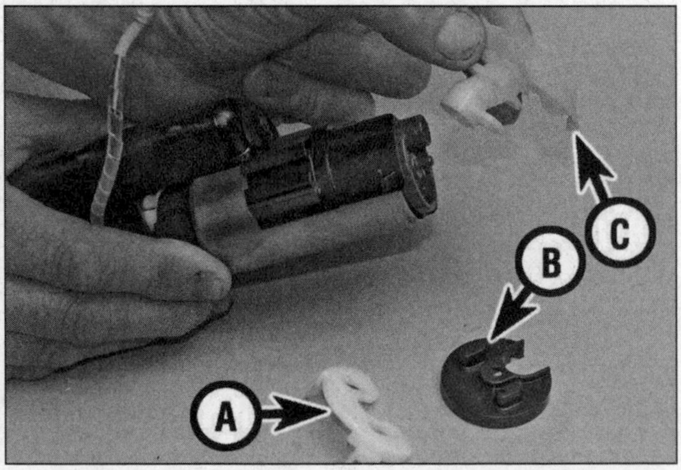

7.4 Remove the clip (A) and rubber cap (B) and pull off the strainer (C)

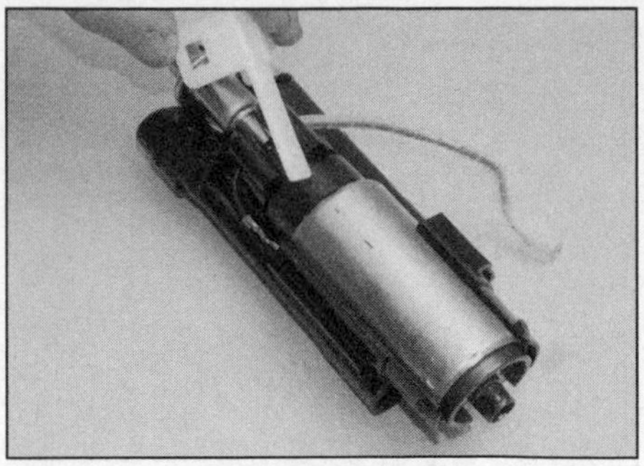
7.9a Release the clip . . .

7.9b . . . then pull off the regulator, noting the O-ring (arrowed)

pressure regulator. However, if it is thought to be faulty, it can be tested as follows.

8 Remove the fuel pump (see Section 6).

9 Release the clip securing the regulator holder to the pump assembly, then pull the regulator out of its socket **(see illustrations)**.

10 The regulator should be closed. If it is stuck open, it will be possible to blow through it with a low pressure air source. Alternatively, use a high pressure air source with a gauge to check the pressure at which the regulator opens, if at all, and compare the result with the specification at the beginning of the Chapter. If the regulator is stuck in either position, a new filter cartridge assembly will have to be fitted – the regulator is not available as a separate component.

11 Before installation, smear the regulator O-ring with engine oil, then secure the regulator with the clip.

12 Install the remaining components in the reverse order of removal.

Fuel level sensor

Note: *When the ignition is switched ON the low fuel warning LED will come on for a few seconds, then either extinguish, flash or remain on according to the model and the level of fuel in the tank. On K5 models onward, the low fuel warning LED will flash when the volume of fuel in the tank drops to approximately 4 litres. Refer to Chapter 9, Section 16 to check the instrument function of the low fuel warning circuit.*

13 Remove the fuel pump (see Section 6).

14 Trace the wire from the sensor to its terminal on the pump base, then undo the nut securing the wire and detach it. **Note:** *K3 and K4 models have one sensor, K5-on models have two sensors.*

15 Undo the screws securing the sensor and remove it, noting how it fits **(see illustration 7.2c)**.

16 Connect a self-powered test light or battery and bulb test circuit as shown, noting the two tests for K5 models onward **(see Part A of the appropriate illustration)**. The bulb should come on after a few seconds if the sensor is good.

17 Now immerse the sensor in water **(see Part B of illustration 7.16a or 16b)**. Note the

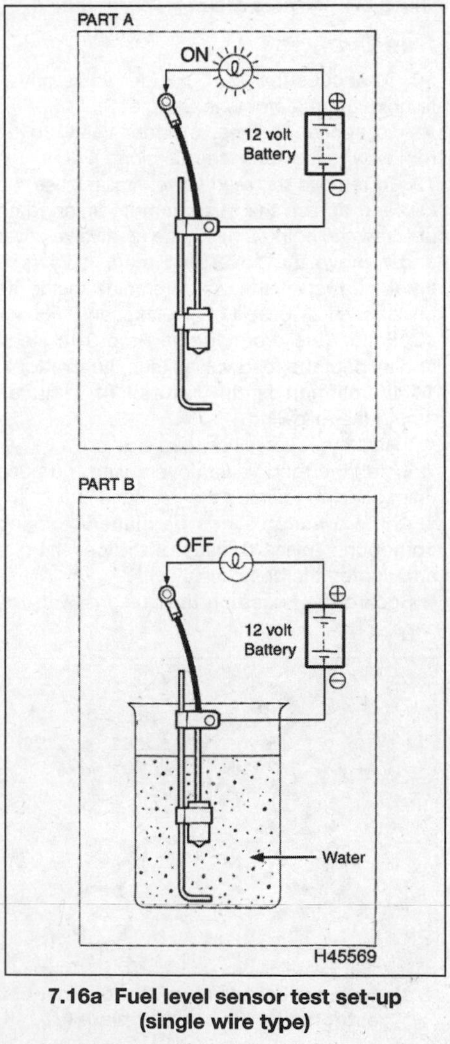

7.16a Fuel level sensor test set-up (single wire type)

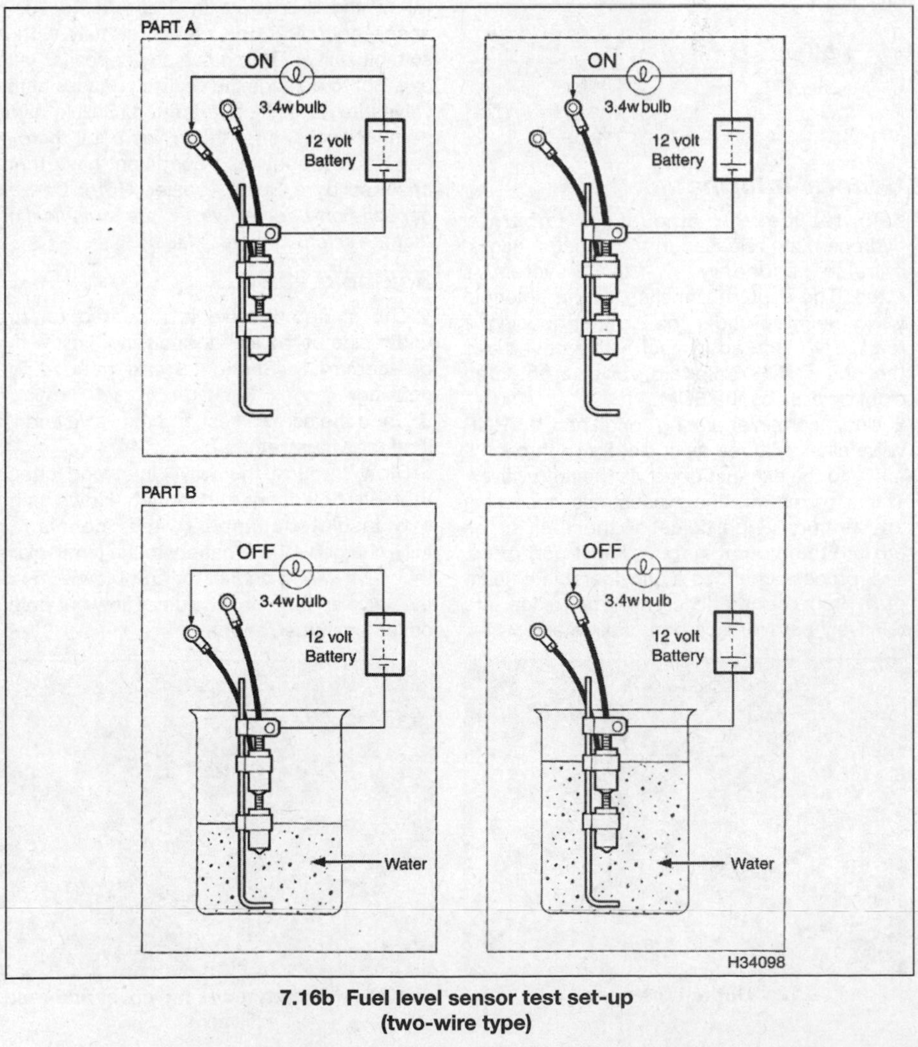

7.16b Fuel level sensor test set-up (two-wire type)

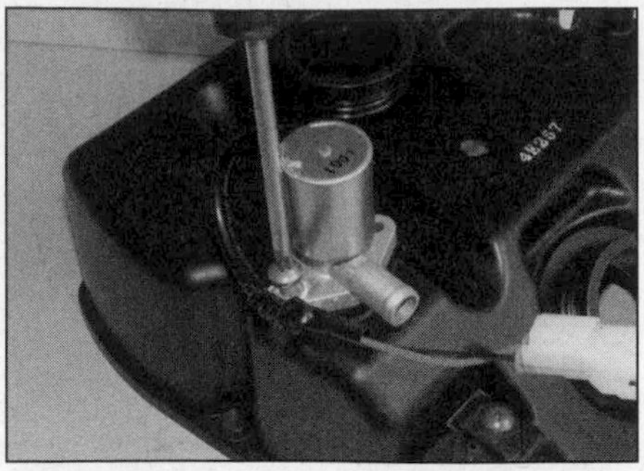

8.5a Undo the screws securing the PAIR solenoid valve

8.5b PAIR solenoid valve – K7-on models

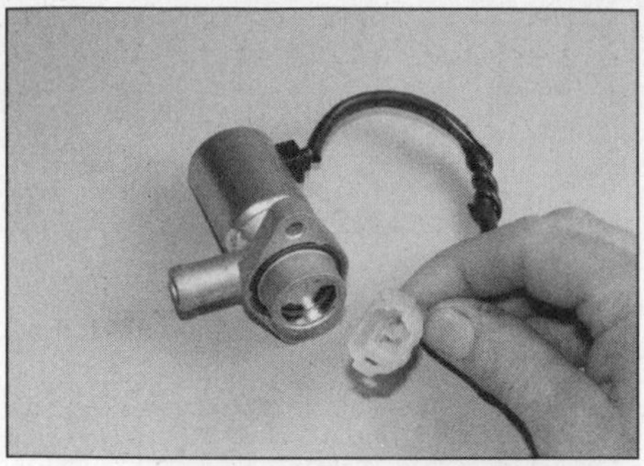

8.6 Connect a 12 volt battery to the wiring terminals as described

different water levels for the sensors on K5 models onward. The bulb should go out when the appropriate sensor is fully immersed.

18 If the tests show the sensor to be good, check the circuit and instruments (see Chap-ter 9). If the sensor is faulty it must be replaced with a new one.

19 Installation is the reverse of removal. If appropriate, take care to wipe all water off the sensor before installing it. Ensure the sensor terminals are connected securely in the correct order.

8 PAIR system

General information

1 To reduce the amount of unburned hydrocarbons released in the exhaust gases, a pulse secondary air (PAIR) system is fitted. The system consists of the solenoid valve mounted under the air filter housing, a reed valve located in each valve cover, and the hoses. The solenoid valve is actuated electronically by the ECM.

2 Under certain operating conditions, the PAIR valve allows filtered air to be drawn through it and into the exhaust ports via the reed valves. The air mixes with the exhaust gases, causing any unburned particles of the fuel in the mixture to be burnt in the exhaust port/pipes. This process changes a considerable amount of hydrocarbons and carbon monoxide into relatively harmless carbon dioxide and water. The reed valves prevent the flow of exhaust gases back into the control valve and air filter housing.

3 The system is not adjustable and requires no maintenance, except to ensure that the hoses are in good condition and are securely connected at each end, and that there is no build-up of gum or carbon fouling the reed valves and stopper plates. Renew any hoses that are cracked, split or generally deteriorated. The access the reed valves, follow the procedure in Steps 10 to 13. If necessary, clean the reeds carefully with a suitable solvent to remove any deposits. Take care not to damage the sealing surfaces of the valves as no gaskets are fitted. Suzuki gives no specifications for the valves but if there is any doubt about their condition, have them checked by a Suzuki dealer. **Note:** *Carbon deposits on the reed valves are an indication that the solenoid valve is faulty.*

Solenoid valve

4 The solenoid valve is mounted on the under-side of the air filter housing. Follow the pro-cedure in Section 3 and remove the housing.

5 Undo the screws securing the valve and lift it off **(see illustrations)**.

6 Blow through the valve inlet and check that air flows out the outlet. Now, using two insulated jumper wires, connect a fully-charged 12 volt battery to the terminals in the valve wiring connector and blow through the valve again – air should not flow out of the outlet **(see illustration)**.

7 If the solenoid valve fails either of these tests it is defective and should be renewed.

8 The solenoid valve is actuated electronically by the ECM. A fault with the valve circuit should be indicated by the fuel injection system diagnostic process (see Section 10). Follow the procedure in Section 11 to check the valve resistance.

9 Installation is the reverse of removal. Ensure the hoses are pushed fully onto their unions and secured with the clips. Ensure the valve wiring connector is securely connected.

Reed valves

10 To access the front cylinder valve cover, remove the radiator (see Chapter 3).

11 To access the rear cylinder valve cover, remove the fuel tank (see Section 2).

12 To remove the reed valve, first release the clip and detach the hose from its union, then unscrew the bolts securing the reed valve cover and remove the cover and reed valve **(see illustrations)**. If the valve remains inside its cover; carefully prise it out, noting how it fits.

13 Follow the procedure in Step 3 to clean and inspect the reed valves **(see illustration)**.

14 Installation is the reverse of removal, noting the following.

- Install the reed valves reed side down.
- Install the reed valve covers with the hose unions facing towards the left-hand side.
- Apply a suitable non-permanent locking compound to the threads of the cover bolts and tighten the bolts securely.
- Secure the hoses on their unions with the clips.

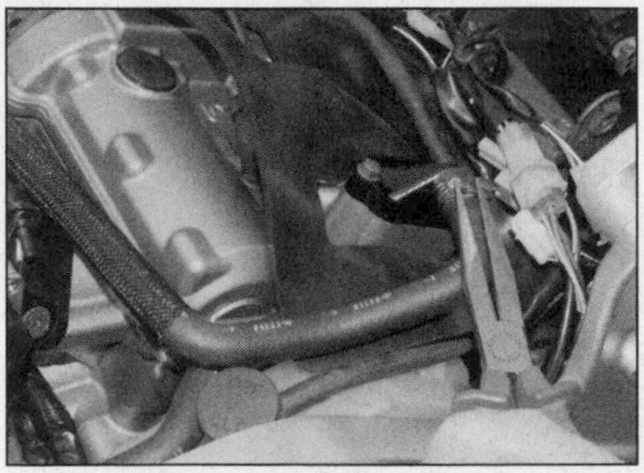

8.12a Detach the hose . . .

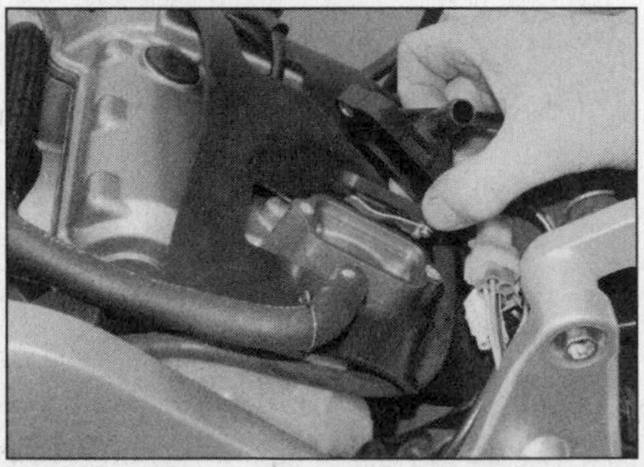

8.12b . . . then remove the cover and reed valve

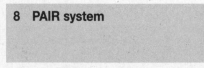

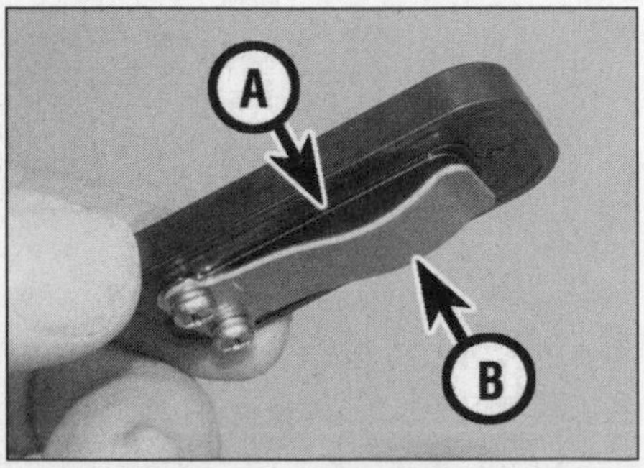

8.13 Note that reed valve (A) movement is restricted by the stopper plate (B)

9 Fuel injection system – description

1 The fuel injection system consists of two main component groups, the fuel supply circuit and the electronic control circuit.

2 The fuel supply circuit consists of the tank, pump and filter, pressure regulator and injectors. Fuel is pumped under pressure from the tank to the fuel rail, from which the individual injectors are fed. When the engine is off, fuel pressure is maintained in the system by a check valve in the pump. When the pump is running, operating pressure is maintained by the pump's pressure regulator which incorporates a pressure relief valve, releasing fuel back into the tank should the system become over-pressurised. The injectors spray pressurised fuel into the throttle bodies where it mixes with air and vaporises, before entering the cylinder where it is compressed and ignited.

3 The electronic control circuit consists of the engine control module (ECM), which operates and co-ordinates both the fuel injection and ignition systems, and the various sensors which provide the ECM with information on engine operating conditions.

4 The ECM monitors signals from the following sensors:

- Intake air temperature (IAT) sensor
- Intake air pressure (IAP) sensor
- Throttle position (TP) sensor
- Secondary throttle position (STP) sensor
- Crankshaft position (CKP) sensor
- Engine coolant temperature (ECT) sensor
- Gear position (GP) sensor
- Tip over (TO) sensor
- Oxygen sensor – K7 models onward

5 Based on the information it receives, the ECM calculates the appropriate ignition and fuel requirements of the engine. By varying the length of the electronic pulse it sends to each injector, the ECM controls the length of time the injectors are held open and thereby the amount of fuel that is supplied to the engine. Fuel supply varies according to the engine's needs for starting, warming-up, idling, cruising and acceleration.

6 In the event of an abnormality in any of the sensor signals, the ECM will determine whether the engine can still be run safely. If it can, a back-up mode replaces the sensor signal with a fixed signal, restricting performance but allowing the bike to be ridden home or to a dealer. When this occurs, the LCD display in the instrument cluster will indicate the letters FI every two seconds, alternating with the coolant temperature reading, the FI symbol will illuminate and the panel warning light will come on. If the fault is too serious, the appropriate system will be shut down and the engine will not run. When this occurs, the LCD display in the instrument cluster will indicate the letters FI continuously and the FI symbol and panel warning light will flash. See Section 10 for fault finding.

7 In the event of no signal being received from the ECM within 3 seconds of the ignition being switched ON, the LCD panel will display the letters CHEC. This is not a fault code in itself, but will occur if the ignition is ON for the stated time but if the kill switch is in the OFF position, or if the starter interlock circuit has a fault (see Chapter 9), or if the ignition fuse has blown (see Chapter 9). It will also occur if a wiring connector between the ECM and instrument cluster has become disconnected.

8 The system incorporates three safety circuits. When the ignition is switched ON, the fuel pump runs for three seconds and pressurises the system. Thereafter the pump automatically switches off until the engine is started. The second circuit incorporates a tip-over sensor, which automatically switches off the fuel pump and cuts the ignition and injection circuits if the motorcycle falls over. The third circuit incorporates a rev limiter signal which cuts the fuel injector circuit when engine rpm reaches the designated safety limit.

10 Fuel injection system – fault finding

1 The system incorporates a self-diagnostic function whereby any faults are stored in the ECM memory. To access the appropriate fault code, and to perform certain tests, the Suzuki mode select switch (Pt. No. 09930-82720) is very useful, though its function can easily be replicated using a short jumper wire with suitable terminals that will fit into the terminals in the fault code connector. The mode select switch is not expensive.

2 Remove the seat cowling (see Chapter 8) and locate the mode select switch wiring connector on the left-hand side of the machine. Remove the connector cover, ensure the ignition and the select switch are OFF, then connect the select switch **(see illustrations)**. If a jumper wire is being used in place of the switch, connect one end of the wire to the white/red wire terminal in the connector, but leave the other end free for the moment.

3 Start the engine, or if it will not start, crank the engine on the electric starter for a few seconds. Turn the mode select switch ON or connect the free end of the jumper wire to the black/white wire terminal. The fault code(s) will be displayed on the LCD panel on the instrument cluster, at two-second intervals and in ascending order if there is more than one. Note the codes and identify the faults from the table opposite. **Note:** *Do not disconnect the ECM wiring connectors, battery leads or main fuse before recording the fault codes. The ECM memory is erased when the connectors are disconnected.*

4 To check the fuel injection system components see Section 11.

5 Once the fault has been corrected, turn the ignition switch ON. If the fault has been cleared, the instrument display with indicate the code C00. Turn the mode select switch OFF and disconnect it, or remove the jumper wire, then turn the ignition switch OFF. Refit the wiring connector cover and install the seat cowling (see Chapter 8).

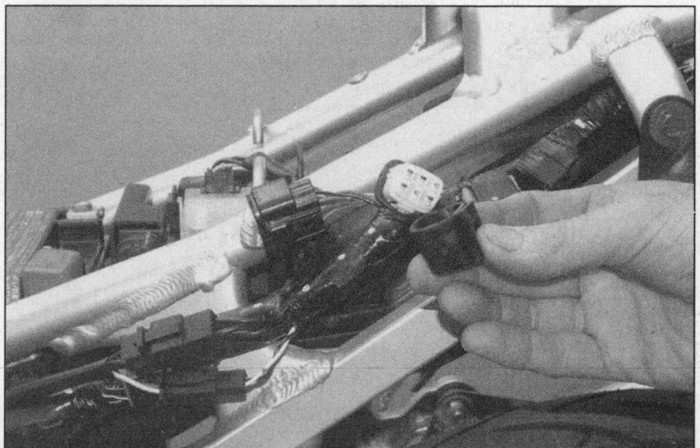

10.2a Remove the mode select switch connector cover . . .

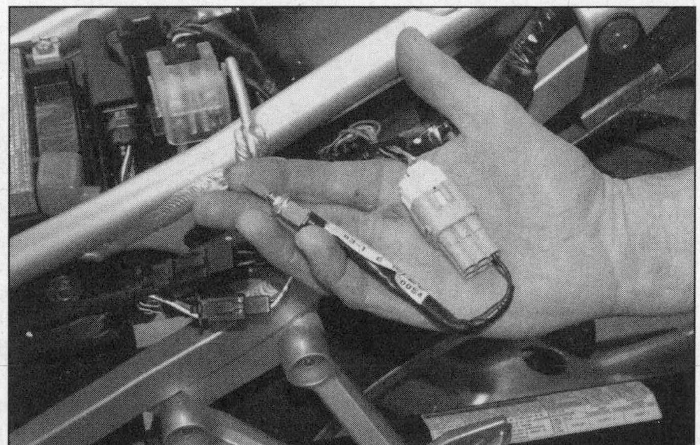

10.2b . . . and connect the select switch

Fault codes – K3 to K6 models

Fault code	Faulty component – symptoms	Possible causes
CHEC	No ECM signal – engine will not run	Kill switch OFF Faulty wiring or wiring connector Faulty ignition safety interlock system (clutch switch, sidestand switch, diode or gear position sensor) Damaged ignition fuse
C00	No fault	System clear
C12	Crankshaft position (CKP) sensor – engine will not run	Faulty wiring or wiring connector Damaged sensor
C13	Intake air pressure (IAP) sensor – engine will run, air pressure signal fixed at 760 mmHg	Faulty wiring or wiring connector Damaged sensor
C14	Throttle position (TP) sensor – engine will run, throttle and secondary throttle valve position signal and ignition timing fixed	Faulty wiring or wiring connector Damaged sensor
C15	Engine coolant temperature (ECT) sensor – engine will run, coolant temperature signal fixed at 80°C	Faulty wiring or wiring connector Damaged sensor
C21	Intake air temperature (IAT) sensor – engine will run, air temperature signal fixed at 40°C	Faulty wiring or wiring connector Damaged sensor
C23	Tip-over (TO) sensor – engine will not run	Faulty wiring or wiring connector Damaged sensor
C24	Front cylinder ignition coil – engine will run on other cylinder, ignition signal to No. 1 cylinder cut	Faulty wiring or wiring connector Damaged ignition coil Faulty power supply for the ignition system (see Chapter 5 for details)
C25	Rear cylinder ignition coil – engine will run on other cylinder, ignition signal to No. 2 cylinder cut	Faulty wiring or wiring connector Damaged ignition coil Faulty power supply for the ignition system (see Chapter 5 for details)
C28	Secondary throttle valve (STV) servo – engine will run, valve fixed in half open position	Faulty wiring or wiring connector Damaged servo motor
C29	Secondary throttle position (STP) sensor – engine will run, sensor fixed in half open position	Faulty wiring or wiring connector Damaged sensor
C31	Gear position (GP) sensor – engine will run, signal fixed to 4th gear	Faulty wiring or wiring connector Damaged sensor Faulty gearchange mechanism
C32	Front cylinder fuel injector – engine will run on other cylinder	Faulty wiring or wiring connector Damaged fuel injector
C33	Rear cylinder fuel injector – engine will run on other cylinder	Faulty wiring or wiring connector Damaged fuel injector
C41	Fuel pump system – engine will not run	Faulty wiring or wiring connector to pump and/or pump relay Faulty pump relay(see Section 5)
C49	PAIR solenoid valve – engine will run	Faulty wiring or wiring connector Faulty solenoid valve

11 Fuel injection system – components

1 If a fault is indicated on any of the system components, first check the wiring and connectors between the appropriate component and the engine control module (ECM); see *Wiring Diagrams* at the end of Chapter 9. A continuity test of all wires will locate a break or short in any circuit. Inspect the terminals inside the wiring connectors and ensure they are not loose or corroded. Spray the inside of the connectors with an electrical terminal cleaner before reconnection.

2 It is possible to undertake some checks on system components using a multimeter and comparing the results with the specifications at the beginning of this Chapter. **Note:** *Different meters may give slightly different results to those specified even though the component being tested is not faulty – do not consign a component to the bin before having it double-checked.* However, some faults will only become evident when a component is tested with a peak voltage tester, in which case the checks should be undertaken by a Suzuki dealer.

3 If after a thorough check the source of a fault has not been identified, it is possible that the ECM itself is faulty. Suzuki provides no test specifications for the ECM. In order

Fault codes – K7 models onward

Fault codes with C prefix will appear on the instrument display. Codes with P prefix can only be read out with Suzuki SDS tester.

Fault code	Faulty component - symptoms	Possible causes
C00	No fault	System clear
C12 (P0335)	Crankshaft position (CKP) sensor – engine will not run	Faulty wiring or wiring connector Damaged sensor
C13 (P1750) C17 (P0105)	Intake air pressure (IAP) sensor for front/rear cylinder – engine will run, air pressure signal fixed at 760 mmHg	Sensor voltage outside of specified range. Check the sensor and its wiring
C14 (P0120)	Throttle position (TP) sensor – engine will run, fixed in full open position	Sensor voltage outside of specified range. Check the sensor and its wiring
C15 (P0115)	Engine coolant temperature (ECT) sensor – engine will run, coolant temperature signal fixed at 70°	Sensor voltage outside of specified range. Check the sensor and its wiring
C21 (P0110)	Intake air temperature (IAT) sensor – engine will run, air temperature signal fixed at 25°C	Sensor voltage outside of specified range. Check the sensor and its wiring
C23 (P1651)	Tip-over (TO) sensor	TO sensor circuit shorted or grounded at some point
C24 (P0351) C25 (P0352)	Ignition signal	Check ignition coil connections and power supply from the battery
C28 (P1655)	Secondary throttle valve (STV) servo – engine will run, valve fixed in any position	Check STV servo motor and its wiring
C29 (P1654)	Secondary throttle position (STP) sensor – engine will run, valve operation stopped	Sensor voltage outside of specified range. Check the sensor and its wiring
C31 (P0705)	Gear position (GP) sensor – engine will run, signal fixed to 4th gear	Check the switch operation and its wiring
C32 (P0201) C33 (P0202)	Fuel injector front/rear cylinder – engine will run on other cylinder	Check wiring connection to the injector and power supply
C40 (P0505, P0506 or P0507)	Idle speed control (ISC) valve – engine will run, valve operation is stopped	Valve hoses pinched or disconnected, power supply to valve failed, valve failed internally, wiring open circuit or shorted to earth. Valve requires resetting to pre-set position
C41 (P0230)	Fuel pump relay	Check fuel pump relay, its wiring and the wiring to the injectors
C42 (P1650)	Ignition (main) switch	Check ignition switch wiring and switch itself
C44 (P0135)	Oxygen sensor – engine will run, signal fixed to 'normal'	Check power supply to the sensor and sensor wiring
C49 (P1656)	PAIR solenoid valve – engine will run, oxygen sensor feedback stopped and PAIR valve fixed in open position	Check PAIR valve resistance and its wiring

to determine conclusively that the unit is defective, it should be substituted with a known good one. If the problem is then rectified, the original unit is proven faulty.

Crankshaft position (CKP) sensor

4 Make sure the ignition is OFF. To access the CKP sensor wiring connector, first remove the seat cowling (see Chapter 8), then trace the wiring from the alternator cover on the left-hand side of the engine and disconnect it at the wiring connector.

5 Using an ohmmeter or multimeter set to the ohms scale, measure the resistance between the terminals on the sensor side of the connector **(see illustration)**. If the result is as specified, check that there is no continuity between each terminal and earth (ground).

6 If the results are not as specified, first check the wiring between the connector and the alternator cover for damage, then follow the procedure in Chapter 9, Section 33, and remove the cover and inspect the sensor. If required, clean the sensor – a build-up of dirt and/or debris can affect the signal sent to the ECM – then check the resistance again. Also check the trigger on the alternator rotor for damage.

7 If the results are good, have the sensor peak voltage tested by a Suzuki dealer.

8 To remove the sensor, see Chapter 9, Section 33 – it is part of the alternator stator assembly and is not available separately.

Intake air pressure (IAP) sensor

9 Make sure the ignition is OFF. Raise the fuel tank (see Section 2). On K3 to K6 models, the IAP sensor is on the rear right-hand side of the air filter housing. K7 models have a sensor on each rear corner of the housing. Check the condition of the vacuum hose between the

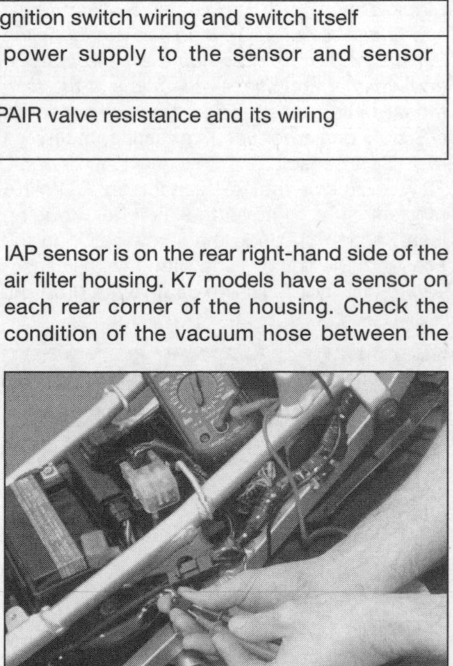

11.5 Measuring CKP sensor resistance

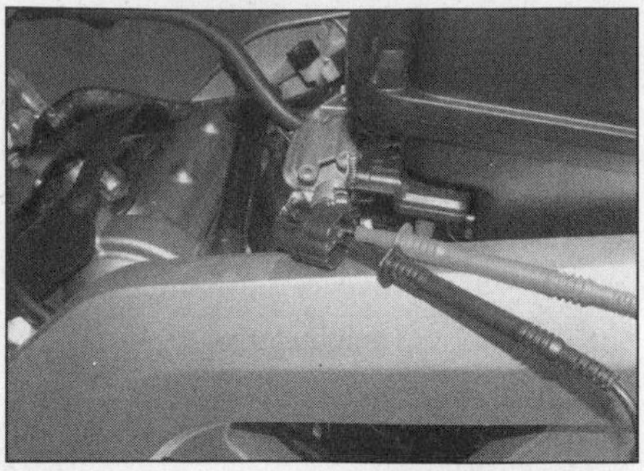

11.10 Checking IAP sensor input voltage

11.11 Backprobe the IAP sensor connector to check the output voltage

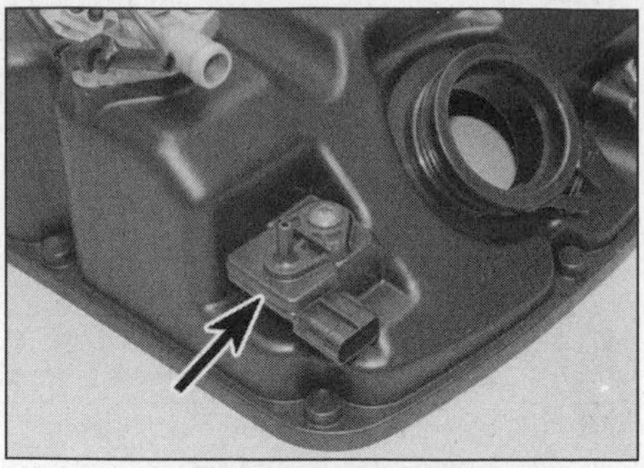

11.12a Location of the IAP sensor on the underside of the housing – K3 to K6

sensor(s) and make sure the hose is a tight fit at each end with no air leaks.

10 To check the input voltage, disconnect the sensor wiring connector and turn the ignition ON. Connect the positive (+ve) probe of a voltmeter to the red wire terminal on the loom side of the wiring connector and the negative (-ve) probe first to earth (ground), then to the black/brown wire terminal **(see illustration)**. Turn the ignition OFF. If the input voltage is not as specified in both cases, check the wiring to the ECM and the ECM connector terminals. On K7 models onward, repeat the test on the other IAP sensor.

11 If the input voltage is good, reconnect the wiring to the sensor(s), then start the engine and allow it idle. Insert the positive (+ve) probe of a voltmeter into the green/black wire terminal in the connector and the negative (-ve) probe into the black/brown wire terminal to check the output voltage **(see illustration)**. On K7 models onward, repeat the test on the other sensor, between the green/yellow and black/brown wire terminals. **Note:** *Suzuki state that the output voltage can vary between 0.1 and 4.8 volts depending on the altitude and weather conditions at the time of the test.* If the result is as specified, take the sensor to a Suzuki dealer for vacuum testing, otherwise renew the sensor.

12 To remove the IAP sensor on K3 to K6 models, first remove the air filter housing (see Section 3). Undo the screw securing the sensor to the housing and withdraw the sensor – take care not to let the captive nut drop out of its holder where fitted **(see illustration)**. On K7 models onward, gently ease the sensor off its tab **(see illustration 3.10b)**, then pull off the vacuum hose and disconnect the wire connector **(see illustration)**. On all models, ensure the wiring connector terminals are clean and that the vacuum hose is a tight fit on the sensor union.

Throttle position (TP) sensor

Note: *The TP sensor is secured by special Torx security screws (single screw on K7 models onward) which have a raised pip in their centres and will require the appropriate Torx key to turn them.*

13 Make sure the ignition is OFF. Raise the fuel tank (see Section 2) – the TP sensor is the lower of the two sensors located on the left-hand side of the rear throttle body. Disconnect the sensor wiring connector. Turn the ignition ON and connect the positive (+ve) probe of a voltmeter to the red wire terminal on the loom side of the wiring connector and the negative (-ve) probe first to earth (ground), and then to the black/brown wire terminal to check the input voltage **(see illustrations)**. Turn the ignition OFF. If the input voltage is not as specified in both cases, check the wiring to the ECM, the multi-pin wiring connector for the injector loom and the ECM connector terminals.

14 If the input voltage is good, remove the air filter housing and check for continuity between the pink/white wire terminal on the sensor and earth (ground). There should be no continuity.

15 Using an ohmmeter set to the K-ohms scale, measure the resistance between the pink/white and black/brown wire terminals on the sensor, first with the throttle closed, then with the throttle fully open. If the results are as specified, reconnect the wiring connector.

16 Turn the ignition ON and connect the positive (+ve) probe of a voltmeter to the pink/white wire terminal and the negative (-ve) probe to the black/brown wire terminal in the connector to check the output voltage, first with the throttle closed, then with the throttle fully open. Turn the ignition OFF. If the results are not as specified, the sensor is faulty.

17 To remove the TP sensor, first disconnect its wiring connector. Mark the position of the sensor to aid installation, then undo the Torx screws (see **Note** above) securing the sensor and remove it (access to the Torx screws is made easier by displacing the throttle bodies – see Section 12). Note how the end of the throttle shaft engages the slot in the sensor.

18 Installation is the reverse of removal. Apply some grease to the seal in the sensor socket in the throttle body. Ensure that the throttle shaft engages correctly in the slot in the sensor and align any register marks before lightly tightening the Torx screws. Ensure the wiring connector terminals are clean.

19 To check and adjust the position of the TP sensor, first check the engine idle speed and on K3 to K6 models adjust it if necessary (see Chapter 1). Turn the engine OFF and connect the mode select switch to the wiring connector (see Section 10).

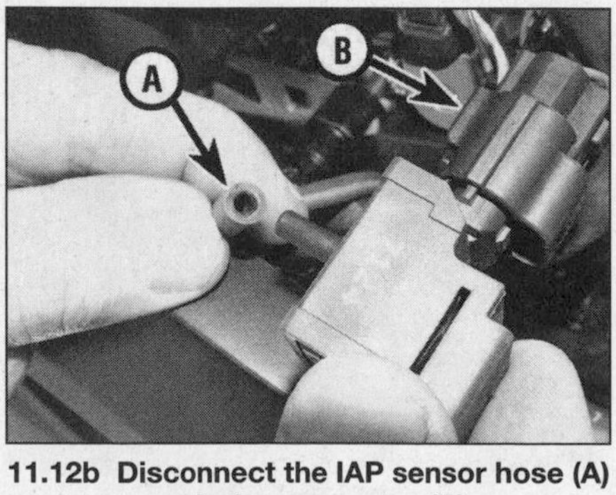

11.12b Disconnect the IAP sensor hose (A) and wire connector (B)

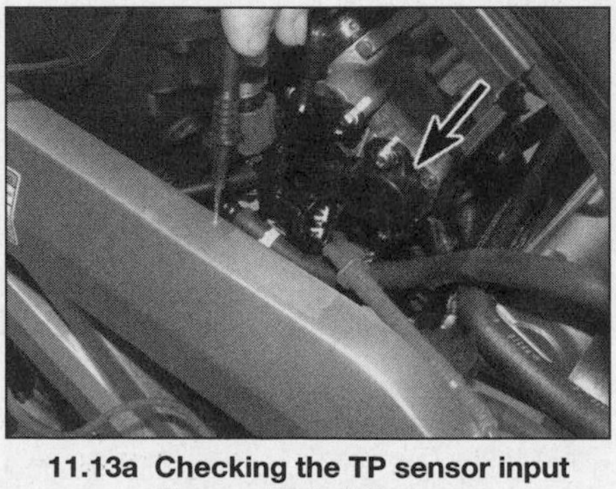

11.13a Checking the TP sensor input voltage – K3 to K6 shown

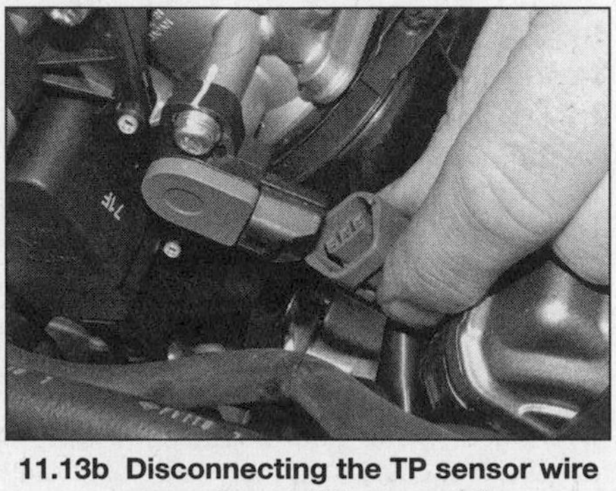

11.13b Disconnecting the TP sensor wire connector on K7-on models

11.22 Check ECT sensor input voltage at the connector (arrowed)

11.25a Disconnect the IAT sensor wiring connector . . .

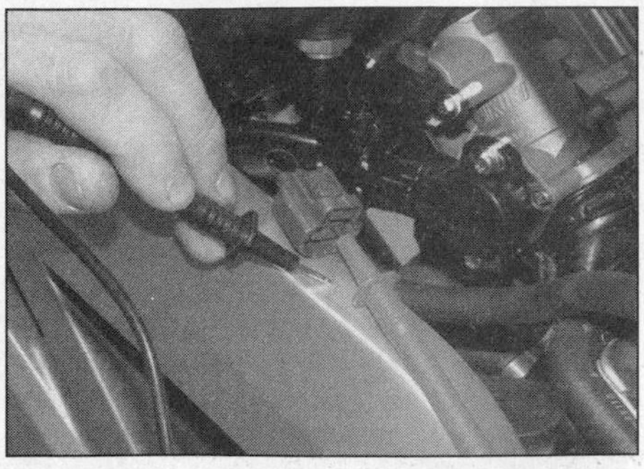

11.25b . . . and check the input voltage as described

20 Turn the select switch ON. A code C00 will be displayed on the LCD panel on the instrument cluster with a line in front of it. If the line is in the mid-way position i.e. -C00, the TP sensor is adjusted correctly. If the line is above or below the mid-way position (_C00 or ¯C00), loosen the Torx screws and carefully rotate the sensor until the line is in the mid-way position. Tighten the Torx screws to the specified torque setting. Lower the fuel tank when the test is complete.

Engine coolant temperature (ECT) sensor

21 The engine coolant temperature (ECT) sensor is mounted in the thermostat housing between the engine cylinders.

22 Disconnect the sensor wiring connector and turn the ignition ON **(see illustration)**. Connect the positive (+ve) probe of a voltmeter to the black/blue wire terminal on the loom side of the connector and the negative (-ve) probe first to earth (ground), then to the black/brown wire terminal to check the input voltage. Turn the ignition OFF. If the input voltage is not as specified in both cases, check the wiring to the ECM and the ECM connector terminals.

23 Using an ohmmeter or multimeter set to the K-ohms scale, measure the resistance between the terminals on the sensor itself with the engine cold. If the result is not as specified, the sensor is faulty.

24 If the sensor is working correctly, the resistance should drop as the engine warms up. A check for sensor performance is described in Chapter 3. Also refer to Chapter 3 for the removal and installation procedure.

Intake air temperature (IAT) sensor

25 Make sure the ignition is OFF. Raise the fuel tank (see Section 2). The IAT sensor is on the rear left-hand side of the air filter housing on K3 to K6 models and centrally in the rear of the housing on K7 models onward **(see illustration 3.10c)** . Disconnect the sensor wiring connector and turn the ignition ON **(see illustration)**. Connect the positive (+ve) probe of a voltmeter to the dark green wire terminal on the loom side of the wiring connector and the negative (-ve) probe first to earth (ground), then to the black/brown wire terminal to check the input voltage **(see illustration)**. Turn the ignition OFF. If the input voltage is not as specified in both cases, check the wiring to the ECM and the ECM connector terminals.

26 Remove the air filter housing. Using an ohmmeter or multimeter set to the K-ohms scale, measure the resistance between the terminals on the sensor itself. If the result is not as specified, the sensor is faulty. **Note:** *The sensor resistance should drop as the engine warms up – the sensor performance can be checked in the same way as the ECT sensor (see Step 24).*

27 On K3 to K6 models, the sensor screws into an insert in the bottom of the air filter housing **(see illustration)**. To remove the sensor, first disconnect the wiring connector, then unscrew the sensor. Note the O-ring on the sensor body and replace it with a new one on installation if it is damaged. Tighten the sensor to the specified torque setting. On K7 models onward, remove the retaining screw and pull the sensor out of the air filter housing **(see illustration)**.

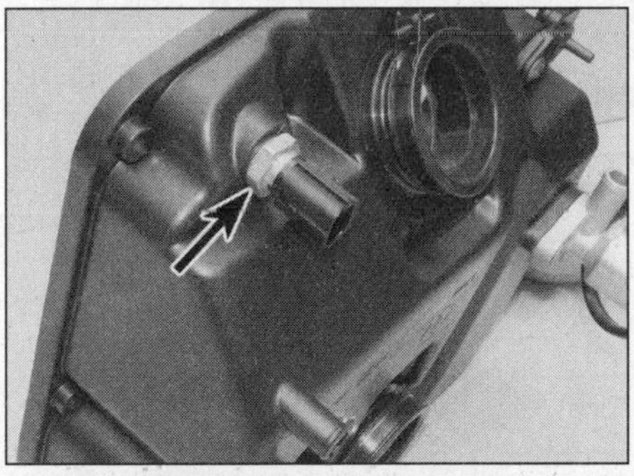

11.27a Location of the IAT sensor on the underside of the housing – K3 to K6

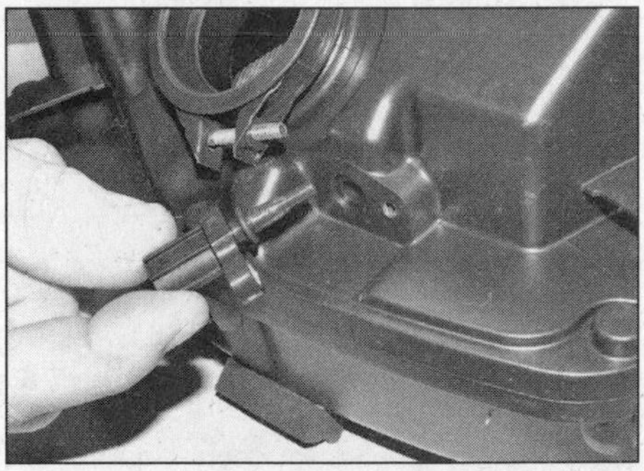

11.27b IAT sensor is retained by a single screw on K7-on models

Tip-over (TO) sensor

28 Make sure the ignition is OFF. Remove the right-hand side panel and rider's seat (see Chapter 8) – the TO sensor is mounted on a bracket behind the rear brake fluid reservoir on K3 to K6 models **(see illustration)** or on the front of the battery carrier on K7 models onward **(see illustration)**. Detach the sensor and its holder from its bracket. Note the TO sensor holder is marked UPPER on its top edge.

29 Disconnect the wiring connector from the sensor. Using an ohmmeter or multimeter set to the K-ohms scale, measure the resistance between the red and black/

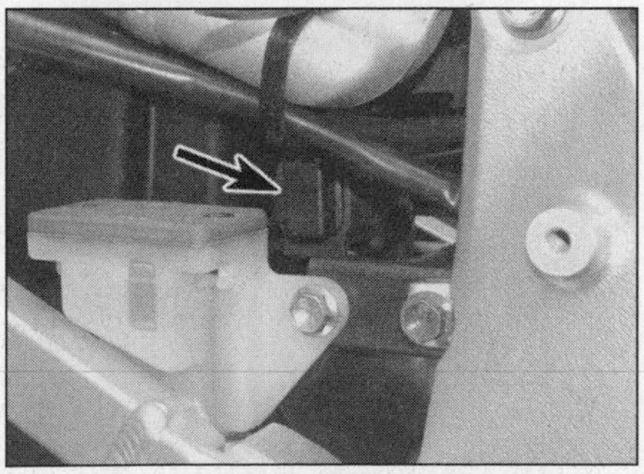

11.28a Location of the TO sensor – K3 to K6

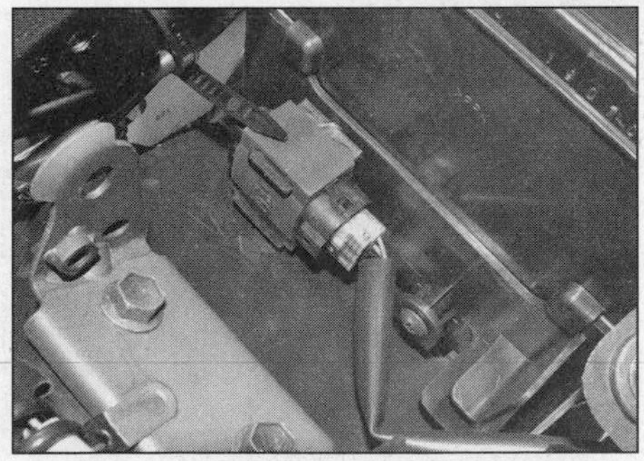

11.28b Location of the tip-over sensor – K7-on models

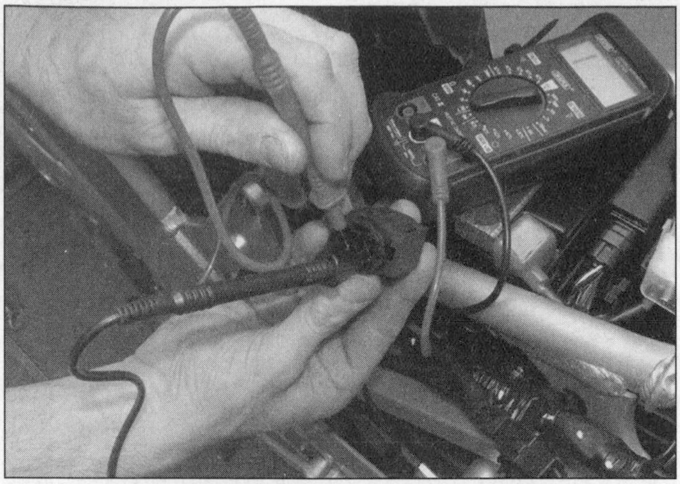

11.29 Checking the TO sensor resistance

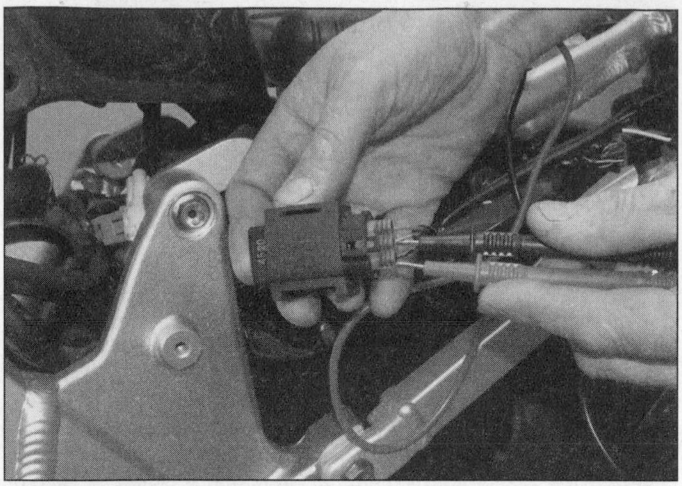

11.30a Checking the voltage with the sensor held horizontally . . .

11.30b . . . and with it tilted 65° or more

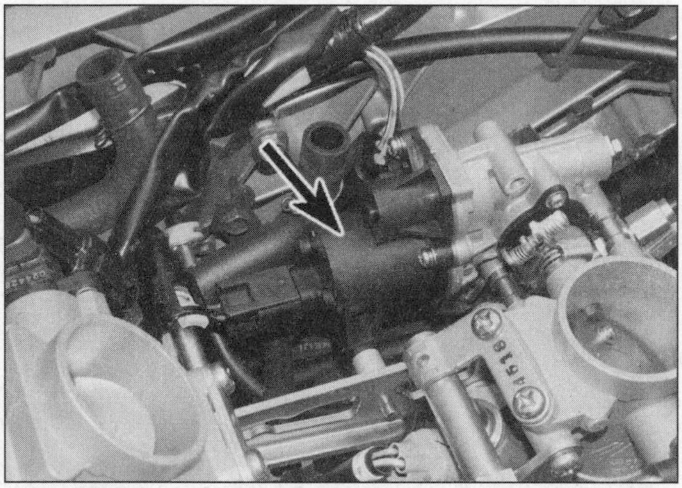

11.32 Location of the STV servo on the front throttle body

brown wire terminals on the sensor **(see illustration)**. Compare the result to that given in the Specifications at the beginning of this Chapter; if the result is good, reconnect the wiring connector.

30 With the connector reconnected, turn the ignition ON and insert the positive (+ve) probe of a voltmeter into the brown/white wire terminal on the loom side of the wiring connector and the negative (-ve) probe into the black/brown wire terminal and check the voltage with the sensor held horizontally **(see illustration)**. Now tilt the sensor 65° or more from the horizontal, first one way and then the other, and note the voltage reading **(see illustration)**. If the results are not as specified the sensor is faulty and must be renewed.

11.33a Check the operation of the front . . .

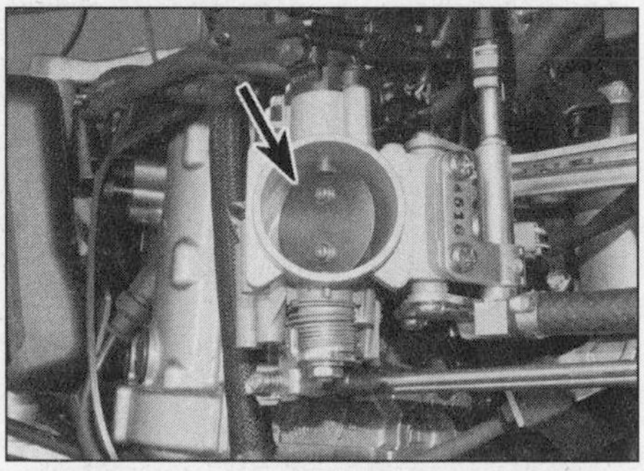

11.33b . . . and rear secondary throttle valves

31 Ensure that the sensor is installed the right way up and that the connector is secure.

Secondary throttle valve (STV) servo – K3 to K6 models

32 Remove the air filter housing (see Section 3). The STV servo is on the left-hand side of the front throttle body **(see illustration)**.

33 Turn the ignition ON and check the operation of the secondary throttle valves in start-up mode. From half-open the valves should open fully and then return to the half-open position **(see illustrations)**. Turn the ignition OFF. If the valves do not move as described, check the wiring from the servo to the ECM and check the ECM connector terminals. **Note:** *The valves should open and close together by the same amount – if not, follow the procedure in Section 14 and synchronise them.*

34 Disconnect the wiring connector from the servo. Check that there is no continuity

11.34 Ensure there is no continuity between the left-hand servo terminal and earth

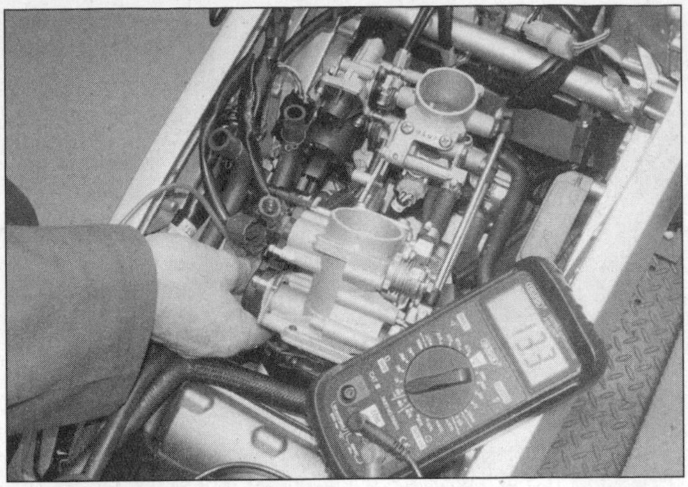

11.35 Checking the resistance between the servo terminals

11.37 Location of the STV servo (arrowed) on the rear throttle body – K7 models on

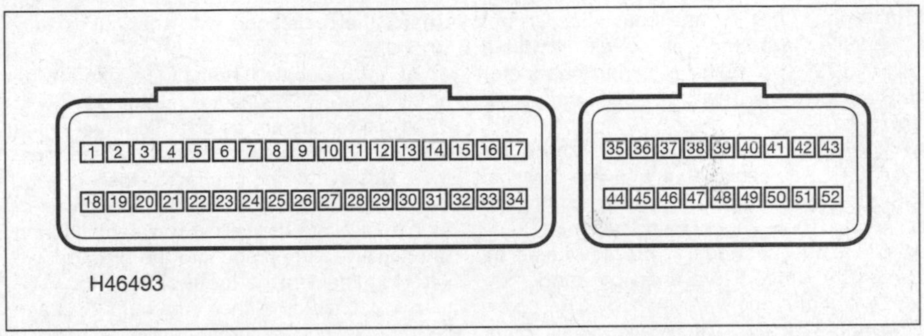

11.38 ECM wire connector (harness side) terminal identification

between the left-hand wire terminal on the servo and earth (ground) **(see illustration)**.

35 Using an ohmmeter or multimeter set to the ohms scale, measure the resistance between the two servo terminals **(see illustration)**. If the result is not as specified, the servo is faulty. If the result is as specified, have the ECM checked by a Suzuki dealer.

36 The servo is not available separately from the front throttle body – if the servo is faulty a new throttle body must be installed (see Sections 12 and 13).

Secondary throttle valve (STV) servo – K7 models onward

37 Remove the air filter housing (see Section 3). The STV servo is on the left-hand side of the rear throttle body **(see illustration)**.

38 Turn the ignition ON and check the operation of the secondary throttle valves in start-up mode. The valves should go from the fully open position to 15° open. Turn the ignition OFF. If the valves do not move as described, check the wiring from the servo to the ECM wire connector – black/light green wire to terminal 35, pink/white wire to terminal 37, green wire to terminal 44 and white/black wire to terminal 46 **(see illustration)**. **Note:** *The valves should open and close together by the same amount – if not, follow the procedure in Section 14 and synchronise them.*

39 Remove the throttle bodies (see Section 12). Using a multimeter set to the ohms function, check for continuity between each pin in the servo connector and earth, making four tests in total – no continuity should be indicated.

40 Now connect the meter probes between terminals 1 and 2, then 3 and 4 – in each case a reading of 7 ohms should be obtained **(see illustration)**.

41 If the results are not as specified the STV servo is most likely faulty, although have your findings confirmed by a Suzuki dealer before fitting a new throttle body assembly.

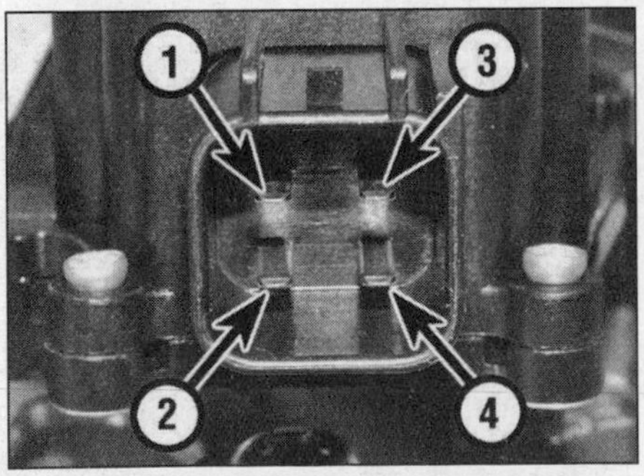

11.40 Servo terminal identification for testing

Secondary throttle position (STP) sensor – K3 to K6 models

Note: *The STP is secured by two special Torx security screws (they have a raised pip in their centres) which will require the appropriate Torx key to turn them.*

42 Remove the air filter housing (see Section 3). The STP sensor is the upper of the two sensors located on the left-hand side of the rear throttle body – disconnect the sensor wiring connector **(see illustration)**. Turn the

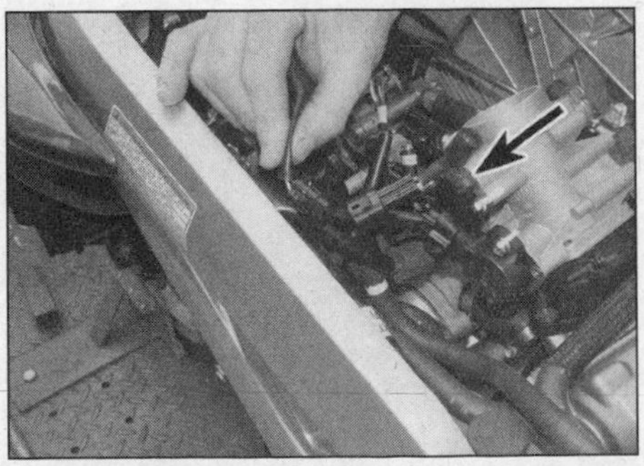

11.42a Disconnect the STP sensor (arrowed) wiring connector – K3 to K6 moels

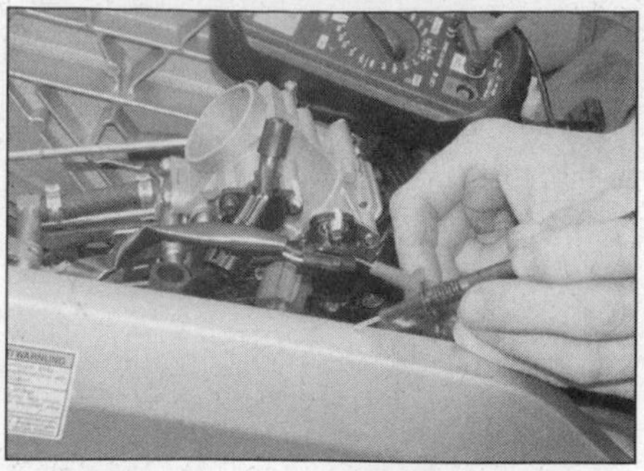

11.42b Checking the STP sensor input voltage

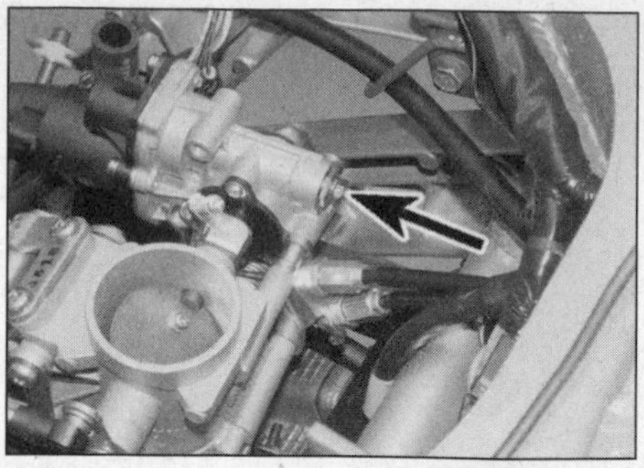

11.44a Close the secondary throttle valves by turning the shaft (arrowed)

11.44b Checking the STP sensor resistance

ignition ON and connect the positive (+ve) probe of a voltmeter to the red wire terminal on the loom side of the wiring connector and the negative (-ve) probe first to earth (ground), and then to the black/brown wire terminal to check the input voltage **(see illustration)**. Turn the ignition OFF. If the input voltage is not as specified in both cases, check the wiring to the ECM, the multi-pin wiring connector for the injector loom and the ECM connector terminals.

43 If the input voltage is good, check for continuity between the yellow wire terminal and earth (ground) on the sensor side of the connector. There should be no continuity.

44 Close the secondary throttle valves by turning the valve servo shaft by hand – do not try to turn the valves themselves **(see illustration)**. Using an ohmmeter or multimeter set to the K-ohms scale, measure the sensor resistance between the yellow and black wire terminals **(see illustration)**. Now open the secondary throttle valves by turning the valve servo shaft and measure the resistance **(see illustration)**.

45 If the results are not as specified, check the sensor adjustment as follows. Ensure the secondary throttle valves are still fully open and loosen the sensor Torx screws. Connect the ohmmeter or multimeter set to the K-ohms scale between the yellow and black wire terminals as before and note the sensor resistance, then carefully rotate the sensor until the resistance reading is within specification. Tighten the sensor screws. Check the resistance with the valves fully closed.

46 If the specified resistance cannot be obtained, the STP sensor is faulty.

47 If the results are as specified, reconnect the sensor wiring connector and disconnect the STP servo wiring connector, then turn the ignition ON. Insert the positive (+ve) probe of a voltmeter into the yellow wire terminal and the negative (-ve) probe into the black/brown wire terminal on the loom side of the STP sensor connector to check the output voltage with the secondary throttle valves fully open and then fully closed **(see illustration)**. Turn the ignition OFF and reconnect the STV servo wiring connector. If the output voltage is not as specified the STP sensor is faulty. If the output voltage is good, have the ECM checked by a Suzuki dealer.

48 To remove the sensor, first disconnect the wiring connector. Mark the position of the sensor to aid installation, then undo the Torx screws (see **Note** above) securing the sensor and remove it. Note how the end of the throttle shaft engages the slot in the sensor.

49 Installation is the reverse of removal. Apply some grease to the seal in the sensor socket in the throttle body. Ensure that the throttle shaft engages correctly in the slot in the sensor and align any register marks before lightly tightening the Torx screws. Ensure the wiring connector terminals are clean. After installation adjust the sensor as described in Step 40.

Secondary throttle position (STP) sensor – K7 models onward

Note: *The STP is secured by a special Torx security screw (with a raised pip in its centre) which will require the appropriate Torx key to turn it.*

50 The STP sensor is the upper of the two sensors located on the left-hand side of the rear throttle body. Raise the fuel tank (see Section 2) and disconnect the sensor wiring connector **(see illustration)**. Turn the ignition ON and connect the positive (+ve) probe of a voltmeter to the red wire terminal on the loom side of the wiring connector and the negative (-ve) probe first to earth (ground), and then to the black/brown wire terminal to check

11.44c Opening the secondary throttle valves

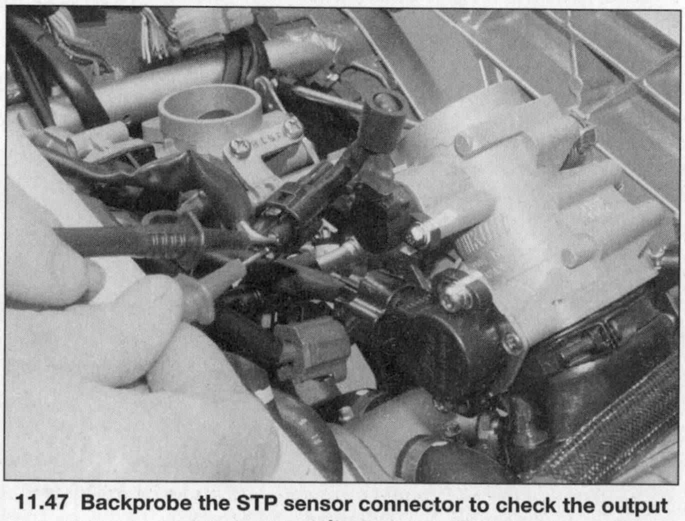

11.47 Backprobe the STP sensor connector to check the output voltage

11.50a Disconnect the STP sensor wire connector (arrowed) – K7 models onward

11.50b Make the input voltage test on the loom side of the wire connector

the input voltage **(see illustration)**. Turn the ignition OFF. If the input voltage is not as specified in both cases, check the wiring to the ECM and the ECM connector terminals for continuity – yellow wire to terminal 4, red wire to terminal 5 and black/brown wire to terminal 12 **(see illustration 11.38)**.

51 Remove the air filter housing (see Section 3). Reconnect the STP sensor wire connector. Back probe the connector with the voltmeter positive probe to the yellow wire terminal and its negative probe to the black/brown wire terminal. Disconnect the wiring connector from the STP servo, then turn the ignition ON. Use finger pressure only to operate the secondary butterfly valve in the throttle body, noting the output voltage shown on the meter – compare this with the value given in the Specifications with valve open and then with the valve closed.

52 If the output voltage is incorrect, adjust the STP sensor position by slackening the sensor mounting screw (see **Note** above) and rotating the sensor body until the voltage reading is 0.6V with the butterfly valve closed **(see illustration)**. Tighten the screw once the correct setting has be achieved. Turn the ignition OFF and reconnect the STP servo connector and refit the air filter housing.

Gear position (GP) switch

53 Support the bike on an auxiliary stand and raise the sidestand. The GP switch is located in the left-hand side of the crankcase below the front sprocket. Raise the fuel tank (see Section 2), then trace the wiring from the switch and disconnect it at the 3-pin connector with blue, pink and black/white wires.

54 Connect the probes of an ohmmeter or continuity tester between the blue and black/white wire terminals on the switch side of the connector. With the transmission in neutral there should be continuity. If not, remove the switch and check the contacts on its inside and the plungers in the end of the selector drum (see Chapter 9, Section 23 for details).

55 Reconnect the wiring connector and ensure the engine kill switch is in the RUN position. Turn the ignition switch ON and insert the positive (+ve) probe of a voltmeter into the pink wire terminal in the connector and connect the negative (-ve) probe to earth (ground) to check the output voltage **(see illustration)**. Select each gear in turn and check that the voltage is above the specified minimum in each gear. Turn the ignition OFF.

56 If the output voltage is not as specified, either the pink wire to the GP switch or the GP switch itself is faulty.

57 If the output voltage is as specified, first check the voltage following the procedure in Chapter 9, Section 23, then check the wiring from the switch to the ECM and check the ECM connector terminals.

Fuel injectors

58 Make sure the ignition is OFF. Remove the air filter housing (see Section 3). Identify the faulty injector by the fault code and disconnect the injector wiring connector. Using an ohmmeter or multimeter set to the ohms scale, measure the resistance between

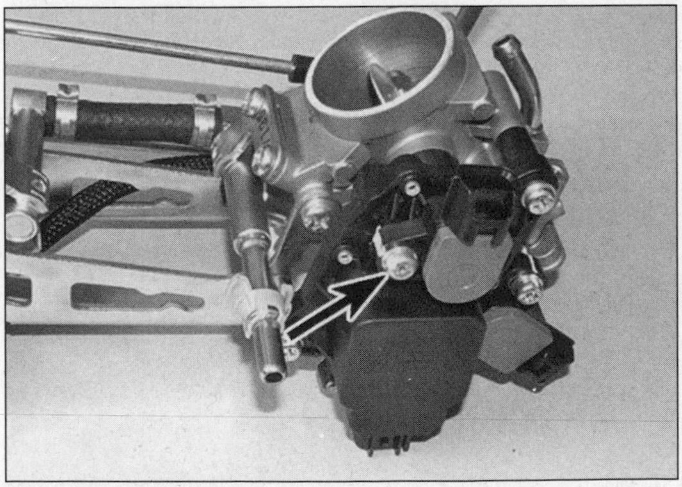

11.52 Slacken the STP screw (arrowed) and move its position to arrive at correct output voltage

11.55 Backprobe the GP switch connector to check the output voltage

11.58a Checking the resistance of the front cylinder fuel injector

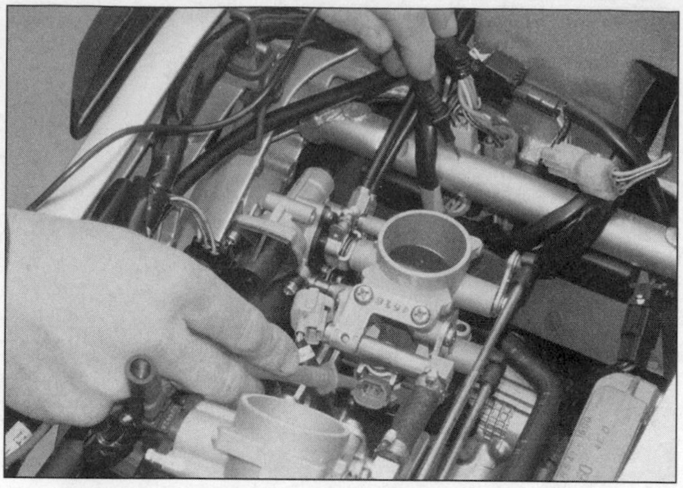

11.58b Ensure there is no continuity between the injector terminals and earth

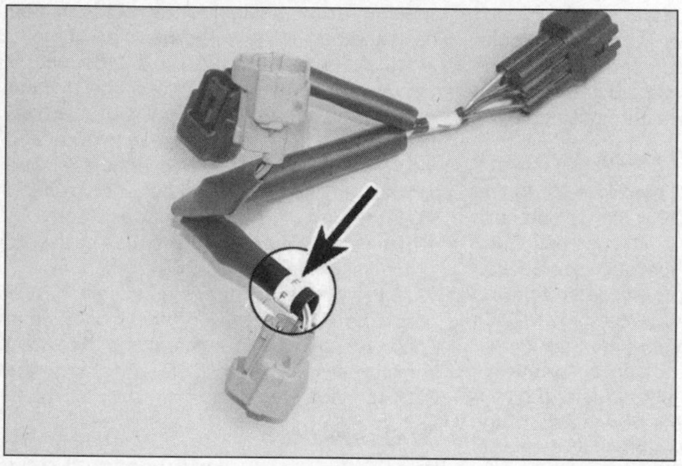

11.60 Test the injector wiring loom as described – note the F mark (arrowed)

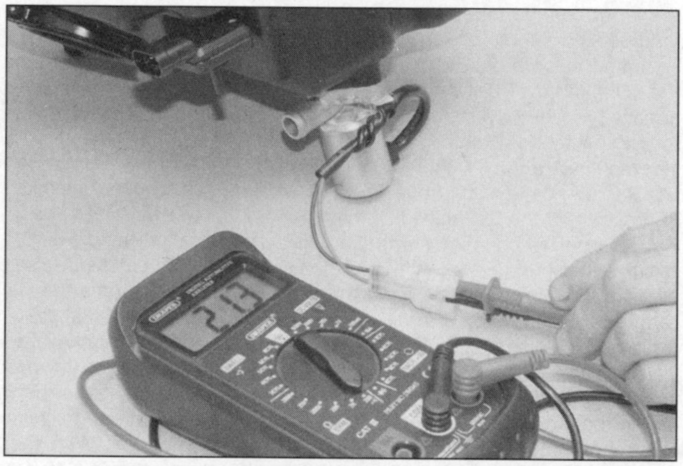

11.65a Checking the resistance of the PAIR solenoid valve

the terminals on the injector **(see illustration)**. If the result is as specified, check that there is no continuity between each terminal and earth (ground) **(see illustration)**. If there is continuity the injector is faulty and a new one must be installed (see Section 13).

59 Turn the ignition ON. Connect the positive (+ve) probe of a voltmeter to the yellow/red wire terminal on the loom side of the wiring connector and the negative (-ve) probe to earth (ground) to check the input voltage. **Note:** *Injector voltage can only be detected for 3 seconds after the ignition has been turned ON.* Turn the ignition OFF. If the input voltage is not as specified, refer to the Wiring Diagrams at the end of Chapter 9 and check for a fault in the yellow/red wire.

60 On K3 to K6 models, if the input voltage is as specified, disconnect the injector wiring connectors and disconnect the STV servo wiring connector – the front fuel injector wiring should be marked with an F – if not, mark it to aid reassembly. Check for continuity between the injector connector wiring terminals and the STV servo connector terminals. There should be continuity on all checks – if not, renew the injector wiring loom **(see illustration)**.

61 On K7 models onward, check the grey/white wire (front cyl) for continuity between the injector connector and terminal 51 of the ECM connector. Check the grey/black wire (rear cyl) for continuity between the injector connector and terminal 42 of the ECM connector **(see illustration 11.38)**.

Fuel pump control system

62 Refer to Section 5 for fuel pump relay checks.

63 Refer to Section 4 for fuel pump and wiring checks.

Note: *A fault with both fuel injectors is also indicated by fault code C41.*

PAIR solenoid valve

64 The solenoid valve is mounted on the underside of the air filter housing. Raise the fuel tank (see Section 2), then trace the wiring from the valve and disconnect it at the 2-pin connector **(see illustration 3.4)** on K3 to K6 models or directly from the solenoid valve body on K7-on models **(see illustration 3.13b)**.

65 Using an ohmmeter or multimeter set to the ohms scale, measure the resistance between the terminals on the valve side of the connector **(see illustration)**. On K7 models onward, the test is made directly across the valve terminals **(see illustration)**. If the result

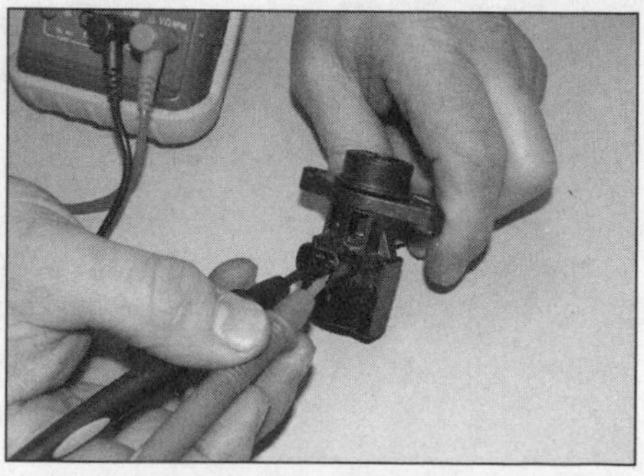

11.65b . . . and on K7 models onward

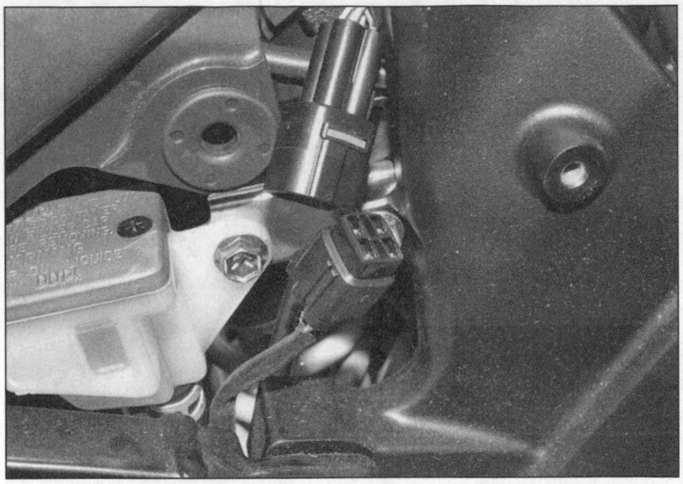
11.67 Oxygen sensor wire connector is under right-hand side panel

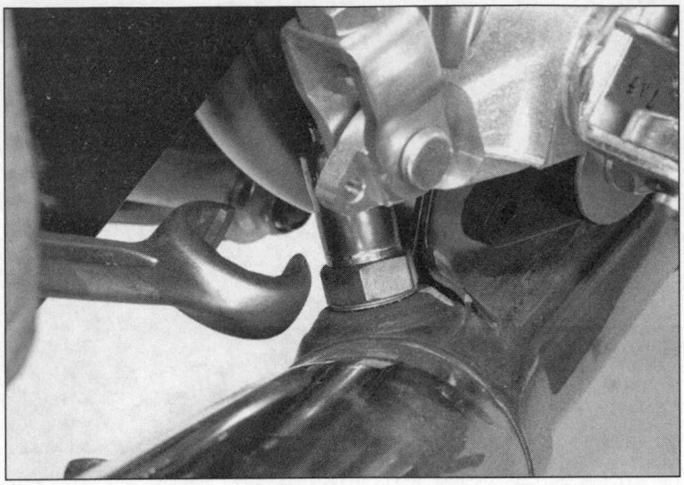
11.70 Ring spanner with cut-out is ideal for unscrewing the oxygen sensor

is not as specified, refer to Section 8 and test the operation of the valve.

66 If the resistance is as specified, connect the wiring connector and turn the ignition ON. Connect the positive (+ve) probe of a voltmeter to the brown wire terminal on the loom side of the wiring connector and the negative (-ve) probe to earth (ground) to check the input voltage. Turn the ignition OFF. If the input voltage is not as specified, check the wiring to the ECM and the ECM connector terminals.

Oxygen sensor (Europe K7 models onward)

67 The heated oxygen sensor is threaded into the exhaust system, just forward of the silencer. Trace its wiring up to the connector under the right-hand side panel and disconnect it **(see illustration)**. To check the sensor's heater element resistance, connect a multimeter set to the ohms function between the two white wire connectors. Compare the reading with the value given in the Specifications.

68 Check the heater element voltage with the connector halves joined. Backprobe the white/black wire terminal on the wire harness side of the connector with the meter positive probe and earth the meter negative probe. Turn the ignition ON – battery voltage should be shown on the meter.

69 Check the white/green wire between the oxygen sensor wire connector (harness side) and terminal 6 the ECM connector for continuity **(see illustration 11.38)**. Check the black/brown wire between the oxygen sensor wire connector (harness side) and terminal 12 the ECM connector for continuity.

70 To remove the sensor, use an open-end spanner (or a ring spanner with cut-out for the wiring) to unscrew it from the exhaust pipe **(see illustration)**. Take care not to damage the sensor tip when refitting and tighten the sensor to the specified torque setting if possible.

12 Throttle bodies – removal, installation

Warning: Refer to the precautions given in Section 1 before starting work.

Removal

1 Remove the fuel tank (see Section 2) and the air filter housing (see Section 3).

2 On K3 to K6 models, disconnect the idle speed adjuster from its holder **(see illustration)**.

3 Disconnect the wire connectors from the throttle position (TP) sensor and the secondary throttle position (STP) sensor **(see illustration)**. On K3 to K6 models, disconnect the common wiring connector for the fuel injectors and secondary throttle valve (STV) servo **(see illustration)**. On K7 models onward, disconnect the separate wiring connectors for the TP and

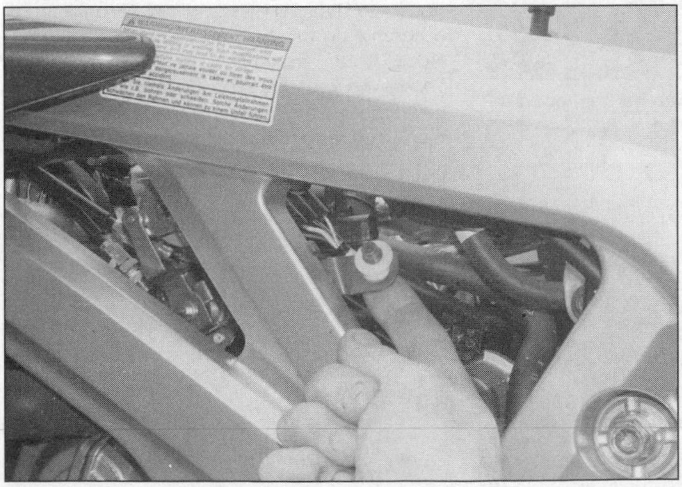
12.2 Detach the idle speed adjuster

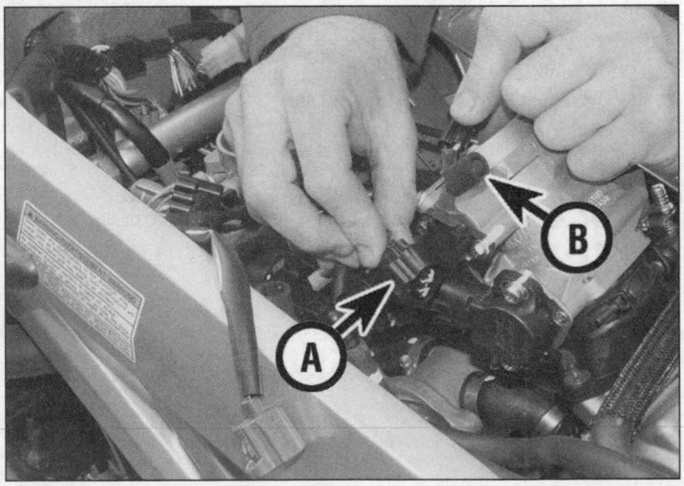

12.3a On K3 to K6 models disconnect the TP sensor (A) and STP sensor (B) wiring connectors . . .

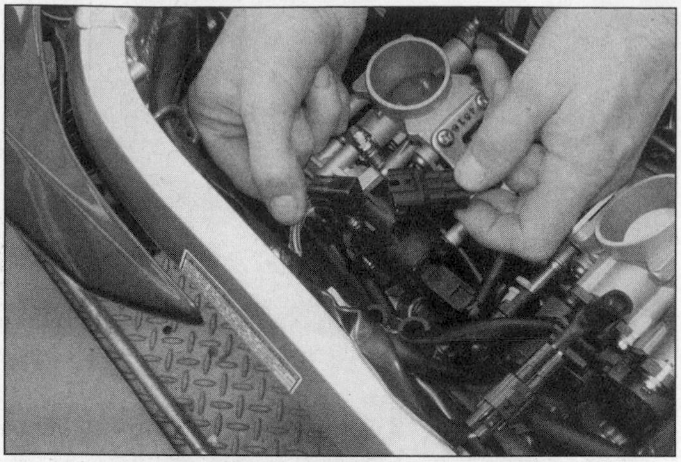

12.3b . . . and disconnect the common fuel injector assembly wiring connector

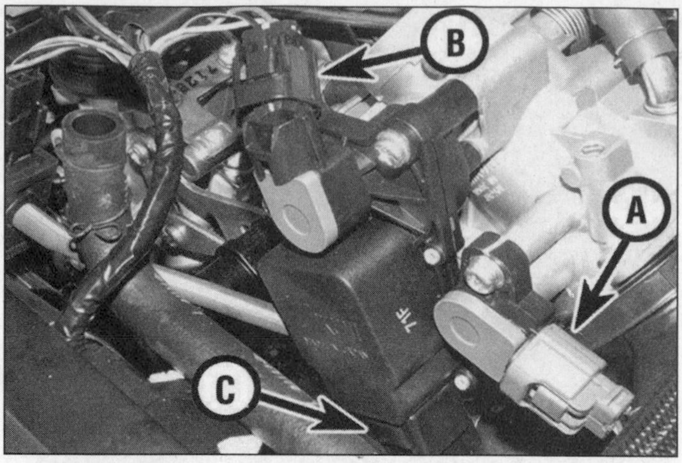

12.3c On K7-on models, disconnect the TP sensor (A), STP sensor (B) and STV servo (C) wiring . . .

12.3d . . . the fuel injector connectors . . .

12.3e . . . the ISC valve hose from the rear throttle body . . .

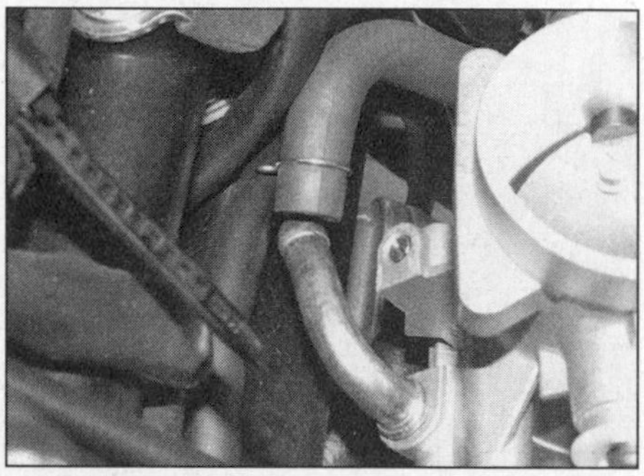

12.3f . . . and from the front throttle body

12.3g Pull the vacuum hose off the underside of the rear body

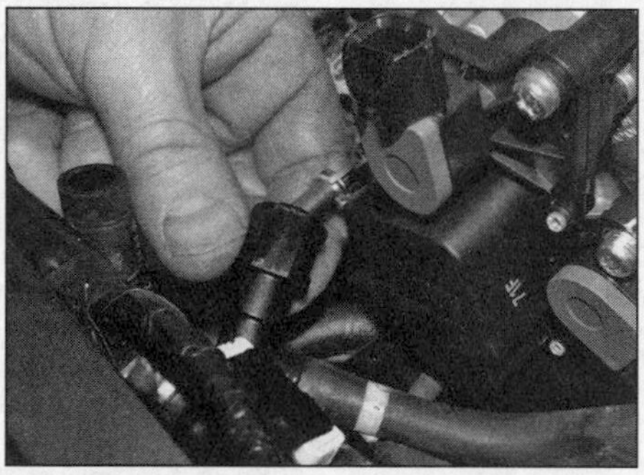

12.3h The fuel hose can be unclipped if required

STP sensors, the fuel injectors and STV servo and pull the two idle speed control (ISC) valve hoses off their unions **(see illustrations)**. On California models, pull the purge hoses off their unions on the throttle bodies. If required, the fuel supply hose can be detached from the throttle bodies at this stage, or removed with them **(see illustration)**.

4 Slacken the clamp screws securing the throttle bodies to the intake stubs, then ease the body assembly up off the stubs **(see illustrations)**. **Note:** *A long screwdriver will be required to access the front throttle body clamp screw.*

5 Disconnect the throttle cables (see Section 16) then lift off the throttle body assembly.

12.4a Slacken the front throttle body clamp (arrowed) . . .

12.4b . . . and the rear throttle body clamp . . .

12.4c . . . then displace the assembly to access the throttle cables

Installation

6 Installation is the reverse of removal, noting the following.

- Connect the throttle cables before installing the throttle body assembly.
- Ensure the throttle bodies are fully engaged with the intake stubs before tightening the clamps.
- Ensure the terminals in the wiring connectors are clean. On K7 models onward, the connector for the TPS is grey and the connector for the STPS is black, the front injector connector is brown and its wiring marked F and the rear injector connector is grey.
- Check the operation of the throttle cables and adjust them as necessary (see Chapter 1).
- Check the operation of the STV servo (see Section 11).
- Check the engine idle speed on K3 to K6 models and adjust if necessary (see Chapter 1).
- If the throttle bodies have been disassembled, synchronise them (see Chapter 1).

13 Throttle bodies – overhaul

Warning: Refer to the precautions given in Section 1 before starting work.

K3 to K6 models

Disassembly

1 Release the clip on the fuel feed hose and disconnect the hose from the fuel rail **(see illustration)**.

2 Detach the intake air pressure vacuum chamber from its bracket and detach the hose from the union on the front throttle body **(see illustrations)**. Note the blanking caps on the other throttle body unions **(see illustration)**.

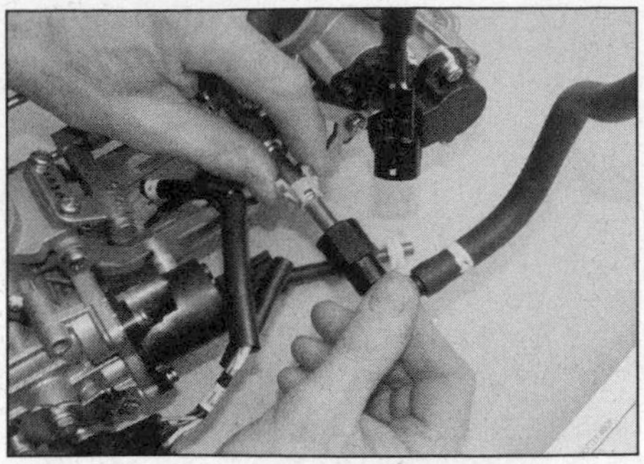

13.1 Disconnect the fuel hose from the fuel rail

3 The front fuel injector wiring should be marked with an F – if not, mark it to aid reassembly, then disconnect both injector connectors. Disconnect the STV servo wiring connector and remove the injector wiring loom **(see illustration)**.

4 Note the location of the throttle link rods,

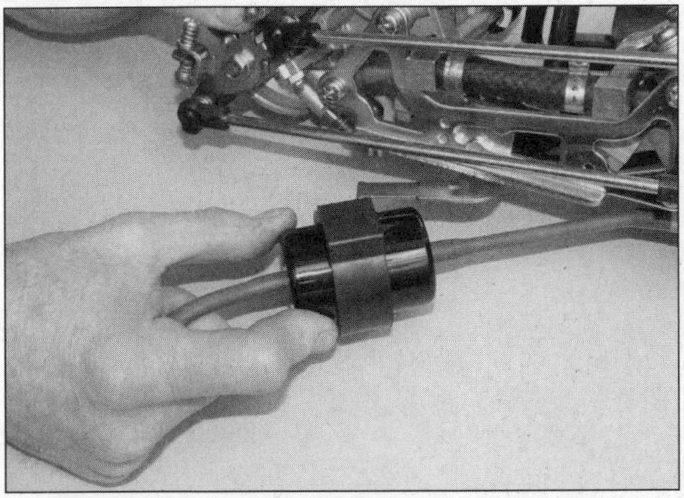

13.2a Detach the vacuum chamber from its bracket . . .

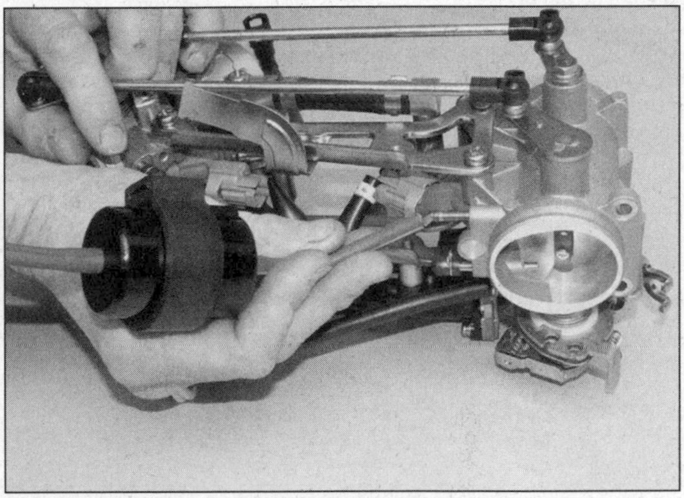

13.2b . . . and detach the hose from the union on the front throttle body

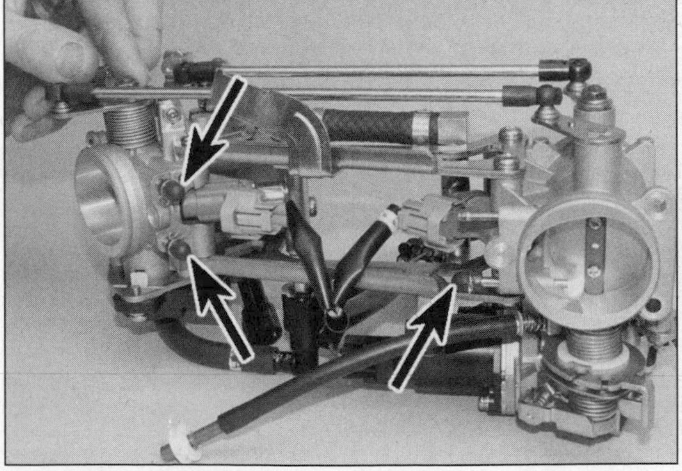

13.2c Note the location of the blanking caps (arrowed)

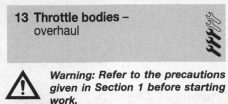

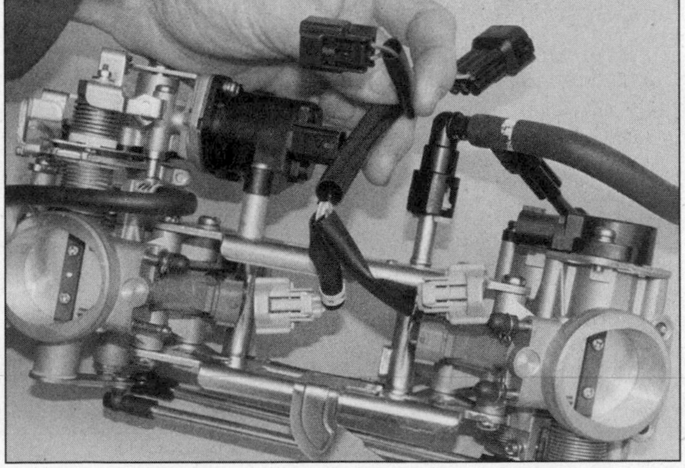

13.3 Remove the fuel injector wiring loom

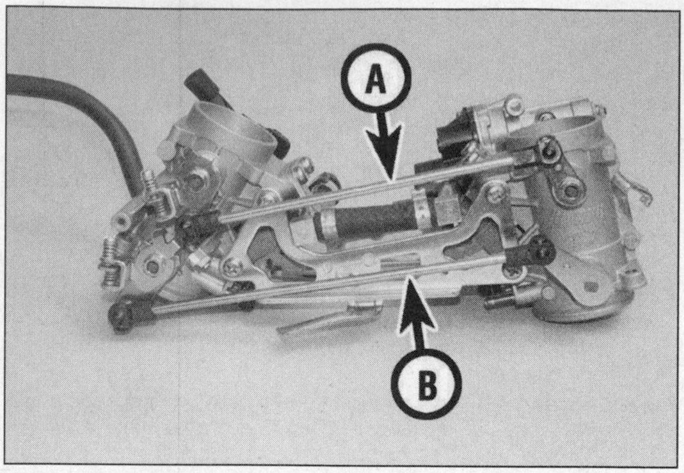

13.4a Note the location of the secondary throttle valve (A) and throttle valve (B) link rods

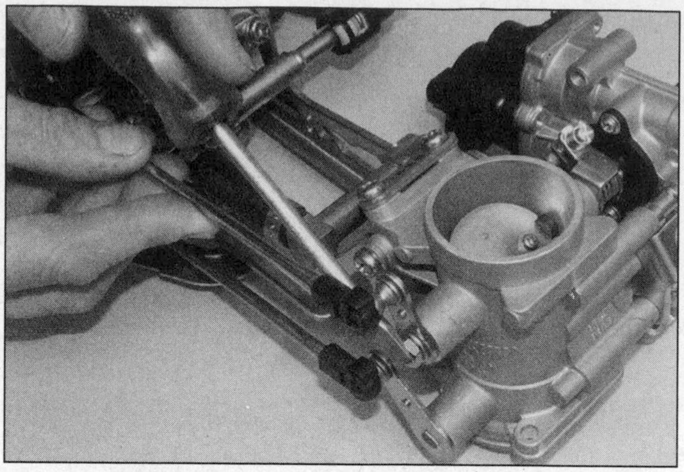
13.4b Unclip the rod ends from the throttle arms

then unclip the rods from the throttle arms – note that the lower (throttle valve) rod is longer than the upper (secondary throttle valve) rod **(see illustrations)**.

5 Measure the spring length on the idle speed adjuster and note it for installation, then unscrew the adjuster **(see illustration)**. Remove the spring and washer for safekeeping.

6 Release the clip(s) securing the fuel hose to the fuel rail **(see illustration)**. Note that unless the hose is being renewed, only one clip need be released.

7 To separate the throttle bodies, undo the bracket screws on one, diagonally opposite, side of each throttle body only, so that one bracket is left attached to the front throttle body and one is attached to the rear throttle body, then separate the throttle bodies **(see illustrations)**.

8 If required, follow the procedure in Section 15 and remove the fuel injectors.

9 The throttle position (TP) sensor and the secondary throttle position (STP) sensor are located on the left-hand side of the rear throttle body **(see illustration)**. If required, follow the procedure in Section 11 to remove

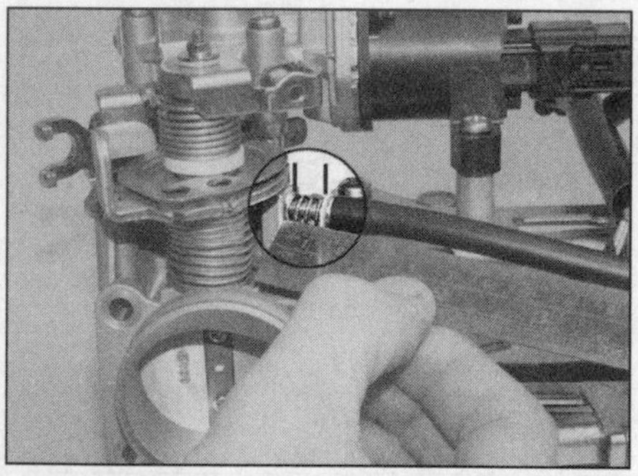
13.5 Measure the idle speed adjuster spring length before unscrewing it

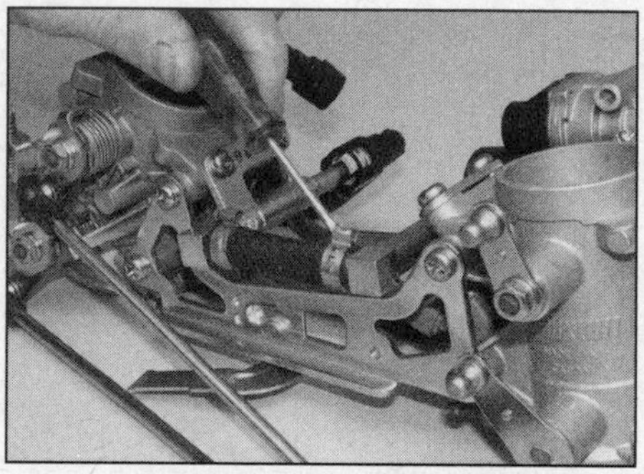
13.6 Release the clips carefully if they are to be reused

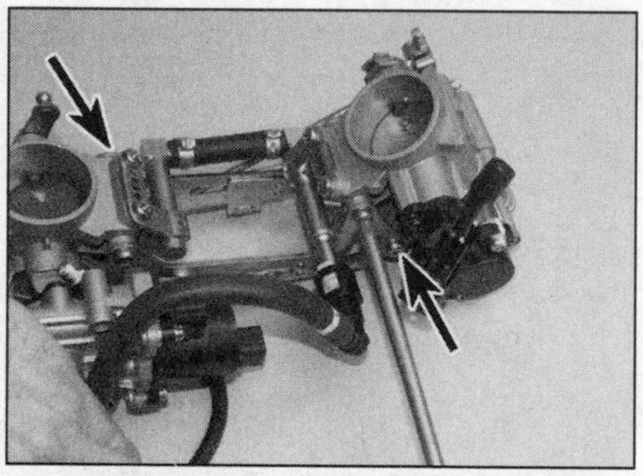
13.7a Remove the diagonally opposite bracket screws . . .

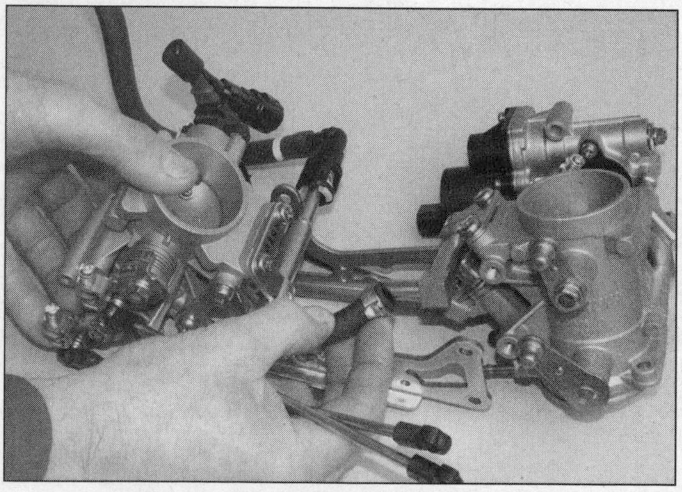
13.7b . . . then separate the throttle bodies

13.9a Location of the throttle position (A) and secondary throttle position (B) sensors

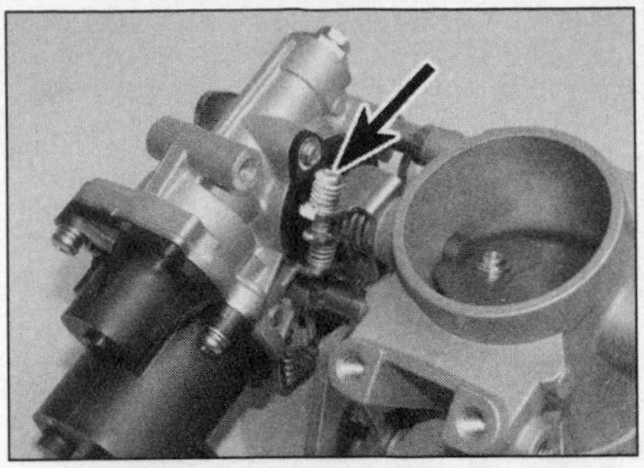
13.9b Do not tamper with the STV screw (arrowed) . . .

13.9c . . . or the throttle stop screw (arrowed)

13.9d Do not remove the throttle valves

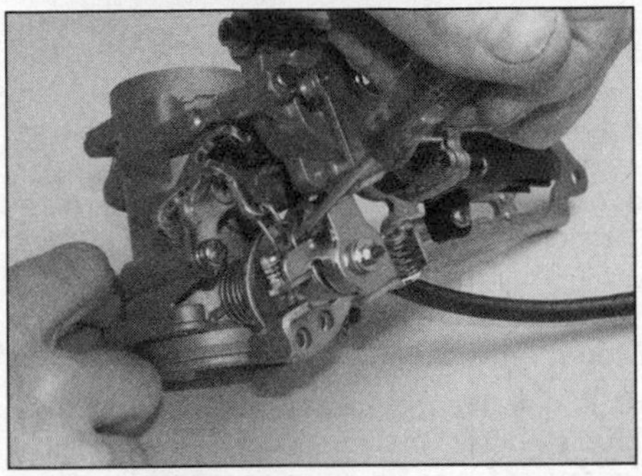
13.10a Release the fast idle link lever return spring . . .

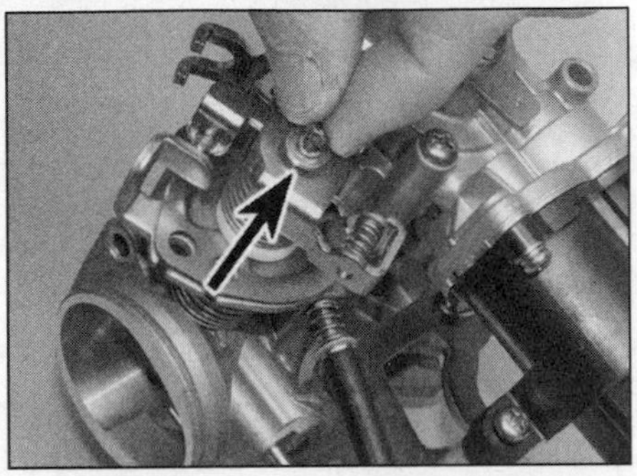
13.10b . . . then undo the centre nut

13.10c Lift off the lever assembly . . .

the sensors. Note: *During disassembly, DO NOT remove the secondary throttle valve (STV) servo from the front throttle body. If the servo is faulty a new throttle body must be installed. DO NOT tamper with the setting of the STV screw or the throttle stop screw on the rear throttle body* ***(see illustrations)****. DO NOT remove the throttle valves or the secondary throttle valves* ***(see illustration)****.*

10 To remove the fast idle link lever, first release the lever return spring, then undo the centre nut **(see illustrations)**. Lift off the spring washer, flat washer, nylon flat washer and the lever assembly, noting the location of the small spring on the lever assembly **(see illustrations)**. Lift off the lever return spring, central spindle and stepped seat, noting how they fit **(see illustrations)**.

Cleaning

Caution: Use only a petroleum based solvent or dedicated injector cleaner for throttle body cleaning. Don't use caustic cleaners.

11 Ensure that only metal components are washed in cleaning solvent and always follow manufacturers recommendations as to cleaning time. If a spray cleaner is used, direct the spray into all passages.

12 After the cleaner has loosened and dissolved most of the varnish and other deposits, use a nylon-bristled brush to remove the stubborn deposits. Rinse the throttle bodies again, then dry them with compressed air.

13 Use compressed air to blow out all of the fuel and air passages.

Caution: Never clean the passages with a piece of wire or a drill bit, as they will be enlarged, causing the fuel and air metering rates to be upset.

Inspection

14 Check the throttle bodies for cracks or any other damage which may result in air getting in.

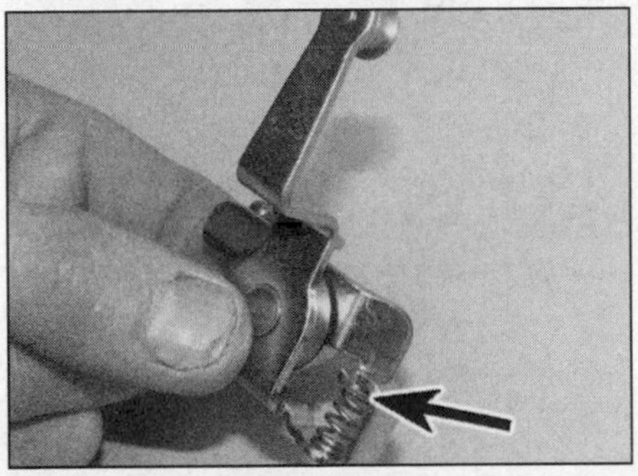
13.10d . . . noting the location of the small spring (arrowed)

13.10e Lift off the lever return spring . . .

13.10f . . . central spindle with castellated top . . .

13.10g . . . and stepped seat (stepped side uppermost)

13.16 Check the terminals in the wiring loom connectors

13.17 Assembled components of the fast idle link lever – note the fast idle screw (arrowed)

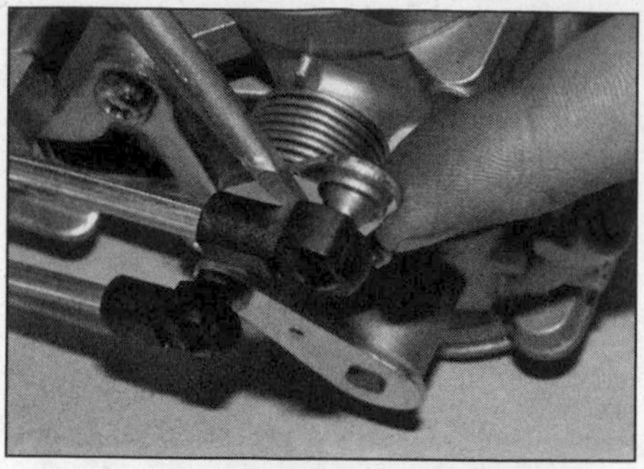

13.19a Use a flat-bladed screwdriver to unclip the rods . . .

15 Check that the throttle valves and linkages move smoothly and freely in the bodies. Inspect the valve shafts and throttle bodies for wear. Check the condition of the valve shaft springs.

16 Check that the terminals in the injector wiring loom are clean and undamaged, then follow the procedure in Section 11, Step 52, and check the injector wiring loom **(see illustration)**.

Reassembly

17 Reassembly is the reverse of removal, noting the following:

13.19b . . . from each end of the throttle arms

- Ensure the components of the fast idle link lever are installed in the correct order (see Step 10) **(see illustration)**.
- If required, follow the procedure in Sec-tion 11 to install the TP sensor and the STP sensor.
- If required, follow the procedure in Sec-tion 15 and install the fuel injectors.
- Ensure the fuel hose is securely clipped to each fuel rail.
- Ensure the washer and spring are correctly installed on the idle speed adjuster and turn the adjuster to set the spring length as noted on removal (see Step 5).

13.21a Do not disturb the throttle valve butterflies . . .

- Ensure the fuel injector and STV servo wiring connectors are securely connected.
- If removed, don't forget to fit the blanking caps on the throttle body unions (see Step 2).
- Check the STV synchronisation (see Sec-tion 14).

K7 models onward

Disassembly

18 If not already disconnected when the throttle bodies were removed, release the clip on the fuel feed hose and disconnect the hose from the fuel rail, then pull the two vacuum hoses off their unions.

19 Note the location of the throttle link rods, then unclip the rods from the throttle arms – note that the lower (throttle valve) rod is longer than the upper (secondary throttle valve) rod **(see illustrations)**.

20 If required, remove the injector assembly as described in Section 15.

21 The TP sensor and STP sensor can be removed from the rear throttle body if required, although their positions must be marked with a felt pen prior to removal to enable them to be returned to their original positions on reassembly – see Section 11. Do not disturb the STV servo – it cannot be obtained separately **(see illustration)**. Equally, the throttle valve

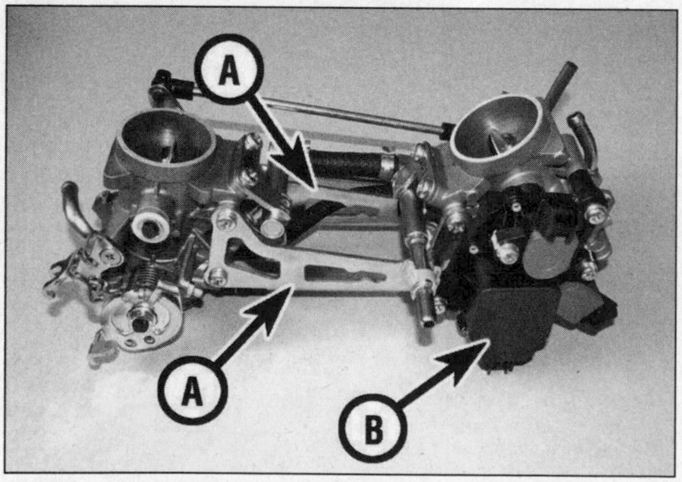

13.21b . . . the brackets linking the bodies (A) or the STV servo (B)

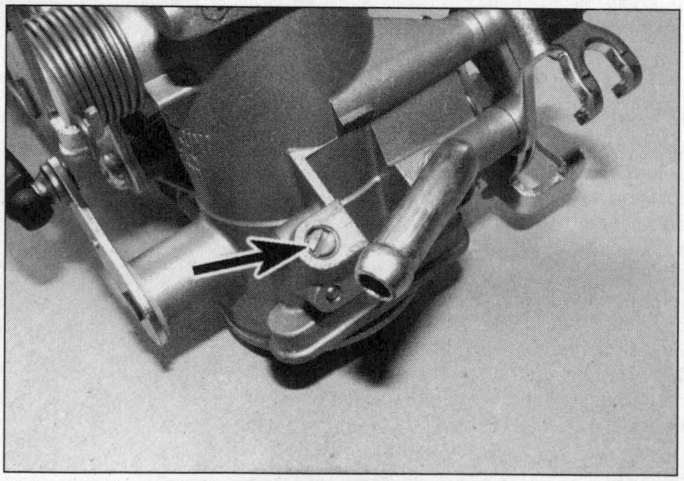

13.21c Air screw location on front . . .

13.21d . . . and rear throttle body (arrowed)

13.25 The lower rod is longer than the upper rod

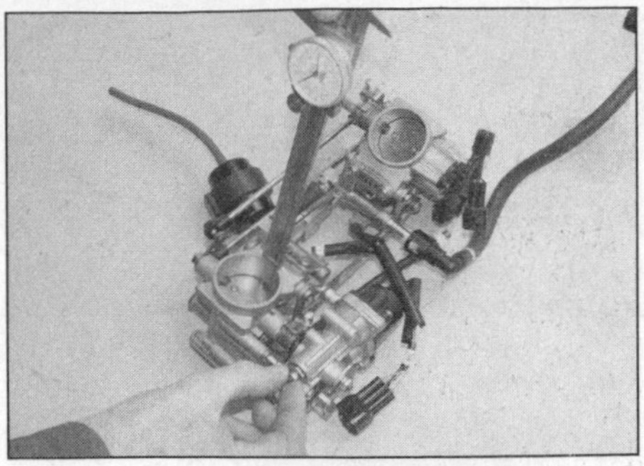

14.2 Level the secondary throttle valve on the front throttle body as described

butterflies, pulley assembly and its adjuster screws, and the large brackets linking the two throttle bodies should not be disturbed – all are pre-set at the factory. The air screws can be removed, although you are advised to first screw them in until they seat lightly, counting the exact number of turns so that they can be returned to roughly the correct position on reassembly **(see illustration)**.

Cleaning and inspection

22 Refer to Steps 11 to 15 of this section.

Reassembly

23 If the TP sensor or STP sensor have been disturbed, apply a smear of grease to their O-rings then fit them so that the cut-out engages the tang of the throttle butterfly shaft. Re-align the marks made on removal and secure the sensor with the retaining screw. Operate each throttle shaft to check that its butterfly valve opens and closes smoothly. Final adjustment of the sensor positions must be made after the throttle bodies are refitted.

24 If the injectors have been removed from the fuel rail, fit a new seal and O-ring to each one. Align the wire connector body with the square section of its holder on the fuel rail, then press the injector into place - do not rotate it once in place. Carefully insert the injectors and fuel rail assembly into the throttle bodies. Secure with the four screws, tightening them to the specified torque.

25 Clip the throttle link rods to the throttle arms, noting that the longer rod is the lower of the two **(see illustration)**.

14 Secondary throttle valve synchronisation – K3 to K6 models

Warning: Refer to the precautions given In Section 1 before proceeding.

1 If this procedure is being undertaken with the throttle bodies installed on the machine, make sure the ignition is OFF. Remove the air filter housing (see Section 3).

2 Work on the front throttle body first. Turn the valve servo shaft by hand until the secondary valve is level with the top rim of the throttle body – use a vernier gauge to measure the distance between the front and back edges of the valve and the rim **(see illustration)**. **Note:** *Do not try to turn the valve itself.*

3 Now make the same measurements on the rear throttle body valve - do this carefully to avoid disturbing the position of the front throttle body valve. The valve should be level with the top edge of the throttle body; if not, turn the adjusting screw on the linkage pulley until it is **(see illustration)**.

4 Open and close the secondary valves using the valve servo shaft and recheck the setting. Note that wear in the clips at the ends of the connecting rod will create excessive freeplay between the front and rear valves, making synchronisation difficult. If necessary, renew the rod.

15 Fuel rail and injectors

Warning: Refer to the precautions given in Section 1 before proceeding.

Removal

Note: *The fuel injectors can be removed with the throttle bodies in place. If the bodies have been removed, ignore the Steps which do not apply.*

1 Remove the air filter housing (see Section 3).

2 Place a rag underneath the fuel supply hose union on the throttle bodies to catch any residual fuel, then release the clip on the hose connector and disconnect it **(see illustration 13.1)**.

3 On K3 to K6 models, the front fuel injector wiring should be marked with an F – if not, mark it to aid reassembly, then disconnect both injector connectors **(see illustration)**.

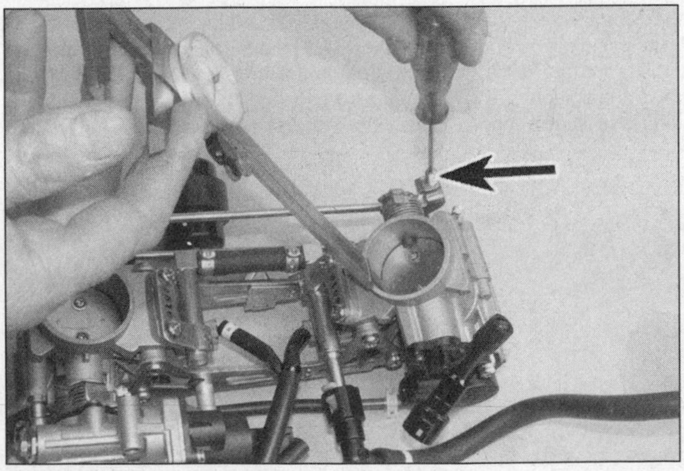

14.3 Turn the linkage pulley screw (arrowed) to adjust the position of the rear throttle body valve

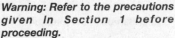

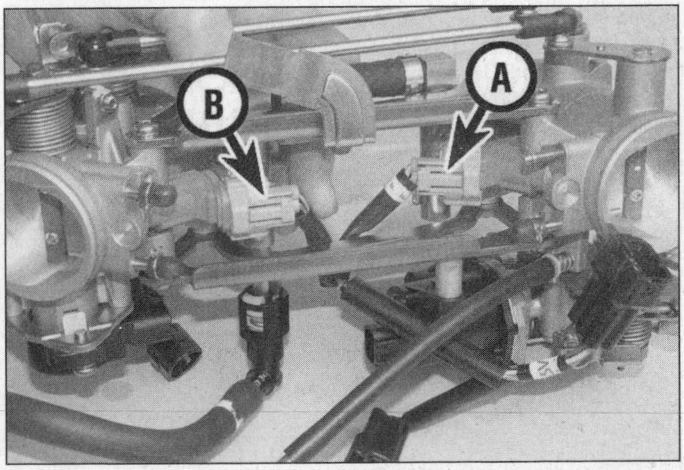

15.3a Disconnect the front (A) and rear (B) injector wiring connectors – K3 to K6 models

15.3b Front injector brown connector (A) and rear injector grey connector (B) - K7 onwards

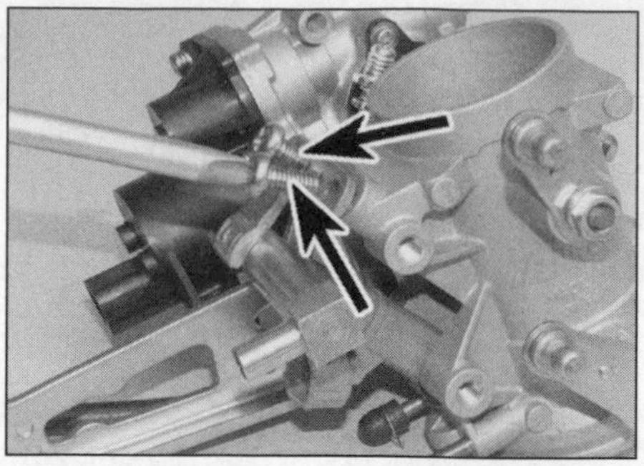

15.5a Remove the screws (arrowed) . . .

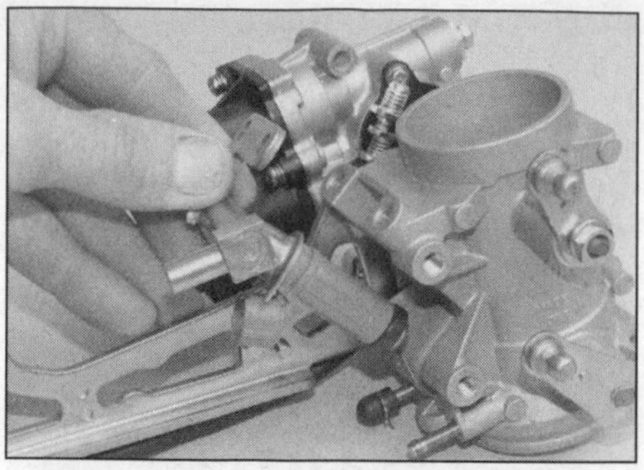

15.5b . . . then lift off the fuel rail carefully

If they are difficult to access, disconnect the STV servo and injector wiring loom connectors now and disconnect the injector connectors after displacing the fuel rail. On K7 models onward, unplug the wiring connector from each injector noting their colour coding – front cyl brown (and wiring marked with an F), rear cyl grey **(see illustration)**.

4 If required, release the clips securing the fuel hose to the fuel rails **(see illustration 13.6)**. The hose can be disconnected once the fuel rails have been removed.

5 Remove the screws securing the fuel rails to the throttle bodies, then carefully lift the fuel rails off the throttle bodies – the injectors should come away with the rail, but if they don't carefully pull them out of the throttle bodies **(see illustrations)**.

6 If they are still in the fuel rails pull each injector out. Discard the injector O-ring and seal as new ones must be fitted on reassembly **(see illustrations)**.

7 Modern fuels contain detergents which should keep the injectors clean and free of gum or varnish from fuel residue. If an injector is suspected of being blocked, clean it through with injector cleaner. If the injector is clean but its performance is suspect, follow the procedure in Section 11 to check it or take it to a Suzuki dealer for assessment.

8 Separate the fuel rails from the hose and ensure that they are thoroughly clean and free of sediment. Inspect the hose and replace it with a new one if there are any signs of cracking or deformation. Renew the clips if they are deformed or corroded.

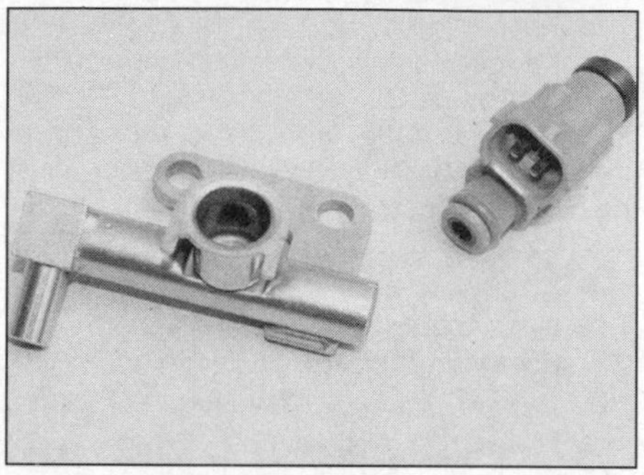

15.6a Separate the injector from the fuel rail . . .

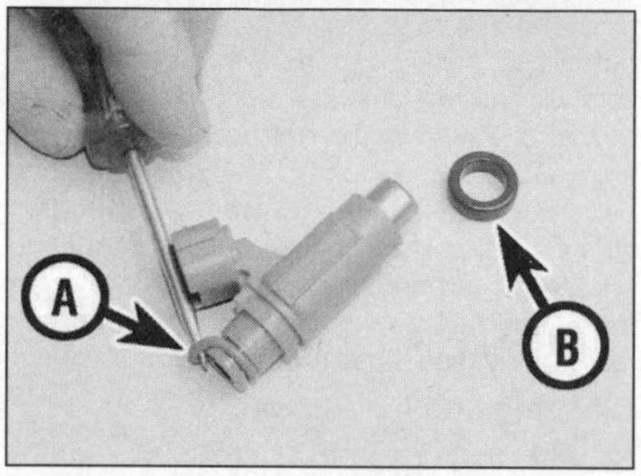

15.6b . . . and discard the O-ring (A) and seal (B)

Installation

Note: *Apply a smear of clean engine oil to all new seals and O-rings before reassembly.*

9 Fit a new seal onto the bottom of each injector and a new O-ring onto the top. Carefully press the injectors into the throttle bodies, aligning them so the wiring connectors face away from the throttle body **(see illustration 15.11)**. **Note:** *Avoid twisting the injectors as this may damage the seals.* If the injectors are difficult to locate in the throttle bodies because of the bottom seals, remove the seals and fit them into the throttle bodies first, then install the injectors.

10 Connect the injector wiring connectors, making sure the connector marked F fits onto the front injector.

11 Install the fuel hose and clips onto the fuel rails, then locate the rails over the injectors and press them down until the O-rings are felt to seat. Install the fuel rail screws and tighten them to the specified torque setting **(see illustration)**.

12 Position the hose clips over the unions on the fuel rails and tighten them securely.

13 Install the remaining components in the reverse order of removal. On completion, start the engine and check carefully that there are no fuel leaks.

16 Throttle cables

Removal

1 Remove the air filter housing (see Section 3). Access to the throttle cable bracket on the front throttle body is extremely restricted – if required, follow the procedure in Section 12 and displace the throttle body assembly.

2 Loosen the upper locknuts securing the throttle cable adjusters in the bracket on the front throttle body, then slip the adjusters out of the bracket **(see illustration)**. Detach

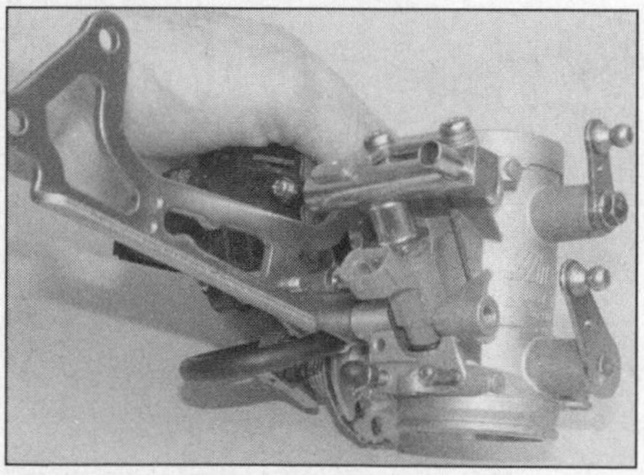

15.11 Assembled fuel rail and injector

16.2a Loosen the cable adjuster upper locknuts (arrowed) . . .

16.2b . . . then slip the adjusters out of the bracket . . .

16.2c . . . and detach the inner cable ends from the pulley

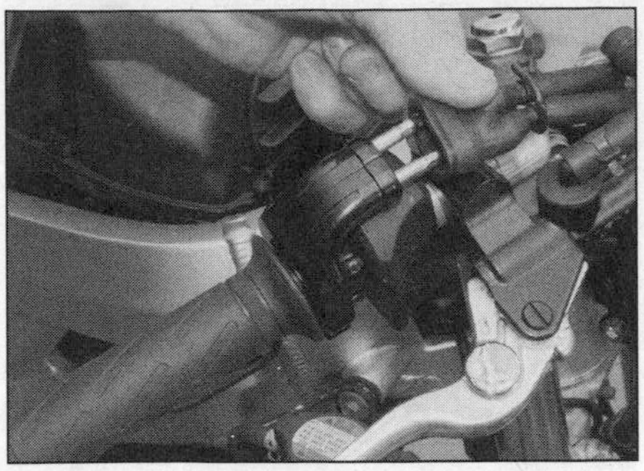

16.3a Pull back the rubber boot . . .

16.3b . . . then undo the housing screws (arrowed) . . .

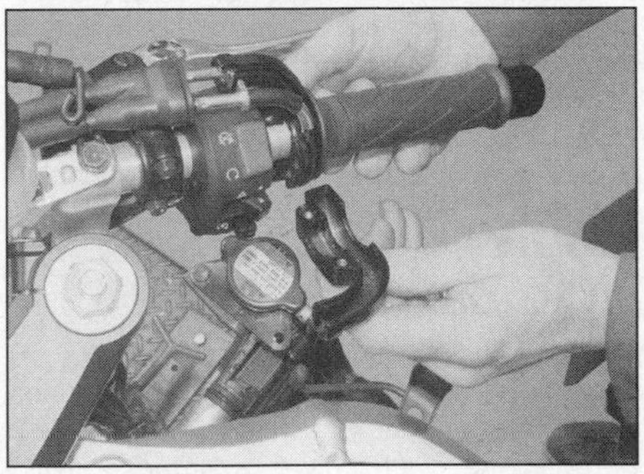

16.3c . . . and separate the housing halves

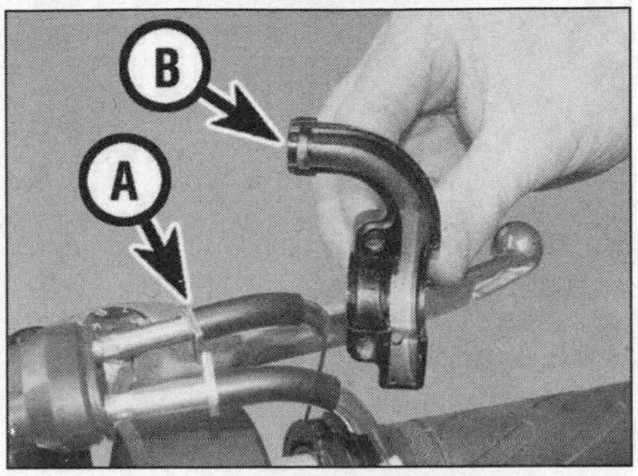

16.3d Note how the D-shape (A) locates in the housing (B)

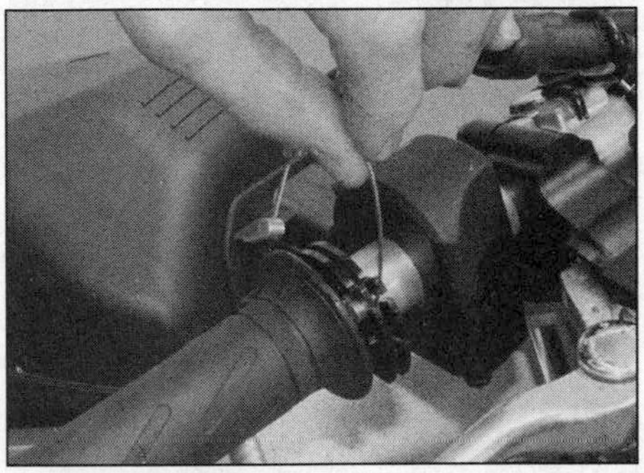

16.3e Detach the cable ends from the twistgrip pulley

the inner cable ends from the throttle pulley, noting how they fit – the upper cable is the throttle opening cable, the lower cable is the throttle closing cable **(see illustration)**.

3 On SV650 models, follow the procedure in Chapter 4A, Section 12, to detach the upper cable ends from the throttle pulley. On SV650S models, pull the rubber boot off the throttle pulley housing on the handlebars **(see illustration)**. Unscrew the housing screws and separate the halves, noting how the D-shape on each outer cable end locates in the housing **(see illustrations)**. Note that the opening cable is colour-coded silver and the closing cable is colour-coded gold. Detach the cable ends from the twistgrip pulley, noting how they fit **(see illustration)**.

4 Remove the cables from the machine, noting their correct routing.

Installation

5 Thread the cables through to the throttle bodies and up to the handlebars, making sure they are correctly routed – they must not interfere with any other component and should not be kinked or bent sharply.

6 Lubricate the cable ends with multi-purpose grease and attach them to the pulley, making sure they are the correct way round (see Step 3). On SV650 models, follow the procedure in Chapter 4A, Section 12, to install the upper cable ends in the throttle pulley. On SV650S models, locate the cables in the housing halves, then join the halves around the handlebar. Align the cables with the guide on the front brake reservoir bracket **(see illustration)**. Install the longer housing screw in the top screw hole and the shorter screw in the lower hole and tighten them securely. Fit the rubber boot.

7 Check that the twistgrip pulley turns freely.

8 Fit the lower end of the inner closing cable onto the throttle pulley – the closing cable goes around the bottom of the pulley **(see illustration)**. Now fit the end of the opening cable – the opening cable goes around the top. Locate the cable adjusters in the bracket, ensuring the adjuster locknuts are located on each side of the plate **(see illustration 16.2a)**. Adjust the cables as described in Chapter 1.

9 If displaced, install the throttle body assembly (see Section 12).

10 Install the air filter housing (see Section 3).

11 Start the engine and check the action of the throttle, and that the idle speed does not rise as the handlebars are turned. If it does, check the routing of the cables and correct the problem before riding the motorcycle.

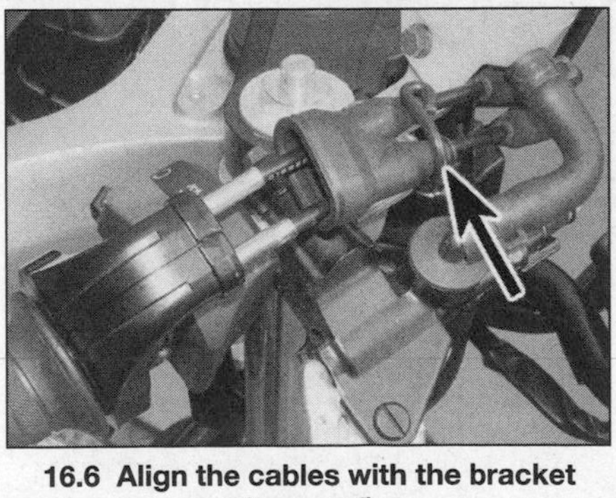

16.6 Align the cables with the bracket (arrowed)

17 Fast idle system – removal, installation and adjustment

K3 to K6 models

Note: *The fast idle mechanism is actuated by the STV servo when the engine is cold and should cancel automatically when engine coolant temperature reaches 40 to 50°C. If the idle speed cannot be adjusted correctly (see Chapter 1), check for a possible fault in the engine coolant temperature sensor or sensor wiring (see Section 10).*

1 The engine should be cold. Start the engine and check the fast idle speed with the

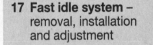

16.8 Install the closing cable around the bottom of the pulley

17.3a Disconnect the STV servo wiring connector . . .

17.3b . . . then fully open the secondary throttle valves

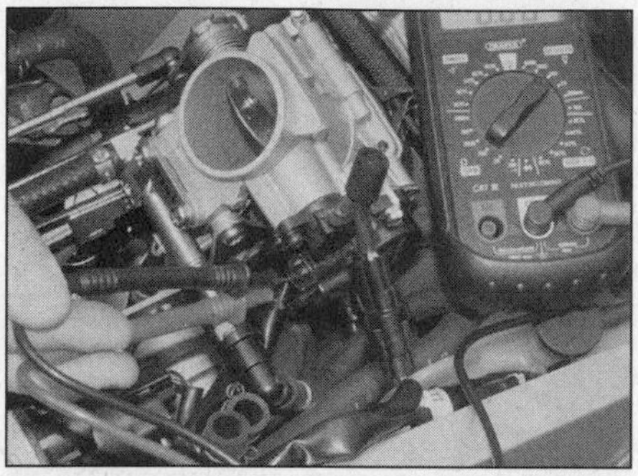
17.4a Backprobe the TP sensor wiring connector to check the output voltage

17.4b Location of the fast idle adjuster screw (arrowed)

specifications given at the beginning of this Chapter. Note that the fast idle speed will rise by 100 to 200 rpm in colder weather.

2 If the fast idle speed is not within the specifications, remove the air filter housing (see Section 3).

3 Disconnect the STV servo wiring connector, then fully open the secondary throttle valves by turning the valve servo shaft by hand – do not try to turn the valves themselves **(see illustrations)**.

17.7a Disconnect the ISC valve wiring connector (arrowed) and hoses

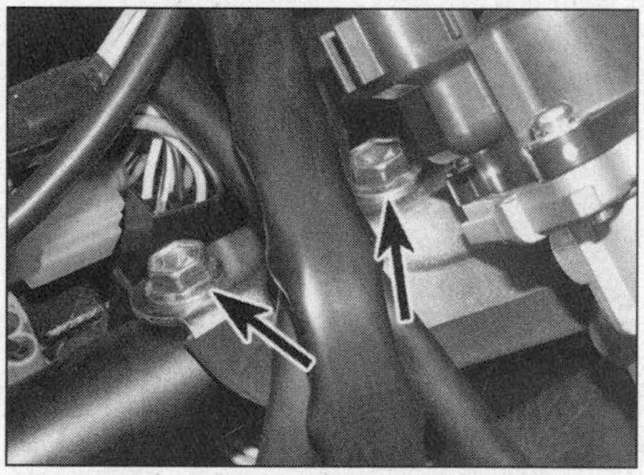
17.7b ISC valve mounting bracket bolts (arrowed)

17.8a Remove the three screws to release the valve cover, then draw the valve out of its body

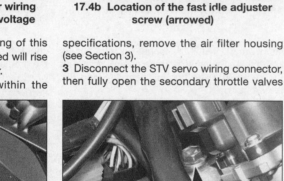

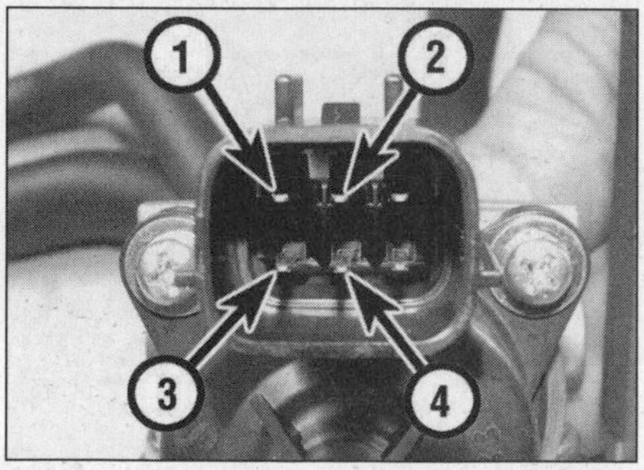

17.8b ISC valve wire terminal identification

4 Turn the ignition ON and connect the positive (+ve) probe of a voltmeter to the pink/white wire terminal and the negative (-ve) probe to the black/brown wire terminal in the throttle position (TP) sensor wiring connector to check the output voltage **(see illustration)**. If the result is not as specified (TP sensor closed), turn the fast idle adjuster on the front edge of the throttle cable pulley below the STV servo until the voltage is within specification **(see illustration)**. Turn the ignition OFF.

5 Connect the STV servo wiring connector and install the air filter housing (see Section 3). Start the engine, leave it running and check that the fast idle setting cancels automatically when the engine coolant temperature reaches 40 to 50°C. At that point the idle speed should fall to the normal (warm engine) specification. If necessary, adjust the engine idle speed (see Chapter 1).

K7 models onward

6 Idle speed is controlled by the idle speed control (ISC) valve – there is no manual means of adjustment. If a C40 fault code is indicated, the idle speed with have deviated from its pre-set value or there may be a problem with the power supply to the ISC motor. Use of the Suzuki SDS tester (available to a dealer) will enable full diagnosis of the ISC valve and also erase the fault code from the ECM memory – refer to a dealer for this service. It is however, possible to remove and refit the valve, test its circuitry and restore it to its preset position using the mode select switch described in Section 10.

7 To remove the valve, check that the ignition is OFF, then remove the air filter housing as described in Section 3. Disconnect the wire connector from the ISC valve, followed by its three hoses – take note of their positions as an aid to refitting - the outer hoses are marked with a spot of blue paint **(see illustration)**. Remove the two bolts which retain the valve mounting bracket to the frame **(see illustration)**.

8 The valve can only be purchased as a complete part, although there is nothing lost by removing its cover to examine the valve unit for damage or a build up of carbon deposits and to check that its sealing O-ring is in good condition **(see illustration)**. Check the internal circuitry using a multimeter set to the ohms function. There should be no continuity between terminals 1 and 3, and no continuity between terminals 2 and 4 **(see illustration)**. Now test between terminals 1 and 2, then between terminals 3 and 4 – a reading of approx. 30 ohms should be indicated. If the readings are wildly different, the ISC valve should be considered faulty.

9 Check the wiring between the ISC valve wire connector and the ECM connector for continuity. Use the wiring diagram at the end of this manual to identify the six wires.

10 If the valve was removed from the machine, install its mounting bracket and reconnect the three hoses, securing them with their wire clips. Reconnect the wiring connector. The valve position must now be restored to its preset mode.
11 With the ignition OFF, connect the mode select switch (see Section 10) and turn it ON, Now turn the ignition switch ON, then OFF. Wait at least five seconds then turn the mode select switch OFF and disconnect it from the wiring plug.

18 Exhaust system

Warning: If the engine has been running the exhaust system will be very hot. Allow the system to cool before carrying out any work.

Removal

Note: *The silencer and main exhaust system are a complete unit – the silencer cannot be removed separately.*
1 Slacken the clamp bolt securing the front cylinder downpipe to the exhaust system **(see illustration)**.
2 Unscrew the front cylinder downpipe flange bolts, then pull the downpipe off **(see illustrations)**. Remove the gasket from the front cylinder head exhaust port and discard it as a new one must be used.
3 Slacken the clamp bolt securing the rear cylinder downpipe to the exhaust system **(see illustration)**.
4 Remove the bolts securing the exhaust system to the underside of the frame and to the lower right-hand side of the frame **(see illustrations)**. On K7 models onward, trace the wiring from the oxygen sensor to its connector under the right-hand side panel and disconnect it **(see illustration)**. Take note of its wiring before pulling it from position.
5 Unscrew the silencer mounting bolt, then support the exhaust system and withdraw the bolt and lower the system away from the machine **(see illustrations)**.
6 Gaskets are fitted in the exhaust system where it joins the front and rear downpipes – remove the gaskets and discard them as new ones must be used.
7 Remove the spacers and check the condition of the system mounting bushes; if the bushes are worn or deteriorated renew them.
8 Clean all corrosion off the mounting bolts and apply a smear of copper grease to the threads to prevent them seizing in the future.

18.1 Slacken the clamp bolt . . .

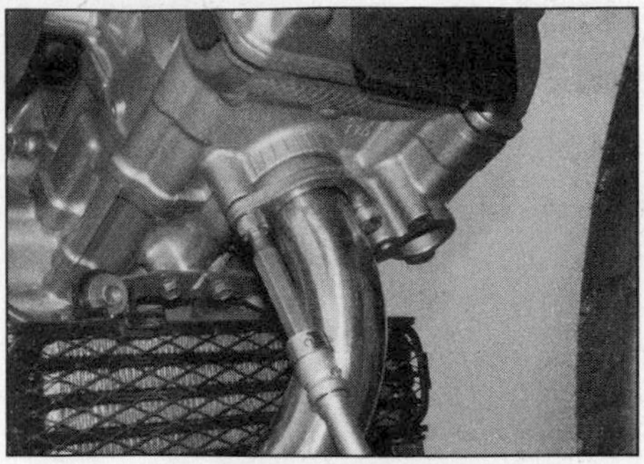

18.2a . . . then unscrew the flange bolts . . .

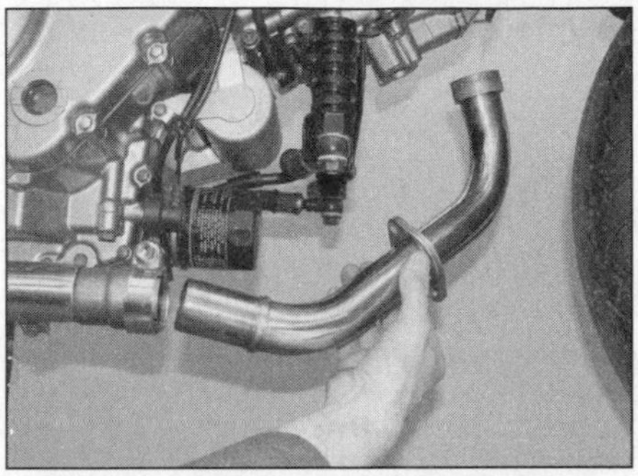

18.2b . . . and pull the front cylinder downpipe off

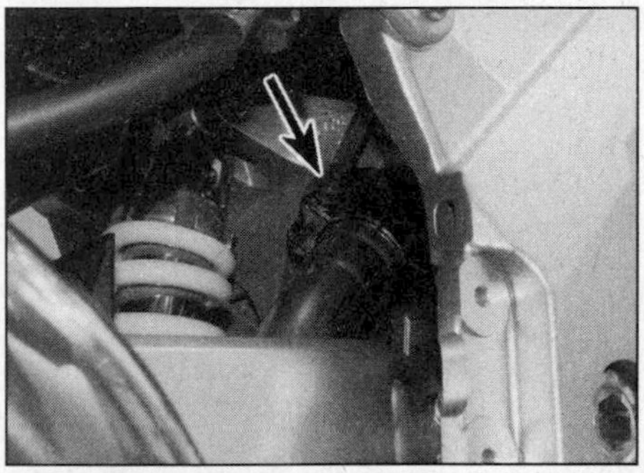

18.3 Slacken the clamp bolt (arrowed) on the rear cylinder downpipe

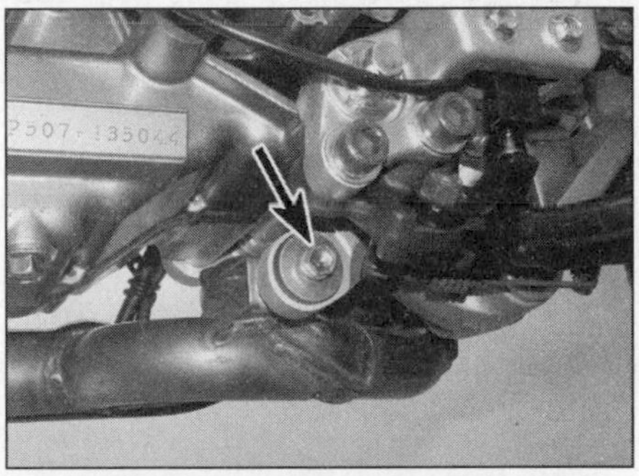

18.4a Remove the bolt (arrowed) on the underside of the frame . . .

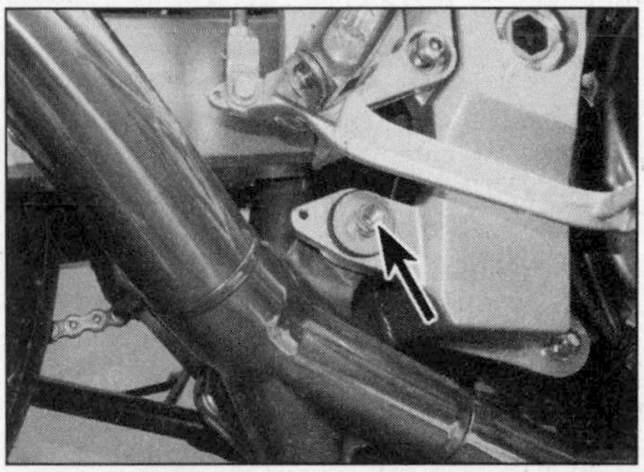

18.4b . . . and on the lower right-hand side

18.4c Disconnect the oxygen sensor wiring connector under the right side panel

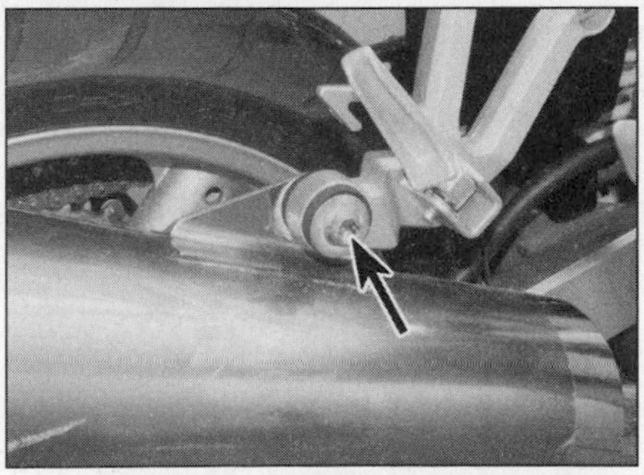

18.5a Unscrew the silencer mounting bolt . . .

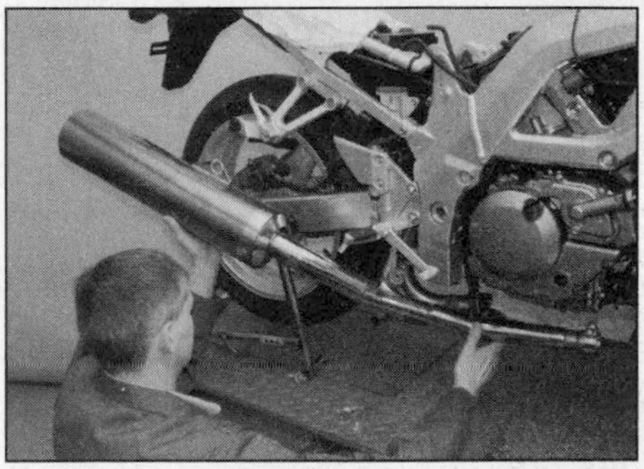

18.5b . . . and lift the exhaust system off

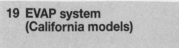

18.9 Ensure the system locates correctly over the rear cylinder downpipe (arrowed)

Installation

9 Apply a suitable exhaust sealant (such as Permatex 1372) to the gaskets and fit them into the system where it joins the front and rear downpipes. Ensure the front and drear clamps are in position, then manoeuvre the system into position so that it locates over the rear cylinder downpipe **(see illustration)**. Push the system into position and align the silencer mounting bracket with the footrest bracket, then install the bolt finger-tight **(see illustration 18.5a)**.

10 Install the remaining system mounting bolts and tighten them finger-tight **(see illustrations 18.4a and 4b)**.

11 Apply a smear of grease to the new front cylinder exhaust port gasket to keep it in place, then fit the gasket in the port. Install the front cylinder downpipe and secure it with the flange bolts **(see illustration 18.2a)**.

12 Once the system is installed and correctly aligned, tighten all the fixings to the torque setting specified at the beginning of the Chapter. Don't forget to tighten the rear cylinder downpipe clamp bolt. Tighten the silencer mounting last.

13 Run the engine and check that there are no exhaust gas leaks.

19 EVAP system (California models)

1 Details of the EVAP system can be found in Chapter 4A, Section 18.

20 Catalytic converter

Note: *A catalytic converter is fitted as standard for European and US market models.*

General information

1 A three-way catalytic converter is incorporated in the silencer to minimise the level of exhaust pollutants released into the atmosphere. From K7 Europe models onward, a heated oxygen sensor is fitted just forward of the silencer, and feeds exhaust gas content information back to the ECM.

2 The catalytic converter consists of a canister containing a fine mesh impregnated with a catalyst material, over which the hot exhaust gases pass. The catalyst speeds up the oxidation of harmful carbon monoxide, unburned hydrocarbons and soot, effectively reducing the quantity of harmful products released into the atmosphere via the exhaust gases.

3 Refer to Section 18 for exhaust system removal and installation information.

Precautions

4 The catalytic converter is a reliable and simple device which needs no maintenance in itself, but there are some facts of which an owner should be aware if the converter is to function properly for its full service life.

- DO NOT use leaded or lead replacement petrol (gasoline) – the additives will coat the precious metals, reducing their converting efficiency and will eventually destroy the catalytic converter.
- Always keep the ignition and fuel systems well maintained in accordance with the manufacturer's schedule – if the fuel/air mixture is suspected of being incorrect have it checked on an exhaust gas analyser.
- If the engine develops a misfire, do not ride the bike at all (or at least as little as possible) until the fault is cured.
- DO NOT use fuel or engine oil additives – these may contain substances harmful to the catalytic converter.
- DO NOT continue to use the bike if the engine burns oil to the extent of leaving a visible trail of blue smoke.
- Remember that the catalytic converter is FRAGILE – handle the exhaust system carefully and do not strike it with tools during servicing work.

Chapter 5
Ignition system

Contents

Degrees of difficulty

Easy, suitable for novice with little experience	**Fairly easy,** suitable for beginner with some experience	**Fairly difficult,** suitable for competent DIY mechanic	**Difficult,** suitable for experienced DIY mechanic	**Very difficult,** suitable for expert DIY or professional

Specifications

General information

Spark plugs	see Chapter 1
Cylinder identification	Front cyl no. 1, rear cyl no. 2

Ignition timing

X, Y, K1 and K2 models	5° BTDC @ 1300 rpm
K3 to K6 models	7° BTDC @ 1300 rpm
K7-on models	8° BTDC @ 1300 rpm

Pulse generator coil – X, Y, K1 and K2 models

Resistance	140 to 230 ohms at 20°C
Minimum peak voltage (see text)	3.0 volts

Crankshaft position sensor – K3-on models

Resistance	130 to 240 ohms at 20°C
Minimum peak voltage (see text)	3.7 volts

Ignition HT coils

Primary winding resistance	
X, Y, K1 and K2 models	3.5 to 5.5 ohms at 20°C
K3 to K6 models	2.0 to 5.0 ohms at 20°C
K7-on models	1.0 to 5.0 ohms @ 20°C
Secondary winding resistance	
X, Y, K1 and K2 models	
With plug cap	20 to 31 K-ohms at 20°C
Without plug cap	15 to 26 K-ohms at 20°C
K3 to K6 models (with plug cap)	24 to 37 K-ohms at 20°C
K7-on models (with plug cap)	25 to 40 K-ohms @ 20°C
Plug cap resistance (X, Y, K1 and K2 models)	approx. 5 K-ohms
Minimum peak voltage (see text)	150 volts

Throttle position sensor – X, Y, K1 and K2 models

Resistance	
Closed	3.5 to 6.5 K-ohms
Open	see Text

Torque settings

Throttle position sensor screws	3.5 Nm
Timing mark inspection cap	23 Nm

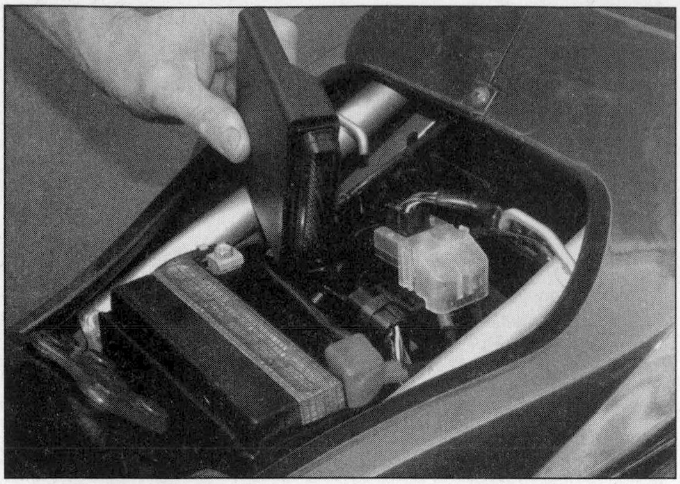

2.2a Disconnect the ECM connector – K3-on models . . .

2.2b . . . and check for battery input voltage on the loom side of the wiring connector

1 General information

All models are fitted with a fully transistorised electronic ignition system, which due to its lack of mechanical parts is totally maintenance free.

On X, Y, K1 and K2 models the system comprises the timing rotor, pulse generator coil, ignition control unit, ignition HT coils, and throttle position sensor. Refer to the wiring diagrams at the end of Chapter 9 for details. The ignition timing rotor triggers are incorporated in the alternator rotor, which is on the left-hand end of the crankshaft. These magnetically actuate the pulse generator coil as the crankshaft rotates. The pulse generator coil sends a signal to the ignition control unit which then supplies the ignition HT coils with the power necessary to produce a spark at the plugs. The system incorporates an electronic advance system. The throttle position sensor supplies the ignition control unit with information on throttle position and rate of opening or closing. Note that there is no provision for adjusting the ignition timing.

On K3 and later models the ignition system is combined with the fuel injection system, both being controlled by the engine control module (ECM). The ignition system comprises the timing rotor, crankshaft position sensor, ECM and ignition HT coils. The ignition timing rotor triggers are incorporated in the alternator rotor, which is on the left-hand end of the crankshaft. These magnetically actuate the crankshaft position sensor as the crankshaft rotates. The crankshaft position sensor sends a signal to the ECM which, in conjunction with information received from the various system sensors, calculates the ignition timing and supplies the ignition HT coils with the power necessary to produce a spark at the plugs. Note that dual spark ignition is fitted to K7 models onward, each coil supplying two plugs per cylinder.

Due to the inter-relation between the ignition and fuel systems, and the comprehensive fault diagnosis system, details of all ignition sensor checks are provided in Chapter 4B.

The ignition system incorporates a safety interlock circuit which will cut the ignition if the sidestand is extended whilst the engine is running and in gear, or if a gear is selected whilst the engine is running and the sidestand is down. The engine should be started with the transmission in neutral and the clutch lever pulled in. It can be started with the transmission in gear, but the sidestand must be up and the clutch lever pulled in.

Note: *Individual ignition system components can be checked but not repaired. If ignition system troubles occur, and the faulty component can be isolated, the only cure for the problem is to renew the part. Keep in mind that most electrical parts, once purchased, cannot be returned. To avoid unnecessary expense, make very sure the faulty component has been positively identified before buying a new part.*

2 Ignition system – check

Warning: The energy levels in electronic systems can be very high. On no account should the ignition be switched on whilst the plugs or plug caps are being held. Shocks from the HT circuit can be most unpleasant. Secondly, it is vital that the engine is not turned over or run with any of the plug caps removed, and that the plugs are soundly earthed (grounded) when the system is checked for sparking. The ignition system components can be seriously damaged if the HT circuit becomes isolated.

1 As no means of adjustment is available, any failure of the system can be traced to failure of a system component or a simple wiring fault. Of the two possibilities, the latter is by far the most likely. In the event of failure, check the system in a logical fashion, as described below.

Note: *Before checking the ignition system ensure that the battery is fully charged and that all fuses are in good condition.*

2 On K3-on models, follow the procedure in Chapter 8 and remove the rider's seat, then disconnect the ECM multi-pin wiring connector **(see illustration)**. Turn the ignition ON. Connect the probes of a voltmeter between the orange/green (Europe) or orange/white (US) and black/white wire terminals on the loom side of the wiring connector and check for battery input voltage (12V approx) **(see illustration)**. Turn the ignition OFF. If the input voltage is not as specified, check the ignition (main) switch, sidestand/turn signal relay and engine stop switch (see Chapter 9).

3 On all models, working on one cylinder at a time, pull the cap off the spark plug and connect a spare spark plug into the cap **(see illustration)**. Lay the plug against the cylinder head so that its threads are contacting it. If necessary hold the spark plug with an insulated tool. On K7 models onwards, note that this applies to both spark plugs relating to that cylinder.

Warning: Do not remove either of the spark plugs from the engine to perform this check – atomised

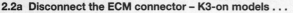

2.3 Pull the cap off the spark plug

fuel being pumped out of the open spark plug hole could ignite, causing severe injury! Make sure the plugs are securely held against the engine – if they are not earthed when the engine is turned over, the ignition system could be damaged.

4 Having observed the above precautions, check that the kill switch is in the RUN position and the transmission is in neutral, then turn the ignition switch ON, pull in the clutch lever and turn the engine over on the starter motor. If the system is in good condition a regular, fat blue spark should be evident at the plug electrode. If the spark appears thin or yellowish, or is non-existent, further investigation will be necessary. Turn the ignition OFF and repeat the check for the other lead.

5 The ignition system must be able to produce a spark which is capable of jumping an 8 mm gap at normal atmospheric pressure. A tool to test this is commercially available – set the required gap on the adjuster, then fit the tool into the spark plug cap and lay the other end against the engine **(see illustration)**. Alternatively a simple testing tool can be made to test the minimum gap across which the spark will jump (see **Tool Tip**).

6 Connect one of the spark plug HT leads from one coil to the protruding electrode on the test tool, and clip the tool to a good earth (ground) on the engine or frame. Check that the kill switch is in the RUN position, turn the ignition switch ON, pull in the clutch lever and turn the engine over on the starter motor. If the system is in good condition a regular, fat blue spark should be seen to jump the gap between the ends. Repeat the test for the other coil. If the test results are good the entire ignition system can be considered good. If the spark appears thin or yellowish, or is non-existent, further investigation will be necessary.

7 Ignition faults can be divided into two categories, namely those where the ignition system has failed completely, and those which are due to a partial failure. The likely faults are listed below, starting with the most

2.5 Using a commercially available spark testing tool

probable source of failure. Work through the list systematically, referring to the subsequent sections for full details of the necessary checks and tests. Note that for K3-on models, details of the integrated fuel injection system fault diagnosis procedure are provided in Chapter 4B.

- Loose, corroded or damaged wiring connections, broken or shorted wiring between any of the component parts of the ignition system (see Chapter 9).
- Faulty HT lead or spark plug cap, faulty spark plug, dirty, worn or corroded plug electrodes, or incorrect gap between electrodes.
- Faulty ignition (main) switch or engine kill switch (see Chapter 9).
- Faulty neutral/gear position, clutch or sidestand switch (see Chapter 9).
- Faulty pulse generator coil or damaged trigger on alternator rotor (X, Y, K1 and K2 models).
- Faulty crankshaft position sensor or damaged trigger on alternator rotor (K3-on models).
- Faulty ignition HT coil(s).
- Faulty throttle position sensor.
- Faulty ignition control unit (X, Y, K1 and K2 models).
- Faulty engine control module (K3-on models).

8 If the above checks don't reveal the cause

TOOL TiP

A simple spark gap testing tool can be made from a block of wood, a large alligator clip and two nails, one of which is fashioned so that a spark plug cap or bare HT lead end can be connected to its end. Make sure the gap between the two nail ends is the same as specified.

of the problem, have the ignition system tested by a Suzuki dealer.

3 Ignition HT coils

Check

1 Raise the fuel tank, and on K3-on models remove the air filter housing (see Chapter 4B). Check the coils visually for loose or damaged terminals, cracks and other damage **(see illustrations). Note:** *On K3-on models access to the ignition HT coils is extremely restricted. The coils are located inside the frame to the left (front cylinder coil) and right (rear cylinder coil) of the engine unit* ***(see illustrations).***

2 Disconnect the battery negative (–ve) lead (see Chapter 9).

3 Disconnect the primary circuit wiring connectors from the coil being tested, noting

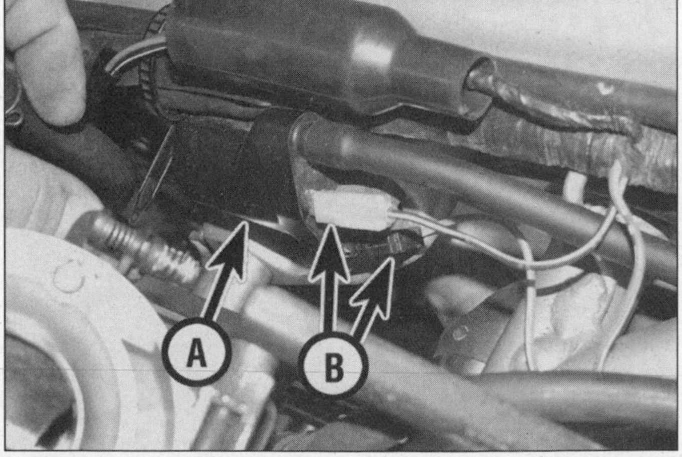

3.1a Front cylinder HT coil (A) and its primary circuit wiring connectors (B) – X, Y, K1 and K2 models

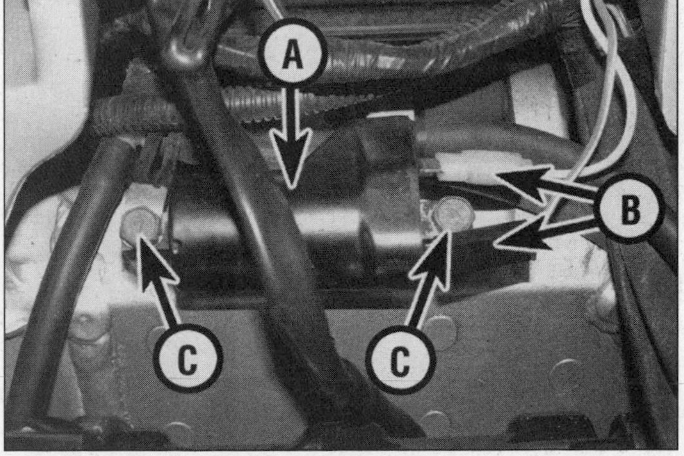

3.1b Rear cylinder HT coil (A), primary circuit wiring connectors (B), mounting bolts (C) – X, Y, K1 and K2 models

3.1c Location of the rear cylinder HT coil – K3 to K6 models

3.1d Front cylinder HT coil – K7-on models

3.1e Rear cylinder HT coil – K7-on models

which fits where, and pull the spark plug cap off the plug **(see illustrations 3.1a and b and 2.3)**.

4 Set an ohmmeter or multimeter to the ohms x 1 scale and measure the resistance between the primary circuit terminals on the coil **(see illustration)**; on K7 models onward make the test at the two-pin wire connector. This will give a resistance reading for the primary windings of the coil and should be consistent with the value given in the Specifications at the beginning of the Chapter.

5 To check the secondary windings, set the meter to the K-ohm scale. On X to K6 models, connect one meter probe to the spark plug socket in the cap and the other probe to a primary circuit terminal on the coil **(see illustration)**. On K7 models onward, connect the meter probes between the spark plug socket in each cap. This will give a resistance reading for the secondary windings of the coil and should be consistent with the value given in the Specifications at the beginning of the Chapter. On X to K2 models, if the reading is not within the specified range, unscrew the cap from the end of the HT lead and repeat the measurement. If the reading is now as specified, then the cap could be faulty. To test the cap, measure the resistance between the lead socket and the plug socket; this should be around 5 K-ohms.

6 The coils can be tested further using a peak voltage adapter (Pt. No. 09900-25008) in conjunction with a multimeter. If this equipment is available, first pull the leads off the spark plugs and connect them to spare plugs that are known to be good. Lay the plugs against the cylinder head with the threads contacting it. Ensure that the primary circuit wiring connectors are securely connected to the coils. On X, Y, K1 and K2 models, to test the front cylinder coil, connect the positive (+) probe of the test equipment to the black/yellow wire terminal on the coil and connect the negative (–) probe to a suitable earth (ground) point. On K3-on models, to test the front cylinder coil, connect the positive (+) probe of the test equipment to the white/blue wire terminal on the coil and connect the negative (–) probe to a suitable earth (ground) point.

7 Check that the kill switch is in the RUN position and the transmission is in neutral, then turn the ignition switch ON. Note the initial voltage reading on the meter, then pull the clutch lever in and turn the engine over on the starter motor. Note the ignition coil peak voltage reading on the meter.

8 Repeat the test for the rear cylinder coil. On X, Y, K1 and K2 models, connect the positive (+) probe of the test equipment to the white wire terminal on the coil and connect the negative (–) probe to a suitable earth (ground) point. On K3-on models, connect the positive (+) probe of the test equipment to the black wire terminal on the coil and connect the negative (–) probe to a suitable earth (ground) point.

9 Once both readings have been noted, turn the ignition switch off and disconnect the meter. If the peak voltage readings are lower than the specified minimum (and the coils have proven good when tested as above) then a fault is present somewhere else in the ignition system circuit (see Section 2); note that the peak voltage readings for each coil can be different but each one must exceed the specified minimum.

10 If the peak voltage readings are as specified but the plug does not spark, then the ignition HT coil, HT lead or plug cap are faulty. In order to determine conclusively that an ignition coil is defective, it should be tested by a Suzuki dealer. If the coil is confirmed to be faulty, it must be renewed; the coil is a sealed unit and cannot therefore be repaired.

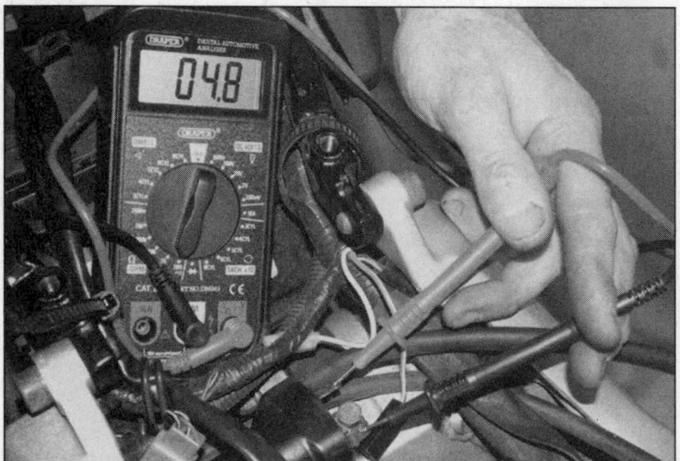

3.4 To test the HT coil primary resistance, connect the multimeter leads between the primary circuit terminals

3.5 To test the HT coil secondary resistance, connect the multimeter leads between the spark plug socket and a primary terminal – X to K6 models

4.2 Coil/sensor wiring connector (arrowed)

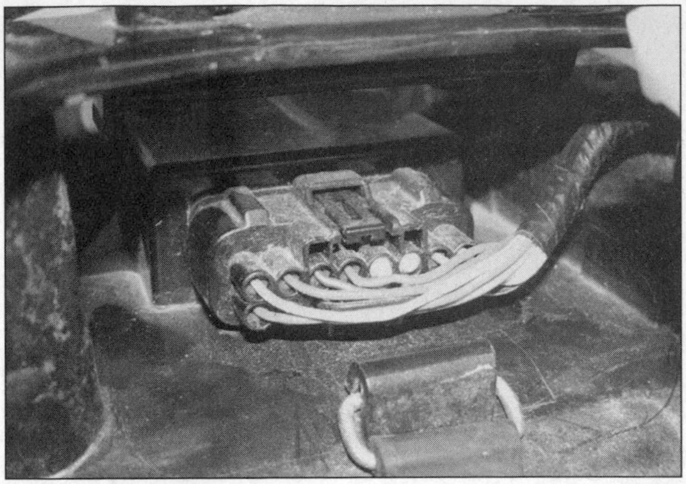

5.3a Disconnect the wiring connector . . .

Removal

11 Raise the fuel tank (see Chapter 4A or 4B).

12 Mark the locations of all wires and leads, then disconnect the primary circuit wiring connectors from the coil and pull the cap off the spark plug **(see illustrations 3.1a and b and 2.3)**.

13 Unscrew the bolts securing the coil and remove it.

Installation

14 Installation is the reverse of removal. Make sure the wiring connectors and HT leads are securely connected.

4 Pulse generator coil and crankshaft position sensor

Note: *The pulse generator coil fitted to X, Y, K1 and K2 models and the crankshaft position sensor fitted to K3-on models perform similar functions in the ignition system. The check and renewal procedures are the same for both, noting the different readings given in the Specifications section of this Chapter.*

Check

1 Remove the seat cowling (see Chapter 8).

2 Trace the wiring back from the coil or sensor, mounted in the alternator cover on the left-hand side of the engine, to the wiring connector and disconnect it **(see illustration)**. Perform the following check(s).

3 Using an ohmmeter check for continuity between each of the connector terminals on the coil/sensor side of the connector and earth (ground). If there is continuity between either terminal and earth (ground) then the coil/sensor is faulty.

4 Measure the resistance between the terminals in the wiring connector (coil/sensor side). If the reading is widely different to that specified at the beginning of the Chapter, first check the connector and the wiring between the connector and the coil/sensor itself (see below to access it). If the wiring is good, the coil/sensor is faulty.

5 The coil/sensor can be tested further using a peak voltage adapter (Pt. No. 09900-25008) in conjunction with a multimeter. If this equipment is available, make the following test on the coil/sensor side of the wiring connector. On X, Y, K1 and K2 models, connect the positive (+) probe of the test equipment to the green wire terminal and the negative (–) probe to the white terminal. On K3-on models, connect the positive (+) probe of the test equipment to the blue wire terminal and the negative (–) probe to the green terminal.

6 Check that the kill switch is in the RUN position and the transmission is in neutral, then turn the ignition switch ON. Note the initial voltage reading on the meter, then pull the clutch lever in and turn the engine over on the starter motor. Note the peak voltage reading on the meter.

7 If this reading is below the specified minimum, the coil/sensor is faulty and must be renewed. If the reading is good, check for a fault in the wiring harness between the coil/sensor connector and the ignition control unit (X, Y, K1 and K2 models) or engine control module (K3-on models). Refer to the *Wiring diagrams* at the end of Chapter 9 and check the wiring for continuity, and check the connectors themselves for loose or broken terminals.

5.3b . . . then undo the screws (arrowed) and remove the ignition control unit – X, Y, K1 and K2 models

Renewal

8 The pulse generator coil/crankshaft position sensor is integral with the alternator stator. If the coil/sensor is faulty, the complete stator assembly must be renewed. Refer to Chapter 9 for details.

5 Ignition control unit (X, Y, K1 and K2 models)

Check

1 If the tests shown in the preceding Sections have failed to isolate the cause of an ignition fault, it is possible that the ignition control unit (ICU) is faulty. No details are available for checking the ICU on home workshop equipment. Take the machine to a Suzuki dealer for testing.

Removal and installation

2 Remove the tail light (see Chapter 9).

3 Disconnect the wiring connector from the ICU, then undo the two screws and remove it **(see illustrations)**.

4 Installation is the reverse of removal. Make sure the wiring connector is correctly and securely connected.

6 Engine control module (K3-on models)

Check

1 If the testing procedures described in this Chapter and Chapter 4B indicate that all ignition and fuel injection system components are functioning correctly , yet a fault exists, take the machine to a Suzuki dealer for testing. No details are available for checking

the engine control module (ECM) on home workshop equipment.

Removal and installation

2 To remove the ECM, first remove the rider's seat (see Chapter 8) and disconnect the battery negative (-ve) lead.

3 The ECM is located to the rear of the battery – disconnect the multi-pin wiring connector from the unit and remove it **(see illustration 2.2a)**. On ABS-equipped models, the ECM is located forward of the battery carrier.

4 Installation is the reverse of removal. Make sure the wiring connectors are clean and secure.

7 Ignition timing (X, Y, K1 and K2 models)

General information

1 Since it is not possible to adjust the ignition timing and since no component is subject to mechanical wear, there is no provision for any checks. While in theory it is possible to check the timing dynamically (engine running) using a stroboscopic lamp, the firing point at idle is not actually marked on the alternator rotor. However if you have a degree disc and feel it is absolutely necessary to check the timing it is possible to mark your own at 5° BTDC (before top dead centre) for the cylinder being checked, i.e. 5° before the F mark for the front cylinder and 5° before the R mark for the rear cylinder – unscrew the timing inspection cap in the alternator cover to see the valve timing marks. Suzuki do not provide a specification for the full advance angle for the timing.

2 The inexpensive neon lamps should be adequate in theory, but in practice may produce a pulse of such low intensity that the timing mark remains indistinct. If possible, one of the more precise xenon tube lamps should be used, powered by an external source of the appropriate voltage. **Note:** *Do not use the machine's own battery as an incorrect reading may result from stray impulses within the machine's electrical system.*

Check

3 Warm the engine up to normal operating temperature then stop it.

4 Unscrew the timing mark inspection cap from the alternator cover **(see illustration)**. Check the condition of the sealing washer and discard it if it is damaged, deformed or deteriorated.

5 The static timing mark with which your own firing point mark should align is a notch in the top of the inspection hole.

HAYNES HiNT ***The rotor timing mark can be highlighted with white paint to make it more visible under the stroboscope light.***

6 Connect the timing light to the front cylinder HT lead as described in the manufacturer's instructions.

7 Start the engine and aim the light at the static timing mark.

8 With the machine idling at the specified speed, your firing point mark should align with the static timing mark.

9 Slowly increase the engine speed whilst observing the timing mark. The timing mark should move clockwise, increasing in relation to the engine speed until it reaches full advance. Perform the same check for the rear cylinder, attaching the light to the rear HT lead.

10 As already stated, there is no means of adjustment of the ignition timing on these machines. If the ignition timing is incorrect, or suspected of being incorrect, one of the ignition system components is at fault, and the system must be tested as described in the preceding Sections of this Chapter.

11 Install the timing inspection cap using a new sealing washer if necessary, and tighten it to the specified torque setting.

8 Throttle position sensor (X, Y, K1 and K2 models)

Note: *For K3-on models, refer to Chapter 4B, Section 11.*

Check

1 The throttle position sensor (TPS) is mounted on the right-hand side of the rear carburettor. Raise the fuel tank for access (see Chapter 4A).

2 Disconnect the sensor wiring connector **(see illustration 8.5)**. Using a multimeter set to the K-ohm scale, connect the probes to the top left and bottom terminals on the sensor wiring connector as shown **(see illustration – meter connections A)**. If the resistance reading obtained is not within the range specified at the beginning of the Chapter, take the sensor to a Suzuki dealer for testing. If it is confirmed to be faulty, a new one must be installed; the sensor is a sealed unit and cannot therefore be repaired.

3 Check the sensor visually for cracks and other damage.

4 Using a multimeter set to resistance or a continuity tester, check for continuity between the terminals of the sensor wiring connector (loom side) and the corresponding terminals on the ignition control unit connector. There should be continuity between each terminal. If not, this is probably due to a damaged or broken wire between the connectors; pinched or broken wires can usually be repaired.

Removal

Caution: Suzuki advise against removing the sensor from the carburettors unless absolutely necessary.

5 The throttle position sensor is mounted on the right-hand side of the rear carburettor. Raise the fuel tank for access (see Section 2).

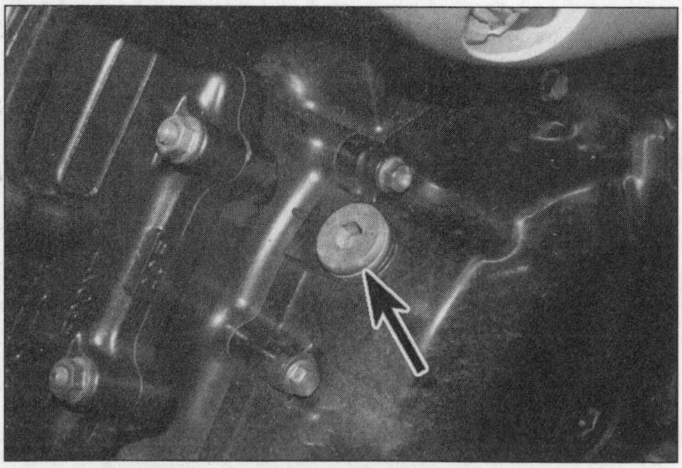

7.4 Unscrew the timing inspection cap (arrowed)

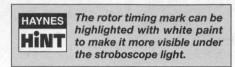

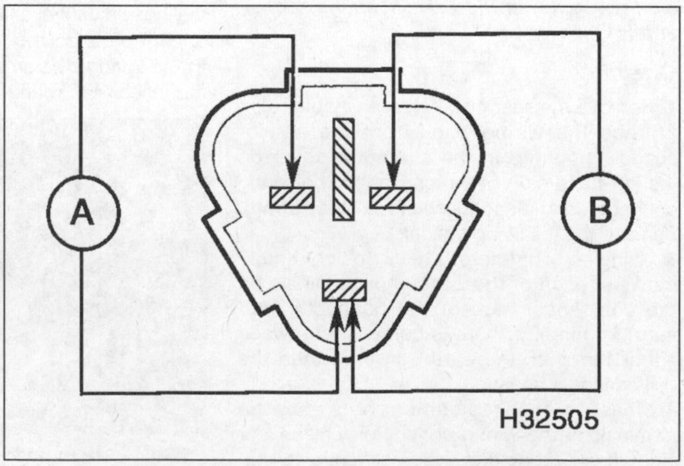

8.2 Throttle position sensor test meter connections

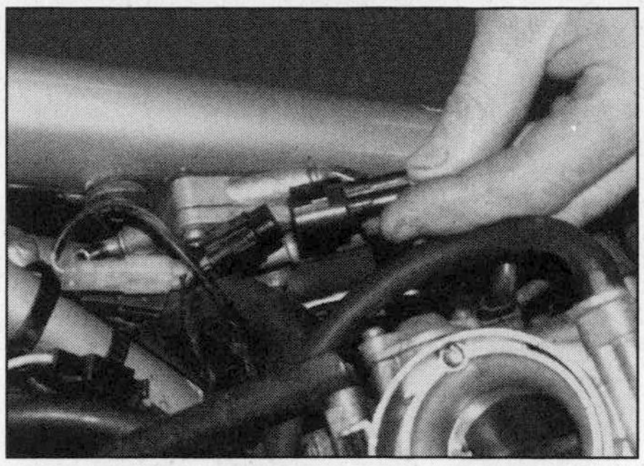

8.5 Disconnect the wiring connector

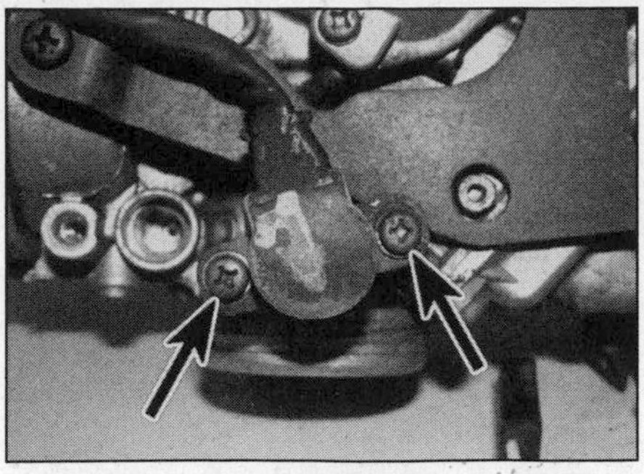

8.6 Throttle position sensor screws (arrowed)

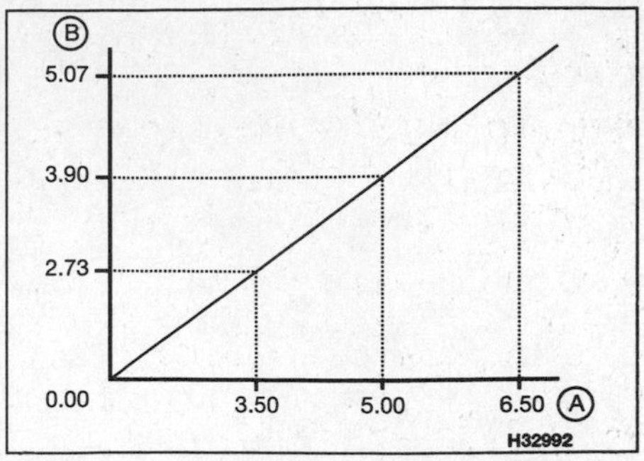

8.8 Throttle position sensor set-up

Disconnect the sensor wiring connector **(see illustration)**.

6 Before removing the mounting screws, mark or scribe lines on the sensor to indicate the exact position of the screws in relation to it **(see illustration)**. Remove the screws and remove the sensor, noting how it fits.

Installation

7 Install the sensor, making sure it engages correctly with the throttle shaft. Thread the two screws into position, but only secure them finger-tight at this stage. If the original sensor is being reinstalled, realign the marks made prior to removal. Before the sensor screws are tightened, the position of the sensor body must be set as follows.

8 Suzuki specify that the resistance value across terminals B should be 78% of the resistance value across terminals A (connect test meter as shown in illustration 8.2) with the throttle held fully open. For example, if value A is 5 ohms with the throttle fully open, then value B should be 3.9 ohms **(see illustration)**. Calculate 78% of value A and compare the result with value B; If necessary, move the sensor body position until value B is correct. Tighten the sensor screws to the specified torque setting, making sure the position of the sensor is not disturbed.

9 Connect the sensor wiring connector **(see illustration 8.5)** and lower the fuel tank.

Chapter 6
Frame, suspension and final drive

Contents

Degrees of difficulty

Easy, suitable for novice with little experience

Fairly easy, suitable for beginner with some experience

Fairly difficult, suitable for competent DIY mechanic

Difficult, suitable for experienced DIY mechanic

Very difficult, suitable for expert DIY or professional

Specifications

Front forks

Fork oil type	10W fork oil or SS8 suspension fluid
Fork oil capacity	
X, Y and K1 models	
US models	491 cc
European models	489 cc
K2 models	
US models	480 cc
European models	478 cc
K3-on models	
SV650 models	490 cc
SV650SX to SK6 models	488 cc
SV650SK7-on models	485 cc
Fork oil level*	
X, Y and K1 models	
US models	102 mm
European models	104 mm
K2 models	
US models	113 mm
European models	115 mm
K3-on models	
SV650 models	92 mm
SV650S models	94 mm
Fork spring free length	
X, Y, K1 and K2 models	
Standard	314.6 mm
Service limit	308 mm
K3-on models	
SV650 models	
Standard	429 mm
Service limit	420 mm
SV650S models	
Standard	437.4 mm
Service limit	428 mm
Fork tube runout limit	0.2 mm

**Oil level is measured from the top of the tube with the fork spring removed and the leg fully compressed.*

Rear suspension

Swingarm pivot bolt runout (max)	0.3 mm

Final drive

Drive chain slack and lubricant	see Chapter 1
Drive chain	
Type	DID 525V8
Length	
SV650 models	110 links
SV650S models	108 links
ABS models	114 links
Sprocket sizes	
SV650 models and SV650SK7-on models	15T front, 45T rear
SV650SX to SK6 models	15T front, 44T rear

Torque settings

Brake hose banjo bolt	23 Nm
Brake torque arm nuts	35 Nm
Clutch lever bracket clamp bolt	10 Nm
Footrest bracket bolts	23 Nm
Footrest holder bolt	39 Nm
Fork damper rod bolt	
X, Y, K1 and K2 models	30 Nm
K3-on models	20 Nm
Fork top bolt	23 Nm
Fork bottom yoke clamp bolts	23 Nm
Fork top yoke clamp bolts	23 Nm
Front brake master cylinder clamp bolts	10 Nm
Front sprocket nut	145 Nm
Handlebar clamp bolts (SV650)	23 Nm
Handlebar clamp bolts (SV650S)	23 Nm
Handlebar holder nuts (SV650)	45 Nm
Handlebar positioning bolts (SV650S)	10 Nm
Rear sprocket nuts	60 Nm
Shock absorber mounting bolts/nut	50 Nm
Side stand bracket bolts (K3-on models)	100 Nm
Steering stem adjuster locknut	80 Nm
Steering stem adjuster nut preload	45 Nm
Steering stem nut	
X, Y, K1 and K2 models	65 Nm
K3-on models	90 Nm
Suspension linkage bolts/nuts	78 Nm
Swingarm pivot bolt	15 Nm
Swingarm pivot bolt locknut	90 Nm
Swingarm pivot bolt nut	100 Nm

1 General information

All models have an aluminium truss frame with the engine acting as a stressed member.

Front suspension is by a pair of 41 mm oil-damped telescopic forks. On K2 -on models, the forks are adjustable for spring pre-load.

At the rear, a box-section aluminium swingarm acts on a single shock absorber via a three-way linkage. The shock absorber is adjustable for spring pre-load on all models.

The drive to the rear wheel is by chain and sprockets.

2 Frame

1 The frame should not require attention unless accident damage has occurred. In most cases, frame renewal is the only satisfactory remedy for such damage. A few frame specialists have the jigs and other equipment necessary for straightening the frame to the required standard of accuracy, but even then there is no simple way of assessing to what extent the frame may have been over stressed.

2 After the machine has accumulated a lot of miles, the frame should be examined closely for signs of cracking or splitting at the welded joints. Loose engine mount bolts can cause ovaling or fracturing of the mounting tabs. Minor damage can often be repaired by welding, depending on the extent and nature of the damage.

3 Remember that a frame which is out of alignment will cause handling problems. If misalignment is suspected as the result of an accident, it will be necessary to strip the machine completely so the frame can be thoroughly checked.

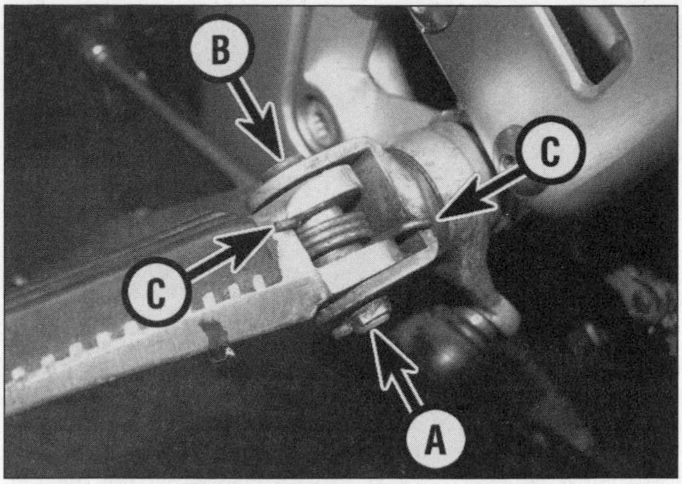

3.1 Remove the split pin and washer (A) and withdraw the pivot pin (B), noting the return spring ends (C)

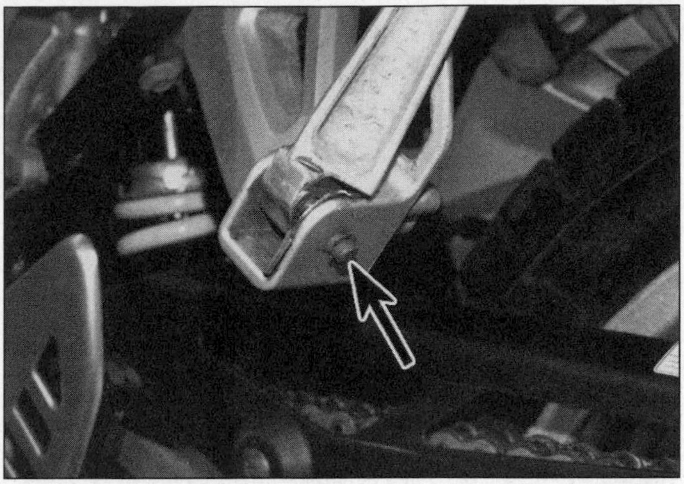

3.2a Remove the E-clip (arrowed) . . .

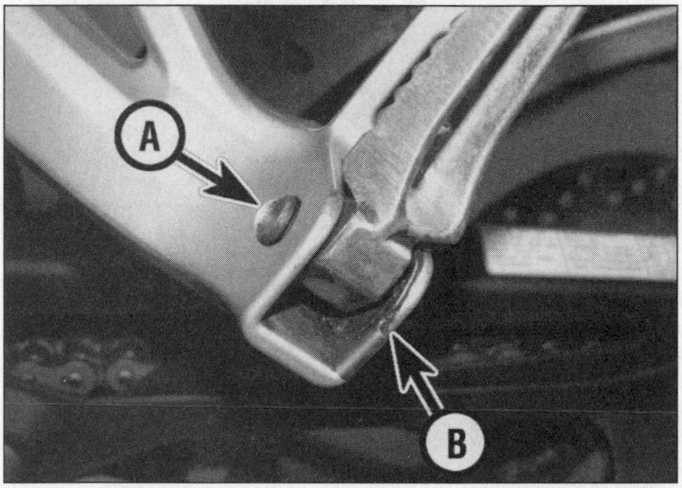

3.2b . . . then withdraw the pivot pin (A) and remove the footrest, noting the detent assembly (B)

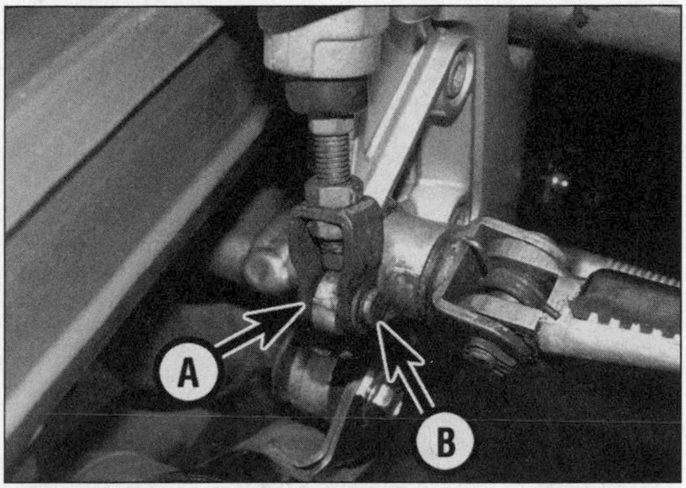

3.4 Remove the split pin and washer (A), then withdraw the clevis pin (B)

3 Footrests, brake pedal and gearchange lever

Footrests

1 On the front footrests, remove the split pin and washer, or E-clip, from the bottom of the pivot pin, then withdraw the pin and remove the footrest, noting how the return spring ends locate **(see illustration)**.

2 On the rear footrests, remove the E-clip from the bottom of the pivot pin, then withdraw the pin and remove the footrest, noting how the detent plate, ball and spring are fitted **(see illustrations)**. Take care not to let the spring and ball ping out.

3 Installation is the reverse of removal. Apply some grease to the pivot pin.

Brake pedal

Removal

4 Remove the split pin and washer from the clevis pin securing the brake pedal to the master cylinder pushrod **(see illustration)**. Withdraw the clevis pin and separate the pushrod from the pedal.

5 Unhook the brake pedal return spring and the brake light switch spring from the hook on the pedal **(see illustration)**.

6 Unscrew the footrest holder bolt on the inside of the bracket **(see illustration 3.5)**. Withdraw the footrest assembly from the bracket, noting how it locates, then remove the thrust washer and slide the pedal off its pivot on the holder.

Installation

7 Installation is the reverse of removal, noting the following:

- Apply grease to the gear lever pivot.
- Make sure the footrest holder locates correctly in the bracket. Tighten the footrest holder bolt to the torque setting specified at the beginning of the Chapter.
- Use a new split pin on the clevis pin securing the brake pedal to the master cylinder pushrod.
- Check the operation of the rear brake light switch (see Chapter 1).

Gearchange lever

Removal

8 Slacken the gearchange lever linkage rod locknuts, then unscrew the rod and separate it from the lever and the arm (the rod is reverse-threaded on one end and so will

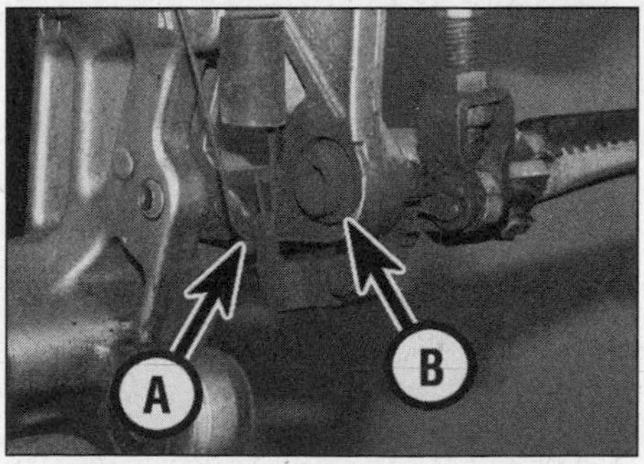

3.5 Unhook the spring ends (A), then unscrew the footrest holder bolt (B)

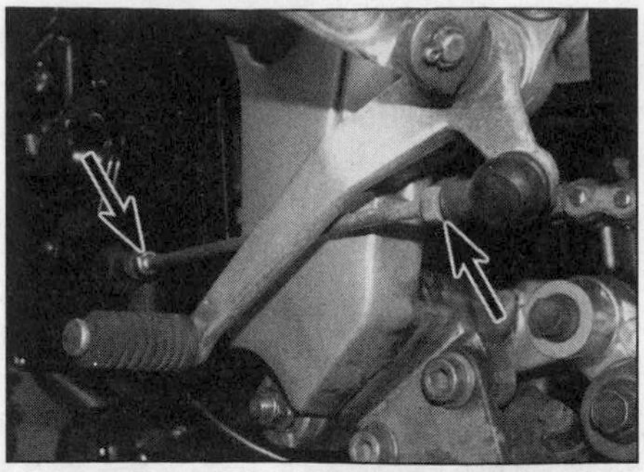

3.8 Slacken the locknuts (arrowed) and thread the rod out of the lever and arm

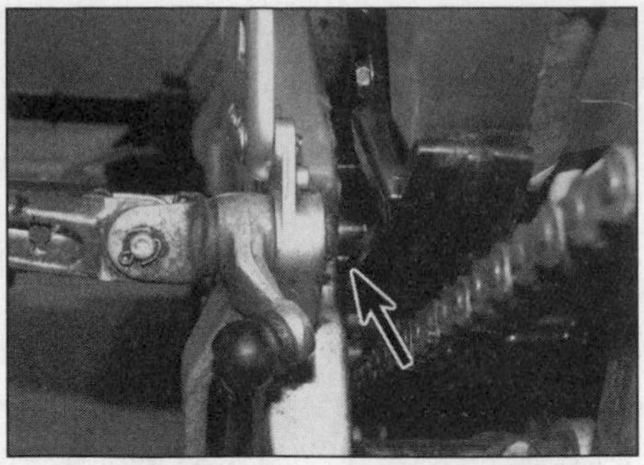

3.9 Unscrew the footrest holder bolt (arrowed)

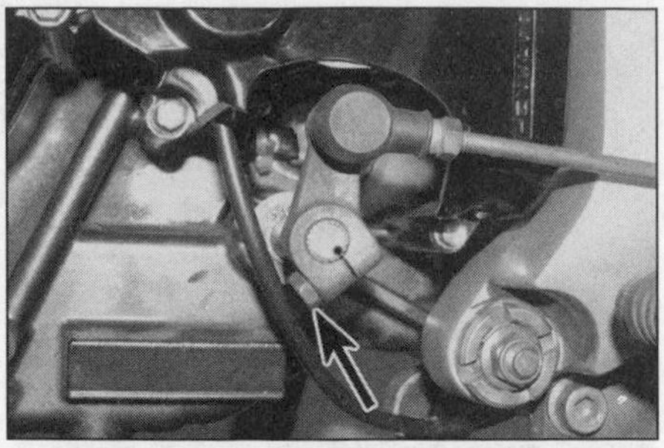

3.10 Note the alignment of the punch mark, then unscrew the bolt (arrowed) and remove the lever

simultaneously unscrew from both lever and arm when turned in the one direction) **(see illustration)**. Note how far the rod is threaded into the lever and arm as this determines the height of the lever relative to the footrest.

9 Unscrew the footrest holder bolt on the inside of the bracket – access is fairly restricted **(see illustration)**. Withdraw the footrest assembly from the bracket, noting how it locates, then slide the lever off its pivot on the holder.

10 To remove the linkage arm, note the alignment of the punch mark on the gearchange shaft end with the slit in the lever clamp, then unscrew the pinch bolt and slide the arm off the shaft **(see illustration)**. If no marks are visible make your own so that the arm can be installed in the correct position.

Installation

11 Installation is the reverse of removal, noting the following:

- If the linkage arm was removed, align the slit in the clamp with the punch mark on the end of the gearchange shaft **(see illustration 3.10)**.
- Apply grease to the gear lever pivot.
- Make sure the footrest holder locates correctly in the bracket. Tighten the footrest holder bolt to the torque setting specified at the beginning of the Chapter.
- Adjust the gear lever height as required by screwing the linkage rod in or out of the lever and arm. Tighten the locknuts securely.

4 Sidestand

Removal

1 The sidestand is attached to a bracket on the frame. Two springs ensure the stand is held in the retracted or extended position.

2 Support the bike on an auxiliary stand.

3 On X, Y, K1 and K2 models, first unhook the stand springs **(see illustration)**. Unscrew the nut from the pivot bolt, then unscrew the bolt and remove the stand **(see illustration)**.

4 On K3-on models, undo the two bolts securing the stand assembly to the frame and remove the stand **(see illustrations)**. If required, unhook the stand springs, noting how they fit **(see illustration)**.

Installation

5 Apply grease to the pivot bolt shank and tighten it securely but not overtight. Install the nut and tighten it securely **(see illustration 4.3b)**.

6 If removed, reconnect the springs and check that they hold the stand securely up when not in use – an accident is almost certain to occur if the stand extends while the machine is in motion **(see illustrations 4.3a and 4.4c)**.

7 On K3-on models, tighten the stand mounting bolts to the specified torque setting.

5 Handlebars and levers

Handlebars – SV650 model

Removal

Note: *The handlebars can be displaced from the top yoke without having to remove the individual assemblies from them – follow Step 8 only. If you do this, cover the instrument cluster with some rag and lay the handlebar assembly on it.*

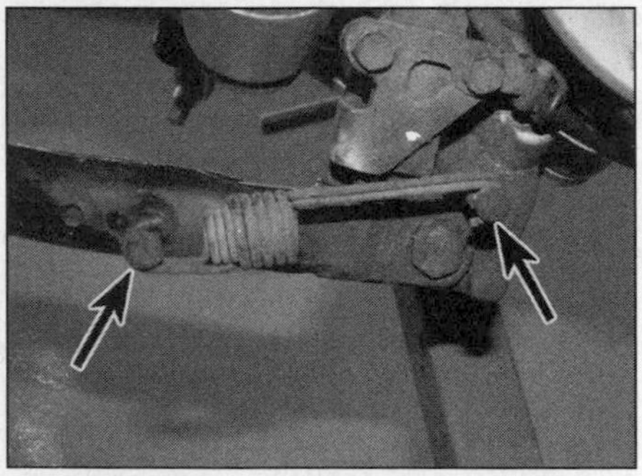

4.3a On X, Y, K1 and K2 models, unhook the spring ends (arrowed) . . .

4.3b . . . then unscrew the nut (arrowed) and the pivot bolt

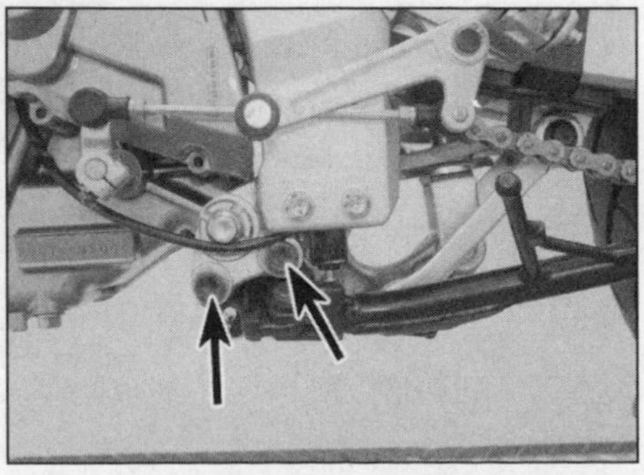

4.4a On K3-on models, undo the stand mounting bolts (arrowed) . . .

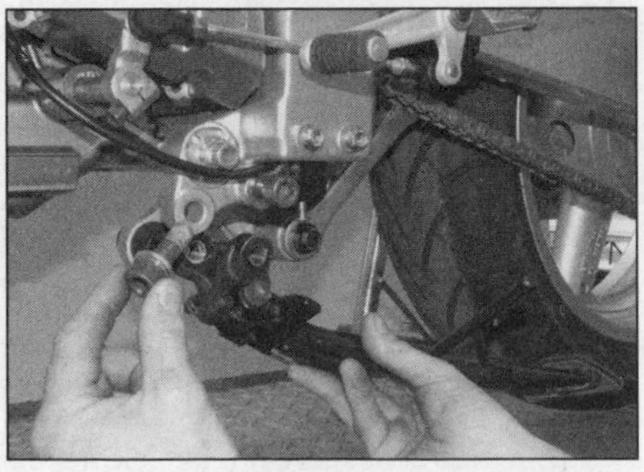

4.4b . . . and remove the stand

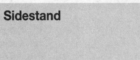

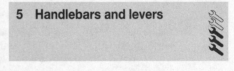

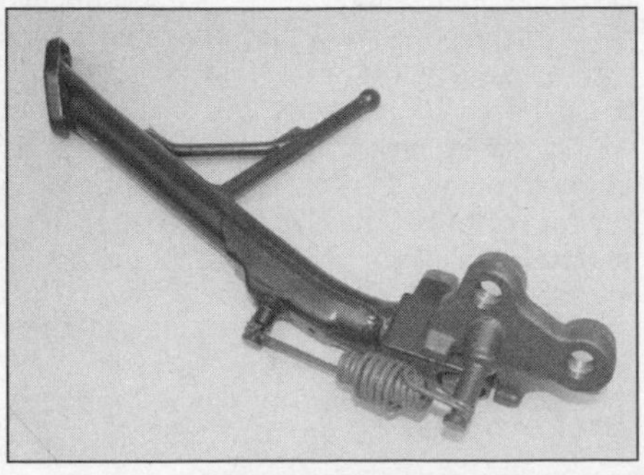

4.4c Location of the stand springs

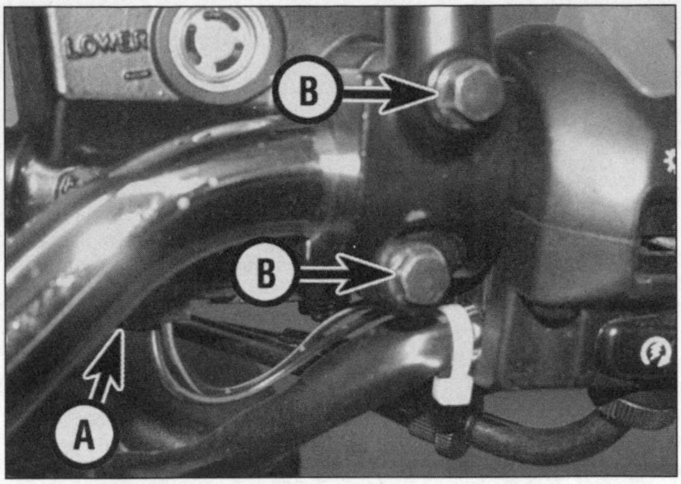

5.3 Disconnect the wiring connectors (A) then unscrew the master cylinder clamp bolts (B) and displace the assembly

5.4 Disconnect the wiring connectors (A) and slacken the clamp bolt (B)

1 Remove the rear view mirrors (see Chapter 8).

2 Refer to Chapter 4A or 4B as applicable and detach the throttle cables and, on X, Y, K1 and K2 models, also the choke cable – these procedures incorporate detaching the handlebar switch housings. Create slack in the throttle cables as necessary using the adjusters (see Chapter 1) to avoid having to detach the cable ends from the throttle cam on the carburettor/throttle body.

3 Disconnect the wires from the brake light switch **(see illustration)**. Unscrew the two front brake master cylinder assembly clamp bolts and position the assembly clear of the handlebar, making sure no strain is placed on the hydraulic hose. Keep the master cylinder reservoir upright to prevent possible fluid leakage.

4 Disconnect the wires from the clutch switch **(see illustration)**. Refer to Chapter 2 and detach the clutch cable from the lever and bracket. Slacken the clutch lever bracket clamp bolt.

5 Unscrew the right handlebar end-weight retaining screw, then remove the weight from the end of the handlebar and slide the throttle twistgrip off the end **(see illustration 5.18)**.

6 Unscrew the left handlebar end-weight retaining screw, then remove the weight from the end of the handlebar and slide off the grip **(see illustration 5.18)**. If the grip has been glued on, you will probably have to slit it with a knife to remove it. Slide the clutch lever assembly off the handlebar.

7 If the handlebar holders are being removed from the top yoke, slacken the nuts securing them on the underside of the yoke now.

8 Carefully prise the blanking caps out of the handlebar clamp bolts **(see illustration)**. Support the handlebars, then unscrew the bolts and remove the clamps and the handlebars **(see illustrations)**. If required, unscrew the nuts on the handlebar holder bolts, then draw the holders out of the top yoke.

Installation

9 Installation is the reverse of removal, noting the following.

- If removed, tighten the handlebar holder nuts after the handlebars are installed, and tighten them to the torque setting specified at the beginning of the Chapter.
- Align the punch mark on the front of the handlebar with the mating surfaces of the left handlebar holder and clamp **(see illustration)**
- On X, Y, K1 and K2 models, fit the handlebar clamps with the punch mark at the back, and tighten the bolts evenly so that the gap between holder and clamp is the same at the front and back, and tighten them to the specified torque setting **(see illustration)**.
- On K3-on models, fit the handlebar clamps with the punch mark at the front. Tighten the

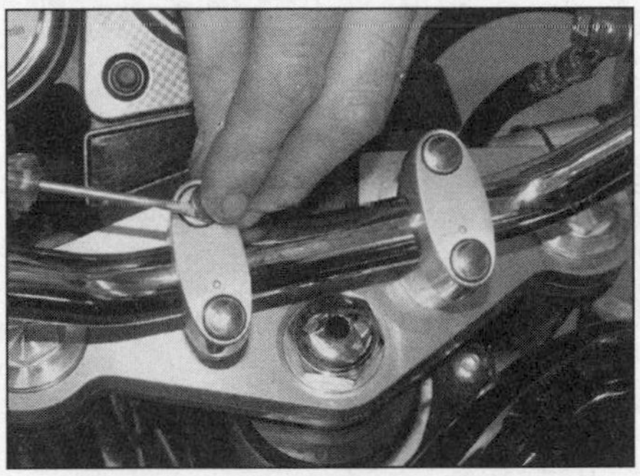
5.8a Prise out the blanking caps . . .

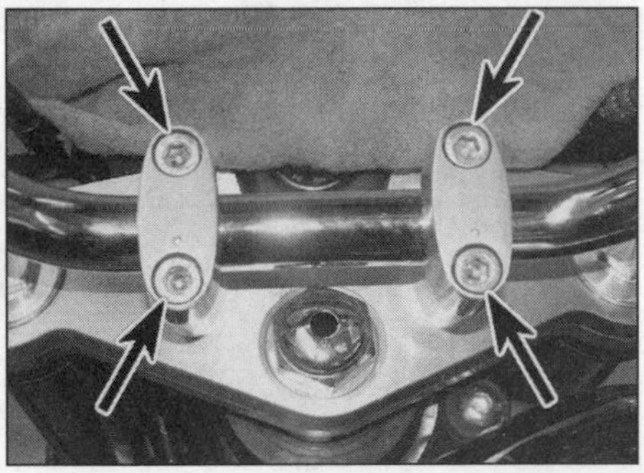
5.8b . . . then unscrew the bolts (arrowed) . . .

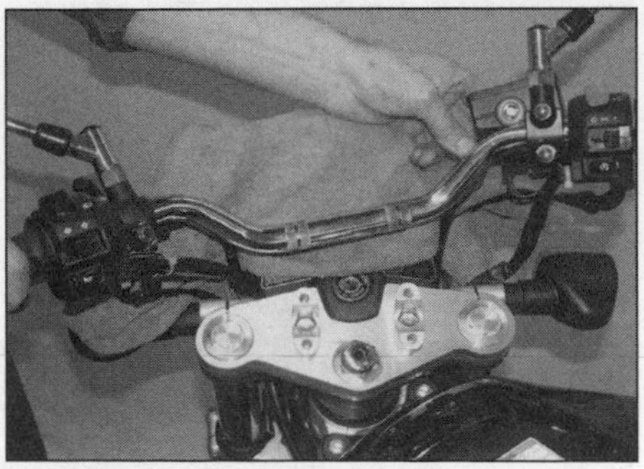
5.8c . . . and displace or remove the handlebars

5.9a Align the punch mark on the handlebar with the mating surface of the holder and clamp

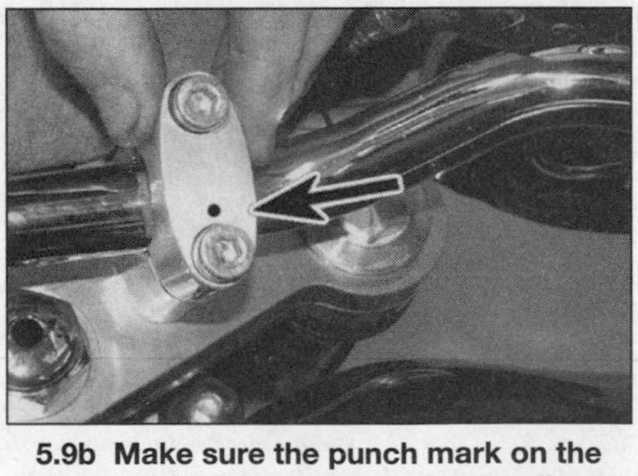
5.9b Make sure the punch mark on the holder is correctly positioned according to model

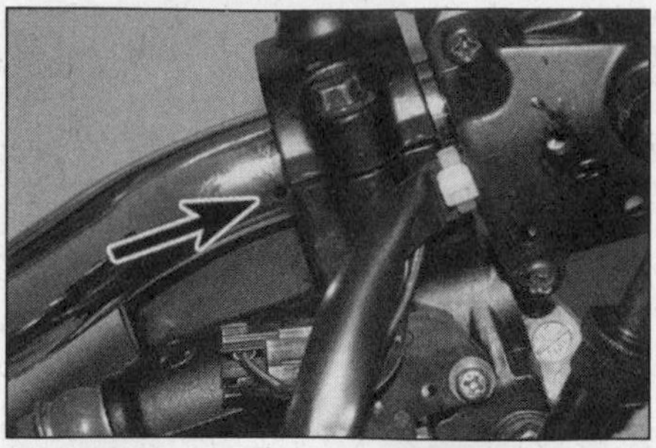

5.9c Align the master cylinder clamp mating surfaces with the punch mark on the handlebar

front bolts first to the specified torque setting, then tighten the rear bolts to the specified torque.

- Apply some grease to the throttle twistgrip section of the handlebar.
- Make sure the front brake master cylinder assembly clamp is installed with the mirror mounting facing up and the clamp mating surfaces aligned with the punch mark on the bottom of the handlebar **(see illustration)**. Tighten the clamp bolts to the specified torque setting, tightening the top bolt first.
- Align the clutch lever bracket clamp mating surfaces with the punch mark on the bottom of the handlebar, and tighten the bolt to the specified torque setting **(see illustration)**.

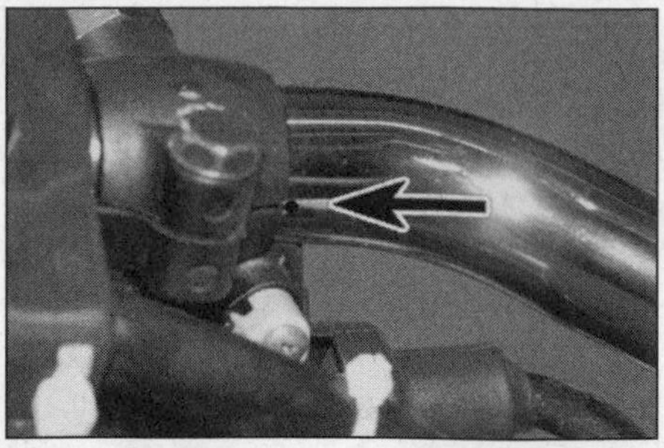

5.9d Align the clutch lever bracket clamp mating surfaces with the punch mark on the handlebar

- Make sure the pin in the top half of each switch housing locates in its hole in the handlebar.
- When installing the handlebar end-weights, use some non-permanent thread locking compound on the screws. If new grips are being fitted, secure them using a suitable adhesive.
- Do not forget to reconnect the front brake light switch and clutch switch wiring connectors.

Handlebars – SV650S model

Right handlebar removal

Note: *The handlebars can be displaced from the top yoke without having to remove all the individual assemblies from them, though the front brake master cylinder must be displaced as there is not enough slack in the brake hose – follow Steps 10, 13, 14 and 15 only.*

10 Disconnect the wires from the brake light switch **(see illustration)**. Unscrew the master cylinder reservoir bracket bolt and the two master cylinder assembly clamp bolts and position the assembly clear of the handlebar, making sure no strain is placed on the hydraulic hose **(see illustration)**. Keep the master cylinder reservoir upright to prevent possible fluid leakage.

11 Unscrew the two handlebar switch housing screws and separate the halves. If required, free the throttle cable ends from the throttle pulley, creating slack in the cable as necessary using the adjusters (see Chapter 1). To avoid having to do this, note that the switch housing and throttle pulley can be slid off the end of the handlebar with the cables still attached after the handlebar has been displaced from the fork.

12 Unscrew the handlebar end-weight retaining screw, then remove the weight from the end of the handlebar **(see illustration 5.18)**. If the throttle cables have been detached, slide the twistgrip off the handlebar.

13 On X, Y, K1 and K2 models, free the handlebar switch wiring from its guide on the top yoke, then unscrew both handlebar

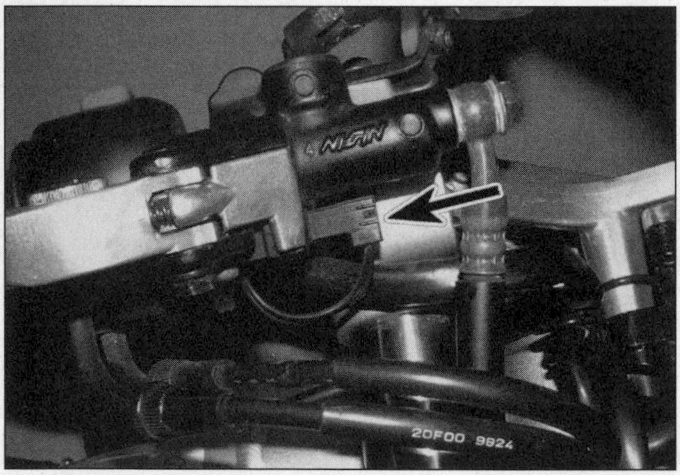

5.10a Disconnect the wiring connectors (arrowed)

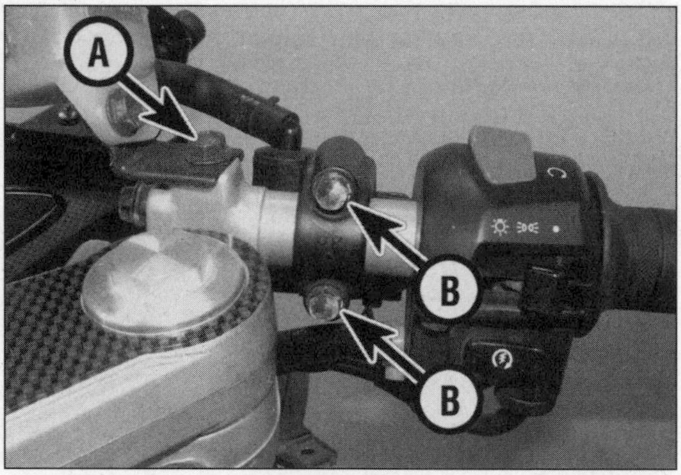

5.10b Unscrew the reservoir bracket bolt (A) and the master cylinder clamp bolts (B)

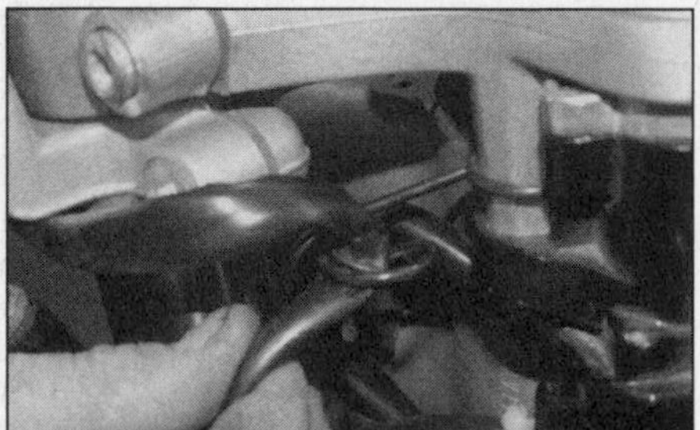

5.13a On X, Y, K1 and K2 models, lift the loom up over the end of the guide . . .

5.13b . . . and slip it out the side . . .

5.13c . . . then unscrew the right . . .

5.13d . . . and the left handlebar positioning bolts

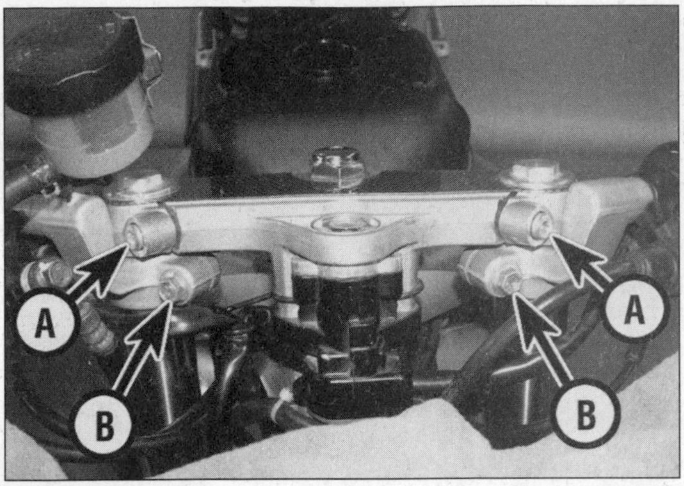

5.14a Slacken the fork clamp bolts (A). Handlebar clamp bolts (B)

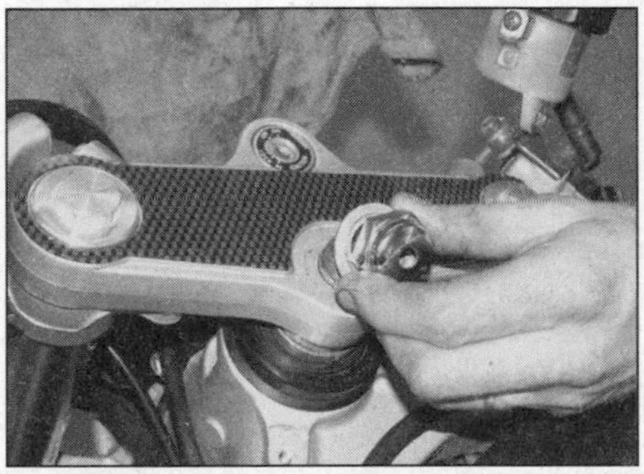
5.14b Unscrew the steering stem nut and remove the washer

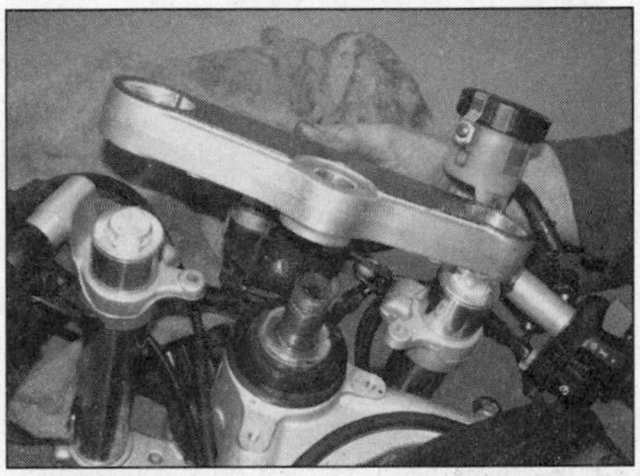
5.14c Ease the yoke up and off the forks

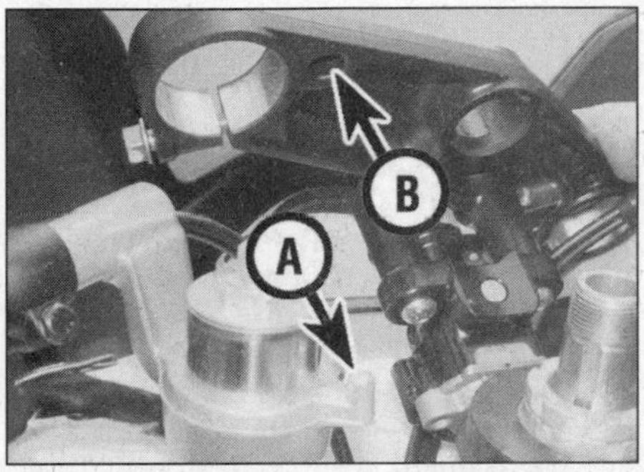

5.14d On K3-on models note how the peg (A) locates in the hole (B)

positioning bolts on the underside of the yoke **(see illustrations)**.

14 Slacken the fork clamp bolts in the top yoke **(see illustration)**. Unscrew the steering stem nut and remove the washer **(see illustration)**. Gently ease the top yoke up and off the forks and position it clear, using a rag to protect other components **(see illustration)**. On K3-on models, note how the peg on the handlebar clamp locates in the underside of the yoke **(see illustration)**.

15 Slacken the handlebar clamp bolt, then ease the handlebar up and off the fork **(see illustrations)**. If required, slide the throttle twistgrip and switch housing assembly off the handlebar.

Left handlebar removal

Note: *The handlebar can be displaced from the top yoke without having to remove the individual assemblies from them – follow Steps 19, 20 and 21 only.*

16 On X, Y, K1 and K2 models, refer to Chapter 4A and detach the choke cable from the lever – this procedure incorporates detaching the handlebar switch housing.

17 Disconnect the wires from the clutch switch **(see illustration)**. Refer to Chapter 2 and detach the clutch cable from the lever and bracket. Slacken the clutch lever bracket clamp bolt **(see illustration)**.

5.15a Slacken the handlebar clamp bolt (arrowed) . . .

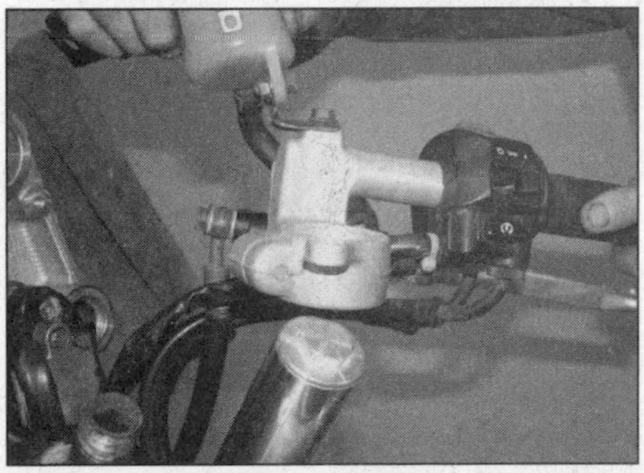
5.15b . . . then ease the handlebar up and off the fork

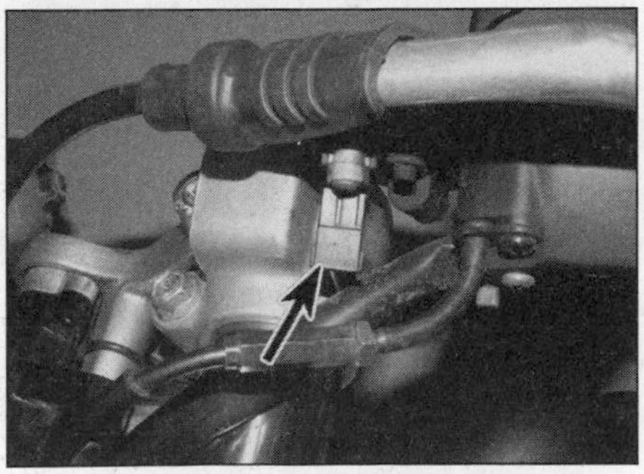
5.17a Disconnect the wiring from the clutch switch (arrowed)

5.17b Slacken the clamp bolt (arrowed)

5.18 Handlebar end-weight screw (arrowed)

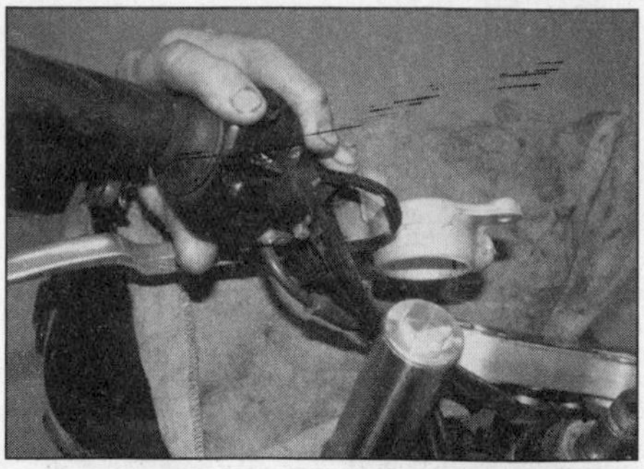

5.21 Ease the handlebar up and off the fork

5.22a Align the master cylinder clamp mating surfaces with the punch mark (arrowed)

5.22b Fit the clamp with its UP mark facing up

18 Unscrew the handlebar end-weight retaining screw, then remove the weight from the end of the handlebar and slide off the grip **(see illustration)**. If the grip has been glued on, you will probably have to slit it with a knife to remove it. Slide the clutch lever assembly off the handlebar.

19 On X, Y, K1 and K2 models, free the handlebar switch wiring from its guide on the top yoke, then unscrew both handlebar positioning bolts on the underside of the yoke **(see illustrations 5.13a, b, c and d)**.

20 Slacken the fork clamp bolts in the top yoke **(see illustration 5.14a)**. Unscrew the steering stem nut and remove the washer **(see illustration 5.14b)**. Gently ease the top yoke up and off the forks and position it clear, using a rag to protect other components **(see illustration 5.14c)**. On K3-on models, note how the peg on the handlebar clamp locates in the underside of the yoke **(see illustration 5.14d)**.

21 Slacken the handlebar clamp bolt **(see illustration 5.14a)**, then ease the handlebar up and off the fork **(see illustration)**.

Installation

22 Installation is the reverse of removal, noting the following.

- Tighten the steering stem nut first, then the fork clamp bolts in the top yoke, then the handlebar positioning bolts if applicable, then the handle-bar clamp bolts, tightening them all to the torque settings specified at the beginning of the Chapter.
- Apply some grease to the throttle twistgrip section of the right handlebar.
- Align the master cylinder clamp mating surfaces with the punch mark on the top of the handlebar **(see illustration)**.
- Make sure the front brake master cylinder assembly clamp is installed with the UP mark facing up **(see illustration)**. Tighten the master cylinder clamp bolts to the specified torque setting, tightening the top bolt first.
- Align the clutch lever assembly clamp mating surfaces with the punch mark on the bottom of the handlebar, and tighten the bolt to the specified torque setting **(see illustration 5.9d)**.
- Make sure the pin in the top half of each switch housing locates in its hole in the handlebar.
- When installing the handlebar end-weights, use some non-permanent thread locking compound on the screws. If new grips are being fitted, secure them using a suitable adhesive.
- Do not forget to reconnect the front brake light switch and clutch switch wiring connectors.

Handlebar levers

23 To free the brake lever, unscrew the nut on the underside of the lever bracket **(see illustration)**. Unscrew the pivot bolt and remove the lever.

24 To free the clutch lever, pull the rubber boot off the clutch cable adjuster. Slacken the adjuster lockring and thread the adjuster fully into the bracket to provide maximum freeplay in the cable **(see illustration)**. Unscrew the nut on the underside of the lever bracket. Unscrew the pivot bolt and remove the lever, detaching the cable end as you do so.

25 Installation of the levers is the reverse of

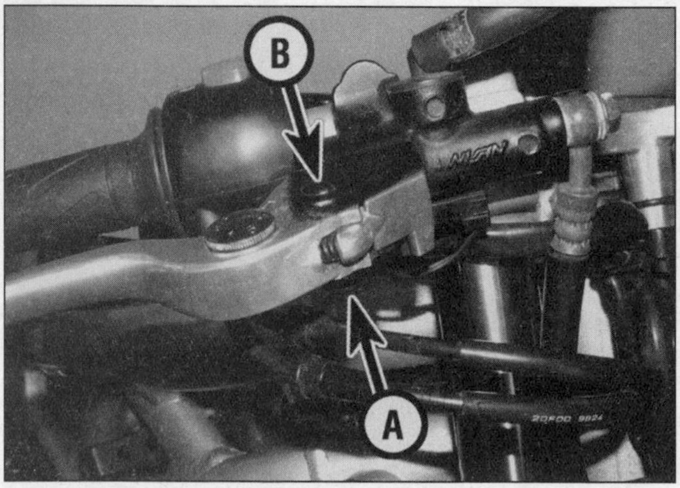

5.23 Unscrew the nut (A), then unscrew the pivot bolt (B) and remove the brake lever

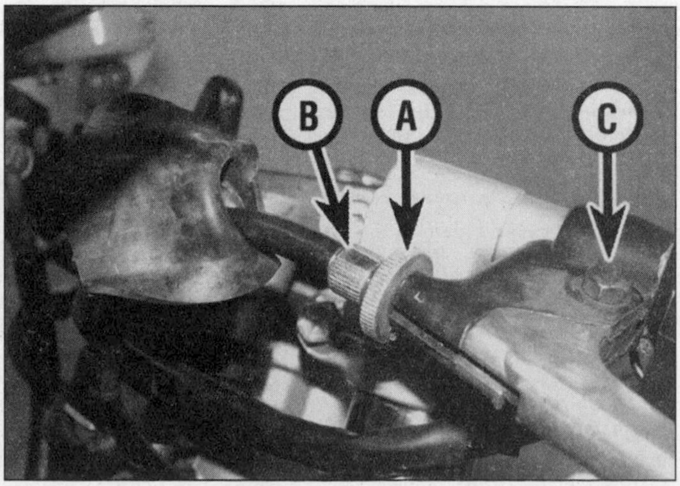

5.24 Slacken the ring (A) and thread the adjuster (B) in. Clutch lever pivot bolt (C)

removal. Apply grease to their pivot bolt shafts and the contact areas between the lever and its bracket. When installing the brake lever, apply silicone grease to the tip of the master cylinder pushrod. When installing the clutch lever apply grease to the cable nipple. Adjust the clutch cable freeplay (see Chapter 1).

6 Forks – removal and installation

Removal

Caution: Although not strictly necessary, before removing the forks it is recommended that the fairing and fairing panels are removed (see Chapter 8). This will prevent accidental damage to the paintwork.

1 On SV650S models, remove the fairing (See Chapter 8).

2 Remove the front wheel (see Chapter 7). Tie the front brake calipers and hoses back so that they are out of the way.

3 Remove the front mudguard (see Chapter 8).

4 On SV650S models, slacken the handlebar clamp bolts **(see illustration 5.14a)**.

5 If applicable, measure the amount of protrusion of the fork tube above the top surface of the top yoke – measure up to the top rim of the tube itself, do not include the top bolt. Record this information as a guide to refitting.

6 Working on one fork at a time, slacken the fork clamp bolt in the top yoke **(see illustration 5.14a)**. If the fork is to be disassembled, or if the fork oil is being changed, it is advisable to slacken the fork top bolt at this stage **(see illustration)**. On K2 models onward, first note the spring pre-load setting, then set it to its minimum amount (see Section 13).

7 Slacken the fork clamp bolts in the bottom yoke, and remove each fork by twisting it and pulling it downwards **(see illustrations)**.

HAYNES HiNT ***If the fork legs are seized in the yokes, spray the area with penetrating oil and allow time for it to soak in before trying again.***

Installation

8 Remove all traces of corrosion from the fork tube and the yokes. Slide the fork up through the bottom yoke, on SV650 models through the headlight assembly holders and on SV650S models through the handlebar clamp, and into the top yoke, making sure all cables, hoses and wiring are routed on the correct side of the fork **(see illustration 6.7b)**.

9 Set the amount of protrusion of the top of the fork tube (not the top of the fork top bolt) above the top yoke as noted on removal. Make sure it is the same on both sides. Note that on X, Y, K1 and K2 SV650 models, Suzuki specify a distance of 3 mm between the top surface of the top yoke and the top of the fork tube for US

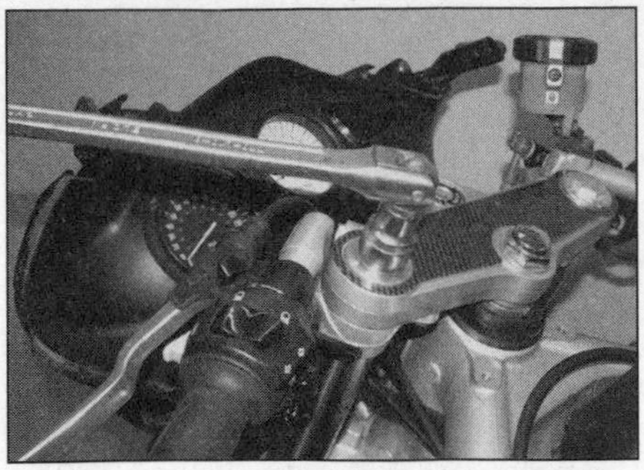

6.6 If required slacken the fork top bolt

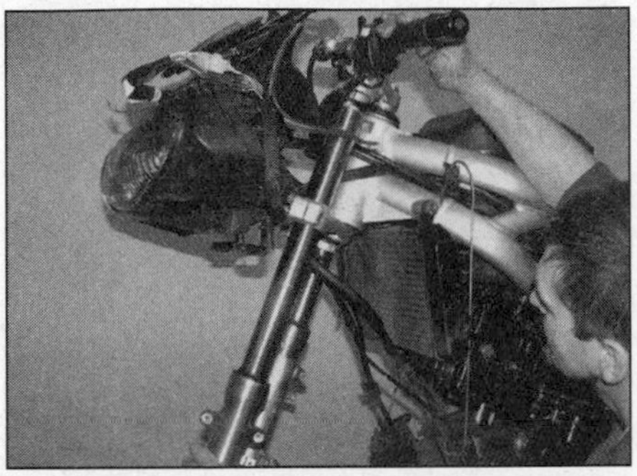

6.7b Draw the fork down and out of the yokes

models, and 6 mm for other market models. On X, Y, K1 and K2 SV650S models and all K3-on models, Suzuki specify that the top of the fork tube should align exactly with the top surface of the top yoke.

10 Tighten the fork clamp bolts in the bottom yoke to the torque setting specified at the beginning of the Chapter **(see illustration 6.7a)**. If the fork has been dismantled or if the fork oil was changed, tighten the fork top bolt to the specified torque setting **(see illustration)**. Now tighten the fork clamp bolt in the top yoke to the specified torque **(see illustration 5.14a)**.

11 On SV650S models, tighten the handlebar clamp bolts to the specified torque setting **(see illustration 5.14a)**.

12 On K2 models onward, set the spring pre-load as required (see Section 13).

13 Install the front mudguard (see Chapter 8), and the front wheel (see Chapter 7). On SV650S models, install the fairing (see Chapter 8).

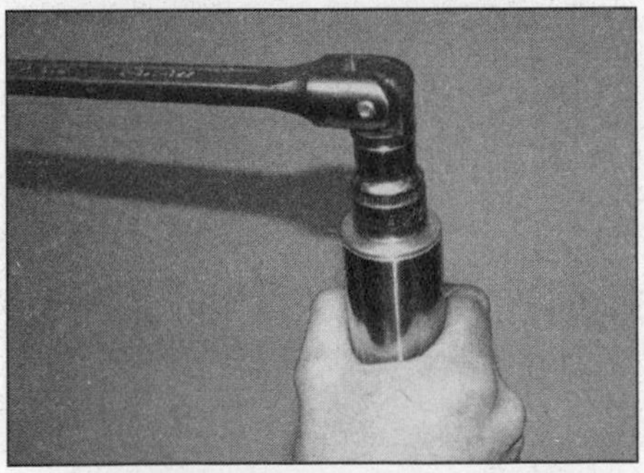

7.2 If not already done, slacken the top bolt

6.7a Bottom yoke fork clamp bolts (arrowed)

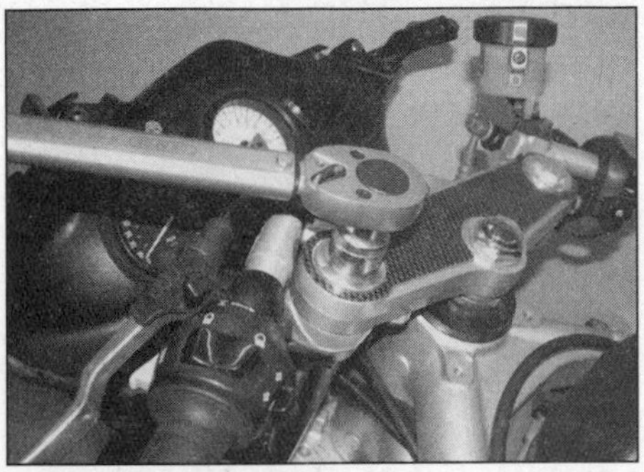

6.10 If required tighten the fork top bolt to the specified torque

14 Check the operation of the front forks and brakes before taking the machine out on the road.

7 Forks – oil change

1 Remove the forks (see Section 6). Always work on the fork legs separately to avoid interchanging parts and thus causing an accelerated rate of wear.

2 If the fork top bolt was not slackened with the fork in situ, carefully clamp the fork tube in a vice equipped with soft jaws, taking care not to overtighten or score its surface, and slacken the top bolt **(see illustration)**.

3 Unscrew the fork top bolt from the top of the fork tube **(see illustration)**. On K2 models onward, remove the pre-load adjuster plate **(see illustration 8.1)**.

7.3 Thread the top bolt out of the tube

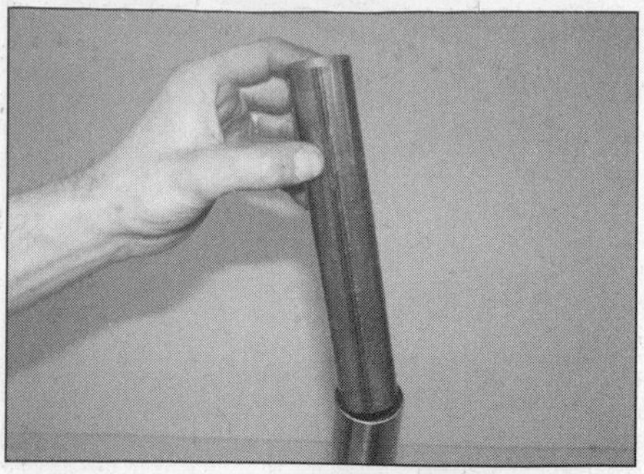
7.4a Remove the spacer . . .

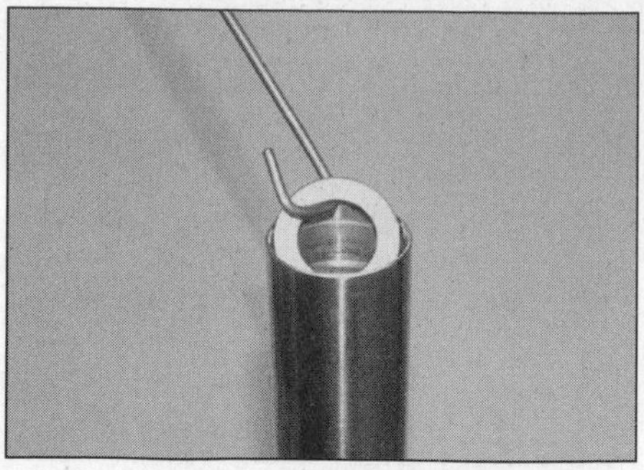
7.4b . . . then hook out the spring seat . . .

7.4c . . . and the spring

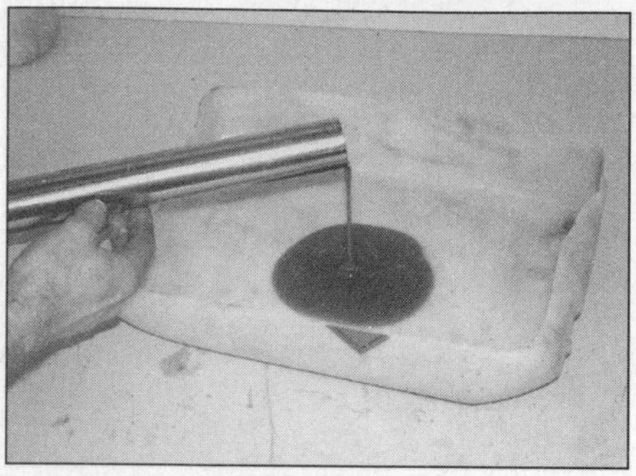
7.5 Invert the fork over a container and pump the tube to expel the oil

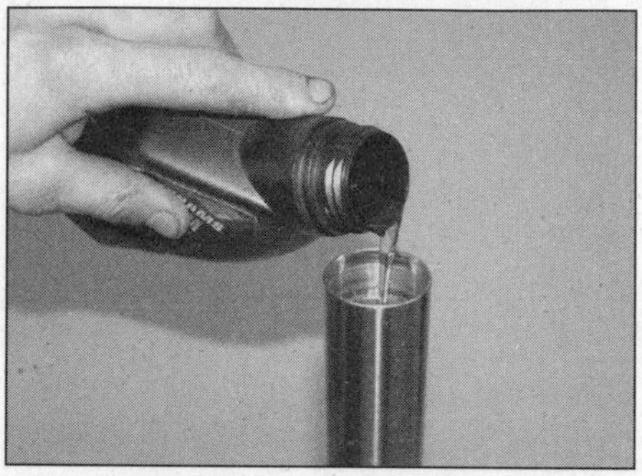
7.6a Pour the oil into the top of the tube

7.6b Measure the oil level and adjust if necessary

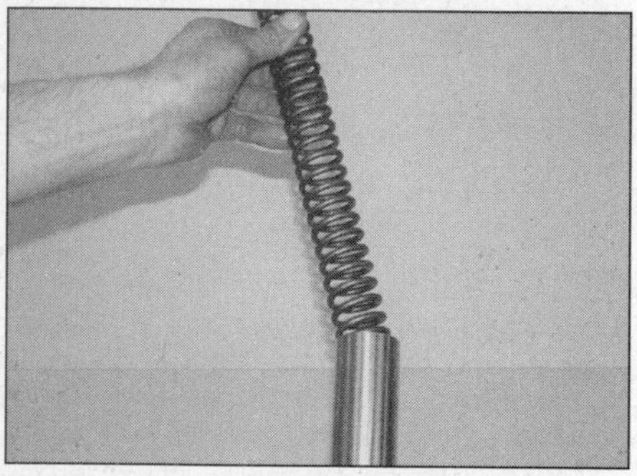
7.7a Install the spring . . .

7.7b . . . the spring seat . . .

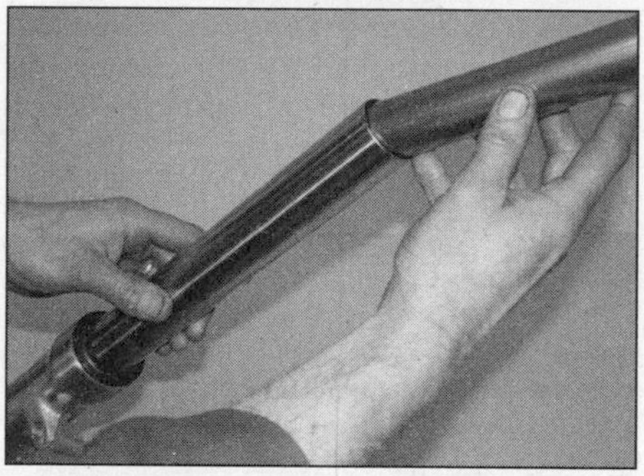
7.7c . . . and the spacer

Warning: The fork spring is pressing on the fork top bolt, though not with any great pressure. Unscrew the bolt carefully, keeping a downward pressure on it and release it slowly.

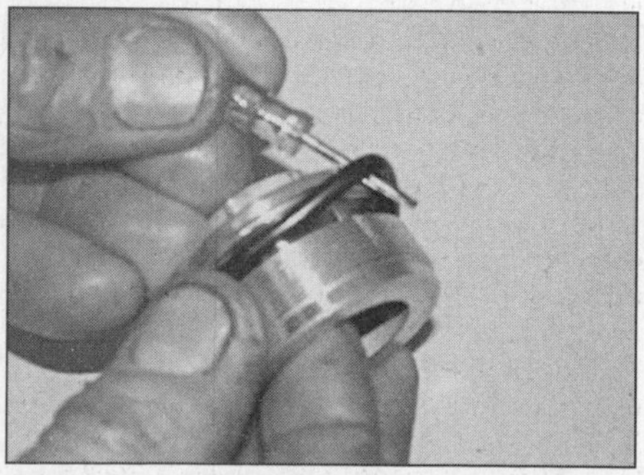
7.8a Fit a new O-ring onto the top bolt . . .

4 Slide the fork tube down into the slider and remove the spacer **(see illustration)**. Using a piece of wire bent over at the end, hook out the spring seat and the spring from the tube **(see illustrations)**.

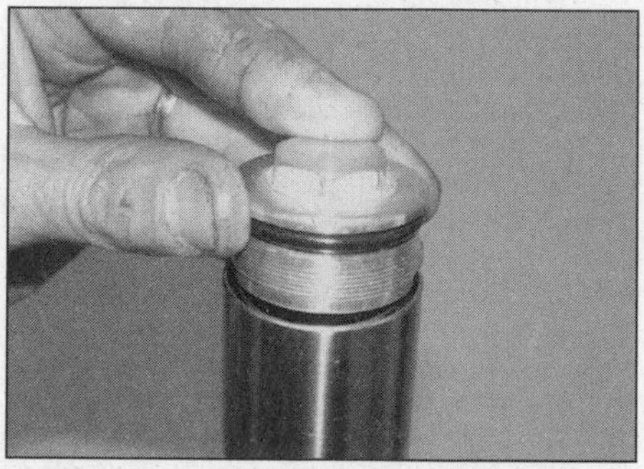
7.8b . . . then thread the bolt into the fork tube

5 Invert the fork over a suitable container and pump the fork tube vigorously to expel as much oil as possible **(see illustration)**. Support the fork upside down in the container for a while to allow as much oil as possible to drain, and pump the fork again.

6 Slowly pour in the specified quantity of the specified grade of fork oil and pump the fork at least ten times to distribute it evenly **(see illustration)**. Fully compress the fork tube into the slider and measure the oil level, and make any adjustment by adding more or tipping some out until the oil is at the level specified at the beginning of the Chapter **(see illustration)**.

7 Clamp the slider in a soft-jawed vice using the brake caliper mounting lugs, taking care not to overtighten and damage them. Pull the fork tube out of the slider as far as possible then install the spring, the spring seat and the spacer **(see illustrations)**. On K2 models onward, fit the pre-load adjuster plate onto the top of the spacer **(see illustration 8.1)**.

8 Fit a new O-ring smeared with fork oil onto the fork top bolt and thread the bolt into the top of the fork tube **(see illustrations)**. Keep the fork tube fully extended whilst doing so. Screw the top bolt carefully into the fork tube making sure it is not cross-threaded. **Note:** *The top bolt can be tightened to the specified torque setting at this stage if the tube is held between the padded jaws of a vice, but do not risk distorting the tube by doing so. A better method is to tighten the top bolt when the fork has been installed in the bike and is securely held in the bottom yoke* ***(see illustration 6.10)****.*

HAYNES HiNT ***Use a ratchet-type tool when installing the fork top bolt. This makes it unnecessary to remove the tool from the bolt whilst threading it in making it easier to maintain a downward pressure on the spring.***

9 Install the forks (see Section 6).

8 Forks – overhaul

Disassembly

1 Remove the forks (see Section 6). Always dismantle the fork legs separately to avoid interchanging parts and thus causing an accelerated rate of wear. Store all components in separate, clearly marked containers **(see illustration)**.

2 Before dismantling the fork, it is advisable to slacken the damper rod bolt now as there is less chance of the damper rotating with it (due to the pressure of the spring). When working on the right-hand fork on X, Y, K1 and K2 models, first remove the axle spacer from the fork. Compress the fork tube in the slider so that the spring exerts maximum pressure on the damper head, then have an assistant slacken the bolt in the base of the fork slider **(see illustration)**. If the bolt does not unscrew, but merely rotates inside the fork tube, note the damper rod can be held as described in Step 7.

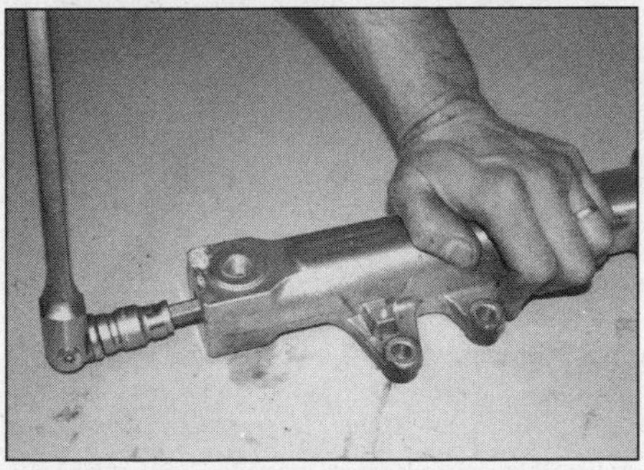

8.2 Slacken the damper rod bolt

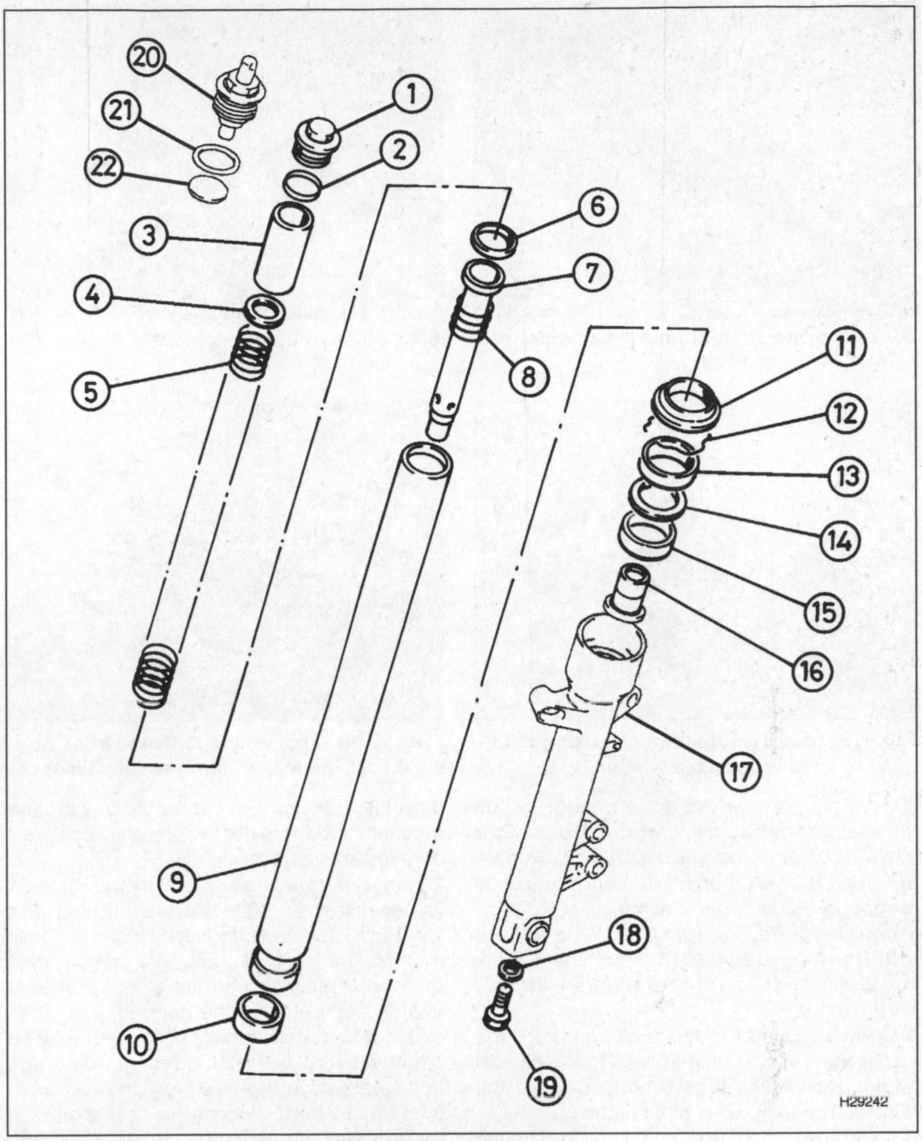

8.1 Front fork components

1 Top bolt (X, Y and K1 models)
2 O-ring (X, Y and K1 models)
3 Spacer
4 Spring seat
5 Spring
6 Piston ring
7 Damper rod
8 Rebound spring
9 Fork tube
10 Bottom bush
11 Dust seal
12 Retaining clip
13 Oil seal
14 Washer
15 Top bush
16 Damper rod seat
17 Slider
18 Sealing washer
19 Damper rod bolt
20 Top bolt (K2-on models)
21 O-ring (K2-on models)
22 Plate (K2-on models)

3 If the fork top bolt was not slackened with the fork in situ, carefully clamp the fork tube in a vice equipped with soft jaws, taking care not to overtighten or score its surface, and slacken the top bolt **(see illustration 7.2)**.

4 Unscrew the fork top bolt from the top of the fork tube **(see illustration 7.3)**. On K2 models onward, remove the pre-load adjuster plate **(see illustration 8.1)**.

Warning: The fork spring is pressing on the fork top bolt, though not with any great pressure. Unscrew the bolt carefully, keeping a downward pressure on it and release it slowly.

5 Slide the fork tube down into the slider and remove the spacer **(see illustration 7.4a)**. Using a piece of wire bent over at the end, hook out the spring seat and the spring from the tube **(see illustrations 7.4b and c)**. Note which way up the spring fits.

6 Invert the fork over a suitable container and pump the fork tube vigorously to expel as much oil as possible **(see illustration 7.5)**.

7 Remove the previously slackened damper rod bolt and its sealing washer from the bottom of the slider **(see illustration)**. Discard the sealing washer as a new one must be used on reassembly. Invert the fork

8.7a Unscrew and remove the damper rod bolt . . .

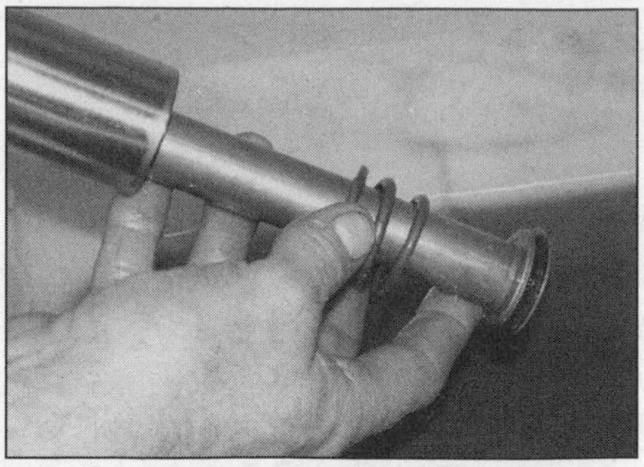
8.7b . . . then tip the damper rod out of the fork

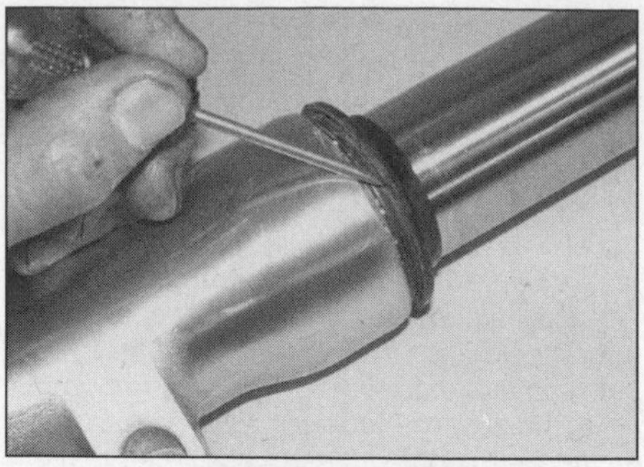
8.8 Prise out the dust seal using a flat-bladed screwdriver

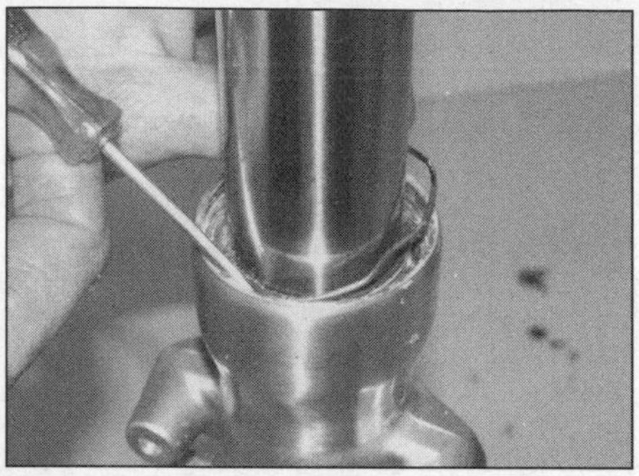
8.9 Prise out the retaining clip using a flat-bladed screwdriver

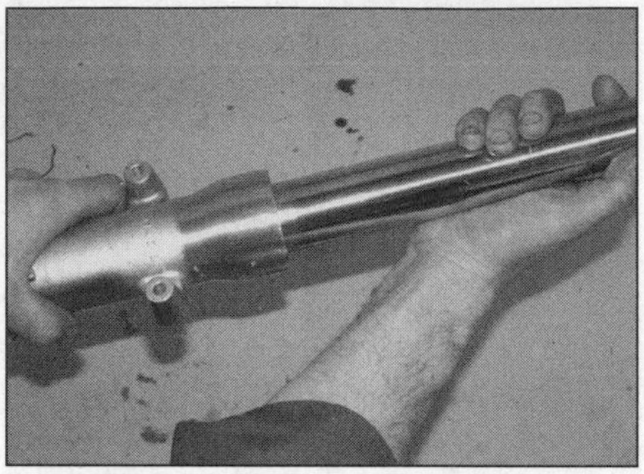
8.10a To separate the fork tube from the slider, pull them apart firmly several times . . .

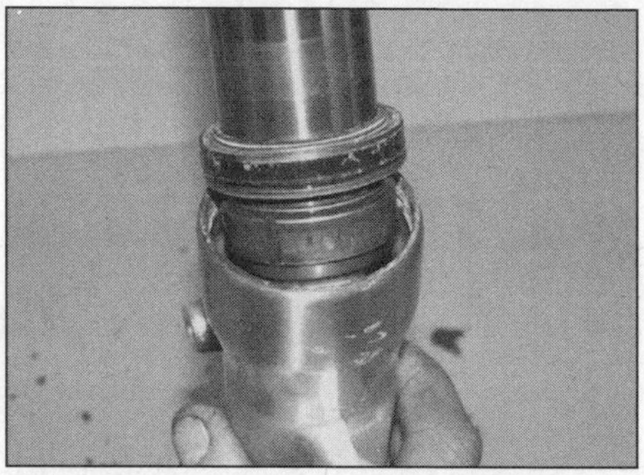
8.10b . . . the slide-hammer effect will displace the oil seal and bush

and tip the damper rod out of the top of the tube **(see illustration)**. **Note:** *If the damper rod bolt couldn't be successfully slackened, the head of the damper rod can be held by passing a holding tool down through the top of the fork tube – Suzuki produce a service tool (Pt. Nos. 09940-34520 for the handle and 09940-34531 for the adapter) for this purpose.*

8 Carefully prise out the dust seal from the top of the slider to gain access to the oil seal retaining clip **(see illustration)**. Discard the dust seal as a new one must be used.

9 Carefully remove the retaining clip, taking care not to scratch the surface of the tube **(see illustration)**. It is advisable to slide the tube fully into the slider to keep any accidental damage above the seal area.

10 To separate the tube from the slider it is necessary to displace the oil seal and top bush. The bottom bush does not pass through the top bush, and this can be used to good effect. Push the tube gently inwards until it stops against the damper seat. Take care not to do this forcibly or the seat may be damaged. Now pull the tube sharply outwards until the bottom bush strikes the top bush **(see illustration)**. Repeat this operation until the top bush and seal are tapped out of the slider **(see illustration)**.

11 With the tube removed, slide off the oil seal, washer and top bush, noting which way up they fit **(see illustration)**. Discard the oil seal as a new one must be used. **Note:** *On K3-on models, fork tube protectors are fitted to the fork sliders – do not remove the protectors unless they are damaged and are going to be renewed.*

Caution: Do not remove the bottom bush from the tube unless it is to be renewed.

12 Remove the damper rod seat from the bottom of the tube if it is there, or tip it out of the slider – you may have to push it from the bottom via the damper bolt hole **(see illustration)**.

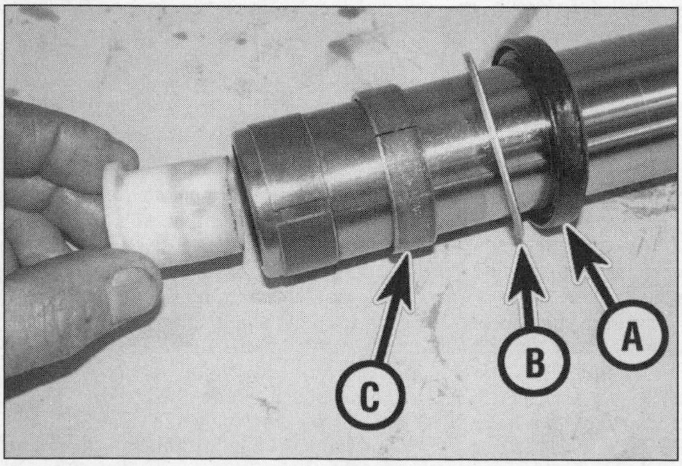

8.11 Slide the oil seal (A), washer (B) and top bush (C) off the top of the tube. Remove the damper rod seat from the bottom of the tube if there . . .

8.12 . . . or tip it out of the slider

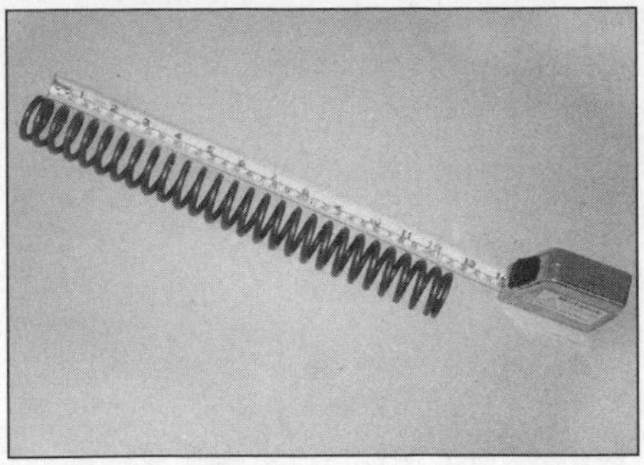

8.15 Check the spring free length

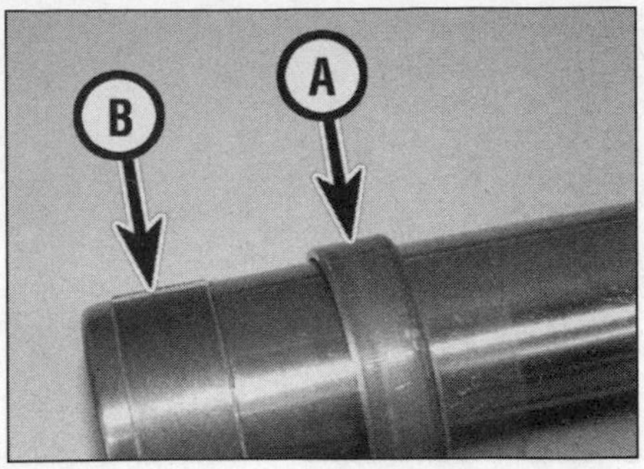

8.16a Check the top bush (A) and bottom bush (B)

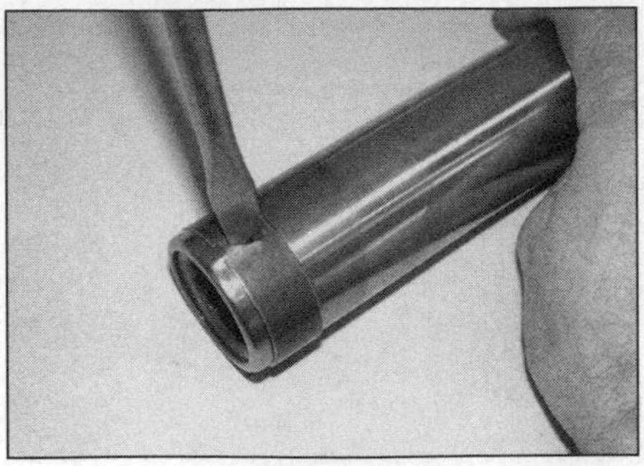

8.16b Carefully lever the ends apart and slide the bush off

Inspection

13 Clean all parts in solvent and blow them dry with compressed air, if available. Check the fork tube for score marks, scratches, flaking of the chrome finish and excessive or abnormal wear. Look for dents in the tube and renew the tube in both forks if any are found. Check the fork seal seat for nicks, gouges and scratches. If damage is evident, leaks will occur. Also check the oil seal washer for damage or distortion and renew it if necessary.

14 Check the fork tube for runout using V-blocks and a dial gauge. If the amount of runout exceeds the service limit specified, the tube should be renewed.

Warning: If the tube is bent or exceeds the runout limit, it should not be straightened; renew it.

15 Check the springs (the main spring and the rebound spring on the damper rod) for cracks and other damage. Measure the main spring free length and compare the measurement to the specifications at the beginning of the Chapter **(see illustration)**. If it is defective or sagged below the service limit, renew the main springs in both forks. Never renew only one spring.

16 Examine the working surfaces of the two bushes; if worn or scuffed they must be renewed – they are worn if the grey Teflon coating has rubbed off to reveal the copper surface **(see illustration)**. To remove the bottom bush from the fork tube, prise it apart at the slit using a flat-bladed screwdriver and slide it off. Make sure the new one seats properly **(see illustration)**.

17 Check the damper rod and its piston ring for damage and wear, and renew them if necessary **(see illustration)**. Do not remove the ring from the top of the rod unless it is being renewed.

Reassembly

18 If removed, fit the piston ring into the groove in the damper rod head, then slide the rebound spring onto the rod **(see illustration 8.17)**. Insert the damper rod into the top of the fork tube and slide it down so that it projects fully from the bottom of the tube **(see illustration)**. Make sure the spring is inside the damper rod seat, then fit the seat onto the bottom of the damper **(see illustrations)**.

19 Oil the fork tube and bottom bush with the specified fork oil and insert the assembly into the slider **(see illustration)**. Fit a new copper sealing washer onto the damper rod bolt and apply a few drops of a suitable non-permanent thread locking compound, then install the bolt into the bottom of the slider **(see illustration)**. Tighten the bolt to the specified torque setting **(see illustration)**. If the damper rod rotates inside the tube, temporarily install the fork spring, spring seat, spacer and top bolt (see

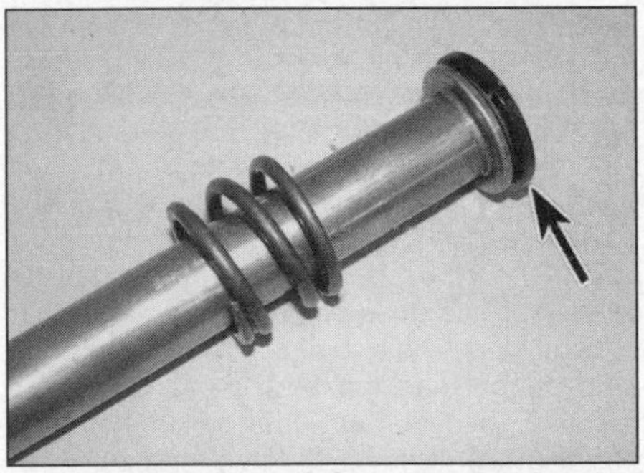

8.17 Check the damper rod, rebound spring and piston ring (arrowed)

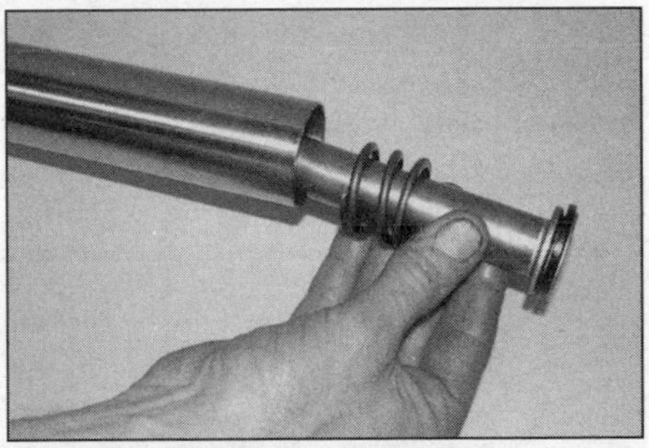

8.18a Slide the damper rod into the tube and all the way down so that it projects from the bottom

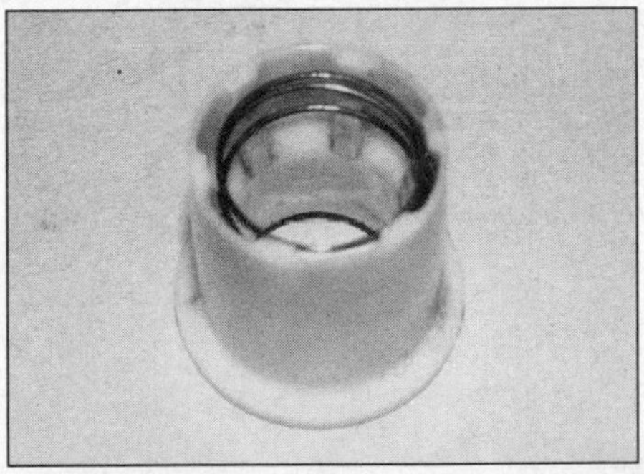

8.18b Check the spring is in the damper rod seat . . .

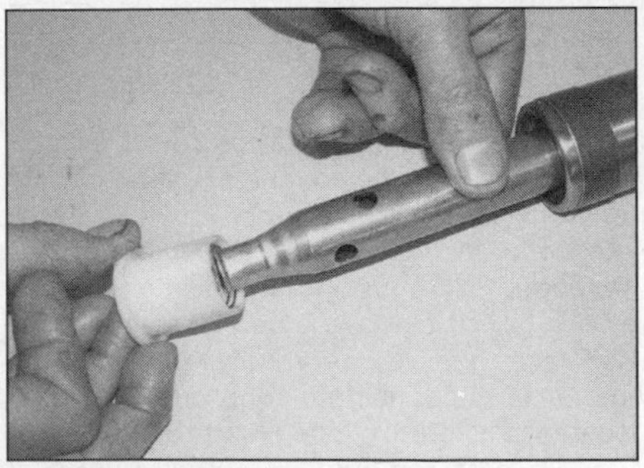

8.18c . . . then fit the seat onto the rod

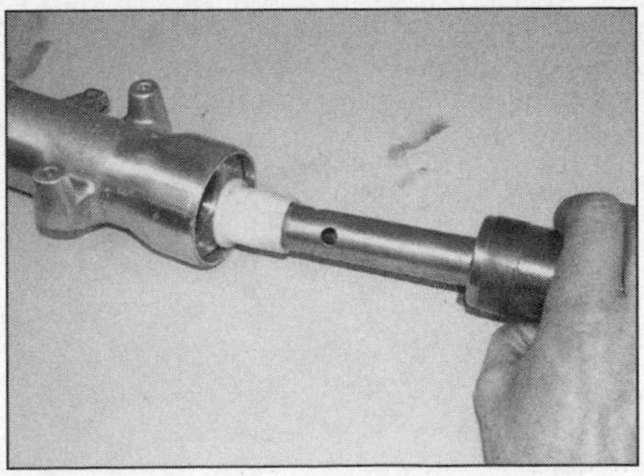

8.19a Slide the tube into the slider . . .

8.19b . . . then fit the bolt using threadlock and a new sealing washer . . .

8.19c . . . and tighten it to the specified torque

8.20a Install the top bush . . .

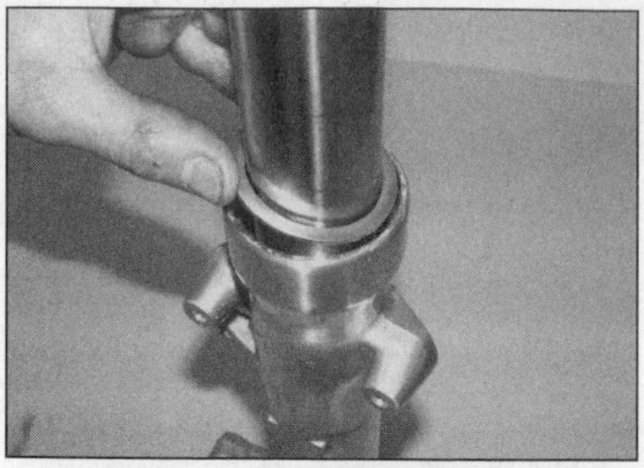

8.20b . . . followed by the washer

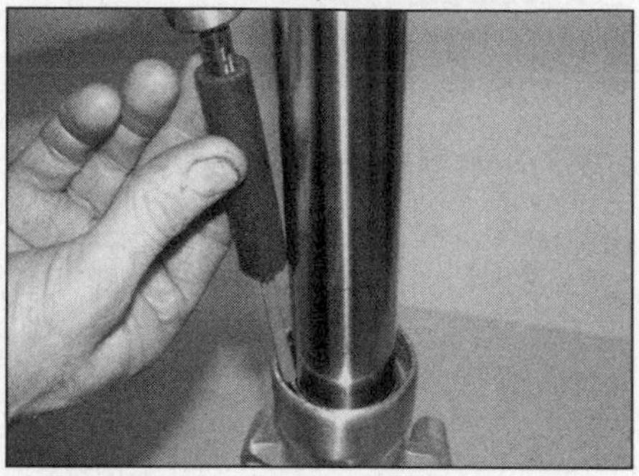

8.20c A drift can be used to tap the bush into place

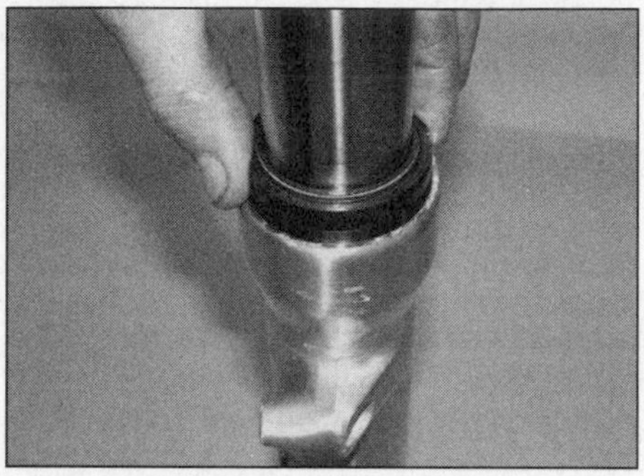

8.22a Smear the oil seal with clean fork oil then slide it down the tube

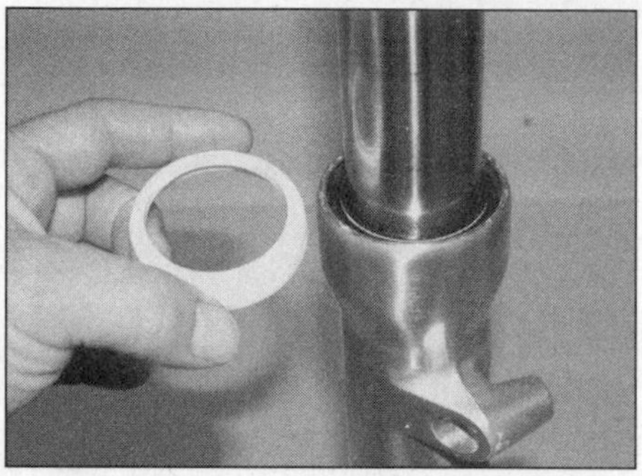

8.22b A piece of plastic tube makes a good tool to protect the seal

Steps 26 and 27) and compress the fork to hold the damper rod. Alternatively, the Suzuki service tool (see Step 7) or a long metal bar or length of wood doweling pressed hard into the damper rod head can be used. On X, Y, K1 and K2 models, if working on the right-hand fork, once the bolt is tightened fit the axle spacer into the axle bore.

20 Push the fork tube fully into the slider, then oil the top bush and slide it down over the tube **(see illustration)**. Press the bush squarely into its recess in the slider as far as possible, then install the oil seal washer with its flat side facing up **(see illustration)**. Use either the Suzuki service tool (Pt. No. 09940-52861), or a suitable piece of plastic tubing to tap the bush fully into place; the tubing must be slightly larger in diameter than the fork tube and slightly smaller in diameter than the bush recess in the slider **(see illustrations 8.22b and d)**. Take care not to scratch the fork tube during this operation; wind insulating tape around the exposed length of tube, and push the tube fully into the slider so that any accidental scratching is confined to the area above the oil seal. A drift or punch can be used, but this does not help the bush enter squarely, and the angle narrows as the bush gets deeper and makes it more difficult to make a good contact with a hammer **(see illustration)**. If using a drift or punch, wrap tape around it to prevent it scratching the tube.

21 Remove the washer to check the bush is seated fully and squarely in its recess in the slider, then wipe the recess clean and fit the washer.

22 Smear the seal's lips with fork oil and slide it over the tube so that its markings face upwards **(see illustration)**. Press the seal into the slider, then drive it fully into place as described in Step 20 until the retaining clip groove is visible above it **(see illustrations)**.

23 Once the seal is correctly seated, fit the retaining clip, making sure it is correctly located in its groove **(see illustration)**.

24 Lubricate the lips of the new dust seal then slide it down the fork tube and press it into position **(see illustrations)**.

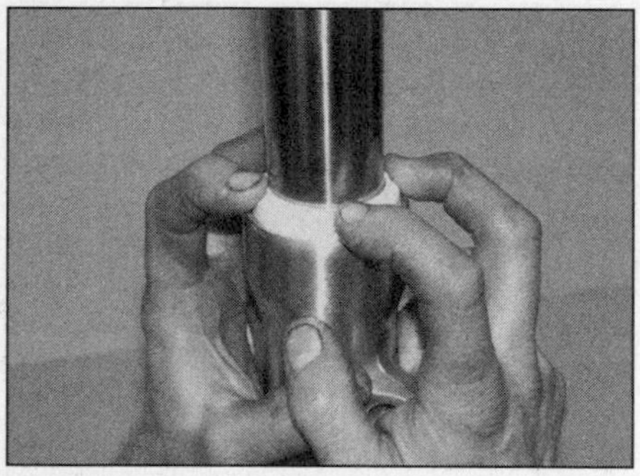

8.22c Press the seal into the top of the slider . . .

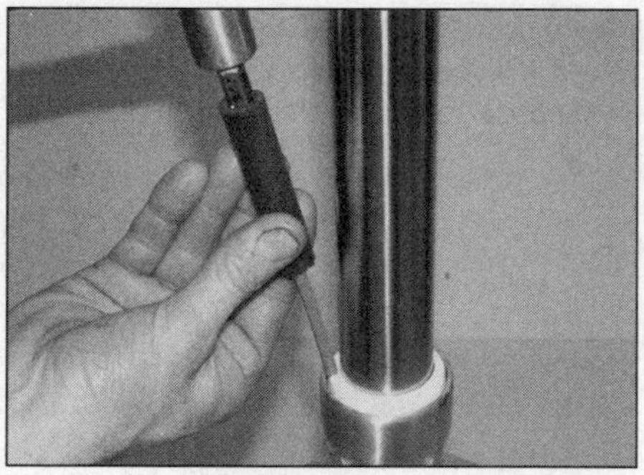

8.22d . . . then drive it in as described

8.23 Install the retaining clip . . .

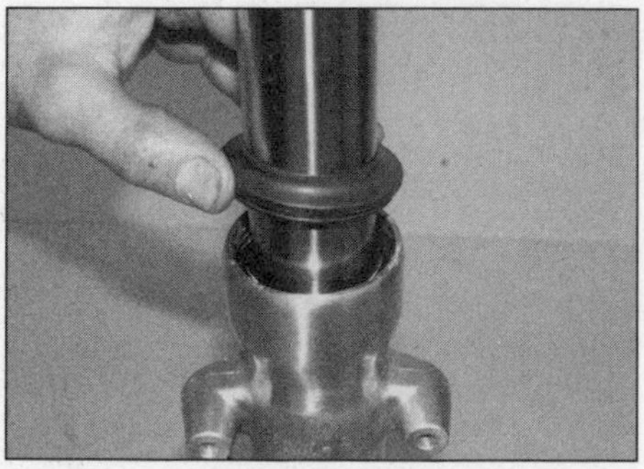

8.24a . . . followed by the dust seal . . .

25 Slowly pour in the specified quantity of the specified grade of fork oil and pump the fork at least ten times to distribute it evenly **(see illustration 7.6a)**. Fully compress the fork tube and damper rod into the slider and measure the oil level, and make any adjustment by adding more or tipping some out until it is at the level specified at the beginning of the Chapter **(see illustration 7.6b)**.

26 Clamp the slider in a soft-jawed vice using the brake caliper mounting lugs, taking care not to overtighten and damage them. Pull the fork tube out of the slider as far as possible then install the spring, the spring seat and the spacer **(see illustrations 7.7a, b and c)**. On K2 models onward, fit the pre-load adjuster plate onto the top of the spacer **(see illustration 8.1)**.

27 Fit a new O-ring smeared with fork oil onto the fork top bolt and thread the bolt into the top of the fork tube **(see illustrations 7.8a and b)**. Keep the fork tube fully extended whilst doing so. Screw the top bolt carefully into the fork tube making sure it is not cross-threaded. **Note:** *The top bolt can be tightened to the specified torque setting at this stage if the tube is held between the padded jaws of a vice, but do not risk distorting the tube by doing so. A better method is to tighten the top bolt when the fork has been installed in the bike and is securely held in the bottom yoke* **(see illustration 6.10)**.

> **HAYNES HiNT** ***Use a ratchet-type tool when installing the fork top bolt. This makes it unnecessary to remove the tool from the bolt whilst threading it in making it easier to maintain a downward pressure on the spring.***

28 Install the forks (see Section 6).

9 Steering stem

Removal

1 On SV650S models, remove the fairing (See Chapter 8).

2 Remove the fuel tank (see Chapter 4A or 4B as applicable). This will prevent the possibility of damage should a tool slip. If the top yoke is being removed from the bike rather than just being displaced, remove the air filter housing, then trace the wiring from the ignition switch and disconnect it at the connector.

3 On all X, Y, K1 and K2 models, remove the horn (see Chapter 9).

4 On SV650 models, remove the headlight assembly (see Chapter 9).

5 On all X, Y, K1 and K2 models, unscrew the bolt securing the front brake hose splitter to the bottom yoke **(see illustration)**.

6 Remove the front wheel (see Chapter 7). Tie the front brake calipers and hoses aside so that they are out of the way.

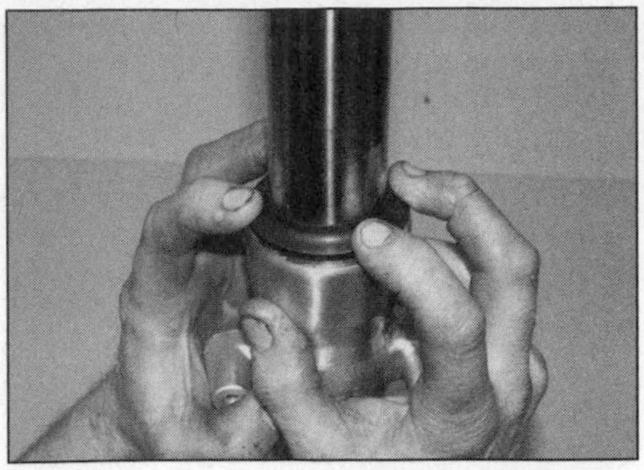

8.24b . . . which can be pressed in using your fingers

7 Remove the front mudguard (see Chapter 8).

8 Remove the front forks (see Section 6).

9 On SV650 models remove the headlight assembly holders, noting how they locate between the top and bottom yokes – if they are tight fit, remove them after slackening the steering stem nut (Step 11). On SV650 models, displace the handlebars (see Section 5).

10 On X, Y, K1 and K2 SV650S models, free the handlebar switch wiring from its guide on the top yoke, then unscrew the handlebar positioning bolts on the underside of the yoke and place the handlebars aside **(see illustrations 5.13a, b, c and d)**.

11 Unscrew the steering stem nut and remove the washer **(see illustration 5.14b)**. Ease the top yoke up and off the steering stem and either remove it or position it clear, using a rag to protect other components **(see illustration 5.14c)**.

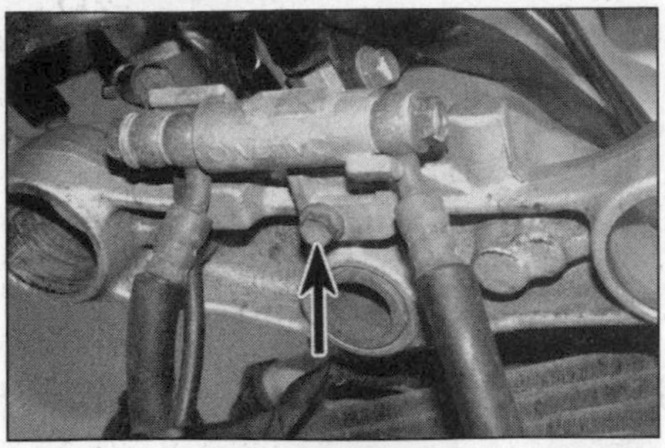

9.5 On X, Y, K1 and K2 models, unscrew the bolt (arrowed) and displace the brake hose splitter

12 On K3-on models, unscrew the adjuster locknut using either a C-spanner, a peg-spanner, or a drift located in one of the notches, then remove the internal tab washer noting how it fits **(see illustration)**. On all models support the bottom yoke and unscrew the adjuster nut **(see illustration)**. Remove the adjuster nut and the grease seal from the steering stem **(see illustration)**. Check the condition of the grease seal and discard it if it is damaged.

13 Gently lower the bottom yoke and steering stem out of the frame **(see illustration)**. Take care not to strain or knock the brake hoses.

14 Remove the inner race and bearing from the top of the steering head **(see illustrations 9.16b and a)**. Remove the bearing from the base of the steering stem **(see illustration 9.15b)**. Remove all traces of old grease from the bearings and races and check them for wear or damage as described in Section 10. **Note:** *Do not attempt to remove the outer*

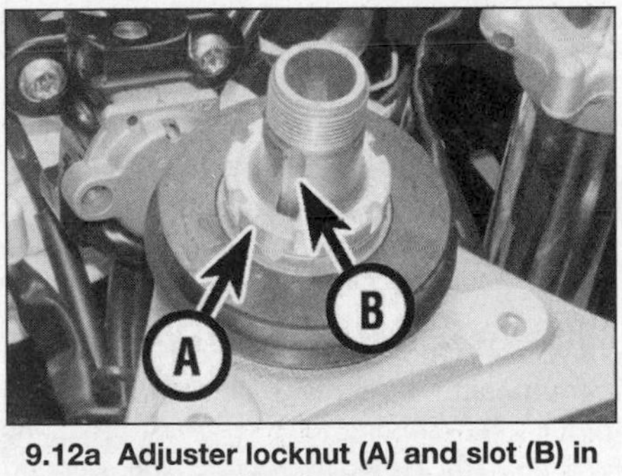

9.12a Adjuster locknut (A) and slot (B) in steering stem for tab washer – K3-on models

9.12b Unscrew the adjuster nut . . .

9.12c . . . and remove the grease seal

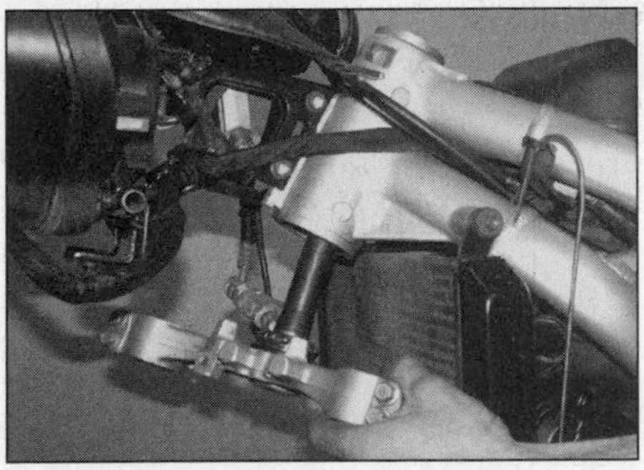

9.13 Draw the bottom yoke/steering stem out of the steering head

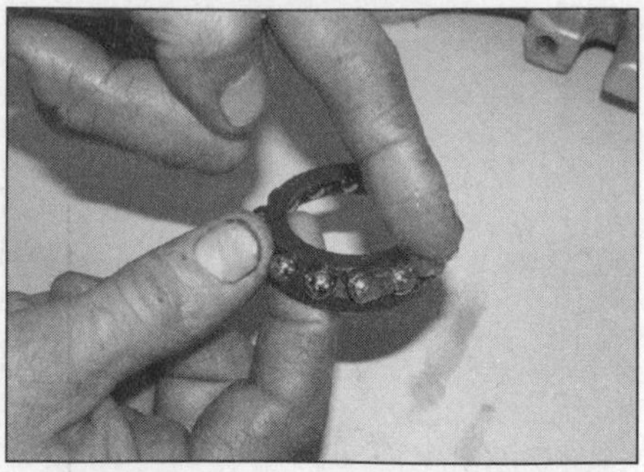

9.15a Grease the bearings and races

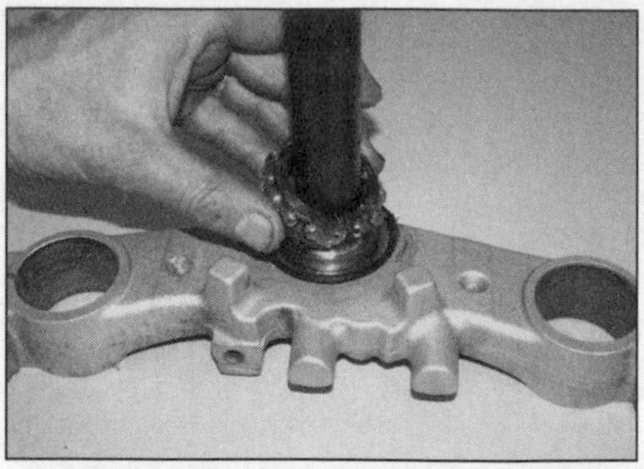

9.15b Fit the lower bearing onto the steering stem

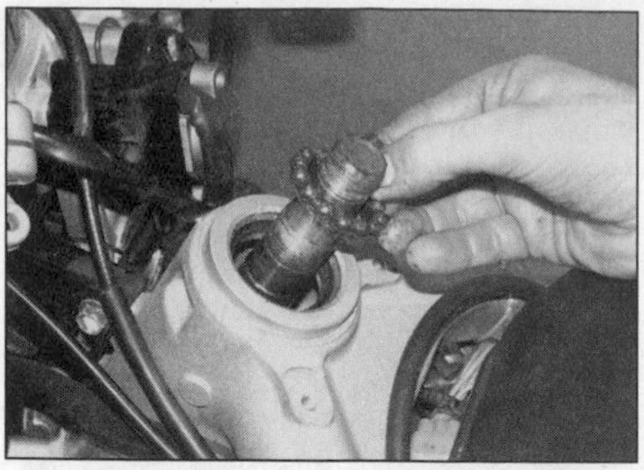

9.16a Fit the upper bearing . . .

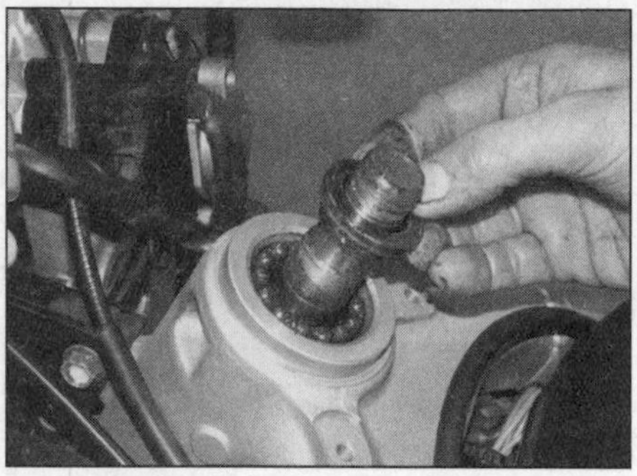

9.16b . . . and the inner race

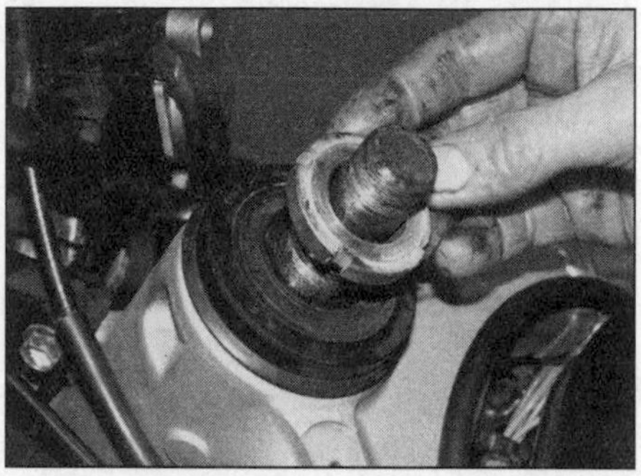

9.16c Thread the adjuster nut onto the stem

races from the steering head or the inner race from the steering stem unless they are to be renewed.

Installation

15 Smear a liberal quantity of multi-purpose grease onto the bearing races, and work some grease well into both the upper and lower bearings **(see illustration)**. Also smear the grease seal lip with grease. Fit the lower bearing onto the steering stem **(see illustration)**.

16 Carefully lift the steering stem/bottom yoke up through the steering head **(see illustration 9.13)**. Fit the upper bearing and its inner race into the top of the steering head **(see illustrations)**. Fit the grease seal **(see illustration 9.12c)**. Thread the adjuster nut onto the steering stem **(see illustration)**.

17 If the correct tools are available, tighten the adjuster nut to the preload torque setting specified at the beginning of the Chapter, then turn the steering stem through its full lock at least five times. Now slacken the adjuster nut by 1/4 to 1/2 a turn. If the correct tools are not available, tighten the nut using a C-spanner or drift to pre-load the bearings, then slacken it off a bit, but not so much that freeplay can be felt **(see illustration)**.

18 On K3-on models, fit the internal tab washer ensuring the tab locates in the slot in the steering stem, then thread the adjuster locknut onto the steering stem. Tighten the locknut to the specified torque setting, making sure the adjuster nut does not turn as you do so.

19 On all models, install the remaining components in a reverse of the removal procedure, referring to the relevant Sections or Chapters. **Note:** *If required, the steering head bearings can be adjusted after the forks, wheel and handlebars have been installed. Always check the bearing adjustment before final tightening of the steering stem nut and fork yoke clamp bolts to the specified torque settings (see Chapter 1, Section 19).*

10 Steering head bearings

Inspection

1 Remove the steering stem (see Section 9).

2 Remove all traces of old grease from the bearings and races and check them for wear or damage.

3 The outer races should be polished and free from indentations. Inspect the bearing balls for signs of wear, damage or discoloration, and examine the ball retainer cage for signs of cracks or splits. If there are any signs of wear on any of the above components both upper and lower bearing assemblies must be renewed as a set. Only remove the outer races in the steering head and the lower bearing inner race on the steering stem if they need to be renewed – do not re-use them once they have been removed.

Renewal

4 The outer races are an interference fit in the steering head and can be tapped from position with a suitable drift **(see illustrations)**. Tap firmly and evenly around each race to ensure that it is driven out squarely. It may prove advantageous to curve the end of the drift slightly to improve access.

9.17 Tighten the adjuster nut as described

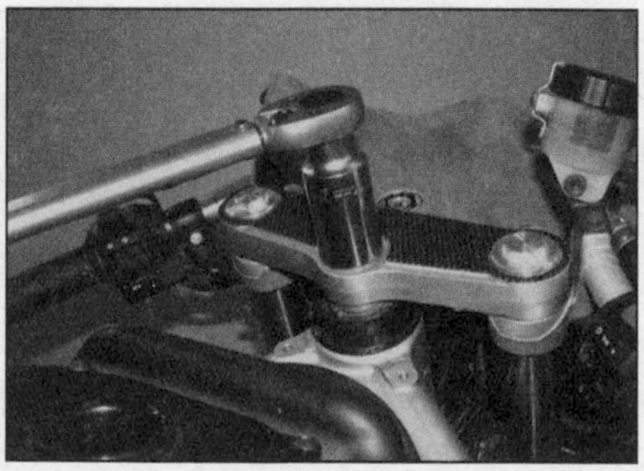

9.18 Tighten the steering stem nut to the specified torque

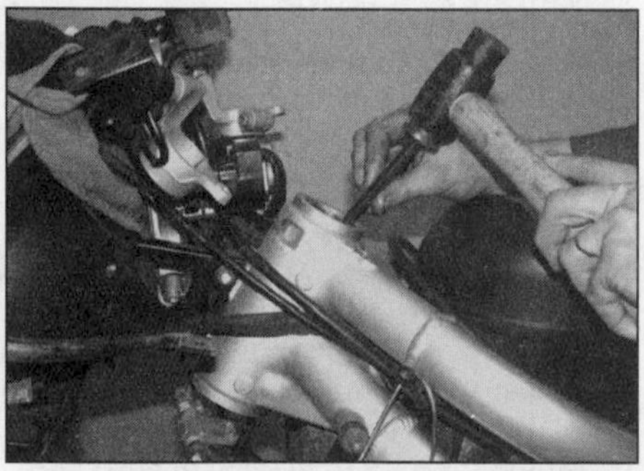

10.4a Drive the bearing races out with a brass drift . . .

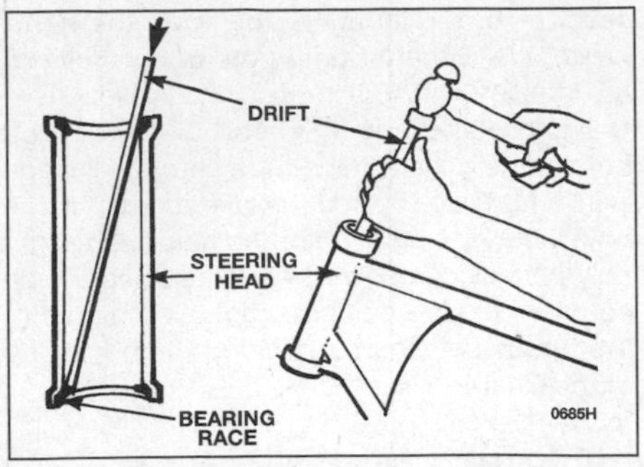

10.4b . . . locating it as shown

5 Alternatively, the races can be removed using a slide-hammer type bearing extractor; these can often be hired from tool shops.

6 The new outer races can be pressed into the head using a drawbolt arrangement **(see illustration)**, or by using a large diameter tubular drift. Ensure that the drawbolt washer or drift (as applicable) bears only on the outer edge of the race and does not contact the working surface. Alternatively, have the races installed by a Suzuki dealer equipped with the bearing race installation tools.

HAYNES HiNT ***Installation of new bearing outer races is made much easier if the races are left overnight in the freezer. This causes them to contract slightly making them a looser fit. Alternatively, use a freeze spray.***

7 The lower bearing inner race should only be removed from the steering stem if a new one is being fitted **(see illustration)**. To remove the race, use two screwdrivers placed on opposite sides to work it free, using blocks of wood to improve leverage and protect the yoke, or tap under it using a cold chisel. If the steering stem is placed on its side on a hard surface, thread a suitable nut onto the top to prevent the threads being damaged. If the race is firmly in place it will be necessary to use a puller **(see illustration)**. Take the steering stem to a Suzuki dealer if required.

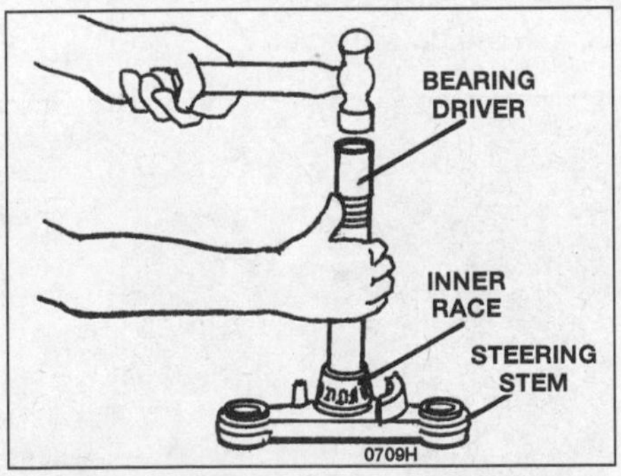

10.9 Drive the new race on using a suitable bearing driver or a length of pipe that bears only against the inner edge of the race

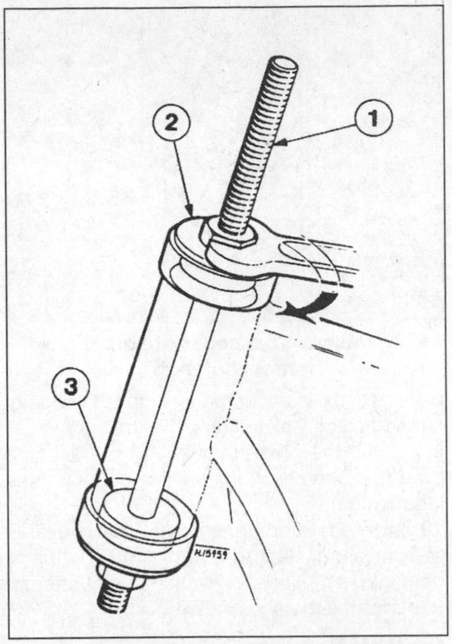

10.6 Drawbolt arrangement for fitting steering stem bearing races

1 Long bolt or threaded bar
2 Thick washer
3 Guide for lower race

8 Remove the dust seal from the bottom of the stem and replace it with a new one **(see illustration 10.7a)**. Smear the new seal with grease.

9 Fit the new lower race onto the steering stem. A length of tubing with an internal diameter slightly larger than the steering stem will be needed to tap the new race into position **(see illustration)**.

10 Install the steering stem (see Section 9).

11 Rear shock absorber

Removal

1 Support the motorcycle on an auxiliary stand that does not take the weight through any part of the rear suspension, or by using a hoist. Position a support under the rear wheel or swingarm so that it does not drop when the shock absorber is removed, but also making sure that the weight of the machine is off the rear suspension so that the shock is not compressed. Make a note of which side the bolts go in from, and make a note of which way round the shock absorber fits.

2 Remove the rider's seat (see Chapter 8) and for best access the exhaust system (see Chapter 4A or 4B as applicable). Depending on the tools you have available, you may also need to remove the fuel tank (to access the top mounting bolt).

3 On X, Y, K1 and K2 models, unscrew the sidestand bracket rear bolt and slacken the front one **(see illustration)**. Pivot the bracket down **(see illustration)**.

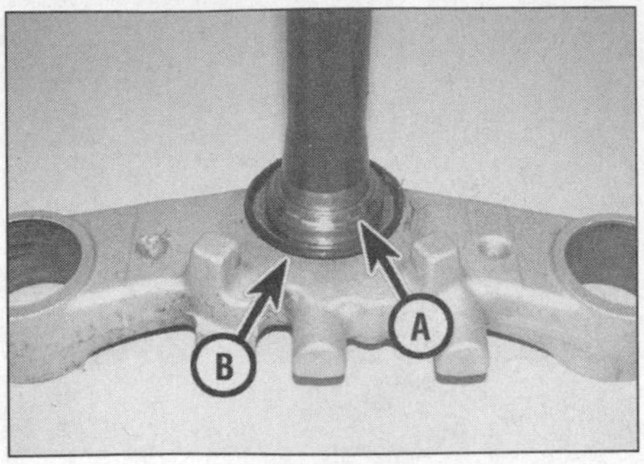

10.7a Remove the lower bearing inner race (A) and dust seal (B) . . .

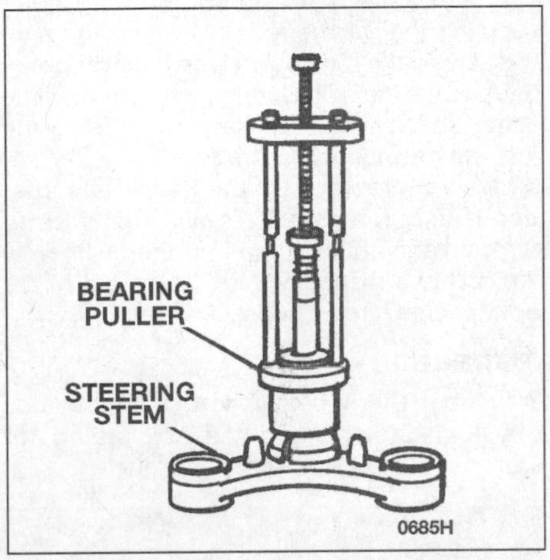

10.7b . . . using a puller if necessary

11.3a Unscrew the rear bolt and slacken the front one . . .

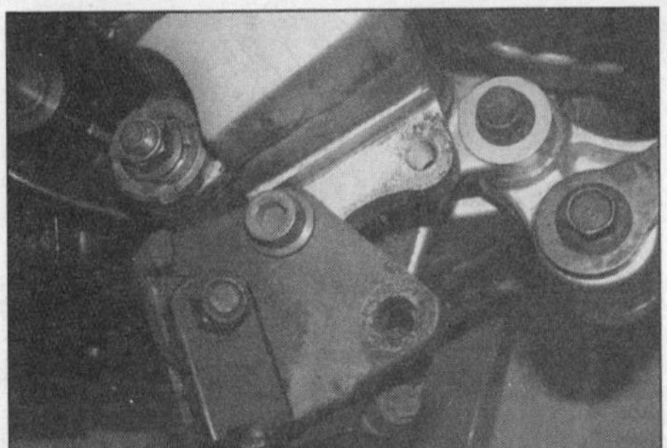

11.3b . . . then pivot the bracket down

11.4 Unscrew the nut and withdraw the linkage rods-to-arm bolt

11.5 Unscrew the shock absorber lower mounting bolt

4 Unscrew the nut and withdraw the bolt securing the linkage rods to the linkage arm, then swing the rods down **(see illustration)**.
5 Unscrew the bolt securing the bottom of the shock absorber to the linkage arm, then swing the arm down **(see illustration)**.
6 Unscrew the nut on the shock absorber upper mounting bolt **(see illustration)**. Support the shock absorber, then withdraw the bolt and manoeuvre the shock out of the bottom **(see illustrations)**.

Inspection

7 Inspect the shock absorber for obvious physical damage and the coil spring for looseness, cracks or signs of fatigue.
8 Inspect the damper rod for signs of bending, pitting and oil leakage **(see illustration)**.
9 Inspect the pivot hardware at the top and bottom of the shock for wear or damage **(see illustration)**.
10 Individual components are not available for the shock absorber, so if it is worn or damaged it must be renewed – do not attempt to dismantle the shock absorber.

Installation

11 Installation is the reverse of removal, noting the following points.
- Apply multi-purpose grease to the shock absorber and linkage pivot points.
- Install the shock absorber with the threaded section for the mounting bolts on the right-hand side. Do not tighten the upper bolt/nut until the lower bolt is in position.
- Tighten the shock absorber lower bolt before fitting the linkage rods onto the linkage arm otherwise the rods block access to the bolt. Install the other bolts and nuts finger-tight only until all components are in position, then counter-hold the bolts and tighten the nuts to the torque settings specified at the beginning of the Chapter.

12 Rear suspension linkage

Removal

1 Support the motorcycle on an auxiliary stand that does not take the weight through any part of the rear suspension, or by using a hoist. Position a support under the rear wheel or swingarm so that it does not drop when the shock absorber lower mounting is detached, but also making sure that the weight of the machine is off the rear suspension so that the shock is not compressed. Make a note of which side the bolts go in from.
2 Remove the exhaust system (see Chapter 4A or 4B as applicable).

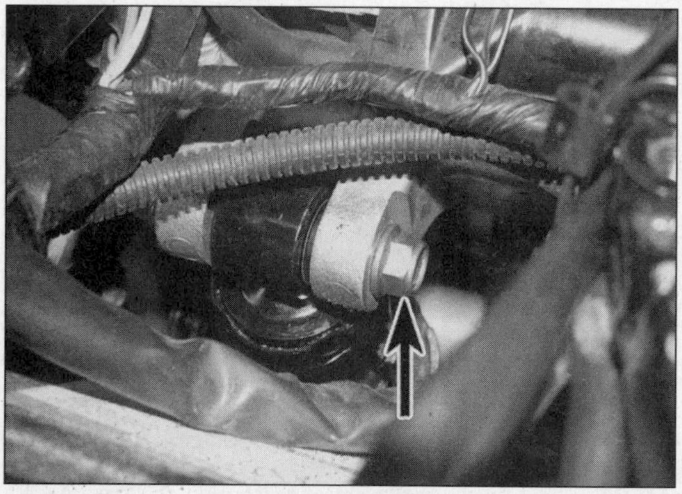

11.6a Unscrew the nut on the bolt (arrowed) . . .

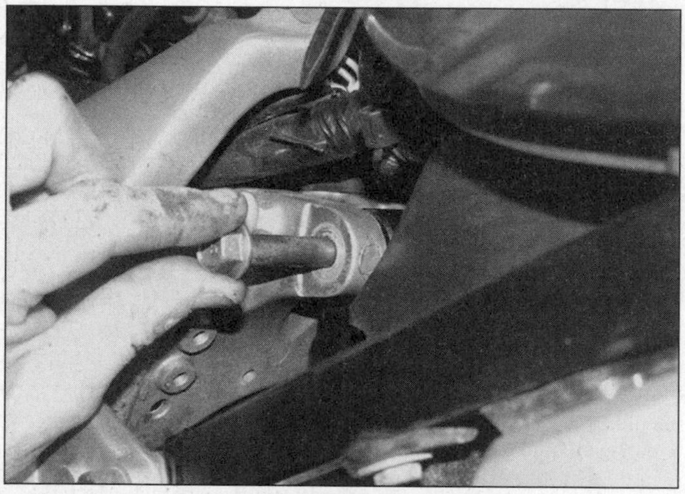

11.6b . . . then withdraw the bolt . . .

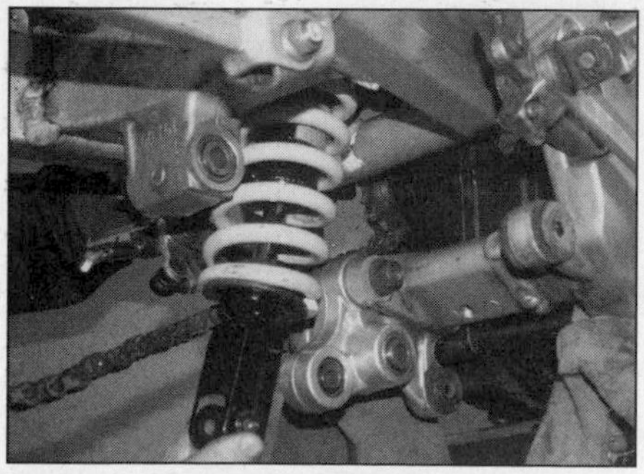

11.6c . . . and remove the shock absorber from the bottom

11.8 Check the damper rod (arrowed) as described

11.9 Check the bush (arrowed) in the bottom pivot for cracks and deterioration

12.4 Unscrew the nut, withdraw the bolt and remove the rods

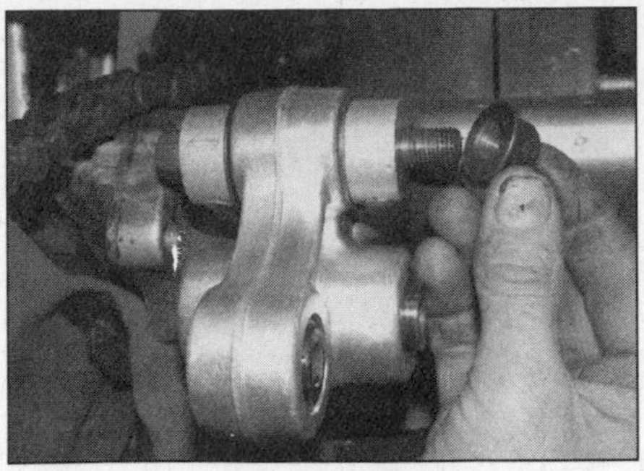

12.6a Unscrew the nut . . .

12.6b . . . then withdraw the bolt and remove the linkage arm and the washers

3 Mark the linkage arm and rods so that they can be installed the same way round.
4 Unscrew the nut and withdraw the bolt securing the linkage rods to the linkage arm, then swing the rods down **(see illustration 11.4)**. Unscrew the nut and withdraw the bolt securing the linkage rods to the swingarm and remove the rods **(see illustration)**.
5 Unscrew the bolt securing the bottom of the shock absorber to the linkage arm, then swing the arm down **(see illustration 11.5)**.
6 Unscrew the nut and withdraw the bolt securing the linkage arm to the frame and remove the arm, noting the washers **(see illustrations)**.

Inspection

7 Withdraw the spacers from the linkage arm and swingarm, noting any difference in sizes **(see illustrations)**. Thoroughly clean all components, removing all traces of dirt, corrosion and grease.
8 Inspect all components closely, looking for obvious signs of wear such as heavy scoring, or for damage such as cracks or distortion. Slip each spacer back into its bearing and check that there is not an excessive amount of freeplay between the two components. Renew any components as required.
9 Check the condition of the needle roller bearings **(see illustrations 12.7a and b)**. Refer to *Tools and Workshop Tips* (Section 5) in Reference for more information on bearings.
10 Worn bearings can be drifted out of their bores, but note that removal will destroy them; new bearings should be obtained before work commences. The new bearings should be pressed or drawn into their bores rather than driven into position. In the absence of a press, a suitable drawbolt tool can be made up as described in *Tools and Workshop Tips* in the Reference section.
11 Lubricate the needle bearings and spacers with multi-purpose grease. Install the spacers **(see illustration 12.7a and b)**.

Installation

12 Installation is the reverse of removal, noting the following points.
- Apply multi-purpose grease to the bearings, spacers and bolts.
- Install the linkage arm ensuring it is fitted

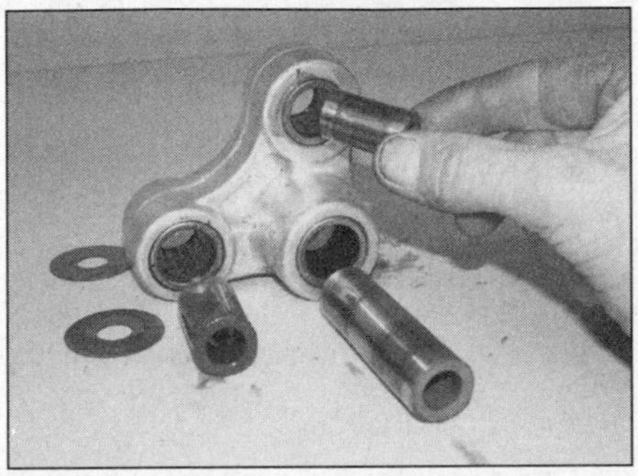

12.7a Withdraw the spacers from the linkage arm . . .

the correct way round (see Step 3). Do not forget the washers between the arm and the frame **(see illustration 12.6b)**.
- Tighten the shock absorber lower bolt before fitting the linkage rods onto the linkage arm otherwise the rods block access to the bolt. Install the other bolts and nuts finger-tight only until all components are in position, then counter-hold the bolts and tighten the nuts to the torque settings specified at the beginning of the Chapter.

13 Suspension adjustments

Front forks – K2-on models

1 The front forks are adjustable for spring pre-load.

13.2 Fork pre-load adjuster (arrowed) – K4 model shown

12.7b . . . and the linkage rod pivot in the swingarm (shown removed)

2 Pre-load is adjusted using a suitable spanner or screwdriver on the top of the adjuster **(see illustration)**. Turn it clockwise to increase pre-load and anti-clockwise to decrease it.
3 The amount of pre-load is indicated by grooves on the adjuster **(see illustration)**. On K2 models, there are seven grooves – if all seven are visible the spring pre-load is at a minimum, and at a maximum with only one groove showing. The standard position is with the 6th groove aligned with the top of the fork bolt. Always make sure both adjusters are set equally. On K3-on models, there are five grooves – if all five are visible the spring pre-load is at a minimum, and at a maximum with no grooves showing. The standard position is with the 3rd groove aligned with the top of the fork bolt. Always make sure both adjusters are set equally.

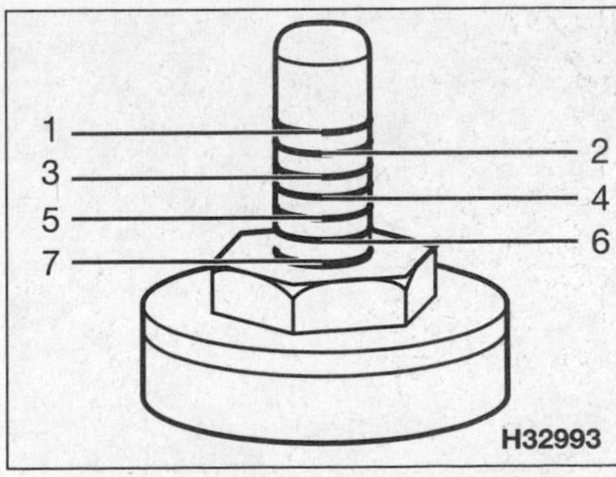

13.3 Fork adjuster pre-load grooves – K2 model shown

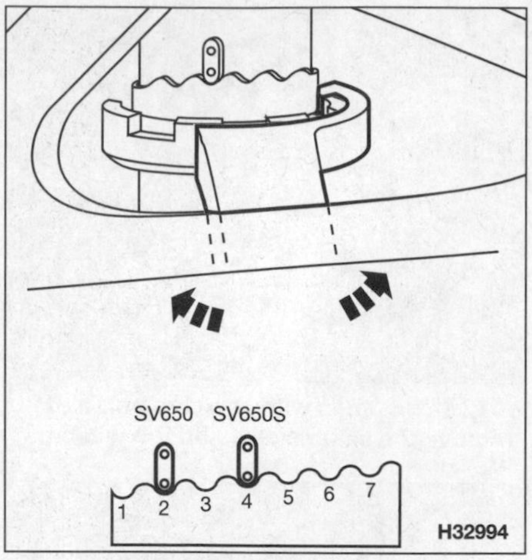

13.5a Adjusting rear pre-load – X, Y, K1 and K2 models

Rear shock absorber – all models

4 The shock absorber is adjustable for spring pre-load.

5 Pre-load is adjusted using a suitable C-spanner (one is provided in the toolkit) on the adjuster on the top of the shock absorber **(see illustrations)**. On X, Y, K1 and K2 models, turn it clockwise to increase pre-load and anti-clockwise to decrease it. On K3-on models, turn it clockwise to decrease pre-load and anti-clockwise to increase it.

6 The amount of pre-load is indicated by the position of the adjuster relative to its stop. There are seven positions – the number 1 position on

14.2 Undo the screws (arrowed) and remove the chainguard

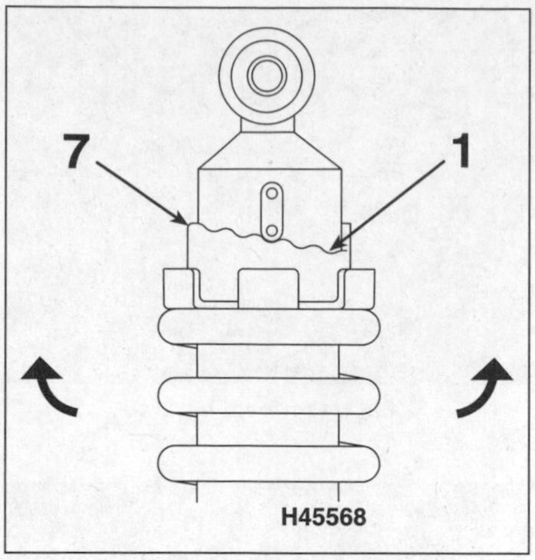

13.5b Adjusting rear pre-load – K3-on models

the adjuster provides minimum pre-load, and the number 7 provides the maximum. On X, Y, K1 and K2 SV650 models the standard setting is number 2; on K3, K4 and K5 SV650 models the standard setting is number 3. On all SV650S models, the standard setting it is number 4. On ABS models it is number 3.

14 Swingarm – removal and installation

TOOL TIP ***A peg spanner is required to slacken and tighten the swingarm pivot bolt locknut. If the Suzuki service tool (Pt. No. 09940-14940) is not available, a suitable one can be made from an old socket (see illustration 14.8a). The socket size required is 27 mm.***

Removal

1 Remove the exhaust system (see Chapter 4A or 4B).

2 Undo the screws securing the chainguard to the swingarm and remove the guard, noting how it locates **(see illustration)**.

3 Note the routing of the brake hose, then unscrew the bolt(s) securing the brake hose holder(s) to the top of the swingarm **(see illustration)**.

4 On X, Y, K1 and K2 models, the rear brake hose is routed through a riveted guide on the inside of the swingarm. Unscrew the brake hose banjo bolt and detach the hose from the rear brake caliper, noting its alignment **(see illustration)**. Draw the hose through the guide **(see illustration)**. Either plug the end using another suitable short piece of hose fitted through the eye of the banjo bolt (it wants to be a fairly tight fit to seal it properly), clamp the hose using a hose clamp, or wrap a plastic bag tightly around to minimise fluid loss and prevent dirt entering the system. Discard the sealing washers as new ones must be used on installation.

Warning: Brake fluid can harm your eyes and damage painted surfaces and plastic parts, so use extreme care when disconnecting the hose.

5 Remove the rear wheel (see Chapter 7). On K3-on models, secure the brake caliper clear of the swingarm, ensuring no strain is put on the brake hose.

6 On X, Y, K1 and K2 models, unscrew the nut and withdraw the bolt securing the brake torque arm to the swingarm and remove the caliper assembly.

7 Remove the rear shock absorber (see Section 11), but unscrew the nut and withdraw the bolt securing the linkage rods to the swingarm instead of the linkage arm, then swing the rods all the way down **(see illustration 12.4)**.

8 Unscrew the locknut on the right-hand end of the swingarm pivot bolt using a suitable peg spanner (see ***Tool Tip*** above) **(see illustration)**. Unscrew the nut on the left-hand end of the pivot bolt **(see illustration)**.

9 Unscrew the pivot bolt, then support the swingarm and withdraw the bolt from the right-hand side **(see illustrations)**. **Note:** *On K3-on models, use a 19 mm Allen socket or hex bar to unscrew the pivot bolt.* Manoeuvre the swingarm out of the frame, noting how the drive chain routes around the front **(see illustration)**.

10 If required, unscrew the bolts securing the mud deflector and chain slider to the swingarm and remove them, noting how they

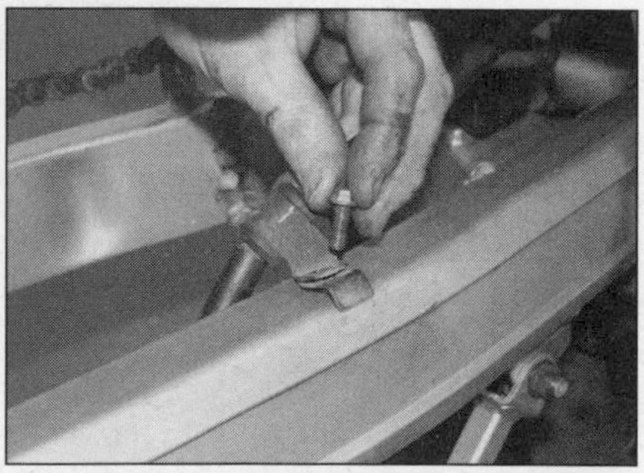

14.3 Unscrew the brake hose holder bolt

14.4a Unscrew the banjo bolt (arrowed) and detach the hose . . .

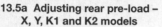

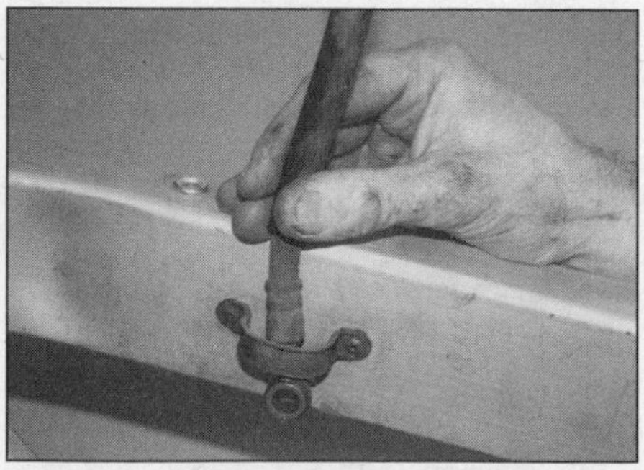

14.4b . . . and draw the hose out of the guide

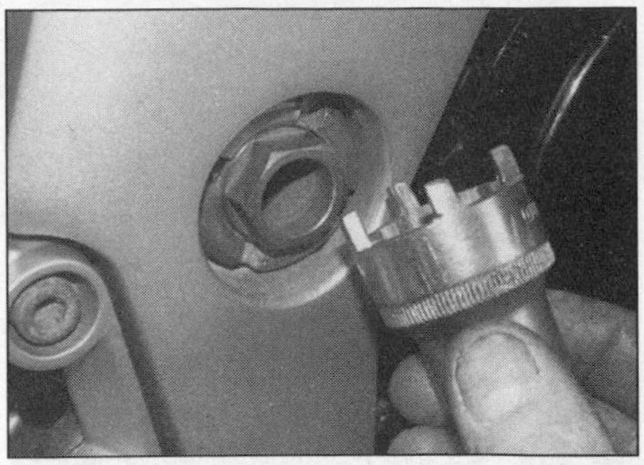

14.8a Using a suitable peg spanner as described . . .

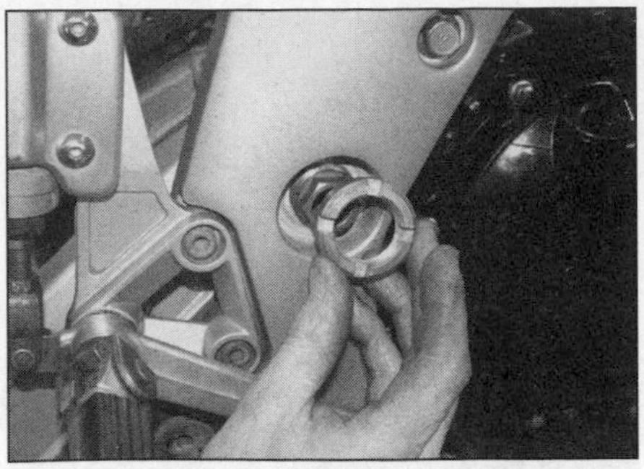

14.8b . . . unscrew the locknut

14.8c Unscrew the nut (arrowed)

14.9a Unscrew the pivot bolt (arrowed) . . .

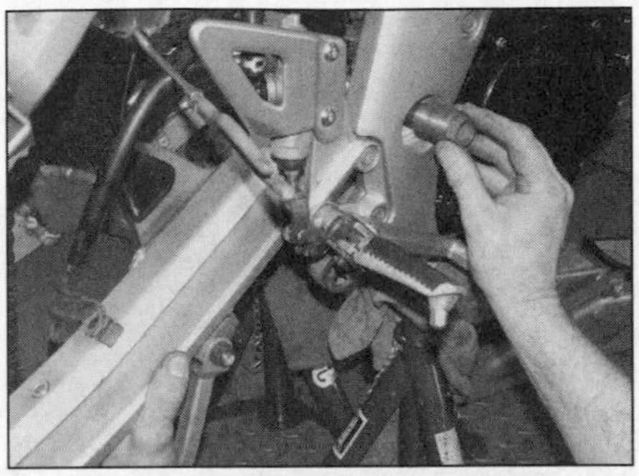

14.9b . . . then withdraw it from the swingarm . . .

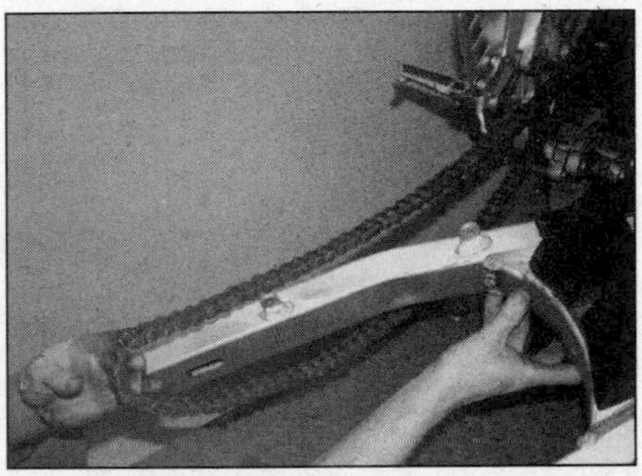

14.9c . . . and manoeuvre the swingarm out

fit **(see illustrations)**. If the chain slider is badly worn or damaged it should be renewed.

11 Inspect all pivot components for wear or damage as described in Section 15.

Installation

12 If removed, install the chain slider, making sure it locates correctly **(see illustration 14.10b)**, then fit the mud deflector, locating the peg on its base in the hole in the swingarm **(see illustration)**.

13 On X, Y, K1 and K2 models, remove the dust cap and thrust washer from each side of the swingarm pivot **(see illustration)**. Withdraw the pivot spacers – note that on K3-on models, the spacers have an integral end cap. Clean off all old grease, then lubricate the bearings, spacers, washers, caps and the pivot bolt with multi-purpose grease. Insert the spacers, then fit the washers and dust caps as applicable.

14 Offer up the swingarm and have an assistant hold it in place **(see illustration)**. Make sure the drive chain is looped over the front of the swingarm. Slide the pivot bolt through from the right-hand side and push it all the way through, then tighten it to the torque setting specified at the beginning of the Chapter **(see illustrations)**.

15 Fit the nut onto the left-hand end of the bolt **(see illustration)**. Counter-hold the head

14.10a If required unscrew the bolt (arrowed) and remove the mud deflector . . .

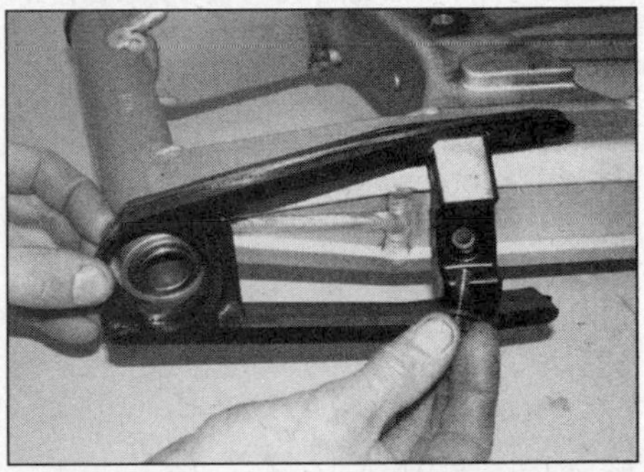

14.10b . . . and the chain slider

14.12 Locate the peg in the hole

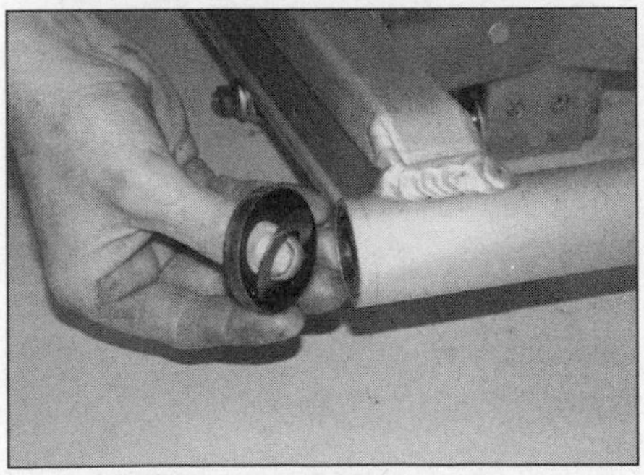

14.13a Remove the dust cap and thrust washer – X, Y, K1 and K2 models

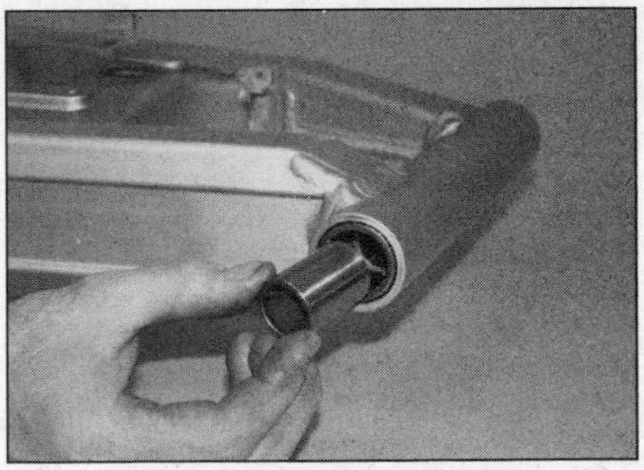

14.13b Withdraw the spacer

14.14a Locate the swingarm in the frame, looping the chain around the front . . .

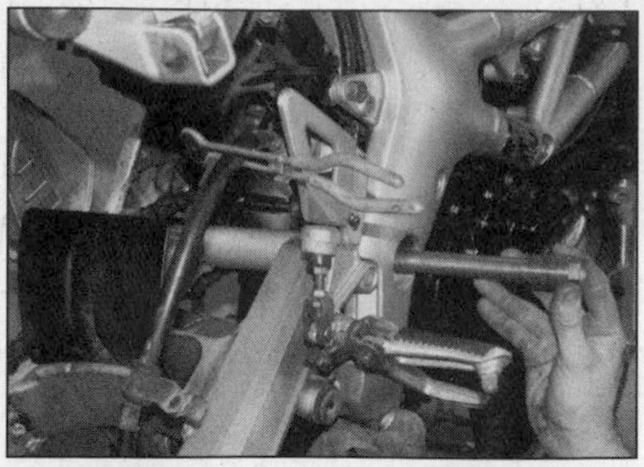

14.14b . . . then slide the pivot bolt through . . .

14.14c . . . and tighten it to the specified torque

14.15a Fit the nut . . .

14.15b . . . and tighten it to the specified torque

14.22 Use a new sealing washer on each side of the union

of the bolt and tighten the nut to the specified torque setting **(see illustration)**.

16 Fit the locknut onto the right-hand end of the bolt and tighten it to the specified torque setting, using the peg-spanner as on removal (see ***Tool Tip***) **(see illustrations 14.8b and a)**.

17 Install the shock absorber (see Section 11).

18 On X, Y, K1 and K2 models, fit the brake torque arm onto the swingarm, then install the bolt and tighten the nut to the specified torque setting. Route the brake hose through its guide on the swingarm **(see illustration 14.4b)**.

19 Fit the brake hose holder(s) and tighten the bolt(s) securely **(see illustration 14.3)**.

20 Install the chainguard, making sure it locates correctly and tighten the screws securely **(see illustration 14.2)**.

21 Install the rear wheel (see Chapter 7).

22 On X, Y, K1 and K2 models, connect the brake hose to the caliper, using new sealing washers on each side of the fitting **(see illustration)**. Align the hose as noted on removal **(see illustration 14.4a)**. Tighten the banjo bolt to the torque setting specified at the beginning of the Chapter. Remove the brake hose clamp if used. Refer to Chapter 7 and bleed the brakes.

23 Check and adjust the drive chain slack (see Chapter 1). Check the operation of the rear suspension and brake before taking the machine on the road.

15.1 Note the UP mark on the adjuster inner face – X, Y, K1 and K2 models

15 Swingarm – inspection, bearing check and renewal

Inspection

1 Remove the swingarm (see Section 14). Remove the chain adjusters if required, noting how they fit – on X, Y, K1 and K2 models, note the UP mark on the inner face **(see illustration)**.

15.6 Check each needle bearing as described

2 Thoroughly clean the swingarm, removing all traces of dirt, corrosion and grease.

3 Inspect the swingarm closely, looking for obvious signs of wear such as heavy scoring, and cracks or distortion due to accident damage. Any damaged or worn component must be replaced.

4 Check the swingarm pivot bolt for straightness by rolling it on a flat surface such as a piece of plate glass (first wipe off all old grease and remove any corrosion using wire wool). If the equipment is available, place the axle in V-blocks and measure the runout using a dial gauge. If the axle is bent or the runout exceeds the limit specified, renew it.

Bearing check and renewal

5 On X, Y, K1 and K2 models, remove the dust cap and thrust washer from each side of the swingarm pivot **(see illustration 14.13a)**. On all models, withdraw the spacers from the swingarm **(see illustrations 14.13b)**. Clean off all old grease from the spacers and bearings.

6 Check the condition of the bearings – a needle roller bearing is fitted on each side **(see illustration)**. Slip each spacer back into its bearing and check that there is not an excessive amount of freeplay between the two components. If the bearings do not run smoothly and freely or if there is excessive freeplay, they must be renewed. Refer to *Tools and Workshop Tips* (Section 5) in the Reference section for more information on bearings.

7 Worn bearings can be drifted out of their bores, but note that removal will destroy them; new bearings should be obtained before work commences. The new bearings should

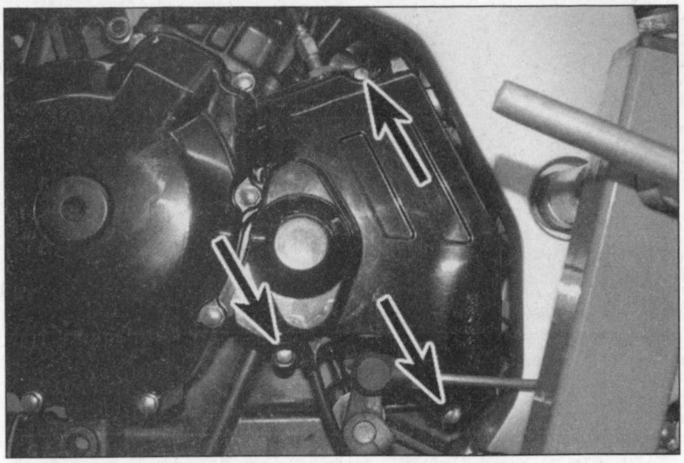
17.1 Unscrew the bolts (arrowed) and remove the cover

17.5 Unscrew the bolts and displace the clutch release mechanism

be pressed or drawn into their bores rather than driven into position. In the absence of a press, a suitable drawbolt tool can be made up as described in *Tools and Workshop Tips* in Reference. A central spacer separates the two bearings – remove it if required, but do not forget to fit it before installing the second bearing.

8 On X, Y, K1 and K2 models, check the condition of the washers and dust caps and renew them if they are damaged, deformed or have deteriorated.

9 Lubricate the bearings and spacers with multi-purpose grease and install the spacers **(see illustration 14.13b)**. On X, Y, K1 and K2 models, smear the washers with grease, then fit the washers and dust caps **(see illustration 14.13a)**.

16 Drive chain

Note: *Inspect the drive chain to determine whether it has a soft joining link (its pin ends will be deeply centre punched rather than peened over as all other chain links). If a soft link is fitted, the chain can be split and rejoined using a new soft link – this must be done using the correct tool (see 'Chains' in the Tools and Workshop Tips section in Reference). If a soft link is not fitted, the chain is effectively endless, and can only be removed as described below.*

Warning: NEVER install a drive chain which uses a clip-type master (split) link.

Removal

1 If the sprockets are also being renewed, slacken the front sprocket nut before removing the rear wheel so that the rear brake can be used to stop the sprocket turning (see Section 17).

2 Remove the swingarm (see Section 14), then remove the chain.

Cleaning

3 Soak the chain in paraffin (kerosene) for approximately five or six minutes, then scrub it vigorously with a stiff-bristled brush.

Caution: Don't use petrol (gasoline), solvent or other cleaning fluids which might damage the chains internal O-ring seals. Don't use high-pressure water. Remove the chain, clean it as described, then dry it with compressed air or clean rag immediately. The entire process shouldn't take longer than ten minutes – if it does, the O-ring seals could be damaged.

Installation

4 Installation is the reverse of removal. On completion adjust and lubricate the chain following the procedures described in Chapter 1.

17 Sprockets

Check

1 Unscrew the three front sprocket cover bolts and remove the cover **(see illustration)**.

2 Check the wear pattern on both sprockets (see Chapter 1, Section 1). If the sprocket teeth are worn excessively, renew the chain and both sprockets as a set. Whenever the sprockets are inspected, the drive chain should be inspected also (see Chapter 1). If you are renewing the chain, renew the sprockets as well.

3 Adjust and lubricate the chain following the procedures described in Chapter 1.

Front sprocket renewal

4 Unscrew the three front sprocket cover bolts and remove the cover **(see illustration 17.1)**.

5 Unscrew the two bolts securing the clutch release mechanism and displace it – there is no need to detach the cable **(see illustration)**.

6 Bend down the tabs on the sprocket nut lockwasher **(see illustration)**. Engage first gear, then have an assistant hold the rear brake on. Unscrew the sprocket nut and remove the washer **(see illustrations)**. Check

17.6a Bend down the lockwasher tabs . . .

17.6b . . . then unscrew the nut . . .

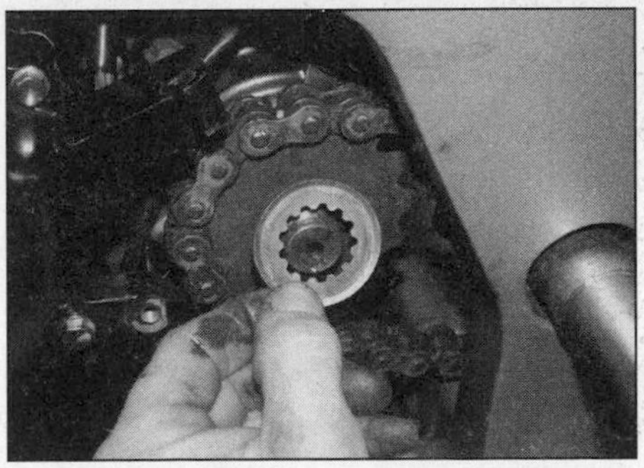
17.6c . . . and remove the washer

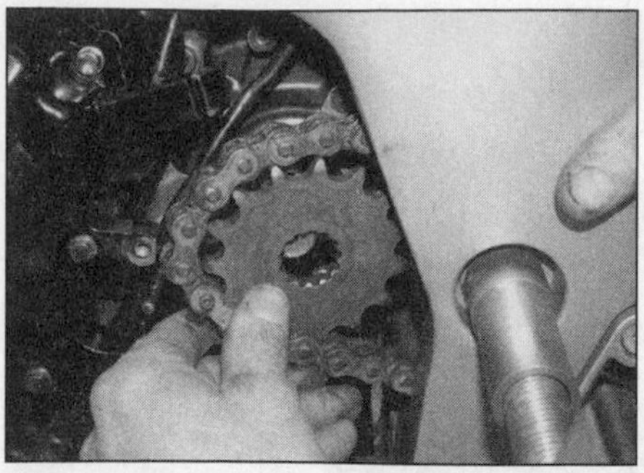

17.8 Disengage the chain and remove the sprocket

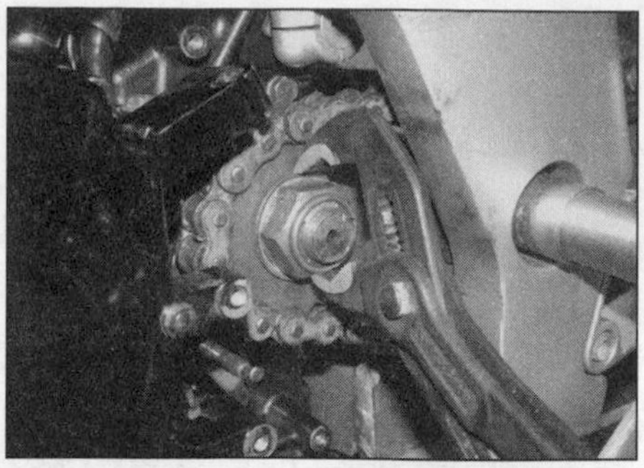

17.10 Bend the rim of the lockwasher up against the nut

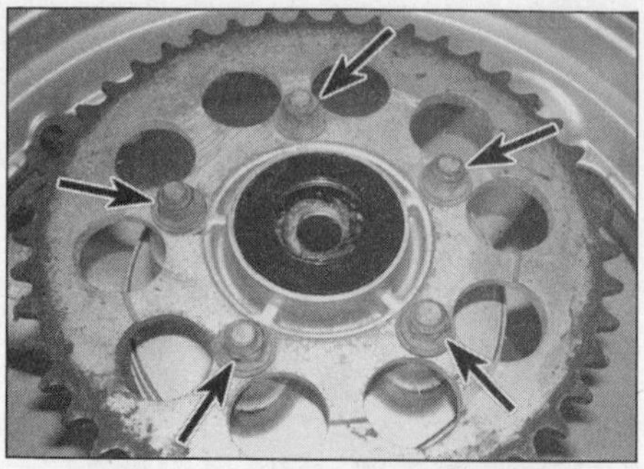

17.13 Rear sprocket bolts (arrowed)

the condition of the washer and discard it if there are any cracks or if it is badly scored or deformed. Otherwise it can be reused.

7 Fully slacken the drive chain as described in Chapter 1. If the rear sprocket is being renewed as well, remove the rear wheel now to give full slack. Otherwise disengage the chain from the rear sprocket.

8 Disengage the chain from the front sprocket then slide the sprocket off the shaft **(see illustration)**.

9 Slide the new sprocket on the shaft, making sure the marked side is facing out, and fit the chain around it **(see illustrations 17.8)**. Fit the chain onto the rear sprocket or install the rear wheel (see Chapter 7), then take up the slack in the chain.

10 Fit a new lockwasher onto the shaft **(see illustration 17.6c)**. Fit the nut and tighten it to the specified torque setting, holding the rear brake on to prevent the sprocket turning (if the rear sprocket is being renewed as well do that now and install the rear wheel so that the brake can be used) **(see illustration 17.6b)**. Bend the lockwasher tab up against one of the nut flats **(see illustration)**.

11 Locate the clutch release mechanism and secure it with the bolts **(see illustration 17.5)**. Check the clutch cable freeplay and adjust if necessary (see Chapter 1). Fit the sprocket cover and tighten its bolts **(see illustration 17.1)**. Adjust and lubricate the chain following the procedures described in Chapter 1.

HAYNES HiNT ***Keep your old front sprocket as it can be used along with a holding tool to lock the transmission input shaft should you ever need to remove the clutch (see Chapter 2).***

Rear sprocket renewal

12 Remove the rear wheel (see Chapter 7).

13 Unscrew the nuts securing the sprocket to the hub assembly, and remove the washers **(see illustration)**. Remove the sprocket, noting which way round it fits. Fit the new sprocket onto the hub with the stamped mark facing out. Install the nuts with their washers, and tighten the nuts evenly and in a criss-cross sequence to the torque setting specified at the beginning of the Chapter.

14 Install the rear wheel (see Chapter 7).

18 Rear sprocket coupling/ rubber dampers

1 Remove the rear wheel (see Chapter 7). ***Caution: Do not lay the wheel down on the disc as it could become warped. Lay the wheel on wooden blocks so that the disc is off the ground.***

2 Lift the sprocket coupling away from the wheel leaving the rubber dampers in position **(see illustration)**. Note the spacer inside the coupling – it should be a tight fit but remove it if it is likely to drop out **(see illustration)**. Check the coupling for cracks or any obvious signs of damage. Also check the sprocket studs for wear or damage.

3 Lift the rubber damper segments from the wheel and check them for cracks, hardening and general deterioration **(see illustration)**. Renew them as a set if necessary.

4 Checking and renewal procedures for the sprocket coupling bearing are described in Chapter 7.

5 Installation is the reverse of removal. Smear some grease around the outside of the left-hand bearing housing where the sprocket coupling fits over it. Make sure the spacer is still correctly installed in the coupling, or install it if it was removed **(see illustration 18.2b)**.

6 Install the rear wheel (see Chapter 7).

18.2a Lift the sprocket coupling out of the wheel . . .

18.2b . . . noting the spacer

18.3 Check the rubber dampers

Chapter 7
Brakes, wheels and tyres

Contents

Degrees of difficulty

Easy, suitable for novice with little experience

Fairly easy, suitable for beginner with some experience

Fairly difficult, suitable for competent DIY mechanic

Difficult, suitable for experienced DIY mechanic

Very difficult, suitable for expert DIY or professional

Specifications

Brakes

Brake fluid type	DOT 4	
Disc minimum thickness	**Standard**	**Service lmit**
Front	4.5 mm	4.0 mm
Rear	5.0 mm	4.5 mm
Disc maximum runout (front and rear)	0.3 mm	
Caliper bore ID		
Front – non-ABS models	30.230 to 30.306 mm	
Front – ABS models	27.000 to 27.076 mm	
Rear		
X, Y, K1 and K2 models	38.180 to 38.256 mm	
K3-on models	38.180 to 38.230 mm	
Caliper piston OD		
Front – non-ABS models	30.150 to 30.200 mm	
Front – ABS models	26.920 to 26.970 mm	
Rear	38.080 to 38.130 mm	
Master cylinder bore ID		
Front – non-ABS models	15.870 to 15.913 mm	
Front – ABS models	14.000 to 14.043 mm	
Rear		
X, Y, K1 and K2 models	12.700 to 12.743 mm	
K3-on models	14.000 to 14.043 mm	
Master cylinder piston OD		
Front – non-ABS model	15.827 to 15.854 mm	
Front – ABS models	13.957 to 13.984 mm	
Rear		
X, Y, K1 and K2 models	12.657 to 12.684 mm	
K3-on models	13.957 to 13.984 mm	
ABS wheel speed sensor air gap	0.3 to 1.5 mm	

Wheels

Maximum wheel runout (front and rear)	
Axial (side-to-side)	2.0 mm
Radial (out-of-round)	2.0 mm
Maximum axle runout (front and rear)	0.25 mm
Rim size	
Front	17 x MT3.50
Rear	17 x MT4.50

Tyres

Tyre pressures	see *Daily (pre-ride)* checks on page 0•16
Tyre sizes*	
Front	120/60-ZR17 55W
Rear	160/60-ZR17 69W

**Refer to the owners handbook or the tyre information label on the chainguard for approved tyre brands.*

Torque settings

Brake caliper bleed valves	7.5 Nm
Brake hose banjo bolts	23 Nm
Brake pipe gland nuts (ABS models)	16 Nm
Front brake caliper mounting bolts	39 Nm
Front brake disc bolts	23 Nm
Front brake master cylinder clamp bolts	10 Nm
Front wheel axle	65 Nm
Front wheel axle clamp bolt	23 Nm
Rear brake caliper body joining bolts (X, Y, K1 and K2 models)	30 Nm
Rear brake caliper mounting bolts	
X, Y, K1 and K2 models	26 Nm
K3-on models	23 Nm
Rear brake caliper sliding pin (K3-on models)	27 Nm
Rear brake caliper pad pin (K3-on models)	18 Nm
Rear brake disc bolts	23 Nm
Rear brake master cylinder bolts	10 Nm
Rear brake torque arm nuts (X, Y, K1 and K2 models)	35 Nm
Rear wheel axle nut	
X, Y, K1 and K2 models	65 Nm
K3-on models	100 Nm

1 General information

All models covered in this manual are fitted with cast alloy wheels designed for tubeless tyres only. Both front and rear brakes are hydraulically operated disc brakes.

On all models the front brakes have twin piston sliding calipers. On X, Y, K1 and K2 models, the rear brake has a single opposed piston caliper and on K3-on models, the rear brake has a single piston sliding caliper.

Caution: Hydraulic disc brake components rarely require disassembly. Do not disassemble components unless absolutely necessary. If a hydraulic brake line is loosened, the entire system must be disassembled, drained, cleaned and then properly filled and bled upon reassembly. Do not use solvents on internal brake components. Solvents will cause the seals to swell and distort. Use only clean brake fluid or denatured alcohol for cleaning. Use care when working with brake fluid as it can injure your eyes and it will damage painted surfaces and plastic parts.

2.2a Unscrew the caliper mounting bolts (arrowed) . . .

2 Brake pad renewal

Warning: The dust created by the brake system may contain asbestos, which is harmful to your health. Never blow it out with compressed air and don't inhale any of it. An approved filtering mask should be worn when working on the brakes. Do not, under any circum-stances, use petroleum-based solvents to clean brake parts. Use clean brake fluid, brake cleaner or denatured alcohol only.

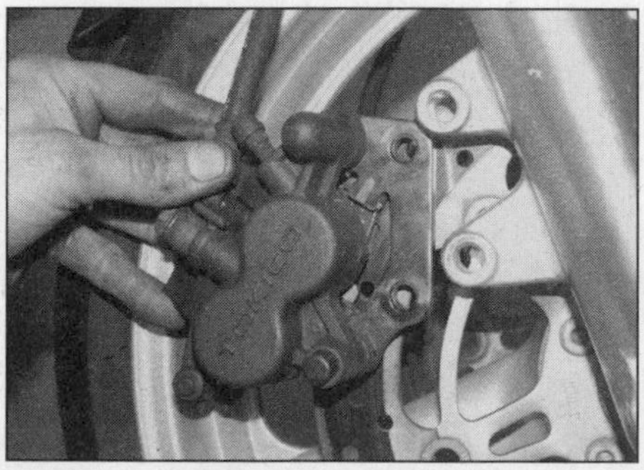

2.2b . . . and slide the caliper off the disc

Front brake pads

1 If new pads are being fitted, push the brake caliper against the disc so that the pistons are forced back into the caliper to allow for the increased friction material thickness. It may be necessary to remove the master cylinder reservoir cover or cap and diaphragm and remove some fluid (see *Daily (pre-ride) checks*). If the pistons are difficult to push back, either attach a length of clear hose to the bleed valve and place the open end in a suitable container, then open the valve and try again, or wait until the caliper has been displaced and the pads removed as it is not good to push too hard against a floating disc (see Step 7). If you open the bleed valve, take great care not to draw any air into the system **(see illustration 9.5a)**. If in doubt, bleed the brakes afterwards (see Section 9).

2 Unscrew the caliper bracket mounting bolts and slide the caliper assembly off the disc **(see illustrations)**.

3 Pull the retaining clip out of the pad pin, then withdraw the pin **(see illustrations)**. Pivot the inner pad out of the caliper until it clears the bracket then slide it sideways off its post **(see illustration)**. Remove the outer pad, noting how it locates against the guide **(see illustration)**. Note the pad spring in the top of caliper and the pad guide on the caliper bracket and remove them if required for cleaning or renewal, noting how they fit **(see illustrations)**. Also note the shim on the back of the outer pad **(see illustration)** – if new pads are being installed, keep the old shim in case the new one doesn't come with it fitted.

4 Inspect the surface of each pad for contamination and check whether the friction

2.3a Remove the clip . . .

2.3b . . . and withdraw the pin

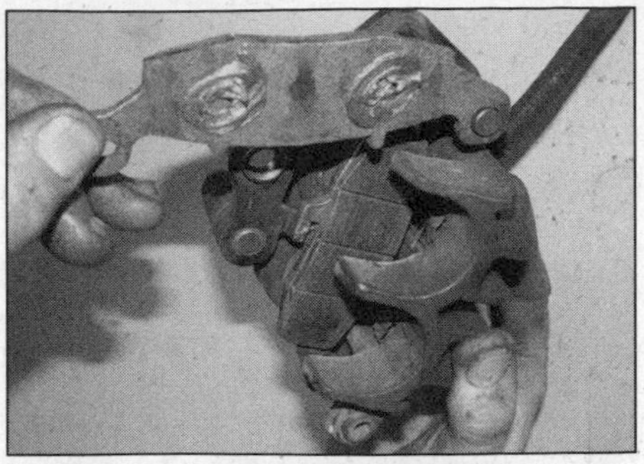
2.3c Remove the inner pad . . .

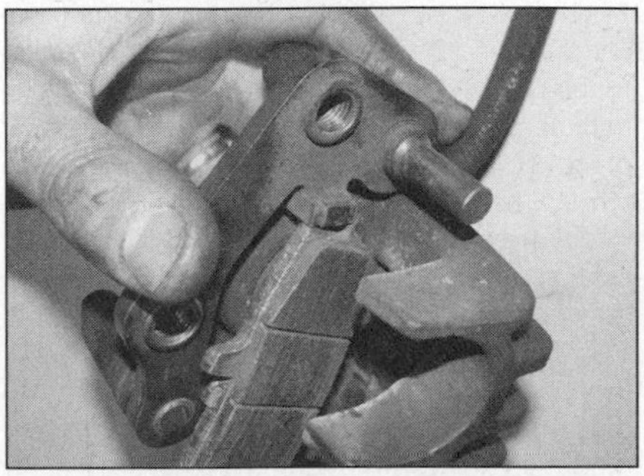
2.3d . . . and the outer pad, noting how they fit

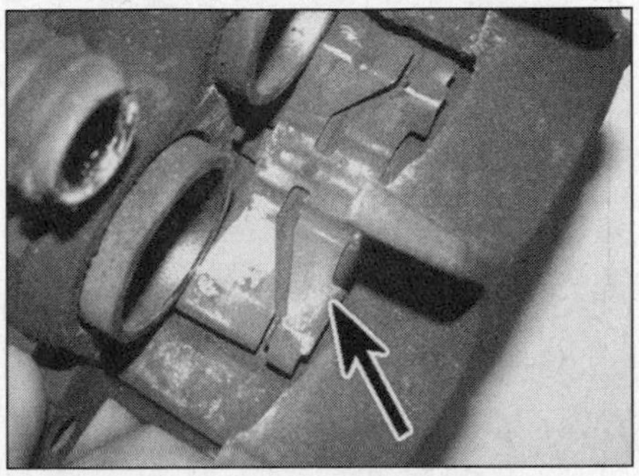
2.3e Note the pad spring (arrowed) . . .

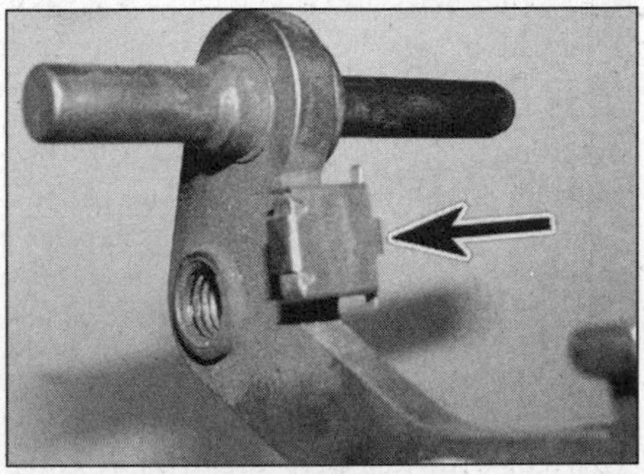
2.3f . . . the pad guide (arrowed) . . .

material has worn beyond its service limit (see Chapter 1, Section 11) **(see illustration)**. If any pad is worn to or beyond the service limit, is contaminated with oil or grease, or is heavily scored or damaged by dirt and debris, both sets of pads must be renewed as a set.

5 If the pads are in good condition clean them carefully, using a fine wire brush which is completely free of oil and grease to remove all traces of road dirt and corrosion. Using a pointed instrument, clean out the grooves in the friction material **(see illustration)**. Any areas of glazing may be removed using emery cloth. Spray with a dedicated brake cleaner to remove any dust. It is also worth spraying the inside of the caliper to remove any dust there, and also to spray the discs.

6 Check the condition of the brake disc (see Section 3).

7 If necessary, push the pistons back into the caliper to create room for the new pads – you can use your hands to do this, though a piece of wood against the pistons in conjunction with some grips and a bit of card to protect the caliper works very well, as does a proper piston-pushing tool **(see illustrations)**.

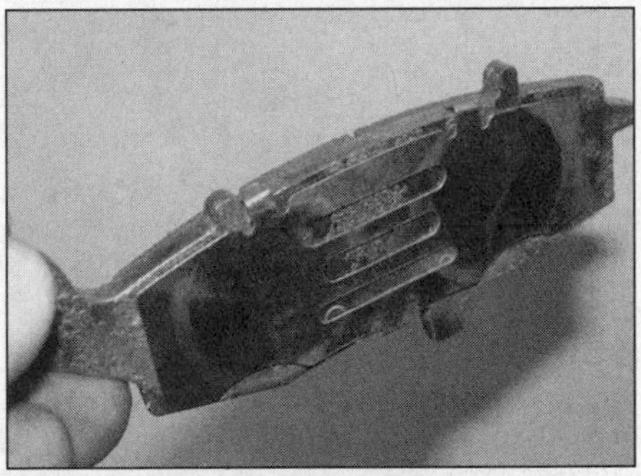
2.3g . . . and the shim on the back of the outer pad

8 Make sure that the pad spring and pad guide are correctly fitted **(see illustrations 2.3e and f)**. If removed, fit the shim onto the back of the outer pad **(see illustration 2.3g)**.

9 Remove all traces of corrosion from the

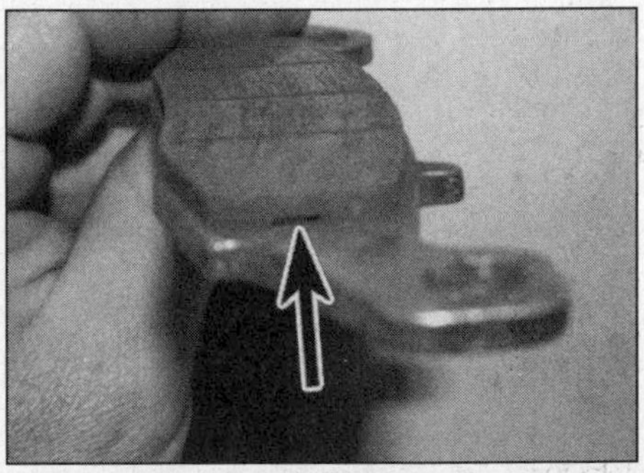
2.4 Friction material wear limit cutout (arrowed)

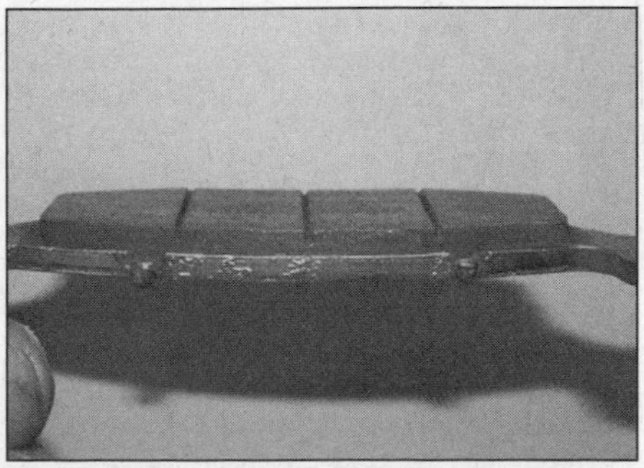
2.5 Clean out the grooves in the friction material

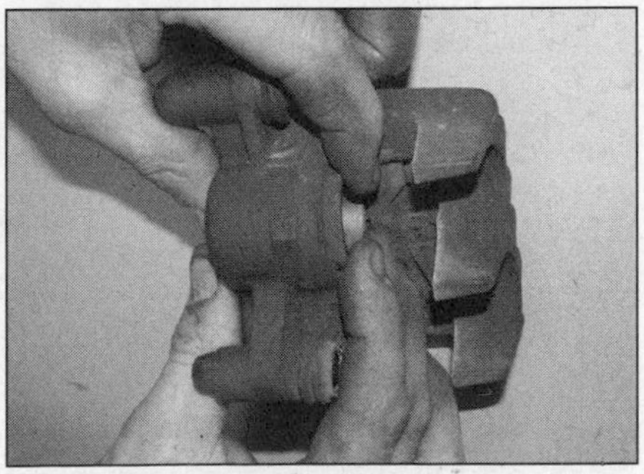
2.7a Push the pistons back using your fingers . . .

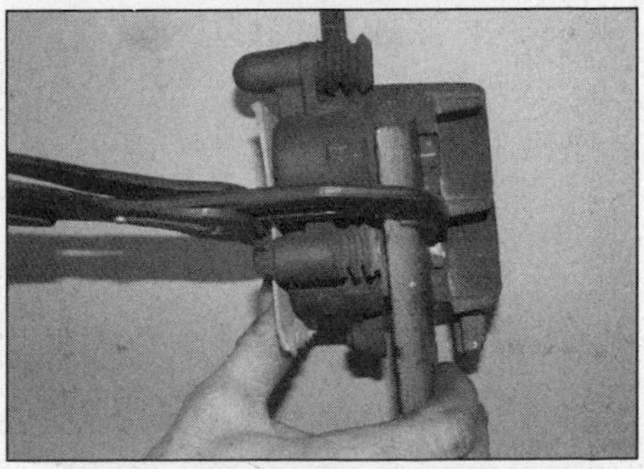
2.7b . . . some grips and a piece of wood . . .

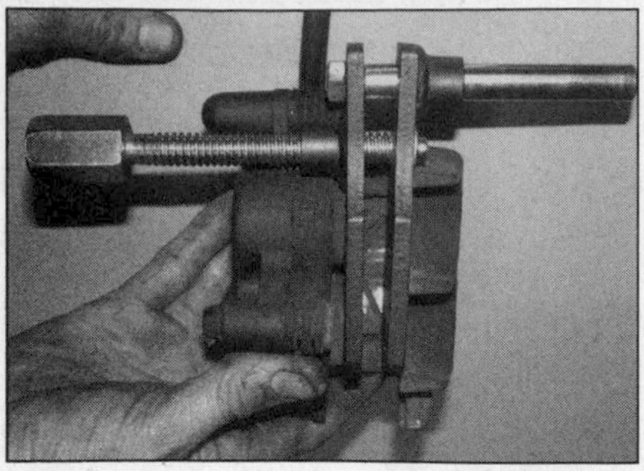

2.7c . . . or a commercially available tool

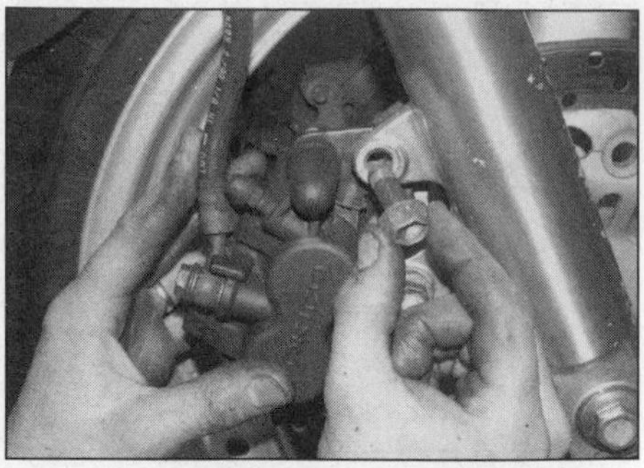

2.11 Slide the caliper onto the disc and tighten the bolts to the specified torque

pad pin and check it is not bent or damaged. Smear the pin and the backs of the pads with copper-based grease, making sure that none gets on the friction material.

10 Fit the outer pad into the caliper so that the shim on the back is against the pistons, making sure the inner end locates correctly against the guide on the bracket **(see illustration 2.3d)**. Fit the inner pad over its post, then slide it across and pivot it down **(see illustration 2.3c)**. Press the pads up against the pad spring to align the holes and insert the pad pin **(see illustration 2.3b)**. Secure the pin with the retaining clip, making sure it fits through the hole in the pin – if necessary rotate the pad pin to align the hole correctly **(see illustration 2.3a)**. Use a new clip if the old one is corroded or deformed in any way.

11 Slide the caliper onto the disc making sure the pads locate on each side **(see illustration)**. Apply a suitable non-permanent thread locking compound to the caliper bolts and tighten them to the specified torque setting.

12 Top up the master cylinder reservoir if necessary (see *Daily (pre-ride) checks*).

13 Operate the brake lever several times to bring the pads into contact with the disc. Check the operation of the brake before riding the motorcycle. Repeat the operation on the pads in the other front brake caliper.

Rear brake pads

X, Y, K1 and K2 models

Note: *If the pad pins have not been previously greased and have not been removed for a while, they could well be very difficult to withdraw (see Step 16). If this is the case, they will have to be driven out from the back of the caliper. To do this you will have to remove the caliper (see Section 5), as otherwise the shock could distort the disc. If you apply penetrating fluid this will help, but make sure none gets on the pads.*

14 Prise off the brake pad cover using a flat-bladed screwdriver **(see illustration)**.

15 Pull the retaining clips out of the pad pins **(see illustration)**. Before removing the pads. Look up into the caliper and note how the pad springs fit.

16 Withdraw the pad pins from the caliper using a suitable pair of pliers and remove the pad springs **(see illustration)**. Withdraw the pads from the caliper body. If required remove the anti-chatter shim from the back of each pad, noting how they fit.

17 If new pads are being fitted, push the pistons as far back into the caliper as possible to allow for the increased friction material thickness. Use a piece of wood as leverage, or place the old pads back in the caliper and use a metal bar or a screwdriver inserted between them, or use grips and a rag or card to protect the caliper body **(see illustrations)**. You can do this with the pads removed, but you should only use wood or your fingers so as not to damage the pistons. It may be necessary to remove the master cylinder reservoir cap and diaphragm and remove some fluid (see *Daily (pre-ride) checks)*. If the pistons are difficult to push back, attach a length of clear hose to the bleed valve and place the open end in a suitable container, then open the valve and try again **(see illustration 9.5b)**. Take great care not to draw any air into the system. If in doubt, bleed the brake afterwards (see Section 9).

18 Refer to Steps 4, 5 and 6 above.

2.14 Remove the pad cover

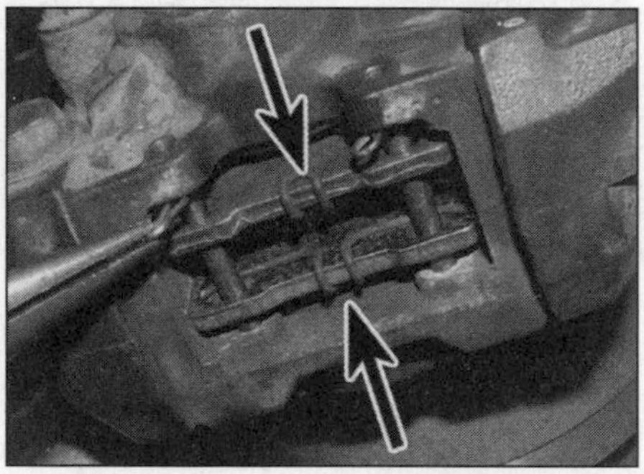

2.15 Withdraw the clips. Note how the springs (arrowed) locate

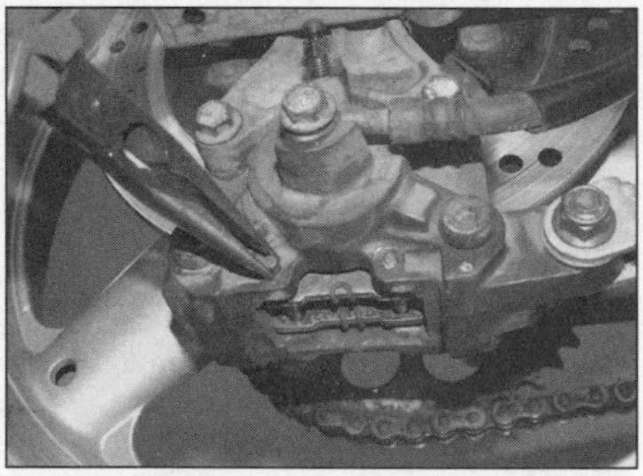

2.16 Withdraw the retaining pins and remove the springs and pads

2.17a Push the pistons back using a bar as leverage . . .

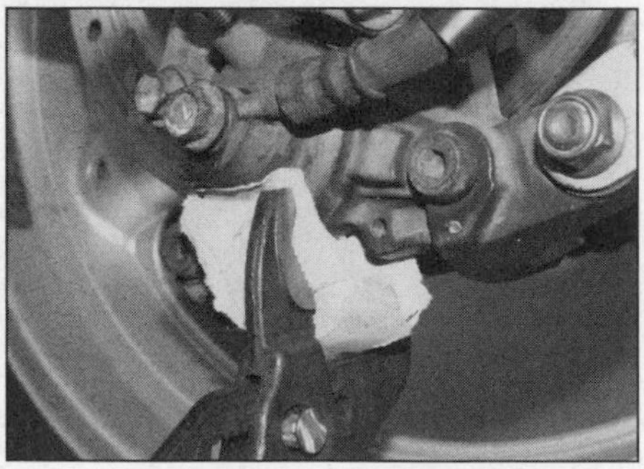

2.17b . . . or grips

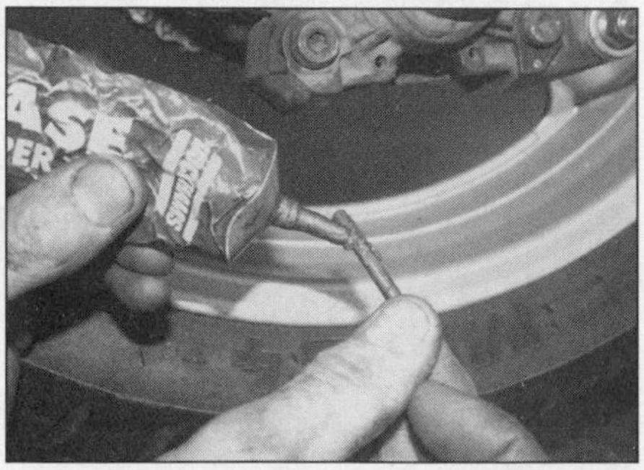

2.19 Smear copper grease on the pins and the back of each pad

2.20a Insert the outer pad and slide one pin part-way through . . .

2.20b . . . then locate the end of one spring under the pin and onto the pad

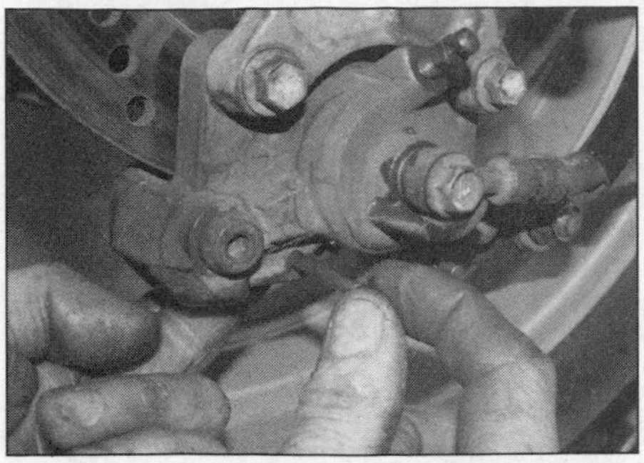

2.20c Push up on the other end of the spring and slide the pin through

2.20d Fit the inner pad . . .

2.20e . . . then locate the spring end under the pin and onto the pad . . .

2.20f . . . and push the other end up and slide the pin through

19 Smear the backs of the pads and the shank of each pad pin with copper-based grease, making sure that none gets on the front or sides of the pads **(see illustration)**. Fit the anti-chatter shim onto the back of each pad with its open end facing forward.

20 Insert the outer pad up into the caliper with the friction material facing the disc, then slide one pad pin, with its holed end on the outside, through the hole in the pad and part-way through the caliper **(see illustrations)**. Fit the pad spring, locating one end under the installed pad pin and onto the edge of the friction material, fitting the central hooked section over the bottom edge of the pad backing **(see illustration)**. Press up on the free end of the pad spring and slide the other pad pin over the spring end **(see illustration)**. Fit the inner pad up into the caliper and repeat the procedure of installing the pad spring and second pin **(see illustrations)**. Secure the pins with the retaining clips, making sure they fit through the holes in the pad pins – if necessary rotate the pad pins to align their holes correctly **(see illustration 2.15)**. Use new clips if the old ones are deformed in any way.

21 Fit the pad cover **(see illustration 2.14)**.

22 Top up the master cylinder reservoir if necessary (see *Daily (pre-ride) checks*).

23 Operate the brake pedal several times to bring the pads into contact with the disc. Check the operation of the brake before riding the motorcycle.

K3-on models

24 Unscrew the plug then slacken the pad pin **(see illustrations)**.

25 Unscrew the caliper mounting bolt, then pivot the caliper up **(see illustrations)**.

26 Withdraw the pad pin then pull the pads out of the caliper **(see illustrations)**. Note the pad spring in the top of caliper and remove it if required for cleaning or renewal, noting how it fits **(see illustration)**. Also note the shims and insulators on the back of each pad **(see illustration)** – if new pads are being installed, keep the old insulators and

2.24a Unscrew the plug . . .

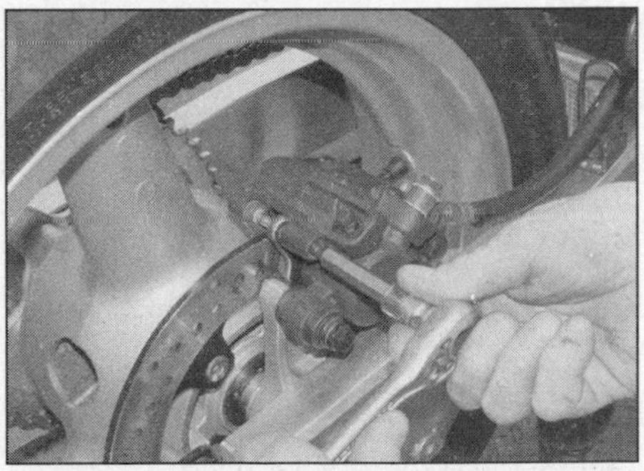

2.24b . . . then slacken the pad pin

2.25a Unscrew the caliper bolt . . .

2.25b . . . and pivot the caliper up

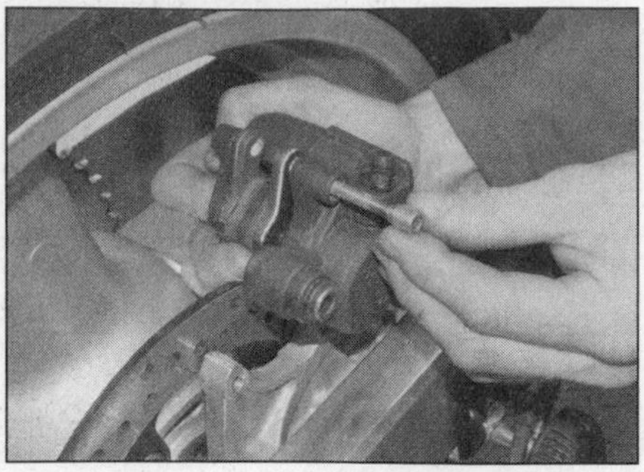

2.26a Remove the pad pin . . .

2.26b . . . and pull out the pads

2.26c Note the location of the pad spring (arrowed)

shims in case the new ones don't come with them fitted.

27 Refer to Steps 4, 5 and 6 above.

28 If necessary, push the piston back into the caliper to create room for the new pads – you can use your hands to do this, though a piece of wood against the piston in conjunction with some grips and a bit of card to protect the caliper works very well, as does a proper piston-pushing tool (see Step 7). **Note:** *Under no circumstances lever against the brake disc to push the piston back into the caliper as damage to the disc will result.* If necessary, remove the master cylinder reservoir cap and diaphragm and remove some fluid (see Step 17).

29 Make sure that the pad spring is correctly fitted **(see illustration 2.26c)**. If removed, fit the insulators and shims onto the backs of the pads **(see illustration 2.26d)**.

30 Remove all traces of corrosion from the pad pin and check it is not bent or damaged. Smear the pin and the backs of the pads with copper-based grease, making sure that none gets on the friction material.

31 Insert the pads into the caliper with the friction material facing the disc. Ensure that the inner ends locate correctly against the guide on the bracket, then secure the pads with the pad pin **(see illustration 2.26a)**.

32 Pivot the caliper down and install the mounting bolt. Tighten the bolt and the pad pin to the specified torque setting, then fit the plug.

33 Top up the master cylinder reservoir if necessary (see *Daily (pre-ride) checks*).

34 Operate the brake pedal several times to bring the pads into contact with the disc. Check the operation of the brake before riding the motorcycle.

3 Brake discs

Warning: The dust created by the brake system may contain asbestos, which is harmful to your health. Never blow it out with compressed air and don't inhale any of it. An approved filtering mask should be worn when working on the brakes. Do not, under any circumstances, use petroleum-based solvents to clean brake parts. Use clean brake fluid, brake cleaner or denatured alcohol only.

Inspection

1 Visually inspect the surface of the disc for score marks and other damage. Light scratches are normal after use and won't affect brake operation, but deep grooves and heavy score marks will reduce braking efficiency and accelerate pad wear. If a disc is badly grooved it must be machined or renewed.

2 To check disc runout, position the bike on an auxiliary stand so that the wheel being checked is off the ground. Mount a dial gauge to a fork slider or on the swingarm, according to wheel, with the plunger on the gauge touching the surface of the disc about 10 mm (1/2 in) from the outer edge **(see illustration)**. Rotate the wheel and watch the gauge needle, comparing the reading with the limit listed in the Specifications at the beginning of the Chapter. If the runout is greater than the service limit, check the wheel bearings for play (see Chapter 1). If the bearings are worn, renew them (see Section 14) and repeat this check. It is also worth removing the disc (see below) and checking for built-up corrosion (see Step 6) as this will cause runout. If the runout is still excessive, the disc must be renewed, although machining by an engineer may be possible. Note: Always renew the front discs as a pair, never singly.

3 The disc must not be machined or allowed to wear down to a thickness less than the service limit as listed in this Chapter's Specifications and as marked on the disc itself

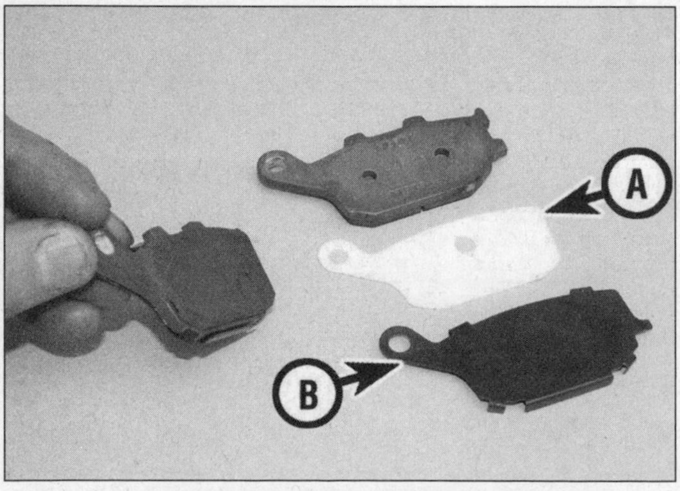

2.26d An insulator (A) and shim (B) are fitted to the back of each pad

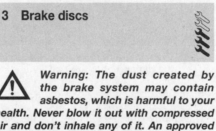

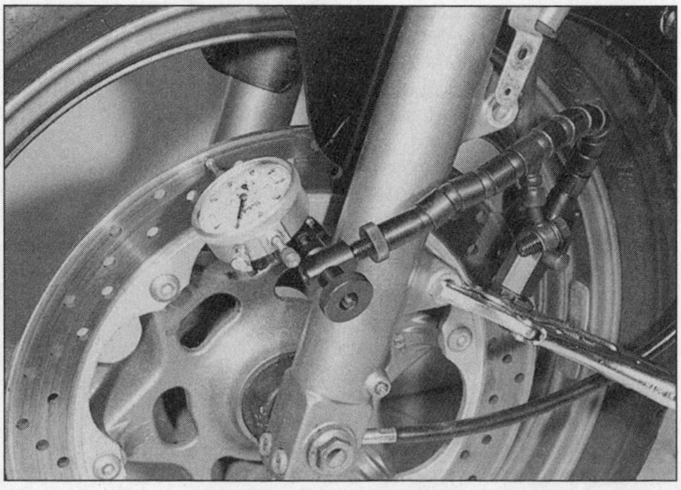

3.2 Checking disc runout

3.3a Front disc minimum thickness markings

3.3b Rear disc minimum thickness markings

3.3c Checking disc thickness

(see illustrations). Check the thickness of the disc using a micrometer **(see illustration)**. If the thickness of the disc is less than the service limit, it must be renewed.

Removal

4 Remove the wheel (see Section 12 or 13). ***Caution: Do not lay the wheel down and allow it to rest on the disc – the disc could become warped. Set the wheel on wood blocks so the disc doesn't support the weight of the wheel.***

5 Mark the relationship of the disc to the wheel, so it can be installed in the same position and on the same side of the wheel in the case of the front discs. Unscrew the disc retaining bolts, loosening them a little at a time in a criss-cross pattern to avoid distorting the disc, then remove the disc from the wheel **(see illustrations)**. On ABS-equipped models, the pulser ring can be detached from the disc by removing its three retaining bolts. Note that the pulser ring must be installed with its 50T marking facing outwards.

Installation

6 Before installing the disc, make sure there is no dirt or corrosion where the disc seats on the hub, particularly right in the angle of the seat, as this will not allow the disc to sit flat when it is bolted down and it will appear to be warped when checked or when using the brake.

7 Install the disc on the wheel, making sure the directional arrow is on the outside and pointing in the direction of normal (i.e. forward) rotation. Also note any R or L marking on the front discs that denotes on which side of the wheel it must be mounted. Align the previously applied matchmarks (if you're reinstalling the original disc).

8 Apply a suitable non-permanent thread locking compound to the threads of the disc bolts, and tighten them evenly in a criss-cross pattern to the torque setting specified at the beginning of the Chapter **(see illustration 3.5a or b)**. Clean off all grease from the brake disc(s) using acetone or brake system cleaner. If a new brake disc has been installed, remove any protective coating from its working surfaces.

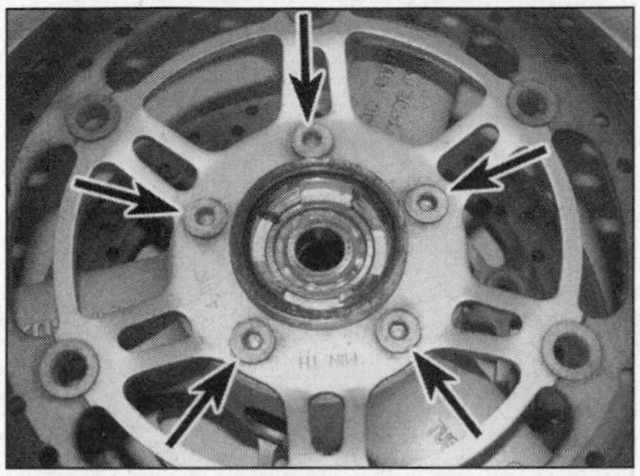

3.5a Front disc . . .

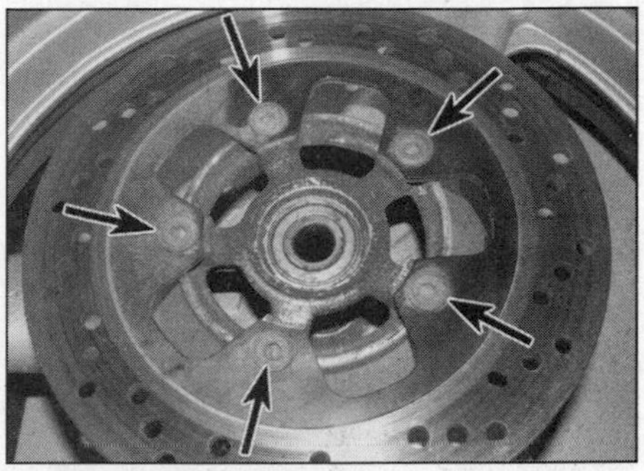

3.5b . . . and rear disc bolts (arrowed)

9 Install the wheel (see Section 12 or 13). Note that when installing a new disc it is advisable to fit new brake pads (see Section 2).

10 Operate the brake lever or pedal (as applicable) several times to bring the pads into contact with the disc. Check the operation of the brakes carefully before riding the bike.

4 Front brake calipers

Warning: If a caliper indicates the need for an overhaul (usually due to leaking fluid or sticky operation), all old brake fluid should be flushed from the system. Also, the dust created by the brake system may contain asbestos, which is harmful to your health. Never blow it out with compressed air and don't inhale any of it. An approved filtering mask should be worn when working on the brakes. Do not, under any circumstances, use petroleum-based solvents to clean brake parts. Use clean brake fluid, brake cleaner or denatured alcohol only.

Warning: Use care when working with brake fluid as it can injure your eyes and it will damage painted surfaces and plastic parts.

Removal

1 If the caliper is just being displaced and not completely removed or overhauled, do not disconnect the brake hose. If the caliper is being completely removed or overhauled, unscrew the brake hose banjo bolt and detach the hose, noting its alignment with the caliper **(see illustration)**. Either plug the hose using another suitable short piece of hose fitted through the eye of the banjo union (it needs to be a fairly tight fit to seal it properly), clamp it using a hose clamp, or wrap a plastic bag tightly around to minimise fluid loss and prevent dirt entering the system. Discard the sealing washers as new ones must be used on installation. **Note:** *If you are planning to overhaul the caliper and don't have a source of compressed air to blow out the pistons, just loosen the banjo bolt at this stage and retighten it lightly. The bike's hydraulic system can then be used to force the pistons out of the body once the pads have been removed. Disconnect the hose once the pistons have been sufficiently displaced.*

2 If required, unscrew the bolt securing

4.1 Brake hose banjo bolt (arrowed)

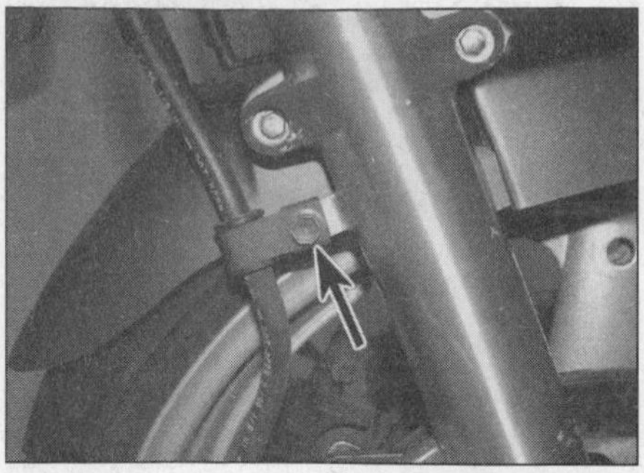

4.2 Brake hose clamp bolt (arrowed)

4.5 Separate the caliper and bracket by sliding them apart

the brake hose clamp to the front fork **(see illustration)**.

3 If the caliper is being overhauled, remove the brake pads (see Section 2).

4 If not already done, unscrew the caliper bracket mounting bolts and slide the caliper assembly off the disc **(see illustrations 2.2a and b)**.

Overhaul

5 Separate the caliper from the bracket by sliding them apart **(see illustration)**. If required, remove the pad spring from the caliper and the guide from the bracket, noting how they fit **(see illustrations 2.3e and f)**.

6 Clean the exterior of the caliper with denatured alcohol or brake system cleaner **(see illustration)**.

7 Remove the pistons from the caliper body, either by pumping them out by operating the brake lever, or by using compressed air. If the compressed air method is used, place a wad of rag over the pistons to act as a cushion, then use compressed air directed into the fluid inlet to force the pistons out of the body. Use only low pressure to ease the pistons out, and make sure they are displaced at the same time. If the air pressure is too high and the pistons are forced out, the caliper and/or pistons may be damaged.

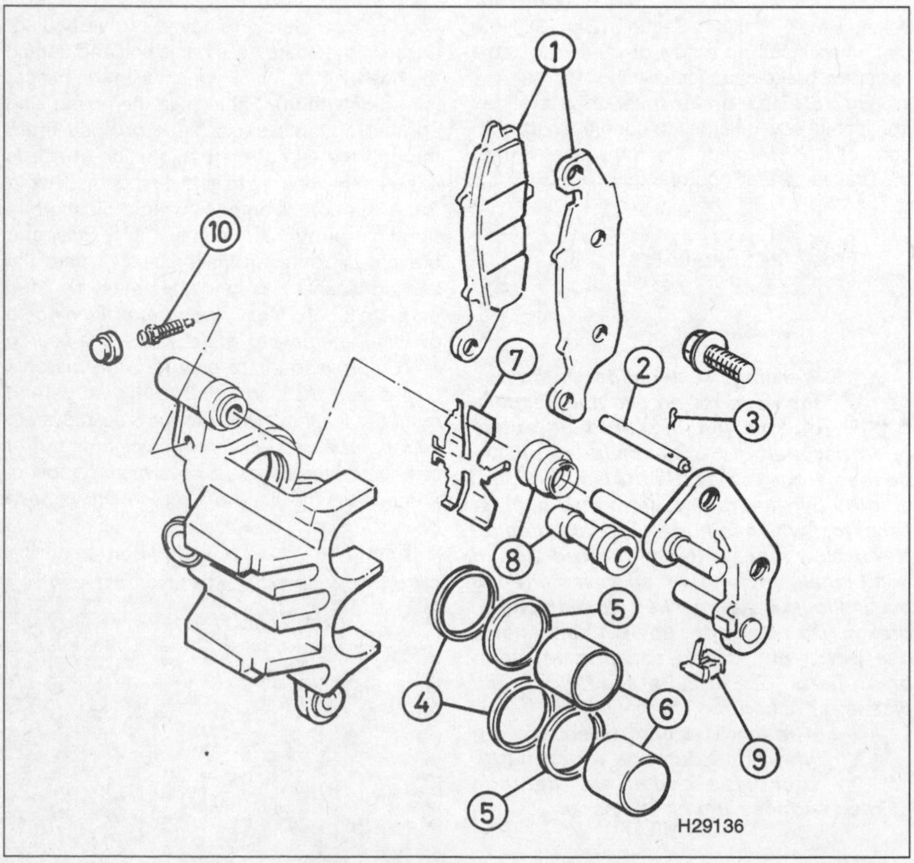

4.6 Front brake caliper components

1 *Brake pads*
2 *Pad pin*
3 *Retaining clip*
4 *Piston seal*
5 *Dust seal*
6 *Piston*
7 *Pad spring*
8 *Rubber boots*
9 *Pad guide*
10 *Bleed valve*

Warning: Never place your fingers in front of the pistons in an attempt to catch or protect them when applying compressed air, as serious injury could result. Place the caliper piston side down on a bench, with the rag between them, and let the air lift the caliper off the piston.

Caution: Do not try to remove the pistons by levering them out, or by using pliers or any other grips.

8 Using a wooden or plastic tool, remove the dust seals from the caliper bores taking great care not to damage the bores. **(see illustration)**. Discard the seals as new ones must be used on installation.

9 Remove and discard the piston seals in the same way.

10 Clean the pistons and bores, paying attention to the seal grooves, with denatured alcohol, clean brake fluid or brake system cleaner. If compressed air is available, use it to dry the parts thoroughly (make sure it's filtered and unlubricated).

Caution: Do not, under any circumstances, use a petroleum-based solvent to clean brake parts.

11 Inspect the caliper bores and pistons for signs of corrosion, nicks and burrs and loss of plating. If surface defects are present, the caliper and/or pistons must be renewed. If the necessary measuring equipment is available, compare the dimensions of the pistons and bores to those given in the Specifications Section of this Chapter, renewing any component that is worn beyond its service limit. If the caliper is in bad shape the master cylinder should also be checked.

12 Remove the slider pin rubber boots from the caliper **(see illustration)**. Clean off all traces of corrosion and hardened grease from the boots and pins. Renew the rubber boots if they are damaged, deformed or deteriorated. Apply a smear of silicone based grease to the boots and fit them into their bores in the caliper.

13 Lubricate the new piston seals with clean brake fluid and fit them in their grooves in the caliper bores. On X, Y, K1 and K2 models, fit the seals with the wider side facing out **(see illustration)**.

14 Lubricate the new dust seals with clean brake fluid and fit them in their grooves in the caliper bore.

4.8 Use a plastic or wooden tool to remove the seals

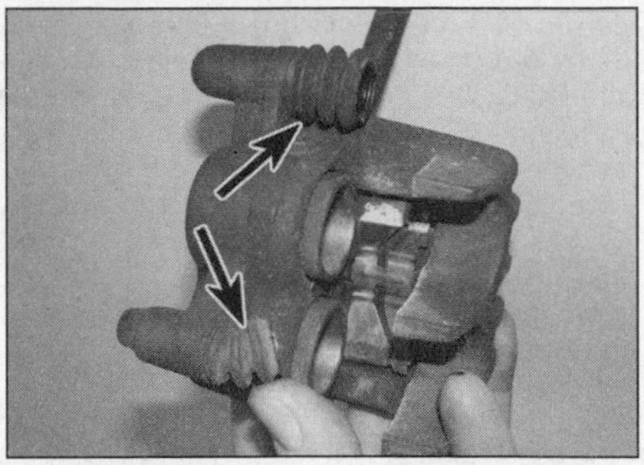

4.12 Remove the rubber boots (arrowed)

15 Lubricate the pistons with clean brake fluid and fit them closed-end first into the caliper bores. Using your thumbs, push the pistons all the way in, making sure they enter the bore squarely.

16 Make sure that the pad spring and pad guide are correctly fitted **(see illustrations 2.3e and f)**. Apply a smear of silicone based grease to the slider pins on the bracket. Slide the caliper and bracket together **(see illustration 4.5)**.

Installation

17 If the caliper has not been overhauled, separate the caliper from the bracket by sliding them apart **(see illustration 4.5)**. Remove the slider pin rubber boots from the caliper **(see illustration 4.12)**. Clean off all traces of corrosion and hardened grease from the boots and pins. Renew the rubber boots if they are damaged, deformed or deteriorated. Apply a smear of silicone based grease to the boots and slider pins. Fit the boots into their bores. Make sure that the pad spring and pad guide are correctly fitted **(see illustrations 2.3e and f)**. Slide the caliper and bracket together.

18 If the caliper has been overhauled, install the brake pads (see Section 2).

19 Slide the caliper onto the disc making sure the pads locate on each side **(see illustration 2.11)**. Apply a suitable non-permanent thread-locking compound to the mounting bolts and tighten them to the torque setting specified at the beginning of the Chapter.

20 If detached, connect the brake hose to the caliper, using new sealing washers on each side of the fitting. Align the hose as noted on removal **(see illustration 4.1)**. Tighten the banjo bolt to the torque setting specified at the beginning of the Chapter.

21 If removed, fit the brake hose clamp onto the front fork and secure it with the bolt **(see illustration 4.2)**.

22 Fill the master cylinder reservoir with DOT 4 brake fluid (see *Daily (pre-ride) checks*) and bleed the hydraulic system as described in Section 9.

23 Check that there are no fluid leaks and thoroughly test the operation of the front brake before riding the motorcycle.

5 Rear brake caliper

Warning: If a caliper indicates the need for an overhaul (usually due to leaking fluid or sticky operation), all old brake fluid should be flushed from the system. Also, the dust created by the brake system may contain asbestos, which is harmful to your health. Never blow it out with compressed air and don't inhale any of it. An approved filtering mask should be worn when working on the brakes. Do not, under any circumstances, use petroleum-based solvents to clean brake parts. Use clean brake fluid, brake cleaner or denatured alcohol only.

Warning: Use care when working with brake fluid as it can injure your eyes and it will damage painted surfaces and plastic parts.

X, Y, K1 and K2 models

Removal

1 If the caliper is just being displaced and not completely removed or overhauled, do not disconnect the brake hose. If the caliper is being completely removed or overhauled, unscrew the brake hose banjo bolt and detach the hose, noting its alignment with the caliper **(see illustration)**. Either plug the hose using another suitable short piece of hose fitted through the eye of the banjo union (it needs to be a fairly tight fit to seal it properly), clamp it using a hose clamp, or wrap a plastic bag tightly around to minimise fluid loss and prevent dirt entering the system. Discard the sealing washers as new ones must be used on installation. **Note:** *If you are planning to overhaul the caliper and don't have a source of compressed air to blow out the pistons, just loosen the banjo bolt at this stage and retighten it lightly. The bike's hydraulic system can then be used to force the pistons out of the body once the pads have been removed. Disconnect the hose once the pistons have been sufficiently displaced.*

2 If the caliper is being overhauled, remove the brake pads (see Section 2). If the caliper body is to be split into its halves for overhaul, slacken the joining bolts now and lightly retighten them **(see illustration)**.

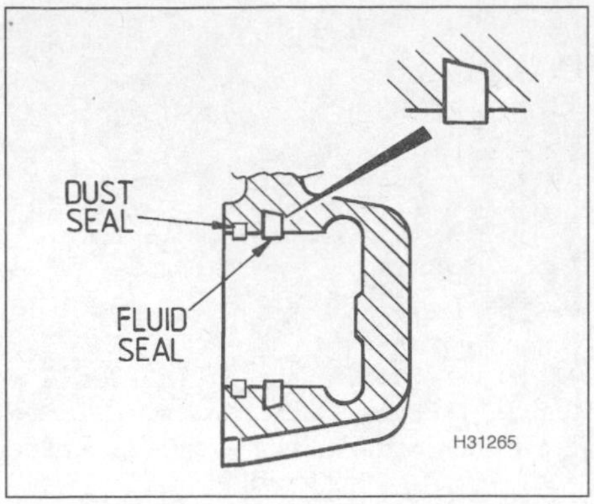

4.13 Note the fitment of the piston fluid seal – X, Y, K1 and K2 models

5.1 Brake hose banjo bolt (arrowed)

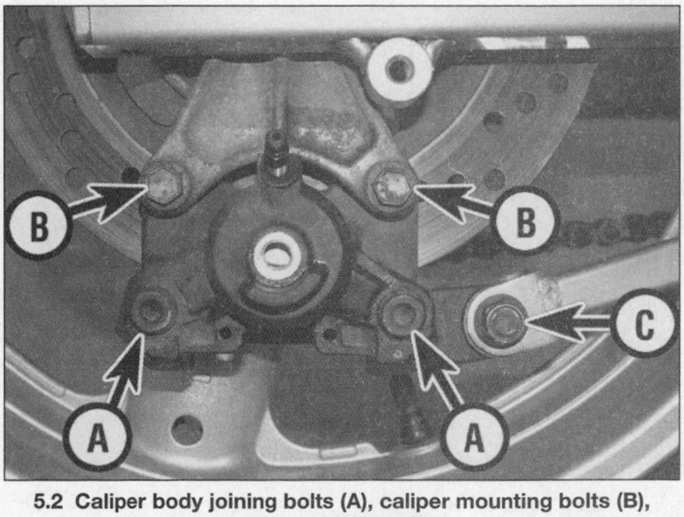

5.2 Caliper body joining bolts (A), caliper mounting bolts (B), torque arm bolt (C)

5.4 Unscrew the bolts and slide the caliper off the disc

3 Slacken the caliper mounting bolts, but do not yet remove them **(see illustration 5.2)**. Unscrew the nut securing the brake torque arm to the caliper, but do not yet remove the bolt.

4 Withdraw the bolt from the torque arm and move the arm off the caliper. Unscrew the caliper mounting bolts and slide the caliper down off the disc **(see illustration)**.

Overhaul

5 Clean the exterior of the caliper with denatured alcohol or brake system cleaner **(see illustration)**.

6 Displace the pistons as far as possible from the caliper body, either by pumping them out by operating the brake pedal, or by forcing them out using compressed air – do not allow the piston heads to touch. If the compressed air method is used, place a wad of rag between the pistons to act as a cushion, then use compressed air directed into the fluid inlet to force the pistons out of the body. Use only low pressure to ease the pistons out. If the air pressure is too high and the pistons are forced out, the caliper and/or pistons may be damaged.

Warning: Never place your fingers in front of either piston in an attempt to catch or protect it when applying compressed air, as serious injury could result.

Caution: Do not try to remove the pistons by levering them out, or by using pliers or any other grips.

7 Unscrew the caliper body joining bolts and separate the body halves. Remove the piston from each half. Mark each piston head and caliper body with a felt marker to ensure that the pistons can be matched to their original bores on reassembly. Extract the caliper seal from whichever body half it is in and discard it as a new one must be used.

8 Using a wooden or plastic tool, remove the dust seals from the caliper bores taking great care not to damage the bores **(see illustration 4.8)**. Discard the seals as new ones must be used on installation.

9 Remove and discard the piston seals in the same way.

10 Clean the pistons and bores, paying attention to the seal grooves, with denatured alcohol, clean brake fluid or brake system cleaner. If compressed air is available, use it to dry the parts thoroughly (make sure it's filtered and unlubricated).

Caution: Do not, under any circumstances, use a petroleum-based solvent to clean brake parts.

11 Inspect the caliper bores and pistons for signs of corrosion, nicks and burrs and loss of plating. If surface defects are present, the caliper and/or pistons must be renewed. If the necessary measuring equipment is available, compare the dimensions of the piston and bore to those given in the Specifications Section of this Chapter, renewing any component that is worn beyond its service limit. If the caliper is in bad shape the master cylinder should also be checked.

12 Lubricate the new piston seals with clean brake fluid and fit them in their grooves in the caliper bores, with the wider side facing out **(see illustration 4.13)**.

13 Lubricate the new dust seal with clean brake fluid and fit it in its groove in the caliper bore.

14 Lubricate the pistons with clean brake fluid and install each one closed-end first into its caliper bore. Using your thumbs, push the pistons all the way in, making sure they enter the bores squarely.

15 Lubricate the new caliper seal and install it into one half of the caliper body. Join the two halves of the caliper body together, making sure that the seal stays correctly seated in its recess. Install the caliper body joining bolts and tighten them to the torque setting specified at the beginning of the Chapter. If it is not possible to tighten the bolts fully at this stage, tighten them as much as possible, then tighten them fully once the caliper has been installed.

Installation

16 Slide the caliper onto the brake disc,

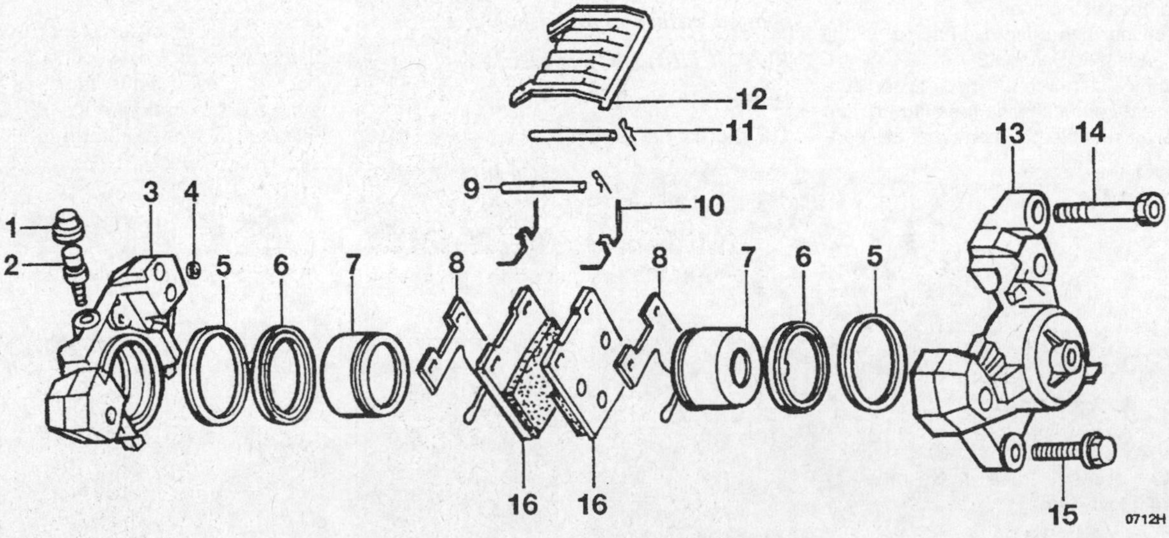

5.5 Rear brake caliper components – X, Y, K1 and K2 models

1 Bleed valve cap
2 Bleed valve
3 Caliper body half
4 Caliper seal
5 Piston seal
6 Dust seal
7 Piston
8 Anti-chatter shim
9 Pad pin
10 Pad spring
11 Retaining clips
12 Brake pad cover
13 Caliper body half
14 Caliper joining bolt
15 Caliper mounting bolt
16 Brake pads

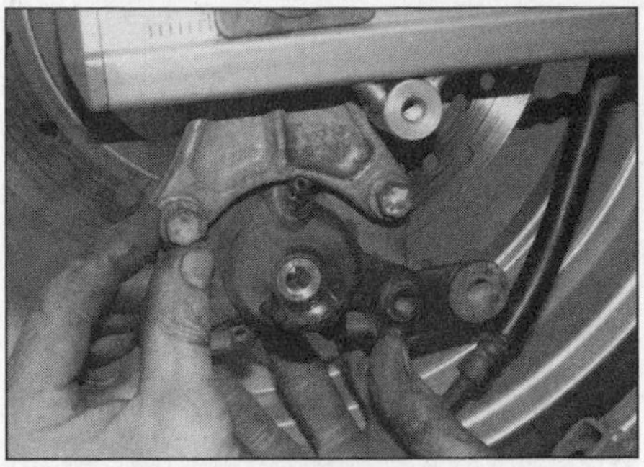

5.16 Install the bolts and tighten them as described

5.20 Use a new sealing washer on each side of the union

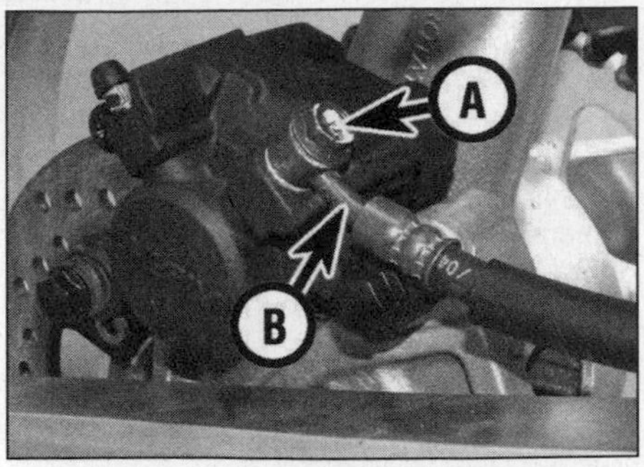

5.22 Unscrew the bolt (A) noting the alignment of the hose union (B)

making sure the pads sit squarely over each side of the disc if they weren't removed **(see illustration 5.4)**. Install the caliper mounting bolts, and tighten them finger-tight **(see illustration)**.

17 Fit the brake torque arm onto the caliper and secure it with its bolt **(see illustration 5.2)**. Tighten the nut to the torque setting specified at the beginning of the Chapter. Now tighten the caliper mounting bolts to the specified torque setting.

18 If the calipers were overhauled and if not already done, tighten the caliper body joining bolts to the specified torque setting **(see illustration 5.2)**.

19 If removed, install the brake pads (see Section 2).

20 If removed, connect the brake hose to the caliper, making sure it is routed through its guide on the swingarm, using new sealing washers on each side of the fitting **(see illustration)**. Align the hose as noted on removal **(see illustration 5.1)**. Tighten the banjo bolt to the torque setting specified at the beginning of the Chapter. Top up the master cylinder reservoir with DOT 4 brake fluid (see *Daily (pre-ride) checks*) and bleed the hydraulic system as described in Section 9.

21 Check that there are no fluid leaks and thoroughly test the operation of the rear brake before riding the motorcycle.

K3-on models

Removal

22 If the caliper is just being displaced and not completely removed or overhauled, do not disconnect the brake hose. If the caliper is being completely removed or overhauled, unscrew the brake hose banjo bolt and detach the hose union, noting its alignment with the caliper **(see illustration)**. Either plug the hose using another suitable short piece of hose fitted through the eye of the banjo union (it needs to be a fairly tight fit to seal it properly), clamp it using a hose clamp, or wrap a plastic bag tightly around to minimise fluid loss and prevent dirt entering the system. Discard the sealing washers as new ones must be used on installation. **Note:** *If you are planning to overhaul the caliper and don't have a source of compressed air to blow out the piston, just loosen the banjo bolt at this stage and retighten it lightly. The bike's hydraulic system can then be used to force the piston out of the body once the pads have been removed. Disconnect the hose once the piston has been sufficiently displaced.*

23 If the caliper is being overhauled, remove the brake pads (see Section 2). If the caliper is just being displaced, unscrew the caliper mounting bolt, then pivot the caliper up.

24 Pull the caliper off the caliper bracket **(see illustration)**. If required, secure the caliper with a cable tie to prevent straining the brake hose. Note the location of the pad guide on the caliper bracket **(see illustration)**.

Overhaul

25 Note the location of the pad spring inside the caliper then remove it **(see illustration)**.

26 Clean the exterior of the caliper with denatured alcohol or brake system cleaner.

27 Remove the spacer and rubber boot from the caliper **(see illustration)**. If the boot is damaged, deformed or deteriorated, renew it. If the spacer is worn or corroded, renew it. Clean the slider pin and inspect it for corrosion or wear; if necessary, unscrew the pin and fit a new one.

28 Remove the piston from the caliper body, either by pumping it out by operating the brake pedal, or by using compressed air. If the compressed air method is used, place a wad of rag over the piston to act as a cushion, then use compressed air directed into the fluid inlet to force the piston out of the body. Use only low pressure to ease the piston out – if the air pressure is too high and the piston is forced out, the caliper and/or piston may be damaged.

Warning: Never place your fingers in front of the piston in an attempt to catch or protect it when applying compressed air, as serious injury could result.

5.24a Pull the caliper off the bracket

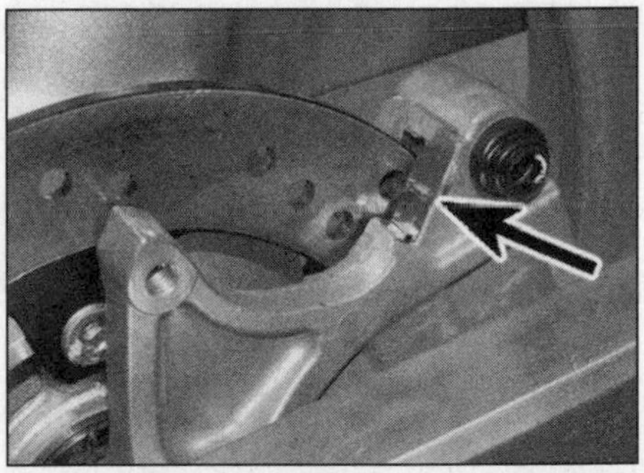

5.24b Note the location of the pad guide

5.25 Location of the pad spring (arrowed)

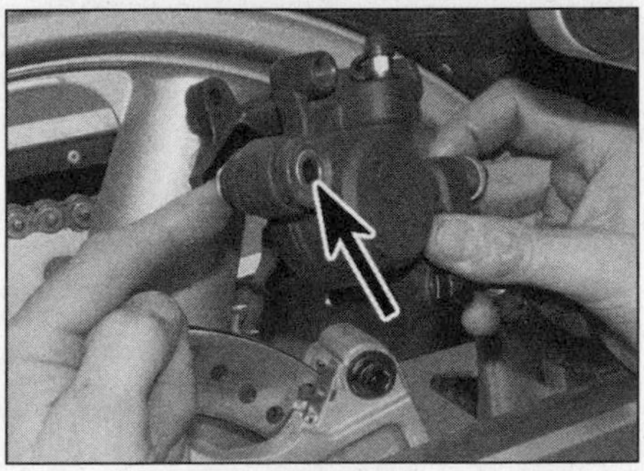

5.27 Push out the spacer and rubber boot (arrowed)

Caution: Do not try to remove the piston by levering it out, or by using pliers or any other grips.

29 Follow the procedure in Steps 8 and 9 and remove the dust and piston seals. Clean the piston and caliper bore, then inspect them for damage and wear (see Steps 10 and 11).

30 Lubricate the new piston seal with clean brake fluid and fit it into its groove in the caliper bore, then lubricate the new dust seal and install it in its groove.

31 Lubricate the piston with clean brake fluid and fit it closed-end first into the caliper bore. Using your thumbs, push the piston all the way in, making sure it enters the bore squarely.

32 If removed, install the slider pin and tighten it to the specified torque setting. Apply a smear of silicone based grease to the slider pin.

33 Apply a smear of silicone based grease to the boot and spacer and fit them into the caliper **(see illustration 5.27)**.

Installation

34 If the caliper has not been overhauled, clean and inspect the rubber boot, spacer and slider pin (see Step 27). Lubricate the components with a smear of silicone based grease. If a new slider pin is fitted, tighten it to the specified torque setting.

35 Ensure the pad guide is in place on the caliper bracket and the pad spring is correctly installed inside the caliper **(see illustrations 5.24b and 5.25)**.

36 Slide the caliper onto the bracket.

37 If removed, install the brake pads (see Section 2).

38 Install the caliper mounting bolt and tighten it to the specified torque setting. Fit the plug.

39 If removed, connect the brake hose to the caliper, top up the master cylinder reservoir and bleed the hydraulic system (see Step 20).

40 Check that there are no fluid leaks and thoroughly test the operation of the rear brake before riding the motorcycle.

6 Front brake master cylinder

Warning: Use care when working with brake fluid as it can injure your eyes and it will damage painted surfaces and plastic parts.

1 If the master cylinder is leaking fluid, or if the lever does not produce a firm feel when the brake is applied, and bleeding the brakes does not help (see Section 9), and the hydraulic hoses and unions are all in good condition, then master cylinder overhaul is recommended.

2 Before disassembling the master cylinder, read through the entire procedure and make sure that you have the correct rebuild kit. Also, you will need some new DOT 4 brake fluid, some clean rags and internal circlip pliers. **Note:** *To prevent damage to the paint from spilled brake fluid, always cover the fuel tank when working on the master cylinder.*

Caution: Disassembly, overhaul and reassembly of the brake master cylinder must be done in a spotlessly clean work area to avoid contamination and possible failure of the brake hydraulic system components.

Removal

Note: *If the master cylinder is being displaced from the handlebar and not being removed completely or overhauled, follow Steps 5, 7 and 8 only.*

3 On SV650 models, loosen, but do not remove, the screws holding the reservoir cover in place **(see illustration)**. On SV650S models, unscrew the reservoir cap clamp screw, then slacken, but do not remove, the reservoir cap **(see illustration)**.

4 Remove the front brake lever (see Chapter 6).

5 Disconnect the electrical connectors from the brake light switch **(see illustration)**.

6 Unscrew the brake hose banjo bolt and separate the hose from the master cylinder, noting its alignment **(see illustration)**. Discard the two sealing washers as they must be renewed. Either plug the hose using another suitable short piece of hose fitted through the eye of the banjo union (it needs to be a fairly tight fit to seal it properly), clamp it using a hose clamp, or wrap a plastic bag tightly around to minimise fluid loss and prevent dirt entering the system.

7 On SV650 models, remove the rear view mirror (see Chapter 8). On SV650S models, unscrew the bolt securing the reservoir bracket to the handlebar **(see illustration)**.

8 Unscrew the master cylinder clamp bolts, then lift the master cylinder and reservoir away from the handlebar, noting how the mating surfaces of the clamp align with the punch

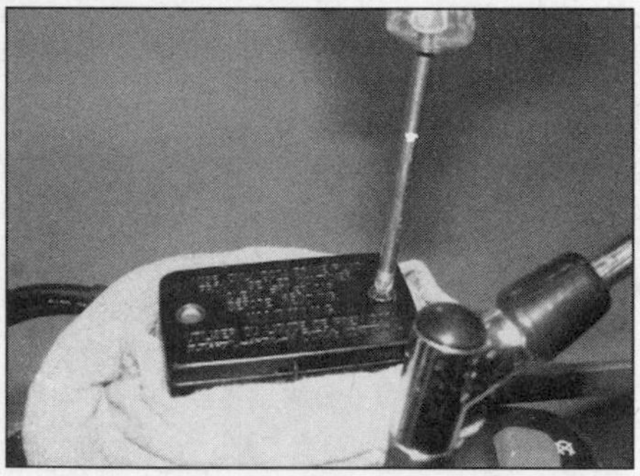

6.3a Slacken the reservoir cover screws

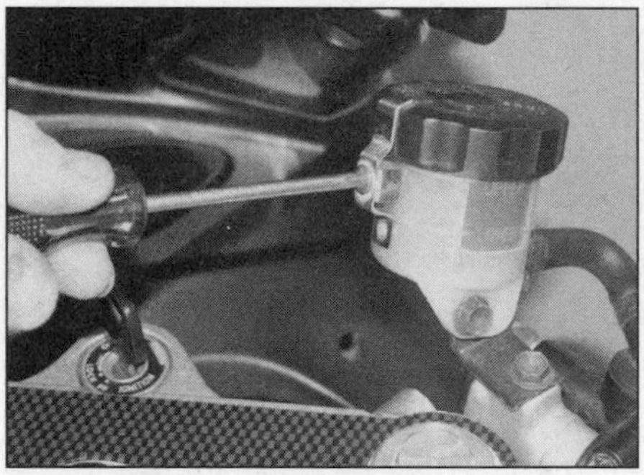

6.3b Release the clamp and slacken the cap

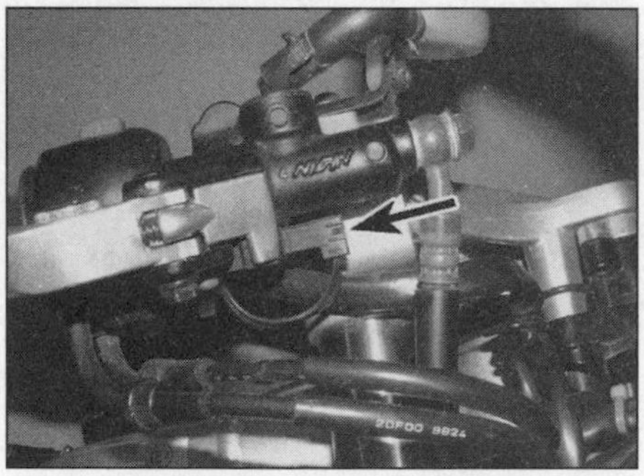

6.5 Disconnect the brake light switch wiring connectors (arrowed)

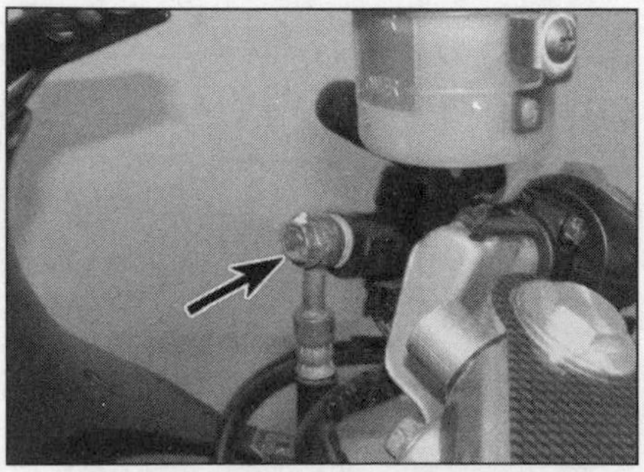

6.6 Brake hose banjo bolt (arrowed)

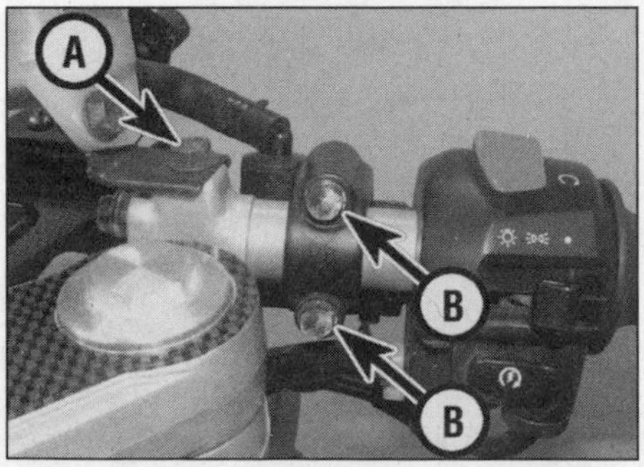

6.7 Reservoir bracket bolt (A), master cylinder clamp bolts (B) – SV650S

6.8 Master cylinder clamp bolts (arrowed) – SV650

mark on the bottom (SV650) or top (SV650S) of the handlebar **(see illustration)**.

Caution: Do not tip the master cylinder upside down or brake fluid will run out.

9 Remove the reservoir cover or cap, diaphragm plate and rubber diaphragm. Drain the brake fluid from the reservoir into a suitable container. Wipe any remaining fluid out of the reservoir with a clean rag. On SV650S models release the clamp securing the reservoir hose to the union on the master cylinder and detach the hose.

10 If required undo the brake light switch screw and remove the switch, noting how it fits.

Overhaul

11 Carefully remove the dust boot from the end of the master cylinder and from around the piston, noting how it locates **(see illustrations)**.

12 Push the piston in and, using circlip pliers, remove the circlip from its groove in the master cylinder and slide out the piston assembly and the spring, noting how they fit. If they are difficult to remove, apply low pressure compressed air to the fluid outlet. Lay the parts out in order as you remove them to prevent confusion during reassembly.

13 On SV650S models, remove the cap from around the base of the reservoir hose union. Remove the circlip, then pull the union out of its bore. Discard the O-ring as a new one must be used.

14 Clean all parts with clean brake fluid or denatured alcohol. If compressed air is available, use it to dry the parts thoroughly (make sure it's filtered and unlubricated).

Caution: Do not, under any circumstances, use a petroleum-based solvent to clean brake parts.

15 Check the master cylinder bore for corrosion, scratches, nicks and score marks. If the necessary measuring equipment is available, compare the dimensions of the piston and bore to those given in the Specifications Section of this Chapter. If damage or wear is evident, the master cylinder must be renewed. If the master cylinder is in poor condition, then the calipers should be checked as well. Check that the fluid inlet and outlet ports in the master cylinder are clear.

16 The dust boot, circlip, piston, seal, cup and spring are included in the rebuild kit. Use all of the new parts, regardless of the apparent condition of the old ones. If the seal and cup are not already on the piston, fit them according to the layout of the old one.

17 Lubricate the cup, seal and piston with clean brake fluid.

18 Locate the narrow end of the spring onto the inner end of the piston. Fit the spring and piston assembly into the master cylinder, with the wide end of the spring going in first. Make sure the lips on the cup and seal do not turn inside out when they enter the bore. Depress the piston and install the new circlip, making sure that it locates in the groove in the master cylinder.

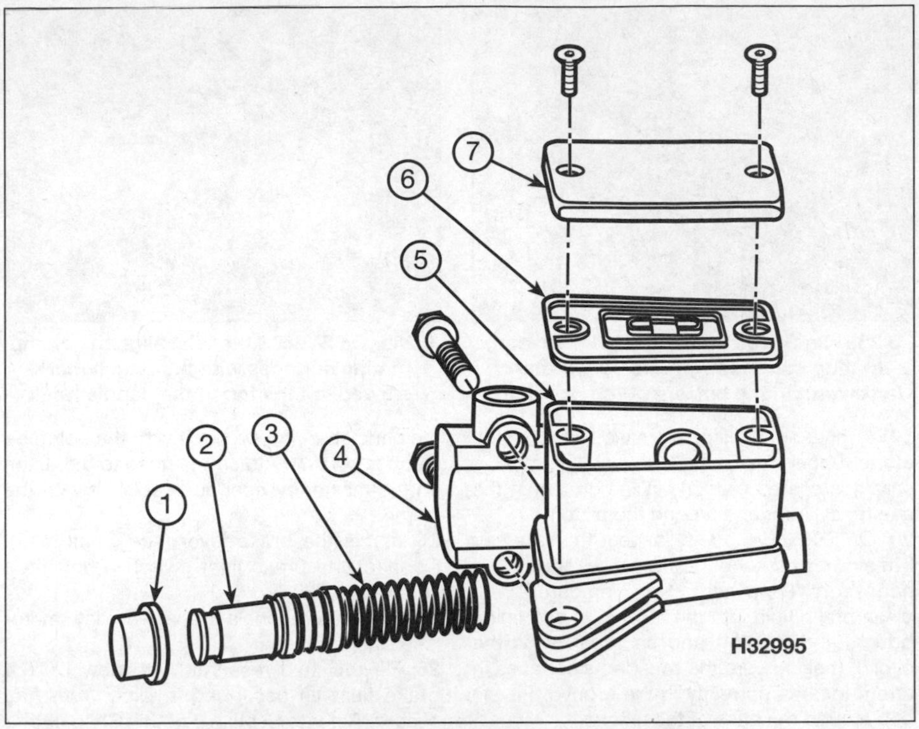

6.11a Front master cylinder components – SV650

1 Rubber boot
2 Piston assembly
3 Spring
4 Clamp
5 Reservoir
6 Diaphragm
7 Cover

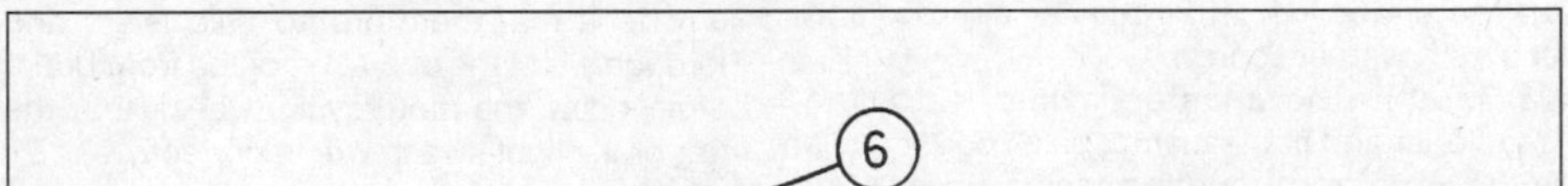

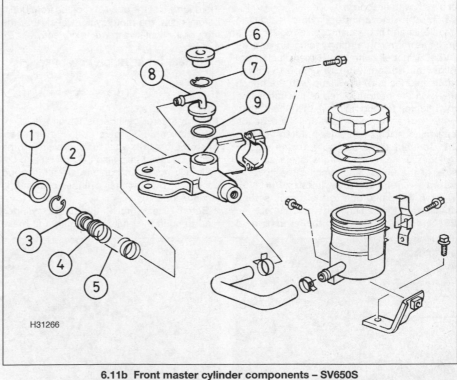

6.11b Front master cylinder components – SV650S

1 Rubber boot
2 Circlip
3 Piston assembly
4 Cup
5 Spring
6 Rubber cap
7 Circlip
8 Union
9 O-ring

6.23a On SV650 models, align the clamp mating surfaces with the punch mark (arrowed) on the bottom of the handlebar

6.23b On SV650S models, align the clamp mating surfaces with the punch mark (arrowed) on the top of the handlebar . . .

6.23c . . . and fit the clamp with the UP mark facing up

19 Apply some silicone grease to the inside of the rubber dust boot, then install it, making sure it is seated properly in the groove in the master cylinder and around the piston.

20 On SV650S models, inspect the reservoir hose for cracks or splits and renew it if necessary. Fit a new O-ring smeared with clean brake fluid into the reservoir hose union bore. Fit the union and secure it with the circlip, making sure the rounded side faces in and it locates correctly in the groove. Fit the cap around the base of the union.

21 Inspect the reservoir rubber diaphragm and renew it if it is damaged or deteriorated.

Installation

22 If removed, locate the brake light switch on the underside of the master cylinder and secure it with the screw.

23 Attach the master cylinder to the handlebar and fit the clamp, on SV650 models with the mirror mounting facing up and on SV650S models with its UP mark facing up. Align the bottom (SV650) or top (SV650S) mating surfaces of the clamp with the punch mark on the bottom or top of the handlebar, then tighten the top bolt first, then the bottom bolt, to the torque setting specified at the beginning of the Chapter **(see illustrations)**.

24 Connect the brake hose to the master cylinder, using new sealing washers on each side of the union, and aligning the hose as noted on removal **(see illustration 6.6)**. Tighten the banjo bolt to the torque setting specified at the beginning of the Chapter.

25 On SV650S models, fit the reservoir onto the handlebar and secure it with the bolt **(see illustration 6.7)**. Attach the hose to the union on the master cylinder and secure it with the clamp.

26 Install the brake lever (see Chapter 6). Connect the brake light switch wiring **(see illustration 6.5)**.

27 On SV650 models fit the rear view mirror (see Chapter 8).

28 Fill the fluid reservoir with new DOT 4 brake fluid as described in *Daily (pre-ride) checks*. Refer to Section 9 of this Chapter and bleed the air from the system.

29 Fit the rubber diaphragm, making sure it is correctly seated, the diaphragm plate and the cover or cap onto the reservoir, not forgetting the cap clamp on SV650S models.

30 Check that there are no fluid leaks and thoroughly test the operation of the front brake before riding the motorcycle. Check that the front brake light switch works correctly.

7 Rear brake master cylinder

1 If the master cylinder is leaking fluid, or if the lever does not produce a firm feel when the brake is applied, and bleeding the brakes does not help (see Section 9), and the hydraulic hoses and unions are all in good condition, then master cylinder overhaul is recommended.

2 Before disassembling the master cylinder, read through the entire procedure and make sure that you have the correct rebuild kit. Also, you will need some new DOT 4 brake fluid, some clean rags and internal circlip pliers. **Note:** *To prevent damage to the paint from spilled brake fluid, always cover the surrounding components when working on the master cylinder.*

Caution: Disassembly, overhaul and reassembly of the brake master cylinder must be done in a spotlessly clean work area to avoid contamination and possible failure of the brake hydraulic system components.

Warning: Use care when working with brake fluid as it can injure your eyes and it will damage painted surfaces and plastic parts.

Removal

3 If available, fit a brake hose clamp onto the master cylinder reservoir hose. Detach the hose from the union on the master cylinder, being prepared to catch any drops of fluid with a rag **(see illustration)**. If a clamp is not available, drain the fluid from the reservoir into a suitable container. If you do this, then undo the two reservoir cover screws and remove the cover and diaphragm to act as a vent **(see illustration)**. Refit the diaphragm, plate and cover afterwards. On X, Y, K1 and K2 models, remove the rear seat to access the reservoir (see Chapter 8). On K3-on models, undo the reservoir mounting bolt and displace the reservoir to access the cover screws **(see illustration)**.

4 Unscrew the brake hose banjo bolt and separate the hose from the master cylinder,

7.3a Reservoir hose clamp (A), brake hose banjo bolt (B)

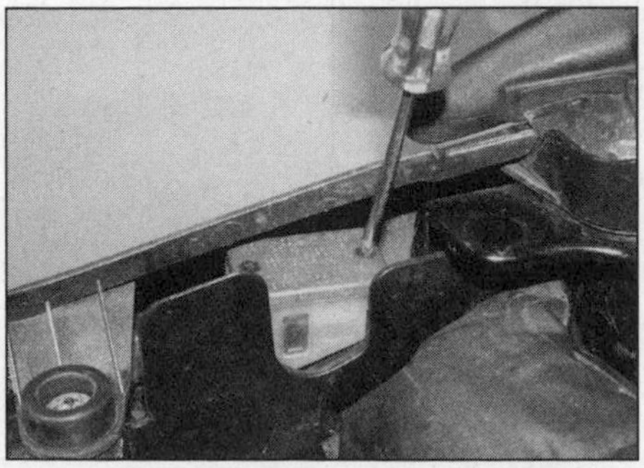

7.3b Undo the screws and remove the cover – X, Y, K1 and K2 models

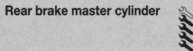

7.3c Displace the reservoir to access the cover screws – K3-on models

noting its alignment **(see illustration 7.3a)**. Discard the two sealing washers as they must be renewed. Either plug the hose using another suitable short piece of hose fitted through the eye of the banjo union (it needs to be a fairly tight fit to seal it properly), clamp it using a hose clamp, or wrap a plastic bag tightly around it to minimise fluid loss and prevent dirt entering the system.

5 Remove the split pin and washer from the clevis pin securing the brake pedal to the master cylinder pushrod, then remove the clevis pin and separate the pedal from the pushrod **(see illustration)**.

6 Unscrew the two bolts securing the master cylinder to the bracket and remove the master cylinder **(see illustration)**.

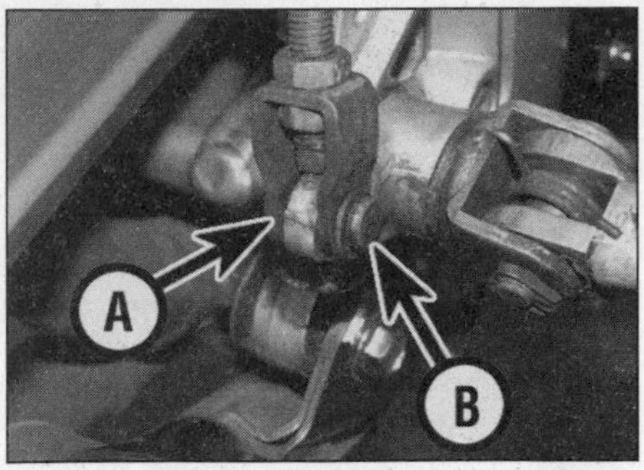

7.5 Remove the split pin and washer (A) then withdraw the clevis pin (B)

7.6 Master cylinder mounting bolts (arrowed)

Overhaul

7 If required, mark the position of the clevis locknut on the pushrod, then slacken the locknut and thread the clevis and its base nut off the pushrod **(see illustration)**.

8 Dislodge the rubber dust boot from the base of the master cylinder and from around the pushrod, noting how it locates, and slide it down the pushrod.

9 Push the pushrod in and, using circlip pliers, remove the circlip from its groove in the master cylinder and slide out the piston assembly and the spring, noting how they fit. If they are difficult to remove, apply low pressure compressed air to the fluid outlet. Lay the parts out in the proper order to prevent confusion during reassembly.

10 If required, remove the screw securing the fluid reservoir hose union and detach it from the master cylinder. Discard the O-ring as a new one must be used. Inspect the reservoir hose for cracks or splits and renew it if necessary.

11 Clean all of the parts with clean brake fluid or denatured alcohol.

Caution: Do not, under any circumstances, use a petroleum-based solvent to clean brake parts. If compressed air is available, use it to dry the parts thoroughly (make sure it's filtered and unlubricated).

12 Check the master cylinder bore for corrosion, scratches, nicks and score marks. If the necessary measuring equipment is available, compare the dimensions of the piston and bore to those given in the Specifications Section of this Chapter. If damage or wear is evident, the master cylinder must be renewed. If the master cylinder is in poor condition, then the caliper should be checked as well.

13 The dust boot, circlip, piston, seal, cup and spring are included in the rebuild kit. Use all of the new parts, regardless of the apparent condition of the old ones. If the seal and cup are not already on the piston, fit them according to the layout of the old one. Slide the new boot onto the pushrod, making sure it is the correct way round.

14 Lubricate the cup, seal and piston with clean brake fluid.

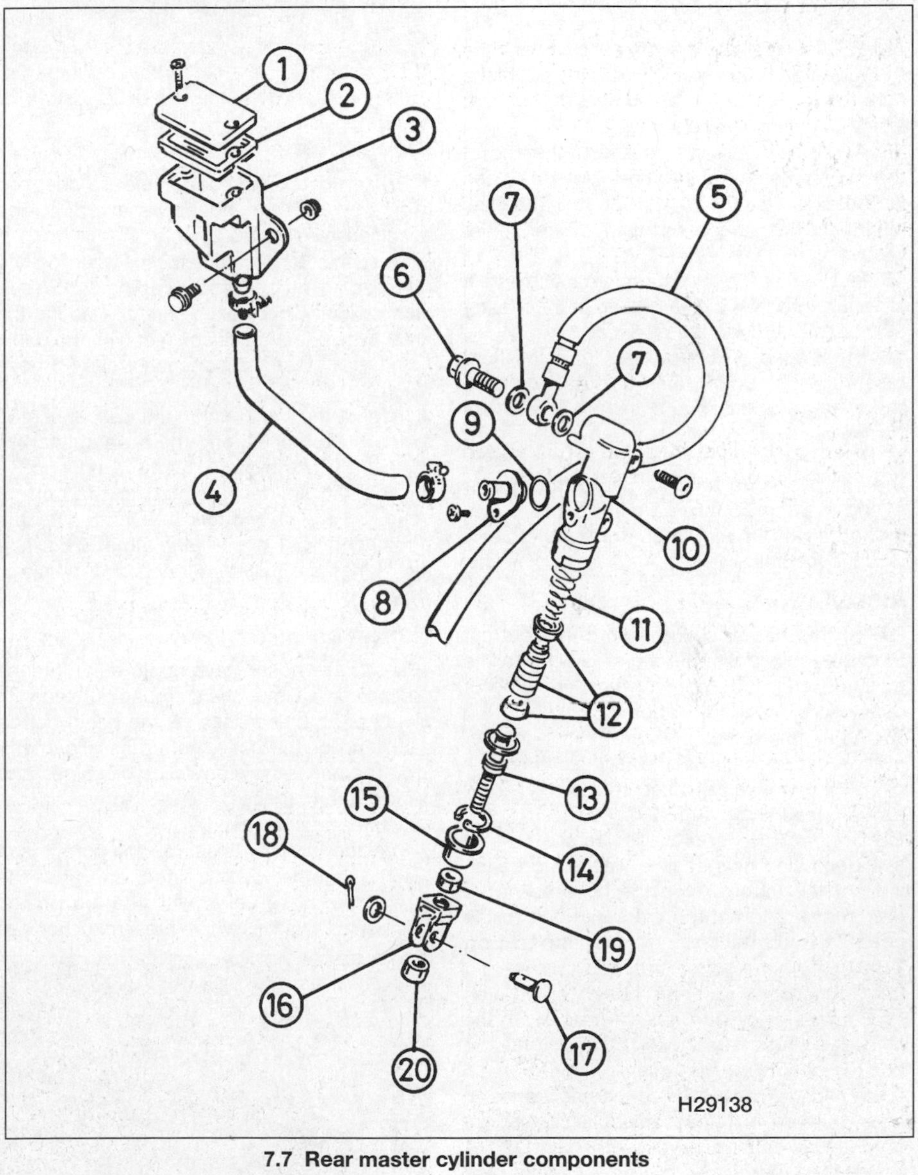

7.7 Rear master cylinder components

1 Reservoir cover
2 Rubber diaphragm
3 Reservoir
4 Reservoir hose
5 Brake hose
6 Banjo bolt
7 Sealing washer
8 Reservoir hose union
9 O-ring
10 Master cylinder
11 Spring
12 Piston assembly
13 Pushrod
14 Circlip
15 Rubber dust boot
16 Clevis
17 Clevis pin
18 Split pin
19 Locknut
20 Clevis base nut

8.2 Flex the brake hoses and check for cracks, bulges and leaking fluid

15 Locate the narrow end of the spring onto the inner end of the piston. Fit the spring and piston assembly into the master cylinder, with the wide end of the spring going in first. Make sure the lips on the cup and seal do not turn inside out when they enter the bore.

16 Apply some silicone grease to the end of the pushrod and fit it into the master cylinder. Depress the pushrod, then install the new circlip, making sure it is properly seated in the groove.

17 Install the rubber dust boot, making sure it is seated properly in the groove in the master cylinder and around the pushrod.

18 If removed, fit a new O-ring to the fluid reservoir hose union, then fit the union onto the master cylinder and secure it with its screw.

19 If removed, thread the clevis locknut, the clevis and its base nut onto the master cylinder pushrod end. Position the clevis as noted on removal, then tighten the clevis locknut securely.

Installation

20 Fit the master cylinder onto the footrest bracket and tighten its mounting bolts to the torque setting specified at the beginning of the Chapter **(see illustration 7.6)**.

21 Align the brake pedal with the master cylinder pushrod clevis, then slide in the clevis pin, fit the washer and secure it using a new split pin **(see illustration 7.5)**.

22 Connect the brake hose to the master cylinder, using new sealing washers on each side of the union. Align the hose as noted on removal and tighten the banjo bolt to the specified torque setting **(see illustration 7.3a)**.

23 Connect the reservoir hose to the union on the master cylinder and secure it with the clip **(see illustration 7.3a)**. Check that the hose is secure at the reservoir end as well. If the clips have weakened, use new ones. If used on removal, release the hose clamp.

24 Fill the fluid reservoir with new DOT 4 brake fluid (see *Daily (pre-ride) checks*) and bleed the system following the procedure in Section 9. If any new parts have been fitted, it is advisable to renew the brake fluid.

25 Check that there are no fluid leaks and check the operation of the brake and brake light carefully before riding the motorcycle.

8.3 Location of the front brake hose splitter – K3-on models

8 Brake hoses and unions

Inspection

1 Brake hose condition should be checked regularly and the hoses renewed at the specified interval (see Chapter 1).

2 Twist and flex the rubber hoses while looking for cracks, bulges and seeping fluid **(see illustration)**. Check extra carefully around the areas where the hoses connect with the banjo fittings, as these are common areas for hose failure.

3 Inspect the banjo union fittings connected to the brake hoses, and the hose splitter for the front brake system. On X, Y, K1 and K2 models the splitter is bolted to the bottom yoke; on K3-on models it is bolted to the right-hand fork slider **(see illustration)**. If the fittings are rusted, scratched or cracked, renew them.

Renewal

4 The brake hoses have banjo union fittings on each end. Cover the surrounding area with plenty of rags and unscrew the banjo bolt at each end of the hose, noting its alignment. Free the hoses from any clips or guides and remove them. Discard the sealing washers as new ones must be used.

5 Position the new hose, making sure it isn't twisted or otherwise strained, and abut the tab on the hose union with the lug on the component casting, where present. Otherwise align the hose as noted on removal. Install the hose banjo bolts using new sealing washers on both sides of the unions **(see illustration 5.20)**. Tighten the banjo bolts to the torque setting specified at the beginning of this Chapter.

6 Make sure the hoses are correctly aligned and routed clear of all moving components. Flush the old brake fluid from the system, refill with new DOT 4 brake fluid (see *Daily (pre-ride) checks*) and bleed the air from the system (see Section 9). Check the operation of the brakes carefully before riding the motorcycle.

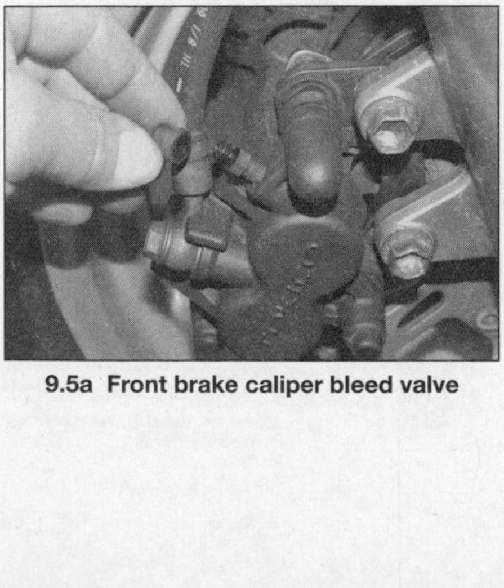

9.5a Front brake caliper bleed valve

9 Brake system bleeding and fluid change

Warning: Use care when working with brake fluid as it can injure your eyes and it will damage painted surfaces and plastic parts.

Bleeding

1 Bleeding the brakes is simply the process of removing all the air bubbles from the brake fluid reservoirs, the hoses and the brake calipers. Bleeding is necessary whenever a brake system hydraulic connection is loosened, when a component or hose is renewed, or when the master cylinder or caliper is overhauled. Leaks in the system may also allow air to enter, but leaking brake fluid will reveal their presence and warn you of the need for repair.

2 To bleed the brakes, you will need some new DOT 4 brake fluid, a length of clear vinyl or plastic tubing, a small container partially filled with clean brake fluid, some rags and a ring spanner to fit the brake caliper bleed valves.

3 Cover the fuel tank, fairing panels (SV650S), front mudguard, seat cowling and other painted components to prevent damage in the event that brake fluid is spilled.

4 Remove the reservoir cover or cap, diaphragm plate and diaphragm (see *Daily (pre-ride) checks*) and slowly pump the brake lever or pedal a few times, until no air bubbles can be seen floating up from the holes in the bottom of the reservoir. Doing this bleeds the air from the master cylinder end of the line. Loosely refit the reservoir cover.

5 Pull the dust cap off the bleed valve **(see illustrations)**. Attach one end of the clear vinyl or plastic tubing to the bleed valve and submerge the other end in the brake fluid in the container **(see illustration)**. Note that the rear caliper has two bleed valves, one on each side of the caliper.

6 Remove the reservoir cap or cover and check the fluid level. Do not allow the fluid level to drop below the lower mark during the bleeding process.

7 Carefully pump the brake lever or pedal three or four times and hold it in (front) or down (rear) while opening the caliper bleed

9.5b Rear brake caliper bleed valve – X, Y, K1 and K2 models

9.5c To bleed the brakes, you need a spanner, a short section of clear tubing, and a clear container half-filled with brake fluid

valve. When the valve is opened, brake fluid will flow out of the caliper into the clear tubing and the lever will move toward the handlebar or the pedal will move down.

8 Retighten the bleed valve, then release the brake lever or pedal gradually. Repeat the process until no air bubbles are visible in the brake fluid leaving the caliper and the lever or pedal is firm when applied. On completion, disconnect the bleeding equipment, then tighten the bleed valve to the torque setting specified at the beginning of the chapter and install the dust cap.

9 Install the diaphragm, plate and cover or cap assembly, wipe up any spilled brake fluid and check the entire system for leaks.

HAYNES HiNT ***If it's not possible to produce a firm feel to the lever or pedal the fluid may be aerated. Let the brake fluid in the system stabilise for a few hours and then repeat the procedure when the tiny bubbles in the system have settled out. Also check to make sure that there are no 'high-spots' in the brake hose in which an air bubble can become trapped – this will occur most often in an incorrectly mounted hose union, but can also arise through bleeding the brakes while some of the brake system components are at such an angle to encourage this. Reversing the angle or displacing and moving the offending component around will normally dislodge any trapped air.***

Fluid change

10 Changing the brake fluid is a similar process to bleeding the brakes and requires the same materials plus a suitable tool for siphoning the fluid out of the reservoir. Also ensure that the container is large enough to take all the old fluid when it is flushed out of the system.

11 Follow Steps 3 and 5, then remove the reservoir cap or cover, diaphragm plate and diaphragm and siphon the old fluid out of the reservoir. Fill the reservoir with new brake fluid, then follow Step 7.

12 Tighten the bleed valve, then release the brake lever or pedal gradually. Keep the reservoir topped-up with new fluid to above the LOWER level at all times or air may enter the system and greatly increase the length of the task. Repeat the process until new fluid can be seen emerging from the bleed valve.

HAYNES HiNT ***Old brake fluid is invariably much darker in colour than new fluid, making it easy to see when all old fluid has been expelled from the system.***

13 Disconnect the hose, then tighten the bleed valve to the specified torque setting and install the dust cap.

14 Top-up the reservoir, install the diaphragm, diaphragm plate and cap or cover, and wipe up any spilled brake fluid. Check the entire system for fluid leaks.

15 Check the operation of the brakes before riding the motorcycle.

10 Wheel inspection and repair

1 Position the motorcycle on an auxiliary stand. Support the bike so that the wheel to be checked is raised off the ground. Clean the wheels thoroughly to remove mud and dirt that may interfere with the inspection procedure or mask defects. Make a general check of the wheels (see Chapter 1) and tyres (see *Daily (pre-ride) checks*).

2 To check axial (side-to-side) runout, attach a dial gauge to the fork slider or the swingarm and position its stem against the side of the rim **(see illustration)**. Spin the wheel slowly and check the amount of runout at the rim. To accurately check radial (out of round) runout with the dial gauge, remove the wheel from the machine, and the tyre from the wheel. With the axle clamped in a vice and the dial gauge positioned on the top of the rim, rotate the wheel and check the runout.

3 An easier, though slightly less accurate, method is to attach a stiff wire pointer to the fork slider or the swingarm and position the end a fraction of an inch from the wheel (where the wheel and tyre join). If the wheel is true, the distance from the pointer to the rim will be constant as the wheel is rotated. **Note:** *If wheel runout is excessive, check the wheel bearings and axle very carefully before assuming the wheel to be distorted.*

4 Visually inspect the wheels for cracks, flat spots on the rim, and other damage. Look very closely for dents in the area where the tyre bead contacts the rim. Dents in this area may prevent complete sealing of the tyre against the rim, which leads to deflation of the tyre over a period of time.

5 If damage is evident, or if runout in either direction is excessive, the wheel will have to be renewed. Never attempt to repair a damaged cast alloy wheel.

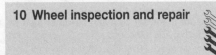

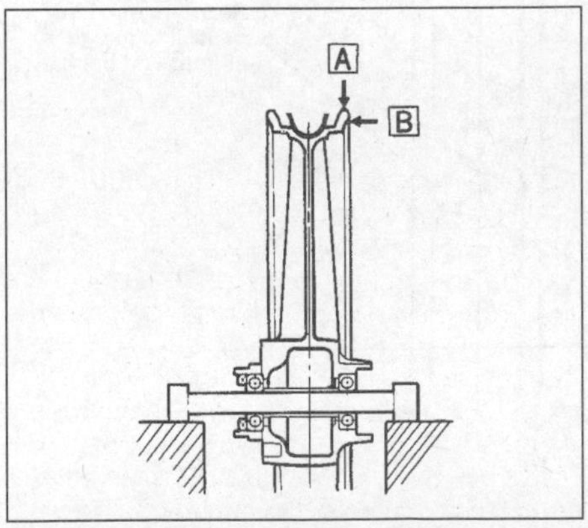

10.2 Check the wheel for radial (out-of-round) runout (A) and axial (side-to-side) runout (B)

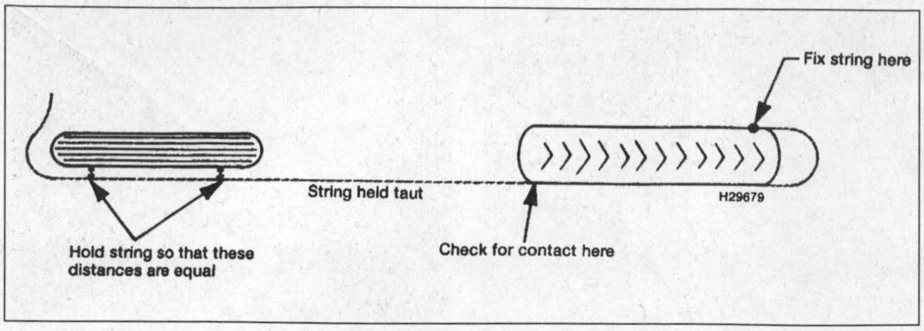

11.5 Wheel alignment check using string

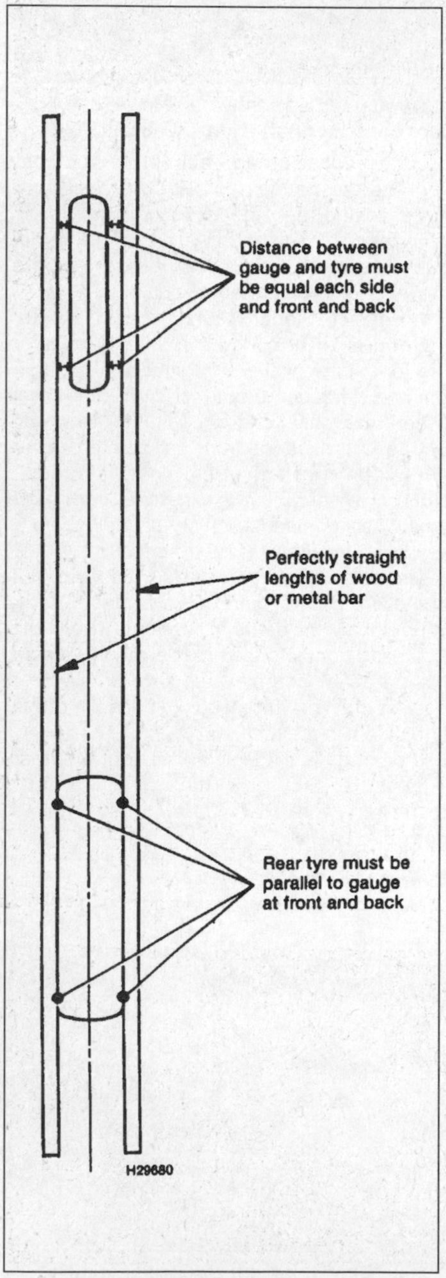

11.7 Wheel alignment check using a straight edge

11 Wheel alignment check

1 Misalignment of the wheels, which may be due to a cocked rear wheel or a bent frame or fork yokes, can cause strange and possibly serious handling problems. If the frame or yokes are at fault, repair by a frame specialist or replacement with new parts are the only alternatives.

2 To check the alignment you will need an assistant, a length of string or a perfectly straight piece of wood and a ruler. A plumb bob or other suitable weight will also be required.

3 Place the bike on an auxiliary stand so the bike is upright. Measure the width of both tyres at their widest points. Subtract the smaller measurement from the larger measurement, then divide the difference by two. The result is the amount of offset that should exist between the front and rear tyres on both sides.

4 If a string is used, have your assistant hold one end of it about halfway between the floor and the rear axle, touching the rear sidewall of the tyre.

5 Run the other end of the string forward and pull it tight so that it is roughly parallel to the floor **(see illustration)**. Slowly bring the string into contact with the front sidewall of the rear tyre, then turn the front wheel until it is parallel with the string. Measure the distance from the front tyre sidewall to the string.

6 Repeat the procedure on the other side of the motorcycle. The distance from the front tyre sidewall to the string should be equal on both sides.

7 As previously mentioned, a perfectly straight length of wood or metal bar may be substituted for the string **(see illustration)**. The procedure is the same.

8 If the distance between the string and tyre is greater on one side, or if the rear wheel appears to be cocked, refer to Chapter 1 and check that the chain adjuster markings are in the same position on each side of the swingarm.

9 If the front-to-back alignment is correct, the wheels still may be out of alignment vertically.

10 Using a plumb bob, or other suitable weight, and a length of string, check the rear wheel to make sure it is vertical. To do this, hold the string against the tyre upper sidewall and allow the weight to settle just off the floor. When the string touches both the upper and lower tyre sidewalls and is perfectly straight, the wheel is vertical. If it is not, place thin spacers under one leg of the stand until it is.

11 Once the rear wheel is vertical, check the front wheel in the same manner. If both wheels are not perfectly vertical, the frame and/or major suspension components are bent.

12 Front wheel

Removal

1 Position the motorcycle on an auxiliary stand and support it so that the front wheel is off the ground. Always make sure the motorcycle is properly supported.

2 Remove the two mounting bolts on each brake caliper and slide the calipers off the discs. Support the calipers with a cable tie or a bungee cord so that no strain is placed on their hydraulic hoses. There is no need to disconnect the hoses from the calipers. **Note**: *Do not operate the front brake lever with the calipers removed.* On models fitted with ABS, remove the ABS wheel speed sensor's mounting bolt and withdraw the sensor from its bracket.

3 Slacken the axle clamp bolt(s) on the bottom of the right-hand fork, then unscrew the axle **(see illustration)**. **Note:** *On K3-on models, there is only 1 axle clamp bolt. Use a 12 mm Allen socket or hex bar to unscrew the axle.*

4 Support the wheel, then withdraw the axle from the right-hand side, using a drift to tap it out if necessary, and carefully lower the wheel **(see illustration)**.

5 Remove the speed sensor from the left-hand side of the wheel, noting how it fits **(see illustration)**. On X, Y, K1 and K2 models, remove the spacer from the right-hand side, noting which way round it fits **(see illustration)** and on ABS-equipped models remove the wheel speed sensor bracket from the right-hand side.

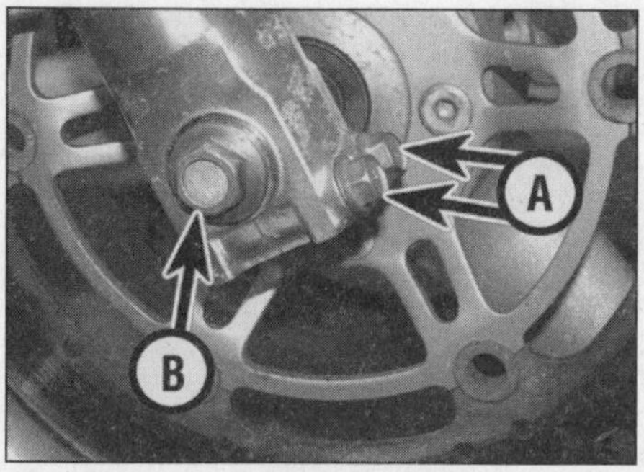

12.3 Slacken the axle clamp bolts (A), then unscrew the axle (B)

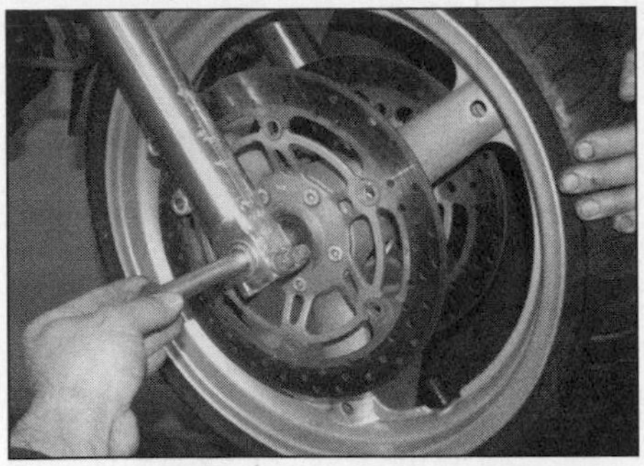
12.4 Withdraw the axle and remove the wheel

12.5a Detach the speed sensor

12.5b Remove the spacer on X, Y, K1 and K2 models

Caution: Don't lay the wheel down and allow it to rest on a disc – the disc could become warped. Set the wheel on wood blocks so the disc doesn't support the weight of the wheel.

6 Check the axle for straightness by rolling it on a flat surface such as a piece of plate glass (first wipe off all old grease and remove any corrosion using wire wool). If the equipment is available, place the axle in V-blocks and measure the runout using a dial gauge. If the axle is bent or the runout exceeds the limit specified, renew it.

7 Check the condition of the wheel bearings (see Section 14). Wipe all old grease off the bearing seals (where fitted), inspect the seals and renew them as described in Section 14 if necessary. Refer to Chapter 9 for checks on the speed sensor.

Installation

8 Apply a smear of grease to the inside of the speed sensor and the wheel spacer, if applicable, and also to the outside where they fit into the wheel. Also apply a thin coat of grease to the axle. On ABS models, also lightly grease the inside of the ABS wheel speed sensor bracket.

9 Manoeuvre the wheel into position between the fork sliders. Fit the speed sensor into the left side of the wheel, locating its tabs into the drive plate cutouts **(see illustration 12.5a)**. On X, Y, K1 and K2 models, fit the spacer into the right-hand side, with its shouldered end on the inside **(see illustration 12.5b)**. On ABS-equipped models, fit the sensor bracket into the right-hand side.

10 Lift the wheel into place, making sure the speed sensor, spacer and ABS sensor bracket (as applicable) remain in position. The speed sensor must be positioned so that it is butted against the back of the lug on the fork slider **(see illustration)**. On ABS-equipped models, locate the lugs on the wheel speed sensor bracket each side of the lug on the fork slider. Slide the axle in from the right-hand side and tighten it finger tight **(see illustration 12.4)**. Check that the wheel spins freely, then tighten the axle to the torque setting specified at the beginning of the Chapter **(see illustration)**.

11 Lower the front wheel to the ground. Slide the calipers onto their discs, make sure the

12.10a Make sure the sensor housing butts against the back of the lug on the fork

pads locate on each side of the disc. Apply a suitable non-permanent thread locking compound to the caliper bolts and tighten them to the specified torque setting.

12 Apply the front brake a few times to bring the pads back into contact with the discs. Move the motorcycle off its stand, apply the front brake and pump the front forks a few times to settle all components in position.

13 Now tighten the axle clamp bolt(s) on the bottom of the right-hand fork to the specified torque setting **(see illustration 12.3)**.

14 On ABS-equipped models, fit the wheel speed sensor back into its bracket and secure it with the bolt. Using a feeler gauge check for the correct air gap between the sensor tip and pulser ring.

15 Check for correct operation of the brake before riding the motorcycle.

12.10b Tighten the axle to the specified torque

13 Rear wheel

Removal

1 Position the motorcycle on an auxiliary stand so that the rear wheel is off the ground. On models equipped with ABS, unbolt the wheel speed sensor and withdraw it from the brake caliper bracket.

2 On X, Y, K1 and K2 models, slacken the nut on the brake torque arm front bolt.

3 On US models, remove the split pin from the axle nut.

4 Slacken the chain adjuster nuts, then unscrew the axle nut and remove the washer (if fitted) and left-hand chain adjustment marker **(see illustrations)**.

5 Support the wheel (a good way to do this is to

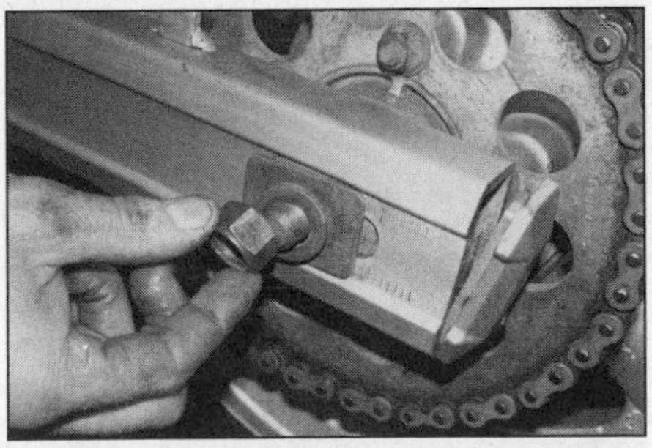
13.4a Unscrew the nut and remove the washer and marker – X, Y, K1 and K2 models shown

13.4b Unscrew the nut and remove the marker – K3, K4 and K5 models shown

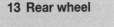

13.5a Withdraw the axle – X, Y, K1 and K2 models shown

13.5b Withdraw the axle – K3-on models shown

13.5c Disengage the chain from the sprocket

13.5d Support the caliper and remove the wheel – K3-on models shown

13.6a Remove the spacer from the right-hand side . . .

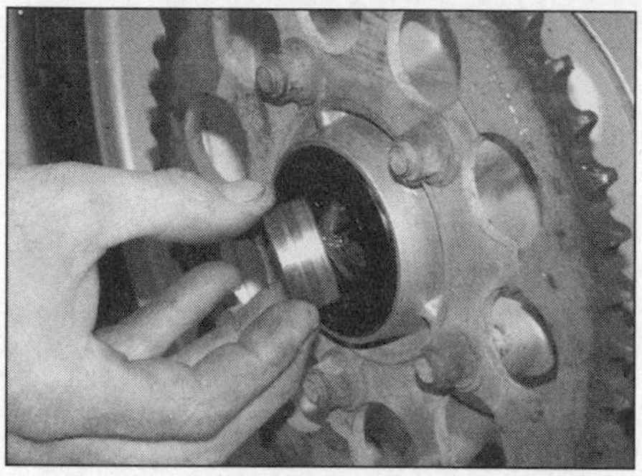
13.6b . . . and from the left-hand side, noting their locations

slide your foot part way under it) then withdraw the axle along with the adjustment marker from the right-hand side **(see illustrations)**. Note how the axle passes through the caliper mounting bracket. Gently lower the wheel to the ground, then disengage the chain from the sprocket **(see illustration)**. Draw the wheel back so the disc is clear of the caliper and remove the wheel **(see illustration)**. If required, secure the caliper to the swingarm with a cable tie to ensure no strain is placed on the brake hose.

6 Remove the spacer from each side of the wheel, noting which fits where **(see illustrations)**.

Caution: Do not lay the wheel down and allow it to rest on the disc or the sprocket – they could become warped. Set the wheel on wood blocks so the disc or the sprocket doesn't support the weight of the wheel. Do not operate the brake pedal with the wheel removed.

7 Check the axle for straightness by rolling it on a flat surface such as a piece of plate glass (if the axle is corroded, first remove the corrosion with wire wool). If the equipment is available, place the axle in V-blocks and check the runout using a dial gauge. If the axle is bent or the runout exceeds the limit specified at the beginning of the Chapter, renew it.

8 Check the condition of the grease seals and wheel bearings (see Section 14).

Installation

9 Apply a smear of grease to the inside of the wheel spacers, and also to the outside where they fit into the seals. Fit the shouldered spacer into the right-hand (disc) side of the wheel – on X, Y, K1 and K2 models the wider end should be innermost, and the plain spacer into the left-hand (sprocket) side **(see illustrations 13.6a and b)**.

10 Push the brake caliper pistons a little way back into the caliper using hand pressure or a piece of wood between the pads as leverage.

11 Slide the right-hand adjustment marker onto the axle, making sure it is the right way round.

12 Manoeuvre the wheel so that it is between the ends of the swingarm and move it forward so that the brake disc slides into the caliper, making sure the pads sit squarely on each side of the disc **(see illustration)**.

13 Engage the drive chain with the sprocket, then lift the wheel into position, making sure the caliper stays on the disc and the caliper bracket is correctly aligned with the wheel and the swingarm, and the spacers remain in place in the wheel.

14 Install the axle from the right, making sure it passes through the caliper mounting bracket, and push it all the way through **(see illustrations)**. On X, Y, K1 and K2 models,

13.12 Slide the disc into the caliper – X, Y, K1 and K2 models shown

13.14a Install the axle from the right – X, Y, K1 and K2 models shown

13.14b Install the axle from the right – K3-on models shown

13.16 Tighten the axle nut to the specified torque

ensure the right-hand adjustment marker locates horizontally in the swingarm. Check that everything is correctly aligned, then fit the left-hand side adjustment marker, the washer (if fitted) and the axle nut, but do not tighten it yet **(see illustration 13.4a or 4b)**. If it is difficult to insert the axle due to the tension of the drive chain, back off the chain adjusters (see Chapter 1).

15 Adjust the chain slack as described in Chapter 1.

16 Tighten the axle nut to the torque setting specified at the beginning of the Chapter, counter-holding the axle head on the other side of the wheel to prevent it turning if necessary **(see illustration)**. On US models, fit a new split pin into the nut and secure its ends correctly.

17 On X, Y, K1 and K2 models, tighten the brake torque arm nut to the specified torque setting.

18 Operate the brake pedal several times to bring the pads into contact with the disc.

19 On ABS-equipped models, fit the wheel speed sensor back into the caliper bracket and secure it with the bolt. Using a feeler gauge check for the correct air gap between the sensor tip and pulser ring.

20 Check for correct operation of the brake before riding the motorcycle.

14 Wheel bearing renewal

Note: *Examine the wheel bearings and sprocket coupling bearing while they are installed in their housings. Once the bearings have been driven out they must never be reused.*

Front wheel bearings

1 Remove the wheel (see Section 12).

2 Rotate the inner race of each bearing using your fingers **(see illustration)**. If either bearing race doesn't turn smoothly, has rough spots or is noisy, renew both bearings – never renew just one wheel bearing.

3 Set the wheel on blocks so as not to allow the weight to rest on either brake disc. On K3 models onward, lever out the right-hand grease seal using a flat-bladed screwdriver and a piece of wood – take care not to damage the hub **(see illustration)**. Discard the seal as a new one must be fitted.

4 Using a metal rod (preferably a brass drift punch) inserted through the centre of the upper bearing, tap evenly around the inner race of the lower bearing to drive it from the hub **(see illustrations)**. The bearing spacer will also come out.

14.2 Check the bearings as described

5 Lay the wheel on its other side so that the remaining bearing faces down. Drive the bearing out of the wheel using the same technique as above.

6 Thoroughly clean the hub area of the wheel. Install the new left-hand bearing into the recess in the hub, with its sealed or marked side facing outwards. Using the old bearing, a bearing driver or a socket large enough to contact the outer race of the bearing, drive it in until it's completely seated **(see illustration)**.

7 Turn the wheel over and install the bearing spacer. Drive the other new bearing into place as described above. On K3-on models, apply

14.3 Lever out the right-hand seal – K3-on models

14.4a Knock out the bearings using a drift . . .

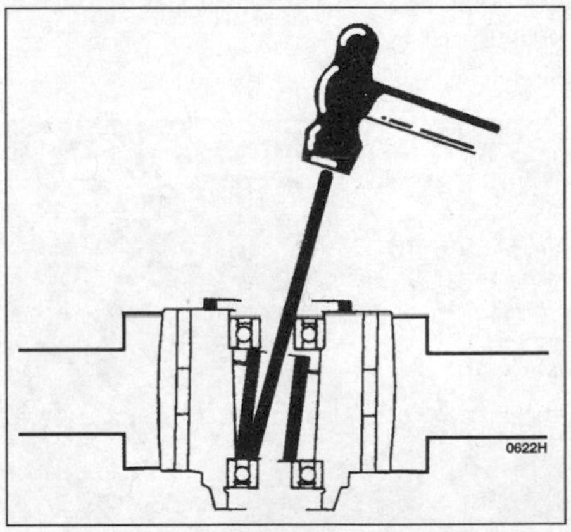

14.4b . . . locating it as shown

14.6 A socket can be used to drive in the bearing

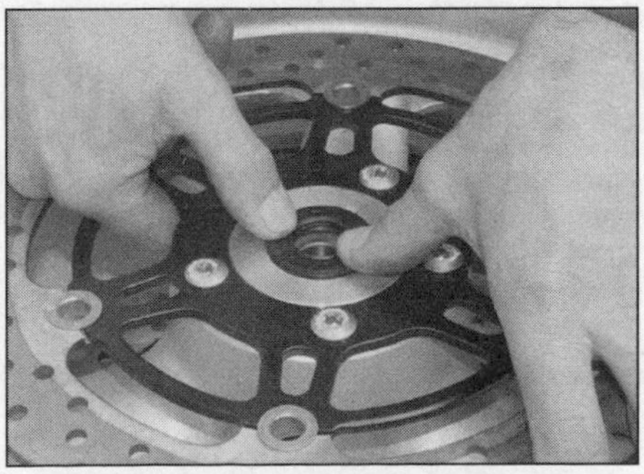

14.7a Level the seal with the rim of the hub . . .

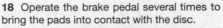

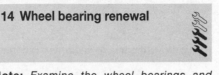

14.7b . . . using a block of wood as described

14.9 Lift the sprocket coupling out of the wheel

14.12 Drive the bearings out as described

14.15 A socket can be used to drive in the bearing

a smear of grease to the new seal, then press it into the hub using a bearing driver or large socket. If necessary, level the seal with the rim of the hub with a small block of wood **(see illustrations)**.

8 Clean off all grease from the brake discs using acetone or brake system cleaner then install the wheel (see Section 12).

Rear wheel bearings

9 Remove the rear wheel (see Section 13). Lift the sprocket coupling out of the left-hand side of the wheel, noting how it fits and its spacer **(see illustration)**.

10 Rotate the inner race of each bearing using your fingers. If either bearing race doesn't turn smoothly, has rough spots or is noisy, renew both bearings – never renew just one wheel bearing.

11 Set the wheel on blocks so as not to allow the weight of the wheel to rest on the brake disc. On K3 models onward, lever out the grease seal on the right-hand side of the hub using a flat-bladed screwdriver and a piece of wood – take care not to damage the hub, disc (or pulser ring on ABS models). Discard the seal as a new one must be fitted.

12 Using a metal rod (preferably a brass drift punch) inserted through the centre of the right-hand bearing, tap evenly around the inner race of the left-hand bearing to drive it from the hub **(see illustration and 14.4b)**. The bearing spacer will also come out.

13 Lay the wheel on its other side so that the remaining bearing faces down. Drive the bearing out of the wheel using the same technique as above.

14 Thoroughly clean the hub area of the wheel. First install the new right-hand bearing into its recess in the hub, with its sealed or marked side facing outwards. Using the old bearing, a bearing driver or a socket large enough to contact the outer race of the bearing, drive it in squarely until it's completely seated **(see illustration 14.6)**. On K3-on models, apply a smear of grease to the new seal, then press it into the hub using a bearing driver or large socket. Level the seal with the rim of the hub with a small block of wood.

15 Turn the wheel over and install the bearing spacer. Drive the new left-hand side bearing into place as described above **(see illustration)**.

16 Smear some grease around the outside of the left-hand bearing housing where the sprocket coupling fits over it.

17 Clean off all grease from the brake disc using acetone or brake system cleaner. Ensure that spacer is in place in the sprocket coupling, then fit the sprocket coupling assembly onto the wheel **(see illustration 14.9)**. Install the wheel (see Section 13).

14.19 Lever out the grease seal

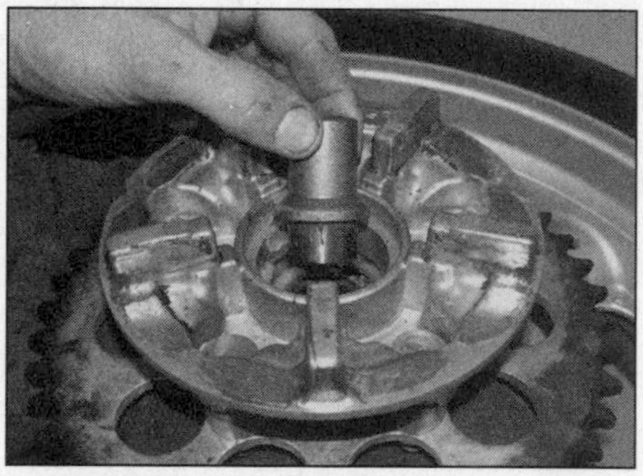

14.20 Remove the spacer from inside the coupling

14.25a Press or drive the seal into the coupling

14.25b Using a piece of wood as shown automatically sets the seal flush

Sprocket coupling bearing

18 Remove the rear wheel (see Section 13). Lift the sprocket coupling out of the wheel, noting how it fits **(see illustration 14.9)**.

19 Using a flat-bladed screwdriver, lever out the grease seal from the outside of the coupling **(see illustration)**.

20 Remove the spacer from the inside of the coupling bearing, noting which way round it fits **(see illustration)**. The spacer could be a tight fit and may have to be driven out from the outside using a suitable socket or piece of tubing. Support the coupling on blocks of wood to do this.

21 Rotate the inner race of the bearing using your fingers. If the bearing race doesn't turn smoothly, has rough spots or is noisy, it must be renewed.

22 Support the coupling on blocks of wood and drive the bearing out from the inside using a bearing driver or socket.

23 Thoroughly clean the bearing recess then fit the new bearing into the coupling, with its sealed or marked side facing out. Using the old bearing, a bearing driver or a socket large enough to contact the outer race of the bearing, drive it in until it is completely seated.

24 Fit the spacer into the inside of the coupling, making sure it is the correct way round and fits squarely into the bearing **(see illustration 14.20)**. Drive it into place if it is tight, supporting the bearing inner race on a suitable socket to prevent it from being damaged or driven out at the same time.

25 Apply a smear of grease to the new seal, then press it into the coupling using a bearing driver or suitable socket; level the seal with the rim of the coupling with a small block of wood **(see illustrations)**.

26 Check the sprocket coupling/rubber dampers (see Chapter 6).

27 Smear some grease around the outside of the left-hand bearing housing on the wheel where the sprocket coupling fits over it.

28 Fit the sprocket coupling into the wheel **(see illustration 14.9)**, then install the wheel (see Section 13).

15 ABS – operation and fault finding (SV650A/SA)

1 The ABS prevents the wheels from locking up under hard braking or on uneven road surfaces. A sensor on each wheel transmits information about the speed of rotation to the ABS control unit; if the unit senses that a wheel is about to lock, it releases brake pressure to that wheel momentarily, preventing skidding **(see illustration)**.

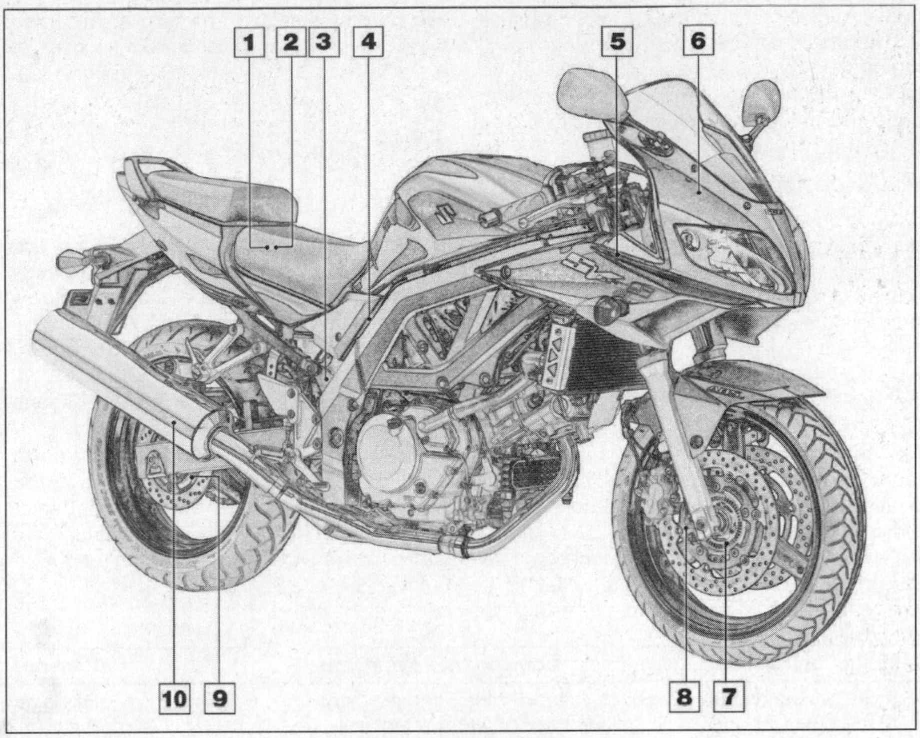

15.1 ABS component location

1 Motor fuse
2 Valve fuse
3 Control unit
4 Rear speed sensor wire connector
5 Front speed sensor wire connector
6 Warning light
7 Front pulser ring
8 Front speed sensor
9 Rear pulser ring
10 Rear speed sensor

2 The ABS is self-checking and is activated when the ignition (main) switch is turned on – the ABS indicator light in the instrument cluster will come on and will remain on until road speed increases above 3 mph (5 kmh) at which point, if the ABS is normal, the light will go off. **Note:** *If the ABS indicator light does not come on initially there is a fault in the indicator light system.*

Fault code output

3 If the indicator light remains on, or starts flashing while the machine is being ridden, there is a fault in the system and the ABS function will be switched off – the brakes will still operate but without the ABS function.

4 If a fault is indicated, details will be stored in the ABS control unit memory in the form of a fault code – up to six codes can be stored. Access the fault code(s) as follows. **Note:** *Don't disconnect the battery or the ABS control unit connector until the fault code has been confirmed – disconnection will erase the control unit memory.*

5 Before reading out the fault code, carry out a general check of the braking system. Check that the fluid level in the front and rear master cylinders is correct, that the pads are not worn down to the wear indicators and that there is no air in the brake system. Note that it is important that the correct size tyres are used for the ABS to function correctly. Also check that the battery is in good condition and fully charged and that both ABS fuses are in good condition and not blown.

6 Remove the rider's seat (see Chapter 8). Ensure the ignition (main) switch is OFF. Trace the orange and black/white wires to the mode select switch connector, located to the left of the ABS fuseholders, and pull the connector out of its holder. If the Suzuki model select switch is available (pt no. 09930-82710) plug it into the connector and set it to the ON position. Note that this tool is inexpensive, although if preferred can be substituted with a short piece of insulated jumper wire to bridge the wire terminals in the connector. Turn the ignition (main) switch ON.

7 The fault code will be represented as a series of flashes of the ABS indicator light – all the two digit fault codes given the accompanying table are displayed as 0.4 second flashes, with a 1.6 pause between the tens and units. Thus the example shown indicates fault code 42 as four 0.4 second flashes, followed by a 1.6 second pause, then two 0.4 second flashes **(see illustration)**. If a second fault

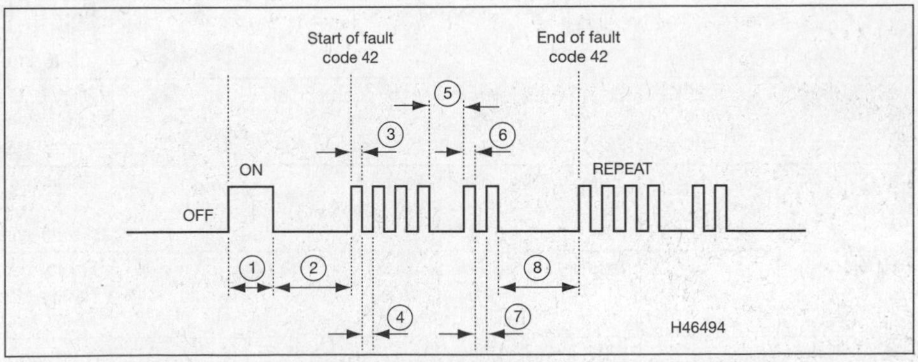

15.7 Example of ABS fault code read-out – code 42 represented

1 2 seconds light on
2 3.6 second light off
3 0.4 second light on
4 0.4 second light off
5 1.6 seconds light off
6 0.4 second light on
7 0.4 second light off
8 3.6 seconds light off

code has been recorded, a 3.6 second pause will separate the two codes. The cycle will repeat until the mode select switch is turned OFF or five minutes have lapsed. Record the code and identify the fault from the table. Turn the ignition (main) switch OFF.

Fault code erasing

8 Once the fault has been corrected, reset the control unit memory as follows. Ensure the ignition (main) switch is OFF. Connect the orange and black/white wire terminals in the mode select switch connector using the mode select switch (set to ON). Turn the ignition (main) switch ON. While the fault codes are being displayed, turn the mode select switch OFF, then after 12.5 seconds, turn it ON then OFF three times, each time leaving it ON for more than one second. After erasing the fault codes, the system will resume its normal self-diagnosis mode.

9 Repeat the fault code output procedure (see Steps 6 and 7) to check that the codes have been erased. Note that if no faults are recorded the indicator light will flash for 3.6 seconds at every 3.6 second interval **(see illustration 15.7)**.

16 ABS – system checks (SV650A/SA)

1 If a fault is indicated in the ABS, first check that the battery is fully charged, then check the two ABS fuses located in separate holders to the rear of the battery.

2 Unless specified otherwise, carry out all checks with the ignition (main) switch OFF.

3 Refer to Chapter 9, Section 2, for general fault finding procedures and equipment.

4 If, after a thorough check, the source of a fault has not been identified, have the ABS control unit tested by a Suzuki dealer equipped with the SDS diagnostic tester.

Note: *Codes with C prefix can only be read out with Suzuki SDS tester.*

ABS indicator light does not come on

5 First check the signal 10A fuse, then check the orange/green wire between the instrument cluster and the fusebox (see Chapter 9).

6 Remove the rider's seat and disconnect the negative (-ve) lead from the battery. Remove the plastic cover from the ABS control unit – it is held by a screw on each side and a screw on the underside. Lower the cover to reveal the control unit large multi-pin wire connector and the hydraulic solenoid unit. Remove the two bolts which retain the battery carrier to the frame top tubes, then lift the carrier complete with battery upwards just sufficiently to pull up the lock lever on the ABS unit multi-pin connector and pull the connector free.

7 Reconnect the negative lead to the battery and turn the ignition ON. Using a multimeter set to the dc volts function, measure the voltage between pin 12 (positive probe) and pin 4 (negative probe) on the wire harness side of the connector **(see illustration)**. Between

Fault code/flashes	Faulty component - symptoms	Possible causes
Light does not come on	No voltage at instrument cluster No voltage at ABS control unit	Damaged signal fuse Faulty wiring or wiring connector Damaged earth (ground) wire
Light stays on continuously	Service check connector No voltage at ABS control unit ABS control unit	Faulty wiring or wiring connector Damaged earth (ground) wire Internal fault
25 (C1625)	Tyre size Speed sensors	Incorrect tyre size/tyre pressure Deformed wheel, wheel spinning, incorrect tooth count Dirty or damaged sensor Damaged pulser ring
35 (C1635)	ABS motor fuse No voltage at ABS control unit ABS control unit	Fuse blown Faulty wiring or wiring connector Internal fault
41 (C1641)	Front wheel speed sensor	Worn or missing teeth on pulser ring, loose wheel speed sensor contact Dirty or damaged sensor ABS control unit failure
42 (C1642)	Front wheel speed sensor circuit open	Dirty or damaged sensor Faulty wiring or wiring connector Input amplifier in ABS control unit failure
44 (C1644)	Rear wheel speed sensor	Dirty or damaged sensor Damaged pulser ring Input amplifier in ABS control unit failure
45 (C1645)	Rear wheel speed sensor circuit open	Dirty or damaged sensor Faulty wiring or wiring connector Input amplifier in ABS control unit failure
47 (C1647)	Supply voltage increased*	Faulty battery Faulty regulator/rectifier Faulty wiring
48 (C1648)	Supply voltage decreased*	Faulty battery or low battery charge Faulty alternator or regulator/rectifier Faulty wiring
55 (C1655)	ABS control unit	Internal fault
61 (C1661)	ABS valve fuse ABS solenoid	Fuse blown Faulty ABS control unit

**The ABS indicator light will extinguish when the voltage returns to the correct level.*

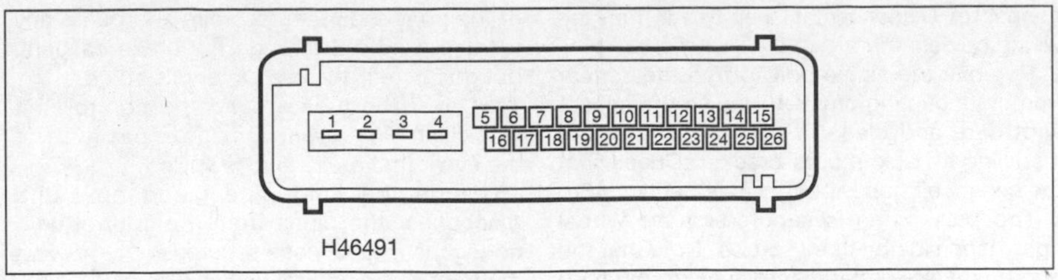

16.7 ABS control unit wire connector (harness side) terminal identification

7.5 and 9.5 V should be shown. If no voltage is shown check the blue wire between the connector and the instruments. If the wiring is good, the ABS indicator light may be faulty. **Note:** *If the indicator light LED has failed a new instrument cluster will have to be fitted (see Chapter 9).* Turn the ignition OFF when the check is complete.

8 If there is voltage in Step 7, test for continuity between terminal 4 and earth (ground). If there is no continuity, check for a fault in the earth wires. If there is continuity it is likely the ABS control unit is faulty – have it tested by a Suzuki dealer.

ABS indicator light stays on continuously

9 First check the ignition 10A fuse (see Chapter 9).

10 If the fuse is good, follow the procedure in Step 6 and disconnect the ABS control unit wiring connector.

11 Reconnect the negative lead to the battery and turn the ignition ON. Using a multimeter set to the dc volts function, measure the voltage between pin 18 (positive probe) and pin 4 (negative probe) on the wire harness side of the connector – battery voltage should be shown. If there is no voltage, inspect the wiring for damage.

12 If there is voltage in Step 11, measure the voltage between terminal 12 (positive probe) and terminal 4 (negative probe) in the harness side of the connector. Between 7.5 and 9.5 V should be shown. If there is no voltage, check the wiring to the instrument cluster and the terminals of the instrument cluster connector. Turn the ignition OFF.

13 If there is voltage it is likely the ABS control unit is faulty – have it tested by a Suzuki dealer.

Code 25 – Speed sensor malfunction

14 Ensure that the tyre size and pressure are correct (see Specifications at the beginning of the Chapter).

15 Check the speed sensor pulser ring condition, particularly that nothing has become trapped between the segments.

16 Follow the procedure in Step 23 (front) or Step 30 (rear) and check the speed sensor air gap.

17 If the checks fail to identify the fault, have the ABS control unit checked by a Suzuki dealer.

Code 35 – ABS motor fuse

18 Turn the ignition ON and listen for any operating noise from the ABS control unit. If there is any noise with the machine at a standstill the fault is likely to be in the ABS control unit - have it checked by a Suzuki dealer.

19 Remove the rider's seat (see Chapter 8). Check the ABS motor 40A fuse (see Chapter 9).

20 If the fuse is good, follow the procedure in Step 6 to access the ABS control unit wiring connector. Ensure that the connector is secure, then disconnect it and check that the contacts are clean and undamaged.

21 Turn the ignition ON. Test for battery voltage between the terminal 2 (positive probe) and terminal 1 (negative probe) in the loom side of the connector. If there is no voltage, inspect the wiring for damage.

Code 41 – Front wheel speed sensor signal malfunction

22 Check that the sensor is mounted securely and the pulser ring is clean and in good condition without anything trapped between its segments.

23 Use feeler gauge blades to measure the air gap between the sensor tip and the pulser ring segments and compare it with the value given in the Specifications. If the gap is outside of this figure, there may be a problem with the pulser ring or disc (which it mounts to) not seating correctly on the wheel hub, or the sensor or its bracket being out of line. Note that there are no shims available to adjust the air gap setting. Refer to Section 17 for sensor removal details.

Code 42 – Front wheel speed sensor circuit open

24 Remove the headlight on SV650A models to access the sensor wiring connector (see Chapter 8). On SV650S models, reach up under the fairing to access the wiring connector. Inspect the sensor wiring for damage and ensure that the wiring connector is secure.

25 Follow the procedure in Step 6 to access the ABS control unit wiring connector. Ensure that the connector is secure, then disconnect it and check that the contacts are clean and undamaged.

26 Test for continuity between terminal 16 and terminal 5 in the loom side of the connector. If continuity is shown, check the wiring between the connector and the sensor for a fault.

27 If no continuity is indicated, test between terminal 16 and earth (ground) – no continuity should be shown. If it is, disconnect the wheel speed sensor connector and test for continuity between the white/red (white) wire terminal and earth on the sensor side of the connector. No continuity should be shown. If continuity is shown, the speed sensor is faulty.

28 Test for continuity between terminal 5 in the loom side of the ABS control unit connector and earth – no continuity should be shown. If it is, disconnect the wheel speed sensor connector and test for continuity between the black/red (black) wire terminal and earth on the sensor side of the connector. No continuity should be shown. If continuity is shown, the speed sensor is faulty.

29 Finally, check the white/red wire between the ABS control unit connector harness side and the wheel speed sensor connector – continuity should be shown.

Code 44 – Rear wheel speed sensor signal malfunction

30 Follow the procedure in Steps 22 and 23 and check the rear wheel speed sensor and pulser ring. Note that the sensor locates directly in the rear caliper bracket.

Code 45 – Rear wheel speed sensor circuit open

31 Follow the procedure in Step 6 to access the ABS control unit wiring connector. Ensure that the connector is secure, then disconnect it and check that the contacts are clean and undamaged.

32 Inspect the speed sensor wiring for damage and ensure that the wiring connector is secure. The wiring connector is located on the left-hand side of the frame, below the side panel.

33 Test for continuity between terminal 19 and terminal 7 in the loom side of the connector. If continuity is shown, check the wiring between the connector and the sensor for a fault.

34 If no continuity is indicated, test between terminal 7 and earth (ground) – no continuity should be shown. If it is, disconnect the wheel speed sensor connector and test for continuity between the white/yellow (white) wire terminal and earth on the sensor side of the connector. No continuity should be shown. If continuity is shown, the speed sensor is faulty.

35 Test for continuity between terminal 19 in the loom side of the ABS control unit connector and earth – no continuity should be shown. If it is, disconnect the wheel speed sensor connector and test for continuity between the black/yellow (black) wire terminal and earth on the sensor side of the connector. No continuity should be shown. If continuity is shown, the speed sensor is faulty.

36 Finally, check the white/yellow wire between the ABS control unit connector harness side and the wheel speed sensor connector – continuity should be shown.

Code 47, 48 – Supply voltage

37 Check the battery voltage (see Chapter 9, Section 3). If the voltage is good, check the output of the charging system (see Chapter 9, Section 32).

38 If the charging system is good, follow the procedure in Step 6 to access the ABS control unit wiring connector. Ensure that the connector is secure, then disconnect it and check that the contacts are clean and undamaged.

39 With the control unit wiring connector disconnected, start the engine and warm it up to normal operating temperature. Switch the headlight main (HI) beam ON and increase the engine speed to 5000 rpm. Measure the voltage between terminal 18 (positive probe) and terminal 4 (negative probe) on the loom side of the connector. If the specified regulated voltage is shown, it is likely the ABS control unit is faulty – have it checked by a Suzuki dealer. If the voltage is outside the specifications, inspect the ABS wiring loom for damage.

Code 55 – Control unit malfunction

40 Follow the procedure in Step 23 to ensure that the front and rear speed sensor air gaps are correct, that the components are not damaged and that the speed sensor and pulser ring fixings are tight.

41 If the checks fail to identify the fault, follow the procedure in Section 15 to reset the control unit memory, then activate the self-checking procedure. If the fault code remains it is likely the ABS control unit is faulty – have it checked by a Suzuki dealer.

Code 61 – ABS solenoid malfunction

42 Remove the rider's seat to access the ABS valve fuse (see Chapter 9). If the fuse is good, follow the procedure in Step 6 and disconnect the ABS control unit wiring connector. Check that the contacts are clean and undamaged.

43 Check for battery voltage between terminal 3 (positive probe) and terminal 4 (negative probe) on the loom side of the connector. If there is no voltage, inspect the wiring for damage.

44 If there is voltage, it is likely the ABS control unit is faulty – have it tested by a Suzuki dealer.

17 ABS component removal and installation

Front speed sensor and pulser ring

1 Remove the headlight on SV650A models to access the sensor wiring connector (see Chapter 8). On SV650S models, reach up under the fairing to access the wiring connector. Disconnect it, then free it from the wiring guides.

2 Remove the single bolt to free the sensor from its mounting bracket. Handle the sensor with care and clean of all road dirt before installing it back into its bracket. Check that the sensor air gap is correct (see Section 16).

3 The pulser ring is secured to the wheel right-hand side by three screws. Note that the ring has a No. of segments marking (50T) on its outer face.

4 Follow the procedure in Chapter 7 to remove the wheel, noting that care must be taken not to knock the sensor tip at any time, and that the cut-out in the sensor bracket must engage the lug on the fork leg on installation. Check the sensor air gap after installing the wheel.

Rear speed sensor and pulser ring

5 The speed sensor wiring connector is located on the left-hand side of the frame, below the side panel. Disconnect it, then free it from the wiring guides.

6 Remove the single bolt to free the sensor from the caliper mounting bracket. Handle the sensor with care and clean of all road dirt before installing it back into its bracket. Check that the sensor air gap is correct (see Section 16).

7 The pulser ring is secured to the wheel right-hand side by three screws. Note that the ring has a No. of segments marking (50T) on its outer face.

8 Follow the procedure in Chapter 7 to remove the wheel, noting that care must be taken not to knock the sensor tip at any time. Check the sensor air gap after installing the wheel.

ABS control unit

Note: *Before the control unit can be removed from the bike, the brake fluid must be drained from the hydraulic system. When refilling and bleeding the ABS-equipped brake system it is essential to use a vacuum-type brake bleeder kit. Alternatively, removal and installation of the control unit should be entrusted to a Suzuki dealer.*

9 Remove the rider's seat (see Chapter 8). Remove the battery (see Chapter 9).

10 The battery carrier must be removed to gain access to the ABS control unit. Free the fusebox, fuel pump relay, the two ABS system fuses and the starter relay from their mountings on the carrier. Lift the rubber matt out of the bottom of the carrier to reveal the relay/diode unit – disconnect its wire connector.

11 Free the ABS control unit wiring connector and the tip-over sensor from their mountings on the battery carrier.

12 Remove the plastic cover from the ABS control unit – it is held by a screw on each side and a screw on the underside. Remove the two bolts which retain the battery carrier to the frame top tubes, then lift the carrier upwards.

13 Refer to the procedure in Section 9 for changing the brake fluid – siphon the fluid out of the front and rear reservoirs and pump any residual fluid out through the brake calipers, but do not refill the system at this stage.

14 Cover the area around the control unit with clean rag prevent damage to paintwork in the event that brake fluid is spilled.

15 Undo the fluid pipe gland nuts and disconnect the pipes from the control unit, noting the flexible hose secured in the hook at the front of the control unit carrier.

16 Pull up the lock lever on the ABS unit multi-pin connector and pull the connector free.

17 Remove the three mounting bolts, two underneath and one at the rear, then lift the control unit out.

18 Installation is the reverse of removal, noting the following:

- *If possible, tighten the fluid pipe gland nuts to the torque setting specified at the beginning of this Chapter. Support the metal pipes whilst the nuts are tightened to prevent them distorting.*
- *Ensure the ABS control unit wiring connector is secure.*
- *Follow the procedure in Section 11 to refill and bleed the brake system.*

18 Tyres – general information and fitting

General information

1 The wheels fitted to all models are designed to take tubeless tyres only. Tyre sizes are given in the Specifications at the beginning of this chapter and are displayed on a label attached to the chainguard. Tyre sizes are also given the machine's owners manual.

2 Refer to the *Daily (pre-ride) checks* listed at the beginning of this manual for tyre maintenance.

Fitting new tyres

3 When selecting new tyres ensure that front and rear tyre types are compatible, the correct size and correct speed rating; if necessary seek advice from a Suzuki dealer or tyre fitting specialist **(see illustration)**.

4 It is recommended that tyres are fitted by a motorcycle tyre specialist rather than attempted in the home workshop. This is particularly relevant in the case of tubeless tyres because the force required to break the seal between the wheel rim and tyre bead is substantial, and is usually beyond the capabilities of an individual working with normal tyre levers. Additionally, the specialist will be able to balance the wheels after tyre fitting.

5 Note that punctured tubeless tyres can in some cases be repaired. Repairs must only be carried out by a motorcycle tyre specialist. Suzuki advise that the motorcycle must not exceed 50 mph (80 km/h) for the first 24 hrs after the repair, and must not exceed 80 mph (130 km/h) thereafter.

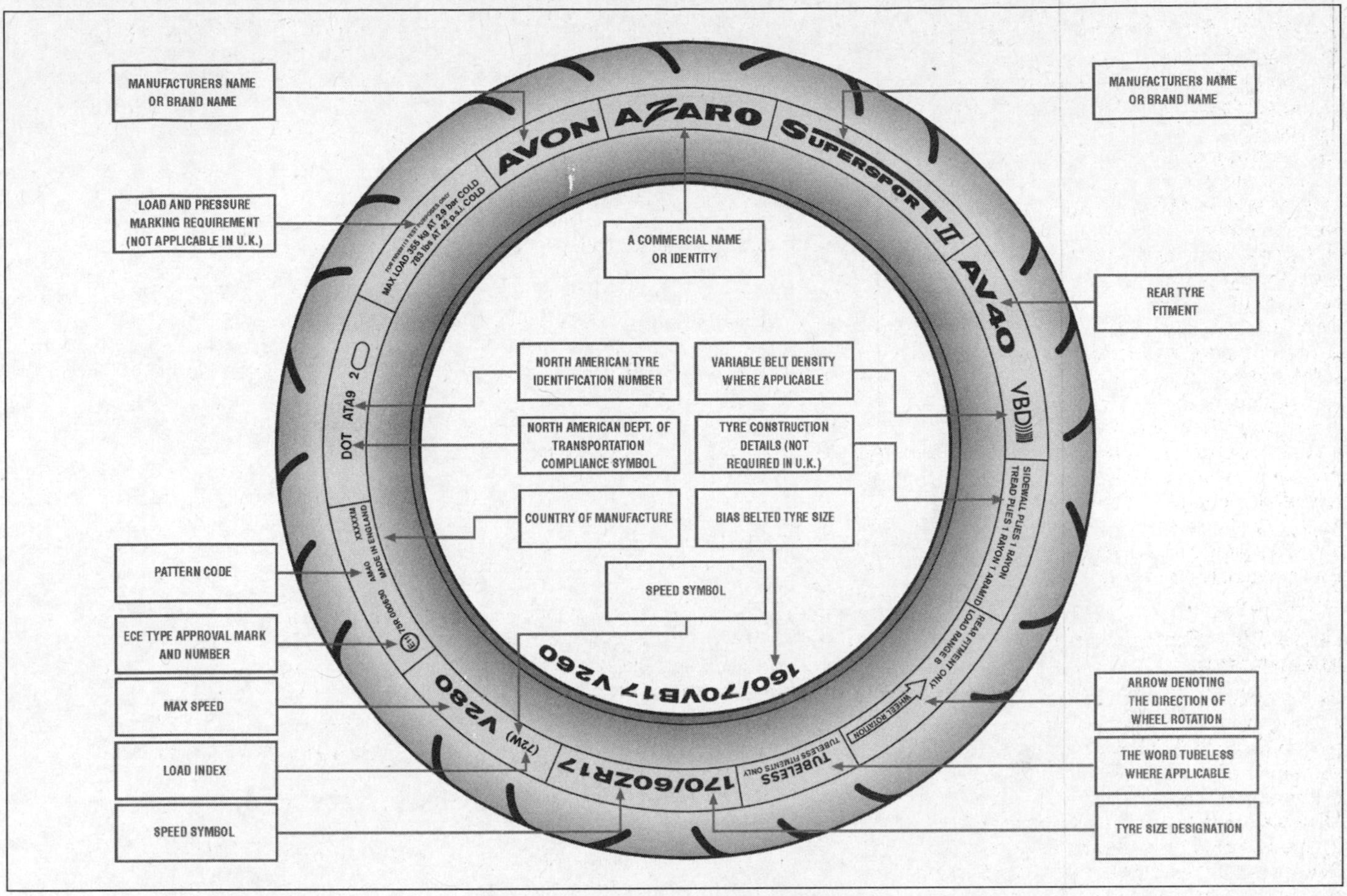
MANUFACTURERS NAME OR BRAND NAME
MANUFACTURERS NAME OR BRAND NAME
LOAD AND PRESSURE MARKING REQUIREMENT (NOT APPLICABLE IN U.K.)
A COMMERCIAL NAME OR IDENTITY
REAR TYRE FITMENT
NORTH AMERICAN TYRE IDENTIFICATION NUMBER
VARIABLE BELT DENSITY WHERE APPLICABLE
NORTH AMERICAN DEPT. OF TRANSPORTATION COMPLIANCE SYMBOL
TYRE CONSTRUCTION DETAILS (NOT REQUIRED IN U.K.)
COUNTRY OF MANUFACTURE
BIAS BELTED TYRE SIZE
PATTERN CODE
SPEED SYMBOL
ECE TYPE APPROVAL MARK AND NUMBER
ARROW DENOTING THE DIRECTION OF WHEEL ROTATION
MAX SPEED
THE WORD TUBELESS WHERE APPLICABLE
LOAD INDEX
SPEED SYMBOL
TYRE SIZE DESIGNATION
AVON
AZARO
SUPERSPORT II
AV40
VBD
MAX LOAD 355 kg AT 2.9 bar COLD
783 lbs AT 42 p.s.i. COLD
DOT ATA9 2
MADE IN ENGLAND
SIDEWALL PLIES 1 RAYON
TREAD PLIES 1 RAYON 1 ARAMID
REAR FITMENT ONLY
LOAD RANGE B
WHEEL ROTATION
160/70VB17 V260
V280
(72W)
170/60ZR17
TUBELESS
TUBELESS FITMENT ONLY

18.3 Common tyre sidewall markings

Chapter 8
Bodywork

Contents

Degrees of difficulty

Easy, suitable for novice with little experience	**Fairly easy,** suitable for beginner with some experience	**Fairly difficult,** suitable for competent DIY mechanic	**Difficult,** suitable for experienced DIY mechanic	**Very difficult,** suitable for expert DIY or professional

1 General information

This Chapter covers the procedures necessary to remove and install the body parts. Since many service and repair operations require the removal of body parts, the procedures are grouped here and referred to from other Chapters.

In the case of damage to the body parts, it is usually necessary to remove the broken component and replace it with a new (or used) one. The material that the body panels are composed of doesn't lend itself to conventional repair techniques. There are however companies who specialise in repair of plastic body panels and there are also a number of kits available for DIY repair of small cracks.

When attempting to remove any body panel, first study it closely, noting any fasteners and associated fittings, to be sure of returning everything to its correct place on installation. In some cases the aid of an assistant will be required when removing panels, to help avoid the risk of damage to paintwork. Once the evident fasteners have been removed, try to withdraw the panel as described but DO NOT FORCE IT – if it will not release, check that all fasteners have been removed and try again. Where a panel engages another by means of tabs, be careful not to break the tab or its mating slot or to damage the paintwork. Remember that a few moments of patience at this stage will save you a lot of money in replacing broken fairing panels!

When installing a body panel, first study it closely, noting any fasteners and associated fittings removed with it, to be sure of returning everything to its correct place. Check that all fasteners are in good condition, including all trim nuts or clips and damping/rubber mounts; any of these must be renewed if faulty before the panel is reassembled. Check also that all mounting brackets are straight and repair or renew them if necessary before attempting to install the panel. Where assistance was required to remove a panel, make sure your assistant is on hand to install it. Tighten the fasteners securely, but be careful not to overtighten any of them or the panel may break (not always immediately) due to the uneven stress.

HAYNES HiNT *Note that a small amount of lubricant (liquid soap or similar) applied to the mounting rubber grommets of the seat cowling will assist the lugs to engage without the need for undue pressure.*

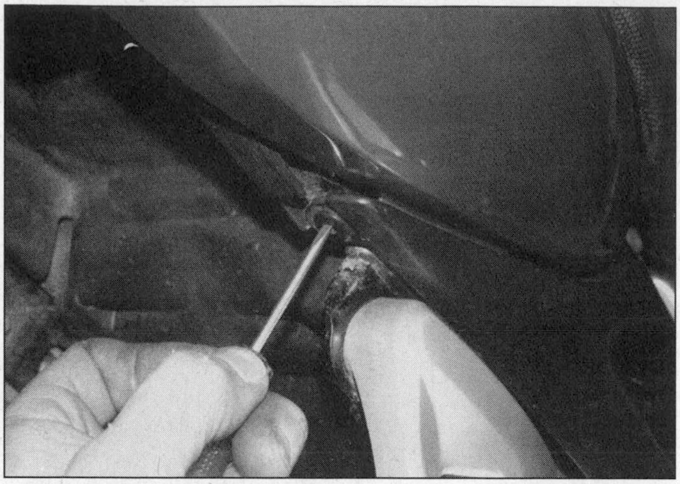

2.1a On X, Y, K1 and K2 models, push the centre of the trim clip in . . .

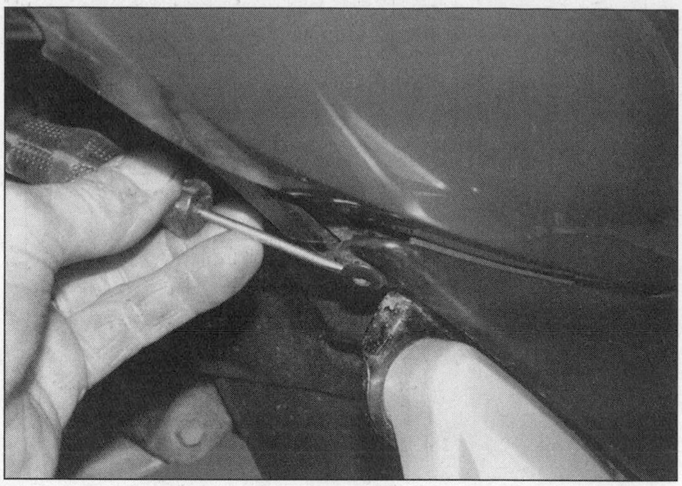

2.1b . . . then draw the body out

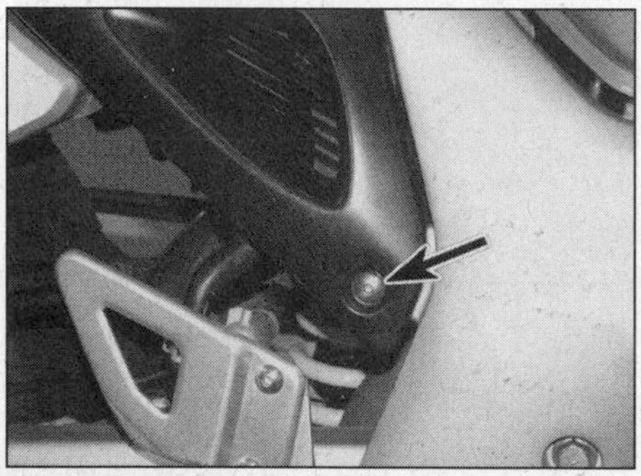

2.2a Undo the screw (arrowed) . . .

2.2b . . . and remove the panel

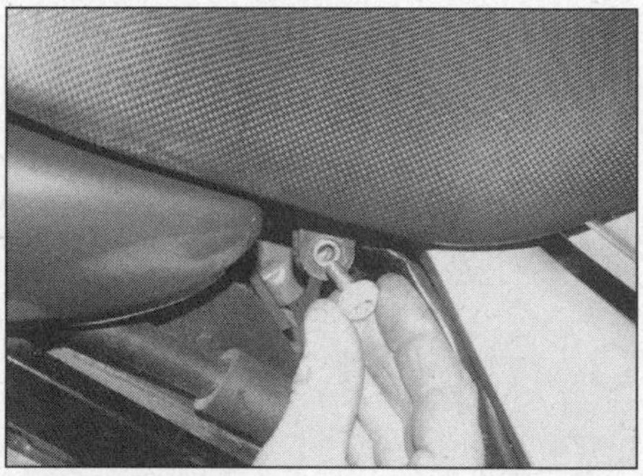

2.3a Unscrew the bolt on each side . . .

2 Seats

Rider's seat

1 On X, Y, K1 and K2 models, first release the trim clip on each side panel – push in the centre then draw the clip out of the panel **(see illustrations)**.

2 On all models, undo the screw securing each side panel and remove the panels **(see illustrations)**.

3 Unscrew the two bolts (one on each side) securing the seat and remove it, noting how the tabs at the rear locate under the bracket **(see illustrations)**.

4 Installation is the reverse of removal. Make sure the tabs locate correctly. On X, Y, K1 and K2 models, to install the side panel trim clips, pull the centre out of the body, then fit the body into the panel and push the centre back in **(see illustrations)**.

Passenger's seat

5 Insert the ignition key into the seat lock

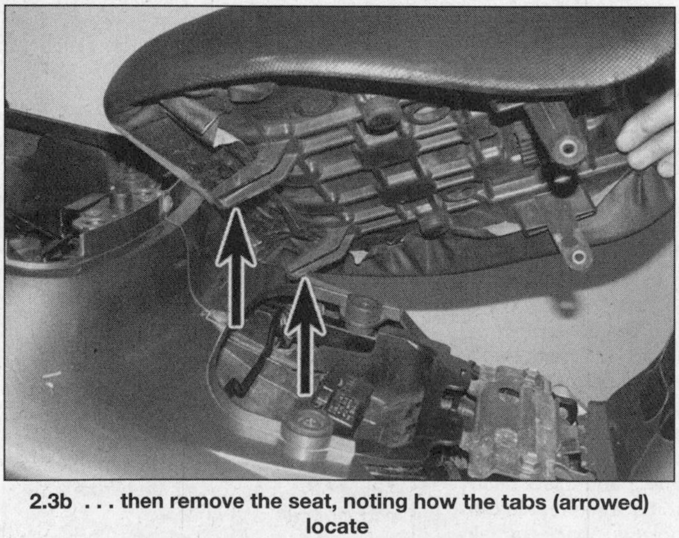

2.3b . . . then remove the seat, noting how the tabs (arrowed) locate

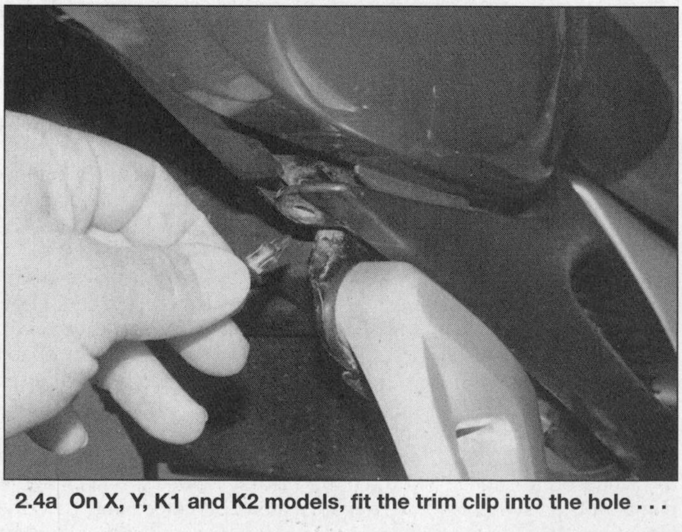

2.4a On X, Y, K1 and K2 models, fit the trim clip into the hole . . .

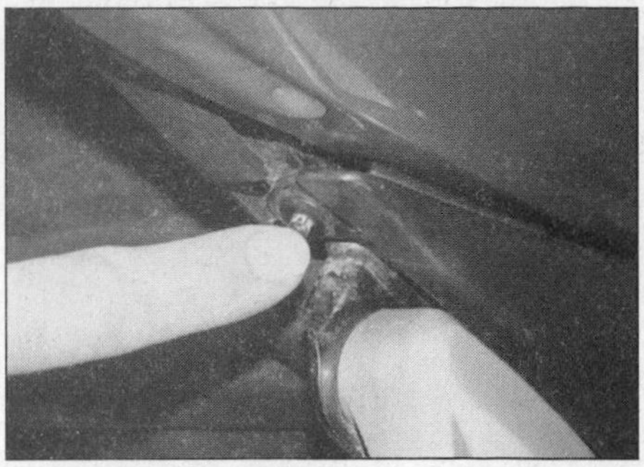

2.4b . . . then push the centre in

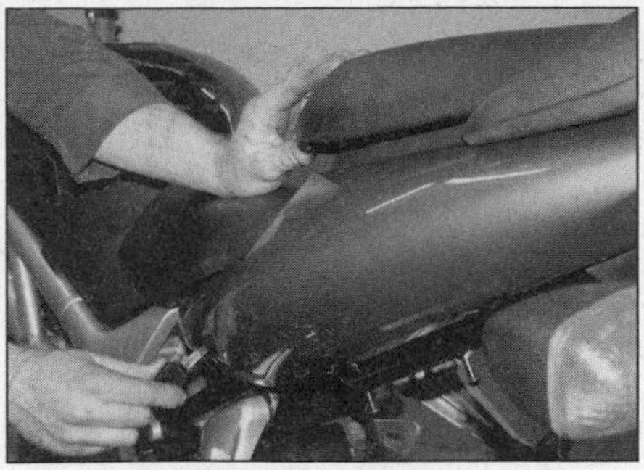

2.5a Unlock the seat, lift it up at the front and remove it . . .

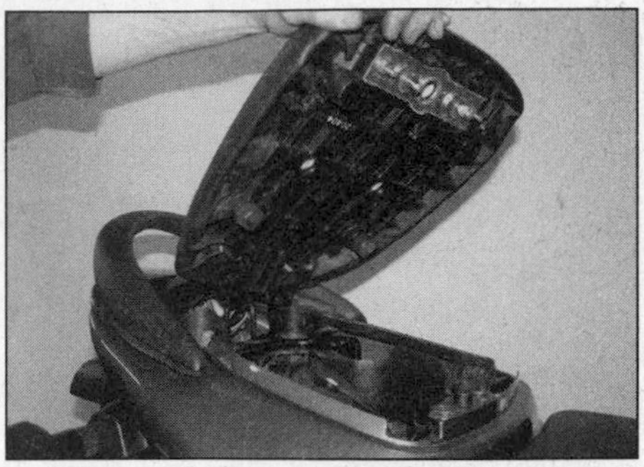

2.5b . . . noting where the tab locates

located in the left-hand seat cowling and turn it clockwise to unlock the seat **(see illustration)**. Remove the seat by lifting the front and drawing it forward, noting how the tab at the rear locates under the bracket **(see illustration)**.

6 Installation is the reverse of removal. Make sure the tab locates correctly. Push down on the front of the seat to engage the latch.

3 Seat cowling

Removal

1 Remove the seats (see Section 2).

2 On X, Y, K1 and K2 models, undo the two screws on the underside of the cowling **(see illustration)**. On K3-on models, follow the procedure in Section 2 and release the four trim clips on the underside of the cowling **(see illustration)**.

3 Undo the two bolts and remove the passenger grab-rail, then remove the four screws securing the cowling **(see illustrations)**.

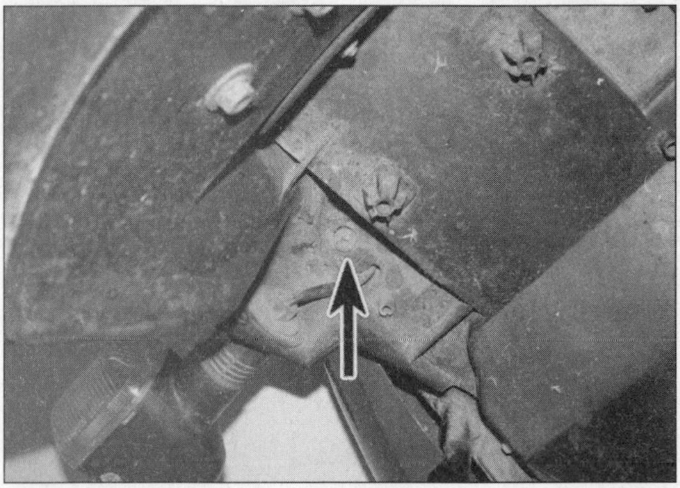

3.2a Undo the screw (arrowed) on each side – X, Y, K1 and K2 models

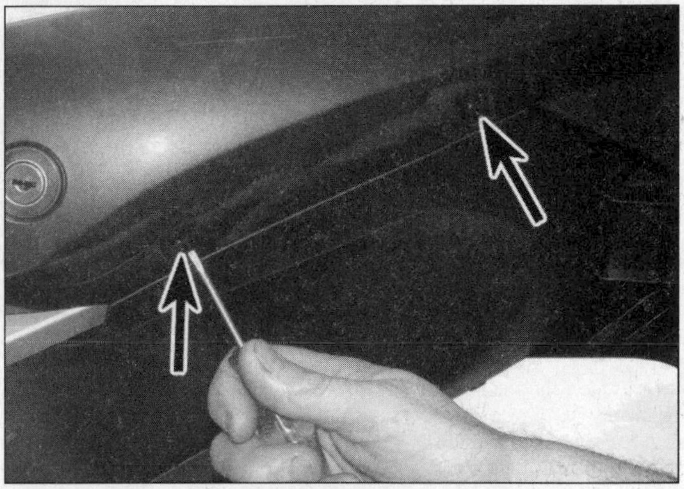

3.2b On X, Y, K1 and K2 models, release two trim clips (arrowed) on each side

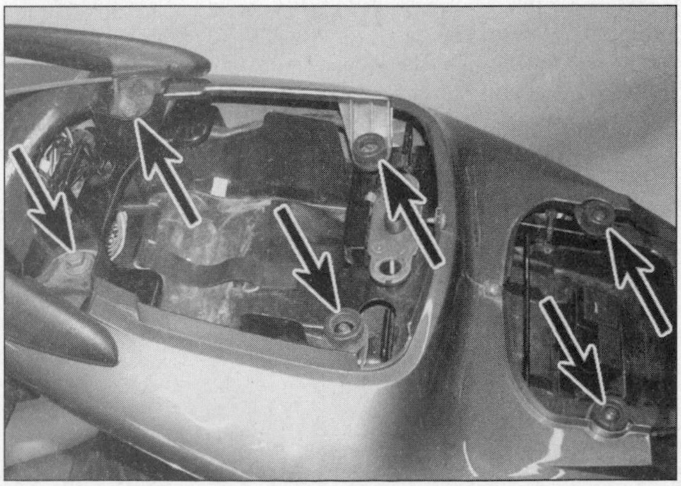

3.3a Undo the screws and bolts (arrowed) . . .

3.3b . . . and remove the grab-rail

3.4a On K3-on models, disconnect the tail light wiring connector . . .

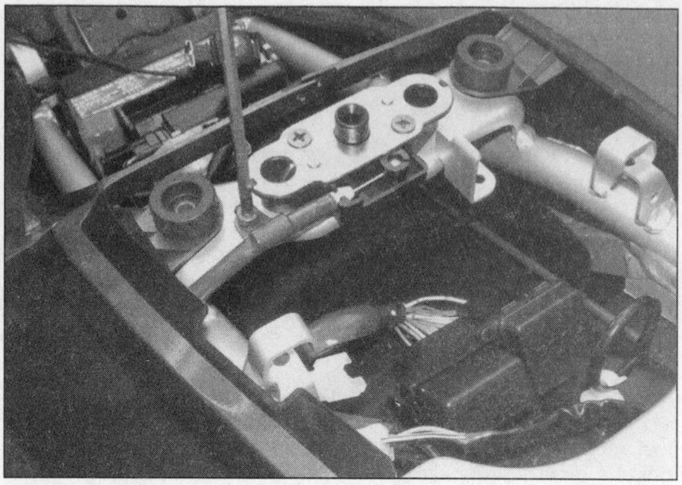

3.4b . . . then unbolt the seat lock cable stop . . .

3.4c . . . and disconnect the inner cable end

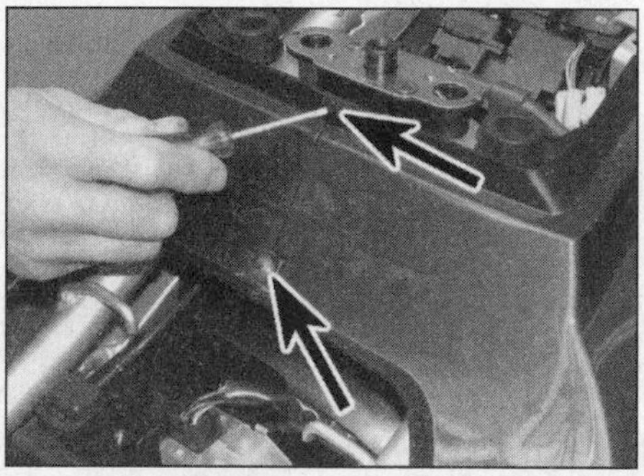

3.5 Remove the fixings (arrowed) that join the halves of the cowling

3.6a On X, Y, K1 and K2 models, release the pegs from the grommets at the front . . .

4 On K3-on models, disconnect the tail light assembly wiring connector, then unbolt the seat lock cable stop and disconnect the inner cable end from the lock **(see illustrations)**.
5 Remove the two screws, or the screw and trim clip, that join the halves of the cowling in the middle **(see illustration)**.
6 On X, Y, K1 and K2 models, carefully pull each side away at the front to release the pegs from the grommets **(see illustration)**. Lift the left-hand side of the cowling up off the rear sub-frame, then move the cowling to the right to free that side. Disengage the seat lock cable from the lock when accessible and lift the cowling off **(see illustrations)**.
7 On K3-on models, lift the rear of the cowling and carefully ease it off **(see illustration)**.

Installation

8 Installation is the reverse of removal. Check the operation of the seat lock before installing the passenger's seat. On K3-on models, check the operation of the brake/ tail light before riding the motorcycle.

4 Front mudguard

Removal

1 Remove the front wheel (see Chapter 7).
2 On X, Y, K1 and K2 models, from the underside of the mudguard, spread the pegs of the speed sensor wiring trim clip body, then push the centre up through the mudguard and

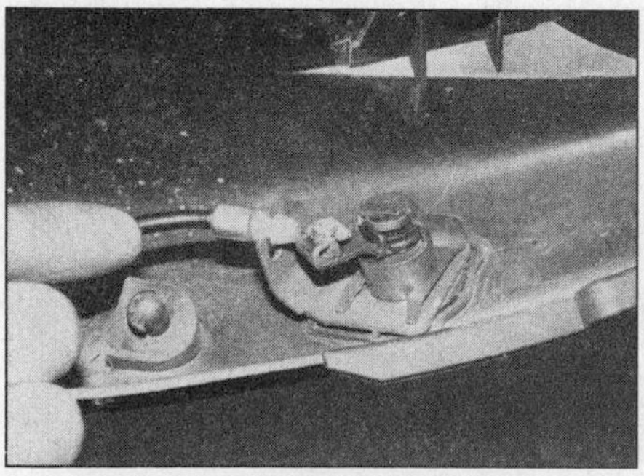

3.6b . . . and detach the lock cable . . .

3.6c . . . then ease off the cowling

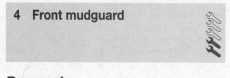

3.7 Draw the cowling to the rear on K3, K4 and K5 models

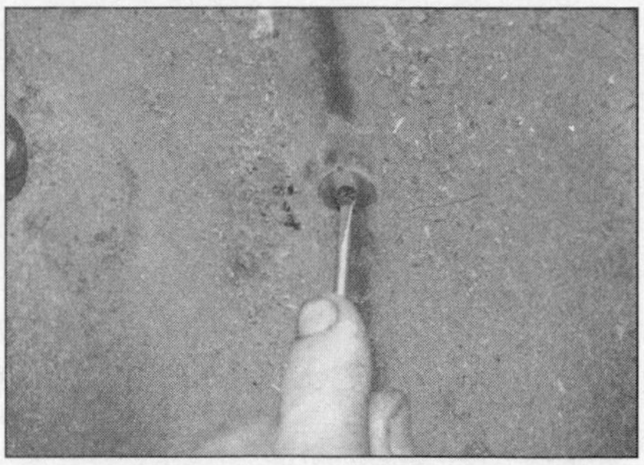
4.2a On X, Y, K1 and K2 models, push the centre up . . .

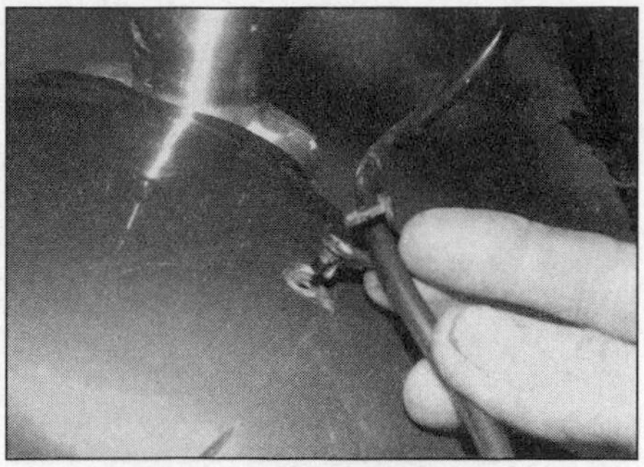
4.2b . . . and pull the body out

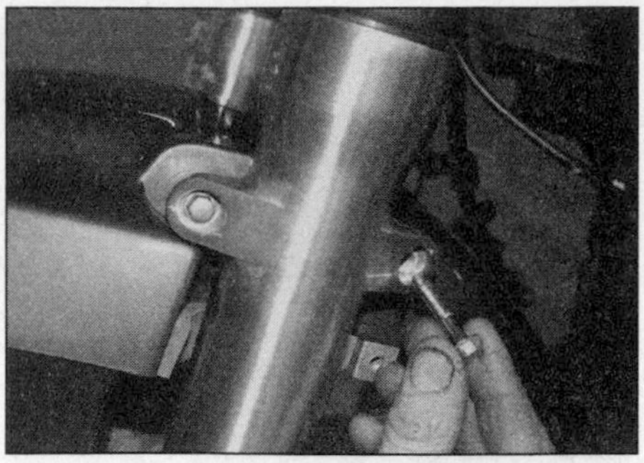
4.2c Unscrew the bolts . . .

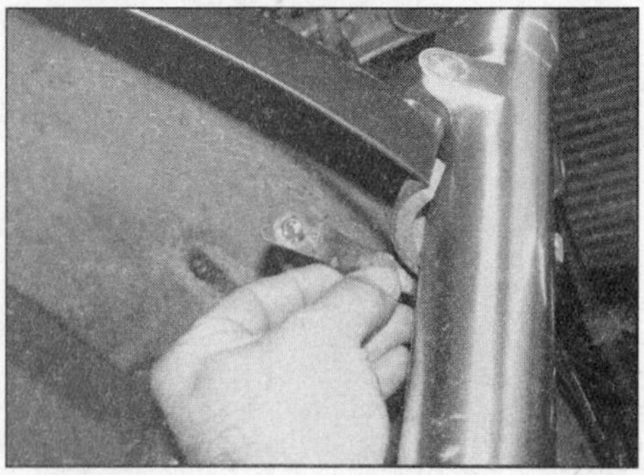
4.2d . . . noting the brackets . . .

4.2e . . . and remove the mudguard

4.3 On K3-on models, undo the two bolts (arrowed) on each side

draw the body out of the top **(see illustrations)**. Unscrew the two bolts on each side and draw the mudguard forwards **(see illustrations)**. Note the brackets on the inside of the mudguard and remove them if they are loose.

3 On K3-on models, undo the two bolts on the front outside and the two bolts on the rear inside of the mudguard and lift the mudguard off **(see illustration)**.

Installation

4 Installation is the reverse of removal. On X, Y, K1 and K2 models, if removed, fit the brackets to the inside of the mudguard, making sure the triangular mark points to the front. To fit the trim clip, fit the body into the hole, then push the centre into the body **(see illustration)**. Install the front wheel (see Chapter 7)

5 Rear view mirrors

SV650

1 The mirrors simply screw into the handlebar mounting – slacken the locknut on the base of the stem then unscrew the mirror **(see illustration)**.

2 Installation is the reverse of removal. The position of the mirror can be adjusted by slackening the locknut, moving the mirror as required, then retightening the locknut.

SV650S

3 On X, Y, K1 and K2 models, undo the screw securing the fairing trim panel and remove the panel, noting how it fits **(see illustrations)**. Unscrew the two sleeve nuts and remove the mirror **(see illustrations)**.

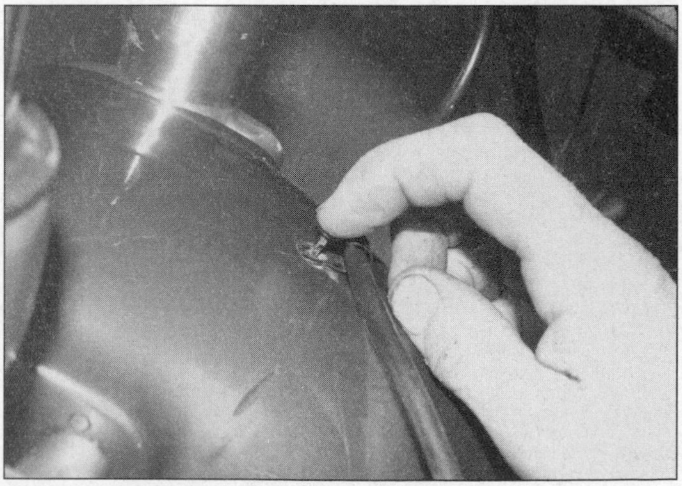
4.4 Fit the trim clip body then press the centre into it

5.1 Slacken the nut (arrowed) then unscrew the mirror

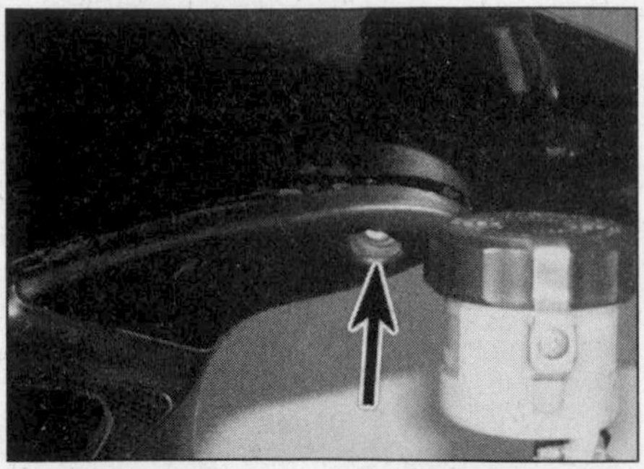
5.3a Undo the screw (arrowed) . . .

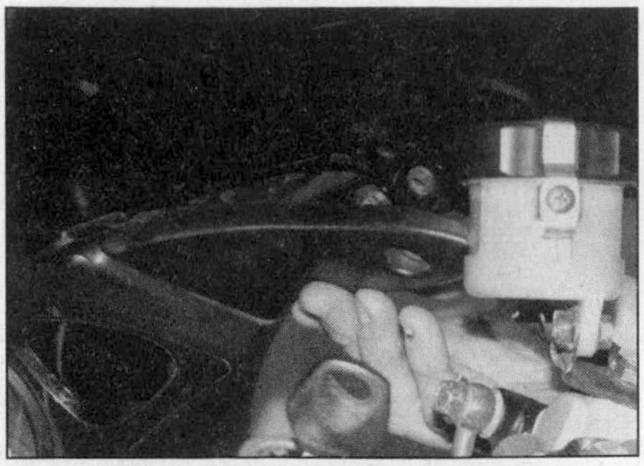
5.3b . . . and remove the panel

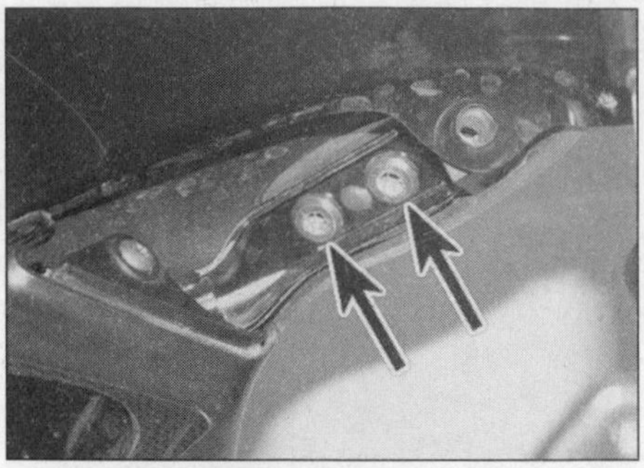
5.3c Unscrew the nuts (arrowed) . . .

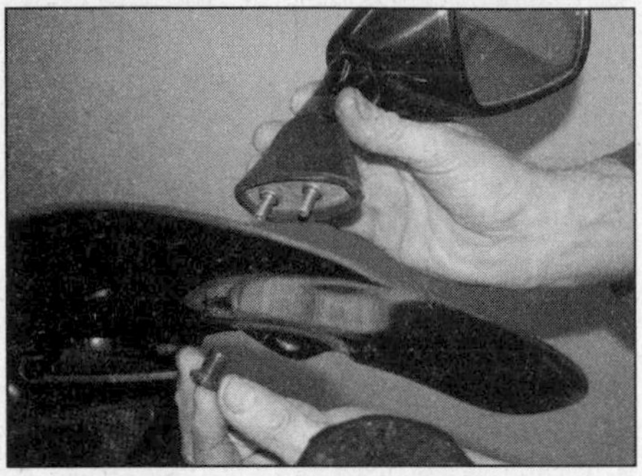
5.3d . . . and remove the mirror

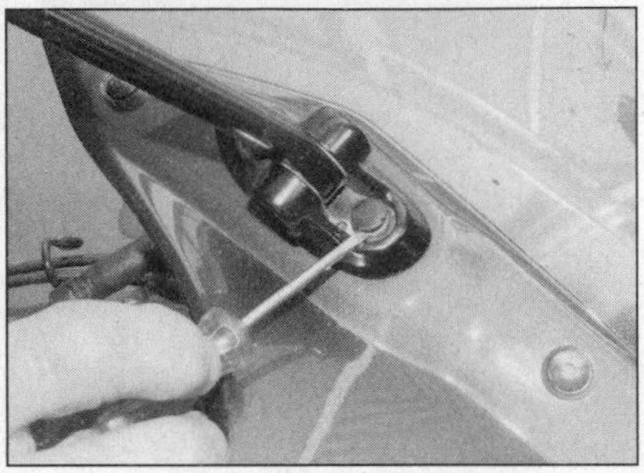
5.4a Prise out the blanking caps . . .

5.4b . . . then unscrew the bolts (arrowed)

4 On K3-on models, undo the two screws and remove the mirror **(see illustrations)**.
5 Installation is the reverse of removal.

6 Fairing panels (SV650S)

X, Y, K1 and K2 models

Fairing side panels

1 Remove the rear view mirror (see Section 5).
2 Each panel is secured by three screws at the front and three on the side **(see illustration)**. Undo the screws, then carefully pull the side of the panel away from the radiator to release the peg from the grommet **(see illustration)**. Disengage the panel from the fairing and the cockpit trim panel and remove it, noting how it fits, and disconnect the turn signal wiring connector when accessible **(see illustrations)**.
3 Installation is the reverse of removal. Check the operation of the turn signals before riding the motorcycle.

Fairing

4 Remove both fairing side panels.
5 Undo the four screws securing the fairing, then draw it forwards off the headlight and disconnect the sidelight wiring connector **(see illustrations)**.
6 Installation is the reverse of removal.

Cockpit trim panel

7 Remove the fairing (see above).
8 Undo the three screws securing the trim panel and lift it off the instrument cluster **(see illustration)**.
9 Installation is the reverse of removal.

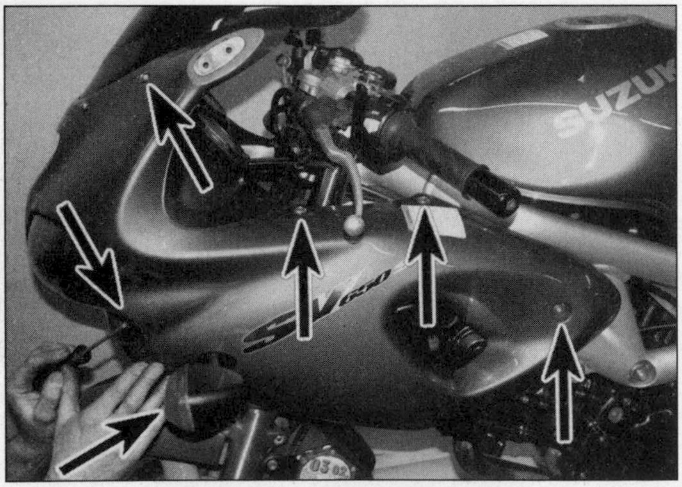
6.2a Undo the screws (arrowed) . . .

6.2b . . . then release the peg (arrowed) from the grommet

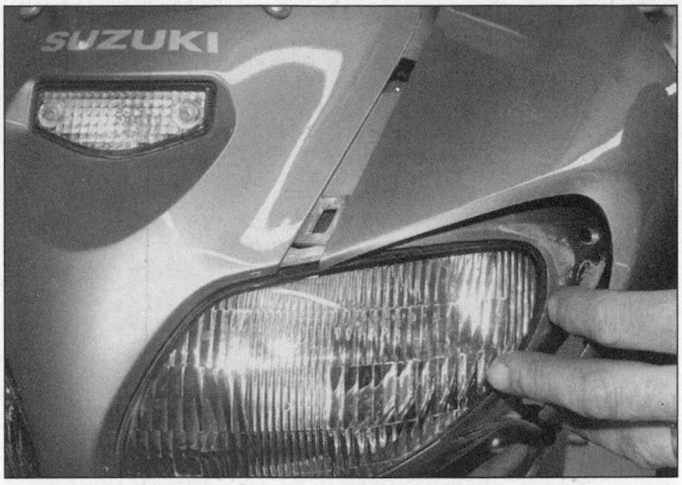

6.2c Free the panel from the fairing, noting how it fits . . .

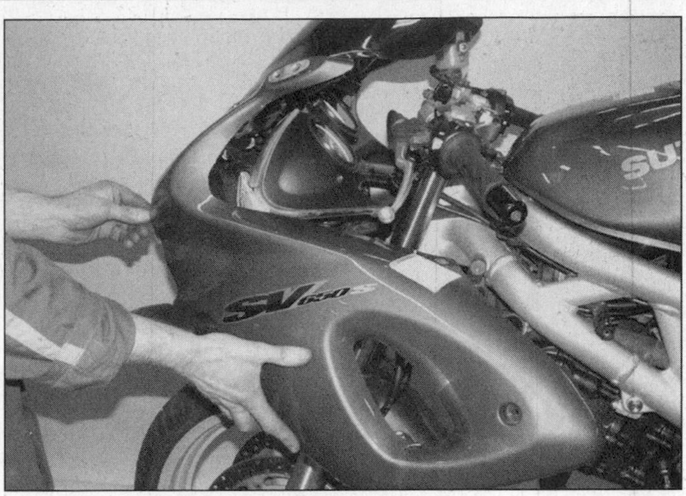

6.2d . . . then draw it off . . .

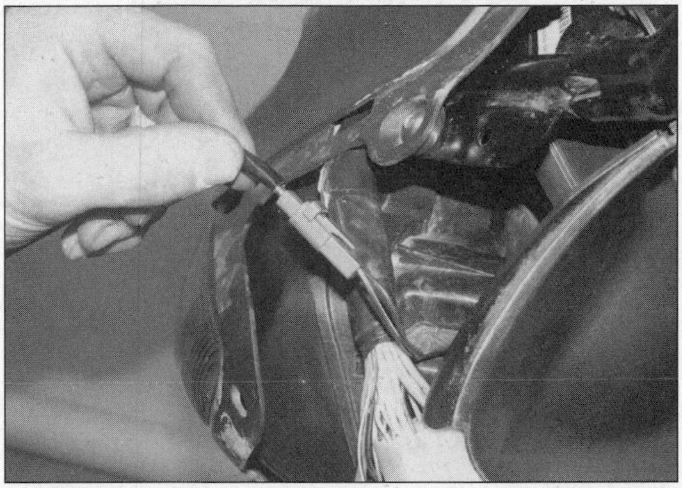

6.2e . . . and disconnect the turn signal wiring connector

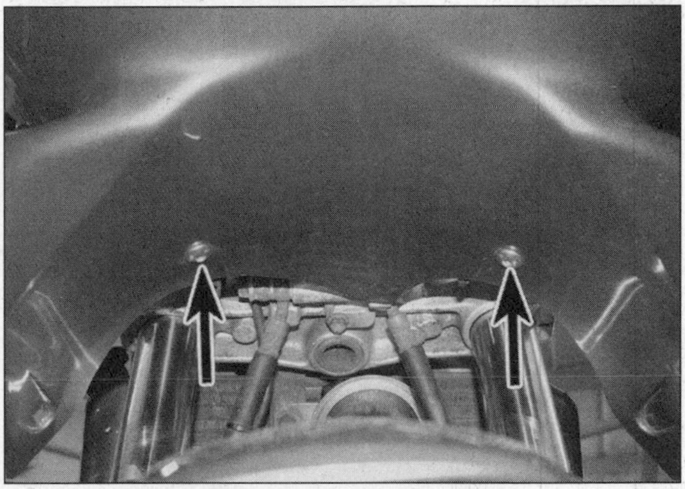

6.5a Undo the lower screws (arrowed) . . .

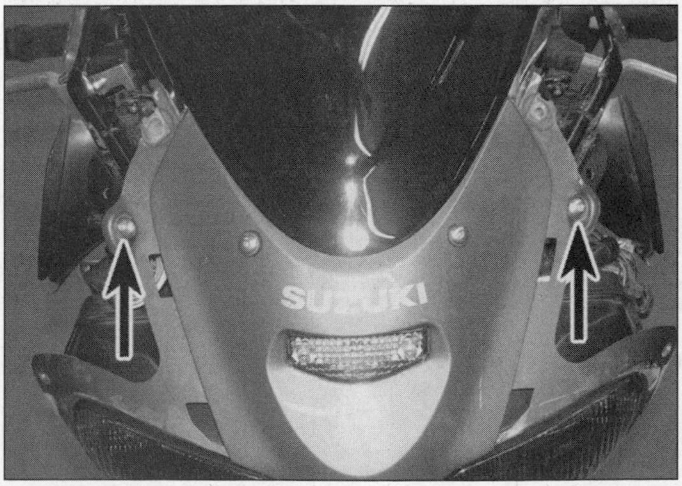

6.5b . . . and the top screws (arrowed) . . .

6.5c . . . then draw the fairing forward . . .

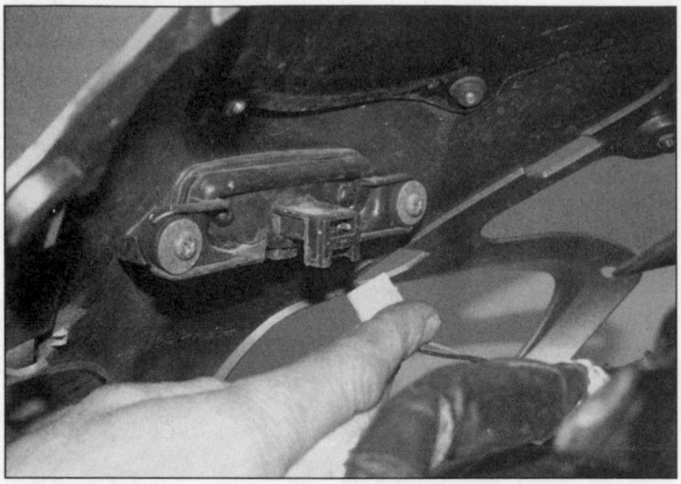

6.5d . . . and disconnect the sidelight wiring connector (where fitted)

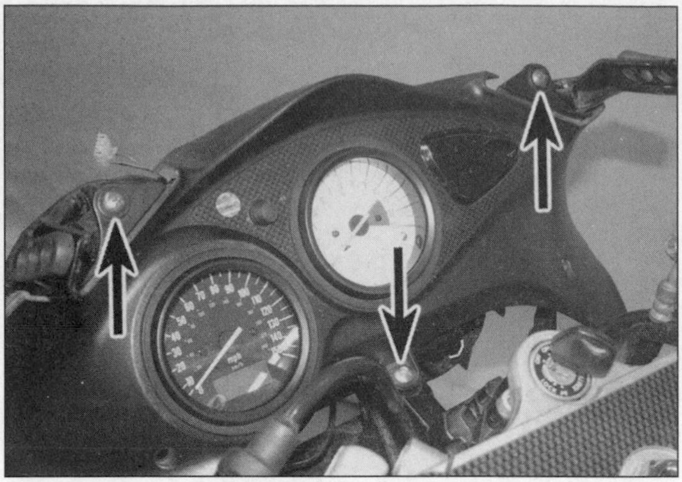

6.8a Undo the screws . . .

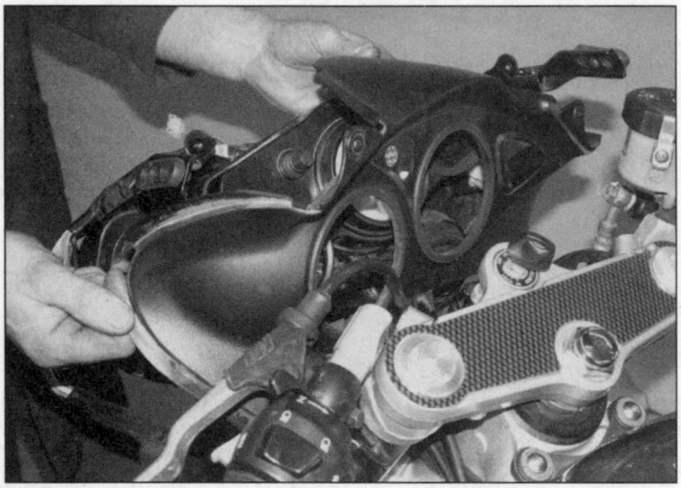

6.8b . . . and remove the cockpit trim panel

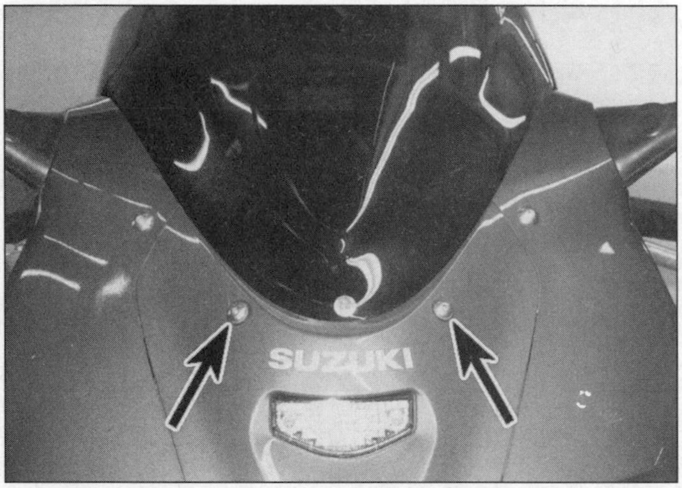

6.11 Windshield screws (arrowed)

Windshield

10 Undo the screw securing each fairing trim panel and remove the panels, noting how they fit **(see illustrations 5.3a and b)**.

11 Undo the two screws securing the windshield to the fairing, noting their washers. Carefully withdraw the windshield from the fairing, noting how it fits **(see illustration)**.

12 Installation is the reverse of removal.

K3-on models

Windshield

13 Undo the two self-tapping screws securing the rear upper edges of the windshield **(see illustration)**.

14 Undo the four screws securing the windshield to the fairing, noting their washers, then withdraw the wellnuts **(see illustrations)**.

15 Carefully withdraw the windshield, noting how it fits between the fairing and the cockpit trim panel **(see illustrations)**.

16 Installation is the reverse of removal. Take care not to overtighten the screws in the wellnuts.

Lower fairing panel

17 The lower fairing inner panel is retained

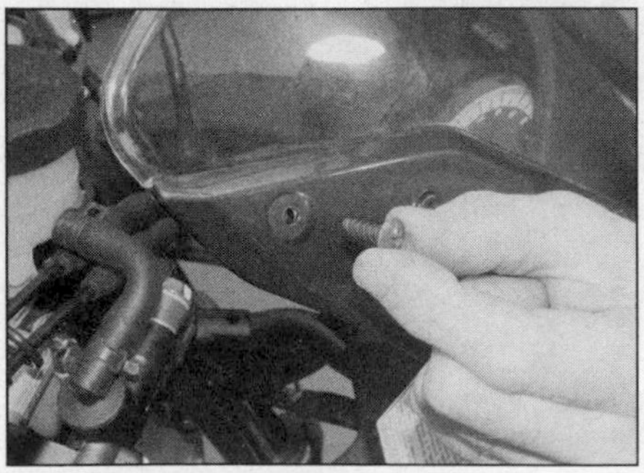

6.13 Undo the self-tapping screw on each side

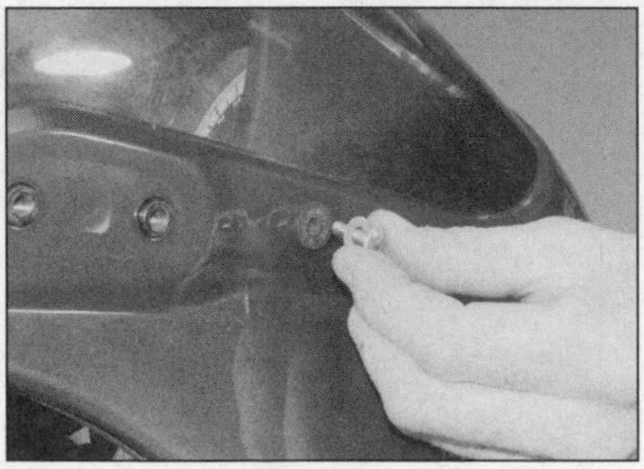

6.14a Undo the windshield screws . . .

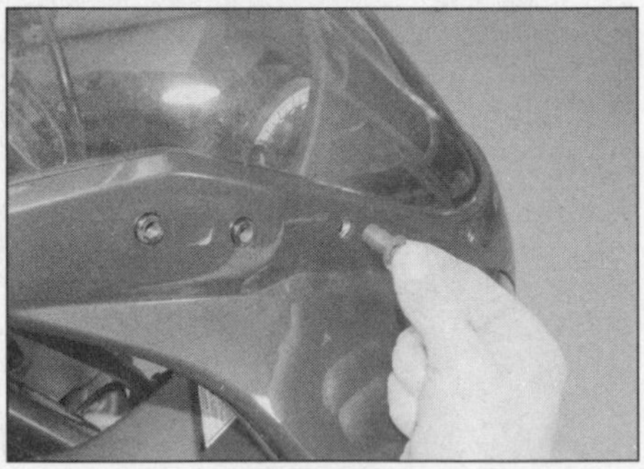

6.14b . . . and withdraw the wellnuts

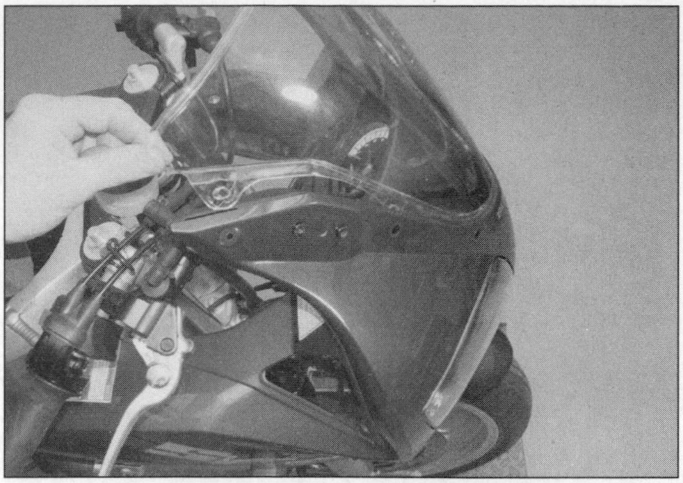

6.15a Withdraw the windshield carefully . . .

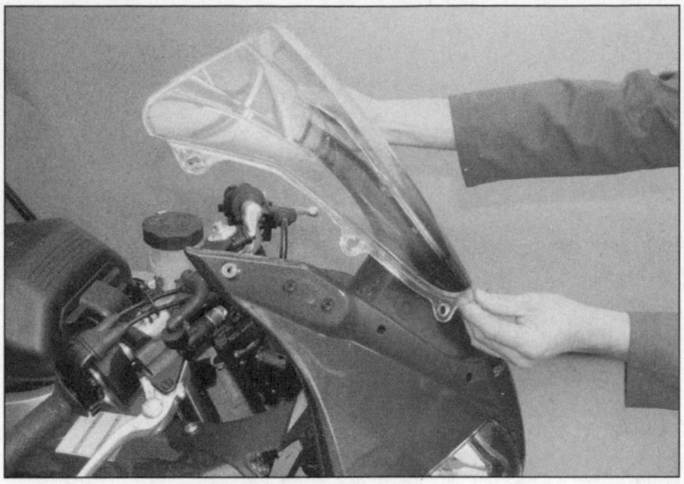

6.15b . . . and lift it off

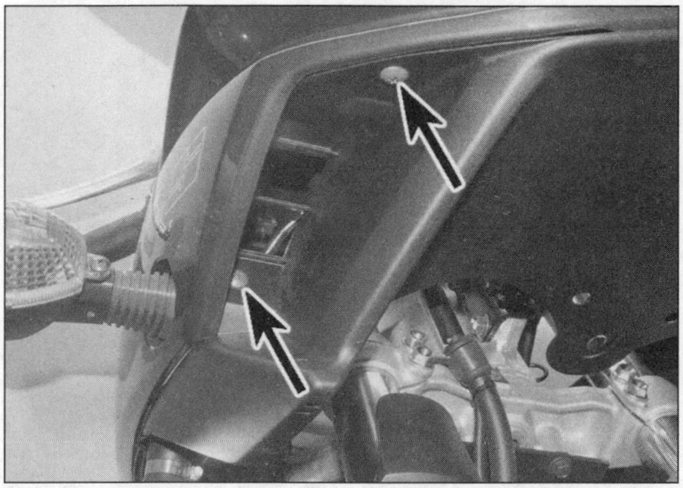

6.17a Lower panel is retained by two screws (arrowed) . . .

6.17b . . . and a trim clip (arrowed) on each side

by two screws and a trim clip on each side **(see illustrations)**. Undo the screws and follow the procedure in Section 2 to remove the trim clips. Carefully unclip the front upper edge of the panel from the lower edge of the fairing and lift off the panel **(see illustration)**.

18 Installation is the reverse of removal. Ensure the front edge is correctly clipped in place before installing the fixings.

Cockpit trim panel

19 Undo the screws securing the left and right-hand inspection panels in the cockpit trim panel and lift them off **(see illustration)**.

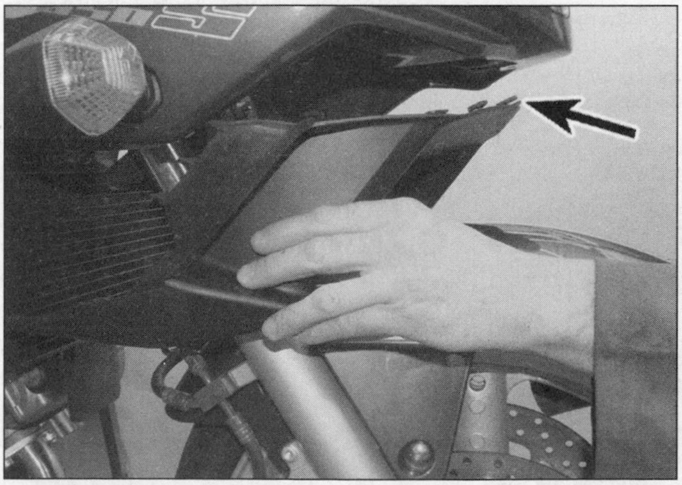

6.17c Note the clips (arrowed) on the front edge of the panel

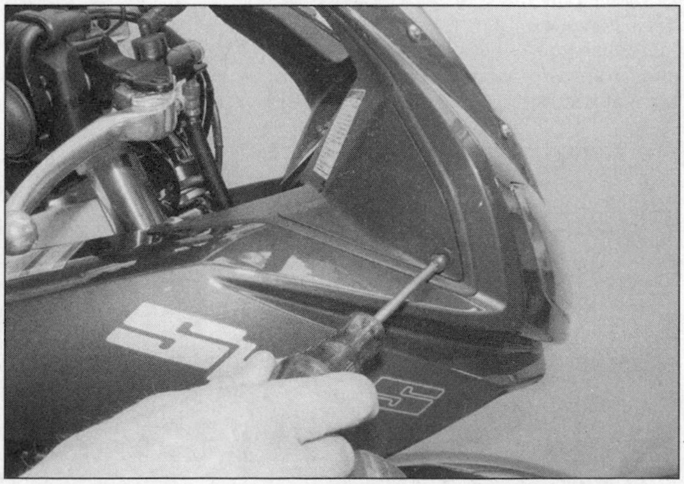

6.19 Inspection panels are retained by a single screw

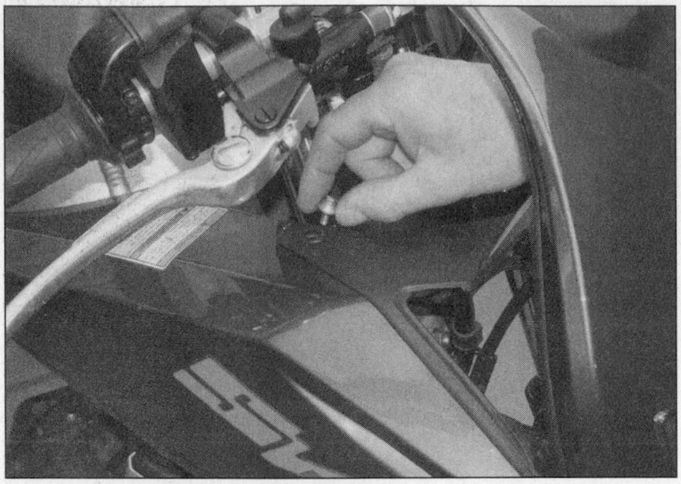

6.21a Remove the trim clips from each side . . .

6.21b . . . and from the centre of the cockpit panel

6.22a Trim panel locates behind tab (arrowed) on each side

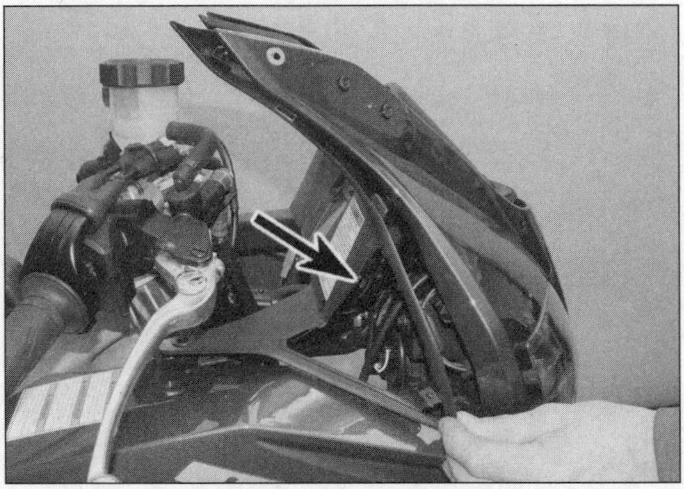

6.22b Release the peg (arrowed) on each side . . .

20 Remove the windshield (see Steps 13 to 15).
21 Follow the procedure in Section 2 to remove the three trim clips **(see illustrations)**.
22 Note how the trim panel locates behind the fixing tabs for the inspection panel screws, then ease the panel back to disengage the pegs from the grommets on the fairing support bracket and lift it off **(see illustrations).**
23 Installation is the reverse of removal.

Fairing

24 Remove the rear view mirrors (see Section 5).
25 Remove the lower fairing panel and the cockpit trim panel (see above).
26 Disconnect the headlight assembly/turn signals wiring connector **(see illustration).**
27 Undo the two screws on each side securing the fairing to the brackets on the frame **(see illustration)**. Carefully pull the fairing forward to disengage the pegs from the grommets on the fairing support bracket and lift the fairing off **(see illustrations)**.

6.22c . . . and lift the panel off

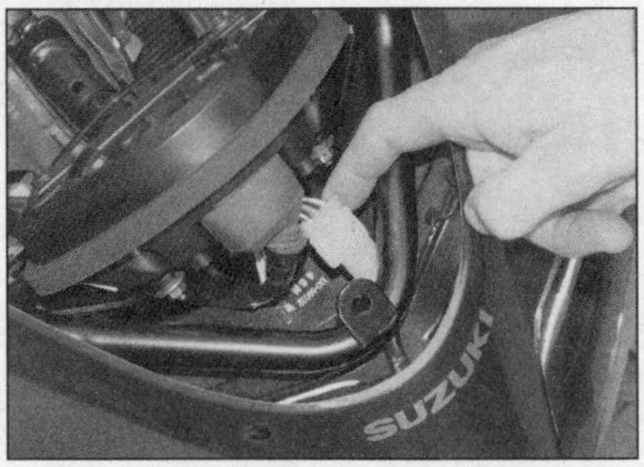

6.26 Disconnect the wiring connector

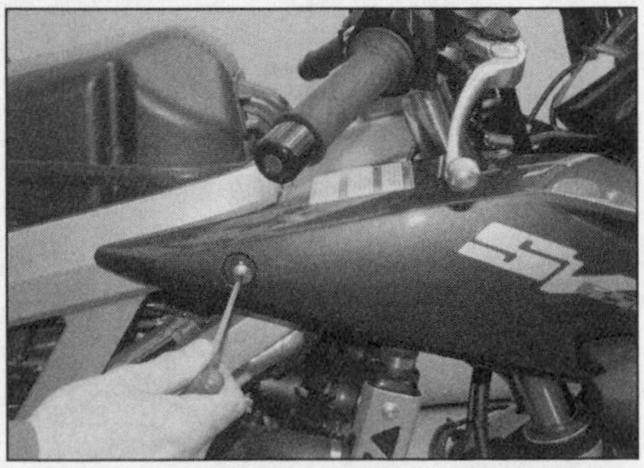

6.27a Undo the screws on each side

6.27b Release the peg (arrowed) on each side . . .

6.27c . . . and lift the fairing off

6.28 Ensure the caps (arrowed) are in place on the support brackets

28 Installation is the reverse of removal. Ensure the rubber caps are in place on the left and right-hand fairing support brackets **(see illustration)**. Check the operation of the headlight and turn signals before riding the motorcycle.

7 Instrument cowl (SV650K5-on)

1 A cowl is fitted over the instrument cluster **(see illustration)**.

2 To remove the cowl, first undo the four screws securing the cowl to the cowl bracket, then withdraw the wellnuts **(see illustrations 6.14a and 14b)**. Note there are no washers fitted to the screws.

3 To remove the cowl brackets, undo the two screws securing each bracket to the headlight brackets and lift them off.

4 Installation is the reverse of removal. Take care not to overtighten the screws in the wellnuts.

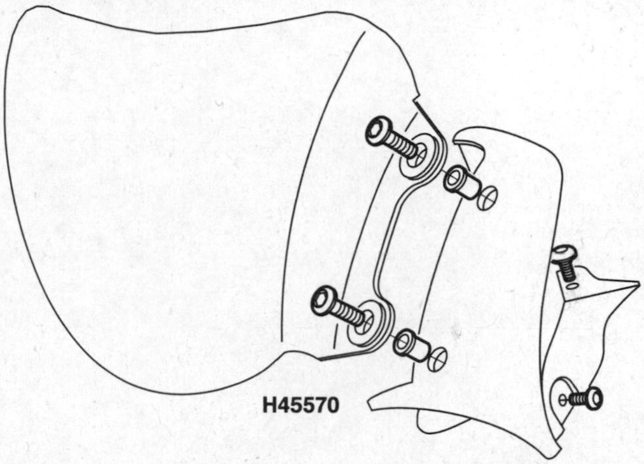

7.1 Arrangement of the instrument cowl fitted to SV650 K5-on models

Chapter 9
Electrical system

Contents

Degrees of difficulty

Easy, suitable for novice with little experience	**Fairly easy,** suitable for beginner with some experience	**Fairly difficult,** suitable for competent DIY mechanic	**Difficult,** suitable for experienced DIY mechanic	**Very difficult,** suitable for expert DIY or professional

Specifications

Battery

Type/capacity	
X to K2 models and ABS equipped K7-on models	YT12A-BS / 9.5 Ah
K3-on models (including non-ABS K7-on models)	YTX12-BS / 10 Ah
Voltage	
Fully charged	13.0 to 13.2 V
Uncharged	below 12.0 V
Charging rate	
Normal	1.2 A for 5 to 10 hrs
Quick	5.0 A for 1.0 hr

Charging system

Current leakage	0.1 mA (max)
Regulated voltage output	13.5 to 15.5 V @ 5000 rpm
No load unregulated voltage output	min 60 V (ac) @ 5000 rpm
Alternator stator coil resistance	0.2 to 0.7 ohms
Alternator output (max)	
X, Y and K1 models	approx. 300 W @ 5000 rpm
K2 model	approx. 275 W @ 5000 rpm
K3-on models	approx. 375 W @ 5000 rpm

Starter relay

Coil resistance	3 to 6 ohms

Fuses

Main	30A
Circuit fuses – X, Y, K1 and K2 models	
Headlight	15A x 2
Signal	15A
Ignition	10A
Instruments	10A
Circuit fuses – K3-on models	
Headlight	
SV650S	15A x 2
SV650	10A x 2
Signal	10A
Fan	15A
Fuel system	10A
Ignition	10A
ABS motor	40A
ABS valve	25A

Bulbs – X, Y, K1 and K2 models

Headlight	
SV650	12V, 60/55W
SV650S	
UK, Canada, Australia and all US models	12V, 45/45W x 2
All other market models	12V, 55W x 2
Sidelight	12V, 5W
Licence plate light	12V, 5W
Brake/tail light	12V, 21/5W x 2
Turn signal lights	12V, 21W x 4
Instrument lights	
SV650	12V, 1.7W x 2
SV650S	14V, 0.84W x 3
Turn signal indicator light	
SV650	12V, 1.7W
SV650S	14V, 3W
Fuel level warning light	12V, 1.7W
High beam indicator light	12V, 1.7W
Neutral indicator light	12V, 1.7W
Oil pressure warning light	
SV650	LED
SV650S	12V, 1.7W
Coolant temperature warning light	LED

Bulbs – K3-on models

Headlight	12V, 60/55W
Sidelight	12V, 5W
Licence plate light	12V, 5W
Brake/tail light	LEDs
Turn signal lights	12V, 21W x 4
Instrument lights	LEDs

Torque settings

Alternator cover bolts	10 Nm
Alternator rotor bolt	120 Nm
Alternator stator bolts	10 Nm
Oil pressure switch	14 Nm
Pulse generator coil bolts	5.5 Nm
Starter motor long bolts	3.5 Nm
Starter motor mounting bolts	6 Nm

1 General information

All models have a 12-volt electrical system charged by a three-phase alternator with a separate regulator/rectifier.

The regulator maintains the charging system output within the specified range to prevent overcharging, and the rectifier converts the ac (alternating current) output of the alternator to dc (direct current) to power the lights and other components and to charge the battery. The alternator rotor is mounted on the left-hand end of the crankshaft.

The starter motor is mounted on the front of the engine. The starting system includes the motor, the battery, the relay and the various wires and switches, and a starter safety interlock system. If the engine kill switch is in the RUN position, the ignition (main) switch is ON and the clutch lever is pulled in, the system prevents the engine from being started if the sidestand is down and the engine is in gear – the engine can be started with the transmission in gear if the sidestand is up.

Note: *Keep in mind that electrical parts, once purchased, often cannot be returned. To avoid unnecessary expense, make very sure the faulty component has been positively identified before buying a new part.*

3.2 On X, Y, K1 and K2 models, lift the fusebox tray off the battery

2 Fault finding

Warning: To prevent the risk of short circuits, the ignition (main) switch must always be OFF and the battery negative (–ve) terminal should be disconnected before any of the bike's other electrical components are disturbed. Don't forget to reconnect the terminal securely once work is finished or if battery power is needed for circuit testing.

1 A typical electrical circuit consists of an electrical component, the switches, relays, etc. related to that component and the wiring and connectors that link the component to the battery and the frame. To aid in locating a problem in any electrical circuit, and to guide you with the wiring colour codes and connectors, refer to the *Wiring Diagrams* at the end of this Chapter.

2 Before tackling any troublesome electrical circuit, first study the wiring diagram (see end of Chapter) thoroughly to get a complete picture of what makes up that individual circuit. Trouble spots, for instance, can often be narrowed down by noting if other components related to that circuit are operating properly or not. If several components or circuits fail at one time, chances are the fault lies in the fuse or earth (ground) connection, as several circuits often are routed through the same fuse and earth (ground) connections.

3 Electrical problems often stem from simple causes, such as loose or corroded connections or a blown fuse. Prior to any electrical fault finding, always visually check the condition of the fuse, wires and connections in the problem circuit. Intermittent failures can be especially frustrating, since you can't always duplicate the failure when it's convenient to test. In such situations, a good practice is to clean all connections in the affected circuit, whether or not they appear to be good. All of the connections and wires should also be wiggled to check for looseness which can cause intermittent failure.

4 If testing instruments are going to be utilised, use the wiring diagram to plan where you will make the necessary connections in order to accurately pinpoint the trouble spot.

5 The basic tools needed for electrical fault finding include a battery and bulb test circuit or a continuity tester, a test light, and a jumper wire. A multimeter capable of reading volts, ohms and amps is a very useful alternative and performs the functions of all of the above, and is necessary for performing more extensive tests and checks where specific voltage, current or resistance values are needed.

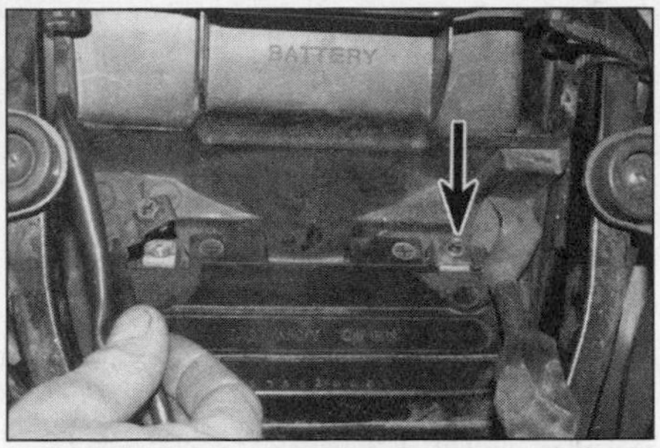

3.3 Disconnect the negative lead first then lift the terminal cover and disconnect the positive lead (arrowed)

HAYNES HiNT ***Refer to Fault Finding Equipment in the Reference section for details of how to use electrical test equipment.***

3 Battery – removal, installation, inspection and maintenance

Caution: Be extremely careful when handling or working around the battery. The electrolyte is very caustic and an explosive gas (hydrogen) is given off when the battery is charging.

Removal and installation

1 Make sure the ignition is switched OFF. Remove the rider's seat (see Chapter 8).

2 On X, Y, K1 and K2 models, lift the fusebox tray off the battery and lay it aside **(see illustration)**.

3 Unscrew the negative (–ve) terminal bolt first and disconnect the lead from the battery **(see illustration)**. Lift up the red insulating cover to access the positive (+ve) terminal, then unscrew the bolt and disconnect the lead.

4 Lift the battery out of its box and remove it **(see illustration)**.

5 On installation, clean the battery terminals and lead ends with a wire brush or knife and emery paper. When reconnecting the leads, connecting the positive (+ve) terminal first. On X, Y, K1 and K2 models, fit the fusebox tray, locating the slots in the front edge over the tabs on the fuel tank bracket. Install the seat (see Chapter 8).

HAYNES HiNT ***Battery corrosion can be kept to a minimum by applying a layer of petroleum jelly to the terminals after the cables have been connected. There are also dedicated sprays commercially available.***

3.4 Lift the battery out of its box

Inspection and maintenance

6 The battery fitted to all models covered in this manual is of the maintenance free (sealed) type, therefore requiring no scheduled maintenance. However, the following checks should still be regularly performed.

7 Check the battery terminals and leads for tightness and corrosion. If corrosion is evident, unscrew the terminal screws and disconnect the leads from the battery, disconnecting the negative (–ve) terminal first, and clean the terminals and lead ends with a wire brush or knife and emery paper. Reconnect the leads, connecting the negative (–ve) terminal last, and apply a thin coat of petroleum jelly to the connections to slow further corrosion.

8 Keep the battery case clean to prevent current leakage, which can discharge the battery over a period of time (especially when it sits unused). Wash the outside of the case with a solution of baking soda and water. Rinse the battery thoroughly, then dry it.

9 Look for cracks in the case and renew the battery if any are found. If acid has been spilled on the frame or battery box, neutralise it with a baking soda and water solution, dry it thoroughly, then touch up any damaged paint.

10 If the motorcycle sits unused for long periods of time, disconnect the cables from the battery terminals, negative (–ve) terminal first. Refer to Section 4 and charge the battery once every month to six weeks.

11 Check the condition of the battery by measuring the voltage present at the battery terminals. Connect the voltmeter positive (+ve) probe to the battery positive (+ve) terminal, and the negative (–ve) probe to the battery negative (–ve) terminal. When fully charged there should be 13.0 to 13.2 volts present. If the voltage falls below 12.3 volts the battery must be removed, disconnecting the negative (–ve) terminal first, and recharged as described in Section 4.

4 Battery – charging

Caution: Be extremely careful when handling or working around the battery. The electrolyte is very caustic and an

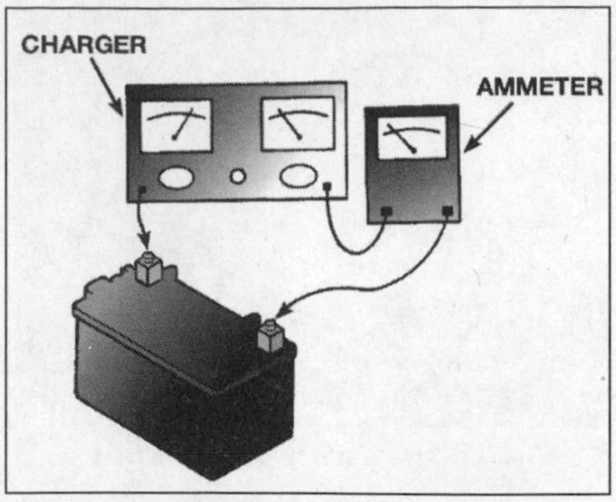

4.2 If the charger doesn't have ammeter built in, connect one in series as shown. DO NOT connect the ammeter between the battery terminals or it will be ruined

explosive gas (hydrogen) is given off when the battery is charging.

1 Remove the battery (see Section 3). Connect the charger to the battery, making sure that the positive (+ve) lead on the charger is connected to the positive (+ve) terminal on the battery, and the negative (–ve) lead is connected to the negative (–ve) terminal.

2 Suzuki recommend that the battery is charged at the normal rate specified at the beginning of the Chapter. Exceeding this figure can cause the battery to overheat, buckling the plates and rendering it useless. Few owners will have access to an expensive current controlled charger, so if a normal domestic charger is used check that after a possible initial peak, the charge rate falls to a safe level **(see illustration)**. If the battery becomes hot during charging **stop**. Further charging will cause damage. **Note:** *In emergencies the battery can be charged at the quick rate specified. However, this is not recommended and the normal charging rate is by far the safer method of charging the battery.*

3 If the recharged battery discharges rapidly if left disconnected it is likely that an internal short caused by physical damage or sulphation has occurred. A new battery will be required. A good battery will tend to lose its charge at about 1% per day.

4 Install the battery (see Section 3).

5 If the motorcycle sits unused for long periods of time, leave the battery disconnected and charge it once every month to six weeks.

5 Fuses

1 The electrical system is protected by fuses of different ratings. All except the main fuse are housed in the fusebox; on X, Y, K1 and K2 models (and ABS K7-on models), the fusebox is located under the rider's seat, on K3 models onward the fusebox is located under the passenger's seat **(see illustrations)**. The main fuse is integral with the starter relay, which is behind the right-hand side panel on X, Y, K1 and K2 models, and under the rider's seat on K3 models onward. ABS equipped models have two fuses for the ABS circuit housed in separate holders to the rear of the starter relay.

2 To access the fusebox fuses remove the appropriate seat (see Chapter 8), then unclip the fusebox lid **(see illustration)**. To access the main fuse, first remove the right-hand side panel or rider's seat as appropriate (see Chapter 8). On all models, remove the starter relay cover **(see illustration)**.

3 The fuses can be removed and checked visually **(see illustration)**. If you can't pull the fuse out with your fingertips, use a pair of suitable pliers. A blown fuse is easily identified by a break in the element **(see illustration)**. Each fuse is clearly marked with its rating and must only be replaced by a fuse of the correct rating. A spare fuse of each rating except the main fuse is housed in the fusebox, and a spare main fuse is housed with the starter relay **(see illustration 5.2b)**. If a spare fuse is used, always renew it so that a spare of each rating is carried on the bike at all times.

Warning: Never put in a fuse of a higher rating or bridge the terminals with any other substitute, however temporary it may be. Serious damage may be done to the circuit, or a fire may start.

4 If a fuse blows, be sure to check the wiring circuit very carefully for evidence of a short-circuit. Look for bare wires and chafed, melted or burned insulation. If the fuse is renewed before the cause is located, the new fuse will blow immediately.

5 Occasionally a fuse will blow or cause an open-circuit for no obvious reason. Corrosion of the fuse ends and fusebox terminals may occur and cause poor fuse contact. If this happens, remove the corrosion with a wire brush or emery paper, then spray the fuse end and terminals with electrical contact cleaner.

5.1a On X, Y, K1 and K2 models, remove the rider's seat to access the fusebox (arrowed)

5.1b On K3-on models, remove the passenger's seat to access the fusebox

5.2a Unclip the lid to access the fuses

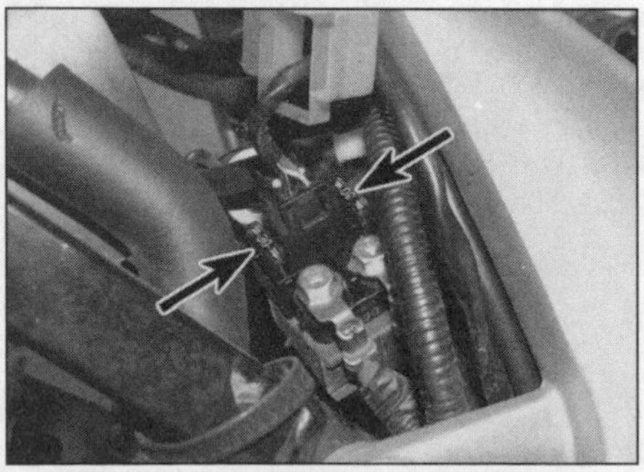

5.2b Lift the relay cover to access the main fuse and its spare (arrowed)

5.3a Remove the fuse and check it visually

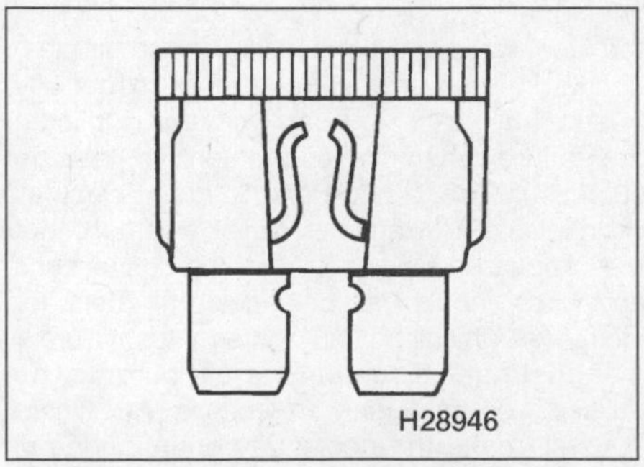

5.3b A blown fuse can be identified by a break in its element

6 Lighting system check

1 The battery provides power for operation of the headlight, tail light, brake light and instrument cluster lights. If none of the lights operate, check the battery first, making sure its terminals are clean and secure and the voltage level is sufficient. Low battery voltage indicates either a neglected or faulty battery or a defective charging system. Refer to Section 3 for battery checks and Sections 31 and 32 for charging system tests. Also, check the fuses. Note that if there is more than one problem at the same time, it is likely to be a fault relating to a multi-function component, such as one of the fuses governing more than one circuit, or the ignition switch.

Headlight

2 If a headlight beam fails to work, first check the fuse (see Section 5), and then the bulb(s) (see Section 7). If they are good, use jumper wires to connect the bulb in question directly to the battery terminals or check it with a multimeter. If the light comes on, or the meter indicates continuity, the problem lies in the wiring or connectors, or the switches in the circuit. Refer to Section 21 for the switch testing procedures, and also to the wiring diagrams at the end of this Chapter.

3 If the low beam does not work, check for battery voltage at the white wire terminal on the headlight wiring connector with the ignition ON, the light switch ON (where fitted) and the dimmer switch set to LO. If voltage is present, check for continuity to earth (ground) in the black/white wire from the wiring connector. Repair or renew the wiring or connectors as necessary. If there is no voltage, check the wiring, connectors and switches.

4 If the high beam does not work, check for battery voltage at the yellow wire terminal on the headlight wiring connector with the ignition ON, the light switch ON (where fitted) and the dimmer switch set to HI. If voltage is present, check for continuity to earth (ground) in the black/white wire from the wiring connector. Repair or renew the wiring or connectors as necessary. If there is no voltage, check the wiring, connectors and switches.

5 When checking the headlights on SV650S models, note that the lighting arrangement differs depending on the country of use. On models with twin filament bulbs, both headlights will come on in the HI or LO switch positions. Where asymmetrical lighting is used, the right-hand headlight will come on in the HI position and the left-hand headlight in the LO position.

Sidelight (where fitted), tail light, licence plate light

6 If the any of the above lights fail to work, first check the fuse (see Section 5), and then the

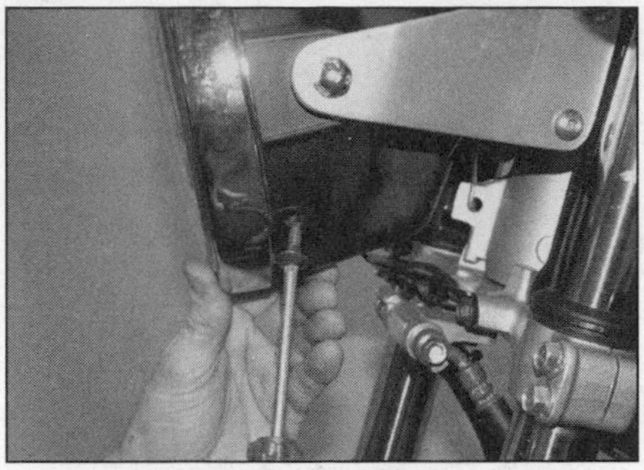

7.1a Undo the screw on each side . . .

bulbs (see Section 9). If they are good, use jumper wires to connect the bulb in question directly to the battery terminals or check it with a multimeter. If the light comes on, or the meter indicates continuity, the problem lies in the wiring or connectors, or the switches in the circuit. Refer to Section 21 for the switch testing procedures, and also to the wiring diagrams at the end of this Chapter. Note that on K3-on models, the tail light/brake light assembly consists of a number of LEDs in a sealed unit. When a single LED fails it cannot be renewed, however the failure of one LED will not affect the function of the others. If the unit fails to work completely, carry out the same checks as for conventional bulbs. When sufficient LEDs have failed so as to impair the safe operation of the motorcycle, renew the tail light/brake light assembly (see Section 10).

7 Check for battery voltage at the brown wire terminal on the light wiring connectors with the ignition switch ON. If voltage is present, check for continuity to earth (ground) in the black/white wire from the wiring connector. If no voltage is indicated, check the wiring and connectors between the light unit and the ignition switch, via the fusebox and the handlebar switch, then check the ignition switch itself (see Section 20).

Brake light

8 If the brake light fails to work, first check the signal fuse (see Section 5), and then the bulbs (see Section 9). If they are good, use jumper wires to connect the bulb in question directly to the battery terminals or check it with a multimeter. If the light comes on, or the meter indicates continuity, the problem lies in the wiring or connectors, or the switches in the circuit. Note that on K3-on models, the tail light/brake light assembly consists of a number of LEDs in a sealed unit (see Step 6).

9 Check for battery voltage at the white/black wire terminal on the tail light wiring connectors, first with the front brake lever on, then with the rear brake pedal on. If voltage is present with one brake on but not the other, then the switch or its wiring is faulty. If voltage is present in both cases, check for continuity to earth (ground) in the black/white wire from the wiring connectors. If no voltage is indicated, check the wiring and connectors

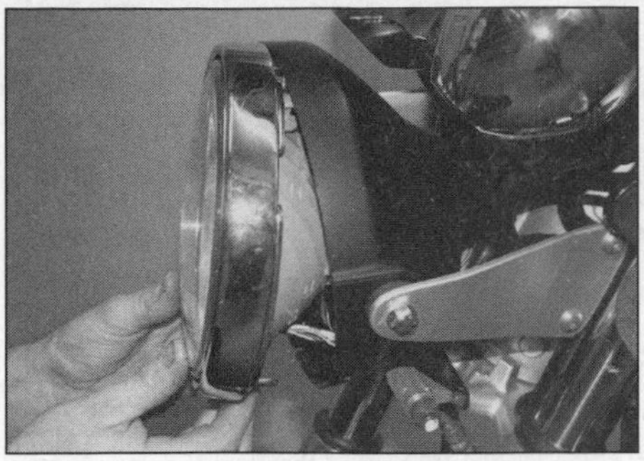

7.1b . . . and draw the rim out of the shell as described

between the brake light and the brake switches, then between the switches and the fusebox. Check the switches themselves (see Section 14).

Instrument and warning lights

10 See Section 17 for instrument and warning light bulb renewal where applicable.

Turn signals

11 See Section 11 for turn signal circuit checks.

7 Headlight bulb(s) and sidelight bulb

Caution: The headlight bulbs are of the quartz-halogen type. Do not touch the bulb glass as skin acids will shorten the bulb's service life. If the bulb is accidentally touched, it should be wiped carefully when cold with a rag soaked in alcohol or soapy water and dried before fitting.

Warning: Allow the bulb time to cool before removing it if the headlight has just been on.

Headlight – SV650 models

1 Undo the screw on each side of the headlight rim **(see illustration)**. Pull the bottom of the rim out of the shell then release the tab at the top, noting how it locates **(see illustration)**.

2 Disconnect the headlight and sidelight wiring connectors **(see illustrations)**.

3 Remove the rubber dust cover, noting how

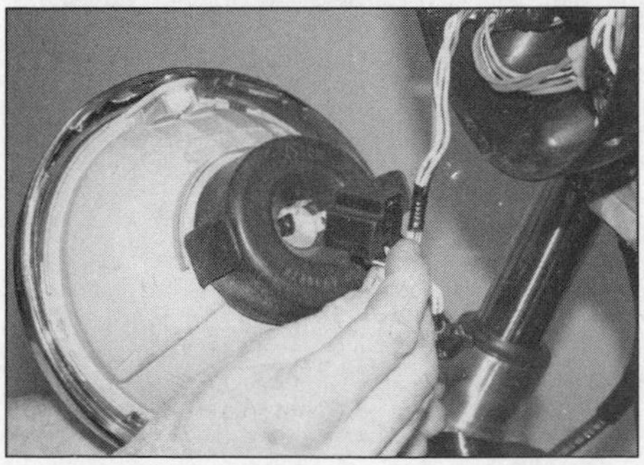

7.2a Disconnect the headlight wiring connector . . .

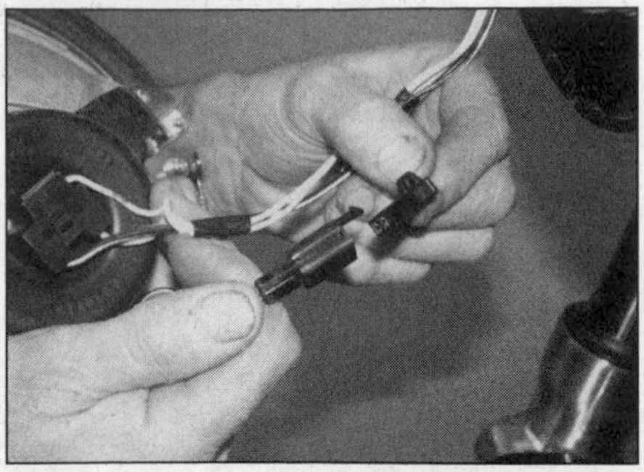

7.2b . . . and if required the sidelight wiring connector

7.3a Remove the dust cover

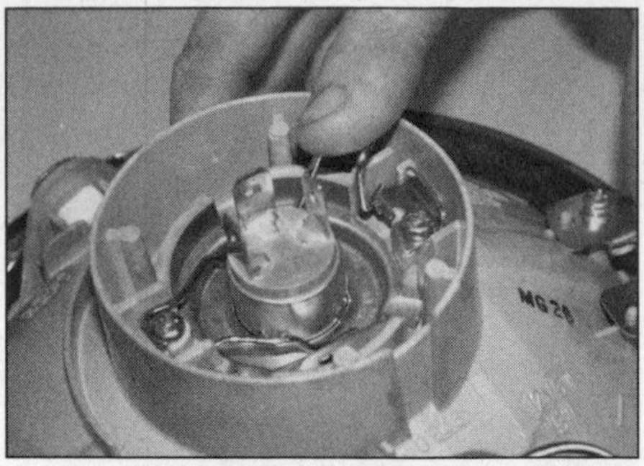

7.3b Release the clip . . .

7.3c . . . and remove the bulb

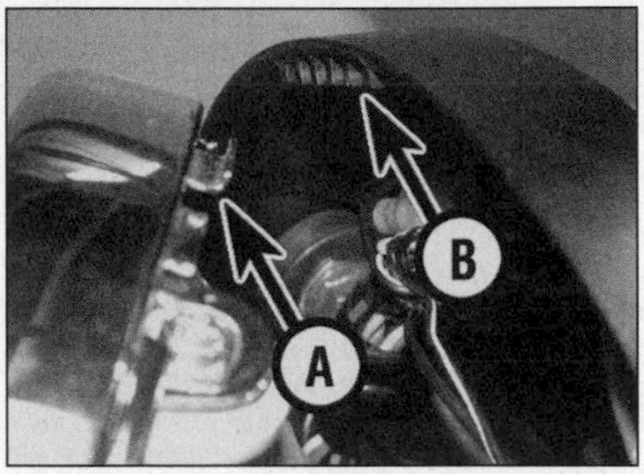

7.7 Locate the tab (A) behind the protrusion (B)

it fits **(see illustration)**. Release the bulb retaining clip, noting how it fits, then remove the bulb **(see illustrations)**.

4 Fit the new bulb, bearing in mind the information in the **Caution** above. Make sure the tabs on the bulb fit correctly in the slots in the bulb housing, and secure it in position with the retaining clip.

5 Install the dust cover, making sure it is correctly seated and with the 'TOP' mark at the top. Connect the wiring connector. Connect the sidelight wiring connector.

6 Check the operation of the headlight.

7 Locate the tab on the top of the headlight rim behind the protrusion on the shell, then push the bottom of the rim in **(see illustration)**. Make sure it is correctly seated all the way round then install the screws.

HAYNES HiNT ***Always use a paper towel or dry cloth when handling new bulbs to prevent injury if the bulb should break and to increase bulb life.***

Headlight – SV650S models

Note: *The lighting arrangement differs depending on the country of use. On models with twin filament bulbs, both headlights will come on in the HI or LO switch positions. Where asymmetrical lighting is used, the right-hand headlight will come on in the HI position and the left-hand headlight in the LO position.*

8 Disconnect the wiring connector from the back of the headlight **(see illustration)**. Remove the rubber dust cover, noting how it fits **(see illustration)**. Release the bulb retaining clip, noting how it fits, then remove the bulb **(see illustrations)**. Where asymmetric headlights are fitted, the left-hand (LO beam) bulb is accessed by removing the rubber dust cover, disconnecting the two wires from the back of the bulb and releasing the wire retaining clip.

9 Fit the new bulb, bearing in mind the information in the **Caution** above **(see illustration 7.8d)**. Make sure the tabs on the bulb fit correctly in the slots in the bulb housing, and secure it in position with the retaining clip **(see illustration 7.8c)**.

10 Install the dust cover, making sure it is correctly seated and with the 'TOP' mark at the top, and connect the wiring connector **(see illustrations 7.8b and a)**.

11 Check the operation of the headlights.

Sidelight – SV650 models

12 Undo the screw on each side of the headlight rim **(see illustration 7.1a)**. Pull the bottom of the rim out of the shell then release the tab at the top, noting how it locates **(see illustration 7.1b)**.

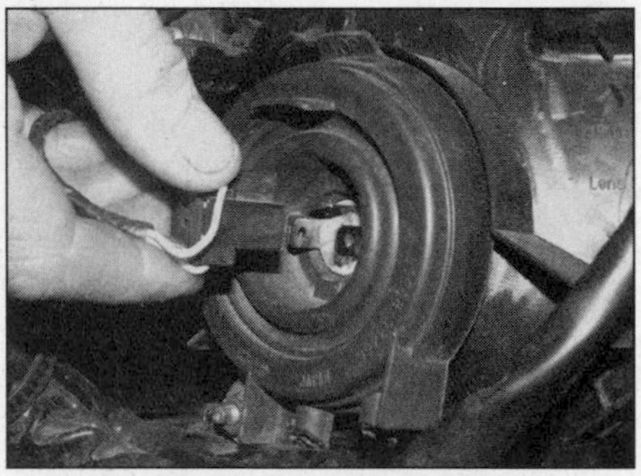

7.8a Disconnect the headlight wiring connector . . .

7.8b . . . then remove the dust cover . . .

7.8c . . . release the clip . . .

7.8d . . . and remove the bulb

7.14a Draw out the bulbholder . . .

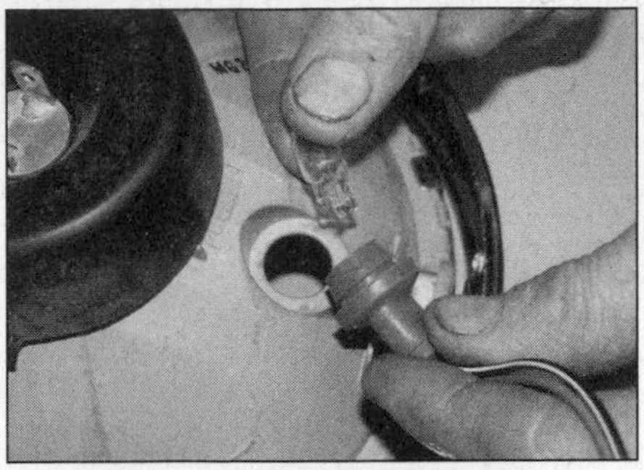

7.14b . . . and remove the bulb

7.17 Undo the screws (arrowed) and remove the lens

13 Disconnect the headlight and sidelight wiring connectors **(see illustrations 7.2a and b)**.

14 Pull the sidelight bulbholder out of the headlight, then remove the bulb **(see illustrations)**. Fit the new bulb in the bulbholder, then fit the bulbholder into the headlight, making sure it correctly seated. Check the operation of the sidelight.

15 Connect the headlight and sidelight wiring connectors **(see illustrations 7.2a and b)**.

16 Locate the tab on the top of the headlight rim behind the protrusion on the shell, then push the bottom of the rim in **(see illustration 7.7)**. Make sure it is correctly seated all the way round then install the screws **(see illustration 7.1a)**.

Sidelight – X, Y, K1 and K2 SV650S models

17 Undo the two screws securing the sidelight lens to the fairing and remove the lens **(see illustration)**.

18 Carefully pull the bulb out of its socket **(see illustration)**. Fit the new bulb. Check the operation of the sidelight.

19 Check the condition of the rubber sealing ring and renew it if it is damaged, deformed or deteriorated **(see illustration)**. Fit the lens, making sure it is correctly seated and the sealing ring stays in place, and secure it with the screws.

Sidelight – K3-on SV650S models

20 Remove the appropriate inspection panel in the cockpit trim panel (see Chapter 8).

7.18 Pull the bulb out of its socket

7.19 Check the condition of the sealing ring (arrowed) before installing the lens

21 Twist and pull the bulbholder out of the headlight, then remove the bulb **(see illustrations)**.

22 Fit the new bulb in the bulbholder, then fit the bulbholder into the headlight, making sure it correctly seated. Check the operation of the sidelight, then install the inspection panel.

8 Headlight assembly

SV650 models

1 Undo the screw on each side of the headlight rim **(see illustration 7.1a)**. Pull the bottom of the rim out of the shell then release the tab at the top, noting how it locates **(see illustration 7.1b)**.

2 Disconnect the headlight and sidelight wiring connectors **(see illustrations 7.2a and b)**.

3 Make a note of the routing of all the wiring in the headlight shell and the location of the wiring connectors **(see illustration)**. Release the wiring from the clips and disconnect the connectors, then feed the wiring out of the back of the shell.

4 Unscrew the two bolts securing the headlight beam height adjuster to the bottom yoke **(see illustration)**. Support the shell, then either unscrew the two nuts, withdraw the bolts and remove the shell from between the brackets **(see illustration)**, or unscrew the bracket bolts and remove the shell with them attached **(see illustration)**. If the shell is separated from the brackets, note the collars in the rubber mounts. Check the rubber mounts for damage, deformation and deterioration and renew them if necessary.

7.21a Remove the bulbholder from the back of the headlight . . .

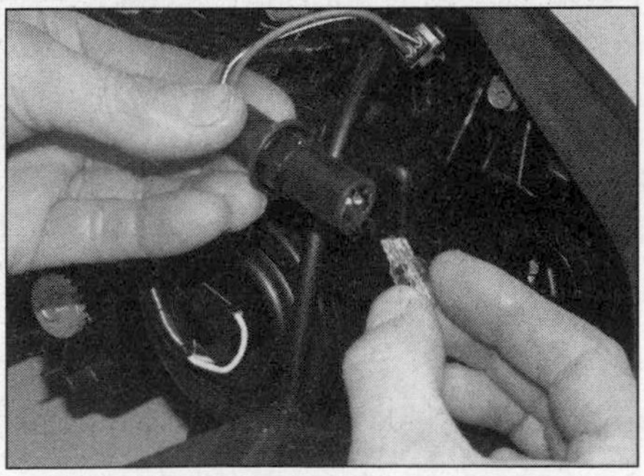

7.21b . . . and pull out the bulb

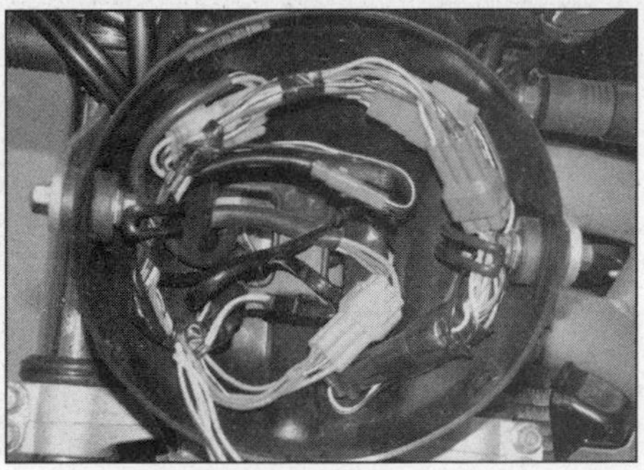

8.3 Release the wiring from the clips and disconnect the connectors

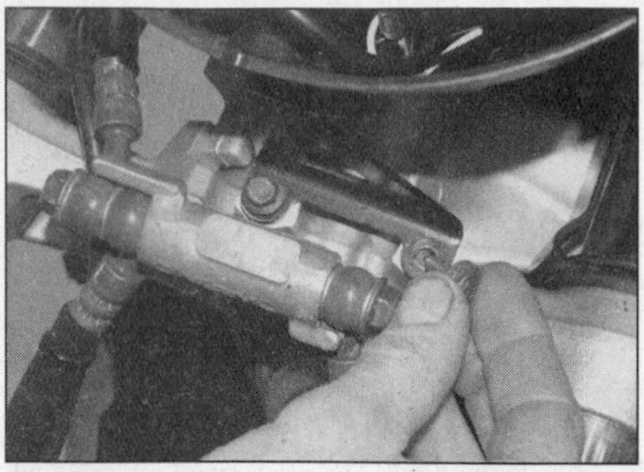

8.4a Unscrew the two bolts

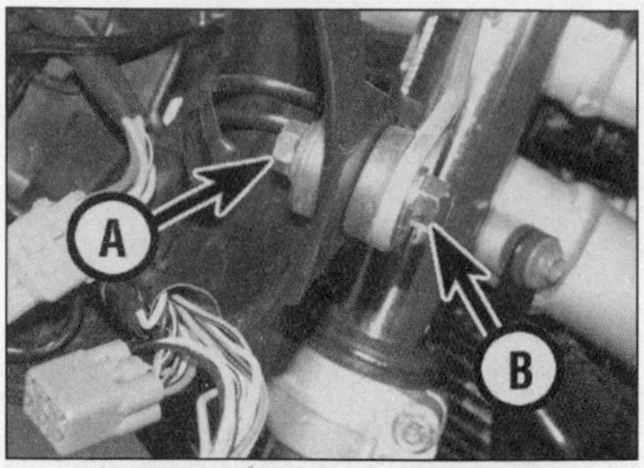

8.4b Either unscrew nut (A) and remove the bolt (B) on each side . . .

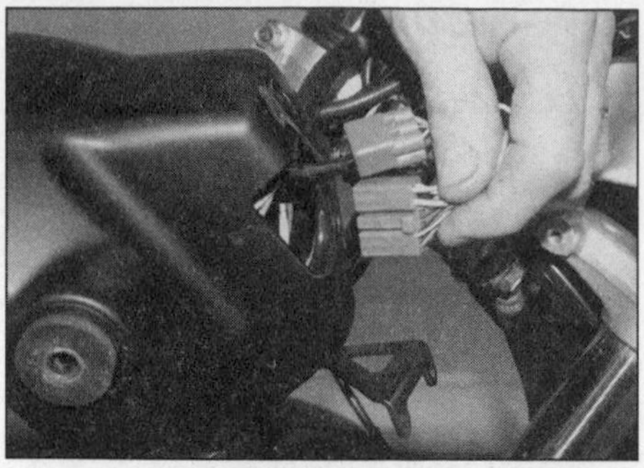

8.4c . . . and remove the shell from the brackets . . .

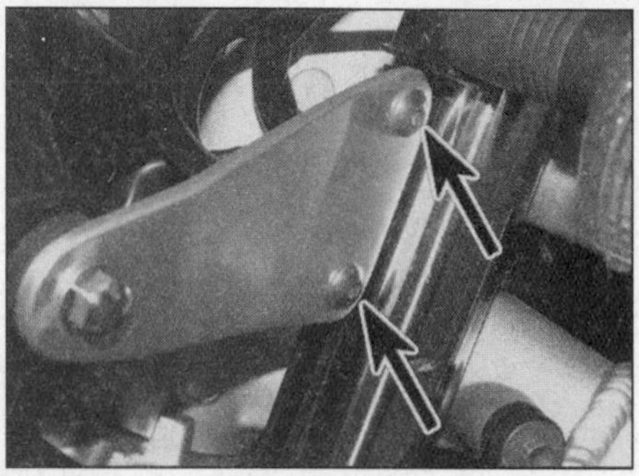

8.4d . . . or unscrew the bracket bolts (arrowed) and remove the headlight assembly

5 Installation is the reverse of removal. Make sure all the wiring is correctly connected and secured. Check the operation of the headlight and sidelight. Check the headlight aim (see Chapter 1).

X, Y, K1 and K2 SV650S models

6 Remove the fairing (see Chapter 8).
7 Disconnect the headlight wiring connectors **(see illustration 7.8a)**. **Note:** *Models with asymmetrical lighting are fitted with a different type bulb on the left-hand side, on which the rubber cover must be removed to access the wiring connectors.*
8 Unscrew the four nuts and remove the

8.8a Unscrew the nuts (arrowed) and remove the washers . . .

washers securing the headlight assembly to the bracket and remove the headlight, noting how it fits **(see illustrations)**.
9 Check the rubber mounting grommets in the bracket for damage, deformation and deterioration and renew them if necessary.
10 Installation is the reverse of removal. Make sure all the wiring is correctly connected and secured. Check the operation of the headlights. Check the headlight aim (see Chapter 1).

K3-on SV650S models

11 Remove the fairing (see Chapter 8).
12 Unscrew the six bolts securing the headlight assembly to the fairing and remove the headlight, noting how it fits **(see illustration)**.
13 Installation is the reverse of removal. Make sure all the wiring is correctly connected and secured. Check the operation of the headlights. Check the headlight aim (see Chapter 1).

9 Brake/tail light bulbs and licence plate light bulb

Brake/tail light – X, Y, K1 and K2 models

Note: *The pins on the bulbs are offset so that the bulbs can only be installed one way. It is a good idea to use a paper towel or dry cloth when handling a new bulb to prevent injury if it breaks, and to increase bulb life.*
1 Undo the two screws securing the tail light lens and remove it **(see illustrations)**.
2 Carefully push the bulb in slightly and twist it anti-clockwise to release it **(see illustration)**.
3 Check the socket terminals for corrosion and clean them if necessary. Check the condition of the rubber sealing ring and renew it if necessary **(see illustration)**. Make sure it is properly seated.

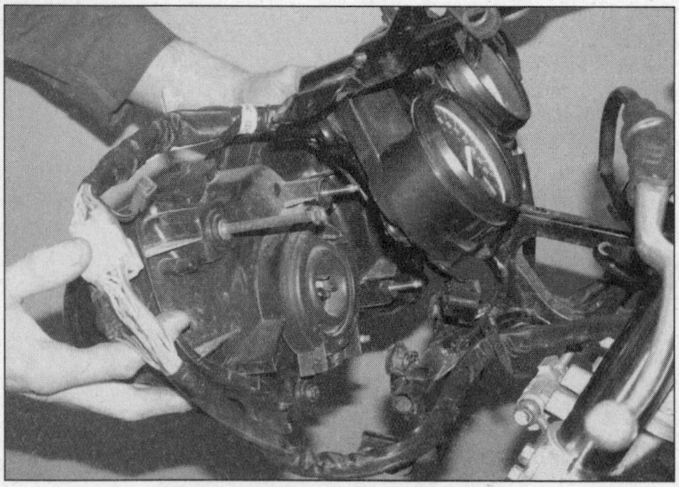

8.8b . . . and remove the headlight

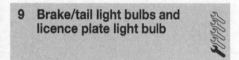

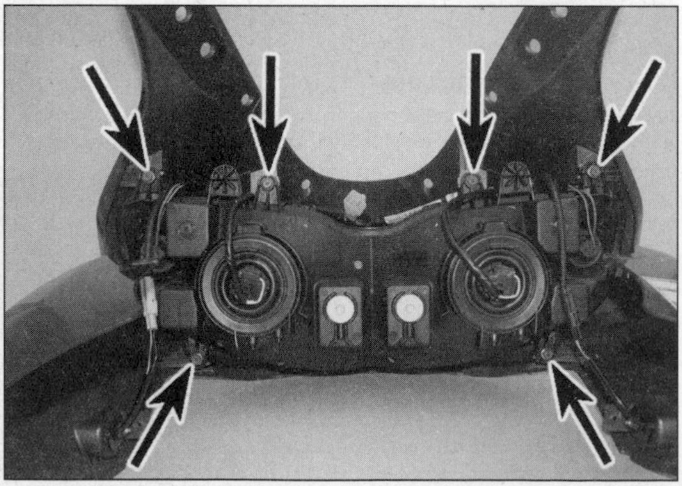

8.12 Headlight assembly is retained by six bolts (arrowed)

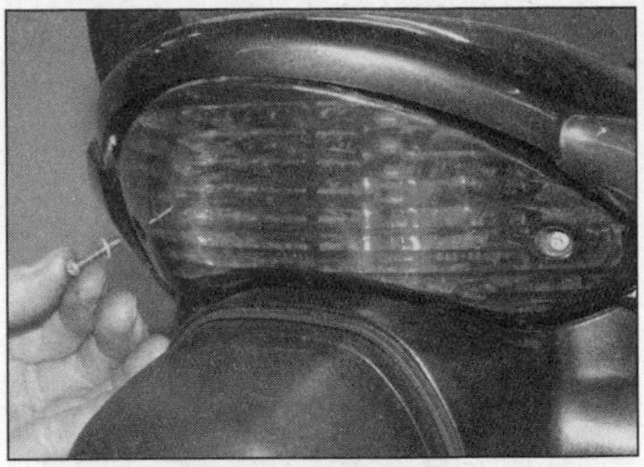
9.1a Undo the screws . . .

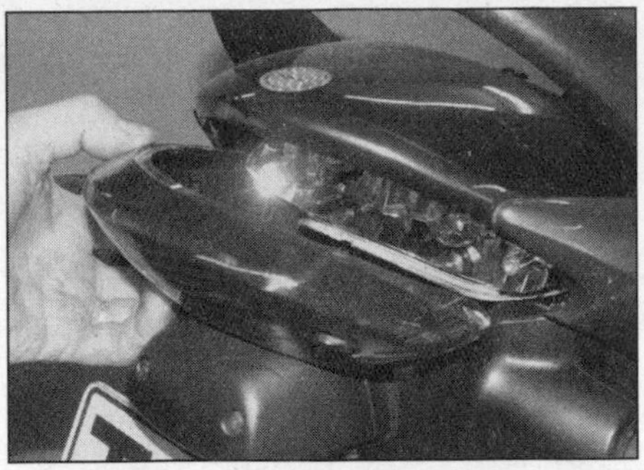
9.1b . . . and remove the lens

9.2 Remove the bulb as described

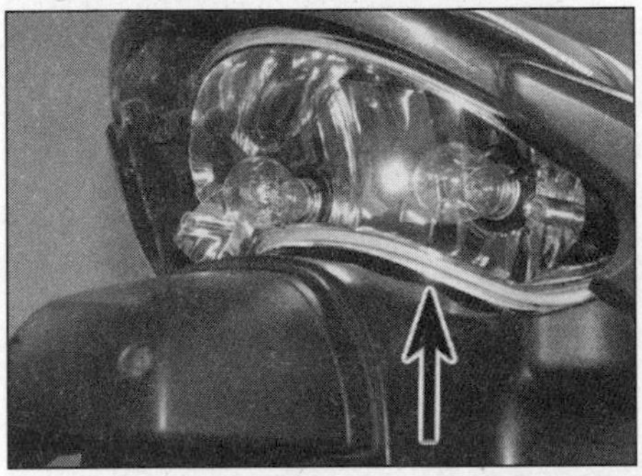
9.3 Check the condition of the sealing ring (arrowed)

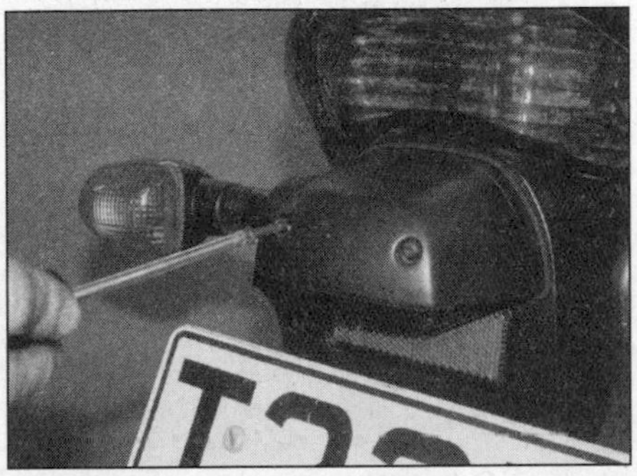
9.7a Undo the screws . . .

9.7b . . . and remove the cover

4 Install the new bulb by aligning its pins with the correct cut-outs, then pushing it into the socket and twisting it clockwise.

5 Fit the lens and secure it with the screws, making sure the ring stays seated, and taking care not to overtighten the screws as the lens threads are easily damaged and the lens easily cracked.

Brake/tail light – K3-on models

6 These models use LEDs in a sealed unit. The LEDs cannot be renewed individually (see Section 6, Step 6).

Licence plate light

7 Undo the two screws securing the cover and remove it **(see illustrations)**.

8 Carefully pull the bulb out of its socket **(see illustration)**.

9 Check the socket terminals for corrosion and clean them if necessary.

10 Install the new bulb by pushing it into the socket – it can be installed either way round.

11 Fit the cover and secure it with the screws.

10 Tail light assembly

X, Y, K1 and K2 models

1 Remove the seat cowling (see Chapter 8).

2 Turn the bulbholders anti-clockwise and withdraw them from the tail light **(see illustration)**.

3 Support the tail light, then unscrew the three bolts and remove the tail light with its mounting bracket **(see illustrations)**.

4 If required, separate the tail light from its bracket by undoing the two screws and the nut. Note the collars in the rubber mounts and remove them if required. Check the condition of the rubbers and renew them if they are damaged, deformed or deteriorated.

5 Installation is the reverse of removal. Check the operation of the tail and brake lights.

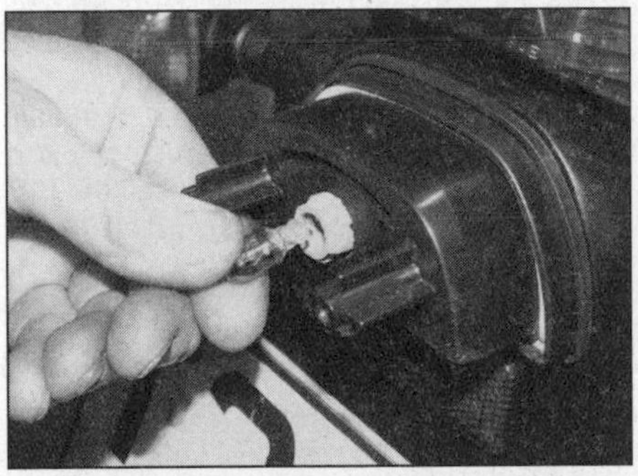
9.8 Pull the bulb out of its socket

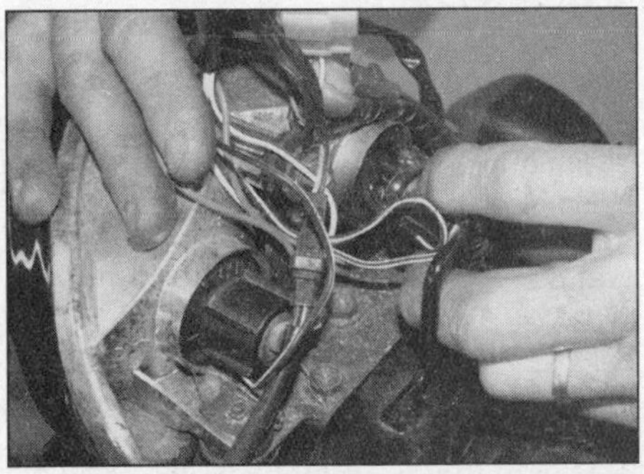
10.2 Remove the bulbholders from the tail light . . .

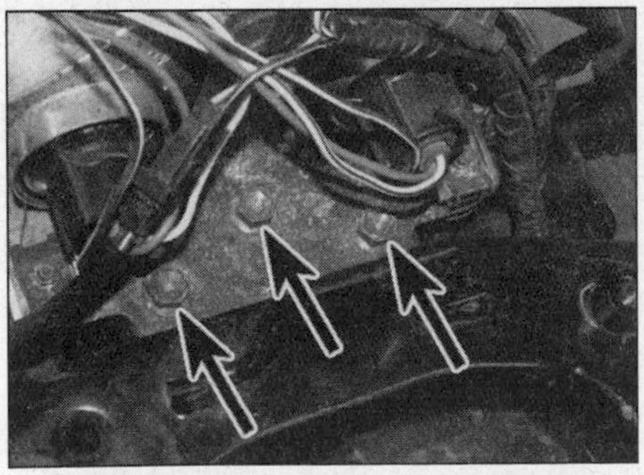
10.3a . . . then unscrew the bolts (arrowed) . . .

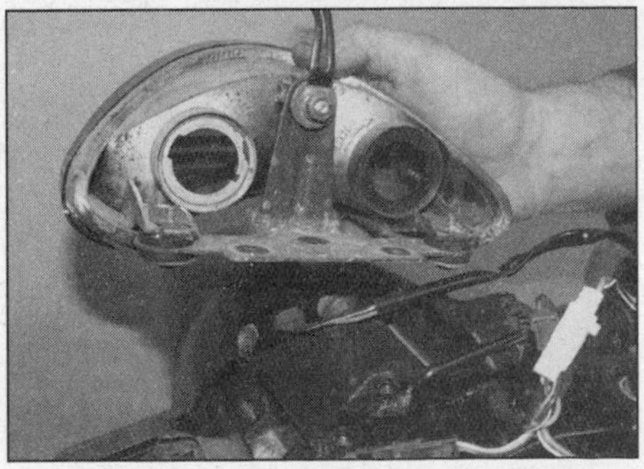
10.3b . . . and remove the tail light

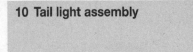

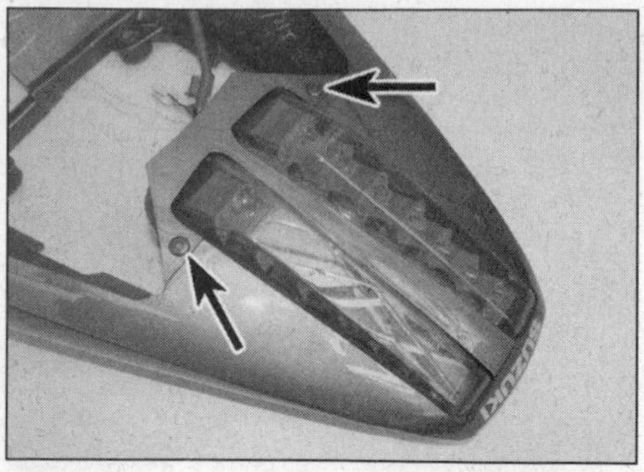

10.7a Release the trim clips (arrowed) . . .

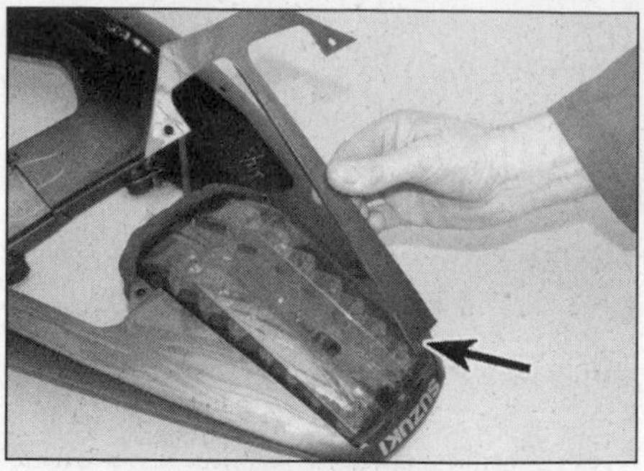

10.7b . . . and lift out the panel noting the tab (arrowed)

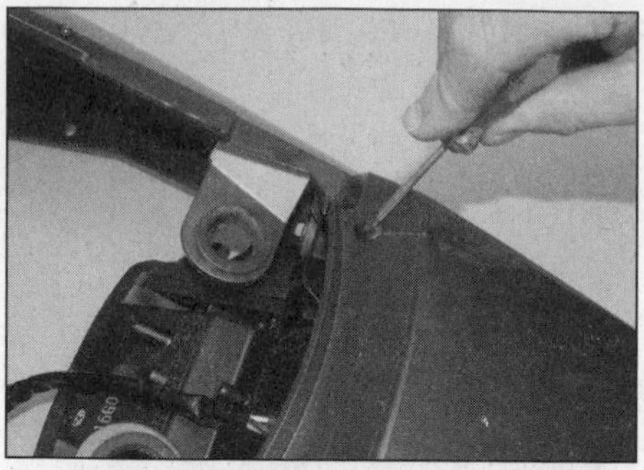

10.8a Release the trim clip on each side

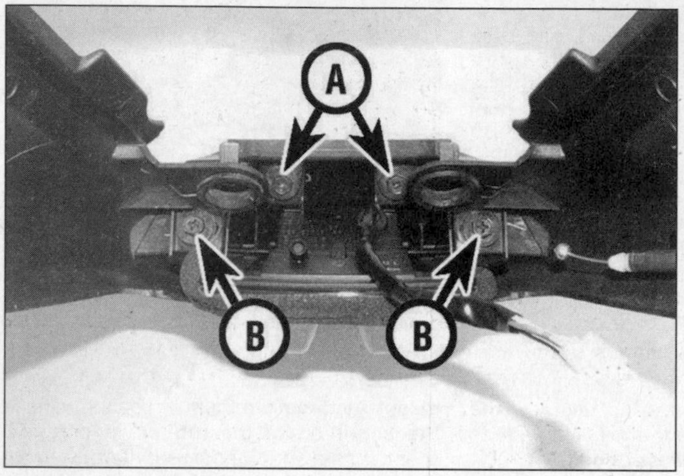

10.8b Bolts (A) secure the top panel; bolts (B) secure the light assembly

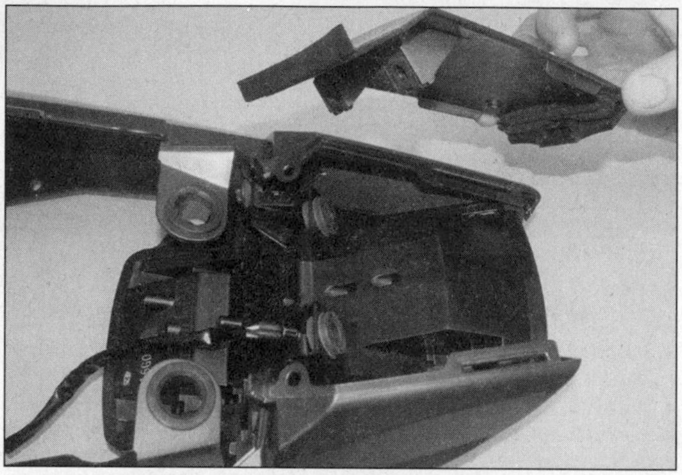

10.8c Note how the tabs locate in the sides of the cowling

K3-on models

6 Remove the seat cowling (see Chapter 8).

7 Release the two trim clips on the underside of the seat cowling, then lift out the panel, noting how the tab on the rear edge locates **(see illustrations)**.

8 Release the two trim clips on the top of the seat cowling **(see illustration)**. Undo the two bolts securing the top panel then lift out the panel, noting the tabs on each side locate **(see illustrations)**.

9 Undo the two bolts securing the tail light assembly **(see illustration 10.8b)**. Ease the two halves of the cowling apart and remove the tail light assembly **(see illustration)**.

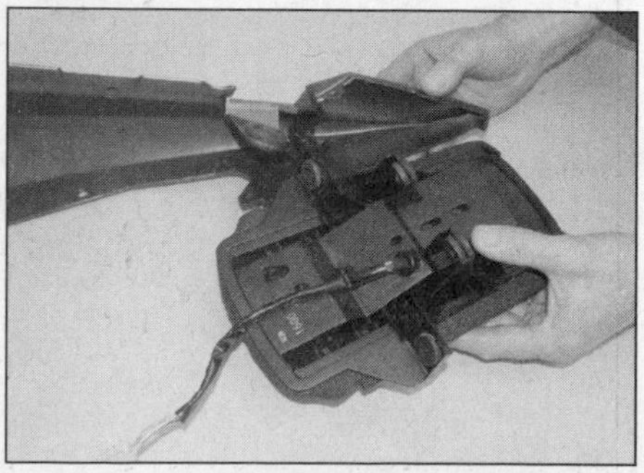

10.9 Separate the tail light assembly from the cowling halves

Check the condition of the rubber grommets and the assembly seal and renew them if they are damaged, deformed or deteriorated.

10 Installation is the reverse of removal. Make sure the tabs locate correctly. Follow the procedure in Chapter 8 to install the trim clips. Check the operation of the tail and brake lights.

11 Turn signal circuit check

1 Most turn signal problems are the result of a burned out bulb or corroded socket. This is especially true when the turn signals function properly in one direction, but fail to flash in the other direction. If this is the case, first check the bulbs, the sockets and the wiring connectors. If all the turn signals fail to work, first check the signal fuse (see Section 5), and then the wiring and connectors, and the switch. Refer to Section 21 for the switch testing procedures, and also to the wiring diagrams at the end of this Chapter.

2 If all the above are good, then the relay is probably faulty. The turn signal relay is integrated in one component with the sidestand relay and diode circuit. Suzuki provide no test details for the turn signal function of the relay, so the best way to determine whether it is faulty is to substitute it with one that is known to be good. If the turn signals then work, the relay is faulty. To access the relay/diode unit, on X, Y, K1 and K2 models remove the rider's seat; on K3 models onward remove the passenger's seat (see Chapter 8). The unit is next to the fusebox and plugs into a socket in the tray **(see illustration)**; pull the relay/diode unit out of its socket and fit the new one **(see illustration)**. Note that on ABS equipped K7-on models, the relay is located in the base of the battery carrier, below the rubber mat.

3 If a substitute is not available, or if it does

11.2a Relay/diode unit (arrowed)

not solve the problem, pull the relay/diode unit out of its socket. Check for battery voltage at terminal G (the orange/green wire terminal on X, Y, K1 and K2 models, and the brown wire terminal on K3-on models) in the socket with the ignition ON. Turn the ignition OFF when the check is complete. If no voltage was present, check the wiring from the socket to the ignition (main) switch (via the fusebox) for voltage and continuity. If voltage was present, check the light blue wire from the socket to the switch for continuity. Continue to check the wiring right through to the bulbs, referring to the appropriate wiring diagram at the end of this Chapter. Repair or renew the wiring or connectors as necessary.

12 Turn signal bulbs

Note: *It is a good idea to use a paper towel or dry cloth when handling the new bulb to prevent injury if the bulb should break and to increase bulb life.*

X, Y, K1 and K2 models

1 Undo the screw securing the lens assembly and detach it from the housing, noting how it fits **(see illustration)**.
2 Turn the bulbholder anti-clockwise and withdraw it from the lens **(see illustration)**.
3 Push the bulb into the holder and twist it anti-clockwise to remove it **(see illustration)**.
4 Check the socket terminals for corrosion and clean them if necessary.

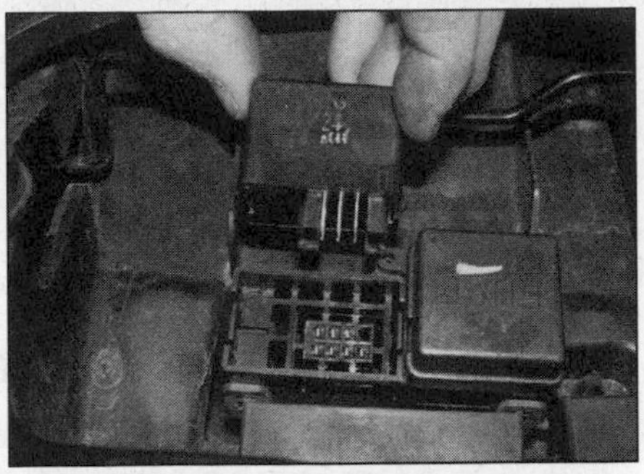

11.2b Pull the unit out of its socket. Each socket terminal is identified by a letter

5 Line up the pins of the new bulb with the slots in the socket, then push the bulb in and turn it clockwise until it locks into place.
6 Fit the bulbholder into the lens and turn it clockwise to secure it.
7 Fit the lens assembly into the housing, making sure the tab on the inner locates correctly, and install the screw **(see illustration)**. Do not overtighten the screw as it is easy to strip the threads or crack the lens. Check that the turn signal works correctly.

K3-on models

8 Undo the screw securing the lens and remove the lens, noting how it fits **(see illustration)**.
9 Push the bulb into the holder and twist it anti-clockwise to remove it **(see illustration)**. Check the socket terminals for corrosion and clean them, if necessary. Line up the pins of the new bulb with the slots in the socket, then

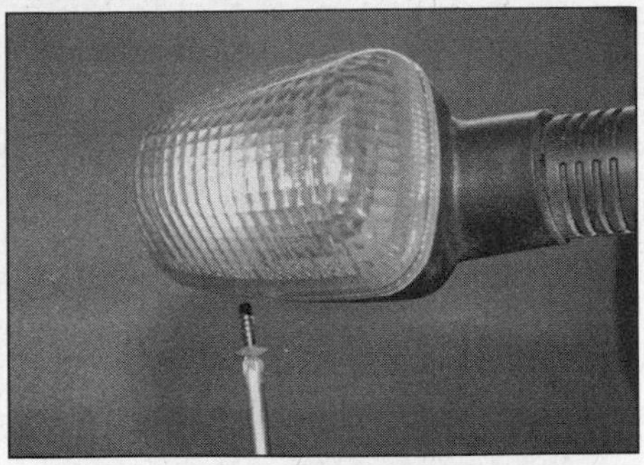

12.1 Undo the screw and remove the lens

push the bulb in and turn it clockwise until it locks into place.
10 Fit the lens onto the holder, making sure the tab locates correctly. Do not overtighten the screw as the lens or threads could be damaged.

13 Turn signal assemblies

Front turn signals – SV650 models

1 Refer to Section 8, Steps 1 and 2 and remove the headlight from the shell.
2 Trace the wiring from the turn signal and disconnect it at the connector **(see illustration)**. Feed the wiring out the back of the headlight shell and through to the turn signal, noting its routing.

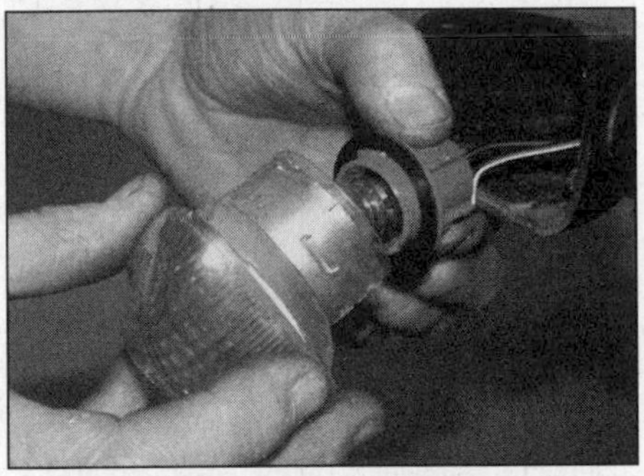

12.2 Release the bulbholder . . .

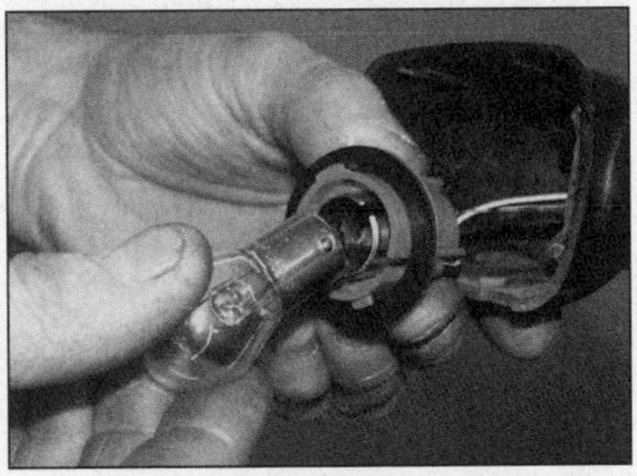

12.3 . . . and remove the bulb

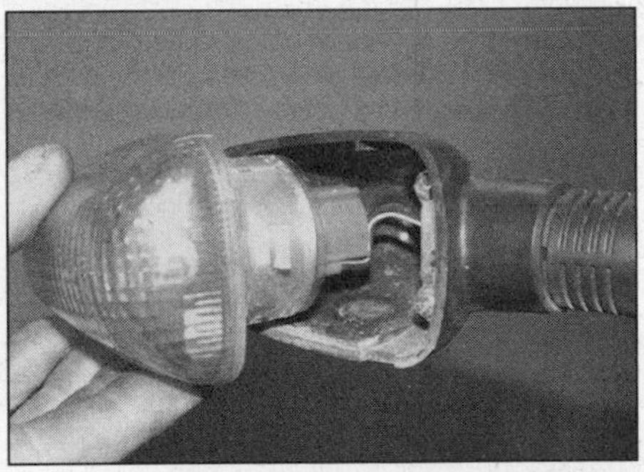

12.7 Make sure the lens locates correctly

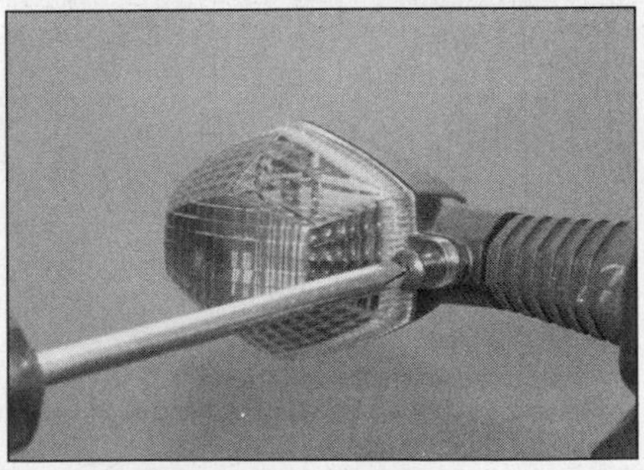

12.8a Undo the screw . . .

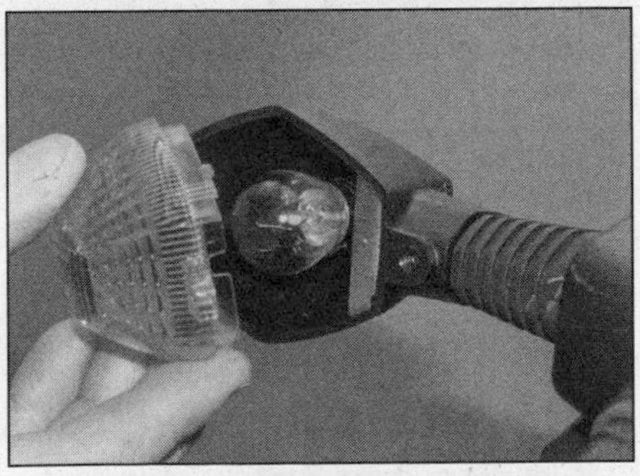

12.8b . . . and remove the lens

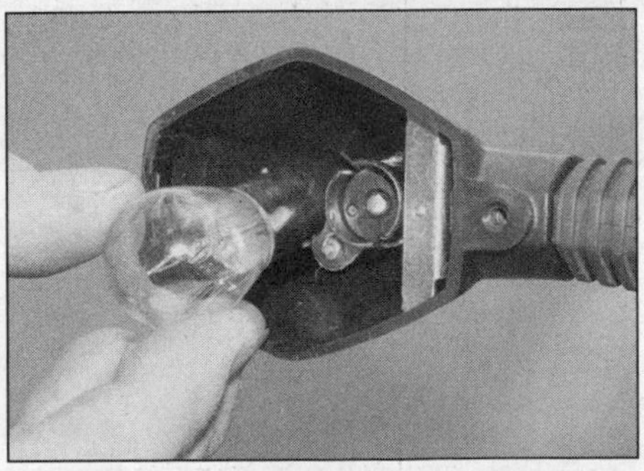

12.9 Twist the bulb anti-clockwise to remove it

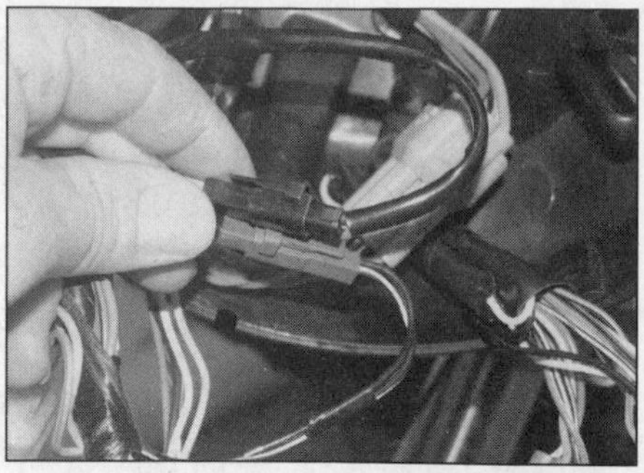

13.2 Disconnect the relevant wiring connector . . .

13.3 . . . then unscrew the nut (arrowed) and remove the turn signal

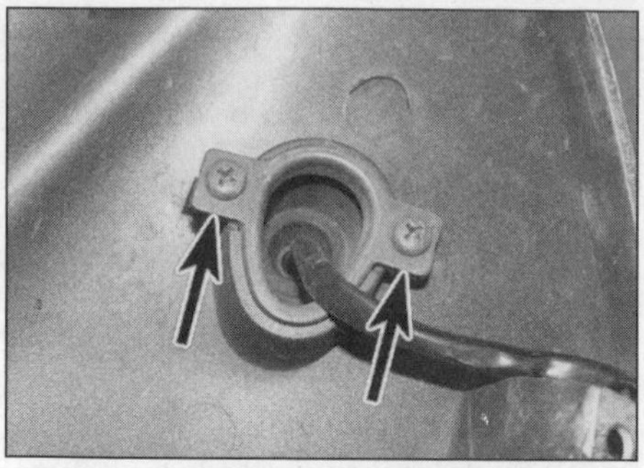

13.6 Undo the screws (arrowed), remove the plate and withdraw the turn signal

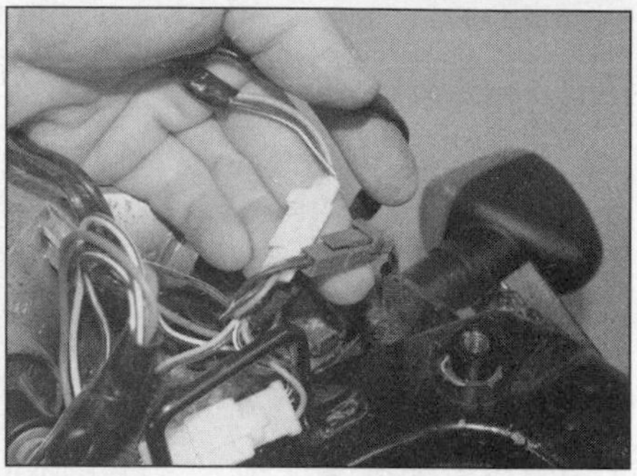

13.13 Disconnect the relevant wiring connector . . .

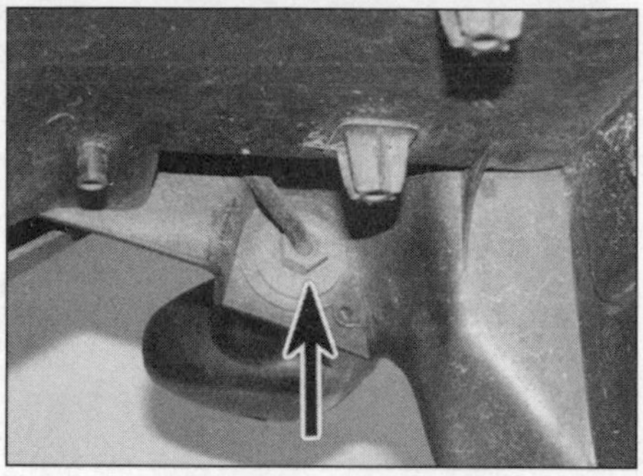

13.14 . . . then unscrew the nut (arrowed) and remove the turn signal

3 Support the turn signal, then unscrew the nut on the inside of the bracket **(see illustration)**. Draw the nut off the wiring, then remove the turn signal, taking care not to snag the connector as you draw it through the bracket.
4 Installation is the reverse of removal. Check the operation of the turn signals.

Front turn signals – X, Y, K1 and K2 SV650S models

5 Remove the fairing side panel (see Chapter 8).
6 Undo the two screws securing the turn signal mounting plate to the inside of the panel **(see illustration)**. Remove the plate and draw the signal off the panel, taking care not to snag the wiring as you draw it through.
7 Installation is the reverse of removal. Check the operation of the turn signals.

Front turn signals – K3-on SV650S models

8 Remove the lower fairing and cockpit trim panels (see Chapter 8).
9 Trace the wiring from the turn signal and disconnect the wiring connector.
10 Unscrew the nut securing the stem, and remove the backing plate. Remove the turn signal, taking care as you draw the wiring through.
11 Installation is the reverse of removal. Check the operation of the turn signals.

Rear turn signals – all models

12 Remove the seat cowling (see Chapter 8).
13 Trace the wiring from the turn signal and disconnect the wiring connector **(see illustration)**. Carefully draw the wiring through to the underside of the mudguard, taking care not to snag it.
14 Unscrew the nut securing the stem, and remove the washer or backing plate **(see illustration)**. Remove the turn signal, again taking care as you draw the wiring through.
15 Installation is the reverse of removal. Check the operation of the turn signals.

14 Brake light switches

Circuit check

1 Before checking the switches, and if not already done, check the brake light circuit (see Section 6, Steps 8 and 9).
2 The front brake light switch is mounted on the underside of the brake master cylinder. Disconnect the wiring connectors from the switch **(see illustration)**. Using a continuity tester, connect the probes to the terminals of the switch. With the brake lever at rest, there should be no continuity. With the brake lever applied, there should be continuity. If the switch does not behave as described, renew it.
3 On X, Y, K1 and K2 models, the rear brake light switch is mounted on the inside of the frame, above the brake pedal. On K3-on models, the rear brake light switch is mounted on the inside of the right-hand footrest bracket. Remove the seat cowling to access the wiring connector (see Chapter 8). Trace the wiring from the switch and disconnect it at the connector **(see illustration)**. Using a continuity tester, connect the probes to the terminals on the switch side of the wiring connector. With the brake pedal at rest, there should be no continuity. With the brake pedal applied, there should be continuity. If the switch does not behave as described, and you have already tried adjusting the switch (see Step 10), renew it with a new one.
4 If the switches are good, check for voltage at the black/red (front) or orange (rear) wire terminal on the connector with the ignition switched ON – there should be battery voltage. If there's no voltage present, check the wiring between the switch and the ignition switch via the fusebox (see the *Wiring Diagrams* at the end of this Chapter). If voltage is present, check the black and white/black (front) or

14.2 Front brake switch wiring connectors (arrowed)

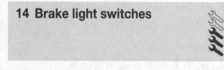

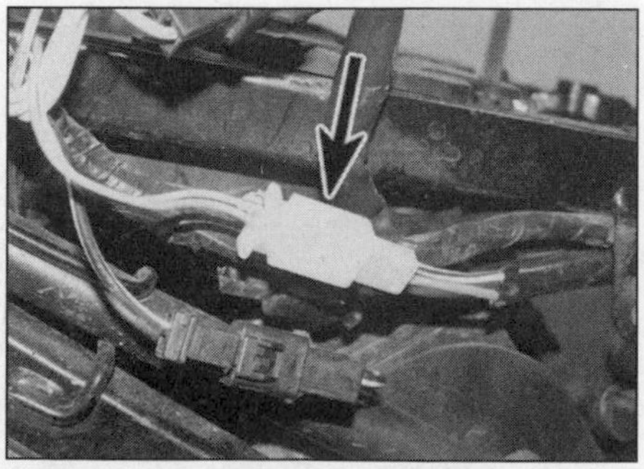

14.3 Rear brake light switch wiring connector (arrowed)

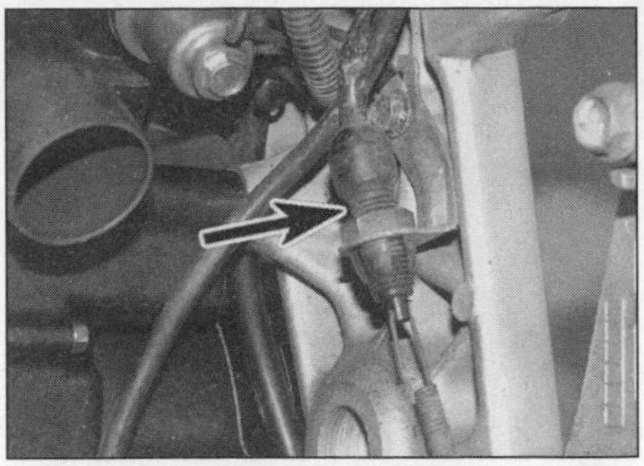

14.8a Rear brake light switch (arrowed) – X, Y, K1 and K2 models

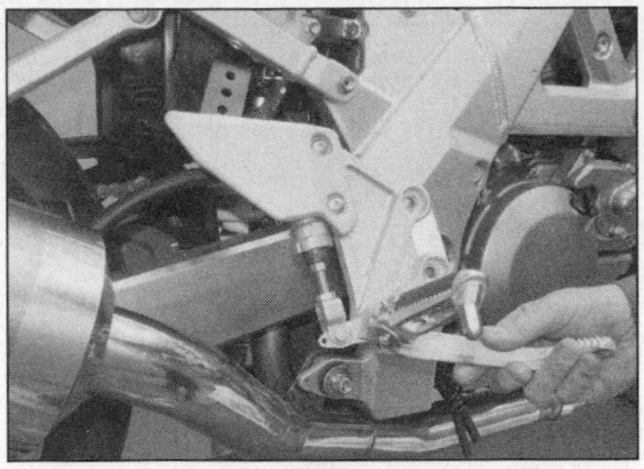

14.8b On K3-on models, displace the footrest assembly . . .

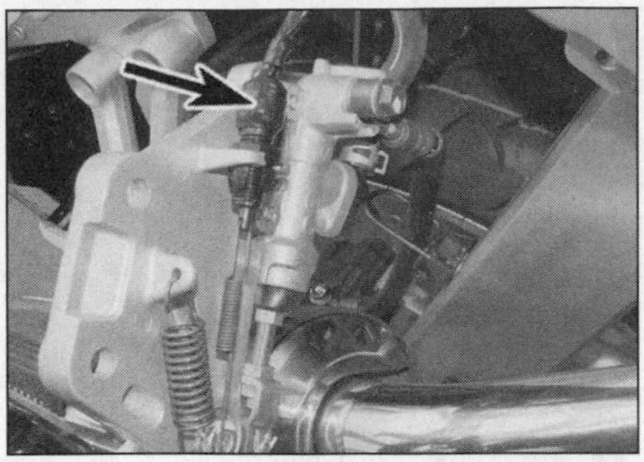

14.8c . . . to access the rear brake light switch (arrowed)

white/black (rear) wire for continuity from the switch to the brake light bulb wiring connector, referring to the relevant *Wiring Diagram*. Repair or renew the wiring as necessary. **Note:** *Front brake light switch wires colour codes change at the main loom wiring connector.*

Front brake lever switch renewal

5 The switch is mounted on the underside of the brake master cylinder. Disconnect the wiring connectors from the switch **(see illustration 14.2)**.

6 Undo the single screw securing the switch to the master cylinder and remove the switch, noting how it fits.

7 Installation is the reverse of removal. The switch isn't adjustable.

Rear brake pedal switch renewal

8 On X, Y, K1 and K2 models, the rear brake light switch is mounted on the inside of the frame, above the brake pedal **(see illustration)**. On K3-on models, the rear brake light switch is mounted on the inside of the right-hand footrest bracket; undo the two bolts securing the bracket to the frame and displace the footrest bracket assembly to access the switch **(see illustration)**.

9 Remove the seat cowling to access the wiring connector (see Chapter 8). Trace the wiring from the switch and disconnect it at the connector **(see illustration 14.3)**.

10 Detach the lower end of the switch spring from the brake pedal, then either release the switch with its adjustment nut from the mounting by squeezing the tabs on the underside of the nut, or thread the switch itself out of the nut, leaving the nut in the mounting.

11 Installation is the reverse of removal. Make sure the brake light is activated just before the rear brake pedal takes effect. If adjustment is necessary, hold the switch body and turn the adjustment nut as required (either raising or lowering the switch) until the brake light is activated correctly.

15 Instrument cluster – removal and installation

X, Y, K1 and K2 SV650 models

1 Remove the headlight assembly (see Section 8).

2 Undo the two bolts, noting the wiring clips where fitted, and remove the instrument cluster, noting how it fits **(see illustrations)**.

3 Installation is the reverse of removal. Check the rubber grommets for damage, deformation and deterioration and renew them if necessary. Make sure that the wiring connectors are correctly routed and secured.

K3-on SV650 models

4 Remove the headlight assembly (see Section 8).

5 Remove the three trim clips securing the lower cover and lift it off.

6 Disconnect the instrument cluster wiring connector.

7 Undo the two nuts and two screws securing the instrument cluster to the bracket and lift it off.

8 Installation is the reverse of removal. Check the rubber grommets for damage, deformation and deterioration and renew them if necessary. Make sure that the wiring is securely connected and correctly routed. Follow the procedure in Section 10, Step 11, to install the trim clips.

X, Y, K1 and K2 SV650S models

9 Remove the fairing and cockpit trim panel (see Chapter 8).

10 Disconnect the wiring connector from the instrument cluster **(see illustration)**.

11 Unscrew the four nuts, noting the washers, and remove the instrument cluster, noting how it fits **(see illustrations)**.

12 Installation is the reverse of removal. Check the rubber grommets for damage, deformation and deterioration and renew them if necessary. Make sure that the wiring connectors are correctly routed and secured.

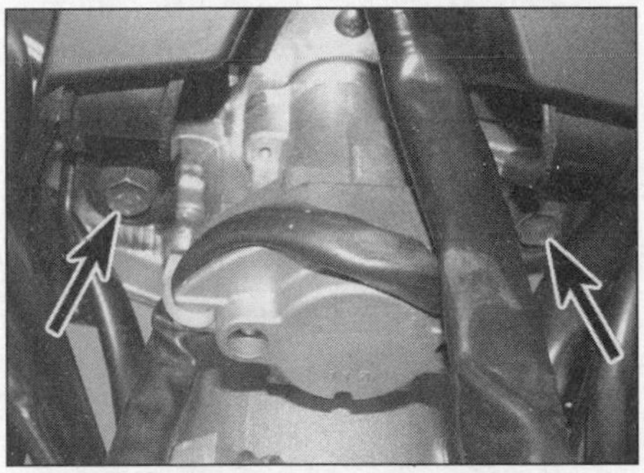

15.2a Unscrew the bolts (arrowed) . . .

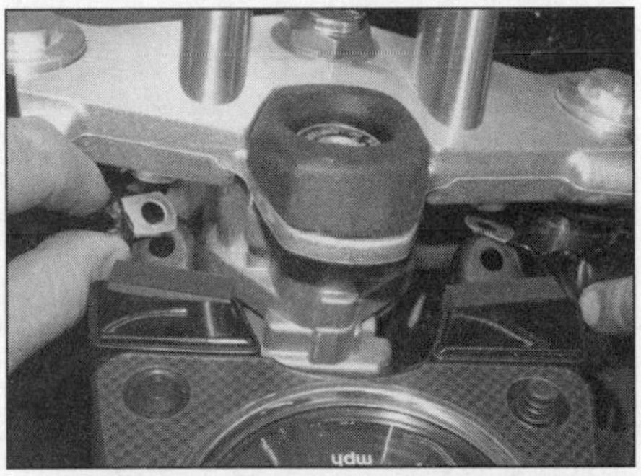

15.2b . . . noting the wiring clips

15.10 On X, Y, K1 and K2 models, disconnect the wiring connector . . .

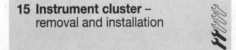

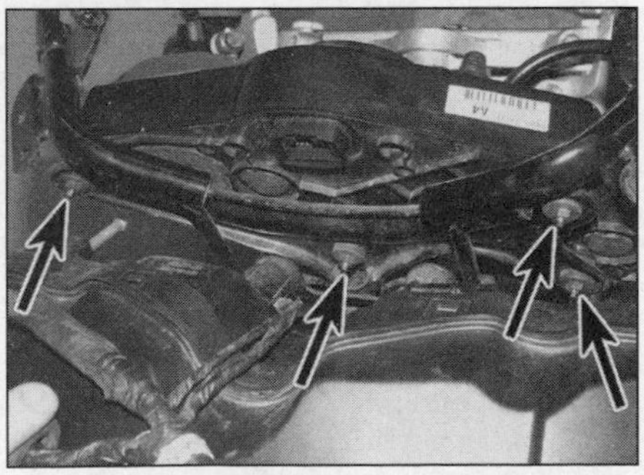

15.11a . . . then unscrew the nuts (arrowed) . . .

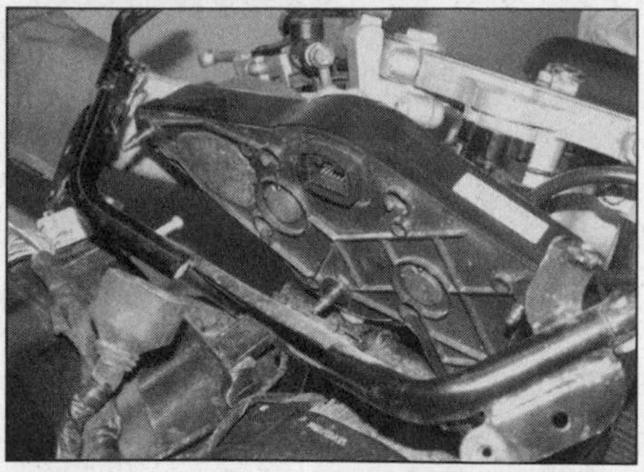

15.11b . . . and remove the instrument cluster

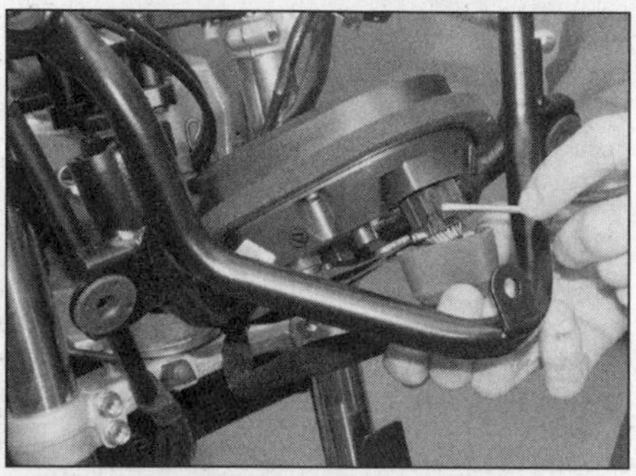

15.14a On K3-on models, disconnect the wiring connector . . .

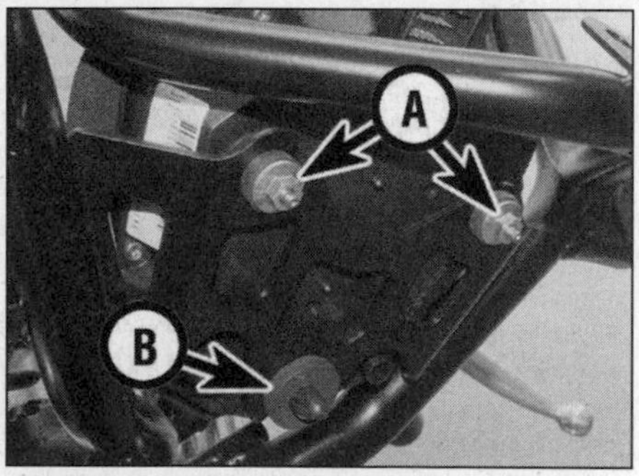

15.14b . . . then unscrew the nuts (A), noting the peg and grommet (B)

16.1 Disconnect the instrument wiring connectors

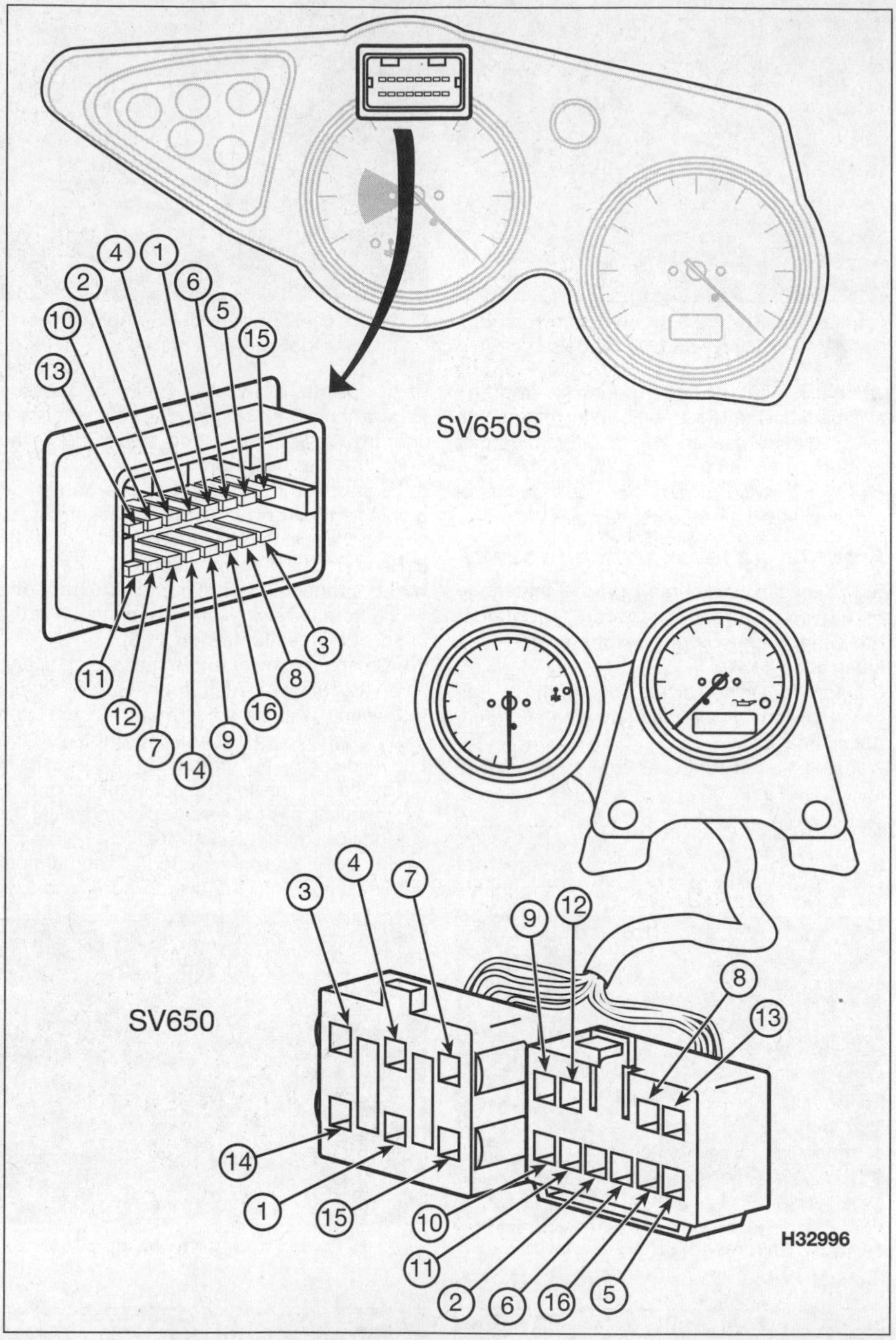

16.3 Instrument cluster terminal identification and test connections – X, Y, K1 and K2 models

Terminal identification

1 *Battery +ve*
2 *Ignition +ve*
3 *Speed sensor +ve*
4 *Ignition coil (signal)*
5 *Fuel level light B*
6 *Fuel level light A*
7 *Oil pressure warning light*
8 *Earth (power)*
9 *Illumination +ve*
10 *High beam indicator light +ve*
11 *Left turn signal indicator light +ve*
12 *Right turn signal indicator light +ve*
13 *Neutral switch*
14 *Speed sensor (signal)*
15 *Coolant temperature sensor*
16 *Earth (signal)*

Test connections	**+ve probe**	**-ve probe**
Left turn signal light	11	8
Right turn signal light	12	8
Fuel level light	2	5, 6
Neutral light	2	13

Test connections	**+ve probe**	**-ve probe**
Hi beam light	10	8
Oil pressure light	2	7
Coolant temperature light	2	15
Instrument illumination	9	8

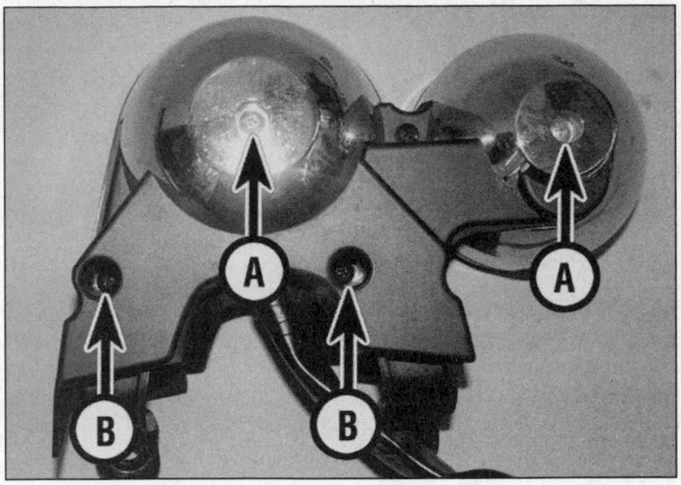

16.8a Undo the shell screws (A) and the rear cover screws (B) . . .

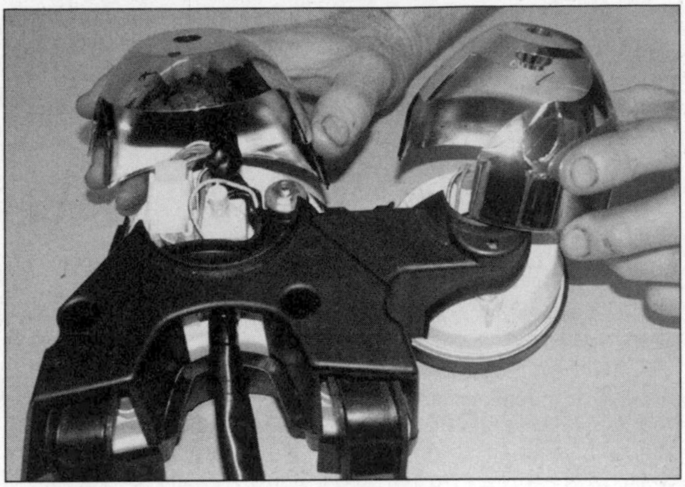

16.8b . . . and remove the shells . . .

K3-on SV650S models

13 Remove the fairing (see Chapter 8).

14 Disconnect the wiring connector **(see illustration)**. Undo the two nuts securing the instrument cluster to the bracket and lift it off, noting how the peg on the back of the cluster locates in the grommet **(see illustration)**.

15 Installation is the reverse of removal. Check the rubber grommets for damage, deformation and deterioration and renew them if necessary. Make sure that the wiring is securely connected and correctly routed.

16 Instruments – check and renewal

X, Y, K1 and K2 models

Circuit check

1 On SV650 models, remove the headlight from its shell (see Section 8). Trace the wiring from the instrument cluster and disconnect it at the connectors **(see illustration)**.

2 On SV650S models, remove the fairing (see Chapter 8). Disconnect the wiring connector from the instrument cluster **(see illustration 15.10)**.

3 Using a multimeter or continuity tester, refer to the relevant wiring diagram for your model and perform the continuity checks between the indicated terminals on the wiring connector(s) **(see illustration opposite)**. If any test reveals no continuity, first remove, check and renew if necessary the relevant bulb (see Section 17). Note that if there is a faulty LED in an instrument, it cannot be removed and so the instrument itself must be renewed.

4 On SV650 models, if there is still no continuity in that circuit, remove the bulbholders from the cluster (see Section 17) and check for continuity in the individual wires between the connectors and the bulb sockets, and then from the socket back to the connectors, to isolate the fault, then repair the wire if possible. Otherwise fit a new wiring sub-loom. If the wiring is good, the circuit board in the cluster is faulty and must be renewed.

5 On SV650S models, if there is still no continuity in that circuit, renew the instrument and circuit board – it is supplied as a unit.

Speedometer check

6 If there is a fault, first check the speed sensor (see Section 18). If the sensor is proved good and the wiring between the sensor and speedometer is unbroken the speedometer head is likely to be faulty. The speedometer head can be purchased separately on SV650 models, but is part of the instrument circuit board on SV650S models.

Speedometer renewal – SV650 models

7 Remove the instrument cluster (see Section 15).

8 Undo the instrument shell screws and remove the shells **(see illustrations)**. Undo the rear cover screws and remove the cover **(see illustration)**. Unscrew the mounting bracket nuts and remove the washers, then remove the bracket **(see illustration)**.

9 Undo the front cover screws on the back of the housing and lift off the front cover **(see illustrations)**.

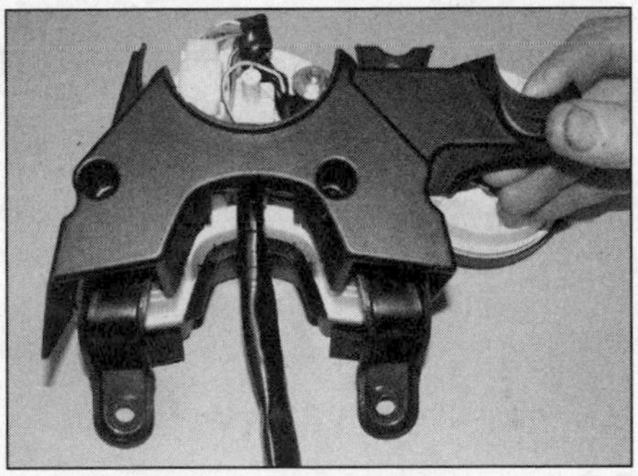

16.8c . . . and the cover

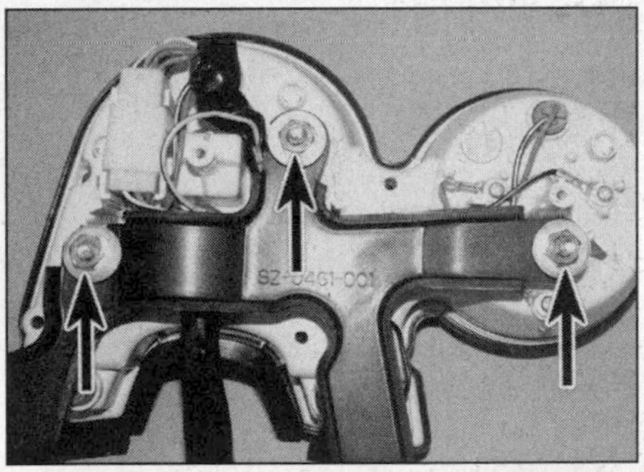

16.8d Unscrew the nuts and remove the bracket

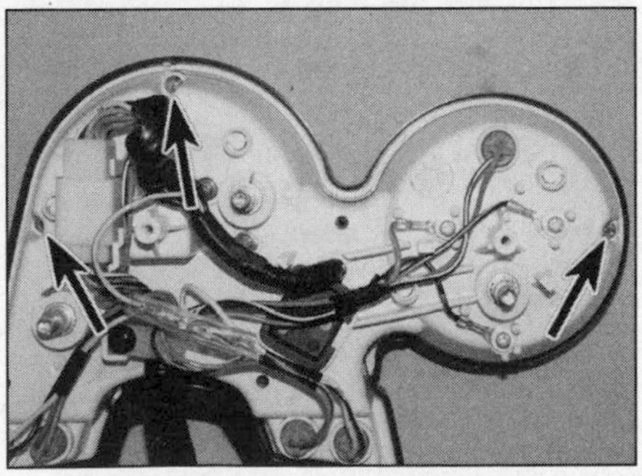

16.9a Undo the screws (arrowed) . . .

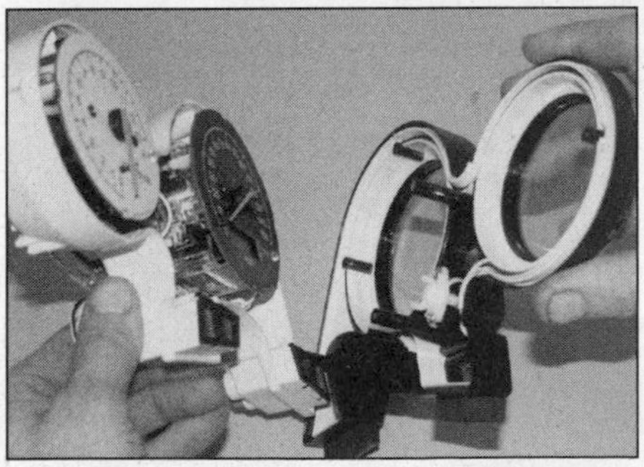

16.9b . . . and remove the front cover

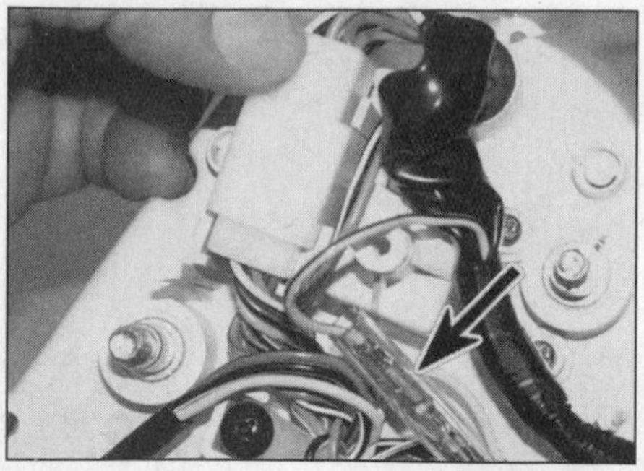

16.10a Disconnect the main wiring connector and the bullet connector (arrowed)

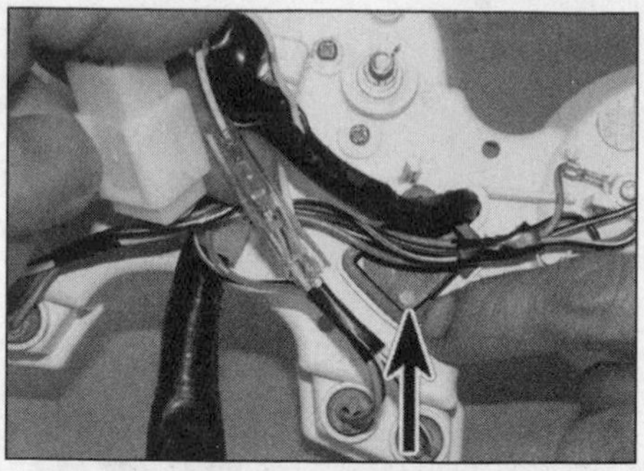

16.10b Remove the blanking plug (arrowed) from the housing

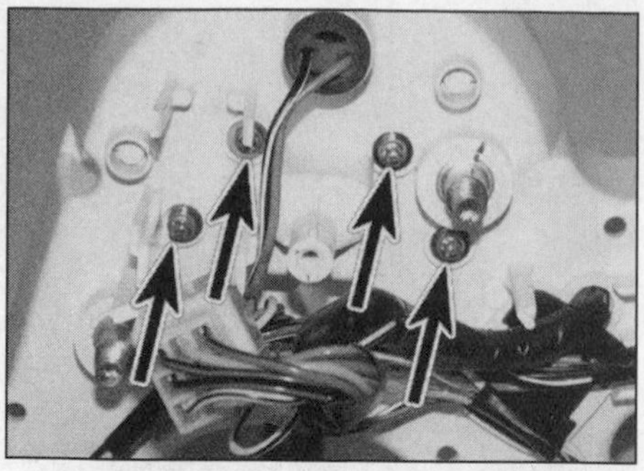

16.10c Speedometer screws (arrowed)

10 Release the speedometer wiring connector from the housing and disconnect it and the single wire bullet connector **(see illustration)**. Remove the blanking plug from the instrument housing **(see illustration)**. Undo the screws securing the speedometer and remove it from the housing, noting how it fits, drawing the wiring and connector through as you do **(see illustration)**.

11 Installation is the reverse of removal.

Speedometer renewal – SV650S models

12 Remove the instrument cluster (see Section 15).

13 Undo the front cover screws on the back of the housing and lift off the front cover **(see illustrations)**.

14 Undo the instrument and circuit board screw on the back of the housing and lift the board out **(see illustrations)**.

15 Installation is the reverse of removal. Check the condition of the rubber sealing ring around the housing and renew it if it is damaged, deformed or deteriorated **(see illustration)**. Make sure the front cover seats correctly onto the sealing ring.

Tachometer check

16 If there is a fault, take the instrument cluster to a Suzuki dealer for assessment. The tachometer head can be purchased separately on SV650 models, but is part of the instrument circuit board on SV650S models.

Tachometer renewal – SV650

17 Remove the instrument cluster (see Section 15).

18 Undo the instrument shell screws and remove the shells **(see illustration 16.8a and b)**. Undo the rear cover screws and remove the cover **(see illustration 16.8c)**. Unscrew the mounting bracket nuts and remove the washers, then remove the bracket **(see illustration 16.8d)**.

19 Undo the front cover screws on the back of the housing and lift off the front cover **(see illustrations 16.9a and b)**.

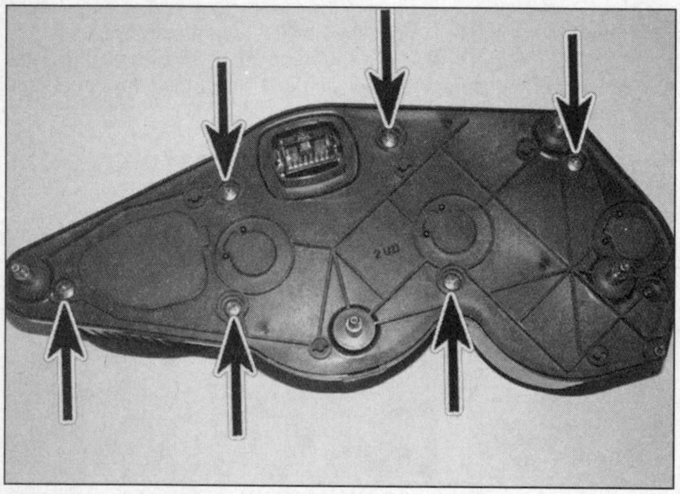

16.13a Undo the screws (arrowed) . . .

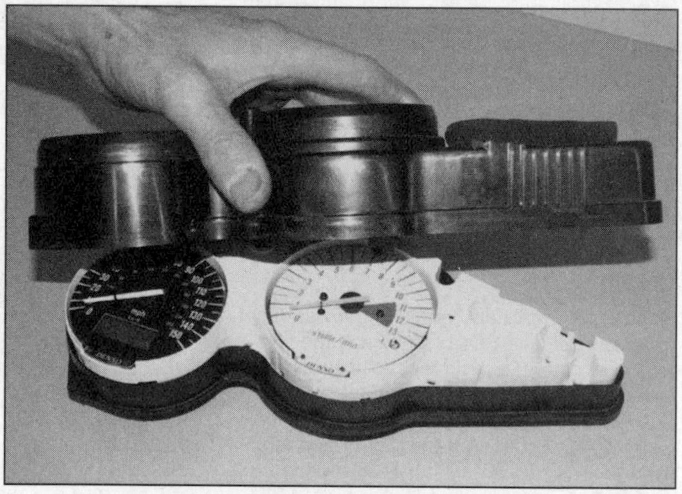

16.13b . . . and remove the front cover

16.14a Undo the single screw . . .

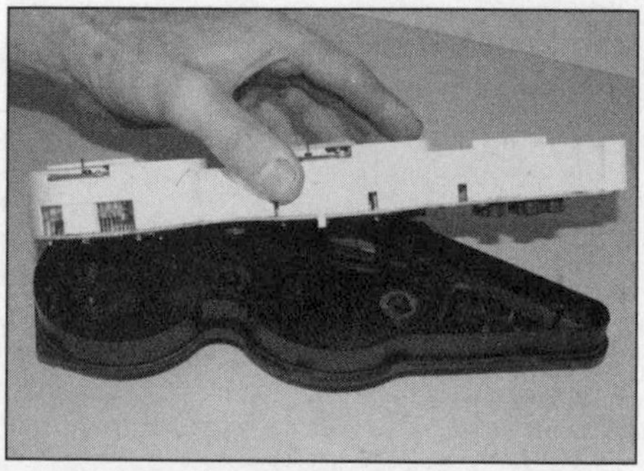

16.14b . . . and lift the instrument and circuit board out

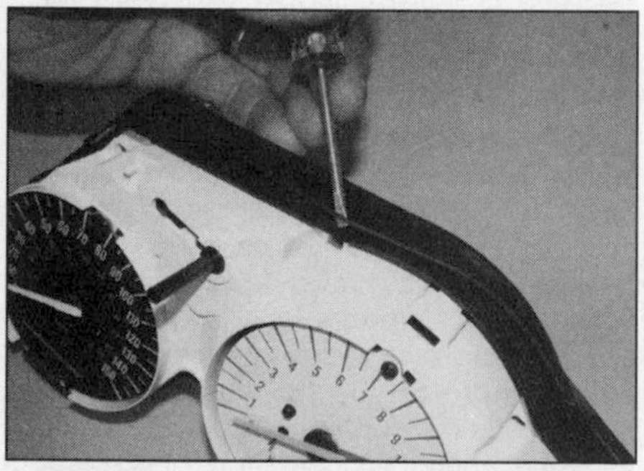

16.15 Check the sealing ring and renew it if necessary

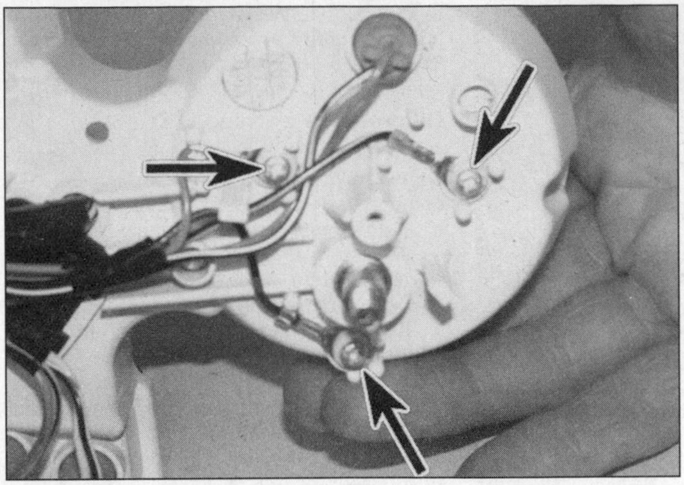

16.20 Undo the screws (arrowed), detach the wires and remove the tachometer

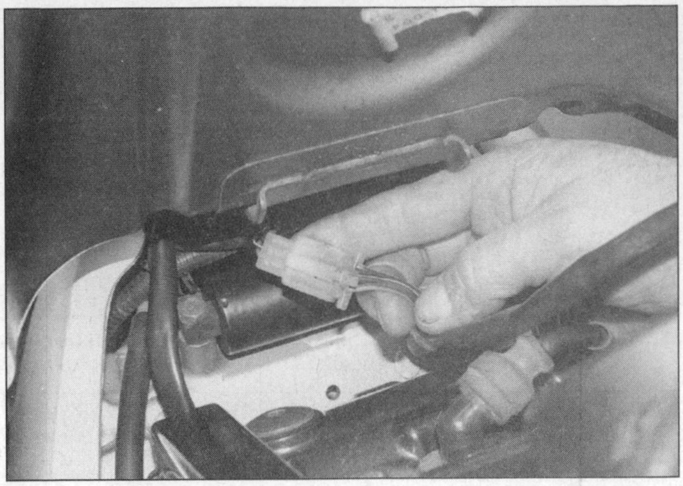

16.30 Disconnect the fuel level sensor wiring connector

20 Undo the screws securing the tachometer and its wiring, noting which wire fits where (though the colour codes of the wires should be marked next to the terminals), and detach the wires **(see illustration)**. Remove the tachometer from the housing, noting how it fits.

21 Installation is the reverse of removal.

Tachometer renewal – SV650S

22 Remove the instrument cluster (see Section 15).

23 Undo the front cover screws on the back of the housing and lift off the front cover **(see illustrations 16.13a and b)**.

24 Undo the instrument and circuit board screw on the back of the housing and lift the board out **(see illustrations 16.14a and b)**.

25 Installation is the reverse of removal. Check the condition of the rubber sealing ring around the housing and renew it if it is damaged, deformed or deteriorated **(see illustration 16.15)**. Make sure the front cover seats correctly onto the sealing ring.

Coolant temperature warning LED

26 See Chapter 3 for checks.

27 The LED is incorporated in the tachometer. If the LED fails, the tachometer must be renewed (see above).

Fuel warning light

28 In normal operation, the fuel level warning light will come on when the ignition is first turned on and extinguish after a few seconds if there is sufficient fuel in the tank – this serves as a check of the warning light system. The light will start to flicker when the volume of fuel remaining in the tank reaches approximately 3.5 litres, and then stay illuminated when the volume falls to approximately 1.5 litres.

29 If it doesn't perform as described above, first carry out the check in Steps 1 to 5.

30 If the circuit and bulb are good, raise the fuel tank (see Chapter 4A). Disconnect the fuel level sensor wiring connector **(see illustration)**.

31 Using a jumper wire, connect between the black/white and red/black wire terminals on the loom side of the connector. With the ignition ON, the warning light should flicker. Disconnect the jumper wire – the light should go out after approximately 30 seconds.

32 Reconnect the jumper wire between the black/white and red/black wire terminals as above. Using a second jumper wire, connect between the black/white and black/light green wire terminals on the loom side of the connector. With the ignition ON, the warning light should be on. Disconnect the jumper wires – the light should go out after approximately 30 seconds.

33 If the light does not behave as described, or is good for one of the tests but not the other, check the relevant wiring between the connector and the instrument cluster for faults, and repair as required. Refer to the *Wiring diagrams* at the end of the Chapter.

34 If no problems have been found so far, yet the fault still exists, the level sensor may be faulty (see Chapter 4A).

35 Refer to Section 17 for details of how to change the warning light bulb.

Oil pressure warning light

36 See Section 19 for checks.

37 On SV650 models, the warning light is an LED that is integral with the speedometer – renew the speedometer if the LED has failed (see above). On SV650S models the warning light bulb can be renewed as described in Section 17.

K3-on models

Note: *The individual instruments and warning LEDs are integral with the instrument cluster circuit board – separate components are not available.*

Circuit check

38 Follow the appropriate procedure in Section 15 and disconnect the instrument cluster wiring connector.

39 Refer to the *Wiring diagrams* at the end of the Chapter and identify the relevant terminals on the instrument cluster for the circuit to be checked. Using a multimeter or continuity tester, perform a continuity check between the indicated terminals. If any check reveals no continuity it is likely the LED or circuit board is faulty – have it tested by a Suzuki dealer. If there is continuity, the fault lies elsewhere in the circuit for the LED in question. Check the signal fuse and wiring, and the operation of the component linked to the LED.

Speedometer check

40 If there is a fault, first check the speed sensor (see Section 18). If the sensor is proved good and the wiring between the sensor and instrument cluster is unbroken, the speedometer LCD is likely to be faulty – have it tested by a Suzuki dealer. The LCD is part of the instrument circuit board.

Speedometer renewal

41 Remove the instrument cluster (see Section 15).

42 Undo the five screws securing the two halves instrument case and separate the halves. Note the location of the seal. Lift the integral circuit board and tachometer out of the case, noting how it fits.

43 Installation is the reverse of removal. Check the condition of the seal around the housing and renew it if it is damaged, deformed or deteriorated.

Tachometer

44 If there is a fault, take the instrument cluster to a Suzuki dealer for assessment. The tachometer head is part of the instrument circuit board. If required, follow the procedure in Steps 41 to 43 to remove and install the circuit board.

Engine coolant temperature warning LED and display

45 When the coolant temperature rises above 120°C, the coolant temperature LCD flashes and the temperature symbol and panel warning LED come on. When the coolant temperature rises above 140°C, the LCD

16.47 Engine coolant temperature sensor wiring connector (arrowed)

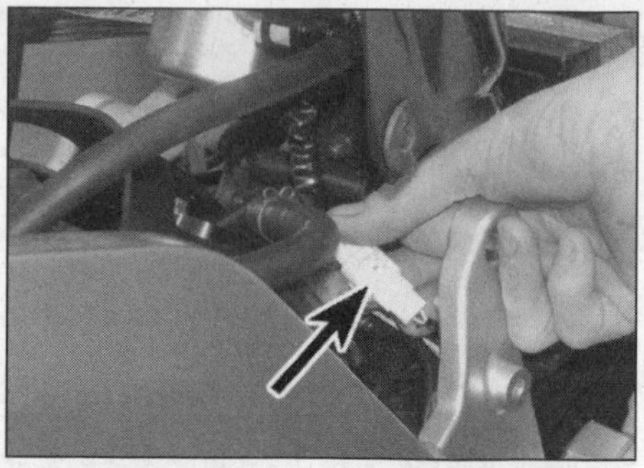

16.52 Fuel level sensor wiring connector (arrowed)

Resistance	2.45 K-ohms or more	0.587 K-ohms approx	0.1 K-ohms and less	Zero ohms
Warning LED	OFF	OFF	ON	ON
Temp. symbol	OFF	OFF	ON	ON
Temp. LCD	OFF	60°C	Flash 120 to 129°C	Flash HI

flashes HI and the temperature symbol and panel warning LED come on.

46 If either the LED or LCD are thought to be faulty, refer to Chapter 3 and check the engine coolant temperature sensor. Note that a sensor fault should be indicated by the fuel injection system diagnostic process (see Chapter 4B). If the sensor is good, check the LED and LCD with a variable resistor or rheostat as follows, or have them tested by a Suzuki dealer.

47 Ensure that the ignition (main) switch is OFF, then disconnect the engine coolant temperature sensor wiring connector **(see illustration)**.

48 Connect the variable resistor between the two terminals on the loom side of the connector and set the resistance to 2.5 K-ohms. Turn the ignition ON, note the instrument cluster display and refer to the accompanying table. The LCD, temperature symbol and panel warning LED should all be OFF. Now gradually reduce the resistance and observe the LCD – at approximately 0.587 K-ohms the LCD should read 60°C. Reduce the resistance further and compare the LCD readings and the point at which the LEDs come on with the table.

49 If the LCD and LEDs do not perform as described in the table above it is likely that the circuit board is faulty and must be renewed.

Fuel warning LED

50 In normal operation, the low fuel level warning LED will come on when the ignition is first turned on and extinguish after a few seconds if there is sufficient fuel in the tank – this serves as a check of the low fuel level warning system. On K3 and K4 models, the LED will stay illuminated when the volume falls to approximately 4.2 litres. On K5-on models, the LED flashes when the volume falls to approximately 4 litres, and stays illuminated at approximately 1.5 litres.

51 If it doesn't perform as described above, first carry out the check in Steps 38 and 39.

52 If the circuit and LED are good, raise the fuel tank (see Chapter 4B). Disconnect the fuel level sensor wiring connector **(see illustration)**.

53 Using a jumper wire, connect between the black/white and yellow/black wire terminals on the loom side of the connector. With the ignition ON, the warning LED should come on after approximately five seconds. Disconnect the jumper wire – the LED should go out after approximately 30 seconds.

54 If the LED does not behave as described, check the relevant wiring between the connector and the instrument cluster for faults, and repair as required. Refer to the *Wiring diagrams* at the end of the Chapter.

55 If the problem cannot be identified, the level sensor may be faulty (see Chapter 4B).

Oil pressure warning LED

56 In normal operation, the oil pressure warning symbol and panel warning LED will come on when the ignition is turned ON and extinguish as soon as the engine is started – this serves as a check of the oil pressure warning system. If they do not come on, first check the signal fuse (see Section 5), and the instrument cluster circuit (Steps 38 and 39).

57 If the warning symbol and panel warning LED come on whilst the engine is running, stop the engine immediately and check the oil level (see *Daily (pre-ride) checks*). If the level is correct, check the operation of the oil pressure switch (see Section 19).

ABS indicator light

58 Refer to Chapter 7, Section 16 for checking procedures.

17 Instrument and warning light bulbs (X, Y, K1 and K2 models only)

Note: *On K3-on models, the individual instrument and warning LEDs are integral with the instrument cluster circuit board –separate components are not available.*

SV650 models

1 Remove the instrument cluster (see Sec-tion 15).

2 Undo the instrument shell screws and remove the shells **(see illustrations 16.8a and b)** – the meter illumination bulbs are now accessible. To access the warning light bulbs, go on to undo the rear cover screws and remove the cover **(see illustration 16.8c)**. Unscrew the mounting bracket nuts and remove the washers, then remove the bracket **(see illustration 16.8d)**.

3 Carefully pull the bulbholder out of the instrument cluster, then pull the bulb out of the bulbholder **(see illustrations)**. If the socket contacts are dirty or corroded, scrape them clean and spray with electrical contact cleaner before a new bulb is installed.

4 Make sure the new bulb is of the correct wattage (see Specifications). Carefully fit the new bulb into the holder, then fit the holder into the housing.

5 Assemble and install the instrument cluster in a reverse of the disassembly and removal procedure.

SV650S models

6 Remove the instrument cluster (see Sec-tion 15). The meter illumination bulbs are behind the small rubber access panels, and the warning light bulbs are behind the large panel **(see illustration)**. Remove the panel(s) as required.

7 Turn the bulbholder anti-clockwise and draw it out of the circuit board **(see illustration)**.

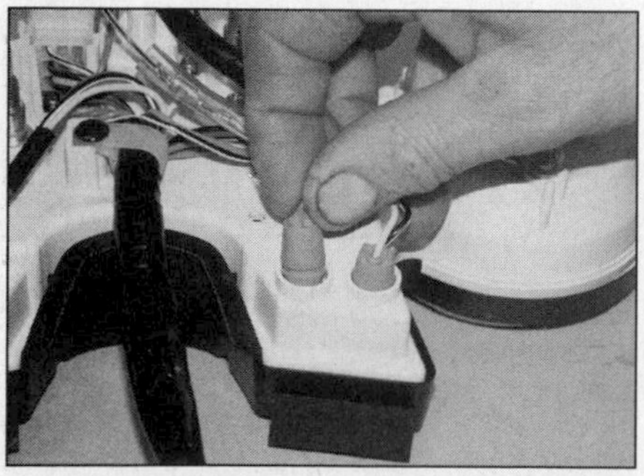

17.3a Carefully pull the bulbholder out of the instrument cluster . . .

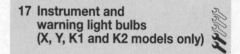

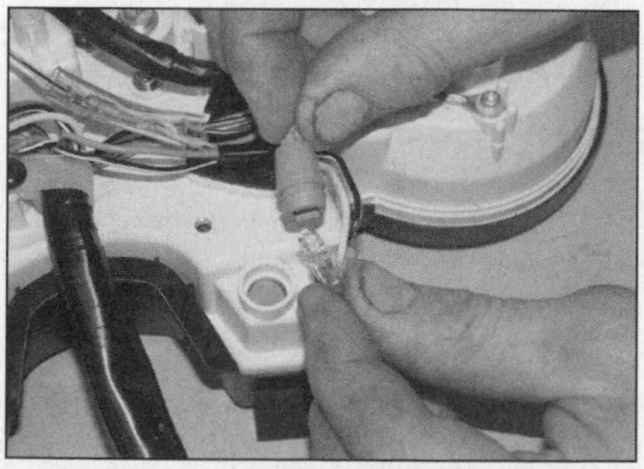

17.3b . . . then pull the bulb out of the holder

Pull the bulb out of the holder. If the socket contacts are dirty or corroded, scrape them clean and spray with electrical contact cleaner before a new bulb is installed.

8 Make sure the new bulb is of the correct wattage (see Specifications). Carefully fit the new bulb into the holder, then fit the holder into the housing and turn it clockwise to secure it in place.

9 Fit the rubber panel(s), then install the instrument cluster.

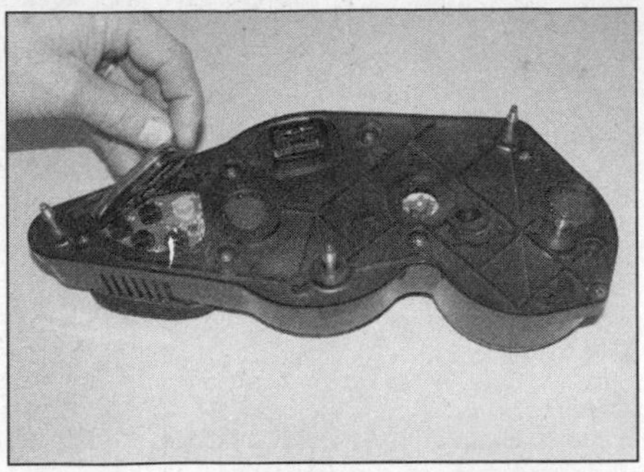

17.6 Remove the relevant rubber access panel . . .

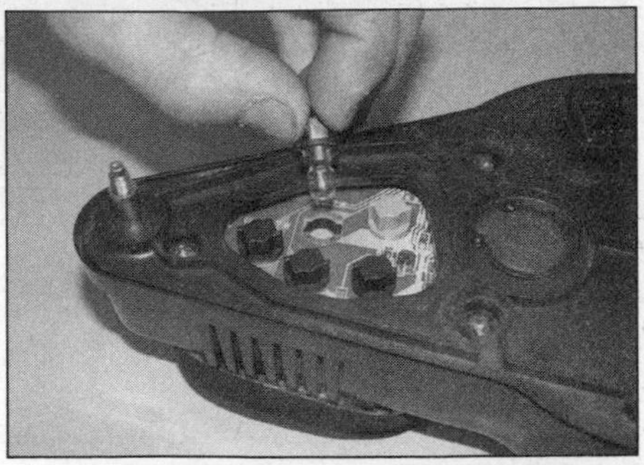

17.7 . . . then remove the bulbholder

18 Speed sensor

Check

Note: *To check the sensor you need four 1.5 V dry cell batteries, a 1 K-ohm resistor, a voltmeter, some wire to make a circuit, a soldering iron and some small crocodile clips.*

1 On SV650 models, refer to Section 8, Steps 1 and 2 and remove the headlight from the shell. Trace the wiring from the speed sensor, located on the left-hand side of the front wheel, and disconnect it at the connector **(see illustration)**.

2 On SV650S models, remove the air filter housing (see Chapter 4A or 4B as applicable). Trace the wiring from the speed sensor, located on the left-hand side of the front wheel, and disconnect it at the connector **(see illustration)**.

3 Place the motorcycle on an auxiliary stand and raise the front wheel off the ground using a jack and piece of wood under the engine.

4 Rig up the batteries, resistor and voltmeter (see **Note** above) as shown in the circuit, and connect to the speed sensor wiring connector **(see illustration)**.

5 Turn the front wheel in its normal direction of rotation and observe the voltmeter. The reading should alternate between zero and 6.0 volts as the wheel spins. If it doesn't, renew the sensor (see below).

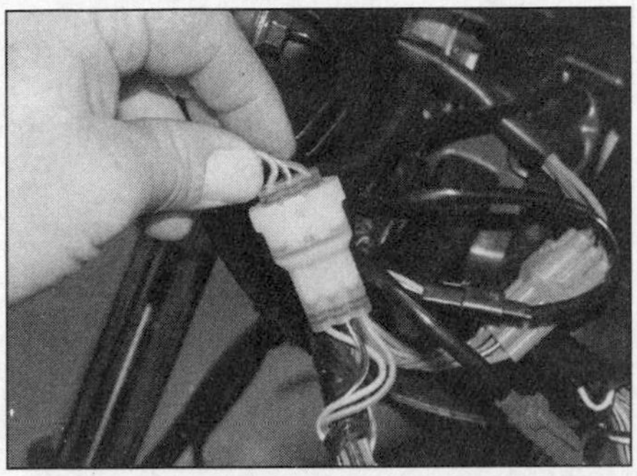

18.1 Speed sensor wiring connector - SV650

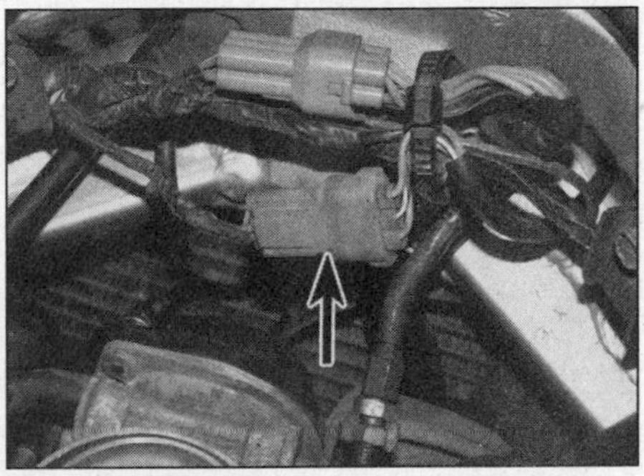

18.2 Speed sensor wiring connector (arrowed) - SV650S

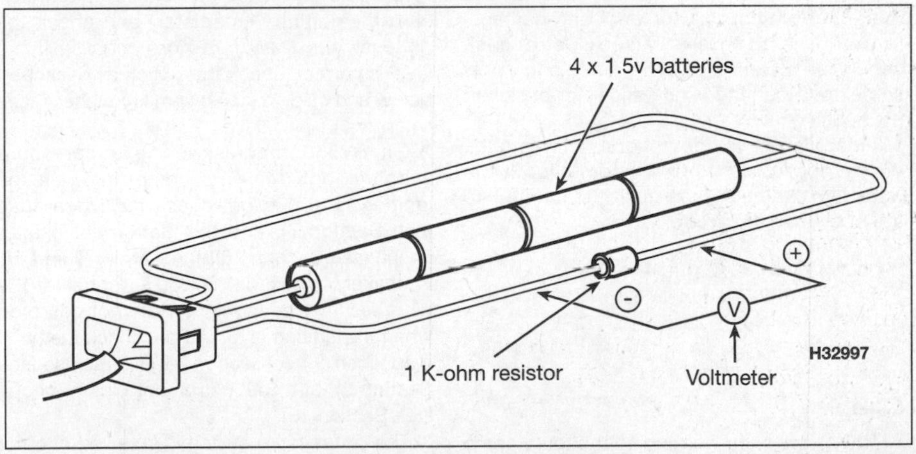

18.4 Speed sensor test set-up

Renewal

6 On SV650 models, refer to Section 8, Steps 1 and 2 and remove the headlight from the shell. Trace the wiring from the speed sensor, located on the left-hand side of the front wheel, and disconnect it at the connector **(see illustration 18.1)**.

7 On SV650S models, remove the air filter housing (see Chapter 4A or 4B as applicable). Trace the wiring from the speed sensor, located on the left-hand side of the front wheel, and disconnect it at the connector **(see illustration 18.2)**.

8 Remove the front wheel (see Chapter 7).

9 Release the speed sensor wiring from the clamps on the front fork, noting its routing **(see illustration)**. On X, Y, K1 and K2 models, spread the pegs of the sensor wiring trim clip from the underside of the mudguard, then push the centre up through the mudguard and draw the clip out of the top **(see illustrations)**. Remove the sensor.

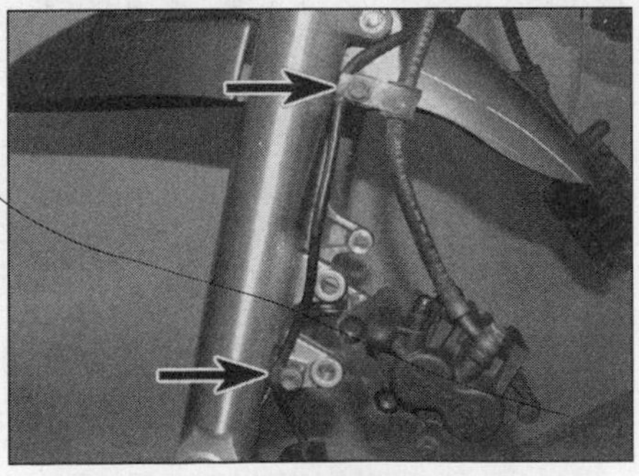

18.9a Release the wiring from the front fork

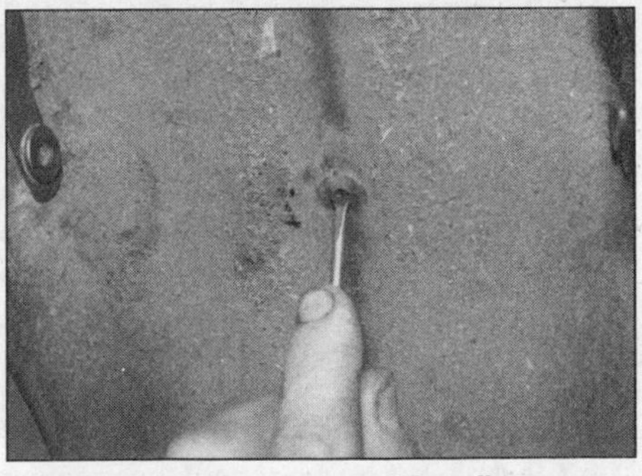

18.9b Push the centre of the clip up . . .

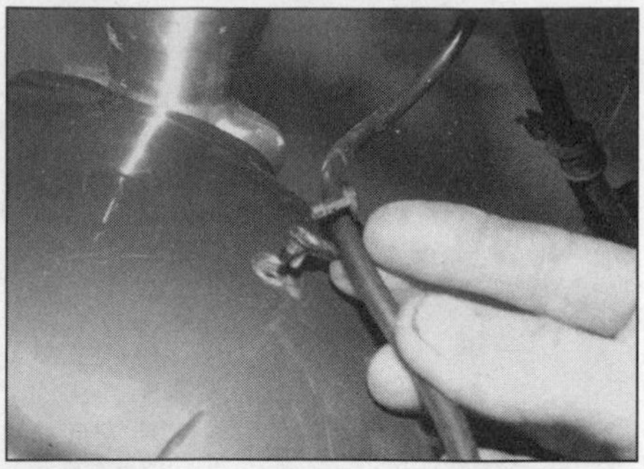

18.9c . . . then draw the clip out of the mudguard

18.10a Remove the rotor and ring . . .

18.10b . . . and check the seal (arrowed)

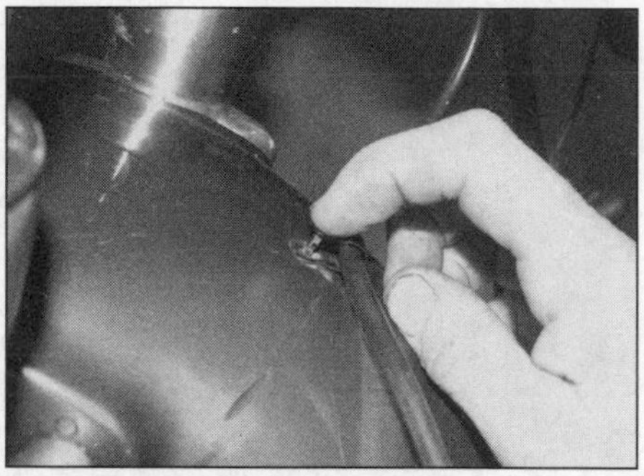

18.11 Fit the body into the mudguard, then press the centre into the body

10 Remove the rotor and ring from the sensor housing and check them and the seal around the rim of the housing for wear and damage, renewing them if necessary **(see illustrations)**. Otherwise clean off all old grease and apply some new, then fit the ring and rotor back into the housing.

11 Installation is the reverse of removal. Where applicable, to fit the trim clip, fit the body into the hole, then push the centre into the body **(see illustration)**.

19 Oil pressure switch

Check

1 The oil pressure warning light should come on when the ignition (main) switch is turned ON and extinguish a few seconds after the engine is started. If the oil pressure warning light comes on whilst the engine is running, stop the engine immediately and check the oil level (see *Daily (pre-ride) checks*). If the level is correct, check the switch as described below and carry out an oil pressure check (see Chapter 1).

2 On SV650 models, if the oil pressure warning light does not come on when the ignition is turned on, check the signal fuse (see Section 5), and the instrument cluster circuit (see Section 16); the warning light LED is unlikely to fail. On SV650S, models if the oil pressure warning light does not come on when the ignition is turned on, check the bulb, if applicable (see Section 17), signal fuse (see Section 5), and the instrument cluster circuit (see Section 16).

3 The oil pressure switch is screwed into the front of the engine on the right-hand side. Pull the rubber cover off the switch and remove the screw securing the wiring connector **(see illustration)**. With the ignition switched ON, earth (ground) the wire on the crankcase and check that the warning light comes on. If the light comes on, the switch is defective and must be renewed.

19.3 Pull back the rubber boot then remove the terminal screw and detach the wiring

4 If the light still does not come on, check for voltage at the wire terminal. If there is no voltage present, check the wire between the switch, the instrument cluster and fusebox for continuity (see the *Wiring diagrams* at the end of the Chapter).

5 If the warning light comes on whilst the engine is running, yet the oil pressure is satisfactory, remove the wire from the oil pressure switch. With the wire detached and the ignition switched ON the light should be out. If it is illuminated, the wire between the switch and instrument cluster must be earthed (grounded) at some point. If the wiring is good, the switch must be assumed faulty and renewed.

Removal

6 Drain the engine oil (see Chapter 1). The oil pressure switch is screwed into the front of the engine on the right-hand side.

7 Pull the rubber cover off the switch, then undo the screw securing the wiring connector.

8 Unscrew the oil pressure switch and withdraw it from the crankcase.

Installation

9 Apply a suitable sealant (such as Suzuki Bond 1207B or equivalent) to the upper portion of the switch threads near the switch body, leaving the bottom half of thread clean. Install the switch and tighten it to the torque setting specified at the beginning of the Chapter.

10 Attach the wiring connector and secure it with the screw, then fit the rubber cover.

11 Replenish the engine with oil (see Chap-ter 1). Run the engine and check that the switch operates correctly without leakage.

20 Ignition (main) switch

Warning: To prevent the risk of short circuits, disconnect the battery negative (–ve) lead before making any ignition (main) switch checks.

Check

1 On X, Y, K1 and K2 SV650 models, refer to Section 8, Steps 1 and 2 and remove the headlight from the shell. Trace the wiring from the ignition switch and disconnect it at the connector **(see illustration)**.

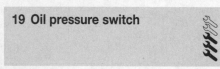

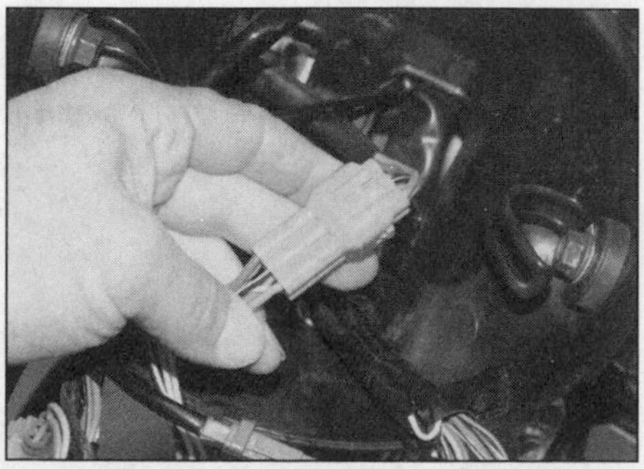

20.1 Ignition switch wiring connector – SV650

2 On K3-on SV650 models and all SV650S models, remove the air filter housing (see Chapter 4A or 4B as applicable). Trace the wiring from the ignition switch and disconnect it at the connector **(see illustration)**.

3 Using an ohmmeter or a continuity tester,

check the continuity of the connector terminal pairs (see the *Wiring diagrams* at the end of the Chapter). Continuity should exist between the terminals connected by a solid line on the diagram when the switch is in the indicated position.

4 If the switch fails any of the tests, renew it.

Removal

5 Disconnect the battery negative (-ve) lead.

6 On X, Y, K1 and K2 SV650 models, remove the headlight assembly (see Section 8). Release the ignition switch wiring from any clips or ties and disconnect the switch wiring at the connector.

7 On K3-on SV650 models and all SV650S models, remove the air filter housing (see Chapter 4A or 4B as applicable). Trace the wiring from the ignition switch and disconnect it at the connector. Release the wiring from any clips or ties. Remove the headlight assembly (see Section 8).

8 Unscrew the two Torx bolts securing the switch and withdraw it from the top yoke **(see illustration)**.

Installation

9 Installation is the reverse of removal. If reusing the old Torx bolts, apply a suitable non-permanent thread locking compound to their threads and tighten them securely. Note that new bolts are already pre-treated with thread locking compound. Make sure the wiring connectors are securely connected and correctly routed. Reconnect the battery negative (-ve) lead.

21 Handlebar switches – check

1 Generally speaking, the switches are reliable and trouble-free. Most troubles, when they do occur, are caused by dirty or corroded contacts, but wear and breakage of internal parts is a possibility that should not be overlooked. If breakage does occur, the entire switch and related wiring harness will have to be replaced with a new one, as individual parts are not available.

2 The switches can be checked for continuity using an ohmmeter or a continuity test light. Always disconnect the battery negative (–ve) lead, which will prevent the possibility of a short circuit, before making the checks.

3 On SV650 models, raise the fuel tank (see Chapter 4A or 4B). Trace the wiring from the switch being tested and disconnect it at the connector.

4 On SV650S models, remove the fairing (see Chapter 8). Trace the wiring from the switch being tested and disconnect it at the connector.

5 Check for continuity between the terminals of the switch connector with the switch in the various positions (i.e. switch off – no continuity, switch on – continuity) – see the *Wiring diagrams* at the end of the Chapter. Continuity should exist between the terminals connected by a solid line on the diagram when the switch is in the indicated position.

6 If the continuity check indicates a problem exists, refer to Section 22, displace the switch housing and spray the switch contacts with electrical contact cleaner (there is no need to remove the switch completely). If they are accessible, the contacts can be scraped clean with a knife or polished with crocus cloth. If switch components are damaged or broken, it will be obvious when the switch is disassembled.

22 Handlebar switches – removal and installation

Removal

1 On SV650 models, if the switch is to be removed from the bike, rather than just displaced from the handlebar, raise the fuel tank (see Chapter 4A or 4B as applicable). Trace the wiring from the switch being removed and disconnect it at the connector. Work back along the harness, freeing it from any clips and ties, noting its correct routing.

2 On SV650S models, if the switch is to be removed from the bike, rather than just displaced from the handlebar, remove the fairing (see Chapter 8). Trace the wiring from the switch being removed and disconnect it at the connector. Work back along the harness, freeing it from any clips and ties, noting its correct routing.

3 Disconnect the wiring from the brake light switch (if removing the right-hand switch) or the clutch switch (if removing the left-hand switch) **(see illustration 14.2 or 25.2)**.

4 To remove the right-hand switch, refer to Chapter 4A or 4B for throttle cable removal and to remove the left-hand switch, refer to Chapter 4A for choke cable removal (X, Y, K1 and K2 models). Note in each case you do not need to detach the cables from the carburettors or throttle body assembly, though you may need to access the adjusters at the lower end to create enough slack to detach them from the twistgrip.

Installation

5 Installation is the reverse of removal. Make sure the locating pin in the switch housing locates in the hole in the handlebar.

23 Neutral/gear position switch

Check

1 Before checking the electrical circuit, check the bulb where applicable (see Section 17), signal fuse (see Section 5), and the instrument cluster circuit (see Section 16).

2 The switch is located in the left-hand side of

20.2 Ignition switch wiring connector (arrowed) – SV650S

20.8 Ignition switch bolts (arrowed)

23.2 Neutral/gear position switch (arrowed)

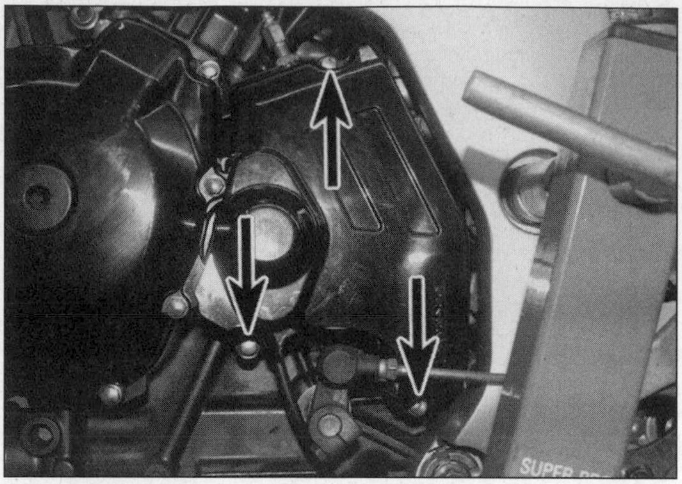
23.7 Unscrew the bolts (arrowed) and remove the cover

the crankcase below the front sprocket **(see illustration)**. Raise the fuel tank (see Chapter 4A or 4B as applicable). Trace the wiring from the switch and disconnect it at the connector. Make sure the transmission is in neutral.

3 With the connector disconnected and the ignition switch ON, the neutral light should be out. If not, the wire between the connector and instrument cluster must be earthed (grounded) at some point.

4 Check for continuity between the blue wire terminal on the switch side of the connector and the black/white (earth/ground) wire terminal. With the transmission in neutral, there should be continuity. With the transmission in gear, there should be no continuity. If the tests prove otherwise, then the switch is faulty.

5 On X, Y, K1 and K2 models, if the continuity tests prove the switch is good, check for voltage at the blue wire terminal on the loom side of the connector with the ignition switch ON. If there's no voltage present, check the wire between the switch, and the instrument cluster via the diodes (see the *Wiring diagrams* at the end of the Chapter). If no faults are found check the diodes (see Section 26).

6 On K3-on models, check the gear position function of the switch as follows. Support the machine upright on an auxiliary stand with the side stand up. Ensure the wiring connector is securely connected. Using a multimeter set to the volts scale, backprobe the pink and black wire terminals on the loom side of the connector and turn the ignition (main) switch ON. Select 1st gear and note the voltage between the wire terminals, then select 2nd to 6th gear in sequence, noting the voltage in each gear. Compare the readings with those shown below. If the results are not as described it is likely that the gear position switch is faulty and must be renewed.

Gear	Voltage (approx)
1st	1.36V
2nd	1.77V
3rd	2.49V
4th	3.23V
5th	4.10V
6th	4.55V

23.9a Undo the screws and remove the switch

23.9b Remove the plungers and springs for safekeeping

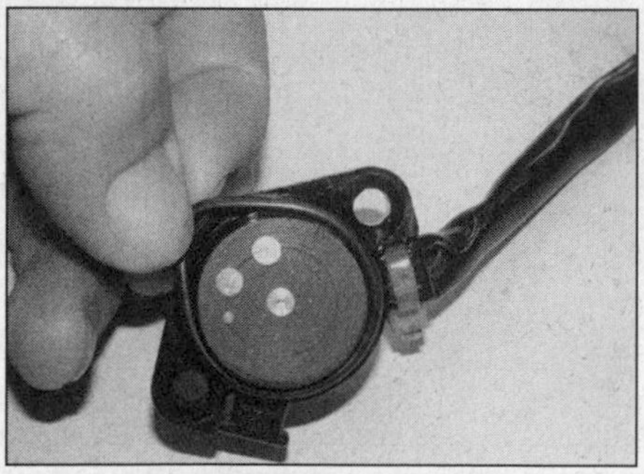
23.10a Fit a new O-ring onto the switch . . .

23.10b . . . and fit it into the crankcase

Removal

7 The switch is located in the left-hand side of the crankcase below the front sprocket. Drain the engine oil (see Chapter 1). Unscrew the front sprocket cover bolts and remove the cover **(see illustration)**.

8 Raise the fuel tank (see Chapter 4A or 4B as applicable). Trace the wiring from the switch and disconnect it at the connector. Free the wiring from any guides or ties, noting its routing.

9 Clean the chain grease and road dirt from the switch area. Undo the switch screws and withdraw it from the crankcase **(see illustration)**. Discard the O-ring as a new one should be used **(see illustration 23.9a)**. Note the contact plungers in the end of the selector drum and remove them with their springs for safekeeping if required **(see illustration)**.

Installation

10 If removed, fit the springs and contact plungers into their bores in the end of the selector drum. Install the switch using a new O-ring smeared with grease and tighten the screws **(see illustrations)**.

11 Route the wiring as noted on removal and connect the wiring connector. Check the operation of the neutral light.

12 Replenish the engine oil (see Chapter 1). Lower the fuel tank and install the sprocket cover.

24 Sidestand switch, relay and diodes

1 The sidestand switch is mounted on the frame behind the sidestand. The switch is part of the safety circuit which prevents or stops the engine running if the transmission is in gear whilst the sidestand is down, and prevents the engine from starting if the transmission is in gear unless the sidestand is up. The sidestand switch relay and diode, and the neutral/gear position switch diode, are integrated into one component with the turn signal relay **(see illustration 24.4)**.

Check

2 Before checking the electrical circuit, check the ignition fuse (see Section 5).

3 To check the switch, raise the fuel tank (see Chapter 4A or 4B). Trace the wiring back from the switch and disconnect it at the wiring connector **(see illustration)**. Connect an ohmmeter or continuity tester between the terminals on the switch side of the wiring connector. With the sidestand up there should be continuity (zero resistance) between the terminals, and with the stand down there should be no continuity (infinite resistance). If the switch does not perform as expected, it is faulty and must be renewed.

4 To access the relay/diode unit, remove the rider's seat on X, Y, K1 and K2 models or the passenger's seat on K3 models onwards (see Chapter 8). The relay/diode unit is next to the fusebox and plugs into a socket in the tray **(see illustration 11.2a)**. Pull the relay/diode unit out of its socket **(see illustration 11.2b)**. Note that on ABS equipped K7-on models, the relay is located in the base of the battery carrier, below the rubber mat. To check the relay, set a multimeter to the ohms x 1 scale and connect it across the unit's D and E terminals as shown **(see illustration)**. There should be no continuity. Using a fully-charged 12 volt battery and two insulated jumper wires, connect the positive (+ve) terminal of the battery to terminal D, and the negative (–ve) terminal to terminal C. At this point the relay should be heard to click and the multimeter read zero ohms (continuity). If this is the case the relay is proved good. If the relay does not click when battery voltage is applied and indicates no continuity (infinite resistance) across its terminals, it is faulty and the unit must be renewed.

5 The diodes allow current flow in one direction only. To check the diodes, first connect the positive (+ve) probe of an ohmmeter or continuity tester to the C terminal on the unit and the negative (-ve)

24.3 Sidestand switch wiring connector (arrowed)

probe to the A terminal **(see illustration 24.4)**. There should be continuity. Now reverse the probes. There should be no continuity. Repeat the test between the B terminal and the A terminal. The same results should be achieved. In either test, if there is continuity in both directions, or no continuity in either direction, the diodes are faulty and the unit must be renewed.

6 If the switch and relay/diode unit are good, check for battery voltage at terminal D in the relay socket with the ignition ON, the transmission in neutral and the engine STOP switch in the RUN position. Turn the ignition OFF when the check is complete. If no voltage was present, check the wiring from the socket to the ignition (main) switch (via the fusebox) for voltage and continuity. If the voltage is good, check the wiring and connectors between the various components in the starter safety circuit using a continuity tester, and check the other components themselves (see the *Wiring diagrams* at the end of the Chapter).

Renewal

7 The sidestand switch is mounted on the frame behind the sidestand. Raise the fuel tank (see Chapter 4A or 4B as applicable). Trace the wiring back from the switch and disconnect it at the wiring connector. Work back along the switch wiring, freeing it from any clips and ties, noting its routing.

8 Unscrew the two bolts securing the switch and remove it, noting how it fits **(see illustrations)**. Fit the new switch onto the

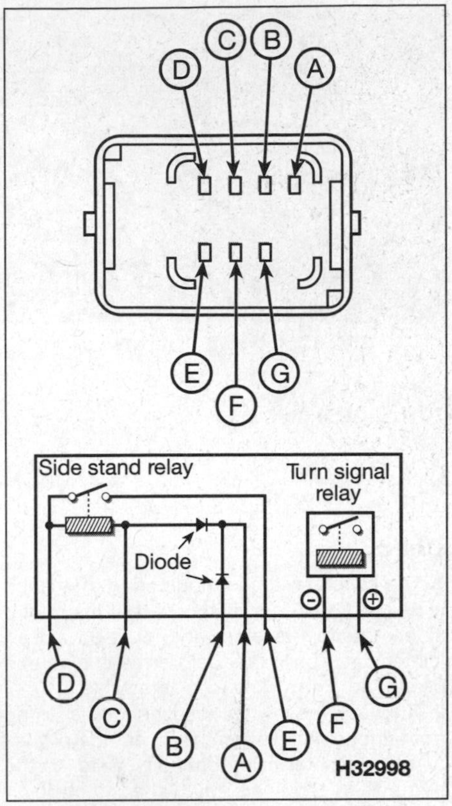

24.4 Relay/diode unit terminal identification and circuit diagram

bracket, making sure the plunger locates correctly against the sidestand when it is raised. Secure the switch with the bolts and tighten them securely. Make sure the wiring is correctly routed up to the connector and retained by any clips and ties, then reconnect the wiring connector.

9 Check the operation of the switch.

10 To access the relay, remove the rider's seat (see Chapter 8). The relay is integrated into one component with the turn signal relay and diode circuit and is next to the fusebox and plugs into a socket in the tray **(see illustration 11.2a)**. Pull the relay/diode unit out of its socket and renew it **(see illustration 11.2b)**.

24.8a Sidestand switch bolts (arrowed) – X, Y, K1 and K2 models

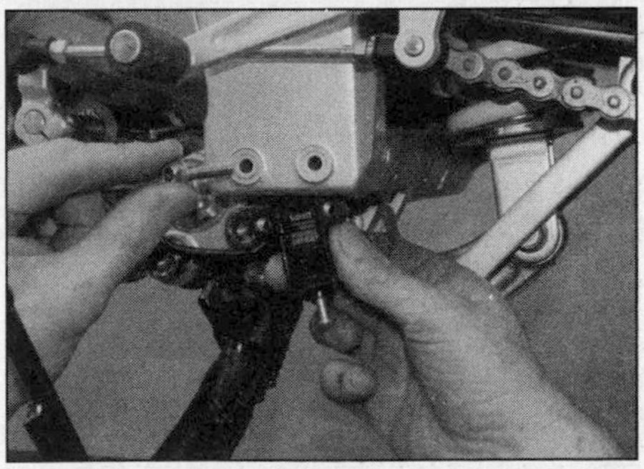

24.8b Remove the sidestand switch – K3-on models

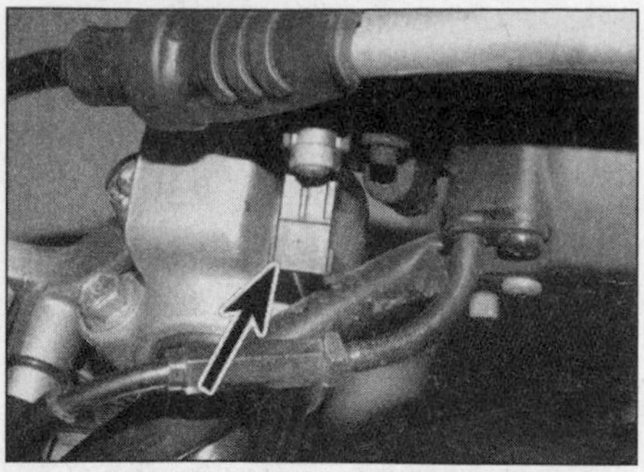

25.2 Clutch switch (arrowed)

25 Clutch switch

Check

1 The clutch switch is mounted in the clutch lever bracket. The switch is part of the starter safety interlock system and must be closed (clutch lever pulled in) before the engine can be started. The switch isn't adjustable.

2 To check the switch, disconnect the wiring from it **(see illustration)**. Connect the probes of an ohmmeter or a continuity tester to the two switch terminals. With the clutch lever pulled in, there should be continuity (zero resistance). With the clutch lever out, there should be no continuity (infinite resistance).

3 If the switch is good, check the other components in the starter circuit as described in the relevant sections of this Chapter. Note that on X, Y, K1 and K2 models, a diode is fitted in the switch circuit (see Section 26). If all components are good, check the wiring between the various components (see the *Wiring diagrams* at the end of this book).

Renewal

4 The clutch switch is mounted on the clutch lever bracket.

5 Disconnect the wiring from the switch. Undo the screws securing the switch to the bracket and remove the switch, noting how it fits.

6 Installation is the reverse of removal.

26 Clutch switch diode (X, Y, K1 and K2 models)

1 The clutch switch diode is part of the starter safety interlock system (see Section 1). The diode plugs into a connector in the wiring loom behind the seat cowling on the right-hand side **(see illustration)**. Refer to the relevant wiring diagram at the end of the Chapter for details.

2 To access the diode, first remove the seat cowling (see Chapter 8), then unwind the insulating tape from around the diode and unplug it from the connector **(see illustration 26.1)**.

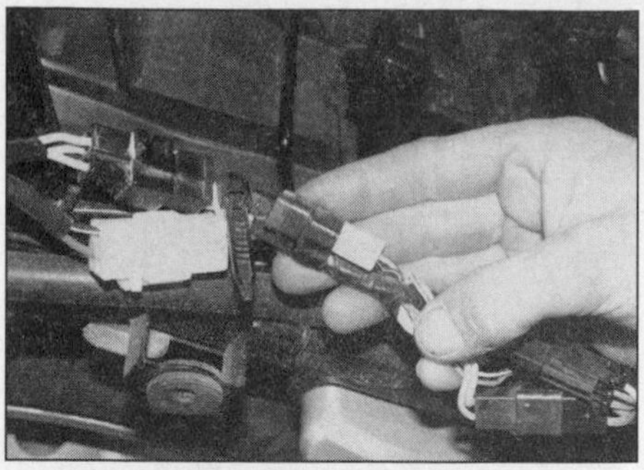

26.1 The clutch switch diode plugs into the loom – X, Y, K1 and K2 models only

3 The diode allows current flow in one direction only. To check the diode, first connect the positive (+ve) probe of an ohmmeter or continuity tester to the black/white wire terminal on the diode and the negative (-ve) probe to the yellow/green terminal. There should be continuity. Now reverse the probes. There should be no continuity. If it doesn't behave as stated, renew the diode. Wrap

4 Ensure the diode is securely plugged into its connector and wrap insulating tape around it to secure it in the wiring loom.

5 If the diode is good, check the other components in the starter circuit as described in the relevant sections of this Chapter. If all components are good, check the wiring between the various components (see the *Wiring diagrams* at the end of the Chapter).

27 Horn

Check

1 On X, Y, K1 and K2 models, the horn is mounted in front of the radiator. On K3-on models, the horn is mounted on the back of the radiator. On X, Y, K1 and K2 SV650S models, remove the left-hand fairing side panel (see Chapter 8).

2 Unplug the wiring connectors from the horn **(see illustration)**. Using two jumper wires, apply battery voltage directly to the terminals on the horn. If the horn doesn't sound, renew it.

3 If the horn sounds, check the switch (see

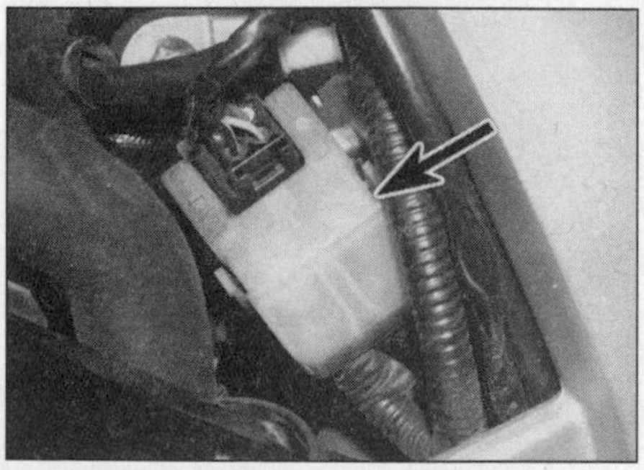

28.2a Starter relay (arrowed) – X, Y, K1 and K2 models

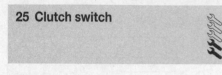

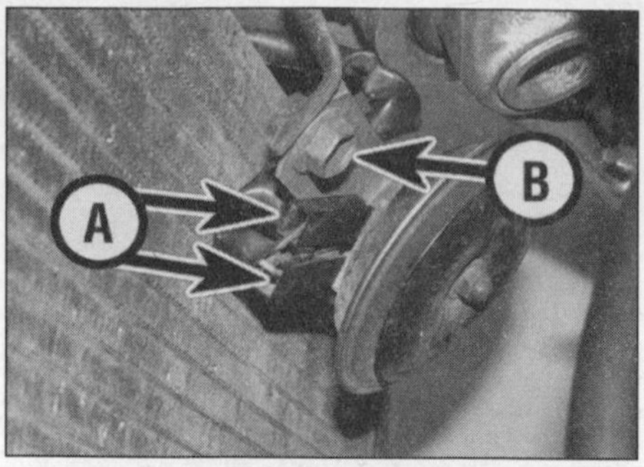

27.2 Horn wiring connectors (A) and mounting bolt (B)

Section 21). Also check for voltage at the orange/green wire connector with the ignition ON, noting that on K3, K4 and K5 models, the horn button must be pressed to complete the circuit. If no voltage was present, check the orange/green wire and the connectors for faults (see the *Wiring diagrams* at the end of the Chapter).

4 If voltage is present, check the other wire for continuity to earth, noting that on X, Y, K1 and K2 models, the horn button must be pressed to complete the circuit. If no continuity was present, locate the fault by systematically working along the circuit (use the wiring diagrams) checking where the continuity breaks down.

Renewal

5 On X, Y, K1 and K2 models, the horn is mounted in front of the radiator. On K3-on models, the horn is mounted on the back of the radiator. On X, Y, K1 and K2 SV650S models, remove the left-hand fairing side panel (see Chapter 8).

6 Unplug the wiring connectors from the horn **(see illustration 27.2)**. Unscrew the bolt securing the horn to its bracket and remove it from the bike.

7 Installation is the reverse of removal. Ensure that the wiring connectors are secure and check that the horn works before riding the motorcycle.

28 Starter relay

Check

1 If the starter circuit is faulty, first check the ignition fuse in the fusebox (see Section 5).

2 On X, Y, K1 and K2 models, the starter relay is behind the right-hand side panel **(see illustration)**. Remove the panel for access (see Chapter 8). On K3-on models, the starter relay is underneath the rider's seat **(see illustration)**.

3 Disconnect the battery negative (–ve) terminal (see Section 3).

4 Lift the insulating cover off the relay and disconnect the wiring connector **(see illustration)**. Unscrew the bolts securing the

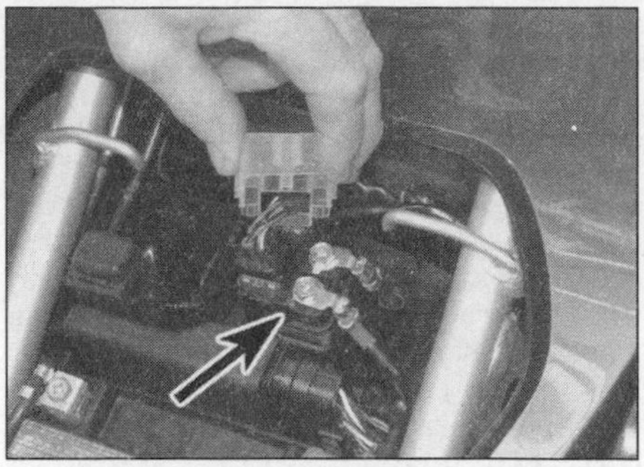

28.2b Starter relay (arrowed) – K3-on models

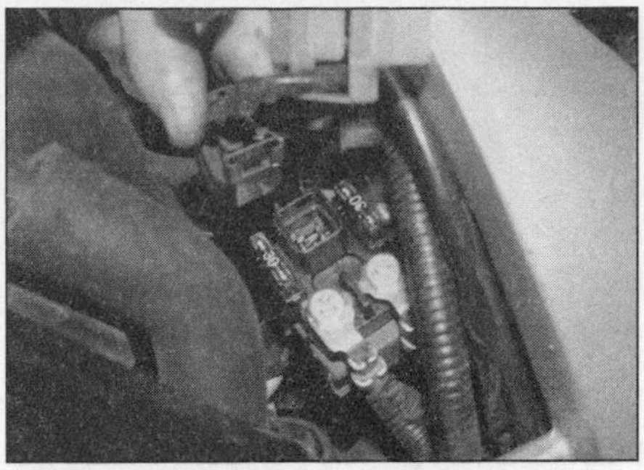

28.4a Disconnect the wiring connector

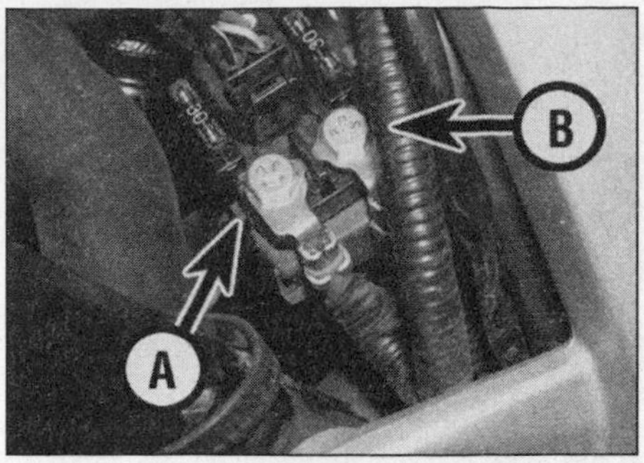

28.4b Starter relay battery lead (A) and starter motor lead (B)

starter motor and battery leads to the relay and detach the leads **(see illustration)**. Move the relay to the bench for testing.

5 Connect a multimeter set to the ohms scale across the relay's starter motor and battery terminals – no continuity should be shown. Now connect a 12V battery across the relay's coil terminals – continuity should now be shown on the meter and the relay should be heard to click **(see illustration)**.

Caution: Do not connect the battery for more than five seconds or the coil may be damaged.

6 If no continuity is shown in the test described above, connect a multimeter set to the ohms x 1 scale across the relay's coil wire terminals **(see illustration)**. The coil resistance should be as specified at the beginning of this Chapter. If no continuity (infinite resistance) is shown, the relay is confirmed faulty and should be renewed.

7 If the relay is good, check for continuity in the main lead from the battery to the relay. Also check that the terminals and connectors at each end of the lead are tight and corrosion-free. Next check the wiring between the relay wiring connector and the other components in the starter circuit, including the starter button in the right-hand handlebar switch and the clutch switch, as described in the relevant sections of this Chapter. If all components are good, check the wiring and connectors between the various components (see the *Wiring diagrams* at the end of this book).

Renewal

8 Follow the appropriate procedure in Step 2 to access the starter relay.

9 Disconnect the battery negative (–ve) terminal (see Section 3).

10 Lift the insulating cover off the relay and disconnect the wiring connector. Unscrew the bolts securing the starter motor and battery leads to the relay and detach the leads. Remove the relay with its rubber sleeve from its mounting lug on the frame. Remove the main and spare fuses, and remove the relay from its sleeve.

11 Installation is the reverse of removal. Make sure the terminal bolts are securely tightened. Do not forget to fit the main and spare fuses into the relay. Connect the negative (–ve) lead last when reconnecting the battery.

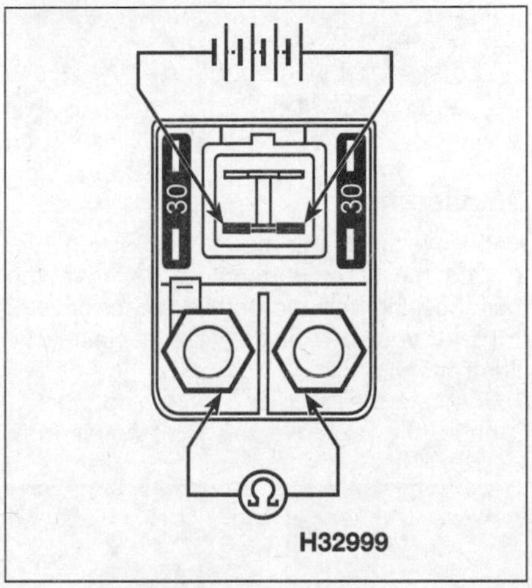

28.5 Starter relay test set-up

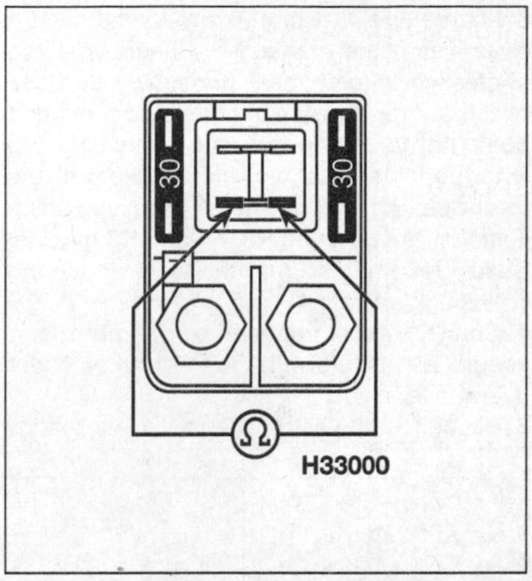

28.6 Measuring the starter relay coil resistance

29 Starter motor – removal and installation

Removal

1 Disconnect the battery negative (–ve) lead (see Section 3). The starter motor is mounted on the front of the engine above the oil filter.

2 Peel back the rubber terminal cover on the starter motor **(see illustration)**. Unscrew the nut securing the starter lead to the motor and detach the lead.

29.2 Pull back the terminal cover then unscrew the nut and detach the lead

3 Unscrew the two bolts securing the starter motor to the crankcase, noting the wiring clip secured by the lower bolt **(see illustration)**. Slide the starter motor out and remove it **(see illustration)**

4 Remove the O-ring on the end of the starter motor and discard it as a new one must be used.

Installation

5 Fit a new O-ring smeared with grease onto the end of the starter motor, making sure it is seated in its groove **(see illustration)**.

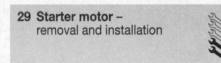

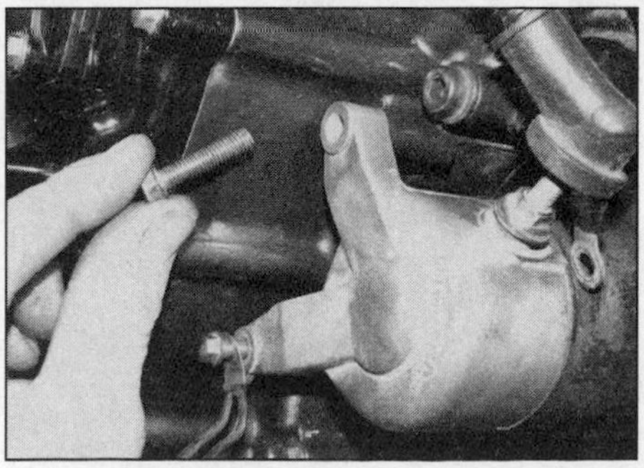

29.3a Unscrew the two bolts . . .

29.3b . . . and slide the starter motor out of the crankcase

6 Manoeuvre the motor into position and slide it into the crankcase. Ensure that the starter motor teeth mesh correctly with those of the starter drive gear. Install the mounting bolts, not forgetting to secure the wiring clip with the lower bolt, and tighten them to the torque setting specified at the beginning of the Chapter. Note that on K3, K4 and K5 models, Suzuki recommend that the lower mounting bolt is tightened first.

7 Connect the starter lead to the motor and secure it with the nut. Fit the rubber cover over the terminal.

8 Reconnect the battery negative (–ve) lead.

29.5 Fit a new O-ring smeared with grease

30 Starter motor – disassembly, inspection and reassembly

Disassembly

1 Remove the starter motor (see Section 29).

2 Note the alignment marks between the main housing and the front and rear covers, or make your own if they aren't clear **(see illustration)**.

3 Unscrew the two long bolts, noting the O-rings, then remove the front cover from the motor along with its sealing ring **(see illustrations)**. Discard the sealing ring as a new one must be used. Remove the tabbed washer from the cover and slide the insulating washer and shim(s) from the front end of the armature, noting the number of shims and their correct fitted order **(see illustrations)**.

4 Remove the rear cover from the motor along with its sealing ring. Discard the sealing ring as a new one must be used. Remove the shim(s) from the rear end of the armature noting how many and their correct fitted positions **(see illustration 30.17a)**.

5 Withdraw the armature from the main housing, noting that it will be held by the pull of the magnets **(see illustration)**.

6 Noting the correct fitted location of each component, unscrew the nut from the terminal bolt and remove the plain washer, the one large and two small insulating washers and the rubber O-ring **(see illustration)**. Remove the brushplate assembly and terminal bolt from the rear cover, noting how it locates, and recover the insulator **(see illustrations)**.

7 Move each brush spring end off its brush and slide the brushes out **(see illustration)**.

Inspection

8 The parts of the starter motor that are most likely to require attention are the brushes.

30.2 Note the alignment marks, or make your own

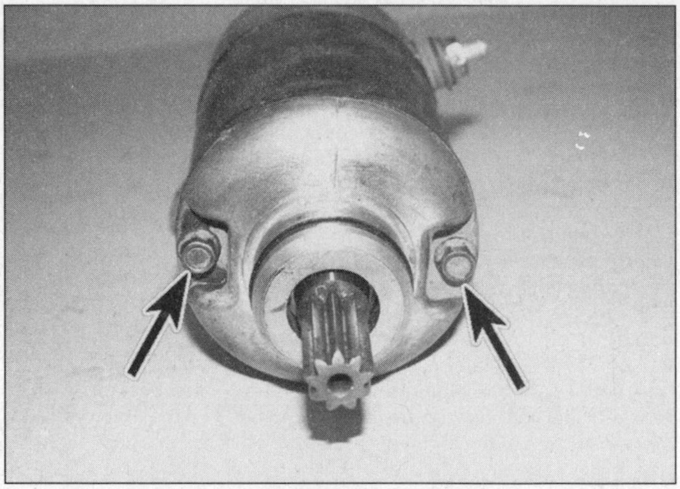

30.3a Unscrew and remove the two bolts (arrowed) . . .

30.3b . . . then remove the front cover and sealing ring (arrowed)

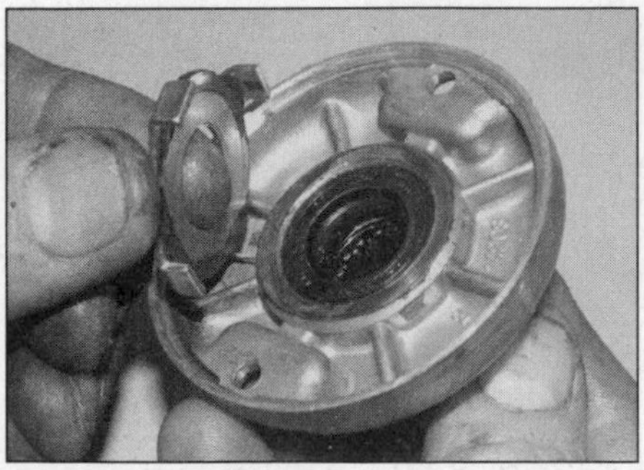

30.3c Remove the tabbed washer . . .

30.3d . . . and the shims

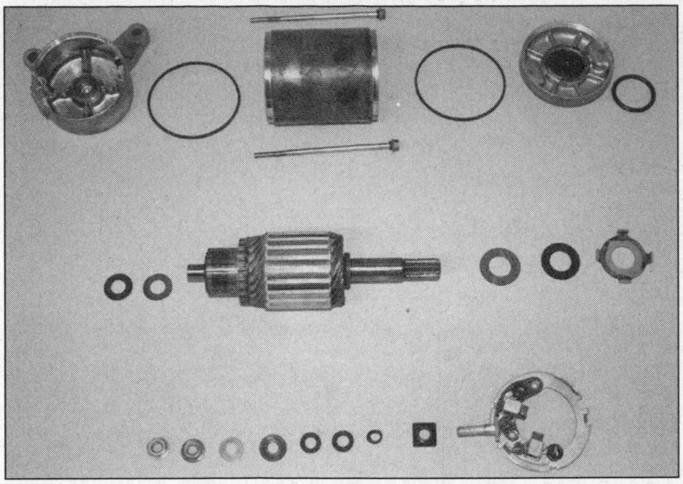

30.5 Starter motor components

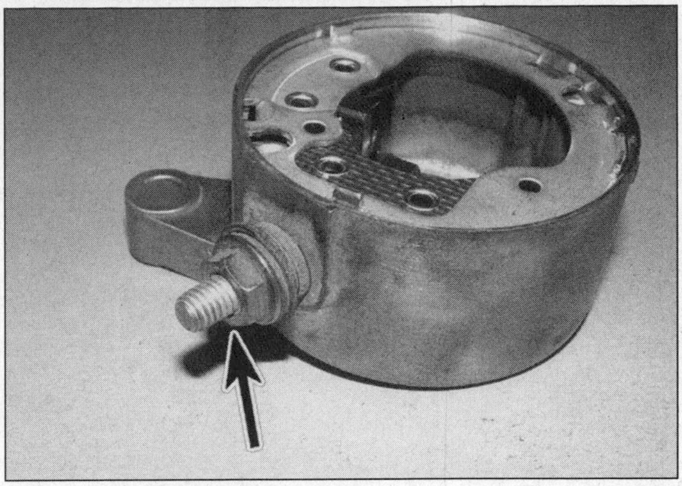

30.6a Unscrew the nut (arrowed) and remove the large and small insulating washers and the O-ring

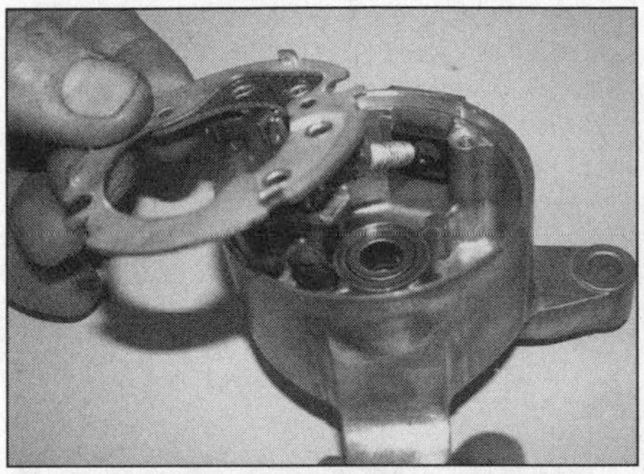

30.6b Remove the brushplate assembly . . .

30.6c . . . and the insulator

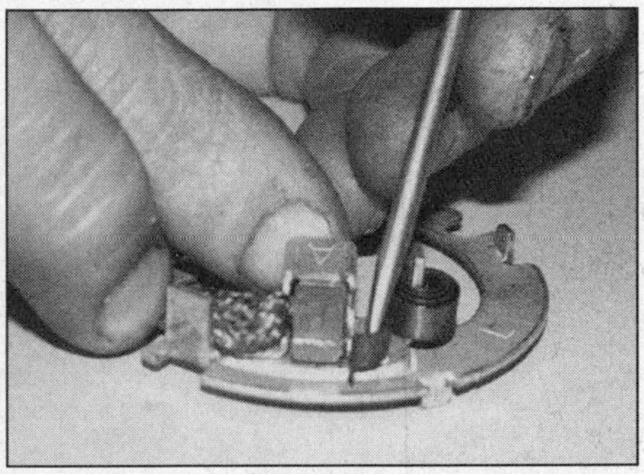

30.7 Move the spring end aside and withdraw the brush

Suzuki give no measurements or wear limits, but if the brushes are worn down to approximately 8 mm, or are damaged, renew the brushplate assembly **(see illustration)**.

9 Inspect the commutator bars on the armature for scoring, scratches and discoloration **(see illustration)**. The commutator can be cleaned and polished with crocus cloth, but do not use sandpaper or emery paper. After cleaning, wipe away any residue with a cloth soaked in electrical system cleaner or denatured alcohol. Make sure the insulating mica that separates the bars is not level with their outer surface. If it is, scrape out the mica using a pointed instrument or hacksaw blade.

10 Using an ohmmeter or a continuity tester, check for continuity between the commutator bars **(see illustration)**. Continuity should exist between each bar and all of the others. Also, check for continuity between the commutator bars and the armature shaft **(see illustration)**. There should be no continuity (infinite resistance) between the commutator and the shaft. If the checks indicate otherwise, the armature is defective.

11 Check for continuity between the terminal bolt and the brush it connects to **(see**

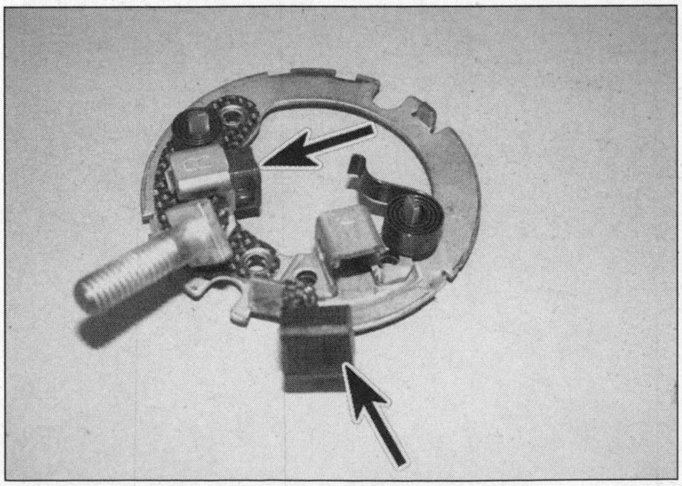

30.8 Check each brush as described

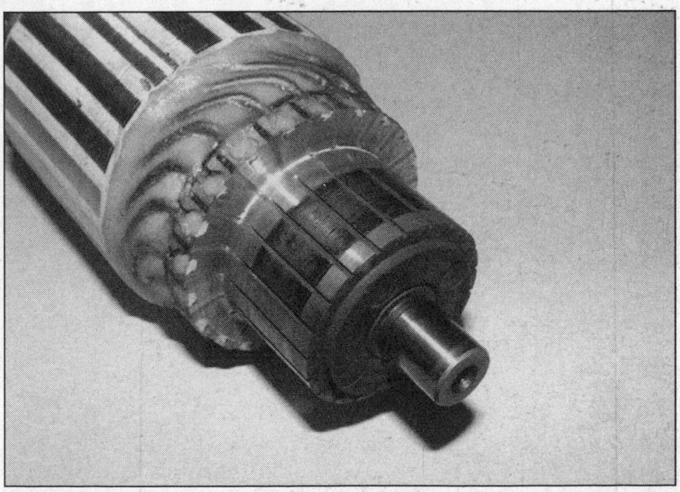

30.9 Check the commutator bars and the insulating mica between them as described

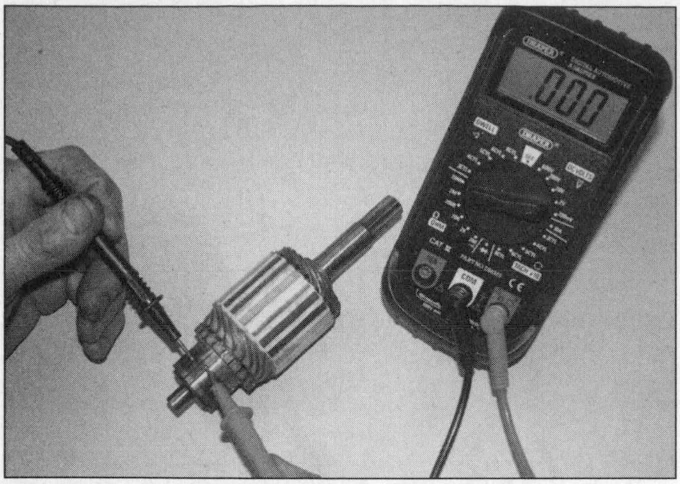

30.10a Continuity should exist between the commutator bars

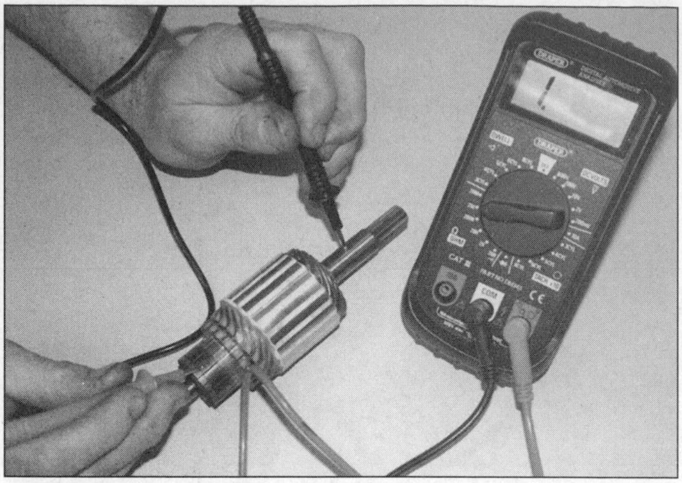

30.10b There should be no continuity between the bars and the shaft

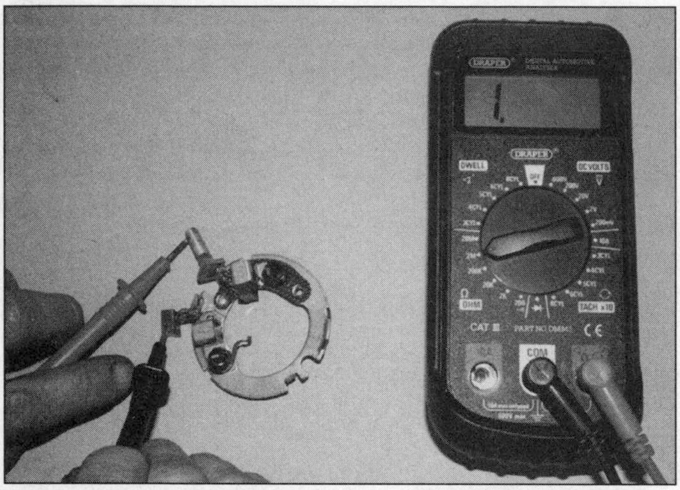

30.11a Check for continuity between the terminal bolt and its brush . . .

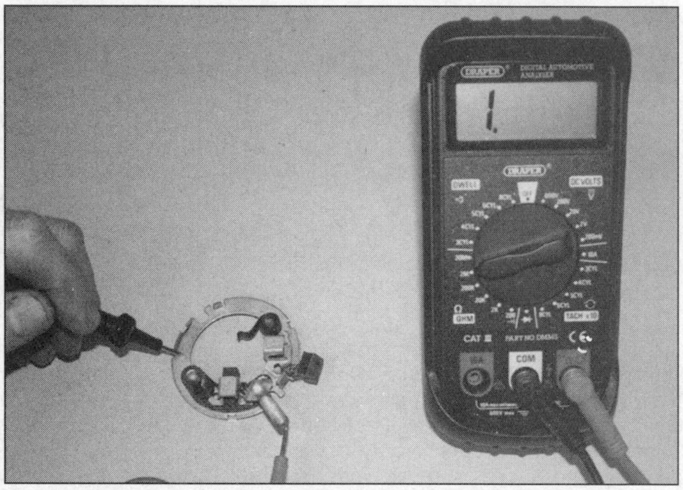

30.11b . . . between the bolt and the brushplate . . .

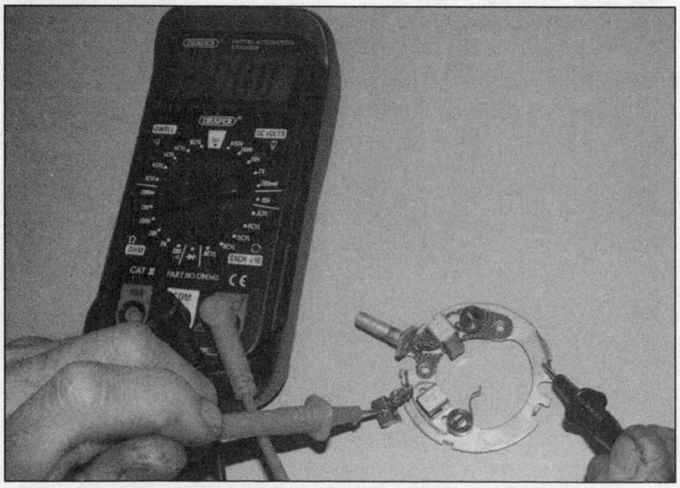

30.11c . . . and between the other brush and the brushplate

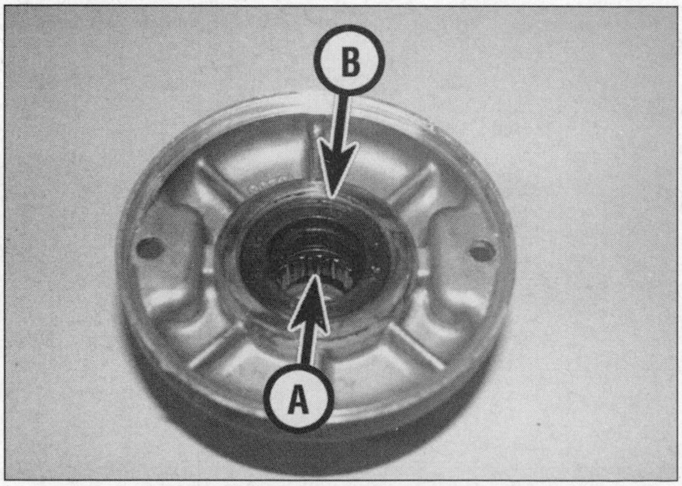

30.13a Check the seal (B) and needle bearing (A) in the front cover . . .

30.13b . . . and the bush (arrowed) in the rear cover

30.16 Fit the O-ring and small insulating washers onto the terminal bolt, followed by the large insulating washer, the plain washer and the nut

illustration). There should be continuity (zero resistance). Check for continuity between the terminal bolt and the brushplate **(see illustration)**. There should be no continuity (infinite resistance). Also check for continuity between the other brush wire and the brushplate **(see illustration)**. There should be continuity (zero resistance). If there is no continuity when there should be or vice versa, identify the faulty component and renew it.

12 Check the starter shaft gear for worn, cracked, chipped and broken teeth. If they are damaged or worn, renew the starter motor – the armature is not available separately.

13 Inspect the end covers for signs of cracks or wear. Check the needle bearing and oil seal in the front cover and the bush in the rear cover for wear and damage **(see illustrations)**. Inspect the magnets in the main housing and the housing itself for cracks.

14 Inspect the insulating washers, O-ring, and sealing rings for signs of damage, deformation and deterioration and renew if necessary.

Reassembly

15 Slide the brushes back into position in their housings and locate the spring ends onto the outer ends of the brushes **(see illustration 30.7)**.

16 Fit the insulator into the rear cover **(see illustration 30.6c)**. Insert the terminal bolt through the insulator and the cover and locate the brushplate, making sure its tab is correctly located in the housing slot **(see illustrations 30.6b and 30.13b)**. Slide the rubber O-ring and small insulating washers onto the terminal bolt, followed by the large insulating washer and the plain washer **(see illustration)**. Fit the nut onto the terminal bolt and tighten it securely.

17 Fit the shims onto the rear of the armature shaft **(see illustration)**. Apply a smear of molybdenum grease to the end of the shaft **(see illustration)**. Insert the armature into the brushplate at an angle so that the brushes locate against the commutator, then straighten the armature, pushing the brushes back into their housings against the springs, and insert it into the rear cover so that the shaft end locates in the bush **(see illustrations)**.

18 Fit the sealing ring onto the rear of the main housing **(see illustration)**. Grasp both the armature and the rear cover in one hand

30.17a Fit the shims . . .

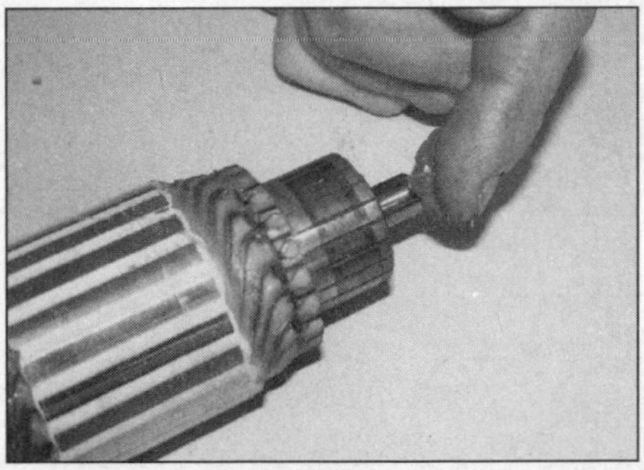

30.17b . . . then smear grease onto the shaft end

30.17c Locate the commutator bars against the brushes . . .

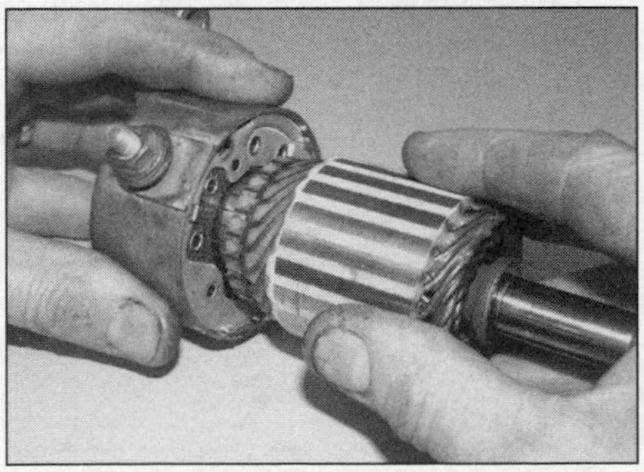

30.17d . . . and slide the armature into the cover

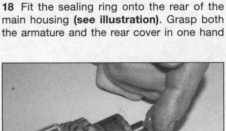

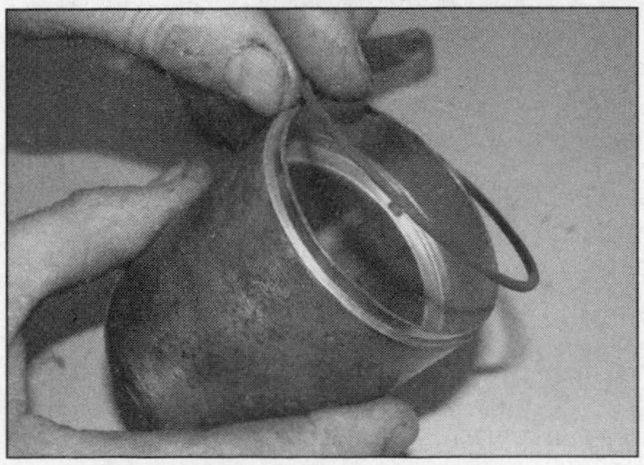

30.18a Fit the sealing ring . . .

30.18b . . . then carefully slide the housing over the armature

30.20 Fit the sealing ring onto the front of the housing

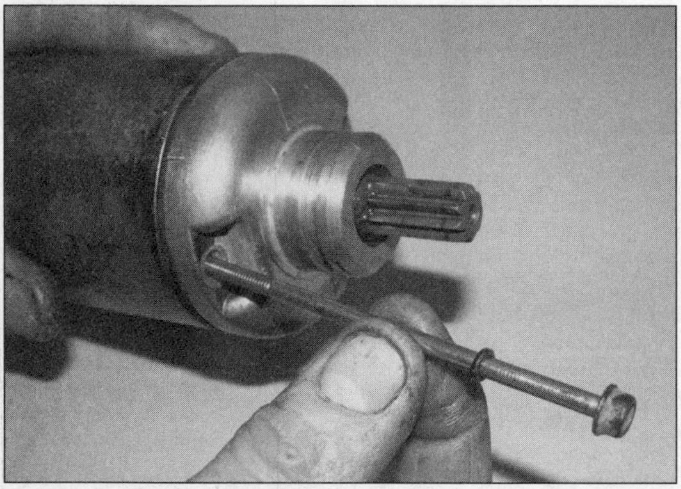

30.21 Fit the long bolts with their O-rings

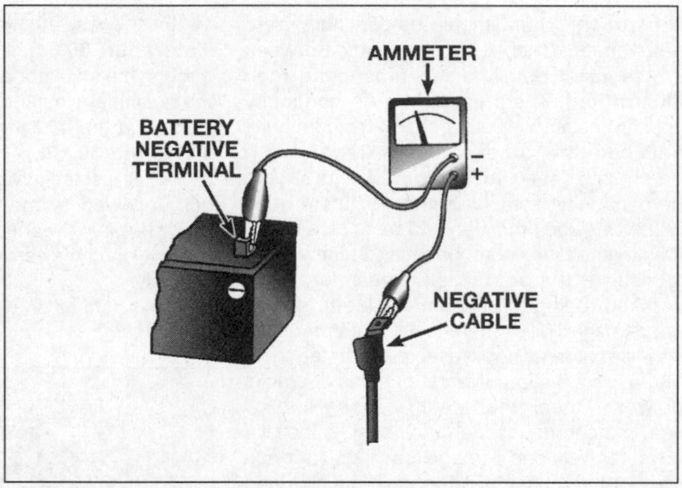

32.3 Checking the charging system leakage rate – connect the meter as shown

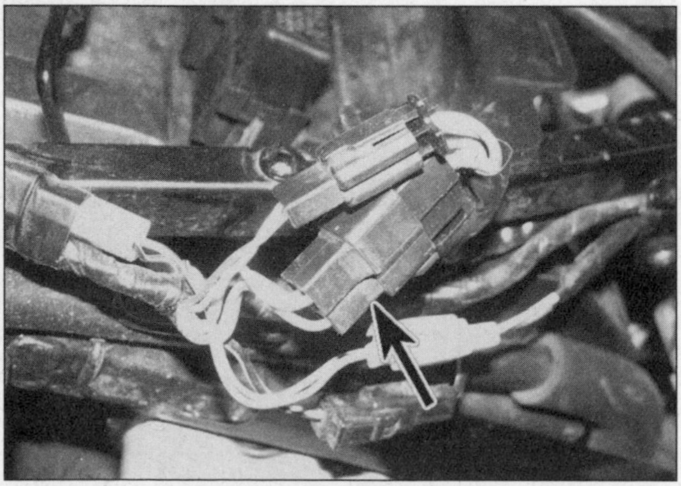

32.8a Alternator wiring connector (arrowed)

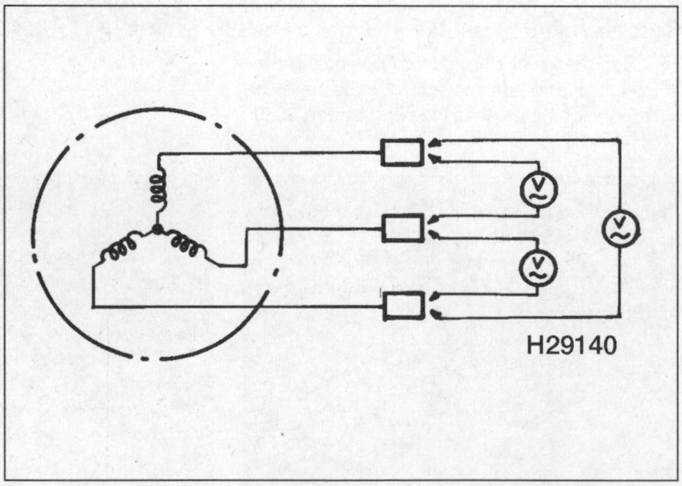

32.8b Alternator no-load voltmeter test connections

and hold them together – this will prevent the armature being drawn out by the magnets in the housing **(see illustration)**. Note however that you should take care not to let the housing be drawn forcibly onto the armature by the magnets. Carefully allow the housing to be drawn onto the armature, making sure the end with the cut-out faces the rear cover and aligns with the brushplate outer tab (aligning the marks between the cover and housing (Step 2) will help).

19 Apply a smear of grease to the front cover oil seal lip **(see illustration 30.13a)**. Fit the tabbed washer into the cover so that its teeth are correctly located with the cover ribs **(see illustration 30.3c)**.

20 Slide the shim(s) onto the front end of the armature shaft then fit the insulating washer **(see illustration 30.3d)**. Fit the sealing ring onto the front of the housing **(see illustration)**. Slide the front cover into position, aligning the marks made on removal **(see illustration 30.3b)**.

21 Check the alignment marks made on removal are correctly aligned **(see illustration 30.2)**. Apply a smear of grease to the long bolt O-rings, using new ones if the old ones are damaged, deformed or deteriorated. Apply a small amount of a suitable non-permanent thread locking compound to the bolts, then fit them and tighten them to the specified torque setting **(see illustration)**.

22 Install the starter motor (see Section 29).

31 Charging system testing – general information and precautions

1 If the performance of the charging system is suspect, the system as a whole should be checked first, followed by testing of the individual components. **Note:** *Before beginning the checks, make sure the battery is fully charged and that all system connections are clean and tight.*

2 Checking the output of the charging system and the performance of the various components within the charging system requires the use of a multimeter (with voltage, current and resistance checking facilities).

3 When making the checks, follow the procedures carefully to prevent incorrect connections or short circuits, as irreparable damage to electrical system components may result if short circuits occur.

4 If a multimeter is not available, the job of checking the charging system should be left to a Suzuki dealer.

32 Charging system – leakage and output test

1 If the charging system of the machine is thought to be faulty, perform the following checks.

Leakage test

2 Turn the ignition switch OFF and disconnect the lead from the battery negative (–ve) terminal (see Section 3).

3 Set a multimeter to the Amps function and connect its negative (–ve) probe to the battery negative (–ve) terminal, and positive (+ve) probe to the disconnected negative (–ve) lead **(see illustration)**. Always set the meter to a high amps range initially and then bring it down to the mA (milli Amps) range; if there is a high current flow in the circuit it may blow the meter's fuse.

Caution: Always connect an ammeter in series, never in parallel with the battery, otherwise it will be damaged. Do not turn the ignition ON or operate the starter motor when the ammeter is connected – a sudden surge in current will blow the meter's fuse.

4 If the current leakage indicated exceeds the amount specified at the beginning of the Chapter, there is probably a short circuit in the wiring. Use the wiring diagrams at the end of this book and systematically disconnect individual electrical components until the source is identified.

5 Disconnect the meter and connect the negative (–ve) lead to the battery, tightening it securely.

HAYNES HiNT ***If an alarm or immobiliser is fitted, its current drain should be taken into account when checking for current leakage.***

Output test

6 Start the engine and allow it to warm up.

7 To check the regulated voltage output, connect a multimeter set to the 0 to 20 volts DC scale (voltmeter) across the terminals of the battery (positive (+ve) lead to battery positive (+ve) terminal, negative (–ve) lead to battery negative (–ve) terminal). Turn the lighting switch on and turn the dimmer switch to the HI position. Slowly increase the engine speed to 5000 rpm and note the reading obtained. The regulated voltage output should be as specified at the beginning of the Chapter. If not, check the unregulated output as follows.

8 To check the no-load unregulated voltage output, remove the seat cowling (see Chap-ter 8). Trace the wiring back from the alternator cover on the left-hand side of the engine and disconnect the wiring connector containing the three yellow wires **(see illustration)**. Start the engine and allow it to idle. Using the multimeter, now set to the AC volts x 100 scale, measure the voltage between each of the yellow wires on the alternator side of the connector, taking a total of three readings, with the engine running briefly at around 5000 rpm **(see illustration)**. The unregulated voltage output should be as specified at the beginning of the Chapter. If it is, but the regulated output was incorrect, then check the regulator (see Section 34). If the voltage is outside these limits, check the alternator stator coil resistance (see Section 33).

HAYNES HiNT ***Clues to a faulty regulator are constantly blowing bulbs, with brightness varying considerably with engine speed, and battery overheating.***

33 Alternator

Check

1 Remove the seat cowling (see Chapter 8). Trace the wiring back from the alternator cover on the left-hand side of the engine and disconnect it the wiring connector containing the three yellow wires **(see illustration 32.8a)**. Check the connector terminals for corrosion and security.

2 To check the stator coil resistance, use a multimeter set to the ohms x 1 (ohmmeter) scale and measure the resistance between each of the yellow wires on the alternator side of the connector, taking a total of three readings, then check for continuity between each terminal and ground (earth). If the stator coil windings are in good condition the three readings should be within the range shown in the Specifications at the start of this Chapter, and there should be no continuity (infinite resistance) between any of the terminals and ground (earth). If not, the alternator stator coil assembly is at fault and should be renewed. **Note:** *Before condemning the stator coils, check the fault is not due to damaged wiring between the connector and the coils.*

Removal

3 Drain the engine oil (see Chapter 1).

4 Remove the seat cowling (see Chapter 8). Trace the wiring back from the alternator cover on the left-hand side of the engine and disconnect it the wiring connector containing the three yellow wires **(see illustration 32.8a)**.

5 Working in a criss-cross pattern, evenly slacken the alternator cover bolts **(see illustration)**. Lift the cover away from the engine, noting that it will be restrained by the pull of the rotor magnets, and be prepared to catch any residual oil. Remove the gasket and discard it – a new one will be required. Remove the dowels from either the cover or the crankcase if they are loose.

6 To remove the rotor bolt it is necessary to stop the rotor from turning. The best way is to use a commercially available rotor strap **(see illustration)**. If one is not available, try placing the transmission in gear and having an assistant sit on the seat and apply the rear brake whilst you unscrew the bolt. Note that the bolt will be very tight. Alternatively, Suzuki

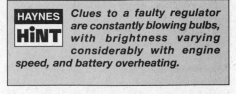

33.5 Alternator cover bolts (arrowed) – note the sealing washer with the bolt (A)

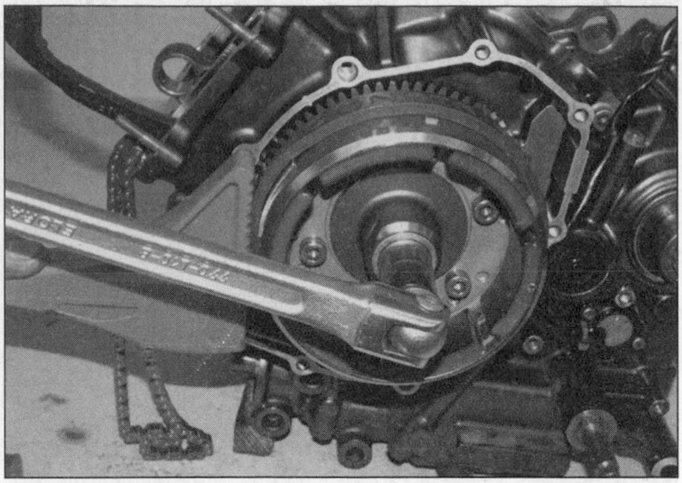

33.6 Using a rotor strap to hold the rotor while unscrewing the bolt

33.7 Remove the Woodruff key if it is loose

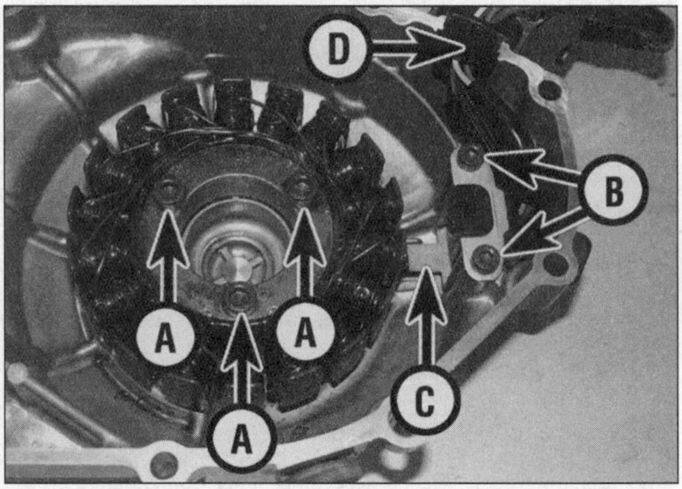

33.8 Unscrew the stator bolts (A) and the pulse generator bolts (B) noting the wiring clamp (C) and the grommet (D)

produce a service tool (Pt. No. 09930-44530) which fits around the inner boss of the rotor and can be held to prevent rotation. Note the washer fitted with the bolt when it is removed.

7 To remove the rotor from the shaft it is necessary to use a rotor puller, either the Suzuki service tool (Pt. No. 09930-30450) or a commercial available equivalent from a motorcycle dealer – do not use a legged puller to remove the rotor. Thread the rotor puller into the centre of the rotor and turn it until the rotor is displaced from the shaft, holding the rotor as described above to prevent the engine turning. Remove the Woodruff key from its slot in the crankcase if it is loose **(see illustration)**.

8 To remove the stator from the cover, unscrew the bolts securing the stator and the bolts securing the pulse generator coil/crankshaft position sensor, then remove the assembly, noting how the wiring clamp and rubber wiring grommet fits **(see illustration)**.

33.10a Fit the Woodruff key into its slot if removed . . .

33.10b . . . then slide the rotor onto the shaft

Installation

9 Fit the stator, wiring clamp and pulse generator coil/crankshaft position sensor into the cover, making sure the clamp is correctly fitted. Apply a suitable non-permanent thread locking compound to the stator and coil bolt threads and tighten them to the appropriate torque settings specified at the beginning of the Chapter. Apply a suitable sealant to the wiring grommet, then press it into the cut-out in the cover.

10 Clean the tapered end of the crankshaft and the corresponding mating surface on the inside of the rotor with a suitable solvent. Fit the Woodruff key into its slot in the crankshaft if removed **(see illustration)**. Make sure that no metal objects have attached themselves to the magnets on the inside of the rotor. Slide the rotor onto the shaft, making sure the groove on the inside is aligned with and fits over the Woodruff key **(see illustration)**.

33.11a Install the lubricated bolt . . .

33.11b . . . and tighten it to the specified torque

33.13a Locate the new gasket onto the dowels (arrowed) . . .

33.13b . . . then install the cover making sure the gear shaft locates in its bore (arrowed)

33.13c Do not forget the sealing washer with the bolt, and use a new one if necessary

Make sure the Woodruff key does not become dislodged.

11 Apply some clean oil to the rotor bolt threads and the underside of the head **(see illustration)**. Install the rotor bolt with its washer and tighten it to the torque setting specified at the beginning of the Chapter, using the method employed on removal to prevent the rotor from turning **(see illustration)**.

12 Lubricate the end of the idle/reduction gear shaft with clean engine oil.

13 Fit the dowels into the crankcase if removed. Install the alternator cover using a new gasket, making sure it locates onto the dowels, and that the bore in the cover locates onto the idle/reduction gear shaft **(see illustrations)** – take care not to trap your fingers as the cover is drawn into place by the pull of the magnets. Tighten the cover bolts evenly in a criss-cross sequence, not forgetting the sealing washer with the bolt below the timing inspection cap – use a new washer if the old one is deformed **(see illustration)**.

14 Reconnect the wiring at the connector and secure it with any clips or ties previously released **(see illustration 32.8a)**. Install the seat cowling (see Chapter 8).

15 Replenish the engine oil (see Chapter 1).

34 Regulator/rectifier

Check

1 Before assuming the regulator/rectifier is faulty, first check all other charging system components as described in Sections 32 and 33.

2 If all appears to be good, check the wiring between the battery, regulator/rectifier and alternator, and the wiring connectors (see the *Wiring diagrams* at the end of the book).

3 If everything else in the circuit is good, it is likely the regulator/rectifier is faulty. Take it to a Suzuki dealer for testing.

Renewal

4 On X, Y, K1 and K2 models, remove the seat cowling (see Chapter 8). The regulator/rectifier is mounted on the right-hand side of the rear sub-frame. Disconnect the wiring connectors, then unscrew the two bolts securing the regulator/rectifier and remove it **(see illustrations)**.

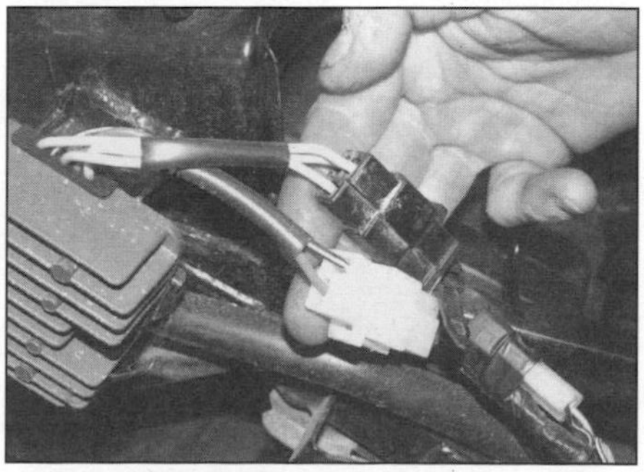

34.4a Disconnect the regulator/rectifier wiring connectors . . .

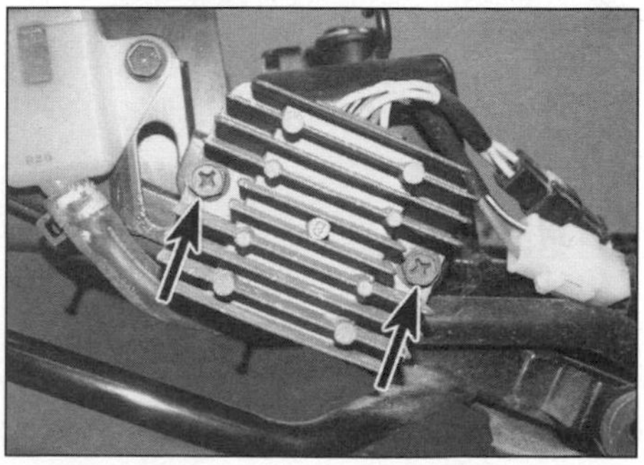

34.4b . . . then unscrew the bolts (arrowed)

34.5 Location of the regulator/rectifier – K3-on models

5 On K3-on models, remove the air filter housing (see Chapter 4B). The regulator/ rectifier is mounted on the right-hand side of the frame **(see illustration)**. Disconnect the wiring connectors, then unscrew the two bolts securing the regulator/rectifier and remove it.

6 Install the new unit and tighten its bolts securely. Connect the wiring connectors.

7 Install the remaining components in the reverse order of removal.

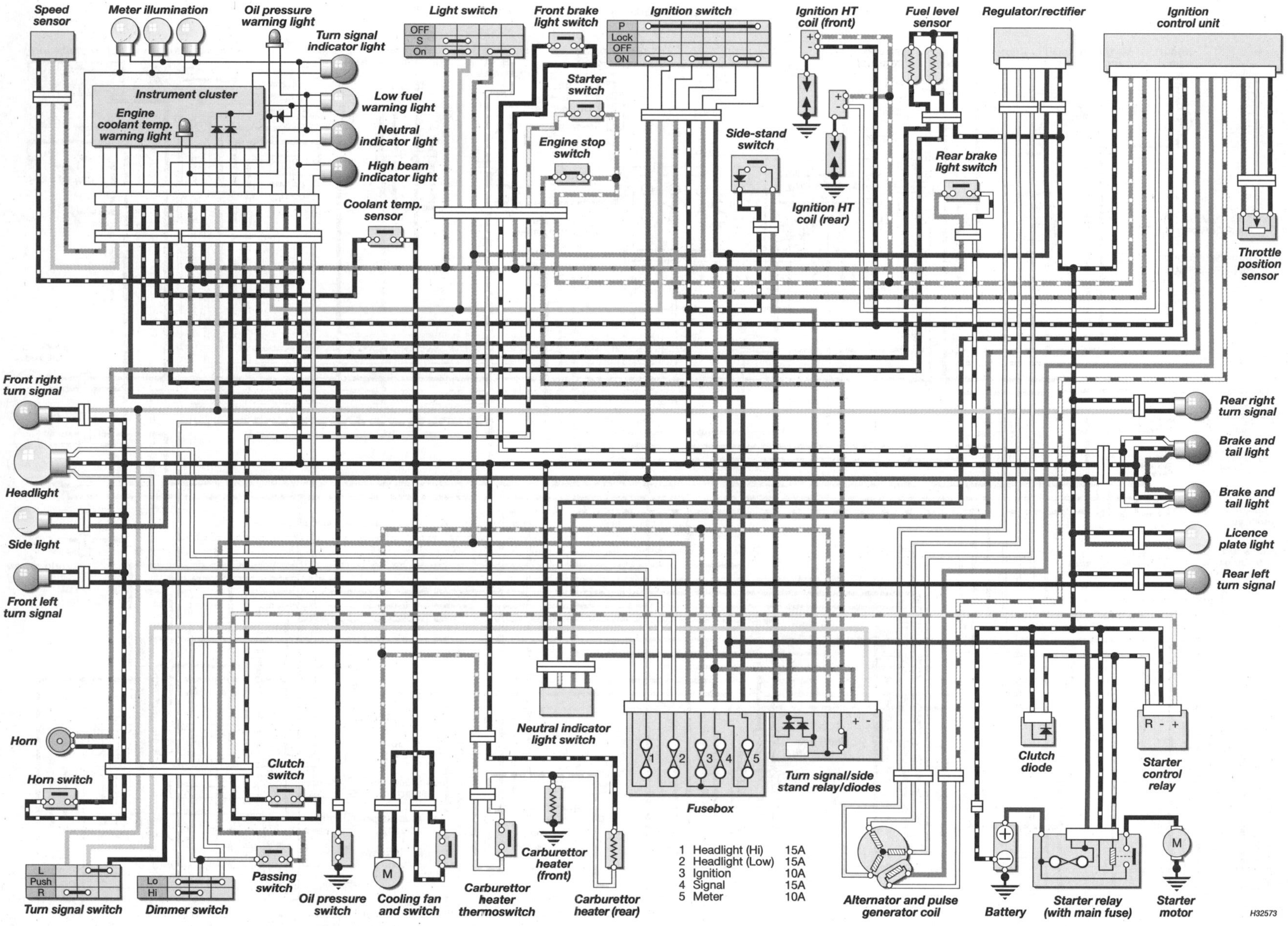

1	Headlight (Hi)	15A
2	Headlight (Low)	15A
3	Ignition	10A
4	Signal	15A
5	Meter	10A

SV650 X and Y European models

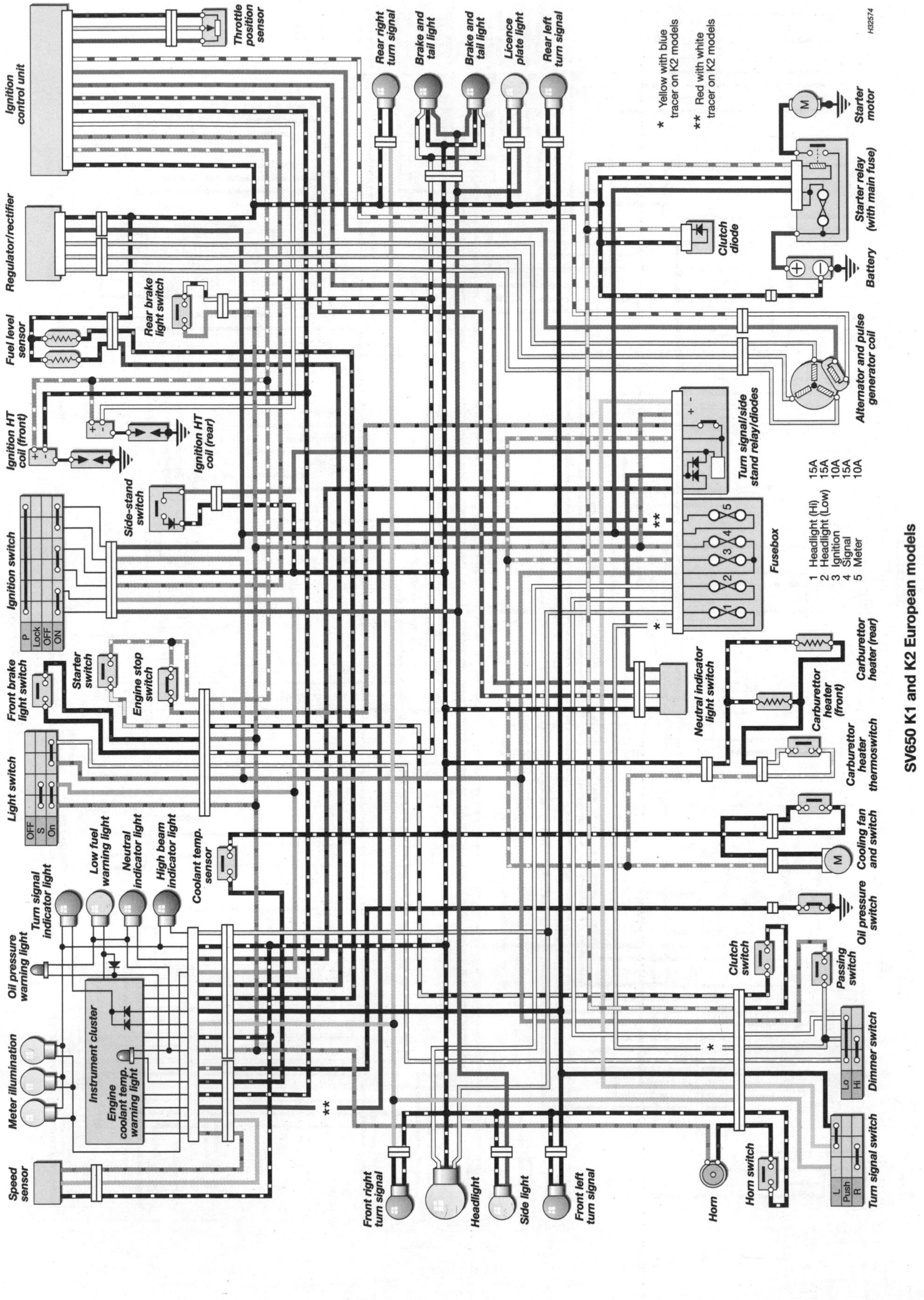
Ignition control unit
Throttle position sensor
Regulator/rectifier
Fuel level sensor
Rear brake light switch
Ignition HT coil (front)
Ignition HT coil (rear)
Side-stand switch
Ignition switch
P
Lock
OFF
ON
Front brake light switch
Starter switch
Engine stop switch
Light switch
OFF
S
On
Turn signal indicator light
Low fuel warning light
Neutral indicator light
High beam indicator light
Coolant temp. sensor
Oil pressure warning light
Meter illumination
Instrument cluster
Engine coolant temp. warning light
Speed sensor
Front right turn signal
Headlight
Side light
Front left turn signal
Horn
Horn switch
Turn signal switch
L
Push
R
Dimmer switch
Lo
Hi
Passing switch
Clutch switch
Oil pressure switch
Cooling fan and switch
Carburettor heater thermoswitch
Carburettor heater (front)
Carburettor heater (rear)
Neutral indicator light switch
Fusebox
1 Headlight (Hi) 15A
2 Headlight (Low) 15A
3 Ignition 10A
4 Signal 15A
5 Meter 10A
Turn signal/side stand relay/diodes
Alternator and pulse generator coil
Battery
Clutch diode
Starter relay (with main fuse)
Starter motor
Rear right turn signal
Brake and tail light
Brake and tail light
Licence plate light
Rear left turn signal
* Yellow with blue tracer on K2 models
** Red with white tracer on K2 models
H32574
SV650 K1 and K2 European models

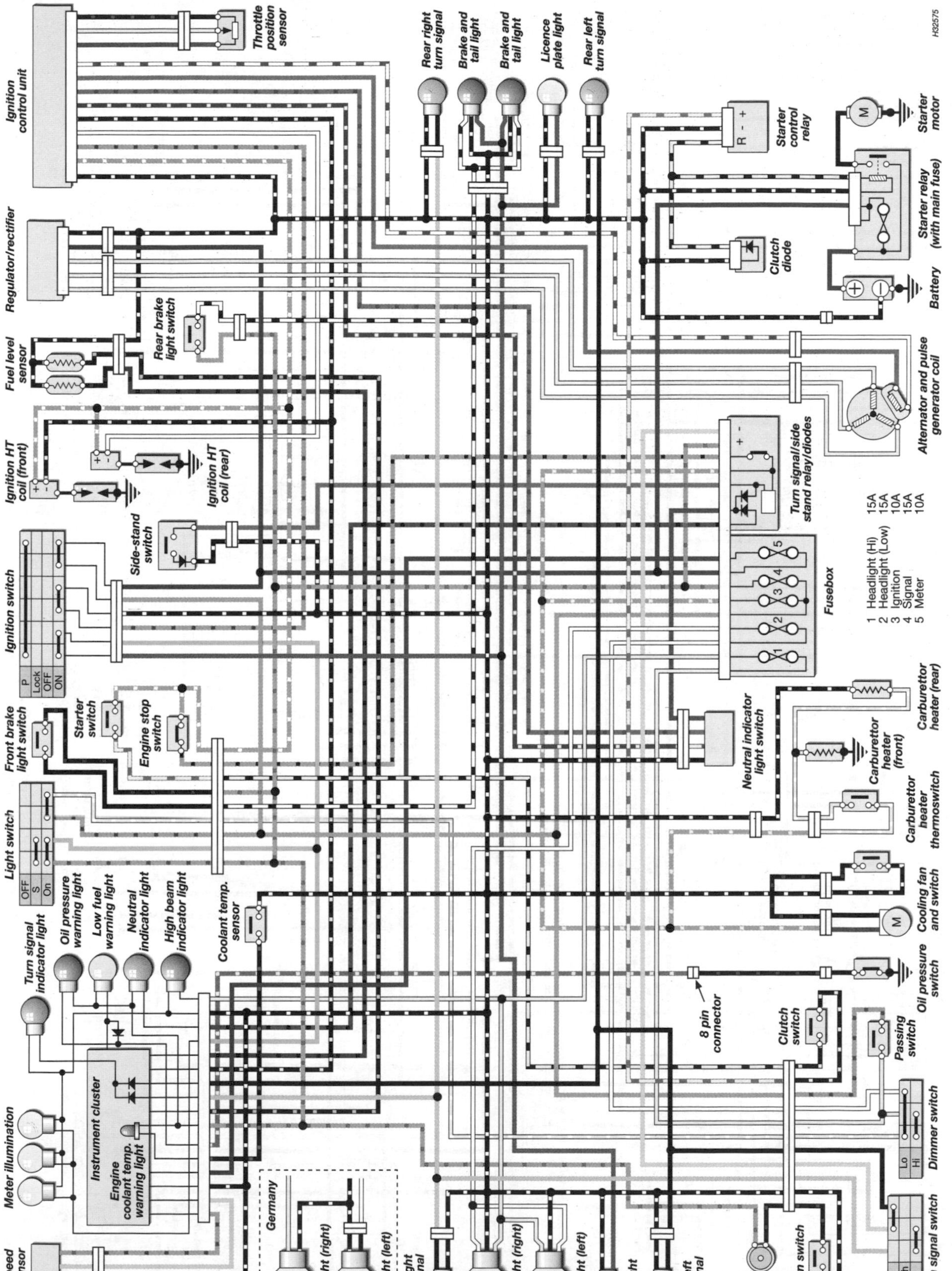

SV650 SX and SY European models

Note: 8-pin and 20-pin block connectors located inside fairing are not shown

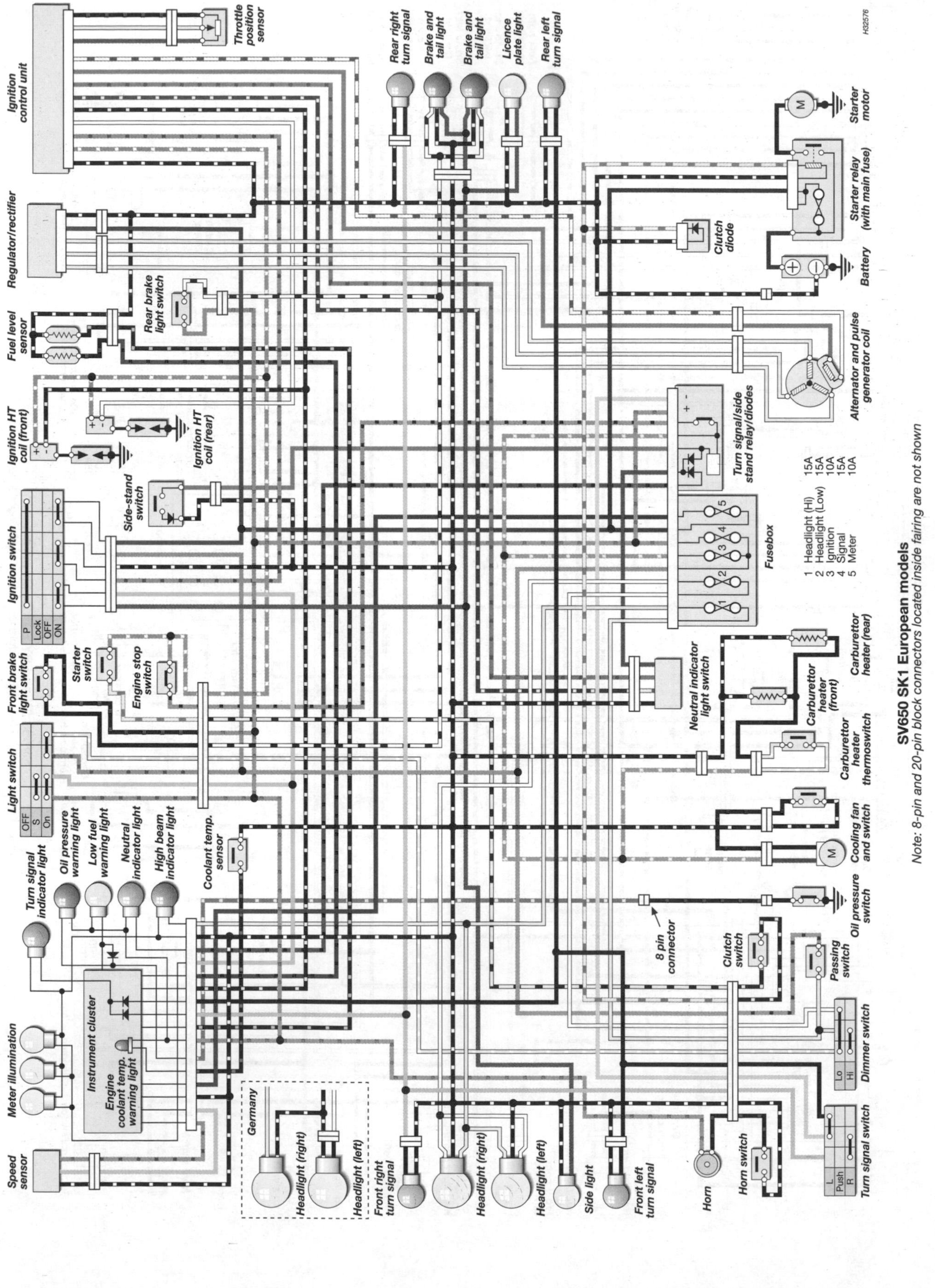

SV650 SK1 European models

Note: 8-pin and 20-pin block connectors located inside fairing are not shown

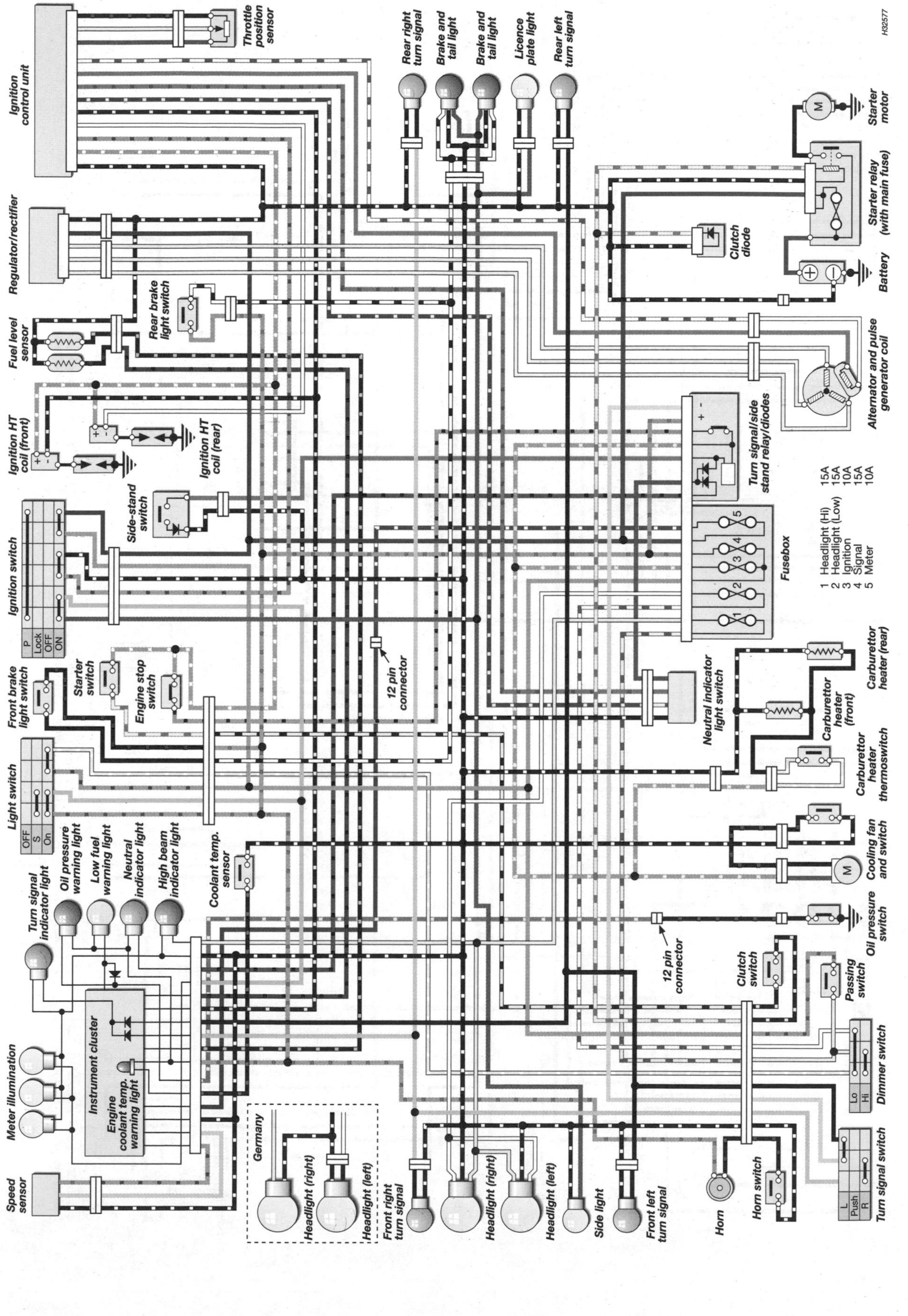

SV650 SK2 European models

Note: 6-pin and 12-pin block connectors located inside fairing are not shown

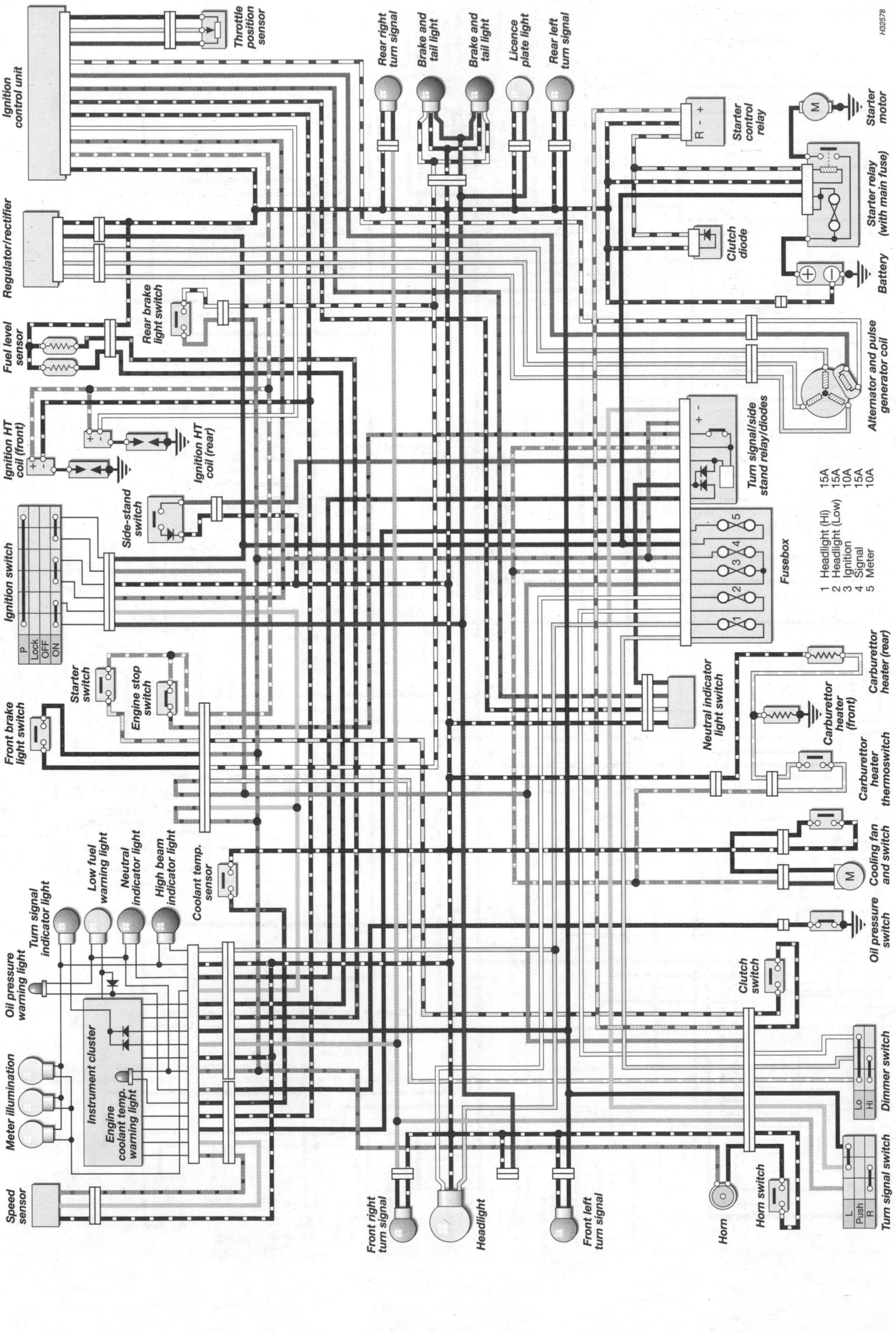

SV650 X and Y US models

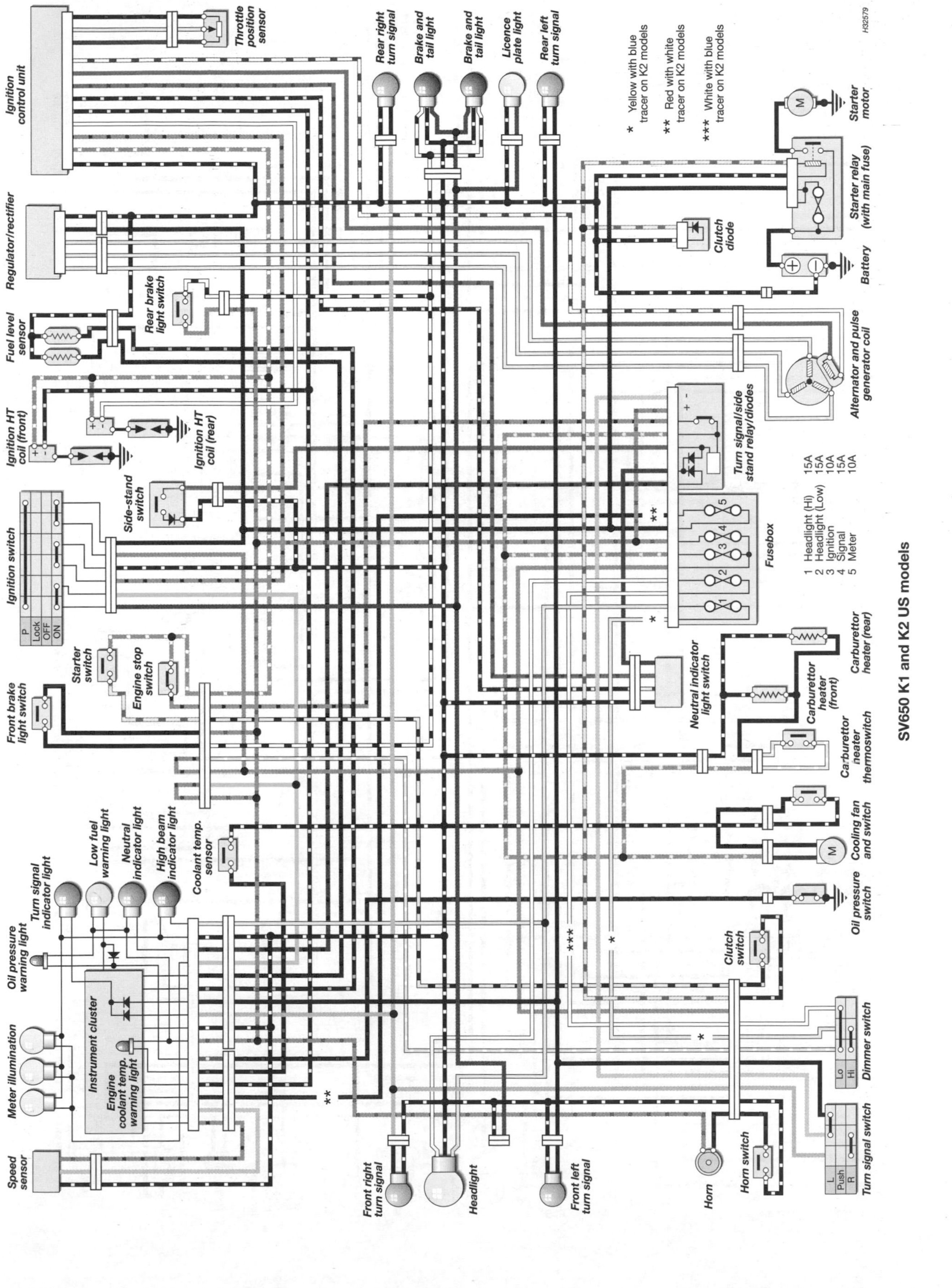
Ignition control unit
Throttle position sensor
Regulator/rectifier
Fuel level sensor
Rear brake light switch
Ignition HT coil (front)
Ignition HT coil (rear)
Side-stand switch
Ignition switch
P
Lock
OFF
ON
Front brake light switch
Starter switch
Engine stop switch
Oil pressure warning light
Turn signal indicator light
Low fuel warning light
Neutral indicator light
High beam indicator light
Coolant temp. sensor
Meter illumination
Instrument cluster
Engine coolant temp. warning light
Speed sensor
Front right turn signal
Headlight
Front left turn signal
Horn
Horn switch
Turn signal switch
L
Push
R
Dimmer switch
Lo
Hi
Clutch switch
Oil pressure switch
Cooling fan and switch
Carburettor heater thermoswitch
Carburettor heater (front)
Carburettor heater (rear)
Neutral indicator light switch
Fusebox
1 Headlight (Hi) 15A
2 Headlight (Low) 15A
3 Ignition 10A
4 Signal 15A
5 Meter 10A
Turn signal/side stand relay/diodes
Alternator and pulse generator coil
Battery
Clutch diode
Starter relay (with main fuse)
Starter motor
Rear right turn signal
Brake and tail light
Brake and tail light
Licence plate light
Rear left turn signal
* Yellow with blue tracer on K2 models
** Red with white tracer on K2 models
*** White with blue tracer on K2 models
H32579
SV650 K1 and K2 US models

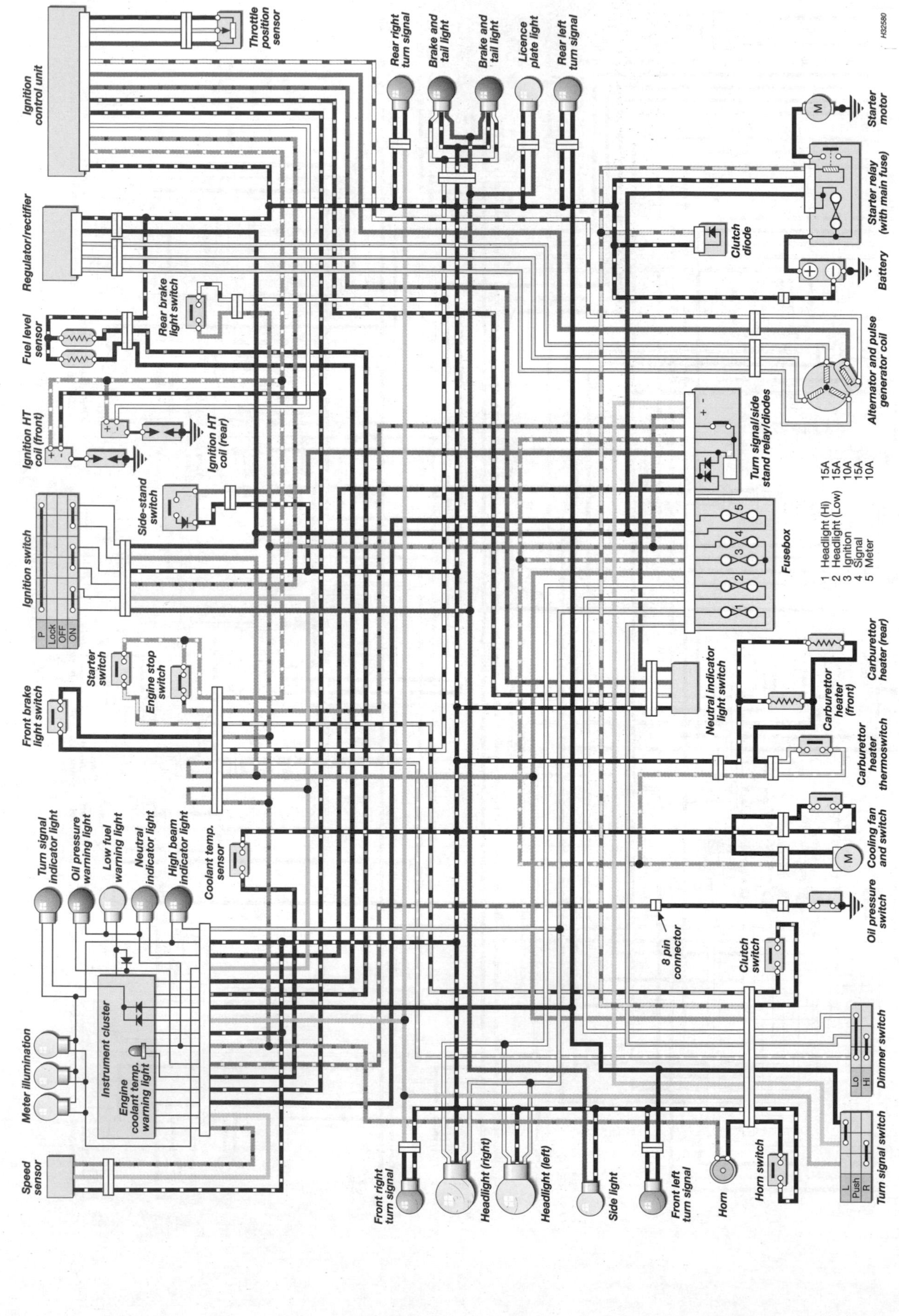

SV650 SK1 US models

Note: 8-pin and 20-pin block connectors located inside fairing are not shown

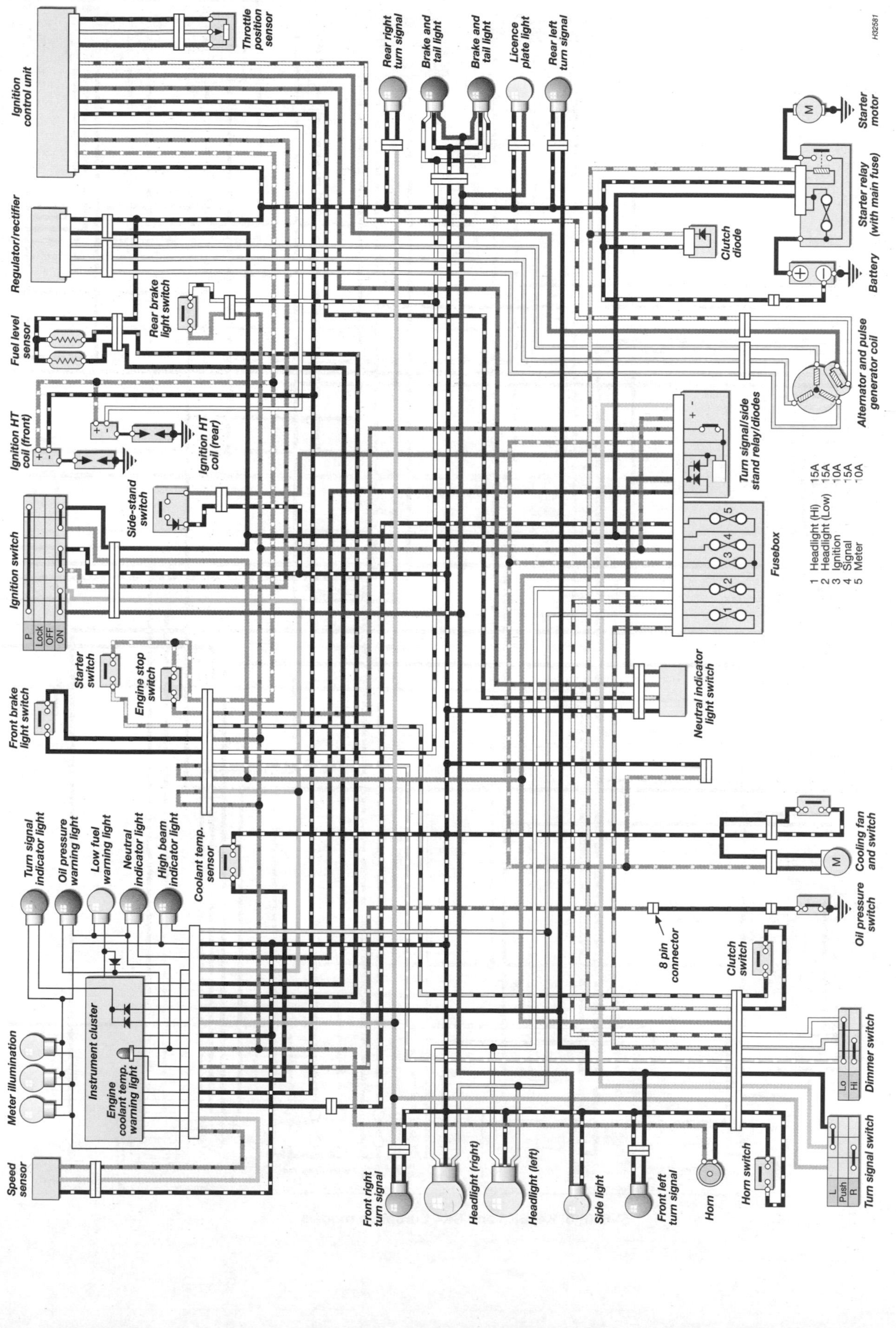

SV650 SK2 US models

Note: 6-pin and 12-pin block connectors located inside fairing are not shown

1	Headlight (Hi)	15A
2	Headlight (Low)	15A
3	Ignition	10A
4	Signal	15A
5	Meter	10A

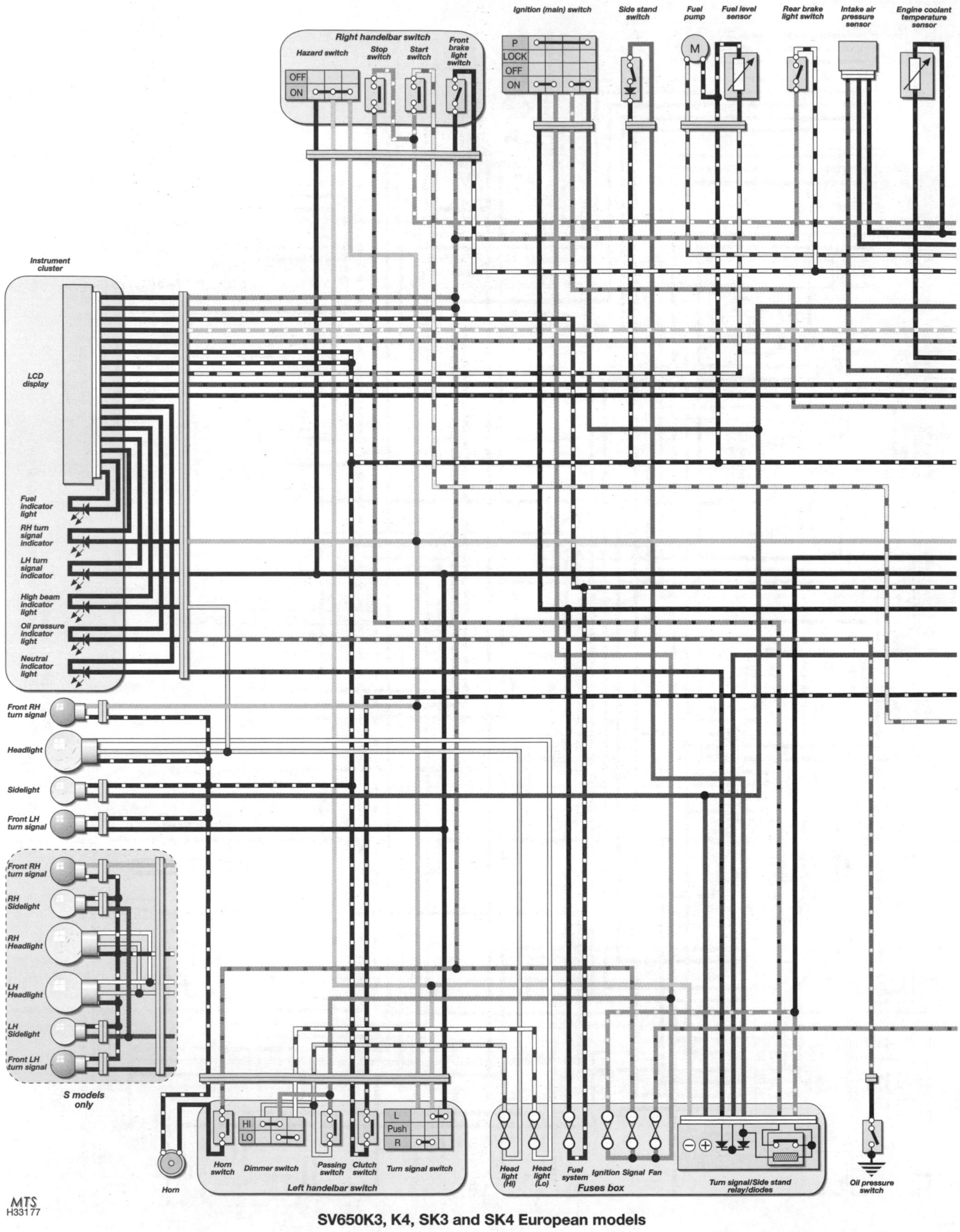

SV650K3, K4, SK3 and SK4 European models

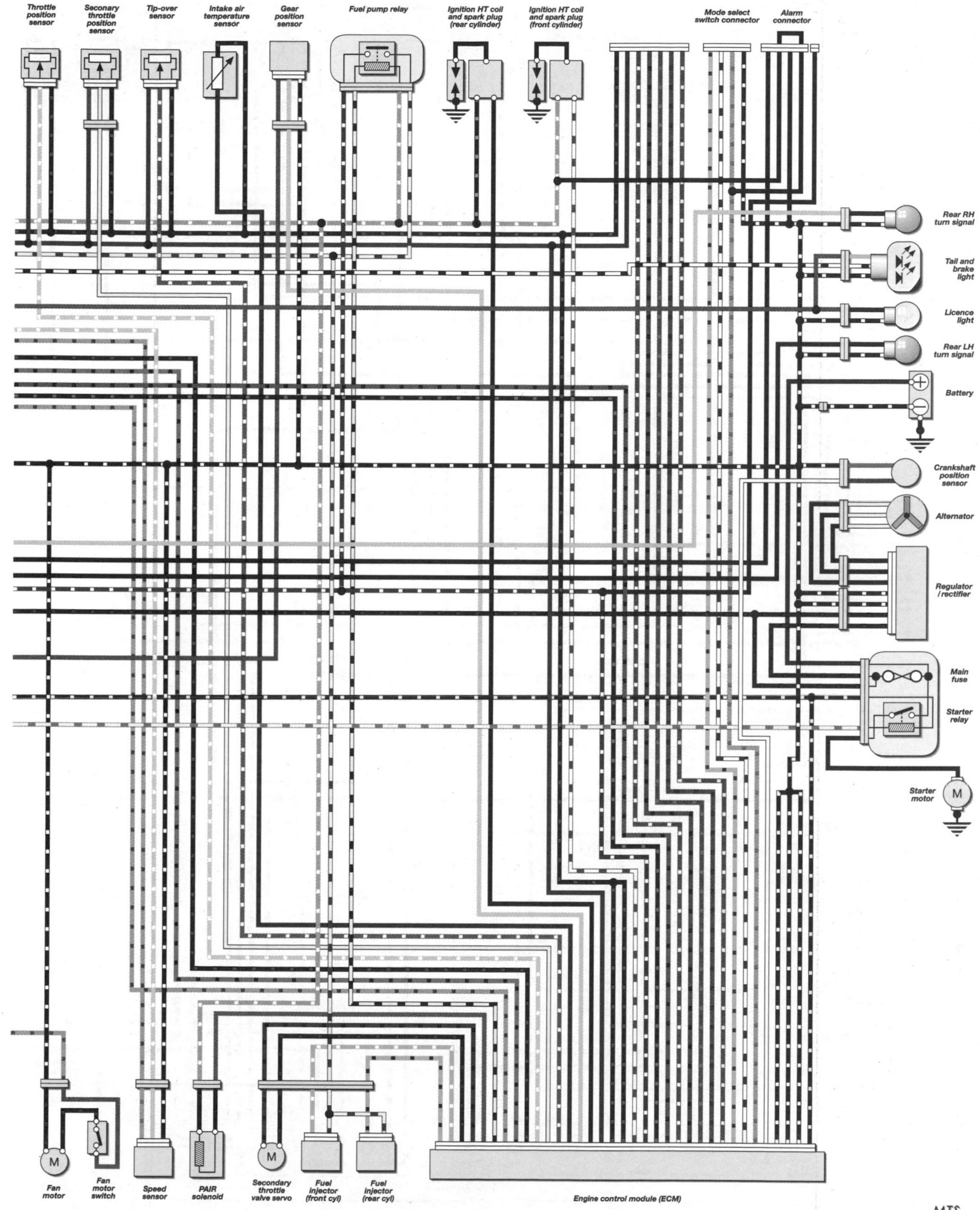
Throttle position sensor
Seconary throttle position sensor
Tip-over sensor
Intake air temperature sensor
Gear position sensor
Fuel pump relay
Ignition HT coil and spark plug (rear cylinder)
Ignition HT coil and spark plug (front cylinder)
Mode select switch connector
Alarm connector
Rear RH turn signal
Tail and brake light
Licence light
Rear LH turn signal
Battery
Crankshaft position sensor
Alternator
Regulator /rectifier
Main fuse
Starter relay
Starter motor
Fan motor
Fan motor switch
Speed sensor
PAIR solenoid
Secondary throttle valve servo
Fuel injector (front cyl)
Fuel injector (rear cyl)
Engine control module (ECM)

SV650K3, K4, SK3 and SK4 European models

MTS
H33178

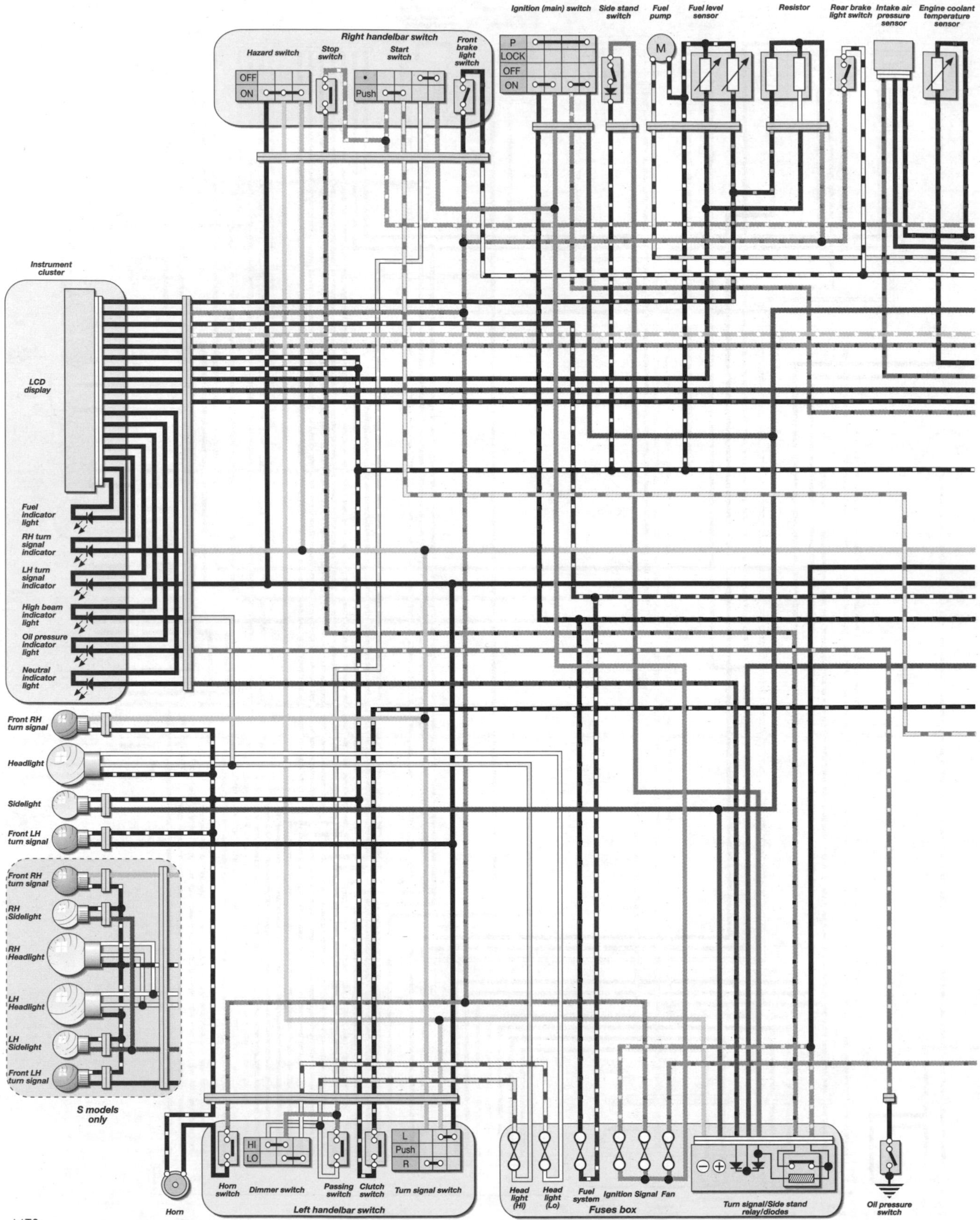

SV650K5, K6, SK5, and SK6 European models

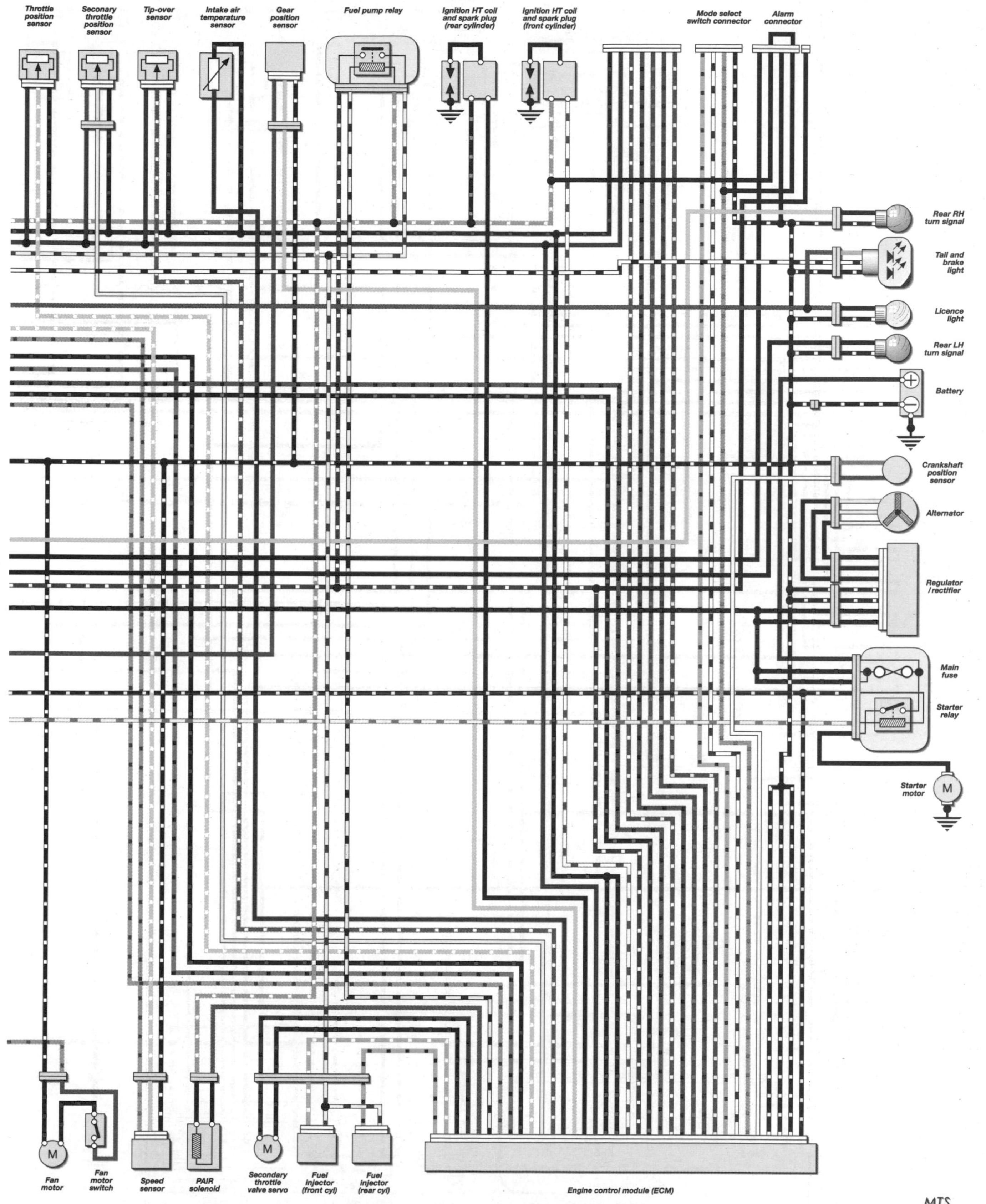

SV650K5, K6, SK5, and SK6 European models

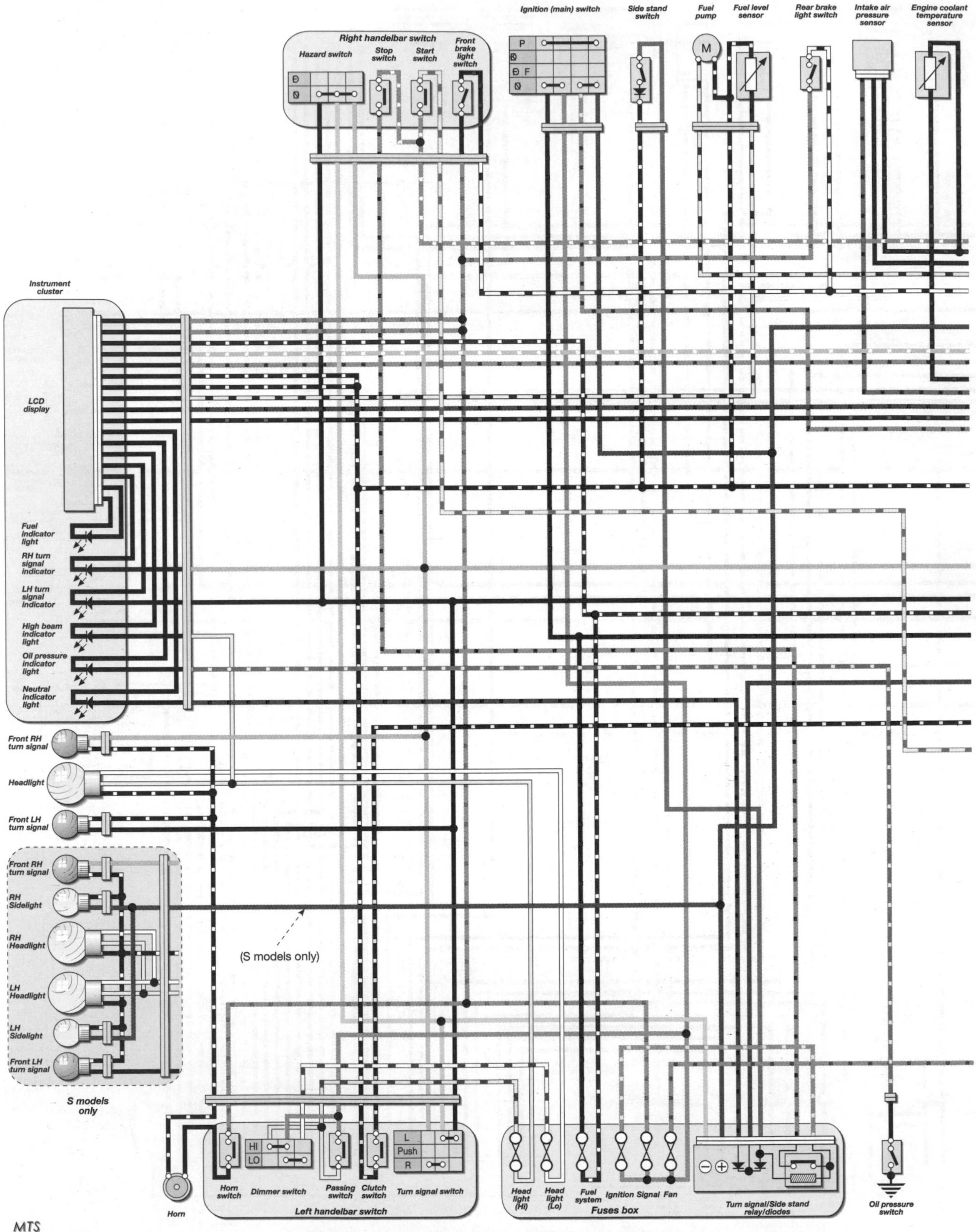

SV650K3, K4, K5, K6, SK3, SK4, SK5 and SK6 US models

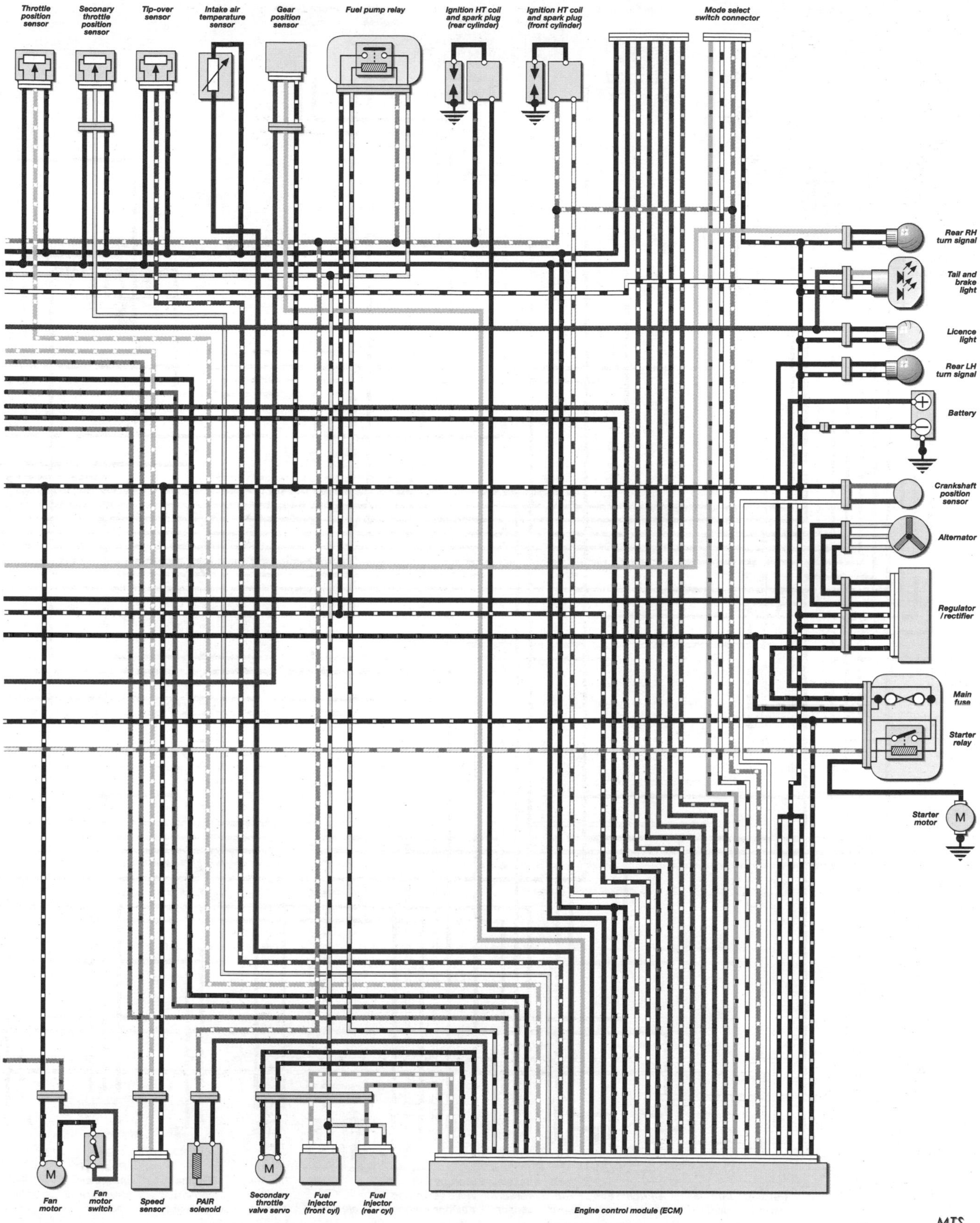

SV650K3, K4, K5, K6, SK3, SK4, SK5 and SK6 US models

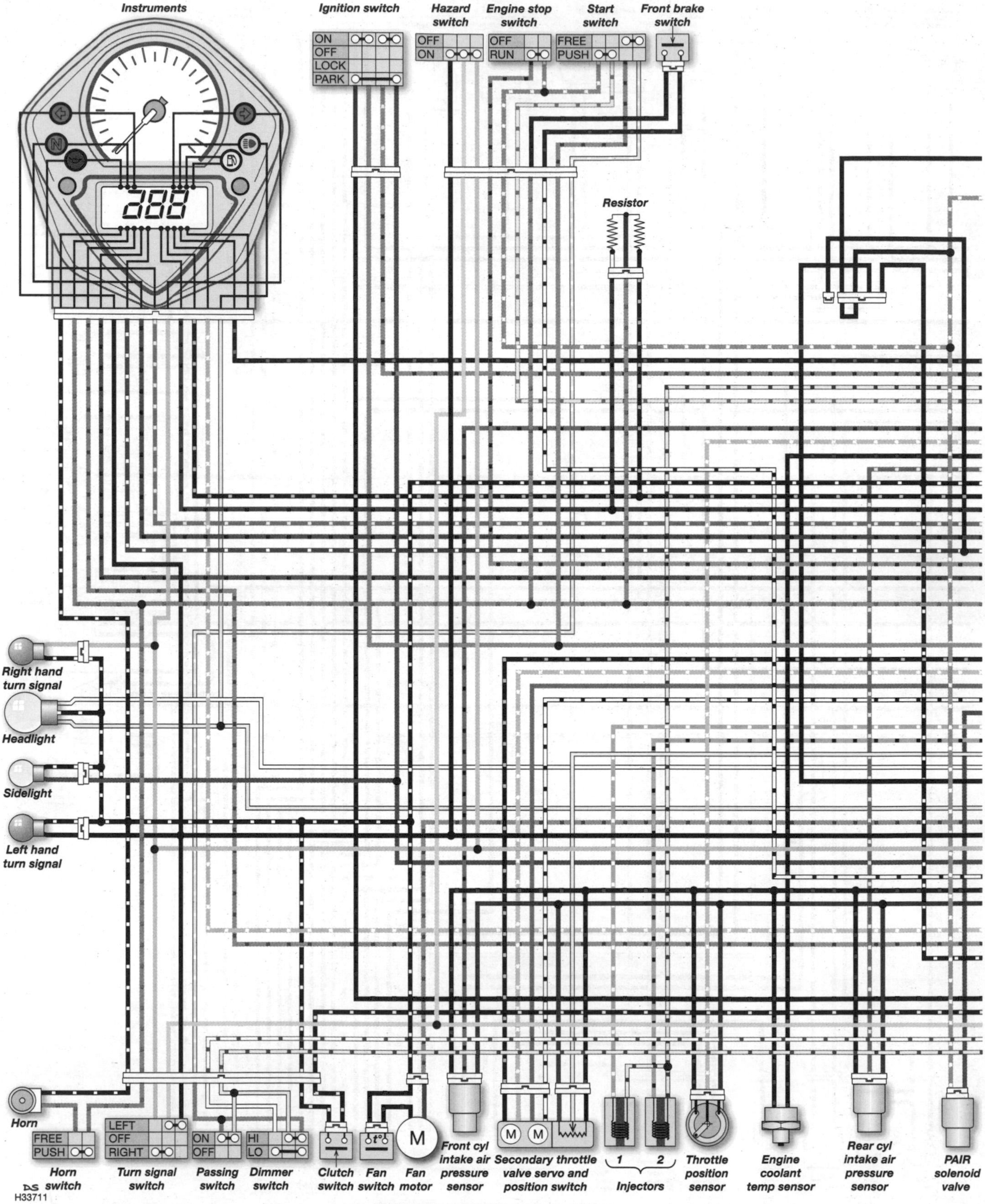
Instruments
Ignition switch
ON
OFF
LOCK
PARK
Hazard switch
OFF
ON
Engine stop switch
OFF
RUN
Start switch
FREE
PUSH
Front brake switch
Resistor
Right hand turn signal
Headlight
Sidelight
Left hand turn signal
Horn
FREE
PUSH
Horn switch
LEFT
OFF
RIGHT
Turn signal switch
ON
OFF
Passing switch
HI
LO
Dimmer switch
Clutch switch
Fan switch
M
Fan motor
Front cyl intake air pressure sensor
M
M
Secondary throttle valve servo and position switch
1
2
Injectors
Throttle position sensor
Engine coolant temp sensor
Rear cyl intake air pressure sensor
PAIR solenoid valve
H33711

SV650K7 and K8 Europe models

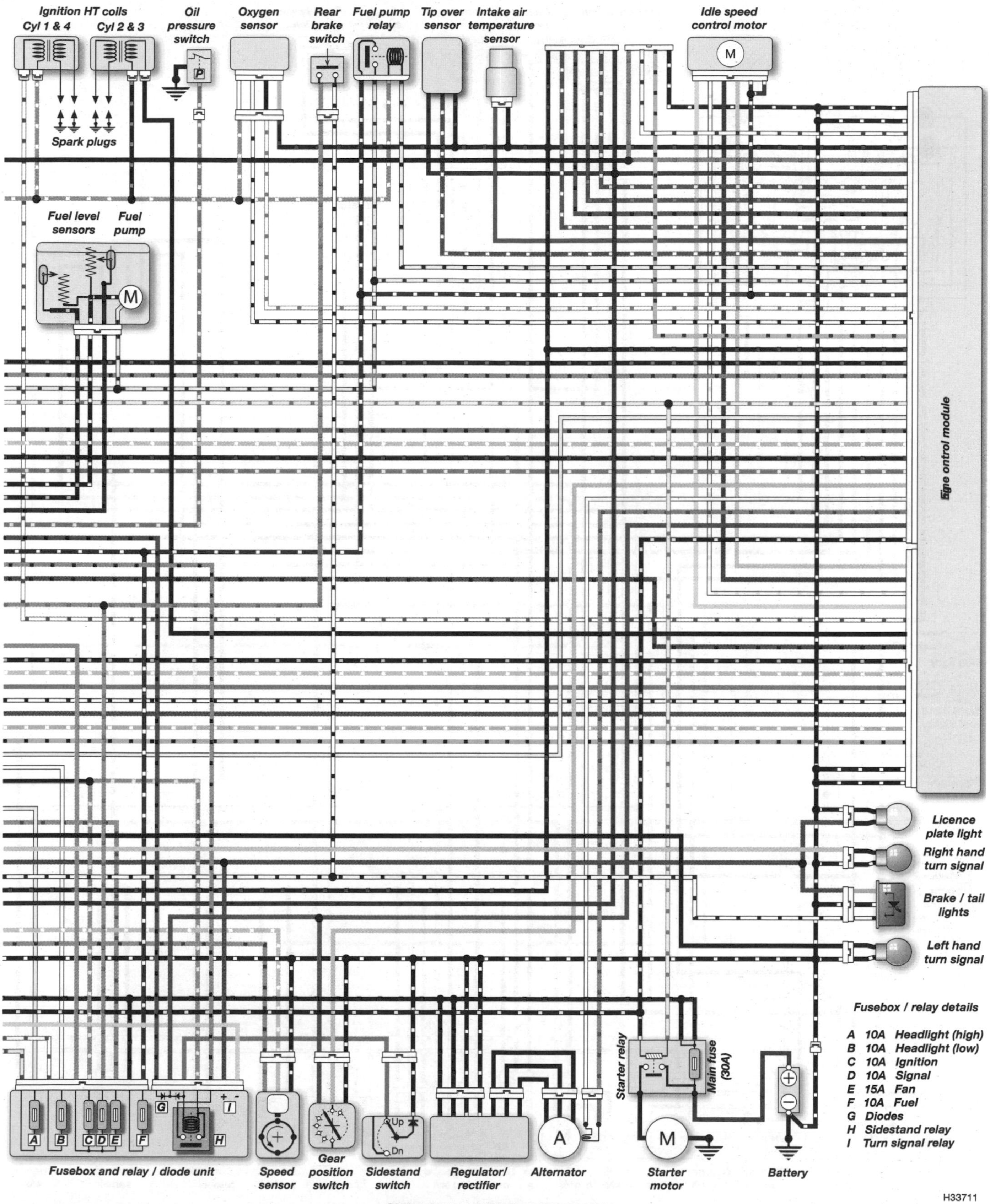

Ignition HT coils
Cyl 1 & 4
Cyl 2 & 3
Oil pressure switch
Oxygen sensor
Rear brake switch
Fuel pump relay
Tip over sensor
Intake air temperature sensor
Idle speed control motor
Spark plugs
Fuel level sensors
Fuel pump
Engine control module
Licence plate light
Right hand turn signal
Brake / tail lights
Left hand turn signal
Fusebox / relay details
A 10A Headlight (high)
B 10A Headlight (low)
C 10A Ignition
D 10A Signal
E 15A Fan
F 10A Fuel
G Diodes
H Sidestand relay
I Turn signal relay
Starter relay
Main fuse (30A)
Fusebox and relay / diode unit
Speed sensor
Gear position switch
Up
Dn
Sidestand switch
Regulator/ rectifier
Alternator
Starter motor
Battery
H33711

SV650K7 and K8 Europe models

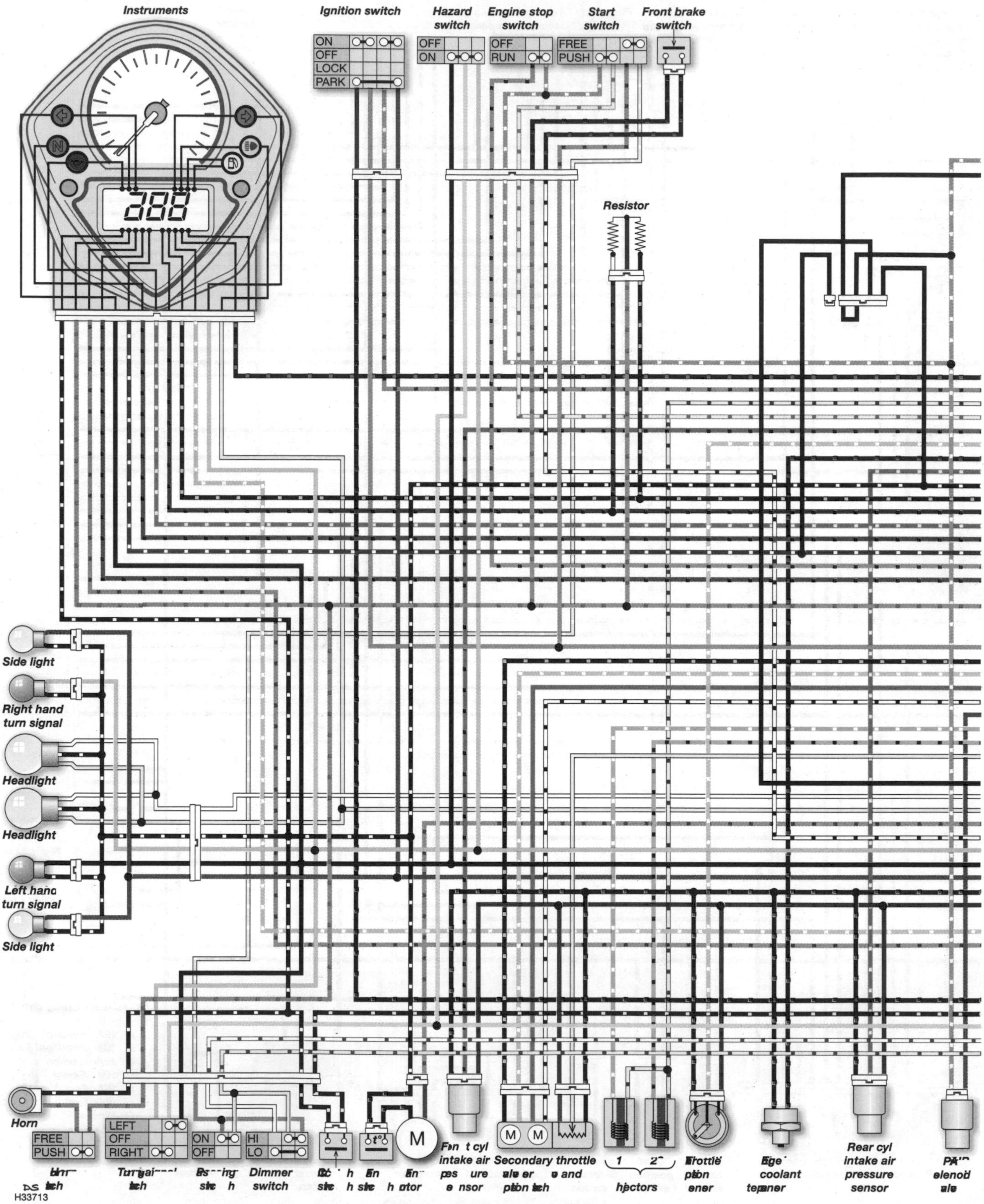

SV650SK7 and SK8 Europe models

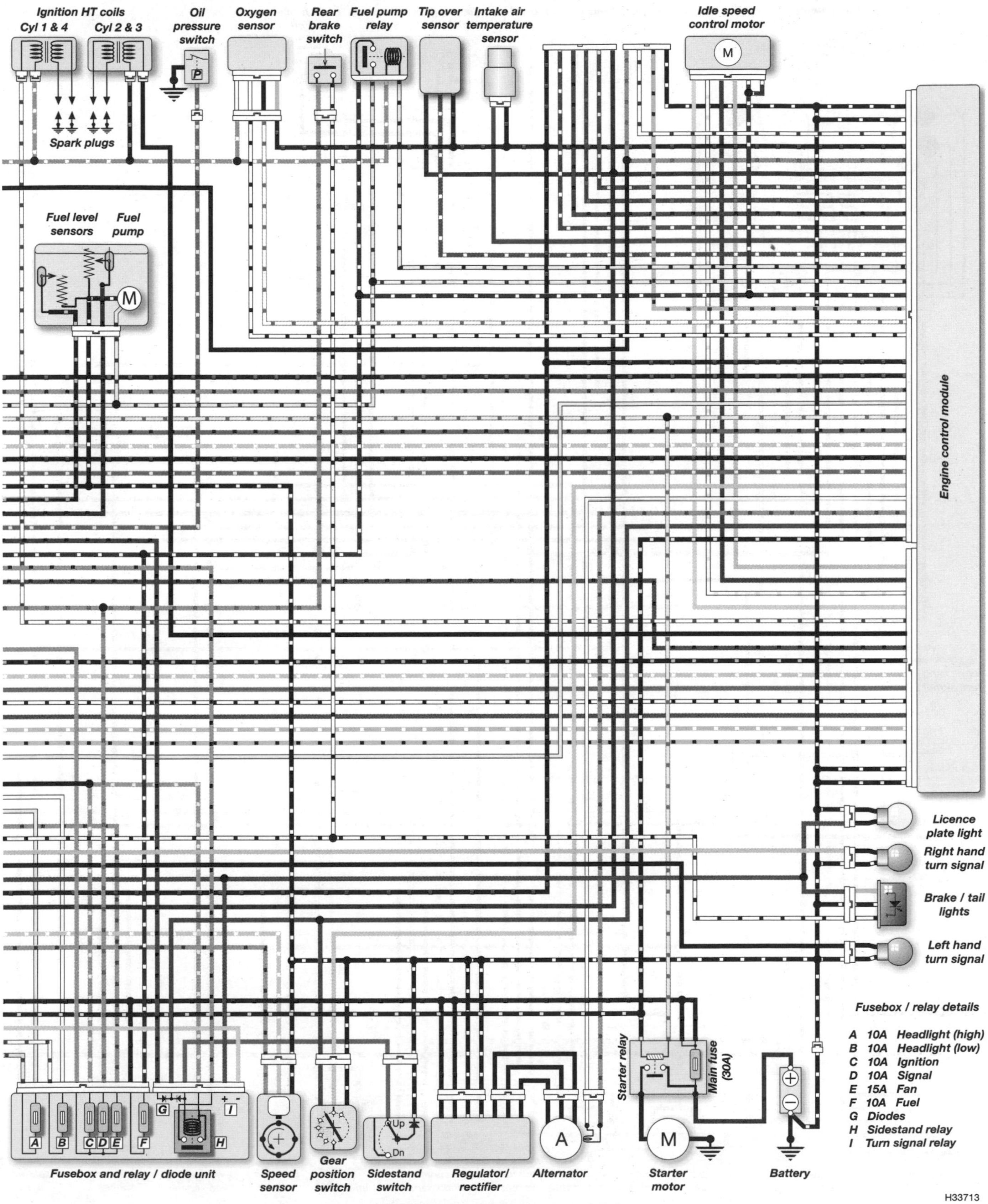

SV650SK7 and SK8 Europe models

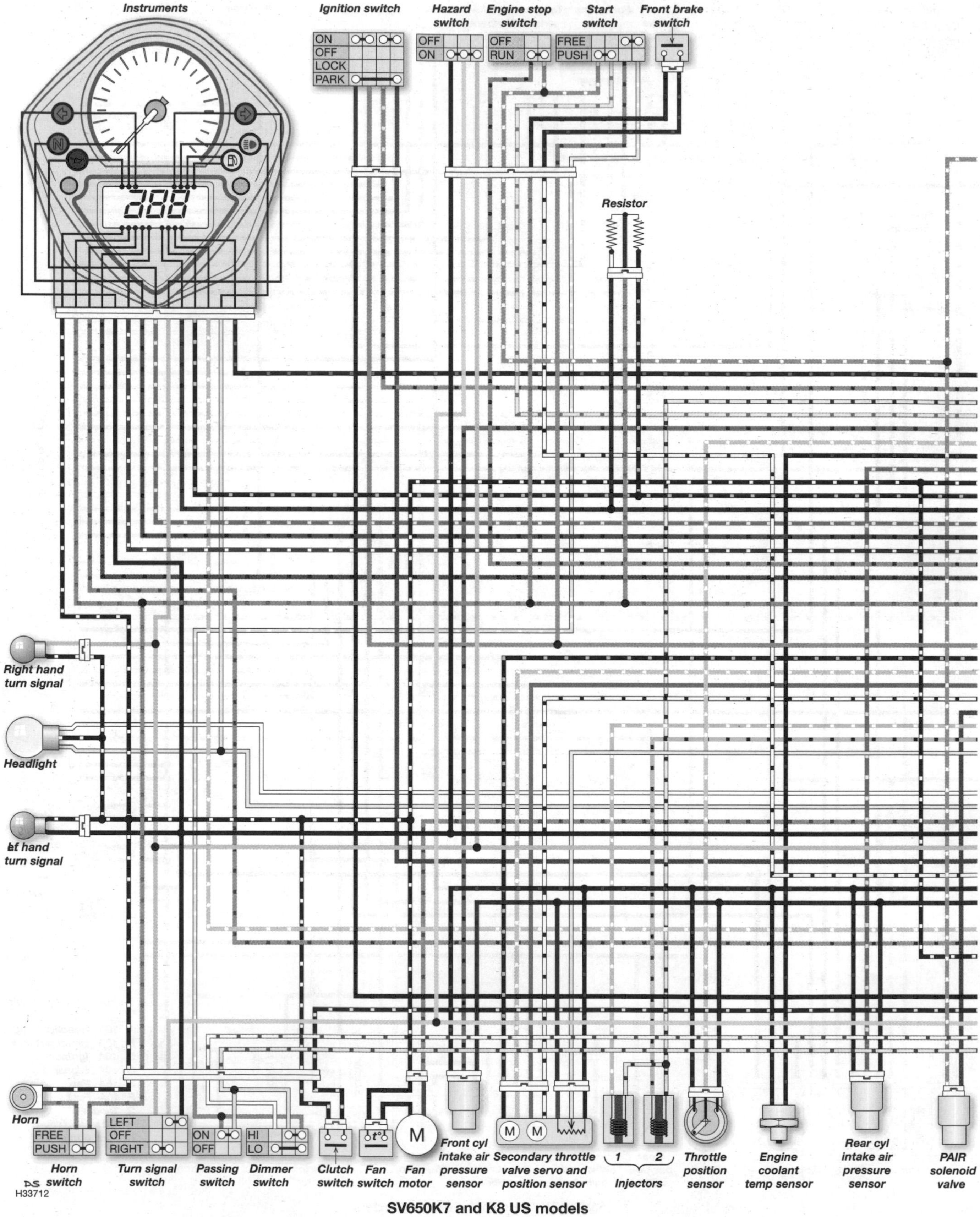

SV650K7 and K8 US models

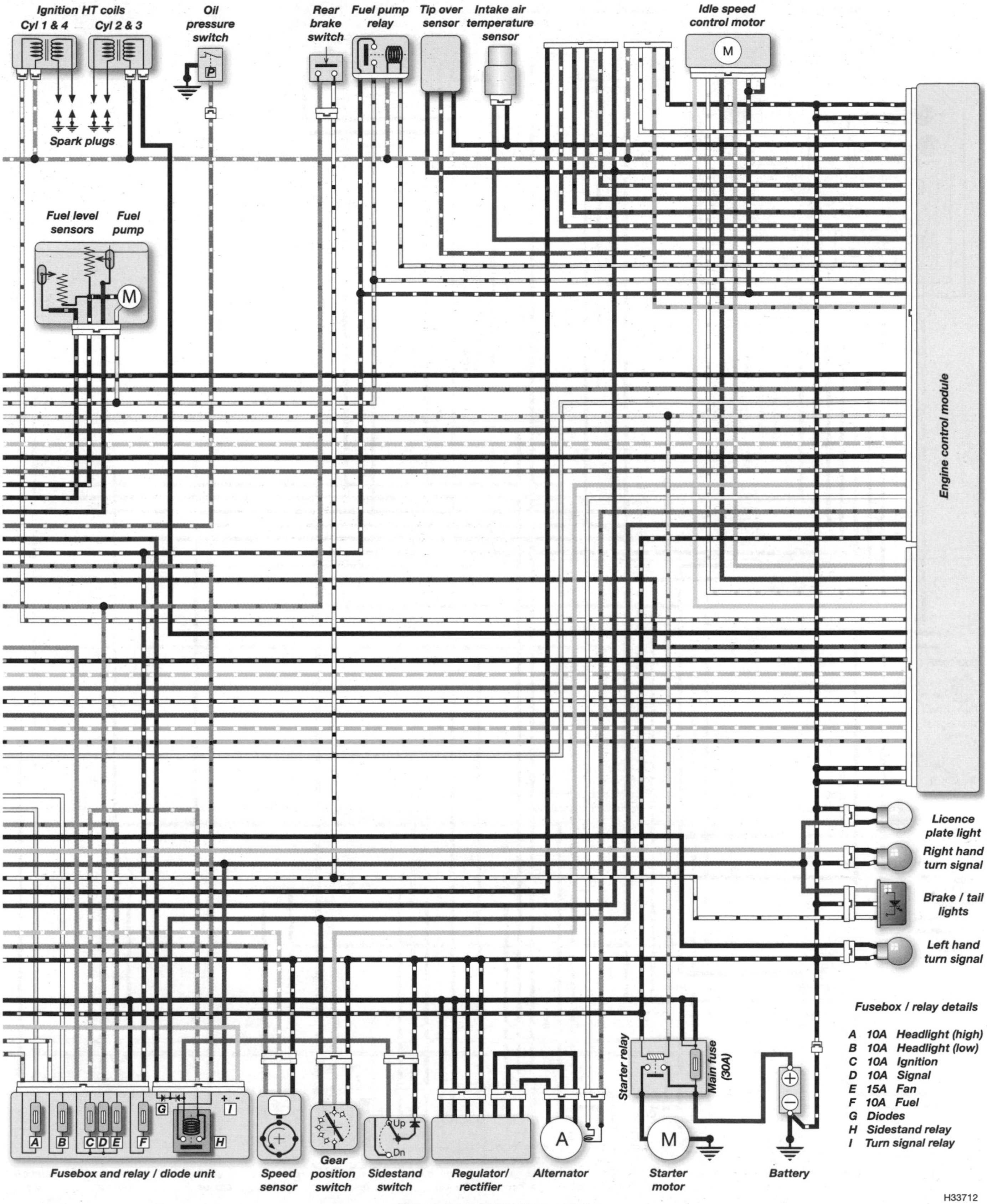

SV650K7 and K8 US models

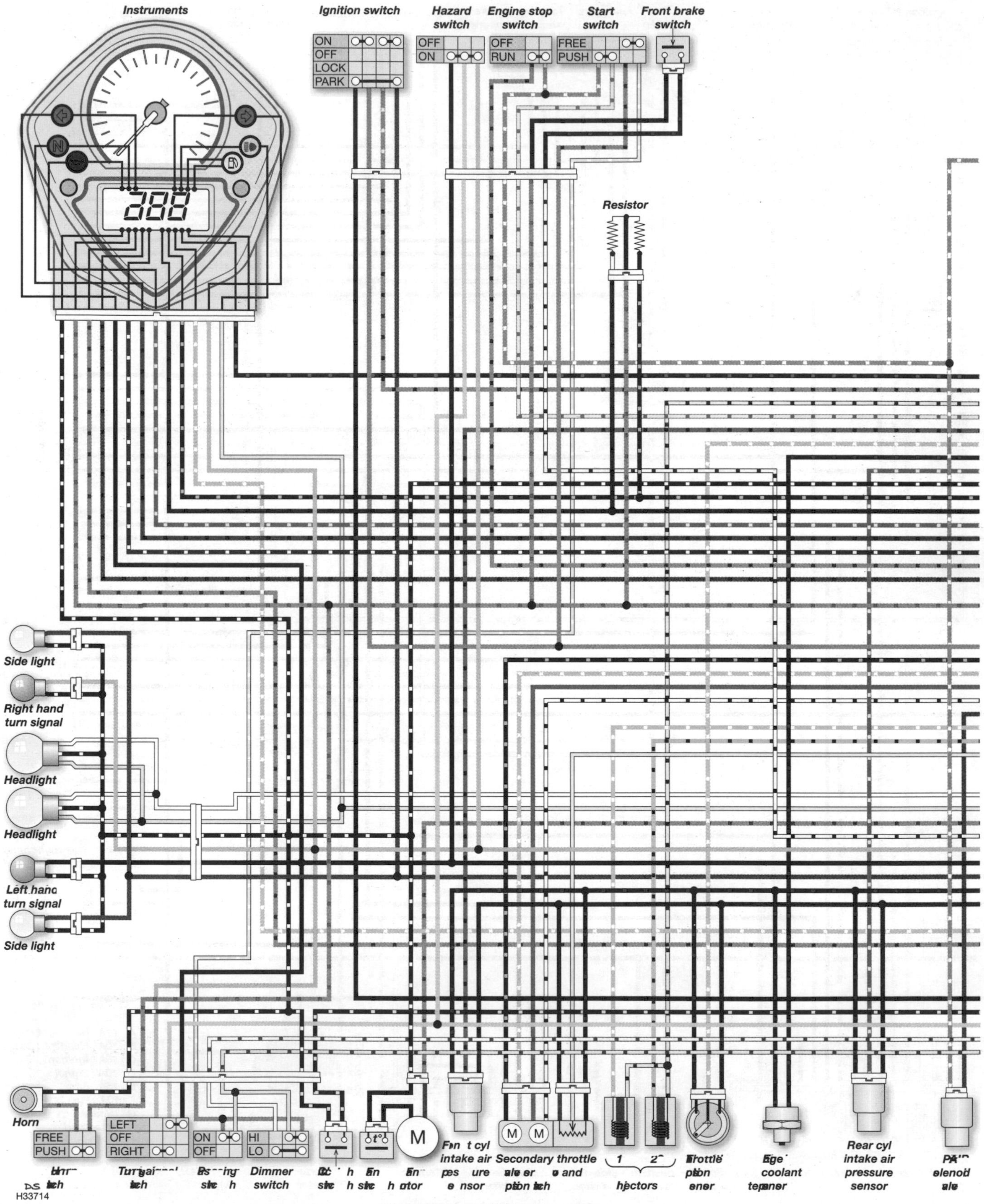

SV650SK7 and SK8 US models

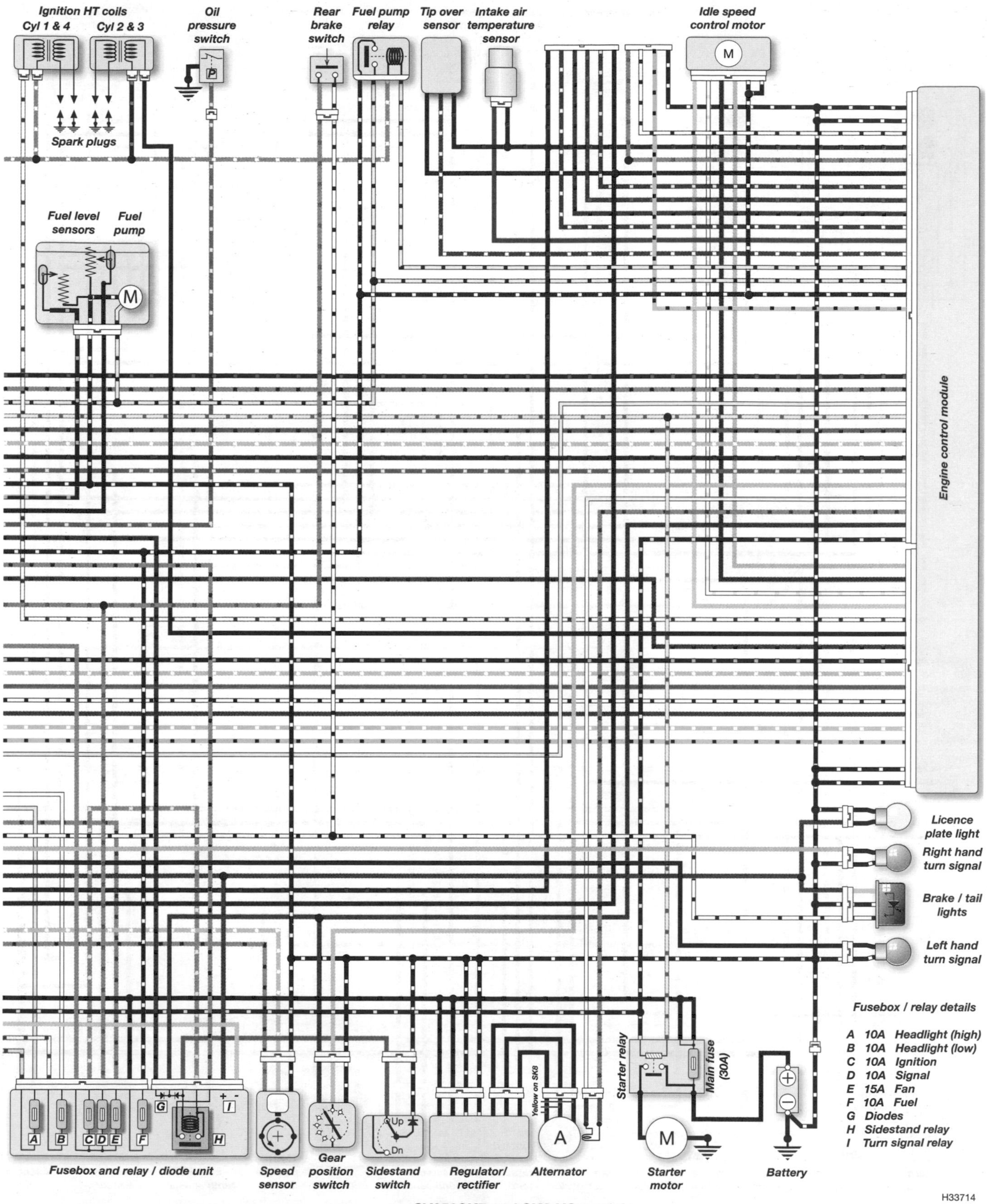

SV650SK7 and SK8 US models

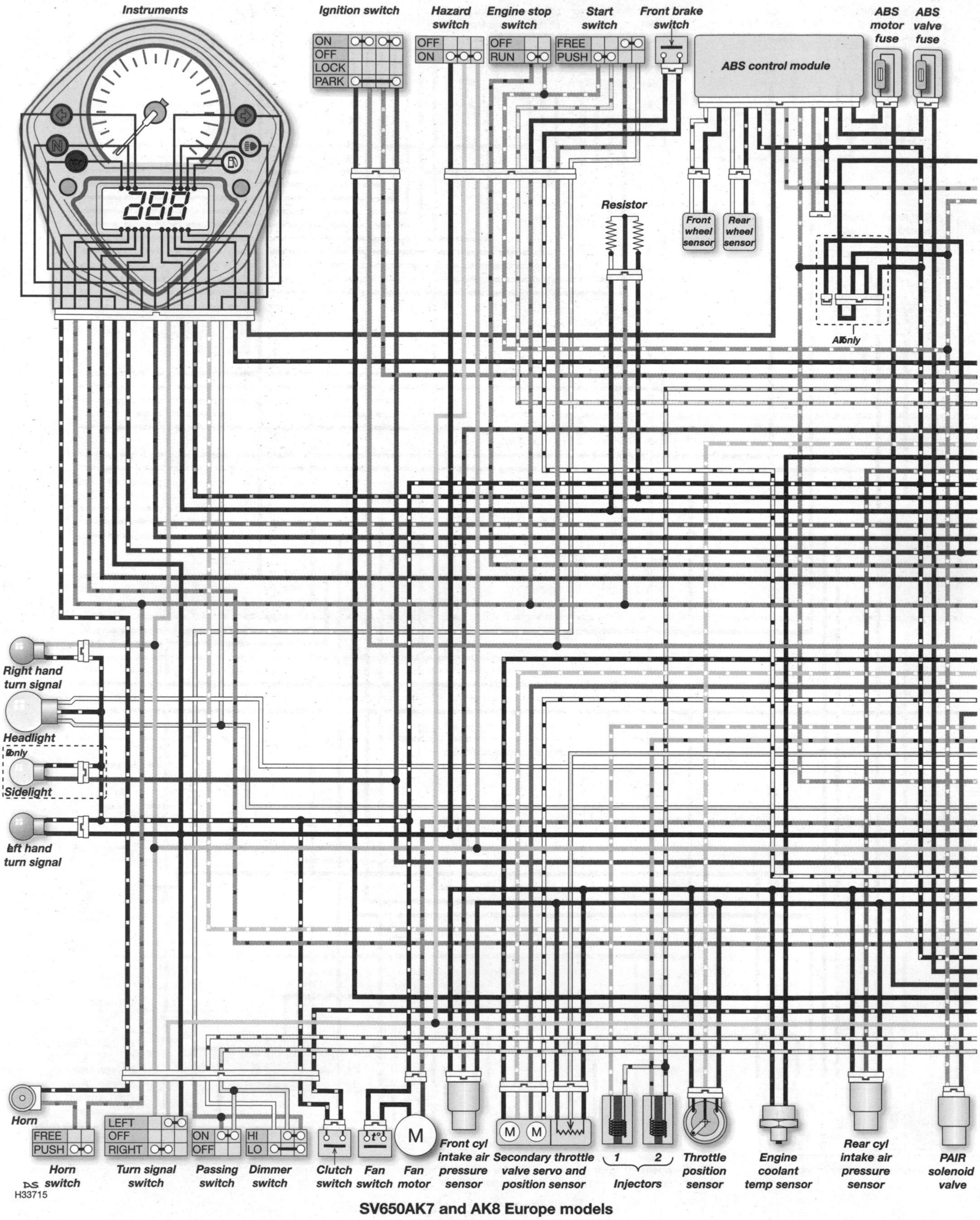

SV650AK7 and AK8 Europe models

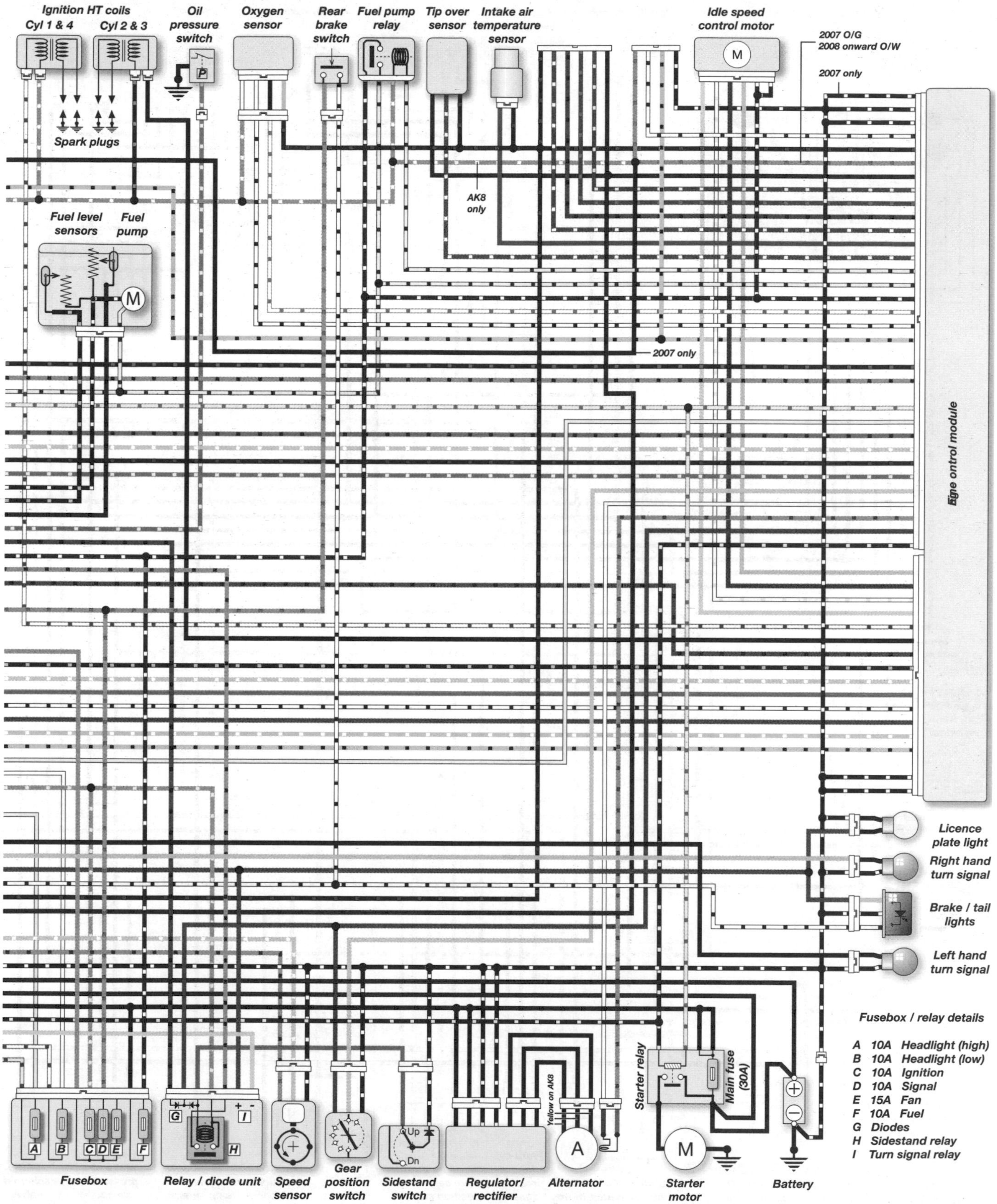

SV650AK7 and AK8 Europe models

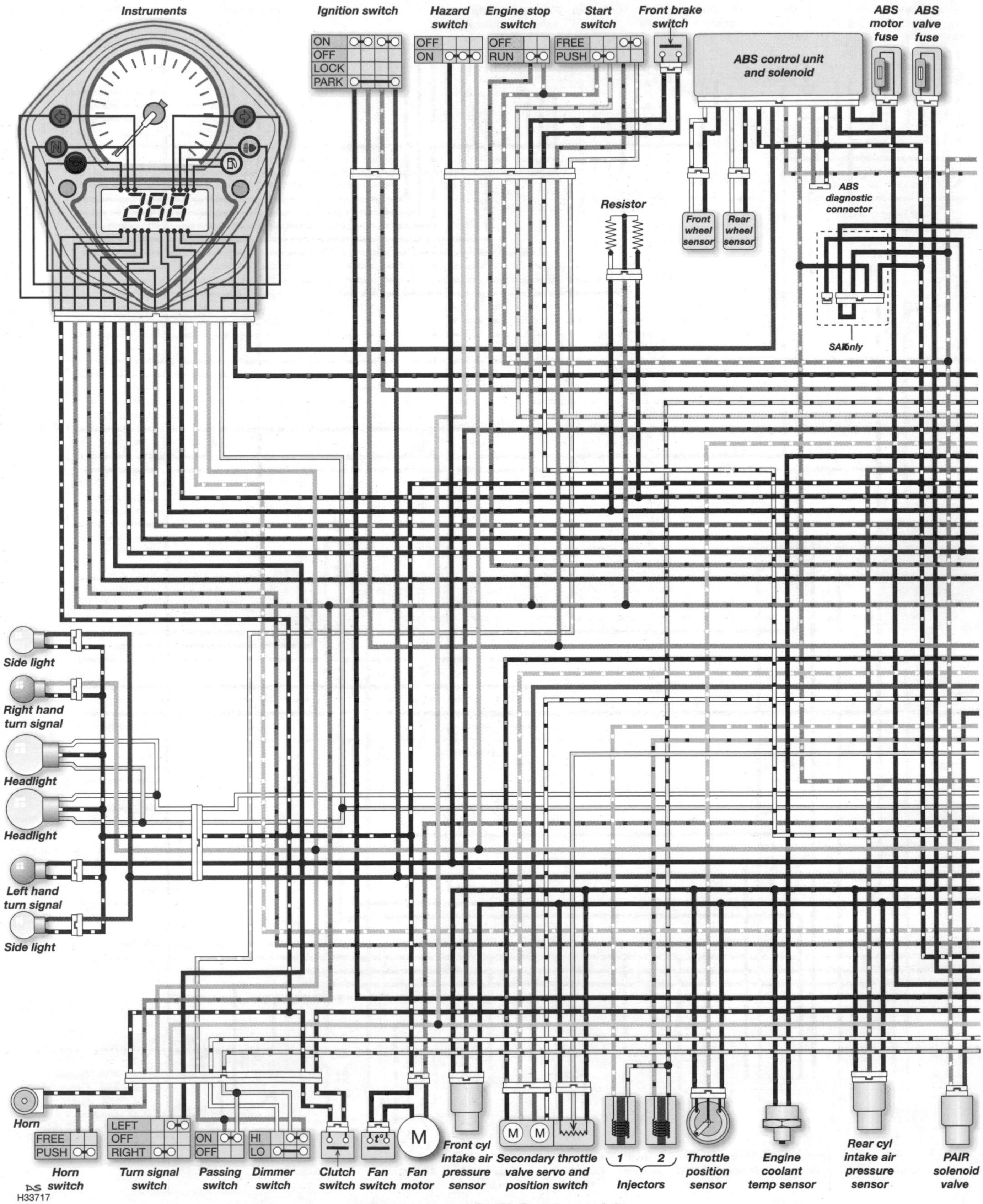

SV650SAK7 and SAK8 Europe models

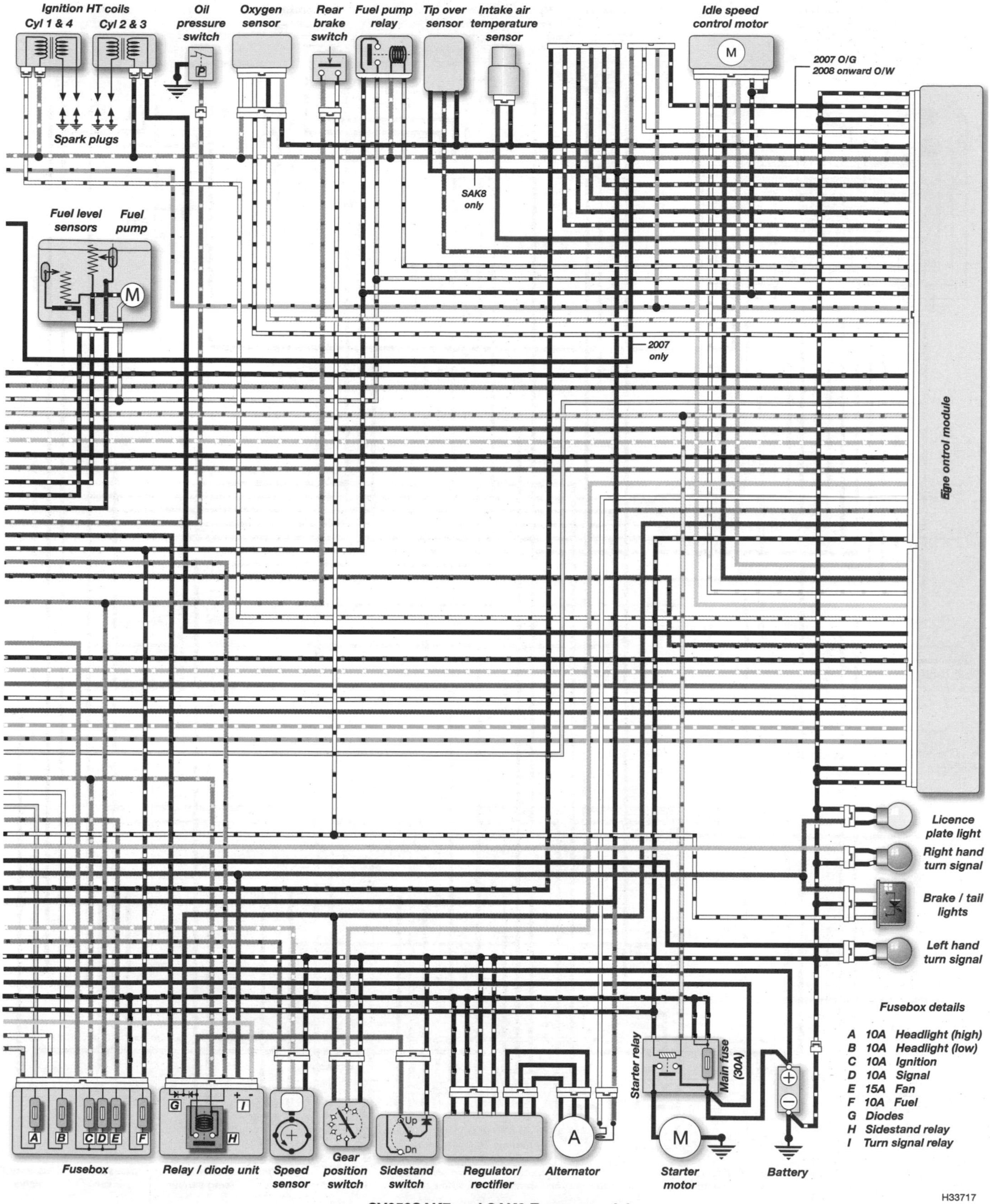

SV650SAK7 and SAK8 Europe models

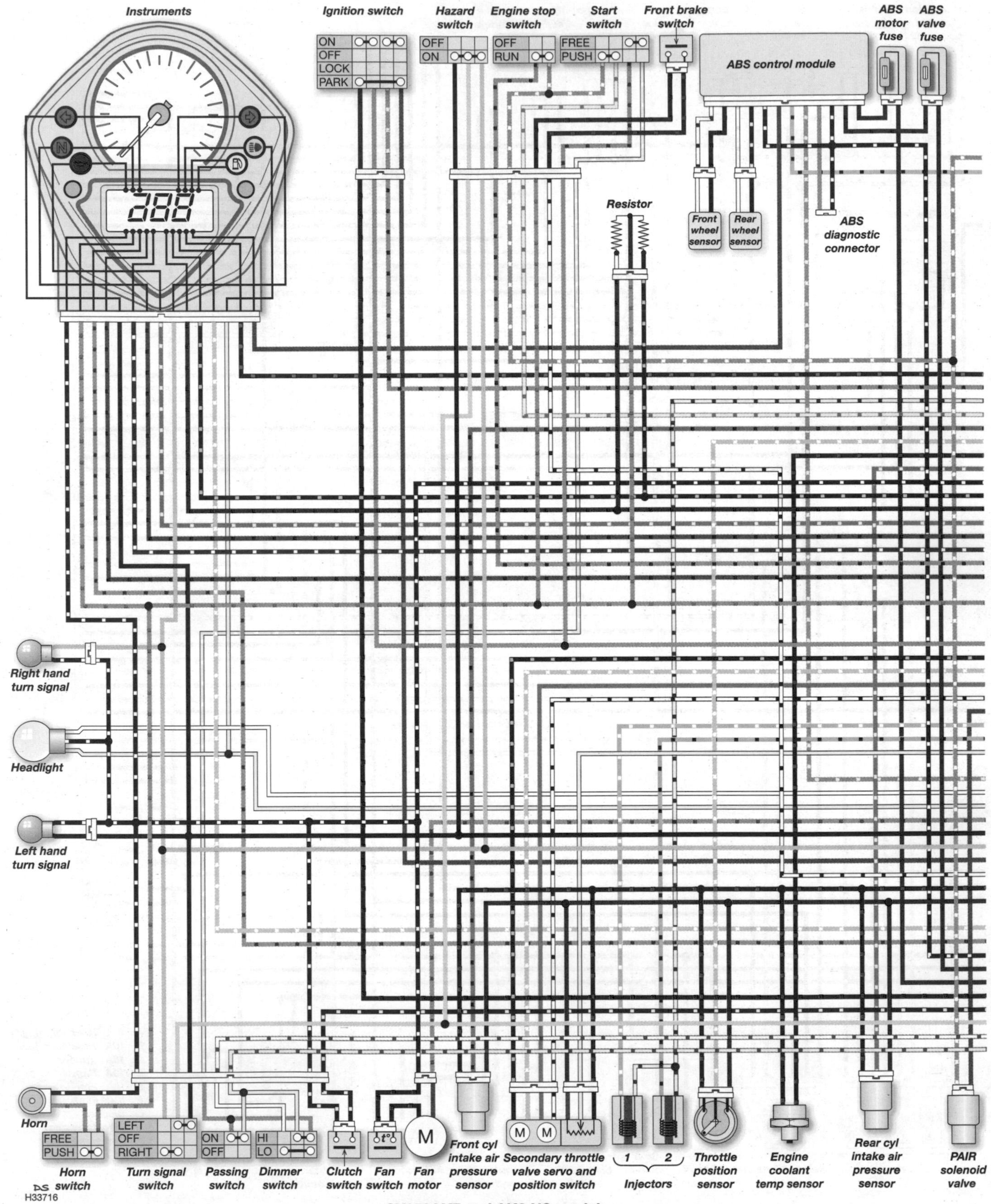

SV650AK7 and AK8 US models

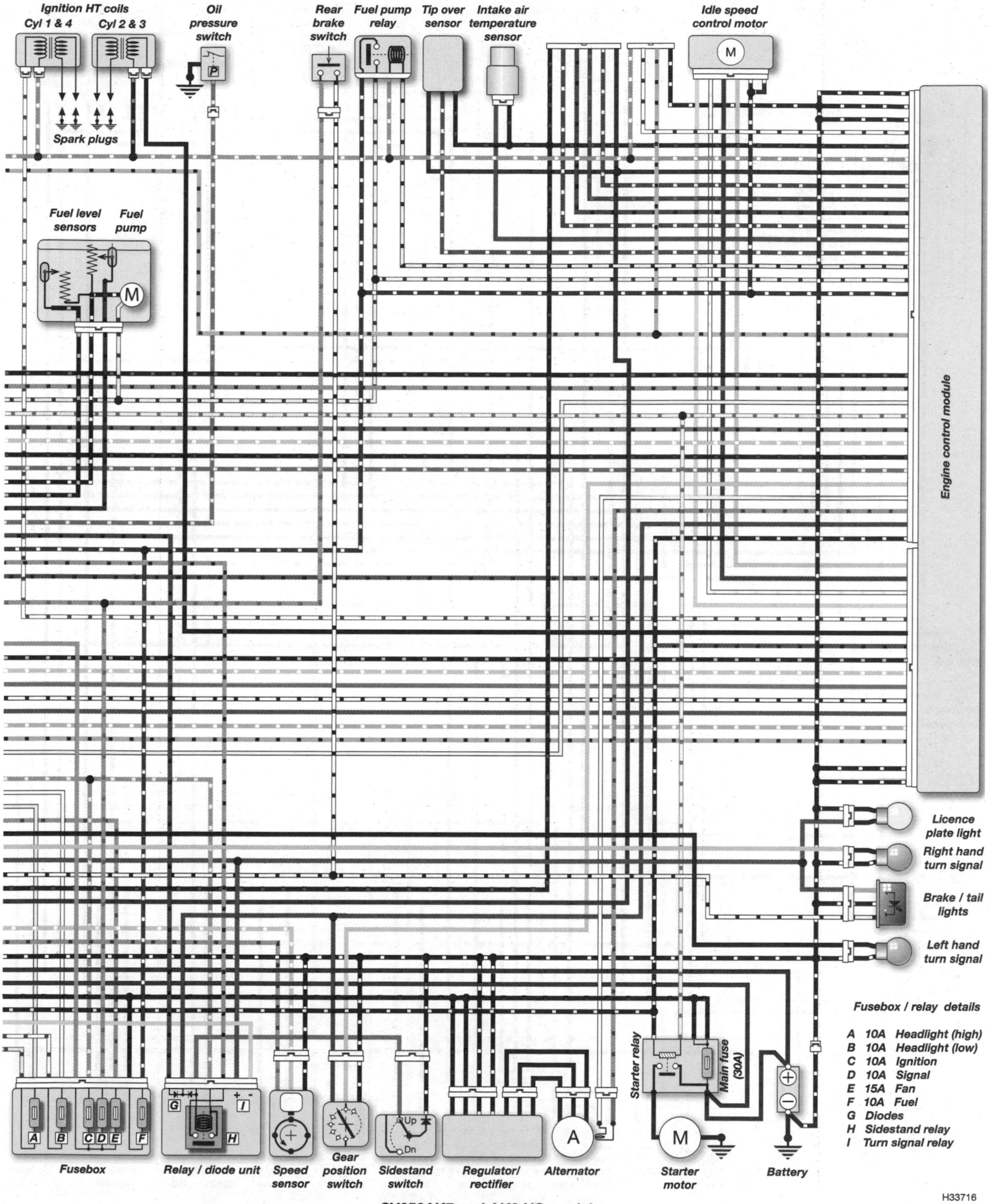

SV650AK7 and AK8 US models

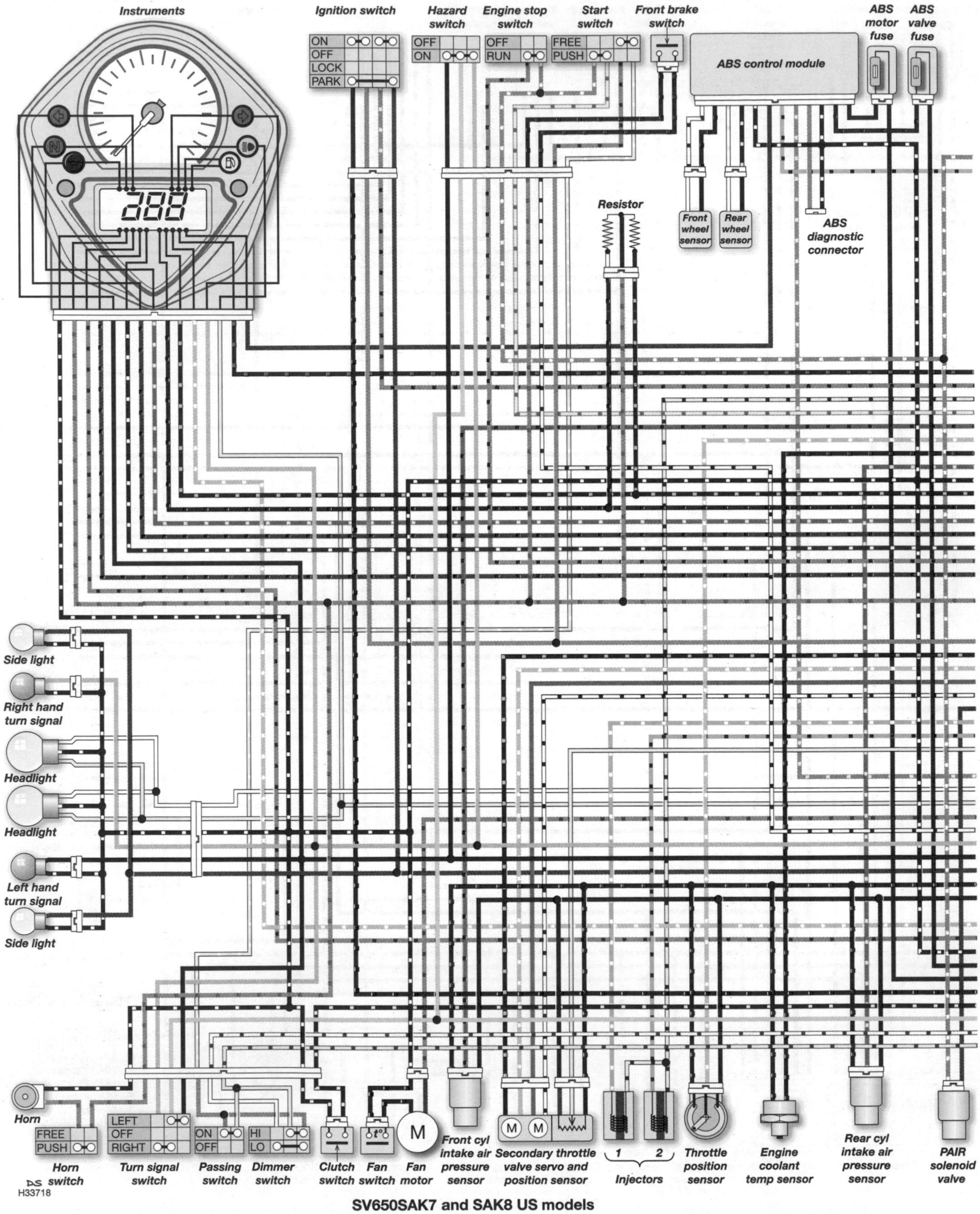

SV650SAK7 and SAK8 US models

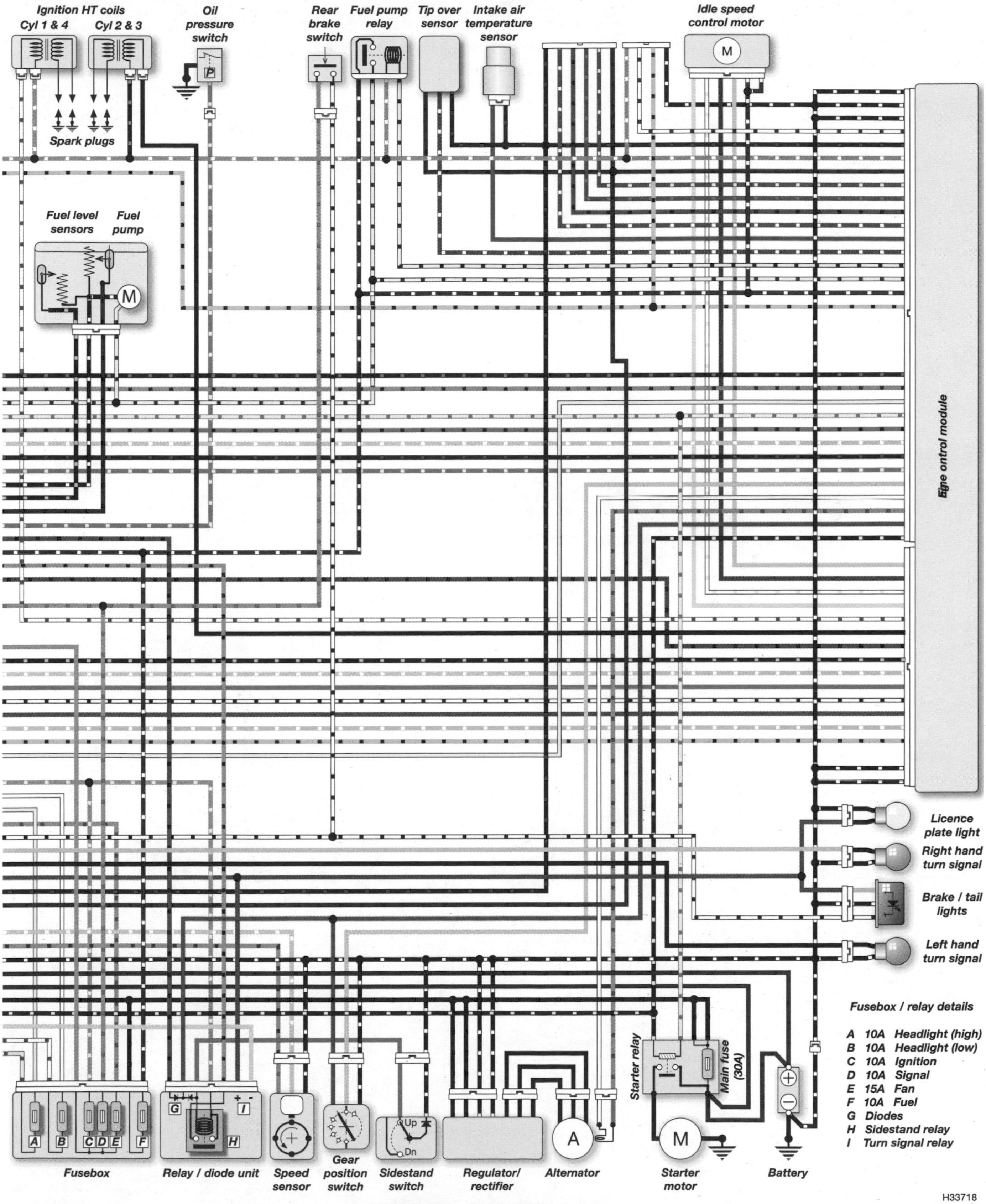

SV650SAK7 and SAK8 US models

Reference

Tools and Workshop Tips

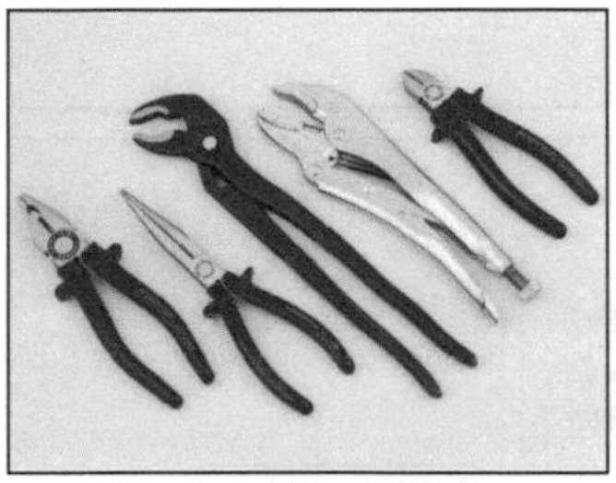

● Building up a tool kit and equipping your workshop ● Using tools ● Understanding bearing, seal, fastener and chain sizes and markings ● Repair techniques

Security

● Locks and chains ● U-locks ● Disc locks ● Alarms and immobilisers ● Security marking systems ● Tips on how to prevent bike theft

Lubricants and fluids

● Engine oils ● Transmission (gear) oils ● Coolant/anti-freeze ● Fork oils and suspension fluids ● Brake/clutch fluids ● Spray lubes, degreasers and solvents

Conversion Factors

$$34 \text{ Nm} \times 0.738 = 25 \text{ lbf ft}$$

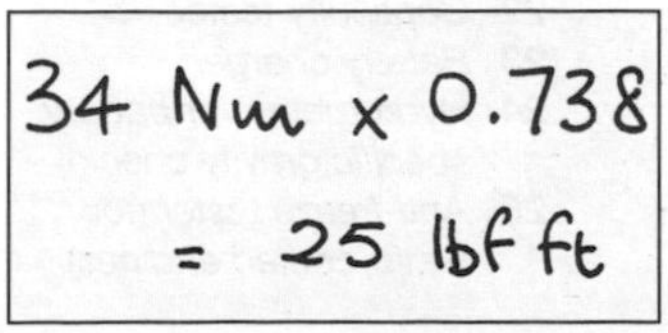

● Formulae for conversion of the metric (SI) units used throughout the manual into Imperial measures

MOT Test Checks

● A guide to the UK MOT test ● Which items are tested ● How to prepare your motorcycle for the test and perform a pre-test check

Storage

● How to prepare your motorcycle for going into storage and protect essential systems ● How to get the motorcycle back on the road

Fault Finding

● Common faults and their likely causes ● How to check engine cylinder compression ● How to make electrical tests and use test meters

Index

Buying tools

A toolkit is a fundamental requirement for servicing and repairing a motorcycle. Although there will be an initial expense in building up enough tools for servicing, this will soon be offset by the savings made by doing the job yourself. As experience and confidence grow, additional tools can be added to enable the repair and overhaul of the motorcycle. Many of the specialist tools are expensive and not often used so it may be preferable to hire them, or for a group of friends or motorcycle club to join in the purchase.

As a rule, it is better to buy more expensive, good quality tools. Cheaper tools are likely to wear out faster and need to be renewed more often, nullifying the original saving.

> ***Warning: To avoid the risk of a poor quality tool breaking in use, causing injury or damage to the component being worked on, always aim to purchase tools which meet the relevant national safety standards.***

The following lists of tools do not represent the manufacturer's service tools, but serve as a guide to help the owner decide which tools are needed for this level of work. In addition, items such as an electric drill, hacksaw, files, soldering iron and a workbench equipped with a vice, may be needed. Although not classed as tools, a selection of bolts, screws, nuts, washers and pieces of tubing always come in useful.

For more information about tools, refer to the Haynes *Motorcycle Workshop Practice Techbook* (Bk. No. 3470).

Manufacturer's service tools

Inevitably certain tasks require the use of a service tool. Where possible an alternative tool or method of approach is recommended, but sometimes there is no option if personal injury or damage to the component is to be avoided. Where required, service tools are referred to in the relevant procedure.

Service tools can usually only be purchased from a motorcycle dealer and are identified by a part number. Some of the commonly-used tools, such as rotor pullers, are available in aftermarket form from mail-order motorcycle tool and accessory suppliers.

Maintenance and minor repair tools

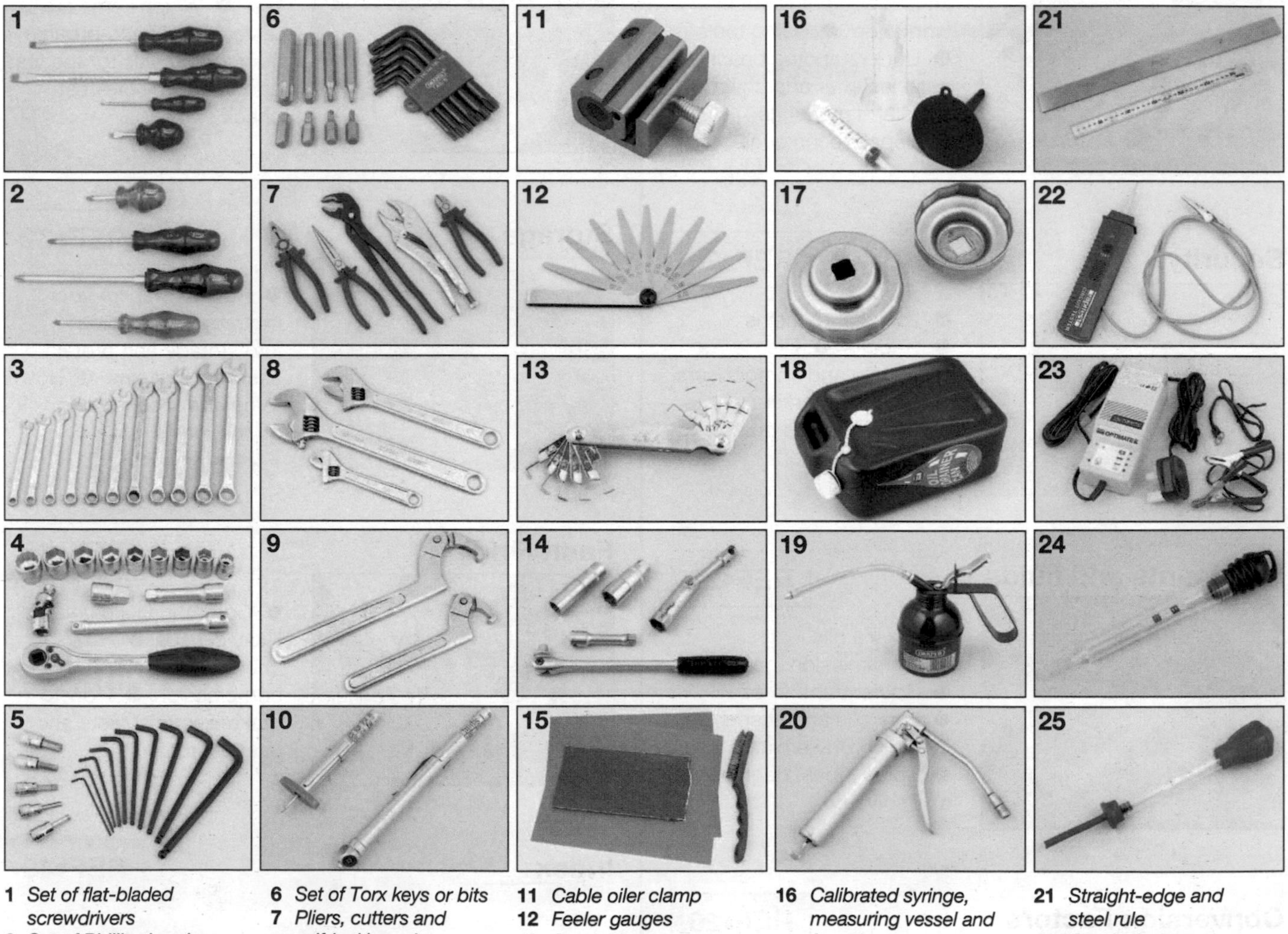

1 *Set of flat-bladed screwdrivers*
2 *Set of Phillips head screwdrivers*
3 *Combination open-end and ring spanners*
4 *Socket set (3/8 inch or 1/2 inch drive)*
5 *Set of Allen keys or bits*
6 *Set of Torx keys or bits*
7 *Pliers, cutters and self-locking grips (Mole grips)*
8 *Adjustable spanners*
9 *C-spanners*
10 *Tread depth gauge and tyre pressure gauge*
11 *Cable oiler clamp*
12 *Feeler gauges*
13 *Spark plug gap measuring tool*
14 *Spark plug spanner or deep plug sockets*
15 *Wire brush and emery paper*
16 *Calibrated syringe, measuring vessel and funnel*
17 *Oil filter adapters*
18 *Oil drainer can or tray*
19 *Pump type oil can*
20 *Grease gun*
21 *Straight-edge and steel rule*
22 *Continuity tester*
23 *Battery charger*
24 *Hydrometer (for battery specific gravity check)*
25 *Anti-freeze tester (for liquid-cooled engines)*

Repair and overhaul tools

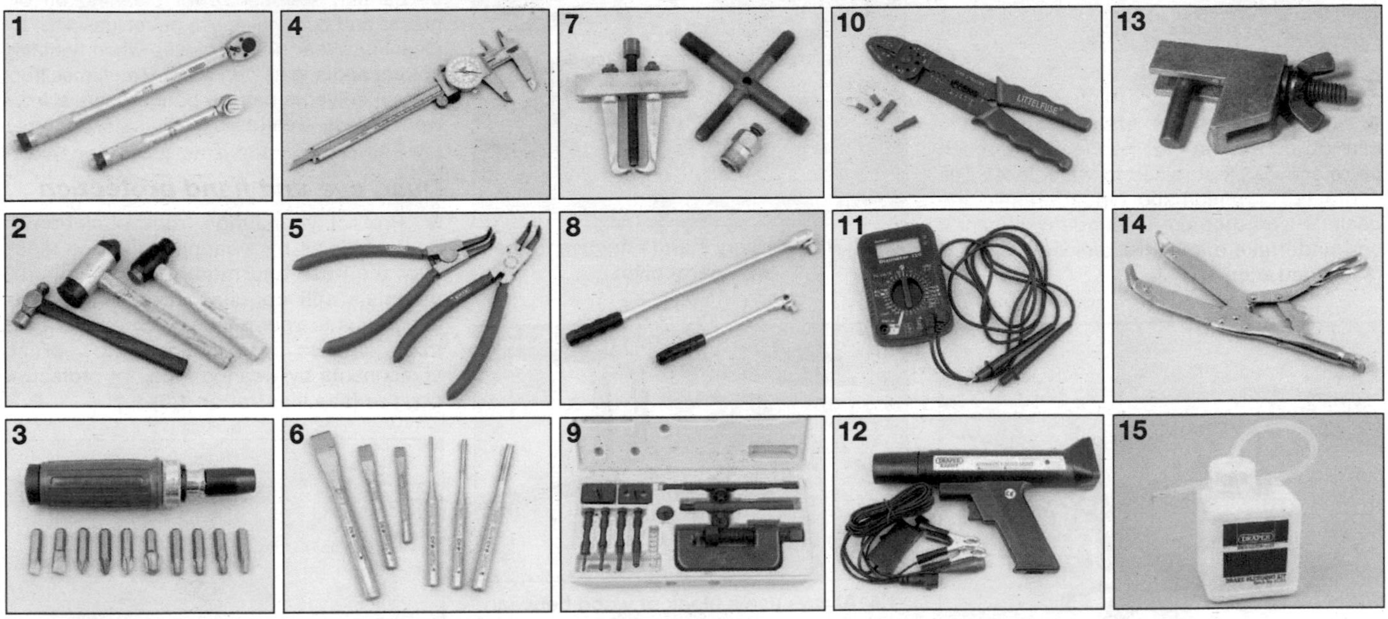

1 *Torque wrench (small and mid-ranges)*
2 *Conventional, plastic or soft-faced hammers*
3 *Impact driver set*
4 *Vernier gauge*
5 *Circlip pliers (internal and external, or combination)*
6 *Set of cold chisels and punches*
7 *Selection of pullers*
8 *Breaker bars*
9 *Chain breaking/ riveting tool set*
10 *Wire stripper and crimper tool*
11 *Multimeter (measures amps, volts and ohms)*
12 *Stroboscope (for dynamic timing checks)*
13 *Hose clamp (wingnut type shown)*
14 *Clutch holding tool*
15 *One-man brake/clutch bleeder kit*

Specialist tools

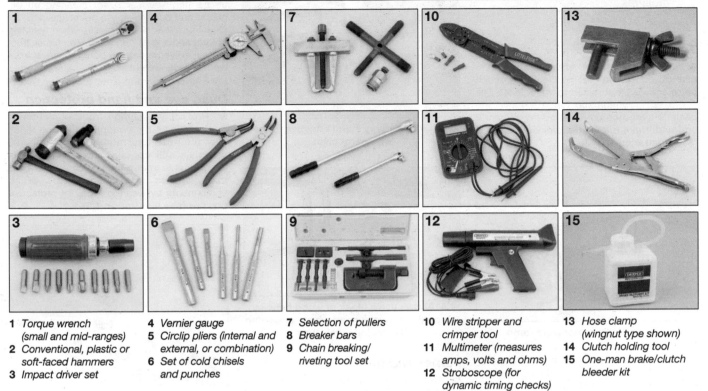

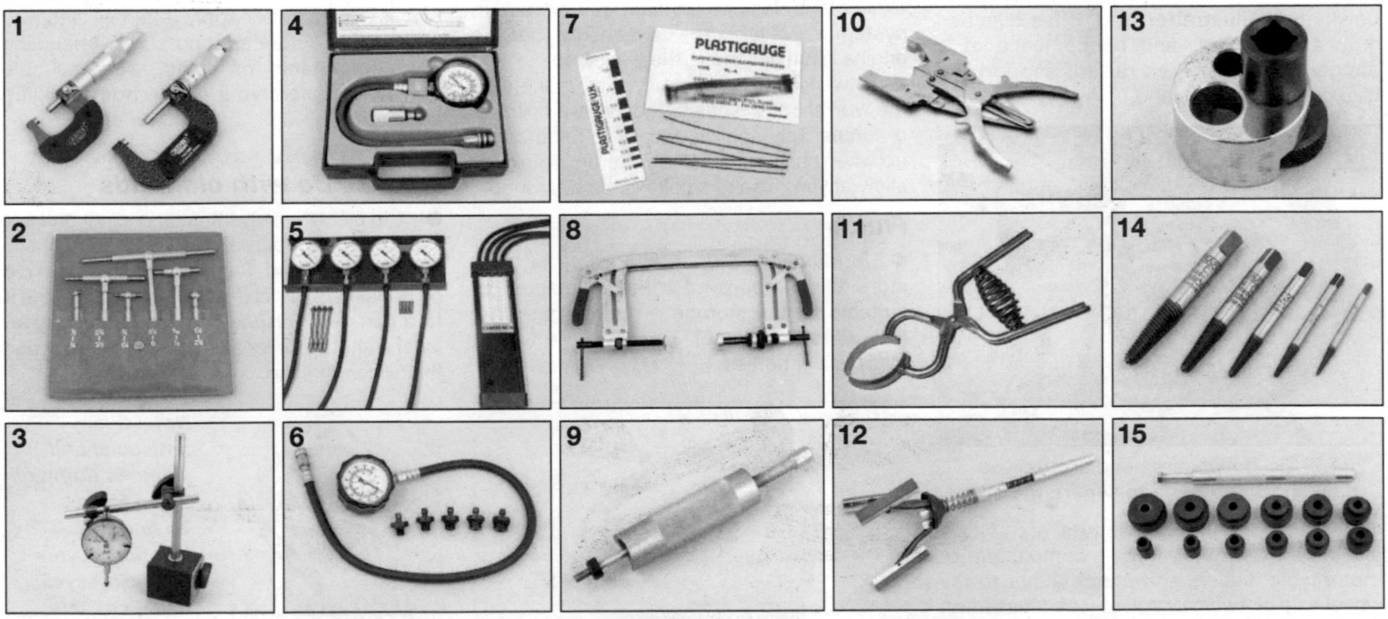

1 *Micrometers (external type)*
2 *Telescoping gauges*
3 *Dial gauge*
4 *Cylinder compression gauge*
5 *Vacuum gauges (left) or manometer (right)*
6 *Oil pressure gauge*
7 *Plastigauge kit*
8 *Valve spring compressor (4-stroke engines)*
9 *Piston pin drawbolt tool*
10 *Piston ring removal and installation tool*
11 *Piston ring clamp*
12 *Cylinder bore hone (stone type shown)*
13 *Stud extractor*
14 *Screw extractor set*
15 *Bearing driver set*

1 Workshop equipment and facilities

The workbench

● Work is made much easier by raising the bike up on a ramp - components are much more accessible if raised to waist level. The hydraulic or pneumatic types seen in the dealer's workshop are a sound investment if you undertake a lot of repairs or overhauls **(see illustration 1.1)**.

1.1 Hydraulic motorcycle ramp

● If raised off ground level, the bike must be supported on the ramp to avoid it falling. Most ramps incorporate a front wheel locating clamp which can be adjusted to suit different diameter wheels. When tightening the clamp, take care not to mark the wheel rim or damage the tyre - use wood blocks on each side to prevent this.

● Secure the bike to the ramp using tie-downs **(see illustration 1.2)**. If the bike has only a sidestand, and hence leans at a dangerous angle when raised, support the bike on an auxiliary stand.

1.2 Tie-downs are used around the passenger footrests to secure the bike

● Auxiliary (paddock) stands are widely available from mail order companies or motorcycle dealers and attach either to the wheel axle or swingarm pivot **(see illustration 1.3)**. If the motorcycle has a centrestand, you can support it under the crankcase to prevent it toppling whilst either wheel is removed **(see illustration 1.4)**.

1.3 This auxiliary stand attaches to the swingarm pivot

1.4 Always use a block of wood between the engine and jack head when supporting the engine in this way

Fumes and fire

● Refer to the Safety first! page at the beginning of the manual for full details. Make sure your workshop is equipped with a fire extinguisher suitable for fuel-related fires (Class B fire - flammable liquids) - it is not sufficient to have a water-filled extinguisher.

● Always ensure adequate ventilation is available. Unless an exhaust gas extraction system is available for use, ensure that the engine is run outside of the workshop.

● If working on the fuel system, make sure the workshop is ventilated to avoid a build-up of fumes. This applies equally to fume build-up when charging a battery. Do not smoke or allow anyone else to smoke in the workshop.

Fluids

● If you need to drain fuel from the tank, store it in an approved container marked as suitable for the storage of petrol (gasoline) **(see illustration 1.5)**. Do not store fuel in glass jars or bottles.

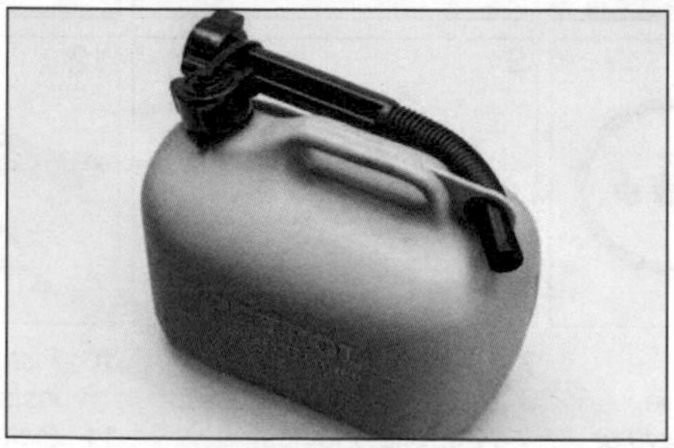

1.5 Use an approved can only for storing petrol (gasoline)

● Use proprietary engine degreasers or solvents which have a high flash-point, such as paraffin (kerosene), for cleaning off oil, grease and dirt - never use petrol (gasoline) for cleaning. Wear rubber gloves when handling solvent and engine degreaser. The fumes from certain solvents can be dangerous - always work in a well-ventilated area.

Dust, eye and hand protection

● Protect your lungs from inhalation of dust particles by wearing a filtering mask over the nose and mouth. Many frictional materials still contain asbestos which is dangerous to your health. Protect your eyes from spouts of liquid and sprung components by wearing a pair of protective goggles **(see illustration 1.6)**.

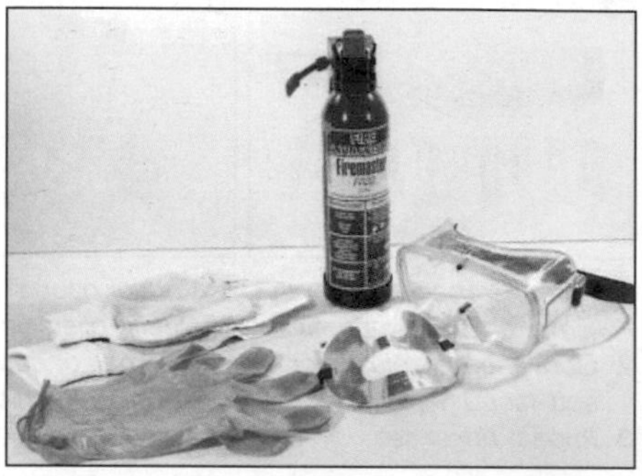

1.6 A fire extinguisher, goggles, mask and protective gloves should be at hand in the workshop

● Protect your hands from contact with solvents, fuel and oils by wearing rubber gloves. Alternatively apply a barrier cream to your hands before starting work. If handling hot components or fluids, wear suitable gloves to protect your hands from scalding and burns.

What to do with old fluids

● Old cleaning solvent, fuel, coolant and oils should not be poured down domestic drains or onto the ground. Package the fluid up in old oil containers, label it accordingly, and take it to a garage or disposal facility. Contact your local authority for location of such sites or ring the oil care hotline.

OIL CARE
FOLLOW THE CODE
OIL BANK LINE
0800 66 33 66
www.oilbankline.org.uk

Note: It is antisocial and illegal to dump oil down the drain. To find the location of your local oil recycling bank, call this number free.

In the USA, note that any oil supplier must accept used oil for recycling.

2 Fasteners - screws, bolts and nuts

Fastener types and applications

Bolts and screws

● Fastener head types are either of hexagonal, Torx or splined design, with internal and external versions of each type **(see illustrations 2.1 and 2.2)**; splined head fasteners are not in common use on motorcycles. The conventional slotted or Phillips head design is used for certain screws. Bolt or screw length is always measured from the underside of the head to the end of the item **(see illustration 2.11)**.

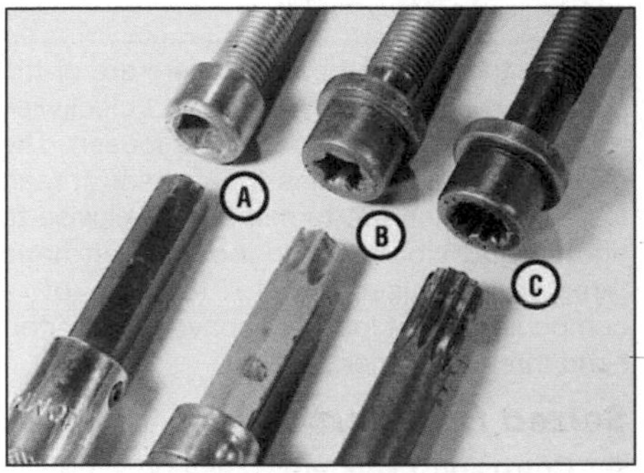

2.1 Internal hexagon/Allen (A), Torx (B) and splined (C) fasteners, with corresponding bits

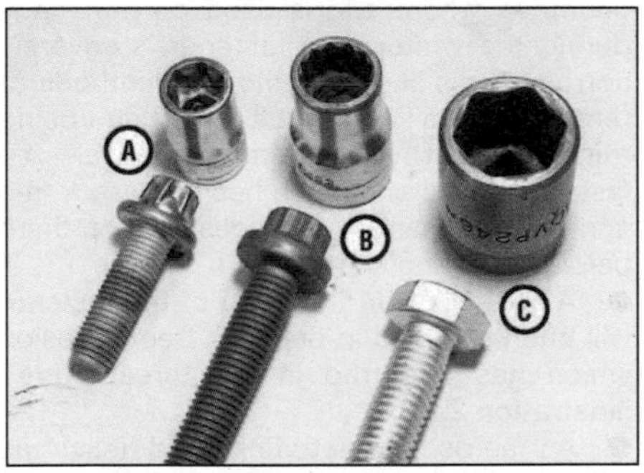

2.2 External Torx (A), splined (B) and hexagon (C) fasteners, with corresponding sockets

● Certain fasteners on the motorcycle have a tensile marking on their heads, the higher the marking the stronger the fastener. High tensile fasteners generally carry a 10 or higher marking. Never replace a high tensile fastener with one of a lower tensile strength.

Washers (see illustration 2.3)

● Plain washers are used between a fastener head and a component to prevent damage to the component or to spread the load when torque is applied. Plain washers can also be used as spacers or shims in certain assemblies. Copper or aluminium plain washers are often used as sealing washers on drain plugs.

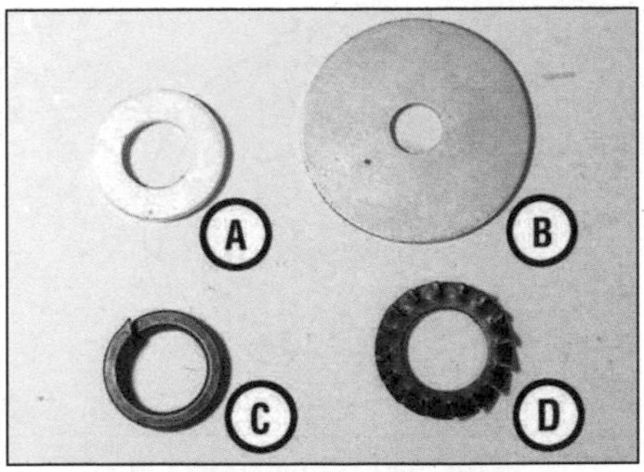

2.3 Plain washer (A), penny washer (B), spring washer (C) and serrated washer (D)

● The split-ring spring washer works by applying axial tension between the fastener head and component. If flattened, it is fatigued and must be renewed. If a plain (flat) washer is used on the fastener, position the spring washer between the fastener and the plain washer.

● Serrated star type washers dig into the fastener and component faces, preventing loosening. They are often used on electrical earth (ground) connections to the frame.

● Cone type washers (sometimes called Belleville) are conical and when tightened apply axial tension between the fastener head and component. They must be installed with the dished side against the component and often carry an OUTSIDE marking on their outer face. If flattened, they are fatigued and must be renewed.

● Tab washers are used to lock plain nuts or bolts on a shaft. A portion of the tab washer is bent up hard against one flat of the nut or bolt to prevent it loosening. Due to the tab washer being deformed in use, a new tab washer should be used every time it is disturbed.

● Wave washers are used to take up endfloat on a shaft. They provide light springing and prevent excessive side-to-side play of a component. Can be found on rocker arm shafts.

Nuts and split pins

● Conventional plain nuts are usually six-sided **(see illustration 2.4)**. They are sized by thread diameter and pitch. High tensile nuts carry a number on one end to denote their tensile strength.

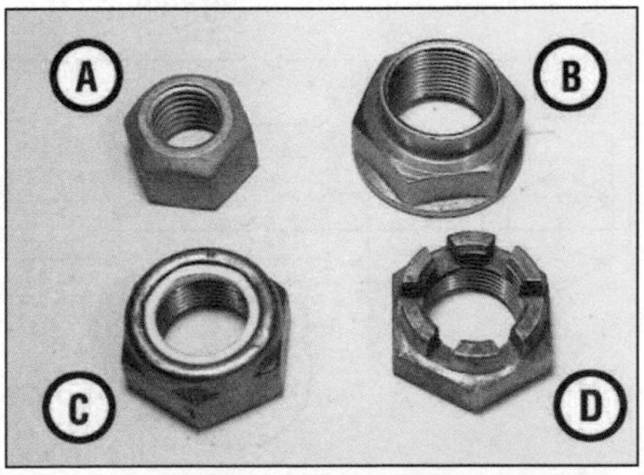

2.4 Plain nut (A), shouldered locknut (B), nylon insert nut (C) and castellated nut (D)

● Self-locking nuts either have a nylon insert, or two spring metal tabs, or a shoulder which is staked into a groove in the shaft - their advantage over conventional plain nuts is a resistance to loosening due to vibration. The nylon insert type can be used a number of times, but must be renewed when the friction of the nylon insert is reduced, ie when the nut spins freely on the shaft. The spring tab type can be reused unless the tabs are damaged. The shouldered type must be renewed every time it is disturbed.

● Split pins (cotter pins) are used to lock a castellated nut to a shaft or to prevent slackening of a plain nut. Common applications are wheel axles and brake torque arms. Because the split pin arms are deformed to lock around the nut a new split pin must always be used on installation - always fit the correct size split pin which will fit snugly in the shaft hole. Make sure the split pin arms are correctly located around the nut **(see illustrations 2.5 and 2.6)**.

2.5 Bend split pin (cotter pin) arms as shown (arrows) to secure a castellated nut

2.6 Bend split pin (cotter pin) arms as shown to secure a plain nut

> ***Caution: If the castellated nut slots do not align with the shaft hole after tightening to the torque setting, tighten the nut until the next slot aligns with the hole - never slacken the nut to align its slot.***

● R-pins (shaped like the letter R), or slip pins as they are sometimes called, are sprung and can be reused if they are otherwise in good condition. Always install R-pins with their closed end facing forwards **(see illustration 2.7)**.

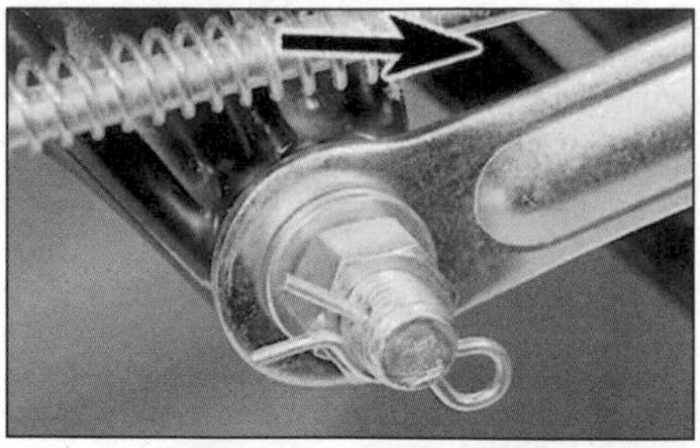

2.7 Correct fitting of R-pin. Arrow indicates forward direction

Circlips (see illustration 2.8)

● Circlips (sometimes called snap-rings) are used to retain components on a shaft or in a housing and have corresponding external or internal ears to permit removal. Parallel-sided (machined) circlips can be installed either way round in their groove, whereas stamped circlips (which have a chamfered edge on one face) must be installed with the chamfer facing away from the direction of thrust load **(see illustration 2.9)**.

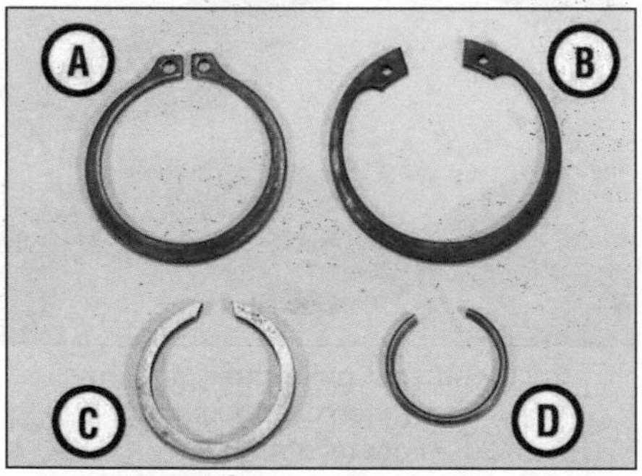

2.8 External stamped circlip (A), internal stamped circlip (B), machined circlip (C) and wire circlip (D)

● Always use circlip pliers to remove and install circlips; expand or compress them just enough to remove them. After installation, rotate the circlip in its groove to ensure it is securely seated. If installing a circlip on a splined shaft, always align its opening with a shaft channel to ensure the circlip ends are well supported and unlikely to catch **(see illustration 2.10)**.

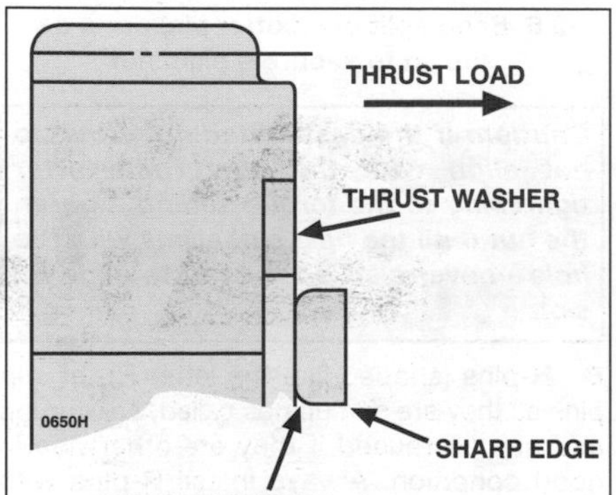

2.9 Correct fitting of a stamped circlip

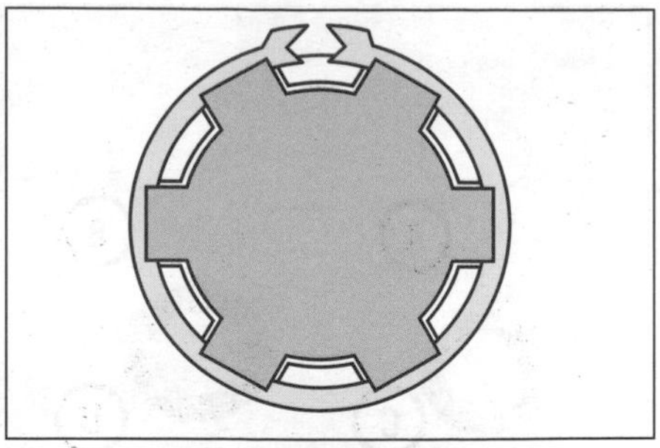

2.10 Align circlip opening with shaft channel

● Circlips can wear due to the thrust of components and become loose in their grooves, with the subsequent danger of becoming dislodged in operation. For this reason, renewal is advised every time a circlip is disturbed.

● Wire circlips are commonly used as piston pin retaining clips. If a removal tang is provided, long-nosed pliers can be used to dislodge them, otherwise careful use of a small flat-bladed screwdriver is necessary. Wire circlips should be renewed every time they are disturbed.

Thread diameter and pitch

● Diameter of a male thread (screw, bolt or stud) is the outside diameter of the threaded portion **(see illustration 2.11)**. Most motorcycle manufacturers use the ISO (International Standards Organisation) metric system expressed in millimetres, eg M6 refers to a 6 mm diameter thread. Sizing is the same for nuts, except that the thread diameter is measured across the valleys of the nut.

● Pitch is the distance between the peaks of the thread **(see illustration 2.11)**. It is expressed in millimetres, thus a common bolt size may be expressed as 6.0 x 1.0 mm (6 mm thread diameter and 1 mm pitch). Generally pitch increases in proportion to thread diameter, although there are always exceptions.

● Thread diameter and pitch are related for conventional fastener applications and the accompanying table can be used as a guide. Additionally, the AF (Across Flats), spanner or socket size dimension of the bolt or nut **(see illustration 2.11)** is linked to thread and pitch specification. Thread pitch can be measured with a thread gauge **(see illustration 2.12)**.

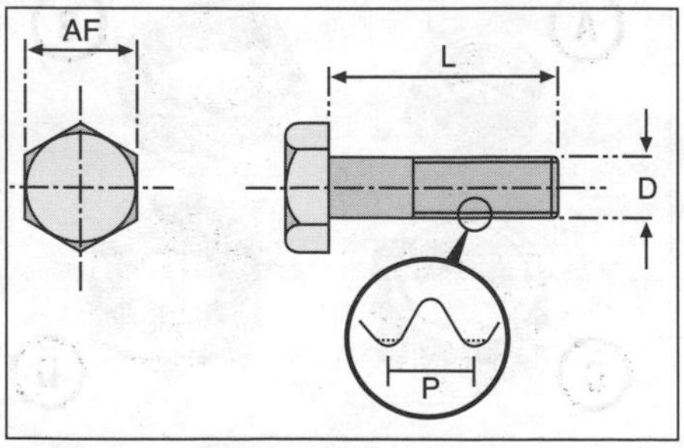

2.11 Fastener length (L), thread diameter (D), thread pitch (P) and head size (AF)

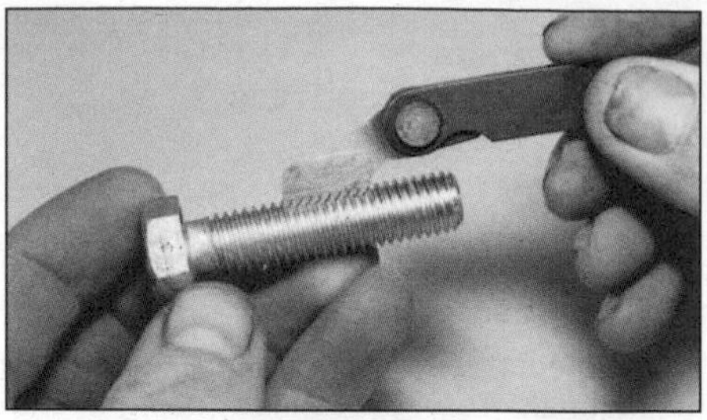

2.12 Using a thread gauge to measure pitch

AF size	Thread diameter x pitch (mm)
8 mm	M5 x 0.8
8 mm	M6 x 1.0
10 mm	M6 x 1.0
12 mm	M8 x 1.25
14 mm	M10 x 1.25
17 mm	M12 x 1.25

● The threads of most fasteners are of the right-hand type, ie they are turned clockwise to tighten and anti-clockwise to loosen. The reverse situation applies to left-hand thread fasteners, which are turned anti-clockwise to tighten and clockwise to loosen. Left-hand threads are used where rotation of a component might loosen a conventional right-hand thread fastener.

Seized fasteners

● Corrosion of external fasteners due to water or reaction between two dissimilar metals can occur over a period of time. It will build up sooner in wet conditions or in countries where salt is used on the roads during the winter. If a fastener is severely corroded it is likely that normal methods of removal will fail and result in its head being ruined. When you attempt removal, the fastener thread should be heard to crack free and unscrew easily - if it doesn't, stop there before damaging something.

● A smart tap on the head of the fastener will often succeed in breaking free corrosion which has occurred in the threads **(see illustration 2.13)**.

● An aerosol penetrating fluid (such as WD-40) applied the night beforehand may work its way down into the thread and ease removal. Depending on the location, you may be able to make up a Plasticine well around the fastener head and fill it with penetrating fluid.

2.13 A sharp tap on the head of a fastener will often break free a corroded thread

● If you are working on an engine internal component, corrosion will most likely not be a problem due to the well lubricated environment. However, components can be very tight and an impact driver is a useful tool in freeing them **(see illustration 2.14)**.

2.14 Using an impact driver to free a fastener

● Where corrosion has occurred between dissimilar metals (eg steel and aluminium alloy), the application of heat to the fastener head will create a disproportionate expansion rate between the two metals and break the seizure caused by the corrosion. Whether heat can be applied depends on the location of the fastener - any surrounding components likely to be damaged must first be removed **(see illustration 2.15)**. Heat can be applied using a paint stripper heat gun or clothes iron, or by immersing the component in boiling water - wear protective gloves to prevent scalding or burns to the hands.

2.15 Using heat to free a seized fastener

● As a last resort, it is possible to use a hammer and cold chisel to work the fastener head unscrewed **(see illustration 2.16)**. This will damage the fastener, but more importantly extreme care must be taken not to damage the surrounding component.

Caution: Remember that the component being secured is generally of more value than the bolt, nut or screw - when the fastener is freed, do not unscrew it with force, instead work the fastener back and forth when resistance is felt to prevent thread damage.

2.16 Using a hammer and chisel to free a seized fastener

Broken fasteners and damaged heads

● If the shank of a broken bolt or screw is accessible you can grip it with self-locking grips. The knurled wheel type stud extractor tool or self-gripping stud puller tool is particularly useful for removing the long studs which screw into the cylinder mouth surface of the crankcase or bolts and screws from which the head has broken off **(see illustration 2.17)**. Studs can also be removed by locking two nuts together on the threaded end of the stud and using a spanner on the lower nut **(see illustration 2.18)**.

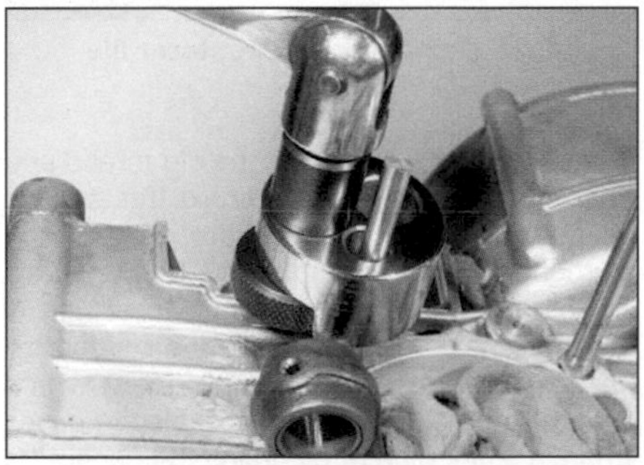

2.17 Using a stud extractor tool to remove a broken crankcase stud

2.18 Two nuts can be locked together to unscrew a stud from a component

● A bolt or screw which has broken off below or level with the casing must be extracted using a screw extractor set. Centre punch the fastener to centralise the drill bit, then drill a hole in the fastener **(see illustration 2.19)**. Select a drill bit which is approximately half to three-quarters the diameter of the fastener and drill to a depth which will accommodate the extractor. Use the largest size extractor possible, but avoid leaving too small a wall thickness otherwise the extractor will merely force the fastener walls outwards wedging it in the casing thread.

2.19 When using a screw extractor, first drill a hole in the fastener . . .

● If a spiral type extractor is used, thread it anti-clockwise into the fastener. As it is screwed in, it will grip the fastener and unscrew it from the casing **(see illustration 2.20)**.

2.20 . . . then thread the extractor anti-clockwise into the fastener

● If a taper type extractor is used, tap it into the fastener so that it is firmly wedged in place. Unscrew the extractor (anti-clockwise) to draw the fastener out.

Warning: Stud extractors are very hard and may break off in the fastener if care is not taken - ask an engineer about spark erosion if this happens.

● Alternatively, the broken bolt/screw can be drilled out and the hole retapped for an oversize bolt/screw or a diamond-section thread insert. It is essential that the drilling is carried out squarely and to the correct depth, otherwise the casing may be ruined - if in doubt, entrust the work to an engineer.

● Bolts and nuts with rounded corners cause the correct size spanner or socket to slip when force is applied. Of the types of spanner/socket available always use a six-point type rather than an eight or twelve-point type - better grip

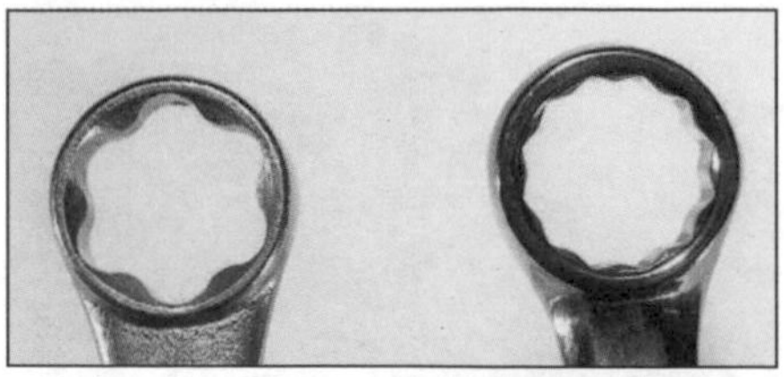

2.21 Comparison of surface drive ring spanner (left) with 12-point type (right)

is obtained. Surface drive spanners grip the middle of the hex flats, rather than the corners, and are thus good in cases of damaged heads **(see illustration 2.21)**.

- Slotted-head or Phillips-head screws are often damaged by the use of the wrong size screwdriver. Allen-head and Torx-head screws are much less likely to sustain damage. If enough of the screw head is exposed you can use a hacksaw to cut a slot in its head and then use a conventional flat-bladed screwdriver to remove it. Alternatively use a hammer and cold chisel to tap the head of the fastener around to slacken it. Always replace damaged fasteners with new ones, preferably Torx or Allen-head type.

HAYNES HiNT

A dab of valve grinding compound between the screw head and screw-driver tip will often give a good grip.

Thread repair

- Threads (particularly those in aluminium alloy components) can be damaged by overtightening, being assembled with dirt in the threads, or from a component working loose and vibrating. Eventually the thread will fail completely, and it will be impossible to tighten the fastener.
- If a thread is damaged or clogged with old locking compound it can be renovated with a thread repair tool (thread chaser) **(see illustrations 2.22 and 2.23)**; special thread

2.22 A thread repair tool being used to correct an internal thread

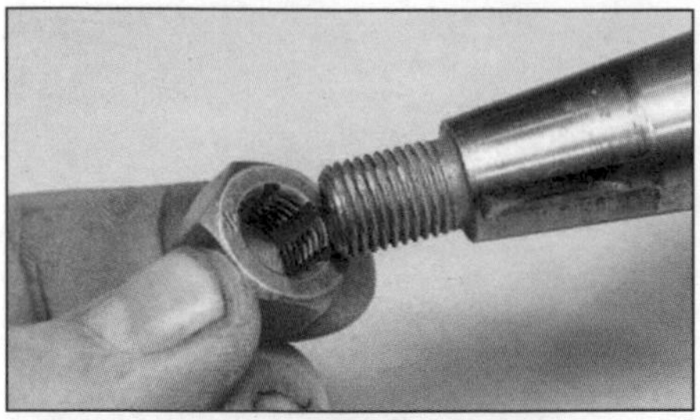

2.23 A thread repair tool being used to correct an external thread

chasers are available for spark plug hole threads. The tool will not cut a new thread, but clean and true the original thread. Make sure that you use the correct diameter and pitch tool. Similarly, external threads can be cleaned up with a die or a thread restorer file **(see illustration 2.24)**.

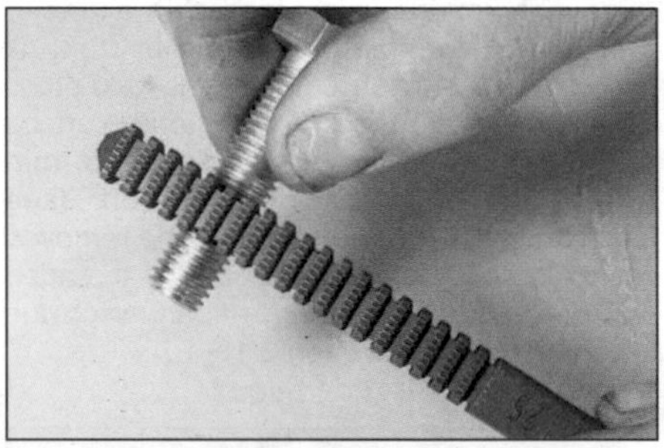

2.24 Using a thread restorer file

- It is possible to drill out the old thread and retap the component to the next thread size. This will work where there is enough surrounding material and a new bolt or screw can be obtained. Sometimes, however, this is not possible - such as where the bolt/screw passes through another component which must also be suitably modified, also in cases where a spark plug or oil drain plug cannot be obtained in a larger diameter thread size.
- The diamond-section thread insert (often known by its popular trade name of Heli-Coil) is a simple and effective method of renewing the thread and retaining the original size. A kit can be purchased which contains the tap, insert and installing tool **(see illustration 2.25)**. Drill out the damaged thread with the size drill specified **(see illustration 2.26)**. Carefully retap the thread **(see illustration 2.27)**. Install the

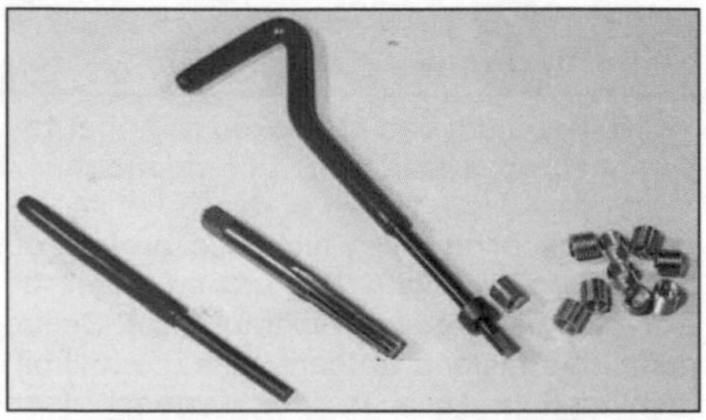

2.25 Obtain a thread insert kit to suit the thread diameter and pitch required

2.26 To install a thread insert, first drill out the original thread . . .

2.27 . . . tap a new thread . . .

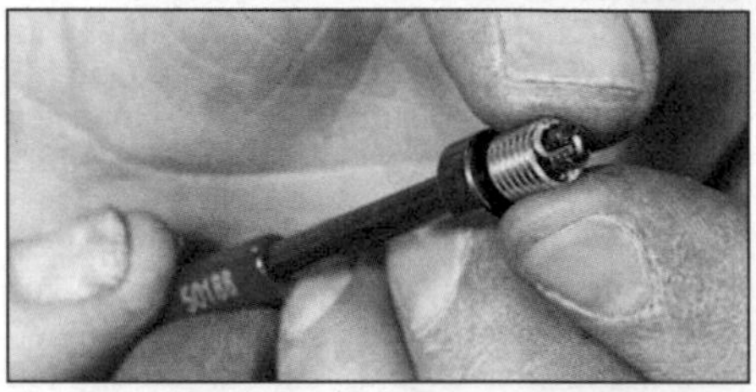

2.28 . . . fit insert on the installing tool . . .

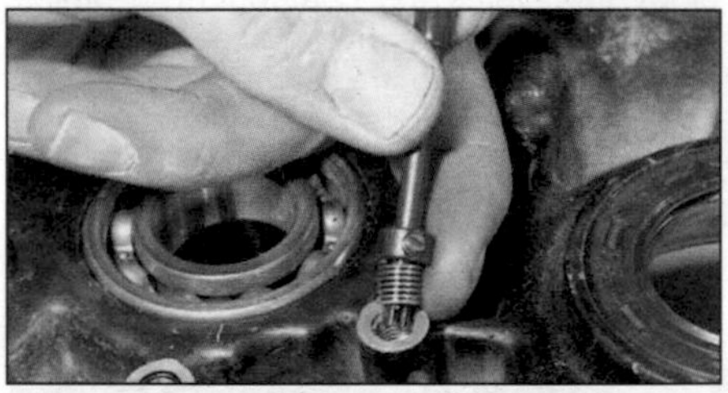

2.29 . . . and thread into the component . . .

2.30 . . . break off the tang when complete

insert on the installing tool and thread it slowly into place using a light downward pressure **(see illustrations 2.28 and 2.29)**. When positioned between a 1/4 and 1/2 turn below the surface withdraw the installing tool and use the break-off tool to press down on the tang, breaking it off **(see illustration 2.30)**.

- There are epoxy thread repair kits on the market which can rebuild stripped internal threads, although this repair should not be used on high load-bearing components.

Thread locking and sealing compounds

● Locking compounds are used in locations where the fastener is prone to loosening due to vibration or on important safety-related items which might cause loss of control of the motorcycle if they fail. It is also used where important fasteners cannot be secured by other means such as lockwashers or split pins.

● Before applying locking compound, make sure that the threads (internal and external) are clean and dry with all old compound removed. Select a compound to suit the component being secured - a non-permanent general locking and sealing type is suitable for most applications, but a high strength type is needed for permanent fixing of studs in castings. Apply a drop or two of the compound to the first few threads of the fastener, then thread it into place and tighten to the specified torque. Do not apply excessive thread locking compound otherwise the thread may be damaged on subsequent removal.

● Certain fasteners are impregnated with a dry film type coating of locking compound on their threads. Always renew this type of fastener if disturbed.

● Anti-seize compounds, such as copper-based greases, can be applied to protect threads from seizure due to extreme heat and corrosion. A common instance is spark plug threads and exhaust system fasteners.

3 Measuring tools and gauges

Feeler gauges

● Feeler gauges (or blades) are used for measuring small gaps and clearances **(see illustration 3.1)**. They can also be used to measure endfloat (sideplay) of a component on a shaft where access is not possible with a dial gauge.

● Feeler gauge sets should be treated with care and not bent or damaged. They are etched with their size on one face. Keep them clean and very lightly oiled to prevent corrosion build-up.

3.1 Feeler gauges are used for measuring small gaps and clearances - thickness is marked on one face of gauge

● When measuring a clearance, select a gauge which is a light sliding fit between the two components. You may need to use two gauges together to measure the clearance accurately.

Micrometers

● A micrometer is a precision tool capable of measuring to 0.01 or 0.001 of a millimetre. It should always be stored in its case and not in the general toolbox. It must be kept clean and never dropped, otherwise its frame or measuring anvils could be distorted resulting in inaccurate readings.

● External micrometers are used for measuring outside diameters of components and have many more applications than internal micrometers. Micrometers are available in different size ranges, eg 0 to 25 mm, 25 to 50 mm, and upwards in 25 mm steps; some large micrometers have interchangeable anvils to allow a range of measurements to be taken. Generally the largest precision measurement you are likely to take on a motorcycle is the piston diameter.

● Internal micrometers (or bore micrometers) are used for measuring inside diameters, such as valve guides and cylinder bores. Telescoping gauges and small hole gauges are used in conjunction with an external micrometer, whereas the more expensive internal micrometers have their own measuring device.

External micrometer

Note: *The conventional analogue type instrument is described. Although much easier to read, digital micrometers are considerably more expensive.*

● Always check the calibration of the micrometer before use. With the anvils closed (0 to 25 mm type) or set over a test gauge (for

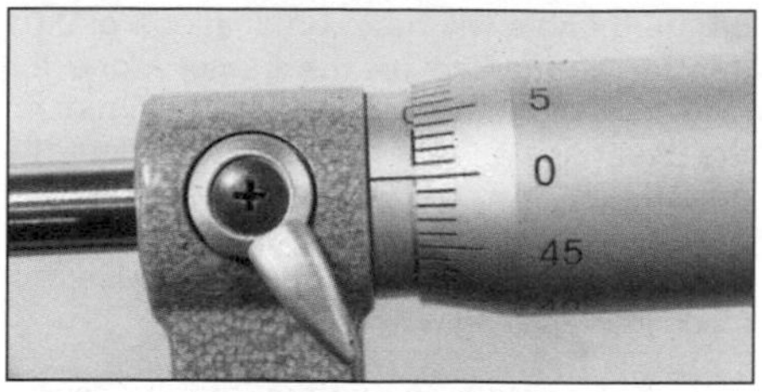

3.2 Check micrometer calibration before use

the larger types) the scale should read zero **(see illustration 3.2)**; make sure that the anvils (and test piece) are clean first. Any discrepancy can be adjusted by referring to the instructions supplied with the tool. Remember that the micrometer is a precision measuring tool - don't force the anvils closed, use the ratchet (4) on the end of the micrometer to close it. In this way, a measured force is always applied.

● To use, first make sure that the item being measured is clean. Place the anvil of the micrometer (1) against the item and use the thimble (2) to bring the spindle (3) lightly into contact with the other side of the item **(see illustration 3.3)**. Don't tighten the thimble down because this will damage the micrometer - instead use the ratchet (4) on the end of the micrometer. The ratchet mechanism applies a measured force preventing damage to the instrument.

● The micrometer is read by referring to the linear scale on the sleeve and the annular scale on the thimble. Read off the sleeve first to obtain the base measurement, then add the fine measurement from the thimble to obtain the overall reading. The linear scale on the sleeve represents the measuring range of the micrometer (eg 0 to 25 mm). The annular scale

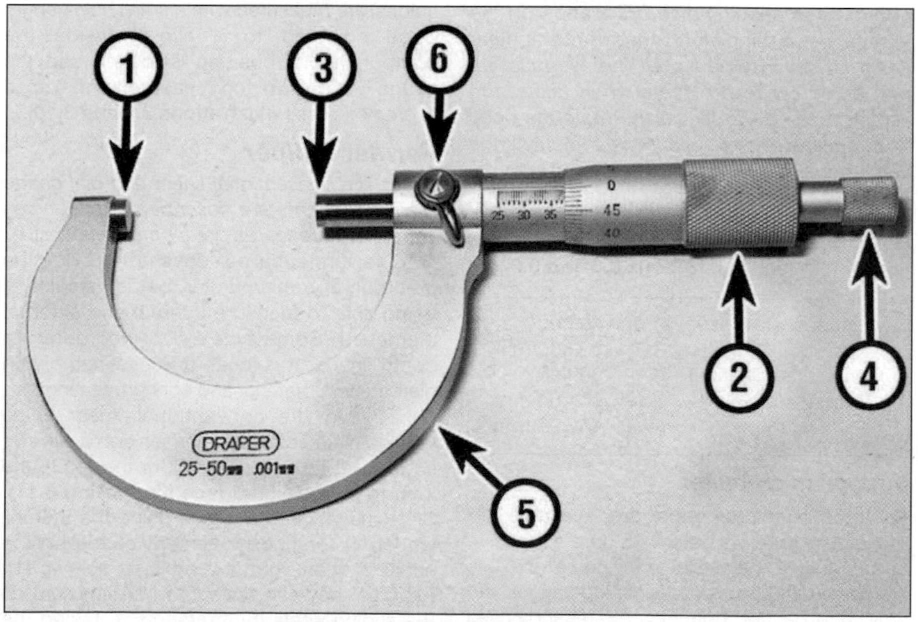

3.3 Micrometer component parts

1 Anvil
2 Thimble
3 Spindle
4 Ratchet
5 Frame
6 Locking lever

on the thimble will be in graduations of 0.01 mm (or as marked on the frame) - one full revolution of the thimble will move 0.5 mm on the linear scale. Take the reading where the datum line on the sleeve intersects the thimble's scale. Always position the eye directly above the scale otherwise an inaccurate reading will result.

In the example shown the item measures 2.95 mm **(see illustration 3.4)**:

Linear scale	2.00 mm
Linear scale	0.50 mm
Annular scale	0.45 mm
Total figure	**2.95 mm**

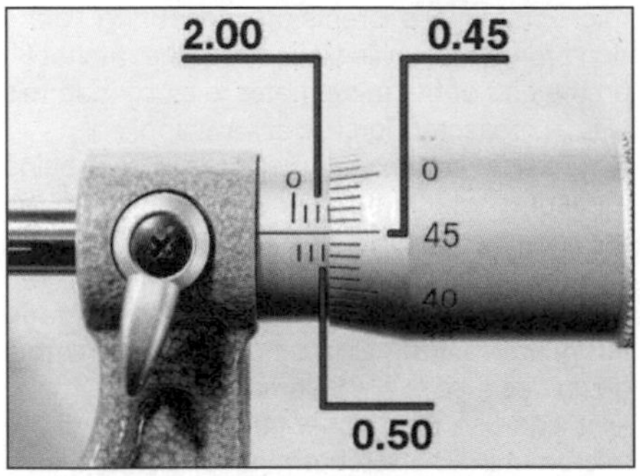

3.4 Micrometer reading of 2.95 mm

Most micrometers have a locking lever (6) on the frame to hold the setting in place, allowing the item to be removed from the micrometer.

● Some micrometers have a vernier scale on their sleeve, providing an even finer measurement to be taken, in 0.001 increments of a millimetre. Take the sleeve and thimble measurement as described above, then check which graduation on the vernier scale aligns with that of the annular scale on the thimble **Note:** *The eye must be perpendicular to the scale when taking the vernier reading - if necessary rotate the body of the micrometer to ensure this.* Multiply the vernier scale figure by 0.001 and add it to the base and fine measurement figures.

In the example shown the item measures 46.994 mm **(see illustrations 3.5 and 3.6)**:

Linear scale (base)	46.000 mm
Linear scale (base)	00.500 mm
Annular scale (fine)	00.490 mm
Vernier scale	00.004 mm
Total figure	**46.994 mm**

Internal micrometer

● Internal micrometers are available for measuring bore diameters, but are expensive and unlikely to be available for home use. It is suggested that a set of telescoping gauges and small hole gauges, both of which must be used with an external micrometer, will suffice for taking internal measurements on a motorcycle.

● Telescoping gauges can be used to measure internal diameters of components. Select a gauge with the correct size range, make sure its ends are clean and insert it into the bore. Expand the gauge, then lock its position and withdraw it from the bore **(see illustration 3.7)**. Measure across the gauge ends with a micrometer **(see illustration 3.8)**.

● Very small diameter bores (such as valve guides) are measured with a small hole gauge. Once adjusted to a slip-fit inside the component, its position is locked and the gauge withdrawn for measurement with a micrometer **(see illustrations 3.9 and 3.10)**.

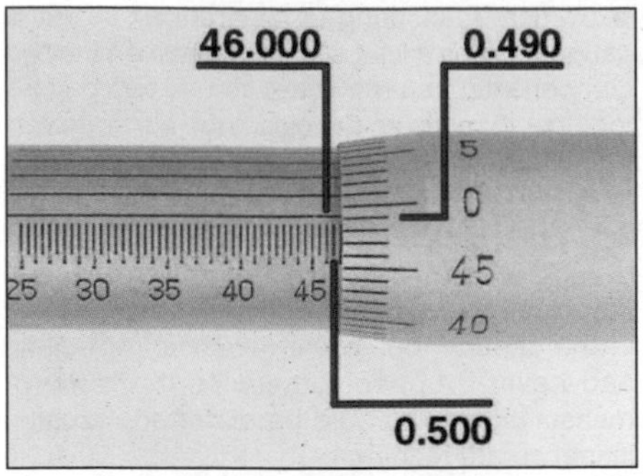

3.5 Micrometer reading of 46.99 mm on linear and annular scales . . .

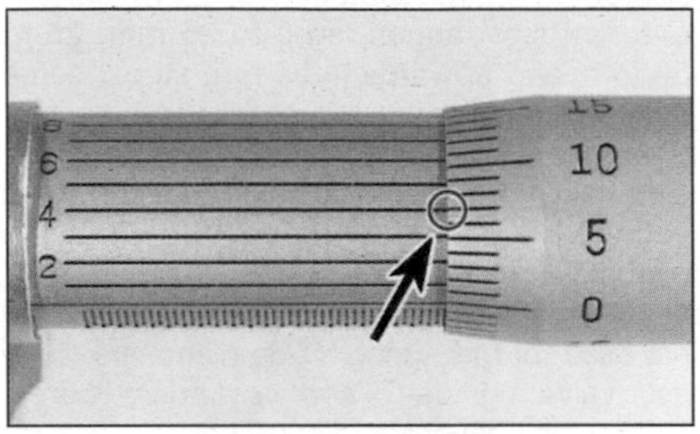

3.6 . . . and 0.004 mm on vernier scale

Vernier caliper

Note: *The conventional linear and dial gauge type instruments are described. Digital types are easier to read, but are far more expensive.*

● The vernier caliper does not provide the precision of a micrometer, but is versatile in being able to measure internal and external diameters. Some types also incorporate a depth gauge. It is ideal for measuring clutch plate friction material and spring free lengths.

● To use the conventional linear scale vernier, slacken off the vernier clamp screws (1) and set its jaws over (2), or inside (3), the item to be measured **(see illustration 3.11)**. Slide the jaw into contact, using the thumb-wheel (4) for fine movement of the sliding scale (5) then tighten the clamp screws (1). Read off the main scale (6) where the zero on the sliding scale (5) intersects it, taking the whole number to the left of the zero; this provides the base measurement. View along the sliding scale and select the division which lines up exactly with any of the divisions on the main scale, noting that the divisions usually represents 0.02 of a millimetre. Add this fine measurement to the base measurement to obtain the total reading.

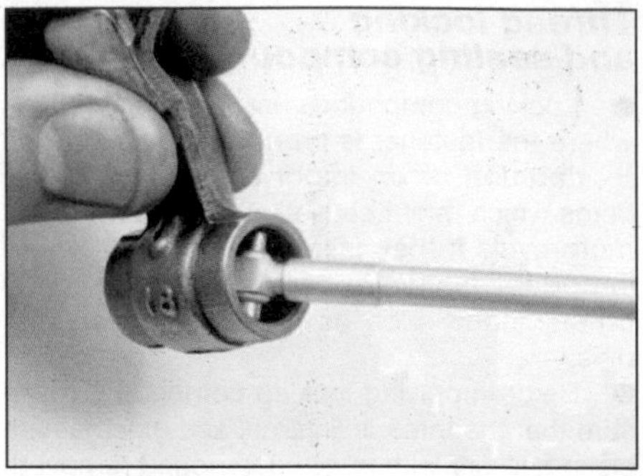

3.7 Expand the telescoping gauge in the bore, lock its position . . .

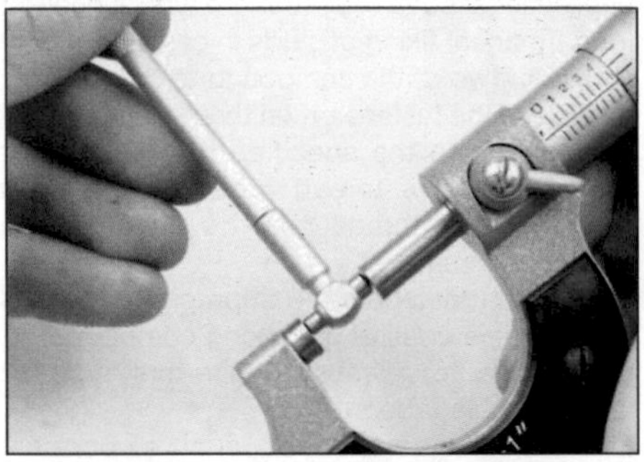

3.8 . . . then measure the gauge with a micrometer

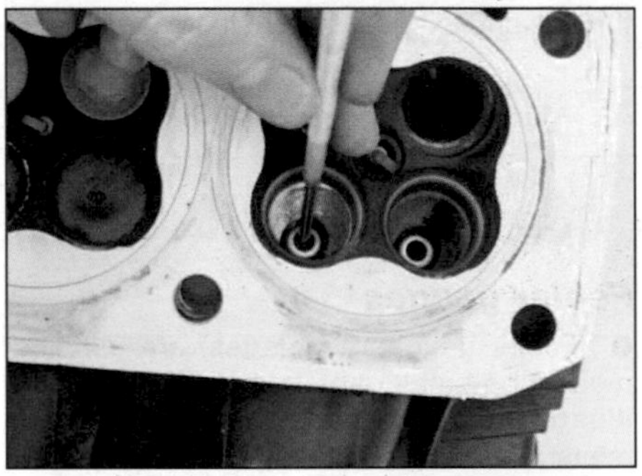

3.9 Expand the small hole gauge in the bore, lock its position . . .

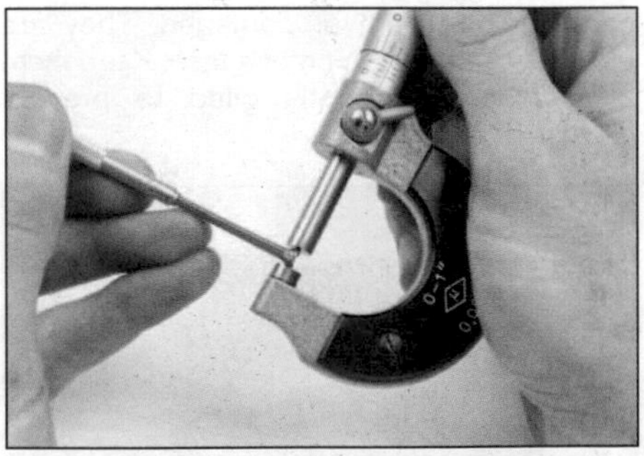

3.10 . . . then measure the gauge with a micrometer

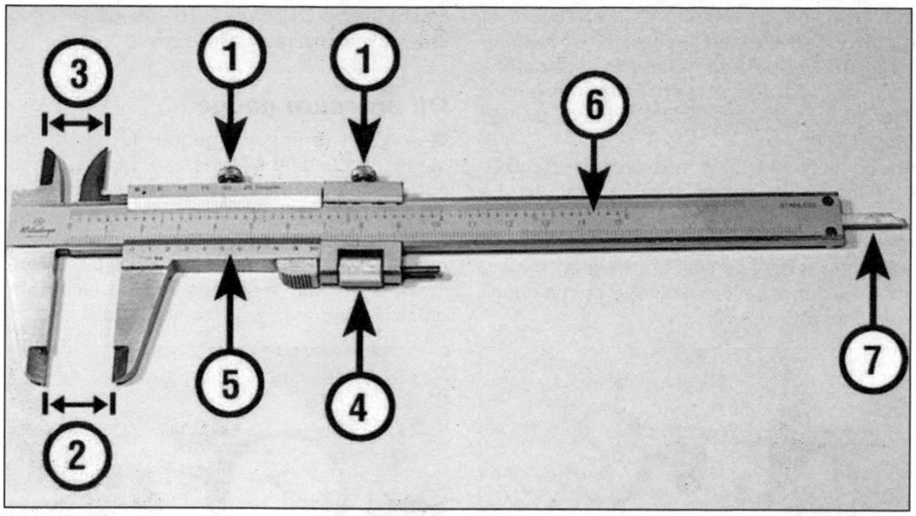

3.11 Vernier component parts (linear gauge)

1 Clamp screws
2 External jaws
3 Internal jaws
4 Thumbwheel
5 Sliding scale
6 Main scale
7 Depth gauge

In the example shown the item measures 55.92 mm **(see illustration 3.12)**:

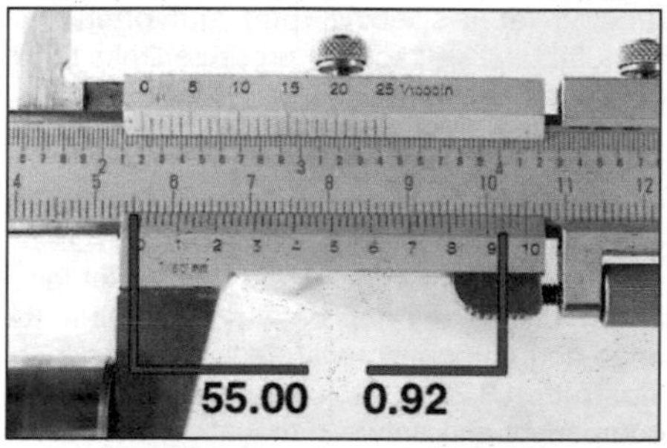

3.12 Vernier gauge reading of 55.92 mm

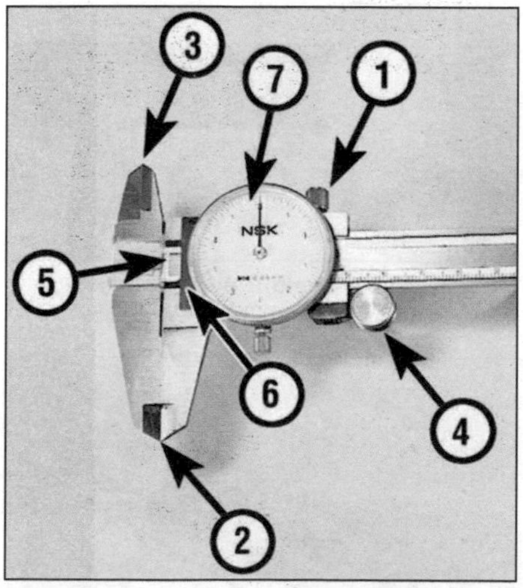

3.13 Vernier component parts (dial gauge)

1 Clamp screw
2 External jaws
3 Internal jaws
4 Thumbwheel
5 Main scale
6 Sliding scale
7 Dial gauge

Base measurement	55.00 mm
Fine measurement	00.92 mm
Total figure	**55.92 mm**

● Some vernier calipers are equipped with a dial gauge for fine measurement. Before use, check that the jaws are clean, then close them fully and check that the dial gauge reads zero. If necessary adjust the gauge ring accordingly. Slacken the vernier clamp screw (1) and set its jaws over (2), or inside (3), the item to be measured **(see illustration 3.13)**. Slide the jaws into contact, using the thumbwheel (4) for fine movement. Read off the main scale (5) where the edge of the sliding scale (6) intersects it, taking the whole number to the left of the zero; this provides the base measurement. Read off the needle position on the dial gauge (7) scale to provide the fine measurement; each division represents 0.05 of a millimetre. Add this fine measurement to the base measurement to obtain the total reading.

In the example shown the item measures 55.95 mm **(see illustration 3.14)**:

Base measurement	55.00 mm
Fine measurement	00.95 mm
Total figure	**55.95 mm**

3.14 Vernier gauge reading of 55.95 mm

Plastigauge

● Plastigauge is a plastic material which can be compressed between two surfaces to measure the oil clearance between them. The width of the compressed Plastigauge is measured against a calibrated scale to determine the clearance.

● Common uses of Plastigauge are for measuring the clearance between crankshaft journal and main bearing inserts, between crankshaft journal and big-end bearing inserts, and between camshaft and bearing surfaces. The following example describes big-end oil clearance measurement.

● Handle the Plastigauge material carefully to prevent distortion. Using a sharp knife, cut a length which corresponds with the width of the bearing being measured and place it carefully across the journal so that it is parallel with the shaft **(see illustration 3.15)**. Carefully install both bearing shells and the connecting rod. Without rotating the rod on the journal tighten its bolts or nuts (as applicable) to the specified torque. The connecting rod and bearings are then disassembled and the crushed Plastigauge examined.

3.15 Plastigauge placed across shaft journal

● Using the scale provided in the Plastigauge kit, measure the width of the material to determine the oil clearance **(see illustration 3.16)**. Always remove all traces of Plastigauge after use using your fingernails.

Caution: Arriving at the correct clearance demands that the assembly is torqued correctly, according to the settings and sequence (where applicable) provided by the motorcycle manufacturer.

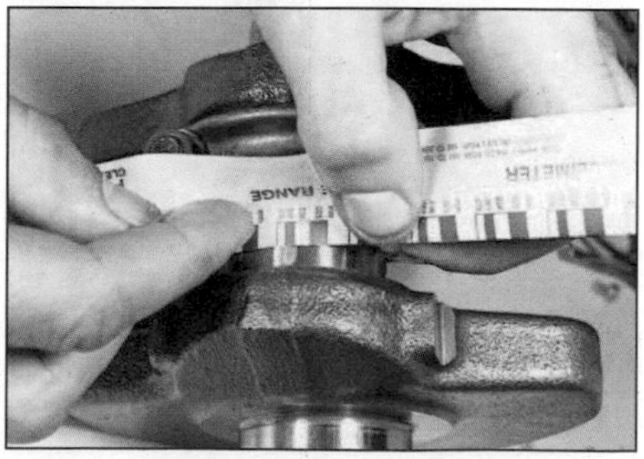

3.16 Measuring the width of the crushed Plastigauge

Dial gauge or DTI (Dial Test Indicator)

● A dial gauge can be used to accurately measure small amounts of movement. Typical uses are measuring shaft runout or shaft endfloat (sideplay) and setting piston position for ignition timing on two-strokes. A dial gauge set usually comes with a range of different probes and adapters and mounting equipment.

● The gauge needle must point to zero when at rest. Rotate the ring around its periphery to zero the gauge.

● Check that the gauge is capable of reading the extent of movement in the work. Most gauges have a small dial set in the face which records whole millimetres of movement as well as the fine scale around the face periphery which is calibrated in 0.01 mm divisions. Read off the small dial first to obtain the base measurement, then add the measurement from the fine scale to obtain the total reading.

In the example shown the gauge reads 1.48 mm **(see illustration 3.17)**:

Base measurement	1.00 mm
Fine measurement	0.48 mm
Total figure	**1.48 mm**

3.17 Dial gauge reading of 1.48 mm

● If measuring shaft runout, the shaft must be supported in vee-blocks and the gauge mounted on a stand perpendicular to the shaft. Rest the tip of the gauge against the centre of the shaft and rotate the shaft slowly whilst watching the gauge reading **(see illustration 3.18)**. Take several measurements along the length of the shaft and record the maximum gauge reading as the amount of runout in the shaft. **Note:** *The reading obtained will be total runout at that point - some manufacturers specify that the runout figure is halved to compare with their specified runout limit.*

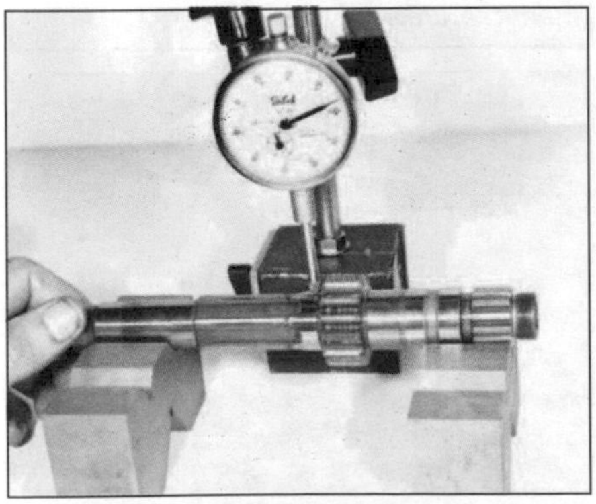

3.18 Using a dial gauge to measure shaft runout

● Endfloat (sideplay) measurement requires that the gauge is mounted securely to the surrounding component with its probe touching the end of the shaft. Using hand pressure, push and pull on the shaft noting the maximum endfloat recorded on the gauge **(see illustration 3.19)**.

3.19 Using a dial gauge to measure shaft endfloat

● A dial gauge with suitable adapters can be used to determine piston position BTDC on two-stroke engines for the purposes of ignition timing. The gauge, adapter and suitable length probe are installed in the place of the spark plug and the gauge zeroed at TDC. If the piston position is specified as 1.14 mm BTDC, rotate the engine back to 2.00 mm BTDC, then slowly forwards to 1.14 mm BTDC.

Cylinder compression gauges

● A compression gauge is used for measuring cylinder compression. Either the rubber-cone type or the threaded adapter type can be used. The latter is preferred to ensure a perfect seal against the cylinder head. A 0 to 300 psi (0 to 20 Bar) type gauge (for petrol/gasoline engines) will be suitable for motorcycles.

● The spark plug is removed and the gauge either held hard against the cylinder head (cone type) or the gauge adapter screwed into the cylinder head (threaded type) **(see illustration 3.20)**. Cylinder compression is measured with the engine turning over, but not running - carry out the compression test as described in *Fault Finding Equipment*. The gauge will hold the reading until manually released.

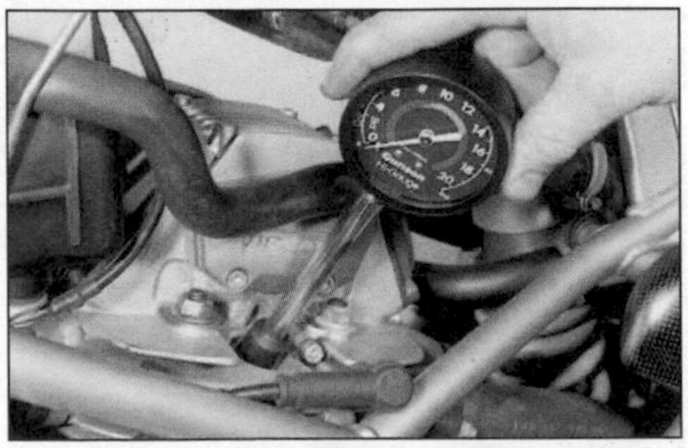

3.20 Using a rubber-cone type cylinder compression gauge

Oil pressure gauge

● An oil pressure gauge is used for measuring engine oil pressure. Most gauges come with a set of adapters to fit the thread of the take-off point **(see illustration 3.21)**. If the take-off point specified by the motorcycle manufacturer is an external oil pipe union, make sure that the specified replacement union is used to prevent oil starvation.

3.21 Oil pressure gauge and take-off point adapter (arrow)

● Oil pressure is measured with the engine running (at a specific rpm) and often the manufacturer will specify pressure limits for a cold and hot engine.

Straight-edge and surface plate

● If checking the gasket face of a component for warpage, place a steel rule or precision straight-edge across the gasket face and measure any gap between the straight-edge and component with feeler gauges **(see illustration 3.22)**. Check diagonally across the component and between mounting holes **(see illustration 3.23)**.

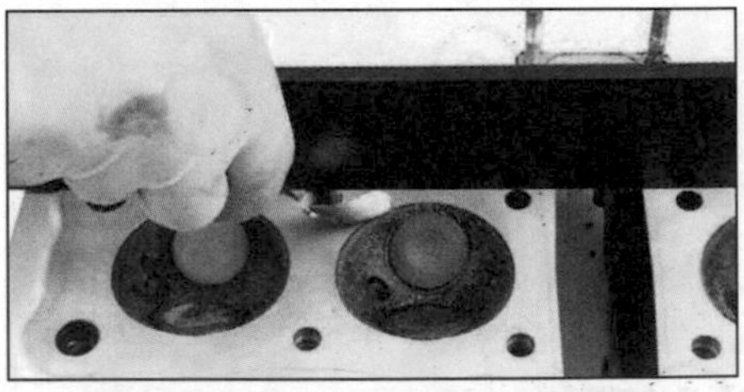

3.22 Use a straight-edge and feeler gauges to check for warpage

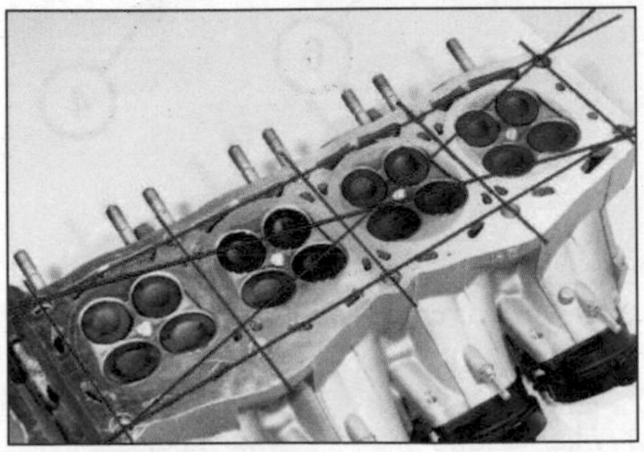

3.23 Check for warpage in these directions

● Checking individual components for warpage, such as clutch plain (metal) plates, requires a perfectly flat plate or piece or plate glass and feeler gauges.

4 Torque and leverage

What is torque?

● Torque describes the twisting force about a shaft. The amount of torque applied is determined by the distance from the centre of the shaft to the end of the lever and the amount of force being applied to the end of the lever; distance multiplied by force equals torque.

● The manufacturer applies a measured torque to a bolt or nut to ensure that it will not slacken in use and to hold two components securely together without movement in the joint. The actual torque setting depends on the thread size, bolt or nut material and the composition of the components being held.

● Too little torque may cause the fastener to loosen due to vibration, whereas too much torque will distort the joint faces of the component or cause the fastener to shear off. Always stick to the specified torque setting.

Using a torque wrench

● Check the calibration of the torque wrench and make sure it has a suitable range for the job. Torque wrenches are available in Nm (Newton-metres), kgf m (kilograms-force metre), lbf ft (pounds-feet), lbf in (inch-pounds). Do not confuse lbf ft with lbf in.

● Adjust the tool to the desired torque on the scale **(see illustration 4.1)**. If your torque wrench is not calibrated in the units specified, carefully convert the figure (see *Conversion Factors*). A manufacturer sometimes gives a torque setting as a range (8 to 10 Nm) rather than a single figure - in this case set the tool midway between the two settings. The same torque may be expressed as 9 Nm ± 1 Nm. Some torque wrenches have a method of locking the setting so that it isn't inadvertently altered during use.

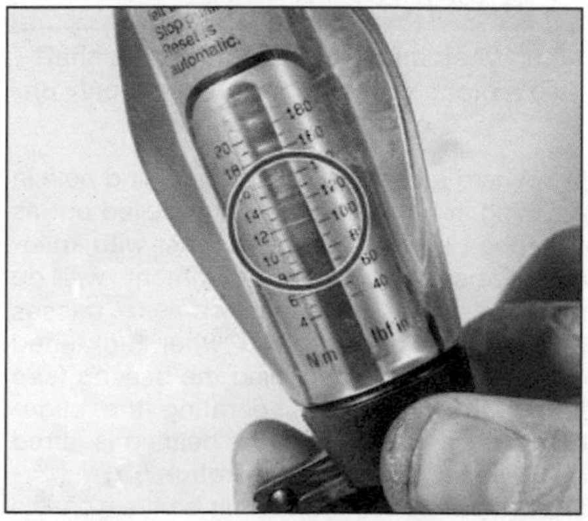

4.1 Set the torque wrench index mark to the setting required, in this case 12 Nm

● Install the bolts/nuts in their correct location and secure them lightly. Their threads must be clean and free of any old locking compound. Unless specified the threads and flange should be dry - oiled threads are necessary in certain circumstances and the manufacturer will take this into account in the specified torque figure. Similarly, the manufacturer may also specify the application of thread-locking compound.

● Tighten the fasteners in the specified sequence until the torque wrench clicks, indicating that the torque setting has been reached. Apply the torque again to double-check the setting. Where different thread diameter fasteners secure the component, as a rule tighten the larger diameter ones first.

● When the torque wrench has been finished with, release the lock (where applicable) and fully back off its setting to zero - do not leave the torque wrench tensioned. Also, do not use a torque wrench for slackening a fastener.

Angle-tightening

● Manufacturers often specify a figure in degrees for final tightening of a fastener. This usually follows tightening to a specific torque setting.

● A degree disc can be set and attached to the socket **(see illustration 4.2)** or a protractor can be used to mark the angle of movement on the bolt/nut head and the surrounding casting **(see illustration 4.3)**.

4.2 Angle tightening can be accomplished with a torque-angle gauge . . .

4.3 . . . or by marking the angle on the surrounding component

Loosening sequences

● Where more than one bolt/nut secures a component, loosen each fastener evenly a little at a time. In this way, not all the stress of the joint is held by one fastener and the components are not likely to distort.

● If a tightening sequence is provided, work in the REVERSE of this, but if not, work from the outside in, in a criss-cross sequence **(see illustration 4.4)**.

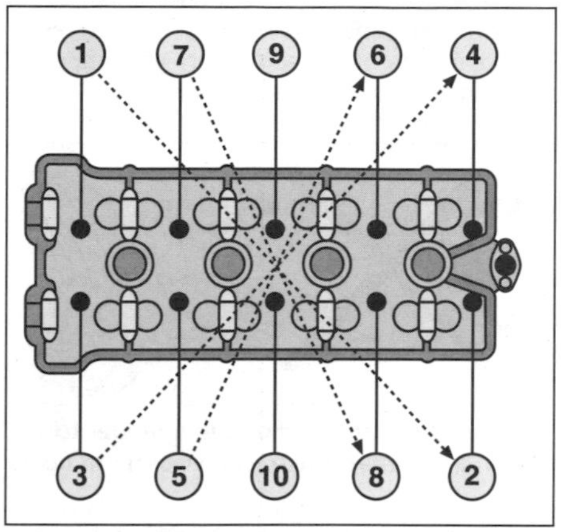

4.4 When slackening, work from the outside inwards

Tightening sequences

● If a component is held by more than one fastener it is important that the retaining bolts/nuts are tightened evenly to prevent uneven stress build-up and distortion of sealing faces. This is especially important on high-compression joints such as the cylinder head.

● A sequence is usually provided by the manufacturer, either in a diagram or actually marked in the casting. If not, always start in the centre and work outwards in a criss-cross pattern **(see illustration 4.5)**. Start off by securing all bolts/nuts finger-tight, then set the torque wrench and tighten each fastener by a small amount in sequence until the final torque is reached. By following this practice,

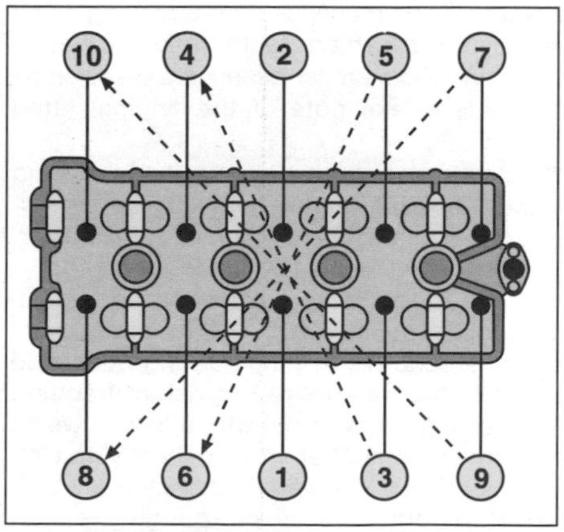

4.5 When tightening, work from the inside outwards

the joint will be held evenly and will not be distorted. Important joints, such as the cylinder head and big-end fasteners often have two- or three-stage torque settings.

Applying leverage

● Use tools at the correct angle. Position a socket wrench or spanner on the bolt/nut so that you pull it towards you when loosening. If this can't be done, push the spanner without curling your fingers around it **(see illustration 4.6)** - the spanner may slip or the fastener loosen suddenly, resulting in your fingers being crushed against a component.

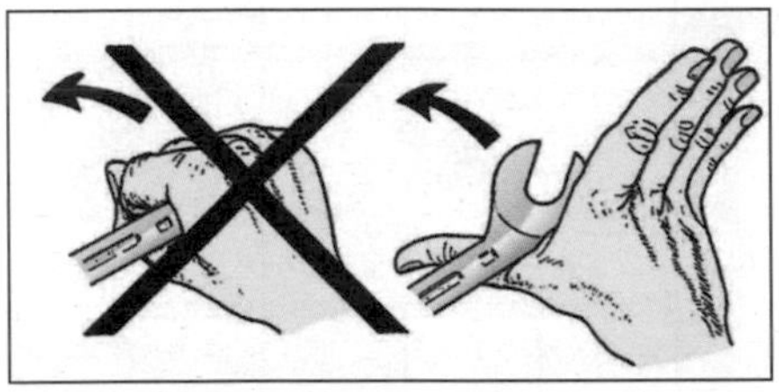

4.6 If you can't pull on the spanner to loosen a fastener, push with your hand open

● Additional leverage is gained by extending the length of the lever. The best way to do this is to use a breaker bar instead of the regular length tool, or to slip a length of tubing over the end of the spanner or socket wrench.
● If additional leverage will not work, the fastener head is either damaged or firmly corroded in place (see *Fasteners*).

5 Bearings

Bearing removal and installation

Drivers and sockets

● Before removing a bearing, always inspect the casing to see which way it must be driven out - some casings will have retaining plates or a cast step. Also check for any identifying markings on the bearing and if installed to a certain depth, measure this at this stage. Some roller bearings are sealed on one side - take note of the original fitted position.
● Bearings can be driven out of a casing using a bearing driver tool (with the correct size head) or a socket of the correct diameter. Select the driver head or socket so that it contacts the outer race of the bearing, not the balls/rollers or inner race. Always support the casing around the bearing housing with wood blocks, otherwise there is a risk of fracture. The bearing is driven out with a few blows on the driver or socket from a heavy mallet. Unless access is severely restricted (as with wheel bearings), a pin-punch is not recommended unless it is moved around the bearing to keep it square in its housing.

● The same equipment can be used to install bearings. Make sure the bearing housing is supported on wood blocks and line up the bearing in its housing. Fit the bearing as noted on removal - generally they are installed with their marked side facing outwards. Tap the bearing squarely into its housing using a driver or socket which bears only on the bearing's outer race - contact with the bearing balls/rollers or inner race will destroy it **(see illustrations 5.1 and 5.2)**.
● Check that the bearing inner race and balls/rollers rotate freely.

5.1 Using a bearing driver against the bearing's outer race

5.2 Using a large socket against the bearing's outer race

Pullers and slide-hammers

● Where a bearing is pressed on a shaft a puller will be required to extract it **(see illustration 5.3)**. Make sure that the puller clamp or legs fit securely behind the bearing and are unlikely to slip out. If pulling a bearing off a gear shaft for example, you may have to locate the puller behind a gear pinion if there is no access to the race and draw the gear pinion off the shaft as well **(see illustration 5.4)**.

5.3 This bearing puller clamps behind the bearing and pressure is applied to the shaft end to draw the bearing off

Caution: Ensure that the puller's centre bolt locates securely against the end of the shaft and will not slip when pressure is applied. Also ensure that puller does not damage the shaft end.

5.4 Where no access is available to the rear of the bearing, it is sometimes possible to draw off the adjacent component

● Operate the puller so that its centre bolt exerts pressure on the shaft end and draws the bearing off the shaft.
● When installing the bearing on the shaft, tap only on the bearing's inner race - contact with the balls/rollers or outer race with destroy the bearing. Use a socket or length of tubing as a drift which fits over the shaft end **(see illustration 5.5)**.

5.5 When installing a bearing on a shaft use a piece of tubing which bears only on the bearing's inner race

● Where a bearing locates in a blind hole in a casing, it cannot be driven or pulled out as described above. A slide-hammer with knife-edged bearing puller attachment will be required. The puller attachment passes through the bearing and when tightened expands to fit firmly behind the bearing **(see illustration 5.6)**. By operating the slide-hammer part of the tool the bearing is jarred out of its housing **(see illustration 5.7)**.
● It is possible, if the bearing is of reasonable weight, for it to drop out of its housing if the casing is heated as described opposite. If this

5.6 Expand the bearing puller so that it locks behind the bearing . . .

5.7 . . . attach the slide hammer to the bearing puller

method is attempted, first prepare a work surface which will enable the casing to be tapped face down to help dislodge the bearing - a wood surface is ideal since it will not damage the casing's gasket surface. Wearing protective gloves, tap the heated casing several times against the work surface to dislodge the bearing under its own weight **(see illustration 5.8)**.

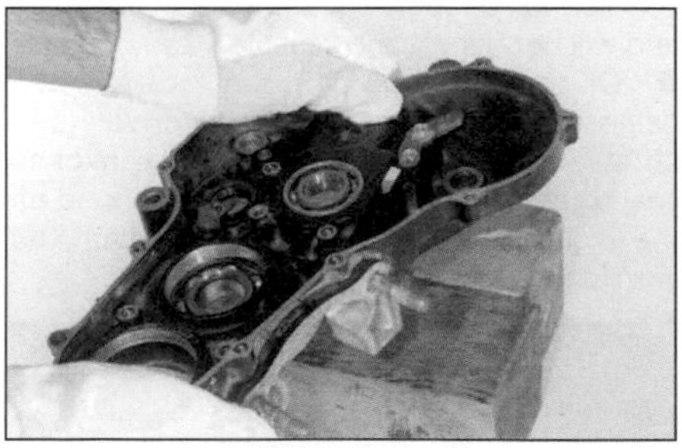

5.8 Tapping a casing face down on wood blocks can often dislodge a bearing

● Bearings can be installed in blind holes using the driver or socket method described above.

Drawbolts

● Where a bearing or bush is set in the eye of a component, such as a suspension linkage arm or connecting rod small-end, removal by drift may damage the component. Furthermore, a rubber bushing in a shock absorber eye cannot successfully be driven out of position. If access is available to a engineering press, the task is straightforward. If not, a drawbolt can be fabricated to extract the bearing or bush.

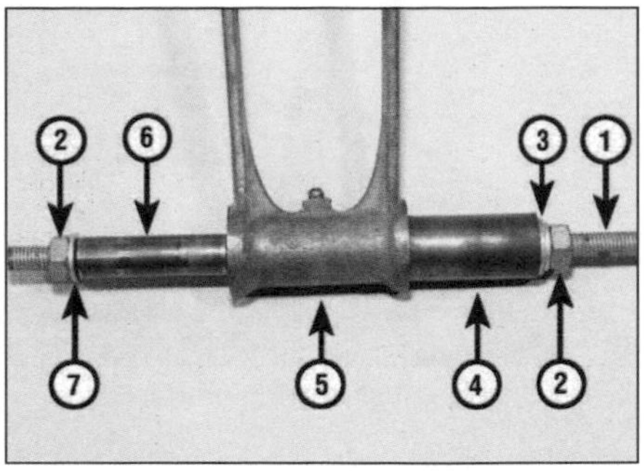

5.9 Drawbolt component parts assembled on a suspension arm

1 *Bolt or length of threaded bar*
2 *Nuts*
3 *Washer (external diameter greater than tubing internal diameter)*
4 *Tubing (internal diameter sufficient to accommodate bearing)*
5 *Suspension arm with bearing*
6 *Tubing (external diameter slightly smaller than bearing)*
7 *Washer (external diameter slightly smaller than bearing)*

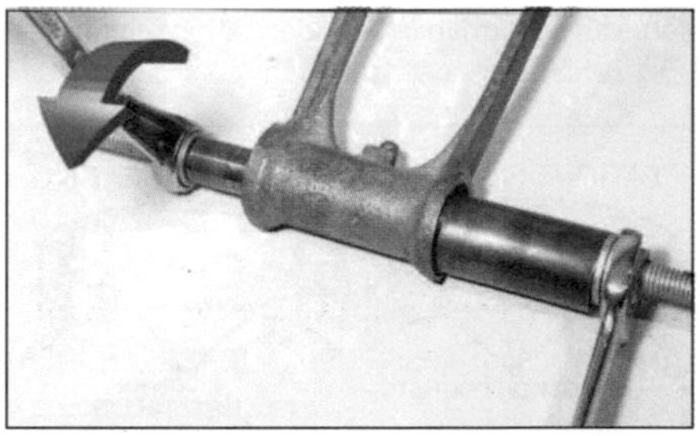

5.10 Drawing the bearing out of the suspension arm

● To extract the bearing/bush you will need a long bolt with nut (or piece of threaded bar with two nuts), a piece of tubing which has an internal diameter larger than the bearing/bush, another piece of tubing which has an external diameter slightly smaller than the bearing/bush, and a selection of washers **(see illustrations 5.9 and 5.10)**. Note that the pieces of tubing must be of the same length, or longer, than the bearing/bush.

● The same kit (without the pieces of tubing) can be used to draw the new bearing/bush back into place **(see illustration 5.11)**.

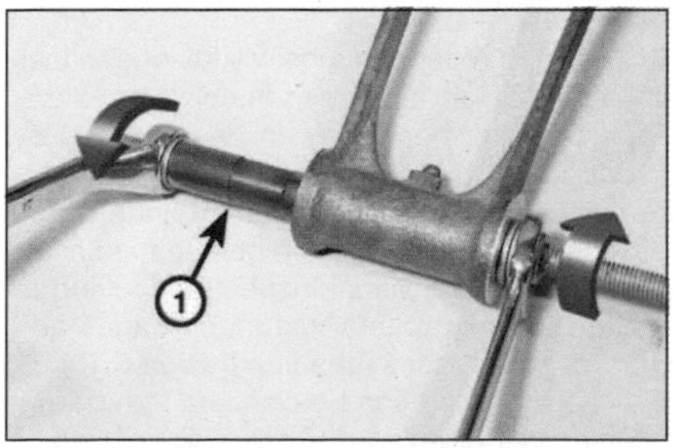

5.11 Installing a new bearing (1) in the suspension arm

Temperature change

● If the bearing's outer race is a tight fit in the casing, the aluminium casing can be heated to release its grip on the bearing. Aluminium will expand at a greater rate than the steel bearing outer race. There are several ways to do this, but avoid any localised extreme heat (such as a blow torch) - aluminium alloy has a low melting point.

● Approved methods of heating a casing are using a domestic oven (heated to 100°C) or immersing the casing in boiling water **(see illustration 5.12)**. Low temperature range localised heat sources such as a paint stripper heat gun or clothes iron can also be used **(see illustration 5.13)**. Alternatively, soak a rag in boiling water, wring it out and wrap it around the bearing housing.

⚠ ***Warning: All of these methods require care in use to prevent scalding and burns to the hands. Wear protective gloves when handling hot components.***

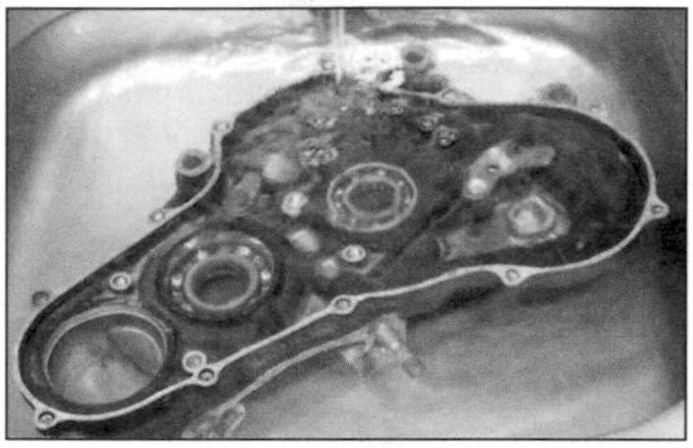

5.12 A casing can be immersed in a sink of boiling water to aid bearing removal

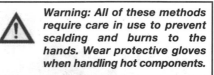

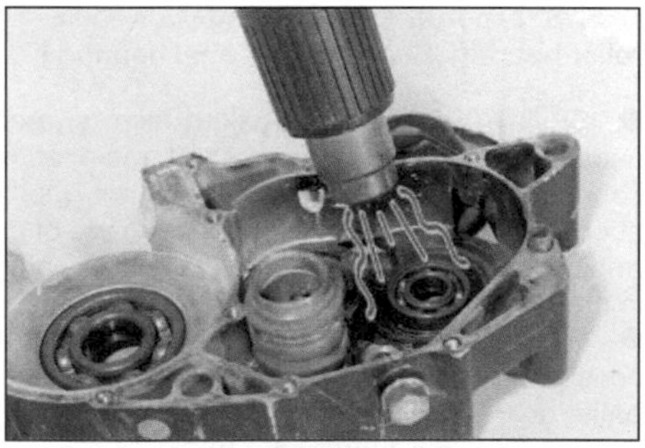

5.13 Using a localised heat source to aid bearing removal

● If heating the whole casing note that plastic components, such as the neutral switch, may suffer - remove them beforehand.

● After heating, remove the bearing as described above. You may find that the expansion is sufficient for the bearing to fall out of the casing under its own weight or with a light tap on the driver or socket.

● If necessary, the casing can be heated to aid bearing installation, and this is sometimes the recommended procedure if the motorcycle manufacturer has designed the housing and bearing fit with this intention.

● Installation of bearings can be eased by placing them in a freezer the night before installation. The steel bearing will contract slightly, allowing easy insertion in its housing. This is often useful when installing steering head outer races in the frame.

Bearing types and markings

● Plain shell bearings, ball bearings, needle roller bearings and tapered roller bearings will all be found on motorcycles **(see illustrations 5.14 and 5.15)**. The ball and roller types are usually caged between an inner and outer race, but uncaged variations may be found.

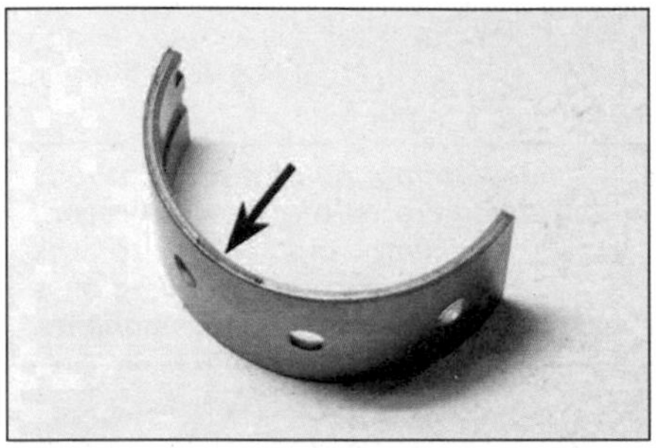

5.14 Shell bearings are either plain or grooved. They are usually identified by colour code (arrow)

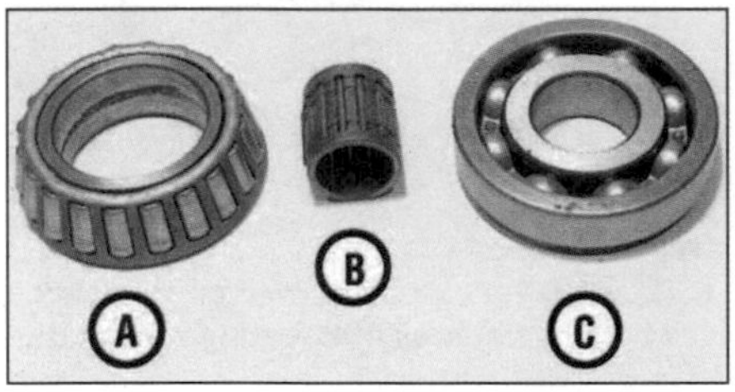

5.15 Tapered roller bearing (A), needle roller bearing (B) and ball journal bearing (C)

● Shell bearings (often called inserts) are usually found at the crankshaft main and connecting rod big-end where they are good at coping with high loads. They are made of a phosphor-bronze material and are impregnated with self-lubricating properties.

● Ball bearings and needle roller bearings consist of a steel inner and outer race with the balls or rollers between the races. They require constant lubrication by oil or grease and are good at coping with axial loads. Taper roller bearings consist of rollers set in a tapered cage set on the inner race; the outer race is separate. They are good at coping with axial loads and prevent movement along the shaft - a typical application is in the steering head.

● Bearing manufacturers produce bearings to ISO size standards and stamp one face of the bearing to indicate its internal and external diameter, load capacity and type **(see illustration 5.16)**.

● Metal bushes are usually of phosphor-bronze material. Rubber bushes are used in suspension mounting eyes. Fibre bushes have also been used in suspension pivots.

5.16 Typical bearing marking

Bearing fault finding

● If a bearing outer race has spun in its housing, the housing material will be damaged. You can use a bearing locking compound to bond the outer race in place if damage is not too severe.

● Shell bearings will fail due to damage of their working surface, as a result of lack of lubrication, corrosion or abrasive particles in the oil **(see illustration 5.17)**. Small particles of dirt in the oil may embed in the bearing material whereas larger particles will score the bearing and shaft journal. If a number of short journeys are made, insufficient heat will be generated to drive off condensation which has built up on the bearings.

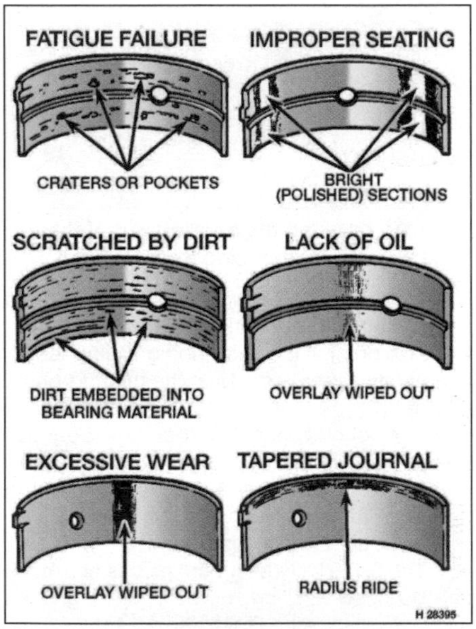

5.17 Typical bearing failures

● Ball and roller bearings will fail due to lack of lubrication or damage to the balls or rollers. Tapered-roller bearings can be damaged by overloading them. Unless the bearing is sealed on both sides, wash it in paraffin (kerosene) to remove all old grease then allow it to dry. Make a visual inspection looking to dented balls or rollers, damaged cages and worn or pitted races **(see illustration 5.18)**.

● A ball bearing can be checked for wear by listening to it when spun. Apply a film of light oil to the bearing and hold it close to the ear - hold the outer race with one hand and spin the inner

5.18 Example of ball journal bearing with damaged balls and cages

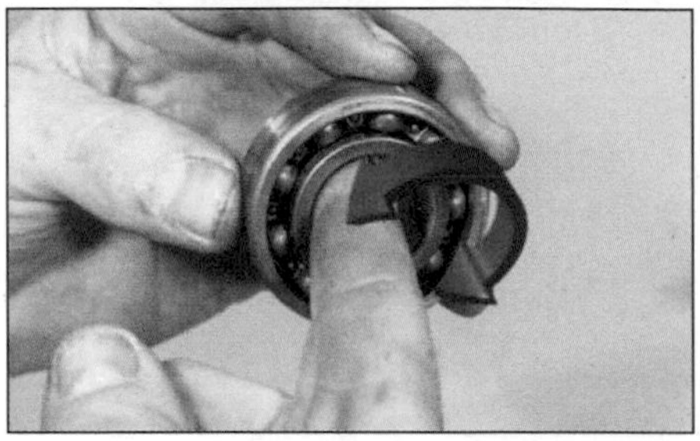

5.19 Hold outer race and listen to inner race when spun

race with the other hand **(see illustration 5.19)**. The bearing should be almost silent when spun; if it grates or rattles it is worn.

6 Oil seals

Oil seal removal and installation

● Oil seals should be renewed every time a component is dismantled. This is because the seal lips will become set to the sealing surface and will not necessarily reseal.

● Oil seals can be prised out of position using a large flat-bladed screwdriver **(see illustration 6.1)**. In the case of crankcase seals, check first that the seal is not lipped on the inside, preventing its removal with the crankcases joined.

6.1 Prise out oil seals with a large flat-bladed screwdriver

● New seals are usually installed with their marked face (containing the seal reference code) outwards and the spring side towards the fluid being retained. In certain cases, such as a two-stroke engine crankshaft seal, a double lipped seal may be used due to there being fluid or gas on each side of the joint.

- Use a bearing driver or socket which bears only on the outer hard edge of the seal to install it in the casing - tapping on the inner edge will damage the sealing lip.

Oil seal types and markings

- Oil seals are usually of the single-lipped type. Double-lipped seals are found where a liquid or gas is on both sides of the joint.
- Oil seals can harden and lose their sealing ability if the motorcycle has been in storage for a long period - renewal is the only solution.
- Oil seal manufacturers also conform to the ISO markings for seal size - these are moulded into the outer face of the seal **(see illustration 6.2)**.

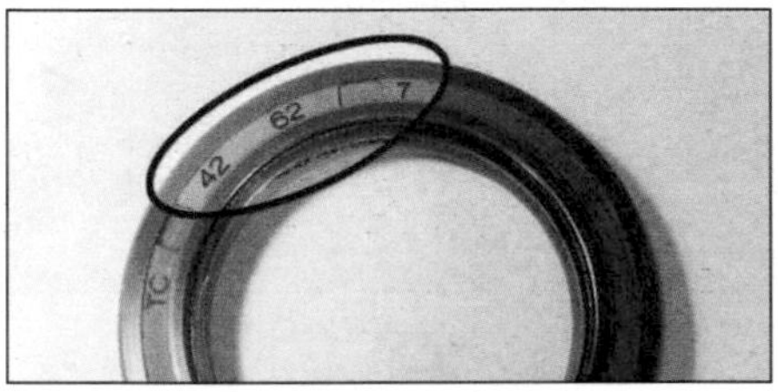

6.2 These oil seal markings indicate inside diameter, outside diameter and seal thickness

7 Gaskets and sealants

Types of gasket and sealant

- Gaskets are used to seal the mating surfaces between components and keep lubricants, fluids, vacuum or pressure contained within the assembly. Aluminium gaskets are sometimes found at the cylinder joints, but most gaskets are paper-based. If the mating surfaces of the components being joined are undamaged the gasket can be installed dry, although a dab of sealant or grease will be useful to hold it in place during assembly.
- RTV (Room Temperature Vulcanising) silicone rubber sealants cure when exposed to moisture in the atmosphere. These sealants are good at filling pits or irregular gasket faces, but will tend to be forced out of the joint under very high torque. They can be used to replace a paper gasket, but first make sure that the width of the paper gasket is not essential to the shimming of internal components. RTV sealants should not be used on components containing petrol (gasoline).
- Non-hardening, semi-hardening and hard setting liquid gasket compounds can be used with a gasket or between a metal-to-metal joint. Select the sealant to suit the application: universal non-hardening sealant can be used on virtually all joints; semi-hardening on joint faces which are rough or damaged; hard setting sealant on joints which require a permanent bond and are subjected to high temperature and pressure. **Note:** *Check first if the paper gasket has a bead of sealant impregnated in its surface before applying additional sealant.*
- When choosing a sealant, make sure it is suitable for the application, particularly if being applied in a high-temperature area or in the vicinity of fuel. Certain manufacturers produce sealants in either clear, silver or black colours to match the finish of the engine. This has a particular application on motorcycles where much of the engine is exposed.
- Do not over-apply sealant. That which is squeezed out on the outside of the joint can be wiped off, whereas an excess of sealant on the inside can break off and clog oilways.

Breaking a sealed joint

- Age, heat, pressure and the use of hard setting sealant can cause two components to stick together so tightly that they are difficult to separate using finger pressure alone. Do not resort to using levers unless there is a pry point provided for this purpose **(see illustration 7.1)** or else the gasket surfaces will be damaged.
- Use a soft-faced hammer **(see illustration 7.2)** or a wood block and conventional hammer to strike the component near the mating surface. Avoid hammering against cast extremities since they may break off. If this method fails, try using a wood wedge between the two components.

Caution: If the joint will not separate, double-check that you have removed all the fasteners.

7.1 If a pry point is provided, apply gently pressure with a flat-bladed screwdriver

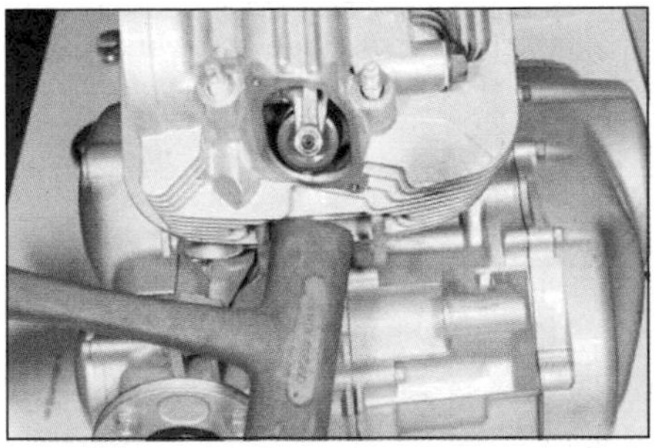

7.2 Tap around the joint with a soft-faced mallet if necessary - don't strike cooling fins

Removal of old gasket and sealant

- Paper gaskets will most likely come away complete, leaving only a few traces stuck on the sealing faces of the components. It is imperative that all traces are removed to ensure correct sealing of the new gasket.
- Very carefully scrape all traces of gasket away making sure that the sealing surfaces are not gouged or scored by the scraper **(see illustrations 7.3, 7.4 and 7.5)**. Stubborn deposits can be removed by spraying with an aerosol gasket remover. Final preparation of

Most components have one or two hollow locating dowels between the two gasket faces. If a dowel cannot be removed, do not resort to gripping it with pliers - it will almost certainly be distorted. Install a close-fitting socket or Phillips screwdriver into the dowel and then grip the outer edge of the dowel to free it.

7.3 Paper gaskets can be scraped off with a gasket scraper tool . . .

7.4 . . . a knife blade . . .

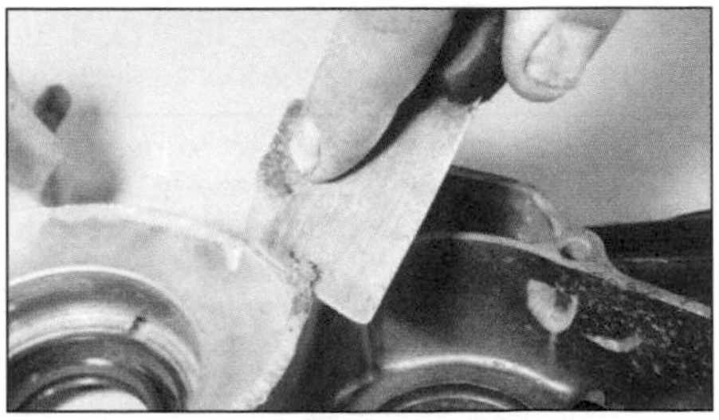

7.5 . . . or a household scraper

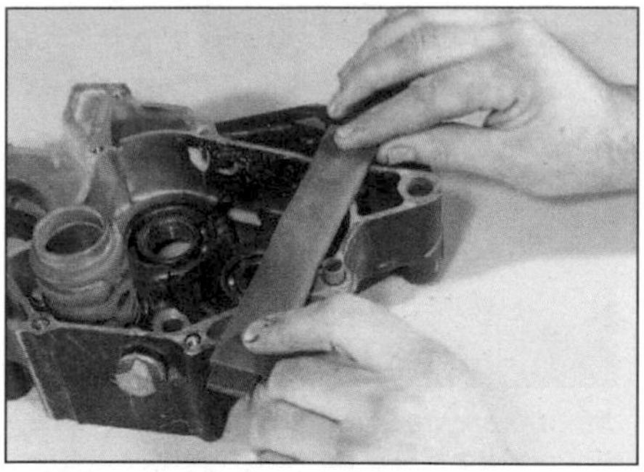

7.6 Fine abrasive paper is wrapped around a flat file to clean up the gasket face

7.7 A kitchen scourer can be used on stubborn deposits

the gasket surface can be made with very fine abrasive paper or a plastic kitchen scourer **(see illustrations 7.6 and 7.7)**.

● Old sealant can be scraped or peeled off components, depending on the type originally used. Note that gasket removal compounds are available to avoid scraping the components clean; make sure the gasket remover suits the type of sealant used.

8 Chains

Breaking and joining final drive chains

● Drive chains for all but small bikes are continuous and do not have a clip-type connecting link. The chain must be broken using a chain breaker tool and the new chain securely riveted together using a new soft rivet-type link. Never use a clip-type connecting link instead of a rivet-type link, except in an emergency. Various chain breaking and riveting tools are available, either as separate tools or combined as illustrated in the accompanying photographs - read the instructions supplied with the tool carefully.

> ***Warning: The need to rivet the new link pins correctly cannot be overstressed - loss of control of the motorcycle is very likely to result if the chain breaks in use.***

● Rotate the chain and look for the soft link. The soft link pins look like they have been deeply centre-punched instead of peened over like all the other pins **(see illustration 8.9)** and its sideplate may be a different colour. Position the soft link midway between the sprockets and assemble the chain breaker tool over one of the soft link pins **(see illustration 8.1)**. Operate the tool to push the pin out through the chain **(see illustration 8.2)**. On an O-ring chain, remove the O-rings **(see illustration 8.3)**. Carry out the same procedure on the other soft link pin.

8.1 Tighten the chain breaker to push the pin out of the link . . .

8.2 . . . withdraw the pin, remove the tool . . .

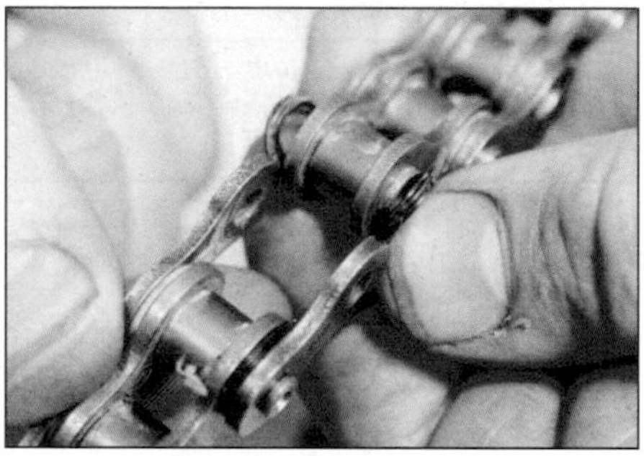

8.3 . . . and separate the chain link

> ***Caution: Certain soft link pins (particularly on the larger chains) may require their ends to be filed or ground off before they can be pressed out using the tool.***

● Check that you have the correct size and strength (standard or heavy duty) new soft link - do not reuse the old link. Look for the size marking on the chain sideplates **(see illustration 8.10)**.

● Position the chain ends so that they are engaged over the rear sprocket. On an O-ring chain, install a new O-ring over each pin of the link and insert the link through the two chain ends **(see illustration 8.4)**. Install a new O-ring over the end of each pin, followed by the sideplate (with the chain manufacturer's marking facing outwards) **(see illustrations 8.5 and 8.6)**. On an unsealed chain, insert the link through the two chain ends, then install the sideplate with the chain manufacturer's marking facing outwards.

● Note that it may not be possible to install the sideplate using finger pressure alone. If using a joining tool, assemble it so that the plates of the tool clamp the link and press the sideplate over the pins **(see illustration 8.7)**. Otherwise, use two small sockets placed over

8.4 Insert the new soft link, with O-rings, through the chain ends . . .

8.5 . . . install the O-rings over the pin ends . . .

8.6 . . . followed by the sideplate

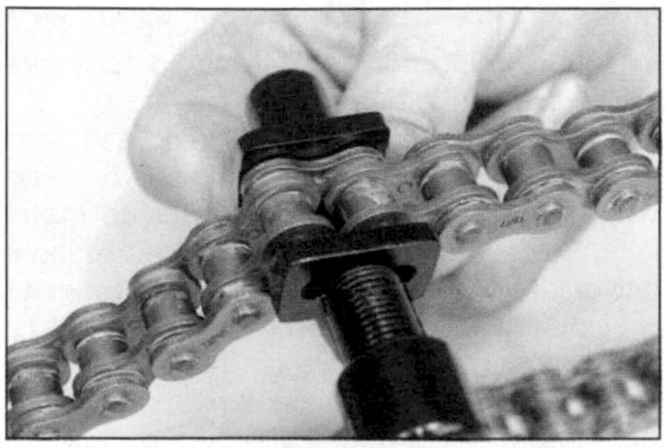

8.7 Push the sideplate into position using a clamp

8.8 Assemble the chain riveting tool over one pin at a time and tighten it fully

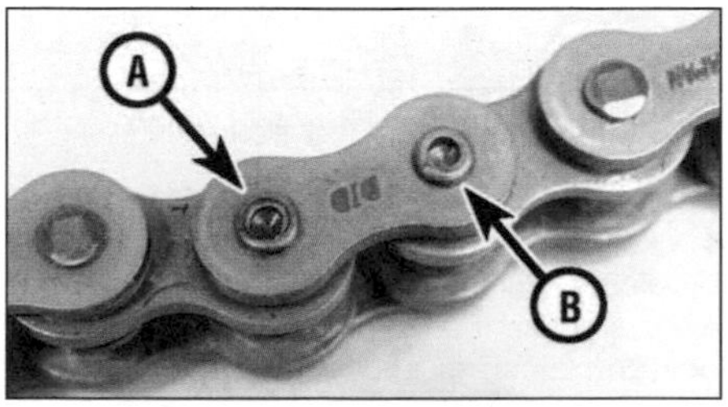

8.9 Pin end correctly riveted (A), pin end unriveted (B)

the rivet ends and two pieces of the wood between a G-clamp. Operate the clamp to press the sideplate over the pins.

- Assemble the joining tool over one pin (following the maker's instructions) and tighten the tool down to spread the pin end securely **(see illustrations 8.8 and 8.9)**. Do the same on the other pin.

> ***Warning: Check that the pin ends are secure and that there is no danger of the sideplate coming loose. If the pin ends are cracked the soft link must be renewed.***

Final drive chain sizing

- Chains are sized using a three digit number, followed by a suffix to denote the chain type **(see illustration 8.10)**. Chain type is either standard or heavy duty (thicker sideplates), and also unsealed or O-ring/X-ring type.
- The first digit of the number relates to the pitch of the chain, ie the distance from the centre of one pin to the centre of the next pin **(see illustration 8.11)**. Pitch is expressed in eighths of an inch, as follows:

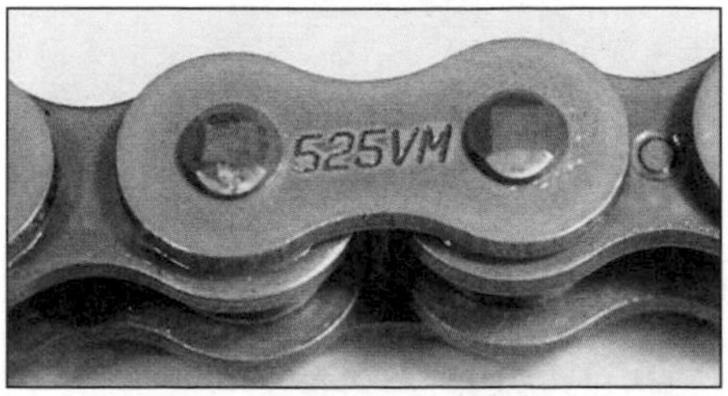

8.10 Typical chain size and type marking

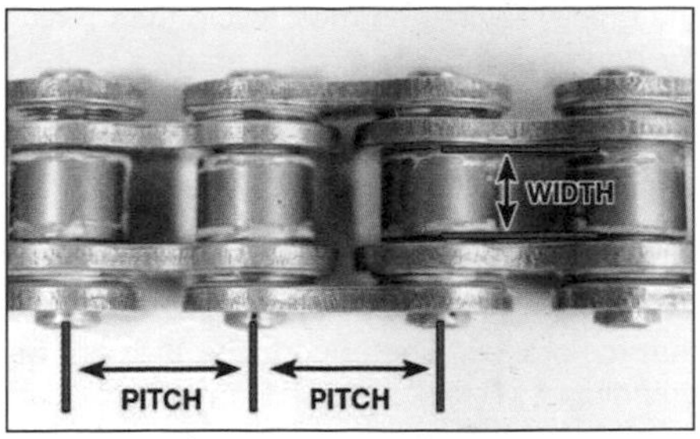

8.11 Chain dimensions

Sizes commencing with a 4 (eg 428) have a pitch of 1/2 inch (12.7 mm)
Sizes commencing with a 5 (eg 520) have a pitch of 5/8 inch (15.9 mm)
Sizes commencing with a 6 (eg 630) have a pitch of 3/4 inch (19.1 mm)

- The second and third digits of the chain size relate to the width of the rollers, again in imperial units, eg the 525 shown has 5/16 inch (7.94 mm) rollers **(see illustration 8.11)**.

9 Hoses

Clamping to prevent flow

- Small-bore flexible hoses can be clamped to prevent fluid flow whilst a component is worked on. Whichever method is used, ensure that the hose material is not permanently distorted or damaged by the clamp.

*a) A brake hose clamp available from auto accessory shops **(see illustration 9.1)**.*
*b) A wingnut type hose clamp **(see illustration 9.2)**.*

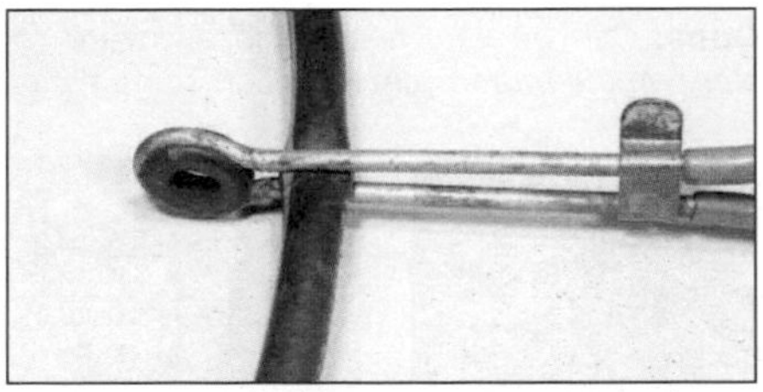

9.1 Hoses can be clamped with an automotive brake hose clamp . . .

9.2 . . . a wingnut type hose clamp . . .

*c) Two sockets placed each side of the hose and held with straight-jawed self-locking grips **(see illustration 9.3)**.*
*d) Thick card each side of the hose held between straight-jawed self-locking grips **(see illustration 9.4)**.*

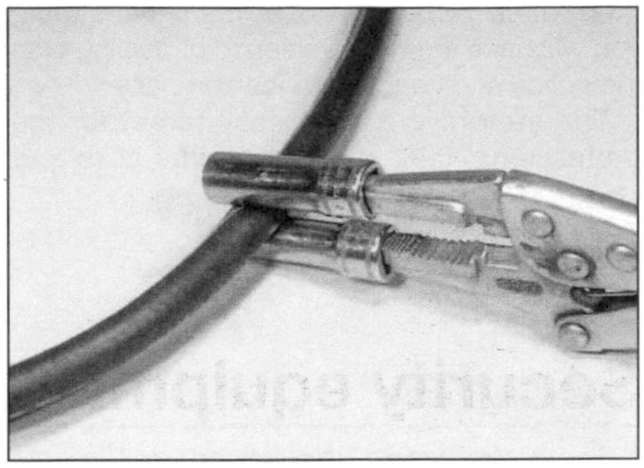

9.3 . . . two sockets and a pair of self-locking grips . . .

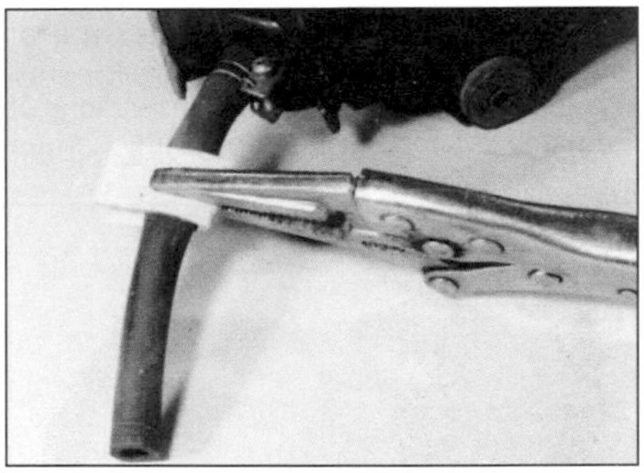

9.4 . . . or thick card and self-locking grips

Freeing and fitting hoses

- Always make sure the hose clamp is moved well clear of the hose end. Grip the hose with your hand and rotate it whilst pulling it off the union. If the hose has hardened due to age and will not move, slit it with a sharp knife and peel its ends off the union **(see illustration 9.5)**.
- Resist the temptation to use grease or soap on the unions to aid installation; although it helps the hose slip over the union it will equally aid the escape of fluid from the joint. It is preferable to soften the hose ends in hot water and wet the inside surface of the hose with water or a fluid which will evaporate.

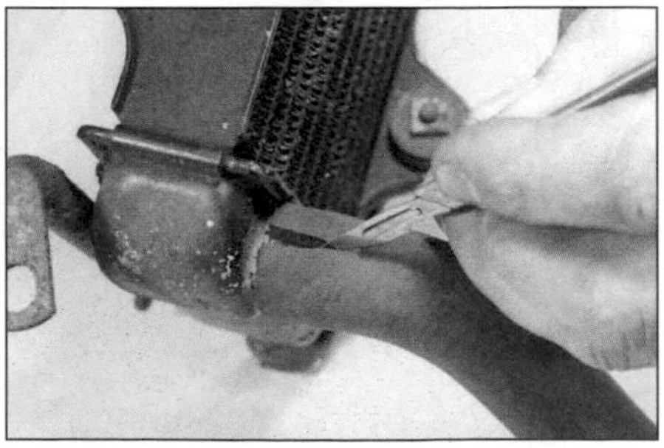

9.5 Cutting a coolant hose free with a sharp knife

Introduction

In less time than it takes to read this introduction, a thief could steal your motorcycle. Returning only to find your bike has gone is one of the worst feelings in the world. Even if the motorcycle is insured against theft, once you've got over the initial shock, you will have the inconvenience of dealing with the police and your insurance company.

The motorcycle is an easy target for the professional thief and the joyrider alike and the official figures on motorcycle theft make for depressing reading; on average a motorcycle is stolen every 16 minutes in the UK!

Motorcycle thefts fall into two categories, those stolen 'to order' and those taken by opportunists. The thief stealing to order will be on the look out for a specific make and model and will go to extraordinary lengths to obtain that motorcycle. The opportunist thief on the other hand will look for easy targets which can be stolen with the minimum of effort and risk.

Whilst it is never going to be possible to make your machine 100% secure, it is estimated that around half of all stolen motorcycles are taken by opportunist thieves. Remember that the opportunist thief is always on the look out for the easy option: if there are two similar motorcycles parked side-by-side, they will target the one with the lowest level of security. By taking a few precautions, you can reduce the chances of your motorcycle being stolen.

Security equipment

There are many specialised motorcycle security devices available and the following text summarises their applications and their good and bad points.

Once you have decided on the type of security equipment which best suits your needs, we recommended that you read one of the many equipment tests regularly carried out by the motorcycle press. These tests compare the products from all the major manufacturers and give impartial ratings on their effectiveness, value-for-money and ease of use.

Ensure the lock and chain you buy is of good quality and long enough to shackle your bike to a solid object

No one item of security equipment can provide complete protection. It is highly recommended that two or more of the items described below are combined to increase the security of your motorcycle (a lock and chain plus an alarm system is just about ideal). The more security measures fitted to the bike, the less likely it is to be stolen.

Lock and chain

Pros: *Very flexible to use; can be used to secure the motorcycle to almost any immovable object. On some locks and chains, the lock can be used on its own as a disc lock (see below).*

Cons: *Can be very heavy and awkward to carry on the motorcycle, although some types will be supplied with a carry bag which can be strapped to the pillion seat.*

- Heavy-duty chains and locks are an excellent security measure **(see illustration 1)**. Whenever the motorcycle is parked, use the lock and chain to secure the machine to a solid, immovable object such as a post or railings. This will prevent the machine from being ridden away or being lifted into the back of a van.

- When fitting the chain, always ensure the chain is routed around the motorcycle frame or swingarm **(see illustrations 2 and 3)**. Never merely pass the chain around one of the wheel rims; a thief may unbolt the wheel and lift the rest of the machine into a van, leaving you with just the wheel! Try to avoid having excess chain free, thus making it difficult to use cutting tools, and keep the chain and lock off the ground to prevent thieves attacking it with a cold chisel. Position the lock so that its lock barrel is facing downwards; this will make it harder for the thief to attack the lock mechanism.

Pass the chain through the bike's frame, rather than just through a wheel . . .

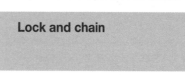

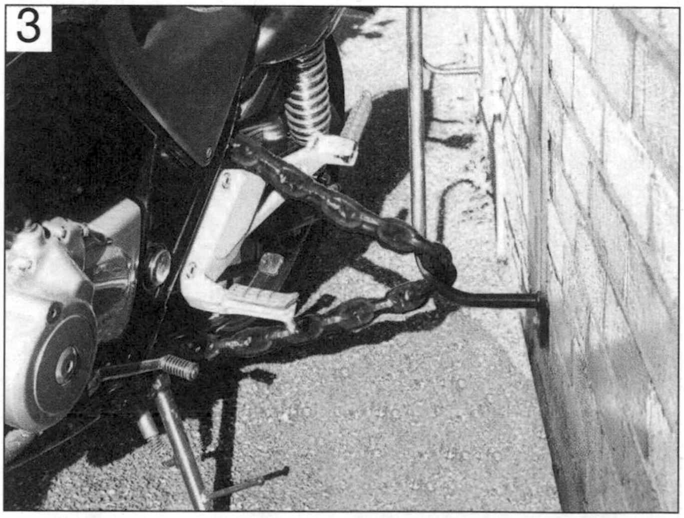

. . . and loop it around a solid object

U-locks

Pros: *Highly effective deterrent which can be used to secure the bike to a post or railings. Most U-locks come with a carrier which allows the lock to be easily carried on the bike.*

Cons: *Not as flexible to use as a lock and chain.*

● These are solid locks which are similar in use to a lock and chain. U-locks are lighter than a lock and chain but not so flexible to use. The length and shape of the lock shackle limit the objects to which the bike can be secured **(see illustration 4)**.

U-locks can be used to secure the bike to a solid object – ensure you purchase one which is long enough

Disc locks

Pros: *Small, light and very easy to carry; most can be stored underneath the seat.*

Cons: *Does not prevent the motorcycle being lifted into a van. Can be very embarrassing if you forget to remove the lock before attempting to ride off!*

A typical disc lock attached through one of the holes in the disc

● Disc locks are designed to be attached to the front brake disc. The lock passes through one of the holes in the disc and prevents the wheel rotating by jamming against the fork/brake caliper **(see illustration 5)**. Some are equipped with an alarm siren which sounds if the disc lock is moved; this not only acts as a theft deterrent but also as a handy reminder if you try to move the bike with the lock still fitted.

● Combining the disc lock with a length of cable which can be looped around a post or railings provides an additional measure of security **(see illustration 6)**.

Alarms and immobilisers

Pros: *Once installed it is completely hassle-free to use. If the system is 'Thatcham' or 'Sold Secure-approved', insurance companies may give you a discount.*

Cons: *Can be expensive to buy and complex to install. No system will prevent the motorcycle from being lifted into a van and taken away.*

● Electronic alarms and immobilisers are available to suit a variety of budgets. There are three different types of system available: pure alarms, pure immobilisers, and the more expensive systems which are combined alarm/immobilisers **(see illustration 7)**.

● An alarm system is designed to emit an audible warning if the motorcycle is being tampered with.

● An immobiliser prevents the motorcycle being started and ridden away by disabling its electrical systems.

● When purchasing an alarm/immobiliser system, check the cost of installing the system unless you are able to do it yourself. If the motorcycle is not used regularly, another consideration is the current drain of the system. All alarm/immobiliser systems are powered by the motorcycle's battery; purchasing a system with a very low current drain could prevent the battery losing its charge whilst the motorcycle is not being used.

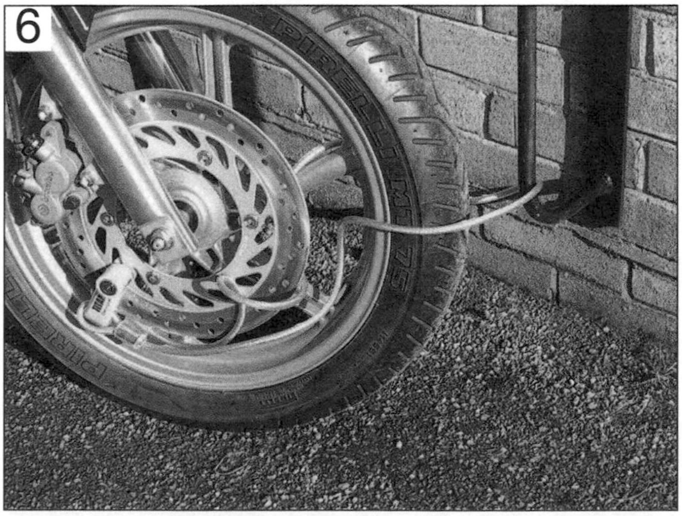

A disc lock combined with a security cable provides additional protection

A typical alarm/immobiliser system

Indelible markings can be applied to most areas of the bike – always apply the manufacturer's sticker to warn off thieves

Security marking kits

Pros: *Very cheap and effective deterrent. Many insurance companies will give you a discount on your insurance premium if a recognised security marking kit is used on your motorcycle.*

Cons: *Does not prevent the motorcycle being stolen by joyriders.*

● There are many different types of security marking kits available. The idea is to mark as many parts of the motorcycle as possible with a unique security number **(see illustrations 8, 9 and 10)**. A form will be included with the kit to register your personal details and those of the motorcycle with the kit manufacturer. This register is made available to the police to help them trace the rightful owner of any motorcycle or components which they recover should all other forms of identification have been removed. Always apply the warning stickers provided with the kit to deter thieves.

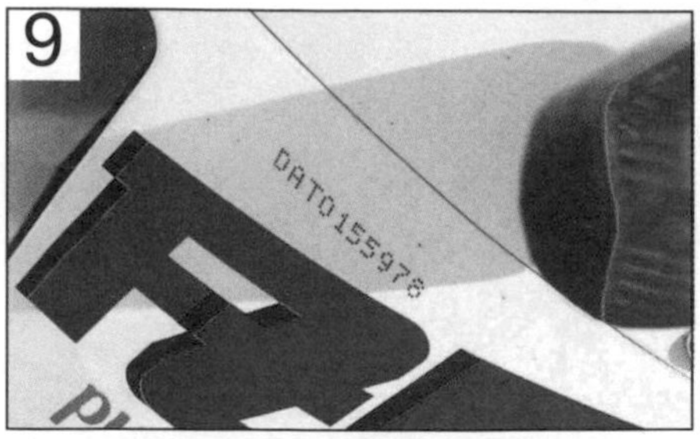

Chemically-etched code numbers can be applied to main body panels . . .

Ground anchors, wheel clamps and security posts

Pros: *An excellent form of security which will deter all but the most determined of thieves.*

Cons: *Awkward to install and can be expensive.*

. . . again, always ensure that the kit manufacturer's sticker is applied in a prominent position

● Whilst the motorcycle is at home, it is a good idea to attach it securely to the floor or a solid wall, even if it is kept in a securely locked garage. Various types of ground anchors, security posts and wheel clamps are available for this purpose **(see illustration 11)**. These security devices are either bolted to a solid concrete or brick structure or can be cemented into the ground.

Permanent ground anchors provide an excellent level of security when the bike is at home

Security at home

A high percentage of motorcycle thefts are from the owner's home. Here are some things to consider whenever your motorcycle is at home:

✔ Where possible, always keep the motorcycle in a securely locked garage. Never rely solely on the standard lock on the garage door, these are usual hopelessly inadequate. Fit an additional locking mechanism to the door and consider having the garage alarmed. A security light, activated by a movement sensor, is also a good investment.

✔ Always secure the motorcycle to the ground or a wall, even if it is inside a securely locked garage.

✔ Do not regularly leave the motorcycle outside your home, try to keep it out of sight wherever possible. If a garage is not available, fit a motorcycle cover over the bike to disguise its true identity.

✔ It is not uncommon for thieves to follow a motorcyclist home to find out where the bike is kept. They will then return at a later date. Be aware of this whenever you are returning home on your motorcycle. If you suspect you are being followed, do not return home, instead ride to a garage or shop and stop as a precaution.

✔ When selling a motorcycle, do not provide your home address or the location where the bike is normally kept. Arrange to meet the buyer at a location away from your home. Thieves have been known to pose as potential buyers to find out where motorcycles are kept and then return later to steal them.

Security away from the home

As well as fitting security equipment to your motorcycle here are a few general rules to follow whenever you park your motorcycle.

✔ Park in a busy, public place.

✔ Use car parks which incorporate security features, such as CCTV.

✔ At night, park in a well-lit area, preferably directly underneath a street light.

✔ Engage the steering lock.

✔ Secure the motorcycle to a solid, immovable object such as a post or railings with an additional lock. If this is not possible, secure the bike to a friend's motorcycle. Some public parking places provide security loops for motorcycles.

✔ Never leave your helmet or luggage attached to the motorcycle. Take them with you at all times.

Lubricants and fluids

A wide range of lubricants, fluids and cleaning agents is available for motor-cycles. This is a guide as to what is available, its applications and properties.

Four-stroke engine oil

● Engine oil is without doubt the most important component of any four-stroke engine. Modern motorcycle engines place a lot of demands on their oil and choosing the right type is essential. Using an unsuitable oil will lead to an increased rate of engine wear and could result in serious engine damage. Before purchasing oil, always check the recommended oil specification given by the manufacturer. The manufacturer will state a recommended 'type or classification' and also a specific 'viscosity' range for engine oil.

● The oil 'type or classification' is identified by its API (American Petroleum Institute) rating. The API rating will be in the form of two letters, e.g. SG. The S identifies the oil as being suitable for use in a petrol (gasoline) engine (S stands for spark ignition) and the second letter, ranging from A to J, identifies the oil's performance rating. The later this letter, the higher the specification of the oil; for example API SG oil exceeds the requirements of API SF oil. **Note:** *On some oils there may also be a second rating consisting of another two letters, the first letter being C, e.g. API SF/CD. This rating indicates the oil is also suitable for use in a diesel engines (the C stands for compression ignition) and is thus of no relevance for motorcycle use.*

● The 'viscosity' of the oil is identified by its SAE (Society of Automotive Engineers) rating. All modern engines require multigrade oils and the SAE rating will consist of two numbers, the first followed by a W, e.g. 10W/40. The first number indicates the viscosity rating of the oil at low temperatures (W stands for winter – tested at –20°C) and the second number represents the viscosity of the oil at high temperatures (tested at 100°C). The lower the number, the thinner the oil. For example an oil with an SAE 10W/40 rating will give better cold starting and running than an SAE 15W/40 oil.

● As well as ensuring the 'type' and 'viscosity' of the oil match the recommendations, another consideration to make when buying engine oil is whether to purchase a standard mineral-based oil, a semi-synthetic oil (also known as a synthetic blend or synthetic-based oil) or a fully-synthetic oil. Although all oils will have a similar rating and viscosity, their cost will vary considerably; mineral-based oils are the cheapest, the fully-synthetic oils the most expensive with the semi-synthetic oils falling somewhere in-between. This decision is very much up to the owner, but it should be noted that modern synthetic oils have far better lubricating and cleaning qualities than traditional mineral-based oils and tend to retain these properties for far longer. Bearing in mind the operating conditions inside a modern, high-revving motorcycle engine it is highly recommended that a fully synthetic oil is used. The extra expense at each service could save you money in the long term by preventing premature engine wear.

● As a final note always ensure that the oil is specifically designed for use in motorcycle engines. Engine oils designed primarily for use in car engines sometimes contain additives or friction modifiers which could cause clutch slip on a motorcycle fitted with a wet-clutch.

Two-stroke engine oil

● Modern two-stroke engines, with their high power outputs, place high demands on their oil. If engine seizure is to be avoided it is essential that a high-quality oil is used. Two-stroke oils differ hugely from four-stroke oils. The oil lubricates only the crankshaft and piston(s) (the transmission has its own lubricating oil) and is used on a total-loss basis where it is burnt completely during the combustion process.

● The Japanese have recently introduced a classification system for two-stroke oils, the JASO rating. This rating is in the form of two letters, either FA, FB or FC – FA is the lowest classification and FC the highest. Ensure the oil being used meets or exceeds the recommended rating specified by the manufacturer.

● As well as ensuring the oil rating matches the recommendation, another consideration to make when buying engine oil is whether to purchase a standard mineral-based oil, a semi-synthetic oil (also known as a synthetic blend or synthetic-based oil) or a fully-synthetic oil. The cost of each type of oil varies considerably; mineral-based oils are the cheapest, the fully-synthetic oils the most expensive with the semi-synthetic oils falling somewhere in-between. This decision is very much up to the owner, but it should be noted that modern synthetic oils have far better lubricating properties and burn cleaner than traditional mineral-based oils. It is therefore recommended that a fully synthetic oil is used. The extra expense could save you money in the long term by preventing premature engine wear, engine performance will be improved, carbon deposits and exhaust smoke will be reduced.

● Always ensure that the oil is specifically designed for use in an injector system. Many high quality two-stroke oils are designed for competition use and need to be pre-mixed with fuel. These oils are of a much higher viscosity and are not designed to flow through the injector pumps used on road-going two-stroke motorcycles.

Transmission (gear) oil

● On a two-stroke engine, the transmission and clutch are lubricated by their own separate oil bath which must be changed in accordance with the Maintenance Schedule.

● Although the engine and transmission units of most four-strokes use a common lubrication supply, there are some exceptions where the engine and gearbox have separate oil reservoirs and a dry clutch is used.

● Motorcycle manufacturers will either recommend a monograde transmission oil or a four-stroke multigrade engine oil to lubricate the transmission.

● Transmission oils, or gear oils as they are often called, are designed specifically for use in transmission systems. The viscosity of these oils is represented by an SAE number, but the scale of measurement applied is different to that used to grade engine oils. As a rough guide a SAE90 gear oil will be of the same viscosity as an SAE50 engine oil.

Shaft drive oil

● On models equipped with shaft final drive, the shaft drive gears are will have their own oil supply. The manufacturer will state a recommended 'type or classification' and also a specific 'viscosity' range in the same manner as for four-stroke engine oil.

● Gear oil classification is given by the number which follows the API GL (GL standing for gear lubricant) rating, the higher the number, the higher the specification of the oil, e.g. API GL5 oil is a higher specification than API GL4 oil. Ensure the oil meets or exceeds the classification specified and is of the correct viscosity. The viscosity of gear oils is also represented by an SAE number but the scale of measurement used is different to that used to grade engine oils. As a rough guide an SAE90 gear oil will be of the same viscosity as an SAE50 engine oil.

● If the use of an EP (Extreme Pressure) gear oil is specified, ensure the oil purchased is suitable.

Fork oil and suspension fluid

● Conventional telescopic front forks are hydraulic and require fork oil to work. To ensure the forks function correctly, the fork oil must be changed in accordance with the Maintenance Schedule.

● Fork oil is available in a variety of viscosities, identified by their SAE rating; fork oil ratings vary from light (SAE 5) to heavy (SAE 30). When purchasing fork oil, ensure the viscosity rating matches that specified by the manufacturer.

● Some lubricant manufacturers also produce a range of high-quality suspension fluids which are very similar to fork oil but are designed mainly for competition use. These fluids may have a different viscosity rating system which is not to be confused with the SAE rating of normal fork oil. Refer to the manufacturer's instructions if in any doubt.

Brake and clutch fluid

● All disc brake systems and some clutch systems are hydraulically operated. To ensure correct operation, the hydraulic fluid must be changed in accordance with the Maintenance Schedule.

● Brake and clutch fluid is classified by its DOT rating with most motorcycle manufacturers specifying DOT 3 or 4 fluid. Both fluid types are glycol-based and can be mixed together without adverse effect; DOT 4 fluid exceeds the requirements of DOT 3 fluid. Although it is safe to use DOT 4 fluid in a system designed for use with DOT 3 fluid, never use DOT 3 fluid in a system which specifies the use of DOT 4 as this will adversely affect the system's performance. The type required for the system will be marked on the fluid reservoir cap.

● Some manufacturers also produce a DOT 5 hydraulic fluid. DOT 5 hydraulic fluid is silicone-based and is not compatible with the glycol-based DOT 3 and 4 fluids. Never mix DOT 5 fluid with DOT 3 or 4 fluid as this will seriously affect the performance of the hydraulic system.

Coolant/antifreeze

● When purchasing coolant/antifreeze, always ensure it is suitable for use in an aluminium engine and contains corrosion inhibitors to prevent possible blockages of the internal coolant passages of the system. As a general rule, most coolants are designed to be used neat and should not be diluted whereas antifreeze can be mixed with distilled water to provide a coolant solution of the required strength. Refer to the manufacturer's instructions on the bottle.

● Ensure the coolant is changed in accordance with the Maintenance Schedule.

Chain lube

● Chain lube is an aerosol-type spray lubricant specifically designed for use on motorcycle final drive chains. Chain lube has two functions, to minimise friction between the final drive chain and sprockets and to prevent corrosion of the chain. Regular use of a good-quality chain lube will extend the life of the drive chain and sprockets and thus maximise the power being transmitted from the transmission to the rear wheel.

● When using chain lube, always allow some time for the solvents in the lube to evaporate before riding the motorcycle. This will minimise the amount of lube which will 'fling' off from the chain when the motorcycle is used. If the motorcycle is equipped with an 'O-ring' chain, ensure the chain lube is labelled as being suitable for use on 'O-ring' chains.

Degreasers and solvents

● There are many different types of solvents and degreasers available to remove the grime and grease which accumulate around the motorcycle during normal use. Degreasers and solvents are usually available as an aerosol-type spray or as a liquid which you apply with a brush. Always closely follow the manufacturer's instructions and wear eye protection during use. Be aware that many solvents are flammable and may give off noxious fumes; take adequate precautions when using them (*see Safety First!*).

● For general cleaning, use one of the many solvents or degreasers available from most motorcycle accessory shops. These solvents are usually applied then left for a certain time before being washed off with water.

Brake cleaner is a solvent specifically designed to remove all traces of oil, grease and dust from braking system components. Brake cleaner is designed to evaporate quickly and leaves behind no residue.

Carburettor cleaner is an aerosol-type solvent specifically designed to clear carburettor blockages and break down the hard deposits and gum often found inside carburettors during overhaul.

Contact cleaner is an aerosol-type solvent designed for cleaning electrical components. The cleaner will remove all traces of oil and dirt from components such as switch contacts or fouled spark plugs and then dry, leaving behind no residue.

Gasket remover is an aerosol-type solvent designed for removing stubborn gaskets from engine components during overhaul. Gasket remover will minimise the amount of scraping required to remove the gasket and therefore reduce the risk of damage to the mating surface.

Spray lubricants

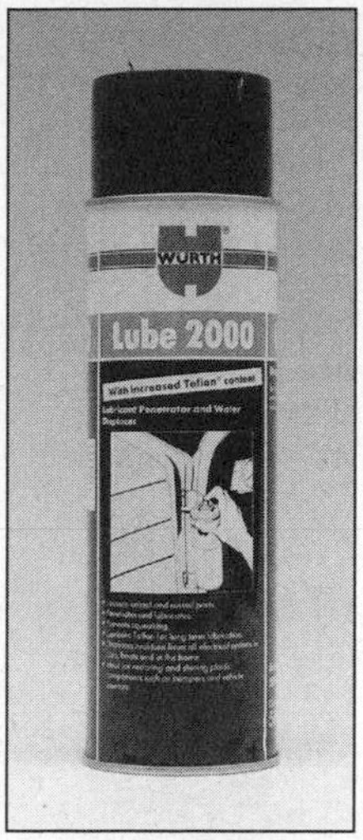

● Aerosol-based spray lubricants are widely available and are excellent for lubricating lever pivots and exposed cables and switches. Try to use a lubricant which is of the dry-film type as the fluid evaporates, leaving behind a dry-film of lubricant. Lubricants which leave behind an oily residue will attract dust and dirt which will increase the rate of wear of the cable/lever.

● Most lubricants also act as a moisture dispersant and a penetrating fluid. This means they can also be used to 'dry out' electrical components such as wiring connectors or switches as well as helping to free seized fasteners.

Greases

● Grease is used to lubricate many of the pivot-points. A good-quality multi-purpose grease is suitable for most applications but some manufacturers will specify the use of specialist greases for use on components such as swingarm and suspension linkage bushes. These specialist greases can be purchased from most motorcycle (or car) accessory shops; commonly specified types include molybdenum disulphide grease, lithium-based grease, graphite-based grease, silicone-based grease and high-temperature copper-based grease.

Gasket sealing compounds

● Gasket sealing compounds can be used in conjunction with gaskets, to improve their sealing capabilities, or on their own to seal metal-to-metal joints. Depending on their type, sealing compounds either set hard or stay relatively soft and pliable.

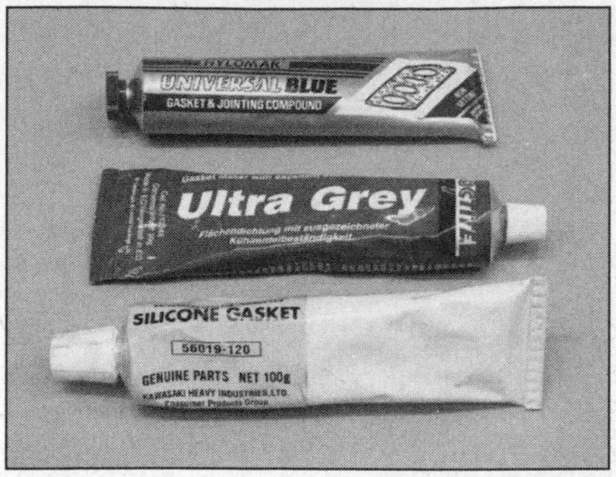

● When purchasing a gasket sealing compound, ensure that it is designed specifically for use on an internal combustion engine. General multi-purpose sealants available from DIY stores may appear visibly similar but they are not designed to withstand the extreme heat or contact with fuel and oil encountered when used on an engine (*see 'Tools and Workshop Tips' for further information*).

Thread locking compound

● Thread locking compounds are used to secure certain threaded fasteners in position to prevent them from loosening due to vibration. Thread locking compounds can be purchased from most motorcycle (and car) accessory shops. Ensure the threads of the both components are completely clean and dry before sparingly applying the locking compound (*see 'Tools and Workshop Tips' for further information*).

Fuel additives

● Fuel additives which protect and clean the fuel system components are widely available. These additives are designed to remove all traces of deposits that build up on the carburettors/injectors and prevent wear, helping the fuel system to operate more efficiently. If a fuel additive is being used, check that it is suitable for use with your motorcycle, especially if your motorcycle is equipped with a catalytic converter.

● Octane boosters are also available. These additives are designed to improve the performance of highly-tuned engines being run on normal pump-fuel and are of no real use on standard motorcycles.

Conversion factors

Length (distance)

Inches (in)	x 25.4	= Millimetres (mm)	x 0.0394	= Inches (in)
Feet (ft)	x 0.305	= Metres (m)	x 3.281	= Feet (ft)
Miles	x 1.609	= Kilometres (km)	x 0.621	= Miles

Volume (capacity)

Cubic inches (cu in; in^3)	x 16.387	= Cubic centimetres (cc; cm^3)	x 0.061	= Cubic inches (cu in; in^3)
Imperial pints (Imp pt)	x 0.568	= Litres (l)	x 1.76	= Imperial pints (Imp pt)
Imperial quarts (Imp qt)	x 1.137	= Litres (l)	x 0.88	= Imperial quarts (Imp qt)
Imperial quarts (Imp qt)	x 1.201	= US quarts (US qt)	x 0.833	= Imperial quarts (Imp qt)
US quarts (US qt)	x 0.946	= Litres (l)	x 1.057	= US quarts (US qt)
Imperial gallons (Imp gal)	x 4.546	= Litres (l)	x 0.22	= Imperial gallons (Imp gal)
Imperial gallons (Imp gal)	x 1.201	= US gallons (US gal)	x 0.833	= Imperial gallons (Imp gal)
US gallons (US gal)	x 3.785	= Litres (l)	x 0.264	= US gallons (US gal)

Mass (weight)

Ounces (oz)	x 28.35	= Grams (g)	x 0.035	= Ounces (oz)
Pounds (lb)	x 0.454	= Kilograms (kg)	x 2.205	= Pounds (lb)

Force

Ounces-force (ozf; oz)	x 0.278	= Newtons (N)	x 3.6	= Ounces-force (ozf; oz)
Pounds-force (lbf; lb)	x 4.448	= Newtons (N)	x 0.225	= Pounds-force (lbf; lb)
Newtons (N)	x 0.1	= Kilograms-force (kgf; kg)	x 9.81	= Newtons (N)

Pressure

Pounds-force per square inch (psi; lbf/in^2; lb/in^2)	x 0.070	= Kilograms-force per square centimetre (kgf/cm^2; kg/cm^2)	x 14.223	= Pounds-force per square inch (psi; lbf/in^2; lb/in^2)
Pounds-force per square inch (psi; lbf/in^2; lb/in^2)	x 0.068	= Atmospheres (atm)	x 14.696	= Pounds-force per square inch (psi; lbf/in^2; lb/in^2)
Pounds-force per square inch (psi; lbf/in^2; lb/in^2)	x 0.069	= Bars	x 14.5	= Pounds-force per square inch (psi; lbf/in^2; lb/in^2)
Pounds-force per square inch (psi; lbf/in^2; lb/in^2)	x 6.895	= Kilopascals (kPa)	x 0.145	= Pounds-force per square inch (psi; lbf/in^2; lb/in^2)
Kilopascals (kPa)	x 0.01	= Kilograms-force per square centimetre (kgf/cm^2; kg/cm^2)	x 98.1	= Kilopascals (kPa)
Millibar (mbar)	x 100	= Pascals (Pa)	x 0.01	= Millibar (mbar)
Millibar (mbar)	x 0.0145	= Pounds-force per square inch (psi; lbf/in^2; lb/in^2)	x 68.947	= Millibar (mbar)
Millibar (mbar)	x 0.75	= Millimetres of mercury (mmHg)	x 1.333	= Millibar (mbar)
Millibar (mbar)	x 0.401	= Inches of water (inH_2O)	x 2.491	= Millibar (mbar)
Millimetres of mercury (mmHg)	x 0.535	= Inches of water (inH_2O)	x 1.868	= Millimetres of mercury (mmHg)
Inches of water (inH_2O)	x 0.036	= Pounds-force per square inch (psi; lbf/in^2; lb/in^2)	x 27.68	= Inches of water (inH_2O)

Torque (moment of force)

Pounds-force inches (lbf in; lb in)	x 1.152	= Kilograms-force centimetre (kgf cm; kg cm)	x 0.868	= Pounds-force inches (lbf in; lb in)
Pounds-force inches (lbf in; lb in)	x 0.113	= Newton metres (Nm)	x 8.85	= Pounds-force inches (lbf in; lb in)
Pounds-force inches (lbf in; lb in)	x 0.083	= Pounds-force feet (lbf ft; lb ft)	x 12	= Pounds-force inches (lbf in; lb in)
Pounds-force feet (lbf ft; lb ft)	x 0.138	= Kilograms-force metres (kgf m; kg m)	x 7.233	= Pounds-force feet (lbf ft; lb ft)
Pounds-force feet (lbf ft; lb ft)	x 1.356	= Newton metres (Nm)	x 0.738	= Pounds-force feet (lbf ft; lb ft)
Newton metres (Nm)	x 0.102	= Kilograms-force metres (kgf m; kg m)	x 9.804	= Newton metres (Nm)

Power

Horsepower (hp)	x 745.7	= Watts (W)	x 0.0013	= Horsepower (hp)

Velocity (speed)

Miles per hour (miles/hr; mph)	x 1.609	= Kilometres per hour (km/hr; kph)	x 0.621	= Miles per hour (miles/hr; mph)

Fuel consumption*

Miles per gallon (mpg)	x 0.354	= Kilometres per litre (km/l)	x 2.825	= Miles per gallon (mpg)

Temperature

Degrees Fahrenheit = (°C x 1.8) + 32

Degrees Celsius (Degrees Centigrade; °C) = (°F - 32) x 0.56

** It is common practice to convert from miles per gallon (mpg) to litres/100 kilometres (l/100km), where mpg x l/100 km = 282*

About the MOT Test

In the UK, all vehicles more than three years old are subject to an annual test to ensure that they meet minimum safety requirements. A current test certificate must be issued before a machine can be used on public roads, and is required before a road fund licence can be issued. Riding without a current test certificate will also invalidate your insurance.

For most owners, the MOT test is an annual cause for anxiety, and this is largely due to owners not being sure what needs to be checked prior to submitting the motorcycle for testing. The simple answer is that a fully roadworthy motorcycle will have no difficulty in passing the test.

This is a guide to getting your motorcycle through the MOT test. Obviously it will not be possible to examine the motorcycle to the same standard as the professional MOT tester, particularly in view of the equipment required for some of the checks. However, working through the following procedures will enable you to identify any problem areas before submitting the motorcycle for the test.

It has only been possible to summarise the test requirements here, based on the regulations in force at the time of printing. Test standards are becoming increasingly stringent, although there are some exemptions for older vehicles. More information about the MOT test can be obtained from the TSO publications, *How Safe is your Motorcycle* and *The MOT Inspection Manual for Motorcycle Testing*.

Many of the checks require that one of the wheels is raised off the ground. If the motorcycle doesn't have a centre stand, note that an auxiliary stand will be required. Additionally, the help of an assistant may prove useful.

Certain exceptions apply to machines under 50 cc, machines without a lighting system, and Classic bikes - if in doubt about any of the requirements listed below seek confirmation from an MOT tester prior to submitting the motorcycle for the test.

Check that the frame number is clearly visible.

Electrical System

Lights, turn signals, horn and reflector

✔ With the ignition on, check the operation of the following electrical components. **Note:** *The electrical components on certain small-capacity machines are powered by the generator, requiring that the engine is run for this check.*

a) Headlight and tail light. Check that both illuminate in the low and high beam switch positions.
b) Position lights. Check that the front position (or sidelight) and tail light illuminate in this switch position.
c) Turn signals. Check that all flash at the correct rate, and that the warning light(s) function correctly. Check that the turn signal switch works correctly.
d) Hazard warning system (where fitted). Check that all four turn signals flash in this switch position.
e) Brake stop light. Check that the light comes on when the front and rear brakes are independently applied. Models first used on or after 1st April 1986 must have a brake light switch on each brake.
f) Horn. Check that the sound is continuous and of reasonable volume.

✔ Check that there is a red reflector on the rear of the machine, either mounted separately or as part of the tail light lens.

✔ Check the condition of the headlight, tail light and turn signal lenses.

Headlight beam height

✔ The MOT tester will perform a headlight beam height check using specialised beam setting equipment **(see illustration 1)**. This equipment will not be available to the home mechanic, but if you suspect that the headlight is incorrectly set or may have been maladjusted in the past, you can perform a rough test as follows.

✔ Position the bike in a straight line facing a brick wall. The bike must be off its stand, upright and with a rider seated. Measure the height from the ground to the centre of the headlight and mark a horizontal line on the wall at this height. Position the motorcycle 3.8 metres from the wall and draw a vertical line up the wall central to the centreline of the motorcycle. Switch to dipped beam and check that the beam pattern falls slightly lower than the horizontal line and to the left of the vertical line **(see illustration 2)**.

1

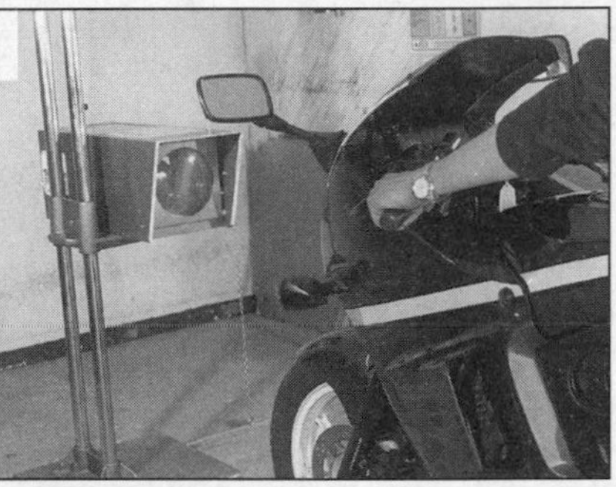

Headlight beam height checking equipment

2

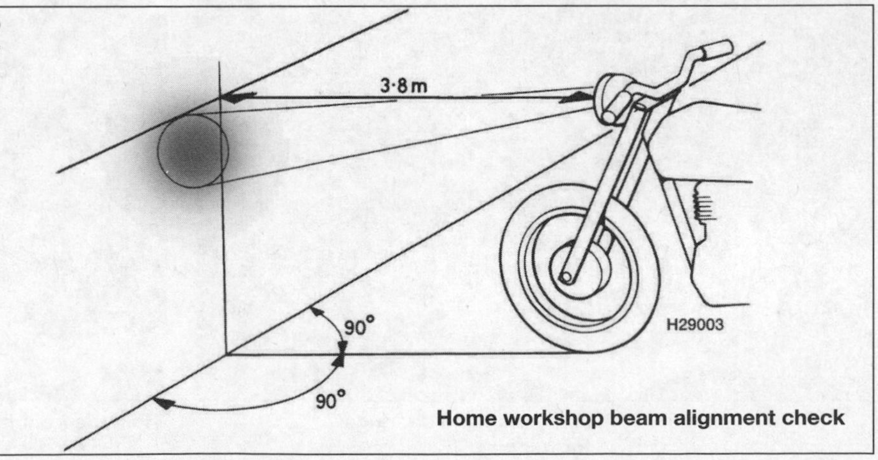

Home workshop beam alignment check

Exhaust System and Final Drive

Exhaust

✔ Check that the exhaust mountings are secure and that the system does not foul any of the rear suspension components.

✔ Start the motorcycle. When the revs are increased, check that the exhaust is neither holed nor leaking from any of its joints. On a linked system, check that the collector box is not leaking due to corrosion.

✔ Note that the exhaust decibel level ("loudness" of the exhaust) is assessed at the discretion of the tester. If the motorcycle was first used on or after 1st January 1985 the silencer must carry the BSAU 193 stamp, or a marking relating to its make and model, or be of OE (original equipment) manufacture. If the silencer is marked NOT FOR ROAD USE, RACING USE ONLY or similar, it will fail the MOT.

Final drive

✔ On chain or belt drive machines, check that the chain/belt is in good condition and does not have excessive slack. Also check that the sprocket is securely mounted on the rear wheel hub. Check that the chain/belt guard is in place.

✔ On shaft drive bikes, check for oil leaking from the drive unit and fouling the rear tyre.

Steering and Suspension

Steering

✔ With the front wheel raised off the ground, rotate the steering from lock to lock. The handlebar or switches must not contact the fuel tank or be close enough to trap the rider's hand. Problems can be caused by damaged lock stops on the lower yoke and frame, or by the fitting of non-standard handlebars.

✔ When performing the lock to lock check, also ensure that the steering moves freely without drag or notchiness. Steering movement can be impaired by poorly routed cables, or by overtight head bearings or worn bearings. The tester will perform a check of the steering head bearing lower race by mounting the front wheel on a surface plate, then performing a lock to lock check with the weight of the machine on the lower bearing **(see illustration 3)**.

✔ Grasp the fork sliders (lower legs) and attempt to push and pull on the forks **(see illustration 4)**. Any play in the steering head bearings will be felt. Note that in extreme cases, wear of the front fork bushes can be misinterpreted for head bearing play.

Front wheel mounted on a surface plate for steering head bearing lower race check

✔ Check that the handlebars are securely mounted.

✔ Check that the handlebar grip rubbers are secure. They should by bonded to the bar left end and to the throttle cable pulley on the right end.

Front suspension

✔ With the motorcycle off the stand, hold the front brake on and pump the front forks up and down **(see illustration 5)**. Check that they are adequately damped.

Checking the steering head bearings for freeplay

Hold the front brake on and pump the front forks up and down to check operation

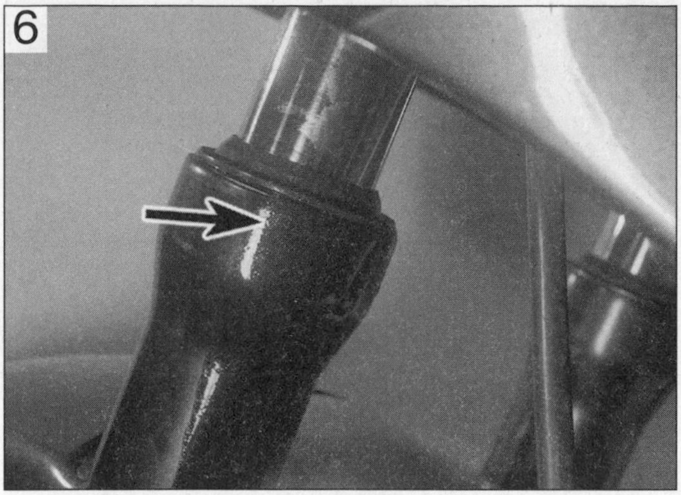

Inspect the area around the fork dust seal for oil leakage (arrow)

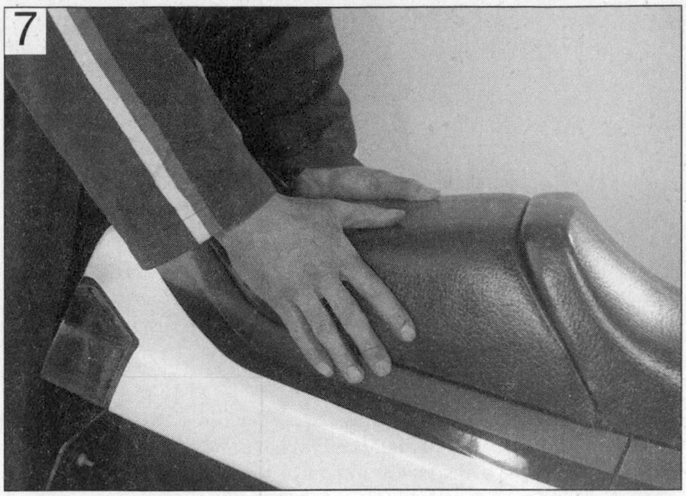

Bounce the rear of the motorcycle to check rear suspension operation

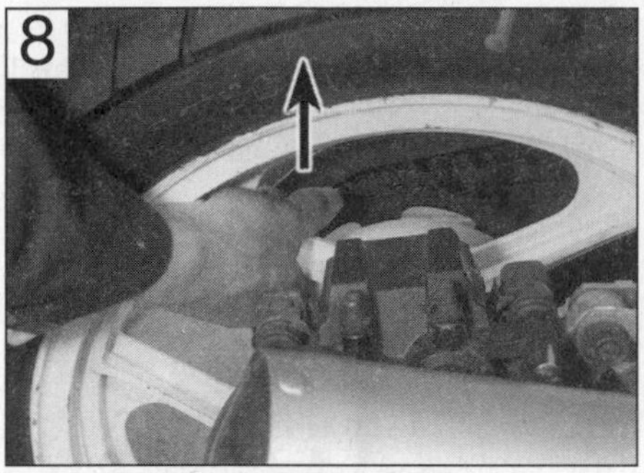

Checking for rear suspension linkage play

✔ Inspect the area above and around the front fork oil seals **(see illustration 6)**. There should be no sign of oil on the fork tube (stanchion) nor leaking down the slider (lower leg). On models so equipped, check that there is no oil leaking from the anti-dive units.

✔ On models with swingarm front suspension, check that there is no freeplay in the linkage when moved from side to side.

Rear suspension

✔ With the motorcycle off the stand and an assistant supporting the motorcycle by its handlebars, bounce the rear suspension **(see illustration 7)**. Check that the suspension components do not foul on any of the cycle parts and check that the shock absorber(s) provide adequate damping.

✔ Visually inspect the shock absorber(s) and check that there is no sign of oil leakage from its damper. This is somewhat restricted on certain single shock models due to the location of the shock absorber.

✔ With the rear wheel raised off the ground, grasp the wheel at the highest point and attempt to pull it up **(see illustration 8)**. Any play in the swingarm pivot or suspension linkage bearings will be felt as movement. **Note:** *Do not confuse play with actual suspension movement.* Failure to lubricate suspension linkage bearings can lead to bearing failure **(see illustration 9)**.

✔ With the rear wheel raised off the ground, grasp the swingarm ends and attempt to move the swingarm from side to side and forwards and backwards - any play indicates wear of the swingarm pivot bearings **(see illustration 10)**.

Worn suspension linkage pivots (arrows) are usually the cause of play in the rear suspension

Grasp the swingarm at the ends to check for play in its pivot bearings

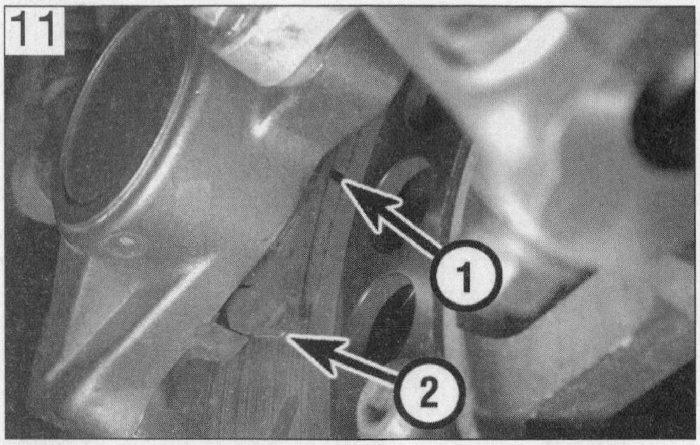

Brake pad wear can usually be viewed without removing the caliper. Most pads have wear indicator grooves (1) and some also have indicator tangs (2)

On drum brakes, check the angle of the operating lever with the brake fully applied. Most drum brakes have a wear indicator pointer and scale.

Brakes, Wheels and Tyres

Brakes

✔ With the wheel raised off the ground, apply the brake then free it off, and check that the wheel is about to revolve freely without brake drag.

✔ On disc brakes, examine the disc itself. Check that it is securely mounted and not cracked.

✔ On disc brakes, view the pad material through the caliper mouth and check that the pads are not worn down beyond the limit **(see illustration 11)**.

✔ On drum brakes, check that when the brake is applied the angle between the operating lever and cable or rod is not too great **(see illustration 12)**. Check also that the operating lever doesn't foul any other components.

✔ On disc brakes, examine the flexible hoses from top to bottom. Have an assistant hold the brake on so that the fluid in the hose is under pressure, and check that there is no sign of fluid leakage, bulges or cracking. If there are any metal brake pipes or unions, check that these are free from corrosion and damage. Where a brake-linked anti-dive system is fitted, check the hoses to the anti-dive in a similar manner.

✔ Check that the rear brake torque arm is secure and that its fasteners are secured by self-locking nuts or castellated nuts with split-pins or R-pins **(see illustration 13)**.

✔ On models with ABS, check that the self-check warning light in the instrument panel works.

✔ The MOT tester will perform a test of the motorcycle's braking efficiency based on a calculation of rider and motorcycle weight. Although this cannot be carried out at home, you can at least ensure that the braking systems are properly maintained. For hydraulic disc brakes, check the fluid level, lever/pedal feel (bleed of air if its spongy) and pad material. For drum brakes, check adjustment, cable or rod operation and shoe lining thickness.

Wheels and tyres

✔ Check the wheel condition. Cast wheels should be free from cracks and if of the built-up design, all fasteners should be secure. Spoked wheels should be checked for broken, corroded, loose or bent spokes.

✔ With the wheel raised off the ground, spin the wheel and visually check that the tyre and wheel run true. Check that the tyre does not foul the suspension or mudguards.

✔ With the wheel raised off the ground, grasp the wheel and attempt to move it about the axle (spindle) **(see illustration 14)**. Any play felt here indicates wheel bearing failure.

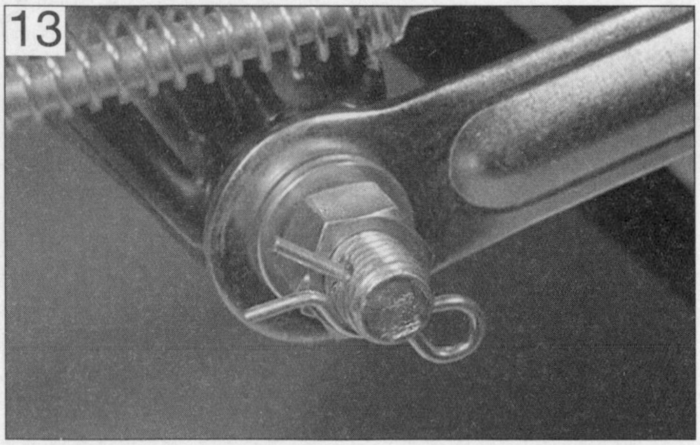

Brake torque arm must be properly secured at both ends

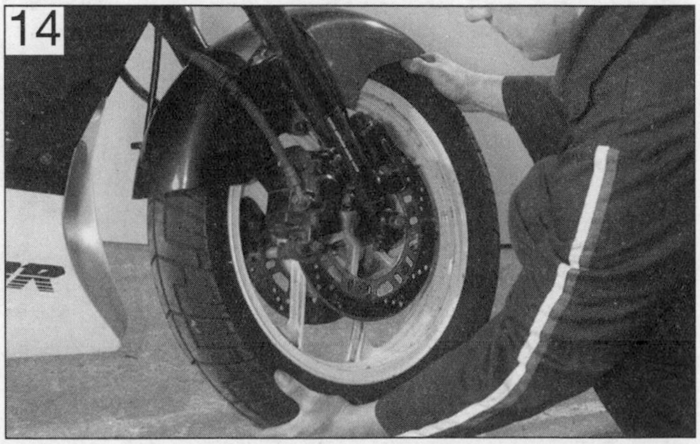

Check for wheel bearing play by trying to move the wheel about the axle (spindle)

15

Checking the tyre tread depth

16

Tyre direction of rotation arrow can be found on tyre sidewall

17

Castellated type wheel axle (spindle) nut must be secured by a split pin or R-pin

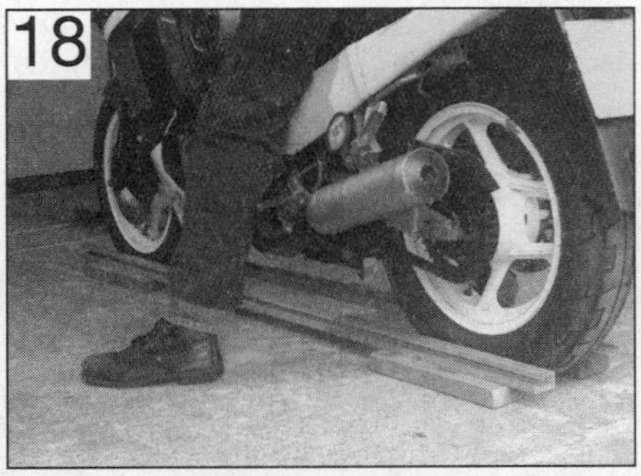
18

Two straightedges are used to check wheel alignment

✔ Check the tyre tread depth, tread condition and sidewall condition **(see illustration 15)**.

✔ Check the tyre type. Front and rear tyre types must be compatible and be suitable for road use. Tyres marked NOT FOR ROAD USE, COMPETITION USE ONLY or similar, will fail the MOT.

✔ If the tyre sidewall carries a direction of rotation arrow, this must be pointing in the direction of normal wheel rotation **(see illustration 16)**.

✔ Check that the wheel axle (spindle) nuts (where applicable) are properly secured. A self-locking nut or castellated nut with a split-pin or R-pin can be used **(see illustration 17)**.

✔ Wheel alignment is checked with the motorcycle off the stand and a rider seated. With the front wheel pointing straight ahead, two perfectly straight lengths of metal or wood and placed against the sidewalls of both tyres **(see illustration 18)**. The gap each side of the front tyre must be equidistant on both sides. Incorrect wheel alignment may be due to a cocked rear wheel (often as the result of poor chain adjustment) or in extreme cases, a bent frame.

General checks and condition

✔ Check the security of all major fasteners, bodypanels, seat, fairings (where fitted) and mudguards.

✔ Check that the rider and pillion footrests, handlebar levers and brake pedal are securely mounted.

✔ Check for corrosion on the frame or any load-bearing components. If severe, this may affect the structure, particularly under stress.

Sidecars

A motorcycle fitted with a sidecar requires additional checks relating to the stability of the machine and security of attachment and swivel joints, plus specific wheel alignment (toe-in) requirements. Additionally, tyre and lighting requirements differ from conventional motorcycle use. Owners are advised to check MOT test requirements with an official test centre.

Preparing for storage

Before you start

If repairs or an overhaul is needed, see that this is carried out now rather than left until you want to ride the bike again.

Give the bike a good wash and scrub all dirt from its underside. Make sure the bike dries completely before preparing for storage.

Engine

- Remove the spark plug(s) and lubricate the cylinder bores with approximately a teaspoon of motor oil using a spout-type oil can **(see illustration 1)**. Reinstall the spark plug(s). Crank the engine over a couple of times to coat the piston rings and bores with oil. If the bike has a kickstart, use this to turn the engine over. If not, flick the kill switch to the OFF position and crank the engine over on the starter **(see illustration 2)**. If the nature on the ignition system prevents the starter operating with the kill switch in the OFF position, remove the spark plugs and fit them back in their caps; ensure that the plugs are earthed (grounded) against the cylinder head when the starter is operated **(see illustration 3)**.

Warning: It is important that the plugs are earthed (grounded) away from the spark plug holes otherwise there is a risk of atomised fuel from the cylinders igniting.

HAYNES HiNT ***On a single cylinder four-stroke engine, you can seal the combustion chamber completely by positioning the piston at TDC on the compression stroke.***

- Drain the carburettor(s) otherwise there is a risk of jets becoming blocked by gum deposits from the fuel **(see illustration 4)**.

- If the bike is going into long-term storage, consider adding a fuel stabiliser to the fuel in the tank. If the tank is drained completely, corrosion of its internal surfaces may occur if left unprotected for a long period. The tank can be treated with a rust preventative especially for this purpose. Alternatively, remove the tank and pour half a litre of motor oil into it, install the filler cap and shake the tank to coat its internals with oil before draining off the excess. The same effect can also be achieved by spraying WD40 or a similar water-dispersant around the inside of the tank via its flexible nozzle.

- Make sure the cooling system contains the correct mix of antifreeze. Antifreeze also contains important corrosion inhibitors.

- The air intakes and exhaust can be sealed off by covering or plugging the openings. Ensure that you do not seal in any condensation; run the engine until it is hot,

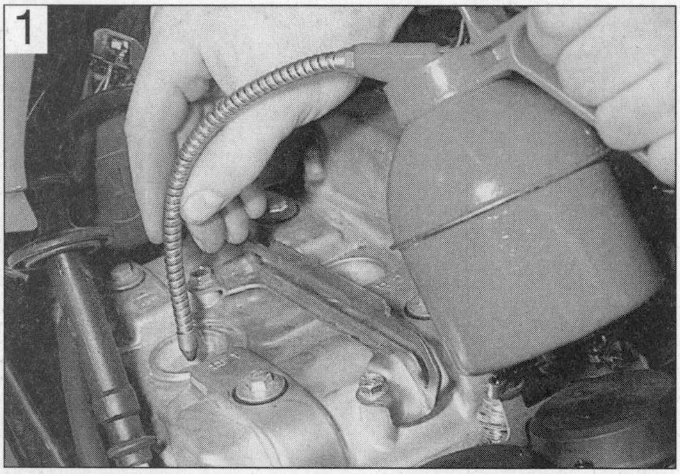

Squirt a drop of motor oil into each cylinder

Flick the kill switch to OFF . . .

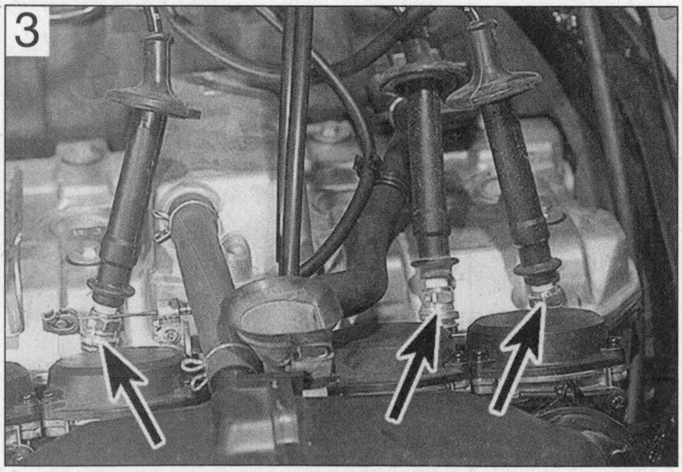

. . . and ensure that the metal bodies of the plugs (arrows) are earthed against the cylinder head

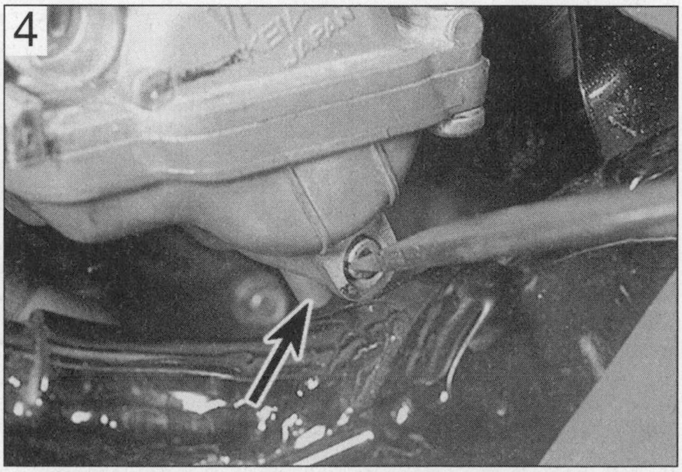

Connect a hose to the carburettor float chamber drain stub (arrow) and unscrew the drain screw

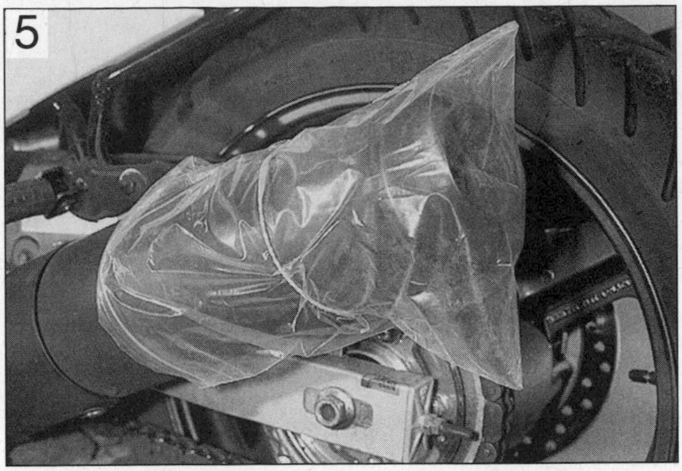

Exhausts can be sealed off with a plastic bag

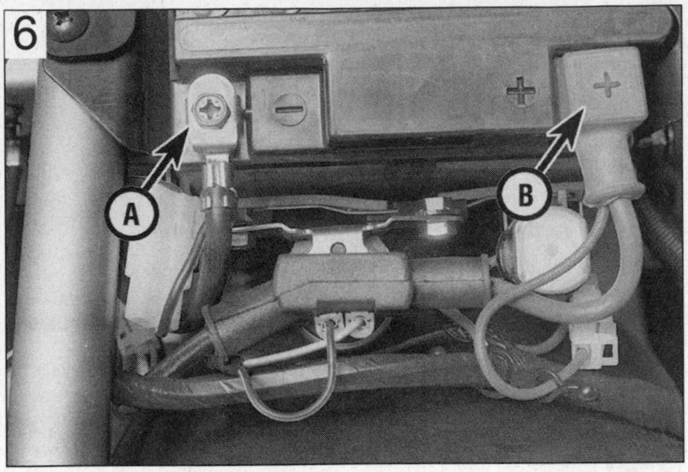

Disconnect the negative lead (A) first, followed by the positive lead (B)

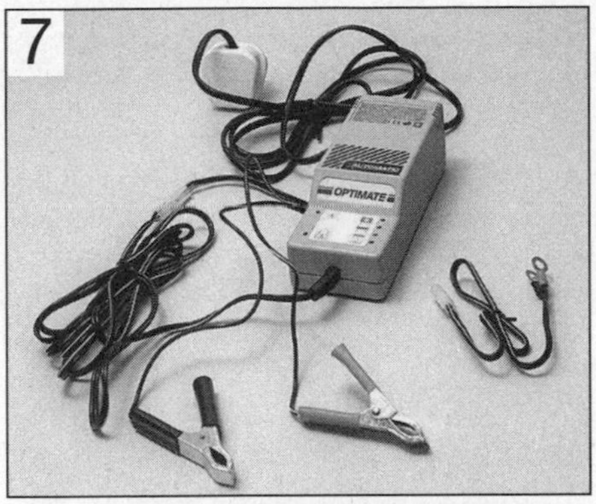

Use a suitable battery charger - this kit also assess battery condition

then switch off and allow to cool. Tape a piece of thick plastic over the silencer end(s) **(see illustration 5)**. Note that some advocate pouring a tablespoon of motor oil into the silencer(s) before sealing them off.

Battery

● Remove it from the bike - in extreme cases of cold the battery may freeze and crack its case **(see illustration 6)**.

● Check the electrolyte level and top up if necessary (conventional refillable batteries). Clean the terminals.

● Store the battery off the motorcycle and away from any sources of fire. Position a wooden block under the battery if it is to sit on the ground.

● Give the battery a trickle charge for a few hours every month **(see illustration 7)**.

Tyres

● Place the bike on its centrestand or an auxiliary stand which will support the motorcycle in an upright position. Position wood blocks under the tyres to keep them off the ground and to provide insulation from damp. If the bike is being put into long-term storage, ideally both tyres should be off the ground; not only will this protect the tyres, but will also ensure that no load is placed on the steering head or wheel bearings.

● Deflate each tyre by 5 to 10 psi, no more or the beads may unseat from the rim, making subsequent inflation difficult on tubeless tyres.

Pivots and controls

● Lubricate all lever, pedal, stand and footrest pivot points. If grease nipples are fitted to the rear suspension components, apply lubricant to the pivots.

● Lubricate all control cables.

Cycle components

● Apply a wax protectant to all painted and plastic components. Wipe off any excess, but don't polish to a shine. Where fitted, clean the screen with soap and water.

● Coat metal parts with Vaseline (petroleum jelly). When applying this to the fork tubes, do not compress the forks otherwise the seals will rot from contact with the Vaseline.

● Apply a vinyl cleaner to the seat.

Storage conditions

● Aim to store the bike in a shed or garage which does not leak and is free from damp.

● Drape an old blanket or bedspread over the bike to protect it from dust and direct contact with sunlight (which will fade paint). This also hides the bike from prying eyes. Beware of tight-fitting plastic covers which may allow condensation to form and settle on the bike.

Getting back on the road

Engine and transmission

● Change the oil and replace the oil filter. If this was done prior to storage, check that the oil hasn't emulsified - a thick whitish substance which occurs through condensation.

● Remove the spark plugs. Using a spout-type oil can, squirt a few drops of oil into the cylinder(s). This will provide initial lubrication as the piston rings and bores comes back into contact. Service the spark plugs, or fit new ones, and install them in the engine.

● Check that the clutch isn't stuck on. The plates can stick together if left standing for some time, preventing clutch operation. Engage a gear and try rocking the bike back and forth with the clutch lever held against the handlebar. If this doesn't work on cable-operated clutches, hold the clutch lever back against the handlebar with a strong elastic band or cable tie for a couple of hours **(see illustration 8)**.

● If the air intakes or silencer end(s) were blocked off, remove the bung or cover used.

● If the fuel tank was coated with a rust

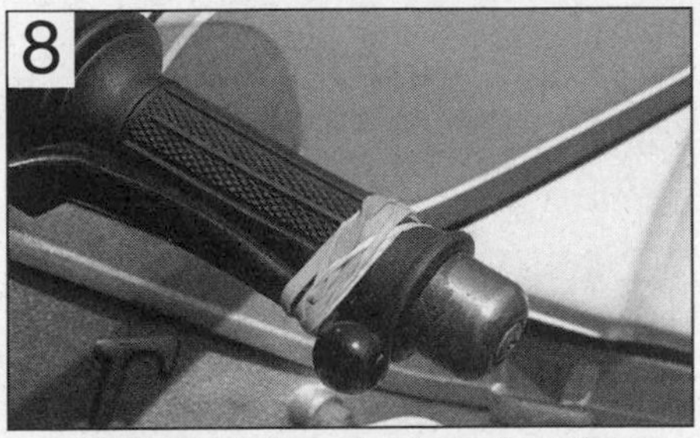

Hold clutch lever back against the handlebar with elastic bands or a cable tie

preventative, oil or a stabiliser added to the fuel, drain and flush the tank and dispose of the fuel sensibly. If no action was taken with the fuel tank prior to storage, it is advised that the old fuel is disposed of since it will go off over a period of time. Refill the fuel tank with fresh fuel.

Frame and running gear

● Oil all pivot points and cables.

● Check the tyre pressures. They will definitely need inflating if pressures were reduced for storage.

● Lubricate the final drive chain (where applicable).

● Remove any protective coating applied to the fork tubes (stanchions) since this may well destroy the fork seals. If the fork tubes weren't protected and have picked up rust spots, remove them with very fine abrasive paper and refinish with metal polish.

● Check that both brakes operate correctly. Apply each brake hard and check that it's not possible to move the motorcycle forwards, then check that the brake frees off again once released. Brake caliper pistons can stick due to corrosion around the piston head, or on the sliding caliper types, due to corrosion of the slider pins. If the brake doesn't free after repeated operation, take the caliper off for examination. Similarly drum brakes can stick due to a seized operating cam, cable or rod linkage.

● If the motorcycle has been in long-term storage, renew the brake fluid and clutch fluid (where applicable).

● Depending on where the bike has been stored, the wiring, cables and hoses may have been nibbled by rodents. Make a visual check and investigate disturbed wiring loom tape.

Battery

● If the battery has been previously removal and given top up charges it can simply be reconnected. Remember to connect the positive cable first and the negative cable last.

● On conventional refillable batteries, if the battery has not received any attention, remove it from the motorcycle and check its electrolyte level. Top up if necessary then charge the battery. If the battery fails to hold a charge and a visual checks show heavy white sulphation of the plates, the battery is probably defective and must be renewed. This is particularly likely if the battery is old. Confirm battery condition with a specific gravity check.

● On sealed (MF) batteries, if the battery has not received any attention, remove it from the motorcycle and charge it according to the information on the battery case - if the battery fails to hold a charge it must be renewed.

Starting procedure

● If a kickstart is fitted, turn the engine over a couple of times with the ignition OFF to distribute oil around the engine. If no kickstart is fitted, flick the engine kill switch OFF and the ignition ON and crank the engine over a couple of times to work oil around the upper cylinder components. If the nature of the ignition system is such that the starter won't work with the kill switch OFF, remove the spark plugs, fit them back into their caps and earth (ground) their bodies on the cylinder head. Reinstall the spark plugs afterwards.

● Switch the kill switch to RUN, operate the choke and start the engine. If the engine won't start don't continue cranking the engine - not only will this flatten the battery, but the starter motor will overheat. Switch the ignition off and try again later. If the engine refuses to start, go through the fault finding procedures in this manual. **Note:** *If the bike has been in storage for a long time, old fuel or a carburettor blockage may be the problem. Gum deposits in carburettors can block jets - if a carburettor cleaner doesn't prove successful the carburettors must be dismantled for cleaning.*

● Once the engine has started, check that the lights, turn signals and horn work properly.

● Treat the bike gently for the first ride and check all fluid levels on completion. Settle the bike back into the maintenance schedule.

This Section provides an easy reference-guide to the more common faults that are likely to afflict your machine. Obviously, the opportunities are almost limitless for faults to occur as a result of obscure failures, and to try and cover all eventualities would require a book. Indeed, a number have been written on the subject.

Successful troubleshooting is not a mysterious 'black art' but the application of a bit of knowledge combined with a systematic and logical approach to the problem. Approach any troubleshooting by first accurately identifying the symptom and then checking through the list of possible causes, starting with the simplest or most obvious and progressing in stages to the most complex.

Take nothing for granted, but above all apply liberal quantities of common sense.

The main symptom of a fault is given in the text as a major heading below which are listed the various systems or areas which may contain the fault. Details of each possible cause for a fault and the remedial action to be taken are given, in brief, in the paragraphs below each heading. Further information should be sought in the relevant Chapter.

1 Engine doesn't start or is difficult to start

Starter motor doesn't rotate

- ☐ Engine kill switch OFF.
- ☐ Fuse blown. Check main fuse and ignition circuit fuse (Chapter 9).
- ☐ Battery voltage low. Check and recharge battery (Chapter 9).
- ☐ Starter motor defective. Make sure the wiring to the starter is secure. Make sure the starter relay clicks when the start button is pushed. If the relay clicks, then the fault is in the wiring or motor.
- ☐ Starter relay faulty. Check it according to the procedure in Chapter 9.
- ☐ Starter button not contacting. The contacts could be wet, corroded or dirty. Disassemble and clean the switch (Chapter 9).
- ☐ Wiring open or shorted. Check all wiring connections and harnesses to make sure that they are dry, tight and not corroded. Also check for broken or frayed wires that can cause a short to ground (earth) (see Wiring Diagrams).
- ☐ Ignition (main) switch defective. Check the switch according to the procedure in Chapter 9. Renew the switch if it is defective.
- ☐ Engine kill switch defective. Check for wet, dirty or corroded contacts. Clean or renew the switch as necessary (Chapter 9).
- ☐ Faulty neutral/gear position, side stand or clutch switch or failed diode. Check the wiring to each switch and the switch itself according to the procedures in Chapter 9.
- ☐ Fuel injection system shutdown due to system fault – K3-on models (see Chapter 4B).

Starter motor rotates but engine does not turn over

- ☐ Starter clutch defective. Inspect and repair or renew (Chapter 2).
- ☐ Damaged idle or starter gears. Inspect and renew the damaged parts (Chapter 2).

Starter works but engine won't turn over (seized)

- ☐ Seized engine caused by one or more internally damaged components. Failure due to wear, abuse or lack of lubrication. Damage can include seized valves, followers, camshafts, pistons, crankshaft, connecting rod bearings, or transmission gears or bearings. Refer to Chapter 2 for engine disassembly.

No fuel flow

- ☐ No fuel in tank.
- ☐ Fuel tank breather hose obstructed.
- ☐ Fuel line clogged. Pull the fuel line loose and carefully blow through it.
- ☐ Fuel tap strainer clogged – X, Y, K1 and K2 models. Remove the tap and clean it (Chapter 4A).
- ☐ Fuel tap vacuum hose split or detached – X, Y, K1 and K2 models. Check the hose (Chapter 4A).
- ☐ Fuel tap diaphragm split – X, Y, K1 and K2 models. Remove the tap and check the diaphragm (Chapter 4A).
- ☐ Float needle valve clogged – X, Y, K1 and K2 models. For both of the valves to be clogged, either a very bad batch of fuel with an unusual additive has been used, or some other foreign material has entered the tank. Many times after a machine has been stored for many months without running, the fuel turns to a varnish-like liquid and forms deposits on the inlet needle valves and jets. The carburettors should be removed and overhauled if draining the float chambers doesn't solve the problem (Chapter 4A).
- ☐ Fuel rail or injector clogged – K3-on models. For both injectors to be clogged, either a very bad batch of fuel with an unusual additive has been used, or some other foreign material has entered the tank. Check the fuel strainer in the fuel pump. In some cases, if a machine has been unused for several months, the fuel turns to a varnish-like liquid which can cause an injector needle to stick to its seat. Drain the tank and fuel system (Chapter 4B).
- ☐ Fuel pump vacuum hose split or detached – X, Y, K1 and K2 models. Check the hose (Chapter 4A).
- ☐ Fuel pump faulty. Check the fuel pump flow and renew the pump if necessary (Chapter 4A or 4B).

Engine flooded

- ☐ Float height too high – X, Y, K1 and K2 models. Check as described in Chapter 4A.
- ☐ Float needle valve worn or stuck open – X, Y, K1 and K2 models. A piece of dirt, rust or other debris can cause the valve to seat improperly, causing excess fuel to be admitted to the float chamber. In this case, the float chamber should be cleaned and the needle valve and seat inspected. If the needle and seat are worn, then the leaking will persist and the parts should be renewed (Chapter 4A).
- ☐ Injector needle valve worn or stuck open – K3-on models. A piece of dirt, rust or other debris can cause the needle to seat improperly, causing excess fuel to be admitted to the throttle body. In this case, the injector should be cleaned and the needle and seat inspected (see Chapter 4B). If the needle and seat are worn, then the leaking will persist and the parts should be renewed.
- ☐ Starting technique incorrect – X, Y, K1 and K2 models. Under normal circumstances (i.e. if all the carburettor functions are sound) the machine should start with little or no throttle. When the engine is cold, the choke should be operated and the engine started without opening the throttle. When the engine is at operating temperature, only a very slight amount of throttle should be necessary. If the engine is flooded, disconnect the fuel tap vacuum hose (see Chapter 4A) and hold the throttle open while cranking the engine. This will allow additional air to reach the cylinders. Remember to attach the vacuum hose afterwards.
- ☐ Starting technique incorrect – K3-on models. Under normal circumstances (i.e. if all the components of the fuel injection system are good) the machine should start with little or no throttle. When the engine is cold, the automatic fast idle should operate and the engine should start without opening the throttle. When the engine is at operating temperature the fast idle should shut off, only a very slight amount of throttle should be necessary for starting (see Chapter 4B).

1 Engine doesn't start or is difficult to start (continued)

No spark or weak spark

- ☐ Ignition switch OFF.
- ☐ Engine kill switch turned to the OFF position.
- ☐ Battery voltage low. Check and recharge the battery as necessary (Chapter 9).
- ☐ Spark plugs dirty, defective or worn out. Locate reason for fouled plugs using spark plug condition chart and follow the plug maintenance procedures (Chapter 1).
- ☐ Spark plug caps or secondary (HT) wiring faulty. Check condition. Renew either or both components if cracks or deterioration are evident (Chapter 5).
- ☐ Spark plug caps not making good contact. Make sure that the plug caps fit snugly over the plug ends.
- ☐ Ignition HT coils defective. Check the coils (Chapter 5).
- ☐ Pulse generator coil/crankshaft position sensor defective. Check the unit (Chapter 5).
- ☐ Ignition control unit defective – X, Y, K1 and K2 models. Check the unit (Chapter 5).
- ☐ Engine control module defective – K3-on models see (Chapter 5).
- ☐ Ignition or kill switch shorted. This is usually caused by water, corrosion, damage or excessive wear. The switches can be disassembled and cleaned with electrical contact cleaner. If cleaning does not help, renew the switches (Chapter 9).
- ☐ Wiring shorted or broken between:
  - *a) Ignition (main) switch and engine kill switch (or blown fuse)*
  - *b) Ignition control unit/engine control module and engine kill switch*
  - *c) Ignition control unit/engine control module and ignition HT coils*
  - *d) Ignition HT coils and spark plugs*
  - *e) Ignition control unit/engine control module and pulse generator coil*
- ☐ Make sure that all wiring connections are clean, dry and tight. Look for chafed and broken wires (Chapters 5 and 9).

Compression low

- ☐ Spark plugs loose. Remove the plugs and inspect their threads. Reinstall and tighten to the specified torque (Chapter 1).
- ☐ Cylinder head(s) not sufficiently tightened down. If a cylinder head is suspected of being loose, then there's a chance that the gasket or head is damaged if the problem has persisted for any length of time. The head bolts should be tightened to the proper torque in the correct sequence (Chapter 2).
- ☐ Improper valve clearance. This means that the valve is not closing completely and compression pressure is leaking past the valve. Check and adjust the valve clearances (Chapter 1).
- ☐ Cylinder and/or piston worn. Excessive wear will cause compression pressure to leak past the rings. This is usually accompanied by worn rings as well. A top-end overhaul is necessary (Chapter 2).
- ☐ Piston rings worn, weak, broken, or sticking. Broken or sticking piston rings usually indicate a lubrication or carburation problem that causes excess carbon deposits or seizures to form on the pistons and rings. Top-end overhaul is necessary (Chapter 2).
- ☐ Piston ring-to-groove clearance excessive. This is caused by excessive wear of the piston ring lands. Piston renewal is necessary (Chapter 2).
- ☐ Cylinder head gasket(s) damaged. If a head is allowed to become loose, or if excessive carbon build-up on the piston crown and combustion chamber causes extremely high compression, the head gasket may leak. Retorquing the head is not always sufficient to restore the seal, so gasket renewal is necessary (Chapter 2).
- ☐ Cylinder head(s) warped. This is caused by overheating or improperly tightened head bolts. Machine shop resurfacing or head renewal is necessary (Chapter 2).
- ☐ Valve spring broken or weak. Caused by component failure or wear; the springs must be renewed (Chapter 2).
- ☐ Valve not seating properly. This is caused by a bent valve (from over-revving or improper valve adjustment), burned valve or seat (improper carburation) or an accumulation of carbon deposits on the seat (from carburation or lubrication problems). The valves must be cleaned and/or renewed and the seats serviced if possible (Chapter 2).

Stalls after starting

- ☐ Improper choke action – X, Y, K1 and K2 models. Make sure the choke linkage shaft is getting a full stroke and staying in the out position (Chapter 4A).
- ☐ Faulty fast idle action – K3-on models. Check the operation of the fast idle mechanism (Chapter 4B).
- ☐ Ignition malfunction (Chapter 5).
- ☐ Carburettor malfunction – X, Y, K1 and K2 models (Chapter 4A).
- ☐ Fuel injection system malfunction – K3-on models (Chapter 4B).
- ☐ Fuel contaminated. The fuel can be contaminated with either dirt or water, or can change chemically if the machine is allowed to sit for several months or more. Drain the tank and fuel system (Chapter 4A or 4B).
- ☐ Intake air leak – X, Y, K1 and K2 models. Check for loose carburettor-to-intake manifold connections, loose or missing vacuum gauge adapter screws or hoses, or loose carburettor tops (Chapter 4A).
- ☐ Intake air leak – K3-on models. Check for loose throttle body-to-intake manifold connections, loose or missing vacuum gauge blanking caps, or loose or damaged PAIR vacuum hose (Chapter 4B).
- ☐ Engine idle speed incorrect. Turn idle adjusting screw until the engine idles at the specified rpm (Chapter 1).

Rough idle

- ☐ Ignition malfunction (Chapter 5).
- ☐ Idle speed incorrect (Chapter 1).
- ☐ Carburettors not synchronised – X, Y, K1 and K2 models. Adjust carburettors with vacuum gauge or manometer set as described in Chapter 1.
- ☐ Throttle valves not synchronised – K3-on models. Adjust them with vacuum gauge or manometer set as described in Chapter 1.
- ☐ Pilot jet or air passage clogged. Remove and overhaul the carburettors, and check jet sizes (Chapter 4A).
- ☐ Fuel injection system malfunction (see Chapter 4B).
- ☐ Fuel contaminated. The fuel can be contaminated with either dirt or water, or can change chemically if the machine is allowed to sit for several months or more. Drain the tank and fuel system (Chapter 4A or 4B).
- ☐ Intake air leak – X, Y, K1 and K2 models. Check for loose carburettor-to-intake manifold connections, loose or missing vacuum take-off point blanking cap (front cylinder), or loose carburettor tops (Chapter 4A).
- ☐ Intake air leak – K3-on models. Check for loose throttle body-to-intake manifold connections, loose or missing vacuum gauge blanking caps, or loose or damaged PAIR vacuum hose (Chapter 4B).
- ☐ Air filter clogged. Renew the air filter element (Chapter 1).

2 Poor running at low speeds

Spark weak

- ☐ Battery voltage low. Check and recharge battery (Chapter 9).
- ☐ Spark plugs fouled, defective or worn out. Refer to Chapter 1 for spark plug maintenance.
- ☐ Spark plug cap or HT wiring defective. Refer to Chapters 1 and 5 for details on the ignition system.
- ☐ Spark plug caps not making contact. Make sure they are securely pushed on to the plugs.
- ☐ Incorrect spark plugs. Wrong type, heat range or cap configuration. Check and install correct plugs listed in Chapter 1.
- ☐ Ignition control unit/engine control module defective (Chapter 5).
- ☐ Pulse generator coil/crankshaft position sensor defective (Chapter 5).
- ☐ Ignition HT coils defective (Chapter 5).

Fuel/air mixture incorrect

- ☐ Air filter clogged, poorly sealed or missing (Chapter 1).
- ☐ Air filter housing poorly sealed. Look for cracks, holes or loose clamps and renew or repair defective parts.
- ☐ Pilot screws out of adjustment – X, Y, K1 and K2 models (Chapter 4A).
- ☐ Pilot jet or air passage clogged – X, Y, K1 and K2 models (Chapter 4A). Remove and overhaul the carburettors (Chapter 4A).
- ☐ Air bleed holes clogged – X, Y, K1 and K2 models. Remove carburettor and blow out all passages (Chapter 4A).
- ☐ Fuel level too high or too low – X, Y, K1 and K2 models. Check the float height (Chapter 4A).
- ☐ Fuel tank breather hose obstructed.
- ☐ Carburettor intake manifolds loose – X, Y, K1 and K2 models. Check for cracks, breaks, tears or loose clamps (Chapter 4A). Renew the rubber intake manifold joints if split or perished.
- ☐ Incorrect carburettor jet sizes – X, Y, K1 and K2 models. Check according to the Specifications in Chapter 4A.
- ☐ Fuel pump faulty, or the fuel strainer is blocked – K3-on models (see Chapter 4B).
- ☐ Fuel rail or injector clogged – K3-on models. For all of the injectors to be clogged, either a very bad batch of fuel with an unusual additive has been used, or some other foreign material has entered the tank. Check the fuel strainer. In some cases, if a machine has been unused for several months, the fuel turns to a varnish-like liquid which can cause an injector needle to stick to its seat. Drain the tank and fuel system (Chapter 4B).
- ☐ Intake air leak – K3-on models. Check for loose throttle body-to-inlet manifold connections, loose or damaged PAIR vacuum hose or missing vacuum gauge blanking caps (Chapter 4B).

Compression low

- ☐ Spark plugs loose. Remove the plugs and inspect their threads. Reinstall and tighten to the specified torque (Chapter 1).
- ☐ Cylinder head(s) not sufficiently tightened down. If a cylinder head is suspected of being loose, then there's a chance that the gasket and head are damaged if the problem has persisted for any length of time. The head bolts should be tightened to the proper torque in the correct sequence (Chapter 2).
- ☐ Improper valve clearance. This means that the valve is not closing completely and compression pressure is leaking past the valve. Check and adjust the valve clearances (Chapter 1).
- ☐ Cylinder and/or piston worn. Excessive wear will cause compression pressure to leak past the rings. This is usually accompanied by worn rings as well. A top end overhaul is necessary (Chapter 2).
- ☐ Piston rings worn, weak, broken, or sticking. Broken or sticking piston rings usually indicate a lubrication or carburation problem that causes excess carbon deposits or seizures to form on the pistons and rings. Top-end overhaul is necessary (Chapter 2).
- ☐ Piston ring-to-groove clearance excessive. This is caused by excessive wear of the piston ring lands. Piston renewal is necessary (Chapter 2).
- ☐ Cylinder head gasket(s) damaged. If a head is allowed to become loose, or if excessive carbon build-up on the piston crown and combustion chamber causes extremely high compression, the head gasket may leak. Retorquing the head is not always sufficient to restore the seal, so gasket renewal is necessary (Chapter 2).
- ☐ Cylinder head(s) warped. This is caused by overheating or improperly tightened head bolts. Machine shop resurfacing or head renewal is necessary (Chapter 2).
- ☐ Valve spring broken or weak. Caused by component failure or wear; the springs must be renewed (Chapter 2).
- ☐ Valve not seating properly. This is caused by a bent valve (from over-revving or improper valve adjustment), burned valve or seat (improper carburation) or an accumulation of carbon deposits on the seat (from carburation, lubrication problems). The valves must be cleaned and/or renewed and the seats serviced if possible (Chapter 2).

Poor acceleration

- ☐ Carburettors leaking or dirty – X, Y, K1 and K2 models. Overhaul the carburettors (Chapter 4A).
- ☐ Throttle bodies leaking or dirty – K3-on models. Overhaul them (Chapter 4B).
- ☐ Fuel flow restricted. Check the tap and its filter or the pump and strainer as applicable, and all the hoses from the tank (Chapter 4A or 4B). If the breather hose is blocked a vacuum can form in the tank which will restrict flow.
- ☐ Timing not advancing – X, Y, K1 and K2 models. The pulse generator coil or the ignition control unit may be defective (Chapter 5). If so, they must be renewed, as they can't be repaired.
- ☐ Timing not advancing – K3-on models. The crankshaft position sensor or the engine control module may be defective (Chapter 5). If so, they must be renewed.
- ☐ Carburettors not synchronised – X, Y, K1 and K2 models. Adjust them with a vacuum gauge set or manometer (Chapter 1).
- ☐ Throttle valves not synchronised – K3-on models. Adjust them with a vacuum gauge set or manometer (Chapter 1).
- ☐ Engine oil viscosity too high. Using a heavier oil than that recommended in Chapter 1 can damage the oil pump or lubrication system and cause drag on the engine.
- ☐ Brakes dragging. Usually caused by debris which has entered the brake piston seals, or from a warped disc or bent axle. Repair as necessary (Chapter 7).

Miscellaneous causes

- ☐ Modification to exhaust system – X, Y, K1 and K2 models. Most aftermarket exhaust systems cause the engine to run leaner, which make them run hotter. When installing an accessory exhaust system, always check whether different carburettor jet sizes are needed and rejet the carburettors accordingly, if necessary (see Chapter 4A).
- ☐ Modification to exhaust system – K3-on models. Most aftermarket exhaust systems cause the engine to run leaner, which make them run hotter. When installing an accessory exhaust system, always check with the manufacturer/supplier as to whether the ECM requires re-mapping.

3 Poor running or no power at high speed

Firing incorrect

- ☐ Air filter restricted. Clean or renew the filter (Chapter 1).
- ☐ Spark plugs fouled, defective or worn out. See Chapter 1 for spark plug maintenance.
- ☐ Spark plug caps or HT wiring defective. See Chapters 1 and 5 for details of the ignition system.
- ☐ Spark plug caps not in good contact (Chapter 5).
- ☐ Incorrect spark plugs. Wrong type, heat range or cap configuration. Check and install correct plugs listed in Chapter 1.
- ☐ Ignition HT coils defective (Chapter 5).
- ☐ Ignition control unit defective – X, Y, K1 and K2 models (Chapter 5).
- ☐ Engine control module defective – K3-on models (Chapter 5).

Fuel/air mixture incorrect

- ☐ Fuel tank breather hose obstructed. If the breather hose is blocked a vacuum can form in the tank which will restrict flow (Chapter 4A or 4B).
- ☐ Air filter clogged, poorly sealed, or missing (Chapter 1).
- ☐ Air filter housing poorly sealed. Look for cracks, holes or loose clamps, and renew or repair defective parts (Chapter 4A or 4B).
- ☐ Main jet clogged – X, Y, K1 and K2 models. Dirt, water or other contaminants can clog the main jets. Clean the fuel tap filter, the float chamber area, and the jets and carburettor orifices (Chapter 4A).
- ☐ Main jet wrong size – X, Y, K1 and K2 models. Check the jet sizes according to the Specifications in Chapter 4. The standard jetting is for sea level atmospheric pressure and oxygen content – if you are constantly running at high altitude (where the oxygen content of the air is reduced), the mixture will be affected Chapter 4A).
- ☐ Air bleed holes clogged – X, Y, K1 and K2 models. Remove and overhaul carburettors (Chapter 4A).
- ☐ Fuel level too high or too low – X, Y, K1 and K2 models. Check the float height (Chapter 4A).
- ☐ Carburettor intake manifolds loose – X, Y, K1 and K2 models. Check for cracks, breaks, tears or loose clamps. Renew the rubber intake manifolds if they are split or perished (Chapter 4A).
- ☐ Fuel pump faulty, or the fuel strainer is blocked – K3-on models (see Chapter 4B).
- ☐ Fuel rail or injector clogged – K3-on models. For both injectors to be clogged, either a very bad batch of fuel with an unusual additive has been used, or some other foreign material has entered the tank. Check the fuel strainer. In some cases, if a machine has been unused for several months, the fuel turns to a varnish-like liquid which can cause an injector needle to stick to its seat. Drain the tank and fuel system (Chapter 4B).
- ☐ Inlet air leak – K3-on models. Check for loose throttle body-to-inlet manifold connections, loose or damaged PAIR vacuum hose or missing vacuum gauge blanking caps (Chapter 4B).

Compression low

- ☐ Spark plugs loose. Remove the plugs and inspect their threads. Reinstall and tighten to the specified torque (Chapter 1).
- ☐ Cylinder head(s) not sufficiently tightened down. If a cylinder head is suspected of being loose, then there's a chance that the gasket and head are damaged if the problem has persisted for any length of time. The head bolts should be tightened to the proper torque in the correct sequence (Chapter 2).
- ☐ Improper valve clearance. This means that the valve is not closing completely and compression pressure is leaking past the valve. Check and adjust the valve clearances (Chapter 1).
- ☐ Cylinder and/or piston worn. Excessive wear will cause compression pressure to leak past the rings. This is usually accompanied by worn rings as well. A top end overhaul is necessary (Chapter 2).
- ☐ Piston rings worn, weak, broken, or sticking. Broken or sticking piston rings usually indicate a lubrication or carburation problem that causes excess carbon deposits or seizures to form on the pistons and rings. Top-end overhaul is necessary (Chapter 2).
- ☐ Piston ring-to-groove clearance excessive. This is caused by excessive wear of the piston ring lands. Piston renewal is necessary (Chapter 2).
- ☐ Cylinder head gasket(s) damaged. If a head is allowed to become loose, or if excessive carbon build-up on the piston crown and combustion chamber causes extremely high compression, the head gasket may leak. Retorquing the head is not always sufficient to restore the seal, so gasket renewal is necessary (Chapter 2).
- ☐ Cylinder head(s) warped. This is caused by overheating or improperly tightened head bolts. Machine shop resurfacing or head replacement is necessary (Chapter 2).
- ☐ Valve spring broken or weak. Caused by component failure or wear; the springs must be renewed (Chapter 2).
- ☐ Valve not seating properly. This is caused by a bent valve (from over-revving or improper valve adjustment), burned valve or seat (improper carburation) or an accumulation of carbon deposits on the seat (from carburation, lubrication problems). The valves must be cleaned and/or renewed and the seats serviced if possible (Chapter 2).

Knocking or pinking

- ☐ Carbon build-up in combustion chamber. Use of a fuel additive that will dissolve the adhesive bonding the carbon particles to the crown and chamber is the easiest way to remove the build-up. Otherwise, the cylinder heads will have to be removed and decarbonised (Chapter 2).
- ☐ Incorrect or poor quality fuel. Old or improper grades of fuel can cause detonation. This causes the knocking or pinking sound. Drain old fuel and always use the recommended fuel grade.
- ☐ Spark plug heat range incorrect. Uncontrolled detonation indicates the plug heat range is too hot. The plug in effect becomes a glow plug, raising cylinder temperatures. Install the proper heat range plug (Chapter 1).
- ☐ Improper air/fuel mixture. This will cause the cylinders to run hot, which leads to detonation. A blockage in the fuel system or an air leak can cause this imbalance. See Chapter 4A or 4B.

Miscellaneous causes

- ☐ Throttle valve doesn't open fully. Adjust the throttle grip freeplay (Chapter 1).
- ☐ Clutch slipping. May be caused by an incorrectly adjusted cable (see Chapter 1), or loose or worn clutch components. Refer to Chapter 2 for clutch overhaul procedures.
- ☐ Timing not advancing. Check as described in Chapter 5.
- ☐ Engine oil viscosity too high. Using a heavier oil than the one recommended in Chapter 1 can damage the oil pump or lubrication system and cause drag on the engine.
- ☐ Brakes dragging. Usually caused by debris which has entered the brake piston seals, or from a warped disc or bent axle. Repair as necessary.
- ☐ Fuel flow restricted. Check the tap and its filter or the pump and strainer as applicable, and all the hoses from the tank (Chapter 4A or 4B). If the breather hose is blocked a vacuum can form in the tank which will restrict flow.
- ☐ Modification to exhaust system – X, Y, K1 and K2 models. Most aftermarket exhaust systems cause the engine to run leaner, which make them run hotter. When installing an accessory exhaust system, always check whether different carburettor jet sizes are needed and rejet the carburettors accordingly, if necessary (see Chapter 4A).
- ☐ Modification to exhaust system – K3-on models. Most aftermarket exhaust systems cause the engine to run leaner, which make them run hotter. When installing an accessory exhaust system, always check with the manufacturer/supplier as to whether the ECM requires re-mapping.

4 Overheating

Engine overheats

- ☐ Coolant level low. Check and add coolant (Chapter 1).
- ☐ Leak in cooling system. Check cooling system hoses and radiator for leaks and other damage. Repair or renew parts as necessary (Chapter 3).
- ☐ Thermostat sticking closed. Check and renew as described in Chapter 3.
- ☐ Faulty radiator cap. Remove the cap and have it pressure tested.
- ☐ Coolant passages clogged. Have the entire system drained and flushed, then refill with fresh coolant.
- ☐ Water pump defective. Remove the pump and check the components (Chapter 3).
- ☐ Clogged radiator fins. Clean them by blowing compressed air through the fins from the rear of the radiator, and straighten any bent fins that restrict air flow.
- ☐ Cooling fan or fan switch fault (Chapter 3).

Firing incorrect

- ☐ Spark plugs fouled, defective or worn out. See Chapter 1 for spark plug maintenance.
- ☐ Incorrect spark plugs.
- ☐ Ignition control unit/engine control module defective (Chapter 5).
- ☐ Faulty ignition HT coils (Chapter 5).

Fuel/air mixture incorrect

- ☐ Fuel tank breather hose obstructed. If the breather hose is blocked a vacuum can form in the tank which will restrict flow (Chapter 4A or 4B).
- ☐ Air filter clogged, poorly sealed, or missing (Chapter 1).
- ☐ Air filter housing poorly sealed. Look for cracks, holes or loose clamps, and replace or repair defective parts.
- ☐ Main jet clogged – X, Y, K1 and K2 models. Dirt, water or other contaminants can clog the main jets. Clean the fuel tap filter, the float chamber area, and the jets and carburettor orifices (Chapter 4A).
- ☐ Main jet wrong size – X, Y, K1 and K2 models. Check the jet sizes according to the Specifications in Chapter 4A. The standard jetting is for sea level atmospheric pressure and oxygen content – if you are constantly running at high altitude (where the oxygen content of the air is reduced), the mixture will be affected.
- ☐ Air bleed holes clogged – X, Y, K1 and K2 models. Remove and overhaul carburettors (Chapter 4A).
- ☐ Fuel level too high or too low – X, Y, K1 and K2 models. Check the float height (Chapter 4A).
- ☐ Carburettor intake manifolds loose – X, Y, K1 and K2 models. Check for cracks, breaks, tears or loose clamps. Renew the rubber intake manifolds if they are split or perished (Chapter 4A).
- ☐ Fuel pump faulty, or the fuel strainer is blocked – K3-on models (see Chapter 4B).
- ☐ Fuel rail or injector clogged – K3-on models. For both injectors to be clogged, either a very bad batch of fuel with an unusual additive has been used, or some other foreign material has entered the tank. Check the fuel strainer. In some cases, if a machine has been unused for several months, the fuel turns to a varnish-like liquid which can cause an injector needle to stick to its seat. Drain the tank and fuel system (Chapter 4B).
- ☐ Inlet air leak – K3-on models. Check for loose throttle body-to-inlet manifold connections, loose or damaged PAIR vacuum hose or missing vacuum gauge blanking caps (Chapter 4B).

Compression too high

- ☐ Carbon build-up in combustion chamber. Use of a fuel additive that will dissolve the adhesive bonding the carbon particles to the piston crown and chamber is the easiest way to remove the build-up. Otherwise, the cylinder heads will have to be removed and decarbonised (Chapter 2).
- ☐ Improperly machined head surface or installation of incorrect gasket during engine assembly.

Engine load excessive

- ☐ Clutch slipping. Can be caused by damaged, loose or worn clutch components. Refer to Chapter 2 for overhaul procedures.
- ☐ Engine oil level too high. The addition of too much oil will cause pressurisation of the crankcase and inefficient engine operation. Check Specifications and drain to proper level (Daily (pre-ride) checks).
- ☐ Engine oil viscosity too high. Using a heavier oil than the one recommended in Chapter 1 can damage the oil pump or lubrication system as well as cause drag on the engine.
- ☐ Brakes dragging. Usually caused by debris which has entered the brake piston seals, or from a warped disc or bent axle. Repair as necessary.

Lubrication inadequate

- ☐ Engine oil level too low. Friction caused by intermittent lack of lubrication or from oil that is overworked can cause overheating. The oil provides a definite cooling function in the engine. Check the oil level (Daily (pre-ride) checks).
- ☐ Poor quality engine oil or incorrect viscosity or type. Oil is rated not only according to viscosity but also according to type. Some oils are not rated high enough for use in this engine. Check the Specifications section and change to the correct oil (Chapter 1).
- ☐ Faulty oil pump causing reduced pressure in system. Check the pump for wear (see Chapter 2).

Miscellaneous causes

- ☐ Modification to exhaust system – X, Y, K1 and K2 models. Most aftermarket exhaust systems cause the engine to run leaner, which make them run hotter. When installing an accessory exhaust system, always check whether different carburettor jet sizes are needed and rejet the carburettors accordingly, if necessary (see Chapter 4A).
- ☐ Modification to exhaust system – K3-on models. Most aftermarket exhaust systems cause the engine to run leaner, which make them run hotter. When installing an accessory exhaust system, always check with the manufacturer/supplier as to whether the ECM requires re-mapping.

5 Clutch problems

Clutch slipping

- ☐ Clutch cable incorrectly adjusted (see Chapter 1).
- ☐ Friction plates worn or warped. Overhaul the clutch assembly (Chapter 2).
- ☐ Plain plates warped (Chapter 2).
- ☐ Clutch springs broken or weak. Old or heat-damaged (from slipping clutch) springs should be renewed (Chapter 2).
- ☐ Clutch release mechanism defective. Renew any defective parts (Chapter 2).
- ☐ Clutch centre or housing unevenly worn. This causes improper engagement of the plates. Renew the damaged or worn parts (Chapter 2).

5 Clutch problems (continued)

Clutch not disengaging completely

- ☐ Clutch cable incorrectly adjusted (see Chapter 1) or faulty. The inner cable could be seizing in outer cable, caused by dirt, kinks or incorrect routing. Check the cable and renew if necessary (see Chapter 2).
- ☐ Clutch plates warped or damaged. This will cause clutch drag, which in turn will cause the machine to creep. Overhaul the clutch assembly (Chapter 2).
- ☐ Clutch spring tension uneven. Usually caused by a sagged or broken spring. Check and renew the springs as a set (Chapter 2).
- ☐ Engine oil deteriorated. Old, thin, worn out oil will not provide proper lubrication for the plates, causing the clutch to drag. Renew the oil and filter (Chapter 1).
- ☐ Engine oil viscosity too high. Using a heavier oil than recommended in Chapter 1 can cause the plates to stick together, putting a drag on the engine. Change to the correct weight oil (Chapter 1).
- ☐ Clutch housing guide seized on input shaft. Lack of lubrication, severe wear or damage can cause the guide to seize on the shaft. Overhaul of the clutch, and perhaps transmission, may be necessary to repair the damage (Chapter 2).
- ☐ Clutch release mechanism defective. Overhaul the components in the clutch cover (Chapter 2).
- ☐ Loose clutch centre nut. Causes housing and centre misalignment putting a drag on the engine. Engagement adjustment continually varies. Overhaul the clutch assembly (Chapter 2).

6 Gearchanging problems

Doesn't go into gear or lever doesn't return

- ☐ Clutch not disengaging. See above.
- ☐ Selector fork(s) bent, worn or seized. Often caused by dropping the machine or from lack of lubrication. Overhaul the transmission (Chapter 2).
- ☐ Gear(s) stuck on shaft. Most often caused by a lack of lubrication or excessive wear in transmission bearings and bushes. Overhaul the transmission (Chapter 2).
- ☐ Selector drum binding. Caused by lubrication failure or excessive wear. Renew the drum and bearing (Chapter 2).
- ☐ Gearchange lever return spring weak or broken (Chapter 2).
- ☐ Gearchange lever broken. Splines stripped out of lever or shaft, caused by allowing the lever to get loose or from dropping the machine. Renew necessary parts (Chapter 2).
- ☐ Gearchange mechanism stopper arm broken or worn. Full engagement and rotary movement of selector drum results. Renew the arm (Chapter 2).
- ☐ Stopper arm spring broken. Allows arm to float, causing sporadic shift operation. Renew spring (Chapter 2).
- ☐ Gearchange mechanism selector arm broken or worn, or missing pins on selector drum. Remove the gearchange mechanism and check the arm and all components (see Chapter 2).

Jumps out of gear

- ☐ Selector fork(s) or selector drum tracks worn or damaged. Overhaul the transmission (Chapter 2).
- ☐ Gear groove(s) worn. Overhaul the transmission (Chapter 2).
- ☐ Gear dogs or dog slots worn or damaged. The gears should be inspected and replaced. No attempt should be made to service the worn parts.

Overselects

- ☐ Stopper arm spring weak or broken (Chapter 2).
- ☐ Gearchange shaft return spring post broken or distorted (Chapter 2).

7 Abnormal engine noise

Knocking or pinking

- ☐ Carbon build-up in combustion chamber. Use of a fuel additive that will dissolve the adhesive bonding the carbon particles to the piston crown and chamber is the easiest way to remove the build-up. Otherwise, the cylinder heads will have to be removed and decarbonised (Chapter 2).
- ☐ Incorrect or poor quality fuel. Old or improper fuel can cause detonation. This causes the knocking or pinking sound. Drain the old fuel and always use the recommended grade fuel (Chapter 4A or 4B).
- ☐ Spark plug heat range incorrect. Uncontrolled detonation indicates that the plug heat range is too hot. The plug in effect becomes a glow plug, raising cylinder temperatures. Install the proper heat range plug (Chapter 1).
- ☐ Improper air/fuel mixture. This will cause the cylinders to run hot and lead to detonation. A blockage in the fuel system or an air leak can cause this imbalance. See Chapter 4A or 4B.

Piston slap or rattling

- ☐ Cylinder-to-piston clearance excessive. Caused by improper assembly. Inspect and overhaul top-end parts (Chapter 2).
- ☐ Connecting rod bent. Caused by over-revving, trying to start a badly flooded engine or from ingesting a foreign object into the combustion chamber. Renew the damaged parts (Chapter 2).
- ☐ Piston pin or piston pin bore worn or seized from wear or lack of lubrication. Renew damaged parts (Chapter 2).
- ☐ Piston ring(s) worn, broken or sticking. Overhaul the top-end (Chapter 2).
- ☐ Piston seizure damage. Usually from lack of lubrication or over-heating. Rebore the cylinders and fit oversize pistons (Chapter 2).
- ☐ Connecting rod upper or lower end clearance excessive. Caused by excessive wear or lack of lubrication. Renew worn parts.

Valve noise

- ☐ Incorrect valve clearances. Adjust the clearances by referring to Chapter 1.
- ☐ Valve spring broken or weak. Check and renew weak valve springs (Chapter 2).
- ☐ Camshaft(s) or cylinder head(s) worn or damaged. Lack of lubrication at high rpm is usually the cause of damage. Insufficient oil or failure to change the oil at the recommended intervals are the chief causes. Since there are no replaceable bearings in the head, the head itself and/or the camshaft will have to be renewed if there is excessive wear or damage (Chapter 2).

Other noise

- ☐ Cylinder head gasket(s) leaking.
- ☐ Exhaust pipe leaking at cylinder head connection. Caused by improper fit of pipe, loose exhaust flange or damaged gasket. All exhaust fasteners should be tightened evenly and carefully. Failure to do this will lead to a leak (Chapter 4A or 4B).
- ☐ Crankshaft runout excessive. Caused by a bent crankshaft (from over-revving) or damage from an upper cylinder component failure.
- ☐ Engine mounting bolts loose. Tighten all engine mount bolts (Chapter 2).
- ☐ Crankshaft bearings worn (Chapter 2).
- ☐ Camshaft drive chain or tensioner defective or worn. Renew according to the procedure in Chapter 2.

8 Abnormal driveline noise

Clutch noise

- ☐ Clutch outer drum/friction plate clearance excessive (Chapter 2).
- ☐ Loose or damaged clutch pressure plate and/or bolts (Chapter 2).

Transmission noise

- ☐ Bearings worn. Also includes the possibility that the shafts are worn. Overhaul the transmission (Chapter 2).
- ☐ Gears worn or chipped (Chapter 2).
- ☐ Metal chips jammed in gear teeth. Probably pieces from a broken clutch, gear or selector mechanism that were picked up by the gears. This will cause early bearing failure (Chapter 2).
- ☐ Engine oil level too low. Causes a whine or howl from transmission. Also affects engine power and clutch operation (Daily (pre-ride) checks).

Final drive noise

- ☐ Chain not adjusted properly (Chapter 1).
- ☐ Front or rear sprocket loose. Tighten fasteners (Chapter 6).
- ☐ Sprockets worn. Renew sprockets (Chapter 6).
- ☐ Rear sprocket warped. Renew sprockets (Chapter 6).
- ☐ Loose or worn rear wheel or sprocket coupling bearings. Check and renew as needed (Chapter 7).

9 Abnormal frame and suspension noise

Front end noise

- ☐ Low fluid level or improper viscosity oil in forks. This can sound like spurting and is usually accompanied by irregular fork action (Chapter 6).
- ☐ Spring(s) weak or broken. Makes a clicking or scraping sound. Fork oil, when drained, will have a lot of metal particles in it (Chapter 6).
- ☐ Steering head bearings loose or damaged. Clicks when braking. Check and adjust or renew as necessary (Chapters 1 and 6).
- ☐ Fork yokes loose. Make sure all clamp pinch bolts are tightened to the specified torque (Chapter 6).
- ☐ Fork tube bent. A possibility if machine has been in an accident. Renew tube(s) (Chapter 6).
- ☐ Front axle or axle clamp nuts loose. Tighten them to the specified torque (Chapter 7).
- ☐ Loose or worn wheel bearings. Check and renew as needed (Chapter 7).

Rear shock absorber noise

- ☐ Fluid level incorrect. Indicates a leak caused by defective seal. Shock will be covered with oil. Renew shock or seek advice on repair from a Suzuki dealer or suspension specialist (Chapter 6).
- ☐ Defective shock absorber with internal damage. This is in the body of the shock and can't be remedied. The shock must be renewed (Chapter 6).
- ☐ Bent or damaged shock body. Renew the shock (Chapter 6).
- ☐ Loose or worn suspension linkage components. Check and renew as necessary (Chapter 6).
- ☐ Loose bolts in suspension assembly. Check all bolts and tighten to the specified torque settings (Chapter 6).

Brake noise

- ☐ Worn brake pads – if there is no friction material left there will be a metal-on-metal grinding sound, and the disc(s) will be damaged.
- ☐ Squeal caused by pad shim not installed or positioned correctly (where fitted) (Chapter 7).
- ☐ Squeal caused by dust on brake pads. Usually found in combination with glazed shoes/pads. Clean using brake cleaning solvent (Chapter 7).
- ☐ Contamination of brake pads. Oil, brake fluid or dirt causing brake to chatter or squeal. Renew the pads (Chapter 7).
- ☐ Pads glazed. Caused by excessive heat from prolonged use or from contamination. Do not use sandpaper, emery cloth, carborundum cloth or any other abrasive to roughen the pad surfaces as abrasives will stay in the pad material and damage the disc. A very fine flat file or wire brush can be used, but pad renewal is recommended as a cure (Chapter 7).
- ☐ Disc warped. Can cause a chattering, clicking or intermittent squeal. Usually accompanied by a pulsating lever and uneven braking. Renew the disc and fit new pads (Chapter 7).
- ☐ Loose or worn wheel bearings. Check and renew as needed (Chapter 7).

10 Oil pressure low

Engine lubrication system

- ☐ Engine oil level low. Inspect for leak or other problem causing low oil level and add recommended oil (Daily (pre-ride) checks).
- ☐ Engine oil viscosity too low. Very old, thin oil or an improper weight of oil used in the engine. Change to correct oil (Chapter 1).
- ☐ Engine oil pump defective, blocked oil strainer gauze or failed relief valve. Carry out oil pressure check (Chapter 1).
- ☐ Camshaft or journals worn. Excessive wear causing drop in oil pressure. Renew cam and/or cylinder head. Abnormal wear could be caused by oil starvation at high rpm from low oil level or improper weight or type of oil (Chapter 2).
- ☐ Crankshaft and/or bearings worn. Same problems as above. Check and renew crankshaft and/or bearings (Chapter 2).

11 Excessive exhaust smoke

White smoke

- ☐ Piston oil ring worn. The ring may be broken or damaged, causing oil from the crankcase to be pulled past the piston into the combustion chamber. Renew the piston rings (Chapter 2).
- ☐ Cylinders worn, cracked, or scored. Caused by overheating or oil starvation. Check the cylinder block, lubrication system and cooling system (see Chapters 2 and 3).
- ☐ Valve stem oil seal damaged or worn. Renew the oil seals (Chapter 2).
- ☐ Valve guide worn. Perform a complete valve job (Chapter 2).
- ☐ Engine oil level too high, which causes the oil to be forced past the rings. Drain oil to the proper level (Chapter 1).
- ☐ Head gasket broken between oil return and cylinder. Causes oil to be pulled into the combustion chamber. Renew the head gasket and check the head for warpage (Chapter 2).
- ☐ Abnormal crankcase pressurisation, which forces oil past the rings. Clogged breather is usually the cause (Chapter 1).

Black smoke

- ☐ Air filter clogged. Clean or renew the element (Chapter 1).
- ☐ Main jet too large or loose – X, Y, K1 and K2 models. Compare the jet size to the Specifications (Chapter 4A).
- ☐ Choke cable or linkage shaft stuck, causing fuel to be pulled through choke circuit – X, Y, K1 and K2 models (Chapter 4A).
- ☐ Fuel level too high – X, Y, K1 and K2 models. Check and adjust the float height(s) as necessary (Chapter 4A).
- ☐ Float needle valve held off needle seat – X, Y, K1 and K2 models. Clean the float chambers and fuel line and renew the needles and seats if necessary (Chapter 4A).
- ☐ Fuel injection system malfunction – K3-on models (Chapter 4B).

Brown smoke

- ☐ Air filter poorly sealed or not installed (Chapter 1).
- ☐ Main jet too small or clogged – X, Y, K1 and K2 models. Lean condition caused by wrong size main jet or by a restricted orifice. Clean float chambers and jets and compare jet size to Specifications (Chapter 4A).
- ☐ Fuel flow insufficient – X, Y, K1 and K2 models. Float needle valve stuck closed due to chemical reaction with old fuel; fuel level incorrect; restricted fuel line; faulty fuel pump (Chapter 4A).
- ☐ Carburettor intake manifold clamps loose – X, Y, K1 and K2 models (Chapter 4A).
- ☐ Fuel injection system malfunction – K3-on models (Chapter 4B).

12 Poor handling or stability

Handlebar hard to turn

- ☐ Steering head bearing adjuster nut too tight. Check adjustment as described in Chapter 1.
- ☐ Bearings damaged. Roughness can be felt as the bars are turned from side-to-side. Renew bearings and races (Chapter 6).
- ☐ Races dented or worn. Denting results from wear in only one position (e.g. straight ahead), from a collision or hitting a pothole or from dropping the machine. Renew races and bearings (Chapter 6
- ☐ Steering stem lubrication inadequate. Causes are grease getting hard from age or being washed out by high pressure car washes. Disassemble steering head and repack bearings (Chapter 6).
- ☐ Steering stem bent. Caused by a collision, hitting a pothole or by dropping the machine. Renew the damaged part. Don't try to straighten the steering stem (Chapter 6).
- ☐ Front tyre air pressure too low (Daily (pre-ride) checks).

Handlebar shakes or vibrates excessively

- ☐ Tyres worn or out of balance (Chapter 7).
- ☐ Swingarm bearings worn. Renew the bearings (Chapter 6).
- ☐ Wheel rim(s) warped or damaged. Inspect wheels for runout (Chapter 7).
- ☐ Wheel bearings worn. Worn front or rear wheel bearings can cause poor tracking. Worn front bearings will cause wobble (Chapter 7).
- ☐ Handlebar clamp bolts loose (Chapter 6).
- ☐ Fork yoke bolts loose. Tighten them to the specified torque (Chapter 6).
- ☐ Engine mounting bolts loose. Will cause excessive vibration with increased engine rpm (Chapter 2).

Handlebar pulls to one side

- ☐ Frame bent. Definitely suspect this if the machine has been dropped. May or may not be accompanied by cracking near the bend. Renew the frame (Chapter 6).
- ☐ Wheels out of alignment. Caused by improper location of axle spacers or from bent steering stem or frame (Chapter 6).
- ☐ Swingarm bent or twisted. Caused by age (metal fatigue) or impact damage. Renew the swingarm (Chapter 6).
- ☐ Steering stem bent. Caused by impact damage or by dropping the motorcycle. Renew the steering stem (Chapter 6).
- ☐ Fork tube bent. Disassemble the forks and renew the damaged parts (Chapter 6).
- ☐ Fork oil level uneven. Check and add or drain as necessary (Chapter 6).

Poor shock absorbing qualities

- ☐ Too hard:
  - *a) Fork oil level excessive (Chapter 6).*
  - *b) Fork oil viscosity too high. Use a lighter oil (see the Specifications in Chapter 6).*
  - *c) Fork tube bent. Causes a harsh, sticking feeling (Chapter 6).*
  - *d) Fork internal damage (Chapter 6).*
  - *e) Shock shaft or body bent or damaged (Chapter 6).*
  - *f) Shock internal damage.*
  - *g) Tyre pressure too high (Chapter 1).*
- ☐ Too soft:
  - *a) Fork or shock oil insufficient and/or leaking (Chapter 6).*
  - *b) Fork oil level too low (Chapter 6).*
  - *c) Fork oil viscosity too light (Chapter 6).*
  - *d) Fork springs weak or broken (Chapter 6).*
  - *e) Shock internal damage or leakage (Chapter 6).*

13 Braking problems

Brakes are spongy, don't hold

- ☐ Air in brake line. Caused by inattention to master cylinder fluid level or by leakage. Locate problem and bleed brakes (Chapter 7).
- ☐ Pad or disc worn (Chapters 1 and 7).
- ☐ Brake fluid leak. See paragraph 1.
- ☐ Contaminated pads. Caused by contamination with oil, grease, brake fluid, etc. Renew the pads. Clean disc thoroughly with brake cleaner (Chapter 7).
- ☐ Brake fluid deteriorated. Fluid is old or contaminated. Drain system, replenish with new fluid and bleed the system (Chapter 7).
- ☐ Master cylinder internal parts worn or damaged causing fluid to bypass (Chapter 7).
- ☐ Master cylinder bore scratched by foreign material or broken spring. Repair or renew the master cylinder (Chapter 7).
- ☐ Disc warped. Renew the disc and fit new pads (Chapter 7).

Brake lever or pedal pulsates

- ☐ Disc warped. Renew the disc and fit new pads (Chapter 7).
- ☐ Axle bent. Renew the axle (Chapter 7).
- ☐ Brake caliper bolts loose (Chapter 7).
- ☐ Brake caliper sliders damaged or sticking (front caliper – all models, rear caliper – K3 models onward), causing caliper to bind. Lubricate the sliders or renew them if they are corroded or bent (Chapter 7).
- ☐ Wheel warped or otherwise damaged (Chapter 7).
- ☐ Wheel bearings damaged or worn (Chapter 7).

Brakes drag

- ☐ Master cylinder piston seized. Caused by wear or damage to piston or cylinder bore (Chapter 7).
- ☐ Lever balky or stuck. Check pivot and lubricate (Chapter 7).
- ☐ Brake caliper binds. Caused by inadequate lubrication or damage to caliper sliders (front) (Chapter 7).
- ☐ Brake caliper piston seized in bore. Caused by wear or ingestion of dirt past deteriorated seal (Chapter 7).
- ☐ Brake pad damaged. Pad material separated from backing plate. Usually caused by faulty manufacturing process or from contact with chemicals. Renew the pads (Chapter 7).
- ☐ Pads improperly installed (Chapter 7).

ABS indicator light comes on

- ☐ If the light remains on or starts flashing while the machine is being ridden, investigate the fault as described in Chapter 7, Section 15.

14 Electrical problems

Battery dead or weak

- ☐ Battery faulty. Caused by sulphated plates which are shorted through sedimentation. Also, broken battery terminal making only occasional contact (Chapter 9).
- ☐ Battery cables making poor contact (Chapter 9).
- ☐ Load excessive. Caused by addition of high wattage lights or other electrical accessories.
- ☐ Ignition (main) switch defective. Switch either grounds (earths) internally or fails to shut off system. Renew the switch (Chapter 9).
- ☐ Regulator/rectifier defective (Chapter 9).
- ☐ Alternator stator coil open or shorted (Chapter 9).
- ☐ Wiring faulty. Wiring grounded (earthed) or connections loose in ignition, charging or lighting circuits (Chapter 9).

Battery overcharged

- ☐ Regulator/rectifier defective. Overcharging is noticed when battery gets excessively warm (Chapter 9).
- ☐ Battery defective. Renew the battery (Chapter 9).
- ☐ Battery amperage too low, wrong type or size. Install manufacturer's specified amp-hour battery to handle charging load (Chapter 9).

Checking engine compression

- Low compression will result in exhaust smoke, heavy oil consumption, poor starting and poor performance. A compression test will provide useful information about an engine's condition and if performed regularly, can give warning of trouble before any other symptoms become apparent.
- A compression gauge will be required, along with an adapter to suit the spark plug hole thread size. Note that the screw-in type gauge/adapter set up is preferable to the rubber cone type.
- Before carrying out the test, first check the valve clearances as described in Chapter 1.

1 Run the engine until it reaches normal operating temperature, then stop it and remove the spark plug(s), taking care not to scald your hands on the hot components.

2 Install the gauge adapter and compression gauge in No. 1 cylinder spark plug hole **(see illustration 1)**.

1

Screw the compression gauge adapter into the spark plug hole, then screw the gauge into the adapter

3 On kickstart-equipped motorcycles, make sure the ignition switch is OFF, then open the throttle fully and kick the engine over a couple of times until the gauge reading stabilises.

4 On motorcycles with electric start only, the procedure will differ depending on the nature of the ignition system. Flick the engine kill switch (engine stop switch) to OFF and turn the ignition switch ON; open the throttle fully and crank the engine over on the starter motor for a couple of revolutions until the gauge reading stabilises. If the starter will not operate with the kill switch OFF, turn the ignition switch OFF and refer to the next paragraph.

5 Install the plugs back into their caps and arrange the plug electrodes so that their metal bodies are earthed (grounded) against the cylinder head; this is essential to prevent damage to the ignition system **(see illustration 2)**. Position the plugs well away from the plug holes otherwise there is a risk of atomised fuel escaping from the plug holes and igniting. As a safety precaution, cover the cylinder head covers with rag and, on K3 models onward, disconnect the fuel pump wiring connector (see Chapter 4B). Turn the ignition switch and kill switch ON, open the throttle fully and crank the engine over on the starter motor for a couple of revolutions until the gauge reading stabilises.

2

All spark plugs must be earthed (grounded) against the cylinder head

6 After one or two revolutions the pressure should build up to a maximum figure and then stabilise. Take a note of this reading and on multi-cylinder engines repeat the test on the remaining cylinders.

7 The correct pressures are given in Chapter 2 Specifications. If the results fall within the specified range and on multi-cylinder engines all are relatively equal, the engine is in good condition. If there is a marked difference between the readings, or if the readings are lower than specified, inspection of the top-end components will be required.

8 Low compression pressure may be due to worn cylinder bores, pistons or rings, failure of the cylinder head gasket, worn valve seals, or poor valve seating.

9 To distinguish between cylinder/piston wear and valve leakage, pour a small quantity of oil into the bore to temporarily seal the piston rings, then repeat the compression tests **(see illustration 3)**. If the readings show a noticeable increase in pressure this confirms that the cylinder bore, piston, or rings are worn. If, however, no change is indicated, the cylinder head gasket or valves should be examined.

3

Bores can be temporarily sealed with a squirt of motor oil

10 High compression pressure indicates excessive carbon build-up in the combustion chamber and on the piston crown. If this is the case the cylinder head should be removed and the deposits removed. Note that excessive carbon build-up is less likely with the used on modern fuels.

Checking battery open-circuit voltage

Warning: The gases produced by the battery are explosive - never smoke or create any sparks in the vicinity of the battery. Never allow the electrolyte to contact your skin or clothing - if it does, wash it off and seek immediate medical attention.

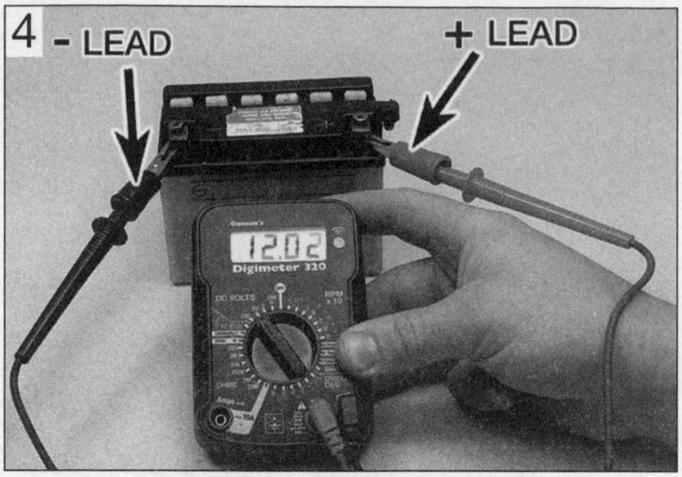

Measuring open-circuit battery voltage

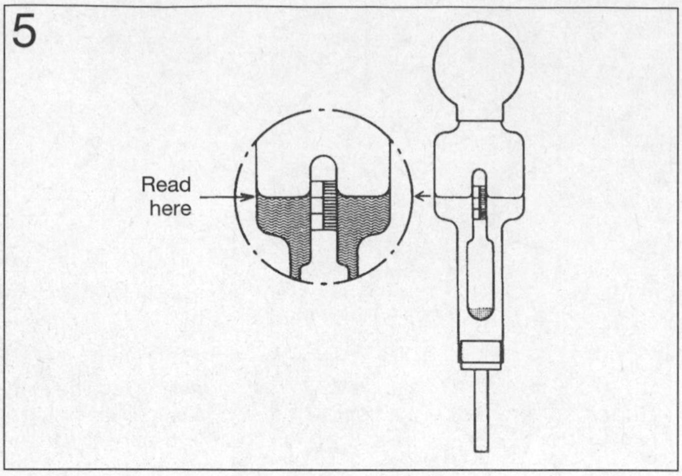

Float-type hydrometer for measuring battery specific gravity

- Before any electrical fault is investigated the battery should be checked.
- You'll need a dc voltmeter or multimeter to check battery voltage. Check that the leads are inserted in the correct terminals on the meter, red lead to positive (+ve), black lead to negative (-ve). Incorrect connections can damage the meter.
- A sound fully-charged 12 volt battery should produce between 12.3 and 12.6 volts across its terminals (12.8 volts for a maintenance-free battery). On machines with a 6 volt battery, voltage should be between 6.1 and 6.3 volts.

1 Set a multimeter to the 0 to 20 volts dc range and connect its probes across the battery terminals. Connect the meter's positive (+ve) probe, usually red, to the battery positive (+ve) terminal, followed by the meter's negative (-ve) probe, usually black, to the battery negative terminal (-ve) **(see illustration 4)**.

2 If battery voltage is low (below 10 volts on a 12 volt battery or below 4 volts on a six volt battery), charge the battery and test the voltage again. If the battery repeatedly goes flat, investigate the motorcycle's charging system.

Checking battery specific gravity (SG)

Warning: The gases produced by the battery are explosive - never smoke or create any sparks in the vicinity of the battery. Never allow the electrolyte to contact your skin or clothing - if it does, wash it off and seek immediate medical attention.

- The specific gravity check gives an indication of a battery's state of charge.
- A hydrometer is used for measuring specific gravity. Make sure you purchase one which has a small enough hose to insert in the aperture of a motorcycle battery.
- Specific gravity is simply a measure of the electrolyte's density compared with that of water. Water has an SG of 1.000 and fully-charged battery electrolyte is about 26% heavier, at 1.260.
- Specific gravity checks are not possible on maintenance-free batteries. Testing the open-circuit voltage is the only means of determining their state of charge.

1 To measure SG, remove the battery from the motorcycle and remove the first cell cap. Draw some electrolyte into the hydrometer and note the reading **(see illustration 5)**. Return the electrolyte to the cell and install the cap.

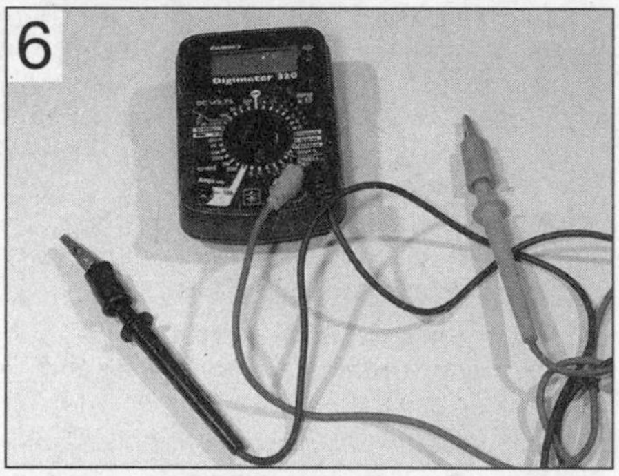

Digital multimeter can be used for all electrical tests

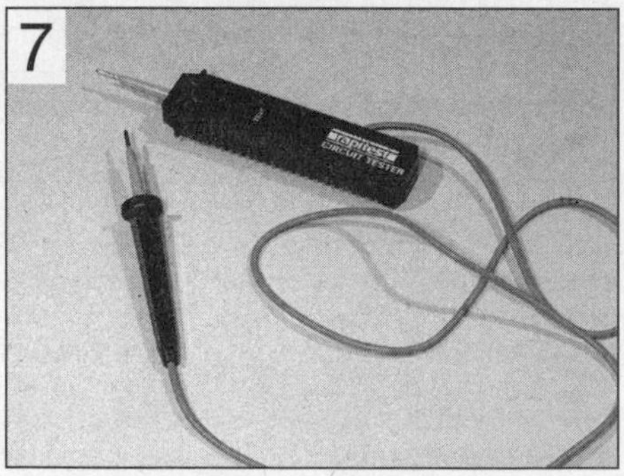

Battery-powered continuity tester

2 The reading should be in the region of 1.260 to 1.280. If SG is below 1.200 the battery needs charging. Note that SG will vary with temperature; it should be measured at 20°C (68°F). Add 0.007 to the reading for every 10°C above 20°C, and subtract 0.007 from the reading for every 10°C below 20°C. Add 0.004 to the reading for every 10°F above 68°F, and subtract 0.004 from the reading for every 10°F below 68°F.

3 When the check is complete, rinse the hydrometer thoroughly with clean water.

Checking for continuity

- The term continuity describes the uninterrupted flow of electricity through an electrical circuit. A continuity check will determine whether an **open-circuit** situation exists.
- Continuity can be checked with an ohmmeter, multimeter, continuity tester or battery and bulb test circuit **(see illustrations 6, 7 and 8)**.

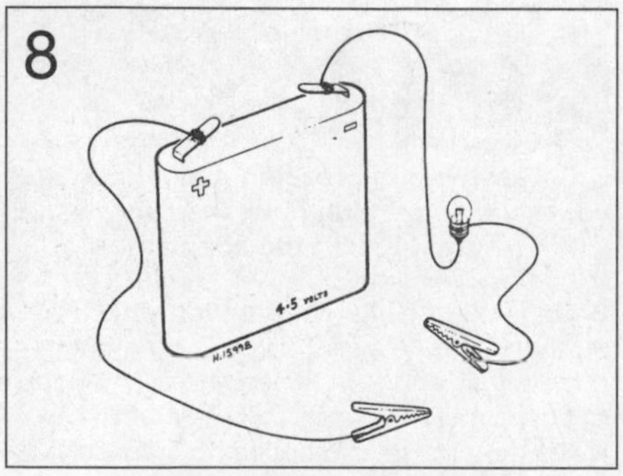

Battery and bulb test circuit

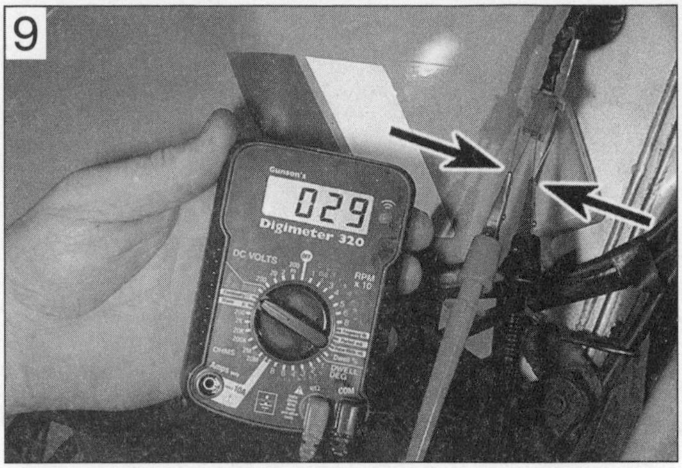

Continuity check of front brake light switch using a meter - note split pins used to access connector terminals

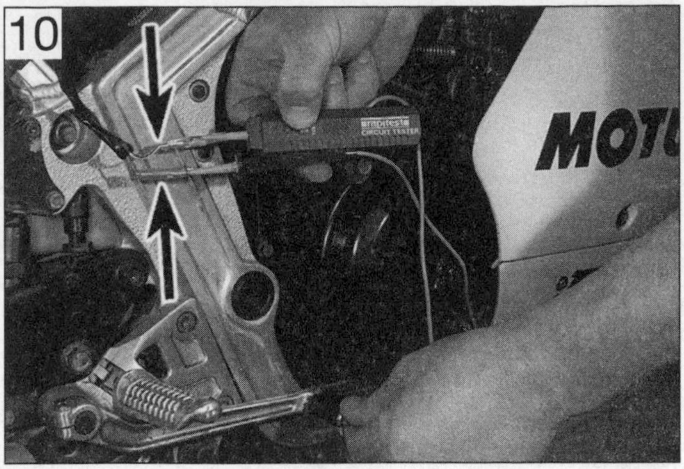

Continuity check of rear brake light switch using a continuity tester

- All of these instruments are self-powered by a battery, therefore the checks are made with the ignition OFF.
- As a safety precaution, always disconnect the battery negative (-ve) lead before making checks, particularly if ignition switch checks are being made.
- If using a meter, select the appropriate ohms scale and check that the meter reads infinity (∞). Touch the meter probes together and check that meter reads zero; where necessary adjust the meter so that it reads zero.
- After using a meter, always switch it OFF to conserve its battery.

Switch checks

1 If a switch is at fault, trace its wiring up to the wiring connectors. Separate the wire connectors and inspect them for security and condition. A build-up of dirt or corrosion here will most likely be the cause of the problem - clean up and apply a water dispersant such as WD40.

2 If using a test meter, set the meter to the ohms x 10 scale and connect its probes across the wires from the switch **(see illustration 9)**. Simple ON/OFF type switches, such as brake light switches, only have two wires whereas combination switches, like the ignition switch, have many internal links. Study the wiring diagram to ensure that you are connecting across the correct pair of wires. Continuity (low or no measurable resistance - 0 ohms) should be indicated with the switch ON and no continuity (high resistance) with it OFF.

3 Note that the polarity of the test probes doesn't matter for continuity checks, although care should be taken to follow specific test procedures if a diode or solid-state component is being checked.

4 A continuity tester or battery and bulb circuit can be used in the same way. Connect its probes as described above **(see illustration 10)**. The light should come on to indicate continuity in the ON switch position, but should extinguish in the OFF position.

Wiring checks

- Many electrical faults are caused by damaged wiring, often due to incorrect routing or chaffing on frame components.
- Loose, wet or corroded wire connectors can also be the cause of electrical problems, especially in exposed locations.

1 A continuity check can be made on a single length of wire by disconnecting it at each end and connecting a meter or continuity tester across both ends of the wire **(see illustration 11)**.

2 Continuity (low or no resistance - 0 ohms) should be indicated if the wire is good. If no continuity (high resistance) is shown, suspect a broken wire.

Checking for voltage

- A voltage check can determine whether current is reaching a component.
- Voltage can be checked with a dc voltmeter, multimeter set on the dc volts scale, test light or buzzer **(see illustrations 12 and 13)**. A meter has the advantage of being able to measure actual voltage.
- When using a meter, check that its leads are inserted in the correct terminals on the meter, red to positive (+ve), black to negative (-ve). Incorrect connections can damage the meter.
- A voltmeter (or multimeter set to the dc volts scale) should always be connected in parallel (across the load). Connecting it in series will not harm the meter, but the reading will not be meaningful.
- Voltage checks are made with the ignition ON.

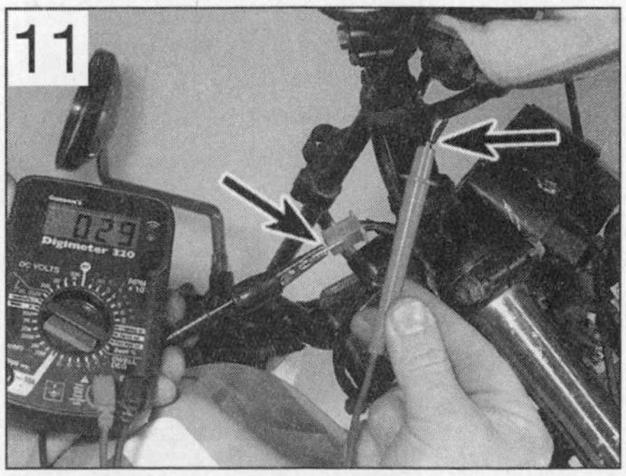

Continuity check of front brake light switch sub-harness

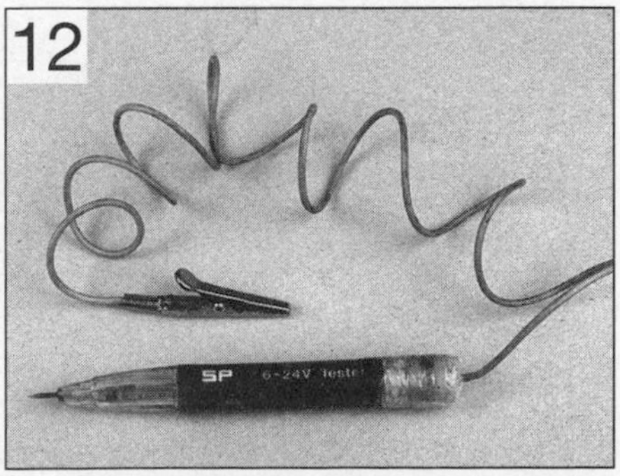

A simple test light can be used for voltage checks

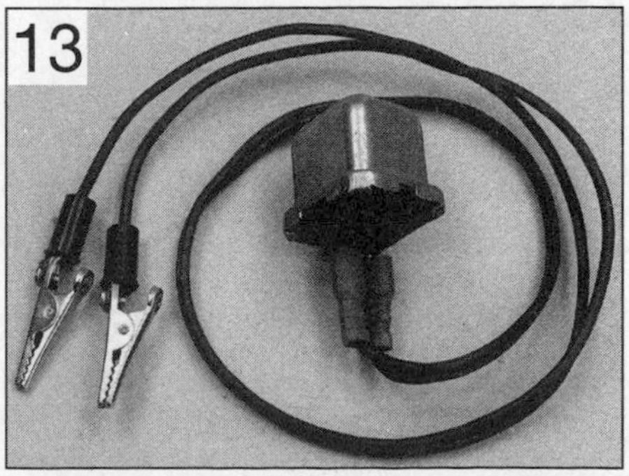

A buzzer is useful for voltage checks

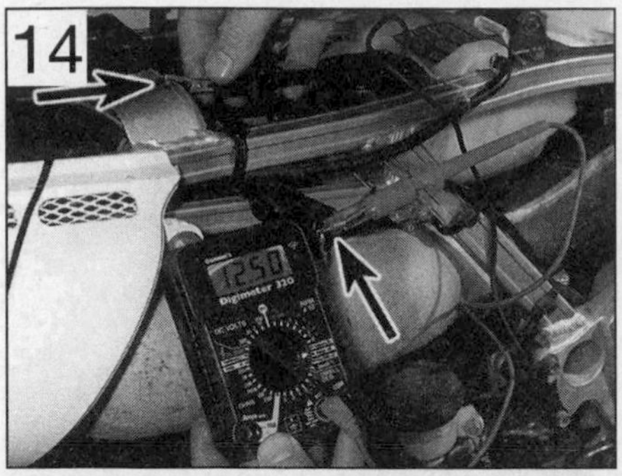

Checking for voltage at the rear brake light power supply wire using a meter . . .

1 First identify the relevant wiring circuit by referring to the wiring diagram at the end of this manual. If other electrical components share the same power supply (ie are fed from the same fuse), take note whether they are working correctly - this is useful information in deciding where to start checking the circuit.

2 If using a meter, check first that the meter leads are plugged into the correct terminals on the meter (see above). Set the meter to the dc volts function, at a range suitable for the battery voltage. Connect the meter red probe (+ve) to the power supply wire and the black probe to a good metal earth (ground) on the motorcycle's frame or directly to the battery negative (-ve) terminal **(see illustration 14)**. Battery voltage should be shown on the meter

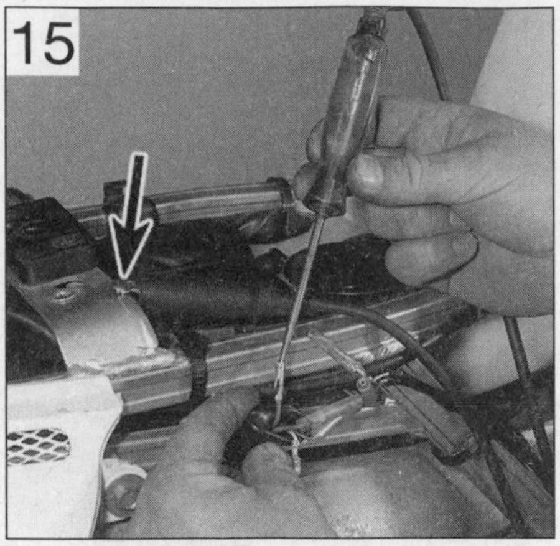

. . . or a test light - note the earth connection to the frame (arrow)

with the ignition switched ON.

3 If using a test light or buzzer, connect its positive (+ve) probe to the power supply terminal and its negative (-ve) probe to a good earth (ground) on the motorcycle's frame or directly to the battery negative (-ve) terminal **(see illustration 15)**. With the ignition ON, the test light should illuminate or the buzzer sound.

4 If no voltage is indicated, work back towards the fuse continuing to check for voltage. When you reach a point where there is voltage, you know the problem lies between that point and your last check point.

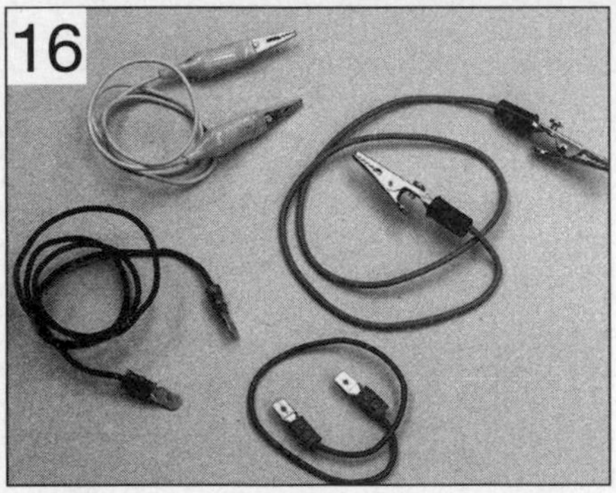

A selection of jumper wires for making earth (ground) checks

Checking the earth (ground)

- Earth connections are made either directly to the engine or frame (such as sensors, neutral switch etc. which only have a positive feed) or by a separate wire into the earth circuit of the wiring harness. Alternatively a short earth wire is sometimes run directly from the component to the motorcycle's frame.
- Corrosion is often the cause of a poor earth connection.
- If total failure is experienced, check the security of the main earth lead from the negative (-ve) terminal of the battery and also the main earth (ground) point on the wiring harness. If corroded, dismantle the connection and clean all surfaces back to bare metal.

1 To check the earth on a component, use an insulated jumper wire to temporarily bypass its earth connection **(see illustration 16)**. Connect one end of the jumper wire between the earth terminal or metal body of the component and the other end to the motorcycle's frame.

2 If the circuit works with the jumper wire installed, the original earth circuit is faulty. Check the wiring for open-circuits or poor connections. Clean up direct earth connections, removing all traces of corrosion and remake the joint. Apply petroleum jelly to the joint to prevent future corrosion.

Tracing a short-circuit

- A short-circuit occurs where current shorts to earth (ground) bypassing the circuit components. This usually results in a blown fuse.
- A short-circuit is most likely to occur where the insulation has worn through due to wiring chafing on a component, allowing a direct path to earth (ground) on the frame.

1 Remove any bodypanels necessary to access the circuit wiring.

2 Check that all electrical switches in the circuit are OFF, then remove the circuit fuse and connect a test light, buzzer or voltmeter (set to the dc scale) across the fuse terminals. No voltage should be shown.

3 Move the wiring from side to side whilst observing the test light or meter. When the test light comes on, buzzer sounds or meter shows voltage, you have found the cause of the short. It will usually shown up as damaged or burned insulation.

4 Note that the same test can be performed on each component in the circuit, even the switch.

Note: *References throughout this index are in the form* **"Chapter number" • "Page number"**. *So, for example, 2•15 refers to page 15 of Chapter 2.*

Note: *References throughout this index are in the form* **"Chapter number" • "Page number"**. *So, for example, 2•15 refers to page 15 of Chapter 2.*

E

F

G

Note: *References throughout this index are in the form* **"Chapter number" • "Page number"**. *So, for example, 2•15 refers to page 15 of Chapter 2.*

H

I

L

M

N

O

P

R

S

Note: *References throughout this index are in the form* **"Chapter number" • "Page number"**. *So, for example, 2•15 refers to page 15 of Chapter 2.*

Haynes Motorcycle Manuals – The Complete List

Title	Book No
APRILIA RS50 (99 - 06) & RS125 (93 - 06)	4298
Aprilia RSV1000 Mille (98 - 03)	◆ 4255
BMW 2-valve Twins (70 - 96)	◆ 0249
BMW K100 & 75 2-valve Models (83 - 96)	◆ 1373
BMW R850, 1100 & 1150 4-valve Twins (93 - 04)	◆ 3466
BMW R1200 (04 - 06)	◆ 4598
BSA Bantam (48 - 71)	0117
BSA Unit Singles (58 - 72)	0127
BSA Pre-unit Singles (54 - 61)	0326
BSA A7 & A10 Twins (47 - 62)	0121
BSA A50 & A65 Twins (62 - 73)	0155
DUCATI 600, 620, 750 and 900 2-valve V-Twins (91 - 05)	◆ 3290
Ducati MK III & Desmo Singles (69 - 76)	◇ 0445
Ducati 748, 916 & 996 4-valve V-Twins (94 - 01)	◆ 3756
GILERA Runner, DNA, Ice & SKP/Stalker (97 - 07)	4163
HARLEY-DAVIDSON Sportsters (70 - 03)	◆ 2534
Harley-Davidson Shovelhead and Evolution Big Twins (70 - 99)	◆ 2536
Harley-Davidson Twin Cam 88 (99 - 03)	◆ 2478
HONDA NB, ND, NP & NS50 Melody (81 - 85)	◇ 0622
Honda NE/NB50 Vision & SA50 Vision Met-in (85 - 95)	◇ 1278
Honda MB, MBX, MT & MTX50 (80 - 93)	0731
Honda C50, C70 & C90 (67 - 03)	0324
Honda XR80/100R & CRF80/100F (85 - 04)	2218
Honda XL/XR 80, 100, 125, 185 & 200 2-valve Models (78 - 87)	0566
Honda H100 & H100S Singles (80 - 92)	◇ 0734
Honda CB/CD125T & CM125C Twins (77 - 88)	◇ 0571
Honda CG125 (76 - 07)	◇ 0433
Honda NS125 (86 - 93)	◇ 3056
Honda CBR125R (04 - 07)	4620
Honda MBX/MTX125 & MTX200 (83 - 93)	◇ 1132
Honda CD/CM185 200T & CM250C 2-valve Twins (77 - 85)	0572
Honda XL/XR 250 & 500 (78 - 84)	0567
Honda XR250L, XR250R & XR400R (86 - 03)	2219
Honda CB250 & CB400N Super Dreams (78 - 84)	◇ 0540
Honda CR Motocross Bikes (86 - 01)	2222
Honda CRF250 & CRF450 (02 - 06)	2630
Honda CBR400RR Fours (88 - 99)	◇ ◆ 3552
Honda VFR400 (NC30) & RVF400 (NC35) V-Fours (89 - 98)	◇ ◆ 3496
Honda CB500 (93 - 01)	◇ 3753
Honda CB400 & CB550 Fours (73 - 77)	0262
Honda CX/GL500 & 650 V-Twins (78 - 86)	0442
Honda CBX550 Four (82 - 86)	◇ 0940
Honda XL600R & XR600R (83 - 00)	2183
Honda XL600/650V Transalp & XRV750 Africa Twin (87 to 07)	◆ 3919
Honda CBR600F1 & 1000F Fours (87 - 96)	◆ 1730
Honda CBR600F2 & F3 Fours (91 - 98)	◆ 2070
Honda CBR600F4 (99 - 06)	◆ 3911
Honda CB600F Hornet & CBF600 (98 - 06)	◇ ◆ 3915
Honda CBR600RR (03 - 06)	◆ 4590
Honda CB650 sohc Fours (78 - 84)	0665
Honda NTV600 Revere, NTV650 and NT650V Deauville (88 - 05)	◇ ◆ 3243
Honda Shadow VT600 & 750 (USA) (88 - 03)	2312
Honda CB750 sohc Four (69 - 79)	0131
Honda V45/65 Sabre & Magna (82 - 88)	0820
Honda VFR750 & 700 V-Fours (86 - 97)	◆ 2101
Honda VFR800 V-Fours (97 - 01)	◆ 3703
Honda VFR800 V-Tec V-Fours (02 - 05)	◆ 4196
Honda CB750 & CB900 dohc Fours (78 - 84)	0535
Honda VTR1000 (FireStorm, Super Hawk) & XL1000V (Varadero) (97 - 00)	◆ 3744
Honda CBR900RR FireBlade (92 - 99)	◆ 2161
Honda CBR900RR FireBlade (00 - 03)	◆ 4060
Honda CBR1000RR Fireblade (04 - 07)	◆ 4604
Honda CBR1100XX Super Blackbird (97 - 07)	◆ 3901
Honda ST1100 Pan European V-Fours (90 - 02)	◆ 3384
Honda Shadow VT1100 (USA) (85 - 98)	2313
Honda GL1000 Gold Wing (75 - 79)	0309
Honda GL1100 Gold Wing (79 - 81)	0669
Honda Gold Wing 1200 (USA) (84 - 87)	2199
Honda Gold Wing 1500 (USA) (88 - 00)	2225
KAWASAKI AE/AR 50 & 80 (81 - 95)	1007
Kawasaki KC, KE & KH100 (75 - 99)	1371
Kawasaki KMX125 & 200 (86 - 02)	◇ 3046
Kawasaki 250, 350 & 400 Triples (72 - 79)	0134
Kawasaki 400 & 440 Twins (74 - 81)	0281
Kawasaki 400, 500 & 550 Fours (79 - 91)	0910
Kawasaki EN450 & 500 Twins (Ltd/Vulcan) (85 - 04)	2053
Kawasaki EX500 (GPZ500S) & ER500 (ER-5) (87 - 05)	◆ 2052
Kawasaki ZX600 (ZZ-R600 & Ninja ZX-6) (90 - 06)	◆ 2146
Kawasaki ZX-6R Ninja Fours (95 - 02)	◆ 3541
Kawasaki ZX-6R (03 - 06)	◆ 4742
Kawasaki ZX600 (GPZ600R, GPX600R, Ninja 600R & RX) & ZX750 (GPX750R, Ninja 750R)	◆ 1780
Kawasaki 650 Four (76 - 78)	0373
Kawasaki Vulcan 700/750 & 800 (85 - 04)	◆ 2457
Kawasaki 750 Air-cooled Fours (80 - 91)	0574
Kawasaki ZR550 & 750 Zephyr Fours (90 - 97)	◆ 3382
Kawasaki Z750 & Z1000 (03 - 08)	◆ 4762
Kawasaki ZX750 (Ninja ZX-7 & ZXR750) Fours (89 - 96)	◆ 2054
Kawasaki Ninja ZX-7R & ZX-9R (94 - 04)	◆ 3721
Kawasaki 900 & 1000 Fours (73 - 77)	0222
Kawasaki ZX900, 1000 & 1100 Liquid-cooled Fours (83 - 97)	◆ 1681
KTM EXC Enduro & SX Motocross (00 - 07)	◆ 4629
MOTO GUZZI 750, 850 & 1000 V-Twins (74 - 78)	0339
MZ ETZ Models (81 - 95)	◇ 1680
NORTON 500, 600, 650 & 750 Twins (57 - 70)	0187
Norton Commando (68 - 77)	0125
PEUGEOT Speedfight, Trekker & Vivacity Scooters (96 - 05)	◇ 3920
PIAGGIO (Vespa) Scooters (91 - 06)	◇ 3492
SUZUKI GT, ZR & TS50 (77 - 90)	◇ 0799
Suzuki TS50X (84 - 00)	◇ 1599
Suzuki 100, 125, 185 & 250 Air-cooled Trail bikes (79 - 89)	0797
Suzuki GP100 & 125 Singles (78 - 93)	◇ 0576
Suzuki GS, GN, GZ & DR125 Singles (82 - 05)	◇ 0888
Suzuki 250 & 350 Twins (68 - 78)	0120
Suzuki GT250X7, GT200X5 & SB200 Twins (78 - 83)	◇ 0469
Suzuki GS/GSX250, 400 & 450 Twins (79 - 85)	0736
Suzuki GS500 Twin (89 - 06)	◆ 3238
Suzuki GS550 (77 - 82) & GS750 Fours (76 - 79)	0363
Suzuki GS/GSX550 4-valve Fours (83 - 88)	1133
Suzuki SV650 & SV650S (99 - 05)	◆ 3912
Suzuki GSX-R600 & 750 (96 - 00)	◆ 3553
Suzuki GSX-R600 (01 - 03), GSX-R750 (00 - 03) & GSX-R1000 (01 - 02)	◆ 3986
Suzuki GSX-R600/750 (04 - 05) & GSX-R1000 (03 - 06)	◆ 4382
Suzuki GSF600, 650 & 1200 Bandit Fours (95 - 06)	◆ 3367
Suzuki Intruder, Marauder, Volusia & Boulevard (85 - 06)	◆ 2618
Suzuki GS850 Fours (78 - 88)	0536
Suzuki GS1000 Four (77 - 79)	0484
Suzuki GSX-R750, GSX-R1100 (85 - 92), GSX600F, GSX750F, GSX1100F (Katana) Fours	◆ 2055
Suzuki GSX600/750F & GSX750 (98 - 02)	◆ 3987
Suzuki GS/GSX1000, 1100 & 1150 4-valve Fours (79 - 88)	0737
Suzuki TL1000S/R & DL1000 V-Strom (97 - 04)	◆ 4083
Suzuki GSX1300R Hayabusa (99 - 04)	◆ 4184
Suzuki GSX1400 (02 - 07)	◆ 4758
TRIUMPH Tiger Cub & Terrier (52 - 68)	0414
Triumph 350 & 500 Unit Twins (58 - 73)	0137
Triumph Pre-Unit Twins (47 - 62)	0251
Triumph 650 & 750 2-valve Unit Twins (63 - 83)	0122
Triumph Trident & BSA Rocket 3 (69 - 75)	0136
Triumph Bonneville (01 - 07)	◆ 4364
Triumph Daytona, Speed Triple, Sprint & Tiger (97 - 05)	◆ 3755
Triumph Triples and Fours (carburettor engines) (91 - 04)	◆ 2162
VESPA P/PX125, 150 & 200 Scooters (78 - 06)	0707
Vespa Scooters (59 - 78)	0126
YAMAHA DT50 & 80 Trail Bikes (78 - 95)	◇ 0800
Yamaha T50 & 80 Townmate (83 - 95)	◇ 1247
Yamaha YB100 Singles (73 - 91)	◇ 0474
Yamaha RS/RXS100 & 125 Singles (74 - 95)	0331
Yamaha RD & DT125LC (82 - 87)	◇ 0887
Yamaha TZR125 (87 - 93) & DT125R (88 - 02)	◇ 1655
Yamaha TY50, 80, 125 & 175 (74 - 84)	◇ 0464
Yamaha XT & SR125 (82 - 03)	◇ 1021
Yamaha Trail Bikes (81 - 00)	2350
Yamaha 2-stroke Motocross Bikes 1986 - 2006	2662
Yamaha YZ & WR 4-stroke Motocross Bikes (98 - 07)	2689
Yamaha 250 & 350 Twins (70 - 79)	0040
Yamaha XS250, 360 & 400 sohc Twins (75 - 84)	0378
Yamaha RD250 & 350LC Twins (80 - 82)	0803
Yamaha RD350 YPVS Twins (83 - 95)	1158
Yamaha RD400 Twin (75 - 79)	0333
Yamaha XT, TT & SR500 Singles (75 - 83)	0342
Yamaha XZ550 Vision V-Twins (82 - 85)	0821
Yamaha FJ, FZ, XJ & YX600 Radian (84 - 92)	2100
Yamaha XJ600S (Diversion, Seca II) & XJ600N Fours (92 - 03)	◆ 2145
Yamaha YZF600R Thundercat & FZS600 Fazer (96 - 03)	◆ 3702
Yamaha FZ-6 Fazer (04 - 07)	◆ 4751
Yamaha YZF-R6 (99 - 02)	◆ 3900
Yamaha YZF-R6 (03 - 05)	◆ 4601
Yamaha 650 Twins (70 - 83)	0341
Yamaha XJ650 & 750 Fours (80 - 84)	0738
Yamaha XS750 & 850 Triples (76 - 85)	0340
Yamaha TDM850, TRX850 & XTZ750 (89 - 99)	◇ ◆ 3540
Yamaha YZF750R & YZF1000R Thunderace (93 - 00)	◆ 3720
Yamaha FZR600, 750 & 1000 Fours (87 - 96)	◆ 2056
Yamaha XV (Virago) V-Twins (81 - 03)	◆ 0802
Yamaha XVS650 & 1100 Drag Star/V-Star (97 - 05)	◆ 4195
Yamaha XJ900F Fours (83 - 94)	◆ 3239
Yamaha XJ900S Diversion (94 - 01)	◆ 3739
Yamaha YZF-R1 (98 - 03)	◆ 3754
Yamaha YZF-R1 (04 - 06)	◆ 4605
Yamaha FZS1000 Fazer (01 - 05)	◆ 4287
Yamaha FJ1100 & 1200 Fours (84 - 96)	◆ 2057
Yamaha XJR1200 & 1300 (95 - 06)	◆ 3981
Yamaha V-Max (85 - 03)	◆ 4072
ATVs	
Honda ATC70, 90, 110, 185 & 200 (71 - 85)	0565
Honda Rancher, Recon & TRX250EX ATVs	2553
Honda TRX300 Shaft Drive ATVs (88 - 00)	2125
Honda TRX300EX, TRX400EX & TRX450R/ER ATVs (93 - 06)	2318
Kawasaki Bayou 220/250/300 & Prairie 300 ATVs (86 - 03)	2351
Polaris ATVs (85 - 97)	2302
Polaris ATVs (98 - 06)	2508
Yamaha YFS200 Blaster ATV (88 - 02)	2317
Yamaha YFB250 Timberwolf ATVs (92 - 00)	2217
Yamaha YFM350 & YFM400 (ER and Big Bear) ATVs (87 - 03)	2126
Yamaha Banshee and Warrior ATVs (87 - 03)	2314
Yamaha Kodiak and Grizzly ATVs (93 - 05)	2567
ATV Basics	10450
TECHBOOK SERIES	
Twist and Go (automatic transmission) Scooters Service and Repair Manual	4082
Motorcycle Basics TechBook (2nd Edition)	3515
Motorcycle Electrical TechBook (3rd Edition)	3471
Motorcycle Fuel Systems TechBook	3514
Motorcycle Maintenance TechBook	4071
Motorcycle Modifying	4272
Motorcycle Workshop Practice TechBook (2nd Edition)	3470

◇ = not available in the USA *◆ = Superbike*

The manuals on this page are available through good motorcycle dealers and accessory shops.
In case of difficulty, contact: **Haynes Publishing**
(UK) **+44 1963 442030** (USA) **+1 805 498 6703**
(SV) **+46 18 124016**
(Australia/New Zealand) **+61 3 9763 8100**

MCL23.12/07

Preserving Our Motoring Heritage

< The Model J Duesenberg Derham Tourster. Only eight of these magnificent cars were ever built – this is the only example to be found outside the United States of America

Almost every … at the Haynes Motor Museum. Ove… …pect of our motoring heritage, from ele… …erg to curiosities like the bug-eyed BMW… …ember the 1959 Ford Popular that yo… …e of classic sports cars including AC, A… Porsche and Triumph.

Each and every v… …nd culture of Motoring. Today, they mak… …e kids, bring Mum and Dad, but abo… …u will also find an impressive array… of the most extensive transport book… …o wholesome, home-made meals or, i… rural surroundings of

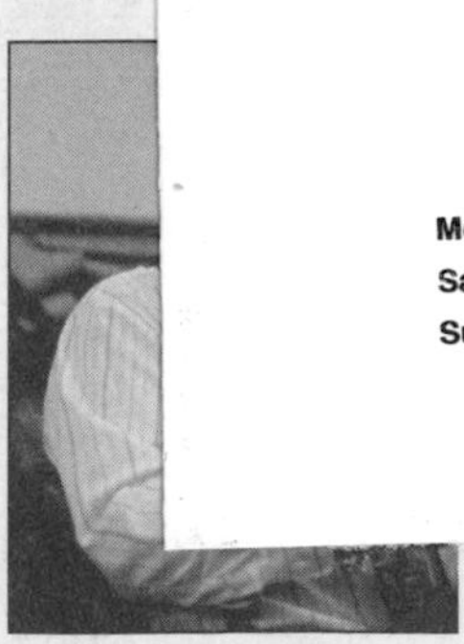

> John Haynes O.B.E., Founder and Chairman of the museum at the wheel of a Haynes Light 12.

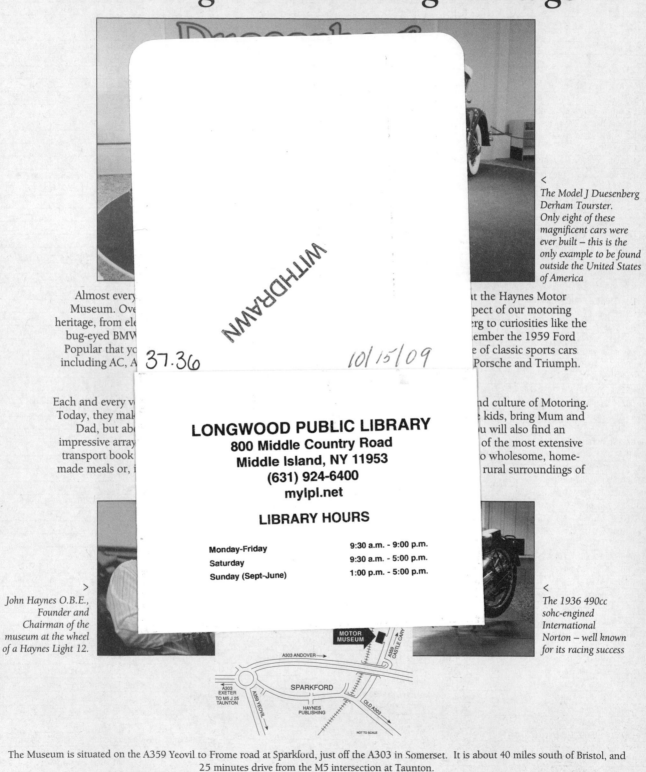

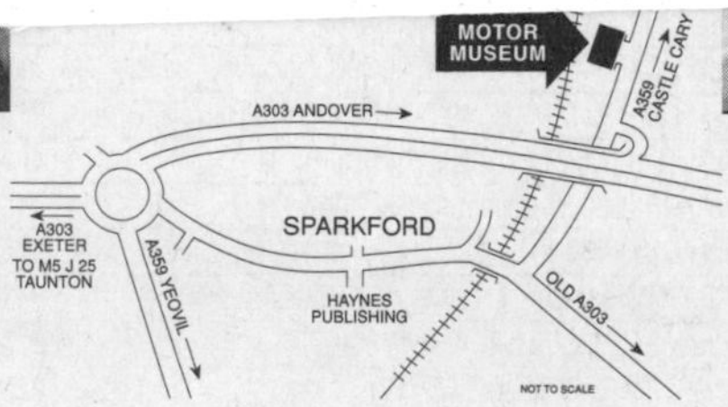

< The 1936 490cc sohc-engined International Norton – well known for its racing success

The Museum is situated on the A359 Yeovil to Frome road at Sparkford, just off the A303 in Somerset. It is about 40 miles south of Bristol, and 25 minutes drive from the M5 intersection at Taunton.

Open 9.30am - 5.30pm (10.00am - 4.00pm Winter) 7 days a week, *except Christmas Day, Boxing Day and New Years Day*

Special rates available for schools, coach parties and outings Charitable Trust No. 292048